League of Nations & United Nations Monthly List of Selected Articles

•

CUMULATIVE 1920 - 1970

•

Edited by
NORMAN S. FIELD
Associate Chief Librarian
United Nations Library, Geneva

Legal Questions

NATIONAL LAW – COUNTRIES

Volume II

1972 Oceana Publications, Inc. Dobbs Ferry, NY

Published with the cooperation of the
United Nations, Geneva.

Series International Standard Book Number (ISBN): 0-379-14150-7

Sub-Series ISBN: 0-379-14156-6 (Legal Questions)

Library of Congress Catalog Card Number: 75-147817

Manufactured in the United States of America

Contents

LEGAL QUESTIONS
(1920 - 1944)

Contents

LEGAL QUESTIONS
(1920 - 1944)

Contents

LEGAL QUESTIONS
(1945 - 1970)

Contents

LEGAL QUESTIONS
(1945 - 1970)

Contents

LEGAL QUESTIONS
(1945 - 1970)

LEGAL QUESTIONS
(1945 - 1970)

National Law – Countries

NATIONAL LAW - COUNTRIES

ARGENTINE

MacDONALD, A.F. : The Government of Argentina. Hispanic America historical review 5 : 52-82, February 1922.
Summary of the Argentine constitution - the executive power - the legislative power, etc.

ZEBALLOS, E.S. : The evolution of law in Latin America. American bar association journal 9 : 633-635, October 1923.

The Argentine Republic's contribution to civilisation. Commercial and financial chronicle 118 - 12-13, January 5, 1924.
Summary of lecture by the late Dr. E.S. Zeballos.

MORENO QUINTANA, Lucio M. : Le système argentin de la nationalité et la prétendue "citoyenneté automatique" des étrangers sans la perte de la nationalité d'origine. Journal du droit international 50 : 244-248, mars-avril 1923.

Proposed Argentine citizenship law contains radical changes. Pan American Union 58 : 375-378, April 1924.
Text of the proposed law.

AUSTRALIA

Constitution alteration. Weakness of Senate. Journal of the parliaments of the empire 1 : 513-514, July 1920.
Proposed amendment of the Arbitration Act.

Nationality act. Journal of the parliaments of the empire 2 : 368-372, May 1921.
Main provisions of the Act - debate.

GARRAN, Robert : The development of the Australian constitution. Law quarterly review 40 : 202-220, April 1924.

AUSTRIA

Der verfassungsentwurf. Österreichische Volkswirt 12 : 902-903, September 4, 1920.
Comment on the draft Constitution of the Republic.

MERKL, Adolf : Die Verfassung der deutsch-österreichischen Republik. Prager Juristische Zeitschrift 2 : 2-30, Heft 1, 1922.
Summary and analysis.

GODSHALL, W. Leon : The constitution of new Austria. Current history 18 : 281-285, May 1923.
Analysis.

WURMBRAND, Norbert : Der österreichische bundesstaatliche Finanzausgleich des Jahres 1922 und seine staatsrechtliche Bedeutung. Zeitschrift für öffentliches Recht 3 : 628-683, 5-6 Heft 1923.
System of financial allocation within Austria.

WITTMAYER, Dr. : Das Staatsrecht des österreichischen Wiederaufbaues. Deutsche Juristen-Zeitung 28 : 387-391, 1 Juli 1923.
Effect of measures of reconstruction on Austrian constitutional law.

KELSEN, Hans : Die Vollendung der österreichischen Bundesverfassung. Zeitschrift für Politik 15 : 301-319, Heft 4, 1925.

AUSTERLITZ, Friedrich : Verfassungsrevision. Kampf 18 : 161-165, Mai 1925.
Comment on proposed constitutional revision.

ADAMOVICH, Ludwig : Zur Judikatur des Verfassungsgerichtshofes. Zeitschrift für öffentliches Recht 4 : 367-444, 5-6tes Heft 1925.

HUGELMANN, Karl : Das österreichische Reichsgericht. Zeitschrift für öffentliches Recht 4 : 458-538, 5-6tes Heft 1925.
Origin - organisation and activity.

DANNEBERG, R. : Revision der Verfassung? Der Kampf 18 : 201-204, Juni 1925.

MERKL, Dr. A. : Epilog zur Verfassungsreform. Oesterreichische Volkswirt 17 : 1241-1243, 8 August 1925.

MERKL, Dr. A. : Epilog zur Verfassungsreform. Österreichische Volkswirt 17 : 1269-1272, 15 august 1925.

LÖWENFELD, W. : Die Reform der Verfassung. Industrie 30 : 3-4, 22 August 1925.

LÖWENFELD, W. : Die Verfassungsreform in Österreich. Wirtschaftliche Nachrichten 2 : 971-972, 25 August 1925.

BELGIUM

ERRERA, Paul : La clause de révision dans la constitution belge et ses deux applications 1893-1921. Revue de droit public et de la science politique 39 : 325-346, July-August-September 1922.

NISOT, Marie Thérèse : La nationalité de la femme mariée d'après la loi belge du 15 mai 1922. Journal du droit international 49 : 970-974, novembre 1922.

Belgique. Nationalité (acquisition et perte de la) Loi du 15 mai 1922. Journal du droit international 49 : 1067-1073, novembre 1922.

Optionsabkommen zwischen Deutschland und Belgien, 11.9.1922. Niemeyers Zeitschrift für internationale Recht 33 : 201-203, 1. bis 4. Heft, 1924/1925.
Text in German.

BOLIVIA

FORTOUL, Gil J. : La Constitución Boliviana. Cultura Venezolana 5 : 24-29, April 1922.

VETANCOURT ARISTEGUIETA, J. : La première constitution de Bolivie. Revue de l'Amérique latine 4 : 199-204, 1 septembre 1925.

BULGARIA

BARBAR, Leo : Zum bulgarischen Fremdenrecht. Niwmeyers Zeitschrift für internationales Recht 30 : 67-109, Heft 1-4, 1922.
Rights of aliens in Bulgaria.

CANADA

Naturalization acts, 1914 and 1920. Journal of the Parliaments of the Empire 2 : 74-80, January 1921.

NATIONAL LAW - COUNTRIES

LOWELL, Lawrence : The treaty-making power of Canada. Foreign affairs (N.Y.) 2 : 12-22, September 1923.
Development of the status of the Dominions.

ROWELL, Newton W. : Recent constitutional developments in Canada. American bar association journal 10 : 427-433, June 1924.

KEITH, B. : The privy council and the Canadian constitution. Journal of comparative legislation and international law 7 : 61-68, February 1925.

MACKENZIE, N.A.M. : The treaty-making power in Canada. American journal of international law 19 : 489-504, July 1925.

CHINA

The United States court for China. Millard's review of the Far East 12 : 254-259, April 3 1920.
Powers of extra-territorial courts created by the United States.

PREMET, Paul : L'extra-territorialité et la juridiction des cours mixtes. L'Europe nouvelle 10 : 396, 3 avril 1920.
Mixed courts the only guarantee of justice in China.

TONG, H.K. : A special court for Shanghai proposed Millard's review 16 : 290-292, 9 April 1921.

CHENG, F.T. : The supreme court in China. Millard's review 16 : 673-674, 28 May 1921.

SOKOLSKY, G.E. : The mixed court. Weekly review of the Far East 21 : 44-47, 10 June 1922.

HSU, Leonard S. : The Chinese legal system. American bar association journal 8 : 765-766, December 1922.

ESCARRA, Jean : Le problème de l'exterritorialité en Chine. Revue de droit international privé 18 : 693-720, 1922-1923.
Evolution of the "Cour mixte internationale".

REINSCH, Paul S. : The Chinese constitution from the American view point. Weekly review 23 : 420-421, February 10, 1923.

HSU, Leonard S. : The Chinese legal system. Weekly review 24 : 12-16, March 3, 1923.

Foreigners in China. Japan weekly chronicle No. 1355 : 829-830, 14 June 1923.

China, a current review. Far East 30 : 7-10, 23 June 1923.
Precarious position of foreigners in China.

The Chinese problem. Herald of Asia 15 : 267, 30 June 1923.
Foreigners in China - residence and travel.

BAU, Mingchien Joshua : The framing and adoption of the Chinese constitution. China weekly review 25 : 175-176, July 7 1923.

WILLIAMS, B.H. : The protection of American citizens in China - cases of lawlessness. American journal of international law 17 : 489-503, July 1923.

Constitution-making in China. China weekly review 25 : 321-322, August 4 1923.

CONLU, Francisco Villanueva : The constitution of China and the constitutional law of the Philippines. China weekly review 26 : 11-14, 55, 90-92, September 1, 8, 15, 1923.

HEDGES, Frank H. : The foreign grip on China. Current history 19 : 288-294, November 1923.
Privileged position of foreigners in China.

Text of the Chinese constitution. Current history 19 : 660-665, January 1924.

ESCARRA, Jean : La législation commerciale chinoise. Annales de droit commercial 33 : 25-33, janvier-mars 1924.

WONG, Hin : The anti-foreign agitation in Canton. China weekly review 27 : 268-269, 19 January 1924.

MacNAIR, H.F. : Chinese nationality in its relation to treaty ports. China weekly review 27 : 349-351, 2 February 1924.

CONLU, F.V. : A criticism of China's new constitution. China weekly review 28 : 254-255, 19 April 1924, 325-326, 3 May 1924.

CONLU, F.V. : China's new constitution - a criticism. China weekly review 28 : 454-456, 24 May 1924.

QUIGLEY, H.S. : The constitution of China. American political science review 18 : 346-350, May 1924.

CONLU, F.V. : A criticism of China's new constitution (contd.). China weekly review 29 : 10-14, 7 June 1924.

CONLU, F.V. : A criticism of China's new constitution (contd.). China weekly review 29 : 88, 21 June 1924.

CONLU, F.V. : The new constitution of China - a criticism (contd.). China weekly review 29 : 117-118, 28 June 1924.
Local government- lack of harmony.

QUIGLEY, H.S. : Some aspects of China's constitutional problem. Political science quarterly 39 : 189-200, June 1924.

CONLU, F.V. The new constitution of China - a criticism. China weekly review 29 : 259-260, 26 July 1924.

VISSIÈRE, A. : L'organisation de la république de Chine d'après la Constitution du 10 octobre 1923. Asia française 24 (Supplément No. 11) 13-14, juillet-août 1924.

La constitution chinoise. Asie française 24 (Supplément no. 11) : 5-12, juillet-août 1924.
Text of Chinese constitution - for introduction by André Dubosq see pages 3-4.

CONLU, V.F. : The new constitution of China - a criticism. China weekly review 29 : 364-365, 16 August 1924.
Passing the budget - financial legislation.

CONLU, V.F. : The new constitution of China, a criticism. China weekly review 30 : 15-16, 6 September 1924.
Critical analysis.

QUIGLEY, H.S. : The Chinese constitution. Chinese social and political science review 9 : 88-98, January 1925.

LIAU SCHANG KUO : Von chinesischen Rechts- und Staatstheorien. Zeitschrift für vergleichende Rechtswissenschaft 40 : 135-173, 1. Heft 1925.

La réforme des codes et de l'organisation judiciaire en Chine. Revue politique et parlementaire 124 : 367-386, 10 septembre 1925.

KAWAKAMI, K.K. : China's battle against foreign control. Current history 22 : 911-916, September 1925.

PADOUX, G. : La cour mixte de la Concession internationale de Shanghai. Journal du droit international 52 : 897-917, juillet-août-septembre-octobre 1925.

QUIGLEY, H.S. : China's constitutional problem. China weekly review 34 : 106-110, 3 October 1925.

The Shanghai affair and after. Foreign affairs 4 : 20-34, October 1925.

Why not a "Hague" court for China? China weekly review 34 : 227-228, 7 November 1925.

QUIGLEY, H.S. : Constitutional and political development in China under the republic. Annals 122 : 8-14, November 1925.

TCHANG YAO-TSENG : Condition du système judiciaire chinois et son avenir. Politique de Pékin 12 : 1224-1227, 27 décembre 1925.
Lecture delivered at Peking by President of the extraterritoriality commission.

COMMONWEALTH

La nouvelle constitution de la Rhodésie méridionale. Colonie autonome, our province de l'Union Sud-Africaine? Afrique française 32 : 309-313, juin 1922.

MOORE, D. Gwyther : Notes on the legislation of the Anglo-Egyptian Sudan. Journal of comparative legislation and international law 6 (I) : February 1924.

COLOMBOS, C.J. : The constitution of Malta. Journal of comparative legislation and international law 7 : 91-95, February 1925.

CONGO (KHINSHASA)

SAN, A.E. de : La réorganisation judiciaire au Congo. Notre colonie 4 : 125-132, ler juin 1923.

GIRAULT, A. : Condition juridique des indigènes dans les pays du protectorat. Congo 4 : 413-417, octobre 1923.

CUBA

BETANCOURT Y AGUERO, Sra Laura : Jurisprudencia Cubana sobre derecho internacional. Revista de derecho internacional 2 : 257-265, 30 junio 1923.

CUETO, J.A. del : Fundamentos del proyecto sobre ciudadania cubana y extranjería presentado a la Sección de Derecho Civil de la Comisión Nacional Codificadora de la República de Cuba. Revista de derecho internacional 3 : 289-300, 30 de junio 1924.

CHAPMAN, C.E. : The futility of the law in Cuba. California law review 13 : 193-206, March 1925.

EVERETT, Guerra : Trading under the laws of Cuba. U.S. trade information bulletin No. 343 : 1-70, April 1925.

CZECHOSLOVAKIA

BROZ, A. : The constitution of the Czechoslovak Republic. New Europe 18 : 61-63, April 29 1920.

The Czechosloval constitution. Contemporary review 657 : 412-423, September 1920.

The law of February 29, 1920, whereby the constitutional charter of the Czechoslovak Republic is introduced. International Conciliation 405-408, October 1922.

The Czechoslovak constitution. Contemporary review 118 : 567-574, 733-737, October and November 1920.

WEYR, Franz : Das Verfassungsrecht der tschechoslowakischen Republik. Zeitschrift für öffentliches Recht 2 : 1-38, 1 und 2. Heft, 1921.
Development and basic principles of the Czechoslovak Constitution.

FIELD, B.F. : A study of the constitution. Czechoslovak review 6 : 57-61, March 1922.

BLOCISZEWSKI, J. : La constitution tchécoslovaque. Revue des sciences politiques 45 : 217-247, avril-juin 1922.
Czechoslovakia and the dissolution of the Austro-Hungarian monarchy.

HAYDEN, R. : New European constitutions in Poland, Czechoslovakia and the kindom of the Serbs, Croates and Slovenes. American political science review 16 : 211-227, May 1922.

HOBZA, A. : La République tchécoslovaque et le droit international. Revue générale de droit international public 29 : 385-409, septembre-octobre 1922.
Juridical aspect of the establishment of the Czechosloval Republic.

JOACHIM, V. : Rules of franchise - the constitutional Court. International Conciliation 391 - 404, October 1922.

HOETZL, Dr. Jiré : The definitive constitution of the Czechoslovak Republic. International Conciliation : 379-390, October 1922.

The constitutional charter of the Czechoslovak Republic. International conciliation : 409-447, October 1922.

NATIONAL LAW - COUNTRIES

Act of the 29 February setting forth the constitution and jurisdiction of the Senate. International conciliation : 454-459, October 1922.

PESKA, E. : Le tribunal électoral de la République Tchécoslovaque. Revue de droit publique et de la science politique 40 : 318-335, avril-mai-juin 1923.

ADLER, F. : Politische Gesetzesvorlagen im tschecho-slowakischen Parlamente. Österreichische Volkswirt 16 : 890-892, 19 April 1924.

ADLER, F. : Die Verfassung der Tschechoslovakischen Republik. Der Österreichische Volkswirt 49 : 1490-1493, 6 September 1924.

ADLER, F. : Die Verfassung der Tschechodlovakischen Republik (contd.). Der Österreichische Volkswirt 50 : 1521-1523, 13 September 1924.

ADLER, F. : Das Verhältnis von Völkerrecht und Landesrecht in der Tschechoslawakischen Republik. Prager juristische Zeitschrift 5 : 131-136, Mai 1925.

WEISS, E. : Tschechoslovakei. Der heutige Rechtszustand. Zeitschrift für osteuropäisches Recht 1 : 1-8, Mai 1926.

VERDROSS, A. : Völkerrecht und innerstaatliches Recht im System des tschechoslowakischen Verfassungsrechtes. Prager Juristische Zeitschrift 5 : 130-131, Mai 1925.

URBAN, Johann : Irrwege des tschechischen Staatsgedankens. Zeitschrift für Politik 14 : 515-531, Heft 6, 1925.

LOENING, O. : Die Rechtsentwicklung in der Freien Stadt Danzig. Blätter für vergleichende Rechtswissenschaft und Volkswirtschaftslehre 18 : 151-175, April-Juni 1924.

Die Rechtssprechung des Danziger Obergerichts 1920-1925. Ostrecht 1 : 240-242, Oktober 1925.

DENMARK

STAËL-HOLSTEIN, L. de : La nationalité, son acquisition et sa perte d'après les nouvelles lois scandinaves. Revue de droit international et de législation comparée 52 : 676-685, No. 4-5, 1925.

DOMINICAN REPUBLIC

Saint-Domingue. Loi No. 61 du 31 octobre 1924 sur la naturalisation. (Gaceta oficial, 22 novembre 1924, no. 3596). Revue de droit international privé 20 : 315-316, No. 2, 1925.

ESTHONIA

CLARK, R.T. : Baltic politics. The Esthonian constitution. New Europe 16 : 104-109, August 12, 1920.

The constitution of the Esthonian Republic. Baltic review 1 : 67-70, September 1920.
Passed by the Constituent Assembly on 15 June 1920.

The constitution of the Esthonian Republic (contd.). Baltic review 1 : 111-113, October 1920.
Passed by the Constituent Assembly on 15 June 1920.

CLARK, R.T. : The constitution of Esthonia. Journal of comparative legislation series III, Vol. 3 : 245-250, October 1921.

FRANCE

ARMINJON, Pierre : La fonction judiciaire. Revue de Paris 27 : 598-626, juin 1, 1920.
Organisation of the magistrature in France.

LAURET, Marc : La réforme démocratique de la constitution. Le Parlement et l'opinion 11 : 117-123, 20 janvier 1921.
M. Séailles' program of constitutional reform.

AUDINET, Eugène : La solution des conflits entre la loi française et la loi locale d'Alsace-Lorrane en matière de droit privé. Journal du droit international 48 : 801-813, novembre 1921.

RADONANT, Jean : La condition juridique actuelle des sociétés de commerce en Alsace-Lorraine. Annales de droit commercial 31 : 56-83, janvier-mars 1922.

DUEZ, P. : La théorie générale de la responsabilité de l'Etat et la loi du 3 mai 1921. Revue du droit public et de la science politique 39 : 190-231, avril-mai-juin 1922.

CHÉRON, M. : Le projet d'introduction des lois françaises de procédure civile et commerciale en Alsace et Lorraine. Revue trimestrielle de droit civil 22 : 347-394, avril-juin 1923.

MORELLET, H. : La haute cour de justice et la révision de la constitution. Revue politique et parlementaire 115 : 5-13, 10 juillet 1923.

ECCARD, F. : L'organisation judiciaire en Alsace et en Lorraine. Alsace française 3 : 684-686, 26 juillet 1923.

CHÉRON, M. : De quelques institutions allemandes de procédure maintenues en vigueur par le projet d'introduction des lois françaises. Revue trimestrielle de droit civil 22 : 669-738, juillet-septembre 1923.

RÉGLADE, M. : L'exception d'illégalité en France. Revue du droit public et de la science politique 40 : 393-425, juillet-septembre 1923.

MARIN, P. : Nature du droit des sinistrés immobiliers. (Purge et transcription en matière de dommages de guerre). Revue trimestrielle de droit civil 22 : 661-668, juillet-septembre 1923.

LUCIUS, M. : Y a-t-il lieu de reviser les lois constitutionnelles? Alsace française 3 : 817-820, 8 septembre 1923.

MALBERG, R. Carré de : Y a-t-il lieu de reviser les lois constitutionnelles? Alsace française 6 : 913-917, 6 octobre 1923.

MARCELLIN, L. : Comment la constitution a été faussée. Il y a une responsabilité présidentielle. Opinion 16 : 6-7, 28 décembre 1923.

MORELLET, H. : Pas de réforme de la haute-coeur de justice sans révision. Revue politique et parlementaire 31 : 289-294, 10 février 1924.

CANTALUPO, Roberto : La riforma costituzionale in Francia. Gerarchia 3 : 96-101, febbraio 1924.

BONNET, J.-L. : La révision de la constitution. Le Parlement et l'opinion 14 : 345-356, 20 février 1924.

ROLLAND, Louis : Le projet du 17 janvier et la question "des décrets-lois". Revue du droit public et de la science politique 31 : 42-74, janvier-février-mars 1924.

GOOCH, R.K. : Modern French views on the doctrine of the separation of powers. Political science quarterly 39 : 19-34, March 1924.

ECCARD, F. : L'introduction des lois françaises en Alsace et en Lorraine. Revue politique et parlementaire 31 : 190-203, 10 mai 1924.

WOLF, G. : L'introduction en Alsace des lois républicaines fondamentales. Europe nouvelle 7 : 985-986, 2 août 1924.

HUDDLESTON, Sisley : The "revolt" of Alsace-Lorraine. New statesman 23 : 514-515, August 9, 1924.

HALLAYS, André : En Alsace et en Lorraine. La protestation contre les lois laïques. Revue des deux mondes 94 : 890-908, 15 août 1924.

MAZEAUD, Henri : La maxime "Error communis facit jus". Revue trimestrielle de droit civil 23 : 815-928, octobre-décembre 1924.

BRÄNDI, F. : Rechtsangleichung und Gesetzkollisionen in Elsass-Lothringen. Niemeyers Zeitschrift für internationales Recht 34 : 281-297, 3. bis 6. Heft 1925.

NAST, M. : L'introduction des lois civiles et commerciales françaises en Alsace et Lorraine (Contd.). Journal du droit international 52 : 351-368, mars-avril 1925.

FRANCE
(International Law, Aliens, Nationality)

COURTS, A.L. : Völkerrecht oder französisches Recht? Die Recht sprechung des französisch-deutschen gemischten Schiedsgerichtshofs in Elass-Lothringen-Sachen. Wirtschafts dienst 7 : 3-5, 19-20, 6 und 13 januar 1922.
The judgment of the French-German Mixed Court in matters relating to Alsace-Lorrains.

NEUMEUER, Dr. K. : Die Staatsangehörigkeit juristischer Personen und das gemischte deutsch-französische Schiedsgericht. Zeitschrift für Völkerrecht 12 : 261-275, Heft 3, 1922.

Le décrets du 8 novembre 1921 sur la nationalité d'origine en Tunisie et au Maroc (zone française) devant la Court permanente de Justice internationale. Revue de droit internationale privé 18 : 1-287, No. 1, 1922-1923.

JORDAN, C. : Quelques considérations sur les conditions de l'application aux étrangers de leurs lois nationales en matière d'état et de capacité, et sur le système de renvoi. Revue de dtoit international privé 18 : No. 1922-1923.

Cour Permanente de Justice Internationale. Le différend franco-anglais relatif à la nationalité des étrangers en Tunis et au Maroc. Journal du Droit international 50 : 186-188, janvier-février 1923.
The French and the British point of view - the decision of the Court.

PRUDHOMME, A. : Les étrangers en France et la propriété immobilière. Journal du droit international 50 : 46-54, janvier-février 1923.

Les décrets de nationalité devant la Cour Permanente de Justice Internationale. Afrique française 33 : 86-96, supplément de mars 1923.

PICARD, Maurice : Le différend franco-anglais relatif aux décrets du 8 novembre 1921 sur la nationalité d'origine en Tunisie et au Maroc devant la Cour permanente de Justice internationale de La Haye. Journal du droit international 50 : 256-266, mars-avril 1923.

Cour permanente de Justice internationale de La Haye. Deuxième session (extraordinaire). Journal du droit international 50 : 430-438, mars-avril 1923.
La nationalité en Tunisie.

PRUDHOMME, A. : La perte de la nationalité française et la prise de service militaire en pays étranger. Journal du Droit international 50 : 488-499, mai-juin-juillet 1923.

L'accord franco-britannique sur les décrets de naturalisation. Afrique française 33 : 271-272, juin 1923.

RUZÉ, R. : Le différend franco-britannique au sujet des décrets de nationalité à Tunis et au Maroc (zône française). Revue de Droit international 50 : 597-627, No. 6, 1923.

L'acquisition de la nationalité française. Correspondance d'Orient 16 : 468-471, août 1923.
The jus soli - the Maltese question.

OLIVIERI, A. : La politique française "Terra Clausa". Revue contemporaine 72 : 67-71, 15 janvier 1924.
Summary of M. A. de Monzie's volume "Terra Clausa".

REDSLOB, R. : Le litige franco-britannique sur les décrets de nationalité en Tunisies et au Maroc. Revue de droit international (Genève) 2 : 5-15, janvier-mars 1924.

HUDSON, M.O. : Opinions of the international courts. American Bar Association Journal 10 : 118-119, February 1924.

GOT, A. : L'assimilation des étrangers. Mercure de France 35 : 601-616, 15 mars 1924.

LAFERRIÈRE, M. : Des voies de recours contre les décrets en matière de nationalité. Revue de droit international privé 19 : 161-191, 1924.

NATIONAL LAW - COUNTRIES

METTGENBERG, Dr. W. : Ein französisches Auslieferungsgesetz. Zeitschrift für Völkerrecht 13 : 295-307, Heft 2, 1925.
Will France institute an extradition legislation?

PAULIEN, André et Adrien : The problem of aliens in France. Nineteenth century 97 : 823-834, June 1925.

GERMANY

METTGENBERG, Dr. W. : Die Auslieferung der Mörder des spanischen Ministerpräsidenten Dato durch das Deutsches Reich (Auslieferungsfall Fall). Zeitschrift für Völkerrecht 12 : 300-321, Heft 3, 1922.

Overseas correspondence. Economist 95 : 936-937, November 18 1922.
Ambassador's Conference to protest treatment of Allied citizens in Germany.

Deutsch-polnisches Abkommen über Staatsangehörigkeits-und Optionsfragen 30.8.1924. Niemeyers Zeitschrift für internationales Recht 33 : 296-341, 1. bis 4. Heft 1924/1925.

Optionsabkommen zwischen Deutschland und Belgien 11.9.1922. Niemeyers Zeitschrift für internationales Recht 33 : 201-203, 1. bis 4. Heft, 1924/1925.

SCHULTZE, Dr. E. : Fremdenverkehrspolitik. Deutsche Ökonomist 43 : 197-200, 25 Oktober 1925.
Criticism of present reception of foreigners in Germany.

GERMANY
(International Law and Practice, Aliens, Naturalization)

SHEPARD, W.J. : The new German constitution. American political science review 14 : 34-52, February 1920.

FREUND, E. : The new German constitution. Political science quarterly 35 : 177-203, June 1920.

HELMS, Landesrat : Die neuen Verfassungen der drei Hansestädte. Hanseatische Rechts-Zeitschrift 4 : 339-346, 1 Mai 1921.

CRUSEN, Dr. G. : Blätter für Gesetzeskunde; die Gesätze des neuen deutschen Reichs und der deutschen Länder in kurzgefaszten Inhaltsangaben. Blätter für Gesetzerkunde 3 : 1221-1337, November 1921.

NEUMEUER, Dr. K. : Die Staatsangehörigkeit juristischer Personen und das gemischte deutsch-französiscje Schiedsgericht. Zeitschrift für Völkerrecht 12 : 261-275, Heft 3, 1922.

HIBSCHMAN, H. : The constitution of the German Republic. Current history 16 : 37-41, April 1922.
Summary and analysis.

AUBRY, M. : Chronique constitutionnelle d'Allemagne. Revue du droit public et de la science politique 39 : 593-606, octobre-décembre 1922.

STIER-SOMLO, Fritz : Die Lehre von der Gewaltenteilung und die neuen deutschen Verfassungen. Zeitschrift für die gesamte Staatswissenschaft, Heft 1-2, 1922-1923, pp. 1-51.

Communication de M.E. Chavegrin sur le président de l'Empire allemand d'après la constitution du 11 août 1919. Bulletin mensuel de la Société de Législation comparée 52 : 67-82, janvier-mars 1923.

PREUSS, H. : Reichsverfassungsmässige Diktatur. Zeitschrift für Politik 13 : 97-113, Heft 2, 1923.

WITTMAYER, Leo : Europäische Organisationsfragen der Weimarer Verfassung. Zeitschrift für Politik 13 : 214-247, Heft 3, 1923.
The international importance of the constitutions of individual states.

BALLOT, A. : Le Reich et les "pays" qui le composent. Revue des sciences politiques 46 : 556-569, octobre-décembre 1923.
Structure juridique du Reich d'après la constitution de Weimar.

REDSLOB, R. : Le régime parlementaire en Allemagne. Revue du droit public et de la science politique 40 : 511-559, octobre-décembre 1923.

GIESE, Friedrich : Das kirkenpolitische System der Weimarer Verfassung. Archiv des öffentlichen Rechts 7 : Heft 1, 1-70, 1924.
Church and State and the Weimar constitution.

WITTMAYER, L. : Europäische Organisationsfragen der Weimarer Reichsverfassung. Zeitschrift für Volkswirtschaft und Sozialpolitik 4 : 74-108, 1-3 Heft 1924.

TRIEPEL, H. : Der Föderalismus und die Revision der Weimarer Reichsverfassung. Zeitschrift für Politik 14 : 193-230, Heft 3, 1924.

HOFFMANN, E.H. : Die Stellung des Staatshauptes zur Legislative und Exekutive im Deutschen Reiche und seinen Ländern. Archiv des öffentlichen Rechts 7 : 257-303, Heft 3, 1924.

STIER-SOMLO, F. : Zeitschrift der Erneuerung der Weimarer Reichsverfassung. Zeitschrift für die gesamte Staatswissenschaft 78 : 496-585, 3/4 Heft 1924.

MEHRMANN, Karl : Der deutsche Staat im Kampf um seine Autorität. Deutsche Rundschau 50 : 195-199, Mai 1924.

SCHOEN, P. : Das Verordnungsrecht und die neuen Verfassungen. Archiv des öffentlichen Rechts 6 : 133-192, 1924.
New German constitutions and the right to issue decree laws.

DUQUESNE, J. : La constitution de Weimar et le droit privé. Bulletin de la Société de Legislation comparée 53 : 247-284, juillet-septembre 1924.

HEILE, W. : Das neue deutsche Wahlgesetz. Der Österreichische Volkswirt 51 : 1544-1547, September 20 1924.

WALZ, Dr. G.A. : Die Bedeutung des Art. 4 der Weimarer Reichsverfassung für das nationale Rechtssystem. Zeitschrift für Völkerrecht 13 : 165-193, Heft 2, 1925.

FLEISSNER, H. : Kulturpolitik und Rechsverfassung. Gesellschaft 2 : 144-154, Februar 1925.
Attitude of German constitution towards schools and religion.

NATIONAL LAW - COUNTRIES

FREYTAGH-LORINGHOVEN, A. Freiherr von : Reichsverfassung und Staatspraxis. Zeitschrift für Politik 15 : 223-262, Heft 3, 1925.

THEISEN, E. : Verfassung und Richter. Archiv des öffentlichen Rechts 8 : 257-282, 3. Heft 1925.

FINGER, A. : Der Staatsgerichtshof als Gericht über Anklagen des Reichstags gegen Reichspräsidenten, Reichskanzler, Reichsminister. Archiv des öffentlichen Rechts 9 : 289-313, 3. Heft 1925.

VERMEIL, E. : Le problème des relazions entre le Reich et la Prusse. Bulletin mensuel de la Société de Législation comparée 54 : 286-320, juillet-septembre 1925.

CARRÉ de MALBERG, M.R. : La question de la délégation de puissance législative et les rapports entre la loi et l'ordonnance selon la constitution de Weimar. Bulletin mensuel de la Société de Législation comparée 54 : 321-347, juillet-septembre 1925.

CARRÉ de MALBERG, M.R. : La question de la délégation puissance législative et les rapports entre la loi et l'ordonnance selon la constitution de Weimar (contd.). Bulletin mensuel de la Société de Législation comparée 10-12 : 398-425, octobre-décembre 1925.

CAVARRETTA, G. : La commissione permanente per gli affari esteri nella costituzione tedesca. Rivista di diritto pubblico 17 : 462-471, novembre 1925.

ZORN, Ph. : Locarnopakt und Reichsverfassung. Deutsche Juristenzeitung 30 : 1758-1759, 1 Dezember 1925.

MENDE, Dr. : Völkerbund und Reichsverfassung. Deutsche Juristenzeitung 30 : 1830-1831, 15 Dezember 1925.

GIESE, F. : Entwicklungsmöglichkeiten im Amte des Reichspräsidenten. Wille und Weg 1 : 347-352, No. 14, 1925.

GREAT BRITAIN

Disfranchisement of commercial votes. Chamber of commerce journal 39 : 281, 2 April 1920.

TEMPLE, M. : English justice. Misdemeanour and felony. New world 3 : 236-239, August 1920.

ROBERS, L. : British liberty and arbitrary power. Weekly review 3 : 613-614, 22 December 1920.

Nationality act. Journal of the Parliaments of the Empire 2 : 368-372, May 1921.

Statute codification. Law journal 66 : 360-361, 1 December 1921.
Activities of the legislative authorities in the codification of English Statute law.

POLLOCK, Sir Frederick : Droit privé anglais (1870-1920). Bulletin mensuel de la Société de législation comparée 51 : 128-149, avril-juin 1922.

JENKS, E. et LION, Thérèse : La loi anglaise de 1922 relative au droit de la propriété. Bulletin mensuel de la Société de Législation comparée 52 : 167-194, avril-juin 1923.

HALDANE, Viscount : The judicial committee of the privy council. Empire review 38 : 713-721, July 1923.

A fool-proof constitution. Saturday review 136 : 158, 11 August 1923.

The development of the British constitution Law journal 58 : 393-396, September 1 1923.
Lord Birkenhead's address, 29 August 1923, to American Bar Association.

BIRKENHEAD, Earl of : Development of the British constitution in the last fifty years. American Bar Association journal 9 : 578-582, September 1923.

ALLEN, C.K. : Bureaucracy triumphant. Quarterly review 240 : 261, October 1923.
Lack of administrative law in England.

Constitutional Conservative (pseud.) : The right to advise a dissolution. Spectator 4983 : 1023-1024, December 29, 1923.

The right of dissolution. Nation (London) 34 : 506, 5 January 1924.

KEITH, Professor B. : Notes on imperial constitutional law. Journal of comparative legislation and international law 6 : 135-142, February 1924.
The international status of the Dominions.

ROGERS, L. : The changing English constitution. North American review 219 : 758-768, June 1924.

ATHERLAY-JONES, L.A. : Law reform. Edinburgh review 240 : 112-130, July 1924.
Survey of British judicial system - critics.

GREAT BRITAIN
(International law, Aliens)

ROSCOE, E.S. : The early history of the English prize court. Edinburgh review 237 : 133-140, January 1923.

BELLOT, H.L. : Les développements récents du droit international privé en Engleterre. Journal du droit international 51 : 904-916, juillet-octobre 1924.
Nationalité et naturalisation.

INDIA

MARTIN, P. : Ou en est l'Inde? La nouvelle constitution de l'Inde. Asie française 22 : 197-210, mai 1922.

MESTON, Lord : The new constitution of India. Journal of comparative legislation and international law 5 : 1-16, February 1923.

STRACHEY, J. St. Loe : The Indian crisis. Spectator 4993 : 356-357, 8 March 1924.

O'DWYER, Sir Michael F. : Three years of reform in India: a plea for the Indian masses. Fortnightly review 115 : 353-369, March 1924.

BENNETT, Sir Thomas : A revision of the Indian reform act. Asiatic review 20 : 203-211, April 1924.
Labour government policy and the Indian nationalist claims.

NATIONAL LAW - COUNTRIES

IRELAND

The Irish constitution. New statesman 19 : 312-313, 24 June 1922.

The new Irish constitution. Nation (London) 31 : 431-432, 24 June 1922.

The outlook in Ireland. Spectator 4904 : 773-774, 24 June 1922.

The new Irish constitution. Literary digest 74, No. 1 : 17, 1 July 1922.
American press comment.

Ireland's constitution. Nation (N.Y.) 115 : 102-107, 26 July 1922.
Text of the draft constitution.

MacNEILL, J.G. Swift : Thoughts on the constitution of the Irish Free State. Journal of comparative legislation and international law 5 : 52-62, February 1923.

Ireland - An Australian impression. Round table 52 : 782-794, September 1923.

FIGGIS, Darrell : Ireland and the Privy Council. Fornightly review 114 : 752-765, November 1923.

SAUNDERS, A.F. : The Irish constitution. American political science review 18 : 340-345, May 1924.
What is the legal status of the document?

FIGGIS, Darrell : Irish Free State and the Commonwealth. A question of constitutional status. Empire review 40 : 147-155, August 1924.

ITALY

RADICE, F.R. : Fiume. Anglo-Italian review 1 : 7-14, January 1921.
Comments on D'Annunzio's constitution.

FURST, Henry : D'Annunzio and the City of Dreams. Nineteenth century 89 : 241-252, February 1921.

TAMBARO, Ignazio : Chronique constitutionnelle d'Italie. Revue du droit publique et de la science politique 39 : 584-592, octobre-décembre 1922.
L'abus des décrets lois par le gouvernement.

MARRACINO, Alessandro : La cittadinanza degli italiana all'estero. Problemi italiana 2 : 49-51, 1 gennaio 1933.

SOLMI, Arrigo : Riforma costituzionale. Gerarchia 2 : 1123-1133, Agosto, 1923.
What the Fascisti would like to reform in the Italian constitution.

MEDA, Filippo : La riforma dei codici. Nuova antologia 59 : 304-313, 1 febbraio 1924.

FABBRI, Silene : Alcune considerazioni pratiche sui Consigli Tecnici. Gerarchia 3 : 40-47, gennaio 1924.

FRANSISCI, Pietro de : In tema di "consigli tecnici". Critica fascista 2 : 377-379, 15 Marzo 1924.

GOVI, Mario : La riforma del consiglio di stato. Critica fascista 2 : 417-419, 15 aprile 1924.
History of the council.

TONELLI, Fabio : Gli enti locali nello stato fascista. Critica fascista 2 : 415-416, 15 aprile 1924.
Discussion of the revision of the communal and provincial law, December 1923.

JAPAN

Legal procedure in Japan. Japan chronicle No. 1343 : 395-397, March 22, 1923.

Dangerous thoughts bill. Japan chronicle 1291 : 425, March 23, 1922.
Text of the bill as approved by a Committee of the House of Peers.

The thought subjugation bill. Government versus popular opinion. Japan chronicle 1292 : 469-470, March 30, 1922.
Press comment on the Dangerous Thoughts bill.

The House of Peers. Japan chronicle 1161 : 459-April 3, 1924.

Composition of the House of Peers - comparison between English House of Lords and Japanese House of Peers.

"Dangerous thought" in Japan. Contemporary review 121 : 788-791, June 1922.
Text of the "Dangerous Thought Bill", with comment.

Editorial paragraphs. Weekly review of the Far East 20 : 122, 25 March 1922.
Text of the Government Anti-Bolshevik Bill.

Law in Formosa. Japan weekly chronicle 1180 : 214-215, August 14 1924.
Severe criticism of the application of the peace police law by Japanese authorities in Formosa.

LATVIA

Text of Latvia's constitution. Current history 17 : No. 3, 486-489, December 1922.

POLLOCK, James K. jr. : The constitution of Latvia. Journal of comparative legislation and international law, 3rd series, vol. 5, 311-312, November 1923.

Costituzione della repubblica Lettone. L'Europe orientale 4 : 623-627, dicembre 15 1924.

GIANNINI, A. : La costituzione Lettone. L'Europe orientale 4 : 607-622, dicembre 15 1924.

LITHUANIA

The provisional constitution of Lithuania. Baltic Review 1 : 383, April 1921.

LAMMERS, Dr. : Die Verfassung des Litanischen Staates deutsche Juristen Zeitung 19-20 : 615-617, October 1 1922.

CLEVEN, N.A.N. : Religious aspects of Mexico's constitution. Current history 16 : 12-16, April 1922.

GAITHER, R.B. : The corporation law of Mexico. Virginia law review 9 : 41-50, November 1922.
Article 27 of the new constitution and its consequences.

NATIONAL LAW - COUNTRIES

MEXICO

CLEVEN, N.A.N. : Religious aspects of Mexico's constitution. Current history 16 : 12-16, April 1922.
The position of the Church under the new constitution.

GAITHER, R.B. : The corporation law of Mexico. Virginia law review 9 : 41-50, November 1922.

GONZALEZ ROA, Fernand : The constitutionality of the subsoil. Inter-America 7 : 10-23, October 1923.

MOROCCO

RUZÉ, R. : Le différend franco-britannique au sujet des décrets de nationalité à Tunis et au Maroc (zône française). Revue de droit international 50 : 597-627, No. 6, 1923.

REDSLOB, R. : Le litige franco-britannique sur les décrets de nationalité en Tunisie et au Maroc. Revue de droit international (Genève) 2 : 5-15, janvier-mars 1924.

HUDSON, M.O. : Opinions of the international courts. American Bar Association Journal 10 : 118-119, February 1924.

PALESTINE

BENTWICH, N. : The law and the courts of Palestine. Cambridge law journal 2 : 37-50, No. 1, 1924.

Palestine citizenship order 1925. New Judaea 1 : 404-405, 4 August 1925.
Text in English.

PHILIPPINE ISLANDS

MALCOLM, G.A. : The Malolos constitution. A Filipino attempt at constitution-making. Political science quarterly 36 : 91-103, March 1921.
History and summary of the Malolos constitution of 1898, with comment.

MELENCIO, J.P. : The constitution of the Philippine Islands. Journal of comparative legislation third series, vol. 3 : 178-183, October 1921.

CONLU, F.V. : The constitution of China and the constitutional law of the Philippines. China weekly review 26 : 11-14, 55, 90-92, September 1, 8 and 15, 1923.

POLAND

Le droit international privé en Pologne. Bulletin de l'institut intermédiaire international 2 : 422, avril 1920.
Confusion in Poland owing to the existence of several codes.

KOHN, A. : Die neue Verfassung der polnischen Republik vom 17 März 1921. Zeitschrift für öffentliches Recht 2 : 419-438, Heft 3-4, 1921.

Constitution of the Republic of Poland. N.Y. times current history 14 : 358-367, May 1921.

MERLAY, Michel : La nouvelle constitution polonaise. Grande revuew 25 : 659-663, juin 1921.

BLOCIOZEWSKI, J. : La constitution polonaise du 17 mars 1921. Revue des sciences politiques 45 : 28-58, janvier-mars 1922.

HAYDEN, R. : New European constitutions in Poland, Czechoslovakia and the Kingdom of the Serbs, Croates and Slovenes. American political science review 16 : 211-227, May 1922.

GOLAB, Dr. S. : The codification of Polish law. Journal of comparative legislation and international law, 6 (I) : 95-109, February 1924.

MONTFORT, de H. : La législation sociale polanaise. L'Europe nouvelle 7 : 1710-1711, décembre 20 1924.

Deutsch-polnisches Abkommen über Staatsangehörigkeits-und Optionsfragen, 30.8.1924. Niemeyers Zeitschrift für internationales Recht 33 : 296-341, 1. bis 4. Heft, 1924/1925.

PORTUGAL

MEREA, P. : Die Erforschung der nationalen Rechtsgeschichte in Portugal. Zeitschrift für vergleichende Rechtswissenschaft 40 : 339-354, 2. bis 3. Heft, 1923.

RUMANIA

Législation roumaine en matière de prises maritimes. Bulletin de l'institut intermédiaire international 5 : 326-361, octobre 1921.

FLORESCO, J.T. : L'unification législative en Roumanie. Bulletin mensuel de la Société de législation comparée 53 : 181-189, avril-juin 1924.
L'organisation du corps des avocats et la nouvelle réforme judiciaire.

SWITZERLAND

SCHINDLER, Dietrich : The administration of justice in the Swiss federal court in intercantonal disputes. American journal of international law 15 : 149-188, April 1921.

SCHUSTER, E.J. : The Swiss civil code. Journal of comparative legislation and international law, 3rd series, vol 5 : 216-226, November 1923.

NINCK, V. : Den schweiziska kulturblandningen med hänsyn till pacifismen. Forum No. 9 : 552-563, november 1923.

CHESHIRE, F.M. : Direct democracy as seen in Switzerland. Young men of India 35 : 274-284, May 1924.

BODOR, F. : Das Individuelle in der Schweizerischen Verfassung. Kelet Nepe No. 12-14 : 39-45, September 1924.

NATIONAL LAW - COUNTRIES

SWITZERLAND
(International Law, Aliens)

SAUSER-HALL : La situation juridique des étrangers en Suisse. Bulletin mensuel de la Société de Législation comparée 50 : 6-45, janvier-mars 1921.

BURCKHARDT, W. : Zur Revision der Niederlassungs-vertrage. Schweizerische Monatshefte für Politik und Kultur 1 : 241-246, September 1921.

ZOPFI, H. : Schweizerische Umschau. Schweizerische Monatsheft 2 : 140-142, Juni 1922.
Naturalisation and deportation.

WYLER, Dr. J. : Die schweizerische Einbürgerungsreform im Lichte der Statistik. Zeitschrift für schweizerische Statistik und Volkswirtschaft 59 : 355-362, No. 4, 1923.
Statistical examination of latest federal reform concerning the naturalisation of aliens.

Décision du tribunal fédéral suisse, du 2 février 1923, concernant la convention de La Haye du 17 juillet 1905 relative à la procédure civile. Bulletin de l'institut intermédiaire international 9 : 31-50, juillet 1923.

WETTSTEIN, Dr. O. : La naturalisation des étrangers en Suisse. Bibliothèque universelle 129 : 257-267, mars 1924.

THAILAND

CHARUVASTRA, Chune : Note sur l'administration de la justice au Siam. Bulletin mensuel de législation comparée 52 : 110-112, janvier-mars 1923.

TUNISIA

Les décrets du 8 novembre 1921 sur la nationalité d'origine en Tunisie et au Maroc (zone française) devant la Cour permanente de justice internationale. Revue de droit international privé 18 : 1-287, No. 1, 1922-1923.

Cour permanente de Justice internationale. Le différend franco-anglais relatif à la nationalité des étrangers en Tunis et au Maroc. Journal du droit international 50 : 186-188, janvier-février 1923.

BERGNER, Georges : Les Maltais en Tunisie. Alsace française 5 : 252-254, 17 mars 1923.

TUMEDEI, C. : La Corte dell'Aja e la nazionalità in Tunisia. Politica 14 : 277-285, 31 marzo 1923.
The origin and importance of the question.

Les décrets de nationalité devant la Cour permanente de Justice international. Afrique française 33 : 86-96, supplément de mars 1923.

PICARD, Maurice : Le différend franco-anglais relatif aux décrets du 8 novembre 1921 sur la nationalité d'origine en Tunisie et au Maroc devant la Cour permanente de Justice internationale de La Haye. Journal du droit international 50 : 256-266, mars-avril 1923.

Cour permanente de Justice internationale de La Haye. Deuxième session (extraordinaire). Journal du droit international 50 : 430-438, mars-avril 1923.
Avis consultatif du 7 février sur la question de la nationalité en Tunisie.

RUZE, R. : Le différend franco-britannique au sujet des décrets de nationalité à Tunis et au Maroc (zône française). Revue de droit international 50 : 597-627, No. 6, 1923.

L'accord franco-britannique sur les décrets de naturalisation. Afrique française 33 : 271-272, juin 1923.

Accordo tra la Francia e la Gran Bretagna relative alla questione dei decreti sulla cittadinanza francese in Tunisia. Rivista di diritto internazionale 15 : 340-342, 1 luglio 1923.

NOBILI, Massuero F. : La nuova fase della questione Tunisina. Politica 5 : 54-73, 31 luglio 1923.
French policy - decision of the League Council and the Permanent Court.

Il progetto per l'acquisito della nazionalità francese in Tunisia. Problemi italiana 2 : 241-249, 15 agosto 1923.

L'acquisition de la nationalité française. Correspondence d'Orient 16 : 468-471, août 1923.
The jus soli - the Maltese question.

HUDSON, M.A. : Opinions of the international courts. American Bar Association journal 10 : 118-119, February 1924.

TURKEY

Le statut anatolien, dispositions fondamentales. Economiste d'Orient 32 : 432-433, 10 novembre 1922.

The sacred law in Turkey. Near East 23 : 13 January 4, 1923.
How the courts administer the law.

Der türkische Nationalpakt vom 28 Januar 1920. Welt des Islams 8 : 16-17, Heft 1, 1923.
French text of the National Pact.

Das türkische Verfassungsgesetz von 20 Januar 1921. Welt des Islams 8 : 18-20, Heft 1, 1923.

PERNOT, M. : La nouvelle Turquie. Du sultanat à la république. Revue des deux mondes 19 : 288-322, 15 janvier 1924.

GOADBY, F.M. : Notes on the law of delicts in the Mejelle. Egypte contemporaine 15 : 493-509, novembre-décembre 1924.

TURKEY
(International Law, Aliens)

MESTRE, A. : L'étranger en Turquie d'après le traité de Lausanne. Revue politique et parlementaire 116 : 179-206, août 1923.

MESTRE, A. : La nouvelle situation juridique de l'étranger en Turquie. Europe nouvelle 6 : 978-979, 4 août 1923.

NATIONAL LAW - COUNTRIES

TÉNÉKIDÈS, C.G. : Contribution à l'étude du régime post-capitulaire en Turquie. Journal du droit international 51 : 339-351, mars-avril 1924.

Foreigners in Turkey. Near East 25 : 376, April 10 1924.

COHEN, A. : L'exécution des jugements étrangers en Turquie. Revue de droit international privé 19 : 434-442, 1924.

U.S.S.R.

Soviet law of marriage and the family. Contemporary review 652 : 571-588, April 1920.

Justice under Bolshevism. Contemporary review 655 : 124-132, July 1920.

A comparison of the responsibility of governors to the governed under Russian Sovietism and American democracy. Advocate of peace 82 : 240-241, July 1920.

CARTER, Allan J. : The Bolshevist substitute for a judicial system. Illinois Law Review 16 : 345-360, January 1922.

VRISSON, I.S. : The new civil and criminal legislation of Soviet Russia Manchester guardian commercial reconstruction in Europe No. 3 XXXII, June 15, 1922.

Property rights in Soviet Russia. Nation (N.Y.) 115 : 132. August 2, 1922.
Text of law adopted on May 22, 1922.

EPSTEIN, A. : The judicial system of Russia. The Nation (N.Y.) 115 : 315-318, September 27 1922.

PIERRE, André : La nouvelle législation russe. Europe nouvelle 5 : 1551-1553, 9 décembre 1922.
The new labour code - the agrarian code - the civil code.

Russia's law courts. Russian information and review 2 : 429-430, April 14, 1923.

Décrets et résolutions de la RSFSR, depuis 1917. Bulletin de l'Institut intermédiaire international 8 : 345-385, avril 1923.

PILENCO, Al. : La fédération soviétique. Revue générale de droit international public 30 : 223-241, mai-août 1923.

HALPERN, A.J. : The civil code of the Russian socialist soviet republic. Russian economist 3; 3233-3242, January-June 1923.
Criticism of the civil code published November 25, 1922, and coming into force on January 1, 1923.

KANTOROVITCH, Jacob : The civil code of Soviet Russia. Yale law journal 32 : 778-783, June 1923.

JIMASCHEFF, N.V. : Das neue russische Zivilgesetzbuch. Prager juristische Zeitschrift 3 : 208-211, Juli-August 1923.

NODLE, Baron B. : Le code civil de la république des Soviets. Bulletin mensuel de la Société de Législation comparée 52 : 231-257, juillet-septembre 1923.

Constitution of the Union of Socialist Soviet Republics. Russian information and review 3 : 37-41, July 21, 1923.

Décrets et résolutions de la RSFSR. Bulletin de l'institut intermédiaire international 9 : 173-201, juillet 1923.

La nouvelle constitution russe. Europe nouvelle 6 : 1153-1157, 8 septembre 1923.

Russia's new constitution. Nation (N.Y.) 117 : 173-176, August 15 1923.

The Moscow provincial court. Russian information and review 3 : 187-188, September 22, 1923.

La CHESNAIS, P.G. : Le droit et les institutions de la Russie soviétique. Action nationale 21 : 169-173, septembre 1923.

TAGER, P. et ELIACHEFF, B. : Notes sur la Russie. Le code civil et la législation ouvrière des Soviets. Revue d'économie politique 37 : 692-711, septembre-octobre 1923.

ENGLÄNDER, H. : Das neue bürgerliche Gesetzbuch der russischen Republik. Berichte aus den neuen Staaten 6 : 1129-1131, 5 Oktober 1923.

Décrets et résolution de la RSFSR. (Suite). 1922. Bulletin de l'Institut intermédiaire international 9 : 399-415, octobre 1923.

Die grundlegenden Bestimmungen des bürgerlichen Gesetzbuches der RSFSR. Aus de Volkwirtschaft der RSFSR. Ergänzungheft : 34-38, 1923.

KOMAR, Bo. M. : The federal constitution of Soviet Russia. Columbia law review 24 : 36-53, January 1924.

ENGLÄNDER, H. : Die Bundesverfassung. Zeitschrift für öffentliches Recht 4 : 58-79, Heft 1 und 2., 1924.
Analysis of Russian Soviet constitution.

MARTCHENKO : La nouvelle législation en Russie soviétique examinée par rapport à celle de la France et des pays occidentaux. Revue d'histoire diplomatique 38 : 170-181, avril-juin 1924.

Loi fondamentale (constitution) de la fédération des rébubliques soviétiques socialistes. Bulletin de l'Institut intermédiaire international 10 et 11 : 432-434 et 27-39, avril et juillet 1924.

KOMAR, B.M. : The legal system of Soviet Russia. American bar association journal 10 : 349-354, May 1924.

BRANDENBURGSKI, J. : Die Sowjetgerichtsbarkeit im 6. jahr der Oktoberrevolution. Das neue Russland 1-2 : 13-15, Mai-Juni 1924.

KOMAR, B.M. : The legal system of Soviet Russia (Contd.). American bar association journal 10 : 434-438, June 1924.

KELLEY, R.F. : Political organisation of the Soviet power. Annals 114 : 62-69, July 1924.

La nuova costituzione dei soviety. Politica 20 : 104-117, 31 luglio - 31 agosto 1924.

SEMENOFF, G. : Russlands föderatives System. Das neue Russland, Heft 7-8, 31-33, November-Dezember 1924.

U.S.S.R.
(International Law and Practice, Aliens and Naturalization)

LENZ, G. : Die völkerrechtliche Stellung der U.d.S.S.R. Das neue Russland 3-4 : 7-11, Juli-August 1924.

PIRONE, M. : I recenti trattati dell'Italia e della Gran Bretagna con la Rùssia sovietista. Vita italiana 24 : 273-280, Novembre 15, 1924.

United Arab Republic

GAUTERO, Franco : Quelques réflexions sur le projet de code pénal égyptien. L'Egypte contemporaine 11 : 1-24, janvier 1920.

HABASHY, Aziz : Notes on the merits and demerits of the draft penal code. L'Egypte contemporaine 11 : 25-46, janvier 1920.

Draft laws for reconstituting the mixed courts. L'Egypte contemporaine 12 : 254-259, mars 1921.
English and French text of chapter VII, powers of consuls.

Draft laws for reconstituting the united courts. L'Egypte contemporaine 11, mars 1920.

FORGEUR, Adrien : De la préemption en droit égyptien. L'Egypte contemporaire 51 : 301-336, avril 1920.

FORGEUR, Adrien : De la préemption en droit égyptien. (Suite et fin). L'Egypte contemporaire 52 : 361-383, mai 1920.

ARMINGJON, Pierre : Note sur le projet de code pénal. L'Egypte contemporaire 52 : 384-409, mai 1920.
Note on Section II - Breaches of public law.

MESINA, Salvatore : Les lacunes de la loi en droit égyptien mixte. L'Egypte contemporaine 12 : 353-384, mai 1921.

BLANCHARD, G. : Le régime des capitulations et les tribunaux mixtes en Egypte. Afrique française, supplément de juin 1922, 157-167.
The history and character of the Egyptian capitulations - the Mixed Tribunals, etc.

Loi egyptien prorogeant les pouvoirs des juridictions mixtes à l'égard des nationaux français et hellenes. Bulletin de l'institut intermédiaire international 7 : 141-142, juillet 1922.

Criminal jurisdiction - Civil jurisdiction - Mixed jurisdiction. Near East 22 : 429-430, October 5, 1922.
Statistical report on activity of courts.

The new Egyptian constitution. Near East 22 : 637-628, November 16, 1922.

MESSINA, M. S. : Les sources du droit égyptien mixte. Egypte contemporaine 13 : 549-583, décembre 1922.

Die ägyptische Verfassung vom 19-4-1923. Niemeyers Zeitschrift für internationales Recht 31 : 73-85, Heft 1-4, 1923.
Text in French.

Egypt's new constitution. Near East 23 : 426, April 26, 1923.

Rescrit royal No. 42 de 1923. Rescrit établissant le régime constitutionnel de l'état égyptien. Egypte contemporaine No. 72 : VI-XXX, avril 1923.

La constitution égyptienne. Afrique française 33 : 220-221, avril 1923.

The struggle round the constitution. Near East 23 : 444, 3 May 1923.

Egypt's constitution. Near East 23 : 471, May 10, 1923.

Constitutional reform in Egypt. New age 33 : 70, 31 May 1923.

La constitution égyptienne. Afrique française, supplément de mai 1923, pp. 167-177, mai 1923.

La nouvelle loi électorale et la question de la nationalité égyptienne. Journal du Droit international 50 : 742-743, mai-juin-juillet 1923.

McILWRAITH, Sir Malcolm : Notes on Egyptian law. Assize courts in Egypt. Journal of comparative legislation and international law, 3rd series, vol. 5 : 270-273, November 1923.

SCHEMEIL, Raymond : Chronique judiciaire des tribunaux mixtes. La jurisprudence en 1921-1923. Egypte contemporaine 14 : 604-615, décembre 1923.

BENTWICH, Norman : The constitution of Egypt. Journal of comparative legislation and international law 6 : 41-49, February 1924.

MESSINA, Salvatore : Les sources du droit égyptien mixte. Egypte contemporaine 15 : 293-371, avril 1924.

McILWRAITH, M. : The law of modern Egypt. The Near East 26 : August 28 - 221-224, and September 4 - 247-248, 1924.

U.S.A.

A comparison of the responsibility of governors to the governed under Russian Sovietism and American democracy. Advocate of peace 82 : 240-241, July 1920.

POWELL, T.R. : The supreme court and the constitution. Political science quarterly 35 : 411-439, September 1920.

CORWIN, E.S. : Constitutional law in 1920-1921. The constitutional decisions of the Supreme Court of the United States in the October term, 1920. American political science review 16 : 22-40, February 1922.

CORWIN, E.S. : Constitutional law in 1919-1920. American political science review 14 : 635-658, November 1920.

U.S. (pseud) : The U.S. constitution and the Senate. Saturday review 131 : 85-86, January 29, 1921.

NATIONAL LAW - COUNTRIES

The political function of the Supreme Court. New republic 29 : 236-238, January 25, 1922.

SPRING, Samuel : A new constitution. Yale review 11 : 574-592, April 1922.

SEVERANCE, C.A. : The proposal to make Congress supreme. American bar association journal 8 : 459-464, August 1922.

BROWN, G.S. : The new "bill of rights" amendment. Virginia law review 9 : 14-24, November 1922.

CORWIN, E.S. : Constitutional law in 1921-1922. American political science review 16 : 612-639, november 1922.

STANGELAND, C.E. : Geist und Zukunft der amerikanischen Verfassung. Zeitschrift für Politik 13 : 41-64, Heft 1, 1923.

Communication de M. Lepaulle sur l'unification des droits aux Etats-Unis. Bulletin mensuel de la Société de Législation comparée 52 : 89-109, janvier-mars 1923.

BAKER, F.E. : Our American constitution. American bar association journal 9 : 142-144, March 1923.

American law institute is organized. American bar association journal 9 : 137-141, March 1923.
First step in movement to simplify the law.

CORWIN, E.S. : The spending power of congress - apropos the maternity act. Harvard law review 36 : 548-582, March 1923.

DODD, W.F. : The growth of national power. Yale law journal 32 : 452-459, March 1923.

BUTLER, R.C. : Super-supreme law. Illinois law review 17 : 567-577, April 1923.

LAMBERT, E. : Les tendances à l'unification du droit aux Etats-Unis. Bulletin mensuel de la société de législation comparée 52 : 135-165, avril-juin 1923.
Constitutional obstacles to unification.

The supreme court of the United States. Mr. Beck's lecture at Gray's Inn. The law journal 58 : 282-284, June 30, 1923.

STONE, H.F. : The significance of a restatement of the law. Proceedings of the academy of political science 10 : 3-6, July 1923.

PARKINSON, T.I. : The relation of administrative procedure to the restatement and clarification of the law. Proceedings of the academy of political science 10 : 35-46, July 1923.

OLIPHANT, HERMAN and LLEWELLYN, Karl NICKERSON : The relation of current economic and social problems to the restatement of the law. Proceedings of the academy of political science 10 : 17-34, July 1923.

LEWIS, W.D. : The restatement of the law by the American Law Institute. Proceedings of the academy of political science 10 : 7-16, July 1923.

HART, J. : Ordinance-making powers of the president. North American review 218: 59-66, July 1923.

HOLLANDER, J.H., HALE, R.L. and LEWISOHN, S.A. : Discussion of the restatement and clarification of the law. Proceedings of the academy of political science 10 : 47-58, July 1923.

POUND, Cuthbert W. : Constitutional aspects of American administrative law. American bar association journal 9 : 409-416, August 1923.

Our chaos of laws. A movement for order and simplicity. American review of reviews 68 : 191-192, August 1923.

NORTON, T.J. : The Supreme Court's five to four decisions. American bar association journal 9 : 417-420, August 1923.

ROSENBERRY, M.B. : Development of the federal idea. North American review 218 : 145-169, August 1923.

Remaking the constitution. Nation (N.Y.) 107 : 286, 19 September 1923.

BARRATT, J.A. : The tendency to unification of law in the United States, 1868-1922. Journal of comparative legislation and international law, 3rd series, vol. 5 : 227-233, November 1923.

LANIER, A.S. : Congress and the Supreme Court. North American review 218 : 577-588, November 1923.

CUSHMAN, R.E. : Constitutional law in 1926-1927. The constitutional decisions of the Supreme Court of the United States in the October term 1926. American political science review 22 : 70-107, February 1928.

NORTON, T.J. : What damage have five to four decisions done? American bar association journal 9 : 721-727, November 1923.

CLARKE, J.J. : The "new federalist series". Judicial power to declare legislation unconstitutional. American bar association journal 9 : 689-692, November 1923.

BROWN, G.S. : The perpetual covenant in the constitution. North American review 219 : 30-40, January 1924.

DRIPPS, R.D. : The Constitution of the American Citizen unafraid. North American review 219 : 187-192, February 1924.

CORWIN, E.S. : Constitutional law in 1922-1923. American political science review 18 : 49-78, February 1924.

WARREN, B.W. : Destroying our "indestructible states". Atlantic monthly 133 : 370-378, March 1924.

HASHAGEN, J. : Zur Entstehungsgeschichte der nordamerikanischen Erklärungen der Menschenrechte. Zeitschrift für die gesamte Staatswissenschaft 78 : 461-495, 3. bis 4. Heft 1924.

SMITH, F. D. : Decisive battles of constitutional law. American bar association journal 10 : 343-346, May 1924.

SMITH, F. D. : Decisive battles of constitutional law (Contd.). American bar association journal 10 : 405-407, June 1924.

NATIONAL LAW - COUNTRIES

FRANKFURTER, Felix, and LANDIS, J.M. : Power of congress over procedure in criminal contempt in "inferior" federal courts. Harvard law review 37 : 1010-1058, June 1924.

SMITH, F.D. : Decisive battles of constitutional law (Contd.). American bar association journal 10 : 505-510, July 1924.

ROSENBERRY, M.B. : Law and the changing order. North American review 824 : 18-30, September 1924.

The red terror of judicial reform. New republic 40 : 110-113, 1 October 1924.

BERDAHL, C.A. : La désignation des candidats à la présidence aux Etats Unis. Revue du droit public et de la science politique 31 : 541-571, octobre-novembre-décembre 1924.

MONROE, A.H. : The supreme court and the constitution. American political science review 18 : 737-759, November 1924.

U.S.A.
(International Law, Aliens, Nationality)

The Anderson decision. New republic 23 : 189-191, July 14 1920.

Amendment, California alien land law, adopted November 2, 1920. Annals (Phil) 93 : 13-16, January 1921.

California's alien land law. N.Y. Times current history 13, pt. 2 : 119-120, January 1921.
Text of the anti-alien land-leasing law.

MALCOLM, R. : American citizenship and the Japanese. Annals (Phil) 93 : 77-81, January 1921.

WRIGHT, Q. : Tho control of foreign relations. American political science review 15 : 1-26, February 1921.

FLOURNOY, R.W. : Dual nationality and election (Contd.). Yale Law journal 30 : 693-709, May 1921.

FLOURNOY, R.W. : Naturalization and expatriation. Yale law review 31 : 702-719, May 1922.

FLOURNOY, R.W. : Naturalization and expatriation. Yale law review 31 : 848-868, June 1922.

PERRY, S.H. : The treaty-making power. North American review 216 : 32-40, July 1922.
A study of the treaty-making machinery.

SCOTT, J.B. : The decision in California relating to the holding of land by Japanese. American journal of international law 16 : 420-423, July 1922.

HARRISON, M.E. : Legal aspects of alien land legislation on the Pacific coats. American bar association journal 8 : 467-469, August 1922.

Naturalization in America. Japan chronicle 1327 : 700-701, November 30, 1922.
Japanese press comment on the decision of the Supreme Court excluding Asiatics from citizenship.

REEVES, J.S. : Nationality of married women. American journal of international law 17 : 97-100, January 1923.

CHAMBERLAIN, J.F. : Married women's naturalization act. American bar association journal 9 : 57-58, January 1923.

An act relative to the naturalisation and citizenship of married women. American journal of international law, supplement 17 : 52-53, January 1923.

An act relative to the naturalisation and citizenship of married women. Columbia law review 23 : 180-182, February 1923.

CRANE, R.N. : Naturalization and citizenship of married women in the United States. Journal of comparative legislation and international law 5 : 47-51, February 1923.

UNDERWOOD, J.J. : Japanese and Hindus ineligible for U.S. citizenship. Weekly review 24 : 6-7, March 3, 1923.

SCOTT, J.B. : Japanese and Hindu naturalization in the United States. American journal of international law 17 : 328-330, April 1923.

MALCOLM, R. : Problem of American-born Japanese. Current history 17, No. 1 : 109-112, April 1923.
The constitutional right of citizenship of all born of American soil.

THOMPSON, L.L. : State sovereignty and the treaty-making power. California law review 11 : 242-258, May 1923.

Does the eighteenth amendment violate international law? Yale law journal 33 : 72-78, November 1923.

FLOURNOY, R.W. jr. : The new married women's citizenship law. Yale law journal 33 : 159-170, December 1923.

WALSH, T.J. : The red deportations of 1920. New republic 37 : 340-341, February 20, 1924.

MacNAIR, H.F. : Chinese acquisition of American nationality. China weekly review 29 : 115-116, June 28, 1924.

TANSILL, C.C. : The treaty-making powers of the Senate. American journal of international law 18 : 459-483, July 1924.

GARNER, J.W. : Recent decisions of the United States supreme court affecting the rights of aliens. Journal of comparative legislation and international law 6 : 210-214, November 1924.

VIET-NAM

La réforme de la justice indigène au Tonkin. Asie française 24 : 29-31, janvier 1924.
Discours de M. Monguillot.

YUGOSLAVIA

Yugoslav unity. Near East 20 : 18, 7 July 1921.
Comment on the new constitution.

MOUSSET, A. : La constitution yougoslave. L'Europe nouvelle 4 : 981-982, 30 juillet 1921.

La constitution du royaume des Serbes, Croates et Slovènes. L'Europe nouvelle 4 : 987-991, 30 juillet 1921.

La constitution du royaume des Serbes, Croates et Slovènes. Texte officiel intégral (suite et fin). L'Europe nouvelle 4 : 1021-1027, 6 août 1921.

Constitution making in Jugoslavia. Eastern Europe 5 : 357-361, August 1921.

The Jugoslav constitution. Current history 15 : 832-847, February 1922.

HAYDEN, R. : New European constitutions in Poland, Czechoslovakia and the Kingdom of the Serbs, Croates and Slovenes. American political science review 16 : 211-227, May 1922.

ROUGIER, A. : La constitution du Royaume serbe, croate, slovène. Bibliothèque universelle 106 : 337-347, juin 1922.

BLOCISZEWSKI, J. : La constitution yougoslave du 28 juin 1921. Revue des sciences politiques 45 : 522-554, octobre-décembre 1922.

PITAMIC, L. : Die Verfassung des Konigreiches des Serben, Kroaten und Slovenen. Zeitschrift für öffentliches Recht 3 : 1-2, 1922.

The Jugoslav constitution. Slavonic review 3 : 166-178, June 1924.

NATIONAL LAW - COUNTRIES

AFGHANISTAN

Le CONTE, R. : L'organisation politique de l'Afghanistan. Revue du droit public et de la science politique 36 : 330-346, avril-juin 1929.

ARGENTINE

RIVAROLA, R. : Los principios de ética política en la organización constitucional argentina. Revista argentina de ciencias politicas 31 : 329-339, 12 de enero; 32 : 329-343, 12 de julio, y 32 : 7-16, 12 de octubre 1926.

RIVAROLA, R. : Los principios de ética política en la organización constitucional argentina (contd.). Revista argentia de ciencias politicas 33 : 12 de enero de 1927.

RIVAROLA, R. : Los principios de ética política en la organización constitucional argentina (contd.). Revista argentina de ciencias politicas 34 : 5-13, 12 de abril de 1927.

CILÉA, D. : Per l'italianità in Argentina - i figli d'italiani, le naturalizzazione degli italiani. Rivista di politica economica 17 : 447-449, 30 maggio 1927.

DEMOGUE, R. : Organisation judiciaire de la République argentine. Bulletin mensuel de la société de législation comparée 56 : 195-206, avril-juin 1927.

RIVAROLA, R. : Principios de ética política en la organización constitucional argentina (contd.). Revista argentina de ciencias politicas 35 : 18-37, 12 de octubre 1927.

RIVAROLA, R. : Los principios de ética política (contd.). Revista argentina de ciencias politicas 18 : 317-356, 12 de enoro de 1928.

AUSTRALIA

GIBLIN, L.F. : Federation and finance. Economic record 2 : 145-160, November 1926.

FOENANDER, O.R. : The new conciliation and arbitration act in Australia. International labour review 19 : 151-174, February 1929.

BAILLEY, K.H. : The constitution of the Commonwealth. Economic record 5 : 289-299, November 1929.

AUSTRIA

ADAMOVITCH, L. : Die Reform der österreichischen Bundesverfassung. Zeitschrift für öffentliches Recht 5 : 228-280, 1 Januar 1926.

WITTMAYER : Die österreichische Verfassungs-und Verwaltungsreform. Deutsche Juristen-Zeitung 31 : 483-487, 1 April 1926.

GALLAIX, de : Quelques observations sur le code civil autrichien révisé. Bulletin mensuel de la Société de Législation comparée 55 : 501-530, octobre-décembre 1926.

WITTMAYER, L. : Oesterreichs Verfassungsentwicklung. Ein Beitrag zur Anschlussfrage. Zeitschrift für die gesamte Staatswissenschaft 83 : 449-473, Heft 3, 1927.

ADAMOVITCH, L. : Der Kremsierer Entwurf und die österreichische Bundesverfassung. Zeitschrift für öffentliches Recht 6 : 561-571, 1 Juli 1927.

EISENMANN, Ch. : Dix ans d'histoire constitutionelle autrichienne (1918-1928). Revue du droit public et de la science politique 35 : 54-122, janvier-février-mars 1928.

RATZENHOFER, G. : Die privatrechtliche Gesetzgebung Österreichs in der Zeit vom 1 März 1927 bis 31 März 1928. Zeitschrift für ausländisches und internationales Privatrecht 2 : 612-637, Heft 4-5, 1928.

METALL, R.A. : Das neue österreichische Gesetz vom 18 April 1928 über den Erwerb des Eigentums und unbeweglichem Sachen durch Ausländer. Gesetzgebung und Rechtspraxis des Auslandes 4 : 119-121, August 1928.

KLUCKI, L. : Das wirtschaftliche Assoziationswesen in Oesterreich (Contd.). Mitteilung des Verbandes österreichischer Banken und Bankiers 10 : 304-309, No. 11-12, 1928.

ENGEL : Die Rechtsentwicklung Österreichs im Jahre 1928. Deutsche Juristenzeitung 34 : 54-57, 1 Januar 1929.

RATZENHOFER, G., und BETTELHEIM, E. : Die privatrechtliche Gesetzgebung Österreichs in der Zeit vom 1 April 1928 bis 30 Juni 1929. Zeitschrift für ausländisches und internationales Privatrecht 3 : 500-521, Heft 4, 1929.

METALL, R.A. : Das neue österreichische Konsulargerichtsgesetz. Gesetzgebung und Rechtpraxis des Auslandes 5 : 46-47, April-Mai 1929.

METALL, A.R. : International-verwaltungsrechtliche Bemerkungen zu den neuen österreichischen Sozialversicherungsgesetzen. Niemeyers Zeitschrift für internationales Recht 40 : 339-387, 5.und 6. Heft 1929.

KELSEN, H. : Die österreichische Verfassungsreform. Deutsche Volkswirt 4 : 110-113, 25. Oktober 1929.

MERKL, A. : Verwässerung oder Verbesserung des Verfassungsentwurfes? Oesterreichische Volkswirt 22 : 130-132, 2 November 1929.

MERKL, A. : Verfassungsreform in Oesterreich. Deutsche Juristen-Zeitung 34 : 1582-1587, Dezember 1, 1929.

MERKL, A. : Epilog zum Verfassungskampf. Oesterreichische Volkswirt 22 : 293-297, 14 Dezember 1929.

KUNZ, J.L. : Das österreichische Fremdenrecht. Zeitschrift für öffentliches Recht 9 : 194-230, 15. Dezember 1929.
Legal status of foreigners in Austria.

NATIONAL LAW - COUNTRIES

BELGIUM

LANGHANS-RATZEBURG, M. : Die belgische Gesetzgebung über Eupen und Malmedy. Zeitschrift für Völkerrecht 15 : 100-101, Heft 1, 1929.

BACCARA, R. : A propos de l'ecécution en Belgique des sentences arbitrales étrangères (Contd.). Institut belge de droit comparé, revue 15 : 49-60, avril-juin 1929.

TROUET : Das Recht der ehemals deutschen Gebiete Eupen-Malmedy. Juristische Wochenschrift 58 : 1530-1536, 25 Mai 1929.

BOLIVIA

BELAUNDE, V.-A. : La constitution bolivienne et la présidence à vie. Revue de l'Amérique latine 14 : 204-224, 1 septembre 1927.

BRAZIL

LARRAIN, L. : Doctrina y jurisprudencia brasileñas en materia de inmunidades y privilegios a los diplomaticos extranjeros. Revista chilena 13 : 422-441, abril-mayo 1929.

BULGARIA

GANEFF, V. : La legislazione in Bulgaria durante il 1925. Annuario di diritto comparato e di studi legislativi 1 : 165-169, 1927.
A survey of Bulgarian legislation during 1925.

KESSIAKOW, B.D. : Tabelle der in der Zeit vom 1 Januar 1926 bis zum 31 Dezember 1928 vom Königreich Bzlgarien abgeschlossen Verträge und anderen Abkommen. Zeitschrift für Ostrecht 3 : 1201-1209, August-September 1929.

How Bulgaria is governed. Bulgarian British review : 3-5, October 1929.
Survey of Bulgarian Constitution.

CANADA

The constitutional crisis in Canada. Economist 103 : 4-5, July 3, 1926.

Canada : The political and constitutional crisis. Round table 64 : 824-836, September 1926.

LAVOIE, Paul. : L'Autonomie du Canada et sa nouvelle situation internationale. Revue générale de droit international public 34 : 171-209, mars-avril 1927.

JOHNSTON, K.V. : Dominion status in international law. American journal of international law 21 : 481-489, July 1927.

SIEGFRIED, A. : Le nouveau statut international du Canada. Revue des deux mondes 98 : 187-202, 1 juillet 1928.

MAYBEE, G.E. : Patent and trade mark problems in Canada. Industrial Canada 29 : 44-45, 44-45, February, March 1929.

BURCHELL, Ch. J. : Canadian admiralty jurisdiction and shipping laws. Law quarterly review 45 : 370-377, July 1929.

Canada - law and custom in the Canadian constitution. Round table : 143-160, December 1929.

CHILE

New constitution for Chile. Advocate of peace 87 : 465-466, August 1925.

Chile - the new constitution - Statist 106 : 1004-1005, 5 December 1925.

KELSEN, H. : Bemerkungen zur Chilenischen Verfassung. Zeitschrift für öffentliches Recht 5 : 616-619, 1 Juli 1926.

FIGUEROA, M. : Die neue Staatsverfassung von Chile. Zeitschrift für öffentliches Recht 5 : 596-616, 1 Juli 1926.

Chilean code of commerce under reform. U.S. Commerce reports : 197-199, 22 April 1929.

CHINA

YAO-TSENG, C. : The present conditions of the Chinese judiciary and its future. Chinese social and political science review 10 : 163-182, January 1926.

LIANG, L. : China's new constitution. Chinese social and political science review 10 : 145-162, January 1926.

New constitution of the Republic of China. Chinese social and political science review 10 : 509-540, April 1926.
Text (in English) of constitution of 11 December 1925.

COUSSIN, J.J. : La question de la constitutionnalité. Politique de Pékin 13 : 419, 2 mai 1926.

COUSSIN, J.J. : La solution du problème constittutionnel. Politique de Pékin 13 : 442-444, 9 mai 1926.

RIASANOVERY, Professor : Fundamental institutions of Chinese civil law. China weekly review 37 : 131-140, 10 July 1926.

La Cina e gli stranieri. Nuova antologia 61 : 198-208, 16 luglio 1926.

KEETON, G.W. : The new Chinese codes. Journal of comparative legislation and international law 8 : 225-238, November 1926.

La question chinoise et l'intérêt commun. Journal des économistes 86 : 300-314, 15 mars 1927.

KENNARD, E.A. : In China to-day. Foreigner's position in the military kaleidoscope. Japan weekly chronicle No. 1552 : 340-342, 24 March 1927.

CHANG, S.H. : The provisional court agreement. China weekly review 40 : 249-251, 7 May 1927.

SMITH, J.N. : Imperialism in China. Foreign affairs (L) 8 : 331-333, June 1927.

NATIONAL LAW - COUNTRIES

A picture of China. Round table No. 67 : 473-497, June 1927.

Provisional agreement for the rendition of the Shanghai mixed court. American journal of international law 21 : 113-116, July 1927.

HUDSON, M.O. : The rendition of the international mixed court at Shanghai. American journal of international law 21 : 451-471, July 1927.

ESCARRA, J. : Droits et intérêts étrangers en Chine. Revue d'économie politique 41 : 1017-1053, juillet-août 1927, et 1304-1325, septembre-octobre 1927, et 1471-1492, novembre-décembre 1927.

Treaty revision in China. Foreign policy association information service 4 : 297-320, September 28, 1928.
Most favoured clause in China's treaties.

LIANG YUENG-LI : The five-power constitution. China weekly review 46 : 158-159, September 29, 1928.

GREENWOOD, T. : Les Anglais en Chine. Bibliothèque universelle et revue de Genève 328-342, septembre 1927.

LIANG YUENG-LI : Judicial reform under the nationalist government. China weekly review (New China edition) 105-108, 10 October 1928.

Text of the organic law of nationalist government. China critic 1 : 421-422, 18 October 1928.

KEETON, G.W. : Chinese law and historical jurisprudence. Chinese social and political science review 12 : 511-515, October 1928.

ESCARRA, J. : La loi organique de la Chine a un caractère provisoire. Europe nouvelle 11 : 1513-1515, 3 novembre 1928.

Le nouveau gouvernement en Chine. Bulletin de l'Institut intermédiaire international 20 : 21-25, janvier 1929.

Organic law of the national government of the Republic of China. Chinese social and political science review (public documents supplement) 13 : 1-7, January 1929.
Text of Chinese constitution of October 1928.

ESCARRA, J. : Les lois organiques du gouvernement chinois. Europe nouvelle 12 : 154-158, 2 février 1929.

China - Gesetzgebung; Staatsangehörigkeitsgesetz. Zeitschift für ausländisches öffentliches Recht und Völkerrecht 2 : 507-513, 1931.
5 Februar 1929.

WANG CHUNG-HUI : The national government from a legal, diplomatic and reconstruction standpoint. China weekly review 47 : 462-463, February 9, 1920.

The Shanghai mixed court. Shanghai publicity bureau, news bulletin 3 : 1-56, February 1929.
Series of articles on the present legal status of this court.

CICCHITTI, A. : Se la concessione italiana di Tien Tsin sia un possedimento coloniale. Rivista di diritto pubblico 21 : 141-157, febbraio-marzo 1929.

MOHR, F.W. : Kuomingtang-Krise. Deutsche Volkswirt 3 : 855-857, 28 März 1929.
The third session of the Kuomingtan (March 1929).

VEE ESSE : The consular deputies of the Shanghai provisional court. China critic 2 : 329-331, April 25, 1929.

WOODHEAD, H.G.W. : Treaty revision in China. National review 93 : 214-218, April 1929.

PAXTON HOWARD, H. : China's new labor laws. China weekly review 48 : 416-422, 4 May 1929.

Text of notes to the British, American and French Ministers requesting termination of extrality. China critic 2 : 377-378, 9 May 1929.

HU HAN-MIN : The new civil code (Contd.). China critic 2 : 371-373, 393-395, May 9, 16, 1929.

China's demand for ending of extraterritoriality. China weekly review 48 : 443-444, 11 May 1929.

The attitude of The Review on extraterritoriality. China weekly review 48 : 486-489, 491-492, 18 May 1929.

QUIGLEY, H.S. : The national government of China. American political science review 23 : 441-449, May 1929.

SOKOLSKY, G.E. : The problem of extraterritoriality. Far Eastern review 25 : 193-195, May 1929.

Gouvernement national de la République de Chine - nationalité. Journal du droit international 56 : 814-817, mai-juin 1929.
Texte de loi du 5 février 1929 sur la nationalité.

KWAN HAI-TUNG : Consular juridiction - its place in the present clamor for the abolition of treaties. Pacific affairs : 347-360, June 1929.

FANG, E.L.T. : The workings of extraterritoriality. China critic 2 : 529-531, 4 July 1929.

AMANN, G. : Chinas neue Gesetzgebung. Geopolitik 6 : 596-603, Juli 1929.

LAMPSON, M.W. : British reply to China's note on extraterritoriality. China weekly review 50 : 47, 7 septembre 1929.

The "Unequal treaties". New statesman 33 : 734-736, September 28, 1929.
Comment on treaties giving British subjects in China special privileges.

TYAU, M.T.Z. : How abolition of extraterritoriality may be accomplished. China critic 2 : 769-772, September 26 1929.

SOKOLSKY, G.E. : Extraterritoriality. Far Eastern review 25 : 385-388, 395, September 1929.
Survey of present internal political situation in China.

TZ-HYUNG, L. : Abolition of extraterritoriality in China. China critic 2 : 829-834, 17 October 1929.

WOODHEAD, H.G.W. : China and extraterritoriality. National review : 387-401, November 1929.

BURTON, W. : China denounces extraterritorial treaties. Current history 31 : 294-299, November 1929.

HU, T.W. : Extraterritoriality - its development and its abolition. China weekly review 51 : 20-22, 31, 7 December 1929.

BURTON, W. : China denounces extra-territorial treaties. China weekly review 51 : 56, 58, 14 December 1929.

COMMONWEALTH

British Guiana. A new era. Statist 112 : 147-148, 28 July 1928.
Comment on the new constitution.

KELLY, I.G. : The Dominions and the judicial committee. Nineteenth century 105 : 190-201, February 1929.
Right of appeal to the Privy Council.

MACKENZIE, N. : Constitutional questions in Nova Scotia. Journal of comparative legislation and international law 11 : 87-95, February 1929.

The Ceylon report. Round Table : 295-324, March 1929.
Report on the constitution.

Dominion status. Law journal 67 : 228-229, March 23, 1929.
The constitution of the British Commonwealth of Nations.

MORESCO, E. : De staatsregeling van Ceylon. Koloniaal Tijdschrift 18 : 374-391, Juli 1929.
The Ceylon Constitution.

CHEVALLIER, J.-J. : Les Dominions britanniques et le droit de traiter. Revue de droit international 3 : 67-134, juillet-août-septembre 1929.

OUDIETTE, J. : Les colonies de la couronne britannique. Revue des sciences politiques 44 : 592-609, octobre-décembre 1929.
Statut juridique.

KEITH, B. : Notes on imperial constitutional law. Journal of comparative legislation and international law 11 : 250-267, November 1929.
Dominions status - ratification of treaties and pact to renounce war.

CUBA

VIDAURRETA, J.M. : El derecho internacional privado en el futuro codigo civil cubano. Revista de derecho internacional 9 : 261-273, 30 junio 1926.

CZECHOSLOVAKIA

MAYR, R. : Das internationale Privatrecht des künftigen B.G.-B. für die Tschechoslowakei. Prager Juristische Zeitschrift 6 : 34-50, Heft 1-2, 1926.

DIWALD, H. : Sprachenrecht der Ausländer im Verkehr mit Gerichten und Behörden in der Tschechoslowakei. Ostrecht 2 : 393-396, April 1926.

MAYR, R. : Das internationale Privatrecht der Tschechoslowakei. Ostrecht 2 : 704-709, Heft 7-8, Juli-August 1926.

BOHACEK, M. : Il movimento legislativo nella Repubblica Cecoslovena nel campo del diritto privato negli anni 1918-1925. Annuario di diritto comparato 1 : 111-119, 1927.
A survey of Czechoslovak civil law.

SIK, L. : Der Rechtshilfevertrag zwischen der Tschechoslovakischen Republik und dem Königreiche der Serben, Kroaten und Slovenen in de Praxis. Prager juristische Zeitschrift 9 : 7-11, 1 Januar 1928.
Comment on 1924 judicial treaty.

SILBERSTEIN, Dr. L. : Die Entstehung des Tsechoslowakischen Staates nach Benesch's Memoiren. Europäische Gespräche 6 : 127-147, März 1928.

NANI, U. : Le basi politiche e giuridiche dello stato cecoslovacco. Politica 10 : 311-340, giugno-agosto 1928.

SCHRANIL, R. : Die Neuorganisation der politischen Verwaltung in der Cechoslovakei. Zeitschrift für Ostrecht 2 : 1289-1320, Oktober 1928.

KALOUSCK, V. : La formation de l'état tchécoslovaque et la jurisprudence. Bulletin du droit tchécoslovaque 2 : 67-96, 1 décembre 1928.

KUCERA, B. : Les fondements internationaux de l'état tchécoslovaque. Bulletin de droit tchécoslovaque 2 : 96-112, 1 décembre 1928.

HEGER, E. : Schlesien und die tschéchoslowakische Verwaltungsreform. Nation und Staat 2 : 158-163, Dezember 1928.

KREJCHI, J. : Die Prüfung der Verfassungsmässigkeit von Gesetzen in der cechoslovakischen Republik. Zeitschrift für Ostrecht 3 : 38-47, Januar 1929.

WEISER, M. Die Unterschiede des Tschekoslowakischen Gesetzes gegen den unlauteren Wettbewerb von dem des deutschen Reiches und Oesterreichs. Prager juristische Zeitschrift 9 : 66-82, 1 Februar 1929.

DOMINIK, R. : Das cêchoslovakische Arbeitsrecht. Zeitschrift für Ostrecht 3 : 388-414, März 1929.

VERIANO-OVECKA, S.I. : La riforma fondaria cecoslovacca (Contd.). Civiltà cattolica 80 : 489-503, 16 marzo 1929.

MEYER-WILD, H. : Zum Vertrag zwischen der tschechoslowakischen Republik und der Schweiz über die Anerkennung und Vollstreckung gerichtlicher Entscheidungen. Prager Juristische Zeitschrift 9 : 366-369, 2. Maiheft 1929.

DANZIG

RICHTER : Gesetzgebung und Verfassung. Danziger juristische Monatsschrift 5 : 105-112, 25 November 1926.

GARGAS, S. : Die Danziger Staatsangehörigkeit. Zeitschrift für vergleichende Rechtswissenschaft 42 : 321-341, 3. Heft, 1927.

NATIONAL LAW - COUNTRIES

REISS : Ein Konflikt zwischen Gesetzgebung und Rechtsprechung in Danzig. Deutsche Juristen-Zeitung 33 : 1580-1582, 1. Dezember 1928.

ECUADOR

Texto de la Constitución política del Ecuador que acaba de ser promulgada. Ecuador comercial 7 : 55-69, abril 1929.
Text of Constitution of 26 March 1929.

ESTHONIA

MADDISON, E. : La legislazione del 1925 in Estonia. Annuario di diritto comparato 1 : 130-142, 1927.

MADDISON, E. : Nationalpolitische Grundsätze der estländuschen Staatsverfassung. Nation und Staat 1 : 416-421, Februar 1928.

KOCH, G. : Ein Dezennium estländischer Rechtsentwicklung 1918-1928. Zeitschrift für ausländisches und internationales Privatrecht 2 : 929-956, Heft 6, 1928.

GIANNINI, A. : La costituzione estone. Europa orientale 9 : 309-347, settembre-ottobre 1929.
Text of Esthonian Constitution (in Italian) annexed.

CZEKEY, S. von : Die rechtliche Stellung des estnischen Staatsältesten. Zeitschrift für öffentliches Recht 9 : 104-113, 1 Oktober 1929.

ETHIOPIA

GARDINER, A.L. : La juridiction concernant les étrangers en Ethiopie. Revue générale de droit international public 35 : 713-729, novembre-décembre 1928.

FINLAND

CASELIUS, J. : Das Recht Finnlands. Der Ursprung des Rechts Finnlands. Zeitschrift für osteuropäisches Recht 1 : 285-290, Juli 1926.

FRANCE

BERTHELÉMY, H. : Les limites du pouvoir législatif. Revue politique et parlementaire 32 : 355-369, 10 décembre 1925.

LARNAUDE, F. : L'inconstitutionnalité des lois et le droit public français. Revue politique et parlementaire 126 : 181-199, 10 février 1926.

WALTON, M.F.P. : Les rapports entre le droit français et le droit écossais. Bulletin mensuel de la société de législation comparée 4-6 : 225-246, avril-juin 1926.

VEGA, J. de la : Cronica constitucional de Francia. Crisis financiera y solucion constitucional. Revista argentina de ciencias políticas 33 : 364-373, 12 de enero de 1927.

LOISEAU, C. : Un plan empirique de réforme constitutionnelle. Correspondant 99 : 758-775, 10 mars 1928.

ESMEIN, P. : Gesetzgebung, Rechtsprechung und Schrifttum in Frankreich im Jahre 1927. Zeitschrift für ausländisches und internationales Privatrecht 2 : 637-729, Heft 4-5, 1928.
Annexed detailed bibliography.

WALINE, M. : Elément d'une théorie de la juridiction constitutionnelle en droit positif français. Revue du droit public 45 : 441-462, juillet-août-septembre 1928.

LAROQUE, P. : Le contrôle juridictionnel de la constitutionnalité des lois. Revue des sciences politiques 51 : 611-619, octobre-décembre 1928.
Etude critique comparative: Etats-Unis-France.

HAURIOU, A. : Les partis politiques et la Constitution. Revue politique et parlementaire 35 : 383-395, 10 décembre 1928.

FRANÇOIS-MARSAL : Les incompatibilités parlementaires. Monde nouveau 10 : 791-795, janvier-février 1929.

PERROUD, J. : The organization of the courts and the judicial bench in France. Journal of comparative legislation and international law 11 : 1-18, February 1929.

CRUPPI, J. : La question du Jury - Une solution. Revue de Paris 36 :781-797, 15 février 1929.
Pour une réforme du jury en France.

DITTE, J. : Le projet de loi sur la presse: un attentat contre la justice et la liberté. Revue hebdomadaire 38 : 155-169, mai 1929.

THERY, J. : La loi sur la liberté de la presse. Mercure de France 212 : 257-276, 1 juin 1929.

DELOBEL, J.-L. : Les associations en France. Revue des sciences politiques 44 : 348-383, juillet-septembre 1929.
Historique - régime légal - situation actuelle.

JÈZE, G. : Le régime des pensions de retraite des fonctionnaires publics en France. Revue de science et de législation financières 27 : 653-702, octobre-novembre-décembre 1929.

FRANCE
(International Law, Aliens, Nationality)

BRÄNDI, F. : Rechtsangleichung und Gesetzeskollisionen in Elsass-Lothringen. Niemeyers Zeitschrift für internationales Recht 34 : 281-297, 3. bis 6. Heft 1925.

CARDAHI, Choucri : Le droit des pays sous mandat français en orient dans ses rapports avec les législations étrangères. Bulletin mensuel de la société de législation comparée 54 : 263-285, juillet-septembre 1925.

GABELLINI, E. : Gli stranieri in Francia. Economia 4 : 423-429, giugno 1926.

RAPHAËL, T. : Le problème des étrangers en France. Grande revue 30 : 184-214, août 1926.

SCHWALB, M. : Elsass-Lothringische Staatsangehörigkeitsfragen. Zeitschrift für Völkerrecht 14 : 30-66, Heft 1, 1927.

NATIONAL LAW - COUNTRIES

BARTIN, E. : Le droit conventionnel envisagé comme source du droit international privé en France. Journal du droit international 54 : 5-33, janvier-février 1927.

DONNEDIEU de VABRES, H. : Le régime nouveau de l'extradition, d'après la loi du 10 mars 1927. Revue de droit international privé 22 : 169-192, No. 2, 1927.

SAUVY, A. : La population étrangère en France et les naturalisations (contd.). Journal de la Société de Statistique de Paris 68 : 89-97, mars 1927.

TRACHTENBERG, B. : Les biens des sociétés russes en France. Revue de droit international privé 22 : 561-565, No. 3, 1927.

TRAVERS, Maurice : La loi française d'extradition du 10 mars 1927. Journal du droit international 54 : 594-610, mai-juin 1927.

MAZEAUD, L. : De la nationalité des sociétés. Journal du droit international 55 : 30-66, janvier-février 1928.

STREIT, G. : La nationalité des sociétés commerciales. Revue de droit international et de législation comparée 55 : 494-521, Nos.4-5, 1928.

NISOT, M. Th. : La nationalité de la femme mariée et la loi française du 10 août 1927. Revue de droit international et de législation comparée 55 : 646-649, No. 4-5, 1928.

MARGHIERI, A. : Introno al "progetto di codice delle obligazioni e dei contratti". Rivista del diritto commerciale 26 : 293-302, maggio-giugno 1928.

LARNAUDE, F. : L'unification législative franco-italienne. Revue de droit international 2 : 873-969, juillet-août-septembre 1928.

DREYFUS, R. : Les conflits de nationalités et la loi sur la nationalité du 10 août 1927. Journal du droit international 54 : 928-951, 4e et 5e livraison, juillet-octobre 1927.

DONNEDIEU de VABRES, M.H. : Les tendances actuelles du droit extraditionel, d'après la loi française du 10 mars 1927 et le projet de la loi allemande sur l'extradition. Revue internationale de droit pénal 5 : 327-362, 3ème trimestre 1928.

DONNEDIEU de VABRES, M.H. : De la réciprocité en matière d'extradition d'après la loi française du 10 mars 1927 et le nouveau projet allemand. Revue générale de droit international public 35 : 555-570, 1928, septembre-octobre.

REINACH, F. : Le rapprochement franco-allemand en matière juridique et en matière de jurisprudence. Bulletin mensuel de la Société de Législation comparée 57 : 628-630, octobre-décembre 1928.

F.P.W. : Franco Italian draft code of obligations. Journal of comparative legislation and international law 10 : 311-314, November 1928.

TAUBERT, L. : Notre convention consulaire avec la France. Revue économique de Belgrade 4 : 214-216, septembre 1929.
Commentaire de la convention consulaire ... du 30 janvier 1929.

AUDINET, E. : La nationalité française dans nos colonies. Journal du droit international 56 : 25-31, janvier-février 1929.

AGHION, R. : La loi française sur les loyers et les étrangers. Institut belge de droit comparé 15 : 164-167, octobre-décembre 1929.
Situation des étrangers bénéficiant de conventions diplomatiques.

PETROVITCH, S.R. : La signification du traité de commerce franco-yougoslave. Bulletin officiel de la chambre de commerce franco-yougoslave 1 : 1-3, novembre 1929.

TAUBERT, L. : La convention consulaire franco-yougoslave 1929. Bulletin officiel de la chambre de commerce franco-yougoslave 1 : 3-5, novembre 1929.

BETTI, E. : Il progetto di un Codice italo-francese delle obbligazioni e dei contratti. Rivista del diritto commerciale 27 : 665-668, novembre-dicembre 1929.

NITTI, G. : La situation juridique des émigrés italiens en France. Revue générale de droit international public 36 : 739-759, novembre-décembre 1929.

GERMANY

HÄNTZSCHEL, K. : Die Verfassungsschranken der Diktaturgewalt des Artikels 48 der Reichsverfassung. Zeitschrift für öffentliches Recht 5 : 205-227, 1 Januar 1926.

WITTMAYER, L. : Preussen im Reichsrat. Zeitschrift für öffentliches Recht 5 : 292-299, 1 Januar 1926.

ANSCHÜTZ, G. : Studien zur Weimarer Reichsverfassung. Zeitschrift für öffentliches Recht 5 : 145-183, 1 Januar 1926.

TATARIN-TARNHEYDEN, Dr. E. : Die rechtliche Stellung des Reichswirtschaftsrats nach der Reichverfassung und seine bevorstehende Reform. Deutsche Wirtschafts Zeitung 23 : 5-7, 21-23, 7, 14 Januar 1926.

HIPPEL, E. von : Zur Auslegung des Artikels 109, Absatz 1 der Reichsverfassung. Archiv des öffentlichen Rechts 10 : 124-152, 1-2. Heft 1926.

BILFINGER, C. : Verfassungsumgehung. Betrachtungen zur Auslegung der Weimarer Verfassung. Archiv des öffentlichen Rechts 11 : 163-191, 2. Heft 1926.

SIMONS, W. : Reichsverfassung und Rechtsprechung. Zeitschrift für die gesamte Staatswissenschaft 81 : 385-409, 3. Heft 1926.

ASCHROTT : 25 Jahre Fürsorgeerziehung in Preussen. Deutsche Juristen-Zeitung 31 : 487-491, 1. April 1926.

HUGELMANN, Dr. K.G. : Zur Reform der Weimarer Verfassung. Wille und Weg 2 : 131-135, 15 Juni 1926.

MOST, O. : Das Reich und die Länder. Gedanken zur Reform der Reichsverfassung. Wirtschaftsliche Nachrichten für Rhein und Ruhr 7 : 777-784, 30 Juni 1926.

NATIONAL LAW - COUNTRIES

JAUP, B.H. : The main features of the constitution of the German Reich of 1919 compared with the constitution of 1871. Journal of comparative legislation and international law 8 : 239-245, November 1926.

HUGELMANN, Dr. K. : Zur Reform der Weimarer Verfassung. Wille und Weg 2 : 490-494, 1. Februar 1927.

SIMONS, W. : Reichsverfassung und Rechtsprechung. Zeitschrift für die gesamte Staatswissenschaft 81 : 385-409, 3. Heft 1926.

KLEIN, F. : Anschluss und Verfassungspolitik. Deutsche Volkswirtschaft 1 : 732-735, 11. März 1927.

BREDT, J.V. : Der Weg der Verfassungsänderung. Zeitschrift für die gesamte Staatswissenschaft 82 : 137-456, 3. Heft 1927.

Anschluss und Verfassungspolitik. Oesterreichische Volkswirt 19 : 637-640, 12 März 1927.

HUGELMANN, R.J. : Zur Lehre von der Reichsexecution nach der Weimarer Verfassung. Zeitschrift für öffentliches Recht 6 : 513-534, 1 Juli 1927.

WITTMAYER, L. : Rückblicke auf acht Jahre Weimarer Verfassung. Zeitschrift für öffentliches Recht 6 : 497-512, 1 Juli 1927.

STIER-SOMLO, F. : Das Gesamtgefüge der deutschen Reichsverfassung und die weltpolitische Lage. Gesellschaft 4 : 10, Juli 1927.

KOELLREUTTER, Professor : Die innerpolitische Gliederung des deutsches Volkes als nationales Problam. Wille und Weg 3 : 471-478, 15 Januar 1928.

SPIELHAGEN, W. : Nach der Länderkonferenz. Das Program der Kommissionsarbeiten zur Verfassungs-und Verwaltungsreform. Wirtschaftsdienst 13 : 125-127, 27 Januar 1928.

LANDAUER, Dr. C. : Die Bewegung für deutschen Einheitstaat - Oesterreichische Volkswirt 20 : 481-483, 28 Januar 1928.

VERMEIL, E. : L'Allemagne en pleine crise politique. Alsace française 8 : 91-92, 29 janvier 1928.

OBST, Erich : Zur Neugliederung des Deutschen Reiches. Zeitschrift für Geopolitik 5 : 27-40, Januar 1928.

KLEIN, F. : Deutscher Einheitsstaat und wir. Oesterreichische Volkswirt 20 : 568-570, 18 Februar 1928.

HAMBURGER, E. : Dem Einheitsstaat entgegen. Gesellschaft 5 : 97-112, Februar 1928.

LUCAS, C. : Justizreform. Zeitschrift für die gesamte Staatswissenschaft 85 : 449-467, 3 Heft 1928.

HEDEMANN, J.W. : Das Recht auf Land nach dem gegenwärtigen deutschen Rechtsverhältnissen. Agrar-Probleme 1 : 497-520, Heft 3, 1928.

RINNER, E. : Finanzpolitische Wege zum Einheitstaat. Die Gesellschaft 5 : 329-342, April 1928.

MAUPAS, J. : Le fédéralisme Rhénan. Le correspondant 100 : 321-341, 10 mai 1928.

SOGEMEIER, Dr. : Zur Frage der Verfassungs-und Verwaltungsreform in Deutschland. Mitteilungen des Verbandes österreichischer Banken und Bankiers 10 : 98-102, 11 Mai 1928.

BOETHKE : Vom inneren Dientbetrieb des Reichsfinanzhofes. Juristische Wochenschrift 57 : 2339-2341, 29. September 1928.

CARRÉ de MALBERG, R. : La distinction des lois matérielles et formelles et le concept de loi dans la constitution de Weimar. Bulletin mensuel de la société de législation comparée 57 : 597-619, octobre-décembre 1928.

ALBRECHT, G. : Die Reformbedürfigkeit des Schlichtungswesens. Jahrbücher für Nationalökonomie und Statistik 129 : 833-852, Dezember 1928.

GERBER, H. : Gesetz und Verfassung. Zeitschrift für Ostrecht 3 : 1-29, Januar 1929.

CARRÉ de MALBERG, R. : La distinction des lois matérielles et formelles et le concept de loi dans la constitution de Weimar (Contd.). Bulletin mensuel de la société de législation comparée 58 : 155-173, janvier-mars 1929.

LINZ : Reichsregierung und Staatsgerichtshof. Deutsche Juristenzeitung 34 : 197-201, 1 Februar 1929.

Ausbau des Reichshaushaltsrechts. Magazin der Wirtschaft 5 : 217-220, 14 Februar 1929.

CAMPE, D. von : Glossen zur preussischen Verwaltungsreform. Deutsche Stimmen 41 : 97-108, 20. Februar 1929.

GERLAND, H.B. : The German draft penal code and its place in the history of penal law. Journal of comparative legislation and international law 11 : 19-33, February 1929.

GERLAND, H.B. : Der deutsche Entwurf zu einem Strafgesetzbuch in seiner histoirschen Bedeutung. Schweizerische Monatshefte 8 : 506-518, Februar 1929.

WUNDERLICH, H. : Der Fortgang der Beratungen im Strafrechtausschuss der Reichstags. Deutsche Juristen-Zeitung 34 : 348-355, 1. März 1929.

LEIFMANN, R. : Einige Bemerkungen zur Aktienrechtsreform. Deutsche Oekonomist 47 : 403-405, 28 März 1929.

STOLBERG-WERNIGERODE, A. : Stärkung der Macht des Reichspräsidenten? Deutsche Stimmen 41 : 217-223, 5. April 1929.

MELCHIOR, G. : Die Selbstbeschränkung des deutschen internationalen Privatrechts. Zeitschrift für ausländisches und internationales Privatrecht 3 : 733-751, Heft 5, 1929.

KESSLER, F. : Das für die Aktiengesellschaft massgebdende Recht. Zeitschrift für ausländisches und internationales Privatrecht 3 : 758-774, Heft 5, 1929.
Joint stock companies in German international private law.

NATIONAL LAW - COUNTRIES

RABEL, E. : Die deutsche Rechtsprechung in einzelnen Lehren des internationalen Privatrechts. Zeitschrift für ausländisches und internationales Privatrecht 3 : 752-757, Heft 5, 1929.

LANDAUER, C. : Verwaltungsreform in Preussen. Oesterreichische Volkswirt 21 : 823-826, 4. Mai 1929.

LOWENFELD, E. : Die Aufgaben des Reichsrechtsausschusses der Deutsch-Oesterreichischen Arbeitsgemeinschaft. Juristische Wochenschrift 58 : 1537-1539, 25 Mai 1929.

SCHMÖLDER : Zur Reform des Aktienrechtes - die amtliche Enquête. Juristische Wochenschrift 58 : 2090-2102, 20. - 27. Juli 1929.

BELING, von : Der amtliche Entwurf eines einführungsgesetzes zum Allgemeinen Deutschen Strafgesetzbuch und zum Strafvollzugsgesetz. Deutsches Juristen-Zeitung 34 : 1165-1171, 15. September 1929.

HUGELMANN, C.G. : Das deutsche Volk als Rechtsbegriff im Reichsstaatsrecht der Gegenwart - kritische Bemerkungen zu Liermanns gleichnamigem Werk. Zeitschrift für öffentliches Recht 9 : 32-43, 1. Oktober 1929.

Die deutsche Rechtsprechung auf dem Geniete des internationalen Privatrechts im Jahre 1928. Zeitschrift für ausländisches und internationales Privatrecht 3 : 8-198, 1929 (Special number).

GERMANY
(International Law and Practice, Aliens and Naturalization)

GOTTSCHALK, E. : Deutschland und das Völkerrecht im Jahre 1926. Archiv für Politik und Gesichts 5 (10) : 514-542, Heft 12, 1927.

Die deutsche Rechtsprechung auf dem Gebiete des internationalen Privatrechts in den Jahren 1926 und 1927. Zeitschrift für ausländisches und internationales Privatrecht 2 : 7-162, 1928 (Sonderheft).

KELMAN, E. : Quelques remarques pratiques sur la base de la convention entre l'Union des Républiques soviétiques socialistes et l'Allemagne sur les arbitrages en matière civile du 12 octobre 1925. Revue soviétique de droit international : 60-72, No. 2-3, 1928.
Russian text with French summary.

RAUCHHAUPT, F.W. von : Die praktische Pflege der modernen ausländischen Rechte in Deutschland. Juristische Wochenschrift 58 : 411-413, 16 Februar 1929.

SCHMIDT, W. : Die Auslieferungsstatistik. Deutsche Juristen-Zeitung 34 : 466-470, 1. April 1929.

NITZSCHE : Der Entwurf eines deutschen Auslieferungsgesetzes. Deutsche Juristen-Zeitung 34 : 887-891, 1. Juli 1929.

HAASE, B. : Das deutsche-polnische Aufwertungsabkommen. Deutsche Juristen-Zeitung 34 : 1177-1179, 15. September 1929.

FREUND, H. : Die Staatsengehörigkeit in Deutschland lebender Personen russisch-polnischer Herkunft. Juristen Wochenschrift 58 : 3455-3458, 21, 28 Dezember 1929.

GREAT BRITAIN

KEITH, B. : Notes on imperial constitutional law. Journal of comparative legislation and international law 7 : 101-109, February 1925.

LASKI, H. : Die englische Verfassung und die Zukunft der Arbeiterpartei. Gesellschaft 11 : 323-332, Oktober 1925.

KEITH, B. : Notes on imperial constitutional law. Journal of comparative legislation and international law 7 : 195-211, November 1925.

WHITEHOUSE, J.H. : The constitutional systems of England and the United States. Contemporary review 730 : 459-468, October 1926.

KEITH, B. : Notes on imperial constitutional law. Journal of comparative legislation and international law 8 : 275-271, November 1926.

PELLERIN, P. : La "private limited company" du droit anglais (Companies Acts 1908 à 1928). Journal du droit international 55 : 917-925, juillet-octobre 1928.

MORGAN, E.B. : Die Rechtsverfolgung in Handelssachen in England. Wirtschaft und das Recht : 653-672, August 1928.

CAUDEL, M. : Le développement des juridictions administratives en Angleterre. Revue des sciences politiques 51 : 522-541 octobre-décembre 1928.

AKZIN, B. : La désuétude en droit constitutionnel. Quelques conséquences pour le droit anglais. Revue du droit public et de la science politique 45 : 697-723, octobre-novembre-décembre 1928.

GOLDSCHMIDT : Die Novelle zum englischen Aktienrecht Magazin der Wirtschaft 4 : 1804-1807, 22 November 1928.
The new English Companies Act.

WEINER, J.L. : Theory of anglo-american dividend law; the English cases. Columbia law review 28 : 1046-1060, December 1928.

CHAMBERLAIN, N. : Local government. Nineteenth century 105 : 1-8, January 1929.

GLEN, R.A. : The local government bill. Law journal 67 : 25-26, 45-46, 12 January 1929.

SEITZ, E. : Le système de la répression en Angleterre. Bulletin mensuel de la Société de Législation comparée 58 : 133-154, janvier-mars 1929.

RAIS, J. : La loi anglaise et la protection de l'épargne. Revue des vivants 3 : 36-42, janvier 1929.

The Companies Act, 1928. Law journal 67 : 114-116, February 9, 1929.

GLEN, R.A. : The local government bill - finance (contd.). Law journal 67 : 140, February 23, 1929.

SABONADIERE, A. : Criminal procedure before magistrates in England and Wales and India. Journal of comparative legislation and international law 11 : 52-67, February 1929.

NATIONAL LAW - COUNTRIES

The Censorship of books. Nineteenth century 105 : 433-450, April 1929.
Series of articles on British press law.

CARR, C.T. : Revised statutes. Law quarterly review 45 : 168-177, April 1929.
The revision in Great Britain.

OPPENHEIMER, L. : Das englische Wechselrecht. Zentralblatt für Handelsrecht 4 : 123-125, April 1929.

Notes on the bankruptcy laws. Bankers' magazine 127 : 599-616, April 1929.

HANBURY, H.G. : La position actuelle de l'équité dans le système juridique de l'Angleterre. Bulletin mensuel de la Société de Législation comparée 58 : 435-505, juillet-septembre 1929.

ROSENDORFF, R. : Die Einwirkung der wirtschaftlichen Konzentrationsbewegung und die Reform des englischen Aktiensrechts nach dem Companies Act vom 3. August 1928. Bank-Archiv 29 : 19-22, 15. Oktober 1929.

FINER, H. : Le gouvernement local en Angleterre et les réformes de 1925-1929. Revue des sciences politiques 44 : 521-550, octobre-décembre 1929.

MARQUIS, H. : L'Industrial Court anglaise. Recueil de droit commercial 1 : 305-307, novembre 1929.

MITCHELL, W. : Criminal procedure reform. Contemporary review : 766-770, December 1929.

GREAT BRITAIN
(International Law, Aliens)

BELLOT, H.H.L. : Les développements récents du droit international privé en Angleterre. Journal du droit international 53 : 5-18, janvier février 1926.

LACHS, R. : Die Vollstrecjung ausländischer Urteile in England und die Grenzen der Jurisdiktion der englischen Gerichte. Juristische Wochenschrift 58 : 3452-3455, 21, 28. Dezember 1929.

GREECE

TÉNÉKIDÈS, C.G. : La naturalisation in globo en Grèce et les traités de paix conclus postérieurement au ler janvier 1913. Journal du droit international 52 : 628-651, mai-juin 1925.

BERTOLA, A. : La cittadinanza italiana nelle isole Egee. Rivista coloniale 21 : 59-68, gennaio-febbraio 1926.

TÉNÉKIDÈS, C.G. : La récente réforme hellénique sur la nationalité. Journal du droit international 54 : 45-51, janvier-février 1927.

SAINT-BRICE : La constitution grecque. Correspondance d'orient 19 : 7-14, juillet 1927.

GMELIN, H. : Die Verfassung der griechischen Republik. Jahrbuch des öffentlichen Rechts 16 : 270-294, 1928.
Annexed the German text of the Greek constitution of June 3, 1927.

TÉNÉKIDÈS, C.G. : Le droit international public envisagé comme source du droit interne hellénique. Revue de droit international et de kégislation comparée 55 : 338-345, No. 3, 1928.

GUATEMALA

Constitutional reform in Guatemala. Pan American Union 62 : 656-660, July 1928.

La reforma de la constitución guatemalteca. Boletín de la Union Panamericana 62 : 693-697, julho 1928.

MATOS, J. : Le statut international de Guatémala. Académie diplomatique internationale : 32-39, juin 1929.

HUNGARY

ANGYAL, P. von : Das Rechtssystem Ungarns. Verfassung und Verwaltung. Zeitschrift für osteuropäisches Recht 1 : 253-256, Juli 1925.

EGYED, S. : Das staatsrechtliche Provisorium Ungarns. Ostrecht 2 : 47-52, Januar 1926.

POLGAR, E. : Les institutions hongroises actuelles de droit public. Revue du droit public et de la science politique 43 : 118-122, janvier-février-mars 1926.

VADASZ : La réorganisation du pouvoir législatif en Hongrie. Bulletin mensuel de la Société de Législation comparée 56 : 304-310, avril-juin 1927.

VADASZ, E. : Le projet de code civil hongrois. Bulletin de la Société de Législation comparée 57 : 375-379, juillet-septembre 1928.

SZLADITZ : Der neue Entwurf des Zivilgesetzbuches für Ungarn. Deutsche Juristenzeitung 33 : 1226-1232, 15. September 1928.

EGYED, S. : Grundgesetze in der ungarischen Verfassung. Zeitschrift für Ostrecht 3 : 58-65, Januar 1929.

PAP, D. : Abschnitte aus dem ungarischen Arbeitsrecht. Zeitschrift für Ostrecht 3 : 329-369, März 1929.

SCHWARTZ, J. : Die internationalen Beziehungen des ungarischen Zivilprozessrechtes. Niemeyers Zeitschrift für internationales Recht 14 : 107-196, 1. bis 4. Heft, 1929.

MAGYARY, G. de : L'organisation judiciaire en Hongrie. Revue hongroise de droit (supplément) 1 : 1-6, avril 1929.

VADASZ, E. : Le législation d'après-guerre en Hongrie. Bulletin mensuel de la société de législation comparée 58 : 275-310, avril-juin 1929.

SCHWARTZ, I. : Das Haager Abkommen über die Ehescheidung vom 12.6.1902 und das ungarische Ehegesetz. Niemeyers Zeitschrift für internationales Recht 41 : 363-381, Heft 5-6, 1929.

SCHWARTZ, I. Die Kollisionsnormen des ungarischen Wechselrechtes. Niemeyers Zeitschrift für internationales Recht 40 : 388-409, 5.und 6. Heft, 1929.

NATIONAL LAW - COUNTRIES

INDIA

ARCHBOLD, W.A.J. : A new Indian constitution. Edinburgh review 242 : 279-290, October 1925.

HOME, E. : The future of constitutional reforms in India. Outlook (L.) 58 : 24-26, 3 July 1926.

India; political and constitutional. Round table 65 : 103-117, December 1926.

OLIVIER of RAMSDEN : The Indian reform question. Review of nations 5 : October 1927.
Working of the Montagu-Chelmsford reform scheme.

JOHNSTON, C. : India a dominion? North American review 225 : 385-393, April 1928.

A constitution for India. Moslem chronicle 58 : 4-6, June 22, 1928.

SCOTT, L. : The crown and the Indian States. Law quarterly review 44 : 267-269, July 1928.

MAHARAJAH of PATIALA : The problem of the Indian States. Journal of the royal institute of international affairs 7 : 388-406, November 1928.

GUPTA, N. : Sidelights on the Simon commission. Modern review 45 : 15-18, January 1929.

COLVIN, I.D. : The Indian princes. National review 93 : 76-85, March 1929.

The report of the Indian States committee. Near East and India 35 : 524-525, April 25, 1929.
Relations between India and the States.

Questions for the Simon Commission. Asiatic review 25 : 177-196, April 1929.
Series of articles on India's constitution.

India and the statutory Commission. Spectator : 676, 4 May 1929.

The report of the Indian States Committee. Near East and India 35 : 715, 6 June 1929.
Result of enquiry of Butler Committee.

VERNEY LOVETT, H. : The Indian states and the future. Edinburgh review 250 : 34-49, July 1929.

ALEXANDER, H.G. : Simla or the Nehru report. Socialist review 23-27, No. 43, August 1929.
Plea for acceptance of the Nehru Constitutional proposals.

RONALDSHAY, Earl of : Constitutional developments and political ideals. Annals of the American Academy of political and social science 145 : 1-8, September 1929.
Constitution of the Indian Empire.

POLE, D.G. : India and Dominion status. Labour magazine 8 : 342-344, December 1929.

IRAN

LEVI, Dr. A. : Streifzüge durch das neue persische Aktienrecht. Zentralblatt für Handelsrecht 1 : 460-463, Dezember 1926.

IRELAND

WILKE, Dr. : Der irische Freistaat. Deutsche Juristen-Zeitung 30 : 930-931, Juni 15, 1925.

KENNEDY, H. : Character and sources of constitution of the Irish Free State. American bar association journal 14 : 437-445, August-September 1928

KOHN, L. : Due Verfassung des Irischen Freistaates Archiv des öffentlichen Rechts 54 : 33-84, Oktober 1928.

KOHN, L. : Die Verfassung des Irischen Freistaates Archiv des öffentlichen Rechts 15 : 269-341, Dezember 1928.

ITALY

PETRACCONE, G. : La riforma dei codici. Revista d'Italia 27 : 343-354, 15 luglio 1924.

NOLVA, R. de : La constituante fasciste. Revue hebdomadaire 34 : 38-47, 3 octobre 1925.
Proposed modifications of constitution by fascist government.

GINI, C. : Sulle riforme legislative proposte della commissione del XVIII. Rivista di politica economical XV : 949-956, 31 dicembre 1925.

GIAQUINTO, A. : Del sindicato della corte di cassazione sulla decisioni delle giurisdizioni speciali Rivista di diritto pubblico 18 : 65-86, febbraio 1926.

ROCCO, A. : La réforme constitutionnelle en Italie Revue politique et parlementaire 33 : 329-345, 10 mars 1926.

MARCHI, T. : Lo statuto Albertino ed il suo sviluppo storico. Rivista di diritto pubblico 18 : 187-207, aprile-maggio 1926.

RANELLETTI, O. : La potesta legislativa del governo. Rivista di diritto pubblico 18 : 165-178, aprile-maggio 1926.

RAUCHBERG, H. : Die Entziehung der italienischen Staatsbürgerschaft. Wille und Weg 2 : 112-118, 1 Juni 1926.

PIOLA CASELLI, M.E. : La législation politique fasciste. Egypte contemporaine 17 : 1-49, janvier 1926.

Les douze lois "fascistissimes". Europe nouvelle 9 : 1178-1193, 21 août 1926.

"ITALICUS" (pseud) : Les lois "fascistissimes". Europe nouvelle 9 : 1170-1172, 21 août 1926.

Législation fasciste. Europe nouvelle (special number) 9 : 1166-1193, 21 août 1926.

ROSSI, I. : La riforma dell'alta corte di giustizia (contd.). Nuova antologia 6 : 453-465, 16 giugno 1927.

ROSSI, I. : La riforma dell'alta corte di giustizi Nuova antologia 62 : 339-350, giugno 1927.

D'ALESSIO, F. : Aspetti attuali del diritto italiano. Revista di diritto pubblico 20 : 8-26, gennaio 1928.

NATIONAL LAW - COUNTRIES

FUBINI, R. : Vers le nouveau code civil italien. Revue trimestrielle de droit civil 27 : 75-98, janvier-mars 1928.

WALSMANN, H. : Das Erkenntnisverfahren des italienischen Entwurfs einer Zivilprozessordnung. Zeitschrift für ausländisches und internationales Privatrecht 2 : 370-397, Heft 3, 1928.

POPESCO-RAMNICEANO, R. : La représentation dans le projet de code des obligations. Bulletin mensuel de la Société de Législation comparée 57 : 190-205, avril-juin 1928.

MARGHIERI, A. : Intorno al "progetto di codice delle obligazioni e dei contratti". Rivista del diritto commerciale 26 : 293-302, maggio-giugno 1928.
Unification of Franco-Italian commercial and obligation law.

ASCARELLI, T. : Währungsrechtliche Fragen in der italienischen Rechtsprechung. Zeitschrift für ausländisches und internationales Privatrecht 2 : 793-812, Heft 6, 1928.

LARNAUDE, R. : L'unification législative franco-italienne. Revue de droit international 2 : 873-969, juillet-août-septembre 1928.

ZANGARA, V. : Il parlamento e la costituzionalizzazione. Critica fascista 6 : 323-325, 1 settembre 1928.

BARDA, E. : Les principales réformes fascistes. Bulletin de la Société de Législation comparée 57 : 279-327, juillet-septembre 1928.

F.P.W. : Franco Italian draft code of obligations. Journal of comparative legislation and international law 10 : 311-314, November 1928.

L'unificazione legislativa nei territori annessi al Regno. Rivista di politica economica 18 : 1051-1058, 31 dicembre 1928.

CARNELUTTI, F. : Grundlinien der Neuordnung des Erkenntnisverfahrens in Italien (Contd). Zeitschrift für ausländisches und internationales Privatrecht 3 : 1-32, Heft 1, 1929.

Réformes constitutionnelles en Italie : représentation politique et économique. Europe nouvelle 12 : 88-94, 19 janvier 1929.
Loi électorale - loi relative à la transformation du grand Conseil fasciste et rapport présenté au Sénat.

MASSARI, E. : Le origini e la elaborazione della Riforma penale fascista. Vita italiana 34 : 1-7, gennaio-febbraio 1929.

LEICHT, P.S. : Note storiche sulla unificazione legislativa. Nuovi studi di diritto economia e politica 2 : 1-6, gennaio-febbraio 1929.
The unification of Italian law.

AUNOS, D.A. : La legislación corporativa italiana (Contd.). Revista social 6 : 15-24, Enero, Febrero y Marzo 1929.

MASSARI, E. : Les origines de l'élaboration de la réforme pénale fasciste. Revue pénitentiaire de Pologne 4 : 133-141, janvier-avril 1929.

LONGHI, S. : I motivi del Gran Consiglio del Fascismo. Gerarchia 9 : 117-123, febbraio 1929.

RODES, J.N. : Consideraciones histórico-legales sobre el régimen corporativo (Contd.). Revista social 6 : 52-62, enero-febrero y marzo 1929.

DALLARI, G. : La funzione consultiva del Gran Consiglio del Fascismo e l'ordinamento sindacale e corporativo. Rivista di diritto pubblico 21 : 81-90, febbraio-marzo 1929.

CICCHITTI, A. : Se la concessione italiana di Tien Tsin sia un possedimento coloniale. Rivista di diritto pubblico 21 : 141-157, febbraio-marzo 1929.

VIVANTE, C. : L'autonomia del diritto commerciale e il sistema corporativo. Commercio 2 : 4-8, marzo 1929.

MERLINO, L. : Riforma dei codici e riforma giudiziaria. Gerarchia 9 : 287-290, aprile 1929.

BAAK, J.C. : L'avant-projet du code pénal italien dans ses rapports avec le droit international. Revue de droit international et de législation comparée 10 : 819-849, No. 4, 1929.

FERRACCIU, A. : La figura costituzionale del Gran Consiglio. Rivista di diritto pubblico 21 : 207-226, aprile 1929.

Italia-Finlandia. Tratto di estradizione e di assistenza giudiziaria in materia penale. Revista di diritto penale 3 : 100-106, 1931.
Helsingfors, 10 luglio 1929.

MANYON, L. : The Italian magistracy of labour - a fascist experiment. Michigan law review 27 : 889-920, June 1929.

RANELETTI, O. : Il gran Consiglio del fascismo e la forma di governo dello Stato italiano. Rivista di diritto pubblico 21 : 320-338, giugno-luglio 1929.

BARNES, J.S. : The new Italian constitution. Edinburgh review 250 : 1-18, July 1929.

BARTILUCCI, J. : Six years of fascist legislation. American bar association journal 15 : 473-475, August 1929.

JEMOLO, A.C. : Natura giuridica del P.N.F. Rivista di diritto pubblico 21 : 544-555, ottobre 1929.

BAAK, J.C. : Fascismus und Völkerrecht. Zeitschrift für öffentliches Recht 9 : 1-31, 1 Oktober 1929.

FERRARI, R. : The Italo-American conflict on naturalization. Current history 31 : 306-311, November 1929.

MANGINI, R. : Profili politici del progetto definitivo di un nuovo codice penale. Gerarchia 9 : 879-884, novembre 1929.

VITTA, C. : Divergenza nella dottrina italiana sui principî fondamentali del diritto internazionale pubblico. Rivista di diritto internazionale 21 : 501-525, 1 ottobre - 31 dicembre 1929.
Italian doctrine of international law.

BETTI, E. : Il progetto di un Codice italiano-francese delle obbligazioni e dei contratti. Rivista del diritto commerciale 27 : 665-668, novembre-dicembre 1929.

JAPAN

MIYAOKA, T. : La loi japonaise sur la nationalité et les droits fonciers des étrangers conformément aux lois du Japon. Bulletin mensuel de la société de législation comparée 54 : 348-359, juillet-septembre 1925.

Korea not a colony. Japan chronicle : 618, 30 May 1929.
Legal status of Korea.

MIYAOKA, T. : Treaty-making power under the constitution of Japan. International conciliation 221 : 297-304, June 1926.

REEVES, J.S. : Japanese draft code of international law. American journal of international law 20 : 767-768, October 1926.

HIRABAYASHI, S. : The new code of civil procedure. Japan chronicle : 136, 1 August 1929.

The new civil code. Japan chronicle : 116-117, August 1, 1929.

LATVIA

PACHE, M.B. : Der Rechtszustand in Lettland. Niemeyers Zeitschrift für internationales Recht 33 : 17-35, 1. bis 4. Heft, 1924/1925.

LOEBER, A. : Die neuere Rechtsentwicklung. Zeitschrift für osteuropäisches Recht 1 : 267-271, Juli 1925.

SCHILLING, C. von : Das interterritoriale Privatrecht Lettlands. Ostrecht 2 : 712-729, Heft 7-8, Juli-August 1926.

LEBANON

CARDAHI, C. : L'accès des étrangers à la propriété foncière dans les Pays sous mandat français du Proche-Orient. Gazette des tribunaux Libano-Syriens 4 : 65-70, août et septembre 1928.

MULETTE, R. : Le régime foncier en Syrie et au Liban. Economiste européen (supplément colonial) 37 : 55-56, 19 octobre 1928.

LIBERIA

THOT, L. : Le droit pénal codifié de Tonga, Samoa, Hawaï et Libéria (Contd.). Bulletin mensuel de la Société de Législation comparée 58 : 221-230, janvier-mars 1929.

LIECHTENSTEIN

WYLER, M. : The new civil law of the principality of Liechtenstein. Journal of comparative legislation and international law 8 : 197-214, November 1926.

LITHUANIA

GIANNINI, A. : La costituzione Lituania. L'Europa orientale 5 : 161-185, marzo 1925.

Legge costituzionale dello stato Lituano. L'Europa orientale 5 : 186-196, marzo 1925.
Text in Italian.

BÜCHLER, O. von : Der Rechtzustand in Litauen. Niemeyers Zeitschrift für internationales Recht 34 : 232-262, 3. bis 6. Heft 1925.

Die Verfassung des Litauischen Staates. Zeitschrift für osteuropäisches Recht 1 : 65-78, Mai 1925.
Text in German.

BÜCHLER, O. von : Kollisions Normen des Privatrechts in Litauen. Niemeyers Zeitschrift für internationales Recht 33 : 33-58, 1-4 Heft 1925-1926.

FINKELSTEIN, O. : Litauisches internationales Privatrecht und Stellung der Ausländer in Litauen. Ostrecht 2 : 729-746, Heft 7-8, Juli-August 1926.

BALOG, E. : Il diritto vigente in Lituania con particolare considerazione del diritto privato. Annuario di diritto comparato e di studi legislativi 1 : 143-164, 1927.
The changes in Lithuanian private law.

ROBINSON, J. : Der litauische Staat und seine Verfassungsentwicklung. Jahrbuch des öffentlichen Rechts 16 : 295-327, 1928.
Annexed the German text of the Lithuanian constitutions of August 1, 1922 and May 15, 1928.

MEXICO

The rights of foreigners in Mexico. Economic review 13 : 341-343, April 16, 1926.

BARKER, F.F. : New laws and nationalism in Mexico. Foreign affairs (N.Y.) 5 : 589-604, July 1927.

BULLINGTON, J.P. : Problems of international law in the Mexican constitution of 1917. American journal of international law 21 : 685-705, No. 4, October 1927.

MENDOZA, S. : Mexico's bold experiment in new criminal code. Current history 31 : 107-111, October 1929.

NETHERLANDS

MAUTNER, W. : Das neue niederländische Aktiengesetz. Der Oesterreichische Volkswirt 20 : 1256-1259, 4. August 1928.
Summary of the new Dutch Company law.

HALLSTEIN, W. : Das niederländische Gesetz über die Aktiengesellschaft vom 2 Juli 1928. Zeitschrift für ausländisches und internationales Privatrecht 2 : 730-761, Heft 4-5, 1928.
The new Dutch Company law: commentary and text (in German).

POLAK, R. : Das neue holländische Aktienrecht. Wirtschaftsdienst 13 : 1551-1553, 21 September 1928.
Summary of the new Dutch Company law.

Die neuen Bestimmungen des holländischen Handelsgesetzbuchs; von der Aktiengesellschaft. Gesetzgebung und Rechtspraxis des Auslandes 4 : 152-160, Oktober 1928.
German text of the new Dutch Company law.

GARGAS, S. : Grundriss der Reform des niederländischen Aktienrechts. Gesetzgebung und Rechtspraxis des Auslandes 4 : 178-185, Dezember 1928.
Summary of the new Dutch Company law.

HARENCARSPEL, G.J. van : Die Neuordnung des niederländischen Seerechts. Zeitschrift für ausländisches und internationales Privatrecht 3 : 549-566, Heft 4, 1929.

GUMPRECHT, K. : Das neue niederländische Aktienrecht. Bank-Archiv 28 : 235-238, 3. April 1929.

OPPENHEIMER, L. : Das Wechselrecht von Niederländisch-Indien-Neue Orient 9 : 29-31, Juli 1929.

VOLLENHOVEN, C. van : Parlamentair stelsel en het regeeren overzee. Koloniaal Tijdschrift 18 : 290-311, Juli 1929.
The constitution of the Dutch East Indies.

NEW ZEALAND

Le CONTE, R. : L'évolution de la constitution néo-zélandaise. Revue de droit publi 43 : 343-358, avril-mai-juin 1926.

PALESTINE

Decreto reale 24 luglio 1925 sulla cittadinanza palestinese ("Palestine citizenship order"). Oriente Moderno 5 : 503-507, ottobre 1925.
Italian translation of Palestine citizenship order.

BENTWICH, N. : Legislation of Palestine (1923 1924). Egypte contemporaine 08 : 365-379, novembre 1925.

BENTWICH, N. : The legislation of Palestine 1918-1925. Journal of comparative legislation and international law 8 : 9-20, February 1926.

BENTWICH, N. : The application of Jewish law in Palestine. Journal of comparative legislation and international law 9 : 59-67, February 1927.

POLAND

Costituzione della repubblica di Polonia. L'Europa orientale 5 : 35-49, gennaio 1925.
Text of constitution of March 17 1921 (in Italian).

GIANNINI, A. : La costituzione Polacca. L'Europa orientale 5 : 1-34, gennaio 1925.

MOSCHZISKER, R. von : The constitutions of the United States and Poland - a comparison. Poland 6 : 517-574, September 1925.

BALINSKI, I. : La constitution polonaise. Revue hebdomadaire 36 : 112-115, septembre 1925.

CHMURSKI, A. : Das Polnische oberste Verwaltungsgericht. Ostrecht 2 : 40-47, Januar 1926.

PERETIATKOWICZ, A. : La révision de la constitution polonaise. Revue du droit public 44 : 124-128, janvier-février-mars 1927.

BABINSKI, L. : L'état actuel de la codification en Pologne. Bulletin mensuel de la Société de Législation comparée 55 : 139-154, janvier-mars 1926.

WAHLE, K. : Die Regelung der Zivilrechtlichen Verhältnisse in Polnisch Arva und Zips. Ostrecht 2 : 396-402, April 1926.

STELMACHOWSKI : Das Problem des interterritorialen Privat-und Prozessrechts in Polen. Ostrecht 2 : 697-704, Heft 7-8, Juli-August 1926.

La constitution de la république polonaise du 17 mars 1921, modifiée et complétée par la loi constitutionelle du 2 août 1926. Est européen 6 : 315-320, août 1926.
Text (French) - ancient and modified.

BUKOWIECKI, S. : La réforme de la constitution polonaise. Est européen 6 : 262-271, août 1926.

MÜLLER, W. : Die Entwicklung s österreichischen bürgerlichen Rechts in Polen. Ostrecht : 1042-1052, November 1926.

FIERICH, X. : I lavori di codificazione in Polonia nell' anno 1925. Annuario di diritto comparato 1 : 120-129, 1927.
A survey of the codification work of civil and commercial law in Poland.

BABINSKI, L. : Le droit international privé en Pologne. Revue de droit international privé 22 : 463-489, No. 3, 1927.

GARGAS, S. : Das Staatsangehörigkeitsproblem im polnisch-russischen Friedensvertrage von Riga. Zeitschrift für vergleichende Rechtswissenschaft 42 : 342-351, 3. Heft 1927.

UDINA, M. : Il diritto internazionale privato della repubblica polacca. Rivista di diritto internazionale 19 : 187-266, 10 aprile- 30 giugno 1927.

BABINSKI, Léon : Aperçu sur la situation juridique des étrangers en Pologne. Journal du droit international 54 : 582-594, mai-juin 1927.

CZAJKOWSKI, E. : The Polish aircraft law. Review of polish law and economics 1 : 377-387, No. 4, 1928.
Czaykowski, S. : Der Schutz des gewerblichen Eigentums.

NEYMARK, E. : The prisons in Poland. Review of Polish laws and economics 1 : 350-360, No. 4, 1928.

HILAROWICZ : Verordnung von 19.1.1928 über die Organisation und die Zuständigkeit der Behörden der allgemeinen Verwaltung. Zeitschrift für Ostrecht 2 : 516-538, April 1928.

HAWLITZKY, W. : Das neue polnische Aktienrecht. Zeitschrift für Ostrecht 2 : 589-626, Mai 1928.

KOSCHEMBAHR-LYKOWSKI, M.I. de : Quelques dispositions générales d'un projet de code civil polonais. Revue trimestrielle de droit civil 27 : 551-578, juillet-septembre 1928.

POHLE : Neu-Regelung des Aktienrechts in Polen. Bank-Archiv 27 : 416-421, 15 August 1928.
Comment on the new Polish Companies Act of 22 March 1928.

LACHES, S. : Das Recht der Niederlassungen ausländischer Aktiengesellschaften und Gesellschaften m.b.H. in Polen, nach polnischem Recht. Wirtschaft und das Recht 3 : 919-932, November 1928.

CAPITANT, H. : La législation de la Pologne depuis sa libération jusqu'à 1928. Bulletin mensuel de la Société de Libération comparée 57 : 411-517, octobre-décembre 1928.

MAKAROV, A.N. : Die russisch-polnischen Rechtsbeziehungen seit 1815 unter spezieller Berücksichtigung der Staatsangehörigkeitsfragen. Zeitschrift für ausländisches öffentliches Recht und Völkerrecht (Teil I) 1 : 330-367, 1929.

BABINSKI, L. : La nouvelle organisation judiciaire en Pologne. Bulletin de l'Institut intermédiaire international 20 : 15-20, janvier 1929.

STARZEWSKI, M. : Gesetze und Verfassung in Polen. Zeitschrift für Ostrecht 3 : 29-38, Januar 1929.

NEYMARK, E. : Le dixième anniversaire du système pébitentiaire en Pologne. Revue internationale de droit pénal 6 : 66-90, ler trimestre 1929.

WITENBERG, J.C. : La loi polonaise sur les Sociétés par actions (1928). Annales de droit commercial 38 : 38-57, janvier-mars 1929.

CAR, S. : Le dixième anniversaire du système pénitentiaire polonais. Revue pénitentiaire de Pologne 4 : 42.58, janvier-avril 1929.

Polend. Die neue polnische Strafprozessordnung. Zeitschrift für Ostrecht 3 : 232-303, Februar 1929.
Text and comment of new Polish code of criminal procedure.

TAUBERT, L. : Notre nouvelle convention avec la Pologne. Revue économique de Belgrade 4 : 35-37, février 1929.
Commentaire de la convention du 4 mai 1923 comcernant les relations juridiques des ressortissants polonais et yougoslaves.

The Polish joint stock company law. Polish economist 4 : 121-123, April 1929.

LACHS, S. : Patent-, Marken- und Musterschutz in Polen. Prager Juristische Zeitschrift 9 : 374-378, 2. Maiheft 1929.

KULSCHEWSKI, E. : Die ausländischen Aktiengesellschaften im polnischen Aktienrecht. Danziger Wirtschaftzeitung 9 : 390-391, 7 Juni 1929.

ROST, H. : Das internationale Aufwertungsrecht Polens. Zeitschrift für Ostrecht 3 : 1301-1319, Oktober 1929.

SULKOWSKI, J. : La loi polonaise sur les sociétés anonymes. Bulletin mensuel de la Société de législation comparée 58 : 595-629, octobre-décembre 1929.

LUDKIEWICZ, Z. : Land reform in Poland. Slavonic review 8 : 315-330, December 1929.

PORTUGAL

ROST, H. : Die Reform des portugiesischen Zivilprozesses. Zeitschrift für ausländisches und internationales Privatrecht 3 : 678-694, Heft 4, 1929.

RUMANIA

SCHWEFELBERG, A. : Traement des étrangers en Roumanie en matière de contributions directes. Journal du droit international 52 : 956-962, juillet-août-septembre-octobre 1925.

NEGREA, C. : Der heutige Rechtzustand. Zeitschrif für osteuropäisches Recht 1 : 307-322, Oktober 1925

PHÉRÉKYDE, G. and PANTAZI, E. : Loi du 6 février 1924 sur les personnes juridiques. Bulletin mensuel de la Société de Législation comparée 10-12 : 477-514, octobre-décembre 1925.

ASCH, Dr. A. : Das rumänische Aktiengesellschaftsrecht. Ostrecht 1 : 465-477, Dezember 1925.

COHEN, G. : La nationalité des sociétés commerciales en Roumanie. Revue de droit international privé 21 : 350-361, No. 3, 1926.

SCHWEFELBERG, A. : La loi roumaine du 23 février 1924 sur l'acquisition et la perte de la nationalité roumaine, par rapport aux traités de paix. Journal du droit international 53 : 300-315, mars-avril 1926.

COHEN, J.G. : La législation roumaine en matière de sociétés. Société belge d'études et d'expansion 58 : 465-471, décembre 1926.

POLINGER, A. : L'unification législative en Roumanie. Bulletin de la Société de Législation comparée 57 : 393-396, juillet-septembre 1928.

RADULESCO, J. : Le projet de code pénal roumain. Bulletin mensuel de la société de législation comparée 57 : 540-596, octobre-décembre 1928.

MARCOVITCH, J. : Das Verhältnis zwischen dem normalen Gesetz und der Verfassung in Rumänien. Zeitschrift für Ostrecht 3 : 55-58, Januar 1929.

BARASCH, M.I. : La protection légale des travailleurs en Roumanie. Recueil de droit commercial et de droit social 1 : 65-70, mars 1929.

SPRINGER, P. : Das rumänische Arbeitsrecht. Zeitschrift für Ostrecht 3 : 415-466, März 1929.

NEGREA, C. : Gesetzgebung und Rechtsprechung in Rumänien in den Jahren 1927 und 1928. Zeitschrift für ausländisches und internationales Privatrecht 3 : 967-987, Heft 6, 1929.
Survey of Rumanian legislation and jurisdiction in 1927 and 1928.

GANE, A.N. : Le conseil législatif en Roumanie. Bulletin mensuel de la Société de Législation comparée 58 : 506-516, juillet-septembre 1929.

Gesetz über Erwerb und Verlust der rumänischen Staatsangehörigkeit vom 23. Februar 1924. Zeitschrift für Ostrecht 3 : 1185-1195, August-Septemb 1929.
German text of Rumanian nationality law of February 23, 1924.

DRAGOMIRESCO, P. : Le futur code de commerce roumain en voie d'élaboration. Institut international du commerce, revue 6 : I-IV, 20 septembre 1929.

FILITTI, I.C., et VRABIESCO, G. : Le conseil législatif de Roumanie. Revue de sciences politiques 44 : 481-498, octobre-décembre 1929.

VELESCU, A. : La procédure civile roumaine. Bulletin mensuel de la Société de législation comparée 58 : 642-665, octobre-décembre 1929.

SOUTH AFRICA

R.F. : Naturalisation of Germans domiciled in South-West Africa. British yearbook of international law 6 : 188-191, 1925.

SPAIN

HARTWIG, A. : Studien zur spanischen Rechtsgeschichte bis zur Einführung des Fuero Juzgo. Zeitschrift für vergleichende Rechtswissenschaft 41 : 241-267, 1/11 Heft 1925.

ROGER, R. : Sources et domaine d'application du droit civil espagnol. Bulletin mensuel de la Société de Législation comparée 54 : 227-243, avril-juin 1925.

El nuevo código de comercio - El proyecto de reforma. Espana económica y financiera 34 : 868-869, 11 de septiembre 1926.

El nuevo código de comercio - el proyecto de reforma. Espana económica y financiera 34 : 892-894, 18 de septiembre 1926.

El nuevo código de comercio - el proyecto de reforma. España económica y financiera 34 : 916-918, 25 de septiembre 1926.

El nuevo código de comercio. El proyecto de reforma. España económica y financiera 34 : 939-942, 2 de octubre 1926.

La reforma del código de comercio y los bancos. España económica y financiera 35 : 1-2, 1 de enero 1927.

La casa comercial. España económica y financiera 33 : 49-51, 17 de enero 1925.
Survey of present commercial code.

TRIAS de BES, Y. : Le droit international privé de l'Espagne. Revue de droit international privé 23 : 48-64, No. 1, 1928.

TRIAS de BES, J.M. : El dret internacional privat d'España. Revista jurídica de Cataluña 34 : julio-agosto 1928.

CUELLO CALÓN, E. : Le nouveau code pénal espagnol. Revue internationale de droit pénal 6 : 193-213, No. 2, 1929.

RAMON, A.R. : De la condition des étrangers en Espagne. Revue de droit international privé 24 : 221-238, No. 2, 1929.

LLORENS, E.L. : Der Entwurf eines spanischen Handelsgesetzbuches. Zeitschrift für ausländisches und internationales Privatrecht 3 : 932-966, Heft 6, 1929.
Spanish draft commercial code.

CADALSO, F. : Le nouveau code pénal et les systèmes pénitentiaires en Espagne. Revista de ciencias jurídicas y sociales 12 : 396-433, julio-septiembre 1929.

GOICOCHEA, J.G.L. de : Le nouveau code pénal espagnol. Bulletin de l'institut intermédiaire international 21 : 210-223, octobre 1929.

BRUCHMÜLLER, W. : Der spanische Verfassungsentwurf. Deutschen-Spiegel 6 : 1616-1618, 11 Oktober 1929.

SWEDEN

ENGSTRÖMER, I. : Der schwedische Entwurf einer Prozessreform. Zeitschrift für ausländisches und internationales Privatrecht 3 : 32-36, Heft 1, 1929.

SWITZERLAND

RUCK, E. : Verfassungsrecht und Verfassungsleben in der Schweiz. Zeitschrift für Politik 14 : 289-322, Heft 4, 1925.

Politik oder Jurisprudenz? Betrachtungen zum Entwurf eines Bundesgesetzes über die eidgenössische Verwaltung und Disziplinarrechtspflege. Wissen und Leben 18 : 945-954, 10 September 1925.

HIRZEL, P. : Eidgenössische Verwaltungs-und Disziplinargerichtsbarkeit. Schweizerische Monatshefte 5 : 353-359, Oktober 1925.

FLEINER, F. : Eidgenössische Verwaltungsgerichtsbarkeit. Schweizerische Blätter für Handel und Industrie 32 : 357-360, 15 November 1925.

STREBEL, Y. : Die Praxis des Schweizerischen Bundesgerichtes auf dem Gebiete des Zivilrechts einschliesslich gewerblichen Rechtsschutzes. Zeitschrift für ausländisches und internationales Privatrecht 2 : 544-579, Heft 4-5, 1928.

HAAB, R. : Gesetzgebung der Schweiz, betreffebd Privatrecht, Arbeitsrecht, gewerblichen Rechtsschutz, Zwangsvollstreckung und Konkurs. Zeitschrift für ausländisches und internationales Privatrecht 2 : 525-543, Heft 4-5, 1928.

GIACOMETTI, Z. : Die Fortbildung des öffentlichen Rechts in der schweizerischen Eidgenossenschaft in den Jahren 1921-1928. Jahrbuch des öffentlichen Rechts 16 : 327-396, 1928.

Der Schutz des Staates gegen landesverräterische Umtriebe. Schweizerische Monatshefte 8 : 518-521, Februar 1929.

HAAB, R. : Gesetzgebung der Schweiz, betreffend Privatrecht, Arbeitsrecht, gewerblichen Rechtsschutz, Zwangsvollstreckung und Konkurs, im Jahre 1928. Zeitschrift für ausländisches und internationales Privatrecht 3 : 567-577, Heft 4, 1929.

CLERIC, G.F. von : Zur Schweizer Strafrechtsreform. Schweizerische Monatshefte für Politik und Kultur 9 : 28-34, April 1929.

SWITZERLAND
(International Law, Aliens)

RASCHLE, H. : Oberste Gewalt im Bund und Aussenpolitik. Betrachtungen zur Grundfrage des schweizerischen Staatsrechtes. Schweizerische Blätter für Politik und Kultur 5 : 81-92, Mai 1925.

SENGER, Max : Zur beruflichen Überfremdung der Schweiz. Wissen und Leben 18 : 889-893, 20 August 1925.

FRITZSCHE, H. : Zivilprozessrecht und internationales Privatrecht der Schweiz im Jahre 1927. Zeitschrift für ausländisches und internationales Privatrecht 2 : 580-602, Heft 4-5, 1928.

BOSCO, G. : Il progetto di legge svizzero sulle norme di diritto internazionale privato in materia cambiaria. Rivista di diritto commerciale 26 : 643-647, 18 gennaio 1929.

HIS, E. : De la compétence des cantons suisses de conclure des traités internationaux, spécialement concernant la double imposition. Revue de droit international et de législation comparée 56 : 454-479, No. 3, 1929.

FRITZSCHE, H. : Zivilprozessrecht und internationales Privatrecht der Schweiz im Jahre 1928. Zeitschrift für ausländisches und internationales Privatrecht 3 : 613-638, Heft 4, 1929.

SYRIA

CARDAHI, C. : L'accès aux étrangers à la propriété foncière dans les pays sous mandat français du Proche-Orient. Revue de droit international privé 23 : 209-221, No. 2, 1928.

CARDAHI, C. : Le problème de l'organisation judiciaire dans les pays du Levant placés sous mandat français. Revue de droit international privé 23 : 417-463, No. 3, 1928.

MULETTE, R. : Le régime foncier en Syrie et au Liban. Economiste européen (supplément colonial) 37 : 55-56, 19 octobre 1928.

CARDAHI, C. : Les sûretés réelles et la vente forcée dans le droit des pays sous mandat du Levant. Bulletin mensuel de la Société de Législation comparée 58 : 563-594, octobre-décembre 1929.

TURKEY

GIANNINI, A. : La costituzione turca. Oriente moderno 5 : 65-80, febbraio 15, 1925.
Text (in Italian) and comment.

Exposé des motifs du code civil turc. Echo de Turquie 2 : 405-408, 25 février 1926.

EARLE, E.M. : The new constitution of Turkey. Political science review 40 : 73-100, March 1925.

BRINTON, J.Y. : Turkey's new system of laws and courts. Current history 25 : 498-503, January 1927.

SECRETAN, R. : Le nouveau code turc. Bulletin mensuel de la Société de Législation comparée 56 : 361-386, juillet-septembre 1927.

TURKEY
(International Law, Aliens)

SCHULTHEISS, T. : Die Türken und die Schweiz. Schweizerische Monatshefte 5 : 257-270, August-September 1925.

ASSABGHY, A. : La protection étrangère est-elle héréditaire? Journal du droit international 52 : 1196-1203, juillet-août-septembre-octobre 1925.

TEYSSAIRE, J. : Les sociétés concessionnaires en Turquie et les dommages de guerre. Revue de droit international 1 : 434-439, avril-juin 1927.

SALEM, E.R. : De l'exécution des jugements étranger en Turquie. Journal du droit international 55 : 30[illegible]-314, mars-avril 1928.

SALEM, R. : La loi nouvelle sur la nationalité turque. Revue de droit international privé 24 : 25-59, No. 1, 1929.

TÉNÉKIDÈS, C.G. : Les conditions de forme du mariage des étrangers en Turquie. Journal du droit international 56 : 50-65, janvier-février 1929.

U.S.S.R.

The Soviet legal system. Private law in the U.S.S.R. Soviet Union review 6 : 56-58, January 17, 1925.

FREUND, H. : Recht und Wirtschaft in Sowjetrussland. Blätter für vergleichende Rechtswissenschaft und Volkswirtschaftslehre 19 : 43-62, Nos. 1-6, Oktober 1924-März 1925.

CONTENSON, de L. : Loi fondamentale de l'Union des républiques socialistes soviétiques. Revue d'histoire diplomatique 39 : 1-8, No. 1, 1925.

ANDERSSEN, W. : Die Entwicklung der grundlegenden Verfassungsgesetze des Russischen Bundes bis zur Gründung des Bundes der sozialistischen Räterepubliken. Zeitschrift für Vergleichende Rechtswissenschaft 41 : 129-146, 1/11 Heft 1925.

MIRKINE-GUETZEVITCH, B. : La constitution de l'U.R.S.S. Revue du droit public et de la science politique 42 : 118-126, janvier-février-mars 1925.

Civil liberty in Russia. New republic 42 : 55-56, 11 March 1925.

The Soviet constitution. Soviet union review 6 : 170-171, February 28, 190-191, March 7 and 211-212, March 14, 1925, and 232-234, 21 March 1925, 249-250, 28 March 1925.

PACHE, M.B, : Das Familienrecht in Sowjetrussland. Niemeyers Zeitschrift für internationales Recht 34 : 263-280, 3. bis 6. Heft 1925.

KORSCH, K. : Die Verfassung der vereinigten sozialistischen Sowjetrepublik. Das neue Russland 2 : 28-34, No. 5-6, 1925.

LENSKI, J. : Zur Frage der Gesetzlichkeit in der Union der SSR. Das neue Russland 2 : 34-36, Nos.5-6, 1925.

NATIONAL LAW - COUNTRIES

Russland. Die neue Verfassung (Grundgesetz) der Russischen sozialistischen Sovietrepublik, bestätigt vom XII. allrussischen Rätecongress am 11. Mai 1925. Zeitschrift für osteuropäisches Recht 1 : 156-175, Juli 1925.
Text (in German).

STEBELSKI, A. : Un projet original de constitution soviétique. L'est européen 5 : 249-267, juillet 1925.

TIMASCHEW, N. : Der Rechtzustand von Sovetrussland. Zeitschrift für osteuropäisches Recht 1 : 147-156, Juli 1925.

MIRKINE-GUETZEVITCH, M. : La théorie générale de l'état soviétique. Revue de droit public et de la science politique 42 : 509-521, juillet-août-septembre 1925.

ENGLÄNDER, Dr. : Ist Russland ein Rechtsstaat geworden? Deutsche Juristen-Zeitung 30 : 1234-1238, 15 August 1925.

MIRKINE-GUETZEVITCH, B. : Le contrôle de constitutionnalité des lois soviétiques. Revue du droit public et de la science politique 42 : 529-602, octobre-novembre-décembre 1925.

VEGA, J. de la : La Rusia sovietica. Origenes constitucionales. Revista argentina de ciencias politicas 31 : 340-350, 12 de enero de 1926.

GOLDSTEIN, J. : Die gemischten Gesellschaften. Aus de Volkswirtschaft der U.S.S.R. 5 : 24-28, Januar 1926.

KLENERT, T. : Russland von heute. Seine Verfassung, seine wirtschaftsein Recht. Schweizerische Monatshefte 6 : 11-17, April 1926.

THAL, L. : Die Schranken des Schutzes von Privatrechten nach Art. 1 des Zivilkodex der U.D.S.S.R. Ostrecht 2 : 402-412, April 1926.

CHAMPCOMMUNAL, M.J. : Le droit des personnes d'après le code de famille soviétique. Bulletin mensuel de la société de Législation comparée Nos. 4-6 : 290-320, avril-juin 1926.

MARCÉ, V. de : La constitution soviétique et le contrôle des finances en Russie. Revue politique et parlementaire 127 : 193-230, 10 mai 1926.

SEMENOFF, J. : Die neue Verfassung der R.S.F.S.R. Ostrecht 2 : 489-499, Mai 1926.

TCHLENEV, S. : Le droit et la révolution. Europe nouvelle 9 : 843-844, 19 juin 1926.

MIRKINE-GUETZEVITCH, M. : Le pouvoir constituant dans le droit soviétique. Revue du droit public 43 : 466-484, juillet-août-septembre 1926.

VÉGA, J. de la : La Russia sovietica (contd.). Revista argentina de ciencias politicas 33 : 17-26, 12 de octubre 1926.

Le fonctionnement des institutions en Russie. Revue politique et parlementaire 129 : 411-435, 10 décembre 1926.

TIMASCHEW, N. : Das Nationalitätenrecht der Union sozialistischer Sowjetrepubliken. Archiv des öffentlichen Rechts 13 : 1-21, 1. Heft 1927.

MIRKINE-GUETZEVITCH, M.B. : Aperçu des principes fondamentaux de l'état soviétique. Bulletin mensuel de la Société de Législation comparée 56 : 133-169, janvier-mars 1927.

GARGAS, S. : Das Staatsangehörigkeitsproblem im polnisch-russischen Friedensvertrage von Riga. Zeitschrift für vergleichende Rechtswissenschaft 42 : 342-351, 3. Heft 1927.

CHAMPCOMMUNAL, M.J. : Le nouveau code de famille soviétique. Bulletin mensuel de la Société de Législation comparée 56 : 254-287, avril-juin 1927.

WOLFF, W. : Die neueste Entwicklung der Handelsgesetzgebung der Sovetunion im Zusammenhang mit der gegenwärtigen Richtung der Handelspolitik. Zeitschrift für Ostrecht 1 : 192-207, Mai 1927.

GUBSKY, N. : Economic law in Soviet Russia. Economic journal 37 : 226-236, June 1927.

BASSECHES, N. : Die Entwicklung des Rechtes in der Sowjetunion. Osterreichische Volkswirt 20 : 17-19, 1 Oktober 1927.

ENOUKIDZÉ, A. : La structure politique de l'U.R.S.S. et sa constitution. Europe nouvelle 10 : 1515-1517, 12 novembre 1927.

JENUKIDSE, A. : Die politische Struktur (Konstitution) der Sowjetunion. Zum kehnten Jahrestag. Neue Russland 4 : 14-16, Dezember 1927.

FREUND, Dr. H. : Economic organization, commercial regulations and concessions in the Soviet Union. Illinois law review 22 : 852-879, April 1928.

BRANDENBURGSKI : Die Sowjetgesetzgebung. Das neue Russland 5 : 26-31, Heft 5, 1928.

VEGA, J. de la : El sistema electoral de Rusia sovietica. Revista argentina de ciencias politicas 36 : 269-280, 12 de julio de 1928.

DURDENEVSKIJ, V. : Verwaltungsgesetzbuch der Ukraine von 1927. Zeitschrift für Ostrecht 2 : 1385-1452, Oktober 1928.
Ukrainian administrative law.

Das Gerichtswesen der U.D.S.S.S.R. Neue Russland 5 : 22-24, Dezember 1928.

TIMASCHEW, N. : Das Wahlrecht der Sowjetunion. Archiv des öffentlichen Rechts 55 : 81-109, 1. Heft 1929.

TCHELIABOW : La structure fédérative de l'U.R.S.S. Vie économique des Soviets 5 : 9-10, 5 mai 1929.

LANDKOF, S. : Scheck und laufende Rechnung in Gesetzgebung und Gerichtspraxis der U.d.S.S.R. Zeitschrift für Ostrecht 3 : 657-671, Mai 1929.

Les bolcheviks et le droit des peuples. Prométhée 4 : 24-27, mai 1929.
La souveraineté des Etats dans l'union soviétique.

OLEKSANDRENKO, G.W. : Grundlinien der ukrainischen Verfassung. Neue Russland 6 : 15-17, mai 1929.

KOTLIAREVSKI, S. : Le droit budgétaire de l'U.R.S.S. Revue de science et de législation financières 27 : 422-429, juillet-août-septembre 1929.

HEIFETZ, J.I. : Le droit d'auteur dans l'U.R.S.S. Droit d'auteur 42 : 86-92, 15 août 1929.

MIRKINE-GUETZEVITCH, B. : La révision de la constitution soviétique. Revue politique et parlementaire 36 : 428-432, 10 septembre 1929.
Les modifications du 18 mai 1929.

RESANOV, A. : Nature de l'organisation soviétique gouvernementale et sociale. Mercure de France 40 : 513-536, 15 septembre 1929.

U.S.S.R.
(International Law and Practice, Aliens and Naturalization)

MIRKINE-GUETZEVITCH, B. : La doctrine soviétique du droit international. Revue générale de droit international public 32 : 313-337, no. 4-5, juillet-octobre 1925.

DURDENEWSKI, W. : Die Staatsverträge im Verfassungsrecht der Union des sozialistischen Sowjetrepubliken. Ostrecht 1 : 201-217, Oktober 1925.

MAKAROW, A. : Die Staatsangehörigkeit in Sowjetrussland- Ostrecht 2 : 3-34, Januar 1926.

KUNZ, J.L. : Sowjet-Russland und das Völkerrecht. Zeitschrift für Völkerrecht 13 : 580-586, Heft 4, 1926.

KOREZKI, W.M. : Probleme des internationalen Handelsrechts im Sowjetrecht. Ostrecht 2 : 746-772, Heft 7-8, July-August 1926.

MAKAROV, A.N. : Das internationale Privatrecht Sowjet-Russlands. Ostrecht 2 : 709-712, Heft 7-8, Juli-August 1926.

KOROVINE, E. : La république des soviets et le droit international. Revue générale de droit international public 32 : 292-312, No. 4-5, juillet-octobre 1926.

MIRKINE-GUETZEVITCH, B. : Le droit consulaire de l'U.R.S.S. Revue générale de droit international public 8 : 373-386, septembre-décembre 1926.

NESTEROFF, P. : La situation juridique des étrangers en Russia des Soviets et le régime des concessions (contd.). Revue de droit international privé 22 : 37-43, No. 1, 1927.

STOUPNITZSKY, A. : Etude sur le droit international privé soviétique. Revue de droit international privé 22 : 418-462, No. 3, 1927.

HABICHT, M. : The application of Soviet laws and the exception of public order. American journal of international law 21 : 238-256, April 1927.

La condition des étrangers dans la République des Soviets. Journal du droit international 54 : 572-581, mai-juin 1927.

KOKOVTZOFF, W. : Le gouvernement des Soviets et les "concessions" aux étrangers. Revue des deux mondes 96 : 158-181, 1 septembre 1926.

WOHL, P. : Das rechtliche Schicksal der Aktiengesellschaftenalten russischen Rechts im Ausland. Niemeyers Zeitschrift für internationales Recht 38 : 244-300, 3. bis 5. Heft 1928.

OLEWSKY, L. : Die juristische Bedeutung eines Rechtsgeschäfts, das unter Übertretung des russischen Regeln über die Monopolstellung des Aussenhandels geschlossen ist. Niemayers Zeitschrift für internationales Recht 38 : 197-214, 3. bis 5. Heft 1928.

MIRKINE-GUETZEVITCH, B. : Les traités internationaux de l'Etat soviétique. Revue de droit international 2 : 1012-1049, octobre-novembre-décembre 1928.

HRABAR, E.V. : La condition juridique des agents diplomatiques selon la législation soviétique et les traités conclus par l'U.R.S.S. Revue de droit international de sciences diplomatiques et politiques 6 : 346-368, octobre-décembre 1928.

PHILONENKO, M. : L'expropriation des biens des particuliers par les Soviets devant la justice allemande. Journal du droit international 56 : 13-24, janvier-février 1929.

HANNA, J. : Russia unrecognized. New republic 59 : 116-119, June 19, 1929.
Legal effect of the non recognition of Russia by the United States.

FILIPUCCI-GIUSTINIANI, G. : Il concetto sovietista di diritto internazionale. Politica 11 : 381-409, giugno-agosto 1929.
Survey of Soviet legal theories.

NOLDE, B. : Les mesures soviétiques d'expropriation devant les tribunaux étrangers. Revue de droit international, de sciences diplomatiques et politiques 7 : 201-213, juillet-septembre 1929.

RABINOVITCH, J.M. : Die Nationalisierung der russischen Aktiengesellschaften durch die Sovietregierung im Spiegel der international Praxis. Zeitschrift für Ostrecht 3 : 1109-1137, August-September 1929.

PETROV, M. : Le régime des spécialistes étrangers dans l'Union soviétique. Vie économique des Soviets 5 : 3-4, 5 octobre 1929.

FILIPUCCI-GIUSTINIANI, G. : Il concetto sovietista di duritto internazionale (Contd.). Politica 12 : 162-196, ottobre-dicembre 1929.

BERNSTEIN, P. : Situation juridique des entreprises concessionnées dans l'U.R.S.S. Bulletin d'information de la société pour les relations culturelles entre l'U.R.S.S. et l'étranger : 25-26, 31 décembre 1929.

UNITED ARAB REPUBLIC

CRABITÈS, P. : The fiftieth anniversary of the Mixed Tribunals of Egypt. Nineteenth century 99 : 364-372, March 1926.

SOUBHI GHALI, bey : Les tribunaux de la réforme et l'Egypte. Revue de droit international 4 : 110-118, Nos. 2-3, avril-septembre 1926.

BRINTON, J.Y. : The mixed courts of Egypt. American journal of international law 20 : 670-688, October 1926.

Text of the constitution of Egypt. Current history 25 : 532-539, January 1927.
Text (English).

NATIONAL LAW - COUNTRIES

BACOS, C. : Le statut juridique des Libanais et Syriens en Egypte. Gazette des tribunaux libano-syriens 3 : 1045-1050, janvier 1928.

La réforme des tribunaux arbitraux mixtes égyptiens. Revue politique et parlementaire 35 : 227-234, 10 mai 1928.

PRESTON GILES, H. : The Egyptian nationality law. Palestine weekly 16 : 285, March 15, 1929.

La nouvelle loi sur le statut personnel musulman. Egyptienne 5 : 22-37, mars 1929.
Legislation Egyptienne.

GEORGE-SAMNÉ : La nouvelle loi sur la nationalité égyptienne. Correspondance d'Orient 21 : 146-147, avril 1929.
Son effet sur les Syriens et Libanais établis en Egypte.

The capitulations in Egypt. Near East and India 35 : 516, April 25, 1929.

PRESTONS GILES, H. : The capitulations in Egypt - Why they should not yet be abolished. Palestine weekly 16 : 443-444, 10 May 1929.

BRAUN, F. : Le décret-loi de 1929 sur la nationalité égyptienne. Journal du droit international 56 ; 627-636, mai-juin 1929.
Texte de la loi et rapport de commission même No. pp. 818-831.

The capitulations in Egypt - why they should not yet be abolished. African world 107 : 241, 1 June 1929.

CRABITÈS, P. : The mixed courts of Egypt. American bar association journal 15 : 378-380, June 1929.

U.S.A.

BUTLER MURRAY, N. : Comment les Etats-Unis ont édifié leur puissance depuis cinquante ans. Revue de Paris 32 : 241-263, janvier 15, 1925.

WESTON, M.F. : Political questions. Harvard law review 38 : 296-333, January 1925.

CUSHMAN, R.E. : Constitutional law in 1923-1924. American political science review 19 : 51-68, February 1925.

MOSCHZISKER, R. von : The constitution of the United States and Poland - a comparison. Poland 6 : 517-574, September 1925.

DENNIS, A.H. : The place of the official lawyer in the constitution. Law quarterly review 41 : 378-388, October 1925.

FRANKFURTER, F. : The business of the Supreme Court of the United States - A study in the federal judicial system. Harvard law review 39 : 325-367, January 1926.

WHITEHOUSE, J.H. : The constitutional systems of England and the United States. Contemporary review 730 : 459-468, October 1926.

WOODY, C.H. : Is the Senate unrepresentative? Political science quarterly 41 : 219-239, June 1926.

KÜLZ, Dr. : Die Verfassung der vereinigten Staaten von Nordamerika. Juristische Wochenschrift 55 : 2805-2806, 11 Dezember 1926.

OHLANDER, L.W. : The way of the law. Advocate of peace through justice 90 : 94-99, February 1928.
The judicial settlement of disputes between States of the U.S.A. in their relation to international law.

SIMONS : Der Oberste Gerichtshof der Vereinigten Staaten, Juristische Woschenschrift 57 : 1966-1967, 4-11, August 1928.

STRAWN, S.H. : Fifty years progress in law. American bar association journal 14 : 419-425, August-September 1928.

STONE, F.H. : Fifty years' work of the United States Supreme Court. American bar association journal 14 : 428-436, August-September 1928.

FRANKFURTER, F., LANDIS, James M. : The supreme Court under the judiciary act of 1925. Harvard Law Review 42 : 1-29, November 1928.

KEEDY, E.R. : The drafting of a code of criminal procedure. American bar association journal 15 : 7-11, January 1929.
American Institute of criminal law and criminology undertakes draft.

WAITE, J.B. : Code of criminal procedure : the problem of bail. American bar association journal 15 : 71-75, February 1929.

MOEEIAON. S. : Workmen's compensation and maritime law. Yale law journal 38 : 472-502, February 1929.

FRANKFURTER, F. : The federal courts. New republic 58 : 273-277, April 24, 1929.
President Hoover and the problem of law enforcement - federal courts and the law of the states.

PERROUX, F. : Le problème juridique des trusts aux Etats-Unis. Revue politique et parlementaire 36 : 188-199, 10 août 1929.

U.S.A.
(International Law, Aliens, Nationality).

OAKLEY, I.B. : When is a citizen not a citizen? Atlantic monthly 135 : 19-27, January 1925.
Naturalized Americans who do not lose their former citizenship.

YANGUAS, J. de : La double nationalité en Amérique. Revue de droit international et de législation comparée 6 : 364-368, No. 3, 1925.

DICKINSON, E.D. : The meaning of nationali[illegible] the recent immigration acts. American j[illegible] international law 19 : 344-347, April 19[illegible]

POTTER, P.B. : Relative authority of int[illegible] nal law and national law in the United Stat[illegible] rican journal of international law 19 : 31[illegible] April 1925.

HYDE, C.C. : The non-recognition and expat[illegible] of naturalized American citizens. American [illegible] of international law 19 : 742-744, October 1[illegible]

BORCHARD, E.M. : Projects of the American institute of international law on immigration, responsibility of governments, diplomatic protection and extradition. American journal of international law 21 : 118-123, January 1927.

DENNIS, W C. : Project No. 27, pacific settlement, and project No. 28, pan-American court of justice, of the American institut of international law. American journal of international law 21 : 137-144, January 1927.

BORCHARD, E.M. : How far must we protect our citizens abroad? New republic 50 : 214-216, April 13, 1927.

HAZAZD, H.B. : The doctrine of res judica in naturalization cases in the United States. American journal of international lae 23 : 50-55, January 1929.

WIGMORE, J.H. : Government by secret diplomacy. Illinois law review 23 : 689-694, March 1929.
Criticism of the way treaties are published by the U.S. Department of State.

PANDIT, S.G. : The Naturalization law of the United States of America. World unity 3 : 369-381, March 1929.

Status of Filipinos for purposes of immigration and naturalization. Harvard law review 42 : 809-816, April 1929.

JACOBSON, J.M. : American or foreigner? Nation (N.Y.) 129 : 193-195, August 21, 1929.
The problem of nationality in the United States.

HEYDE, C.C. : The interpretation of treaties by the Supreme Court of the United States. American journal of international law 23 : 824-828, October 1929.

HAZARD, H.B. : "Attachment to the principles of the constitution" as judicially construed in certain naturalization cases in the United States. American journal of international law 23 : 783-808, October 1929.

VATICAN STATE

JEMOLO, A.C. : Carattere dello Stato della Città del Vaticano. Rivist di diritto internazionale 21 : 188-196, 1 aprile- 30 giugno 1929.

YUGOSLAVIA

YOVANOVITCH, N. : L'origine de la constitution [illegible]u Royaume des Serbes, Croates et Slovènes. Revue [illegible] Balkans 7 : 5-11, juillet 1925.

[illegible] G. : Grundzüge des Verfassungsrechts des [illegible]reichs der Serben, Kroaten und Slovenen. Zeit[illegible]ft für osteuropäisches Recht 1 : 323-364, Ok[illegible]er [illegible]25.

[illegible]EISNER, B. : Der heutige Rechtszustand in Bosnien [illegible]nd der Herzegovina. Zeitschrift für osteuropäisches [illegible]echt 1 : 365-380, Oktober 1925.

GIVANOVITCH, Th. : L'état du droit et de la science juridique serbes et le travail législatif dans le royaume des Serbes, Croates et Slovèves. Bulletin mensuel de la Société de Législation comparée 10-12 : 437-451, octobre-décembre 1925.

LACHNER, H. : Das Recht der Aktiengesellschaft in Yugoslawien. Mitteilungen des verbandes österreichischen Banken und Bankiers 7 : 327-341, 31 Dezember 1925.

KREK, G. : Grundzüge der Verfassungsrechtes des Königsreichs der Serben, Kroaten und Slovenen (Contd.). Zeitschrift für osteuropäisches Recht 2 : 86-123, Februar 1926.

PÉRITCH, M.J. : Le droit international privé en Yougoslavie. Bulletin de l'Institut intermédiaire international 14 : 232-252, avril 1926.

WERK, H. : Ueberblick über die im Königreiche der Serben, Kroaten und Slovenen bestehende Zivil, Handels-und Wechselrechtliche Gesetzgebung.

KONSTANTINOVITCH, M. : Die Staatsangehörigkeit in Jugoslawien unter besonderer Berücksichtigung der Friedensverträge. Ostrecht 2 : 783-809, Heft 2-3, Juli-August 1926.

PÉRITCH, M.J. : Les dispositions sociales et économiques dans la constitution yougoslave. Revue du droit public 43 : 485-494, juillet-août 1926.

PÉRITCH, M.J. : Le droit international privé dans la constitution du Royaume des Serbes, Croates et Slovènes. Revue de droit international privé 21 : 362-380, November 1926.

PÉRITCH, M.J. : De l'unification du droit civil en Yougoslavie. Bulletin mensuel de la Société de Législation comparée 55 : 477-500, octobre-décembre 1926.

STAHL, K. : Südslawien. Die Schwierigkeit des vielfältigen Rechts. Wirtschaftsdienst 12 : 1587-1588, 14 Oktober 1927.

SIK, L. : Der Rechtshilfevertrag zwischen der Tschoslovakischen Republik und dem Königreiche der Serben, Kroaten und Slovenen in demPraxis. Prager juristische Zeitschrift 9 : 7-11, 1 Januar 1928.
Comment on 1924 judicial treaty.

FUMAGALLI, P. : La costituzione del Vidov-Dan (contd.). Europe orientale 8 : 371-393, novembre-décembre 1929.

PÉRITCH, J. : Principaux traits caractéristiques de la constitution du royaume des Serbes, Croates et Slovènes (Yougoslavia) du 28 janvier 1921. Bulletin mensuel de la Société de Législation comparée 57 : 518-539, octobre-décembre 1928.

JOVANOVIC, D.B. : Das Verhältnis zwischen der Staatsverfassung und dem normalen Gesetze in Jugoslavien. Zeitschrift für Ostrecht 3 : 47-55, Januar 1929.

FUMAGALLI, P. : La costituzione del Vidov-Dan (Contd). Europa orientale 9 : 56-68, gennaio-febbraio 1929.

PÉRITCH, J. : Principaux traits caractéristiques de la constitution du royaume des Serbes, Croates et Slovènes (Yougoslavie) du 28 janvier 1921 (Contd.). Bulletin mensuel de la Société de Législation comparée 58 : 174-193, janvier-mars 1929.

TAUBERT, L. : Notre nouvelle convention avec la Pologne. Revue économique de Belgrade 4 : 35-37, février 1929.
Commentaire de la convention du 4 mai 1923 concernant les relations juridiques des ressortissants polonais et yougoslaves.

SUMAN, J. : Des modifications apportées à la loi yougoslave sur la protection de la propriété industrielle. Propriété industrielle 45 : 41-45, 38 février 1929.

BILIMOVIC, A. : Arbeitsrecht des Königreichs der Serben, Kroaten und Slovenen (Jugoslavien). Zeitschrift für Ostrecht 3 : 369-388, März 1929.

FUMAGALLI, P. : La costituzione del Vidov-Dan (Contd.). Europa orientale 9 : 118-148, marzo-aprile 1929.

FUMAGALLI, P. : La costituzione del Vidov-Dan (Contd.). Europa orientale 9 : 214-235, maggio-giugno 1929.

TAUBERT, L.T. : Le projet de loi contre la concurrence déloyale. Revue économique de Belgrade 4 : 117-119, mai 1929.

SKERLI, M. : Das jugoslavische Scheckgesetz. Zeitschrift für Ostrecht 3 : 684-710, May 1929.
For German text of cheques law see same number pp. 710-715.

GRAHAM, M.W. : The "Dictatorship" in Yugoslavia. American political science review 23 : 449-459, May 1929.

SIK, L. : Die Durchführung von Exekutionen in Jugoslawien auf Grund des tschechoslowakischen jugoslawischen Rechthilfevertrages. Prager Juristische Zeitschrift 9 : 369-373, 2. Maiheft 1929.

STEFANOVITCH, Y. : Les règles fondamentales de la justice administrative yougoslave. Revue générale du droit de la législation et de la jurisprudence 53 : 53-59, 110-122, 199-204, janvier-février-mars, avril-mai-juin, juillet-août-septembre, 1929.

Das Staatsangehörigkeitsgesetz. Jugoslaviens vom 21. September 1929. Zeitschrift für Ostrecht 3 : 1107-1184, August-September 1929.
German text of Jugoslav nationality law of September 21, 1928, annexed.

Le nouveau régime en Yougoslavie. Monde slave 6 : 454-480, septembre 1929.
Texte français des lois et décrets constitutifs.

PÉRITCH, P. : Le droit de succession en droit international privé yougoslave. Institut belge de droit comparé 15 : 145-158, octobre-décembre 1929.

CHATAIGNEAU, Y. : La réorganisation administrative du royaume de Yougoslavie. Monde Slave 6 : 321-341, décembre 1929.

NATIONAL LAW - COUNTRIES

AFGHANISTAN

GIANNINI, A. : La costituzione afghana. Oriente moderno 11 : 265-274, giugno 1931.

ALBANIA

GIANNINI, A. : La costituzione dell'Albania. Europa orientale 10 : 297-321, novembre-dicembre 1930.

STAVRO-STAVRI : Le statut international de l'Albanie. Académie diplomatique internationale, Séances et travaux 6 : 160-163, octobre-décembre 1932.

LEFCOPARIDIS, X. : L'organisation de l'Etat. Balkans 6 : 42-54, juillet 1934.

ANDORRA

ANDERSSEN, W. : Verfassungsgeschichte von Andorra. Zeitschrift für vergleichende Rechtswissenschaft 48 : 6-92, 1./2. Heft, 1933.

LOEWENSTEIN, K. : Eine Verfassung im Mikroskop (Staatsrechtliche Betrachtungen zu den Verfassungswirren in Andorra). Zeitschrift für öffentliches Recht 14 : 417-444, 20. September 1934.

ARGENTINE

ALCORTA, C.A. : El derecho penal internacional en la legislación argentina. Revista argentina de derecho internacional 1 : 65-89, abril-junio 1930.

SCHLEGELBERGER, F. : Zur Neuordnung des argentinischen internationalen Privatrechts. Zeitschrift für ausländisches und internationales Privatrecht 4 : 741-769, Heft 5, 1930.

REBORA, J.C. : El matrimonio argentino ante la ley extranjera y el matrimonio extranjero ante la ley argentina. Revista argentina de derecho internacional 1 : 91-120, julio-septiembre 1930.

ALCORTA, C.A. : De la aplicación del derecho extranjero en el código civil argentino. Revista argentina de derecho internacional 1 : 141-157, julio-septiembre 1930.

ALCORTA, C.A. : El derecho internacional y la reforma de la constitución. Revista argentina de derecho internacional 1 : 211-227, octubre-diciembre 1930.
The Argentine Constitution.

SINA, E. : Die Grundlagen des ergentinischen Staatrechts. Jahrbuch des öffentlichen Rechts: 410-473, Band 19, 1931.

FONTANARROSA, R.O. : La capacidad del heredero en el sistema argentino de derecho internacional privado. Revista del Colegio de abogados de Rosaria 5 : 43-49, No. 1, 1934.

AUSTRALIA

Australia - The Royal Commission on the constitution. Round table : 408-415, March 1930.

BRENNAN, A. : Nationality of married women. Mid-Pacific magazine 40 : 113-116, August 1930.
The legislation in Australia.

HOLMAN, W.A. : Constitutional relations in Australia-commonwealth and states. Law quarterly review 46 : 502-521, October 1930.

MILLS, S. : Thirty years' working of the Australian Constitution. Journal of comparative legislation and international law 15 : 1-17, February 1933.

AUSTRIA

SLAMA, F. : Osterreich. Juristische Wochenschrift 59 : 19-23, 4. Januar 1930.
Survey of Austrian legislation in 1929.

MIRKINE-GUETZÉVITCH, B. : La révision constitutionnelle en Autriche. Europe nouvelle 13 : 126-135, 18 janvier 1930.
Texte revisé de la constitution en annexe.

MERKL, A. : Der "entpolitisierte" Verfassungsgerichtshof. Oesterreichische Volkswirt 22 : 509-511, 8. Februar 1930.

La révision de la constitution autrichienne. Monde slave 7 : 161-204, février 1930.

MIRKINE-GUETZÉVITCH, B. : La révision de la constitution autrichienne. Revue politique et parlementaire 37 : 485-492, 10 mars 1930.

WITTMAYER, L. : Die österreichische Verfassungsreform von 1929. Zeitschrift für die gesamte Staatswissenschaft 88 : 449-497, Mai 1930.

WASCHING, F. : La nouvelle loi autrichienne sur la protection de la liberte du travail. Internationale syndicale chrétienne 8 : 134-138, juillet-août 1930.

MERKL, A. : Der rechtliche Gehalt der österreichischen Verfassungsreform vom 7. Dezember 1929. Zeitschrift für öffentliches Recht 10 : 161-212, 15 September 1930.

KOESSLER, M. : Le mariage dit "Dispensehe" en Autriche. Institut belge de droit comparé 16 : 177-179, octobre-décembre 1930.

MERKL, A. : Die Entscheidung über die Zukunft der Verfassung. Oesterreichische Volkswirt 23 : 141-142, 8. November 1930.
Recent development of the Austrian constitution.

KELSEN, H. : Die Verfassung Osterreichs. Jahrbuch des öffentlichen Rechts 18 : 130-185, 1930.

RATZENHOFER, G., BETTELHEIM, E. : Die privatrechtliche Gesetzgebung Osterreichs in der Zeit vom 1 Juli 1929 bis zum 31. Dezemeber 1930. Zeitschrift für ausländisches und internationales Privatrecht 5 : 86-114, Heft 1, 1931.

HAUSSLEITER, O. : Zur Organisation der inneren Verwaltung in Osterreich. Zeitschrift für die gesamte Staatswissenschaft 90 : 82-96, 1. Heft 1931.

ROLLER : Die nächsten Aufgaben der Osterreichischen Rechtsangleichung. Deutsche Juristen-Zeitung 36 : 116-120, 15. Januar 1931.

NATIONAL LAW - COUNTRIES

STIER-SOMLO, F. : Die Ausnahmeverordnung des Reichspräsidenten und die Notverordnung des österreichischen Bundespräsidenten. Zeitschrift für öffentliches Recht 11 : 62-88, 15. März 1931.

Questions de droit posées par l'accord douanier austro-allemand. Affairs étrangères 1 : 71-73, avril 1931.

ZESSNER-SPITZENBERG, H.K. : Bodenreform im Sinne der Bundesverfassung. Österreichisches Verwaltungsblatt 2 : 89-96, 16 April 1931.

TOUSSAINT, A. : Der Plan einer deutsch-oesterreichischen "Zollunion" in seiner völkerrechtlichen Bedeutung. Revue de droit international, de sciences diplomatiques et politiques 9 : 161-170, avril-juin 1931.

KLINGHOFFER, H. : Der Schutz der Grundrechte in der deutschen Reichsverfassung und der Österreichischen Bundesverfassung. Zeitschrift für öffentliches Recht 11 : 378-401, 10. Oktober 1931.

BETZ, R. : Die Wahl des Bundespräsidenten. (Gesetz vom 27. März 1931). Österreichisches Verwaltungsblatt 2 : 249-257, 16. Oktober 1931.

RATZENHOFER, G. : Die privatrechtliche Gesetzgebung Österreichs im Jahre 1932. Zeitschrift für ausländisches und internationales Privatrecht 7 : 36-65, Heft 1, 1933.

STRELE, K. : Das Notverordnungsrecht im österreichischen, reichsdeutschen und italienischen Staatsrecht. Zeitschrift für vergleichende Rechtswissenschaft 48 : 382-409, 3. Heft, 1934.

RATZENHOFER, G. : Die privatrechtliche Gesetzgebung Österreichs im Jahre 1933. Zeitschrift für ausländisches und internationales Privatrecht 8 : 451-476, Heft 3/4, 1934.

RASCHHOFER, H. : Österreichs neue Verfassung 1934. Zeitschrift für ausländisches öffentliches Recht und Völkerrecht (Abhandlungen) 4 : 846-857, No. 4, 1934.

JÄCKL, H. : Die Verfassung 1934. Österreichisches Verwaltungsblatt 5 : 105-108, 16. Mai 1934.

WAHLE, K. : Das österreichische internationale Scheidungsrecht und das Konkordat mit dem heiligen Stuhl. Zeitschrift für ausländisches und internationales Privatrecht 8 : 681-715, Heft 5, 1934.

MERKL, A. : Das neue Verfassungsrecht. Juristische Blätter 63 : 201-206, 225-232, 265-270, 19.Mai, 2. Juni, 2. Juli 1934.

TORGGLER, K. : Die österreichischen Notverordnungen und das Hypothekenrecht. Prager juristische Zeitung 14 : 432-439, 1. Juliheft 1934.

MERKL, A. : Das neue Verfassungsrecht, (Contd.). Juristische Blätter 63 : 309-315, 28. Juli 1934.

RABI, K.O. : Die Verfassungsrechtliche Lage Österreichs. Zeitschrift für Politik 24 : 437-450, Juli-August 1934.

TRICAUD, M., et PERRIN, B. : Le Chancelier Dollfuss et la Constitution autrichienne de 1934. Revue des sciences politiques 49 : 353-373, juillet-septembre 1934.

WEISER, M. : Strafrechts-und Strafprozessreformen in Österreich. Prager juristische Zeitschrift 14 : 496-505, 1. Septemberheft, (?) 1934.

EISENMANN, C. : La constitution autrichienne de 1934. Europe nouvelle 17 : 895-898, 8 septembre 1934.

SATTER, K. : Das österreichische Eherecht nach dem Konkordat. Juristische Blätter 63 : 333-339, 8. September 1934.

MIRKINE-GUETZÉVITCH, B. : Le néo-absolutisme corporatif (Autriche et Portugal). Année politique française et étrangère 9 : 251-272, octobre 1934.

AMBROSINI, V. : Ordinamento coporativo e nuova costituzione in Austria. Echi e commenti 15 : 1216-1218, 15 novembre 1934.

ALTER, W. : Das neue österreichische Wasserrechtsgesetz. Wasserwirtschaft und Technik 1 : 69-73, November 1934.

HELLBLING, E. : Die Einrichtung und das Verfahren des Bundesgerichtshofes. Österreiches Verwaltungsblatt 5 : 300-302, 16. Dezember 1934.

HERRNRITT, R. : L'évolution de la vie constitutionnelle en Autriche en 1933. Annuaire de l'Institut international de droit public : 182-190, 1934.

BELGIUM

LOUIS-LUCAS, P. : La nouvelle convention franco-belge sur les conflits en matière de recrutement militaire. Revue de droit international privé 25 : 193-217, No. 2, 1930.

DREYFUS, R. : Convention relative à la nationalité de la femme mariée conclue entre la France et la Belgique. Journal du droit international 57 : 911-916, juillet-octobre 1930.

BOURQUIN, M. : Les principales transformations du droit public belge depuis 1914. Jahrbuch des öffentlichen Rechts 18 : 186-207, 1930.

MOSCATO, A. : Le sorti della neutralizzazione belga dopo la guerra ed i principi vigenti per la modificazione della costituzione della communità internazionale. Rivista di diritto internazionale 22 : 526-541, 1 ottobre-31 dicembre 1930.

SCHELLING, F.W. von : Die belgische Gesetzgebung in den Jahren 1928 und 1929. Zeitschrift für ausländisches und internationales Privatrecht 5 : 194-201, Heft 1, 1931.

POULLET : Le statut juridique international de la Belgique et ses antécédents historiques. Académie diplomatique internationale : 13-19, janvier-mars 1931.

HOBLEY, C.W. : The Congo Basin Treaties. African world 114 : 381-382, April 4 1931.

Das internationale Statut Belgiens. Zeitschrift für ausländisches öffentliches Recht und Völkerrecht 3 : 211-221, No. 1, (Teil 2), 1932.

MUULS, F. : Le traité international et la Constitution belge. Revue de droit international et de législation comparée 61 : 451-491, No. 3, 1934.

Das belgische Gesetz von 30. Juli 1934 betreffend die Aberkennung der Staatsangehörigkeit. Zeitschrift für ausländisches öffentliches Recht und Völkerrecht (Abhandlungen) 4 : 899-903, No. 4, 1934.

PEETERS, J.B. : La convention conclue le 16 mai 1931 entre la Belgique et la France pour éviter les doubles impositions et régler certaines autres questions en matière fiscale. Bulletin de l'Institut intermédiaire international 26 : 253-260, avril 1932.

WILLE, M. : Législation belge, années 1930 et 1931. Revue trimestrielle de droit civil 31 : 595-602, avril-juin 1932.

BERNARD, A. : L'exécution des sentences arbitrales étrangères en Belgique et en France. Institut belge de droit comparé, Revue trimestrielle 18 : 139-157, avril-septembre 1932.

WIRTHS : Der belgische Ausbürgerungs-Gesetz-Antrag. Nation und Staat 7 : 550-553, Juni 1934.

BOLIVIA

SALINAS, C.A. : La Confederación Bolivariana. Revista argentina de derecho internacional 2 : 327-339, abril-junio 1931.

URQUIDI, J.M. : La condición juridica de la mujer en Bolivia. Revista de derecho internacional 12 : 44-134, 30 septiembre 1933.

URQUIDI, J.M. : La condición juridica de la mujer en Bolivia (Contd.). Revista de derecho internacional 12 : 244-285, diciembre 1933.

BRAZIL

OCTAVIO, R. : La codification du droit civil au Brésil. Revue trimestrielle de droit civil 29 : 727-750, juillet-septembre 1930.

OCTAVIO, R. : Le codification du droit civil au Brésil. Revue trimestrielle de droit civil 29 : 1011-1033, octobre-décembre 1930.

VALLADO, H. : Force exécutoire des jugements étrangers au Brésil. Journal du droit international 58 : 590-609, mai-juin 1931.

SANTOS, J.M. dos : La dernière constitution brésilienne - la constitution du 24 février 1891. France-Amérique 23 : 283-288, septembre 1932.

CAVALCANTI, T.B. : L'avant-projet de constitution soumis à l'Assemblée constituante brésilienne. Législation brésilienne 1 : 5-12, mars 1934.

Código de aguas. Brazil-ferro-carril 47 : 57-58, 85-86, 15, 31 de agosto de 1934.
Text of the Brazilian code, dated July 10, 1934, relating to navigable and other waters.

BULGARIA

GANEFF, V. : Rassegna di legislazione bulgara (anno 1927 e primo semestre del 1928). Annuario di diritto comparato vol. 4 e 5, parte 2 : 206-212, 1930.

BARBAR, L. : Die internationalen Beziehungen des neuen bulgarischen Zivilprozessgesetzes. Zeitschrift für internationales Recht 42 : 257-279, Heft 4-6, 1930.

GANEFF, V. : Rassegna di letteratura giuridica bulgara (anno 1927). Annuario di diritto comparato vol. 4 e 5, parte 1, 489 - 490, 1930.

ALTINOFF, I. : La question de la prétendue existence des capitulations en Bulgarie. Journal du droit international 58 : 352-361, mars-avril 1931.

GIANNINI, A. : La costituzione bulgara. Europa orientale 10 : 133-163, maggio-giugno 1930.

DANEFF, S. : La procédure civile bulgare et le droit international privé. Bulletin de l'Institut intermédiaire international 25 : 1-7, juillet 1931.

LAMOUCHE, L. : Notice générale sur les lois promulguées en 1931. Annuaire de législation étrangère 59 : 545-560, 1931.

VLACHOV, I. : Il regimo degli stranieri nella legislazione bulgara. Europa orientale 13 : 146-153, fasc. 3-4, 1933.

GANEFF, V., RADULOVA, V. : Bulgaria. Istituto di studi legislativi, Legislazione internazionale 1 : 687-690, fasc. 4, 1932.

Lois promulguées du 1 juillet au 31 décembre 1931. Bulletin mensuel de la Société de législation comparée 61 : 286-287, avril-juin 1932.

WLAHOFF, S. : Le régime des étrangers d'après la législation bulgare. Bulletin de l'Institut juridique international 30 : 1-12, janvier 1934.

Liste des lois des principaux pays promulguées en 1933 - Bulgarie. Bulletin trimestriel de la Société de Législation comparée 63 : 158-159, janvier-février-mars 1934.

Le régime des étrangers d'après la législation bulgare. Bulgarie 12 : 1, 1, 1, 5, 6, 7 juin 1934.

Les successions en Bulgarie. Bulgarie 12 : 1, 1, 1-2, 1-2, 1, 1-2, 25, 26, 28 juin, 6, 9, 10 juillet 1934.

Bulgarie - Lois promulgées du 1 janvier au 30 juin 1934. Bulletin trimestriel de la Société de législation comparée 63 : 386-388, juillet-août-septembre 1934.

LAMOUCHE, L. : Bulgarie - Notice générale sur les lois promulguées de 1934 à 1936. Annuaire de législation étrangère 62 : 524-573, 1934/1936.

CANADA

KEITH, B. : The ratification of treaties. Journal of comparative legislation and international law 12 : 99-100, February 1930.
Debate in the House of Commons commented.

O'HEARN, W.J. : Extradition. Canadian bar review 8 : 175-183, March 1930.
The Canadian law.

ROWELL, N.W. : Canada's position in the British Commonwealth of Nations. Canadian bar review 8 : 570-628, October 1930.

MACDONALD, V.C. : Canada's power to perform treaty obligations. Canadian bar review 11 : 581-599, 664-680, November, December 1933.

The St.Lawrence waterway. Round table : 548-562, June 1934.

CHILE

SCHLEGELBERGER, F. : Chilenisches Bankrecht. Zeitschrift für ausländisches und internationales Privatrecht 5 : 1-31, Heft 1, 1931.

CHINA

WEI YUNG : The provisional Court Conference. China critic 3 : 7-11, January 2, 1930.
Shanghai Court and extraterritoriality.

HUANG, R.T. : The legal status of the international settlement in Shanghai. China weekly review 51 : 252-254, January 18, 1930.

ESCARRA, J. : La loi chinoise sur les effets de commerce du 30 octobre 1929. Annales de droit commercial 39 : 47-72, janvier-mars 1930.
Texte français annexé.

LIU-YU-YIN : The essential aspect of abolition of extraterritoriality. China weekly review 51 : 428-431, February 22, 1930.

YEN, H. : The Shanghai provisional court. Pacific affairs 8 : 294-298, March 1936.
Text of Court Regulations annexed.

ESCARRA, J. : Le nouveau régime des cours mixtes de Changhaï. Europe nouvelle 13 : 552-555, 5 avril 1930.
Textes des accords et de l'ordre de service annexés.

WRIGHT, Q. : Some legal consequences if extraterritoriality is abolished in China. American journal of international law 24 : 217-227, April 1930.

TSENG YU-HAO : China's new treaties. Pacific affairs 3 : 370-382, April 1930.

The provisional Court settlement. Pacific affairs 3 : 383-389, April 1930.
Text of agreement.

CHANG CHI-TAI : Historical notes on the Shanghai international settlement. China critic 3 : 463-468, May 15, 1930.
Legal status of the Settlement.

CHANG CHI TAI : Proposed solution of the Shanghai international settlement problems. China critic 8 : 487-490, May 22, 1930.

Breaking the diplomatic phalanx. China critic 3 : 677, July 17, 1930.
The privileges of the Doyen of the diplomatic corps in China.

GROENMAN, F.E.H. : La nouvelle organisation judiciaire à Shanghaï. Bulletin de l'Institut intermédiaire international 23 : 11-13, juillet 1930.

National government of the Chinese Republic. Chinese social and political review 14 : 313-330, July 1930.
Organisation and functions.

ESCARRA, J. : Le nouveau régime des cours mixtes de Chang-Haï. Revue de droit international 4 : 326-335, juillet-août-septembre 1930.

ESCARRA, J. : Communication sur la codification contemporaine du droit chinois. Bulletin mensuel de la Société de législation comparée 59 : 407-436, juillet-septembre 1930.

Legislation under the Chinese national government. Chinese social and political science review 14 : 403-424, October 1930.

The law of family relations. China critic 3 : 1182-1183, December 11, 1930.
New Chinese marriage law.

The Chinese civil and commercial code. Chinese economic journal 8 : 1-14, January 1931.

MENG, C.Y.W. : Modern judicial reform in China. China weekly review 55 : 214,235, 256-258, 281-283, January 10, 17, 24, 1931.

ESCARRA, J. : La législation maritime chinoise. Revue de droit maritime comparé 23 : 1-28, janvier-juin 1931.

CHEN TSUNG-HSI : Some peculiarities of the new Chinese civil code. China weekly review 55 : 390, February 14, 1931.

VOGEL, W. : Zur modernen Gesetzgebung Chinas. Ostasiatische Rundschau 12 : 201-202, 1. April 1931.

ESCARRA, J. : La codification chinoise et l'extraterritorialité. Affaires étrangères 1 : 76-84, avril 1931.

Salient points in the Chinese civil and commercial code (Contd.). Chinese economic journal 8 : 401-409, April 1931.

The Shanghai report. Saturday review 151 : 633-634, May 2, 1931.
The future constitution of Shanghai.

Chine - une constitution provisoire. Société d'études et d'informations économiques, bulletin quotidien No. 108 : C-1-4, 16 mai 1931.

Salient points of the Chinese civil and commercial Code (Contd.). Chinese economic journal 8 : 525-532, May 1931.

YOUNG, C.K. : Real property rights of aliens in China and the United States. Chinese social and political science review 15 : 184-228, July 1931.

Salient points in the Chinese civil and commercial code (Contd.). Chinese economic journal 9 : 895-908, August 1931.

HUANG, Y.J. : Nationality and protection of oversea Chinese (contd.). China critic 4 : 895-899, September 17, 1931.

VOGEL, W. : Modern Chinese law and jurisdiction. Pacific affairs 4 : 975-979, November 1931.

NATIONAL LAW - COUNTRIES

CHANG, C. : Die staatsrechtliche Krisis der chinesischen Republik. Jahrbuch des öffentlichen Rechts : 316-355, Band 19, 1931.

PADOUX, G. : Lois de 1931. Annuaire de législation étrangère 59 : 561-573, 1931.

BOURBOUSSON, E. : La nouvelle législation sur le mariage, les régimes matrimoniaux et les successions en Chine. Annuaire de législation étrangère 59 : 457-464, 1931.

Le statut juridique de la Mandchourie du Sud d'après C. Walter Young. Affaires étrangères 2 : 144-154, 25 mars 1932.

Le conflit sino-japonais et les tierces puissances : la doctrine de la porte ouverte. Affaires étrangères 2 : 197-201, 25 avril 1932.

Le leggi vigenti al 1 gennaio 1932, in materia di procedura penale. Giustizia penale 38 : 533-535, marzo-aprile-maggio-giugno-luglio 1932.

CHIU, T. : The treaty-making power of China. Chinese social and political science review 16 : 514-518, October 1932.

BREITZKE, W. : Materialen zum öffentlichen Recht-Chinas. Zeitschrift für vergleichende Rechtwissenschaft 47 : 379-402, 2/3 Heft, 1933.
Text of constitution annexed.

La constitution permanente permanente chinoise. Revue nationale chinoise 13 : 39-44, 14 mars 1933.
Travaux préparatoires.

BENTWICH, N. : Le domicile dans la concession internationale de Shanghai. Journal du droit international 60 : 299-307, mars-avril 1933.

VOGEL, W. : Promissory Notes und Schecks nach chinesischem Recht. Ostasiatische Rundschau 14 : 180-181, 1. Mai 1933.

China's permanent Constitution now in shape. China weekly review 65 : 190-192, July 1, 1933.

YEN-YING LU : Comment le Gouvernement national de Nankin fonctionne. Politique de Pékin 20 : 1398-1405, 15 novembre 1933.

YUEN-LI LIANG : Tendances internationales du projet de constitution chinoise. Revue nationale chinoise 16 : 25-30, 14 décembre 1933.

Nouveau projet de Constitution permanente de la République de Chine. Revue nationale chinoise 17 : 297-314, 14 avril 1934.

The permanent Constitution. Oriental affairs 1 : 26-31, April 1934.

BÜNGER, K. : Neue Entscheidungen des Obersten Gerichtshofes in Nanking. Zeitschrift für ausländisches und internationales Privatrecht 8 : 851-853, Heft 5, 1934.

BÜNGER, K. : Mandschurei - Das geltende Recht. Zeitschrift für ausländisches und internationale Privatrecht 8 : 997-Heft 6, 1934.

A propos des changements à apporter au texte préliminaire de la constitution chinoise. Revue nationale chinoise 18 : 336-338, 14 août 1934.

CHEN CHIN-MAI : The Revised Draft of the Constitution. China critic 7 : 852-854, August 30, 1934.

COMMONWEALTH

ANDERSON, J.C. : Dominion status. Canadian bar review 8 : 32-48, January 1930.

MACKINTOSH, J. : Limitations on free testamentary disposition in the British Empire. Journal of comparative legislation and international law 12 : 13-22, February 1930.

EWART, J.S. : Excerpts from the Imperial Conferences 1923, 1926 and 1929. Canadian bar review 8 : 91-100, February 1930.

PETRIE, C. : The constitution of the Empire. Saturday review 149 : 254-255, March 1930.

WOODS, W. : Ceylon's proposed new constitution. United Empire 21 : 322-329, June 1930.

ELLIOTT, W. : A written constitution for the British Commonwealth? Political quarterly 1 : 386-409, July-September 1930.

The results of the Imperial conference. Law journal 70 : 307, November 22, 1930.
Summary of the results as affecting the Constitutional relations of the Dominions with Great Britain.

BATY, T. : The structure of the Empire. Journal of comparative legislation and international law 12 : 157-167, November 1930.

ELLIOTT, W.V. : The sovereignty of the British Dominions : law overtakes practice. American political science review 24 : 971-989, November 1930.

JENNINGS, I. : La Conférence impériale de 1930. Revue de droit international et de législation comparée 58 : 181-219, No. 2, 1931.

LO VERDE, G. : La forma costituzionale dell'Impero Britannico. Rivista di diritto pubblico 23 : 255-269, maggio 1931.

WITTE, L. von : Die rechtliche Stelling der Dominien innerhalb des britischen Weltreichs. Rigasche Zeitschrift für Rechtswissenschaft 5 : 73-94, Juli 1931.

A note on the Statute of Westminster. Bulletin of international news 8 : 9-10, December 3, 1931.
The inter-imperial relations.

The Statute of Westminster. Bulletin of international news 8 : 339-348, December 17, 1931.

MORGAN, J.H. : The Statute of Westminster. United Empire 22 : 653-664, December 1931.
Inter-imperial relations.

CHEVALLIER, J.-J. : Le droit de représentation diplomatique distincte des Dominions britanniques et de l'Etat libre d'Irlande. Revue de droit international et de législation comparée 59 : 277-301, No. 2, 1932.

JEBB, R. : The Statute of Westminster. Nineteenth century 111 : 61-72, January 1932.

EWART, J.S. : The Statute of Westminster, 1931, as a climax in its relation to Canada. Canadian bar review 10 : 111-122, February 1932.

NATIONAL LAW - COUNTRIES

KENNEDY, W.P.M. : The Imperial Conferences, 1926 -1930 - The Statute of Westminster. Law quarterly review 48 : 191-216, April 1932.

MacRAY, R.A. : The problem of a Commonwealth tribunal. Canadian bar review 10 : 338-348, June 1932.

CHEVALLIER, J.-J. : L'évolution du statut de Dominion. Revue générale de droit international public 39 : 458-497, juillet-août 1932.

LAVOIE, P. : La Conférence impériale de 1930 et la politique des Dominions. Revue générale de droit international public 39 : 776-828, novembre-décembre 1932.

HUDSON, M.O. : Notes on the Statute of Westminster, 1931. Harvard law review 46 : 261-289, December 1932.

LOREN van THEMAAT, H. ver : The equality of status of the Dominions and the sovereignty of the British Parliament. Journal of comparative legislation and international law 15 : 47-53, February 1933.

Foreign law in the British Empire. Round table : 362-382, March 1933.

WILLIAMS, W.L. : The British Commonwealth - a constitutional survey. Foreign policy reports 9 : 26-36, April 12, 1933.

MAHAFFY, R.P. : The Statute of Westminster. Journal of the Royal united service institution 78 : 353-368, May 1933.

DENDIAS, M. : L'île de Chypre dans le droit international. Revue de droit international 7 : 130-159, juillet-août-septembre 1933.

KEITH, B. : The report of the Newfoundland Royal Commission. Journal of comparative legislation and international law 16 : 25-39, February 1934.
The default and British control.

BASTEDO, F.L. : Amending the British North America Act. Canadian bar review 12 : 209-226, April 1934.

SCHÜLE, A. : Neufundland im britischen Weltreich. Zeitschrift für ausländisches öffentliches Recht und Völkerrecht (Abhandlungen) 4 : 858-877, No. 4, 1934.

FABVIER, R. : Administration et politique indigènes dans les colonies britanniques d'Afrique occidentale. Revue politique et parlementaire 41 : 87-100, 10 octobre 1934.

TREDGOLD, C. : The constitutional position of the South African Protectorates. Journal of the African Society 33 : 382-397, October 1934.

BENTWICH, N. : An imperial link? Fortnightly : 407-415, October 1934.
The Judicial Committee of the Privy Council.

CUBA

Nueva ley constitucional de la República de Cuba. Boletín de la unión Panamericana 68 : 475-478, junio 1934.

La nueva Ley Constitucional de la República de Cuba. Revista parlamentaria (Buenos Aires) 3 : 108-111, octubre 1934.

CHEDIAK, N. : Principios de derecho internacional aplicados por los tribunales cubanos (nacionalidad). Revista de derecho internacional 13 : 184-261, 31 diciembre 1934.

CZECHOSLOVAKIA

REINER, P. : Die privatrechtliche Gesetzgebung, Rechtsprechung und Literatur in der Tschechoslowakei in den Jahren 1928-1929. Zeitschrift für ausländisches und internationales Privatrecht 5 : 157-184, Heft 1, 1931.

HORAČEK, C. : Les principes du droit électoral tchécoslovaque. Bulletin de droit tchécoslovaque 3 : 18-26, 1 mai 1931.

SCHEUNER, U. : Die Gleichheit vor dem Gesetz im tschechoslowakischen Verfassungsrecht. Prager juristische Zeitschrift 11 : 391-402, No. 10/11, 1931.

LEGAL, A. : Les conflits de lois en Tchécoslovaquie. Revue de droit international privé 25 : 52-60, No. 1, 1930.

BEDRICH, A. : Rassegna di legislazione cecoslovacca (anno 1927). Annuario di diritto comparativo vol. 4 e 5, parte 2 : 213-240, 1930.

JANŠAK, S. : The land question in Slovakia. Slavonic review 8 : 612-626, March 1930.

PESKA, M.Z. : Après dix années - le développement de la constitution tchécoslovaque. Revue du droit public 47 : 224-250, avril-mai-juin 1930.

SANDER, F. : Die Gültigkeit der Gesetze nach der Verfassungsurkunde der tschechoslowakischen Republik. Zeitschrift für öffentliches Recht 9 : 542-576, 15 April 1930.

KROUAK, R. : President republiky a mezinà rodni smlouvy. Moderni stat 3 : 144-154, čislos 5, 1930.
The President of the Republic and international conventions.

SATTER, K. : Die Anerkennung ausländischer Urteile in Ehesachen tschechoslowakischer Staatsangehöriger. Prager juristische Zeitschrift 10 : 345-351, 1. Maiheft 1930.

WEISS, E. : Čechoslovakei - Übereinkommen zwischen der čechoslovakischen Republik und dem Königreiche Ungarn, betreffend die Regelung der in alten österreichischen und ungarischen Kronen entstandenen Schulden und Forderungen. Zeitschrift für Ostrecht 4 : 961-962, Oktober 1930.
(Text of treaty annexed).

LASTOVKA, K. : La nouvelle organisation de l'administration publique en Tchécoslovaquie. Bulletin de droit tchécoslavaque 3 : 113-140, 1 mars 1932.

REINER, P. : Die privatrechtliche Gesetzgebung, Rechtsprechung und Literatur in der Tschechoslowakei im Jahre 1931. Zeitschrift für ausländisches und internationales Privatrecht 6 : 431-458, Heft 3, 1932.

SVOBODA, E. : Der Entwurf des Bürgerlichen Gesetzbuches für die Tschechoslovakische Republik. Prager Rundschau 11 : 314-322, Heft 4, 1932.

LEMKIN, R. : La réforme du droit pénal en Tchécoslovaquie. Revue pénitentiaire et de droit pénal 56 : 449-457, avril-septembre 1932.

HENRICH, W. : Das Verhältnis des Staatsvertrages zum Gesetz nach tschechoslowakischem Verfassungsrecht. Zeitschrift für Völkerrecht 16 : 795-805, Het 4/5, 1932.

Ergänzungstabelle der von der Tschechoslovakischen Republik bis 31. XII. 1926 abgeschlossenen Staatsverträge. Zeitschrift für Ostrecht 6 : 609-638, August-September 1932.

MAYR-HARTING : Der Entwurf eines Bürgerlichen Gesetzbuches für die Tschechoslowakei. Deutsche Juristen-Zeitung 37 : 1250-1256, 15. Oktober 1932.

SOBOTA, E. : Fünfzehn Jahre Entwicklung der tschechoslovakischen Verfassung. Prager Rundschau 3 : 321-333, Heft 5, 1933.

La loi des pleins pouvoirs en Tchécoslovaquie. Europe centrale 8 : 358-359, 8 juin 1933.

HEXNER, E. : Das neue tschechoslowakische gesetz über Kartelle und Privatmonopole. Kartell-Rundschau 31 : 551-564, Heft 8, 1933.

BEUVE-MÉRY, H. : Le renforcement du pouvoir exécutif en Tchécoslovaquie. Europe nouvelle 17 : 72-80, 20 janvier 1934.
Textes de lois en annexe.

BEUVE-MÉRY, H. : Les tendances générales de la constitution tchécoslovaque. Annales de l'institut de droit comparé de l'Université de Paris 1 : 75-91, 1934.

TANDLER, W. : Die privatrechtliche Gesetzgebung der Tschechoslovakischen Republik in den Jahren 1932-1933. Zeitschrift für ausländisches und internationales Privatrecht 8 : 477-481, Heft 3/4, 1934.

HOCHBERGER, E. : Die privatrechtliche Gesetzgebung in der Tschechoslovakei in den Jahren 1932 und 1933. Zeitschrift für ausländisches und internationales Privatrecht 8 : 482-521, Heft 3/4, 1934.

KÖRNER, A. : Das tschechoslowakische Gemeindewahlsystem nach der Novelle der Gemeindewahlordnung vom 12. Juli 1933. Zeitschrift für öffentliches Recht 14 : 634-641, Heft 5, 1934.

HERMANN-OTAVSKY, K., et KIZLINK, K. : Chronique de législation en matière de droit commercial - République tchécoslovaque (1923-1933). Annales de droit commercial 43 : 217-223, juillet-septembre 1934.

MATEJKA, J. : La responsabilité de l'Etat du point de vue du droit tchécoslovaque. Bulletin de droit tchécoslovaque 4 : 14-23, 1 septembre 1934.

WEYR, F. : Tchécoslovaquie - l'année 1933. Annuaire de l'Institut international de droit public : 747-757, 1934.

DANZIG

BÖHMERT, V. : Die Rechtsgrundlagen der Beziehungen zwischen Danzig und Polen. Zeitschrift für Völkerrecht 15 : 694-702, Heft 4, 1930.

ROSENBAUM : Verfassungsfragen. Danziger juristische Monatsschrift 9 : 65-69, 25. Juli 1930.
Coming into force of the Danzig constitution.

LEWINSKY : Die Reform der Ehescheidung. Danziger juristische Monatsschrift 9 : 70-79, 25. Juli 1930.
Divorce legislation in Danzig.

GIANNINI, A. : La costituzione di Danzica. Europa orientale 10 : 229-251, luglio-ottobre 1930.

RICHTER : Internationales Privatrecht in Danzig. Zeitschrift für ausländisches und internationales Privatrecht 5 : 500-510, Heft 2/3, 1931.

MOEBES : Gesetzesänderungen in der Freien Stadt Danzig. Deutsche Juristen Zeitung 36 : 541-544, 15. April 1931.

RICHTER : Internationales Privatrecht in Danzig. Zeitschrift für ausländisches und internationales Privatrecht 7 : 895-919, Heft 6, 1933.

DENMARK

Quelques observations sur la base de la discussion entre le Danemark et l'Allemagne relative à la compréhension de l'étendue de la notion "la nation la plus favorisée". Nordisk Tidsskrift for international ret 1 : 65-68, fasc.1, 1930.

MENZEL, C. : Das neue dänische Aktiengesellschafts- sowie das neue Bankgesetz. Zeitschrift für ausländisches und internationales Privatrecht 4 : 656-665, Heft 3-4, 1930.

MADSEN, C.M. : Das neue dänische Strafgesetzbuch. Revue der internationalen juristischen Vereinigung 1 : 78-80, No. 5-6, 1930.

RASMUSSEN, G. : La souveraineté du Danemark sur le Groenland. Revue de droit international et de législation comparée 58 : 220-233, No. 2, 1931.

MOLLÈR, J. : Danemark - Lois les plus importantes votées de 1934 à 1936. Annuaire de législation étrangère 62 : 181-184, 1934-1936.

ESTONIA

SAARMANN, C. : Il codice penale estone del 1929. Annuario di diritto comparato vol. 6, parte 1 (fasc. 1) : 447-458, 1930.

MADDISON, E. : Rassegna di letteratura giuridica estone (anni 1927-1929). Annuario di diritto comparato vol. 4 e 5, parte I : 491-503, 1930.

KORSAKOFF, T. : Le système constitutionnel de la République d'Esthonie. Société de législation comparée, bulletin mensuel 59 : 190-212, janvier-mars 1930.

MADDISON, E. : Rassegna di legislazione estone (anni 1927, 1928 e 1929). Annuaria di diritto comparato vol. 4 e 5, parte 2 : 241-288, 1930.

NATIONAL LAW - COUNTRIES

CSEKEY, S.V. : Das Staatsangehörigkeitsrecht in Estland. Zeitschrift für Ostrecht 4 : 225-249, März 1930.

KOCH, G. : Die Gesetzgebung Estlands im 1. Halbjahr 1930. Rigasche Zeitschrift für Rechtswissenschaft 4 : 189-199, Oktober 1930.

KOCH, G. : Die Gesetzgebung Estlands im II. Halbjahr 1930. Risasche Zeitschrift für Rechtswissenschaft 5 : 55-63, I. Heft 1931.

KORSAKOFF, T. : L'organisation administrative de la République d'Esthonie. Revista de drept public 6 : 15-48, januarie-junie 1931.

KOCH, G. : Die Gesetzgebung Estlands im 1. Halbjahr 1931. Rigasche Zeitschrift für Rechtswissenschaft 5 : 170-181, November 1931.

KOCH, G. : Die Gesetzgebung Estlands im II. Halbjahr 1931. Rigasche Zeitschrift für Rechtswissenschaft 6 : 34-42, 1. Heft 1932.

PUSTA, R.C. : Le statut international de l'Estonie. Académie diplomatique internationale, Séances et travaux 6 : 34-43, janvier-mars 1932.

MADDISON, E. : Estonia. Istituto di studi legislativi, Legislazione internazionale 1 : 697-727, fasc. 4, 1932.

SAARMANN, K. : Die Strafrechtsreform in Estland. Zeitschrift für Ostrecht 6 : 371-380, Mai 1932.

KOCH, G. : Die Gesetzgebung Estlands im I. Halbjahr 1932. Rigasche Zeitschrift für Rechtswissenschaft 6 : 104-111, Dezember 1932.

KOCH, G. : Die Gesetzgebung Estlands in der ersten drei Quartalen 1933. Rigasche Zeitschrift für Rechtswissenschaft 7 : 41-48, 1. Heft 1933/1934.

MEDER, W. : Die neue Verfassung Estlands. Rigasche Zeitschrift für Rechtswissenschaft 7 : 127-149, 3. Heft 1933/1934.

KOCH, G. : Die Gesetzgebung Estlands im IV. Quartal 1933. Rigasche Zeitschrift für Rechtswissenschaft 7 : 175-178, 3. Heft 1933/1934.

La nouvelle Constitution. Affaires étrangères 4 : 54-56, 10 janvier 1934.

GIANNINI, A. : La riforma della costituzione estone. Europa orientale 14 : 1-16, fasc. 1-2, 1934.

MADDISON, E. : Rassegna di legislazione estone. (Anni 1930-1931). Annuario di diritto comparate e di studi legislativi (Parte IV) 8 : 27-77, 1934.

CSEKEY, S. v. : Die Verfassungsänderung in Estland. Zeitschrift für ausländisches öffentliches Recht und Völkerrecht (Abhandlungen) 4 : 582-596, Juli 1934.

Übersicht über die wesentliche Gesetzgebung Estlands für das Jahr 1933 und das I. Halbjahr 1934. Zeitschrift für osteuropäisches Recht 1 : 140-144, September 1934.

STOECKLIN, P. de : A propos d'une nouvelle constitution. Cahiers des droits de l'homme 34 : 680-683, 30 octobre 1934.

MEDER, W. : Die neue Verfassung Estlands. Zeitschrift für ost-europäisches Recht 1 : 186-203, Oktober 1934.

MEDER, W. : Die Gesetzgebung Estlands im II. Quartal 1934. Rigasche Zeitschrift für Rechtswissenschaft 8 : 118-123, November 1934.

MEDER, W. : Das Dekretrecht des Staatspräsidenten in Estland. Rigasche Zeitschrift für Rechtswissenschaft 8 : 97-102, November 1934.

KOCH, G. : Die Gesetzgebung Estlands im I. Quartal 1934. Rigasche Zeitschrift für Rechtswissenschaft 8 : 46-51, I. Heft 1934-1935.

ETHIOPIA

Progress in Abyssinia. Near East and India 40 : 87, July 23, 1931.
The Constitution.

RALZ, O. : La costituzione dell'Etiopia. Gerarchia 11 : 831-843, ottobre 1931.

PIGLI, M. : L'Ethiopia e la sua prima costituzione. Rassegna italiana 14 : 897-902, ottobre 1931.

GIANNINI, A. : La Costituzione etiopica. Oriente moderno 12 : 1-11, gennaio 1932.

LEONE, E. de : La Costituzione etiopica. Oltremare 6 : 13-15, gennaio 1932.

VANDAMME, J. : La nouvelle loi abyssinienne sur les sociétés. Revue de l'Institut belge de droit comparé 20 : 60-63, avril-juin 1934.

VANDAMME, J. : Ethiopie - Loi sue les sociétés (1932). Bulletin trimestriel de la Société de Législation comparée 63 : 368-371, juillet-août-septembre 1934.

CERULLI, E. : Il nuovo codice penale etiopico ed i suoi principii fondamentali. Oriente moderno 12 : 392-405, agosto 1932.

FINLAND

HERNBERG, A. : Gesetzgebung, Rechtsprechung und Schrifttum in Finnland in den Jahren 1926-1928. Zeitschrift für ausländisches und internationales Privatrecht : 164-188, Heft 1, 1930.

BROTHERUS, K. R. : Stat och kyrka i Finland. Statsvetenskaplig tidskrift 33 : 446-462, December 1930.

GIANNINI, A. : La Costituzione Finlandese. Europa orientale 11 : 7-48, gennaio-febbraio 1931.

PROCOPÉ, H.J. : Le statut international de la Finlande. Académie de droit international, Séances et travaux 6 : 44-46, janvier-mars 1932.

Rapports sur le mouvement de la législation en matière pénale et pénitentiaire dans divers pays - Finlande. Recueil de documents en matière pénale et pénitentiaire 2 : 1-8, mars 1932.

WREDE, R.A. : La situation des îles d'Aland en droit international. Nordisk tidsskrift for international ret (Acta scandinavica juris gentium) 3 : 123-143, Fasc.4, 1932.

HERNBERG, A. : Gesetzgebung, Rechtsprechung und Schrifttum in den Jahren 1929-1931. Zeitschrift für ausländisches und internationales Privatrecht 7 : 66-135, Heft 1, 1933.

Ministeriets för utenriksärendena meddelande angående tillämpningsområdet för i Finland den 1 januari 1933 gällande internationella konventioner. Finlands författningssamlings fördragsserie : 59-127, 31 mars 1933.
International conventions in force in Finland on 1 January 1933.

Ministeriets för utrikesärendena meddelande angående tillämpningsområdet för i Finland den 1 januari 1934 gällande internationella komventioner. Finlands författningssamlings fördragsserie : 161-232, 9 maj 1934.
International conventions in force in Finland on 1 January 1934.

HAKULINEN : Gesetzgebung in Finnland in den Jahren 1932 und 1933. Zeitschrift für ausländisches und internationales Privatrecht 8 : 846-850, Heft 5, 1934.

FRANCE

LÉVY, E. : La simplification de l'état civil en France de 1919 à 1930. Bulletin de l'Institut intermédiaire international 22 : 11-16, janvier 1930.
Simplification concernant l'état civil et en particulier le mariage.

HOUYET, A. : L'organisation politique, administrative et judiciaire de l'Afrique française du Nord. Congo 10 : 580-602, novembre 1929, et 11 : 220-249, février 1930.

BERTHÉLEMY, H. : The "Conseil d'Etat " in France. Journal of comparative legislation and international law 12 : 23-32, February 1930.

TROTABAS, L. : Liability in damages under French administrative law. Journal of comparative legislation and international law 12 : 44-57, February 1930.

AUFERMANN : Wandlungen des französischen Wertpapierrechts. Bank-Archiv 29 : 313-317, 15. Mai 1930.

ESMEIN, P. : Gesetzgebung, Rechtsprechung und Schrifttum in Frankreich im Jahre 1929. Zeitschrift für ausländisches und internationales Privatrecht 4 : 937-985, Heft 6, 1930.

ROSENDORFF, R. : Die legislatorische Behandlung der Stimmrechtsaktien (actions à vote plural) in Frankreich und die deutsche Reform. Bank-Archiv 30 : 179-184, 15. Januar 1931.

NORDEN, F. : L'empire du Code Napoléon. Deutsch-französische Rundschau 4 : 312-325, April 1931.

DUPEYROUX, H. : Du système français de revision constitutionnelle. Revue du droit public 38 : 445-472, juillet-août-septembre 1931.

ANDRÉADÈS, S. : Le Conseil d'Etat en France et en Grèce - organisation et procédure. Revue de droit public 38 : 613-641, juillet-août-septembre 1931.

ANDRÉADÈS, S. : Etude comparative du Conseil d'Etat en France et en Grèce. Revista de drept public 6 : 265-285, julie-decembrie 1931.

WOODS, D.C. : The French Court of Assizes. Journal of criminal law and criminology 22 : 325-334, September 1931.

BONNET, G. : Contre la réforme électorale. Europe nouvelle 14 : 1681-1682, 19 décembre 1931.
Le droit électoral français.

MILLIOT, L. : Une réforme du statut de la femme kabyle. Afrique française, Renseignements coloniaux 41 : 681-686, décembre 1931.

Congrès national de droit pénal colonial, Paris, 29 et 30 septembre 1931. Revue pénitentiaire et de droit pénal 56 : 3-166, janvier-mars 1932.
Rapports et comptes rendus.

Avant-projet de Code pénal français. Revue internationale de droit pénal 9 : 281-311, Nos. 3-4, 1932.

L'incapacité civile de la femme mariée - un projet de loi. Cahiers des droits de l'homme 32 : 435-440, 30 juillet 1932.

VOLLAEYS, M. : La capacité civile de la femme mariée. Cahiers des droits de l'homme 32 : 531-541, 20 septembre 1932.

ESMEIN, P. : Gesetzgebung, Rechtsprechung und Schrifttum in Franreich im Jahre 1932. Zeitschrift für ausländisches und internationales Privatrecht 7 : 368-442, Heft 2/3, 1933.

DOERNER : Der Vorentwurf eines französischen Strafgesetzbuchs. Deutsche Juristen-Zeitung 38 : 333-338, 1 März 1933.

MIRKINE-GUETZÉVITCH, B. : La revision constitutionnelle. Revue politique et parlementaire 40 : 339-349, 10 mai 1933.
La situation en France.

ANFEL, M. : Le projet français sur la capacité de la femme et les enseignements du droit comparé. Annales de l'Institut de droit comparé et l'Université de Paris I : 145-168, 1934.

Réforme de l'Etat. Annales du droit et des sciences sociales 2 : 1-448, Nos. 2-3, 1934.
Numéro spécial.

ESMEIN, P. : Gesetzgebung, Rechtsprechung und Schrifttum in Frankreich im Jahre 1933. Zeitschrift für ausländisches und internationales Privatrecht 8 : 527-603, Heft 3/4, 1934.

GATINE, P. : Les décrets-lois du 4 avril 1934 - incohérences - violations de contrats - atteintes au droit du travail. Cahiers des droits de l'homme 34 : 245-248, 10-15 avril 1934.

MIRKINE-GUETZÉVITCH, B. : La révision de la Constitution française. Année politique française et étrangère 9 : 1-30 avril 1934.

ALLEMÈS, F. : Nationality under French law. Law quarterly review 50 : 243-259, April 1934.

VOIRIN, P. : La suppression de l'incapacité de la femme mariée d'après le rapport de la Commission de législation du Sénat. Recueil hebdomadaire de jurisprudence (Dalloz) 11 : 65-68, 19 juillet 1934.

NATIONAL LAW - COUNTRIES

BASDEVANT : Le régime des protectorats nord-africains. Recueil de législation, de doctrine et de jurisprudence coloniales 37 : 111-125, septembre-octobre 1934.

La réforme de l'Etat - Le projet de M. Jacques Bardoux. Société d'études et d'informations économiques, Bulletin quotidien 15 : A.1 - A.2 six., 30 octobre 1934.

La réforme constitutionnelle. Europe nouvelle documentaire : I-VIII, 10 novembre 1934.
Textes.

BARTHÉLEMY, J. : La constitution Doumergue. Revue politique et parlementaire 41 : 225-248, 10 novembre 1934.

LAVERGNE, B. : La chute du Cabinet Doumergue et la dissolution automatique de la Chambre. Année politique française et étrangère 9 : 392-403, décembre 1934.

FRANCE
(International law, Aliens, Nationality)

Progetto di codice unico delle obbligazioni per l'Italia et la Francia. Anuario di diritto comparato vol. 4 e 5, parte I : 111-395, 1930.
Series of articles.

PERROUD, J. : Principes de droit international privé selon la loi et la jurisprudence française. Journal du droit international 57 : 5-15, janvier-février 1930.

LOUIS-LUCAS, P. : La nouvelle convention franco-belge sur les conflits en matière de recrutement militaire. Revue de droit international privé 25 : 193-217, No. 2, 1930.

LARNAUDE, F. : L'unification législative entre la France et l'Italie (obligations et contrats). Société de législation comparée, bulletin mensuel 59 : 81-156, janvier-mars 1930.

La nazionalità della donna e i matrimoni misti. Minerva 40 : 166-168, 13 marzo 1930.
New French nationality law commented.

RAYNAUD, B. : Les étrangers devant la loi du 30 avril 1930 sur les assurances sociales. Journal du droit international 57 : 917-919, juillet-octobre 1930.

DREYFUS, R. : Convention relative à la nationalité de la femme mariée conclue entre la France et la Belgique. Journal du droit international 57 : 911-916, juillet-octobre 1930.

LOUIS-LUCAS, P. : La convention franco-belge sur la nationalité de la femme mariée. Revue de droit international privé 26 : 87-99, No. 1, 1931.

KAYSER, P. : L'autonomie de la volonté en droit international privé dans la jurisprudence française. Journal du droit international 58 : 32-57, janvier-février 1931.

AUDINET, E. : La convention entre la France et l'Italie sur l'exécution des jugements en matière civile et commerciale (3 juin 1930). Revue de droit international privé 26 : 627-641, No. 4, 1931.

ANFREVILLE de la SALE, L. d' : Naturalisation et francisation en Afrique du NORD. Afrique française 41 : 111-113, février 1931.
Les lois de nationalité.

BOURBOUSSON, E. : La nationalité françcaise. Revue de droit international, de sciences diplomatiques et politiques 9 : 262-268, juillet-septembre 1931.

RAUCHHAUPT, F.W. von : Zur deutsch-französischen Rechtangleichung. Deutsch-französische Rundschau 4 : 741-753, September 1931.

BOURBOUSSON, E. : La nationalité française. Bulletin de l'Institut intermédiaire international 25 : 260-268, octobre 1931.

VESEY-FITZGERALD, S.G. : The Franco-Italian Draft code of obligations, 1927. Journal of comparative legislation and international law 14 : 1-19, February 1932.

LEVEL, M. : La question de la nationalité des sociétés au regard du droit français. Revue de droit international privé 27 : 405-431, No. 3, 1932.

PEETERS, J.B. : La convention conclue le 16 mai 1931 entre la Belgique et la France pour éviter les doubles impositions et régler certaines autres questions en matière fiscale. Bulletin de l'Institut intermédiaire international 26 : 253-260, avril 1932.

BERNARD, A. : L'exécution des sentences arbitrales étrangères en Belgique et en France. Institut belge de droit comparé, Revue trimestrielle 18 : 139-157, avril-septembre 1932.

The Clipperton Island case, France v. Mexico. Cumulative digest of international law and relations 2 : 94-98, November 18, 1932.
With text of award.

BOURBOUSSON, E. : La nacionalidad francesa. Revista de derecho internacional 11 : 276-282, 31 de diciembre 1932.

BRAULT, M. : Les successions mobilières des Français domiciliés à l'étranger. Journal du droit international 60 : 308-316, mars-avril 1933.

La liquidation des sociétés russes en France. Travaux du Comité français de droit international privé 1 : 130-163, 1934.

Le statut des sociétés. Travaux du Comité français de droit international privé 1 : 67-100, 1934.

BASTID, P. : Les garanties internationales des droits de l'homme d'après la tradition de la France. Académie diplomatique internationale, Séances et travaux 8 : 13-16, No. 1, 1934.

TAGER, P. : L'Etat russe commerçant et le traité franco-soviétique. Journal du droit international 61 : 22-35, janvier-février 1934.

TRACHTENBERG, B. : Le statut de la représentation commerciale de l'U.R.S.S. en France, d'après l'accord franco-soviétique du 11 janvier 1934. Nouvelle revue de droit international 1 : 32-45, janvier-février-mars 1934.

NIBOYET, J.-P. : Tableau des accords internationaux de la France. Revue critique de droit international 29 : 181-232, janvier-mars 1934.

NATIONAL LAW - COUNTRIES

BATIFOL, H. : Chronique de jurisprudence française : conflits de lois, Revue critique de droit international 29 : 607-645, No. 3, 1934.

COSENTINI, F. : Le code international des obligations et le projet de code franco-italien des contrats et des obligations. Bulletin trimestriel de la Société de Législation comparée 63 : 181-192, avril-mai-juin 1934.

MAKAROV, A.N. : Die Bestimmungen des russisch-französischen Handelsabkommens vom 11. Januar 1934 über die Rechtsstellung der Handelsvertretung der UdSSR. Zeitschrift für ausländisches öffentliches Recht und Völkerrecht 4 : 344-348, Mai 1934.

ANCEL, M. : De l'autorisation nécessaire à la femme pour solliciter la naturalisation. Revue critique de droit international 29 : 595-606, juillet-septembre 1934.

RIVIÈRE, P.-L. : Le projet de code franco-italien des obligations et des contrats. Bulletin trimestriel de la société de législation comparée 63 : 438-466, octobre-novembre-décembre 1934.

La question des étrangers devant la Chambre. Cahiers des droits de l'homme 34 : 771-775, 10 décembre 1934.

GERMANY

SAENGER, A. : Probleme einer GmbH-Reform (Contd.). Magazin der Wirtschaft 6 : 179-183, 24. Januar 1930.
Revision of German Company law advocated.

KAHN, R. : Arbitration in England and Germany. Journal of comparative legislation and international law 12 : 58-78, February 1930.

SCHAFER, E. : Der Stand der Strafrechtsreform. Juristische Wochenschrift 59 : 873-874, 29 März 1930.
German criminal law reform.

HARTUNG, F. : Reform des Strafverfahrens nach dem Einführungsgesetz zum Strafgesetzbuch. Juristische Wochenschrift 59 : 2498-2504, 16. August 1930.
Réforme de la procédure pénale en Allemagne.

Ein neues Aktienrecht. Magazin der Wirtschaft 6 : 1615-1622, 29. August 1930.
Draft of new German companies law commented.

LANSBURGH, A. : Zur Reform des deutschen Aktienrechts. Bank 23 : 1331-1337, 30. August 1930.

SINTENIS, G. : Der Aktienrechts-Entwurf. Bank-Archiv 29 : 461-471, 1. September 1930.

MEZGER, F.L. : Organisation and Finanzierung der Aktiengesellschaft im Aktienrechtsentwurf. Wirtschaftdienst 15 : 1528-1531, 5. September 1930.

WIETHAUS, K.W. : Aktiensrechtsreform und Goldbilanzverordnungen. Bank-Archiv 29 : 495-498, 15. September 1930.

MEYER, L. : Die neuen Gesetze und Verordnungen auf dem Gebiete der Industriebelastung und der Aufbringung. Wirtschaft und das Recht 5 : 378-389, September 1930.

La réforme de la législation allemande sur les sociétés anonymes. Comptoir d'escompte de Genève, bulletin économique et financier 11 : 155-163, novembre 1930.

KREY, F. : Aktienrechtsreform? Ruhr und Rhein 11 : 1633-1637, 24. Dezember 1930.
Series of articles on German joint stock company law.

LEO, M. : Änderung des ehelichen Güterrechts? Magazin der Wirtschaft 7 : 287-289, 6. Februar 1931.

NAWIASKY, H. : Wahlrechtsfragen im heutigen Deutschland- Archiv des öffentliches Rechts 20 : 161-193, 2. Heft 1931.

SCHETTER : Die Wiederaufnahme der Strafrechtsreformarbeit. Deutsche Juristen-Zeitung 36 : 329-332, 1. März 1931.
German penal law reform.

MULLER, J. : Die wirtschaftliche und soziale Gesetzgebung des Deutschen Reiches. Jahrbücher für Nationalökonomie 134 : 393-403, März 1931.

MARKULL, W. : Das Reichsrecht der Landes- und Gemeindesteuern. Vierteljahresschrift für Steuer- und Finanzrecht 5 : 482-528, Heft 3, 1931.

KARDEN : Die zweite Verordnung des Reichspräsidenten zur Sicherung von Wirtschaft und Finanzen v. 5. Juni 1931. Deutsche Juristenzeitung 36 : 861-876, 1. Juni 1931.

KLINGHOFFER, H. : Der Schutz der Grundrechte in der deutschen Reichsverfassung und der österreichischen Bundesverfassung. Zeitschrift für öffentliches Recht 11 : 378-401, 10. Oktober 1931.

HULA, E. : Deutscher und englischer Parlamentarismus. Zeitschrift für öffentliches Recht 11 : 368-377, 10. Oktober 1931.

MITTERMAJER, W. : Il progetto di codice penale tedesco (Contd.). Giustizia penale 37 : 1426-1433, 31 ottobre 1931.

ZARDEN : Die vierte Notverordnung des Reichspräsidenten vom 8. Dezember 1931. Deutsche Juristen-Zeitung 37 : 125-132, 15. Januar 1932.

CASTIGLIONE, V. : Natura giuridica e carateristische costituzionali del Reich. Economia (Roma) 10 : 22-53, luglio 1932.
Followed by a bibliography.

SCHMITT, C. : Die Verfassungsmässigkeit der Bestellung eines Reichskommissars für das Land Preussen. Deutsche Juristen-Zeitung 37 : 953-958, 1. August 1932.

HETTNER, R. : Wahlrechtsänderung. Deutsche Juristen-Zeitung 37 : 1081-1088, 15. September 1932.

GLUM, F. : Vorschläge zur Aenderung des organisatorischen Teils der Reichsverfassung. Deutsche Juristen-Zeitung 37 : 1309-1315, 1. November 1932.

KAISENBERG : Das Ermächtigungsgesetz. Deutsche Juristen-Zeitung 38 : 458-461, 1. April 1933.

DÖLLE, H. : Das bürgerliche Recht im nationalsozialistischen deutschen Staat - Ein Vortrag. Schmollers Jahrbuch 57 : 3-30, 5. Heft, 1933.

NATIONAL LAW - COUNTRIES

ROTH, A. : Zum Erbhofrecht. Juristische Wochenschrift 62 : 1372-1373, 17. Juni 1933.

HOCHE : Die Durchführungsvorschriften zum Gesetz zur Wiederherstellung des Berufsbeamtentums. Deutsche Juristen-Zeitung 38 : 720-726, 1. Juni 1933.

SONNEN : Die Vereinheitlichung des Wechselrechts und das neue deutsche Wechselgesetz. Deutsche Juristen-Zeitung 38 : 1082-1086, 15. August 1933.

STRAUSS, W. : Die neue deutsche Kartellgesetzgebung. Kartell-Rundschau 31 : 497-539, Heft 8, 1933.

ZSCHUCKE : Auf dem Wege zur Verfassung des Dritten Reiches. Deutsche Juristen-Zeitung 38 : 997-1002, 1. August 1933.

SAUER, W. : Nationalsozialistisches Strafrecht nach der Denkschrift des preussischen Justizministers. Deutsche Juristen-Zeitung 38 : 1462-1467, 15. November 1933.

MÜLLER, J. : Die wirtschaftliche und soziale Gesetzgebung des Deutschen Reiches (Die Zeit vom 1. Juli bis 30. September 1933 umfassend.). Jahrbücher für Nationalökonomie und Statistik 139 : 865-873, Dezember 1933.

MIRKINE-GUETZÉVITCH, B. : La future Constitution allemande. Affaires étrangères 4 : 14-22, 10 janvier 1934.

SCHNEIDER-NEUENBURG : Die Gesetzgebung des Jahres 1933 auf dem Gebiete des Strafrechts. Juristische Wochenschrift 63 : 257-262, 3. Februar 1934.

MÜNSTER : Deutsche Strafrechtsreform. Juristische Wochenschrift 63 : 461-463, 24. Februar 1934.

CONRAD : Reichskonkordat, Reichsrecht und Landesrecht. Deutsche Juristen-Zeitung 39 : 320-323, 1. März 1934.

STRELE, K. : Das Notverordnungsrecht im österreichischen, reichsdeutschen und italienischen Staatsrecht. Zeitschrift für vergleichende Rechtswissenschaft 48 : 382-409, 3. Heft, 1934.

Amt für die Rechtsbetreuung des deutschen Volkes. Juristische Wochenschrift 63 : 1031-1033, 28 April 1934.

EISENMANN, C. : L'organisation constitutionnelle du IIIe Reich : de Weimar à Potsdam. Comité alsacien d'études et d'informations, Office d'informations allemandes 14 : 194-202, 20 juin 1934.

AMBROSINI, G. : La soppressione dei residni di sovranità nei Laender tedeschi e l'instaurazione nel Reich del sistema unitaria. Rivista di diritto pubblico 26 : 321-326, giugno 1934.

AUBRY, M. : Les modifications apportées par le régime national-socialiste aux institutions politiques du Reich et des Pays allemands. Revue de droit public et de la science politique 41 : 466-502, juillet-août-septembre 1934.

KÜHNE, R. : Devisengesetzgebung und Wertpapierverkehr. Juristische Wochenschrift 63 : 2013-2018, 18.-25. August 1934.

PREUSS, L. : Germanic law versus Roman law in national socialist legal theory. Journal of comparative legislation and international law 16 : 269-280, November 1934.

Loi du 24 avril 1934 apportant des modifications aux prescriptions du droit pénal et de la procédure pénale (Reichsgesetzblatt I, p. 341). Recueil de documents en matière pénale et pénitentiaire 3 : 365-368, novembre 1934.
Résumé.

OPENKOWSKI, B.v. : Reichserbhofgesetz und nationale Minderheiten. Kulturwehr 10 : 643-651, Dezember 1934.

JELLINEK, W. : Le droit public de l'Allemagne en 1933. Annuaire de l'Institut international de droit public : 43-76, 1934.

GERMANY
(International law and practice, Aliens and Naturalization)

DEIKE, F. : Die deutsche Rechtsprechung auf dem Gebiete des internationalen Privatrechts im Jahre 1929. Zeitschrift für ausländisches und internationales Privatrecht 4 : 1-254, Sonderheft, 1930.

KUSTER, K. : Wert und Bedeutung der im Einführungsgesetze zum Bürgerlichen Gesetzbuche für das Deutsche Reich enthaltenen international-privatrechtlichen Norman. Zeitschrift für internationales Recht 42 : 231-256, Heft 4-6, 1930.

BESTREBUNGEN ZUR Einführung des Domizilprinzips bei Statusfragen im deutschen Recht. Zeitschrift für ausländisches und internationales Privatrecht 4 : 390-405, Heft 2, 1930.

BECKER, W. : Das Problem der mehrfachen Staatsangehörigkeit mit besonderer Berücksichtigung des Auslanddeutschtums. Zeitschrift für Völkerrecht 15 : 478-517, Heft 3, 1930.
German nationality law and comparative legislation.

LORENZEN, E.G. : The conflict of laws of Germany. Yale law journal 39 : 804-836, April 1930.

ULLMANN, F. : Das deutsch-polnische Aufwertungsabkommen. Zeitschrift für Ostrecht 4 : 337-359, April 1930.

HELCZYNSKI, B. : Das deutsch-polnische Aufwertungsabkpmmen. Zeitschrift für Ostrecht 4 : 360-374, April 1930.

ERBE : Das neue Gesetz zum Schutze der Republik. Deutsche Juristen-Zeitung 35 : 453-459, 1. April 1930.

NORMANN, A. van : Das internationale Erbrecht des Einführungsgesetzes zum bürgerlichen Gesetzbuch. Juristische Wochenschrift 59 : 975-977, 5. April 1930.

ZWEHL : Das deutsch-polnische Liquidations-Abkommen. Deutsche Juristen-Zeitung 35 : 584-588, 1. Mai 1930.

HENRYCHOWSKI : Das deutsche polnische Aufwertungsabkommen. Juristische Wochenschrift 59 : 1791-1796, 7. - 14. Juni 1930.

NATIONAL LAW - COUNTRIES

ZWEHL : Die deutsche polnische Uebereinkunft vom 31. Oktober 1929. Die Entschädigung vom 31. Oktober 1920. Die Entschädigung nach dem Polenabkommen und die internationale Rechtsprechung- Juristische Wochenschrift 59 : 1792-1796, 7-14. Juni 1930.

JONAS; MEYER-WILD : Das deutsch-schweizerische Vollstreckungsabkommen vom 2. November 1929. Juristische Wochenschrift 59 : 3284-3287, 1.-8. November 1930.

TOPF, E. : Die Kündigung von Verträgen des Deutschen Reichs mit auswärtigen Staaten. Archiv des öffentlichen Rechts 20 : 343-358, 3. Heft 1931.

KLEINFELLER, G. : Internationales Strafrecht nach dem neuen italienischen und dem künftigen deutschen Strafgesetzbuch. Neimeyers Zeitschrift für internationales Recht 43 : 172-188, 2. bis 6. Heft 1931.

DEIKE, F. : Die deutsche Rechtsprechung auf dem Gebiete des internationalen Privatrechts im Jahre 1930. Zeitschrift für ausländisches und internationales Privatrechts im Jahre 1930. Zeitschrift für ausländisches und internationales Privatrecht : 1-288, Sonderheft 1931.

BOSCHAN : Deutsches zwischenstaatliches Personenstandsrecht. Zeitschrift für ausländisches und internationales Privatrecht 5 : 327-354, Heft 2/3, 1931.

KRAUSS, G. : De l'effet international en Allemagne des jugements étrangers et des sentences arbitrales étrangères. Journal du droit international 58 : 66-80, janvier-février 1931.

METTGENBERG, W. : Ein neuer Auslieferungsvertrag mit den Vereinten Staaten von Amerika. Juristische Wochenschrift 60 : 706-707, 14. März 1931.

SCHÄFER, E. : Loi allemande du 23 décembre 1929 sur l'extradition. Recueil de documents en matière pénale et pénitentiaire 1 : 4-11, mars 1931.

Questions de droit posées par l'accord douanier austro-allemand. Affaires étrangères 1 : 71-73, avril 1931.

TOUSSAINT, A. : Der Plan einer deutsch-oesterreichischen "Zollunion" in seiner völkerrechtlichen Bedeutung. Revue de droit international, de sciences diplomatiques et politiques 9 : 161-170, avril-juin 1931.

SILZ, E. : La réforme allemande et l'évolution du droit pénal international. Revue pénitentiaire et de droit pénal 55 : 276-370, juillet-décembre 1931.

RAUCHHAUPT, F.W. von : Zur deutsch-französischen Rechtsangleichung. Deutsch-französische Rundschau 4 : 741-753, September 1931.

KOCH-WESER, E. : Reform des deutschen Staatsangehörigkeitsgesetzes. Auslanddeutsche 14 : 658-667, 1. Novemberheft 1931.

SCHMITZ, E. : Die Methode des Abschlusses internationaler Verträge nach deutschem Recht. Zeitschrift für ausländisches öffentliches Recht und Völkerrecht (Abhandlungen) 3 : 313-385, No. 3, 1932.

SCHADE, H. : Ersatz der Zustimmung des Reichstags zu Staatsverträgen im Wege des Art. 48 RV. Archiv des öffentlichen Rechts 21 : 364-384, 3. Heft 1932.

GERLAND, H. : Internationales Strafrecht nach den Bestimmungen des deutschen Strafgesetzbuchs und den Vorschlägen des Entwurfs. Zeitschrift für ausländisches und internationales Privatrecht 6 : 177-184, Sonderheft 1932.

PRUD'HOMME, A., et GALLAIX, M. de : L'accord polono-allemand du 31 octobre 1930 et les créances pour dommages de guerre. Journal du droit international 59 : 57-64, janvier-février 1932.

SAUSER-HALL, G. : Les conventions germano-suisses sur les hypothèques avec clause d'or. Journal du droit international 59 : 340-366, mars-avril 1932.

MEILICKE, H. : Die Ausbürgerung. Juristische Wochenschrift 62 : 1916-1919, 2. September 1933.

DEIKE, F. : Die deutsche Rechtsprechung auf dem Gebiete des internationalen Privatrechts im Jahre 1932. Zeitschrift für ausländisches und internationales Privatrecht : 1-310, Sonderheft 1933.

SCELLE, G. : A propos de la loi allemande du 14 juillet 1933 sur la déchéance de la nationalité. Revue critique de droit international 29 : 63-76, janvier-mars 1934.

WALZ, G.A. : Das Verhältnis von Vlkerrecht und staatlichen Recht nach nationalsozialistischer Rechtsauffassung. Zeitschrift für Völkerrecht 18 : 145-154, Heft 2, 1934.

WALZ, G.A. : Völkerrecht und Reichsjustizausbildungsordnung. Zeitschrift für Völkerrecht 18 : 323-330, Heft 3, 1934.

METTGENBERG, W. : Das deutsche Ausbürgerungsgesetz. Völkerbund und Völkerrecht 1 : 155-161, Heft 3, 1934.

MOSES, F. : Protection of trade with Soviet Russia by treaty - Germany's experience. American bar association journal 20 : 207-211, April 1934.

JACOB, G. : "L'ordre public" en droit international allemand. Boletin da Faculdade de direito (Coimbra) 13 : 227-246, 1932-1934.

GREAT BRITAIN

FINER, H. : Recent reforms in English local government. Jahrbuch des öffentlichen Rechts 18 : 208-232, 1930.

HUNT, C. : Recent English Company law reform. Harvard business review 8 : 170-183, January 1930.

FINER, H. : Le local Government Act de 1929. Revue des sciences politiques 45 : 77-88. janvier-mars, 1930.

KOCH, F.C. : Das neue englische Aktienrecht und die deutsche Aktienrechtsreform. Zentralblatt für Handelsrecht 5 : 84-90, März 1930.

The referendum. Law journal 69 : 183-184, March 15, 1930.
Mr. Baldwin's proposal of a referendum to settle the future commercial relations of different parts of the Empire.

HANSCHER, V.M. : Oxford and American legal education: a contrast. American bar association journal 16 : 523-529, August 1930.

LASKI, H.J. : Why electoral reform was wanted. Labour magazine 9 : 439-443, February 1931.
An analysis of the new British bill.

HEYER, F. : Die wirtschaftliche Gesetzgebung Grossbritanniens in den Jahren 1928/29 und 1929/30. Weltwirtschaftliches Archiv 33 : 620-627, April 1931.

HULA, E. : Deutscher und englischer Parlamentarismus. Zeitschrift für öffentliches Recht 11 : 368-377, 10. Oktober 1931.

STALLYBRASS, W.T.S. : A comparison of the general principles of criminal law in England with the "Progetto definitivo di un nuovo codice penale" of Alfredo Rocco (Contd.). Journal of comparative legislation and international law 14 : 45-61, February 1932.

Englische Gesetzgebung 1931. Zeitschrift für ausländisches und internationales Privatrecht 6 : 586-629, Heft 4, 1932.

WITTE, E.E. : British trade union law since the trade disputes and Trade Union Act of 1927. American political science review 26 : 341-351, April 1932.

GARDNER, J.C. : The study of comparative law in Great Britain. Journal of comparative legislation and international law 14 : 201-206, November 1932.

GRAHAM, R.B. : British and Russian criminal jurisprudence. Canadian bar review 12 : 1-13, January 1934.

MACCOL, J.E., and WELLS, W.T. : The Incitement to Disaffection Bill 1934. Political quarterly 5 : 352-364, July-September 1934.

GREAT BRITAIN
(International law, Aliens)

The nationality of married women. Law journal 69 : 7-8, 4 January 1930.
The British law.

WEISER, F. : Privates Feindesvermögen im englischen Recht. Niemeyers Zeitschrift für internationales Recht 42 : 208-230, 1.-3. Heft 1930.

MONSARRAT, R. : Le Companies Act 1929 et les sociétés étrangères. Journal du droit international 57 : 82-89, janvier-février 1930.

La Grande-Bretagne et lexterritorialité. Europe nouvelle 13 : 386-387, 1 mars 1930.

Le società straniere nel Companies Act inglese 1929. Rivista del diritto commerciale 28 : 619-622, agosto-settembre 1930.

Tha nationality of married women. Law journal 70 : 144, 6 September 1930.
The law in Great Britain.

MONSARRAT, R. : Le Finance Act 1930 et la double imposition. Journal du droit international 57 : 949-955, juillet-octobre 1930.

Nationality and marriage. Law journal 70 : 390-391, December 20, 1930.
British bill to alter the law as to nationality of married women.

ADAIR, E.A. : The Law of Nations and the Common Law of England. Journal of comparative legislation and international law 13 : 133-137, February 1931.

LEPOINTE, G., et PETCHORINE, D. : L'évolution de la jurisprudence anglaise concernant les sociétées russes nationalisées. Journal du droit international 59 : 853-866, juillet-octobre 1932.

DOBRIN, S. : The English doctrine of the renvoi and the Soviet law of succession. British yearbook of international law 15 : 36-45, 1934.

WADE, E.C.S. : Act of State in English law - its relations with international law. British year-book of international law 15 : 98-112, 1934.

KEETON, G.W. : Foreign currency questions in recent English decisions. Iowa law review 19 : 218-224, January 1934.

MENZEL, E. : Der Wirkungsgrad der Völkerrechtsnorman im englischen Recht. Zeitschrift für Völkerrecht 18 : 155-180, Heft 2, 1934.

GREECE

ANASTASIADIS, E., et LOGOTHETIS, P. : Le fonti del diritto privato greco. Annuario di diritto comparato vol. 4 e 5, parte 1, 35-36, 1930.

ANASTASIADIS, E. : Rassegna di letteratura giuridica greca (anni 1925-1927). Anuario di diritto comparato vol. 4 e 5, parte 1, 527-530, 1930.

SPOURGITIS, R.N. : Quelques remarques sur la loi grecque visant les sociétés anonymes. Société belge d'études et d'expansion, bulletin périodique : 51-56, février 1930.

ANASTASIADIS, E. Rassegna di legislazione greca (anni 1925-1927). Annuario di diritto comparato vol. 4 e 5, parte 2 : 423-429, 1930.

HARIDAKIS, G.S. : Die Vollstreckbarkeit ausländischer Urteile in Griechenland. Zeitschrift für ausländisches und internationales Privatrecht 4 : 506-512, Heft 3-4, 1930.

MILONOPULO, S.P.A. : Sull'esecutorietà delle sentenze e degli atti straniere in Grecia. Rivista di diritto internazionale 23 : 67-71, 1 gennaio-31 marzo 1931.

ANDRÉADÈS : Le Conseil d'Etat en France et en Grèce - organisation et procédure. Revue de droit public 38 : 613-641, juillet-août-septembre 1931.

ANDRÉADÈS, S. : Etude comparative du Conseil d'Etat en France et en Grèce. Revista de drept public 6 : 265-285, julie-decembrie 1931.

ANASTASIADIS, E., LOGOTHETIS, P., ZORAS, G. : Grecia. Istituto di studi legislativi. Legislazione internazionale 1 : 255-319, fasc. 2, 1932.

ZEPOS, P.J. : Aktienrechtsreform in Griechenland. Zeitschrift für ausländisches und internationales Privatrecht 6 : 571-575, Heft 4, 1932.

TÉNÉKIDÈS, C.-G. : La loi étrangère et le droit hellénique. Journal du droit international 59 : 589-605, mai-juin 1932.

TÉNÉKIDÈS, C. : Les sociétés anonymes dans le droit hellénique. Bulletin de l'Institut intermédiaire international 27 : 1-18, juillet 1932.

SÉFÉRIADÈS, S. : La question du rapatriement des "marbres d'Elgin" considérée plus spécialement au point de vue du droit des gens. Revue de droit international 6 : 52-81, juillet-août-septembre 1932.

VALLINDAS, P. : Vorbereitungsarbeiten und Bedeutung der zivilrechtlichen Kodifikation Griechenlands. Zeitschrift für ausländisches und internationales Privatrecht 7 : 161-163, Heft 1, 1933.

FRAGISTAS, Ch. N. : Griechische Rechtsprechung auf dem Gebiet des internationalen Privatrechts (1927 bis 1931). Zeitschrift für ausländisches und internationales Privatrecht 7 : 294-305, Heft 2/3, 1933.

TÉNÉKIDÈS, C.G. : Le divorce des étrangers en Grèce. Bulletin de l'Institut juridique international 31 : 2-7, juillet 1934.

HYDE, C.C. : The extradition case of Samuel Insull, Sr., in relation to Greece. American journal of international law 28 : 307-312, April 1934.

TSIRINTANIS, A.N. : Ein Dezennium griechischer Handelsgesetzgebung. Zeitschrift für ausländisches und internationales Privatrecht 8 : 604-614, Heft 3/4, 1934.

RECHID, A. : L'affaire Samuel Insull. Revue générale de droit international public 41 : 687-710, novembre-décembre 1934.

GUATEMALA

SALAZAR, F.O. : Proyecto del libro 4° del Código civil de la República de Guatemala. Gaceta de los tribunales, Guatemala 50 : 1-171 (annexe), enero 1932.

HAITI

DANTÈS-BELLEGARDE : La situation internationale de la République d'Haïti. Académie diplomatique internationale 5 : 24-25, janvier-mars 1931.

The new constitution of Haiti. Bulletin of the Pan American Union 67 : 133-137, February 1933.

HUNGARY

KUNCZ, E. : Die Bedeutung des neuen ungarischen Gesetzes über die Gesellschaften mit beschränkter Haftung für die Aktienrechtsreform. Zeitschrift für ausländisches und internationales Privatrecht: 48-68, Heft 1, 1930.

CSEKEY, S. v. : Die Verwaltungsreform in Ungarn. Zeitschrift für ausländisches öffentliches Recht und Völkerrecht (Abt.1) 2 : 268-276, Nr. 1-2, 1930.

KUNCZ, E. : Das ungarische Handelsgesetzbuch und seine Reform. Rigasche Zeitschrift für Rechtswissenschaft 4 : 93-110, 2. Heft 1930.

BALOGH, E. : Rassegna di legislazione ungherese (anno 1927). Annuario di diritto comparato vol. 4 e 5, parte 2 : 873-880, 1930.

KUNCZ, E. : Übersicht über das neue ungarische Gesetz betreffend die Gesellschaften mit beschränkter Haftung und die stillen Gesellschaften. Zeitschrift für Ostrecht 4 : 375-388, April 1930.

EGYED, S. : Ungarische Staatsgehörigkeitsgesetz. Zeitschrift für Ostrecht 4 : 495-506, Mai 1930. German text of nationality law annexed.

AUER : Neuere Massnahmen zwecks Vereinfachung des ungarischen Gerichtsverfahrens. Deutsche Juristen-Zeitung 10 : 671-674, 15. Mai 1930.

HAJNAL, H. : La loi hongroise concernant les sociétés à responsabilité limitée et l'association en participation. Annales de droit commercial 39 : 197-219, juillet-septembre 1930.

HAJNAL, H. : Le droit international hongroise en matière de mariage et de divorce. Journal du droit international 57 : 891-910, juillet-octobre 1930.

SCHWARTZ, I. : Die internationalen Beziehungen des ungarischen Zivilprozessrechtes. Niemeyers Zeitschrift für internationales Recht 43 : 168-171, 2. bis 6. Heft 1931.

DORNING, H., et HAJNAL, H. : Le droit pénal international hongrois. Revue de droit international et de législation comparée 58 : 576-606, No. 3, 1931.

EGYED, E. : La réforme de la procédure en matière de mariage en Hongrie. Bulletin de l'Institut intermédiaire international 24 : 225-229, avril 1931.

GOELLNER, H. de : Notice sur les lois promulguées en 1931. Annuaire de législation étrangère 59 : 431-446, 1931.

CSEKEY, S. v. : Die Entwicklung des öffentlichen Rechts in Ungarn seit 1926. Jahrbuch des öffentliche Rechts : 199-315, Band 19, 1931.

TOMCSÁNYI, M. de : L'évolution constitutionnelle de la Hongrie et sa situation actuelle en droit public. Acta juris hungarici 1 : 5-32, janvier-mars 1932.

SZÁSZY, E. de : Le droit international privé hongrois. Acta juris hungarici 1 : 106-120, janvier-mars 1932.

HALÁSZ, Z. : Ungheria. Istituto di studi legislativi, Legislazione internazionale 1 : 157-185, fasc. 2, 1932.

SZLADITS, C. : Le projet de code civil hongrois. Acta juris hungarici 1 : 213-221, septembre-décembre 1932.

SZENTE, A. : Die privatrechtliche Gesetzgebung Ungarns nach dem Kriege. Ungarische Jahrbücher 13 : 126-136, Juli 1933.

URBACH, L. : Ungarisches Luftrecht. Zetschrift für Ostrecht 7 : 1029-1039, Dezember 1933.

EGYED, E. : Le droit électoral hongrois. Nouvelle revue de Hongrie 27 : 25-30, janvier 1934.

BALÁS, E.P. e EGYED, S. : Rassegna di legislazione ungherese (anni 1929 e 1930). Annuario di diritto comparato e di studi legislativi (Parte IV) 8 : 316-401, 1934.

RACZ, G. : Rapport concernant le développement de la législation pénale hongroise d'après-guerre. Recueil de documents en matière pénale et pénitentiaire 3 : 315-332, mai 1934.

ROSSI, L. : Potere personale e potere rappresentativo nella "Sacra Corona d'Ungheria". Rivista di diritto pubblico 26 : 653-675, dicembre 1934.

RÁCZ, G. : Ungarn - Übersicht über die wesentliche Gesetzgebung für das Jahr 1933-1934. Zeitschrift für osteuropäisches Recht 1 : 325-326, Dezember 1934.

DUPUIS, R. : Les grandes étapes du droit public hongrois. Annales de l'Institut de droit comparé de l'Université de Paris 1 : 113-143, 1934.

ICELAND

ARNÓRSSON, E. : Einige Bemerkungen über die Völkerrechtliche Stellung Islands. Acta scandinavica juris gentium 2 : 63-78, fasc. 2, 1931.

ARNÓRSSON, E. : Nogle Bemaerkninger om Islands folkeretlige Stilling. Nordisk tidsskrift for international ret 2 : 67-80, fasc. 2, 1931.

INDIA

Documents concerning the origin and purpose of the Indian statutory commission. International conciliation : 129-187, March 1930.

The constitutional development of India, 1917-1930. Bulletin of international news 6 : 3-10, 19 June 1930.

GARATT, G.T. : A new constitution for India. Labour magazine 9 : 102-105, July 1930.

HOLDSWORTH, W.S. : The Indian States and India. Law quarterly review 46 : 407-446, October 1930.
Analysis of the report of the Indian States Committee.

SRINAVASA SASTRI, V.S. : The Indian States problem. Servant of India 13 : 548-552, November 13, 1930.

The constitutional development of India. Bulletin of international news 7 : 9-12, November 20, 1930.

BISSON, T.A. : The crisis in India - its constitutional basis. Foreign policy association, Information service 6 : 345-358, November 26, 1930.

The United States of India. New statesman 36 : 228-229, November 29, 1930.
Work of the Round Table Conference.

CHANDY, K. : On a Dominion Constitution for India. Indian affairs 1 : 103-202, December 1930.

Le développement constitutionnel de l'Inde depuis 1917 et la conférence de la Table Ronde. Société d'études et d'informations économiques, supplément au Bulletin quotidien No. 23 : 1-13, 31 janvier 1931.

A Supreme Court for Federal India. Near East and India 39 : 354, 26 March 1931.

Indian States and the Federal Constitution. Indian affairs 2 : 11-15, April 1931.

MARRIOTT, J. : A constitution for a continent - the problem of India. Fortnightly review 129 : 754-765, June 1931.

MOLSON, A.H.E. : The constitutional position of the Indian States (Contd.). Asiatic review 46 : 487-495, July 1931.

Un projet de constitution pour la Birmanie. Société d'études et d'informations économiques, bulletin quotidien 14 : G.-1 - G. 4, 10 et 11 août 1933.

MARTIN, P. : Le projet de nouvelle constitution de l'Inde anglaise. Asie française 34 : 9-17, janvier 1934.

IRELAND

JACQUEMARD, L. : Situation internationale de l'Etat libre d'Irlande. Revue de droit international 4 : 205-224, juillet-août-septembre 1930.

ITALY

GEMMA, S. : Notes de droit international privé relatives aux réformes législatives italiennes. Revue de droit international privé 25 : 33-51, No. 1, 1930.

GEMMA, S. : Réformes législatives italiennes (Contd). Revue de droit international privé 25 : 251-269, No. 2, 1930.

JEMOLO, A.C. : El nuevo derecho matrimonial italiano. Revista de derecho y legislación 19 : 33-34, febrero 1930.
New Italian marriage law.

SALEMI, G. : Il Consiglio di Stato e i Corpi consultativi analoghi nella legislazione fascista. Archivio di studi corporativi 1 : 453-471, fasc. 3, 1930.

KEETMANN : Die Gesetzgebung Italiens im Jahre 1928. Zeitschrift für ausländisches und internationales Privatrecht 4 : 535-563, Heft 3-4, 1930.

Rechtsprechung und Literatur Italiens im Jahre 1928. Zeitschrift für ausländisches und internationales Privatrecht 4 : 564-609, Heft 3-4, 1930.

BETTI, E. : Sul progetto di un codice italo-francese delle obbligazioni e dei contratti. Rivista del diritto commerciale 28 : 184-189, marzo-aprile 1930.

Progetto di codice unico delle obbligazioni per l'Italia e la Francia. Annuario di diritto comparato vol. 4 e 5, parte I : III-395, 1930.
Series of articles.

DONNEDIEU de VABRES, H. : Il diritto penale internazionale secondo il progetto definitivo di Codice penale italiano. Annuario di diritto comparato vol. 6, parte 1 (fascicolo 1) : 193-237, 1930.

RHEINSTEIN, M. : Gesetzgebung, Rechtsprechung und Rechtsliteratur Italiens im Jahre 1929. Zeitschrift für ausländisches und internationales Privatrecht 4 : 986-1032, Heft 6, 1930.

WOLFF, M. : Das neue italienische Eherecht. Zeitschrift für ausländisches und internationales Privatrecht 4 : 915-929, Heft 6, 1930.

NATIONAL LAW - COUNTRIES

SMITH, H.A. : Aspetti internazionali del progetto di Codice penale italiano. Anuario di diritto comparato vol. 6, parte 1 (fascicolo 1) : 59-62, 1930.

Il progetto di legge sul fallimento e sul concordato preventivo. Rivista di diritto, economia e commercio 3 : 319-369, giugno-luglio 1930.

PACINOTTI, G. : Studi sui contratti collettivi di lavoro. Rivista del diritto commerciale 28 : 549-564, agosto-settembre 1930.

UDINA, M. : Le recenti annessioni territoriale al Regno d'Italia. Rivista di diritto internazionale 22 : 301-341, 1 luglio-30 settembre 1930.

BOSCO, G. : Le nuove leggi sul matrimonio e la loro influenza nel diritto internazionale privato italiano. Rivista di diritto internationale 22 : 363-378, 1 luglio - 30 settembre 1930.

COSTAMAGNA, C. : Il congresso di scienze amministrative di Madrid e il diritto pubblico italiano. Rivista di diritto pubblico 23 : 36-40, gennaio 1931.
Fourth international congress of administrative science, Madrid, October 1930.

BRESCH, M. : Die unregelmässigen Handelsgesellschaften nach italienischem Recht. Mitteilungen des Verbandes österreichischer Banken und Bankiers 12 : 325-335, Dezember 1930.

SIOTTO-PINTOR, M. : Die Erledigung der "Römischen Frage" durch die Lateranverträge und das neue Kirchenrecht in Italien. Jahrbuch des öffentliches Rechts 18 : 233-260, 1930.

FERRARA, F. : La teoria delle persona giuridiche nel progetto di Codice Civile italiano. Rivista di diritto pubblico 23 : 12-25, gennaio 1931.

RENDE, D. : Il nuovo codice penale italiano e il suo primo commento. Rivista internazionale di filosofia del diritto 11 : 72-77, gennaio-febbraio 1931.

BALDASSARRI, A. : L'estradizione nella nuova legislazione penale italiana. Rivista di diritto internazionale 23 : 3-31, 1 gennaio-31 marzo 1931.

STEINER, N.A. : The treaty-making power in fascist Italy. American political science review 25 : 146-152, February 1931.

MARINO, F. : La corporazione provinciale e la riforma della legislazione del lavoro. Rivista di diritto, economia e commercio 4 : 93-95, febbraio 1931.

KLEINFELLER, G. : Internationales Strafrecht nach dem neuen italienischen und dem künftigen deutschen Strafgesetzbuch. Niemeyers Zeitschrift für internationales Recht 43 : 172-188, 2. bis 6. Heft 1931.

CAVAGLIERI, A. : Les règles de droit international privé de l'école italienne. Revue de droit international privé 25 : 397-411, No. 3, 1930.

LONGHI, S. : Le nuove leggi penali. Gerarchia 11 : 229-232, marzo 1931.
Fascist legislation.

BUNGE : Der Fortgang der italienischen Strafrechtsreform. Deutsche Juristen-Zeitung 36 : 332-337, 1. März 1931.

Il matrimonio in Italia (Contd.). Civiltà cattolica 82 : 481-492, 21 marzo 1931.

AUDINET, E. : La convention entre la France et l'Italie sur l'exécution des jugements en matière civile et commerciale (3 juin 1930). Revue de droit international privé 26 : 627-641, No. 4, 1931.

CAEMMERER, v. : Gesetzgebung, Rechtsprechung und Rechtsliteratur Italiens im Jahre 1930. Zeitschrift für ausländisches und internationales Privatrecht 5 : 806-879, heft 5, 1931.

COMBA, M. : La figura del Governatore delle colonie Italiane. Oltremare 5 : 203-210, maggio 1931.

TREVES, G. : Figura giuridica del Sindicato fascista. Rivista di politica economica 21 : 689-704, 30 giugno 1931.

OLIVETTI, A.O. : La nuova legge fallimentare. Commercio 4 : 345-350, luglio 1931.

BERTOLA, A. : L'ordinamente giuridico di Rodi. Oltremare 5 : 282-286, luglio 1931.

FEDOZZI, P. : Appunti sul progetto di riforma del diritto internazionale privato italiano. Rivista italiana di diritto internazionale privato e processuale 1 : 9-55, luglio-agosto 1931.

AGO, R. : Le norme di diritto internazionale privato nel progetto di Codice Civile. Rivista di diritto internazionale 23 : 297-351, 1 luglio-30 settembre 1931.

CRECCHIO, G. : La riforma penitenziaria. Vita italiana 19 : 176-184, agosto 1931.

GABRIELI, F.P. : Esposizione dei principi direttivi e spiegazione pratica del nuovo Codice penale italiano (pubblicato con R.D. 19 ottobre 1930 n. 1938 e in vigore dal 1 luglio 1931) (Contd.). Giustizia penale 37 : 1401-1426, 31 ottobre 1931.

FERRARA, A. : Il rapporto d'impiego nell'Istituto Internazionale di Agricoltura ed il potere di giurisdizione dello Stato italiano. Rivisto di diritto pubblico 23 : 531-540, ottobre 1931.

BALDASSARI, A. : L'estradizione nella nuova legislazione penale italiana. Rivista di diritto internazionale, Vol. X : 3-31, 1931.

Trattato di estradizione e di assistenza Giuridizaria in materia penale. Rivista di diritto internazionale, Vol. X : 100-106, 1931.

ANZILOTTI, D. : Sui limiti della giuridizione italiana sulle persone giuridiche straniere. Rivista di diritto pubblico 24 : 8-19, gennaio 1932.

VESEY-FITZGERALD, S.G. : The Franco-Italian Draft Code of obligations, 1927. Journal of comparative legislation and international law 14 : 1-19, February 1932.

VALÉRY, J. : Observations sur les dispositions contenues dans le projet de réforme du Code civil itali[e] qui intéressent le droit international privé. Revue de droit international privé 27 : 213-227, No. 2, 1932.

ROCCO : La législation fasciste. Revue économique internationale 24 : 231-258, février 1932.

NATIONAL LAW - COUNTRIES

STALLYBRASS, W.T.S. : A comparison of the general principles of criminal law in England wit the "Progetto definitivo di un nuovo codie penale" of Alfredo Rocco (Contd.). Journal of comparative legislation and international law 14 : 45-61, February 1932.

Rapports sur le mouvement de la législation en matière pénale dans divers pays - Italie. Recueil de documents en matière pénale et pénitentiaire 2 : 9-131, mars 1932.

LEIBHOLZ, G. : Der Abschluss und die Transformation von Staatsverträgen in Italien. Zeitschrift für Völkerrecht 16 : 353-376, Heft 3, 1932.

GABRIELI, F. : Le projet définitif d'un nouveau code pénal italien (Contd.). Revue pénitentiaire et de droit pénal 56 : 439-448, avril-septembre 1932.

PALOPALI, N. : Individuo e stato nella concezione corporativa. Economia italiana 17 : 298-306, maggio-giugno 1932.

GASLINI, P. : La natura giuridica del Partito Fascista. Economia italiana 17 : 306-312, maggio-giugno 1932.

CAEMMERER, E. v. : Gesetzgebung Italiens im Jahre 1931. Zeitschrift für ausländisches und internationales Privatrecht 6 : 983-1001, Heft 6, 1932.

SCHIFALACQUA, G.B. : La réforme pénale en Italie. Europe nouvelle 15 : 1032-1036, 27 août 1932.

AZARA, A. : La preparazione dei nuovi codici. Echi e commenti 13 : 2-3, 25 ottobre 1932.

MARRACINO, Alessandro : La cittadinanza degli italiani 2 : 49-51, 1 gennaio 1933.

GIURIATI, G. : Il progetto del Codice penale militare di guerra. Nuova antologia 68 : 491-512, 16 febbraio 1933.

RIEZLER, E. : Der Entwurf eines neuen italienischen Zivilgesetzbuches. Zeitschrift für ausländisches und internationales Privatrecht 7 : 207-279, Heft 2/3, 1933.

ZENNARO, T. : Le norme di diritto internazionale privato nei progetti di riforma legislativa in Italia (Contd.). Annali della R. Università degli studi economici e commerciali di Trieste 3 : 1-17, 1933.

SANGIACOMO, V.O. : L'esenzione degli stati esteri dalla giurisdizione locale e i rapporti italo-russi. Studi senesi 46 : 507-529, fascicolo 5, 1933.

KAAS, L. : Der Konkordatstyp des faschistischen Italien. Zeitschrift für ausländisches öffentliches Recht und Völkerrecht (Abhandlungen) 3 : 488-522, No. 4, 15. Juli 1933.

TOSCANO, M. : Di alcuni particolari modi di acquisto volontario della cittadinanza italiana. Rivista di diritto internazionale 25 : 428-452, 1 ottobre - 31 dicembre 1933.

Elenco dei trattati di commercio fra l'Italia e gli altri Stati al 1 gennaio 1934 - XII. Bollettino di legislazione doganale e commerciale 51 : 1-39, gennaio 1934 (supplemento).

BERTOLA, A. : Confessione religiose e statuto personale dei cittadini italiani dell'Egeo e libici. Rivista di diritto pubblico 26 : 100-107, febbraio 1934.

STRELE, K. : Das Notverordnungsrecht im österreichischen, reichsdeutschen und italianischen Staatsrecht. Zeitschrift für vergleichende Rechtswissenschaft 48 : 382-409, 3. Heft, 1934.

DEPEIGES, J. : Le code de procédure pénale du Royaume d'Italie du 19 octobre 1930. Bulletin trimestriel de la société de législation comparée 63 : 77-122, janvier-février-mars 1934.

BERTOLA, A. : Confessione religiosa e statuto oersonale dei cittadini italiani nell-Egeo e libici. Oriente moderno 14 : 105-111, marzo 1934.
On the Italian decree of October 19, 1933.

COSENTINI, F. : Le code international des obligations et le projet de code franco-italien des contrats et des obligations. Bulletin trimestrial de la Société de législation comparée 63 : 181-192, avril-mai-juin 1934.

GATTA, E. : Il nuovo testo unico della legge comunale e provinciale (Contd.). Rivista di diritto pubblico 26 : 299-310, maggio 1934.

APOLLONJ, F.M. : Die Korporationen - Das Gesetz über die Errichtung der korporativen Organe des faschistischen Staates. Zeitschrift für ausländisches öffentliches Recht und Völkerrecht (Abhandlungen) 4 : 193-207, 547-581, Mai, Juli 1934.

BALZARINI, R. : Sulla natura giuridica del Partito Nazionale Fascista. Diritto del lavoro 8 : 365-371, agosto.

GABRIELLI, A. : Il nuovo ordinamento organico per l'Eritrea e le sue norme giuridiche. Oltremare 8 : 379-384, novembre 1934.

LONGHI, S. : I problemi più urgenti della riforma fascista dei codici. Rivista di diritto pubblico 26 : 589-602, novembre 1934.

RIVIERE, P.-L. : Le projet de code franco-italien des obligations et des contrats. Bulletin trimestriel de la Société de législation comparée 63 : 438-466, octobre-novembre-décembre 1934.

COTTINO, M. : Le concordat avec le Saint-Siège et le droit matrimonial italien. Annales de l'Institut de droit comparé de l'Université de Paris 1 : 25-39, 1934.

JAPAN

Revising the criminal code. Japan chronicle : 43 -44, January 16, 1930.

TAKAYANAGI, K. : Occidental legal ides in Japan. Pacific affairs 3 : 740-753, August 1930.
Their reception and their influence.

PERRIS, G. : Rassegna di legislazione giapponese (anni 1924-1927). Anuario di diritto comparato vol. 4 e 5, parte 2 : 359-421, 1930.

COLEGROVE, K.W. : The treaty-making power in Japan. American journal of international law 25 : 270-297, April 1931.

COLEGROVE, K. : The Japanese privy council. American political science review 25 : 589-615, August 1931.

OHGUSHI, T. : Die Entwicklung des japanischen Konstitutionalismus seit dem Weltkriege. Jahrbuch des öffentlichen Rechts : 356-409, Band 19, 1931.

JENKS, E. : The Japanese Commercial Code. Journal of comparative legislation and international law 14 : 62-65, February 1932.

RICHTER, O. : Japan - Die gesetzgeberische Tätigkeit des Parlaments in der Frühjahrstagung. Ostasiatische Rundschau 14 : 207-208, 16. Mai 1933.

Regulations for bills and cheques. Japan chronicle : 53-55, January 11, 1934.
Summary of the two new laws in force from January 1, 1934.

COLEGROVE, K. : Powers and functions of the Japanese Diet (Contd.). American political science review 28 : 23-39, February 1934.

PERRIS, G. : Rassegna di legislazione giapponese (anno 1928). Annuario di diritto comparato e di studi legislativi (Parte IV) 8 : 78-98, 1934.

MIYASAWA, T. : Le droit public du Japon de 1931 à 1934. Annuaire de l'Institut international de droit public : 576-581, 1934.

KURIHARA et SUZUKI : Japon - Notice sur le mouvement législatif de 1934 à 1936. Annuaire de législation étrangère 62 : 507-523, 1934/1936.

LATVIA

WITTE, L. v. : La costituzione della Repubblica lettone. Annuario di diritto comparato vol. 4 e 5, parte I : 57-71, 1930.

LOEBER, A. : Fonti e lineamenti della legislazione lettone in materia di diritto comparato vol. 4 e 5, parte I : 73-83, 1930.

LOEBER, A. : Fonti e lineamenti di diritto commerciale lettone. Annuario di diritto comparato vol. 4 e 5, parte I : 85-106, 1930.

KALNIN, K. : Die Agrarreform in Lettland. Gesellschaft 7 : 104-111, Febuar 1930.

MINTZ, P. : Rassegna di legislazione lettone (anni 1918-1927). Annuaria di diritto comparato vol. 4 e 5, parte 2 : 581-602, 1930.

MUELLER, W. : Die Gesetzgebung Lettlands im II. Halbjahr 1929. Rigasche Zeitschrift für Rechtswissenschaft 4 : 40-48, März 1930.

MUELLER, W. : Die Gesetzgebung Lettlands im Iv. Quartal 1930. Rigasche Zeitschrift für Rechtswissenschaft 4 : 274-280, 4. Heft 1930.

MINTZ, P. : Lettlands neues Strafgesetzbuch und sein Strafensystem. Rigasche Zeitschrift für Rechtswissenschaft 4 : 217-230, 4. Heft 1930.

MUELLER, W. : Die Gesetzgebung Lettlands im II. und III. Quartal 1930. Rigasche Zeitschrift für Rechtswissenschaft 4 : 199-207, Oktober 1930.

SCHIEMANN, P. : Acht Jahre lettländische Verfassung. Jahrbuch des öffentlichen Rechts 18 : 262-273, 1930.

MUELLER, W. : Die Gesetzgebung Lettlands im 1. Quartal 1931. Rigasche Zeitschrift für Rechtswissenschaft 5 : 121-128, Juli 1931.

NEUMANN, W. : Die Gründung der Aktiengesellschaft nach geltendem lettländischen Recht. Rigasche Zeitschrift für Rechtswissenschaft 5 : 1-110, Sonderbeilage 1931.

MUELLER, W. : Die Gesetzgebung Lettlands in den drei letzten Quartalen des Jahres 1931. Rigasche Zeitschrift für Rechtswissenschaft 5 : 220-234, April 1932.

MUELLER, W. : Die Gesetzgebung Lettlands im I. Quartal 1932. Rigasche Zeitschrift für Rechtswissenschaft 6 : 28-33, 1. Heft 1932.

MUELLER, W. : Die Gesetzgebung Lettlands im II. und III. Quartal 1932. Rigasche Zeitschrift für Rechtswissenschaft 6 : 97-104, Dezember 1932.

BERENT, B. : Ehescheidung in Lettland. Juristische Wochenschrift 61 : 3802, 31. Dezember 1932.

MINTZ, P., and FREYMANN, R. : Rassegna di legislazione lettone (anno 1929). Annuario di diritto comparato e di studi legislativi (Parte II) 6 : 306-319, 1933.

EHLERS, H. : Gesetzgebung und Kodifikation im früheren Russland und in Lettland. Rigasche Zeitschrift für Rechtswissenschaft 6 : 153-164, 3. Heft 1933.

MUELLER, W. : Die Gesetzgebung Lettlands im I. Quartal 1933. Rigasche Zeitschrift für Rechtswissenschaft 6 : 223-230, Juli 1933.

MINTZ, P. : Das neue Strafgesetzbuch Lettlands. Rigasche Zeitschrift für Rechtswissenschaft 7 : 7-20, 1. Heft 1933/1934.

MUELLER, W. : Die Gesetzgebung Lettlands im II. Quartal 1933. Rigasche Zeitschrift für Rechtswissenschaft 7 : 30-41, 1. Heft 1933/1934.

MUELLER, W. : Die Gesetzgebung Lettlands im III. Quartal 1933. Rigasche Zeitschrift für Rechtswissenschaft 7 : 112-121, 2. Heft 1933/1934.

MINTZ, P. : Das neue Strafgesetzbuch Lettlands. Rigasche Zeitschrift für Rechtswissenschaft 7 : 91-104, 2. Heft 1933/1934.

WITTE, L.v. : Bestrebungen der Verfassungsänderung Lettlands. Rigasche Zeitschrift für Rechtswissenschaft 7 : 63-76, 2. Heft 1933/1934.

MUELLER, W. : Die Gesetzgebung Lettlands im IV-Quartal 1933. Rigasche Zeitschrift für Rechtswissenschaft 7 : 168-175, 3. Heft 1933/1934.

MINTZ, P., and FREYMAN, R. : Rassegna di legislazione lettone (anno 1930). Annuario di diritto comparato e di studi legislativi 7 : 237-248, parte IV, 1934.

MINTZ, P. e FREYMANN, R.v. : Rassegna di legislazione lettone (anno 1931). Annuario di diritto comparato e di studi legislativi (Parte IV) 8 : 265-283, 1934.

NATIONAL LAW - COUNTRIES

MUELLER, W. : Die Ehescheidung nach lettländischem Recht. Zeitschrift für osteuropäisches Recht 1 : 66-83, August 1934.

MUELLER, W. : Die Gesetzgebung Lettlands in II. Quartal 1934. Rigasche Zeitschrift für Rechtswissenschaft 8 : 107-118, November 1934.

SCHILLING, K. von : Zu einer Reform der Einleitung zum lettländischen B.G.B. Rigasche Zeitschrift für Rechtswissenschaft 8 : 102-107, November 1934.

MUELLER, W. : Die Gesetzgebung Lettlands im I. Quartal 1934. Rigasche Zeitschrift für Rechtswissenschaft 8 : 37-46, 1. Heft 1934/1935.

LIECHTENSTEIN

BECK, W. : La constitution de la société anonyme dans la principauté de Liechtenstein. Bulletin de l'Institut intermédiaire international 24 : 215-224, avril 1931.

TRACHTENBERG, B. : Le droit international privé de la Principauté de Liechtenstein. Revue de droit international privé 28 : 464-474, No. 3, 1933.

TRACHTENBERG, B. : La législation de la Principauté de Liechtenstein. Bulletin trimestriel de la Société de législation comparée 62 : 414-431, juillet-septembre 1933.

LITHUANIA

BALOGH, E. : Rassegna di legislazione lituana (anno 1927). Annuario di diritto comparato vol. 4 e 5, parte 2 : 603-606, 1930.

BALOGH, E. : Rassegna di letteratura giuridica (anno 1927). Annuario di diritto comparato vol. 4 e 5, parte 1 : 561-562, 1930.

BERENT, B. : Die Sprachenfrage in Lettland. Zeitschrift für Ostrecht 4 : 22-44, Januar 1930.

KAVOLIS, M. : Das Eherecht in Lituaen. Zeitschrift für Ostrecht 5 : 17-39, Januar 1931.

FREUND, H. : Erster Kongress der baltischen Juristen in Kaunas. Deutsche Juristen-Zeitung 36 : 820-821, 15. Juni 1931.

KLIMAS, P. : Le statut juridique international de Lithuanie. Académie diplomatique internationale, Séances et travaux 6 : 47-54, janvier-mars 1932.

HESSE : Die privatrechtliche Gesetzgebung im Memelgebiet seit dem Jahre 1927. Zeitschrift für ausländisches und internationales Privatrecht 6 : 659-675, Heft 4, 1932.

FRIDSTEIN, V. : Der Einfluss der litauischen Verfassung auf die übernommene russische Gesetzgebung. Zeitschrift für Ostrecht 6 : 567-582, August-September 1923.

HESSE : Das litauische Gesetz betr. die Wahl des Präsidenten der Republik (vom 24. November 1931). Zeitschrift für Ostrecht 6 : 792-795, November 1932.

RÖMED'IS, M. de : L'évolution constitutionelle de la lithuanie. Revista de drept public 8 : 155-171, junie-septembrie 1933.

Tabelle der bis Ende 1932 von Litauen abgeschlossenen Staatsverträge in chronologischer Reihenfolge. Zeitschrift für Ostrecht 7 : 789-813, August-September 1933.

BALOGH, E. : Rassegna di legislazione lituana (anni 1928-1930). Anuario di diritto comparate e di studi legislativi 7 : 249-276, parte IV, 1934.

RITTERBUSCH : Die litauische Gerichtsverfassung und das Memelgebiet. Zeitschrift für osteuropäisches Recht 1 : 109-123, September 1934.

LUXEMBOURG

BRASSEUR, R. : La Société anonyme dans le Grand-Duché de Luxembourg au point de vue fiscal. Bulletin de l'Institut intermédiaire international 23 : 1-10, juillet 1930.

MEXICO

ALMAREZ, J. : La libération conditionnelle et la condamnation conditionnelle dans le nouveau Code pénal fédéral mexicain. Revue internationale de droit pénal 7 : 387-389, No. 4, 1930.

REYES, J.A. : El nuevo código mejicano. Nueva democracia 11 : 19-20, 27-28, mayo 1930.

Recent tendencies in Mexican criminal procedure. Pan-American Union, bulletin 64 : 433-438, May 1930.

MENDOZA, S. : The new Mexican system of criminology. Journal of criminal law and criminology 21 : 15-25, May 1930.

ALMARAZ, J. : New Mexican penal principles. Pacific affairs 13 : 531-540, June 1930.

MENDOZA, S. : El nuevo código penal de Mexico. Cultura venezolana 13 : 189-200, noviembre 1930.

PHILLIPS, G.G. : The Anglo-Mexican Special Claims Commission. Law quarterly review 49 : 226-239, April 1933.

The Clipperton Island case, France v. Mexico. Cumulative digest of international law and relations 2 : 94-98, 18 November 1932.
With text of award.

MONACO

ROUSSEL-DESPIERRES, F. : La condition juridique de la Principauté de Monaco. Académie diplomatique internationale : 223-233, octobre-décembre 1930.

ROUSSEL-DESPIERRES, F. : La condition juridique de la Principauté de Monaco. Revue de droit international 4 : 531-543, octobre-novembre-décembre 1931.

MOROCCO

STRUPP, K. : Die Rechtstellung von Angehörigen der Mittlemächte in Marokko nach den Friedensverträgen und Ergänzungsrecht. Nordisk tidsskrift for internationa rel (Acta scandinavica juris gentium) 2 : 101-108, fasc. 3, 1931.

NOULENS, J. : Le statut international du Maroc. Académie diplomatique internationale. Séances et travaux 5 : 165-170, juillet-septembre 1931.

HARDY, G. : La justice indigène au Maroc. Europe nouvelle 14 : 1220-1221, 5 septembre 1931.

NETHERLANDS

BREGSTEIN, M.H. : Rassegna di legislazione (anni 1925-1927). Anuario di diritto comparato vol. 4 e 5, parte 2 : 631-680, 1930.

HUART, F.J.A. : Die Entwicklung des öffentlichen Rechts in den Niederlanden seit 1922. Jahrbuch des öffentlichen Rechts 18 : 274-323, 1930.

RHEINSTEIN : Gesetzgebung und Rechtsliteratur der Niederlande 1928. Zeitschrift fürausländisches und internationales Privatrecht 4 : 1033-1043, Heft 6, 1930.

RHEINSTEIN, M. : Gesetzgebung und Rechtsliteratur der Niederlande 1929. Zeitschrift für ausländisches und internationales Privatrecht 5 : 185-193, Heft 1, 1931.

GARGAS, S. : The new company law of Holland. Journal of comparative legislation and international law 13 : 72-78, February 1931.

MORESCO, E. : Die Verfassungsreform in Niederländisch-Indien. Zeitschrift für ausländisches öffentliches Recht und Völkerrecht 2 : 484-520, No. 3/4 1931.

BOER, C. de : De jongste beperkingen der poenale sanctie in Nederlandsch-Indië. Economiscthe statistische berichten 16 : 754-756, 26 Augustus 1931.

Die völkerrechtliche Stellung der Niederlande im Falle eines Krieges. Zeitschrift für ausländisches öffentliches Recht und Völkerrecht 3 : 200-211, No. 1 (Teil 2), 1932.

Paesi bassi. Istituto di studi legislativi, Giurisprudenza comparata di diritto internazionale privato 1 : 245-267, fasc. 2, 1932.
Private international law cases.

BAAK, J.C. : Rassegna di legislazione olandese (anni 1928-1930). Annuario di diritto comparato e di studi legislativi (Parte II) : 375-398, 1933.

MARCHAL, A. : Le Volksraad indonésien. Annales du droit et des sciences sociales 2 : 285-300, No. 4, 1934.

HUART, F.J.A. : De Rechtspositie van den vreemdeling in Nederland. Volkenbond 9 : 260-265, Juni-Juli 1934.

DUDEN, K. : Gesetzgebung der Niederlande, 1.1. 1930-30.6.1934. Zeitschrift für ausländisches und internationales Privatrecht 8 : 901-936, Heft 6, 1934.

NEW ZEALAND

HALL, T.D.H. : Status of aliens in New Zealand. Pacific affairs 4 : 700-710, August 1931.

NICARAGUA

DEBAYLE, L.M. : The status of women in Nicaragua. Mid-Pacific magazine 45 : 237-239, March 1933.

NORWAY

CASTBERG, F. : Aperçu sur la législation pendant l'année 1931. Annuaire de législation étrangère 59 : 166-175, 1931.

IRGENS, J. : Le statut international de la Norvège. Académie diplomatique internationale, Séances et travaux 6 : 164-167, octobre-décembre 1932.

KRUSE-JENSEN, C. : Norske dommer vedrørende internasjonal privatret. Nordisk tidsskrift for international ret 3 : 53-58, Fasc. 1, 1932.

ANKER, P. : Rassegna di legislazione norvegese (anni 1925-1929). Annuario di diritto comparato e di studi legislativi (Parte II) : 361-375, 1933.

CASTBERG, F. : Norvège - Aperçu sur la législation 1934-1936. Annuaire de législation étrangère 62 : 359-410, 1934/1936.

PALESTINE

KOHN, H. : Die Rechtsstellung der Ausländer in Palästina. Archiv des öffentlichen Rechts 20 : 359-375, 3. Heft 1931.

HILB, K. : Die Grundlagen der Rechtsentwicklung in Palästina. Palästina 15 : 160-166, Mai-Juni-Juli 1932.

BENTWICH, N. : The legislation of Palestine 1931. Palestine and Near East economic magazine 7 : 321-323, August 15, 1932.

PERU

MOORE, R.D. : Elements of Peruvian commercial law. Tulane law review 5 : 574-600, June 1931.

POLAND

ROSTWOROWSKI, M. : La codification du droit international et interprovincial privé en Pologne. Revue de droit international et de législation comparée 57 : 1-61, No. 1, 1930.

MAKOWSKI, W.: Verfassungsfragen in Polen. Review of Polish laws and economics (deutscher Teil) : 10-13, vol. 2, 1930.

ROSTWOROWSKI, M. : La codification du droit international et inter-provincial privé en Pologne. Revue de droit international et de législation comparée 57 : 376-412, No. 2, 1930.

STANIEWICZ, W. : Die Agrarreformarbeiten in Polen im Jahre 1928 und 1929. Vierteljahrshefte der polnischen Landwirtschaft 1 : 5-52, April 1930.

ROSTWOROWSKI, M. : La codification du droit international et interprovincial privé en Pologne (Contd.) Revue de droit international et de législation comparée 57 : 794-828, No. 4, 1930.

ALLERHAND, M. : Probleme des jüdisch-polnischen Eherechts. Zeitschrift für Ostrecht 4 : 449-472, Mai 1930.

ZWEHL : Das deutsch-polnische Liquidations-Abkommen. Deutsche Juristen-Zeitung 35 : 584-588, 1. Mai 1930.

ANDRÉ-PRUDHOMME, PALEWSKI, J.P. : Protection des biens et intérêts privés appartenant à des individus devenus polonais par l'effet du traité de Versailles. Journal du droit international 57 : 577-588, mai-juin 1930.

BIANCO, F. : La nuova legge polacca sulle società anonime. Rivista del diritto commerciale 28 : 627-630, agosto-settembre 1930.

ARIO, C. : Die Verfassungsfrage in Polen. Nation und Staat 4 : 19-38, Oktober 1930.

Pologne - vers la revision constitutionnelle. Société d'études et d'informations économiques, bulletin quotidien 11, No. 279 : D. - 1, 9 décembre 1930.
Plan d'une revision de la Constitution polonaise dans l'esprit d'un système présidentiel.

LIEBESKIND, A. : La legislazione in Polonia negli anni 1925-1927. Annuario di diritto comparato vol. 4 e 5, parte 2 : 681-721, 1930.

STEINBERG, J. : Die neue polnische Zivilprozessordnung. Zeitschrift für ausländisches und internationales Privatrecht 5 : 515-520, Heft 2/3, 1931.

SULKOWSKI, J. : Das Aufwertungsproblem in Oberschlesien - Studium aus dem Gebiete des internationalen Privatrechts. Review of Polish law and economics, deutscher Teil 3 : 35-47, vol. 3 (March 1930-February 1931).

MAKOWSKI, J. : Die Schiedsgerichtsabkommen Polens. Review of Polish law and economics, deutscher Teil 3 : 15-24, vol. 3, (March 1930-February 1931).

KOSCHEMBAHR-LYSKOWSKI : Entwurf eines polnischen Zivilgesetzbuches. Review of Polish law and economics, deutscher Teil 3 : 75-82, vol. 3 (March 1930-February 1931).

BABINSKI, L. : La solution des conflits de lois en Pologne (application de la loi du 2 août 1926). Journal du droit international 58 : 18-31, janvier-février 1931.

Pologne - Le projet de réforme de la Constitution. Société d'études et d'informations économiques, bulletin quotidien 12 : D 1-2, No. 39, 26 février 1931.

La Pologne et la révision de la Constitution. Société d'études et d'informations économiques, Bulletin quotidien 12, No. 59 : C 1-4, 16 mars 1931.

STANISTAW, G. : Projekt Kodeksu Postępowania Cywilnego. (Entwurf einer Zivilprozessordnung). Bulletin international de l'Académie polonaise des sciences et des lettres : 58-66, avril-juin 1931.
Draft of Polish civil procedure Code.

CYBICHOWSKI, Z. : Das polnische Verordnungsrecht. Zeitschrift für Ostrecht 5 : 481-488, Juli 1931.

RAPPAPORT, E.S. : Les travaux de la commission de codification de la République de Pologne (1919-1931). Pologne 12 : 495-504, 1 juillet 1931.

CLASER, S. : Les tendances actuelles du droit pénal et la réforme en Pologne. Revue pénitentiaire et de droit pénal 55 : 195-223, juillet-décembre 1931.

PRUD'HOMME, A., et GALLAIX, M. de : L'accord polono-allemand du 31 octobre 1930 et les créances pour dommages de guerre. Journal du droit international 59 : 57-64, janvier-février 1932.

MAKOWSKI, J. : Ergänzungstabelle der von Polen bis 31-12-1926 abgeschlossenen Verträge - Verträge vom 1- 1-1927 bis 15-11-1931. Zeitschrift für Ostrecht 6 : 115-129, Februar 1932.

FENICHEL, S. : Das polnische internationale Prozessrecht nach der neuen Zivilprozessordnung. Zeitschrift für Ostrecht 6 : 401-427, Juni 1932.

Das Recht der ehemals deutschen Gebiete (Contd.). - Polnisch-Oberschlesien. Juristische Wochenschrift 62 : 26-27, 7, Januar 1933.

KANN, R. : Die polnische Zivilprozessordnung. Zeitschrift für Ostrecht 7 : 1-231, Januar 1933.

MAKAREWICZ, J. : Das Strafgesetzbuch für die Republik Polen. Zeitschrift für Ostrecht 7 : 315-331, März 1933.
See also pp. 331-347, GLEISPACH, W. : Das polnische Strafgesetzbuch.

HIPPEL, R. v. : Das neue polnische Strafgesetzbuch. Deutsche Juristen-Zeitung 38 : 660-662, 15. Mai 1933.

FREUND, H. : Fünfzehn Jahre polnischer Rechtsentwicklung. Ost-Europa 8 : 530-541, Juni 1933.

BOSSOWSKI, F. von : Die Neugestaltung des in Ostpolen unter der russischen Herrschaft geltenden Privatrechts durch die polnische Gesetzgebung. Zeitschrift für Ostrecht 7 : 874-913, Oktober 1933.

KANN, R. : Die neue Polnische Zivilprozessordnung. Deutsche Juristen-Zeitung 38 : 1540-1544, 1. Dezember 1933.

Rapport transmis par M. le Professor E.-S. Rappaport et élaboré par M. Raphaël Lemkin, concernent le Code pénal polonais de 1932. Recueil de documents en matière pénale et pénitentiaire 3 : 127-137, décembre 1933.

SMOGORZEWSKI, C. : La revision constitutionnelle en Pologne. Pologne 15 : 1-4, 1 janvier 1934.

PERNOT, M. : La réforme constitutionnelle en Pologne. Europe nouvelle 17 : 36-38, 13 janvier 1934.

PAPIEROWSKI, Z. : Die politischen Delikte im Lichte des polnischen Strafrechts und der Judikatur des Obersten Gerichtes. Zeitschrift für Ostrecht 8 : 98-110, Februar 1934.

SILZ, E. : Le droit pénal international d'après les nouveaux codes polonais. Revue de droit international et de législation comparée 15 : 325-352, No. 2, 1934.

SILZ, E. : Le droit pénal international d'après les nouveaux codes polonais (Contd.). Revue de droit international et de législation comparée 61 : 531-549, No. 3, 1934.

CYBICHOWSKI, S. : Der Entwurf der neuen polnischen Verfassung. Archiv des öffentlichen Rechts 25 : 316-340, 3. Heft 1934.

KAWAN, L. : La nuova costituzione della Polonia. Rivista di diritto pubblico 26 : 141-145, marzo 1934.

RUKSER, U. : Das neue polnische Obligationenrecht. Zeitschrift für ausländisches und internationales Privatrecht 8 : 342-375, Heft 3/4, 1934.

MAZEAUD, H. : Chronique de jurisprudence polonaie. Revue trimestrielle de droit civil 33 : 475-486, avril-juin 1934.

FREUND, H. : Die Vereinheitlichung des Rechts in Polen. Ost-Europa 9 : 451-461, Mai 1934.

CYBICHOWSKI, Z. : Die Entwicklung der polnischen Verfassung. Zeitschrift für osteuropäisches Recht 1 : 21-35, Juli 1934.

POTULICKI, M. : Le projet de la nouvelle constitution polonaise. Bulletin interparlementaire 14 : 151-161, juillet-août 1934.

DNISTRJANSKYJ, S. : Die leitenden Grundsätze des neuen polnischen Obligationenrechts. Zeitschrift für osteuropäisches Recht 1 : 123-139, September 1934.

RODER : Der polnische Verfassungsentwurf. Zeitschrift der Akademie für deutsches Recht 1 : 226-230, Dezember 1934.

GIANNINI, A. : La riforma della costituzione Polacca. Europe orientale 14 : 369-397, n. 7-10, 1934.
Text of draft constitution annexed.

PORTUGAL

Portugal-Gesetzgebung: Änderung des Staatsangehörigkeitsgesetzes durch Neufassung der Art.18-20 des Bürgerlichen Gesetzbuchs. Zeitschrift für ausländisches öffentliches Recht und Völkerrecht 2 : 708-710, 1931.
16. Dezember 1930.

HUHLEIN, F.E. : Summary process for small civil and commercial actions in Portugal. U.S. Commerce reports No. 3 : 179-January 19 1931.

GERSTMEYER, J. : Die neuen verfassungsrechtlichen Bestimmungen für die portugiesischen Kolonien. Koloniale Rundschau : 152-156, Heft 7-8, 1931.

BATAILLON, M. : La nouvelle Charte organique de l'Empire colonial portugais. Outre-mer 6 : 283-293, septembre 1934.

MIRKINE-GUETZÉVITCH, B. : Le néo-absolutisme corporatif (Autriche et Portugal). Anné politique française et étrangère 9 : 251-272, octobre 1934.

RUMANIA

RADULESCU, A. : Rassegna di legislazione rumena (anni 1925-1928). Annuario di diritto comparato vol. 4 e 5, parte 2 : 723-752, 1930.

LAPRADELLE, A. de : La législation relative à la propriété foncière dans la nouvelle Dobroudja (Dobroudja du Sud), et le droit international. Revue de droit international 4 : 160-274, janvier-février-mars 1930.

RADULESCU, A. : L'introduction de la législation roumaine en Bessarabie. Bulletin mensuel de la Société de législation comparée 59 : 321-339, avril-juin 1930.

PENACOV, I.S. : La loi sur le complètement de la loi sur l'organisation de la nouvelle Dobroudja. Revue bulgare 2 : 227-238, septembre-octobre-novembre-décembre 1930.

DECUSARA, E.C. : Dare de Seamă asupra statisticei judiciare a României pe anii 1925-1928. Bulletin statistique de la Roumanie : 3-125, octobre-décembre 1930.

BOILA, R. : Die Verfassung und Verwaltung Rumäniens seit dem Weltkrieg. Jahrbuch des öffentlichen Rechts 18 : 324-354, 1930.

COHEN, J.G. : Principes du projet de code de commerce roumain. Bulletin mensuel de la Société de législation comparée 60 : 123-278, janvier-mars 1931.

POULOPOL, A.-A. : La justice administrative roumaine - examen critique des textes des lois du 3 août et du 3 janvier 1930, portant création et organisation des comités de révision. Bulletin mensuel de la Société de législation comparée 60 : 387-403, avril-juin 1931.

ROUCEK, J.S. : Reorganization of the Governmental structure of Roumania. American political science review 25 : 700-703, August 1931.

KAUSCHANSKY, D.M. : Übersicht über den heutigen Rechtzustand in Rumänien (1918-1930). Zeitschrift für Ostrecht 5 : 778-783, November 1931.

IONASCO, T.R. : Les associations et les fondations en droit civil roumain. Revue générale du droit, de la législation et de la jurisprudence 55 : 266-285, octobre-novembre-décembre 1931.

LUBENOFF, G. : Die Organisation der Lokalverwaltung in Rumänien. Zeitschrift für ausländisches öffentliches Recht und Völkerrecht 3 : 118-153, No. 1, (Tel 1), 1932.

LADAY, S. : Die Gesetzgebung Rumäniens in den Jahren 1929, 1930 und 1931. Zeitschrift für ausländisches und internationales Privatrecht 6 : 459-473, Heft 3, 1932.

RADULESCU, A., Sachelarie, O. : Romania. Istituto di studi legislativi, Legislazione internazionale 1 : 581-606, fasc. 4, 1932.

LADAY, S. : Die internationalprivatrechtlichen Bestimmungen im Entwurf eines bürgerlichen Gesetzbuches für Rumänien. Zeitschrift für ausländisches und internationales Privatrecht 6 : 741-753, Heft 5, 1932.

ANTONESCO, E.E. : Observations sur l'avant-projet de code civil roumain en matière de droit international privé. Revue de droit international privé 28 : 155-172, No. 1, 1933.
Traduction française des textes annexés.

NATIONAL LAW - COUNTRIES

ANGELESCO, A.C. : Avant-projet de code civil roumain. Bulletin mensuel de la Société de législation comparée 62 : 141-185, janvier-mars 1933.

KAUSCHANSKY, D.M. : Die Unifizierungsgesetze Rumäniens (1923-1933). Zeitschrift für Ostrecht 7 : 506-520, Mai 1933.

SCHWAMM, H. : Über den Erwerb von Grundeigentum durch Ausländer in Rumänien. Zeitschrift für Ostrecht 7 : 585-588, Juni 1933.

Législation de la femme mariée (présenté par la Princesse A. Cantacuzène à la 3e Conférence balkaniques). Balkans 4 : 311-320, juillet 1933.

La situationde la femme mariée dans la législation roumaine (présenté par A. Costin à la 3e Conférence balkanique). Balkans 4 : 321-324, juillet 1933.

VALLIMARESCO, A. : Jurisprudence roumaine en matière de droit civil. Revue trimestrielle de droit civil 32 : 1321-1322, octobre-décembre 1933.

LADAY, S. : Rumänische Gesetzgebung und Rechtsprechung in den Jahren 1932-1933. Zeitschrift für ausländisches und internationales Privatrecht 8 : 615-623, Heft 2/3, 1934.

RADULESCU, A. : Rassegna di legislazione romena (anno 1929). Annuario di diritto comparato e di studi legislativi (Parte IV) 8 : 284-306, 1934.

SALVADOR

ANDERSON, L. : Estatus del Gobierno que preside en la República de el Salvador el General D. Maximiliano Hernandez Martinez, conforme a la constitución y a los tratados de Washington. Revista de derecho internacional 11 : 17-32, 3o septiembre 1932.

SPAIN

Le nouveau code pénal espagnol et le code espagnol de l'enfance. Revue pénitentiaire et le droit pénal 54 : 24-47, janvier-mars 1930.

CIFUENTES, F. : Letteratura giuridica spagnola (anni 1927 e 1928). Annuario di diritto comparato vol. 4 e 5, parte 1 : 577-589, 1930.

CIFUENTES, F. : Rassegna di legislazione spagnola (anni 1927 e 1928). Annuario di diritto comparato vol. 4 e 5, parte 2 : 753-784, 1930.

El movimimiento legislativo en materia de seguros sociales durante el año 1930. Anales del Instituto nacional de previsión 23 : 47-55, enero-febrero 1931.

ROLLIN, L. : La future Constitution espagnole. Europe nouvelle 14 : 1041-1042, 1 août 1931.

TRIAS de BES, J.M. : La nationalité espagnole, d'après les dernières dispositions constitutionnelles et législatives du Gouvernement de la République. Revue de droit international et de législation comparée 59 : 429-435, No. 2, 1932.

JIMÉNEZ de ASÚA, L. : Die Verfassung der Spanischen Republik. Zeitschrift für ausländisches öffentliches Recht und Völkerrecht 3 (Abhandlungen) : 251-295, No. 2, 1932.

CAEMMERER, E. v. : Das neue spanische Scheidungsrecht. Zeitschrift für ausländisches und internationales Privatrecht 6 : 474-502, Heft 3, 1932.

POLO, A. : Das spanische Zivilrecht vor, durch und seit der Verfassung der spanischen Republik. Zeitschrift für ausländisches und internationales Privatrecht 6 : 630-658, Heft 4, 1932.

MIRKINE-GUETZÉVITCH, B. : La nouvelle constitution espagnole. Revue politique et parlementaire 39 : 127-142, 10 janvier 1932.

GARCIA OVIEDO, C. : La nuova Costituzione spagnola. Rivista di diritto pubblico 24 : 186-221, aprile 1932.

MIRKINE-GUETZÉVITCH, B. : La Constitution espagnole. Cahiers des droits de l'homme 32 : 223-225, 10-20 avril 1932.

POSADA, A. : La Constitution de la République espagnole du 9 décembre 1931. Revue du droit public et de la science politique 49 : 359-380, avril-mai-juin 1932.

RUYSSEN, T. : Le statut de la Catalogne. Minorités nationales 5 : 58-62, mai-septembre 1932.

HUDSON, M.O. : The Spanish constitution of 1931. American journal of international law (section one) 26 : 579-582, July 1932.

GARCIA de la BARGA, C. : Avant-projet pour le réforme du Code pénal de 1870. Recueil de documents en matière pénale et pénitentiaire 2 : 162-171, juillet 1932.

GAY de MONTELLA, R. : El estatuto de Cataluña y las obras públicas y servicios de ejecución delegada. Revista nacional de economía 17 : 157-166, julio-octubre 1932.

STRUPP, K. : Völkerrechtliche Vorschriften in der Verfassung der spanischen Republik. Friedenswarte 32 : 264-265, September 1932.

CARENA, A. : Tendenze federali e decentramento politico nella Costituzione della Repubblica spagbola. Annali di scienze politiche 5 : 165-181, settembre 1932.

La doble ciudadanía en la Constitución Española. Revista de las Española. Revista de las Españas 7 : 466-472, septiembre-octubre 1932.

MIRKINE-GUETZÉVITCH, B. : Le droit interne de la paix dans la nouvelle constitution espagnole. Affaires étrangères 2 : 682-688, 25 décembre 1932.

MÉTALL, A. : Die Regelung der zwischenstaatlichen und völkerrechtlichen Beziehungen in der neuen spanischen Verfassung. Zeitschrift für Politik 22 : 682-691, Januar 1933.

MIRKINE-GUETZÉVITCH : Communication sur la nouvelle Constitution espagnole. Bulletin mensuel de la Société de législation comparée 62 : 84-101, janvier-mars 1933.

JOANNIS, J. de : Les droits de l'homme et du citoyen en Espagne. Méditerranée 5 : 40-42, 1 février 1933.

Código Penal español reformado de 1932 (Contd.). Razón y fe 33 : 535-547, abril 1933.
Text.

GMELIN, H. : Die Entwicklung des Verfassungsrechts in Spanien von 1913-1932. Jahrbuch des öffentlichen Rechts 21 : 335-465, 1933/1934.
Contains German translation of the Spanish Constitution of December 9, 1931, and of the Statute of Catalonia of September 15, 1932.

La doble ciudadanía en la constitución española (Contd.). Revista de las Españas : 173-176, abril-mayo-junio 1934.

SWEDEN

PAPPENHEIM, W. : Die Gesetzgebung Schwedens vom. 1. Januar 1926 bis zum 1. Juli 1930. Zeitschrift für ausländisches und internationales Privatrecht 4 : 610-642, Heft 3-4, 1930.

PAPPENHEIM, M. : Die Neuordnung des schwedischen Erbrechts II. Zeitschrift für ausländisches und internationales Privatrecht 5 : 289-307, Heft 2/3, 1931.

HERLITZ, N. : Charakteristische Züge des schwedischen öffentlichen Rechts. Zeitschrift für ausländisches öffentliches Recht und Völkerrecht 3 : 95-117, No. 1 (Teil 1), 1932.

BLOCH, J.-D. : Der Abschluss von Staatsverträgen nach schwedischem Recht. Zeitschrift für ausländisches öffentliches Recht und Völkerrecht (Abhandlungen) 4 : 25-52, Januar 1934.

SWITZERLAND

HAAB, R. : Gesetzgebung der Schweiz betreffend Privatrecht, gewerblichen Rechtsschutz, Arbeitsrecht, Zwangsvollstreckung und Konkurs im Jahre 1929. Zeitschrift für ausländisches und internationales Privatrecht 4 : 826-830, Heft 5, 1930.

BOREL, E. : Le régime légal et fiscal des sociétés anonymes en Suisse. Bulletin de l'Institut intermédiaire international 24 : 1-6, janvier 1931.

Les emprunts obligatoires et la revision du Code suisse des obligations. Union financière de Genève, Bulletin juridique et financier 4 : 1-23, février 1931.

BURCKHARDT, W. : Die Verwaltungsgerichtsbarkeit in der schweizerischen Eidgenossenschaft. Zeitschrift für die gesamte Staatswissenschaft 90 : 225-248, März 1931.

Die schweizerische Gesetzgebung auf dem Gebiet des Arbeitsrechts und der Sozialversicherung im Jahr 1930. Wirtschaftliche und sozialstatistische Mitteilungen : 1-132, Sonderheft 1, 2 August 1931.

SPRECHER, A. von : Grundsätzliches zum eidgenössischen Strafrecht. Schweizer Monatshefte 11 : 239-252, August-September 1931.

Die schweizerische Gesetzgebung auf dem Gebiet des Arbeitsrechts und der Sozialversicherung im Jahre 1931. Volkswirtschaft (Switzerland) : 1-84, Sonderheft 14, 1932.

MEYER-WILD : Die Gesetzgebung der Schweiz im Jahre 1930, 1931 und 1932. Juristische Wochenschrift 62 : 28-29, 7. Januar 1933.

Totalrevision der Bundesverfassung. Neue Schweizer Rundschau 2 : 129-207, Juli 1934.
Special number.

SWITZERLAND
(International law, Aliens)

SAUSER-HALL, G. : Les conventions germano-suisses sur les hypothèques avec clause d'or. Journal di droit international 59 : 340-366, mars-avril 1932.

PESTALOZZI, A. : Zivilprozessrecht und internationales Privatrecht der Schweiz im Jahre 1931. Zeitschrift für ausländisches und internationales Privatrecht 6 : 818-838, Heft 5, 1932.

SYRIA

MURR, D.I., et BOURBOUSSON, E. : Du statut personne en Syrie et au Liban. Bulletin de l'Institut intermédiaire international 26 : 261-270, avril 1932.

HAKIM, V. : La condition des étrangers en Syrie et au Liban. Gazette des tribunaux libano-syriens 8 : 275-278, novembre 1933.

THAILAND

La nouvelle constitution du Siam. Mois : 51-56, 1 janvier - 1 février 1933.

U.S.S.R.

DANILOVA, E.N. : Diritto sovjètico de lavoro. Annuario di diritto comparato vol. 4 e 5, parte 1 : 699-900, 1930.

MAKAROV, A.N. : Ergänzungstabelle der von den Soviet-Republiken und der U.d.S.S.R. abgeschlossenen Verträge. Zeitschrift für Ostrecht 4 : 44-53, Januar 1930.
Survey of Russian treaties.

GIANNINI, A. : La costituzione dell'U.R.S.S. Europa orientale 10 : 1-33, gennaio-febbraio 1930.

KROUGLIAKOFF, A. : New law on cheques in Soviet Russia. Law journal 69 : 75-76, February 1, 1930.

Das neue Scheckgesetz der UdSSR. Zeitschrift für Ostrecht 4 : 184-190, Februar 1930.

FREUND, H. : Das neue Scheckgesetz der Sowjetunion Wirtschaft und das Recht 5 : 78-83, No. 2-3, 1930.

HANSTEEN, V. : Om rettens utvikling i Sowjet-Samfundet. Tidsskrift for Retsvidenskap 9 : 225-244, Hefte 3, 1930.

ZETKIN, A. : Das neue Scheckrecht der UdSSR. Volkwirtschaft der Union der sozialistischen Sowjet-Republiken 9 : 17-21, 1. März 1930.

NATIONAL LAW - COUNTRIES

KARADŽE-ISKROV, N.P. : Die Bildung der neuen Sovietbundesrepublik Tadshikistan. Zeitschrift für Ostrecht 4 : 389-396, April 1930.

GRODSINSKY, M. : Die Kameradengerichte und Schlichtungskammern im Sovetrecht. Zeitschrift für Ostrecht 4 : 951-960, Oktober 1930.

MIRKINE-GUETZÉVITCH, B. : The public law system of the Sovietic dictatorship. Journal of comparative legislation and international law 12 : 248-268, November 1930.

GRODZINSKY, M. : Die Privatklage im Sovietrecht. Zeitschrift für Ostrecht 4 : 1055-1063, November 1930.

VAVIN, N.G. : Das neue Vereinsgesetz der RSFSR, Zeitschrift für Ostrecht 5 : 104-107, Februar 1931.

GRAVE, K. : Die rechtlichen Elemente der Rekonstruktion des Binnenhandels und der Industrie der UdSSR. Zeitschrift für Ostrecht 5 : 81-98, Februar 1931.

WOLFSOHN, F. : Die Grundprinzipien der Sowjetgesetzgebung im Erfindungswesen. Sowjetwirtschaft und Aussenhandel 10 : 28-24, 2. Maiheft 1931.

MAURACH, R. : Das Sovietstrafrecht 1919-1931. Zeitschrift für Ostrecht 5 : 410-432, Juni 1931.

LAKHTINE, V. : Cinq années d'activité de la Section de droit aérien en U.R.S.S. Droit aérien : 341-349, juillet-août-septembre 1931.

BUKOVSKY, V. : Die Fortentwicklung des russischen Zivilprozessrechts in Lettland. Zeitschrift für Ostrecht 5 : 596-605, August-September 1931.

Justice punishment and legislation in Soviet Russia. (Contd.). Law journal 72 : 180, September 26, 1931.

NAPOLITANO, T. : Evoluzione del diritto penale sovietico dall'ottobre 1917 ai giorni nostri. (Contd.). Giustizia penale 37 : 1433-1442, 31 ottobre 1931.

KARADZE-ISKROV, N.P. : Die öffentlichen Sachen nach Sovietrecht. Zeitschrift für Ostrecht 5 : 849-870, Dezember 1931.

NESTEROFF, P. : Notice sur les textes législatifs promulgués en 1930 et 1931. Annuaire de législation étrangère 59 : 206-268, 1931.

MAURACH, R. : Das internationale Zivilprozessrecht der Sowjetunion. Niemeyers Zeitschrift für internationales Recht 47 : 1-48, 1. Heft 1932.

FRANSSEN, M. : Règlement du chèque du 4 décembre 1929 de l'Union des Républiques Soviétiques Socialistes. Annales de droit commercial 41 : 94-95, janvier-mars 1932.

NEMIROVSKIJ, E. : Das neue Strafgesetzbuch der RSFSR. Zeitschrift für Ostrecht 6 : 81-104, Februar 1932.

MAXWELL, B.W. : Civil service in Soviet Russia. American political science review 26 : 318-324, April 1932.

GRODSINSKY, M. : Das Rechtsmittelverfahren im Soviet-Strafprozess. Zeitschrift für Ostrecht 6 : 241-257, April 1932.

Mesures législatives du Gouvernement soviétique publiées dans les "Izvestia" d'octobre 1931 à mars 1932. Bulletin mensuel de la Société de législation comparée 61 : 287-292, avril-juin 1932.

VAVIN, N.G. : Die Praxis der RSFSR in Fragen des Erbrechts. Zeitschrift für Ostrecht 6 : 739-761, Oktober 1932.

RAPOPORT, A. : Das Zentralkomitee der kommunistischen Partei als Gesetzgebungsorgan der Sovietunion. Zeitschrift für Ostrecht 7 : 238-253, Februar 1933.

NOLDE, B. de : Le droit civil de la Russie des Soviets. Vie intellectuelle 5 : 87-101, 10 juillet 1933.

BLUMENFELD, R. : Fragen des gewerblichen Rechtsschutzes in der Sovietunion. Zeitschrift für Ostrecht 7 : 639-651, Juli 1933.

NOLDE, B. : Le droit soviétique et ses transformations. Revue de l'Université de Bruxelles 39 : 36-67, octobre-novembre 1933.

DURDENEVSKY, W.N. : Das Luftgesetz dee UdSSR und die Gesetzgebung der Bundesrepubliken. Zeitschrift für Ostrecht 7 : 948-952, November 1933.

KARADZE-ISKROV : Die juristische Personen des öffentlichen Rechts nach Sovietrecht. Zeitschrift für Ostrecht 7 : 999-1024, Dezember 1933.

GRAHAM, R.B. : British and Russian criminal jurisprudence. Canadian bar review 12 : 1-13, January 1934.

Übersicht über die wesentliche Gesetzgebung der UdSSR und RSFSR für das Jahr 1933 und das 1. Vierteljahr 1934. Zeitschrift für osteuropäisches Recht 1 : 47-50, Juli 1934.

GALLI, P. : Le persone giuridiche di diritto pubblico nel diritto sovietico. Rivista di diritto pubblico 26 : 488-496, agosto-settembre 1934.

MAURACH : Gesetz des Zentralvollzugsausschusses der UdSSR über die Abänderung der geltenden Strafprozessordnungen der Bundesrepubliken vom 1. Dezember 1934 (Lex Kirov). Zeitschrift für osteuropäisches Recht 1 : 326-328, Dezember 1934.

MAURACH : Wann sind in Sovetrussland "religiös" geschlossene Ehen rechtsgültig? Zeitschrift für osteuropäisches Recht 1 : 289-295, Dezember 1934.

U.S.S.R.
(International law and practice, Aliens and Naturalization)

VERDROSS, A. : Die völkerrechtliche Verantwortlichkeit der Sowjetunion für die Handlungen der russischen kommunistischen Partei und der 3. Internationale. Zeitschrift für öffentliches Recht 9 : 577-582, 15 April 1930.

Russian law in the conflict of laws. Michigan law review 28 : 750-755, April 1930.

NEBOLSINE, G. : The recovery of foreign assets of nationalized Russian corporations. Yale law journal 39 : 1130-1162, June 1930.

NATIONAL LAW - COUNTRIES

DURDENEVSKI, W. : Die völkerrechtliche bedingten Gesetze in der UdSSr. Zeitschrift für Ostrecht 4 : 582-596, Juni 1930.

FREUND : Das neue Staatsangehörigkeitsgesetz der UDSSR. Zeitschrift für Ostrecht 4 : 707-710, Juli 1930.

DUFOUR, R. : La nationalité dans l'U.R.S.S. Revue générale de droit international public 37 : 511-520, juillet-octobre 1930.

La nouvelle loi soviétique sur la nationalité. Revue de droit international 4 : 643-648, octobre-novembre-décembre 1930.

SLEXEIEW, N. : Sowjetstaat und Völkerrecht. Zeitschrift für Völkerrecht 16 : 72-99, Heft 1, 1931.

ALEXEIEW, N.N, and ZAITZEFF, L. : Sowjetstaat und Völkerrecht (Contd.). Zeitschrift für Völkerrecht 16 : 177-225, Heft 2, 1931.

The perplexing problem of Soviet recognition. China weekly review 55 : 383-384, February 14, 1931.
China and Moscow.

MÜCKENBERGER : Die nationalism russischen Aktiengesellschaften, ihre Rechtspersönlichkeit und ihr Vermögen im Auslände. Juristische Wochenschrift 60 : 781-783, 21 März 1931.

Sowjet-Union-Gesetzgebung : Gesetz über die Staatsangehörigkeit. Zeitschrift für ausländisches öffentliches Recht und Völkerrecht 2 : 739-745, 1931.
22 April 1931.

Sovetunion - Neuregelung des Konzessionswesens. Zeitschrift für Ostrecht 5 : 376-381, Mai 1931.

DURDENEVSKI, W.N. : Sovetstaatsengehörigkeit und ihre Neuregelung im Jahre 1930. Zeitschrift für Ostrecht 5 : 332-352, Mai 1931.

SCHEFTEL, J. : Des effets des décrets de nationalisation sur les sociétés russes ayant conservé de biens à l'étranger. Journal du droit international 58 : 565-589, mai-juin 1931.

LANDAU, B. : La question de la nationalité des sociétés dans le droit soviétique. Journal du droit international 58 : 610-618, mai-juin 1931.

Foreign merchantmen within USSR coastal waters and ports. USSR Chamber of commerce, Quarterly review : 66-87, July-December 1931.

La nazionalità delle società nel diritto sovietico. Rivista di diritto commerciale 29 : 665-667, settembre-ottobre 1931.

DICKINSON, E.D. : The recognition of Russia. Michigan law review 30 : 181-196, December 1931.

LE FUR, L. : La géorgie et le droit des gens. Revue générale de droit international public 39 : 437-457, juillet-août 1932.

WORMS, A.E. : Zum interterritorialen Privatrechte der UdSSR. Zeitschrift für Ostrecht 6 : 700-713, Oktober 1932.

MILIOUKOV, P. : Le statut de la Russie de la guerre mondiale à nos jours. Académie diplomatique internationale. Séances et travaux 6 : 142-147, octobre-décembre 1932.

DOBRIN, S. : A propos the Soviet maritime code. Law quarterly review 49 : 249-267, April 1933.

LANDAU, B. : Das Seeschiedsgericht in der UdSSR. Zeitschrift für Ostrecht 7 : 782-789, August-September 1933.

FREUND : L'Etat soviétique et le statut de ses représentations commerciales. Journal du droit international 61 : 5-21, janvier-février 1934.

TAGER, P. : L'Etat russe commerçant et le traité franco-soviétique. Journal du droit international 61 : 22-35, janvier-février 1934.

TRACHTENBERG, B. : Le statut de la représentation commerciale de l'U.R.S.S. en France, d'après l'accord franco-soviétique du 11 janvier 1934. Nouvell revue de droit international 1 : 32-45, janvier-février-mars 1934.

MOSES, F. : Protection of trade with Soviet Russia by treaty - Germany's experience. American bar association journal 20 : 207-211, April 1934.

CONSTANTINOFF, B. : Les institutions soviétiques devant les tribunaux. Nouvelle revue de droit international privé 1 : 248-297, avril-mai-juin 1934.

GROSSMAN, A.W. : Effect given to Soviet decrees in the United States. Californian law review 22 : 439-443, May 1934.

MAKAROV, A.N. : Die Bestimmung des russisch-französischen Handelsabkommens von 11. Januar 1934 über die Rechtsstellung der Handelsvertretung der UdSSR. Zeitschrift für ausländisches öffentliches Recht und Völkerrecht 4 : 344-348, Mai 1934

BROWN, P.M. : The Russian Soviet Union land the law of nations. American journal of international law 28 : 733-736, October 1934.

DOBRIN, S. : The Soviet maritime code 1929. Journal of comparative legislation and international la 16 : 252-268, November 1934.

DOBRIN, S. : The English doctrine of the renvoi and the Soviet law of succession. British yearbook of international law 15 : 36-45, 1934.

UNITED ARAB REPUBLIC

GIRAUD, F. : Les arrêts du 2 mai 1929 des Chambre réunies de la Cour d'appel mixte d'Alexandrie disant justiciables des tribunaux mixtes les étranger non capitualires, sauf les Turcs, Syriens et Palestniniens. Revue de droit international privé 25 : 150-159, No. 1, 1930.

GIRAUD, F. : Les capitulations, les tribunaux mix et le statut des Français en Egypte. Revue pénitentiaire et de droit pénal 54 : 193-217, avril-août 1930.

Jurisdiction in Egypt. Law journal 69 : 366-367, 31 May 1930.

CHÉRON, A. : Les innovations législatives égyptiennes en matière de sociétés. Annales de droit commercial 39 : 186-196, juillet-septembre 1930.

NATIONAL LAW - COUNTRIES

BRION, H. : Le statut des étrangers en Egypte. Méditerranée 2 : 181-184, 1 août 1930.

GIRAUD, F. : Les tribunaux mixtes et le statut des Français en Egypte. Revue politique et parlementaire 144 : 218-223, 10 août 1930.

SAINT-BRICE : La refonte de la constitution égyptienne. Correspondance d'Orient 22 : 193-198, novembre 1930.

WACYF BOUTROS GHALI PACHA : Le statut international de l'Egypte. Académie diplomatique internationale 5 : 19-24, janvier-mars 1931.

La Constitution égyptienne : objet de la réforme. Europe nouvelle 14 : 242-252, 21 février 1931.

SMYRDIADIS, B. : Les conflits de lois en Egypte. Revue de droit international privé 26 : 259-291, No. 2, 1931.

SMYRNIADIS, B. : Les conflits de lois en Egypte (Contd.). Revue de droit international privé 26 : 463-503, No. 3, 1931.

McBARNET, A.C. : Egypt and judicial reform. Quarterly review 257 : 46-62, July 1931.

PERCIVAL, J.H. : The Mixed Courts of Egypt. Law quarterly review 48 : 78-89, January 1932.

'ABD EL FATTAH YEHIA PACHA : L'Egypte et les capitulations. Europe nouvelle 15 : 1510-1511, 31 décembre 1932.

KOHN, H. : Die ägyptische Verfassung vom 22. Oktober 1930. Jahrbuch des öffentlichen Rechts Band 20 : 431-445, 1932.

DEMOGUE, R. : Jurisprudence des juridictions mixtes d'Egypte. Revue trimestrielle de droit civil 33 : 253-260, janvier-mars 1934.

HANSSON, M. : Les tribunaux mixtes en Egypte. Nordisk tidsskrift for international ret, Acta scandinavica juris gentium 5 : 104-122, fasc. 4, 1934.

The Mixed Courts in Egypt. Near East and India 43 : 355, 10 May 1934.

DEMOGUE, R. : Jurisprudence des juridiction mixtes d'Egypte. Revue trimestrielle de droit civil 33 : 695-702, juillet-septembre 1934.

U.S.A.

Responsibility of the United States on maritime claims arising out of the operation of government-owned vessels. Yale law journal 39 : 1189-1196, June 1930.

JACKSON, G. : Wickersham and his Commission. Nation (N.Y.) 132 : 63-64, January 21, 1931.
Activity of American Commission on Law observance and enforcement.

LAMBERT, J. : Les origines du contrôle judiciaire de constitutionnalité des lois fédérales aux Etats-Unis - Marbury v. Madison. Revue de droit public et de la science politique 38 : 5-69, janvier-février-mars 1931.

SHAW, A. : Research in law and justice. Review of reviews : 36-43, May 1931.
A new American research institute.

COSENTINI, F. : The integral unification of American civil law. Tulane law review 5 : 515-534, June 1931.

Reports of the National Commission on law observance and enforcement. Michigan law review 30 : 1-132, November 1931.
Comments on the various reports of the National Commission on law observance and enforcement.

20th amendment to the Constitution of the United States. American foreign service journal 10 : 86-88, March 1933.

BRUNYATE, W. : The American draft code of criminal procedure, 1930. Law quarterly review 49 : 192-214, April 1933.

ELDER, C.B. : Some constitutional aspects of the National Industrial Recovery Act. Illinois law review 28 : 636-661, January 1934.

BARROWS, D.P. : Der Präsident der Vereinigten Staaten. Zeitschrift für Politik 24 : 99-106, Februar-März 1934.

BEARDSLEY, A.S. : A selected bibliography of legal and other materials relating to the National Industrial Recovery Act. Index to legal periodicals and law library journal 27 : 15-31, April 1934.

PFANKUCHEN, L. : La constitution des Etas-Unis et les "National Recovery Act". Revue des sciences politiques 49 : 199-220, avril-juin 1934.

Legal aspects of National Recovery program. American bar association journal 20 : 369-289 (sic), May 1934.
Series of articles.

SELLIN, T. : Rapport d'ensemble sur la législation pénale en 1932. Recueil de documents en matière pénale en pénitentiaire 3 : 255-305, mai 1934.

State legislation in support of the N.I.R.A. Columbia law review 34 : 1077-1090, June 1934.

LUFFT, H. : Staatsrechtliche Problems im Rooseveltschen USA - Reichssaufbau. Zeitschrift für Politik 24 : 540-559, September 1934.

McFARLAND, C. : Administrative agencies in government and the effect thereon of constitutional limitations. American bar association journal 20 : 612-617, 623, October 1934.

PINTO, R. : La loi nationale de rétablissement industriel aux Etats-Unis. Revue du droit public 51 : 605-628, octobre-novembre-décembre 1934.
N.I.R.A.

U.S.A.
Patents, Trade-marks, Copyright)

Le nouveau projet de loi américain sur le droit d'auteur (Contd.). Droit d'auteur 44 : 13-20, 15 février 1931.

NATIONAL LAW - COUNTRIES

U.S.A.
(International law, Aliens, Nationality)

KOHLER, M. : Legal disabilities of aliens in the United States. American bar association journal 16 : 113-117, February 1930.
Most disabilities arise in connection with legislation for exclusion or expulsion.

Exclusive federal jurisdiction over suits against foreign consuls and vice-consuls - actions for divorce. Michigan law review 28 : 591-599, March 1930.

Exterritorial recognitions of injunctions against suit. Yale law journal 39 : 719-727, March 1930.

MILLER, H. : Proposed new editions of the treaties of the United States. American journal of international law 24 : 241-263, April, 1930.

The interpretation of treaties by United States courts. Columbia law review 30 : 521-527, April 1930.

OCTAVIO, R. : L'Amérique et la codification du droit international privé. Revue de droit international 4 : 492-522, avril-mai-juin 1930.

FLEMING, D.F. : The advice of the Senate in treaty-making. Current history 32 : 1090-1094, September 1930.

FELLER, A.H. : Procedure in cases involving immunity of foreign states in courts of the United States. American journal of international law 25 : 83-96, January 1931.

Courts - jurisdiction of State Court over vice-consul in divorce suit. Illinois law review 25 : 823-825, Match 1931.
United States jurisdiction.

TENNANT, J.S. : Recognition cases in American Courts, 1923-1930. Michigan law review 29 : 708-741, April 1931.

YOUNG, C.K. : Real property rights of aliens in China and the United States. Chinese social and political science review 15 : 184-228, July 1931.

McCLENDON, R.E. : The two thirds rule in Senate action upon treaties, 1789-1901. American journal of international law 26 : 37-56, January 1932.

BAAK, J.C. : Le droit international américain et le droit international universel.. Revue de droit international et de législation comparée 59 : 307-397, No. 2, 1932.

KORENZEN, E.G. : Exécution aux Etats-Unis des jugements étrangers condamnant au paiement de sommes d'argent. Revue de droit international privé 27 : 228-253, No. 2, 1932.

Proposed revision of the citizenship laws of the United States. Foreign language information service, Interpreter release clip sheet 9 : 4-8, February 20, 1932.

SPROUT, H.H. : Theories as to the applicability of international law in the federal courts of the United States. American journal of international law 26 : 280-295, April 1932.

GARNER, J.W. : The Senate reservations to the Inter-American general treaty of arbitration. American journal of international law 26 : 333-336, April 193.

BORCHARD, E.M. : The unrecognised Government in American courts. American courts. American journal of international law 26 : 261-271, April 1932.

HOVER, E.J. : Citizenship of women in the United States. American journal of international law 26 : 700-719, October 1932.

MacKRACKEN, L. : The status of the foreign student in the United States. Cumulative digest of international law and relations 2 : 67-68, October 19, 1932.

LORENZEN, E.G. : Probleme des internationalen Erbrachts in den Vereinigten Staaten. Zeitschrift für ausl/andisches und internationales Privatrecht 7 : 495-525, Heft 4/5, 1933.

CHANDLER, W.D. : Stateless persons in the United States. Cumulative digest of international law and relations 3 : 63-64, May 18, 1933.

JESSUP, P.C. : Revising our nationality laws. American journal of international law 28 : 104-108, January 1934.
The United States law.

HYDE, C.C. : The extradition case of Samuel Insull, Sr., in relation to greece. American journal of international law 28 : 307-312, April 1934.

HOVER, E.J. : Derivate citizenship in the United States. American journal of international law 28 : 235-273, April 1934.

GROSSMAN, A.W. : Effect given to Soviet decrees in the United States. Californian law review 22 : 439-443, May 1934.

MUELLER, R. : Die Geschäftsfähigkeit natürlicher Personen in der international-privatrechtlichen Rechtsprechung der Vereinigten Staaten. Zeitschrift für ausländisches und internationales Privatrecht 8 : 88-896, Heft 6, 1934.

The St. Lawrence waterway. Round table : 548-562, June 1934.

POTTER, P.B. : Inhibitions upon the treaty-making power of the United States. American journal of international law 28 : 456-474, July 1934.

FLEMING, D.F. : The rôle of the Senate in treaty-making - a survey of four decades. American political science review 28 : 583-598, August 1934.

McGOVNEY, D.O. : Our non-citizen nationals, who are they? California law review 22 : 396-635, September 1934.

IRIZARRY y PUENTE : Principes fondamentaux de droit international public appliqués par la "Circuit cour of appeals" de New-York. Revue générale de droit international public 41 : 537-565, septembre-octobre 1934.

HUDSON, M.O. : The treaty-,aking power of the United States in connection with the manufacture of arms and ammunition. American journal of international law 28 : 736-739, October 1934.

NUSSBAUM, A. Comparative and international aspects of American gold clause abrogazion. Yale law journal 44 : 53-89, November 1934.

LENOIR, J.J. : Piracy cases in the Supreme Court. Journal of criminal law and criminology 25 : 532-553, November-December 1934.

RECHID, A. : L'affaire Samuel Insull. Revue générale de droit internationale public 41 : 687-710, novembre-décembre 1934.

HAZARD, H.B. : Nationality from the legislative, administrative and judicial points of view. Cumulative digest of international law and relations 4 : 14-17, December 19, 1934.

FLOURNOY, R.W. : Proposed codification of our chaotic nationality laws. American bar association journal 20 : 780-783, December 1934.

JESSUP, P.C. : Revising our nationality laws. American journal of international law 28 : 104-108, 1934.

VATICAN STATE

ROUSSEAU, C. : Etat de la Cité du Vatican. Revue générale de droit international public 37 : 145-153, janvier-avril 1930.

LIERMANN, H. : Staat und Kirche in den Lateranverträgen zwischen dem Heiligen Stuhl und Italien vom 11 Februar 1929. Archiv des öffentlichen Rechts 18 : 379-410, 3. Heft 1930.

STRUPP, K. : Die Regelung der römischen Frage durch die Lateranverträge vom 11 Februar 1929. Zeitschrift für Völkerrecht 15 : 531-622, Heft 4, 1930.

OESCHEY, R. : Lo stato della Città del Vaticano. Zeitschrift für Völkerrecht 15 : 623-693, Heft 4, 1930.

OTTOLENGHI, G. : Sulla condizione giuridica della Città del Vaticano. Rivista di diritto internazionale 22 : 180-195, 1 aprile-30 giugno 1930.

CHECCHINI, A. : La natura giuridica della Città del Vaticano e del "Trattato" Lateranse. Rivista di diritto internazionale 22 : 196-211, 1 aprile- 30 giugno 1930.

CHECCHINI, A. : La qualificazione giuridica delle relazioni fra lo Stato italiano e la Chiesa. Rivista di diritto pubblico 22 : 583-601, dicembre 1930.

VALÉRY, J. : La nationalité vaticane- Revue de droit international privé 26 : 1-37, No. 1, 1931.

GIANNINI, A. : La codificazione del diritto canonico orientale. Oriente moderno 11 : 65-74, febbraio 1931.

Compétence juridictionnelle de l'Etat de la Cité du Vatican. Revue générale de droit international public 38 : 344-346, mai-juin 1931.

BALLADORE PALLIERI, G. : Die völkerrechtliche Rechtspersönlichkeit des Staates Città del Vaticano. Zeitschrift für öffentliches Recht 11 : 505-525, 10 Dezember 1931.

ANGELINI, D. : Le caractère indivisible des accords du Latran. Revue générale de droit international public 39 : 512-521, juillet-août 1932.

SCHOEN, P. : Die rechtliche Natur der Vatikanstadt und des politischen Lateranvertrages. Zeitschrift für öffentliches Recht 14 : 1-25, Heft 1, 1934.

TRICAUD, M., et PERRIN, B. : Le régime administratif de la Cité du Vatican. Revue de droit international 8 : 508-520, avril-mai-juin 1934.

COTTINO, M. : Le concordat avec le Saint-Siège et le droit maritime italien. Annales de l'Institut de droit comparé de l'Université de Paris 1 : 25-39, 1934.

VENEZUELA

UZCÁTEGUI, G. : Critica a la ley de naturalización. Revista de derecho y legislación 19 : 65-70, marzo 1930.
Nationality law of Venezuela.

FARRERA, C. : El código Bustamente y nuestro derecho positivo. Revista de derecho y legislación 19 : 88-94, abril 1930.

FARRERA, C. : El códifo Bustamente y nuestro derecho positivo. Revista de derecho internacional 17 : 284-309, 30 junio 1930.

FARRERA, C. : El código Bustamente y nuestro derecho positivo (Contd.). Revista de derecho y legislación 19 : 187-197, setiembre 1930.
International private law of Venezuela.

FARRERA, C. : El código Bustamente y nuestro derecho positivo (Contd.). Revista de derecho internacional 9 : 27-55, 30 septiembre 1930.

FARRERA, C. : El Código Bustamente y nuestro derecho positivo (Contd.). Revista de derecho y legislación 19 : 253-259, diciembre 1930.
The law of Venezuela.

Estudio sobre la letra de cambio en el código de comercio venezolano. Revista juridica 3 : 93-100, marzo 1932.

FARRERA, C. : El derecho penal internacional en la legislación de Venezuela. Revista juridica (Venezuela) 3 : 250-265, julio, agosto y setiembre 1932.

VIET NAM

CORDEMOY, P. : Le statut des étrangers en Indochine. Bulletin de l'Agence économique de l'Indochine 6 : 94-101, mars 1933.

YUOSLAVIA

TAUBERT, L. : Les lois sur le change et la chèque. Revue économique de Belgrade 5 : 9-12, janvier 1930.

PÉRITCH, J. : La nouvelle loi yougoslave du 21 septembre 1928. Revue de droit international privé 25 : 1-32, No. 1, 1930.

LACHNER, H. : Das neue jugoslavische Wechselgesetz im Vergleich mit dem deutschen. Zeitschrift für Ostrecht 4 : 17-22, Januar 1930.

SAJOVIC, R. : Rassegna di letteratura giuridica jugolava (anni 1925-1928). Annuario di diritto comparato vol 4 e 5, parte 1 : 545-560, 1930.

LUBENOFF, G. : Die königliche Diktatur in Jugoslawien. Zeitschrift für ausländisches öffentliches Recht und Völkerrecht (Abt.1) 2 : 252-267, No. 1-2, 1930.

SPILLER, K. : Die neue jugoslavische Zivilprozesordnung vom 13.7. 1929. Gesetzgebung und Techtspraxis des Auslandes 6 : 15-22, Januar-Februar 1930.

PÉRITCH, J. : Le droit de succession en droit international privé yougoslave. Institut belge de droit comparé 16 : 1-18, janvier-mars 1930.

STEFANOVITCH, Y. : Les règles fondamentales de la justice administrative yougoslave (Contd.). Revue gégérale du droit, de la législation et de la jurisprudence 54 : 16-21, janvier-février-mars 1930.

ZEBJĆ, M. : Vergleichende Betrechtungen über das Aktienrecht Jugoslaviens. Zeitschrift für Ostrecht 4 : 113-143, Februar 1930.

SAJOVIC, R. : Rassegna du legislazione jugoslava (anni 1925-1928). Annuario di diritto comparato vol. 4 e 5, parte 2 : 511-580, 1930.

Loi sur le chèque. Bulletin officiel de la chambre de commerce franco-yougoslave 2 : 1-4, mars 1930.
Dispositions essentielles de la loi yougoslave.

PÉRITCH, J.M. : Application du principe de territorialité des lois (statut réel) aux différents instituts du droit privé suivant le droit international privé en Yougoslavie. Journal du droit international 57 : 332-351, mars-avril 1930.

TAUBERT, L. : La nouvelle loi sur les faillites. Revue économique de Belgrade 5 : 179-183, juillet-août 1930.

La loi yougoslave contre la concurrence déloyale. Revue économique de Belgrade 5 : 183-185, juillet-août 1930.

ŠUMAN, J. : Die Urheberrechtsgesetzgebung in Jugoslavien. Zeitschrift für Ostrecht 4 : 799-816, August-September 1930.

PÉRITCH, J. : Basic rules of the Yugoslav law concerning nationality. American journal of international law 24 : 728-737, October 1930.

PERUCIO, S. : Das neue jugoslawische Losratengesetz. Mitteilungen des Verbandes österreichischer Banken und Bankiers 12 : 341-344, Dezember 1930.

STOYKOVITCH, S. : Bibliographie d'ouvrages et d'articles d'intérêt juridique, parus en langue française, di 1er janvier 1919 jusqu'au 1er janvier 1930. Annuaire de l'Association yougoslave de droit international 1 : 397-405, 1931.
Ouvrages et articles d'auteurs yougoslaves traitant n'importe quel sujet d'intérêt juridique - ouvrages et articles d'auteurs étrangers se rapportant aux questions d'intérêt juridique pour la Yugoslavie.

SOURBBOTITCH, I.V. Bibligraphie des ouvrages et articles de revues parus en langue allemande dans les années 1919-1929 et concernant le droit yougoslave. Annuaire de l'Association yougoslave de droit international 1 : 409-418, 1931.

PRZIC, I.A. : La bibliographie yougoslave de droit international (1918-1929). Annuaire de l'Association yougoslave de droit international 1 : 351-393, 1931.

PÉRITCH, J. : Les droits international et interprovincial dans les nouvelles lois yougoslaves sur la lettre de change et sur le chèque du 29 novembre 1928. Annuaire de l'Association yougoslave de droit international 1 : 177-213, 1931.

ANDRASSY, G. : Les traités d'arbitrage et de conciliation conclus par la Yougoslavie. Annuaire de l'Association yougoslave de droit international 1 : 75-95, 1931.

TAUBERT, L. : Notre nouvelle convention avec le royaume de Hongrie. Revue économique de Belgrade 6 : 10-12, janvier 1931.
Convention du 11 november 1929 relative à certaines questions de procédure civile et de droit privé.

PÉRITCH, J. : Le mariage civil des ressortissants serbes a l'étranger. Institut belge de droit comparé 17 : 1-6, janvier-mars 1931.

PÉRITCH, J. : De la condition juridique des étrangers dans le royaume de Yougoslavie au point de vue des droits publics. Zeitschrift für Völkerrecht 16 : 226-236, Heft 2, 1931.

PÉRITCH, J.M. : De la condition juridique des étrangers au Monténégro. Bulletin mensuel de la Société de législation comparée 60 : 376-386, avril-juin 1931.
Le droit du Monténégro.

DOLENC, M. : Die Einstellung Jugoslaviens zum zwischenstaatlichen Strafrechte. Zeitschrift für Ostrecht 5 : 401-405, Juni 1931.

MOUSSET, A. : En Yougoslavie - la Constitution du 3 septembre 1931. Europe centrale 6 : 782-783, 12 septembre 1931.

CAPARELLI, F. : Per la nuova costituzione jougoslava. Gerarchia 11 : 844-852, ottobre 1931.

LUBENOFF, G. : Die Verfassung Jugoslawiens vom 3. September 1931. Zeitschrift für ausländisches öffentliches Recht und Völkerrecht (Abhandlungen) 3 : 402-443, No. 3, 1932.

GIANNINI, A. : La costituzione jugoslava del 1931. Europa orientale 12 : 129-168, marzo-aprile 1932.

DOLENC, M. : Die neuesten Änderungen in den strafrechtlichen Gesetzen Jugoslaviens. Zeitschrift für Ostrecht 6 : 427-432, Juni 1932.

KAUSCHANSKY, D.M. : Das internationale Eherecht Jugoslawiens in seinen Beziehungen zu anderen europäischen und ausseuropäischen Rechten. Revue de droit international, de sciences diplomatiques et politiques 11 : 35-46, janvier-mars 1933.

KAUSCHANSKY, D.M. : Das international Eherecht Jugoslawiens in seinen Beziehungen zu anderen europäischen und aussereuropäischen Rechten. Revue de droit international, de sciences diplomatiques et politiques 11 : 118-126, avril-juin 1933.

NATIONAL LAW - COUNTRIES

PÉRITCH, J. : Responsabilité civile de l'Etat comme personne juridique en droit yougoslave (Contd.). Revue du droit public 40 : 291-301, avril-mai-juin 1933.

GORŠIĆ, F. : Zum neuen jugoslavischen Zivil prozessgesetz. Zeitschrift für Ostrecht 7 : 559-584, Juni 1933.

GOTJEVATZ, A. : Nationalité de la femme mariée dans la nouvelle loi yougoslave. Balkans 4 : 515-520, août 1933.

KAUSCHANSKY, D.M. : Das internationale Eherecht Jugoslawiens in seinen Beziehungen zu anderen europäischen und aussereuropäischen Rechten (Contd.). Revue de droit international, de sciences diplomatiques et politiques 11 : 267-276, octobre-décembre 1933.

MILIČ, I. : Erwerb von Grundeigentum in Jugoslavien durch Ausländer. Zeitschrift für Ostrecht 7 : 1024-1029, Dezember 1933.

GODYÉVATZ, A. : Liste des traités et des engagements internationaux de la Serbie, y compris les lois et les règlements internes d'ordre international. Annuaire de l'Association yougoslave de droit international 2 : 307-308, 1934.
1878-1914.

BARTOŠ, M. : Le droit international sur la faillite en Yougoslavie. Annuaire de l'association yougoslave de droit international 2 : 241-258, 1934.

BÉGOVITCH, M. : Législation relative à l'organisades affaires religieuses des musulmanes en Yougoslavie. Annuaire de l'association yougoslave de droit international 2 : 265-270, 1934.

BLAGOYÉVITCH, B.T. : Exequatur des jugements étrangers selon la loi yougoslave sur les exécutions et saisies. Annuaire de l'association yougoslave de droit international 2 : 275-289, 1934.

TCHIRKOVITCH, S. : Liste des traités et des engagements internationax du Royaume de Yougoslavie, y compris les lois et les règlements internes d'ordre international de 1919-1935. Annuaire de l'association yougoslave de droit international 2 : 347-349, 1934.

PÉRITCH, J. : De la compétence judiciaire en matière matrimoniale dans le royaume de Yougoslavie. Annuaire de l'association yougoslave de droit international 2 : 217-229, 1934.

SOUBBOTITCH, I. : Le nouveau régime juridique du secteur du Danube dit des Cataractes et des Portes-de-Fer. Annuaire de l'Association yougoslave de droit international 2 : 77-111, 1934.

SAJOVIC, R. : Rassegna di legislazione jugoslava (anno 1929). Annuario di diritto comparato e di studi legislativi 7 : 154-236, parte IV, 1934.

SAJOVIC, R. : Rassegna di letteratura giuridica jugoslava (anno 1930). Annuario di diritto comparato e di studi legislativi 8 : 218-236, fascicolo V, 1933.

SAJOVIC, R. : Rassegna di legislazione jugoslava (anno 1930). Annuario di diritto comparate et di studi legislativi (Parte IV) 8 : 186-264, 1934.

SACCHI, P. : La costituzione jugoslava e la pace. Vita internazionale 37 : 11-113, settembre-ottobre 1934.

PHILONENKO, M. : Le refus d'extradition des terroristes croates. Journal du droit international 61 : 1157-1169, novembre-décembre 1934.

NATIONAL LAW - COUNTRIES

AFGHANISTAN

DOLLOT, R. : Coup d'oeil sur l'Afghanistan. Affaires étrangères 7 : 187-192, mars 1937.

ALBANIA

L'unione doganale italo-albanese. Relazioni internazionali 5 : 372, 13 maggio 1939.

RIZZO, G. : La unione dell'Albania con l'Italia. Rivista di diritto pubblico 31 : 497-522, agosto-settembre 1939.

RIZZO, G. : La unione dell'Albania con l'Italia. Rivista di diritto pubblico 31 : 651-677, novembre 1939.

ANDORRA

PIESOLD, W. : Andorra und sein Staatsrecht. Geopolitik 12 : 422-434, Juli 1935.

ARGENTINA

VIOLA, L. : La jurisprudencia argentina en materia de gobierno "de facto". Revista de derecho y legislación 24 : 49-56, marzo y abril 1935.

Convenciones multilaterales vigentes en la República Argentina (por orden cronológico). Anales diplomáticos 3 : 462-464, febrero-marzo 1936.

BELFORT de MATTOS, J.D.F. : O código civil Argentino em face do direito Brasileiro. Revista da faculdade de direito 32 : 259-288, maio-agosto 1936.

CORNEJO, V.A. y GÓMEZ, A.A. : Constitución - Ley Electoral - Ley Orgánica Municipal de la Provincia de Buenos Aires. Revista de derecho y administración municipal : 64-98, diciembre 1936.

SOLF y MURO, A. : La nueva codificación civil en la Argentina. Revista de derecho y ciencias politicas 1 : 169-170, No. 2, 1937.

Un año de gobierno sometido al juicio del país. Revista parlamentaria (Buenos Aires) 5 : 14-75, febrero 1937.
Survey of legislation in 1936.

BIELSA, R. : Il problema del decentramento amministrativo in Argentina. Annuario di diritto comparato e di studi legislativi 12 : 225-248, fasc. 4, 1937.

La elección presidencial. Revista parlamentaria 6 : 3-120, septiembre 1937.
Series of articles and legal texts.

La consesión de la ciudadanía argentina. Revista parlamentaria 6 : 7-10, noviembre 1937.

MAYER, J.M. : Contralor des Estado sobre admisión de los extranjeros. Revista parlamentaria 6 : 11-34, noviembre 1937.

GRECA, A. : La obligaciones en el proyecto de reforma del código civil. Revista de ciencias jurídicas y sociales 1 : 5-14, núm. 20, 1937.

DELAGE : Un projet nouveau de Code pénal argentin. Revue de science criminelle et de droit pénal comparé 3 : 176-181, janvier-mars 1938.

LINARES, J.F. : La teoria de la "anulción" y "revocación por ilegitimidad" de los contratos administrativos, en frente a la Constitución Federal. Revista de derecho y administración municipal : 3-23, febrero 1938.

La ciudadanía Argentina. Revista parlamentaria 7 : 12-13, abril 1938.

VILLEGAS, A.W. : La ciudadania Argentina. Revista parlamentaria 7 : 10-16, junio 1938.
Text of bill annexed.

ALCORTE, C.A. : El régimen jurídico de la nacionalidad en el Brasil y en la Argentina. Revista argentina de derecho internacional 1 : 27-47, julio-agosto-septiembre 1938.

CASTRO, J.S. : La reforma del Código de comercio. Revista de ciencias económicas 26 : 1039-1082, octubre 1938.

COLL, J.E., y GOMEZ, E. : Exposición de motivos del proyecto de código penal para la República Argentina. Revista jurídica 2 : 22-32, noviembre 1938.

La reforma del código civil - Opinion del colegio de abogados de Buenos Aires. Revista parlamentaria 7 : 11-31, diciembre 1938.

GOWLAND, G.D. : Avant-projet de code de commerce - abordages - relâche forcée - assistance et sauvetage - naufrages. Revue de droit maritime comparé 39 : 359-364, janvier-juin 1939.

BUONCORE, D. : La concesión de minas y la concesión de servicios públicos. Revista de ciencias jurídicas y sociales 4 : 43-55, No.26, 1939.

MOUCHET, C. : Se ha constituido el Instituto Argentino de derecho internacional. Revista de derecho internacional 35 : 112-113, 31 marzo 1939.

HOFMANNSTHAL, E. de : La igualdad del extranjero con el nacional. Revista argentina de derecho internacional 2 : 278-282, julio-agosto-septiembre 1939.

FRIAS, J.H. : Le projet de code pénal pour la République Argentine. Recueil de documents en matière pénale et pénitentiaire 8 : 397-410, décembre 1939.

AUSTRALIA

LATHAM, R.T. E. : The power of investigation in the Commonwealth. Australian law journal 9 : 213-218, October 15, 1935.

STEINWALLNER, B. : Das australische Strafrecht. Zeitschrift für vergleichende Rechtswissenschaft 50 : 160-164, 8. November 1935.

GARRAN, R.R. : The law of the Territories of the Commonwealth. Australian law journal 9 : 28-42, November 15, 1935.

STEINWALLNER, B. : Das australische Strafrecht. Zeitschrift für vergleichende Rechtswissenschaft 50 : 160-164, I./II. Heft 1935.

The South Australian centenary of legis lation. Journal of comparative legislation and international law 18 : 21-39, February 1936.

NATIONAL LAW - COUNTRIES

HARPER, A.M. : The new South Wales Companies Act, 1936. Australian law journal 10 : 85-88, July 15, 1936.

HARPER, A.M. : The New South Wales Companies Act, 1936. Australian law journal 10 : 136-138, August 15, 1936.

The Australian constitution. Law journal 82 : 183-184, 19 September 1936.

Australian legal convention, 1936. Supplement to the Australian law journal 10 : 1-2, 15 October 1936.

HANNAN, A.J. : The common law as a bulwark against executive tyranny. Supplement to the Australian law journal 10 : 9-21, 15 October 1936.

HARPER, A.M. : The New South Wales Companies Act 1936 (Contd.). Australian law journal 10 : 228-230, 15 October 1936.

GARRAN, R. : The Australian aviation case. Journal of air law 8 : 27-32, January 1937.
Federal power to legislate with respect to external affairs.

EVATT, H.V. : The judiciary and administrative law in Australia. Canadian bar review 15 : 247-269, April 1937.

Nationality Act (Status of married women). Journal of the parliaments of the Empire 18 : 364-366, April 1937.

STARKE, J.G. : The Privy Council and the competence of federal legislatures to legislate pursuant to international obligations. Australian law journal 2 : 45-50, 87-92, June 15, July 16, 1937.

NAWIASKY, H. : Grundlegende Rechtsfragen der berufständischen Ordnung. Monatsschrift für Kultur und Politik 2 : 708-717, August 1937.

WYNES, W.A. : The judicial power of the Commonwealth. Australian law journal 11 : 250-253, November 12, 1937.

BAILEY, K.H. : Australia - Federal States in external relations. British year book of international law 18 : 175-177, 1937.

EASTMAN, A.J. : Australian nationality legislation - Nationality of married women. British year book of international law 18 : 179-181, 1937.

STEWART, R.B. : International labour convention in Australia. Canadian journal of economics and political science 4 : 34-46, February 1938.

MAYO, H. : The future of the Law council of Australia. Australian law journal 13 : 183-196, August 15, 1939.

AUSTRIA

VOGEL, E.H. : Ständeverfässung und Demokratie. Oesterrechische Volkswirt 27 : 323-325, 26 Jänner 1935.

STEINER, H.A. : The Austrian Constitution of 1934. American journal of international law 20 : 125-129, January 1935.

KÖSTLER, R. : Das neue österreichische Konkordat. Zeitschrift für öffentliches Recht15 : 1-33, Heft 1, 1935.

RATZENHOFER, G., und KOLLROSS, K. : Die privatrechtliche Gesetzgebung Österrechs im Jahre 1934. Zeitschrift für ausländisches und internationales Privatrecht 9 : 92-116, Heft 1-2, 1935.

SPERL : Das neue österreichische Eherecht. Deutsche Juristen-Zeitung 40 : 341-347, 15. März 1935.

KÖSTLER, R. : Grundfragen des Konkordats-Eherechts. Juristische Blätter 64 : 113-138, 157-162, 30-März, 13. April 1935.

DNISTRJANSKYJ, S. : Die Rezeption des österreichischen Privatrechts in der Tschechoslowakei und in Jugoslavien. Zeitschrift für osteuropäisches Recht 1 : 463-490, März 1935.

SPANNER, H. : Der österreichische Bundesgerichtshof. Zeitschrift für öffentliches Recht 15 : 195-240, 15. April 1935.

SPANNER, H. : Das Recht zur Erlassung von Verordnungen nach der Verfassung 1934. Österreichisches Verwaltungsblatt 6 : 138-148, 16. Mai 1935.

STROSS, W. : Die Entwicklung der Kapitulationsrechte in Ägypten seit Abschluss der Friedensverträge. Zeitschrift für öffentliches Recht 15 : 394-407, 21. Juni 1935.

ROSENBERG, K. : L'organisation corporative autrichienne. Affaires étrangères 5 : 329-344, juin 1935.

STRELE, K. : Die Erlassung genereller Normen nach der österreichischen Verfassung 1934. Zeitschrift für öffentliches Recht 15 : 417-445, 20. September 1935.

GÜRKE, N. : Die Verfassung Österreichs. Jahrbuch des öffentlichen Rechts 22 : 339-410, 1935.

Die im Jahre 1936 veröffentlichten österreichischen Entsheidungen zum Privat- Straf- und Prozessrecht. Jahrbuch höchstrichterlicher Entscheidungen (Beiheft der Juristischen Blätter) 9 : 1-93, lief.1, 1936.

BARTSCH, R. : Zur Kodifikation des Verwaltungsrechtes. Osterreichisches Verwaltungsblatt 6 : 257-260, 16. Oktober 1935.

LOHSING, E. : Bemerkungen zu den Strafrechtsänderungen vom Dezember 1935. Juristischer Blätter 65 : 49-52, 8. Februar 1936.

KOSTLER, R. : Die katholische Kirche Österreichs. Zeitschrift für öffentliches Recht 16 : 58-67, 20. Februar 1936.

ADAMOVITCH, L. : Die Gesetzgebung zur Vorbereitung des berufständischen Aufbaues in Österreich. Österreichisches Verwaltungsblatt 7 : 25-27, 16. Februar 1936.

SATTER, K. : Die Anerkennung ausländischer Urteile in Ehesachen nach dem neuen österreichischen Eherecht. Zeitschrift für ausländisches und internationales Privatrecht 9 : 551-557, Heft 4/5, 1935.

ADAMOVICH, L. : Die Gesetzgebung zur Vorbereitung des berufständischen Ausbaues in Östereich. Österreichisches Verwaltungsblatt 7 : 73-77, 17. April 1936.

ADAMOVICH, L. : Die Gesetzgebung zur Vorbereitung des berufständischen Ausbaues in Österreich (Contd.). Österreichisches Verwaltungsblatt 7 : 105-106, 129-132, 17. Mai, 17. Juni 1936.

WAHLE, K. : Übersicht über die Rechtsprechung des österreichischen Obersten Gerichtshofes in Zivilsachen im Jahre 1934. Zeitschrift für ausländisches und internationales Privatrecht 10 : 736-795, Heft 5/6, 1936.

MEZGER, E. : Les conflits de lois dans la loi autrichienne sur le droit d'auteur du 9 avril 1936. Geistiges Eigentum 2 : 105-114, August-September 1936.

FISCHMANN, L. : Les dispositions concernant la radiphonie dans la nouvelle loi autrichienne sur le droit d'auteur. Revue internationale de la radioélectricité 12 : 241-244, juillet-août-septembre 1936.

ADAMOVICH, L. : Die Gesetzgebung zur Vorbereitung des berufständischen Aufbaues in Österreich. Österreichisches Verwaltungsblatt 7 : 153-155, 177-179, 201-202, 17. Juli, 15. August, 17. September 1936.

BERGEL, E. : Das österreichische Urheberrechtsgesetz 1936. Geistiges Eigentum 2 : 81-105, August-September 1936.

SCHNEK, F. : Das Staatsschutzgesetz. Juristische Blätter 65 : 359-363, 19. September 1936.

NEMECEK, C. : Die Selbstverwaltung der Berufsstände. Zeitschrift für öffentliches Recht 16 : 522-531, 6. Oktober 1936.

La nouvelle loi autrichienne sur le droit d'auteur. Droit d'auteur 49 : 110-112, 15 octobre 1936.

ADAMOVICH, L. : Die Gesetzgebung zur Vorbereitung des berufständischen Aufbaues in Österreich (Contd.). Österreichisches Verwaltungsblatt 7 : 225-234, 16. Oktober 1936.

PÍLZ, A. : Die Rechtsentwicklung im neuen Österreich. Zeitschrift der Akademie für deutsches Recht 4 : 2-5, 1. Januar 1937.

ADAMOVICH, L. : Die Gesetzgebung zur Vorbereitung des berufständischen Aufbaues in Österreich (Contd.). Österreichisches Verwaltungsblatt 8 : 1-5, 17. Janner 1937.

ADAMOVICH, L. : Die Gesetzgebung zur Vorbereitung des berufständischen Aufbaues in Österreich (Contd.). Österreichisches Verwaltungsblatt 8 : 25-27, 16. Februar 1937.

Sidelights on family legislation in Austria. New era in home and school 18 : 41-46, February 1937.

NEIDL, W. : Das Budgetrecht der Landtage (Contd.). Österreichisches Verwalungsblatt 8 : 105-112, 16. Mai 1937.

KLANG, H. : Das Goldklauselgesetz. Juristische Blätter 66 : 225-228, 225-228, 29. Mai 1937.

RITTLER, T. : Die Abgrenzung des Hochverrates von den Verbrechen nach dem Staatsschutzgesetz. Juristische Blätter 66 : 265-269, 26. Juni 1937.

ADAMOVICH, L. : Parlamentarische Unvereinbarkeit und berufsständische Ordnung. Zeitschrift für öffentliches Recht 17 : 491-501, 25. September 1937.

MERKL, A. : Vollendung des Verfassungswerkes und der Ständeordnung. Österreichische Volkswirt 30 : 11-13, 2. Oktober 1937.

AUFRICHT, H. : Völkerrecht und Staatsrecht in der Verfassung 1934. Juristische Blätter 66 : 380-386, 2. Oktober 1937.

METALL, R.A. : Zur Auslegung des Artikels 67 : Absatz 3, der Verfassung 1934. Österrechisches Verwaltungsblatt 8 : 258-261, No. 10, 1937. The language of Treaty texts rectified.

ENDER, O. : Gedanken zur Vollendung der Verfassung. Monatsschrift für Kultur und Politik 11 : 965-968, November 1937.

SPANNER, H. : Die Abänderung von Bundesverfassungsgesetzen durch einfache Bundesgesetze und Verordnungen- Österreichisches Verwaltungsblatt 8 : 273-284, 14. November 1937.

GÜRKE, N. : Die Verfassung Österreichs. Jahrbuch des öffentlichen Rechts der Gegenwart 24 : 166-250, 1937.

KLANG, H. : Die Rechtsprechung des Obersten Gerichtshofes in Zivilsachen. Juristische Blätter 67 : 7-9, 8. Januar 1938.

MAYRHOFER-GRÜNBÜHEL, H. : Heimatlosigkeit nach dem Paragraph 1 der H.R.N. 1925. Österreichisches Verwaltungsblatt 9 : 7-13, 16. Jänner 1938.

ADAMOVICH, L. : Ständische Verwaltung und Staatsverwaltung. Monatsschrift für Kultur und Politik 3 : 5-14, Jänner 1938.

HUEBER, F. : Grundfragen der Rechtsangleichung. Zeitschrift der Akademie für deutsches Recht 5 : 220-222, 1. April 1938.

MERKL, A. : Rechtsprobleme der Wiedervereinigung Österreichs mit dem Deutschen Reiche. Österreichisches Verwaltungsblatt 9 : 81-88, 113-119, 20. April, 17. Mai, 1938.

RANCHIN, J. : L'Anschluss. Revue de droit international 12 : 317-338, avril-mai-juin 1938

HULA, E. : The corporative experiment in Austria. Social research 6 : 40-57, February 1939.

BRANDT : Die Regelung der österreichischen Bundesschulden. Zeitschrift für ausländisches öffnetliches Recht und Völkerrecht 9 : 127-147, April 1939.

KEITH, F. : Werdegang und Ende des österreichischen Konkordats. Zeitschrift der Akademie für deutsches Recht 6 : 478-483, 15. Juli 1939.

BELGIUM

ANCEL, M. : Loi belge concernant la déchéance de la nationalité (30 juillet 1934). Revue critique de droit international 30 : 591-593, avril-octobre 1935.

QUADEN, P. : L'abrogation de la clause-or - L'arrêté du 11 avril 1935. Belgique judiciaire 93 : 322-327, 1 juin 1935.

BUTTGENBACH, A. : L'extension des pouvoirs de l'exécutif en temps de guerre et la revision de la constitution belge. Belgique judiciaire 93 : 385-448, 1 juillet - 15 juillet 1935.

NATIONAL LAW - COUNTRIES

MOREAU, L. : Les sociétés de personnes à responsabilité limitée. Vie économique et sociale 12 : 361-369, septembre-octobre 1935.
La loi du 9 juillet 1935.

GRIMM : Der belgische Ausbürgerungsprozess. Deutsche Justiz 97 : 1454-1460, 4. Oktober 1935.

HASSELBLATT, W. : Das belgische Ausbürgerungsverfahren. Deutsche Juristen-Zeitung 40 : 1342-1346, 15. November 1935.

HASSELBLATT, W. : Die erste Anwendung der lex Eupen-Malmedy. Völkerbund und Völkerrecht 2 : 531-536, Dezember 1935.

WAHL, E. : Die belgische Rechtsprechung in den Jahren 1932-1935. Zeitschrift für ausländisches und internationales Privatrecht 10 : 362-384, Heft 1/3, 1936.

Gesetzgebung in Belgien 1932-1935. Zeitschrift für ausländisches und internationales Privatrecht 10 : 319-361, Heft 1/3, 1936.

La protection des missions religieuses et les actes internationaux. Congo 1 : 161-186, février 1936.
Le bassin conventionnel du Congo.

PIÉRARD, A. : Etude sur la loi du 14 décembre 1935, modifiant la procédure en matière de divorce et de séparation de corps (titre VI du livre 1er du Code civil). Belgique judiciaire 94 : 161-171, 15 mars 1936.

BRODMANN, E. : Das belgische Gesetz über Gesellschaften m.b.H. : Zeitschrift für ausländisches und internationales Privatrecht 9 : 867-875, Heft 6, 1935.

CONSTANT, J. : Le régime des armes en Belgique. Revue internationale de droit pénal 13 : 105-131, 2e trimestre 1936.

JOFÉ, B. : La dissolution des mariages autant confessionnels que civils devant les tribunaux civils de Belgique. Revue trimestrielle de l'Institut belge de droit comparé 22 : 118-145, juillet-décembre 1936.

DOR, G., et MOUREAU, L. : Les tendances actuelles du droit public et du droit privé. Revue trimestrielle de l'Institut belge de droit comparé 22 : 99-117, juillet-décembre 1936.

Liste des lois des principaux pays, promulguées en 1936 - Belgique. Bulletin trimestriel de la Société de législation comparée 65 : 478-480, octobre-décembre 1936.

La convention franco-belge sur les doubles impositions. Dalloz, Recueil hebdomadaire de jurisprudence 13 : 57-60, 61-64, 5, 19 novembre 1936.

ROLIN, H. : Belgique. Annuaire de l'Institut international de droit public : 157-162, 1937.
Le droit public en 1936.

HYDE, C.C. : Belgium and neutrality. American journal of international law 31 : 81-85, January 1937.

HILLE, W. van : Commentaire de la convention anglo-belge du 2 mai 1934 sur l'exécution réciproque des jugements. Belgique judiciaire 95 : 66-92, 1-15 février 1937.

BERTAUX, L. : Théorie générale nouvelle du droit de vote dans les sociétés anonymes. Belgique judiciaire 95 : 130-142, 1 mars 1937.

CLÉMENS, R. : Le corporatisme dans l'organisation de l'Etat moderne - Belgique. Institut belge de droit comparé 23 : 1-29, janvier-mars 1937.

Die Gesetzgebung von Belgisch-Kongo in den Jahren 1935 und 1936. Afrika Rundschau 2 : 359-362, April 1937.

GRAULICH, L., et LALOUX, P. :Jurisprudence belge en matière de droit civil (1934-1935). Revue trimestrielle de droit civil 36 : 413-465, avril-juin 1937.

ARMENGAUD : La neutralité volontaire de la Belgique et les progrès de l'armement aérien. Revue des deux mondes 107 : 101-113, 1 juillet 1937.

VAN DER KERKEN, G. : La nationalité du Congolais ou sujets belges du Congo. Institut belge de droit comparé, Revue trimestrielle 23 : 168-188, octobre-décembre 1937.

Réflexions sur l'instance et la procédure de cassation en matière répressive. Belgique judiciaire 96 : 1-17, 1 janvier 1938.

VAN DER KERKEN, G. : Le statut des "sans netionalité" ("heimatlosen") et de leurs descendants en droit congolais. Institut belge de droit comparé, revue trimestrielle 24 : 1-19, janvier-mars 1938.

SASSERATH, S. : Réforme de l'instruction préparatoire en Belgique. Revue internationale de doctrine et de législation pénale comparée 2 : 28-46, No. 2, 1938.

HILLE, W. van : Notes sur la jurisprudence belge en matière de droit international. Revue de droit international et de législation comparée 65 : 294-340, No. 2, 1938.

DEHOUSSE, F. : La conclusion des traités d'après la pratique constitutionnelle et diplomatique belge. Annales de l'Institut de droit comparé de l'université de Paris 3 : 87-143, 1938.

Belgio - Anni 1933-1936. Istituto di studi legislativi, giurisprudenza comparata di diritto internazionale privato 3 : 265-361, 1938.

VAN HOUTTE, M.J. : Les accords de clearing. Pandectes périodiques 45 : 109-155, mars 1938.
Numéro spécial.

L'Etat fédéral en Belgique. Revue de droit international 12 : 412-422, avril-mai-juin 1938.

DOLLOT, R. : La crise des neutralités permanentes. Affairs étrangères 8 : 351-370, juin 1938.
La Belgique.

COLLARD, C. : Les étrangers en Belgique. Service social 17 : 93-110, juillet-août 1938.

DEL MARMOL. C. : Les projets de réforme du statut des sociétés anonymes en Belgique. Annales de droit commercial 57 : 211-243, juillet-septembre 1938.

BERNARD, A., et BIZET, A. : Revue semestrielle de législation. Institut belge de droit comparé, Revue trimestrielle 24 : 110-132, juillet-décembre 1938.

PIRET, R. : Le società anonime nel diritto belga - Norme vigenti e riforme progettate. Rivista del diritto commerciale 36 : 508-519, settembre-ottobre 1938.

MOUREAU, L. : Les principes fondamentaux du droit relatif aux fonctionnaires et l'arrêté royal du 2 octobre 1937 portant statut des agents de l'Etat. Belgique judiciaire 96 : 450-471, 1-15 octobre 1938.

GRAULICH, L., et RENARD, C. : Chronique de droit belge. Revue trimestrielle de droit civil 38 : 231-247, janvier-mars 1939.
Bibliographie, jurisprudence, législation.

BUTTGENBACH, A. : La pratique des pouvoirs spéciaux et le droit constitutionnel de la Belgique. Revue de droit public 46 : 80-154, janvier-mars 1939.

GUINN, P.S. : Belgian company law. U.S. Department of commerce, Comparative law series 2 : 87-97, February 1939.

HOUTTE, J. van, and DEL MARMOL, C. : Synthèse de la littérature juridique belge (1936-1938). Annuario di diritto comparato et di studi legislativi 14 : 439-462, fasc. 4, 1939.

HILLE, W. van : Chronique de la jurisprudence belge en matière de droit international privé en 1938-39. Revue de droit international et de législation comparée 66 : 748-764, No. 4, 1939.

VAN DER KERKEN, G. : La situation des étrangers au Congo belge. Revue trimestrielle de l'Institute belge de droit comparé 25 : 49-56, avril-juin 1939.

SIBELLE, P. : L'expropriation pour cause d'utilité publique par voie d'extrême urgence. Pandectes périodiques 46 : 201-218, mai 1939.

DOCHY, M. : L'exécution en Belgique des obligations alimentaires sanctionnées à l'étranger. Institut belge de droit comparé. Revue trimestrielle 25 : 136-138, juillet-décembre 1939.

WIGNY, P. : Chronique de jurisprudence et de législation (1937-1938). Droit international privé. Belgique judiciaire 97 : 503-610, 1 décembre 1939.

BOLIVIA

NEWHALL, B. : The new Constitution of Bolivia. Pan American Union, Bulletin 73 : 100-106, February 1939.

NEWHALL, B. : La nueva constitución de Bolivia. Boletín de la Unión Panamericana : 275-283, mayo 1939.

BRAZIL

BEVILAQUA, C. : Legitimate inheritance under the Brazilian civil law. Iowa law review 20 : 402-410, January 1935.

ARRUDA, J. : Reforma constitucional Revista da faculdade de direito (Universidade de São Paolo) 31 : 181-219, abril-junho 1935.

EÇA, R. d' : The Brazilian constitution of 1934. Bulletin of the Pan American unio 69 : 621-631, August 1935.

BELFORT de MATTOS, J.D.F. : O Codigo civil Argentino em face do direito Brasileiro. Revista da faculdade de direito 32 : 259-288, maio-agosto 1936.

WYLER, M. : Les voies d'exécution au Brésil (procès d'exécution, saisie, distribution par contribution, faillite, concordat). Bulletin trimestriel de la Société de législation comparée 65 : 282-296, juillet-septembre 1936.

WYLER, M. : La nouvelle Constitution des Etats-Unis de Brésil du 16 juillet 1934. Revue de droit public 43 : 706-722, octobre-novembre-décembre 1936.

AZEVEDO, P. : Der Verlagsvertrag nach brasilianischem Recht. Zeitschrift für ausländisches und internationales Privatrecht 11 : 77-82, Heft 1-2, 1937.

SAMPAIO, R., e AZEVEDO, N. : Paracer sobre o projecto de codigo criminal dos Estados Unidos do Brasil. Revista da faculdade de direito (Universidade de São Paolo) 33 : 613-630, setembre-dezembro 1937.

FARIA, A. de : Da competencia de justiça federal nas questões testamentarias do direito internacional privado. Revista de direito civil, commercial e criminal 126 : 230-246, outubro-novembro-dezembro 1937.

WYLER, M. : La constitution du Brésil di 10 novembre 1937. Nulletin trimestriel de la Société de législation comparée 66 : 322-336, octobre-décembre 1937.

PALOPOLI, N. : La nuova costituzione brasiliana. Echi e commenti 18 : 1003-1005, 25 novembre 1937.

CRAWFORD, H.P. : The new Brazilian Constitution. U.S. Commerce reports : 939, 946, 27 November 1937.

Le projet de Code pénitentiaire du Brésil. Revue de science criminelle et de droit pénal comparé 3 : 182-183, janvier-mars 1938.

MESSINEO, A. : La nuova costituzione brasiliana. Civiltà cattolica 89 : 429-441, 5 marzo 1938.

CHIMIENTI, P. : La nuova costituzione degli Stati Uniti del Brasile. Rivista di diritto pubblico 30 : 133-142, marzo 1938.

WYLER, M. : Le statut des étrangers aux Etats-Unis du Brésil. Nouvelle revue de droit international privé 5 : 239-255, avril-mai-juin 1938.

MACHADO, A. : Projeto do codigo criminal brasileiro. Revista da faculdade de direito 34 : 193-494, maio-agosto 1938.

ALCORTE, C.A. : El régimen jurídico de la nacionalidad en el Brasil y en la Argentina. Revista argentina de derecho internacional 1 : 27-47, julio-agosto-septiembre 1938.

Brazilian law on nationality. Bulletin of the Pan American Union 72 : 489-490, August 1938.

Ley brasilena sobre nacionalidad. Boletín de la Unión Panamericana 72 : 602, octubre de 1938.

NATIONAL LAW - COUNTRIES

MOSCOTE, J.D. : La nueva Constitución Brasileña. Universidad de Panama : 73-88, octubre 1938.

WYLER, M. : Le droit des successions au Brésil. Bulletin trimestriel de la Société de législation comparée 67 : 365-401, octobre-décembre 1938.

GUERIOS, J.F.M. : Comentarios á lei de nacionali - dade. Revista de direito 130 : 25-31, outubro a dezembro 1938.

WYLER, M. : La séparation des époux en droit brésilien (desquite). Nouvelle revue de droit international privé 6 : 70-84, janvier-juin 1939.

Décret-loi No. 479 du 9 juin 1938, modifiant celui du 25 avril 1938, relatif à l'expulsion des étrangers (arch. Judiciario LXVII, p. 84). Nouvelle revue de droit international privé 5 : 675-676, juillet-août-septembre 1939.

BULGARIA

Bulgarien - Übersicht über die wesentliche Gesetzgebung 1933/1934. Zeitschrift für osteuropäisches Recht 1 : 421-423, Februar 1935.

Décrets-lois promulgués du ler juillet au 31 décembre 1934. Bulletin trimestriel de la Société de législation comparée 64 : 274-278, avril-juin 1935.

Bulgarien - Übersicht über die wesentliche Gesetzgebung in den ersten 3 Vierteljahren 1935. Zeitschrift für osteuropäisches Recht 2 : 326-330, Dezember 1935.

STAINOF, P. : La situation constitutionnelle en Bulgarie après le coup d'État de mai 1934. Annuaire de l'Institut international de droit public : 577-586, 1935.

BRAUNIAS, K. : Die öffentlich-rechtliche Gesetzgebung des unparteilichen nationalen Regimes in Bulgarien (Contd.). Archiv des öffentlichen Rechts 27 : 81-109, Heft 1, 1936.
Contians German translation of relevant recent Bulgarian laws.

Tabelle der vom Königreich Bulgarien abgeschlossen internationalen Verträge vom 1. 1. 1929-31.12.1935. Zeitschrift für osteuropäisches Recht 2 : 469-478, Februar 1936.

DIKOW, L. : Die verfassungsrechtliche Lage Bulgariens nach dem Staatsstreich vom 19. Mai 1934. Zeitschrift der Akademie für deutsches Recht 3 : 558-562, Juni 1936.

VENEDIKOV, P. : Der strafrechtliche Schutz des Staates in Bulgarien. Zeitschrift für osteuropäisches Recht 3 : 135-148, September 1936.

Bulgarien - Übersicht über die Gesetzgebung im 4. Vierteljahr 1935 und in den ersten 3 Vierteljahren 1936. Zeitschrift für osteuropäisches Recht 3 : 404-409, Dezember 1936.

SLIVENSKY, I.G. : La nouvelle loi bulgare sur l'extradition. Revue de droit international et de législation comparée 18 : 184-194, No. 1, 1937.

KOJUCHAROFF, A. : Gerichtlicher und aussergerichtlicher Vergleich - Eine rechtsvergleichende Studie mit besonderer Berücksichtigung des bulgarischen Rechts. Zeitschrift für vergleichende Rechtswissenschaft 52 : 154-171, Heft 1, 1937.

VENEDIKOV, P. : Das bulgarische Gesetz über den Arbeitsvertrag vom 8. September 1936. Zeitschrift für osteuropäisches Recht 3 : 497-505, Februar 1937.

GORANOW, I.B. : Die Gesetzgebung in Bulgarien im Jahre 1936. Internationales Anwaltsblatt 23 : 28-29, März 1937.

JOHNSTONE, W.C. : The status of foreign concessions and settlements in the treaty ports of China. American political science review 31 : 942-947, October 19 1937.

Das neue Wahlgesetz in Bulgarien. Europäische Stimmen 11 : 647-649, Erstes Novemberheft 1937.

Bulgarien - Übersicht über die wesentliche Gesetzgebung im 4. Vierteljahr 1936 und in den ersten 3 Vierteljahren 1937. Zeitschrift für osteuropäisches Recht 4 : 296-300, November 1937.

STAÏNOV, P. : Le droit public en Bulgarie en 1935-1936. Annuaire de l'Institut international de droit public : 163-171, 1937.

STAÏNOV, P. : Das Staatsrecht Bulgariens nach dem Weltkrieg. Jahrbuch des öffentlichen Rechts der Gegenwart 24 : 251-265, 1937.

DANEFF, S. : Le mariage en Bulgarie. Bulletin de l'Institut juridique international 38 : 5-6, janvier 1938.

KOJUCHAROFF, A. : Interkonfessionnelle und internationalprivatrechtliche Betrachtung zum Eherecht in Bulgarien (mit einem Überblick über die Rechtslage der bulgarischen Kirche). Zeitschrift für osteuropäisches Recht 4 : 401-415, Januar 1938.

STAÏNOV, P. : Das bulgarische Wahlgesetz vom 22. Oktober 1937. Zeitschrift für osteuropäisches Recht 4 : 537-543, März 1938.

Bulgarien - Übersicht über die wesentliche Gesetzgebung im 4. Vierteljahr 1937 und in den ersten 3 Vierteljahren 1938. Zeitschrift für osteuropäisches Recht 5 : 306-308, November 1938.

DIKOFF, L. : Neue Entwicklungstendenzen des bulgarischen orthodoxen Eherechtes. Zeitschrift für vergleichende Rechtswissenschaft 53 : 291-310, 3./4. Heft 1939.

KOJUCHAROFF, A. : Die Scheriatsgerichte in Bulgarien. Zeitschrift für osteuropäisches Recht 5 : 671-680, Mai 1939.

RUSCOFF, D. : Bulgaria - anno 1939. Istituto italiano di studi legislativi, Legislazione internazionale 8 : 1129-1141, tomo 11, 1939.
Index of laws and summaries.

Bulgarien - Übersicht über die wesentliche Gesetzgebung im 4. Vierteljahr 1938 und in den ersten 3 Vierteljahren 1939. Zeitschrift für osteuropäisches Recht 6 : 208-209, November-Dezember 1939.

NATIONAL LAW - COUNTRIES

CANADA

"I'm alone" case. U.S. Department of State Press releases 12 : 16-20, January 12, 1935.

JENKS, C.W. : The constitutional capacity of Canada to give effect to international labour conventions. Journal of comparative legislation and international law 17 : 12-30, February 1935.

STEVENSON, J.A. : An urgent Canadian reform. Fortnightly 138 : 308-318, March 1935.
Revision of the Constitution.

JENKS, C.W. : The Dominion jurisdiction in respect of criminal law as a basis for social legislation in Canada. Canadian bar review 13 : 270-280, May 1935.

FABRE-SURVEYER, E. : La conception du droit international privé d'après la doctrine et la pratique au Canada. Académie de droit international, Recueil des cours 53 : 181-282, III, 1935.

DEMOGUE, R., et LEPAULLE, P. : Jurisprudence des cours du Canada. Revue trimestrielle de droit civil 35 : 565-575, avril-juin 1936.

BATY, T. : The history of Canadian nationality. Journal of comparative legislation and international law 18 : 195-203, November 1936.

SIEGFRIED, A. : Le statut international du Canada. Revue d'histoire politique et constitutionnelle 1 : 39-54, janvier-mars 1937.

HENEMAN, H.J. : Dominion disallowance of provincial legislation in Canada. American political science review 31 : 92-96, February 1937.

RAY, J. : La structure fédérative du Canada et les conventions internationales du travail. Affaires étrangères 7 : 79-82, février 1937.

ROWELL, N.W. : The place and functions of the judiciary in our Canadian Constitution. Canadian bar review 15 : 57-67, February 1937.

The Privy Council and Canada. Fortnightly 141 : 464-475, April 1937.

DEMOGUE, R., et LEPAULE, P. : Jurisprudence des cours du Canada. Revue trimestrielle de droit civil 36 : 507-514, avril-juin 1937.

MacDONALD, C.V. : The Canadian Constitution seventy years after. Canadian bar review 15 : 401-427, June 1937.

MacKENZIE, N.A.M. : Canada and the treaty-making power. Canadian bar review 15 : 436-454, June 1937.

HYDE, C.C. : Canada's "water-tight compartments". American journal of international law 31 : 466-468, July 1937.
The carrying out of commitments accepted by treaty.

FENWICK, C.G. : The wuestion of Canadian participation in Inter-American Conferences. American journal of international law 31 : 473-476, July 1937.

JENNINGS, W.I. : Constitutional interpretation - The experiences of Canada. Harvard law review 51 : 1-39, November 1937.

MacKENZIE, N. : Canada - The treaty-making power. British year book of international law 18 : 172-175, 1937.

Report of the Ontaria Commissioners on uniformity of legislation. Canadian bar review 16 : 43-51, January 1938.

STEWART, R.B. : Canada and international labour conventions. American journal of international law 32 : 36-62, January 1938.

WILLIS, J. : Statute interpretation in a nutshell. Canadian bar review 16 : 1-27, January 1938.

SPENCER, R.C. : The unicameral legislature of Ontario. American political science review 32 : 67-80, February 1938.

FALCONBRIDGE, J.D. : Canadà - Anni 1933-1936. Istituto di studi legislativi; giurisprudenza comparata di diritto internazionale privato 3 : 149-263, 1938.

DAGGETT, A.P. : Treaty legislation in Canada. Canadian bar review 16 : 159-184, March 1938.

RICHARDSON, B.V. : The Canadian law of civil aviation. Journal of air law 9 : 201-219, April 1938.

McWILLIAMS, R.F. : The amendment of the Constitution. Canadian bar review 16 : 466-475, June 1938.

SIMSARIAN, J. : The diversion of waters affecting the United States and Canada. American journal of international law 32 : 488-518, July 1938.

LEPAULLE, P. : Chronique de jurisprudence canadienne. Revue trimestrielle de droit civil 37 : 511-514, juillet-septembre 1938.

NICHOLLS, G.V.V. : The Bills of Exchange Act and novation in the Province of Quebec. Canadian bar review 16

NICHOLLS, G.V.V. : Mediation, conciliation and arbitration of labor disputes in Canada. Arbitration journal 2 : 375-287 (sic), October 1938.

DAS, S.K. : The Canadian experience and the treaty-making power in the Government of India Act, 1935. Journal of comparative legislation and international law 20 : 204-209, November 1938.

PALMER, K.B. : Securities legislation in Canada. Journal of comparative legislation and international law 20 : 230-241, November 1938.

NICHOLLS, G.V.V. : The Canadian law and practice with regard to arbitration clauses. Arbitration journal 3 : 60-68, January 1939.

KENNEDY, W.P.M. : "The Kingdom of Canada". Canadian bar review 17 : 1-6, January 1939.

JOHNSON, W.S. : De l'usage ou coutume en matière de contrats. Revue critique de droit international 34 : 35-49, janvier-mars 1939.

NICHOLLS, G.V.V. : The law governing conditional sales in Canada. Journal of comparative legislation and international law 21 : 1-10, February 1939.

MacDONALD, V.C. : Constitutional interpretation and extrinsic evidence. Canadian bar review 17 : 77-93, February 1939.

NATIONAL LAW - COUNTRIES

DEL MARMOL, C. : L'administration de la faillite au Canada. Annuario di diritto comparato e di studi legislativi 14 : 257-310, fasc. 3, 1939.

EWART, T.S. : The Kingdom of Canada. Canadian bar review 17 : 178-180, March 1939.

GETTYS, L., and KEY, V.O. : Dominion grants to the Canadian provinces. State government 12 : 63-65, 74, April 1939.

GRAY, V.E. : "The O'Connor Report" on the British North America Act, 1867. Canadian bar review 17 : 309-337, May 1939.

POWER, K.W. : The Office of Attorney-General. Canadian bar review 17 : 416-429, June 1939.

LEPAULLE, P. : Chronique de jurisprudence canadienne. Revue trimestrielle de droit civil 38 : 831-843, juillet-septembre 1939.

MONTGOMERY, W.S. : Noteworthy changes in statute law, 1930. Canadian bar review 17 : 513-540, September 1939.

O'CONNOR, K.E. : A review of Canadian legislation 1939. U.S. Department of State, Comparative law series 2 : 397-405, September 1939.

McWILLIAMS, R.F. : The Privy Council and the Constitution. Canadian bar review 17 : 579-582, October 1930.

HOPKINS, E.R. : Administrative justice in Canada. Canadian bar review 17 : 619-637, November 1939.

WILLIS, J. : Administrative law and the British North America Act. Harvard law review 53 : 251-281, December 1939.

CHILE

IZGUIERDO, G. : Le droit public chilien dans la décade de 1925 à 1935. Annuaire de l'Institut international de droit public : 138-158, 1936.

ALESSANDRI RODRIGUEZ, A. : Le régime matrimonial de droit commun au Chili. Semaine internationale de droit, Travaux : 63-97 (section 4), 1937.

IZQÚIERDO, A. : Chili - Chronique constitutionelle de l'année 1936. Annuaire de l'Institut international de droit public 172-178, 1937.

MARCHANT, A. : Aviation in Chile. Air law review 9 : 160-180, April 1938.

SCHNIEDERKÖTTER, T. : Der chilenisch-peruanische Auslieferungsvertrag und das interamerikanische Strafrecht. Zeitschrift für Völkerrecht 23 : 165-177, Heft 2, 1939.

CHINA

CHANG, T.C. : Inheritance in China. Iowa law review 20 : 411-415, January 1935.

LIANG, L. : Le développement du droit en Chine depuis 1900. Orient et occident 1 : 24-33, 1935.

PADOUX, G. : Le nouveau code pénal chinois. Revue internationale de droit pénal 12 : 211-226, Nos. 2-3, 1935.

WANG, S.Y. : The revised criminal code. China critic 9 : 37-39, April 11, 1935.

BÜNGER : Die Rechtsstellung der Ausländer in China. Zeitschrift für ausländisches öffentliches Recht und Völkerrecht (Berichte und Urkunden) 5 : 477-488, Mai 1935.

China - The new criminel code. Oriental affairs 4 : 5-6, July 1935.

La première conférence judiciaire chinoise. Revue nationale chinoise 23 : 165-175, 14 octobre 1935.

BRITTON, R.S. : Chinese interstate intercourse before 700 B.C. American journal of international law 29 : 616-635, October 1935.

China's new stamp-taxlaw - A question of liability. Oriental affairs 4 : 161-163, October 1935.

PING-SHEUNG, F. : Les principes du Kuomintang et la récente législation chinoise. Revue nationale chinoise 23 : 355-360, 14 novembre 1935.

CHAN, H. : Principles of international law as incorporated in the Chinese municipal law. China law review 8 : 255-266, February 1936.

WULLWEBER, H. : Rückblick auf die Gesetzgebung Chinas im Jahre 1935. Orient et occidental 2 : 251-252, février 1936.

WULLWEBER, H. : Probleme des Chinesischen Strafrechts. Orient et occident 2 : 383-386, Nos. 11-12, 1936.

WULLWEBER, H. : Der Geltungsbereich des chinesischen Strafgesetzbuches. Ostasiatische Rundschau 17 : 72-74, 1. Februar 1936.

The United States court for China. Harvard law review 49 : 793-797, March 1936.

WULLWEBER, H. : Die chinesische Reichsjustizkonferenz 1935. Ostasiatische Rundschau 17 : 126-128, 1. März 1936.

BÜNGER, K. : Die wirtschaftsrechtliche Gesetzgebung der chinesischen Nationalregierung im Jahre 1935. Ostasiatische Rundschau 17 : 209-210, 15. April 1936.

ESCARRA, J. : Le gouvernement de la Chine moderne. Année politique 11 : 1-29, avril 1936.

Chine - Lois et règlements principaux édictés par le Gouvernement national de la République de Chine en 1934. Bulletin trimestriel de la Société de législation comparée 65 : 269-273, avril-juin 1936.

L'arbitrage en Chine. Revue nationale chinoise 25 : 129-132, 1 mai 1936.

The revised draft constitution. China critic 13 : 151-152, 14 May 1936.

BÜNGER, K. : Das Verhältnis zwischen Partei und Staat in China. Zeitschrift für ausländisches öffentliches Recht und Völkerrecht 6 : 286-302, Mai 1936.

The draft constitution of the Republic of China. Council of international affairs. Information bulletin 1 : 1-33, 11 May 1936.

NATIONAL LAW - COUNTRIES

LAVAGNA, A. : Il nuovo codice penale della Repubblica della Cina. Asiatica 2 : 118-133, maggio-giugno 1936.

CHAN, H. : Citizenship in China. China law review 9 : 38-46, June 1936.

L'assemblée des représentants du peuple du 12 novembre prochain: son fonctionnement et sa composition. Revue nationale chinoise 25 : 319-321, ler juin 1936.

KAHN, R.E. : Foreign justice persons in the contemplation of Chinese law. China law review 10 : 1-14, June 1936.

PADOUX, G. : Le nouveau code pénal chinois. Revista de direito civil, commercial e criminal 121 : 3-16, julho 1936.

SHEN, N. : The local government of China. Chinese social and political science review 20 : 163-201, July 1936.

LIU, S.F.F. : Laws and courts in China. China critic 14 : 13-16, July 1936.

CHAN, H. : Modern legal education in China. China law review 9 : 142-148, September 1936.

RIASANOVSKY, V.A. : The code of Northern Mongolia "Khalkha Djirom". Chinese social and political review 20 : 335-368, October 1936.

Le droit chinois - Conception et évolution - Institutions législatives et judiciaires - Science et enseignements. Revue nationale chinoise 8 : 32-38, 1 octobre 1936.

CHEN CHANG HENG : China's legislation - Past and future. People's tribune 25 : 147-151, November 1, 1936.

TANG, E.C. : Judicial reforms in China - Council of International Affairs. Information bulletin 3 : 1-27, January 11 1937.

La conception chinoise de la loi. Europe nouvelle 20 : 70-71, 16 janvier 1937.

PHILLIPS, G.G. : Municipal government of international settlement in Shanghai. China law review 9 : 403-413, March 1937.

SHENG, R.C.W. : The Legislative Yuan of China to-day. China law review 9 : 297-305, March 1937.

PEAKE, C.H. : Recent studies on Chinese law. Political science quarterly 52 : 117-138, March 1937.

BÜNGER, K. : Das mandschurische Patentgesetz. Ostasiatische Rundschau 18 : 129-131, 1. März 1937.

HSIA, C.L. : Background and features of the draft constitution of China. Council of international affairs. Information bulletin 3 : 195-219, April 11, 1937.

BETZ, H. : Der Stand der Justizreform in China. Zeitschrift der Akademie für deutsches Recht 4 : 244-245, 15. April 1937.

CHEN, C.-M. : The Chinese executive. Chinese social and political science review 21 : 34-64, April 1937.

CHIANG, H.-C. : Hauptbestimmung des chinesischen Wahlgesetzes für die Volksvertretung in der Nationalversammlung. Ostasiatische Rundschau 18 : 236-238, 1. Mai 1937.

CHIANG, H.C. : Chinas Weg zu einer eigenen Verfassung. Zeitschrift der Akademie für deutsches Recht 4 : 304-306, 15. Mai 1937.

LÉVY, R. : Le droit chinois. Affaires étrangères 7 : 315-320, mai 1937.

SUN FO : Les récents travaux du yuan législatif. Revue nationale chinoise 29 : 223-236, ler juin 1937.

WANG SHAN-YU : We demand the abolition of extraterritoriality. China critic 17 : 296-298, 24 June 1937.

NYI, T.Y. : The present system of notaries in China. China law review 10 : 91-99, June 1936.

RIASANOVSKY, V.A. : Customary law of the Kirghiz. Chinese social and political science review 21 : 190-220, July 1937.

RIASANOVSKY, M.A. : Le droit mongol. Bulletin trimestriel de la société de législation comparée 66 : 237-262, juillet-septembre 1937.

WULLWEBER, H. : Neue Mandschurische Gesetze. Ostasiatische Rundschau 18 : 409-410, 1. August 1937.

BÜNGER, K. : Die chinesischen Vorschriften über Patente und industrieförderung. Ostasiatische Rundschau 18 : 407-409, 1. August 1937.

Shanghai in torment. Oriental affairs 8 : 126-140, September 1937.

WANG, C.C. : Extraterritoriality in China. Quarterly review 269 : 246-257, October 1937.

WULLWEBER, H. : Entwurf einer Zivilprozessordnung in der Mandschurei (Nach dem Stande vom 9. September 1937). Ostasiatische Rundschau 18 : 562-563, 1. November 1937.

The judicial system of Manchoukuo. Contemporary Manchuria 1 : 29-47, November 1937.

Judicial system of Manchoukuo. Manchuria 2 : 846-847, December 15 1937.

CHIANG H.C. : Zur Frage der zukünftigen politischen und rechtlichen Stellung des Staatsoberhauptes der Republik China auf Grund des Verfassungsentwurfs vom 5. Mai 1936. Archiv des öffentlichen Rechts 29 : 191-204, Heft 2, 1938.

Die Verfassung der "vorläufigen" Regierung. Ostasiatische Rundschau 19 : 58, 1. Februar 1938.

The legal systems of old and new China. Bombay law journal 16 : 70-79, July 1938.

Constitution du Conseil Uni de la République Chinoise. Politique de Pékin 25 : 617-619, 1 octobre 1938.

KEETON, G.W. : The progress of law reform in China (Contd.). Journal of comparative legislation and international law 20 : 210-221, November 1938.

Chinese courts in the Settlement. Oriental affairs 10 : 251-254, November 1938.
Shanghai.

PRATT, J.T. : The international settlement and the French concession at Shanghai. British year book of international law 19 : 1-18, 1938.

Das Handelsgesellschaftgesetz von Manchukuo. Ostasiatische Rundschau 20 : 65-69, 1. Februar 1939.

FRASER, C.F. : The status of the international settlement at Shanghai. Journal of comparative legislation and international law 21 : 38-53, February 1939.

HU, H.Y. : Marriage and divorce in Chinese civil code with reference to the rules of conflict of laws. Chinese social and political science review 22 : 400-427, January-March 1939.

Law reform in Manchoukuo - Progress since 1934, with particular reference to land laws. Manchuria 4 : 1329-1339, August 1, 1939.

BÜNGER, K. : Gesetzgebung und Rechtspflege in Manchukuo. Ostasiatische Rundschau 20 : 402-403, 5. September 1939.

KU TZE HSIAN : Governmental administration of Manchoukuo. Pan Pacific 3 : 22-27, October-December 1939.

COLOMBIA

BACKUS, R.C. : Legislative trends in Colombia. Tulane law review 12 : 534-551, June 1938.

Latest amendments to the Colombian Constitution. Bulletin of the Pan American union 70 : 895-898, November 1936.

La reforma penale in Colombia - I. precedenti legislativi - II. progetto di Codice penale del 1935. Giustizia penale 43 : 393-405, marzo 1937.

YEPES, J.M. : La réforme constitutionnelle colombienne. Annuaire de l'Institut international de droit public : 179-189, 1937.

HOUDOT, A. : Les mesures de sûreté dans le droit pénal de la République colombienne. Revue internationale de droit pénale 16 : 66-101, No. 1, 1939.

MEJÍA, R.G. : La reforma agraria y el Código Civil colombiano. Revista de la Academia colombiana de jurisprudencia 12 : 163-175, enero-junio 1937.

RENDÓN, G.G. : El intervencionismo de Estado en Colombia. Estudios de derecho : 39-62, abril 1939.

MATÉUS, G.N. : La reforma del código civil. Revista de la Academia colombiana de jurisprudencia 14 : V-VIII, julio y agosto 1939.

COMMONWEALTH

WADE, E.C.S. : Constitutional law. Law quarterly review 51 : 235-248, January 1935.

L'adoption en Grande-Bretagne. Bulletin de l'Institut juridique international 32 : 7-8, janvier 1935.

Englische Gesetzgebung 1933. Zeitschrift für ausländisches Recht und internationales Privatrecht 9 : 428-461, Heft 3, 1935.

Interpretation of a foreign commercial usage. Law journal 79 : 268-269, April 20 1935.

Claim of the British ship "I'm alone" v. United States. American journal of international law 29 : 326-331, April 1935.

ERDSIEK, G. : Das uneheliche Kind im englischen Recht. Deutsche Juristen-Zeitung 40 : 735-739, 15. Juni 1935.

KEITH, A.B. : The privy council and the Irish Free State. Spectator : 1056-1057, 21 June 1935.

Appeals to the Privy Council. Law journal 79 : 428-429, 22 June 1935.

MAZÉ, J. : La législation anglaise du mariage des indigènes dans l'Afrique orientale en regard du droit canonique et des coutumes des tribus. Outre-mer 7 : 172-200, juin-septembre 1935.

ASQUITH, C. : The Dominions and the Privy Council. Nineteenth Century 118 : 1-12, July 1935.

AUDINET, E. : L'exécution des jugements étrangers en Angleterre d'après la loi du 13 avril 1933 et la convention franco-britannique du 18 janvier 1934. Journal du droit international 62 : 805-824, juillet-octobre 1935.

KENNEDY, W.P.M. : Annual survey of books on the constitutional and administrative law of the British Commonwealth. Canadian historical review 16 : 309-317, September 1935.

ROBERTS, C.C. : Witchcraft and colonial legislation. Africa 8 : 488-494, October 1935.

ORDE-BROWNE, G.S.J. : Witchcraft and British colonial law. Africa 8 : 481-487, October 1935.

DIXON, O. : The law and the constitution. Law quarterly review 51 : 590-614, October 1935.

BUCKLAND, W.W. : The duty to take care. Law quarterly review 9 : 637-649, October 1935.

MANNHEIM, H. : Neuere Entwicklungstendenzen im englischen Pressrecht. Geistiges Eigentum 1 : 283-294, Oktober-November 1935.

KEITH, B. : Notes on imperial constitutional law. Journal of comparative legislation and international law 17 : 269-280, November 1935.

CRAWFORD, J.D. : A ministry of justice? Nineteenth century 118 : 617-627, November 1935.

CASTBERG, F. : Britisch-norwegische Divergenzen über die Ausdehnung des norwegischen Küstenmeeres. Völkerbund und Völkerrecht 2 : 441-446, November 1935.

KEITH, B. : Change from protectorate to colony status. West African review 6 : 7-8, December 1935.

JENKS, C.W. : The proposed peace act. Grotius society, Problems of peace and war 21 : 1-21, 1935.
The proposed British Act.

NATIONAL LAW - COUNTRIES

SCHAPERA, I. : Land tenure among the natives of Bechuanaland Protectorate. Zeitschrift für vergleichende Rechtswissenschaft 51 : 130-159, Heft 1-2, 1936.

BOYD, T.S. : The law and constitution of Sarawak. Journal of comparative legislation and international law 18 : 60-70, February 1936.

LEE, R.W. : Cases on the conflict of laws from the law reports of the British dominions, 1933-1934. Journal of comparative legislation and international law 18 : 101-109, February 1936.

JENNINGS, W.I. : The statute of Westminster and appeals to the Privy Council. Law quarterly review 52 : 173-188, April 1936.

DIXON, O. : The Statute of Westminster, 1931. Supplement to the Australian law journal 10 : 96-112, October 15 1936.

WINFIELD, P.H. : Recent legislation on the English law of tort. Canadian bar review 14 : 639-662, October 1936.

The Public Order bill. Law journal 82 : 346, November 21 1936.

KEITH, B. : Notes on imperial constitutional law. Journal of comparative legislation and international law 18 : 277-288, November 1936.

HENNESSY, J. : Comment l'Angleterre empêche la diffamation. Europe nouvelle 19 : 1160-1162, 21 novembre 1936.
La loi britannique.

SASTRY, K.R.R. : Foreign judgments and proceedings. Bombay law journal 14 : 245-250, November 1936.

GUPTA, D.C. : Juristic conception of Dominion Status. Calcutta review 61 : 219-230, 339-352, November, December 1936.

Debate in British House of Commons on Public Order Bill, 16 November 1936. International conciliation : 5-110, No. 326, January 1937.

HILLE, W. van : Commentaire de la convention anglo-belge du 2 mai 1934 sur l'exécution réciproque des jugements. Belgique judiciaire 95 : 66-92, 1-15 février 1937.

PHILLIPS, G.G. : Since the statute of Westminster. Cambridge law journal 6 : 182-192, No. 2, 1937.

FOSTER, J. : Abdication and Commonwealth. Legal and constitutional problems. Nineteenth century 121 : 234-249, February 1937.

GRAVESON, R.H. : The doctrine of evasion of the law in England and America. Journal of comparative legislation and international law 19 : 21-31, February 1937.
Domiciliary prohibitions against marriages.

STRICKLAND, P. : A comparative study of the anti-trust laws of the British Dominions and of their administration (Contd.). Journal of comparative legislation and international law 19 : 52-76, February 1937.

JENNINGS, W.I. : The abdication of King Edward VIII. Politica 2 : 287-311, March 1937.

COOKE, C.A. : The reform of the law - The problem of civil litigation. Nineteenth century 121 : 383-393, March 1937.

GUTTERIDGE, H.C. : La Convention franco-britannique pour l'exécution réciproque des jugements. Revue critique de droit internationa 32 : 369-392, avril-juin 1937.

JENNINGS, W.I. : The abdication and the constitution. Political quarterly 18 : 165-179, April-June 1937.

AMOS, M.S. : The common law and the civil law in the British Commonwealth of Nations. Harvard law review 50 : 1249-1274, June 1937.

COREA, G.C.S. : Ceylon's present constitution. Asiatic review 33 : 653-656, July 1937.

BROWN, R.J. : The constitutional law and history of broadcasting in Great Britain. Air law review 8 : 177-200, July 1937.

A blunt bodkin. New statesman and nation 14 : 271-272, 21 August 1937.
On the Report of Department Committee on joint stock system.

MOLTKE : Verfassungsrechtliche Fragen des Empire im Zusammenhang mit dem Thronwechsel, insbesondere in der Süd-Afrikanischen Union. Zeitschrift für ausländisches öffentliches Recht und Völkerrecht 7 : 634-643, August 1937.

LATEY, J. : The Matrimonial Causes Act, 1937 (Contd.). Law journal 84 : 154-155, September 4 1937.

RENÉ-LECLERC, C. : La suppression des capitulations britanniques au Maroc. Correspondance d'Orient 30 : 397-402, septembre 1937.

WADE, E.C.S. : The reform of the law (Contd.) - Administrative tribunals. Nineteenth century 122 : 304-316, September 1937.

KENNEDY, W.P.M. : Annual survey of the literature of constitutional and administrative law and of Empire history. Canadian historical review 18 : 313-323, September 1937.

HENEMAN, H.J. : Ministers of the Crown and the British Constitution. American political science review 31 : 929-937, October 1937.

GORELL : Church, State and divorce. Quarterly review 269 : 189-202, October 1937.

STEWART, R.B. : The Great Seal and treaty-making in the British Commonwealth. Canadian bar review 15 : 745-759, December 1937.

EASTWOOD, R.A. : The reform of the law - Legal education. Nineteenth century 123 : 53-64, January 1938.

Gesetzgebung von Hongkong im Jahre 1936. Ostasiatische Rundschau 19 : 16-19, 1. Januar 1938.

MENZIES, R.G. : The Statute of Westminster. Australian law journal 11 : 368-377, 18 February 1938.

AMOS, M. : Le Statut de Westminster. Annales de l'Institut de droit comparé de l'université de Paris 3 : 9-21, 1938.

NATIONAL LAW - COUNTRIES

STEWART, R.B. : Treaty-making procedure in the British Dominions. American journal of international law 32 : 467-487, July 1938.

STARK, W. : Staatsangehörigkeit in den britischen Dominions. Deutsche Justiz 100 : 1717-1720, 28. Oktober 1938.

BATTELLI, M. : Le premier ministre en Grande-Bretagne (Contd.). Revue d'histoire politique et constitutionnelle 2 : 477-527, octobre-décembre 1938.

BUXTON, C.R. : The government of Crown Colonies - The development of self-government. Political quarterly 9 : 516-528, October-December 1938.

JENNINGS, W.I. : The Constitution of the British Commonwealth. Political quarterly 9 : 465-479, October-December 1938.

DECUGIS, H. : L'influence des juges et des membres du barreau dur l'évolution de l'Empire britannique. Bulletin trimestriel de la Société de legislation comparée 67 : 326-335, octobre-décembre 1938.

Das Schiedsgerichtsverfahren in den Straits Settlements. Ostasiatische Rundschau 19 : 533-536, 16. November 1938.

CHEVALLIER, J.-J. : La Société des Nations britanniques. Académire de droit international, Recueil des cours 64 : 237-345, 1938, tome II.

BENTWICH, N. : Arbitration of disputes between the nations of the British Commonwealth. Arbitration journal 3 : 56-60, January 1939.

NORMAND, W.G. : Consideration of law in Scotland. Law quarterly review 55 : 358-374, July 1939.

MAUGHAN, D. : Statute of Westminster. Australian law journal 13 : 152-165, August 15 1939.

ROBBINS, R.R. : The legal status of Aden Colony and the Aden Protectorate. American journal of international law 33 : 700-715, October 1930.

LAING, L.H. : The struggle for the recognition of Dominion authority. American journal of international law 33 : 747-753, October 1939.

WILLIAMS, G.L. : Dominion legislation relating to libel and slander. Journal of comparative legislation and international law 21 : 161-178, November 1939.

The abolition of British capitulatory rights in the French Zone of Morocco. British yearbook of international law 20 : 58-82, 1939.

CUBA

ZAYDÍN, R. : El proyecto de ley presentado al consejo de estado sobre sociedades anónimas nacionales y extranjeras. Revista de derecho internacional 14 : 189-206, 30 junio 1935.

RODRIGUEZ ALVAREZ, J.R. : Transformaciones operadas en el derecho civil cubano por los gobiernos revolucionarios. Revista cubana de derecho (sección doctrinal) 12 : 164-183, julio-septiembre 1935.

DÍAZ PAIRÓ, A. : El régimen de los derechos reales y de las obligaciones en los dos ultimos años. Revista Cubana de derecho (sección doctrinal) 12 : 201-227, julio-septiembre 1935.

CORUJO, E.H. : Las transformaciones del derecho constitucional cubano desde el 12 de agosto de 1933. Revista cubana de derecho (sección doctrinal) 12 : 276-313, octubre-diciembre 1935.

Reformas de 23 de enero de 1936, a la ley constitucional de 11 de enero de 1935. Revista cubana de derecho 8 : 1-4, enero 1-31, 1936.

DÍAZ PAIRÓ, A. : Efectos de la declaración de nulidad del matrimonio por razón de ligamen anterior de uno de los cónyuges (aclarando y concluyendo). Revista Cubana de derecho (sección doctrinal) 13 : 70-100, enero-junio 1936.

CESPEDES, C.-M. de : Le statut de Cuba. Académie diplomatique internationale, Séances et travaux 9 : 54-60, Nos. 3-4, 1936.

CRAWFORD, H.P. : The corporation law of Cuba. Tulane law review 10 : 568-588, June 1936.

CHEDIAK, N. : El derecho internacional y la constitución Cubana. Revista de derecho internacional 15 : 112-135, 30 septiembre 1936.

CARRICARTE, A. de : Cuba su territorio y jurisdicción. Revista de derecho internacional 15 : 92-111, 30 septiembre 1936.

VIEITES, M.A. : Quelques mots sur le code de défense sociale de la République de Cuba. Revue internationale de droit pénale 13 : 407-413, No. 4, 1936.

MORAN, C.M. : La cuestion social en la constitución. Revista Cubana de derecho (Sección doctrina) 13 : 222-253, julio-septiembre 1936.

CORUJO, E.H. : Equilibrio entre el poder legislativo y el ejecutivo en Cuba. Revista de derecho internacional 31 : 100-124, 31 marzo 1937.

Una ley cubana de ciudadanía y extranjeria. Revista de derecho internacional 16 : 235-297, 30 junio 1937.

CZECHOSLOVAKIA

KORKISCH, F. : Die privatrechtliche Gesetzgebung in der Tsechoslowakischen Republik im Jahre 1934. Zeitschrift für ausländisches und internationales Privatrecht 9 : 238-248, Heft 1-2, 1935.

DNISTRJANSKYJ, S.: Die Rezeption des österreichischen Privatrechts in der Tschechoslovakei und im Jugoslavien. Zeitschrift für österupäisches Recht 1 : 463-490, März 1935.

DNISTRJANSKYJ, S. : Die Rezeption des österreichischen Privatrechts in der Tschechoslowakei und im Jugoslawien (Contd.). Zeitschrift für osteuropäisches Recht 1 : 561-581, 618-634, Mai, Juni 1935.

SCHWELD, E. : Die Judikatur des Obersten Verwaltungsgerichtes in Administrativsachen. Prager Juristische Zeitschrift 15 : 490-489 (sic), 1. Juliheft 1935.

HEXNER, E. : La loi tchécoslovaque sur les cartels. Bulletin de droit tchécoslovaque 4 : 50-68, ler octobre 1935.

HEDRICH : Gesetz vom 28. März 1935 über den Aufenhalt der Ausländer. Zeitschrift für osteuropäisches Recht 2 : 229-231, Oktober 1935.

OSWALD : Zuständigkeitsfragen im Verhältnis zwischen Deutschland und der Tschechoslowakei. Zeitschrift für ausländisches und internationales Privatrecht 10 : 85-88, Heft 1/3, 1936.

KORKISCH, F, F. : Die privatrechtliche Rechtsprechung in der Tschechoslowakei im Jahre 1934. Zeitschrift für ausländisches und internationales Privatrecht 10 : 140-176, Heft 1/3, 1936.

REINOLD, K. : Die Entwicklung des Pressrechts in der Tschechoslowakei. Zeitschrift für osteuropäisches Recht 2 : 449-464, 499-516, Februar, März, 1936.

SCHMIED. E. : Le jury et l'échevinage en Tchécoslovaquie. Revue internationale de droit pénal 13 : 255-269, No. 3, 1936.

CHARMATZ, H. : Die juristische Literatur in der Tschechoslowakei in den Jahren 1934-1935, und dem ersten Halbjahr 1936. Zeitschrift für ausländisches und internationales Privatrecht 10 : 606-619, Heft 4, 1936.

ADLER, F. : Verfassungsrechtliche Betrachtung anlässlich des Präsidentenwechsels. Prager juristische Zeitschrift 16 : 194-199, 1. Aprilheft 1936.

NOVACEK, V. : La Tchécoslovaquie assure sa sécurité. Europe centrale 11 : 293-295, 9 mai 1936.
Projets de lois sur la défense de l'Etat.

SWOBODA, E. : Das Eigentumsrecht im neuesten tschechoslowakischen Entwurf eines bürgerlichen Gesetzbuches. Zeitschrift der Akademie für deutsches Recht 3 : 569-571, Juni 1936.

SCHAFER, H. : Das tschechoslovakische "Staatsverteidigunggesetz". Militärwissenschaftliche Mitteilungen 67 : 467-469, Juni 1936.

GRAZIAN : Tschechoslowakei unter Ausnahmerecht. Volk und Reich 12: 456-464, Heft 6, 1936.

LEUFKE, F. : Der arbeitsrechtliche Inhalt des Gesetzes vom 13. Mai 1936 über die Verteidigung des Staates. Prager juristische Zeitschrift 16 : 445-476, 2. Juliheft 1936.

POHLE, R. : Zur Vollstreckung tschechoslowakischer Forderungen und Urteile in Deutschland. Juristische Wochenschift 65 : 1873-1975, 11. Juli 1936.

SWOBODA, E. : Der tschechoslowakische Entwurf eines allgemeines bürgerlichen Gesetzbuches in der Neufassung vom Jahre 1936. Zeitschrift für osteuropäisches Recht 3 : 7-19, Juli 1936.

SCHMIED, E. : Der strafrechtliche Schutz des Staates in der Tchechoslowakei. Zeitschrift für osteuropäisches Recht 3 : 190-206, September 1936.

DANINGER, E. : Zur Praxis des Zivilprozessrechtes in der tschechoslowakischen Republik. Internationales Anwaltsblatt 22 : 75-78, September 1936.

NEUNER, R. : Die Zivilprozessnovelle vom 16. Juni 1936. Prager juristische Zeitschrift 14 : 494-504, 1. September 1936.

Tschechoslowakei - Ubersicht die wesentliche Gesetzgebung für das 2. Halbjahr 1935 und das 1. Halbjahr 1936. Zeitschrift für osteuropäisches Recht 3 : 245-249, Oktober, 1936.

OSWALD, F. : Wechselhingabe und Eigentumsvorbehalt nach tschechoslowakischem Recht. Zeitschrift für osteuropäisches Recht 3 : 240-245, Oktober 1936.

OSWALD, F. : Die Bindung der Verwaltungsbehörden an die verwaltungsgerichtliche Rechtsprechung in der Tschechowakei. Deutsche Juristen-Zeitung 41 : 1351-1352, 15. November 1936.

KIER, H. : Das tschecoslowakische Staatsverteidigungsgesetz. Zeitschrift für ausländisches öffentliches Recht und Völkerrecht 6 : 803-828, November 1936.

WEISS, E. : Der gegenwärtige Stand der Arbeiten am Bürgerlichen Gesetzbuch. Prager Juristische Zeitschrift 16 : 686-688, 1. Dezemberheft 1936.

SANDER, F. : Das tschechoslowakische Verfassungsrecht in den Jahren 1929-1935. Jahrbuch des öffentlichen Rechts 23 : 262-342, 1936.

WEYR, F. : Tchécoslovaquie. Annuaire de l'Institut international de droit public : 459-473, 1936.
Evolution du droit constitutionnel.

GLAHN : Das Staatsverteidigungsgesetz der tschechoslowakischen Republik vom 13. Mai 1936 (Gesetzsammlung, S. 461) - Ein Beitrag zum Wehrrecht des Auslands. Zeitschrift für Wehrrecht 1 : 393-400, Januar 1937.

SWOBODA, E. : Die Reform des bürgerlichen Rechts in der Tschechoslowakei. Annuario di diritto comparato e di studi legislativi 13 : 16-29, fasc. 1, 1937.

KORKISCH, F. : Privatrechtliche Gesetzgebung der Tschechoslowakei in den Jahren 1935 und 1936. Zeitschrift für ausländisches und internationales Privatrecht 11 : 243-264, Heft 1-2, 1937.

KLEIN, O. : Die Judikatur des Obersten Verwaltungsgerichtes in Administrativsachen. Prager Juristische Zeitschrift 17 : 134-142, 1. Märzheit 1937.

SCHMIDT, H. : Wirtschaftsspionage - Bemerkungen zum Gesetz Slg. Nr. 71/1935. Prager Juristische Zeitschrift 17 : 163-179, 2. Märzheft 1937.

VESELÁ, J. : Loi du 9 avril 1935 sur l'espionage économique. Bulletin de droit tchécoslovaque 4 : 69-84, ler avril 1937.

HOCH, E. : Das tschechoslowakische Staatsverteidigungsgesetz. Wissen und Wehr : 247-260, Heft 4, 1937.

Staatsbürgerschaftsgesetz. Prager Juristische Zeitschrift 17 : 235-238, 2. Aprilheft 1937.
The Czechoslovak draft.

WÜNSCH, H. : Die Bedeutung des Begriffes "Unternehmung" und "Betrieb" im Staatsverteidigungsgesetz. Prager Juristische Zeitung 17 : 263-266, 1. Maiheft 1937.

BYSTŘICKÝ, N. : L'unification du droit privé en Tchécoslovaquie. Europe centrale 12 : 344-346, 29 mai 1937.

MASSFELLER : Die Ehescheidung von tschechoslowakischen Staatsangehörigen. Juristische Wochenschrift 66 : 1297-1299, 15/22. Mai 1937.

SWOBODA, E. : Die Gesetzanträge der Sudetendeutschen zur Sicherung der verfassungsrechtlich verbürgten Gleichberechtigung. Völkerbund und Völkerrecht 4 : 133-139, Juni 1937.

WEISS, E. : Der Entwurf einer Zivilprozessordnung und die Neuerungen im Rechtsmittelverfahren. Prager Juristische Zeitschrift 17 : 354-358, 1. Juniheft 1937.

THIELE, R. : Die verwaltungsrechtlichen Bestimmungen des tschechoslowakischen. Staatsverteidigungsgesetzes. Zeitschrift für osteuropäisches Recht 4 : 1-38, Juli 1937.

KLING, L. : Zur Reform der Verwaltungsgerichtsbarkeit in der Tschechoslowakischen Republik. Internationales Anwaltsblatt 23 : 85-89, Oktober 1937.

SCHMIED, E. : Das neue tschechoslowakische Verwaltungsstrafrecht. Prager Juristische Zeitschrift 17 : 622-626, 1. Novemberheft 1937.

KLUBEŠ, V. : Le projet du nouveau code civil en Tchécoslovaquie. Bulletin de droit tchécoslovaque 4 : 107-135, ler novembre 1937.

LAŠTAKOVA, K. : Les contrôles de l'administration publique en Tchécoslovaquie. Bulletin de droit tchécoslovaque 4 : 136-150, ler novembre 1937.

Der Pressburger Unifikationskongress. Prager Juristische Zeitschrift 17 : 666-667, 2. Novemberheft 1937.

BRAUNIAS, K. : Karpathorussische und sudetendeutsche Autonomie. Völkerbund und Völkerrecht 4 : 487-493, Dezember 1937.

SOLNAŘ, V. : L'unification du droit pénal en Tchécoslovaquie. Revue internationale de doctrine et de législation pénale comparée 2 : 24-29, No. 1, 1938.

FOLTIN, E. : Der tschechoslowakische Strafgesetzentwurf. Juristische Blätter 67 : 10-12, 8. Januar 1938.

BEUVE-MÉRY, H. : Le régime de la presse en Tchécoslovaquie. Annales de l'Institut de droit comparé de l'université de Paris 3 : 229-243, 1938.

REINOLD, K. : Die rechtliche Stellung der Ausländer im tschechoslowakischen Erwerbsleben. Zeitschrift für osteuropäisches Recht 4 : 566-579, März 1938.

RAUCHBERG, H. : Das neue Gesetz über due tschechoslowakische Staatsbürgerschaft. Prager Juristische Zeitschrift 18 : 226-235, 2. Aprilheft 1938.

HOCHBERGER, E. : Das tschechoslowakische internationale und interprovinziale Privatrecht im Lichte der Rechtsprechung des tschechoslowakischen Obersten Gerichtes (mit Berücksichtigung der Bestimmunggen des Entwurfes zum ABGB). Zeitschrift für osteuropäisches Recht 4 : 620-649, April 1938.

FLOREAN, C. : Apropos du projet de code de commerce unifié pour la Tchécoslovaquie. Annales de droit commercial 47 : 175-180, avril-juin 1938.

WESTPHALEN-FÜRSTENBERG, E. : Eine Frage über die Selbstverwaltung der Gemeinden. Prager Juristische Zeitschrift 18 : 322-326, 1. Juniheft 1938.

BRAUNAIS, K. : Das tschechoslowakische Verfassungsleben im Spiegel der Demokratie. Zeitschrift für Politik 28 : 348-370, Juni/Juli 1938.

SCHMIED, E. : Das neue Militärstrafgesetzbuch. Prager juristische Zeitschrift 18 : 428-492, 2. Juliheft 1938.

SWOBODA, E. : Der tschechoslowakische Entwurf über Erwerb und Verlust der Staatsbürgerschaft. Zeitschrift der Akademie für deutsches Recht 5 : 556-557, 1. August 1938.

OSWALD : Praktische Fragen aus dem Ehescheidungsrechte im Verhältnis zwischen dem Deutschen Reiche und der Tschechoslowakei. Juristische Wochenschrift 67 : 2119-2123, 13./20. August 1938.

LAŠTOVKA, K. : L'administration public de la République tchéchoslovaque dans les vingt premières années de son existence. Bulletin de droit tchécoslovaque 5 : 10-24, 1 octobre 1938.

NEMBANER, Z. : L'évolution du droit constitutionnel tchécoslovaque jusqu'à fin juillet 1938. Bulletin de droit tchécoslovaque 5 : 1-9. ler octobre 1938.

La Tchécoslovaquie de Versailles à Munich. Revue de droit international 12 353-749, octobre-novembre-décembre 1938.

FÉAUX de la CROIX, E. : Der deutsch-tschechoslowakische Staatsangehörigkeits- und Optionsvertrag vom 20. November 1938. Deutsche Justiz 100 : 1940 -1948, 9. Dezember 1938.

La loi constitutionnelle sur l'autonomie de la Slovaquie, adoptée le 19 novembre 1938 par l'Assemblée Nationale de la République tchécoslovaque. Europe centrale 13 : 735-736, 15 décembre 1938.

VENTURINI, G.C. : La nuova situazione giuridica dei territori della Cecoslovacchia. Diritto internazionale : 74-82, 1938.

BRAUNIAS, K. : Die verfassungsrechtliche Stellung der Slowakei. Nation und Staat 12 : 217-236, Januar 1939.

OSWALD : Der deutsch-tschechoslowakische Staatsvertrag über Staatsangehörigkeits-und Optionsfragen- Juristische Wochenschrift 68 : 473-476, 25. Februar 1939.

February 18, 1939. Budapesti közlöny : 2-4, február 28, 1939.
Convention au sujet du règlement des questions de nationalité en relation avec la réunion du territoire adjugé à la Homgrie en vertu de la décision arbitrale de Vienne du 2 novembre 1938. (Texte français et hongrois).

GLOBKE, H. : Die Regelung der Staatsangehörigkeitsverhältnisse und der Schutz der Volksgruppen nach den deutsch-tschecho-slowakischen Vereinbarungen v. 20. November 1938. Zeitschrift für osteuropäisches Recht 5 : 473-486, Februar 1939.

RAUPACH, H. : Staat, Gesellschaft und Fridensordnung in Böhmen. Zeitschrift für gesamte Staatswissenschaft 99 : 721-737, Heft 4, 1939.

Tscheko-Slovakei - Ergänzungstabelle der von der Tschecho-Slovakei bis zum 31. Dezember 1931 abgeschlossenen Verträge. Zeitschrift für osteuropäisches Recht 5 : 728-739, Mai 1939.

RABL, K.O. : Zur jüngsten Entwicklung der slowakischen Frage. Zeitschrift für ausländisches öffentliches Recht und Völkerrecht 9 : 284-321, Juli 1939.

Attività dello Stato slovacco - La nuova costituzione. Relazioni internazionali 5 : 613-614, 12 agosto 1939.

SCHMIED, E. : Das Strafrecht im Protektorat Böhmen und Mähren. Zeitschrift für osteuropäisches Recht 6 : 69-96, August 1939.

HOCHBERGER, E. : Die deutsche Gerichtsbarkeit im Protektorat Böhmen und Mähren. Zeitschrift für osteuropäisches Recht 6 : 121-128, September/Oktober 1939.

Protektorat Böhmen und Mähren. Ubersicht über die wesentliche Gesetzgebung vom 15. März 1939 bis zum 30. Juni 1939. Zeitschrift für osteuropäisches Recht 6 : 132-134, September/Oktober 1939.

TRÖGER, K. : Zum Aufbau der deutschen Gerichtsbarkeit im Protektorat Böhmen und Mähren. Deutsches Recht 2 : 319-321, Oktober-November 1939.

BEITZKE, G. : Die Scheldung von Angehörigen des Protektorats Böhmen und Mähren. Deutsches Recht 9 : 1902-1904, 4. November 1939.

MARKUS, J. : Le traité germano-tchécoslovaque du 15 mars 1939 à la lumière du droit international. Revue générale de droit international public 46 : 653-665, novembre-décembre 1939.

LORENZ, M. : Die Neuregelung der Strafgerichtsbarkeit im Protektorat Böhmen und Mähren. Deutsche Justiz 101 : 1821-1823, 8. Dezember 1939.

DENMARK

BRÜEL, E. : Lillebaeltsbroen og folkeretten. Nordisk tidsskrift for international ret 6 : 129-142, fasc. 2-3, 1935.

BRÜEL, E. : Die Brücke über den Kleinen Belt uns das Völkerrecht. Zeitschrift für Völkerrecht 19 : 327-332, Heft 3, 1935.

FAVILLI, V. : Le nouveau pont sur le Petit-Belt du point de vue du droit international. Revue de droit international et de législation comparée 63 : 633-644, No. 3, 1936.

DELMAR, W. : Die dänischen Vertragsbestimmungen verglichen mit den Bestimmungen des Bürgerlichen Gesetzbuchs. Zeitschrift der Akademie für deutsches Recht 3 : 729-737, August 1936.

Danemark - Commission de la Constitution - Loi du 3 février 1937 (Résumé). Informations constitutionnelles et parlementaires 2 : 168-169, 31 mars 1937.

POULSEN, P.C. : Fra den danske Højesterets Praksis i 1937. Tidsskrift for Rettsvidenskap 51 : 315-339, Hefte 3, 1938.

RASTING, C. : Det Danske Forfatningsudkast af 1938. Tidsskrift for Rettsvidenskap 51 : 531-549, Hefte 5, 1938.

HARMS, E. : Die dänische Anordnung über die Anerkennung von deutschen Urteilen vom 13. April 1938. Juristische Wochenschrift 67 : 1942-1943, 30. Juli 1938.

Le Danemark se donne une nouvelle Constitution. Informations internationales 16 : 192-193, 24 mars 1939.

GOODMAN, R. : The new Danish Constitution. Politica 4 : 124-138, June 1939.

DANZIG

CRUSEN, G. : Die Novelle zum Danziger Staatsangehörigkeitsgesetz. Zeitschrift für osteuropäisches Recht 5 : 350-363, Dezember 1938.

ECUADOR

GREAVES, V.E. : The judicial status of non-registered foreign corporations in Ecuador. Tulane law review : 409-415, April 1935.

La elección de ministros en la nueva Carta Constitucional debe hacerse según el sistema ejecutivo, segun el sistema parlamento, o según el sistema de Gabinete? Revista de la Universidad de Guayaquil 6 : 516-532, setiembre-diciembre 1935.

OQUENDO, J.L. : Codificación de leyes y ordenanzas municipales. Anales de la Universidad central del Ecuador 55 : 307-454, octubre-diciembre 1935. and 56 : 5-203, enero-marzo 1936.

OQUENDO, J.L. : Codificación de leyes y ordenanzas municipales. Anales de la Universidad Central 57 : 95-202, julio-setiembre 1936.

INSUA RODRIGUEZ, R. : La capacidad de la mujer casada en el derecho civil ecuatoriano. Revista de la Universidad de Guayaquil 10 : 377-421, num. 3, 1939.

McDONOUGH, D.C. : Ecuadoran law of aliens. U.S. Department of commerce, Comparative law series 1 : 136-138, April 1939.

ESTONIA

MUELLER, W. : Die Zivilprozessreform vom Jahre 1935 Rigasche Zeitschrift für Rechtswissenschaft 9 : 20-28, 1. Heft 1935.

MEDER, W. : Die Gesetzgebung Estlands im 1. Halbjahr 1935. Rigasche Zeitschrift für Rechtswissenschaft 9 : 42-47, 1. Heft 1935.

SKOTTSBERG, B. : Estlands nya författning. Statsvetenskaplig tidsskrift 38 : 246-256, häft 3, 1935.

MEDER, W. : Die Gesetzgebung Estlands im III. Quartal 1934. Rigasche Zeitschrift für Rechtswissenschaft 8 : 193-199, 3. Heft 1935.

JUCUM, H. : Der Strafvollzug in Estland nach dem Strafvollzugsgesetz von 1931/1935. Zeitschrift für osteuropäisches Recht 2 : 26-39, Juli 1935.

PIIP, A. : Estlands Weg zur neuen Verfassung. Ost-Europa 10 : 605-618, Juli 1935.

MEDER, W. : Die Gesetzgebung Estlands im IV. Quartal 1934. Rigasche Zeitschrift für Rechtswissenschaft 8 : 267-274, August 1935.

Ubersicht über die wesentliche Gesetzgebung Estlands für das II. Halbjahr 1934 und das I. Halbjahr 1935. Zeitschrift für osteuropäisches Recht 2 : 218-223, Oktober 1935.

CSEKEY, S. v. : Die Verfassungsentwicklung Estlands 1924-1934. Jahrbuch des öffentliches Rechts 22 : 411-458, 1935.

MEDER, W. : Die Gesetzgebung Estlands im II. Halbjahr 1935. Rigasche Zeitschrift für Rechtswissenschaft 9 : 122-129, 2. Heft, 1935/1936.

MEDER, W. : Das Kirchenrecht Estlands. Rigasche Zeitschrift für Rechtswissenschaft 9 : 90-110, 2. Heft 1935/1936.

MEDER, W. : Die Beschäftigung von Ausländern in Estland nach dem Gesetz vom 3. April 1935. Zeitschift für osteuropäisches Recht 2 : 464-468, Februar 1936.

Estonie - Plébiscite des 23-25 février relatif à la convocation d'une Assemblée nationale. Bulletin interparlementaire 16 : 42-44, avril-mai 1936.

ROUCEK, J.S. : Constitutional changes in Estonia. American politicak science review 30 : 556-558, June 1936.

CSEKEY, S. v. : La revision de la Constitution de la République estonienne. Revue du droit public 53 : 543-596, juillet-août-septembre 1936.

MEDER, W. : Die Gesetzgebung Estlands im I. Quartal 1936. Rigasche Zeitschrift für Rechtswissenschaft 9 : 186-192, September 1936.

MEDER, W. : Estland - Gesetz betreffend den Ausnahmezustand vom 10. Juli in der Fassung der Novellen von 1934, 1935 und 1936. Zeitschrift für osteuropäisches Recht 3 : 249-252, Oktober 1936.

MEDER, W. : Die Gesetzgebung Estlands im II. Quartal 1936. Rigasche Zeitschrift für Rechtswissenschaft 9 : 255-257, Oktober 1936.

Estland - Übersicht über due wesentliche Gesetzgebung für das II. Halbjahr 1935 und dad I. Halbjahr 1936 (Contd.).. Zeitschrift für osteuropäisches Recht 3 : 322-326, November 1936.

MEDER, W. : Die Gesetzgebung Estlands im II. Halbjahr 1936. Rigasche Zeitschrift für Rechtswissenschaft 10 : 52-58, Heft 1, 1937.

MEDER, W. : Die Verwaltungsreform in Estland. Zeitschrift für osteuropäisches Recht 3 : 505-517, Februar 1937.

KLIMANN, A.T. : Diritto processuale amministrativo dell'Estonia. Annuario comparato e di studi legislativi 13 : 77-97, fasc. 2, 1937.

Estland - Der Verfassungsentwurf. Nation und Staat 10 : 371-377, März 1937.

MEDER, W. : Die berufsständischen Kammern in Estland. Zeitschrift für osteuropäisches Recht 3 : 611-619, April 1937.

MEDER, W. : Estländische Juristentagung in Dorpart im April 1937. Zeitschrift für osteuropäisches Recht 3 : 782-784, Juni 1937.

Estland - Übersicht über die wesentliche Gesetzgebung für das 2. Halbjahr 1936 und das 1. Halbjahr 1937. Zeitschrift für osteuropäisches Recht 4 : 240-244, Oktober 1937.

MEDER, W. : Die Verfassung Estlands vom 17. August 1937. Zeitschrift für osteuropäisches Recht 4 : 205-219, Oktober 1937.

NOTTBECK, H. von : Der Entwurf des estländischen Zivilgesetzbuches von 1936. Zeitschrift für osteuropäisches Recht 4 : 269-282, November 1937.

MEDER, W. : Die Gesetzgebung Estlands im Iv. Quartal 1937. Rigasche Zeitschrift für Rechtswissenschaft 10 : 197-201, Heft 1937-1938.

MEDER, W. : Die Gesetzgebung Estlands in den ersten drei Quartalen 1937. Rigasche Zeitschrift für Rechtswissenschaft 10 : 132-140, Januar 1938.

MEDER, W. : Das innerstaatliche Nationalitätenrecht Estlands. Zeitschrift für Völkerrecht 22 : 201-216, Heft 2, 1938.

Das Staatsangehörigkeitsgesetz. Zeitschrift für ausländisches öffentliches Recht und Völkerrecht 8 : 547-552, No. 3, 1938.

MADDISON, E. : Les traits généreux de l'histoire constitutionnelle estonienne jusqu'à l'Assemblée nationale de 1937. Revue d'histoire politique et constitutionnelle 2 : 164-216, avril-juin 1938.

MEDER, W. : Die Selbstverwaltung in Estland. Zeitschrift für ausländisches öffentliches Recht und Völkerrecht 8 : 552-560, August 1938.

KOCH, G. : Estland - Übersicht über die wesentliche Gesetzgebung im 2. Halbjahr 1937 und 1. Halbjahr 1938. Zeitschrift für osteuropäisches Recht 5 : 247-252, Oktober 1938.

MEDER, W. : Die neuen staats-und verwaltungsrechtlichen Gesetze in Estland. Zeitschrift für osteuropäisches Recht 5 : 205-217, Oktober 1938.

KOCH, G. : Estland - Tabelle der von Estland in der Zeit vom 1. Januar 1931 bis zum 31. August 1938 abgeschlossenen Staatsverträge. Zeitschrift für osteuropäisches Recht 5 : 319-331, November 1938.

MEDER, W. : Die Gesetzgebung Estlands im Jahre 1938. Rigasche Zeitschrift für Rechtswissenschaft 11 : 61-75, 1. Heft 1939.

LE FUR, L. ; Democracy and parliamentarianism with reference to a new constitution. Baltic and Scandinavian countries 5 : 1-8, January 1939.

KOCH, G. : Das estländische Gesetz über das Erbrecht von Ausländern. Zeitschrift für osteuropäisches Recht 5 : 405-427, Januar 1939.

MEDER, W. : Neue völkerrechtlichen bedeutsame Gesetze in Estland. Zeitschrift für Völkerrecht 23 : 178-188, Heft 2, 1939.

NOTTBACK, H. von. : Die zwischen Estland, Lettland und Litauen abgeschlossenen Konventionen vom 9.4.1938 über die Vereinheitlichung des Wechsel- und Scheckkrechts, unter besonderer Berücksichtigung Estlands. Zeitschrift für osteuropäisches Recht 5 : 604-612, März-April 1939.

MEDER, W. : Staatsangehörigkeitsgesetz vom 11. April 1938. Zeitschrift für osteuropäisches Recht 5 : 618-621, März-April 1939.

MEDER, W. : Gesetz vom 6. 4. 1938 betr. das Verfahrem der Ratifizierung völkerrechtlicher Verträge. Zeitschrift für osteuropäischen Recht 5 : 614-616, März-April 1939.

LENDER, U. : La reconnaissance et l'exécution des sentences judiciaires étrangères en Estonie. Journal du droit international 66 : 373-377, mars-avril 1939.

LE FUR, L. : Démocratie et parlementarisme. A propos d'une constitution nouvelle. Revue d'histoire politique et constitutionnelle 3 : 429-450, octobre-décembre 1939.

ETHIOPIA

SCHMIDT, F.V.: Die Sklaverei in Abessinien und ihre gesetzliche Aufhebung. Afrika-Rundschau 1 : 232-233, Dezember 1935.

Abessinisches Verfassungsrecht. Afrika Rundschau 1 : 233-234, Dezember 1935.

BOSCO, G. : Conseguenze giuridiche dell'annessione dell'Etiopia. Rivista di diritto pubblico 29 : 141-151, marzo 1937.

MONACO, R. : Carateri della sudditanza dell'Africa orientale italiana. Rivista di diritto pubblico 29 : 239-247, maggio 1937.

UDINA, M. : Il Governatorato di Addis Abeba. Rivista di diritto pubblico 29 : 404-414, agosto-settembre 1937.

FOLCHI, A.E. : La figura del Governatore Generale Vicerè d'Etiopia. Rivista di diritto pubblico 29 : 466-487, ottobre 1937.

MAROI, F. : I diritti consuetudinari delle genti etiopiche e il diritto coloniale italiano. Civiltà fascista 4 : 820-839, novembre 1937.

REALE, E. : L'activité legislative en 1936 et l'organisation de l'Empire italien de l'Afrique orientale. Annuaire de l'Institut international de droit public : 395-409, 1937.

NOVA, R. de : L'annessione dell'Etiopia nella giurisprudenza. Rivista di diritto internazionale 30 : 360-426, 1 luglio - 31 dicembre 1938.

Les actions du chemin de fer franco-éthiopien. Journal des tribunaux mixtes 18 : 5-6, 1-2 mars 1939.

FINLAND

Das finnische Sterilisierungsgesetz vom 13. Juni 1935. Juristische Wochenschrift 64 : 2472-2473, 31. August 1935.

HAKULINEN : Die finnische Aktiennovene vom 15. November 1935. Zeitschrift für ausländisches und internationales Privatrecht 10 : 97-100, Heft 1/3, 1936.

HOSTIE, J. : La sentence arbitrale de M. Bagge dans le différend anglo-finlandais. Revue générale de droit international public 43 : 327-357, mai-juin 1936.

METTGENBERG, W. : Zum deutsch-finnischen Auslieferungsvertrag. Deutsche Justiz 99 : 1526-1528, 1. Oktober 1937.

Ålands självstyrelse. Statsvetenskaplig tidskrift 42 : 64-93, häft 1, 1939.

HAKULINEN, Y.J. : Finnische Gesetzgebung in den Jahren 1936-1937. Zeitschrift für ausländisches und internationale Privatrecht 12 : 133-138, Heft 1/2, 1939.

FRANCE

ESMEIN, P. : Gesetzgebung, Rechtsprechung und Schrifttum in Frankreich im Jahre 1934. Zeitschrift für ausländisches und internationales Privatrecht 9 : 117-199, Heft 1-2, 1935.

BONNARD, R. : La Présidence du Conseil. Revue du droit public 42 : 74-89, janvier-février-mars 1935.

GUILLIEN, R. : La modification du règlement de la Chambre des députés. Revue du droit public 42 : 137-171, janvier-février-mars 1935.

MILHAUD, A. : L'avenir de la réforme électorale. Revue politique et parlementaire 42 : 209-218, 10 février 1935.

GOOCH, R.K. : Constitutional reform in France. American political science review 29 : 84-91, February 1935.

Modifications à la loi de 1867 sur les sociétés anonymes. Revue politique et parlementaire 42 : 475-481, 10 mars 1935.

BLANCKAERT, L. : L'organisation corporative - La semaine sociale d'Angers. Politique 9 : 735-744, septembre 1935.

GIGNOUX, J. : La politique des décrets-lois. Revue politique et parlementaire 42 : 3-15, 10 octobre 1935.

KAHN, E. : Les décrets-lois du 31 octobre. Cahiers des droits de l'homme 35 : 697-705, 10 novembre 1935.

MANTILLA, S. : La organización corporativa en la semana social de Angers. Razón y fe 35 : 289-298, noviembre 1935.

VINCENT, J. : Französische Aktienrechtsreform. Deutsche Juristen-Zeitung 40 : 1406-1411, 1. Dezember 1935.

CAPITANT, H. : L'interprétation des lois d'après les travaux préparatoires. Recueil hebdomadaire de jurisprudence 12 : 77-80, 5 décembre 1935.

SMITH, J.D. : Impossibility of performance as an excuse in French law - The doctrine of force majeure. Yale law journal 45 : 452-467, January 1936.

PIRET, R. : Les mofifications récentes du droit des sociétés anonymes en France. Institut belge de droit comparé 22 : 1-16, janvier-mars 1936.

VIZIOZ, H. : Chronique de jurisprudence marocaine. Revue trimestrielle de droit civil 35 : 285-297, janvier-mars 1936.

DOMINIQUE, P. : La proportionnelle. Vu 9 : 196-187, 12 février 1936.

DIETZ, J. : Jules Ferry - La revision de la Constitution et le scrutin de liste. Revue politique et parlementaire 43 : 514-532, 10 mars 1936.

McCAFFERY, E.M. : The Franco-American convention relative to double taxation. Columbia law review 36 : 382-405, March 1936.

LELOIR, G. : Les décrets-loi et le code d'instruction criminelle. Recueil hebdomadaire de jurisprudence 13 : 21-24, 19 mars 1936.

HAMEL, J. : Le nouveau régime des obligations. Revue politique et parlementaire 43 : 264-282, 10 mai 1936.

Projet de complément à la déclaration des droits de l'homme présenté par le comité central. Cahiers des droits de l'homme 35 : 387-388, 10 juin 1936.

Le système hypothécaire français. Recueil hebdomadaire de jurisprudence 13 : 45-48, 8 juillet 1936.

GORDONNIER, P. : Quelques faiblesses du nouveau statut des obligataires. Recueil hebdomadaire de jurisprudence 13, 53-56, 23 juillet 1936.

DARESTE, P. : Le régime des décrets auc colonies. Quinzaine coloniale 40 : 333-335, 25 août 1936.

PIC, P. : Autour de la loi du 24 juin 1936 sur les conventions collectives de travail - Etude comparative du "New Deal" français et du corporatisme totalitaire. Revue politique et parlementaire 43 : 393-420, 10 septembre 1936.

L'oeuvre législative de la nouvelle Chambre. Europe nouvelle documentaire nos. 42, 43 : I-VIII, I-XII, 29 août, 12 septembre 1936.
Sélection de textes.

DARESTE, P. : Le régime des décrets aux colonies. Quinzaine coloniale 40 : 365-368, 25 septembre 1936.

TCHERNOFF, J. : La loi du 19 août tendant à réprimer la hausse injustifiée des prix. Dalloz, Recueil hebdomadaire de jurisprudence 13 : 61-64, 22 octobre 1936.

BOMPARD, R. : La diffamation envers les hommes publics, les corps constitués et les fonctionnaires. Politique 10 : 680-698, septembre 1936.

La question des cumuls. Cahiers des droits de l'homme 36 : 726-731, 31 octobre 1936.
Traitements publics et pensions.

Chronique administrative française - Le statut des fonctionnaires publics. Revue du droit public 43 : 68-702, octobre-novembre-décembre 1936.

Pouvoir du gouvernement de prononcer la dissolution de ligues politiques. Revue du droit public 43 : 658-670, octobre-novembre-décembre 1936.

BUISSON, A. : L'occupation des usines et le droit français. Revue des deux mondes 106 : 35-50, 1 novembre 1936.

LALOU, H. : Déclaratifs? ou attributifs? Dalloz, Recueil hebdomadaire de jurisprudence 13 : 69-72, 12 novembre 1936.
Caractère des jugements rendus en matière de responsabilité civile.

DOMINIQUE, P. : La loi sur la presse. Europe nouvelle 19 : 1134, 28 novembre 1936.

HERCHENRODER, M.F.P. : Study of the law applicable to native Christians in the French Dependencies and India. Journal of comparative legislation and international law 18 : 186-194, November 1936.

LANDRE, R. : La nouvelle loi sur la convention collective. Politique 10 : 870-883, novembre 1936.

GARÇON, M. : Le projet de loi sur le droit d'auteur. Revue des deux mondes 106 : 509-526, 1er décembre 1936.

LOEWEL, P. : Le projet de loi sur la Presse. Europe nouvelle 19 : 1201-1202, 5 décembre 1936.

LE CORMIER, P.: La capacité civile de la femme mariée au Sénat. Politique 10 : 1021-1023, décembre 1936.

AUDINET, A. : La loi applicable à la capacité de la femme mariée. Travaux du Comité français de droit international privé 4 : 89-117, 1936-37.

CAPITANT, R. : La crise et la réforme du parlementarisme en France - Chronique constitutionnelle française (1931-1936). Jahrbuch des öffentlichen Rechts 23 : 1-71, 1936.

BARTHELÉMY, J. : Le projet contre la Presse. Revue politique et parlementaire 44 : 3-27, 10 janvier 1937.
Le projet de loi français.

MAUNIER, R. : Loi orale et loi écrite aux colonies françaises. Zeitschrift für schwizerisches Recht 56 : 140-154, Heft 1, 1937.

GARÇON, M. : La loi sur la Presse. Revue des deux mondes 107 : 369-393, 15 janvier 1937.

BARTHELÉMY, J. : Le présidence du conseil. Revue d'histoire politique et constitutionnelle 1 : 86-151, janvier-mars 1937.

SALINGARDES, B. : La protection de la liberté individuelle et les lois du 7 février 1933 et du 25 mars 1935, (Contd.). Revue générale du droit, de la législation et de la jurisprudence 61 : 35-48, janvier-février-mars 1937.

CAZALS de FABEL, J. : La nouvelle organisation de la radiodiffusion française. Revue internationale de la radioélectricité 13 : 5-12, janvier-février-mars 1937.

DENOYER, C. : Recent modifications of French Company Law. Journal of comparative legislation and international law 19 : 32-37, February 1937.

ROCHEFOUCAULD, de la : Le projet René Renoult. Revue de Paris 44 : 303-314, 15 mais 1937.
Le code de la femme mariée.

STIEFEL, E. : Les conflits interprovinciaux entre la loi française sur le contrat d'assurance et les lois locales d'Alsace et de Lorraine. Journal du droit international 64 : 205-225, mars-avril 1937.

DAWSON, J.P. : Economic duress and the fair exchange in French and German law. Tulane law review 11 : 345-376, April 1937.

CAPITANT, R. : Le conflit scolaire en Alsace ou comment on légifère pour les départements recouvrés. Dalloz, Recueil hebdomadaire de jurisprudence 14 : 25-28, 15 avril 1937.

PERROUX, F. : La crise de l'Etat et l'Etat de demain. Vie intellectuelle 9 : 367-381, 25 juin 1937.

LAPIE, P.O. : Le projet français de code du droit d'auteur. Geistiges Eigentum 3 : 45-57, Juni-Juli 1937.

PAVIE, A. : L'évolution de la législation et de la jurisprudence relatives au mariage en France depuis cinquante ans. Séances et travaux de l'Académie des sciences morales et politiques 95 : 110-139, juillet-aout 1937.

BRAUNIAS, K. : Die französische Staatsreform im Schrifttum. Zeitschrift für ausländisches öffentliches Recht und Völkerrecht 7 : 644-673, August 1937.

LAROQUE, P. : L'arbitrage obligatoire dans les conflits du travail en France. Sciences politiques 52 : 225-238, 3 août 1937.

JÈZE, G. : Le régime juridique des entreprises de fabrication ou de vente de matériels d'armement. Revue de droit public et de la science politique 54 : 456-500, juillet-août-septembre 1937.

BRUNSCHVIGG, C. : Le suffrage des femmes devant le Parlement. Revue d'histoire politique et constitutionnelle 1 : 497-502, juillet-septembre 1937.

PICARD, R. : Faut-il instituer en France l'Etat corporatif? Cahiers des droits de l'homme 37 : 587-592, 15 septembre 1937.

ELSTER, A. : Persönlichkeit und Sozialgebundenheit im Urheberrecht nach deutscher und französischer Rechtsauffassung. Zeitschrift für ausländisches und internationales Privatrecht 11 : 528-541, Heft 3/4, 1937.

JÈZE, G. : Aptitude légale des femmes aux emplois publics. Revue du droit public et de la science politique 54 : 684-696, octobre-novembre-décembre 1937.

BONNECASE, J. : Facultés de droit et école d'administration. Revue générale du droit, de la législation et de la jurisprudence 61 : 161-186, 241-285, juillet-août-septembre, octobre-novembre-décembre 1937.

REUTER, P. : L'expropriation des usines de guerre. Revue politique et parlementaire 44 : 239-250, 10 novembre 1937.
L'expropriation en France.

KRAEMER-BACH, M. : La capacité de la femme mariée en droit français (loi du 18 février 1938) et en droit comparé. Revue pratique de droit international 4 : 3-30, octobre-novembre-décembre 1937.

CORDIER, M.Y. : De la notion de domicile en droit comparé (France et Angleterre). Journal du droit international 64 : 969-989, novembre-décembre 1937.

REUTER, P. : L'expropriation des usines de guerre (Contd.). Revue politique et parlementaire 44 : 437-453, 10 décembre 1937.

BESSON, A. : La généralisation du contrôle sur les sociétés d'assurances (décret-loi du 25 août 1937). Dalloz, Recueil hebdomadaire de jurisprudence 15 : 1-4, 6 janvier 1938.

BONNECASE, J. : Une ère nouvelle dans la structure de la vie de famille (loi du 18 février 1938). Revue générale du droit, de la législation et de la jurisprudence 62 : 1-19, janvier-février-mars 1938.

A propos de la loi du 18 février 1938 relative à l'incapacité de la femme mariée et de ses conséquences dans le droit des affaires. Annales de droit commercial 47 : 40-43, janvier-mars 1938.

SAVATIER, R. : Les rayons et les ombres d'une expérience sociale - l'arbitrage obligatoire des conflits collectifs de travail. Dalloz, recueil hebdomadaire de jurisprudence 15 : 9-15, 3 février 1938.

FERAL, P. de : La réforme du régime de l'interdiction de séjour. Sciences politiques 53 : 55-65, février 1938.

DONNEDIEU de VABRES, M.H. : Quelques observations sur le rôle du préjudice en droit pénal français. Revue internationale de doctrine de législation pénale comparée 2 : 5-16, No. 2, 1938.

GARRAUD, P. : La suppression, en France, de la transportation coloniale et le projet de loi du 30 décembre 1936. Revue internationale de doctrine et de législation pénale comparée 2 : 71-95, No. 2, 1938.

HUGUENEY, P. : Du tribunal compétent pour juger les infractions de droit commun commises en temps de paix par les militaires ou des marins. Revue internationale de doctrine et de législation pénale comparée 2 : 22-27, No. 2, 1938.

La MORANDIÈRE, L.J. de : Loi du 18 février 1938 sur la capacité de la femme mariée. Dalloz, Recueil hebdomadaire de jurisprudence 15 : 25-28, 24 mars 1938.

CARDIÈGES, P. : A propos de l'Ecole d'administration. Politique 12 : 262-269, mars 1938.

HAMEL, J. : Répercussions de l'économie dirigée sur les institutions de droit privé en France. Revue roumaine de droit privé 1 : 48-59, avril-septembre 1937.

LAGARDE, G. : Les tendances actuelles du droit français. Annuario di diritto comparato e di studi legislativi 13 : 281-296, fasc. 5, Pt. 1, 1938.

DEBEYRE, G. : Le recours pour excès de pouvoir et le contrat. Revue du droit public 55 : 215-254, avril-mai-juin 1938.

JÈZE, G. : Responsabilité de l'Etat en raison du refus de la police de faire cesser les occupations illégales d'usines. Revue du droit public 55 : 374-396, avril-mai-juin 1938.

Le glissement de l'Etat (Contd.) - Les chances perdues et retrouvées. Revue des deux mondes 108 : 769-781, 15 juin 1938.

Une enquête sur l'Ecole Nationale d'Administration. Etat moderne 11 : 325-384, juin 1938.
Numéro spécial.

VOIRIN, P. : Notes parlementaires de droit civil (du 15 mai au 17 juillet 1938). Revue trimestrielle de droit civil 37 : 597-669, juillet-septembre 1938.

DUPOND, O. : A propos du décret du 17 juin 1938 relatif à la répression de l'espionnage. Revue de science criminelle et de droit pénal comparé 3 : 625-632, octobre-décembre 1938.

HERZOG, J.L. : La loi et le règlement d'administration publique - Les effets suspensifs de la délégation législative. Revue de droit public et de la science politique 55 : 643-692, octobre-décembre 1938.

HERCHENRODER, M.F.P. : The capacity of married women in French law. Journal of comparative legislation and international law 20 : 196-203,

UHLER, A. : The doctrine of administrative trespass in French law - An analogue of duc process. Michigan law review 37 : 209-235, December 1938.

HUGUENEY, P. : La répression en France de l'espionnage en temps de paix. Revue internationale de doctrine et de législation pénale comparée 3 : 25-33, No. 1, 1939.

LACHAPELLE, G. : La représentation proportionnelle. Politique 13 : 13-25, janvier 1939.

La Cour supérieure d'arbitrage en France. Bulletin de l'Institut juridique international 40 : 24-28, janvier 1939.

LADREIT de LACHARRIÈRE, R. : Le système des décrets-lois et le régime parlementaire. Revue d'histoire politique et constitutionnele 3 : 122-150, janvier-mars 1939.

ANCELY, R. : Rapport sur la loi du 25 mars 1935 modifiant celle du 7 février 1933 sur les garanties de la liberté individuelle. Revue pénitentiaire et de droit pénal 63 : 60-103, janvier-avril 1939.

CHAUVEAU, P. : La femme commerçante et la loir du 18 février 1938 sur la capacité des femmes mariées. Dalloz, Recueil hebdomadaire de jurisprudence 16 : 5-8, (chronique II), 2 février 1939.

RÉGLADE, M. : La notion d'arbitrage spécialement dans les conflits sociaux. Revue du droit public et de la science politique 56 : 213-239, avril-mai-juin 1939.

BARTHÉLEMY, J. : Un tournant dans les conceptions françaises sur la loi. Revue d'histoire politique et constitutionnelle 3 : 161-168, avril-juin 1939.

MARÉCHAL, G. : L'exercice du contrôle parlementaire par les commissions. Europe nouvelle 22 : 661-663, 17 juin 1939.

Le décret du 29 juillet 1939 portant codification des dispositions relatives aux crimes et délits contre la sûreté extérieure de l'Etat. Recueil de documents en matière pénale et pénitentiaire 8 : 411-415, décembre 1939.

FRANCE
(International law, Aliens, Nationality)

GONZALEZ de ANDIA, M. : L'application et la preuve de la loi étrangère en France et spécialement de la loi espagnole. Nouvelle revue de droit international privé 2 : 22-28, janvier-février-mars 1935.

ROUSSEAU, C. : Jurisprudence française en matière de droit international public. Revue générale de droit international public 42 : 203-230, mars-avril 1935.

GUILHOT, J. : La convention franco-américaine du 27 avril 1932 relative à la double imposition. Journal du droit international 62 : 325-332, mars-avril 1935.

AGHION, R. : Les effets de la convention franco-italienne d'établissement du 3 juin 1930. Journal du droit international 62 : 564-578, mai-juin 1935.

La PRADELLE, A. de : La nouvelle condition du naturalisé d'après la loi et le jurisprudence. Nouvelle revue de droit international privé 2 : 161-208, avril-septembre 1935.

MEZGER, E. : Le divorce des étrangers dont la loi nationale ne reconnaît pas le jugement français. Nouvelle revue de droit international privé 2 : 234-249, avril-septembre 1935.

SAVATIER, R. : Le sort des biens des anciennes sociétés russes en France. Revue critique de droit international 30 : 663-686, octobre-décembre 1935.

BATTIFOL, H. : Chronique de jurisprudence française en matière de conflits de lois. Revue critique de droit international 30 : 613-632, octobre-décembre 1935.

LABOURET, H. : Afrique Orientale française - L'accession des indigènes à la citoyenneté française. Afrique française 45 : 721-725, décembre 1935.

MICHEL, J. : La convention fiscale franco-américaine du 27 avril 1932. Journal du droit international 63 : 1-104, janvier-février 1936.

AUDINET, A. : Chronique de jurisprudence française sur la condition des étrangers 1925-1935. Revue critique de droit international 31 : 40-66, janvier-mars 1936.

Tableau des accords internationaux de la France. Revue critique de droit international 31 : 191-293, janvier-mars 1936.

ANCEL, M. : The French law of naturalization. Tulane law review 10 : 231-245, February 1936.

MOREL, R. : Les articles 14 et 15 du Code civil. Travaux du Comité français de droit international privé 3 : 44-53, 1936.
La compétence des tribunaux français à l'égard d'étrangers.

DEVAUX, J. : La conclusion des traités internationaux en forme s'écartant des règles constitionnelles et dite "conclusion en forme simplifiée". Revue internationale française du droit des gens 1 : 299-309, 15 mars - 15 avril 1936.

A few practical comments on the Franco-American treaty. Foreign law series : 18-21, No. 4, 1936.
Double taxation.

FATOU, R. : Le problème soulevé par la présence en France des étrangers indésirables. Nouvelle revue de droit international privé 1 : 263-275, avril-mai-juin 1936.

PERROUD, J. : La convention franco-britannique sur l'effet extraterritorial des jugements. Revue critique de droit international 32 : 333-343, avril-juin 1936.

NIBOYET, J.-P. : De quelques mises au point que comporterait la législation française sur la nationalité. Revue critique de droit international 32 : 384-391, avril-juin 1936.

La convention franco-américaine sur les doubles impositions. Recueil hebdomadaire de jurisprudence 13 : 33-36, 14 mai 1936.

GUILHOT, J. : L'instance en exequatur des jugements étrangers et ses conséquences fiscales. Journal du droit international 63 : 571-580, mai-juin 1936.

NIBOYET, J.-P. : Un pas appréciable vers le respect des traités. Recueil hebdomadaire de jurisprudence 13 : 41-44, 11 juin 1936.
La primauté des traités et la jurisprudence française.

MEZGER, E. : Mariage et divorce des Français en Allemagne et des Allemands en France. Nouvelle revue de droit international privé 3 : 507-526, juillet-août-septembre 1936.

FLIER, M.-J. van der : Cassation en cas d'application des lois étrangères. Journal du droit international 63 : 1053-1057, juillet-octobre 1936.

GUILHOT, J. : La loi du 30 juillet 1936 sur les avoirs à l'étranger. Journal du droit international 63 : 821-833, juillet-octobre 1936.

NIBOYET, J.-P. : Les immunités de juridiction, en droit français, des Etats etrangers engagés dans des transactions privées. Revue générale de droit inter national public 43 : 525-545, septembre-octobre 1936.

La convention franco-belge sur les doubles impositions. Dalloz, Recueil hebdomadaire de jurisprudence 13 : 57-60, 61-64, 5, 19 novembre 1936.

MAZAS, P. : L'accession des indigènes algériens à la qualité de citoyens français. Terre d'Islam 11 : 363-373, novembre-décembre 1936.

HAMEL : La protection des porteurs d'obligations étrangères. Travaux du Comité français de droit international privé 3 : 105-126, 1936.

STOUPNITZKY, A. : Die Rechtsstellung der Handelsvertretung der UdSSR in Frankreich. Zeitschrift für osteuropäisches Recht 3 : 453-468, Januar 1937.

GUILHOT, J. : La déduction du passif héréditaire en droit fiscal international français. Journal du droit international 64 : 41-52, janvier-février 1937.

Tableau des accords internationaux de la France. Revue critique de droit international 32 : 209-290, janvier-mars 1937.

JAPIOT, R. : Jurisprudence française en matière de procédure civile. Revue trimestrielle de droit civil 36 : 193-197, janvier-mars 1937.

ROUSSEAU, C. : Lois et décrets français en matière de droit international - La vie internationale de la France en 1936. Revue générale de droit international public 44 : 218-229, mars-avril 1937.

Immunité des agents diplomatiques. Documents politiques 18 : 149-151, avril 1937.
Cour de Cassation, 27 février 1937.

BATIFOL, H. : Chronique de jurisprudence française 1935-1936. Conflit des lois. Revue critique de droit international 32 : 419-442, avril-juin 1937.

GUTTERIDGE, H.C. : La Convention franco-britannique pour l'exécution réciproque des jugements. Revue critique de droit international 32 : 369-392, avril-juin 1937.

ROUSSEAU, Ch. : Jurisprudence française en matière de droit international public (1935). Revue générale de droit international public 44 : 465-491, juillet-août 1937.

MICHEL, J. : La convention fiscale franco-allemande du 9 novembre 1934. Revue critique de droit international 32 : 585-645, juillet à décembre 1937.

MAUPAS, J. : Les pouvoirs des tribunaux en matière de réintégration des Alsaciens-Lorrains dans la nationalité française. Nouvelle revue de droit international privé 4 : 697-703, octobre-novembre-décembre 1937.

BATIFOL, H.: Le profit qu'on peut tirer en France des règles américaines de solution des conflits de lois sur les contrats. Travaux du Comité français de droit international privé 5 : 48-62, 1937-1938.

LEVEN, M. : Le statut des étrangers en France. Travaux du Comité français de droit international privé 5 : 101-124, 1937-1938.

LOUIS-LUCAS : La réforme de la législation sur la perte de la nationalité française. Travaux du Comité français de droit international privé 5 : 9-29, 1937-1938.

NIBOYET : Le statut des étrangers en France. Travaux du Comité français de droit international privé 5 : 75-84, 1937-1938.

GUILHOT, J. : Les filiales de sociétés étrangères la notion de fraude à la loi en matière fiscale. Journal du droit international 65 : 21-35, janvier-février 1938.

DUCLOS, P. : L'accession des naturalisés aux fonctions publiques et le droit français. Revue de droit public et de la science politique 55 : 5-86, janvier-février-mars 1938.

NATIONAL LAW - COUNTRIES

STAUFFENBERG, B.S. von : Das Prisenrecht der französischen Instruktionen vom 8. März 1934. Zeitschrift für ausländisches öffentliches Recht und Völkerrecht 8 : 23-47, Februar 1938.

DENOYER, C. et J. : Les Anglais doivent-ils la caution "judicatum solvi"? Journal du droit international 65 : 258-264, mars-avril 1938.

DAVID, F. : De la reconnaissance des sentences pénales étrangères en France au point de vue de la récidive et du sursis. Revue internationale de droit pénal 15 : 321-350, No. 4, 1938.

NIBOYET, J.P. : La distinction rationnelle des problèmes de compétence interne et internationale des tribunaux en France. Revue roumaine de droit privé 1 : 39-53, No. 4, 1938.

Commission chargée d'étudier le statut des étrangers en France. Rapport présenté au nom de la Commission par Henri Battifol. Nouvelle revue de droit international privé 5 : 470-479, avril-mai-juin 1938.

LÉCRIVAIN, A. : A propos de la situation de l'étranger en France et du droit d'expulsion. Revue de science criminelle et de droit pénal comparé 3 : 273-277, avril-juin 1938.

GUILHOT, J. : La convention fiscale franco-allemande du 9 novembre 1934. Journal du droit international 65 : 439-452, mai-juin 1938.

La convention franco-italienne sur les doubles impositions. Dalloz, Recueil hebdomadaire de jurisprudence 15 : 29-32, 12 mai 1938.

ROUSSEAU, Ch. : Jurisprudence française en matière de droit international public (1936). Revue générale de droit international .blic 45 : 457-506, juillet -août 1938.

MORICE, B. : La publicité en France des actes de l'etat civil des Français à l'étranger. Nouvelle revue de droit international privé 5 : 512-526, juillet-août-septembre 1938.

STOUPNITZKY, A. : Le service militaire en France des jeunes gens "ne justifiant d'aucune nationalité". Revue critique de droit international 33 : 394-406, juillet-septembre 1938.

TARDY, M. : La nationalisation et le contrôle des industries de guerre. Revue de Franc 18 : 89-108, 1 septembre 1938.

PHILONENKO, M. : L'expulsion des heimatlos sous le régime du décret-loi sur la police des étrangers du 2 mai 1938 et le décret du 17 juin 1938. Journal du droit international 65 : 723-736, juillet-octobre 1938.

GUILHOT, J. : La Convention franco-suédoise en matière d'impôts sur les successions. Journal du droit international 65 : 708-722, juillet-octobre 1938.

LEROUGE, G. : Le nouveau régime des étrangers au regard de l'impôt général sur le revenu en France. Revue internationale française du droit des gens 3 : 196-199, octobre-novembre 1938.

ANCEL, M. : La nationalité française et le décret-loi du 12 novembre 1938. Nouvelle revue de droit international privé 5 : 723-761, octobre-novembre-décembre 1938.

Commission chargée d'étudier le statut des étrangers en France. Nouvelle revue de droit international privé 5 : 940-952, octobre-novembre-décembre 1938.
Rapport présenté par M. Ancel.

ANCEL, M. : Chronique de jurisprudence en matière de nationalité. Revue critique de droit international 33 : 614-626, octobre-décembre 1938.

Chambre de Commerce de Paris - La situation des étrangers en France. Revue critique de droit international 33 : 702-703, octobre-décembre 1938.

La situation des étrangers en France. Bulletin de la Chambre de Commerce de Paris 45 : 1068-1094, 10 décembre 1938.

AMBROSINI, G. : L'Algéria e l'attribuzione della cittadinanza francese. Civiltà fascisza 5 : 1093-1110, dicembre 1938.

DONNEDIEU de VABRES, J. : Le renvoi et l'affaire de Marchi della Costa. Revue de droit international et de législation comparée 66 : 167-188, No. 1, 1939.
Succession d'un étranger.

LEFEBVRE, R. : L'octroi de délais aux étrangers pour le paiement des sommes dues au trésor public. Journal du droit international 66 : 29-31, janvier-février 1939.

LOUIS-LUCAS, P. : La nouvelle règlementation de la nationalité française. Revue critique de droit international 34 : 1-34, janvier-mars 1939.

LAMPUÉ, P. : Le régime législatif des pays de protectorat. Revue de droit public 46 : 5-37, janvier-mars 1939.

CAMERLYNCK, G.H. : Le mariage entre Français et Annamites. Revue critique de droit international 34 : 50-85, janvier/mars 1939.

Loi (3 février 1939) autorisant la naturalisation des protégés et anciens protégés français. Journal officiel de la République française 71 : 1690-1691, 5 février 1939.

DENNERY, R. : Les conflits de lois et de juridictions intéressant les indigènes à l'intérieur de l'Union Indochinoise. Revue indochinoise : 507-542, No. 3, 1939.

METTERTAL, R. : Exercice en France, par les réfugiés étrangers, des droits qu'ils tiennent de leur activité commerciale antériaure. Journal du droit international 66 : 257-268, mars-avril 1939.

TAGER, P. : Statut des étrangers d'après les récents décrets-lois. Journal du droit international 66 : 278-336, mars-avril 1930.

La vie internationale de France en 1938. Revue générale de droit international public 46 : 167-179, mars-avril 1939.
Traités et lois d'intérêt international.

BARBEY, J. : Des crimes et délits commis à l'étranger aux dépens de l'Etat français. Revue de science criminelle et de droit pénal comparé 4 : 270-282, avril-juin 1939.

MILLET, R. : La situation nouvelle des étrangers en France. Europe nouvelle 22 : 514-515, 13 mai 1939.

COSTE-FLORET, P. : Jus sanguinis, jus soli et statut personnel dans les rapports de la Métropole, de l'Algérie et de l'étranger. Revue critique de droit international 34 : 201-214, avril-juin 1939.

ROUSSEAU, C. : Jurisprudence française en matière de droit international public. Revue générale de droit international public 46 : 390-471, juillet-août 1939.

L'exequatur en France des décisions des tribunaux mixtes d'Egypte. Journal des tribunaux mixtes 18 : 6, 18 et 19 août 1939.

HERCHENRODER, M.F.P. : The aliens regulations in France. Journal of comparative legislation and international law 21 : 220-229, November 1939.

BASSANO, U. : Sulla convenzione italo-francese per l'utilizzazione delle acque del fiume Roja. Foro italiano 64 : 1035-1042, fasc. 14, 1939.

FRANCE
(French community)

COUZINET, P. : La structure juridique de l'Union indochinoise (Contd.). Revue indochineoise : 329-354, No. 10, 1939.

GERMANY

HELMER, E. : Allemagne - Notice sur le mouvement législatif en 1934, 1935 et 1936. Annuaire de législation étrangère 62 : 1-100, 1934/1936.

MAUNZ, T. : Das Ende des subjektiven öffentlichen Rechts. Zeitschrift für die gesamte Staatswissenschaft 96 : 71-111, 1. Heft, 1935.

GLEISPACH : Grundsätzliches zum kommenden deutschen Strafrecht. Deutsche Juristen-Zeitung 40 : 5-11, 1. Januar 1935.

Reichseinheit - Jusizeinheit - Zum 2. Gesetz zur Überleitung der Rechtspflege auf das Reich vom 5. Dezember 1934. Juristische Wochenschrift 64 : 2-3, 5. Januar 1935.

NADELMANN, K.H. : La nouvelle loi allemande sur la liquidation judiciaire (Vergleichsordnung) du 26 février 1935. Annales de droit commercial 44 : 54-67, janvier-mars 1935.

NIEMEYER, T. : Neuester Stand des positiven internationalen Privatrechts im Gebiet der Ehescheidung. Niemeyers Zeitschrift für internationales Recht 51 : 206-208, 1.-3. Heft, 1935.

ZURCHER, A.J. : The Hitler referenda. American political science review 29 : 91-99, February 1935.

HUBER, E.R. : Das Staatsoberhaupt des Deutschen Reiches. Zeitschrift für die gesamte Staatswissenschaft 95 : 202-229, 2. Heft 1935.

HUBER, E.R. : Das Reichstatthaltergesetz vom 30. Januar 1935. Deutsche Juristen-Zeitung 40 : 257-264, 1. März 1935.

HARTENSTEIN : Das neue Devisenrecht (Contd.). Juristische Wochenschrift 64 : 736-744, 9. März 1935.

HAIDN, C. : Das Gesetz gegen heimtückische Angriffe auf Staat und Partei und zum Schutze der Parteiuniform vom 20. Dezember 1934. Juristische Wochenschrift 64 : 897-899, 23. März 1935.

SCHAFER, K. : Zur Regelung des Gnadenwesens. Juristische Wochenschrift 64 : 900-909, 23. März 1935.

Strafrecht. Zeitschrift der Akademie für deutsches Recht 2 : 90-112, März 1935.
Series of articles.

ROGGE, H. : Wehrmacht, Frieden und Völkerrecht. Deutsche Juristen.Zeitung 40 : 387-391, 1. April 1935.

Die 6. Vollsitzung der Akademie für Deutsches Recht, am 27. Februar 1935. Zeitschrift der Akademie für Deutsches Recht 2 : 183-201, April 1935.

JELLINEK, W. : Le droit public de l'Allemagne en 1934. Revue du droit public 52 : 346-353, avril-mai-juin 1935.

RUTTKE : Erb und Rassenpflege in Gesetzgebung und Rechtsprechung des 3. Reiches. Juristische Wochenschrift 64 : 1369-1376, 11. Mai 1935.

FRICK, W. : Das Deutsche Reich als Einheitsstaat. Europäische Revue 11 : 287-289, Mai 1935.

Ergebnisse der Rechtsprechung und Rechtslehre aus Zeitschriften und Entscheidungssammlungen. Deutsche Justiz 6 : 422-490, 29. Juni 1935.
The new German legislation.

MOSSMER, F. : Volk und Ehe im Scheidungsrecht. Juristische Wochenschrift 64 : 1828-1829, 29 Juni 1935.

Ministerpräsident Göring über die Abwehr des politischen Katholizmus - Runderlass an die Oberpräsidenten und Regierungspräsidenten. Deutsche Justiz 97 : 1053-1054, 26. Juli 1935.

Ergebnisse der Rechtsprechung und Rechtslehre aus Zeitschriften und Entscheidungssammlungen. Deutsche Justik (Monatsbeilage das Recht) 39 : 521-528, 26. Juli 1935.

Richtlinien für das Strafverfahren-Allgemeine Verfügung des Reichsministers der Justiz vom 13. April 1935. Amtliche Sonderveröffentlichungen der Deutschen Justiz : 7-194, No. 7, 1935.

ROUSSEL, G. de : L'évolution du pouvoir exécutif en Allemagne (1919-1934). Revue du droit public et de la science politique 42 : 393-481, juillet-août-septembre 1935.

THIERACK : Neues deutsches Strafrecht. Deutsche Juristen-Zeitung 40 : 913-919, 1. August 1935.

SCHWARZ : Der neue Strafprozess auf Grund des Gesetzes vom 28. Juni 1935. Deutsche Juristen-Zeitung 40 : 925-931, 1. August 1935.

FREISLER, R. : Hoch- und Landesverrat im Lichte des Nationalsozialismus. Deutsche Juristen-Zeitung 40 : 906-913, 1. August 1935.

REUSS, R. : Partie und Staat im Dritten Reich. Juristische Wochenschrift 64 : 2314-2320, 17. August 1935.

NATIONAL LAW - COUNTRIES

FREISLER, R. : Der Wandel der politischen Grundanschauungen in Deutschland und sein Einfluss auf die Erneuerung von Strafrecht, Strafprozess und Strafvollzug. Deutsche Justiz 97 : 1247-1254, 30. August 1935.

WELLS, R.H. : Municipal government in National Socialist Germany. American political science review 29 : 652-658, August 1935.

FREISLER, R. : Vom Majestätsverbrechen zum Volksverret - Die Entwicklung des Hochs- und Landesverratsverbrechen. Deutsche Juristen-Zeitung 40 : 997-1004, 1. September 1935.

Die Nürnberger Judengesetz und die Haager Konvention von 1902. Jewish central information office : 1-18, 1. Oktober 1935.

SAAGE, E. : Das neue Grundbuchrecht - Zweck und wesentlicher Inhalt der neuen Vorschriften. Juristische Wochenschrift 64 : 2769-2779, 5. Oktober 1935.

KUHN : Passive Beleidigungsfähigkeit der Gliederungen der NSDAP. Deutsches Justiz 97 : 1494-1497, 11. Oktober 1935.

SCHÄFER, E. : Der "Allgemeine Teil" des kommenden deutschen Strafrechts nach den Ergebnissen der zweiten Lesung der amtlichen Strafrechtskommission. Deutsche Justiz 97 : 1515-1519, 18. Oktober 1935.

FREISLER, R. : Der Wandel der politischen Grundanschauungen in Deutschland und sein Einfluss auf die Erneuerung von Strafrecht, Strafprozess und Strafvollzug. Sonderbeilage der Zeitschrift der Akademie für deutsches Recht : 7-14, Oktober 1935.

Die Strafrechtsnovellen vom 28. Juli 1935 und die amtlichen Begründungen zu diesen Gesetzen. Amtliche Sonderveröffentlichungen der Deutschen Justiz : 1-86, No. 10.

MASSFELLER : Das Gesetz zum Schutze der Erbgesundheit des deutschen Volkes vom 18. Oktober 1935 (Ehegesundheitsgesetz). Juristische Wochenschrift 64 : 3065-3072, 2. November 1935.

LEPEL, V. : Änderungen des Militärstrafgesetzbuches. Militär-Wochenblatt 120 : 718-727, 4. November 1935.

Sondernummer zum Reichsbauerntag. Deutsche Justiz 97 : 1605-1645, 8. November 1935.
Series of articles on land legislation.

EISENMANN, C. : Le gouvernement de l'Allemagne nationale-socialiste. Comité alsacien d'études et d'informations, Bulletin mensuel jaune 16 : 282-296, 20 novembre 1935.

MANNHEIM, H. : The German prevention of crime Act, 1933. Journal of criminal law and criminology 26 : 517-537, November 1935.

ROSSI, L. : Germanesimo "giuridico"? Rivista di diritto pubblico 27 : 567-575, novembre 1935.

LITTAUER, R. : Case law and systematic law - A descriptive comparison of American and German legal thinking. Social research 2 : 481-502, November 1935.

MEINHOF, C.G. : Rasse und Recht. Juristische Wochenschrift 64 : 3072-3080, November 1935.

RIEGNER, G. : Le pouvoir du "Führer"-Chancelier en Allemagne. Revue du droit public et de la science politique 42 : 701-711, octobre-novembre-décembre 1935.

TRACHTENBERG, B. : La nouvelle législation allemande concernant la citoyenneté et la situation des Israélites. Nouvelle revue de droit international privé 2 : 487-492, octobre-novembre-décembre 1935.

FRICK : Das Reichsbürgergesetz und das Gesetz zum Schutz des deutschen Blutes und der deutschen Ehre vom 15. September 1935. Deutsche Juristen-Zeitung 40 : 1390-1394, 1. Dezember 1935.

MASSFELLER : Das Reichsbürgergesetz und das Gesetz zum Schutze des deutschen Blutes und der deutschen Ehre. Juristische Wochenschrift 64 : 3417-3428, 7 Dezember 1935.

KNOTHE, H.A. : Heilung der Ehenichtigkeit trotz Nichtigkeitsurteil? Juristische Wochenschrift 64 : 3428-3430, 7. Dezember 1935.

POETZSCH-HEFFTER, F., ULE, C.-H., und DERNEDDE, C. : Vom deutschen Staatsleben (vom 30. Januar bis 31. Dezember 1933). Jahrbuch des öffentlichen Rechts 22 : 1-272, 1935.

JELLINEK, W. : Le droit public en Allemagne. Annuaire de l'Institut international de droit public : 350-363, 1935.

KRÜGER, H. : Die Verfassung der Gemeinde im nationalsozialistischen Staat. Zeitschrift für die gesamte Staatswissenschaft 97 : 113-146, Heft 1, 1936.

HUBERNAGEL : Die Neuordnung des Zivilprozesses. Deutsche Juristen-Zeitung 41 : 1. Januar 1936.

FRICK, W. : Die Rassepolitik des Dritten Reiches. Zeitschrift der Akademie für deutsches Recht : 2-5, Januar 1936.
Followed by a series of articles on German marriage laws.

CROHNE : Ein Jahr deutscher Strafrechtspflege. Deutsche Justiz 98 : 6-7, 3. Januar 1936.

VOLKMAR : Die Rechtsentwicklung des vergangenen Jahres auf dem Gebiet des bürgerlichen und Verfahrensrechts. Deutsche Justiz 98 : 8-10, 3. Januar 1936.

WAGNER, D. : Der Rechtsbegriff Soldat. Deutsche Juristen-Zeitung 41 : 82-88, 15. Januar 1936.

FREISLER, R. : Deutsches Rechtsleben 1935 und 1936. Deutsche Justiz 98 : 50-54, 90-97, 129-136, 10, 17, 24. Januar 1936.

Nouvelle législation allemande en matière de mariage. Bulletin de l'Institut juridique international 34 : 25-37, janvier 1936
Textes annexés.

STUDENTKOWSKI, W. : Partei und Staat. Zeitschrift für Politik 26 : 22-33, Januar 1936.

STUCKART, W. : Die staatsrechtlichen Grundlagen des Reiches. Zeitschrift für Politik 26 : 1-11, Januar 1936.

WOLGAST, E. : L'amniste et le traité de Versailles. Revue de droit international, de sciences diplomatiques et politiques 14 : 1-29, janvier-mars 1936.

RAEKE, W. : Die Neugestaltung des deutschen Rechts im Sinne des Parteiprogramms seit dem 30. Januar 1933. Juristische Wochenschrift 65 : 289-290, 1. February 1936.

MÖSSMER, F. : Neugestaltung des Ehescheidungsrechtes. Juristische Wochenschrift 65 : 353-354, 8. Februar 1936.

NIESSEL, A. : Les lois militaires allemandes. Revue des deux mondes 106 : 862-880, 15 février 1936.

MEYER, H. : Die Schöpferpersönlichkeit im kommenden deutschen Urheber- und Verlagsrecht. Zeitschrift der Akademie für deutsches Recht 3 : 155-160, Februar 1936.

MEUDON, L. : La situation juridique des Juifs allemands. Affaires étrangères 6 : 82-94, février 1936.

NEESZE, G. : Verfassungsrechtliches Schrifttum. Zeitschrift für die gesamte Staatswissenschaft 96 : 388-414, Heft 2, 1936.
Annotated bibliography.

OETKER : Zur Reform der Strafprozessordnung. Zeitschrift der Akademie für deutsches Recht 3 : 215-220, Februar 1936.

TODT, F. : Das Recht der deutschen Strassen. Deutsche Juristen-Zeitung 41 : 274-278, 1. März 1936.

WENDEL, F. : La constitution du troisième Reich. Allemagne contemporaine 17 : 45-49, 20 mars 1936.

PREUSS, L. : Punishment by analogy in national socialist penal law. Journal of criminal law and criminology 26 : 847-856, March 1936.

HAMBURGER, E. : La conception de la loi écrite dans le fascisme et la national-socialisme. Affaires étrangères 6 : 161-164, mars 1936.

LOEWENSTEIN, K. : Law in the Third Reich. Yale law journal 45 : 779-815, March 1936.

HONIG, F. : Recent changes in German criminal law. Journal of criminal law and criminology 26 : 857-861, March 1936.

WAGNER, M. : Juristische Streitfragen im Wehrrecht. Deutsche Juristen-Zeitung 41 : 466-471, 15. April 1936.
Error and military service.

LEPAWSKY, A. : The Nazis reform the Reich. American political science review 30 : 324-350, April 1936.

Nouvelle législation allemande en matière de mariage (Contd.). Bulletin de l'Institut juridique international 34 : 214-223, avril 1936.

WELLS, R.H. : The liquidation of the German Länder. American political science review 30 : 350-361, April 1936.

KÜHLEWEIN, R. R. : German legislation since 1933. Tulane law review 10 : 425-433, April 1936.

BONNARD, R. : Le droit et l'Etat dans la doctrine nationale-socialiste. Revue du droit public et de la science politique 53 : 205-238, avril-mai-juin 1936.

RUMPF : Die Prozessfähigkeit des Unfruchbarzumachenden. Deutsche Juristen-Zeitung 41 : 535-539, 1. Mai 1936.

SCHÄFER, K. : Das Gesetz über die Gewährung von Straffreiheit vom 23. April 1936. Deutsche Justiz 98 : 672-679, 1. Mai 1936.

CAPITANT, R. : Les lois de Nuremberg. Revue politique et parlementaire 43 : 283-293, 10 mai 1936.

SOMMER, W. : Partei und Staat. Deutsche Juristen-Zeitung 41 : 594-597, 15. Mai 1936.

SCHÖNKE, A. : Grundsätze des Zivilprozesses in rechtsvergleichender Betrachtung. Zeitschrift der Akademie für deutsches Recht 3 : 411-448, 15. Mai 1936.

MASSFELLER : Nationalsozialistische Neugestaltung des Eherechts. Deutsche Juristen-Zeitung 41 : 607-615, 15. Mai 1936.

WEBER, v. : Die neueste Entwicklung des Strafrech[illegible] in Deutschland. Prager juristische Zeitschrift 16 339-352, 1. Juniheft 1936.

SCHAUWECKER : Der Volksgerichtshof für das Deutsc[illegible] Reich. Juristische Wochenschrift 65 : 1569-1570, 6. u. 13. Juni 1936.

SCHWARZ : Die Rassenschande in der strafrechtlich[illegible] Praxis. Deutsche Juristen-Zeitung 41 : 721-728, 15. Juni 1936.

WOLF, G. : Zur deutschen Rechtsprechung in Sachen russischer Emigranten. Juristische Wochenschrift 65 : 1643-1648, 20. Juni 1936.

GROSCHUFF : Firmenwert einst und jetzt mit einem Beitrag zum Firmenzusatz "deutsch". Juristische Wochenschrift 65 : 1722-1726, 27. Juni 1936.

MULLER, H. : Das Gesetz über die Anwendung deutschen Rechts bei der Ehescheidung vom 24. Januar 1935. Zeitschrift für ausländisches und internatio[illegible]nales Privatrecht 9 : 876-890, Heft 6, 1935.

KUHN : Das Blutschutzgesetz in der strafrechtlich[illegible] Praxis. Deutsche Justiz 98 : 1005-1008, 3. Juli 1936.

STEDTFELD, F. : Die Ein- und Ausfuhr von inländis[illegible]chen Geldsorten (Reichsmarknoten, inländische Schei[illegible]demünzen). Juristische Wochenschrift 65 : 1810-1813, 4. Juli 1936.

DOUBLET, J. : La loi communale allemande du 30 janvier 1935. Revue politique et parlementaire 43 56-63, 10 juillet 1936.

Nouvelle législation allemende en matière de maria[illegible]ge (Contd.). Bulletin de l'Institut international 35 : 76-85, juillet 1936.

RITTAU : Zur Ausländerfrage im Wehrrecht. Zeitschrift für Wehrrecht 1 : 116-118, Juli 1936.

NATIONAL LAW - COUNTRIES

PREUSS, L. : La répression par analogie dans le droit pénal national-socialiste. Revue internationale française du droit des gens 1 : 36-48, 15 juillet 1936.

THIERACK : Der Wirtschaftsverrat. Deutsche Juristen-Zeitung 41 : 849-853, 15. Juli 1936.

FISCHDICK, W. : Der Wirtschaftsschutz im kommenden Strafgesetzbuch. Deutsche Volkswirt 10 : 2137-2140, 24-Juli 1936.

La constitution du IIIe Reich. Europe nouvelle documentaire no. 40 : I-VIII, 25 juillet 1936. Collection de textes.

BRAUNS, E. : Wehrdienst und Wehrpflicht. Deutsche Juristen-Zeitung 41 : 930-934, 1. August 1936.

BLUMHAGEN, H.G. : Zur Wehrpflicht der Reichsdeutschen, die ausser der deutschen noch eine fremde Staatsangehörigkeit besitzen. Deutsche Wehr 40 : 101-102, 20. August 1936.

DIETZ, H. : Zum begriff der Wehrunwürdigkeit - Ausländer in der deutschen Wehrmacht. Zeitschrift für Wehrrecht 1 : 167-177, August 1936.

BONNARD, R. : Le droit et l'Etat dans la doctrine nationale-socialiste. Revue de droit public 53 : 415-440, juillet-août-septembre 1936.

STOLL, H. : Die Rechtsprechung des Reichsgerichts in Zivilsachen. Deutsche Juristen-Zeitung 41 : 977-983, 1. September 1936.

HARMENING, R. : Zwei Jahre Reichserbhofgericht. Zeitschrift der Akademie für deutsches Recht 3 : 754-759, Septemberheft 1936.

LANGE, H. : Das Judentum und die deutsche Rechtswissenschaft. Deutsche Juristen Zeitung 41 : 1130-1134, 1. Oktober 1936.

ZELLER, O. : Drei Jahre Akademie für Deutsches Recht - Zum Gründungstage am 2. Oktober 1933. Juristische Wochenschrift 65 : 2769-2770, 3. Oktober 1936.

TRUNK, H. : Die freiwillige Entmannung. Deutsche Justiz 98 : 1519-1525, 9. Oktober 1936.

SCHMITT, C. : Die duetsche Rechtswissenschaft im Kampf gegen den jüdischen Geist. Deutsche Juristen-Zeitung 41 : 1194-1199, 15. Oktober 1936.

GERLAND, H. : Das Reichskriegsgericht und die deutsche Rechtseinheit. Zeitschrift für Wehrrecht 1 : 264-284, Oktober-November 1936.

KÜCHENHOFF, G. : Führung und Verwaltung im Dritten Reich. Deutsche Justiz 98 : 1682-1687, 6 November 1936.

MERKL, A. : Die Verwaltung des neuen Deutschland (Contd.), Österreichisches Verwaltungsblatt 7 : 245-259, 15. November 1936.

SAEMISCH : Einheitliches Haushaltsrecht im Reich und in den Ländern. Deutsche Juristen-Zeitung 41 : 1386-1391, 1. Dezember 1936.

MENZEL, E. : Das Ende der institutionellen Garantien. Archiv des öffentlichen Rechts 28 : 32-76, Dezember 1936.

KOENIGS, G. : Die Staatshoheit über die deutschen Ströme. Zeitschrift der Akademie für deutsches Recht 4 : 9-11, 1. Januar 1937.

MASSFELLER : Die Gesetz der Vererbung, die Grundlage der deutschen Erb- und Rassenpflege. Juristische Wochenschrift 66 : 8-13, 4./9. Januar 1937.

ADAMI, F.W. : Der besondere Teil der Nationalsozialistischen Leitsätze für ein neues deutsches Strafrecht. Juristische Wochenschrift 66 : 129-131, 23. Januar 1937.

TATARIN-TARNHEYDEN, E. : Grundgedanken des neuen deutschen Staatsrechts. Zeitschrift für öffentliches Recht 17 : 37-54, Heft 1, 1937.

BALLARATE, G. : Il partito nazionalsocialista nella sua organizzazione giuridica e nel suo significato politico. Civiltà fascista 4 : 15-41, gennaio -febbraio 1937.

CEGHINI, C. : Il fronte tedesco del lavoro. Diritto del lavoro 11 : 20-33, gennaio-febbraio 1937.

SCHEUNER, U. : Le peuple, l'Etat, le droit et la doctrine nationale-socialiste. Revue du droit public et de la science politique 54 : 38-57, janvier-février-mars 1937.

HERBIG, GESSLER und HEFERMEHL : Das neue Aktiengesetz. Deutsche Justiz 99 : 184-197, 5. Februar 1937.

STEFFEN, W. : Schiedsgerichte oder Staatsgerichte? Juristische Wochenschrift 66 : 292-294, 6. Februar 1937.

KOFFKA : Gesetz über das Verfahren in Binnenschiffahrtssachen vom 30. Januar 1937. Deutsche Justiz 99 : 225-227, 12. Februar 1937.

WITTLAND : Das deutsche Beamtengesetz vom 26 Januar 1937 (RGBl. I, 39). Juristische Wochenschrift 66 : 345-362, 13. Februar 1937.

FABRICIUS : Das Deutsche Beamtengesetz. Zeitschrift der Akademie für deutsches Recht 4 : 98-101, 15. Februar 1937.

BERNARD, Th. : La réforme du droit allemand. Europe nouvelle 20 : 185-186, 2o février 1937.

RUPPERT : Das deutsche Beamtengesetz - Deutsche Justiz 99 : 305-311, 26. Februar 1937.

Das Aktiengesetz vom 26. Januar 1937. Juristische Wochenschrift 66 : 497-513, 27. Februar 1937. Series of articles.

DEGEN, R. : Zur Strafrechtsreform. Weg 8 : 1-15, Nr. 1, 1937. (Beilage zur "Caritas" 42, Februar 1937).

LOBE, A. :Das richterliche Prüfungsrecht und die Entwicklung der gesetzgebenden Gewalt im neuen Reich. Archiv des öffentlichen Rechts 28 : 194-220, Heft 2, 1937.

WERTHEIMER, L. : Die Reform des Aktienrechts in Deutschland und der Schweiz. Annuario di diritto comparato e di studi legislativi 13 : 157-184, ser. 2, fasc. 3, 1937 (parte prima).

NATIONAL LAW - COUNTRIES

DIETRICH, H. : Zum neuen Aktiengesetz. Juristische Wochenschrift 66 : 649-654, 13. März 1937.

BECKER, E. : Die Rechtstellung der deutschen Länder in der Gegenwart. Zeitschrift für die gesamte Staatswissenschaft 97 : 462-498, Heft 3, 1937.

UHLMAN, E., and RUPP, H.G. : The German system of administrative courts - A contribution to the discussion of the proposed federal administrative court. Illinois law review 31 : 847-878, March 1937.

ELSTER, A. : Persönlichkeit und Sozialgebundenheit im Urheberrecht nach deutscher und französischer Rechtsauffassung. Zeitschrift für ausländisches und internationales Privatrecht 11 : 528-541, Heft 3/4, 1937.

DIETZ, G. : la nouvelle législation allemande sur les sociétés par actions. Journal du droit international 64 : 265-271, mars-avril 1937.

UHLMAN, R.E., and RUPP, H.G. : The German system of administrative courts: A contribution to the discussion of the proposed federal administrative court. Illinois law review 31 : 1028-1046, April 1937.

DAWSON, J.P. : Economic duress and the fair exchange in French and German law. Tulane law review 11 : 345-376, April 1937.

BRINKMANN, W. : Die Ehrengerichte der NSDAP und ihre Beziehungen zu den ordentlichen Gerichten. Deutsche Justiz 99 : 848-852, 4. Juni 1937.

SCHLOSKY : Täterschaft und Teilnahme im kommenden Strafrecht. Deutsche Justiz 99 : 961-967, 25. Juni 1937.

KÜHLEWEIN, R.R. : Recent German legislation. Tulane law review 11 : 601-605, June 1937.

Law and life in the Third Reich. Contemporary review : 55-61, July 1937.

LACHMANN, C. : Le retour à la responsabilité personelle dans le droit commercial allemand. Bulletin trimestriel de la Société de législation comparée 66 : 263-271, juillet-septembre 1937.

DROEGE, H. : Zur Neugestaltung des deutschen Eherechts. Juristische Wochenschrift 66 : 2009-2012, 7. August 1937.

HOPP, K. : Die Genehmigungspflicht nach der Ersten Durchführungsverordnung zum Gesetz über die Sicherung der Reichsgrenze und über Vergeltungsmassnahmen vom 17. August 1937 (RGBl. I, S. 905). Deutsche Justiz 99 : 1344-1346, 3. September 1937.

GLAHN : Das Wehrrecht - Grundsätzliches zu seiner planmässigen Darstellung. Zeitschrift für Wehrrecht 2 : 185-207, September 1937.

ROQUETTE : Familienstand und Familienstandsklagen. Juristiche Wochenschrift 66 : 2553-2559, 9. Oktober 1937.

Führer e costituzione. Stato 8 : 517-531, ottobre 1937.

PLATZ, A. : La nouvelle loi allemande sur les sociétés par actions. Bulletin de l'Institut juridique international 37 : 197-213, octobre 1937.

MARX, F.M. : Germany's new Civil Service Act. American political science review 31 : 878-883, October 1937.

MASSFELLER : Das neue deutsche Personenstandsgesetz. Deutsche Justiz 99 : 1768-1774, 12. November 1937.

KISCH, W. : Anerkennung ausländischer Urteile als Gesetzgebungsproblem. Zeitschrift der Akademie für deutsches Recht 4 : 705-709, 1. Dezember 1937.

BONNARD, R. : Constitution et administration du IIIe Reich allemand. Revue du droit public et de la science politique 54 : 603-617, octobre-novembre-décembre 1937.

LEPPIN, R. : Der Schutz des deutschen Blutes und der deutschen Ehre - Ein Überblick über Rechtsprechung und Schrifttum. Juristische Wochenschrift 66 : 3076-3082, 4. Dezember 1937.

KÖTTGEN, A. : Vom deutschen Staatsleben (vom 1. Januar 1934 bis zum 30. September 1937). Jahrbuch des öffentlichen Rechts der Gegenwart 24 : 3-165, 1937.

Gesetz über die Vernehmung von Angehörigen der Nationalsozialistischen deutschen Arbeitspartei und ihrer Gliederungen vom 1. Dezember 1936 miz Ausführungsbestimmungen. Amtliche Sonderveröffentlichungen der deutschen Justiz : 3-26, Nr. 16, 1937.

HEITZ : Das Reichskriegsgericht. Zeitschrift der Akademie für deutsches Recht 5 : 7-9, 1. Januar 1938.

METHNER : Fünf Jahre nationalsozialistische Gesetzgebung in Deutschland. Danziger Juristen-Zeitung 17 : 1-6, 15. Januar 1938.

RIETZSCH : Die Abwehr des Gewohnheitsverbrechertums - Deutsche Gesetze und Gesetzentwürfe bis zur Machtübernahme. Deutsche Justiz 100 : 134-142, 28. Januar 1938.

WEIMAR, W. : Die Aufnahme von Währungsschutzklauseln verstösst gegen die Berufspflicht. Juristiche Wochenschrift 67 : 216, 29 Januar 1938.

Nouvelle législation allemande en matière de mariage (Contd.). Bulletin de l'Institut juridique international 36 : 41-47, janvier 1938.

BAUDOUIN-BUGNET : La loi allemande du 30 janvier 1937 relative aux sociétés par actions. Bulletin trimestrial de la Société de législation comparée 67 : 8-37, janvier-mars 1938.

ZANGARA, V. : Il partito unico e il nuovo Stato rappresentativo in Italia e in Germania. Rivista di diritto pubblico 30 : 88-111, febbraio 1938.

HUBER, E.R. : Der Schutz der Verfassung. Zeitschrift der Akademie für deutsches Recht 5 : 78-81, 1. Februar 1938.

ZINSER, H.W. : Verfassungs- und verwaltungs rechtliche Fragen des Vierjahresplanes. Archiv des öffentlichen Rechts 29 : 204-219, Heft 2, 1938.

HUBER, E.R. : Einheit und Gliederung des völkischen Rechts - Ein Beitrag zur Überwindung des Gegensatzes von öffentlichem und privatem Recht. Zeitschrift für die gesamte Staatswissenschaft 98 : 310-358, Heft 2, 1938.

ROSENBERG, A. : Die nationalsozialistische Weltanschauung und das Recht. Deutsche Justiz 100 : 357-363, 11. März 1938.

DERNEDDE, C. : Die Praxis der Ämterverbindungen in der Verfassung und Verwaltung des Reiches. Zeitschrift für die gesamte Staatswissenschaft 98 : 535-560, Heft 3, 1938.

ERBE : Das Gesetz über die Gewährung von Entschädigungen bei der Einziehung oder dem Übergang von Vermögen. Juristische Wochenschrift 67 : 993-998, 16-23 April, 1938.

Begründung zu dem Gesetz über die Änderung und Ergänzung familienrechtlicher Vorschriften und über die Rechtsstellung der Staatenlosen vom 12. April 1938 (RGBl. IS. 380). Deutsche Justiz 100 : 619-625, 22. April 1938.

GROSSMANN, C.G. : Present status of German aeronautical law. Air law review 9 : 129-159, April 1938.

KOHLRAUSCH, E. : Rasseverrat im Ausland. Zeitschrift der Akademie für deutsches Recht 5 : 335-338, 15. Mai 1938.

MASSFELLER : Das Gesetz über die Änderung und Ergänzung familienrechtlicher Vorschriften und über die Rechtsstellung der Staatenlosen vom 12. April 1938. Juristische Wochenschrift 67 : 1281-1293, 21. Mai 1938.

GRAU, F. : Zur Einführung des deutschen Wehrmachtstrafrechts in Österreich. Zeitschrift für Wehrrecht 3 : 1-5, Mai-Juni 1938.

VERMEIL, E. : Le droit national-socialiste. Europe nouvelle 21 : 589-591, 621-623, 4, 11 juin 1938.

HUGELMANN, K.G. : Fragen des österreichischen Verwaltungsrechts. Zeitschrift der Akademie für deutsches Recht 5 : 422-424, 15. Juni 1938.

DUQUESNE, J. : L'incorporation constitutionnelle et administrative de l'Autriche au IIIe Reich. Allemagne contemporaine 19 : 113-118, 20 juin 1938.

FREISLER, R. : Fragen der Sicherungswahrung in der deutschen Praxis. Deutsche Justiz (Sonderbeilage) : 41-51, 21. Juni 1938.

SIEBERT, W. : Principi fondamentali dell'ordine nazionalsocialista del lavoro. Stato 9 : 321-338, giugno 1938.

KREBS, G. : A step towards Reichsreform in Germany. American political science review 32 : 536-541, June 1938.

SANDER, P. : Das Wesen des Führer-Staates. Zeitschrift für öffentliches Recht 18 : 161-223, 15. Juli 1938.

VOGELS, W. : Vorarbeiten zur Neuregelung der Gesetzlichen Erfolge. Zeitschrift der Akademie für deutsches Recht 5 : 479-499, 15. Juli 1938.

VOLKMAR : Das neue Eheschliessungs- und Ehescheidungsrecht. Deutsche Justiz 100 : 1118-1121, 1145-1149, 15, 22 Juli 1938.

VOGELS, W. : Die Einführung des Erbhofrechtes im Lande (Österreich). Deitsche Justiz 100 : 1224-1227, 5. August 1938.

MONTREMY, P. de : Le parti national-socialiste. Revue politique et parlementaire 45 : 193-216, 10 août 1938.

REXROTH, E.L. : Das neue Recht der Ehescheidung. Juristische Wochenschrift 67 : 2080-2094, 13./20. August 1938.

WALZ, G.A. : Der Gegensatz von öffentlichem und privatem Recht - Eine Frage des national-sozialistischen Rechtsaufbaus. Zeitschrift der Akademie für deutsches Recht 5 : 581-583, 1. September 1938.

PELCOVITS, N.A. : The social honor courts of Nazi Germany. Political science quarterly 53 : 350-371, September 1938.

LÄMMLE : Die Rechtstellung des Volksgerichtshofs in der deutschen Rechtspflege. Juristische Wochenschrift 67 : 2569-2572, 8. Oktober 1938.

Zweifelsfragen des neuen Eherechts. Juristische Wochenschrift 67 : 2706-2709, 22.-29 Oktober 1938.

SCHNITZER, A.F. : La production des preuves en justice en droit suisse et en droit allemand. Bulletin trimestriel de la Société de législation comparée 67 : 336-364, octobre-décembre 1938.

HENKEL, H. : Bemerkungen zum Bericht der amtlichen Strafprozesskommission. Zeitschrift der Akademie für deutsches Recht 5 : 757-761, 15. November 1938.

HÜLLE : Die Tagung der Gesellschaft für Deutsches Strafrecht. Zeitschrift für Wehrrecht 3 : 291-298, November/Dezember 1938.

STEIMLE, T. : Die Neugestaltung des öffentlichen Rechts und die Verwaltungsgerichtsbarkeit. Zeitschrift für öffentliches Recht 18 : 457-466, 1. Dezember 1938.

BOOR, O. de : Die Funktion des Zivil prozesses in der völkischen Rechtsordnung. Zeitschrift der Akademie für deutsches Recht 5 : 834-838, 15. Dezember 1938.

GOZARD, G. : La nouvelle législation des sociétés par actions en Allemagne. Allemagne contemporaine 19 : 242-243, 20 décembre 1938.

BOERNER, A.V. : The position of the NSDAP in the German constitutional order. American political science review 32 : 1059-1081, December 1938.

MAUPAS, J. : L'Etat national-socialiste. Sciences politiques 53 : 506-531, décembre 1938.

KÖTTGEN, A. : Die Stellung des Beamtentums im völkischen Führerstaat. Jahrbuch des öffentlichen Rechts 25 : 1-65, 1938.

MARKULL, F. : Zur Durchführung der Deutschen Gemeindeordnung. Jahrbuch des öffentlichesn Rechts 25 : 66-279, 1938.

Richtlinien für die Tätigkeit der Justizpressestellen vom 1. Juni 1938. Amtliche Sonderveröffentlichungen der Deutschen Justiz : 5-30, No. 17, 1938.

GROSSMANN-DOERTH : Kampf um die Einmanngesellschaft m.b.H. Deutsches Recht 9 : 9-17, 15. Januar 1939.

Nouvelle législation allemande en matière de mariage (Contd.). Bulletin de l'Institut juridique international 40 : 92-94, janvier 1939.
Les effets exterritoriaux.

GARNER, J.W. : The Nazi proscription of German professors of international law. American journal of international law 33 : 112-119, January 1939.

SCHMITT, C. : Das "allgemeine deutsche Staatsrecht" als Beispiel rechtswissenschaftlicher Systembildung. Zeitschrift für die gesamte Staatswissenschaft 100 : 3-24, 1. un d 2. Heft 1939.

DIETZ, G.W. : La nouvelle législation allemende sur le mariage. Journal du droit international 66 : 52-57, janvier-février 1939.

HASELHOFF : Zum neuen Eherecht. Deutsche Justiz 101 : 216-219, 3. Februar 1939.

BEST, W. : Due Schutzstaffel der NSDAP und die Deutsche Polizei. Deutsches Recht 9 : 44-48, 15. Februar 1939.
Political police.

DRESCH, J. : La conception hitlérienne du droit. Allemagne contemporaine 20 : 25-27, 20 février 1939.

SCHEUNER, U. : Der Gleichheitsgedanke in der völkischen Verfassungsordnung. Zeitschrift für die gesamte Staatswissenschaft 99 : 245-278, Heft 2, 1939.

BUEHLER : Nationalsozialistische Strafrechtspolitik. Zeitschrift der Akademie für deutsches Recht 6 : 232-233, 1. April 1939.

WEH : Die Klagen auf Feststellung der blutsmässigen Abstammung. Deutsches Recht 9 : 132-137, 1. April 1939.

SPANNER, H. : Zur Neuordnung und Rechtsangleichung in der ostmärkischen Verwaltung. Zeitschrift für öffentliches Recht 19 : 465-501, Heft 4, 1939.

NADELMANN, K.H. : De la preuve judiciaire en droit allemand. Bulletin trimestriel de la Société de législation comparée : 169-180, avril-juin 1939.

MANNLICHER, E. : Die neuen Reichsgaue in der Ostmark und im Sudetenland. Zeitschrift der Akademie für deutsches Recht 6 : 337-339, 15. Mai 1939.

ENGERT, K. : Stellung und Aufgaben des Volksgerichtshofes. Deutsches Recht 2 : 177-178, 20. Mai 1939.

Les spoliations raciales et les tribunaux mixtes. Journal des tribunaux mixtes 18 : 4-5, 24 et 25 mai 1939.

Der deutsche Rechtswahrerteg 1939. Deutsche Justiz 101 : 886-908, 21. Mai 1939.

WALTZOG : Kriegsgefangenenrecht unterbesonderer Berücksichtigung der Rechtsprechung des Reichs militärgerichts. Zeitschrift für Wehrrecht 4 : 10-23, Mai-Juni 1939.

HUBER, E. : Der Reichsgau. Zeitschrift der Akademie für deutsches Recht 6 : 364-367, 1. Juni 1939.

GÜRTNER : Grundgedanken des kommenden deutschen Strafrechts und Strafvollzugs. Deutsche Justiz 101 : 977-980, 9. Juni 1939.

FRICK : Entwicklung und Aufbau der öffentlichen Verwaltung in der Ostmark und in den sudetendeutschen Gebieten. Deutsche Verwaltung 16 : 321-330, 10. Juni 1939.

STUCKART : Neubau des Reichs. Deutsches Recht 8 : 819-824, 17. Juni 1939.

STEINWENTER, A. : Das neue Reichsrecht in der Ostmark und sein Verhältnis zum allgemeinen bürgerlichen Gesetzbuch. Zeitschrift der Akademie für deutsches Recht 6 : 441-444, 1. Juli 1939.

STEIMLE, T. : Die Neugestaltung des öffentlichen Rechts und die Verwaltungsgerichtsbarkeit. Deutsche Justiz 101 : 1134-1137, 7. Juli 1939.

FRIEDRICH, W. : Zur Verordnung über tilgbare Aktien und Genusscheine bei den Aktiengesellschaften in der Ostmark und im Sudetenland vom 29. Juni 1939. Deutsche Justiz 101 : 1162-1170, 14. Juli 1939.

ROESTEL, G. : Freizügigkeitsrecht und völkische Ordnung. Deutsche Verwaltung 16 : 421-424, 25. Juli 1939.

BARBAY, G. : Le divorce en droit allemand. Institut belge de droit comparé. Revue trimestrielle 25 : 89-101, juillet-décembre 1939.

FRIEDRICH, E. : Zur Frage der Abschaffung des Zivilprozesses. Zeitschrift der Akademie für deutsches Recht 6 : 524-527, 1. August 1939.

HOCHE : Die Durchführung des Ostmark- und des Sudetengaugesetzes. Deutsche Verwaltung 16 : 481-485, 25. August 1939.

EMIG, K. : Das Polizeiverordnungsrecht der Reichsminister. Archiv des öffentlichen Rechts 31 : 61-89, August 1939.

HEDEMANN, W. : Der Krieg und das bürgerliche Rechtsleben. Deutsche Justiz 101 : 1516-1523, 22. September 1939.

SCHMITT, C. : "Inter pacem et bellum nihil medium". Zeitschrift der Akademie für deutsches Recht 6 : 594-595, 1. Oktober 1939.

KUHNEMANN, H. : Erweiterungen des Geltungsbereichs der deutschen gewerblichen Schutzrechte. Deutsche Justiz 101 : 1626-1628, 20. Oktober 1939.

FEHR, J.C. : Work of the mixed claims commission. American bar association journal 25 : 845-848, October 1939.

BOERNER, A.V. : Toward Reichsreform - The Reichsgaue. American political science review 33 : 835-859, October 1939.

KLEMM, W. : Die Lösung deutsch-jüdischer Mischehen (Contd.). Deutsches Recht 2 : 313-316, Oktober-November 1939.

BECKER, W. : Rundfunkstrafrecht im Kriege. Rundfunkarchiv 12 : 401-404, Oktober-November 1939.

KLEMM, W. : Die Lösung deutsch-jüdischer Mischehen. Deutsches Recht 9 : 1899-1902, 4. November 1939.

FREISLER, R. : Verdunkelung und Dunkelheit. Deutsche Justiz 101 : 1705-1708, 10. November 1939.

NATIONAL LAW - COUNTRIES

TEGTMEYER, W. : Zur Frage der Rechtsstellung der NSDAP. Deutsches Recht 9 : 1998-2001, 25. November 1939.

GLADISCH, W. : Die Praxis des Prisenrechts. Wissen und Wehr : 721-735, 11. Heft 1939.

EMGE, C.A. : Die rechtspolitische Arbeit der Akademie für Deutsches Recht im Kriege. Zeitschrift der Akademie für deutsches Recht 6 : 661-664, 1. Dezember 1939.

MIRKINE-GUETZÉVITCH, B. : L'Etat allemand. Revue politique et parlementaire 46 : 289-296, 10 décembre 1939.

GERMANY
(International law and practice, Aliens, Naturalization)

OSWALD : Zuständigkeitsfragen im Verhältnis zwischen Deutschland und der Tschechoslowakei. Zeitschrift für ausländisches und internationales Privatrecht 10 : 85-88, Heft 1/3, 1935.

HELD, H.J. : Vorbehalt und Verweisung im deutschen internationalen Privatrecht. Nordisk tidsskrift for international ret, Acta scandinavica juris gentium 6 : 73-80, fasc. 2-3, 1935.

PREUSS, L. : The position of aliens in national socialist penal law reform. American journal of international law 29 : 206-218, April 1935.

BRUNS, G. : Rechtsprechung in Auslieferungssachen se seit Erlass des Auslieferungsgesetzes vom 23. Dezember 1939. Zeitschrift für ausländisches öffentliches Recht und Völkerrecht 5 : 721-733, Juli 1935.

PREUSS, L. : National socialist conceptions of international law. American political science review 29 : 594-609, August 1935.

Einzelfragen aus dem deutschen internationalen Ehescheidungsrecht. Juristische Wochenschrift 64 : 2665-2469, 31. August 1935.

PREUSS, L. : La conception raciale nationale-socialiste du droit international. Revue générale de droit international public 42 : novembre-décembre 1935.

Extradition to Germany. Grotius society, Problems of peace and war 21 : 191-194, 1935.

MÜLLER, H. : Die deutsche Rechtsprechung auf dem Gebiete des internationalen Privatrechts im Jahre 1934 : Zeitschrift für ausländische und internationales Privatrecht : 5-317, Sonderheft, 1935.

Extradition to Germany. Grotius society, Probelms of peace and war 21 : 191-194, 1935.

GARNER, J.W. : Recent German nationality legislation. American journal of international law 30 : 96-99, January 1936.

VORTISCH, F. : Die gegenseitige Anerkennung der Gerichtsbarkeit in Ehesachen zwischen dem Deutschen Reich und der Schweizerischen Eidgenossenschaft. Zeitschrift für ausländisches und internationales Privatrecht 10 : 17-39, Heft 1/3, 1936.

BOSCHAN : Die Tätigkeit der deutschen Konsulate in Vormundschafts- und Pflegschaftssachen. Zeitschrift für ausländisches und internationales Privatrecht 10 : 89-96, Heft 1/3, 1936.

SCHMITT, C. : Die nationalsozialistische Gesetzgebung und der Vorbehalt des "ordre public" im Internationalen Privatrecht. Zeitschrift für deutsches Recht 3 : 204-211, Februar 1936.

Einige Bemerkungen zu den zwischenstaatlichen Bestimmungen des Ehegesundheitsgesetzes vom 18. Oktober 1935. Juristische Wochenschrift 65 : 772-776, 21. März 1936.

Deutsche Rechtsprechung in Auslieferungssachen. Deutsche Justiz 98 : 556-586, 3. April 1936.

REISNER, P. : Mehrfache gerichtliche Entschedungen in einem Auslieferungsfall. Deutsche Justiz 98 : 546-551, 3. April 1936.

SCHIFFER, W. : Treaty-making in post-war Germany. American journal of international law 30 : 216-232, April 1936.

CHKLAVER, G. : L'Hitlérisme et le droit des gens. Revue de droit international 17 : 560-564, avril-mai-juin 1936.

SCHIEFFER, E. : Zur Frage der Anerkennung der neuen deutschen Ehegesetze in den übrigen europäischen Ländern. Paneuropa 12 : 128-130, Mai 1936.

SCHÜLE, A. : Die Umwandlung völkerrechtlicher Verträge des deutschen Reichs in deutsches Landesrecht. Zeitschrift für ausländisches öffentliches Recht und Völkerrecht 6 : 269-285, Mai 1936.

METTGENBERG, W. : Deutsche Konsulargerichtsbarkeit. Deutsche Justiz 98 : 858-861, 1. Juni 1936.

FÉAUX de la CROIX, E. : Die Neugestaltung des konsularischen Notariatsrechts. Deutsche Justiz 98 : 959-963, 25. Juni 1936.

FÉAUX de la CROIX, E. : Zur Neuordnung des konsularischen Beurkundungswesens. Juristische Wochenschrift 65 : 1736-1740, 27. Juni 1936.

POHLE, R. : Zur Vollstreckung tschechoslowakischer Forderungen und Urteile in Deutschland. Juristische Wochenschrift 65 : 1873-1875, 11. Juli 1936.

HARTENSTEIN, H. : Dollarbondurteil und Auslandsanleihengesetz. Juristische Wochenschrift 65 : 2017-202o, 25. Juli 1936.

AMMON, W. : Deutscher Auslieferungsverkehr in den Jahren 1927 bis 1935. Deutsche Justiz 98 : 1149-1156, 31. Juli 1936.

MASSFELLER, A. : Mischehen und Grenztrauungen. Juristische Wochenschrift 65 : 2433-2439, 29. August 1936.

NADELMANN, K.H. : Le droit allemand et les effets d'une faillite étrangère. Bulletin trimestriel de la Société de législation comparée 65 : 404-412, octobre-décembre 1936.

MEZGER, E. : Mariage et divorce des Français en Allemagne et des Allemands en France. Nouvelle revue de droit international privé 3 : 507-526, juillet-août-septembre 1936.

NATIONAL LAW - COUNTRIES

AMMON, W. von : Die Strafbarkeit von Ausländern nach paragraph 5 Abs. 2 Blutschutzg. Juristische Wochenschrift 65 : 2962-2965, 24. Oktober 1936.

BEITZKE, G. : Die Reichsbahn vor ausländischen Gerichten. Deutsche Juristen-Zeitung 41 : 1269-1275, 1. November 1936.

THOMAS, W. : Die ausländischen Abwertungen im deutschen Recht. Juristische Wochenschrift 65 : 3438-3441, 12. Dezember 1936.

SCHNIEDERKÖTTER, T. : Deutsche Rechtsprechung in Auslieferungssachen. Zeitschrift für Völkerrecht 21 : 87-93, Heft 1, 1937.

LEVIS, D. : Deutsch-schweizerischer Vollstreckungsvertrag. Zeitschrift für schweizerisches Recht 56 : 352-388, Heft 2, 1937.

DOMKE, M. : La législation allemande sur les devises en droit international privé. Journal du droit international 64 : 226-243, mars-avril 1937.

SCHRODER, W.M. : La législation allemande concernant la race et le mariage vue sous l'angle du droit international privé néerlandais. Nouvelle revue de droit international privé 4 : 275-301, avril-juin 1937.

JONAS : Das deutsch-italienische Vollstreckungsabkommen vom 9. März 1936. Deutsche Justiz 99 : 888-893, 11. Juni 1937.

MICHEL, J. : La convention fiscale franco-allemande du 9 novembre 1934. Revue critique de droit international 32 : 585-645, juillet à décembre 1937.

VANSELOW : Sind für Deutschland Neutralitätsvorbereitungen nach Art des neuen U.S.A.-Neutralitätsgesetzes nötig? Wissen und Wehr : 491-495, August 1937.

SÜSS, T. : Ehescheidung polnischer Staatsangehöriger in Deutschland. Zeitschrift der Akademie für deutsches Recht 4 : 558-561, 15. September 1937.

METTGENBERG, W. : Zum deutsch-finnischen Auslieferungsvertrag. Deutsche Justiz 99 : 1526-1528, 1. Oktober 1937.

RIESENFELD, S. : Decision of the German Supreme Cour on termination of treaties of the German States. American journal of international law 31 : 720-725, October 1937.

BEITZKE, G. : L'autorisation pour le commerce des sociétés étrangeres en Allemagne. Journal du droit international 64 : 1001-1005, novembre-décembre 1937.

FABRICIUS, H. : Zur Vollstreckung ausländischer Schiedssprüche im Inland. Juristische Wochenschrift 66 : 3134-3136, 11. Dezember 1937.

LEDERLE, A. : Das Auslieferungsrecht und die neue Rechtsgestaltung. Archiv des öffentlichen Rechts 30 : 71-92, 1. Heft 1938.

Zur Entwicklung des Goldklauselproblems in Deutschland. Niemeyers Zeitschrift für Internationales Recht 52 : 262-295, Heft 3-4, 1938.

GIESE, F. : La forma esterna dello Stato Germanico. Rivista di diritto pubblico 30 : 189-198, aprile 1938.

GUILHOT, J. : La convention fiscale franco-allemande du 9 novembre 1934. Journal du droit international 65 : 439-452, mai-juin 1938.

BEITZKE, G. : Das Verhältnis zwischen deutschem und österreichischem BGB - Interlokal- und international privatrechtliche Fragen nach der Wiedervereinigung. Zeitschrift der Akademie für deutsches Recht 5 : 368-370, 1. Juni 1938.

STUCKART : Probleme des Staatsangehörigkeitsrechts. Zeitschrift der Akademie für deutsches Recht 5 : 401-403, 15. Juni 1938.

CIOFFI, A. : Collaborazione giuridica italo-germanica. Echi e commenti 19 : 585-587, 5 luglio 1938.

Begründung zu dem Gesetz über die Vereinheitlichung des Rechts der Eheschliessung und der Ehescheidung im Lande Österreich und im übrigen Reichsgebiet vom 6. Juli 1938. Deutsche Lustiz 100 : 1102-1114, 15. Juli 1938.

HUEBER : Die Rechtsangleichung auf dem Gebiete des Zivil- und Strafrechtes zwischen Österreich und dem Altreich. Duetsche Justiz 100 : 1169-1176, 29. Juli 1938.

HARMS, E. : Die dänische Arordnung über die Anerkennung von deutschen Urteilen vom 13. April 1938. Juristische Wochenschrift 67 : 1942-1943, 30. Juli 1938.

GARNER, J.W. : Questions of state succession raised by the German annexation of Austria. American journal of international law 32 : 421-438, July 1938.

I lavori del Comitato per le relazioni giuridiche italotedeschi (Roma, 20-26 giugno 1938-XVI). Stato 9 : 385-420, luglio 1938.

Il comitato giuridico italo-germanico per la riforma del diritto delle obbligazioni. Rivista del diritto commerciale 36 : 435-439, luglio-agosto 1938.

PERRIN, B. : L'Anschluss et la confiscatiion des valeurs mobilières appartenant aux émigrés. Nouvelle revue de droit international privé 5 : 527-544, juillet-août-septembre 1938.

WEBER, W. : Das Reichskonjordat in der deutschen Rechtsentwicklung. Zeitschrift der Akademie für deutsches Reich 5 : 532-536, 1. August 1938.

OSWALD : Praktische Fragen aus dem Ehescheidungsrechte im Verhältnis zwischen dem Deutschen Reiche und der Tschechoslowakei. Juristische Wochenschrift 67 : 2119-2123, 13/20. August 1938.

METTGENBERG, W. : Die Verträge und Vereinbarungen des Deutschen Reiches mit den Oststaaten über strafrechtliche Angelegenheiten - Eine Bestandsaufnahme. Zeitschrift für osteuropäisches Recht 4 : 69-88, August 1937.

THEES : Bemerkungen zu dem Gesetz über die Umwandlung der inländischen Fremdwährungsversicherungen. Deutsche Justiz 100 : 1516-1518, 23. September 1938.

GARNER, J.W. : Germany's responsibility for Austria's debts. American journal of international law 32 : 766-775, October 1938.

NIPPERDEY, H.C. : Die Vereinheitlichung des Rechts der Schuldverhältnisse in Italien und Deutschland. Zeitschrift der Akademie für deutsches Recht 5 : 721-725, 1. November 1938,

Deutsche Rechtsprechung in Auslieferungssachen. Deutsche Justiz 100 : 1825-1849, 18. November 1938.

FÉAUX de la CROIX, E. : Der deutsch-tschecho-slowakische Staatsangehörigkeits- und Optionsvertrag vom 10. November 1938.

FEUTH : Internationales Privatrecht oder deutsche Rechtsbereich-Normen? Zeitschrift der Akademie für deutsches Recht 6 : 20-21, 1.Januar 1939.

WALZ, G.A. : Das Völkerrecht in der neuen Reichsjustiz-Ausbildungsordnung. Zeitschrift für Völkerrecht 23 : 108-110, Heft 1, 1939.

BUMKE, E. : Die Jahrestagung der Arbeitsgemeinschaft für die deutsch-polnischen Rechtsbeziehungen in Warschau. Zeitschrift der Akademie für deutsches Recht 6 : 73-78, 1. Februar 1939.

KREISSL, A. : Rechtsfragen der Gemeindeverwaltung im Zusammenhang mit der Eingliederung der sudetendeutschen Gebiete. Zeitschrift der Akademie für deutsches Recht 6 : 85-88, 1. Februar 1939.

Verordnung (von 12. Februar 1939) über die deutsche Staatsangehörigkeit in den sudetendeutschen Gebieten. Reichsgesetzblatt (Teil I) : 205-206, 14. Februar 1930.

OSWALD : Der deutsch-tschechoslowakische Staatsvertrag über Staatsangehörigkeits- und Optionsfragen. Juristische Wochenschrift 68 : 473-476, 25. Februar 1939.

GLOBKE, H. : Die Regelung der Staatsangehörigkeitsverhältnisse und der Schutz der Volksgruppen nach den deutsch-tschecho-slowakischen Vereinbarungen v. 20. November 1938. Zeitschrift für osteuropäisches Recht 5 : 473-486, Februar 1939.

COHN, E.J. : Foreign awards and exchange restrictions under German law. Journal of comparatibe legislation and international law 21 : 75-82, February 1939.

REISNER, P. : Überleitung der Strafrechtspflege und Einführung des deutschen Auslieferungsrechts in den sudetendeutschen Gebieten. Deutsche Justiz 101 : 370-376, 3. März 1939.

KOELLREUTTER, O. : Der Ausbau der rechtswissenschatlichen Beziehungen zwischen Deutschland und Japan. Zeitschrift der Akademie für deutsches Recht 6 : 188-190, 15. März 1939.

December 10, 1938. Gazzetta ufficiale del Regno d'Italia (Parte la) 80 : 1354-1355, 16 marzo 1939.
Exchange of notes concerning reciprocal notification of naturalisation of citizens of one State in the other. (Text in German and Italian).

Razza e diritto al Convegno italo-tedesco di Vienna. Stato 10 : 129-167, marzo 1939.
Series of articles.

CALLE, A. : La nazificación del derecho internacional público. Estudios de derecho : 33-37, abril 1939.

SCHMITT, C. : Der Reichsbegriff im Völkerrecht. Deutsches Recht 9 : 341-344, 29. April 1939.

REISNER, P. : Einführung des deutschen Auslieferungsrechts in der Ostmark. Deutsche Justiz 101 : 829-835, 17. Mai 1939.

FRANKENSTEIN, E. : La législation raciste allemande et la convention de La Haye sur le mariage. Nouvelle revue de droit international privé 6 : 54-69, janvier-juin 1939.

FIEDOROWICZ, G. de : Nationalité des Israélites de Pologne domiciliés en Allemagne. Nouvelle revue de droit international privé 6 : 7-53, janvier-juin 1939.

GLOBKE, H. : Der deutsch-litauische Vertrag über die Staatsangehörigkeit der Memelländer. Zeitschrift für osteuropäisches Recht 6 : 105-113, September-Oktober 1939.

KRIEGE, W. : Die neue deutsche Prisenordnung. Zeitschrift der Akademie für Deutsches Recht 6 : 625-627, 664-666, 1. November, 1. Dezember 1939.

KUNERT, W. : Das deutsches Kriegsrecht - Kriegs-Verwaltungsrecht. Deutsches Recht 9 : 1961-1963, 18. November 1939.

MARKUS, J. : Le traité germano-tchécoslovaque du 15 mars 1939 à la lumière du droit international. Revue générale de droit international public 46 : 653-665, novembre-décembre 1939.

WILLEMS, H. : Die neue Prisenordnung. Deutsche Verwaltung 16 : 589-595, 25. Dezember 1939.

GERMANY
(Copyrights, Patents, Trademarks)

Gewerblicher Rechtsschutz und Urheberrecht. Zeitschrift der Akademie für deutsches Recht 3 : 501-549, 2. Mai-Heft 1936.
Special number.

KLAUER, G. : Die Neugestaltung des deutschen Patentrechts. Juristische Wochenschrift 65 : 1489-1492, 30. Mai 1936.

HEDEMANN, J.W. : Deutschlands neues Patentgesetz. Deutsche Juristen-Zeitung 41 : 658-666, 1. Juni 1936.

VOLKMAR : Die Bedeutung des neuen Patentgesetzes für das Verfahren in Patentverletzungsstreitigkeiten. Deutsche Justiz 98 : 851-856, 1. Juni 1936.

The German copyright Bill 1933/1939. Copyright 5 : 93-102, August/September 1939.

GREAT BRITAIN

HOLLOND, H.A. : Pleading and proof at common law. Cambridge law journal 6 : 1-15, No. 1, 1936.

MULLINS, C. : Summary courts law and procedure - The need for codification (Contd.). Law journal 81 : 90-91, February 8, 1936.

KEMPT, G. : Die Stellung des Solicitors und Barristers im englischen Rechtsleben. Archiv des öffentlichen Rechts 27 : 284-325, Heft 3, 1936.

NATIONAL LAW - COUNTRIES

CARR, C.T. : Ignorance of the law is avoided in England by a method which might apply in the American States. State government 149 : 149-151, July 1936.

BUTTERWORTH, A.K. : Compensation for road accidents. Nineteenth century 120 : 365-376, September 1936.

KEMPT, G. : Die Stellung des Solicitors und Barristers im englischen Rechtsleben. Archiv des öffentlichen Rechts 28 : 1-21, Dezember 1936.

GIBB, A.D. : The inter-relation of the legal systems of Scotland and England. Law quarterly review 53 : 61-79, January 1937.

SCHÜLE, A. : Verfassungsrechtliche Bermerkung zur Abdankung König Eduards VIII. Zeitschrift der Akademie für deutsches Recht 4 : 20-22, 1. Januar 1937.

WEIDENBAUM, P. : British constitutional law and the recent crisis. New York University law quarterly review 14 : 341-357, March 1937.

MANNHEIM, H. : Zum englischen Pressrecht. Geistiges Eigentum 4 : 333-344, März-April 1937.

End immoral mariage. Time and tide 18 : 536-537, April 24 1937.
Reform proposals.

FAIRLIE, J.A. : The doctrine of "stare decisis" in British courts of last resort. Michigan law review 35 : 946-967, April 1937.

WORTLEY, B.A. : The reform of the law (Contd.). - Codification. Nineteenth century 121 : 622-635, May 1937.

The future of divorce. New statesman and nation 14 : 209-210, 7 August 1937.

WORTLEY, B.A. : The reform of the law (Contd.) - Commercial arbitration. Ninteenth century 122 : 738-751, December 1937.

IWI, E.F. : A plea for an Imperial Privy Council and Judicial Committee. Grotius society Transactions 23 : 127-146, 1937.

LATEY, W. : The Matrimonial Causes Act, 1937 (Contd.). Law journal 85 : 47-49, January 15 1938.

ROTHSCHILD, V.H. : Government regulation of trade unions in Great Britain. Columbia law review 38 : 1-48, January 1938.

DOMKE, W. : Grundzüge der englischen Rechtsreform 1936-1938. Zeitschrift für vergleichende Rechtswissenschaft 52 : 205-255, Heft 2/3, 1938.

NORMAND : The law of defamation in Scotland. Cambridge law journal 6 : 327-338, No. 3, 1938.

BAILEY, K.H. : The abdication legislation in the United Kingdom and in the dominions. Politica 3 : 1-26, March 1938.

PELLERIN, P., et J. : La nouvelle loi anglaise sur le divorce, la séparation de corps et la nullité du mariage. Journal du droit international 65 : 232-243, mars-avril 1938.

BINNEY, C. : Military courts and the Judge-Advocate-General. Nineteenth century 123 : 475-485, April 1938.

JENNINGS, W.I. : Principes généraux de droit administratif anglais. Revista de drept public 13 : 163-217, Aprilie-Mai-Junie 1938.

O'SULLIVAN, R. : The bill to amend the law of libel. Law journal 65 : 440-441, 25 June 1938.

STONE, J. : The Evidence Act, 1938. Law journal 65 : 441-443, 25 June 1938.

FOSTER, J. : Law revision. Modern law review 2 : 14-21, June 1938.
The law revision committee.

HAYNES, E. : Contemporary English judges. California law review 26 : 564-578, July 1938.

BATTELLI, M. : Le premier ministre en Grande-Bretagne. Revue d'histoire politique et constitutionnelle 2 : 387-428, juillet-septembre 1938.

VAN MUYSEWINCKEL, J. : La nouvelle loi anglaise en matière de divorce, séparation et nullité de mariage. Institut belge de droit comparé, Revue trimestrielle 24 : 101-109, juillet-décembre 1938.

HARDING, R. : The legalisation of voluntary euthanasia. Nineteenth century 74 : 238-248, August 1938.

CHANEY, W.S. : Amend the bankruptcy law! Nineteenth century 24 : 200-211, August 1938.

Penal reform. Law journal 86 : 360-361, 26 November 1938.

Insanity and divorce. Law journal 86 : 380, 3 December 1938.

GORDON, E. : La confection d'une loi en Angleterre Annales de l'Institut de droit comparé de l'université de Paris 3 : 245-256, 1938.

WINDER, W.H.D. : Equity in the courts of great sessions. Law quarterly review 55 : 106-121, January 1939.

Reporting the law. Law quarterly review 55 : 29-36, January 1939.

FRY, M. : The "Penal Reform" bill. Forntightly 145 : 8-18, January 1939.

RANKIN, G. : The Judicial Committee of the Privy Council. Cambridge law journal 7 : 2-22, No. 1, 1939.

DEPITRE, M. : Les récentes réformes anglaises relatives à la dissolution du mariage. Bulletin trimestrial de la Société de législation comparée 68 : 112-122, janvier-mars 1939.

RUCK, S.K. : The need for the criminal justice bill. Political quarterly 10 : 22-40, January-March 1939.

PATON, G.W. : Reform and the English law of defamation. Illinois law review 33 : 669-684, February 1939.

The Criminal Justice Bill. Howard journal 5 : 143-144, No. 3, 1939.

RADZINOWICZ, L. : The present trend of English penal policy. Law quarterly review 55 : 273-288, April 1939.

Defence measures. Economist 136, 1939. Summary of new Defence Regulations published in every issue since September 2, 1939.

Repair of war damage. Law journal 88 : 191, 23 September 1939.

Defence regulations : amendments. Law journal 88 : 192-193, 23 September 1939.

COHN, E.J. : Currency restrictions and the conflict of laws (Contd.). Law quarterly review 55 : 552-564, October 1939.

GREAT BRITAIN
(International law, Aliens)

GORDON, E. : La théorie des "acts of State" en droit anglais. Revue du droit public 53 : 5-40, janvier-février-mars 1936.

Affreightment and the law of the flag. Law journal 81 : 219, 28 March 1936.

Die Vollstreckung ausländischer Urteile in Grossbritannien. Niemeyers Zeitschrift für internationales Recht 51 : 299-309, Heft 3-4, 1936.

BATY, T. : The nationality of a married woman at common law. Law quarterly review 52 : 247-252, April 1936.

PERROUD, J, : La convention franco-britannique sur l'effet extraterritorial des jugements. Revue critique de droit international 32 : 333-343, avril-juin 1936.

HOSTIE, J. : La sentence arbitrale de M. Bagge dans le différend anglo-finlandais- Revue générale de droit international public 43 : 327-357, mai-juin 1936.

The law and foreign volunteers. New statesman and nation 12 : 1021-1022, 19 December 1936.
The Foreign Enlistment Act.

CORDIER, M.Y. : De la notion de domicile en droit comparé (France et Angleterre). Journal du droit international 64 : 969-989, novembre-décembre 1937.

MORRIS, J.H.C. : Capacity to make a marriage settlement contract in English private international law. Law quarterly review 54 : 78-86, January 1938.

HONIG, F. : Le régime des successions applicable aux étrangers domiciliés en Angleterre. Journal du droit international 65 : 5-20, janvier-février 1938.

CHARTERIS, A.H. : Scotland and the common law system of private international law. Australian law journal 11 : 378-388, 18 February 1938.

STEWART, R.B. : Treaty-making procedure in the United Kingdom. American political science review 32 : 655-669, August 1938.

PINNA, L.A. da : Infants and foreign guardians. Law journal 86 : 195-196, 24 September 1938.

FRANZEN, H. : Irland und Grossbritannien seit 1919 - Ein Beitrag zur Verfassungslehre. Jahrbuch des öffentlichen Rechts 25 : 280-375, 1938.

BECKETT, W.E. : International law in England. Law quarterly review 55 : 257-272, April 1939.

ATWATER, E. : British control over the export of war materials. American journal of international law 33 : 292-317, April 1939.

LAUTERPACHT, H. : Is international law part of the law of England? Law journal 87 : 398-399, 3 June 1939.

SINGTON, D. : Alien tribunals. Time and tide 20 : 1484-1485, November 25 1939.

LAUTERPACHT, H. : The form of Foreign Office certificates. British yearbook of international law 20 : 125-128, 1939.

GREECE

CARABIBER, C. : Chronique de la récente jurisprudence grecque en matière de droit international privé. Revue critique de droit international 30 : 76-83, janvier-mars 1935.

VALLINDAS, P. : Die vorläufige Inkraftsetzung völkerrechtlicher Verträge in Griechenland. Zeitschrift für ausländisches öffentliches Recht und Völkerrecht (Berichte und Urkunden) 5 : 210-214, Februar 1935.

FRAGISTAS, C.N. : Das Eherecht im Entwurf des griechischen B.G.B. Zeitschrift für ausländisches und internationales Privatrecht 9 : 384-404, Heft 3, 1935.

TÉNÉKIDÈS, C.G. : Le divorce des Hellènes à l'étranger et des étrangers en Grèce en l'état actuel du droit hellénique. Journal du droit international 62 : 305-324, mars-avril 1935.

TÉNÉKIDÈS, C.G. : Les tendances du droit hellénique et les principes du droit des gens. Revue de droit international et de législation comparée 62 : 765-808, No. 4, 1935.

MACRIS, T.D. : Die Grundgedanken für die Ausarbeitung des Entwurfs eines griechischen Zivilgesetzbuches. Zeitschrift für ausländisches und internationales Privatrecht 9 : 586-614, Heft 4/5, 1935.

LEONTIADES, L. : Der griechisch-türkische Bevölkerungsaustausch. Zeitschrift für ausländisches öffentliches Recht und Völkerrecht 5 : 546-576, Juli 1935.

ARGYROPOULO, P.A. : La réforme constitutionnelle en Grèce. Revue des sciences politiques 51 : 8-34, janvier-mars 1936.

TRIANTAPHYLLOPOULOS, K. : Der griechische Entwurf eines Obligationenrechts. Zeitschrift für ausländisches und internationales Privatrecht 10 : 53-66, Heft 1/3, 1936.

FRAGISTAS, C.N. : Griechische Rechtsprechung auf dem Gebiete des internationalen Privatrechts (1932-1935). Zeitschrift für ausländisches und internationales Privatrecht 10 : 636-650, Heft 4, 1936.

TÉNÉKIDÈS, C.-G. : La faillite d'après le système de droit international privé en vigueur en Grèce. Journal du droit international 63 : 761-792, juillet-octobre 1936.

SVOLOS, A.-J. : Grèce - Chronique constitutionnelle. Annuaire de l'Institut de droit public : 304-323, 1936.

ANASTASIADIS, E., LOGOTHETIS, P. e ZORAS, G. : Rassegna di legislazione greca (anni 1928-1929-1930 -1931). Annuario di diritto comparato e di studi legislativi (Parte IV) 9 : 113-220, 1936.

MARIDAKIS, G.S. : Die internationalprivatrecht lichen Bestimmungen im Entwurf eines griechischen bürgerlichen Gesetzbuches. Zeitschrift für ausländisches und internationales Privatrecht 11 : 111-130, Heft 1-2, 1937.

BALTATZIS, A. : Die Behandlung des ausländischen Rechts im griechischen Zivilprozess. Zeitschrift für ausländisches und internationales Privatrecht 11 : 131-136, Heft 1-2, 1937.

STASINÒPULOS, M. : I diritti locali in Grecia. Annuario di diritto comparato e di studi legislativi 13 : 145-156, ser. 2, fasc. 3, 1937 (parte prima).

VALLINDAS, P. : Il diritto internazionale privato nel progetto del codice greco. Annuario di diritto comparato e di studi legislativi 13 : 197-201, ser. 2, fasc. 3, 1937 (parte prima).

ANASTASIADIS, E. : I cento anni del codice di commercio greco. Annuario di diritto comparato e di studi legislativi 12 : 265-276, fasc. 5, 1937.

VALLINDAS, P. : El derecho internacional privado en el proyecto de código civil helénico. Revista de derecho internacional 16 : 304-311, 30 junio 1937.

TÉNÉKIDÈS, C.G. : Le mariage en droit international privé hellénique. Bulletin de l'Institut juridique international 37 : 40-47, juillet 1937.

DASKALAKIS, G.D. : Die Verfassungsentwicklung Griechenlands. Jahrbuch des öffentlichen Rechts der Gegenwart 24 : 266-334, 1937.

MARIDAKIS, G.S. : Le projet du Code civil grec et le droit international privé. Revue critique de droit international 33 : 346-350, avril-juin 1938. Texte annexé.

MARIDAKIS, G.S. : Le projet du Code civil grec et le droit international privé. Revue critique de droit international 33 : 346-350, avril-juin 1938.

MICHAÉLIDÈS-NOUAROS, G. : La protection de la propriété artistique et littéraire en Grèce. Geistiges Eigentum 3 : 439-454, Mai/Juin 1938.

SIMANTIRAS, J. : Das Personenrecht im griechischen Entwurf. Zeitschrift für ausländisches und internationales Privatrecht 11 : 761-785, Heft 5/6, 1937.

TÉNÉKIDÈS, C.G. : Le droit international privé en Grèce d'après le Traité de Droit international privé de MM. Georges Streit et Pierre Vallinda. Journal du droit international 65 : 468-479, mai-juin 1938.

DERTILIS, P.B. : Le droit budgétaire en Grèce (Contd.). Revue de science et de législation financières 36 : 344-362, juillet-août-septembre 1938.

La Commission pour la préparation des lois au Ministère de la justice. Messager d'Athènes 60 : 3, 23 novembre 1938.

LIGEROPOULO, A. : Das Kaufrecht im Entwurf des Griechischen Bürgerlichen Gesetzbuchs. Zeitschrift für ausländisches und internationales Privatrecht 12 : 75-101, Heft 1/2 1939.

VALLINDAS, P. : Les nouveaux codes grecs. Revue trimestrielle de l'Institut belge de droit comparé 25 : 34-37, janvier-mars 1939.

DAMASCHINO, D.N. : Grèce - Mouvement législatif des années 1938-1939. Revue internationale de droit pénal 16 : 208-216, No. 2, 1939.

RANKIN, K.L. : Commercial arbitration in Greece. U.S. Department of commerce, Comparative law series 11 : 120-126, March 1939.

VALLINDAS, P. : Les nouveaux codes et l'activité du ministère de la Justice en Grèce. Bulletin trimestriel de la Société de législation comparée 68 : 223-230, avril-juin 1939.

ARGYROPOULO, P.-A. : L'évolution constitutionnelle en Grèce au XXe siècle. Revue d'histoire politique et constitutionnelle 3 : 186-214, avril-juin 1939.

SIMANTIRAS, C.J. : Das Erbrecht im Griechischen Entwurf. Zeitschrift für ausländisches und internationales Privatrecht 12 : 734-771, Heft 5/6, 1939.

GEORGOPOULOS, C.L. : Grèce - années 1937-1939. Istituto italiano di studi legislativi, Legislazione internazionale 8 : 705-918, tomo II, 1939. Index de législation et traductions.

PATRINOS, E. : La nouvelle loi grecque sur les marques. Propriété industrielle 55 : 204-205, décembre 1939.

GUATEMALA

SCHUSTER, E. : The judicial status of non-registered foreign corporations in Guatemala. Tulane law review 12 : 74-107, December 1937.

AREVALO, I.G. : Condition juridique des étrangers au Guatemala. Nouvelle revue de droit international privé 5 : 781-784, octobre-novembre-décembre 1938.

HUNGARY

SCHWARTZ, I. : Die ungarische Gerichtspraxis in Sachen des internationalen Erbrechtes. Niemeyers Zeitschrift für internationales Recht 50 : 60-71, 1.-3. Heft, 1935.

RÁCZ, G. : Internationales aus dem ungarischen Strafrecht. Zeitschrift für osteuropäisches Recht 1 : 365-375, 405-420, Januar, Februar 1935.

RÁCZ, G. : Die vom Königreich Ungarn abgeschlossene und ratifizierten internationalen Staatsverträge. Zeitschrift für osteuropäisches Recht 1 : 530-541, April 1935.

NATIONAL LAW - COUNTRIES

DEMMER, O. : Das ungarische Eherecht und die ungarische Zivilprozessordnung. Juristische Blätter 64 : 271-275, 22. Juni 1935.

LUKACS, G. : Loi hongroise pour la sauvegarde des propriétaires agricoles endettés. Revue générale du droit, de la législation et de la jurisprudence 59 : 174-186, juillet-août-septembre 1935.

ALMASI, A. : Die Bedeutung des Gerichtsgebrauchs für das ungarische Privatrecht. Zeitschrift für osteuropäisches Recht 2 : 195-217, Oktober 1935.

HAELLER, O. : Das ungarische Eherecht und die ungarische Zivilprozessordnung. Juristische Blätter 64 : 450-454, 16. November 1935.

EGYED, E. : L'organisation de l'administration hongroise. Nouvelle revue de Hongrie 28 : 394-401, novembre 1935.

MEDER, W. : Ungarn - Übersicht über die wesentliche Gesetzgebung für das 2. Halbjahr 1934 und die ersten drei Vierteljahre 1935. Zeitschrift für osteuropäisches Recht 2 : 281-283, November 1935.

KUSSBACH, F. : Aktuelle Rechtsprobleme der ungarischen Reform-Ausbauarbeit. Zeitschrift der Akademie für deutsches Recht : 58-60, Januar 1936.

EGYED, S. : The modern corporative system and the Hungarian Constitution. Hungarian quarterly 2 : 74-83, No. 3, 1936.

SZAKTS, C. von : Die Grundprinzipien der neueren ungarischen Rechtschaffung. Zeitschrift der Akademie für deutsches Recht 3 : 491-498, 15. Mai 1936.

SZIGETI, L. : Grundprinzipien einer modernen Prozessordnung und das ungarische Recht. Internationales Anwaltsblatt 22 : 79-81, September 1936.

RÁCZ, G. : Der strafrechtliche Schutz des Staates in Ungarn. Zeitschrift für osteuropäisches Recht 3 : 206-217, September 1936.

HALÁSZ, Z. : Rassegna di legislazione ungherese (anno 1931). Annuario di diritto comparato e di studi legislativi (Parte IV) 9 : 65-111, 1936.

SZÁSZY, S. von : Die ungarische internationalprivatrechtliche Rechtsprechung in den Jahren 1930 bis 1934. Zeitschrift für ausländisches und internationales Privatrecht 11 : 168-193, Heft 1-2, 1937.

UJLAKI, N. : Die rechtsvereinheitlichenden Bestrebungen der Nachfolgestaaten und das ungarische Privatrecht. Zeitschrift für osteuropäisches Recht 3 : 561-583, März 1937.

MAGYARY, Z. : Die starke Exekutive. Zeitschrift für die gesamte Staatswissenschaft 97 : 688-704, Heft 4, 1937.

SILLAY, A. : Le droit aérien hongrois. Revue générale de droit aérien 6 : 206-237, avril-mai-juin 1937.

CHELARD, R. : La réforme de la constitution hongroise. Europe centrale 12 : 392-393, 19 juin 1937.

PETHÖ, A. : L'idée de Saint Etienne et la continuité juridique. Nouvelle revue de Hongrie 30 : 99-103, août 1937.

FELES, M. : Über die Ehetrennung. Internationales Anwaltsblatt 23 : 73-80, September 1937.

EGYED, E. : L'équilibre du pouvoir législatif et du pouvoir exécutif en Hongrie. Nouvelle revue de Hongrie 57 : 217-224, septembre 1937.

SZÁSZY, E. de : Questions et solutions pratiques - Les effets juridiques des accords de clearing en droit privé hongrois. Journal du droit international 64 : 738-748, juillet-octobre 1937.

EGYED, E. : L'institution hongroise de la régence et son développement. Nouvelle revue de Hongrie 57 : 394-399, novembre 1937.

UNGARN. Übersicht über die wesentliche Gesetzgebung im letzten Vierteljahre 1936 und in den ersten drei Vierteljahren 1937. Zeitschrift für osteuropäisches Recht 4 : 364-365, Dezember 1937.

SZLADITS, C. : Some features of Hungarian private international law. Grotius society, Transactions 23 : 25-39, 1937.

CSEKEY, S. von : Übersicht über die verfassungsrechtliche Gesetzgebung und Literatur in Ungarn im Jahre 1937. Jog 5 : 3-19, Januar-Februar 1938.

BETHLEN, E. : Le droit de suffrage au scrutin secret. Nouvelle revue de Hongrie 58 : 108-118, février 1938.

CSEKEY, S. von : Die verfassungsrechtlichen Reformen in Ungarn. Zeitschrift für osteuropäisches Recht 4 : 489-505, Februar 1938.

OTTLIK, L. : The Hungarian Jewish law. Hungarian quarterly 4 : 399-412, No. 3, 1938.

SZLADITS, C. de : Le nouveau projet de code civil en Hongrie. Annales de l'Institut de droit comparé de l'Université de Paris 3 : 259-268, 1938.

HELLER, E. : Fünf Jahre der Gesetzgebung und des Schrifttums auf dem Gebiete des Strafrechts in Ungarn (1933-1937). Jog 5 : 89-111, März-April 1938.

GALLIA, B. : La protection légale du brevet d'invention en Hongrie. Journal du droit international 65 : 201-231, mars-avril 1938.

BOZÓKY, G. von : Die Entwicklung des Handelsrechts in Ungarn im Jahre 1937. Jog 5 : 197-220, Mai-Juni 1938.

MIKECZ, E. : La "Loi juive". Nouvelle revue de Hongrie 59 : 17-28, juillet 1938.

TUNYOGHI, K. von : Die Gestaltung des ungarischen Bodenrechts in der neueren Zeit. Jog 5 : 285-327, September-Dezember 1938.

ARATÓ, I. : Das neue ungarische Gesetz über das Verfahren gegen exterritoriale Personen. Zeitschrift für osteuropäisches Recht 5 : 243-247, Oktober 1938.

ARATÓ, I. : Ungarn - Gesetz vom 29-5-1938 zur Sicherung des Gleichgewichts im wirtschaftlichen und gesellschaftlichen Leben (Judengesetz). Zeitschrift für osteuropäisches Recht 5 : 311-316, November 1938.

EGYED, E. : La nouvelle loi électorale hongroise. Nouvelle revue de Hongrie 59 : 515-518, décembre 1938.

Deutsche Auszüge ungarischer wissenschaftlicher Zeitschriften. Rechtswissenschaft. Ungarische Jahrbücher 18 : 88-95, Dezember 1938.

Ungarn - Übersicht über die wesentliche Gesetzgebung im letzten Vierteljahr 1937 und in den ersten drei Vierteljahren 1938. Zeitschrift für osteuropäisches Recht 5 : Dezember 1938.

MECSÉR, E. von : Ungarische Bodenbesitzpolitik. Volk und Reich 15 : 89-105, Heft 2, 1939.
Text of Bill annexed.

ARATÓ, I. : Die Einführung des ungarischen Rechts auf die mit Ungarn wiedervereinigten Gebiete. Zeitschrift für osteuropäisches Recht 5 : 501-514, Februar 1939.

KARTSOKE, A. : Unlauterer Wettbewerb und gewerbliche Eigentumsrechte in Ungarn. Zeitschrift für ausländisches und internationales Privatrecht 12 : 465-495, Heft 3/4, 1939.

BEST, W. : Die Verfassung und Verwaltung des Königreichs Ungarn. Deutsche Verwaltung 16 : 353-355, 25.Juni 1939.

Die Lehre von der "Heiligen Krone". Deutsches Recht 9 : 1292-1296, 5. August 1939.

ICELAND

BERLIN, K. : Islands völkerrechtliche Stellung. Zeitschrift für öffentliches Recht 15 : 572-599, 15. Dezember 1935.

INDIA

Indian constitutional reform. Economist 120 : 1-20, February 2, 1935 (supplement).

BANERJI, A. : Indian States and the constitution Bill. Contemporary review 147 : 313-320, March 1935.

Le statut futur de l'Inde. Affaires étrangères 5 : 70-74, février 1935.

BISSON, T.A. : A new constitution for India. Foreign policy reports 11 : 118-128, July 17, 1935.

MARTIN, P. : La nouvelle constitution de l'Inde. Asie française 35 : 289-292, novembre 1935.

FITZGERALD, S.V. : Indian and Far Eastern cases on the conflict of laws 1934. Journal of comparative legislation and international law 17 : 220-226, November 1935.

BILFINGER, C. : Rechtsprobleme der Verfassung Indiens. Zeitschrift für ausländisches öffentliches Recht und Völkerrecht 5 : 819-850, November 1935.

SETHI, L.R. : India in the community of nations. Canadian bar review 14 : 36-49, January 1936.

GILLET, E. : La nouvelle loi constitutionnelle de l'Inde. Outre-mer 8 : 53-63, mars 1936.

COELHO, W. : Indian states in the new constitution. New review 3 : 226-236, March 1936.

COLIN, H. : La nouvelle constitution de l'Inde. Revue des sciences politiques 51 : 226-234, avril-juin 1936.

BASTIDE, C. : La nouvelle constitution de l'Inde. Outre-mer 8 : 119-132, juin 1936.

The Indian States and the Goverment of India Act, 1935. Bombay law journal 14 : 117-131, August 1936.

CLOKIE, Mc.D. H. : The new constitution for India. American political science review 30 : 1152-1165, December 1936.

GUPTA, D.C. : The States and the Federal Court. Bombay law journal 14 : 291-300, December 1936.

Men and methods in the Indian Legislative Assembly. New review 5 : 36-48, January 1937.

AMOS, M.S. : Le constitution de l'Inde. Revue d'histoire politique et constitutionnelle 1 : 71-85, janvier-mars 1937.

DAVAR, S.R. : Observations on the Indian Companies (amendment) Act of 1936. Bombay law journal 14 and 15 : 335-340, 379-384, 430-435, 477-483, 518-526, 11-16, 103-116, January-June, August 1937.

Inde britannique - Nouvelle Constitution entrée en vigueur le ler avril 1937. Informations constitutionnelles et parlementaires 2 : 173-176, 31 mars 1937.
(Résumé).

LAVIGNE, R. : Les difficultés constitutionnelles aux Indes britanniques. Europe nouvelle 20 : 319-320, 3 avril 1937.

ANSTEY, V. : The Indian Companies (amendment) Act 1936. Asiatic review 33 : 642-647, July 1937.

Governor's provinces. Bo,bay law journal 15 : 63-65, July 1937.

SETHNA, M.J. : The merits of the Indian Companies Act of 1913 as amended by the Act of 1936. Bombay law journal 15 : 117-125, August 1937.

Custom and its proof. Bombay law journal 15 : 311-329, January 1938.
Muhammadan law.

MODY, R.R. : The code of civil procedure - Order XXX. Bombay law journal 15 : 229-236, 278-283, 330-338, November, December 1937, January 1938.

LINDSAY, B. : Indian States in the Federation. Journal of comparative legislation and international law (Pt.I) 20 : 91-98, February 1938.

SASTRY, R.K.R. : India and "International law ". Bombay law journal 15 : 450-452, April 1938.

The Indian naturalisation (amendment) bill - (British and Indian naturalisation acts; subjects of Great Britain or European States; migrants from Portuguese territory; racial dangers; position in the Dominions). Journal of the parliaments of the Empire 19 : 398-403, April 1938.

IVER, C.S.S. : The rule of law in Indian States. Triveni 10 : 37-47, June 1938.

NATIONAL LAW - COUNTRIES

GOMES, A.A. : Tenancy legislation in Bengal. New review 8 : 247-255, September 1938.

DAS, S.K. : The Canadian experience and the treaty-making power in the Government of India Act, 1935. Journal of comparative legislation and international law 20 : 204-209, November 1938.

RAHMAN, F. : Legislative privileges under the new India Constitution. Modern review 64 : 698-700, December 1938.

GEJENDRSGADKAR, K.B. : The Child Marriage Restraint Act and the punishment. Bombay law journal 17 : 30, January 1939.

CHETTY, S. : Indian States and Federation - The new Cochin Constitution. Asiatic review 35 : 17-41, January 1939.

MARTIN, P. : La nouvelle constitution de l'Inde (Contd.). Asie française 39 : 13-16, janvier 1939.

The Hindu conception of law. Bombay law journal 17 : 41-44, 80, February 1939.

Development of Muslim law. Bombay law journal 17 : 45-50, February 1939.

RUTHNASWAMY, M. : Preamble to an Indian State constitution. New review 9 : 393-399, May 1939.

SHAH, S.H. : Some interesting bills in the Bombay legislature. Bombay law journal 17 : 201-212, June 1939.

MARTIN, P. : La nouvelle constitution de l'Inde (Contd.). Asie française 39 : 193-196, juin 1939.

IRAN

AMIRIAN, A.M. : Dans quelle mesure le droit civil iranien s'est-il inspiré du code civil français? Bulletin trimestriel de la Société de législation comparée 66 : 66-93, janvier-mars 1937.

IRELAND

KEITH, A.B. : The privy council and the Irish Free State. Spectator : 1056-1057, 21 June 1935.

SMITH, J.D. : The Irish Free State and the treaty. Law journal 80 : 286-287, 2 November 1935. The Privy Council decisions.

BATTELLI, M. : Problèmes constitutionnels irlandais. Revue du droit et de la science politique 53 : 365-401, avril-mai-juin 1936.

The Irish Free State and the King. Irish jurist 3 : 24, April-June 1937.

La nuova costituzione irlandese. Relazioni internazionali 3 : 343-344, 8 maggio 1937.

STOYE, J. : Der Irische Freistaat als republikanisches Königreich - Was bedeutet die neue irische Verfassung? Zeitschrift für Politik 27 : 453-458, Juli-August 1937.

BEERS, W.A. : The administration of justice in the Irish Free State. Nineteenth century 122 : 203-213, August 1937.

STOYE, J. : Die Grundgedanken der neuen irischen Verfassung. Völkerbung und Völkerrecht 4 : 278-284, August 1937.

BROMAGE, A.W. : Constitutional developments in Saorstát Eireann and the Constitution of Éire - I. External affairs. American political science review 31 : 842-861, October 1937.

MESSINEO, A. : La nuova costituzione irlandese. Civiltà cattolica 88 : 239-250, 6 novembre 1937.

BROMAGE, A.W. : Constitutional developments in Saorstát Eireann and the constitution of Éire (Contd.). American political science review 31 : 1050-1070, December 1937.

The Constitution of Eire. Irish jurist 4 : 2, January-March 1938.

PRINGLE, D. : Eire. Journal of comparative legislation and international law 21 : 27-32, May 1939.

ITALY

DEAN, V.M. : The economic situation in Italy - the corporative system. Forein policy reports 10 : 294-304, 16 January 1935.

FACCHINETTI, G. : I provvedimenti di amnistia, d'indulto e di grazia in relazione all'art 22 del trattato 11 febbraio 1929 fra la S. Sede e l'Italia. Echi e commenti 16 : 85-86, 25 gennaio 1935.

DUDEN, K. : Internationalprivatrechtliche Rechtsprechung Italiens in den Jahren 1932, 1933, 1934. Zeitschrift für ausländisches und internationales Privatrecht 9 : 200-237, Heft 1-2, 1935.

SENIGALLIA, A. : Sur le projet du Code maritime italien (1931). Revue de droit maritime comparé 31 : 12-42, janvier-juin 1935.

AGHION, R : Les effets de la convention frano-italienne d'établissement du 3 juin 1930. Journal du droit international 62 : 564-578, mai-juin 1935.

UDINA, M. : La législation et la jurisprudence italiennes en matière de droit international privé de 1930 à 1934. Revue critique de droit international 30 : 357-379, avril-octobre 1935.

CAPPELLO, F.M. : Il matrimonio in Italia secondo il diritto concordatario. Civiltà cattolica 86 : 358-371, 18 maggio 1935.

VERNARECCI di FOSSOMBRONE, C. : Die Vollstreckung der ausländischen Gerichtsurteile in Italien. Zeitschrift der Akademie für deutsches Recht 2 : 27-30, Mai 1935.

LAMPIS, G. : Le nuove norme sulla concessione della cittadinanza italiana. Rivista di diritto pubblico 27 : 309-313, maggio 1935.

ZENNARO. T. : Le norme di diritto internationale privato nei progetti di riforma legislativa in Italia (Contd.). Annali della R. università degli studi economici e commerciali di Trieste 5 : 301-317, 1935.

BALZARINI, R. : Il principio corporativo nel nuovo diritto costituzionale. Diritto del lavoro 9 : 188-210, maggio 1935.

PRÉLOT, M. : Le corporatisme italien. Vie intellectuelle 7 : 469-490, 25 juin 1935.

Socialism, fascism and democracy. Annals of the American academy of political and social science 180 : 1-203, July 1935.
Special number.

ROSSI, C. : Local government in Italy under Fascism. American political science review 29 : 658-663, August 1935.

BISCARETTI di RUFFIA, P. : La capacità di diritto pubblico della donna. Echi e commenti 16 : 889-890, 25 agosto 1935.

FRANCK, L.R. : Fascism and the corporate state. Political quarterly 6 : 355-368, July-September 1935.

AZARA, A. : La réforme des codes en Italie. Bulletin trimestriel de la société de législation comparée 64 : 307-328, juillet-septembre 1935.

SCRIMALI, A. : Quelques nouveaux aperçus sur l'accession de la nationalité italienne des sujets de l'ancien empire austro-hongrois habitant les provinces rattachées à l'Italie par le Traité de paix. Journal du droit international 62 : 1108-1114, juillet-octobre 1935.

Chronique de jurisprudence italienne. Revue trimestrielle de droit civil 34 : 887-900, octobre-décembre 1935.

TAMBARO, I. : Le colonie italiane e il loro carattere giuridico. Africa italiana 53 : 305-309, ottobre-dicembre 1935.

UDINA, M. : La législation et la jurisprudence italiennes en matière de droit international privé de 1930 à 1934. Revue critique de droit international 30 : 687-732, octobre-décembre 1935.

CAMPOLONGO,F. : Sul segreto di Stato. Echi e commenti 16 : 1246-1247, 21 dicembre 1935.

CASELLI, E.P. : Il lavoro dei tribunali e le "sanzioni". Echi e commenti 16 : 1244-1245, 21 dicembre 1935.
For simplification of the legal machinery in Italy.

SIOTTO-PINTOR : Der Ausbau des obrigkeitlichen Regierungssystems in Italien (1928-1934). Jahrbuch des öffentlichen Rechts 22 : 459-526, 1935.

REALE, E. : L'évolution de la vie constitutionnelle en Italie en 1934. Annuaire de l'Institut international de droit public : 736-751, 1935.

SFORZA, W.C. : Preliminari sul diritto collettivo. Archivo di studi corporativi 7 : 27-45, fasc. 1, 1936.

WENGLER, W. : Die Kollisionsnormen im Recht der italienischen Kolonien. Zeitschrift für ausländisches und internationales Privatrecht 10 : 71-84, Heft 1/3, 1936.

KLAUER, G. : Das neue italienische Gesetz zum Schutze des gewerblichen Eigentums. Zeitschrift für ausländisches und internationales Privatrecht 10 : 1-16, Heft 1/3, 1936.

BALDONI, C. : La législation corporative en Italie et le droit international privé. Revue critique de droit international 31 : 21-39, janvier-mars 1936.

CAMPOLONGO, F. : Il segreto di stato e sua protezione nell' ora presente. Giustizia penale 42 : 139-150, febbraio 1936.

FRANKENSTEIN, E. : Osservazioni sulle disposizioni di diritto internazionale privato nel Progetto del 1° Libro del Codice Civile Italiano. Annuario di diritto comparato e di studi legislativi 12 : 107-115, fascicolo II, 1936.

HAMBURGER, E. : La conception de la loi écrite dans le fascisme et le national-socialisme. Affaires étrangères 6 : 161-164, mars 1936.

MONACHESI, E.D. : The Italian surveillance judge. Journal of criminal law and criminology 26 : 811-820, March 1936.

CHIARELLI, G. : Il comitato corporativo centrale. Archivio di diritto pubblico 1 : 1-11, gennaio-aprile 1936.

PANUNZIO, S. : Teoria e pratica delle corporazioni. Politica sociale 8 : 102-105, aprile 1936.
Comments to M. Mussolini's speech of 23 March 1936.

PANUNZIO, S. : Teoria generale della dittatura (Contd.). Gerarchia 16 : 303-316, maggio 1936.

CORSO, P. : L'ordinamento corporativo e il nuove diritto pubblico italiana. Diritte del lavoro 10 : 149-167, maggio 1936.

ROSSI, L. : L'ordinamento dello stato d'assedio nelle ultime leggi italiano. Rivista di diritto pubblico 28 : 261-277, giugno 1936.

GUARNIERI-VENTIMIGLIA, A. : La civiltà del lavoro nel mondo giuridico - I codici Mussolini - Principi fondamentali, direttive, finalità. Diritto del lavoro 10 : 221-230, giugno-luglio 1936.

ERCOLE, F. : Il contributo del pensiere italiano alla formazione dello stato moderno. Civiltà fascista 3 : 397-416, luglio 1936.

SALEMI, G. : L'organizzazione nazionale del Partito fascista e i suoi rapporti con lo stato. Rivista di diritto pubblico 28 : 309-330, luglio 1936.

SOLMI, A. : La giustizia nello stato fascista: Rivista internazionale di filosofia del diritto 16 : 329-342, luglio-ottobre 1936.

CASABIANCA, P. : Le nouveau code de procédure pénale d'Italie. Revue internationale de droit pénal 13 : 132-139, 2e trimestre 1936.

RUSSO, G. : La riforma del codice civile - Le successioni e le donazioni. Echi e commenti 17 : 744-743, 5 settembre 1936.

BRUCCULERI, A. : I presupposti teorici del corporativismo. Civiltà cattolica 87 : 474-479, 19 settembre 1936.

CIANCARINI, O. : Nuovi orientamenti nel sistema penale e disciplinare delle forze armate dello stato. Rivista di fanteria 3 : 1166-1174, settembre 1936.

CAPPELLO, F.M. : Il nuovo "progetto" del codice civile italiano. Civiltà cattolica 87 : 17-25, 3 ottobre 1936.

STEINER, H.A. : The government of Italian East Africa. American political science review 30 : 884-902, October 1936.

LA TORRE, M. : Il decennale del sistema podestarile. Gerarchia 16 : 764-768, novembre 1936.

MARPICATI, A. : Il partito Fascista nello stato. Nuova antologia 71 : 271-290, 1 dicembre 1936.

Disegni di legge presentati dal Capo del Governo Primo Ministra Segretario di Stato e Ministro degli affari esteri Benito Mussolini, dal 28 aprile 1934 - Anno XII all'giugno 1936 - Anno XIV. Bollettino parlamentare 10 : 27-208 (supplemento al N. 3) dicembre 1936.
Survey of recent treaties.

STEINER, H.A. : The Fascist conception of law. Columbia law review 36 : 1267-1283, December 1936.

BOTTAI, G. : Il corporativismo e i giovani. Diritto del lavoro 10 : 393-396. dicembre 1936.

CAPPELLO, F.M. : Il nuovo "progetto" del Codice civile italiano. Civiltà cattolica 88 : 112-126, 16 gennaio 1937.

BIGIAVI, W. : La convenzione sui conflitti di leggi in materia di cambiale è penetrata nell' ordinamento interno italiano? Rivista del diritto commerciale 35 : 1-25, gennaio-febbraio 1937.

TEDESCHI, G. : Osservazioni e proposte sul progetto del IIIe libro del codice civile. Studi senesi 50 : 65-99, fasc. 2-3, 1936.

GUILLAUME, A.-E. : L'organisation de l'Afrique orientale italienne. Europe nouvelle 20 : 232-234, 6 mars 1937.

DONATI, D. : Sulla posizione costituzionale della corona nel governo monarchico presidenziale. Archivio di diritto pubblico 2 : 5-12, gennaio-aprile 1937.

GUICCIARDI, E. : Concetti tradizionali e principii ricostruttivi nella giustizia amministrativa. Archivio di diritto pubblico 2 : 50-70, gennaio-aprile 1937.

TOSATO, E. : L'impugnativa dei decreti reali di annullamento. Archivio di diritto pubblico 2 : 13-50, gennaio-aprile 1937.

BIGIAVI, W. : Dal codice di commercio alla legge cambiaria uniforme - Prolegomeni. Rivista del diritto commerciale 35 : 105-130, marzo-aprile 1937.

Il pensiero corporativo, sua affermazione e suoi sviluppi dalla Carta del Lavoro ad oggi. Critica fascista 15 : 181-224, 15 aprile 1937.
Special number.

EULA, E. : Problemi giuridici per la construzione dell' Impero. Echi e commenti 18 : 323-326, 15 aprile 1937.

STEINER, H.A. : The constitutional position of the "Partito Nazionale Fascista". American political science review 31 : 227-242, April 1937.

RASELLI, A., e ILARDI, S. : Osservazioni e proposte della Facoltà di Giuriprudenza della R. Università di Siena sul progetto del III. Libro del Codice Civile. Studi senesi 50 : 263-272, Fasc. 4-5, 1937.

BERNARDI, G. : Die Aufwertung deutscher Forderungen in Italien. Zeitschrift der Akademie für deutsches Recht 4 : 270-273, 1. Mai 1937.

MOSSA, L. : Per la nuova legge italiana sullo check. Rivista del diritto commerciale 35 : 241-268, maggio-giugno 1937.

DUDEN, K., und WINTZINGERODE, R.v. : Internationalprivatrechtliche Rechtsprechung Italiens in den Jahren 1935 und 1936. Zeitschrift für ausländisches und internationales Privatrecht 10 : 978-998, Heft 5/6, 1936.

JONAS : Das italienisch-deutsche Vollstreckungsabkommen vom 9. März 1936. Deutsche Justiz 99 : 888-893, 11. Juni 1937.

CELENTANO, F. : La giustizia amministrativa nell' Eritrea. Rivista di diritto pubblico 29 : 301-309, giugno 1937.

DEGNI, F. : Osservazioni sul progetto preliminare di riforma del III° libro del Codice civile (successioni e donazioni). Annuario di diritto comparato e di studi legislativi 12 : 321-359, fasc. 6, 1937.

AGRESTI, A. : I principi generali del diritto e il principio corporativo nell'ordinamento costituzionale italiano. Diritto del lavoro 11 : 210-221, giugno-luglio 1937.

LA TORRE, M. : La riforma del procedimento civile - Giudice unico o collegio? Gerarchia 17 : 471-476, luglio 1937.

Disegni, proposte di legge e documenti, decretilegge presentati al Parlamento, leggi pubblicate nella XXIX legislatura (28 aprile 1934 - XII - 25 giugno 1934- XV). Bollettino parlamentare XI : suppl. no. 2, 7-311, luglio 1937.

RODIÈRE, R. : La vocation successorale "ab intestat" dans le projet italien de code civil. Bulletin trimestriel de la société de législation comparée 66 : 200-236, juillet-septembre 1937.

MADIA, T. : Mussolini penalista (Le ultime correzioni del Duce sul nuovo Codice Penele). Gerarchia 17 : 523-532, agosto 1937.

WEINBERGER, O. : Der Entwurf der italienischen Zivilprozessordnung. Internationales Anwaltsblatt 23 : 82-84, September 1937.

MAZZONE, R. : Il diritto commerciale nel sistema del diritto fascista. Stato 8 : 449-459, settembre 1937.

ESPOSITO, C. : Lo stato e la nazione italiana. Archivio di diritto pubblico 2 : 409-485, settembre-dicembre 1937.

GENET, R. : La nouvelle réglementation italienne des lois de la guerre et de la neutralité. Revue internationale française du droit des gens 2 : 123-129, octobre-novembre 1937.

MARSICO, A. de : Il diritto penale fascista al Congresso internazionale di Parigi. Gerarchia 17 : 769-773, novembre 1937.

COSTAMAGNA, C. : Les principes constitutionnels du fascisme dans la Charte du Travail. Revue d'histoire politique et constitutionnelle 1 : 665-676, octobre-décembre 1937.

FRANK, H. : L'intesa italo-germanica per gli studi legislativi Stato 8 : 577-583, novembre-dicembre 1937.

LO VERDE, G. : Die Stellung des Monarchen im Italienischen Staatsrecht. Zeitschrift der Akademie für deutsches Recht 4 : 737-740, 15. Dezember 1937.

LA TORRE, M. : Nuovi sviluppi dell'ordinamento corporativo. Gerarchia 17 : 860-864, dicembre 1937.

BERTOLA, A. : Giurisprudenza coloniale nel primo anno di Impero. Rivista di diritto pubblico 30 : 50-55, gennaio 1938.

CAPITANI, U. : Les tendances du droit italien en matière de sociétés. Bulletin trimestriel de la Société de législation comparée 67 : 38-65, janvier-mars 1938.

BATTELLI, M. : Le chef du gouvernement en Italie. Revue d'histoire politique et constitutionnelle 2 : 41-86, janvier-mars 1938.

DONATI, D. : Divisione e coordinamento dei poteri nello Stato fascista. Archivio di diritto pubblico 3 : 5-19, gannaio-aprile 1938.

SERENI, A.P. : L'annessione dell'Etiopia nella giurisprudenza. Rivista di diritto internazionale 30 : 102-141, 1 gennaio-30 giugno 1938.

ZANGARA, V. : Il partito unico e il nuovo Stato rappresentativo in Italia e in Germania. Rivista di diritto pubblico 30 : 88-111, febbraio 1938.

MONACO, R. : L'efficacia esecutiva in Italia delle cambiali emesse all'estero. Istituto di studi legislativi, giurisprudenza comparata di diritto internazionale privato 3 : 44-51, 1938.

SCERNI, M. : La convenzione italo-svizzera del 3 gennaio 1933 e la giurisdizione in materia di stato. Istituto di studi legislativi; giurisprudenza comparata di diritto internazionale privato 3 : 62-65, 1938.

MAURY, J. : De la compétence des tribunaux étrangers pour questions d'état entre ressortissants italiens. Istituto di studi legislativi, giurisprudenza comparata di diritto internazionale privato 3 : 13-19, 1938.

TEDESCHI, G. : Osservazioni e proposte sul progetto de II. libro del Codice Civile. Studi senesi 52 : 378-410, fasc. 3-4, 1938.

BRACCI, M. e RASELLI, A. : Sul progetto preliminare del codice di procedura civile. Studi senesi 51 : 163-206, fasc. 3-5, 1937.

Les tendances nouvelles du droit des sociétés par actions en Italie. Annales de droit commercial 47 : 119-137, avril-juin 1938.

La convention franco-italienne sur les doubles impositions. Dalloz, Recueil hebdomadaire de jurisprudence 15 : 29-32, 12 mai 1938.

LA TORRE, M. : La riforma del codice civile. Gerarchia 18 : 307-312, maggio 1938.

TAMBARO, I. : Lineamenti della costituzione dell'Africa Orientale Italiana. Africa 56 : 289-303, maggio 1938.

GUIDOTTI, F. : Sulla qualifica corporativa dello Stato italiano (Contd.). Studi senesi 52 : 427-480, fasc. 5, 1938.

NOVELLI, G. : Theorie und Praxis der sichernden Massregeln in Italien. Deutsche Justiz (Sonderbeilage) : 7-40, 21.Juni 1938.

PERGOLESI, F. : Il diritto del lavoro. Rivista di diritto pubblico 30 : 357-373, giugno 1938.

MOFFA, G. : Il controllo della Corte dei Conti sulla gestione finanziaria dello Stato ed i suoi rapporti con le supreme gerarchie del Fascismo. Rivista di diritto pubblico 30 : 374-384, giugno 1938.

HORA, V. : Einige Bemerkungen zum Entwurfe der neuen italienischen Z.P.O. Annuario di diritto comparato e di studi legislativi 13 : 361-367, fasc. 6, Pt. 1, 1938.

CIOFFI, A. : Collaborazione giuridica italo-germanica. Echi a commenti 19 : 585-587, 5 luglio 1938.

CHIMIENTI, P. : La qualifica costituzionale di "Duce" al Capo del Governo in regime fascista. Gerarchia 18 : 443-449, luglio 1938.

I lavori del Comitato per le relazioni giuridiche italotedesche (Roma, 20-26 giugno 1938-XVI). Stato 9 : 385-420, luglio 1938.

Chroniques de droit italien. Revue trimestrielle de droit civil 37 : 514-595, juillet-septembre 1938. Bibliographie, jurisprudence, législation.

SPERDUTI, G. : Limiti della giurisdizione italiana in materia di sequestro conservativo e di provvedimenti cautelari in generale. Rivista di diritto internazionale 30 : 310-359, 1 luglio - 31 dicembre 1938.

KORKISCH, und WENGLER : Die Technik des italienischen Wehrwirtschaftsrechts. Zeitschrift für ausländisches öffentliches Recht und Völkerrecht 8 : 561-580, August 1938.

Del GIUDICE, R. : Per una riforma fascista della giurisdizione. Stato 9 : 452-456, agosto-settembre 1938.

Lo Statuto del P.N.F. dell'anno XVI. Archivio di diritto pubblico 3 : 557-609, settembre-dicembre 1938.

MARTINENGHI, F. : Diritto azionario. Ragioniere professionista 13 : 217-223, ottobre 1938.

La difesa del diritto romano. Stato 9 : 513-517, ottobre 1938.

AMBROSINI, G. : L'organizzazione politica, amministrativa ed economica dell'Impero. Rivista di diritto pubblico 30 : 538-564, ottobre 1938.

NIPPERDEY, H.C. : Die Vereinheitlichung des Rechts der Schuldverhältnisse in Italien und Deutschland. Zeitschrift der Akademie für deutsches Recht 5 : 721-725, 1. November 1938.

NATIONAL LAW - COUNTRIES

DELLE DONNE, M. : Decadenza ed azione di danni in materia di concessioni amministrative. Rivista di diritto pubblico 30 : 637-641, novembre 1938.

UMBERTO di BLASI, F. : Nel nuovo codice civile - l'"affiliazione". Echi e commenti 19 : 1000-1001, 25 novembre 1938.

Grundsätze des italienischen Rasserechts - Auszug aus den Beschlüssen des Faschistischen Grossrats vom 6. Oktober 1938. Zeitschrift der Akademie für deutsches Recht 5 : 797-799, 1. Dezember 1938.

Soppressione dei tribunali confessionali nelle isole italiane dell'Egeo. Relazioni internazionali 4 : 833, 3 dicembre 1938.

MONACO, R. : L'efficacia in Italia dei provvedimenti stranieri di giurisdizione volontaria. Diritto internazionale : 53-73, 1938.

BETTI, E. : Il quarto libro nel progetto del codice civile italiano. Rivista del diritto commerciale 36 : 537-570, novembre-dicembre 1938.

LA TORRE, M. : Le commissioni legislative nella Camera dei Fasci e delle Corporazioni. Stato 9 : 641-656, dicembre 1938.

BALLADORE-PALLIERI, G. : Il matrimonio religioso degli stranieri in Italia. Diritto internazionale : 3-8, 1938.

Il comitato giuridico italo-germanico per la riforma del diritto delle obbligazioni. Rivista del diritto commerciale 36 : 435-439, luglio-agosto 1938.

GOLDSCHMIDT, J. : Bemerkungen zum italienischen Zivilprozessentwurf. Annuario di diritto comparato e di studi legislativi 13 : 229-277, pt. 1, série 2, fasc. 4, 1938.

NOVELLI, G. : Delitti e pene nella morale fascista. Gerarchia 18 : 170-176, marzo 1938.

La riforma dei codici penali militari. Nazione militare 13 : 120-122, febbraio 1938.

SETTE, F. : Pubblicazione del primo libro del codice civile fascista. Echi e commenti 20 : 9-12, 5 gennaio 1939.

FOLCHI, A.E. : Cittadinanza e sudditanza nell' espansione imperiale italiana. Rivista di diritto pubblico 31 : 53-69. gennaio 1939.

RANELLETTI, O. : Il Partito nazionale fascista nello Stato italiano. Rivista di diritto pubblico 31 : 30-42, gennaio 1939.

STEINER, H.A. : Italian war and neutrality legislation. American journal of international law 33 : 151-157, January 1939.

AMBROSINI, G. : Ragioni e caraterre della grande riforma civile in Libia. Libia 17 : 5-11, gennaio 1939.

SANDIFORD, R. : Il diritto aeronautico nella legge italiana di guerra e di neutralità. Rivista di diritto aernautico 8 : 114-126, n. 1-2, 1939.

RIEZLER, E. : Der Entwurf eines italienisches Sachenrechts. Zeitschrift für ausländisches und internationales Privatrecht 12 : 1-65, Heft 1/2, 1939.

BIGGINI, C.A. : La camera dei fasci e delle corporazioni nel nuovo ordinamento costituzionale. Archivio di studi corporativi 10 : 31-69, fasc. 1-2, 1939.

CAPPELLO, F.M. : Il nuovo codice civile italiano. Civiltà cattolica 90 : 292-301, 18 febbraio 1939.

FACCHINETTI, G. : La legge per la difesa della razza e il concordato. Civiltà fascista 6 : 110-115, febbraio 1939.

ROCCHI, G.S. : L'esecuzione in Italia delle sentenze di divorzio emesse in Stati non aderenti alla convenzione dell'Aja del 12 giugno 1902. Rivista di diritto internazionale 31 : 100-107, 1 gennaio-31 marzo 1939.

CANSACCHI, G. : L'interpretazione dottrinale e giurisprudenziale degli accordi 6 aprile 1922 fra l'Italia e gli Stati successori della Monarchia austro-ungarica in materia di delibazione. Rivista di diritto internazionale 31 : 31-88, 1 gennaio - 31 marzo 1939.

PUGLIATTI, S. : Immobili e pertinenze nel progetto del secondo libro del codice civile. Rivista di diritto agrario 18 : 32-44, gennaio-marzo 1939.

Accordi internazionali fra l'Italia ed altri Stati resi esecutivi nel 1938. Rivista di diritto internazionale 31 : 121-125, 1 gennaio - 31 marzo 1939.

LA TORRE, M. : La camera dei Fasci e delle corporazioni. Echi e commenti 20 : 264-265, 25 marzo 1939.

BORNHAK, C. : Die italienische Verfassungsreform. Archiv des öffentlichen Rechts 30 : 257-273, 3. Heft 1939.

Razza e diritto al Convegno italo-tedesco di Vienna. Stato 10 : 129-167, marzo 1939.
Series of articles.

LO VERDE, G. : Die verfassungsrechtliche Stellung der neuen faschistischen Kammer. Zeitschrift der Akademie für deutsches Recht 5 : 257-260, 15. April 1939.

VASSALI, G. : Per un diritto unico delle obbligazioni. Stato 10 : 203-216, aprile 1939.

SPAVENTA, J. : Giustizia nell'amministrazione. Rivista di diritto pubblico 31 : 222-250, aprile 1939.

Dispositions de droit international privé contenues dans le code civil italien du 12 décembre 1938. Nouvelle revue de droit international privé 6 : 325-332, janvier-juin 1939.

VACCHINI, A. : La Chambre des faisceaux et des corporations. Revue internationale des sciences administratives 12 : 259-269, avril-mai-juin 1939.

BOLAFFI, R. : La production de la preuve en droit italien. Bulletin trimestriel de la Société de législation comparée 68 : 159-168, avril-juin 1939.

VERDROSS, A. von : Das neue italienische Kriegs- und Neutralitätsrecht. Zeitschrift für öffentliches Recht 19 : 193-315, Mai 1939.

JAMALIO, A. : L'"interpretazione autentica" del Duce. Rivista di diritto pubblico 31 : 302-325, maggio 1939.

BRUNI, G.U. : Sul concetto di Stato totalitario. Stato 10 : 257-289, maggio 1939.

SALEMI, G. : La Camera dei Fasci e delle Corporazioni. Rivista di diritto pubblico 31 : 289-301, maggio 1939.

Riforma costituzionale italiana - Le Commissioni-legislative. Relazioni internazionali 5 : 542, 15 luglio 1939.

UDINA, M. : Il nuovo ordinamento costituzionale dello Stato fascista. Rivista di diritto pubblico 31 : 460-473, luglio 1939.

CUTELLI, S.M. : Critica razzista al disegno di legge sulla tutela penale del prestigio di razza. Vita italiana 27 : 80-92, luglio 1939.

UDINA, M. : Die konstitutionelle Neuordnung des faschistischen Staates. Deutsches Recht 2 : 247-251, 20. Juli 1939.

SCADUTO, G. : Introduzione al libro primo del nuovo Codice civile. Rivista del diritto commerciale 37 : 321-332, luglio-agosto 1939.

Il nuovo codice di commercio romeno ed il diritto commerciale italiano. Rivista del diritto commerciale 37 : 321-332, luglio-agosto 1939.

AMATI, R. : Le droit des personnes et le droit de famille dans le nouveau code civil italien. Bulletin trimestriel de la Société de législation comparée 68 : 329-344, juillet-septembre 1939.

La delibazione, in Italia, delle sentenza di divorzio pronunziate in Stati non aderenti alla Convenzione dell'Aja. Giustizia penale (Parte terza) 45 : 714-7'5. luglio-novembre 1939.

VOLLWEILER, H. : Die faschistische Parlamentsreform. Deutsche Verwaltung 16 : 458-460, 20. August 1939.

RIZZO, G. : La unione dell'Albania con l'Italia. Rivista di diritto pubblico 31 : 497-522, agosto-settembre 1939.

BISCARETTI di RUFFIA, P. : La qualificazione giuridica della forma di Governo dell'Italia. Rivista di diritto pubblico 31 : 523-541, agosto-settembre 1939.

SANDIFORD, R. : Das italienische Kriegs- und Neutralitätsgesetz. Zeitschrift für ausländisches öffentliches Recht und Völkerrecht 9 : 605-619, Oktober 1939.

CASABIANCA, P. de : La tutelle des mineurs dans le nouveau code civil italien. Bulletin trimestriel de la Société de législation comparée 68 : 409-419, octobre-décembre 1939.

ASCOLI, A. : La capacité suivant le nouveau code civil italien. Bulletin trimestriel de la Société de législation comparée 68 : 449-471, octobre-décembre 1939.

MOSSA, L. : Per la società anonima italiana. Rivista di diritto commerciale 37 : 509-522, novembre-dicembre 1939.

CORDOVA, A. : Diritto coloniale e cittadinanza coloniale. Rivista di diritto pubblico 31 : 642-650, novembre 1939.

AZARA, A. : La riforma fascista del diritto di successione. Nuova antologia 74 : 219-228, 1 dicembre 1939.

GRANDI, D. : La riforma fascista dei codici. Foro italiano (parte II) 64 : 241-256, fasc. 21, 1939.

BASSANO, U. : Sulla convenzione italo-francese per l'utilizzazione delle acque del fiume Roja. Foro italiano 64 : 1035-1042, fasc. 14, 1939.

JAPAN

KATAOKA, N. : Japanese air navigation regulations. Journal of air law 7 : 95-107, January 1936.

SUGUYAMA : Les transformations du droit civil japonais et l'influence du droit français. Annales de l'Institut de droit comparé de l'Université de Paris 2 : 195-219, 1936.

TANAKA, K. : La riforma della legislazione sulle società anonime in Giappone. Annuario di diritto comparato e di studi legislativi 12 : 129-136, fasc. 3, 1936.

TANIGUCHI, T. : Uber das heutige japanische "Familien-System". Zeitschrift für ausländisches und internationales Privatrecht 10 : 477-491, Heft 4, 1936.

SONDA, H. : Gemeinschaftsgedanken im japanischen Rechtsleben. Zeitschrift der Akademie für deutsches Recht 3 : 453-458, 15. Mai 1936.

TABOUILLOT, V. : Zur Frage der rechtlichen Bezirhungen Japans zu den Mandatsgebieten. Zeitschrift für ausländisches öffentliches Recht und Völkerrecht 6 : 365-369, Mai 1936.

WERTHEIM, B. : The Russo-Japanese fisheries controversy. Pacific affairs 8 : 185-198, June 1935.

BÜNGER, K.: Das japanische Steuerrecht. Ostasiatische Rundschau 17 : 348-352, 1. Juli 1936.

COLEGROVE, K. : The Japanese cabinet. American political science review 30 : 903-923, October 1936.

SUGIYAMA, N. : Le droit comparé et la mission du droit japonais. Bulletin trimestriel de la Société de législation comparée 64 : 281-306, juillet-septembre 1935.

SCHÜTZ, A. : Tomoo Otakas Grundlegung der Lehre vom sozialen Verband. Zeitschrift für öffentliches Recht 17 : 64-84, Heft 1, 1937.

HOZUMI, S. : Le régime matrimonial de droit commun au Japon. Semaine internationale de droit, Travaux : 187-191 (section 4), 1937.

TAKAYANAGI, K. : La fiducie en droit japonais contemporain. Semaine internationale de droit, Travaux : 71-82 (section 5), 1937.

48 laws passed by 70th session of Imperial Diet. Contemporary opinions on current topics : 12-15, April 15, 1937.

TANIGUCHI, T. : De quelques caractéristiques du droit de mariage au Japon. Bulletin trimestriel de la Société de législation comparée 66 : 136-156, avril-juin 1937.

NATIONAL LAW - COUNTRIES

TANAKA, K. : La protection des obligataires en droit japonais. Semaine internationale de droit, Travaux : 101-109 (section 6), 1937.

Die Gesetzgebung für das japanische Mandatsgebiet in der Südsee. Ostasiatische Rundschau 18 : 238-239, 1. Mai 1937.

COLEGROVE, K. : The Japanese constitution. American political science review 31 : 1027-1049, December 1937.

HUDSON, M.O. : The liquidation of perpetual leases in Japan. American journal of international law 32 : 113-116, January 1938.

Die allgemeinen Vorschriften des japanischen Handelsgesetzbuchs. Ostasiatische Rundschau 19 : 220-221, 1. Mai 1938.

Die allgemeinen Vorschriften des japanischen Handelsgesetzbuchs (Contd.). Ostasiatische Rundschau 19 : 271-272, 1. Juni 1938.

Déclaration du Ministère de la Guerre japonais sur la loi de mobilisation générale nationale. Politique de Pékin 25 : 378-379, 15 juin 1938.

SCHERER, J.A.B. : Behind the Mikado's throne. Current history 48 : 27-29, June 1938.

BARKMEIER, J.H. : Summary of some recent Japanese legislation. U.S. Department of commerce, Comparative law series 1 : 265-269, July 1938.

OKADA, K. : Der Einfluss des deutschen Rechts auf die japanische Gesetzgebung und Kultur. Zeitschrift der Akademie für deutsches Recht 5 : 829-831, 15. Dezember 1938.

KOELLREUTTER, O. : Der Ausbau der rechtswissenschaftlichen Beziehungen zwischen Deutschland und Japan. Zeitschrift der Akademie für deutsches Recht 6 : 188-190, 15. März 1939.

MINEMURA, M. : Important economic legislations approved by the 74th diet. Contemporary opinions on current topics : 4-6, 13 April 1939.

TSAI, W.P. : The Soviet-Japanese fisheries controversy. China forum 3 : 296-300, 10 June 1939.

LATVIA

LUBBE, K. : Die Valutagesetzgebung in Lettland. Rigasche Zeitschrift für Rechtswissenschaft 9 : 15-20, 1. Heft 1935.

MUELLER, W. : Die Gesetzgebung Lettlands im 1. Halbjahr 1935. Rigasche Zeitschrift für Rechtswissenschaft 9 : 29-42, 1. Heft 1935.

MUELLER, W. : Die Gesetzgebung Lettlands im III. Quartal 1934. Rigasche Zeitschrift für Rechtswissenschaft 8 : 181-193, 3. Heft 1935.

SCHILLING, C.v. : Handelsrechtliche Entwürfe für Lettland. Rigasche Zeitschrift für Rechtswissenschaft 8 : 133-156, 3. Heft 1935.

Übersicht über die wesentliche Gesetzgebung Lettlands im Jahre 1933. Zeitschrift für osteuropäisches Recht 1 : 634-639, Juni 1935.

MUELLER, W. : Gesetzgebung Lettlands im Iv. Quartal 1934. Rigasche Zeitschrift für Rechtswissenschaft 8 : 258-267, August 1935.

Übersicht über die wesentliche Gesetzgebung im Jahre 1934. Zeitschrift für osteuropäisches Recht 2 : 152-162, September 1935.

MAURACH, R. : Das Recht der Schwangerschaftsunterbrechung in Lettland nach den Novellen von 1935. Zeitschrift für osteuropäisches Recht 2 : 365-376, Januar 1936.

MUELLER, W. : Die Gesetzgebung Lettlands im II. Halbjahr 1935. Rigasche Zeitschrift für Rechtswissenschaft 9 : 110-112, 2. Heft, 1935/1936.

MINTZ, P. : La nuova legislazione penale della Kettonia. Annuario di diritto comparato e di studi legislativi 12 : 215-223, fasc. 4, 1936.

SCHILLING, C. : Der amtliche Reformentwurf zu einem internationalen Privatrecht Lettlands. Zeitschrift der Akademie für deutsches Recht 3 : 466-473, 15. Mai 1936.

SCHILLING, C.v. : Der lettländische amtliche Entwurf zu einer Reform des Ehegüterrechts und der persönlichen Beziehungen der Ehegatten. Zeitschrift für ausländisches und internationales Privatrecht 10 : 733-735, Heft 5/6, 1936.

Lettland - Übersicht über die wesentlich Gesetzgebung im Jahre 1935. Zeitschrift für osteuropäisches Recht 2 : 730-734, Juni 1936.

SCHILLING, C.v. : Rechtsprechung und Reformfragen auf dem Gebiet des interterritorialen und internationalen Privatrechts Lettlands. Zeitschrift für osteuropäisches Recht 2 : 704-722, Juni 1936.

MUELLER, W.: Die Gesetzgebung Lettlands im 1. Quartal 1936. Rigasche Zeitschrift für Rechtswissenschaft 9 : 179-186, September 1936.

MUELLER, W. : Die Gesetzgebung Lettlands im 1. Quartal 1936. Rigasche Zeitschrift für Rechtswissenschaft 9 : 250-155 (sic), Oktober 1936.

FREYMANN, R. von : Il procedimento civile nella Lettonia. Annuario di diritto comparato e di studi legislativi 12 : 61-106, fascicolo II, 1936.

GRINBERGS, J. : Strukturprobleme im lettländischen Konnossementsrecht. Rigasche Zeitschrift für Rechtswissenschaft 10 : 37-52, Heft 1, 1937.

ZWINGMANN, O. : Die Vormerkung nach ausländischem und lettländischem Recht. Rigasche Zeitschrift für Rechtswissenschaft 10 : 1-20, Heft 1, 1937.

BERENT, B. : Le divorce des étrangers en Lettonie. Nouvelle revue de droit international privé 4 : 24-28, janvier-février-mars 1937.

BLAESE, H. : Die Zivilprozessnovelle von 1937. Rigasche Zeitschrift für Rechtswissenschaft 10 : 161-181, Heft 3, 1937-1938.

MUELLER, W. : Die Gesetzgebung Lettlands im Jahre 1937. Rigasche Zeitschrift für Rechtswissenschaft 10 : 182-196, Heft 3, 1937-1938.

BERENT, B. : Le divorce des étrangers en Lettonie. Annuario di diritto comparato e di studi legislativi 13 : 202-205, ser. 2, fasc. 3, 1937 (parte prima).

SCHILLING, von : Lettlands neues Zivilgesetzbuch. Zeitschrift für ausländisches und internationales Privatrecht 11 : 484-527, Heft 3/4, 1937.

FINCK, V. : Das neue Genossenschaftsrecht Lettlands. Rigasche Zeitschrift für Rechtswissenschaft 10 : 211-234, Heft 4, 1937/1938.

Lettland. Übersicht über die wesentliche Gesetzgebung im Jahre 1936. Zeitschrift für osteuropäisches Recht 3 : 699-702, Mai 1937.

SCHILLING, C. von : Die Einleitung zum neuen lettischen Zivilgesetzbuch. Zeitschrift für osteuropäisches Recht 4 : 219-240, Oktober 1937.

TAMME, W. : Der Einfluss des Staates auf die Wirtschaft Lettlands. Osteuropa 13 : 100-109, November 1937.

SAMSON-HIMMELSTJERNA, H. von : Die Bedeutung des Schiffsregisters nach lettländischem Recht. Rigasche Zeitschrift für Rechtswissenschaft 10 : 9-79, (Sonderbeilage) 1937.

BLAESE, H. : Die Gesetzgebung Lettlands im II. Halbjahr 1936. Rigasche Zeitschrift für Rechtswissenschaft 10 : 120-131, Januar 1938.

LOEBER, A. : Die Gesellschaft (G) nach dem lettländischen Ziwilgesetzbuch vom Jahre 1937 (ZGB). Rigasche Zeitschrift für Rechtswissenschaft 10 : 67-83, Januar 1938.

GALLAIX, de : Die Staatsangehörigkeit von Handelsgesellschaften. Rigasche Zeitschrift für Rechtswissenschaft 10 : 97-120, Januar 1938.

BERENT, B. : Das Eherecht im neuen Zivilgesetzbuch Lettlands. Zeitschrift für osteuropäisches Recht 4 : 415-432, Januar 1938.

MEDER, W. : Das innerstaatliche Nationakitätenrecht Estlands. Zeitschrift für Völkerrecht 22 : 201-216, Heft 2, 1938.

LOEBER, A. : Das lettische Aktiengesetz vom 28. Dezember 1937. Zeitschrift für osteuropäisches Recht 4 : 698-717, Mai 1938.

STRITZKY, A. : Lettland - Übersicht über die wesentliche Gesetzgebung im Jahre 1937. Zeitschrift für osteuropäisches Recht 4 : 718-721, Mai 1938.

HEERWAGEN, A. : Lettland - Gesetz vom 11.2.1938 betr. Ordnung und öffentliche Sicherheit im Staat. Zeitschrift für osteuropäisches Recht 4 : 798-802, Juni 1938.

BÉRENT, B. : Le droit international privé de la Lettonie. Nouvelle revue de droit international privé 5 : 493-511, juillet-août-septembre 1938.

Die gesetzlichen Massnahmen gegen eine Überfremdung in Lettland. Zeitschrift für osteuropäisches Recht 5 : 84-89, August 1938.

NOLDE, B. : Code civil de la Lettonie du 28 janvier 1937. Bulletin trimestriel de la Société de législation comparée 67 : 402-415, octobre-décembre 1938.

MUELLER, W. : Die Gesetzgebung Lettlands im I. Halbjahr 1938. Rigasche Zeitschrift für Rechtswissenschaft 11 : 51-60, 1. Heft 1939.

FINCK, V. : Das neue Genossenschaftsrecht Lettlands (Contd.). Rigasche Zeitschrift für Rechtswissenschaft 11 : 20-50, 1. Heft 1939.

HEERWAGEN, A. : Lettland - Gesetz vom 20.9.1938 betr. Änderung des Staatsangehörigkeitgesetzes. Zeitschrift für osteuropäisches Recht 5 : 450-454, Januar 1939.

La nouvelle législation eugénique en Lettonie. Revue de science criminelle et de droit pénal comparé 4 : 201-203, janvier-mars 1939.

BLAESE, H. : Lettlands neue Zivilgesetzbuch. Zeitschrift für osteuropäisches Recht 5 : 487-500, Februar 1939.

MINTZ, P. : Notice sur les lois promulguées en Lettonie en 1938. Revue internationale de droit pénal 16 : 216-220, No. 2, 1939.

LOEBER, A. : Das neue lettische Gesetz über die Handelsvollmachten. Zeitschrift für osteuropäisches Recht 5 : 568-577, März-April 1939.

Lettland - Übersicht über die wesentliche Gestzgebung im Jahre 1938. Zeitschrift für osteuropäisches Recht 5 : 766-769, Juni 1939.

KRAH, G. : Die lettländische Strafrechtsnovelle vom 25. Juli 1939. Zeitschrift für osteuropäisches Recht 6 : 113-121, September-Oktober 1939.

LIECHTENSTEIN

La naturalisation dans la principauté de Liechtenstein. Bulletin de l'Institut juridique international 36 : 1, 3 janvier 1937.

LUXEMBURG

MARES, R. : Le grand-duché de Luxembourg et son statut international. Revue de Paris 43 : 635-646, 1 août 1936.

SOLUS, H. : Les transformations du droit civil luxembourgeois depuis 1804. Bulletin trimestriel de la Société de législation comparée 66 : 41-65, janvier-mars 1937.

BUMILLER : Die völkerrechtliche Stellung Luxemburgs. Zeitschrift für Völkerrecht 22 : 34-70, Heft 1, 1938.

23 January 1937 (30 June 1938). Finlands författningsamlings fördragsserie: 154-167, No. 25, 1938. Traité d'extradition et d'assistance judiciaire en matière pénale (Texte français et suédois).

LITHUANIA

Litauen - Übersicht über die wesentliche Gesetzgebung 1933/1934. Zeitschrift für osteuropäisches Recht 1 : 375-379, Januar 1935.

FREYTAGH-LORINGHOVEN, F. : Das litauische Statut-Gesetz vom 13. März 1935. Zeitschrift für osteuropäisches Recht 1 : 520-525, April 1935.

Lithuanie - Modifications aux lois électorales. Annuaire de l'Institut international de droit public : 377-383, 1936.

Litauen - Übersicht über die wesentliche Gesetzgebung im Jahre 1935. Zeitschrift für osteuropäisches Recht 2 : 413-417, Januar 1936.

TABOUILLOT, W.v. : Das litauische Statusgerichtsgesetz vom 13. März 1935. Archiv des öffentlichen Rechts 27 : 109-117, Heft 1, 1936.

HESSE : Die privatrechtliche Gesetzgebung und Rechtsprechung im Memelgebiet seit dem Jahre 1932. Zeitschrift für ausländisches und internationales Privatrecht 10 : 123-148, Heft 1/3, 1936.

KARGE, F. : Die Rechtslage der Presse in Litauen. Zeitschrift für osteuropäisches Recht 2 : 661-671, Mai 1936.

THOLL, K. v. : Das neue litauische Vereingesetz. Zeitschrift für osteuropäisches Recht 2 : 722-729, Juni 1936.

SWETSCHIN, A. : Der strafrechtliche Schutz des Staates in Litauen. Zeitschrift für osteuropäisches Recht 3 : 164-173, September 1936.

TABOUILLOT, W.V. : Das neue litauische Militärstatut. Deutsches Juristen-Zeitung 41 : 1288-1289, 1. November 1936.

ROMER'IS, M. : La juridiction dite "Statutaire" en Lithuanie en ce qui concerne le territoire autonome de Memel. Revue internationale française du droit des gens 1 : 361-376, 31 décembre 1936.

Memelgebiet - Übersicht über die wesentliche Gesetgebung im Jahre 1936. Zeitschrift für osteuropäisches Recht 3 : 520-521, Februar 1937.

Litauen - Übersicht über die wesentliche Gesetzgebung im Jahre 1936. Zeitschrift für osteuropäisches Recht 3 : 517-520, Februar 1937.

HESSE : Das litauische Grundbuchrecht nach dem Gesetz vom 4. Dezember 1936. Zeitschrift für osteuropäisches Recht 3 : 619-630, April 1937.

Schiedsspruch über eine Meinungsverschiedenheit zwischen der Regierung des Deutschen Reiches und der Regierung der Republik Litauen betreffend die Staatsangehörigkeit verschiedener Personen. Zeitschrift für ausländisches öffentliches Recht und Völkerrecht 7 : 881-919, November 1937.

Litauen - Übersicht über die wesentliche Gesetzgebung im Jahre 1937. Zeitschrift für osteuropäisches Recht 4 : 438-441, Januar 1938.

SWETSCHIN, A. : Abänderung des verläufigen Gesetzes betr. die litauische Staatsangehörigkeit vom 18.11.1937. Zeitschrift für osteuropäisches Recht 4 : 458-460, Januar 1938.

Memelgebiet - Übersicht über die wesentliche Gesetzgebung im Jahre 1937. Zeitschrift für osteuropäisches Recht 4 : 506-507, Februar 1938.

MEYER, H. : Das litauische Enteignungsgesetz für das Memelgebiet. Zeitschrift für osteuropäisches Recht 4 : 473-478, Februar 1938.

SAENGER, A. : Entwicklung des Zivilrechtes in Litauen. Internationales Anwaltsblatt 24 : 2-4, Februar 1938.

MEYER, H. : Die Entwicklung des litauischen Verfassungsrechts. Zeitschrift für osteuropäisches Recht 5 : 235-242, Oktober 1938.

HEERWAGEN, A. : Lettland - Gesetz vom 20.9.1938 betr. Änderung des Staatsangehörigkeitgesetzes. Zeitschrift für osteuropäisches Recht 5 : 450-454, Januar 1939.

HESSE : Die privatrechtliche Gesetzgebung und Rechtsprechung im Memelgebiet in den Jahren 1936 und1937. Zeitschrift für ausländisches und internationales Privatrecht 12 : 115-132, Heft 1/2, 1939.

Litauen - Übersicht über die wesentliche Gesetzgebung im Jahre 1938. Zeitschrift für osteuropäisches Techt 5 : 447-449, Januar 1939.

Memelgebiet - Übersicht über die wesentliche Gesetzgebung im Jahre 1938. Zeitschrift für osteuropäisches Recht 5 : 514-515, Februar 1939.

GUSTAINIS, V. : Lithuania - The first twenty years. Slavonic and East European review 17 : 606-617, April 1939.

HASTAD, E. : Litauens nya författning. Statsvetenskaplig tidskrift 42 : 376-388, Häft 4, 1939.

STRAVINSKAS, P. : Die Rechtslage ausländischer Aktiengesellschaften in Litauen. Zeitschrift für osteuropäisches Recht 5 : 680-692, Mai 1939.

RAČKAUSKAS, K. : Das neue litauische Wechsel- und Scheckrecht. Zeitschrift für osteuropäisches Recht 5 : 743-750, Juni 1939.

SWETSCHIN, A. : Gesetz vom 8.8.1939 über die litauische Staatsangehörigkeit. Zeitschrift für osteuropäisches Recht 6 : 134-135, September-Oktober 1939.

GLOBKE, H. : Der deutsch-litauische Vertrag über die Staatsangehörigkeit der Memelländer. Zeitschrift für osteuropäisches Recht 6 : 105-113, September-Oktober 1939.

MEXICO

BAUERREISS, W. : Das mexikanische Gesetz über den Versicherungsvertrag vom 31. August 1935. Zeitschrift für ausländisches und internationales Privatrecht 11 : 137-167, Heft 1-2, 1937.

The Mexican expropriation law. Bulletin of the Pan American Union 71 : 286-288, March 1937.

CRAWFORD, H.P. : Expropriation of petroleum companies in Mexico. Tulane law review 12 : 495-508, June 1938.

McKERNAN, L.W. : Special Mexican claims. American journal of international law 32 : 457-466, July 1938.

WOOLSEY, L.H. : The expropriation of oil properties by Mexico. American journal of international law 32 : 519-526, July 1938.

HYDE, C.C. : Confiscatory expropriation. American journal of international law 32 : 759-766, October 1938.

RIVERA, J. : Necesidad jurídica de la expropriación petrolera. Revista jurídica 2 : 9-21, noviembre 1938.

RIGALT, A.F. : Legislación aérea Mexicana (Contd.). Revista jurídica 4 : 42-46, enero 1939.

CRAWFORD, H.P. : The Mexican limited liability company. Tulane law review 13 : 258-265, February 1939.

FRIEDE, W. : Der neue mexikanische Erdölstreit. Zeitschrift für ausländisches öffentliches Recht und Völkerrecht 9 : 31-54, April 1939.

AGUILAR, E.O. : Nuestra Suprema Corte de Justicia y el rezago de asuntos civiles. Revista jurídica (Mexico) 4 : 13-22, abril 1939.

ROBLES, A.G. : La question des matières premières au Mexique et le droit des gens. Revue de droit international 13 : 514-538, avril-mai-juin 1939.

RIVERA SILVA, M. : Hacia un nuevo código penal. Revista jurídica (Mexico) 4 : 5-9, mayo 1939.

AGUILAR, E.O. : Ley de reformas e los artículos 13, 14, 15, 16, 17, 18, 19, 20, fracciones I, III, VI, VIII y X, 21, 22, 23, 94, 104 fracción 1 y 107 de la constitución de la República (contd.). Revista jurídica (Mexico) 4 : 19-35, mayo 1939.

MONACO

AUREGLIA, L. : Le régime fiscal de la Principauté de Monaco. Bulletin de l'Institut juridique international 32 : 1-2, janvier 1935.

LA PRADELLE, A. de : Le statut personnel d'une famille souveraine au XXe siècle - Les Princes de Monaco devant la justice. Nouvelle revue de droit international privé 4 : 704-752, octobre-novembre-décembre 1937.

LA PRADELLE, A. de : Les Princes de Monaco devant la justice (Contd.). Nouvelle revue de droit international privé 5 : 300-315, avril-mai-juin 1938.

MOROCCO

MEYLAN, M. : Les mariages mixtes au Maroc. Revue critique de droit international 30 : 35-50, janvier-mars 1935.

RIVIÈRE, P.L. : Le statut juridique de la colonisation au Maroc. Revue des travaux de l'Académie des sciences morales et politiques 97 : 5-18, janvier-février 1937.

RENÉ-LECLERC, C. : La suppression des capitulations britanniques au Maroc. Correspondance d'Orient 30 : 397-402, septembre 1937.

VISIOZ, H. : Chronique de jurisprudence marocaine. Revue trimestrielle de droit civil 38 : 537-551, avril-juin 1939.

The abolition of British capitulatory rights in The French Zone of Morocco. British yearbook of international law 20 : 58-82, 1939.

NETHERLANDS

VERSCHAVE, P. : Pays-Bas - Notice sur le mouvement législatif de 1933 à 1936. Annuaire de législation étrangère 62 : 411-444, 1934/1936.

RONART, O. : Le renforcement du pouvoir exécutif en Hollande. Europe nouvelle 18 : 139-141, 9 février 1935.

DONKER CURTIUS, F. : La clause de paiement en or de la "Royal Dutch". Journal du droit international 62 : 541-563, mai-juin 1935.

FLIER, J. van der : Aperçu de la jurisprudence néerlandaise en matière de droit international privé, 1933-1934. Journal du droit international 63 : 105-131, janvier-février 1936.

HELD, H.J. : Staats-, Gemeinde- und Beamtenhaftung nach niederländischem Recht. Zeitschrift für vergleichende Rechtswissenschaft 50 : 243-255, 3. Heft 1936.

VAN DER AA, J.S., and CLUYSENAER, O.J. : Rapport concernant la loi du 19 juillet 1934, contenant des dispositions supplémentaires pour la protection de l'ordre public (Staatsblad No. 405). Recueil de documents en matière pénale et pénitentiaire 5 : 169-176, mars 1936.

SCHILLER, A.A. : Native customary law in the Netherlands East Indies. Pacific affairs 9 : 254-263, June 1936.

TELDERS, B.-M. : Le droit des gens dans la jurisprudence des Pays-Bas. Bulletin de l'Institut juridique international 35 : 1-28, juillet 1936.

MEYER-COLLINGS, J.J. : Die niederländische Rechtsprechung auf dem Gebiete des internationalen Privatrechts in den Jahren 1933-1936. Zeitschrift für ausländisches und internationales Privatrecht 11 : 194-242, Heft 1-2, 1937.

VAN BRAKEL, S. : Le régime matrimonial de droit commun en Hollande. Semaine internationale de droit, Travaux : 99-112 (section 4), 1937.

MEYER-COLLINGS : Die juristische Ausbildung in den Niederlanden. Deutsche Justiz 99 : 579-583, 16. April 1937.

KAN : Privatrechtliche Regelung des Lufttransportrechts in Holland. Archiv für Luftrecht : 177-182, April-September 1937.
Texte de la loi en allemand, pp. 183-196.

STOPPELAAR, J.W. de : Nederlanderschap en Nederlansch-onderdaanschap. Koloniaal tijdschrift 26 : 268-272, Mei 1937.

Wetten van 21 December 1936, houdende goedkeuring van het verdrag van 12 April 1930 nopens zekere vragen betreffende wetsconflicten inzake nationaliteit Wetgevingsbijlage van het Indisch tijdschrift van het Recht 146, afl. 6 : 1-34, 1937.
Text of government memorandum annexed.

FLIER, M.J. van der : Aperçu de la jurisprudence néerlandaise en matière de droit international privé 1935-1936. Annuaire Grotius : 155-181, 1937.

PRINS, W.F. : Nederlander of inheemsch onderdaan - niet-Nederlander? Indisch tijdschrift van het Recht : 741-753, Afl. 6, 1938.

Volksraad 1918-1938. Koloniall Studien 22 : 251-394, Juni 1938.

TELDERS, B.M. : Aperçu des faits internationaux d'ordre juridique. Annuaire Grotius : 97-124, 1938.

Jurisprudence néerlandaise en matière de droit international privé. Institut belge de droit comparé, Revue trimestrielle 24 : 145-149, juillet-décembre 1938.

RONART, O. : Le danger aérien et la sauvegarde des objets d'art aux Pays-Bas. Revue générale de droit aérien 8 : 68-75, janvier-fêvrier-mars 1939.

VAN EYSINGA, W.J.M. : Les amendements de la constitution néerlandaise de 1938. Revue d'histoire politique et constitutionnelle 3 : 17-22, janvier-mars 1939.

FONTEIN, A. : A century of codification in Holland. Journal of comparative legislation and international law 21 : 83-88, February 1939.

WESTRA, H. : Die Rechtslage der Landschaftem mit Selbstverwaltung in Niederländisch-Indien. Zeitschrift für vergleichende Rechtswissenschaft 53 : 222-225, 2. Heft, 1939.

TRENITE, G.J.N. : Het Indische strafrecht, wet en adat. Koloniaal tijdschrift 28 : 360-366, Juli 1939.

WELCH, R. : Netherlands War Risk Insurance Act. U.S. Department of State, Comparative law series 2 : 359-363, August 1939.

SCHRIEKE, J.J. : The administrative system of the Netherlands Indies (Contd.). Bulletin of the Colonial Institute of Amsterdam 2 : 245-266, August 1939.

FLIER, M.J. van der : Aperçu de la jurisprudence néerlandaise en matière de droit international privé en 1937 ez 1938. Annuaire Grotius : 187-213, 1939.

NEW ZEALAND

CHRISTIE, J. : New Zealand. Journal of comparative legislation and international law 21 : 86-90, May 1939.

NORWAY

KOCHMANN, G. : Über das Verbot des Paragraph 112 der norwegischen Verfassung, die Prinzipien und den Geist der Verfassung zu verändern. Zeitschrift für öffentliches Recht 15 : 120-135, Heft 1, 1935.

CASTBERG, F. : Britisch-norwegische Divergenzen über die Ausdehnung des norwegischen Küstenmeeres. Völkerbund und Völkerrecht 2 : 441-446, November 1935.

GAARDER, K. : Om de norske internasjonalprivatrettslige regler om "uekte barns" rettsstilling overfor faren. Tidsskrift for rettsvidenskap 15 : 78-108, Hefte 1-2, 1936.

LEIVESTAD, T. : Custom as a type of law in Norway. Law quarterly review 54 : 95-115, January 1938.

LEIVESTAD, T. : Custom as a type of law in Norway (Contd.). Law quarterly review 54 : 266-268, April 1938.

CASTBERG, F. : State and individual in Norwegian public law. Nord : 284-304, No. 3, 1939.

Guerre civile - Droit à la détention des archives d'une légation - Décisions des Cours norvégiennes. Revue de droit international et de législation comparée 66 : 411-422, No. 2, 1939.
Légation d'Espagne en Norvège.

HAMBRO, E. : Den Norske Straffelovs paras. 85 og 95 i folkerrettslig belysning. Tidsskrift for rettsvidenskap 52 : 361-375, Hefte 4, 1939.
Security of the State.

PALESTINE

The Criminal Code of Palestine. Law journal 83 : 390-391, 5 June 1937.

PANAMA

MOSCOTE, J.D. : Estudio del Proyecto de nueva constitución del Licenciado Fabian Velarde. Universidad de Panama : 1-72, octubre 1938.

PERU

APARICIO y GOMEZ SANCHEZ, G. : Código de procedimientos civiles. Revista del foro 22 : 54-63, enero-marzo 1935.
A bibliography.

VILLARÁN, M.V. : Posición constitucional de los Ministros en el Perú. Revista de derecho y ciencias políticas 1 : 9-43, No. 1, 1936.

CARPI, A.R. : Derecho administrativo peruano en materia de finanzas y presupuesto (Contd.). Revista del foro 23 : 113-127, enero-junio 1936.

Leyes, decretos y resoluciones, julio a setiembre, 1936. Revista del foro 23 : 422-427, julio-setiembre 1936.
Index of Peruvian legislation.

La reforma del Código de Comercio. Revista del foro 23 : 585-586, octubre-diciembre 1936.

Administración de justicia en el Perú. Revista de derecho y legislación 25 : 94-99, noviembre-diciembre 1936.

Anteproyecto de código de procedimientos penales, elaborado por el Presidente de la Comisión Reformadora y Catedrático de la Facultad, Sr. Dr. Dn. Carlos Zavala Loayza. Revista de derecho y ciencias politicas 2 : 195-233, Núm. 1, 1937.

El nuevo código civil. Revista de derecho y ciencias políticas 2 : 177-195, Núm. 1, 1937.

Exposición de motivos del libro IV del proyecto de Código civil. Revista de derecho y ciencias políticas 1 : 171-199, No. 2, 1937.

CORNEJO, A.G. : El Nuevo Código Civil Revista de derecho y ciencias políticas 1 : I-XXVIII, no. 2, 1937.

El nuevo código civil. Revista de derecho y ciencias políticas 1 : 413-434, No. 3, 1937.

Leyes, decretos y resoluciones (enero, febrero y marzo de 1937). Revista del foro 24 : 109-151, enero a marzo 1937.

NATIONAL LAW - COUNTRIES

CORNEJO, L. : El matrimonio y el divorcio en el Código Civil y en la legislación anterior. Revista del foro 24 : 399-401, julio-setiembre 1937.

El nuevo código civil del Perú. Revista de derecho y legislación 26 : 79-84, julio-diciembre 1937.

BARANDIARÁN, J.L. : Comentarios al Código civil Peruano. Revista de derecho y ciencias politicas 2 : 323-492, núm. 2, 1938.

VILLARÁN, M.V. : Posición constitucional de los ministros en el Perú. Revista de derecho y ciencias políticas 2 : 271-305, Núm. 2, 1938.

Leyes, decretos y resoluciones (Enero, febrero y marzo de 1938). Revista del foro 25 : 81-82, enero-marzo 1938.

Comentarios al Código Civil Peruano (Derecho de obligaciones). Revista de derecho y ciencias políticas 2 : 537-698, Núm. 3, 1938.

OLAECHEA, M.A. : La reforma del Código Civil. Revista del foro 25 : 186-213, abril-junio 1938.

LA ROSA, P.M. : El certificado médico prenupcial en el nuevo Código Civil peruano. Revista del foro 25 : 376-380, julio-octubre 1938.

Leyes, decretos y resoluciones (Julio, agosto y setiembre de 1938). Revista del foro 25 : 542-586, julio-octubre 1938.

La reforma del Código Civil (Actas de las sesiones de la comisión) (Contd.). Revista del foro 25 : 441-509, julio-octubre 1938.

La reforma del Código civil. Revista del foro 25 : 751-825, noviembre-diciembre 1938.

Peru. - Leyes, decretos y resoluciones - Octubre, noviembre y diciembre de 1938. Revista del foro 25 : 845-863, noviembre-diciembre 1938.
Síntesis de las leyes publicadas en el diario oficial "El Peruano".

PALACIOS, M.S. : Apuntes sobre la ley 7566. Revista de derecho y ciencias políticas 3 : 35-169, no. 1, 1939.
The law of bankruptcy.

BARANDARÁN, J.H. : Comentarios al código civil peruano - Derecho de obligaciones. Revista de derecho y ciencias políticas 3 : 3-34, no. 1, 1939.

SCHNIEDERKÖTTER, T. : Der chilenisch-peruanische Auslieferungsvertrag und das interamerikanische Strafrecht. Zeitschrift für Völkerrecht 23 : 165-177, Heft 2, 1939.

BARANDIARÁN, J.L. : Comentarios al código civil peruano (Contd.). Revista de derecho y ciencias politicas 3 : 320-394, núm. 2, 1939.

PHILIPPINES

STEINWALLNER, B. : Das neue philippinische Strafrecht. Zeitschrift für vergleichende Rechtswissenschaft 50 : 152-159, I./II. Heft 1935.

REEVES, J.S. : The constitution of the Philippines. American journal of international law 29 : 476-478, July 1935.

STEINWALLNER, B. : Das neue philippinische Strafrecht. Zeitschrift für vergleichende Rechtswissenschaft 50 : 152-159, 8. November 1935.

FRIEDE ; Rechtstellung und Verfassung der Philippinen. Zeitschrift für ausländisches öffentliches Recht und Völkerrecht 6 : 172-188, Februar 1936.

MERRILL, F.T. : The outlook for Philippine independence. Foreign policy reports 15 : 154-164, September 15, 1939.

POLAND

BEREZOWAY : Pologne - Notice sur le mouvement législatif 1934-1936. Annuaire de législation étrangère 62 : 308-358, 1934/1936.

LISOWSKI, Z. : Das Recht der Schuldverhältnisse in Polen. Zeitschrift für osteuropäisches Recht 1 : 345-365, Januar 1935.

RAPPAPORT, E.S. : La media via du code pénal polonais. Revue internationale de droit pénal 12 : 227-256, nos. 2-3, 1935.

MAZEAUD, H. : Chronique de jurisprudence polonaise. Revue trimestrielle de droit civil 34 : 201-211, janvier-mars 1935.

KURATOW-KURATOSWKI, R. : L'arbitrage dans le nouveau code de procédure polonais. Bulletin trimestriel de la Société de législation comparée 64 : 68-92, janvier-mars 1935.

LEERS, J. v. : Die neue polnische Verfassung. Deutsche Juristen-Zeitung 40 : 332-338, 15. Mars 1935.

SCHLÜTER, F. : Die Bedeutung der neuen polnischen Strafprozessordnung für das deutsche Strafverfahrensrecht. Zeitschrift der Akademie für deutsches Recht 2 : 113-118, März 1935.

MOLINIÉ, J. : La nouvelle constitution polonaise. Europe orientale 5 : 137-138, mars-avril 1935.

STANIENDA, H. : Das Verhältnis von Völkerrecht und Landesrecht in Polen. Zeitschrift für Völkerrecht 19 : 385-402, Heft 4, 1935.

STELMACHOWSKI, B. : Das neue polnische Konkursrecht. Zeitschrift für osteuropäisches Recht 1 : 601-618, Juni 1935.

STANIENDA, H. : Polens neue Verfassung. Ost-Europa 10 : 535-552, Juni 1935.

PODKOMORSKI, J. und MUSZALSKI, E. : Praktische Fragen des kongress-polnischen Erbrechts. Danziger Juristen-Zeitung 14 : 65-69, 15. Juli 1935.

LONGCHAMPS de BERIER, E. : Le nouveau code polonais des obligations. Bulletin trimestriel de la Société de législation comparée 64 : 329-347, juillet-septembre 1935.

MIRKINE-GUETZÉVITCH, B. : La nouvelle constitution polonaise. Revue politique et parlementaire 42 : 332-342, 10 août 1935.

PIASECKI, A.V. : Polens neue Verfassung. Zeitschrift für osteuropäisches Recht 2 : 57-71, August 1935.

NATIONAL LAW - COUNTRIES

Polen - Übersicht über die wesentliche Gesetzgebung für das 2. Halbjahr 1934 und das 1. Halbjahr 1935. Zeitschrift für osteuropäisches Recht 2 : 79-80, August 1935.

WEGENER, H. : Das polnische Verfassungsgesetz vom 23. März 1935. Zeitschrift für Politik 25 : 552-557, August 1935.

CYBICHOWSKI, S. : Die Entwicklung des polnischen Staatsrechts in den Jahren 1921-1934. Jahrbuch des öffentlichen Rechts 22 : 527-576, 1935.

ZIELENIEIEWSKI, L. : Le problème des minorités nationales dans la constitution polonaise. Questions minoritaires 8 : 1-15, 1935.

STONE, J.F. : Summary of the Polish commercial code. U.S. General legal bulletin : 1-8, January 7, 1936.

WENDORFF, W.v. : Ausländische Währungen im polnischen Recht. Zeitschrift für osteuropäisches Recht 2 : 439-449, Februar 1936.

MAZEAUD, H. : Chronique de jurisprudence polonaise. Revue trimestrielle de droit civile 35 : 298-310, janvier-mars 1936.

ROSSECK, H. : Das polnische Schuldrecht- Danziger Juristen-Zeitung 15 : 25-29, 15. März 1936.

RAPPAPORT, E.-S. : Le Code pénal de 1932 et la nouvelle constitution polonaise. Revue internationale de droit pénal 13 : 209-247, No. 3, 1936.

ZOLL : Dekret des Staatspräsidenten vom 14.1.1936 über den Schutz der Interessen des polnischen Staates und Bürger in internationalen Verhältnissen. Zeitschrift für osteuropäisches Recht 2 : 618-620, April 1936.

KOSCHEMBAHR-LYSKOWSKI, I. von : Die Feststellung und die Aufgabe der leitenden Grundsätze einer Zivilgesetzgebung. Zeitschrift der Akademie für deutsches Recht 3 : 477-480, 15. Mai 1936.

MEYER, H. : Polen - Dekret des Staatspräsidenten vom 26. April 1936 über den Geldverkehr mit dem Auslande sowie den Verkehr mit ausländischen und inländischen Zahlungsmitteln. Zeitschrift für osteuropäisches Recht 2 : 734-735, Juni 1936.
Translation of decree annexed.

Das neue polnische Scheckrecht. Danziger Wirtschaftszeitung 16 : 383-385, 26. Juni 1936.

PAPINI, U.B. : I principi informativi della nuova Costituzione polucca 23 aprile 1935. Rivista di studi politici internazionali 3 : 255-270, luglio-dicembre 1936.

FELDE, L. : Le droit maritime en Pologne. Revue de droit maritime comparé 34 : 26-32, juillet-décembre 1936.

Übersicht über die wesentliche Gestzgebung für das. 2. Halbjahr 1935 und das 1. Halbjahr 1936. Zeitschrift für osteuropäisches Recht 3 : 110-114, August 1936.

LANE, A. : Übersicht über die Rechtsentwicklung des Auslandes - Polen. Zeitschrift der Akademie für deutsches Recht 3 : 828-829, Septemberheft 1936.

WOLTER, W. : Der strafrechtliche Schutz des Staates in Polen. Zeitschrift für osteuropäisches Recht 3 : 174-190, September 1936.

STANIENDA, H. : Das neue Wahlrecht in Polen. Archiv des öffentlichen Rechts 28 : 220-241, Heft 2, 1937.

MEYER, H. : Die Rechtstellung der Evangelisch-Augsburgischen Kirche in Polen nach dem neuen Kirchengesetz. Zeitschrift für osteuropäisches Recht 3 : 485-496, Februar 1937.

LANGROD, G.S. : La nuova costituzione della Repubblica di Polonia. Rivista di diritto pubblico 29 : 64-85, febbraio 1937.

Polonia - anno 1932. Istituto di studi legislativi, Legislazione internazionale 1 : 395-449, fasc. 3, 1932 (1937).
Survey of legislation.

MASSFELLER : Die Ehescheidung von polnischen Staatsangehörigen. Juristische Wochenschrift 66 : 780-783, 27. März 1937.

WERTHEIM, B. : Cenni sui cartelli nella legislazione e nella giurisprudenza Polacca. Annuario di diritto comparato e di studi legislativi 12 : 183-192, fasc. 3, 1937.

Entente juridique roumano-polonaise. Revue roumaine de droit privé 1 : 382-385, avril-septembre 1937.

PRADZYŃSKI, W. : Die autoritäre Idee als Grundlage der neuen polnischen Staatsverfassung. Zeitschrift der Akademie für deutsches Recht 4 : 369-372, 15. Juni 1937.

MEYER, H. : Das polnische Grenzzonenrecht. Zeitschrift für osteuropäisches Recht 3 : 721-736, Juni 1937.

GLASER, S. : Über die Entwicklungsrichtungen im Strafrecht und die polnische Strafrechtsreform. Revue internationale de doctrine et de législation pénale comparée 2 : 54-71. No. 1, 1938.

MAZEAUD, H. : Le nouveau pénal code polonais des obligations. Annales de l'Institut de droit comparé de l'université de Paris 3 : 269-283, 1938.

MAZEAUD, H. : Chronique de jurisprudence polonaise. Revue trimestrielle de droit civile 37 : 129-136, janvier-mars 1938.

PRZYBYTOWSKY, K. : Grund probleme des internationalen Obligationenrechts im Lichte der polnischen Gesetzgebung und Rechtsprechung. Zeitschrift für osteuropäisches Recht 4 : 552-566, März 1938.

MASSFELLER : Die Ehescheidung von polnischen Staatsangehörigen. Juristische Wochenschrift 67 : 640-643, 12. März 1938.

Regänzungstabelle über die von Polen bis zum 15. September 1931 abgeschlossenen Staatsverträge - Tabelle über die von Polen in der Zeit vom 15. September 1931 bis zum 31. Dezember 1937 abgeschlossenen Staatsverträge. Zeitschrift für osteuropäisches Recht 4 : 658-670, April 1938.

RAPPAPORT, E.S. : La réforme de la procédure pénale en Pologne dans ses rapports avec le Code polonais de 1932. Revue de science criminelle et de droit pénal comparé 2 : 163-181, avril-juin 1938.

Tabelle der von Polen in der Zeit vom 15. September 1931 bis zum 31. Dezember 1937 abgeschlossenen Staatsverträge. Zeitschrift für osteuropäisches Recht 4 : 722-737, Mai 1938.

Polen Gesetz vom 31. März 1938 über die Entzirhung der Staatsangehörigkeit. Zeitschrift für osteuropäisches Recht 4 : 805-806, Juni 1938.

TÜRCKE, A. von : Das Schulrecht der Volksgruppen in Polen. Zeitschrift für osteuropäisches Recht 5 : 27-45, Juli 1938.

STANIENDA, H. : Zur verfassungsrechtlichen Lage der religiösen Minderheiten in Polen. Zeitschrift für osteuropäisches Recht 5 : 137-175, September 1938.

SOSNICKI, C. : Les tendances de la nouvelle Constitution polonaise de 1935. Revue de droit public et de la science politique 55 : 867-877, octobre-décembre 1938.

WOLTER, W. : Polen - Dekret des Staatspräsidenten vom 22.11.1938 über den Schutz einiger Staatsinteressen. Zeitschrift für osteuropäisches Recht 5 : 380-384, Dezember 1938.

BEREZOWSKI, K. : Chronique législative - Notice sur les lois pénales promulguées en Pologne en 1938. Revue internationale de droit pénal 16 : 102-111, No. 1, 1939.

BUMKE, E. : Die Jahrestagung der Arbeitsgemeinschaft für die deutsch-polnischen Rechtsbeziehungen in Warschau. Zeitschrift der Akademie für deutsches Recht 6 : 73-78, 1. Februar 1939.

RATHJE, H.U. : Das polnische Grenzzonengesetz. Osteuropa 14 : 383-386, February 1939.

MAZEAUD, H. : Chronique de jurisprudence polonaise. Revue trimestrielle de droit civil 38 : 221-229, janvier-mars 1939.

FIEDOROWICZ, G. de : Nationalité des Israélites de Pologne domiciliés en Allemagne. Nouvelle revue de droit international privé 6 : 7-53, janvier-juin 1939.

Ankieta na temat reformy ordynacji wyborczej do Sejmu i i Senatu. Ruch prawniczy ekonomiczny i socjologiczny 19 : 129-155, avril-mai-juin 1939.
Reform of electoral law.

PERETIATKOWICZ, A. : Le césarisme démocratique et la nouvelle constitution de Pologne. Revue de droit public et de la science politique 56 : 309-325, avril-mai-juin 1939.

WITENBERG, J.C. : Aperçu sur la preuve en droit polonais. Bulletin trimestriel de la Société de législation comparée 68 : 181-196, avril-juin 1939.

KORKISCH, F. : Das Privatrecht im ehemals polnischen Staatsgebiet. Zeitschrift für ausländisches und internationales Privatrecht 12 : 850-879, Heft 5/6, 1939.

Polen. Übersicht über die wesentliche Gesetzgebung im 2. Halbjahr 1938 und im 1. Halbjahr 1939. Zeitschrift für osteuropäisches Recht 6 : 87-95, August 1939.

SIEDECKI, L. : Aperçu sur le procès civil en Pologne. Bulletin trimestriel de la Société de législation comparée 68 : 307-328, juillet-septembre 1939.

LEPENIES, W. : Neues Devisenrecht in Danzig und den besetzten ehemals polnischen Gebieten. Deutsches Recht 39 : 1938-1942, 11. November 1939.

HUBRICH, G. : Gliederung und Verwaltung der Ostgebiete. Deutsche Verwaltung 16 : 605-609, 10. Dezember 1939.

BEST, W. : Die neue Gliederung und Verwaltung des ehemaligen polnischen Staatsgebietes. Deutsches Recht 9 : 2089-2090, 16. Dezember 1939.

PORTUGAL

Le nouveau code administratif. Portugal : 3-5, no. 21, 31 janvier 1937.

LOUREIRO, F.-M. de : Le problème de l'inconstitutionnalité des lois au Portugal. Revue du droit public 53 : 441-463, juillet-août-september 1936.

LARA, C. : El nuevo estado corporativo portugués. Revista Javeriana 8 : 276-288, octubre 1937.

COSTA, A. (fils) : Le droit public au Portugal en 1935-1936. Annuaire de l'Institut international de droit public : 451-497, 1937.

VIANELLO, C.A. : Il nuovo diritto pubblico portoghese. Gerarchia 18 : 108-116, febbraio 1938.

AMORIM GIRAO, A. de : A divisão provincial do novo código administrativo. Biblos 14 : 1-38, 1938.

MARTIN, K. : Die Verwaltungsorganisation des portugiesischen Kolonialrechts. Zeitschrift für vergleichende Rechtswissenschaft 53 : 109-143, 2. Heft 1939.

Da CAMARA PINTO COELHO, L. : Portogallo, anno 1939. Istituto italiano di studi legislativi, Legislazione internazionale 8 : 375-393, 1939.

RUMANIA

ROSETTI BALANESCO, J. : Roumanie - Notice sur le mouvement législatif 1934-1935. Annuaire de législation étrangère 62 : 445-467, 1934/36.

ANTONESCO, E.E. : Chronique législative et jurisprudentielle du droit international privé en Roumanie. Revue critique de droit international 30 : 51-75, janvier-mars 1935.

STANCIU, V.V. : Considérations générales sur le projet du code pénal roumain. Revue internationale de droit pénal 12 : 285-325, Nos. 2-3, 1935.

IONESCO, T.R. : Législation civile roumaine (de 1931-1935). Revue trimestrielle de droit civile 34 : 484-498, avril-juin 1935.

NATIONAL LAW - COUNTRIES

BRANDSCH, R. : Das Sprachenrecht in Rumänien. Zeitschrift für Völkerrecht 20 : 277-289, Heft 3, 1936.

Übersicht über die wesentliche Gesetzgebung für das Jahr 1935. Zeitschrift für osteuropäisches Recht 2 : 536-538, März 1936.

KLEIN, W. : Das rumänische Entschuldungsgesetz vom 7. April 1934. Zeitschrift für osteuropäisches Recht 2 : 528-536, März 1936.

LUKAS, W. : Die Bankgesetzgebung Rumäniens. Zeitschrift für osteuropäisches Recht 2 : 602-614, April 1936.

GÜNDISCH, K. : Rumänien - Das Gesetz über die Regelung des Konsignationsvertrages vom 30. Juli 1934 in der Fassung vom 1. April 1936. Zeitschrift für osteuropäisches Recht 2 : 744-746, Juni 1936.
Translation of decree annexed.

DIMITRESCO, G. : La crise juridique du crédit - Les nouvelles tendances législatives en Roumanie. Bulletin trimestriel de la Société de législation comparée 65 : 277-281, juillet-septembre 1936.

SCHWAMM, H. : Das neue rumänische Strafgesetz und seine international-rechtlichen Bestimmungen. Internationales anwaltsblatt 22 : 82-87, September 1936.

FLEISCHER, E. : Rumänien - Die Bestimmungen des neuen rumänischen Strafgesetzbuches vom 18. März 1936 über Hoch- und Landesverrat und Spionage. Zeitschrift für osteuropäisches Recht 3 : 217-219, September 1936.

VALLIMARESCO, A. : Chronique de jurisprudence roumaine. Revue trimestrielle de droit civil 34 : 991-1003, octobre-décembre 1936.

PETRESCO, G.A. : Le régime juridique des lois d'assainissement des dettes agricoles dans le droit public roumain. Revista de drept public 11 : 331-354, octobre-décembre 1936.

PELLA, V.V., et VASILU, C.G. : Rapport concernant les nouveaux codes pénal et de procédure pénale promulgués le 17 mars 1936. Recueil de documents en matière pénale et pénitentiaire 5 : 419-431, novembre 1936.

BRAUNIAS : Rumänien - Zehn Jahre Consiliu Legislativ. Zeitschrift für osteuropäisches Recht 3 : 349-351, November 1936.

MEITANI, R. : L'extradition dans les nouveaux codes roumains. Revue de droit international et de législation comparée 18 : 34-87, No. 1, 1937.

DOCAN, G.P. : Der Verlagsvertrag nach rumänischem Recht. Zeitschrift für ausländisches und internationales Privatrecht 11 : 53-76, Heft 1-2, 1937.

POSSA, M. : Le droit international privé dans l'avant-projet du code civil roumain. Revue roumaine de droit privé 1 : 192-195, janvier-mars 1937.

STOÏCESCO : Le régime matrimonial en droit roumain. Semaine internationale de droit, Travaux : 125-131, (section 4), 1937.

Entente juridique roumano-polonaise. Revue roumaine dr droit privé 1 : 382-385, avril-septembre 1937.

NEGREA, C., et IONESCO, A.R. : Droit civil applicable en Transylvanie et en Bukovine. Revue roumaine de droit privé 1 : 246-253, avril-septembre 1937.

SIPSOM, C. : Inutilité et danger de la revision générale du code civil. Revue roumaine de droit privé 1 : 21-34, 79-92, janvier-mars, avril-septembre 1937.

PETIT, E., und GHIMPA, N.D. : Die neue rumänische Strafprozessordnung Carols II. Zeitschrift für osteuropäisches Recht 3 : 673-698, Mai 1937.

Rumänien. Übersicht über die wesentliche Gesetzgebung für die Jahre 1935, 1936 und 1937. Zeitschrift für osteuropäisches Recht 3 : 756-762, Juni 1937.

IONASCO, A.R. : Les mesures prises en Roumanie en faveur des débiteurs pour l'exécution de leurs obligations à la suite de la crise économique. Bulletin trimestriel de la société de législation comparée 66 : 175-188, juillet-septembre 1937.

ANGELESCU, C.C. : Jurisdicţiile administrative faţă de articolul 107 din constituţie. Revista de drept public 12 : 217-239, Julie-Septembrie 1937.

Die Vereinheitlichung der Gezetzgebung in Rumänien. Zeitschrift der Akademie für deutsches Recht 4 : 500-501, 15. August 1937.

KESCHMANN, F. : Rumänien - Tabelle der vom Königreich Rumänien 1926-1937 abgeschlossenen Staatsverträge. Zeitschrift für osteuropäisches Recht 4 : 182-192, September 1937.

NEGULESCU, P. : Durata mandatului deputaţilor şi senatorilor - Interpretarea articolului 62 din Constituţie. Revista de drept public 12 : 483-487, Octumbrie-Decembrie 1937.

HOZOC, D. : Contenciosul adminiatrativ Român. Revista de drept public 12 : 564-595, Octombrie-Decembrie 1937.

GRUIA, I.V. : Durata funcţionărei deputaţilor şi senatorilor. Revista de drept public 12 : 493-520, Octombrie-Decembre 1937.

MORUZI, J. : Le nouveau code roumain de procédure pénale. Revue internationale de doctrine et de législation pénale comparée 2 : 82-94, No. 1, 1938.

POPOVICI, J. : L'influence française sur les constitutions roumaines. Revue d'histoire politique et constitutionnelle 2 : 125-144, janvier-mars 1938.

RĂDULESCO, A. : La nouvelle Constitution. Revue de Transylvanie 4 : 3-13, janvier-juin 1938.

MORUZI, J. : Remarques sur la nouvelle législation pénitentiaire en Roumanie. Revue internationale de doctrine et de législation pénale comparée 2 : 134-142, No. 2, 1938.

BOROS, R.C. : Le stato della legislazione aeronautica in Romania. Rivista di diritto aeronautico 6 : 146-153, n. 2-3, 1938.

GOUNAUD, J. : La nouvelle constitution roumaine. Europe centrale 13 : 182-183, 19 mars 1938.

LAPEDATU, A. : Le régime parlementaire en Roumanie d'après la nouvelle Constitution du 24 février 1938. Bulletin interparlementaire 18 : 55-58, avril-mai 1938.

NATIONAL LAW - COUNTRIES

ANTONESCU, E. : Chronique législative et jurisprudentielle de droit international privé en Roumanie. Revue critique de droit international 33 : 191-219, avril-juin 1938.

Die neue Verfassung vom 27. Februar 1938. Zeitschrift für ausländisches öffentliches Recht und Völkerrecht 8 : 373-391, Mai 1938.

GUNDISCH, C. : Rumänien - Übersicht über die wesentliche Gesetzgebung im Jahre 1937/38. Zeitschrift für osteuropäisches Recht 4 : 786-792, Juni 1938.

BRAUNIAS, K. : Die rumänische Verfassungsentwicklung 1923-1938. Zeitschrift für osteuropäisches Recht 4 : 771-785, Juni 1938.

La nouvelle constitution de la Roumanie. Annuario di diritto comparato e di studi legislativi 13 : 421-431, fasc. 6, Pt. 1, 1938.
Texte annexé.

GÜNDISCH, K. : Das Dekretgesetz vom 21. Januar 1938 betr. die Überprüfung der rumänischen Staatsbürgerschaft. Zeitschrift für osteuropäisches Recht 5 : 50-58, Juli 1938.
Suivi du texte de la loi.

RARINCESCU, C.G. : La nouvelle organisation administrative de l'Etat roumain (Loi administrative du 14 août 1938). Revista de drept public 13 : 453-506, Julie-Decembrie 1938.

Etude sur la Constitution sociale et politique de la Roumanie, dù 27 février 1938. Revista de drept public 13 : 375-452, Julie-Decembrie 1938.

VALLIMARESCO, A. : Chronique de droit roumain pour 1937. Revue trimestrielle de droit civile 37 : 845-870, octobre-décembre 1938.

BUSSE : Die rumänische Staatsverfassung vom 27. Februar 1938. Deutsche Justiz 100 : 1988-1993, 16. Dezember 1938.

WITTSTOCK, O. : Die Neugestaltung des rumänischen Staatsrechts. Zeitschrift für osteuropäisches Recht 5 : 364-375, Dezember 1938.

ANDERSSEN, W. : Die Entwicklung des öffentlichen Rechts in Rumänien vom 1. Juli 1930 bis 30. Juni 1938. Jahrbuch des öffentlichen Rechts 25 : 376-417, 1938.

COHEN, J. : La protection des obligatoires en droit roumain. Semaine internationale de droit, Travaux : 111-122 (section 6), 1938.

MORUZI, J. : Nouvelles modifications apportées à la législation pénale roumaine "Roi Charles II". Revue internationale de doctrine et de législation pénale comparée 3 : 105-119, No. 1, 1939.

DEMETRESCU, P.I. : Die Reform des rumänischen Handelsrechts. Zeitschrift für vergleichende Rechtswissenschaft 53 : 73-93, Heft 1, 1939.

DEMETRESCU, P.I. : Die Reform des rumänischen Handelsrechts. Zeitschrift für vergleichende Rechtswissenschaft 53 : 73-93, Heft 1, 1939.

RADULESCU, A., et SACHELARIE, O. : Romania - anno 1939. Istituto italiano disstudi legislativi, Legislazione internazionale 8 : 1053-1128, tomo II, 1939.
Index of laws and summaries.

TOMASSINI, F. : La nuova costituzione rumena. Vita italiana 27 : 323-335, Marzo 1939.

VOICULET, P. : Die landwirtschaftliche und städtische Schuldenregelung in Rumänien und ihre Verfassungsmässigkeit. Zeitschrift für ausländisches und internationales Privetrecht 12 : 630-642, Heft 3/4, 1939.

ALEXIANU, G. : Fragen des interprovinziellen Rechts in Rumänien. Zeitschrift für vergleichende Rechtswissenschaft 53 : 311-326, 3./4. Heft, 1939.

MEITANI, R. : La nationalité en Roumanie. Revue de droit international et de législation comparée 66 : 632-699, No. 4, 1939.

DJUVARA, M. : La nouvelle constitution roumaine et son esprit. Revue de droit public et de la science politique 56 : 277-308, avril-mai-juin 1939.

PETIT, E., and GHIMPA, N. : Die Novelle zum rumänischen Szrafgesetzbuch. Zeitschrift für osteuropäisches Recht 5 : 693-700, Mai 1939.

KESCHMANN, F. : Gesetz vom 16. 1. 1939 über den Erwerb und Verlust der rumänischen Staatsbürgerschaft Zeitschrift für osteuropäisches Recht 5 : 710-716, Mai 1939.

GÜNDISCH, K. : Rumänien - Übersicht über die wesentliche Gestzgebung im Jahre 1938-1939. Zeitschrift für osteuropäisches Recht 5 : 700-709, Mai 1939.

RADULESCU, A. : Doveri e diritti nella nuova costituzione della Romania. Rivista internazionale di filosofia del diritto 19 : 240-250, maggio-agosto 1939.

WITTSTOCK, O. : Das neue Wahlgesetz Rumäniens. Zeitschrift für osteuropäisches Recht 5 : 759-766, Juni 1939.

Il nuovo codice di commercio romeno ed il diritto commerciale italiano. Rivista del diritto commerciale 37 : 321-332, luglio-agosto 1939.

LONASCO, A.R. : La nouvelle constitution roumaine. Bulletin trimestriel de la Société de législation comparée 68 : 345-373, juillet-septembre 1939.

SALVADOR

CRAWFORD, H.P. : The 1939 constitution of ElSalvador. U.S. Department of commerce, Comparative law series 2 : 205-209, May 1929.

The new constitution of El Salvador. Bulletin of th Pan American Union 73 : 353-361, June 1939.

SA'UDI ARABIA

BLEIBER, F. : Die völkerrechtliche Stellung der Staaten Arabiens. Zeitschrift für öffentliches Recht 19 : 137-163, Heft 1, 1939.

SOUTH AFRICA

BROOKES, E.H. : The South African native bills. Journal of the Royal African Society 35 : 65-70, January 1936.

NATIONAL LAW - COUNTRIES

MARAIS, J.S. : A history of the native franchise in South Africa. Zeitschrift für vergleichende Rechtswissenschaft 51 : 175-182, Heft 1-2, 1936.

BUNGER, K. : Die Gesetzgebung der Südafrikanischen Union im Jahre 1935. Afrika Rundschau 2 : 31-35, Juni 1936.

E.E. : Nationality in the Union of South Africa. British yearbook of international law 17 : 187-189, 1936.

SPIRO, E. : The hire purchase agreement in South African law and its problems. Journal of comparative legislation and international law 21 : 11-26, February 1939.

SPAIN

SALA, I.B. : Sobre la accessión o adhesión de España al Código Americano de derecho internacional privado denominado "Código Bustamente". Revista de derecho internacional 28 : 163-175, 30. septiembre 1935.

ALVAREZ, E. : El Código internacional privado (Código Bustamente) y la adhesión de España. Revista de derecho internacional 28 : 176-200, 30 septiembre 1935.

ZAMORA, N.-A. : L'élaboration de la constitution espagnole du 10 décembre 1931. Revue d'histoire politique et constitutionnelle 1 : 20-34, janvier-mars 1937.

CORVINGTON, H. : Una opinión de professor sobre la extensión del campo de aplicación del Código Bustamente y la oportunidad de su adopción por el gobierno de España. Revista de derecho internacional 31 : 88-99. 31 marzo 1937.

LASALA LLANAS, M. de : Il diritto civile interregionale in Spagna. Annuario di diritto comparato e di studi legislativi 12 : 201-214, fasc. 4, 1936.

SIBERT, M. : La guerre civile d'Espagne et les droits des particuliers. Revue générale de droit international public 44 : 505-551, septembre-octobre 1937.

ZAMORA, N.A. : Les tentatives de revision de la constitution espagnole. Revue d'histoire politique et constitutionnelle 2 : 10-22, janvier-mars 1938.

GENET, R. : The charcge of piracy in the Spanish civil war. American journal of international law 32 : 253-263, April 1938.

ZWEIGERT, K. : Französische Urteile zu Ereignissen des Spanienkrieges. Zeitschrift für ausländisches und internationales Privatrecht 11 : 939-944, Heft 5/6, 1937.

L'affaire de l'or de la Banque d'Espagne. Journal des tribunaux mixtes 17 : 7-9, 22/23, juin 1938.

MONTEMAYOR, L. de : Verso il nuovo Stato spagnolo - La legge sulla stampa. Stato 9 : 421-427, luglio 1938.

ALCALA-ZAMORA y CASTILLO, N. : Justice pénale de guerre civile. Revue de science criminelle et de droit pénal comparé 3 : 633-671, octobre-décembre 1938.

ANDIA, M.G. de : La nouvelle législation minière de l'Espagne nationale. Nouvelle revue de droit international privé 5 : 762-780, octobre-novembre-décembre 1938.

Elenco delle disposizioni in materia penale promulgate nella Spagna Nazionale. Giustizia penale (Parte terza) 45 : 118. gennaio-febbraio 1939.

GUIDOTTI, F. : L'organizzazione nazional-sindacalista spagnola. Rivista del lavoro 8 : 31-37, 28 febbraio 1939.

MENDES-FRANCE, P. : La question de l'or espagnol. Cahiers des droits de l'homme 39 : 164-165, 15 mars 1939.

GARRIGUES, J. : Il nuovo ordine in Spagna - Sindacati verticali e corporazioni. Archivio di studi corporativi 10 : 163-187, fasc. 3, 1939.

COSTAMAGNA, C. : Dottrina spagnola dello Stato totalitario. Stato 10 : 168-170, marzo 1939.

ERBLER, H. : El fuero del trabajo - Nationalspaniens sozialpolitisches Grundgesetz. Archiv des öffentlichen Rechts 30 : 274-293, 3. Heft 1939.

GOLDSCHMIDT, J. : La révolution judiciaire en Espagne. Bulletin trimestriel de la Société de législation comparée 68 : 213-222, avril-juin 1939.

LASALA LLANAS, M. de : La restauración del derecho anterior a la constitución de la República de 1931 y la revisión futura del sistema de derecho civil internacional en España. Bulletin de l'Institut juridique internacional 40 : 196-209, avril 1939.

GARRIGUES, J. : Il rapporto di lavoro secondo il nazionalsindacalismo spagnolo. Archivio di studi corporativi 10 : 307-338, fasc. 4, 1939.

SWEDEN

MALMAR, T. : Jugements suédois en matière de droit international privé. Nordisk tidsskrift for international ret (Acta scandinavica juris gentium) 6 : 41-48, fasc. 1, 1935.

MALMAR, F. : Svenske domme vedrerende international privatrecht. Nordisk tidsskrift for international Ret 7 : 152-161, fasc. 2-3, 1936.

BLOCH, J.D. : Das schwedische Gesetz über die Schuldverschreibungen vom 27. März 1936. Zeitschrift für ausländisches und internationales Privatrecht 10 : 523-533, Heft 4, 1936.

Jugement suédois en matière de droit international privé. Nordisk tidsskrift for international ret (Acta scandinavica juris gentium) 7 : 107-116, Fasc. 4, 1936.

SEIDEL, H. : Der schwedische Zivilprozess. Deutsche Jutiz 99 : 814-816, 28. Mai 1937.

MALMAR, F. : Svenske Domme vedrørende International Privatret. Nordisk Tidsskrift for international ret 8 : 188-193, Fasc. 3, 1937.

MALMAR : Le régime matrimonial en droit suédois. Semaine internationale de droit, Travaux : 133-137, (section 4), 1937.

MYRBERG, I. : Till frågan om gränsen mellan konungens i statsrådet och i regeringsrätten kompetens. Statsvetenskaplig tidskrift 40 : 393-425, häft 5, 1937.

PAPPENHEIM, W. : Die Gesetzgebung Schwedens in den Jahren 1930-1936. Zeitschrift für ausländisches und internationales Privatrecht 10 : 899-964, Heft 5/6, 1936.

UDDGREN, L. : Ausgewählte Entscheidungen des Schwedischen Höchsten Gerichts 1926-1934. Zeitschrift fur ausländisches und internationales Privatrecht 10 : 965-977, Heft 5/6, 1936.

BLOCH, J.-D. : Das schwedische Gesetz über internationale Rechtsverhältnisse in Nachlassachen vom 5. März 1937. Zeitschrift für ausländisches und internationales Privatrecht 11 : 929-938, Heft 5/6, 1937.

ENG, B. : Tillämpningen av internationelle överenskommelser i intern svensk rätt. Nordisk Tidsskrift for international Ret 9 : 94-109, Fasc. 1-2, 1938.

DIX, H. : Das schwedische Gesetz über die internationalen Rechtsverhältnisse von Nachlässen vom 5. März 1937. Juristische Wochenschrift 67 : 1509-1510, 11. Juni 1938.

STRAHL, I. : Les nouvelles lois suédoises contre la criminalité juvénile. Revue de sciences criminelle et de droit pénal comparé 2 : 433-437, juillet-septembre 1938.

BELLQUIST, E.C. : Constitutional monarchy in Sweden. Baltic and Scandinavian coutries 4 : 297-300, September 1938.

GUILHOT, J. : La Convention frano-suédoise en matière d'impôts sur les successions. Journal du droit international 65 : 708-722, juillet-octobre 1938.

ALFSEN, F.A.M. : The Swedish share company law. U.S. Department of commerce, Comparative law series 1 : 529-530, December 1938.

GÄRDE, N. : Processreform i Sverige. Tidsskrift for rettsvidenkap 52 : 3-33, Hefte 1, 1939.

WOLGAST, E. : Auswärtige Gewalt. Zeitschrift für öffentliches Recht 19 : 1-43, Heft 1, 1939.
Foreign affairs administration in Sweden.

HULT, P. : Det utomäktenskapliga barnets rättsställning i förhallande till fadern enligt svensk internationell privaträtt. Tidsskrift for rettsvidenskap 52 : 376-401, Hefte 4, 1939.

Survey of the economic defense measures in Sweden. U.S. Department of Commerce, Comparative law series 2 : 527-538, November 1939.

SWITZERLAND

HIS, E. : Cantons suisses - Notice sur le mouvement législatif pendant les annees 1934 à 1936. Annuaire de législation étrangère 62 : 232-237, 1934/36.

CHRIST, A. : Gesetzgebung der Schweiz betreffend Privatrecht, Arbeitsrecht, gewerblichen Rechtsschutz und Urheberrecht, Zwangsvollstreckung und Konkurs im Jahre 1935. Zeitschrift für ausländisches und internationales Privatrecht 10 : 550-563, Heft 4, 1936.

RIGGENBACH, B. : Schrifttum der Schweiz im Jahre 1935. Zeitschrift für ausländisches und internationales Privatrecht 10 : 595-605, Heft 4, 1936.

THILO, E. : Jurisprudence du Tribunal fédéral suisse en 1934 et 1935. Revue trimestrielle de droit civil 35 : 541-564, avril-juin 1936.

MEYER-WILD, H. : Das schweizerische Bundesgesetz über die Banken und Sparkassen. Juristische Wochenschrift 64 : 1539, 25. Mai 1935.

BISE, P. : Rejet par le peuple suisse de la notion de revision constitutionnelle. Revue du droit public et de la science politique 42 : 619-621, juillet-août-septembre 1935.

Schweiz - Vollendung der Revision des Obligationenrechts. Zeitschrift für ausländisches und internationales Privatrecht 10 : 1010, Heft 5/6, 1936.

MEYER-WILD, H. : Die Folgen der Abwertung nach schweizerischem Recht. Juristische Wochenschrift 65 : 3165-3167, 14. November 1936.

SCHNEIDER, M. : Das neue schweizerische Aktienrecht. Zeitschrift der Akademie für deutsches Recht 3 : 1089-1095, Dezember 1936.

WIELAND, A. : Das neue schweizerische Aktienrecht. Zeitschrift für ausländisches und internationales Privatrecht 11 : 83-93, Heft 1-2, 1937.

WERTHEIMER, L. : Die Reform des Aktienrechts in Deutschland und der Schweiz. Annuario di diritto comparato e di studi legislativi 13 : 157-184, ser. 2, fasc. 3, 1937 (parte prima).

RIGGENBACH, B. : Schrifttum der Schweiz im Jahre 1936. Zeitschrift für ausländisches und internationales Privatrecht 11 : 671-682, Heft 3/4, 1937.

HAAB, R., und STAEHELIN, M. : Gesetzgebung der Schweiz betreffend Privatrecht, Arbeitsrecht, gewerblichen Rechtsschutz und Urheberrecht, Zwangsvollstreckung und Konkurs im Jahre 1936. Zeitschrift für ausländisches und internationales Privatrecht 11 : 542-590, Heft 3/4, 1937.

HENGGELER, J. : Die Abwertung des Schweizerfrankens und ihr Einfluss auf die zivilrechtlichen Verhältnisse. Zeitschrift für zweizerisches Recht 56 : 158a-259a, Heft 4, 1937.

GUISAN, H. : La dévaluation du franc suisse et ses effets de droit civil. Zeitschrift für schweizerisches Recht 56 : 260a-346a, Heft 4, 1937.

LIEBESKIND, W.A. : Le droit de cité cantonal et communal. Zeitschrift für schweizerisches Recht 4 : 347a-430a, Heft 5, 1937.

Übersicht über die schweizerische Rechtsgesetzgebung des Jahres 1936. Zeitschrift für schweizerisches Recht 56 : 445-567, Heft 6, 1937.

RIGGENBACH, B. : Übersicht der Literatur über schweizerisches Recht vom Jahre 1936. Zeitschrift für schweizerisches Recht 56 : 411-443, Heft 6, 1937.

THILO, E. : Jurisprudence du Tribunal fédéral suisse en 1936 et 1937. Revue trimestrielle de dr civil 36 : 883-957, octobre-décembre 1937.

COQUOZ, R. : L'hypothèque aérienne - L'état actuel du droit en Suisse et les projets de règlementation internationale. Zeitschrift für schweizerisches Recht 57 : 100-111, Heft 1, 1938.

WYLER, M. : The Swiss company limited by shares. Journal of comparative legislation and international law (Pt. 1) 20 : 85-90, February 1938.

SCHMIED, E. : Das neue Schweizerische Strafrecht. Prager Juristische Zeitschrift 18 : 119-122, 2. Feberheft 1938.

GRAVEN, J. : Le jury et les tribunaux d'échevins en Suisse. Zeitschrift für schweizerisches Recht 57 : 1a-202a, Heft 3, 1938.

GOETSCHEL, E. : Aperçu du droit commercial suisse revisé. Journal du droit international 65 : 244-257, mars-avril 1938.

COMMENT, A. : Les atteintes portées au droit civil par des mesures législatives exceptionnelles. Zeitschrift für schweizerisches Recht 57 : 217a-480a, Heft 4, 1938.

CARRY, P. : La nouvelle législation suisse sur la société anonyme. Bulletin trimestrial de la Société de législation comparé 67 : 177-196, avril-septembre 1938.

OFTINGER, K. : Gesetzgeberische Eingriffe in das Zivilrecht. Zeitschrift für schweizerisches Recht 4 : 481a-695a, Heft 5, 1938.

DOMKE, M. : Le projet suisse sur le conflit de lois en matière de cautionnement. Journal du droit international 65 : 417-438, mai-juin 1938.

PFENNINGER, H.F. : Schwur- und Schöffengericht in der Schweiz. Zeitschrift für schweizerisches Recht 57 : 697a-747a, Heft 6, 1938.

Übersicht über schweizerische Rechtsgesetzgebung des Jahres 1937.

RIGGENBACH, B. : Übersicht der Literatur über schweizerisches Recht vom Jahre 1937. Zeitschrift für schweizerisches Recht 57 : 445-476, Heft 7, 1938.

CHAPUISAT, E. : Démocratie directe et "Landsgemeinde". Revue d'histoire politique et constittutionnelle 2 : 438-443, juillet-septembre 1938.

SCHÖNKE, A. : Das neue schweizerische Strafgesetzbuch. Deutsche Justiz 100 : 1360-1362, 26 August 1938.

HUBER, H. : Über Foederalismus. Neue schweizer Rundschau 6 : 237-244, August 1938.

BATELLI, M. : L'équilibre entre le pouvoir législatif et le pouvoir exécutif en Suisse. Revue du droit public et de la science politique 45 : 605-626, juillet-août-septembre 1938.

COQUOZ, R. : L'hypothèque aérienne. Revue générale de droit aérien 7 : 570-579, octobre-novembre-decembre 1938.
L'état actuel du droit en Suisse.

SCHNITZER, A.F. : La production des preuves en justice en droit suisse et en droit allemand. Bulletin trimestriel de la Société de législation comparée 67 : 336-364, actobre-décembre 1938.

STAEHELIN, M. : Die Bedeutung der Materialien für die Auslegung des neuen Obligationenrechtes. Zeitschrift für schweizerisches Recht 58 : 19-40, Heft 1, 1939.

HAFTER, E. : Das eidgenössische Strafrecht und die Vorbehalte zugunsten der Kantone im Sinne des Art. 335 des schweizerischen Strafgesetzbuches. Zeitschrift für schweizerisches Recht 58 : 1a-54a, Heft 3, 1939.

PANCHAUD, A. : Le droit pénal réservé aux cantons par l'art. 335 du Code pénal suisse. Zeitschrift für schweizerisches Recht 58 : 55a-115a, Heft 3, 1939.

CLERC, F. : Le nouveau Code pénal suisse. Revue de science criminelle et de droit pénal comparé 4 : 238-255, avril-juin 1939.

The Swiss Federal criminal code of December 21, 1937. Journal of criminal law and criminology 30 : 1-17, May-June 1939 (supplement).

KIRCHHOFER, E. : Eigentumsgarantie, Eigentumsbeschränkung und Enteignung. Zeitschrift für schweizerisches Recht 58 : 139-177, 3. Juni 1939.

RÖTHLISBERGER, J.W. : Le nouveau code pénal suisse. Police criminelle internationale 2 : 8, 10 août 1939.

RIGGENBACH, B. : Übersicht der Literatur über schweizerisches Recht vom Jahre 1938. Zeitschrift für schweizerisches Recht 58 : 383-413, Heft 5, 1939.

Übersicht über die schweizerische Rechtsgesetzbung des Jahres 1938. Zeitschrift für schweizerisches Recht 58 : 4414-531, Heft 5, 1939.

CLERC, F. : Le code pénal suisse du 21 décembre 1937. Recueil de documents en matière pénale et pénitentiaire 8 : 309-321, septembre 1939.

SWITZERLAND
(International law, Aliens)

FRITZSCHE, H., und PESTALOZZI, A. : Zivilprozessrecht und internationales Privatrecht der Schweiz im Jahre 1934. Zeitschrift für ausländisches und internationales Privatrecht 9 : 694-727, Heft 4/5, 1935.

GOUY, L. : Les divorces étrangers en Suisse. Tribune des nations 2 : 6 (supplément suisse), 7 novembre 1935.

SCHINDLER, D. : Die schweizerische Neutralität und die Sanktionen. Völkerbund und Völkerrecht 2 : 524-530, Dezember 1935.

Le conflit italo-éthiopien et le statut de la neutralité helvétique (Rapport à l'Assemblée fédérale du 2 décembre 1935). Revue internationale française du droit des gens 1 : 40-50, 15 janvier 1936.

VORTISCH, F. : Die gegenseitige Anerkennung der Gerichtsbarkeit in Ehesachen zwischen dem Deutschen Reich und der Schweizerischen Eidgenossenschaft. Zeitschrift für ausländisches und internationales Privatrecht 10 : 17-39, Heft 1/3. 1936.

FRITZSCHE, H., und PESTALOZZI, A. : Zivilprozessrecht und internationales Privatrecht der Schweiz im Jahre 1935. Zeitschrift für ausländisches und internationales Privatrecht 10 : 564-594, Heft 4, 1936.

KOUTAISSOFF, P. : Chronique de jurisprudence suisse en matière de nationalité et de conflits de lois : 1930-1935. Revue critique de droit international 31 : juillet-novembre 1936.

CLERC, B. : La vie internationale de la Suisse en 1934-1935. Revue générale de droit international public 43 : 631-638, septembre-octobre 1936.

CUTTAT, J.-A. : La représentation diplomatique et consulaire de la Suisse. Archives diplomatiques et consulaires : 196-198, octobre 1936.

LEVIS, O. : Deutsch-schweizerische Vollstreckungsvertrag. Zeitschrift für schweizerisches Recht 56 : 352-388, Heft 2, 1937.

Das Schweizerbürgerrecht. Zeitschrift für schweizerisches Recht 56 : 1-156a, Heft 3, 1937.

ZÜRCHER, E. : Das Asylrecht der Schweiz. Völkerbund (Lausanne) 15 : 45-57, 1. April 1937.

CLERC, B. : La vie internationale de la Suisse en 1936. Revue générale de droit international public 44 : 586-597, septembre-octobre 1937.

LA BRUYÈRE, R. : La fonction stratégique de la neutralité et le droit d'asile suisse. Journal de Genève : 1, 13 février 1938.

SCHINDLER, D. : Die Wiederherstellung der umfassenden Neutralität der Schweiz. Völkerbund und Völkerrecht 4 : 689-698, März 1938.

SCHINDLER, D. : La neutralité suisse de 1920 à 1938. Revue de droit international et de législation comparée 65 : 433-472, No. 3, 1938.

FRITZSCHE, H. : Zivilprozessrecht und internationales Privatrecht der Schweiz im Jahre 1936. Zeitschrift für ausländisches und internationales Privatrecht 11 : 641-670, Heft 3/4, 1937.

DOLLOT, R. : La crise des neutralités permanentes (Contd.) - La neutralité suisse. Affaires étrangères 8 : 396-410, juillet 1938.

Il riconoscimento della neutralità svizzera. Relazioni internationali 4 : 479-480, 2 luglio 1938.

PAGANI, B. : Le nuove tendenze di neutralità e la neutralità svizzera. Rassegna di politica internazionale 5 : 417-431, agosto 1938.

SCHINDLER, D. : Die schweizerische Neutralität 1920 -1938. Zeitschrift für ausländisches öffentliches Recht und Völkerrecht 8 : 413-444, August 1938.

KEPPLER, K.: Die neue Neutralität der Schweiz. Zeitschrift für öffentliches Recht 18 : 505-545, 31. Dezember 1938.

SCERNI, M. : La Convenzione italo-svizzera del 3 gennaio 1933 e la giurisdizione in materia di stato. Istituto di studi legislativi : giurisprudenza comparata di diritto internazionale privato 3 : 62-65, 1938.

FRITZSCHE, H., und PESTALOZZI, A. : Zivilprozessrecht und internationales Privatrecht der Schweiz im Jahre 1937. Zeitschrift für ausländisches und internationales Privatrecht 12 : 577-604, Heft 3/4, 1939.

STEINBUCH, H.C. : Die Stellung der Bank für Internationalen Zahlungsausgleich im öffentlichen Rechte der schweizerisches Eidgenossebschaft und des Kantons Basel-Stadt. Zeitschrift für schweizerisches Recht 58 : 244-262, 3. Juni 1939.

SWITZERLAND
(Patents, Trademarks, Copyrights)

GILLIÉRON, C. : La radio diffusion de disques en droit suisse. Revue internationale de la radioélectricité 13 : 13-19, janvier-février-mars 1937.

SYRIA

CARDAHI, C. : Le code de procédure libanais, sa place dans le mouvement juridique contemporain. Bulletin trimestriel de la Société de Législation comparée 64 : 435-470, octobre-décembre 1935.

DUPOND, O. : La collaboration criminelle et le tentative dans le "Code pénal des pays sous mandat de la France". Revue de science criminelle et de droit pénal comparé 4 : 256-262, avril-juin 1939.

L'exequatur en Egypte des décisions rendues par les juridictions syriennes. Journal des tribunaux mixte 18 : 4-5, 17 et 18 mai 1939.

THAILAND

MÉNARD, A. : Questions de droit international privé dans la zone spécial de Tanger. Revue critique de droit international 31 : 647-665, juillet-novembre 1936.

HUTASINGHA, P. : Die Verfassung des Königreichs Siam. Jahrbuch des öffentlichen Rechts 23 : 376-389, 1936.

EYGOUT, H. : La nouvelle Constitution siamoise. Revue indochinoise juridique et économique : 150-161, No. 3, 1937.

EYGOUT, H. : Le droit pénal siamois. Revue indochinoise juridique et économique : 29-57, No. 1, 1938.

BUNGER, K. : Das Recht der Handelsgesellschaften in Siam. Ostasiatische Rundschau 19 : 68-69, 119-120, 1. Februar, 1 März 1938.

Das Kaufrecht Siams. Ostasiatische Rundschau 19 : 172-174, 222-223, 1. April, 1. Mai 1938.

JOHNSTONE, W.C. : The new commercial treaty with Siam. American journal of international law 32 : 796-799, October 1938.

LA BROSSE, P.B. de : Le traité franco-siamois. Asie française 39 : 17-18, janvier 1939.

HASNA, B. : Structure administrative du Protectorat français en Tunisie - L'administration centrale. Afrique française 47 : 472-476, octobre 1937.

HASNA, B. : Structure administrative du Protectorat français en Tunisie (Contd.). Afrique française 47 : 545-550, novembre 1937.

TURKEY

MARTINELLI, P. : Leggi della nuova Turchia. Azione coloniale 5 : 7, 24 gennaio 1935.
Law on the costume of religious orders.

MOUTAL, A. : Turquie - La concession de service public - Les recours contentieux. Revue du droit public et de la science politique 42 : 791-799, octobre-novembre-décembre 1935.

SALEM, E.R. : Contribution à l'étude de la législation turque sur les sociétés anonymes. Bulletin trimestriel de la Société de législation comparée 65 : 373-403, octobre-décembre 1936.

ZEKERIVA, S. : Changements constitutionnels en Turquie. Voix européennes 2 : 1 au 15 mai 1937.

WEIGERT, O. : The new Turkish labour code. International labour review 35 : 753-774, June 1937.

HIRSCH, E.E. : Der Zentralbegriff des Handelsrechts - Eine Vorstudie zur Reform des türkischen Handelsgesetzbuchs. Annuario di diritto comparato e di studi legislativi 13 : 369-420, fasc. 6, Pt. 1, 1938.

SALEM, M.E.R. : Contributions à l'étude de la législation turque sur les sociétés anonymes. Bulletin trimestriel de la Société de législation comparée 67 : 214-260, avril-septembre 1938.

MIRAS, T. : Le Conseil d'Etat et la juridiction administrative en Turquie. Revue de droit public et de la science politique 55 : 693-701, octobre-décembre 1938.

GOADBY, F.M. : The Moslem law of civil delict as illustrated by the Mejelle. Journal of comparative legislation and international law 21 : 62-74, February 1939.

TURKEY
(International law, Aliens)

LEONTIDES, L. : Der griechisch-türkische Bevölkerungsaustausch. Zeitschrift für ausländisches öffentluches Recht und Völkerrecht 5 : 546-576, Juli 1935.

BLONDEL, A. : La conférence de Montreux et le nouveau régime des Détroits, 20 juillet 1936 (Contd.). Revue de droit maritime comparé 36 : 18-39, juillet-décembre 1937.

SALEM, E.R. : Les sociétés anonymes turques et étrangères exerçant la profession bancaire en Turquie. Journal du droit international 65 : 681-707, juillet-octobre 1938.

U.S.S.R.

Das politische Vertragssystem der UdSSR. Ost-Europa 10 : 247, Januar 1935.
A diagram.

HOLMAN, B. : The law of succession in Soviet jurisprudence since 1922. Iowa law review 20 : 389-401, January 1935.

Rapport de V. Molotoff, Président du Conseil des Commissaires du peuple, présenté au VIIe Congrès des Soviets. Journal de Moscou 2 : 1, 3, 9 février 1935.
Importants changements à la Constitution soviétique.

MAURACH : Gesetz der UdSSR über die Bekämpfung der Kriminalität der Jugendlichen vom 7. April 1935 (Izevstija 1935, Nr. 84). Zeitschrift für osteuropäisches Recht 1 : 585-587, Mai 1935.

LEONTOVITSCH, V. : Das Musterstatut der landwirtschaftlichen Artels (Kollektive) der Sovetunion vom 17. Februar 1934. Zeitschrift für osteuropäisches Recht 1 : 551-560, Mai 1935.

Übersicht über die wesentliche Gesetzgebung der UdSSR - 2.-4. Vierteljahr 1934. Zeitschrift für osteuropäisches Recht 2 : 40-42, Juli 1935.

Übersicht über die wesentliche Gesetzgebung der RSFSR - 2.-4. Vierteljahr 1934. Zeitschrift für osteuropäisches Recht 2 : 43-44, Juli 1935.

KAOUCHANSKY, D.M. : Evolution du droit matrimonial en Russie soviétique. Le mariage dans la loi et la jurisprudence. Journal du droit international 62 : 857-879, juillet-octobre 1935.

Fragen der Strafrechtsreform in der Sitzung der Kommunistischen Akademie und des Kriminalpolitischen Institutes. Zeitschrift für osteuropäisches Recht 2 : 107-109, August 1935.

SCHWEITZER, R. : Die Verwaltungsorganisation der UdSSR (Rayonierung). Ost-Europa 10 : August-September 1935.

MAURACH, R. : Strafrechtsumbruch in der Sovetunion. Zeitschrift für osteuropäisches Recht 2 : 119-138, September 1935.

MAURACH, R. : Erbrechtsnovellen in der Sovenunion. Zeitschrift für osteuropäisches Recht 2 : 183-194, Oktober 1935.

MAURACH, R. : Sovetunion - Novellen auf dem Gebiet des Jugendrechts. Zeitschrift für osteuropäisches Recht 2 : 339-342, Dezember 1935.

TEICHMÜLLER, G. : Zur Neufassung des Luftverkehrsgesetzes der UdSSR im Jahre 1935. Zeitschrift für osteuropäisches Recht 2 : 365-376, January 1936.

HOLMAN, A.B. : The law of succession in Soviet jurisprudence. Iowa law review 21 : 487-537, March 1936.

La nouvelle constitution de l'U.R.S.S. Revue de droit international 17 : 670-688, avril-mai-juin 1936.
Texte annexé.

MAURACH, R. : Grundlagen und Tendenzen der Strafprozessreform in der Sovetunion. Zeitschrift für osteuropäisches Recht 2 : 637-661, Mai 1936.

IZGOIEV, N. : La nouvelle constitution. Journal de Moscou 3 : 1, 9 juin 1936.

Über den Entwurf der Verfassung der UdSSR. Sowjetwirtschaft und Aussenhandel 15 : 3-13, 2. Juniheft 1936.

RADEK, K. : Le projet de la nouvelle constitution de l'URSS. Journal de Moscou 3 : 2-3, 16 juin 1936.

FISCHER, L. : The new Soviet constitution. Nation 142 : 772-774, 17 June 1936.

KROUGLIAKOFF, A. : New Soviet constitution. Law journal 81 : 449-450, 27 June 1936.

PIERRE, A. : Le projet de constitution de l'U.R.S.S. Affaires étrangères 6 : 332-343, juin 1936.

FISCHER, L. : The new Soviet abortion law. Nation 143 : 65-67, 97-99, 18, 25 July 1936.

RIBARD, A. : Réflexions sur le projet de nouvelle constitution soviétique. Cahier du bolchévisme 13 : 843-892, 25 juillet 1936.

Übersicht über die wesentliche Gesetzgebung der RSFSR 2.-4. Vierteljahr 1935. Zeitschrift für osteuropäisches Recht 3 : 35-36, Juli 1936.

The constitution of the land of victorious socialism. World economics and politics : 5-12, July 1936.
(Text in Russian).

DOBRIN, S. : Soviet jurisprudence and socialism. Law quarterly review 52 : 402-424, July 1936.

Sovetunion - Übersicht über die wesentliche Gesetzgebung der UdSSR 2.-4. Vierteljahr 1935. Zeitschrift für osteuropäisches Recht 3 : 33-34, Juli 1936.

MAURACH, R. : Die Entwicklung der Kollektivwirtschaften in Gesetzgebung, Verwaltungspraxis und Rechtsprechung. Zeitschrift für osteuropäisches Recht 3 : 20-32, Juli 1936.

MARKERT, W. : Der Entwurf einer neuen Sowjetverfassung. Osteuropa 11 : 676-690, Juli 1936.

UEXKULL, F, : Die neue Sowjet verfassung und die Nationalität. Nation und Staat 9 : 668-676, Juli-August 1936.

FISCHER, L. : Soviet democracy. New statesman and nation 12 : 148-150, 1 August 1936.
The new constitution.

PIERRE, A. : La constitution de l'U.R.S.S. et le referendum populaire. Europe nouvelle 19 : 803-806, 8 août 1936.

MAURACH, R. : Das Familienschutzgesetz der Sovetunion. Zeitschrift für osteuropäisches Recht 3 : 100-110, August 1936.

MADIA, T. : La donna nel codice penale dei Sovieti. Gerarchia 16 : 546-552, agosto 1936.

APPERT, B. : La réforme constitutionnelle de l'Union soviétique. Revue des sciences politiques 51 : 389-408, juillet-septembre 1936.

MAURACH, R. : Sowjetdemokratie? Zur Verfassungsreform der Sowjetunion. Osteuropa 11 : 713-725, August-September 1936.

MAURACH, R. : Sovetunion - Das Gesetz über den Vaterlandsverrat vom 8. 6. 1934 (G.S. UdSSR, 1934, Nr. 33, Art. 255). Zeitschrift für osteuropäisches Recht 3 : 223-228, September 1936.

BARTHÉLEMY, J. : La nouvelle constitution soviétique ou les modernes droits de l'homme. Revue de Paris 43 : 5-32, 1 septembre 1936.

TCHÉLIAPOV, N. : La question des deux Chambres. Journal de Moscou 3 : 2, 17, novembre 1936.
Le problème en U.R.S.S.

BRAUNIAS, K. : Die neue Sowjetverfassung und das Nationalitätenproblem. Geopolitik 13 : 749-757, November 1936.

Rapport de J. Staline sur le projet de Constitution de l'U.R.S.S. Journal de Moscou 13 : 1-5, 1 décembre 1936.

BRAUNIAS, K. : Die Grund- und Freiheitsrechte nach dem Entwurf der neuen Sowjetverfassung. Zeitschrift für öffentliches Recht 16 : 609-618, 10. Dezember 1936.

HAZARD, J.N. : Soviet law: an introduction. Columbia law review 36 : 1236-1266, December 1936.

STARR, J.R. : The new constitution of the Soviet Union. American political science review 30 : 1143-1152, December 1936.

DOBRIN, S. : The new Soviet constitution. Grotius Society, Problems of peace and war 22 : 99-116 1936.

PIERRE, A. : Le projet de Constitution de l' U.R.S.S. Europe nouvelle documentaire : I-III, No. 38, 1936.

KARADSHE-ISKROW, N. : Das Verwaltungsrecht in der Sowjetunion (Russland) seit 1917. Jahrbuch des öffnetlichen Rechts 23 : 136-261, 1936.

MIRKINE-GUEDZÉVITCH, B. : La nouvelle constitution soviétique. Europe nouvelle 20 : 67-70, 16 janvier 1937.

KAUSCHANSKY, D.M. : Grundsätze des sowjetrussischen Adoptionsrechts. Revue de droit international, de sciences diplomatiques et politiques 15 : 29-35, janvier-mars 1937.

PARES, B. : The new constitution of the U.S.S.R. International conciliation : 135-163, February 1937.

MAURACH, R. : Die Sowjet-Gesetzgebung in den Jahren 1935 und 1936. Osteuropa 12 : 391-402, März 1937.

MAURACH, B. : Das Wahlrecht nach der Verfassung der Sovietunion vom 5. Dezember 1936. Zeitschrift für osteuropäisches Recht 3 : 547-561, März 1937.

NATIONAL LAW - COUNTRIES

DEAN, V.M. : The new constitution of the U.S.S.R. Foreign policy reports 13 : 30-40, 15 April 1937.

OATMAN, M.E. : The new constitution of the Soviet Union. International law and relations 6 : 1-5, 16 April 1937.

COLENS, A. : La nouvelle constitution en U.R.S.S. Institut belge de droit comparé 23 : 49-71, avril-juin 1937.

BRECHT, A. : The new Russian constitution. Social research 4 : 157-190, May 1937.

MAKOWSKI, W. : La nuova costituzione sovietica vista da un giurista polacco. Stato 8 : 257-274, maggio 1937.

LEONTOVITSCH, V. : Die neue Verfassung der Sowjetunion. Zeitschrift für ausländisches öffentliches Recht und Völkerrecht 7 : 374-393, Mai 1937.

MAURACH, R. : Zur neuesten Wandlung in der allgemeinen Rechtslehre, in Strafrecht und Völkerrecht der Sovetunion. Zeitschrift für osteuropäisches Recht 3 : 737-755, Juni 1937.

Règlement des élections au Conseil suprême de l'U.R.S.S. - Projet approuvé par le présidium du Comité exécutif central de l'U.R.S.S. pour être soumis à à la délibération de la IVme session du Comité exécutif central de l'U.R.S.S. Journal de Moscou 4 : 3-4, 6 juillet 1937.

PIERRE, A. : La nouvelle loi électorale de l'U.R.S.S. Europe nouvelle 20 : 683-684, 17 juillet 1937.

Le projet de "Règlement des élections au Conseil suprême de l'U.R.S.S." Journal de Moscou 4 : 3-4, 13 juillet 1937.

Sovetunion - Übersicht über die wesentliche Gesetzgebung der UdSSR 2.-4. Vierteljahr 1936. Zeitschrift für osteuropäisches Recht 4 : 39-43, Juli 1937.

WERTHER, K. : Die juristen "Kader" in der Sovetunion. Zeitschrift für osteuropäisches Recht 4 : 104-109, August 1937.

Le règlement des élections au Conseil Suprême de l'U.R.S.S. et les tâches des Soviets. Journal de Moscou 4 : 2, 7 septembre 1937.

FRIDIEFF, M. : L'organisation actuelle de la justice pénale en U.R.S.S. Revue de science criminelle et de droit pénal comparé 1 : 519-541, octobre-décembre 1937.

RIVIÈRE, P.L. : La loi soviétique. Revue des travaux de l'Académie des sciences morales et politiques 98 : 30-56, janvier-février 1938.

HAZARD, J.N. : Moscow's Law Institute. American bar association journal 24 : 130-131, February 1938.

ENGLÄNDER, H. : Sowjetrussland - Übersicht über die Gesetzgebung des Jahres 1937. Internationales Anwaltsblatt 24 : 8-9, Februar 1938.

SCHLESINGER, R. : Neue sowjetrussische Literatur zur Sozialforschung (Contd.) - Juristisch-ökonomische Duskussion. Zeitschrift für Sozialforschung 7 : 388-403, Heft 3, 1938.

AVERNA, G. : Diritto penale sovietico. Rivista internazionale di filosofia del diritto 18 : 201-209, marzo-aprile 1938.

STOUPNITZKY, A. : Revues de langue russe. Revue de science criminelle et de droit pénal comparé 3 : 374-377, avril-juin 1938.
Le droit pénal en U.R.S.S.

KAUSCHANSKY, D. : Hauptzüge des Ukrainischen Eherechts. Revue de droit international, de sciences diplomatiques et politiques 6 : 83-87, avril-juin 1938.

Sovetunion. Übersicht über die wesentliche Gesetzgebung der UdSSR, 2.-4. Vierteljahr 1937. Zeitschrift für osteuropäisches Recht 5 : 45-49, Juli 1938.

HAZARD, J.N. : Reforming Soviet criminal law. Journal of criminal law and criminology 29 : 157-169, July-August 1938.

COCO, N. : La Costituzione sovietica e le sue contraddizioni. Echi e commenti 19 : 771-774, 15 settembre 1938.

ELIACHEVITCH, M.B. : Le droit contractuel dans le système du droit soviétique. Revue trimestrielle de droit civil 37 : 403-421, juillet-septembre 1938.

BRAUNIAS, K. : Die Grund- und Freiheitsrechte nach der neuen Sowjetverfassung. Zeitschrift für öffentliches Recht 18 : 347-352, 1. Oktober 1938.

MAKAROV, A.N. : Die neue Gerichtsverfassung der Sovetunion. Zeitschrift für osteuropäisches Recht 5 : 297-306, November 1938.

KENT, M.E. : The court system in the Soviet Union. U.S. Department of commerce, Comparative law series 11 : 130-137, March 1939.

MAURACH, R. : Das neue Gerichtsverfassungsrecht der Sowjetunion. Zeitschrift der Akademie für deutsches Recht 6 : 409-413, 15. Juni 1939.

WERTHER, K. : Die neueste Entwicklung der Kollektivwirtschaften in der Gesetzgebung, der Verwaltungspraxis, der Rechtsprechung und im Schrifttum der UdSSR, Zeitschrift für osteuropäisches Recht 6 : 16-35, Juli 1939.

TAVGAZOV, K. : L'analogia è incompatibile con la costituzione dell'U.R.S.S. Giustizia penale (parte seconda) 45 : 956-957, luglio 1939.

Sowjetunion - Übersicht über die wesentliche Gesetzgebung 1938/1939. Zeitschrift für osteuropäisches Recht 6 : 35-39, Juli 1939.
U.S.S.R. and R.S.F.S.R.

HAZARD, J.N. : In the Soviet Law School. Asia : 565-567, October 1939.

U.S.S.R.
(International law and practice, Aliens and Naturalization)

Verordnung des Zentralvollzugausschusses der UdSSR betr. die Unterschriftsleistung bei Aussenhandelgeschäften, vom 26. Dezember 1935. Zeitschrift für osteuropäisches Recht 2 : 539-541, März 1936.

MAKAROV, A.N. : Übersicht der Judikatur ausländischer Gerichte in russischen Sachen. Zeitschrift für osteuropäisches Recht 2 : 563-587, April 1936.

ANDERSON, C.P. : Russian claims negotiations. American journal of international law 29 : 290-295, April 1935.

WERTHEIM, B. : The Russo-Japanese fisheries controversy. Pacific affairs 8 : 185-198, June 1935.

MAKAROV, A.N. : Die Völkerrechtswissenschaft in Sorjetrussland. Zeitschrift für ausländisches öffentliches Recht und Völkerrecht 6 : 479-495, Juli 1936.

Sowjetrussland und das Völkerrecht. Völkerbund und Völkerrecht 3 : 365-370, September-Oktober 1936.

SANDIFER, D.V. : Soviet citizenship. American journal of international law 30 : 614-631, October 1936.

MAURACH, R. : Die Sojetjetunion - ein Mitglied der Völkerrechtsgemeinschaft? Zeitschrift für Völkerrecht 21 : 19-45, Heft 1, 1937.

TACACOUZIO, T.A. : International cooperation of the U.S.S.R. in legal matters. American journal of international law 31 : 55-65, January 1937.

BÖHMERT : Die russische Fischereigrenze. Zeitschrift für Völkerrecht 21 : 441-495, Heft 4, 1937.

BÖHMERT, V. : Die russische Fischereigrenze. Zeitschrift für Völkerrecht 22 : 257-306, Heft 3, 1938.

MAKAROV, A.N. : La rappresentanza russa per il commercio con l'estero e la giurisdizione dei diversi Stati Istituto di studi legislativi; giurisprudenza comparata di diritto internazionale privato 3 : 1-12, 1938.

HAZARD, J.N. : Cleansing Soviet international law of anti-Marxist theories. American journal of international law 32 : 244-253, April 1938.

SCHEFTEL, J. : La reconnaissance internationale du Gouvernement soviétique et ses répercussions sur la jurisprudence américaine. Journal du droit international 65 : 453-467, mai-juin 1938.

MAKAROV, A.N. : Gesetz über die Staatsangehörigkeit, vom 19. August 1938. Zeitschrift für ausländisches öffentliches Recht und Völkerrecht 8 : 801-805, Dezember 1938.

Sovetunion - Gesetz vom 19.8.1938 über die Staatsangehörigkeit der UdSSR. Zeitschrift für osteuropäisches Recht 5 : 389-392, Dezember 1938.

Sovetunion - Gesetz vom 20.8.1938 betr. Ratifizierung und Kündigung von zwischenstaatlichen Verträgen der UdSSR. Zeitschrift für osteuropäisches Recht 5 : 392-394, Dezember 1938.

SACK, A. : Les réclamations diplomatiques contre les Soviets (1918-1938). Revue de droit international et de législation comparée 66 : 6-40, No. 1, 1939.

TARACOUZIO, T.A. : The Soviet citizenship law of 1938. American journal of international law 33 : 157-159, January 1939.

JESSUP, P.C. : The Pacific Coast fisheries. American journal of international law 33 : 129-138, January 1939.

SACK, A.N. : Les réclamations diplomatiques contre les Soviets (1918-1938) (Contd.). Revue de droit international et de législation comparée 66 : 286-322, No. 2, 1939.

HAZARD, J.N. : Soviet commercial arbitration. Arbitration journal 3 : 148-154, April 1939.

TSAI, W.P. : The Soviet-Japanese fisheries controversy. China forum 3 : 296-300, 10 June 1939.

UNITED ARAB REPUBLIC

Egypte - Principales lois de 1934 à 1936. Annuaire de législation étrangère 62 : 238-257, 1934/1936.

La question des Tribunaux mixtes d'Égypte. Journal de droit international 62 : 5-44, janvier-février 1935.

DEMOGUE, R. : Jurisprudence des juridictions mixtes d'Égypte. Revue trimestrielle de droit civil 34 : 213-218, janvier-mars 1935.

DESSERTEAUX, M. : Jurisprudence étrangère - Cour d'appel mixte d'Alexandrie, 13 juin 1934. Annales de droit commercial 44 : 184-196, avril-juin 1935.

STROSS, W. : Die Entwicklung der Kapitulationsrechte in Ägypten seit Abschluss der Friedensverträge. Zeitschrift für öffentliches Recht 15 : 394-407, 21. Juni 1935.

DEMOGUE, R. : Jurisprudence des juridictions mixtes d'Égypte. Revue trimestrielle de droit civil 34 : 693-702, juillet-septembre 1935.

La loi égyptienne sur le cours forcé - Son application aux conventions de droit interne et aux rapports internationaux. Journal du droit international 62 : 1102-1107, juillet-octobre 1935.

PETER-PIRKHAM, O. : Die gemischte Gerichtsbarkeit in Ägypten. Zeitschrift für öffentliches Recht 15 : 470-484, 20. September 1935.

WENGLER, W. : Die staats- und völkerrechtliche Stellung Ägyptens. Afrika Rundschau 1 : 159-161, Oktober 1935.

DEMOGUE, R. : Jurisprudence des juridictions mixtes d'Égypte. Revue trimestrielle de droit civil 35 : 311-319, janvier-mars 1936.

COSTAZ, L. : Les capitulations et le traité anglo-égyptien. Terre d'Islam 11 : 291-307, septembre-octobre 1936.

SIMONS, W. : Die Fremdengerichtsbarkeit in Ägypten. Zeitschrift der Akademie für deutsches Recht 3 : 94-947, Oktoberheft 1936.

Le traité anglo-égyptien et la modification du régime des étrangers en Égypte. Journal du droit international 64 : 60-65, janvier-février 1937.

GORDON, E. : Le traité anglo-égyptien du 26 août et le statut international nouveau de l'Égypte. Revue de droit international et de législation comparée 64 : 228-284, No. 2, 1937.

NATIONAL LAW - COUNTRIES

WATHELET, J. : Le traité d'alliance anglo-égyptien du 26 août 1936 et la convention de Montreux du 8 mai 1937 concernant la suppression des capitulations en Égypte. Revue de droit international et de législation comparée 64 : 391-437, No. 2, 1937.

GEORGE-SAMNÉ : La nationalité égyptienne. Correspondance d'Orient 30 : 107-108, mars 1937.

HERZ, H. : Das Meerengenstatut von Montreux. Friedens-Warte 37 : 126-144, Nr. 3/4, 1937.

Conferenza di Montreux - Progetto di regolamento d'organizzazione giudiziaria. Relazioni internazionali 3 : 299-301, 24 aprile 1937.

Capitulations d'Égypte. Documentation internationale 4 : 57-70, mai-juin 1937.
Textes annexés.

GROS, A. : La Conférence de Montreux et le nouveau statut des étrangers en Égypte. Recueil hebdomanaire Dalloz 14 : 57-60, 22 juillet 1937.

Autour d'un droit égyptien. Terre d'Islam 12 : 213-216, juillet-août 1937.

TABOUILLOT, W. von : Die Abschaffung der Kapitulationen in Ägypten. Zeitschrift für ausländisches öffentliches Recht und Völkerrecht 7 : 511-535, August 1937.

LADREIT de LACHARRIÈRE, J. : En Egypte - Après la Conférence de Montreux. Afrique française 47 : 506-510, novembre 1937.

Les modifications apportées au statut des Tribunaux mixtes par les accords de Montreux. Journal du droit international 64 : 1006-1011, novembre-décembre 1937.

MORELLI, G. : L'abolizione delle capitolazioni in Egitto. Rivista di diritto internazionale 29 : 324-332, 1 ottobre - 31 dicembre 1937.

DEMOGUE, R. : Jurisprudence des juridictions mixtes d'Égypte. Revue trimestrielle de droit civile 37 : 137-141, janvier-mars 1938.

De quelques effets de la nouvelle législation pénale égyptienne mixte sur les infractions et sur les condamnations antérieures à sa promulgation. Journal des tribunaux mixtes 17 : 3-5, 31 janvier et 1 février 1938.

Le problème du renvoi en droit international privé et sa solution en Égypte par les Accords de Montreux. Journal des tribunaux mixtes 17 : 3-6, 21 et 22 mars 1938.

La question de l'extradition des étrangers depuis la suppression des capitulations. Journal des tribunaux mixtes 17 : 3-4, 6 et 7 avril 1938.

BRAUN, F. : La Convention de Montreux et ses difficultés d'application. Nouvelle revue de droit international privé 5 : 287-299, avril-mai-juin 1938.

LAPRADELLE, A. de : La suppression des capitulations en Egypte. Nouvelle revue de droit international privé 5 : 456-470, avril-mai-juin 1938.

LAPRADELLE, A. de : La suppression des capitulations en Égypte. Bulletin trimestriel de la Société de législation comparée 67 : 110-176, avril-sept. 1938.

CHRÉTIEN, M. : La suppression des capitulations en Égypte. Revue générale de droit international public 45 : 302-372, mai-juin 1938.

Les formes et conditions de l'expulsion des étrangers. Journal des tribunaux mixtes 17 : 5, 29-30 juin 1938.

ARMINJON : La suppression des capitulations en Égypte. Nouvelle revue de droit international privé 5 : 677-707, juillet-août-septembre 1938.

THÉBAULT, E.P. : La Conférence de Montreux et l'abolition des capitulations en Égypte. Revue critique de droit international 33 : 406-428, juillet-septembre 1938.

AGHION, R. : La question du renvoi et la clause de non-discrimination dans les Accords de Montreux. Journal des tribunaux mixtes 17 : 3-5, 17-48, août 1938.

LEDERER, Z.J. : Das kommende Rechtsregime des Suezkanals. Zeitschrift für öffentliches Recht 18 : 353-366, 1. Oktober 1938.

CHÉRON, A. : Le chèque sans provision et l'article 337 du nouveau Code pénal égyptien. Annales de droit commercial 47 : 327-332, octobre-décembre 1938.

De la compétence des juridictions mixtes en matière de délit commis à bord d'un navire étranger mouillé dans les eaux territoriales. Journal des tribunaux mixtes 18 : 3-4, 28-29, décembre 1938.

The Suez Canal Company. Bulletin of international news 15 : 1237-1239, 31 December 1938.

Abolition of the capitulation in Egypt. British year book of international law 19 : 161-197, 1938.

De l'autorité de la chose jugée des décisions rendues par la justice répressive nationale à l'égard des tribunaux mixtes. Journal des tribunaux mixtes 18 : 4, 20-21 février 1939.

Le code pénal et le code d'instruction criminelle mixte du 31 juillet 1937 (lois Nos. 57-58). Recueil de documents en matière pénale et pénitentiaire 8 : 8-33, mars 1939.

LE GOFF, M. : Le statut aérien du canal de Suez d'après le traité anglo-égyptien du 26 août 1936. Revue générale de droit international public 46 : 142-158, mars-avril 1939.

Le chapitre du domicile dans un projet de code civil égyptien. Bulletin de l'Institut de droit comparé de Lyon 2 : 1-57, mars-juin 1939.

Du défaut de juridiction pénale des tribunaux mixtes à l'égard des membres et des fonctionnaires des forces britanniques en Égypte. Journal des Tribunaux mixtes 18 : 6-7, 17 et 18 avril 1939.

Le nouveau projet de loi portant réorganisation des juridictions égyptiennes de statut personnel pour les nonmusulmans. Journal des tribunaux mixtes 18 : 3-4, 1 et 2 mai 1939.

Le projet de loi relatif aux mesures exceptionnelles à prendre pour la sécurité du pays. Journal des tribunaux mixtes 18 : 4-5, 19 et 20 mai 1939.

CHEVALLIER, J. : Jurisprudence des juridictions mixtes d'Égypte. Revue trimestrielle de droit civil 38 : 553-567, avril-juin 1939.

Le problème du statut personnel de non-musulmans. Journal des tribunaux mixtes 18 : 3-6, 3-5, 29 et 30 mai, 5 et 6 juillet 1939.

Le sursis en droit égyptien. Journal des tribunaux mixtes 18 : 3-4, 14 et 15 août 1939.

La législation égyptienne de guerre. Journal des tribunaux mixtes 18 : 3-4, 11 et 12 septembre 1939.

L'application de l'interdiction du commerce en ce qui concerne les ressortissabts du Reich et les habitants des territoires occupés par l'Allemagne. Journal des tribunaux mixtes 18 : 3, 25 et 26 septembre 1939.

De l'exacte portée du décret-loi no. 109 de 1939 réglementant les opérations sur les monnaies et devises étrangères. Journal des tribunaux mixtes 18 : 3-4, 4 et 5 octobre 1939.

De la portée de la règle "locus regit actum" pour les actes passés en Égypte entre étrangers de la même nationalité, avant les Accords de Montreux. Journal des tribunaux mixtes 18 : 4-5, 9 et 10 octobre 1939.

La séquestration des biens allemands en Égypte. Journal des tribunaux mixtes 18 : 3-4, 16 et 17 octobre 1939.

L'interdiction du commerce avec le Reich allemand et ses ressortissants et ses garanties législatives en Égypte. Journal des tribunaux mixtes 18 : 3-4, 18 et 19 octobre 1939.

U.S.A.

AUBERTIN, A. : Notstand und Verfassung - Eine Entscheidung des Obersten Bundesgerichts der Vereinigten Staaten. Deutsche Juristen-Zeitung 40 : 84-87, 15. Januar 1935.

BOOTS, Č.F. and O'BRIEN, J. : Federal legislation 1934. American bar association journal 21 : 25-29, January 1935.

PERCEROU, A. : Les arrêts de la Cour Suprême des Etats-Unis sur les "clauses-or". Annales de droit commercial 44 : 29-53, janvier-mars 1935.

CUSHMAN, R.E. : The constitutional decisions of the Supreme Court of the United States in the October term, 1933. American political science review 29 : 36-59, February 1935.

DAWSON, J.P. : The gold clause decisions. Michigan law review 33 : 647-684, March 1935.
Decisions of 18 February 1935.

MÜGEL : Die Goldklausel-Entscheidung des Obersten Gerichtsfofs der Vereinigten Staaten. Deutsche Juristen-Zeitung 40 : 460-466, 15. April 1935.

La constitutionnalité de la loi américaine annulant la clause-or (Contd.). Revue de science et de législation financières 33 : 264-291, avril-mai-juin 1935.

One hundred and forty-six years of federal laws. United States news 3 : 1, 10 June 1935.

CLARK, C.E. : The supreme court and the N.R.A. New republic 83 : 120-122, 12 June 1935.

DARVALL, F. : The Supreme Court versus the New Deal. Contemporary review 148 : 31-37, July 1935.

BROGAN, D.W. : The American constitutional crisis. Fornightly 138 : 1-11, July 1935.

The State constitution of the future. Annals of the American Academy of political and social science 181 : 1-187, September 1935.
Series of articles on a revision of the American Constitution.

McDERMOTT, G.T. : The work of the American Law Institute. American bar association journal 21 : 600-603, September 1935.

Should the Congress enact a federal sedition law? Congressional digest 14 : 225-253, October 1935.
Series of articles.

SCHMECKEBIER, L.F. : Development of national administration in the United States 1932-35. American political science review 29 : 842-856, October 1935.

PFANKUCHEN, L. : Le Président Roosevelt et la Cour suprême. Revue des sciences politiques 50 : 508-543, octobre-décembre 1935.

ISAACS, N. : Liability of the lawyer for bad advice. California law review 24 : 39-47, November 1935.

LITTAUER, R. : Case law and systematic law - A descriptive comparison of American and German legal thinking. Social research 2 : 481-502, November 1935.

BURDICK, C.K. : Constitutional aspects of the New Deal in the United States. Canadian bar review 13 : 699-719, December 1935.

HUGES, C.E. : The genesis of our supreme tribunal. Congressional digest monthly 14 : 293. December 1935.
The Supreme Court.

KRESS, H.J. : The Banking Act of 1935. Michigan law review 34 : 155-199, December 1935.

ROHRLICH, C. : The New Deal in corporation law. Columbia law review 35 : 1167-1195, December 1935.

Should the powers of the U.S. Supreme Court be modified? Congressional digest monthly 14 : 289-292, December 1935.
Series of articles.

WOLFF, R. : Die Wirtschaftsdiktatur des Präsidenten Roosevelt vor dem Obersten Bundesgericht der Vereinigten Staaten. Archiv des öffentlichen Rechts 26 : 176-186, 1935.

POWELL, T.R. : Constitutional overtones in 1936. Yale review 26 : 37-56, No. 1, 1936.

MOLODOVSKY, N. : La mort de la triple A. Europe nouvelle 19 : 59-64, 18 janvier 1936.
Décisions de la Cour suprême.

NATIONAL LAW - COUNTRIES

The constitution and social progress. Proceedings of the Academy of political science 16 : 1-138, January 1936.
Series of articles.

SCHMIDT-KLEVENOW : Die nordamerikanische Sterilisationsgesetzgebung bis 1934. Juristische Wochenschrift 65 : 239-242, 25. Januar 1936.

CUSHMAN, R.E. : Constitutional law in 1934-1935. The constitutional decisions of the Supreme court of the United States in the October term, 1934. American political science review 30 : 51-89, February 1936.

MOORE, J.W., and LEVI, E.H. : Federal intervention - The right to intervene and reorganization. Yale law journal 45 : 565-607, February 1936.

YNTEMA, H.E. : What should the American Law Institution do? Michigan law review 34 : 461-473, February 1936.
Legal reform in the United States.

HAINES, C.G. : Judicial review of acts of Congress and the need for constitutional reform. Yale law journal 45 : 816-856, March 1936.

MARTIG, R.R. : Congress and the appellate jurisdiction of the Supreme Court. Michigan law review 34 : 650-670, March 1936.

CHARLTON, C.B. : Constitutional regulations of legislative procedure. Iowa law review 21 : 538-551, March 1936.

DOWLING, N.T., CHEATHAM, E.E., and HALE, R.L. : Mr. Justice Stone and the constitution. Columbia law review 36 : 351-381, March 1936.
The United States constitution.

COOK, W.C. : Equity jurisdiction for the construction of wills. Iowa law review 21 : 552-572, March 1936.

RUSSELL, J.T. : Business conditions in presidential election years. American political science review 30 : 269-287, April 1936.

ROBINSON, G.H. : "Contract" jurisdiction in Admiralty. Tulane law review 10 : 359-400, April 1936.

ROALFE, W.R. : American lawyers and their books. American bar association journal 22 : 241-244, April 1936.
American law libraries.

BENSON, G.C.S. : American state and local government - State constitutional development in 1936. American political science review 31 : 280-285, April 1936.

GARRISON, L.K. : The constitution and social progress. Tulane law review 10 : 333-358, April 1936.

The constitution in the 20th century. Annals of the American academy of political and social science 185 : 1-211, May 1936.
Special number.

ORFIELD, L.B. : Federal criminal appeals. Yale law journal 45 : 1223-1234, May 1936.

The Honorable Supreme Court. Fortune 13 : 79-85, 170, 172, May 1936.

ORFIELD, L.B. : The procedure of appeal in criminal cases. California law review 24 : 403-427, May 1936.

CUMMINGS, H. : Progress towards a modern administration of criminal justice in United States. American bar association journal 22 : 345-349, May 1936.

Amend the constitution? Nation 142 : 696-697, 3 June 1936.

American law institute holds fourteenth annual meeting. American bar association journal 22 : 373, June 1936.

CRAVEN, L., and FULLER, W. : The 1935 amendments of the railroad bankruptcy law. Harvard law review 49 : 1254-1285, June 1936.

FAIRLIE, J. : The legislature and the administration - Methods of legislative supervision. American political science review 30 : 494-506, June 1936.

JACOBY, S.B. : Delegation of powers and judicial review - A study in comparative law. Columbia law review 36 : 871-907, June 1936.

STEVENS, R. : Uniform corporation laws through interstate compacts and federal legislation. Michigan law review 34 : 1063-1092, June 1936.

VANNEMAN, H.W. : Trusts - restated and rewritten. Michigan law review 34 : 1109-1134, June 1936.

BEARD, C.A. : Little Alice looks at the constitution. New republic 87 : 315-317, 22 July 1936.
Constitution and Supreme Court.

CLARK, C.E. : The proposed Federal rules of civil procedure. American Bar Association journal 22 : 447-451, 491, July 1936.

CHESNUT, W.C. : Analysis of proposed new federal rules of civil procedure. American bar association journal 22 : 533-541 and 572-574, August 1936.

United States of America - Federal legislation. Journal of comparative legislation and international lae 18 : 190-198, August 1936.

REED, S. : The constitution of the United States. American bar association journal 22 : 601-608, September 1936.

GORDON, T.M. : Robinson-Patman anti-discrimination Act - The meaning of sections 1 and 3. American bar association journal 22 : 593-600, 649-651, September 1936.

GODWARD, W. W. : Constitutional law - Privileges or immunities of the fourteenth amendment. California law review 24 : 728-732, September 1936.

KALLENBACH, J.E. : American government and politics - Recent proposals to reform the electoral college system. American political science review 30 : 924-929, October 1936.

American bar association journal 22 : 663-748, October 1936.
Proceedings of the annual meeting 1936 of the American bar association.

STONE, H.F. : The common law in the United States. Harvard law review 50 : 4-26, November 1936.

DODD, E.M. : Statutory development in business corporation law, 1886-1936. Harvard law review 50 : 27-50, November 1936.

DONOVAN, W.J. : The need for revision of the anti-trust laws. American bar association journal 22 : 797-803, November 1936.

WINFIELD, P.H. : The American restatement of the law of contracts. Journal of comparative legislation and international law 18 : 179-183, November 1936.

MILLAR, R.W. : The old régime and the new in civil procedure. New York University law quarterly review 14 : 1-27, November 1936.

Legislation and decisions on inheritance rights of adopted children. Iowa law review 22 : 145-154, November 1936.

FRIEDRICH, C.J. , und KRAUS, W. : Zum gegenwärtigen Stand der Föderalismus in den Vereinigten Staaten. Jahrbuch des öffentlichen Rechts 23 : 343-375, 1936.

La Cour Suprême et le programme de redressement national en 1935. Annuaire de l'Institut international de droit public : 200-262, 1936.

MORDEN, K.G. : The American Law Institute's restatement of the law of trusts. Canadian bar review 15 : 21-31, January 1937.

Removal of Federal judges - A proposed plan. Illinois law review 31 : 631-643, January 1937.

A symposium on state income taxation. Iowa law review 22 : 181-436, January 1937.
Special number.

OPPENHEIMER, R. : The Supreme Court and administrative law. Columbia law review 37 : 1-42, January 1937.

STEINER, H.A. : Problemi attuali del diritto costituzionale americano. Rivista internazionale di filosofia del diritto 17 : 1-22, gennaio-febbraio 1937.

The President and the Court. Christian century 54 : 206-208, 17 February 1937.

President Roosevelt and the United States Supreme Court. Bulletin of international news 13 : 707-714, 20 February 1937.

GRAVESON, R.A. : The doctrine of evasion of the law in England and America. Journal of comparative legislation and international law 19 : 21-31, February 1937.
Domiciliary prohibitions against marriage.

POUND, R. : Fifty years of jurisprudence. Harvard law review 50 : 559-582, February 1937.

LASKI, H.J. : The President and the Supreme Court. Time and tide 18 : 185-186, February 1937.

WARNER, S.B., and CABOT, H.B. : Changes in the administration of criminal justice during the past fifty years. Harvard law review 50 : 583-615, February 1937.

CORWIN, E.S. : National-state cooperation - Its present possibilities. Yale law journal 46 : 599-623, February 1937.

FRAENKEL, O.K. : What can be done about the Constitution and the Supreme Court? Columbia law review 37 : 212-226, February 1937.

COOPER, R.M. : The proposed United States administrative court (Contd.). Michigan law review 35 : 565-596, February 1937.

MANGOLDT, H.v. : Ärzte und Heilpraktiker in Rechtsprechung und Gesetzgebung der Vereinten Staaten von Amerika. Archiv des öffentlichen Rechts 28 : 155-193, Heft 2, 1937.

Note on the U.S. Supreme Court. Bulletin of international news 13 : 757-758, 6 March 1937.

LANGUEPIN : Le Président Roosevelt et la Cour Suprême. Affaires étrangères 7 : 178-186, mars 1937.

MILLER, J. : Reciprocal legislation in the field of criminal law. New York University law quarterly review 14 : 330-340, March 1937.

Sit-down strikes - A new problem for government. Illinois law review 31 : 942-959, March 1937.

Roosevelt's Supreme Court plan. Congressional digest 16 : 65-96, March 1937.
Series of articles.

WILLISTON, S. : The law of contracts since the restatement. American bar association journal 23 : 172-177, March 1937.

WEINER, J.L. : Municipal home rule in New York. Columbia law review 37 : 557-580, April 1937.

SMITH, T.V. : Political liberty to-day - Is it being restricted or enlarged by economic regulation? American political science review 31 : 243-252, April 1937.

GULICK, L. : The recent movement for better government personnel. American political science review 31 : 292-301, April 1937.

CUSHMAN, R.E. : The Constitutional decisions of the Supreme Court of the United States in the October term, 1935. American political science review 31 : 253-279, April 1937.

BEALE, J.H. : The conflict of laws, 1886-1936. Harvard law review 50 : 887-896, April 1937.

American Bar Association journal 23 : 233-290, April 1937.
Series of articles on the Supreme Court.

CUSHMAN, R.E. : Constitutional law in 1936-37. The constitutional decisions of the Supreme Court of the United States in the October term, 1936. American political science review 32 : 278-310, April 1937.

ADAMS, J.T. : The American constitutional crisis. Contemporary review 151 : 399-403, April 1937.

McGOVNEY, D.O. : Reorganization of the Supreme Court. California law review 25 : 389-412, may 1937.

Association's views on the Supreme Court issue presented to Senate Committee. American bar associatic journal 23 : 315-318, May 1937.

NATIONAL LAW - COUNTRIES

SMITH, S.C. : The present situation in the fight to save the Court. American bar association journal 23 : 401-405, June 1937.

MARTIG, R.R. : Amending the Constitution - Article five : The keystone of the arch. Michigan law review 35 : 1253-1285, June 1937.

GREENBURG, L. : Must Louisiana resign to the common law? Tulane law review 11 : 598-601, June 1937.

LEACH, W.B. : The restatements as they were in the beginning, are now, and perhaps henceforth shall be. American bar association journal 23 : 517-521, July 1937.

GRANT, J.A.C. : State constitutional law in 1936-1937. American political science review 31 : 659-679, August 1937.

Unicameral legislatures. Congressional digest 16 : 197-198, August-September 1937.

The work of the Missouri Supreme Court for the year 1936. Missouri law review 2 : 393-514, November 1937.

Civil Service reform. Congressional digest 16 : 259-288, November 1937.

GIBBONS, A.O. : Legal aid in the United States. Canadian bar review 15 : 709-711, November 1937.

DIAMOND, Z.N. : The new Frazier-Lemke Act - A study. Columbia law review 37 : 1092-1135, November 1937.
Bankruptcy.

HORACK, F.E. : The common law of legislation. Iowa law review 23 : 41-56, November 1937.

NUTTING, C.B. : Definitive standards in federal obscenity legislation. Iowa law review 23 : 24-40, November 1937.

CALLAHAN, C.C., and FERGUSON, E.E. : Evidence and the new federal rules of civil procedure (Contd.). Yale law journal 47 : 194-213, December 1937.

REED, T.H. : Les récentes transformations du droit public aux États-Unis (Contd.). Revue de l'Université de Bruxelles 43 : 119-141, décembre 1937-janvier 1938.

FIELD, O.P. : La liberté économique aux États-Unis - La nouvelle organisation dans la législation et la juridiction. Annuaire de l'Institut international de droit public : 96-143, 1937.

GRANT, J.A.C. : États-Unis - Principales décisions rendues par la Cour suprême fédérale sur des questions de droit constitutionnel en 1936. Annuaire de l'Institut international de droit public : 281-311, 1937.

GRANT, J.A.C. : Principales décisions rendues par les Cours suprêmes des États sur des questions de droit constitutionnel en 1935 et 1936. Annuaire de l'Institut international de droit public : 312-341, 1937.

WILLIS, H.E. : The part of the United States constitution made by the Suprême Court. Iowa law review 23 : 165-214, January 1938.

SCHULZ, E.B. : The effect of the contract clause and the fourteenth Amendment upon the power of the states to control municipal corporations. Michigan law review 36 : 385-408, January 1938.

WEINFELD, A.C. : Power of Congress over State ratifying conventions. Harvard law review 51 : 473-506, January 1938.

POUND, R. : Fifty years of jurisprudence, (Contd.). Harvard law review 51 : 444-472, January 1938.

ANDREWS, C.O. : Reorganization of Federal Courts by constitutional amendment. American bar association journal 24 : 29-30, January 1938.

The Federal anti-lynching bill. Columbia law review 38 : 199-207, January 1938.

HALL, J.M. : Preserving liberty of the press by the defense of privilege in libel actions. California law review 26 : 226-239, January 1938.

DAGGETT, H.S. : Legal controls in family law. Iowa law review 23 : 215-231, January 1938.

HERRING, E.P. : The experts on five federal commissions. American political science review 32 : 86-93, February 1938.

FRANKFURTER, F., and FISCHER, A.S. : The business of the Supreme Court at the October terms, 1935 and 1936. Harvard law review 51 : 577-637, February 1938.

FLETCHER, M. : Bicameralism as illustrated by the Ninetieth General Assembly of Ohio ; A technique for studying the legislative process. American political science review 32 : 80-85, February 1938.

The war referendum. Congressional digest 17 : 37-38, February 1938.
The Ludlow resolution.

Supreme Court adopts rules for civil procedure in Federal District Courts. American bar association journal 24 : 97-104, February 1938.

SHORT, L.M. : Studies of administrative management in the Federal Government. American political science review 32 : 93-104, February 1938.

BORCHARD, E. : Report on the study and investigation of the work, activities, personnel and functions of protective and reorganization committees. Columbia law review 38 : 376-383, February 1938.

A discussion of current developments in administrative law. Yale law journal 47 : 515-674, February 1938.
Series of articles.

POWELL, T.R. : From Philadelphia to Philadelphia. American political science review 32 : 1-27, February 1938.
The United States Constitution.

DODD, E.M. Jr. : The Securities and Exchange Commission's reform program for bankruptcy reorganizations. Columbia law review 38 : 223-255, February 1938.

HYNEMAN, C.S. : Tenure and turnover of the Indiana General Assembly. American political science review 32 : 51-67, February 1938.

NATIONAL LAW - COUNTRIES

TOLMAN, E.B. : Review of recent Supreme Court decisions. American bar association journal 24 : 222-234, March 1938.

POUND, R. : Fifty years of jurisprudence (Contd.). Harvard law review 51 : 777-812, March 1938.

JACOBSON, J.M. : Federalism and property rights. New York University law quarterly review 15 : 319-369, March 1938.

BODFISH, J.B. : The destructive effect of the 1937 amendment of section 42 of the probate code of California upon the limitations regarding testamentary dispositions to charity. California law review 26 : 309-328, March 1938.

TEN BROEK, J. : Admissibility and use by the United States Supreme Court of extrinsic aids in constitutional construction. California law review 26 : 287-308, March 1938.

VANDERBILT, A.T. : The place of the administrative tribunal in our legal system. American bar association journal 24 : 267-273, April 1938.

MONROE, M.L. : The implied resolutory condition for non-performance of a contract. Tulane law review 12 : 376-400, April 1938.

LEVI, E.H., and MOORE, J.W. : Federal intervention (Contd.). - The procedure, status and federal jurisdictional requirements. Yale law journal 47 : 898-943, April 1938.

GOEBEL, J. : Constitutional history and constitutional law. Columbia law review 38 : 555-577, April 1938.

JAFFE, L.A. : Publication of administrative rules and orders. American bar association journal 24 : 393-398, May 1938.

How long should a United States President hold office? Congressional digest 17 : 133-160, May 1938.

BORCHARD, E. : The Supreme Court and private rights. Yale law journal 47 : 1051-1078, May 1938.

AGGER, C. : The Government and its employees. Yale law journal 47 : 1109-1135, May 1938.

AUBURTIN, A. : Präsident Roosevelts Versuch einer Reform des Obersten Bundesgerichts der Vereinigten Staaten. Zeitschrift für ausländisches öffentliches Recht und Völkerrecht 8 : 263-281, Mai 1938.

De LONG, E.H. : State's rights and the State executive. Illinois law review 33 : 45-56, May 1938.

SEARS, K.C. : Constitutional revision in Illinois. Illinois law review 33 : 2-14, May 1938.

CLARK, J.P. : Interdependent federal and state law as a form of federal-state cooperation. Iowa law review 23 : 539-564, May 1938.

GRAVES, W.B. : Influence of congressional legislation on legislation in the States. Iowa law review 23 : 519-538, May 1938.

TENBROEK, J. : Use by the United States Supreme Court of extrinsic aids in constitutional construction - Debates and proceedings of the constitutional and ratifying conventions. California law review 26 : 437-454, May 1938.

Symposium on the proposed Louisiana mineral code. Tulane law review 12 : 552-606, June 1938.

DUNLAP, F.L. : Constitutional law - Power of States to prevent entry of paupers from other States. California law review 26 : 603-610, July 1938.

CALDWELL, L.G. : Legal restrictions on the contents of broadcast programs. Air law review 9 : 229-249, July 1938.

Work of the American Law Institute. American bar association journal 24 : 723-725, 25-29 July 1938.

GRANT, J.A.C. : State constitutional law in 1937-1938. American political science review 32 : 670-693, August 1938.

POLETTI, C. : First steps in streamlining a constitution. State government 11 : 148-149, 157, August 1938.

RYAN, O. : Federal and state coöperation under the Federal Power Act. State government 11 : 139-140, August 1938.

CLARK, G. : The prospects for civil liberty. American bar association 24 : 833-836, October 1938.

Recent limitations on free speech and free press. Yale law journal 48 : 54-80, November 1938.

LLEWELLYN, K.N. : On our case-law of contract - offer and acceptance. Yale law journal 48 : 1-36, November 1938.

GERDES, J. : Corporate reorganizations - changes effected by chapter X of the Bankruptcy Act. Harvard law review 52 : 1-39, November 1938.

ALBERTSWORTH, E.F. : Streamlining the Constitution. New York University law quarterly review 16 : 1-18, November 1938.

MILLER, J.D. : The federal rules of civil procedure. Tulane law review 13 : 99-105, December 1938.

BOUDIN, L.B. : Truth fiction about about the fourteenth amendment. New York University law quarterly review 16 : 19-82, November 1938.

KESSLER, R.R. : An analysis of constitutional change in New York State. New York University law quarterly review 16 : 101-113, November 1938.

HARBESON, R.W. : The public interest concept in law and in economics. Michigan law review 37 : 181-208, December 1938.

GRANT, J.A.C. : The search for uniformity of law. American political political science review 32 : 108[illegible]-1098, December 1938.

GRAHAM, H.J. : The "conspiracy theory" of the fourteenth amendment (Contd.). Yale law journal 48 : 17[illegible]-194, December 1938.

FUCHS, R.F. : Procedure in administrative rule-maki[illegible] Harvard law review 52 : 259-280, December 1938.

COTTRELL, E.A. : Twenty-five years of direct legislation in California. Public opinion quarterly 3 : 30-45, January 1939.

Mr. Justice Cardozo. Harvard law review 52 : 353-489, January 1939.
Special number.

NATIONAL LAW - COUNTRIES

TEN BROEK, J. : Use by the United States Supreme Court of extrinsic aids in constitutional construction. California law review 27 : 157-181, January 1939.

RICE, W.B. : A constructive patent law. New York University law quarterly review 16 : 179-201, January 1939.

NUTTING, C.B. : Legislative practice regarding tort claims against the State. Missouri law review 4 : 1-18, January 1939.

FORKOSCH, M.D. : The lie detector and the Courts. New York University law quarterly review 16 : 202-231, January 1939.

Études sur l'évolution constitutionnelle des États-Unis d'Amérique. Revue d'histoire moderne 14 : 4-205, janvier-mai 1939.
Série d'articles.

RUBIN, S.J., and WILLNER, S.J. : Obligatory jurisdiction of the Supreme Court - Appeals from State Courts under Section 237(a) of the Judicial Code. Michigan law review 37 : 540-563, February 1939.

TOLMAN, E.B. : Review of recent Supreme Court decisions. American bar association journal 25 : 137-147, February 1939.

SHORT, L.M. : An investigation of the executive agencies of the United States Government. American political science review 33 : 60-66, February 1939.

CAPLAN, J. : The measure of recovery in actions for the infringement of copyright. Michigan law review 37 : 564-588, February 1939.

MORLEY, F. : The States in present-day government. State government 12 : 23-25 , 33, February 1939.

Monthly periodical index. Michigan law review 37 : 685-690, February 1939.
Subject index of articles in leading law reviews.

A symposium on the techniques in the introduction of evidence. Iowa law review 24 : 411-536, March 1939.
Special number.

The Negro citizen in the Supreme Court. Harvard law review 52 : 823-832, March 1939.

FOX, J. : Recent developments in criminal law. Journal of criminal law and criminology 29 : 799-821, March-April 1939.

PAGE, W.T. : The path of a bill through the House and the Senate. Congressional digest 18 : 121-122, April 1939.

MOSES, L. : A short history of the development of the statutory definition and classification of an oil, gas and mineral lease as a real right. Tulane law review 13 : 416-422, April 1939.

HORACK, C.H. : Admission to the bar - Many are chosen. Illinois law review 33 : 891-913, April 1939.

HALE, R. L. : Our equivocal constitutional guaranties. Columbia law review 39 : 563-594, April 1939.

CUSHMAN, R.E. : Constitutional law in 1937-1938. American political science review 33 : 234-266, April 1939.

DULLES, J.D. : Administrative law - A practical attitude for lawyers. American bar association journal 25 : 275-282, 352-353, April 1939.

Constitutional immunity for federal competition. Illinois law review 33 : 948-961, April 1939.

WEIHOFEN, H. : Legislative pardons. California law review 27 : 371-386, May 1939.

TEN BROEK, J. : Use by the United States Supreme Court of extrinsic aids in constitutional construction. California law review 27 : 399-421, May 1939.

American law institute undertakes code of evidence. American bar association journal 25 : 380-382, May 1939.

McGUIRE, O.E. : Administrative law and American democracy. American bar association journal 25 : 393-399, 435, May 1939.

HYNEMAN, C.S. and RICKETTS, E.F. : Tenure and turnover of the Iowa legislature. Iowa law review 24 : 673-696, May 1939.

The Tenth amendment as a limitation on the powers of Congress. Harvard law review 52 : 1342-1356, June 1939.

JAFFE, L.L. : Invective and investigation in administrative law. Harvard law review 52 : 1201-1245, June 1939.

The long term ground lease - A survey. Yale law journal 48 : 1400-1414, June 1939.

American law institute completes monumental task in torts and projects two important new activities. American bar association journal 25 : 469-476, 486-487, June 1939.

Legislative attempts to eliminate racial and religious minorities. Columbia law review 39 : 986-1003, June 1939.

LANGMAID, S.I. : Contracts for the benefit of third persons in California. California law review 27 : 497-534, July 1939.

STARK, F.C. : Politics and the State Department of Justice. Journal of criminal law and criminology 30 : 182-195, July-August 1939.

HOGAN, F.J. : Important shifts in constitutional doctrines. American bar association journal 25 : 629-638, August 1939.

GRANT, J.A.C. : State constitutional law in 1938-1939. American political science review 33 : 615-633, August 1939.

PINNEY, H. : The legal status of federal Government corporations. California law review 27 : 712-736, September 1939.

JACKSON, R.H. : Back to the constitution. American bar association journal 25 : 745-749, September 1939.

GREEN, P.W. : Duties of the asylum state under the Uniform Criminal Extradition Act. Journal of criminal law and criminology 30 : 295-324, September-October 1939.

Une décision de principe aux États-Unis en matière d'emprunt - Supreme Court, New York County, special term, part III by Mr. Justice Noonan (1939). - Barnes V. United Steel works Corporation (Vereinigte Stahlwerke A.G.) Bulletin de l'Institut juridique international 41 : 206-208, octobre 1939.

BLUNT, I.L. : American commercial arbitration. Arbitration journal 3 : 299-322, October 1939.

TUNKS, L.K. : Categorization and federalism, "Substance" and "procedure" after Erie railroad v. Tompkins. Illinois law review 34 : 271-302, November 1939.

STIMSON, E.S. : Retroactive applications of law - a problem in constitutional law. Michigan law review 38 : 30-56, November 1939.

POUND, R. : A generation of law teaching. Michigan law review 38 : 16-29, November 1939.

SWISHER, C.B. : Federal organization of legal functions. American political science review 33 : 973-1000, December 1939.

U.S.A.
(International law, Aliens, Nationality)

The problem of American neutrality. United States in world affairs : 255-270, 1934-1935.

"I'm alone" case. U.S. Department of State Press releases 12 : 16-20, 12 January 1935.

BECKER, W.G. : Das amerikanische Staatsangehörigkeitsgesetz vom 24. Mai 1934. Zeitschrift für ausländisches und internationales Privatrecht 9 : 261-266, Heft 1-2, 1935.

WRIGHT, B.F. and LATHAM, G. : Some legislative and constitutional aspects of the American recovery policies. Zeitschrift für ausländisches öffentliches Recht und Völkerrecht (Abhandlungen) 5 : 88-108, Februar 1935.

FRANCOIS, J.P.A. : Wijziging in de Amerikanische neutraliteits-politiek? Volkenbond 10 : 133-138, Februari 1935.

YAO, T.S. : La législation américaine et l'immigration chinoise. Politique de Pékin 22 : 235-238, 2 mars 1935.

GUILHOT, J. : La convention franco-américaine du 27 avril 1932 relative à la double imposition. Journal du droit international 62 : 325-332, mars-avril 1935.

BRIGGS, H.W., and BUELL, R.L. : American neutrality in a future war. Foreign policy reports 11 : 26-36, 10 April 1935.

FENWICK, C.G. : The "gold clause" decision in relation to foreign bondholders. American journal of international law 29 : 310-313, April 1935.

Claim of the British ship "I'm alone" v. United States. American journal of international law 29 : 326-331, April 1935.

FLOURNOY, R.W. : Proposed codification of our chaotic nationality laws. American foreign service journal 12 : 260-264, 285, May 1935.

HARPER, F.V. : Das "Restatement of conflict of laws" des amerikanischen " Law Institute". Zeitschrift für ausländisches und internationales Privatrecht 9 : 821-854, Heft 6, 1935.

YNTEMA, H.E. : The enforcement of foreign judgements in Anglo-American law. Michigan law review 33 : 1129-1168, June 1935.

KALAW, M.M. : The new constitution of the Philippine Commonwealth. Foreign affairs 13 : 687-694, July 1935.

GARNER, J.W. : Acts and joint resolutions of Congress as substitutes for treaties. American journal of international law 29 : 482-488, July 1935.

BORCHARD, E.M. : The citizenship of native-born American women who married foreigners before March 2, 1907, and acquired a foreign domicile. American journal of international law 29 : 396-422, July 1935.

Résolution votée par le Congrès américain le 24 août 1935. Esprit international 9 : 547-552, 1 octobre 1935.
Les États-Unis et la neutralité.

JESSUP, P.C. : The new neutrality legislation. American journal of international law 29 : 665-670, October 1935.

La nouvelle législation américaine de la neutralité. Affaires étrangères 5 : 453-456, octobre 1935.

SCOTT, J.B. : Neutrality of the United States. American journal of international law 29 : 644-652, October 1935.

NIELSEN, F.K. : Our methods of giving effect to international law and treaties. American foreign service journal 12 : 616-618, 656-661, November 1935.

The alien deportation controversy in Congress. Congressional digest 14 : 257-288, November 1935.

FAIRMAN, C. : La loi américaine de neutralité du 31 août 1935 appliquée au conflit italo-éthiopien. Revue générale de droit international public 42 : 678-696, novembre-décembre 1935.

BRADLEY, P. : Current neutrality problems - Some precedents, an appraisal, and a draft statute. American political science review 29 : 1022-1041, December 1935.
U.S. neutrality.

NIELSON, F.K. : Our methods of giving effect to international laws and treaties (Contd.). American foreign service journal 12 : 708-712, December 1935.

GARNER, J.W. : Recent American nationality legislation. British yearbook of international law 16 : 176-177, 1935.

MENDELSSOHN BARTHOLDY, A. : The American restatement of the law of conflict of laws. Grotius society, Problems of peace and war 21 : 161-176, 1935.

MILLIS, W. : What does neutrality mean? (Contd.). Nation 3 : 125-127, 29 January 1936.
The U.S. neutrality.

NATIONAL LAW - COUNTRIES

A study of neutrality legislation. International conciliation : 5-61, January 1936.
Official texts annexed.

REIFF, H. : The proclaiming of treaties in the Unites States. American journal of international law 30 : 63-79, January 1936.

BUELL, R.L. : The new American neutrality. Foreign policy reports 11 : 278-292, January 1936.

MICHEL, J. : La convention fiscale franco-américaine du 27 avril 1932. Journal du droit international 63 : 1-104, janvier-février 1936.

NOLDE, B : La codification du droit international privé aux Etats-Unis. Nouvelle revue de droit international privé 3 : 7-19, janvier-février 1936.

NEKAM, A. : L'entr'aide judiciaire aux États-Unis. Nouvelle revue de droit international privé 3 : 36-73, janvier-février-mars 1936.

WIGNY, P. : Le "restatement" américain de droit international privé. Revue critique de droit international 31 : 67-85, janvier-mars 1936.

ATWATER, E. : Examinations for the American service. International law and relations 5 : 1-8, 3 February 1936.

Les États-Unis et la neutralité. Europe nouvelle documentaire No. 31 : III-VIII, 8 février 1936.
Texte des actes législatifs et du message présidentiel annexés.

BUELL, R.L. : Retreat from neutrality. Foreign policy bulletin 15 : 1-2, 21 February 1936.
The U.S. neutrality legislation.

STOWELL, E.C. : The legal adviser of the Department of State. International law and relations 5 : 1-53, 26 February 1936.

HYDE, C.C. : The United States as a neutral. Yale law journal 45 : 608-621, February 1936.

GRASKE, T.W. : Some aspects of treaty interpretation in the United States 1930-1935. Tulane law review 10 : 246-262, February 1936.

United States neutrality policy. Bulletin of international news 12 : 631-639, 7 March 1936.

EAGLETON, C. : La législation sur la neutralité aux Etats-Unis. Revue de droit international et de législation comparée 63 : 461-474, No. 3, 1936.

WEINFELD, A.C. : Are labour conditions a proper subject of international conventions and may the United States government become a party to such conventions though they regulate matters ordinarily reserved to the States? Californian law review 24 : 275-287, March 1936.

McCAFFERY, E.M. : The Franco-American convention relative to double taxation. Columbia law review 36 : 382-405, March 1936.

The United States court for China. Harvard law review 49 : 793-797, March 1936.

Neutralité américaine et Monroisme. Affaires étrangères 6 : 133-137, mars 1936.

BROWN, P.M. : Neutrality legislation. World affairs 99 : 18-20, March 1936.

LECHARTER, G. : Neutralité et politique extérieure aux Etats-Unis. Esprit international 10 : 236-257, 1 avril 1936.

SCHOOP, H. : Kann Amerika neutral bleiben? Völkerbund (Lausanne) 14 : 38-40, 15. April 1936.

A few practical comments on the Franco-American treaty. Foreign law series : 18-21, No. 4, 1936.

DOMKE, M. : La portée européenne des "gold clause cases" américains. Bulletin de l'Institut juridique international 34 : 198-213, avril 1936.

WOOLSEY, L.H. : The fallacies of neutrality. American journal of international law 30 : 256-262, April 1936.

FRASER, H.S. : Research in international law affiliates with American law institute. American bar association journal 22 : 253, 266, April 1936.

JESSUP, P.C. : Towards further neutrality legislation. American journal of international law 30 : 262-265, April 1936.

GETTYS, L. : "Preliminary hearings" in naturalization administration. American political science review 30 : 288-294, April 1936.

VREELAND, H. : The validity of foreign divorces. Tulane law review 10 : 416-425, April 1936.

La convention franco-américaine sur les doubles impositions. Recueil hebdomadaire de jurisprudence 13 : 33-36, 14 mai 1936.

JESSUP, P.C. : Versuch einer Neutralitätsgesetzgebung in den Vereinigten Staaten. Europäische Revue 12 : 298-303, Mai 1936.

SURO, G.A. : La ley de neutralidad de los Estados Unidos. Boletin de la Unión Panamericana 70 : 362-367, mayo 1936.

Treaties and agreements of the United States containing the most-favored-nation clause. U.S. Treaty information bulletin : 17-20, May 1936.

ANGELL, M.E. : The nonresident alien - A problem in federal taxation of income. Columbia law review 36 : 908-919, June 1936.

Concerning continuity of residence for naturalization purposes. Interpreter releases 13 : 219-221, 13 July 1936.

GARNER, J.W. : Non-extradition of American citizens. The Neidecker case. American journal of international law 30 : 480-486, July 1936.

Jurisprudence américaine en matière de droit international (1933-1935). Revue générale de droit international public 43 : 589-630, septembre-octobre 1936.

MORROW, R.L. : The early American attitude toward naturalzed Americans abroad. American journal of international law 30 : 647-663, October 1936.

NATIONAL LAW - COUNTRIES

BORCHARD, E. : Effect of naturalization abroad of American citizens on their minor children born in the United States. American journal of international law 30 : 694-701, October 1936.

BATIFOL, H. : La Cour suprême des États-Unis et le droit international privé. Revue critique de droit international 31 : 597-624, juillet-novembre 1936.

Constitutional law - Termination of treaties. Michigan law review 35 : 88-119, November 1936.

The neutrality issue. United States in world affairs : 129-152, 1936.

FITZMAURICE, G.G. : The case of the "I'm alone". British year book of international law 17 : 82-111, 1936.

WHITTON, J.B. : Is American neutrality possible? Geneva, Institute of international relations, "Problems of peace" ser. 10 : 57-81, 1936.

BRADLEY, P. : The U.S.A. and neutrality. Peace year book : 61-68, 1936.

HINTON, H.B. : Neutrality - with bated breath. North American review 244 : 9-23, No. 1, 1937.

KUNZ, J.L. : Das Neutralitätsproblem in den Vereinigten Staaten. Zeitschrift für öffentliches Recht 17 : 85-121, Heft 1, 1937.

ATWATER, E. : Neutrality revision before Congress. International law and relations 6 : 1-6, January 1937.

The Department of State - Marriage of foreign service officers with foreign wives. American journal of international law (official documents) 31 : 50-51, January 1937.

REINHARDT, G.F. : Rectification of the Rio Grande in the El Paso-Juarez valley. American journal of international law 31 : 44-54, January 1937.

STOWELL, E.C. : The ban on alien marriages in the foreign service. American journal of international law 31 : 91-94, January 1937.

KRUGER, E. : Grundzüge der Organisation und Leitung der auswärtigen Angelegenheiten in den Vereinigten Staaten von Amerika. Niemeyers Zeitschrift für internationales Recht 52 : 5-35, 1. Heft, 1937.

MILLER, H. : Treaties and the Constitution. U.S. Press releases 16 : 49-60, 23 January 1937.

KNAUTH, A.W. : Les règles de La Haye aux États-Unis d'Amérique. Revue de droit maritime comparé 35 : 15-33, janvier-juin 1937.

BRADLEY, P. : Neutrality - as of 1936 and 1937. American political science review 31 : 100-113, February 1937.

COUDERT, F.R. : Can present legislation guarantee future neutrality? International conciliation : 169-191, February 1937.

PITAMIC, L. : Observations sur la question de la nationalité aux États-Unis. Annuaire de l'Association yougoalave de droit international 3 : 124-128, 1937.

HAZARD, H.B. : The use of United States passports during 1935 and 1936. International law and relations 6 : 1-4, 8 March 1937.

The United States' neutrality legislation. Bulletin of international news 13 : 795-800, 20 March 1937.

PREUSS, L. : Jurisprudence américaine relative à la reconnaissance de l'U.R.S.S. par les États-Unis (1933-1935). Revue générale de droit international public 44 : 199-217, mars-avril 1937.

New developments in the U.S.A. neutrality policy. New Commonwealth Institute, Information bulletin : 6-10, 3 April 1937.

BORCHARD, E. : "Neutrality" and civil war. American journal of international law 31 : 304-306, April 1937.

DUMBAULD, E. : Neutrality laws of the United States. American journal of international law 31 : 258-270, April 1937.

GARNER, J.W. : Executive discretion in the conduct of foreign relations. American journal of international law 31 : 289-293, April 1937.

JESSUP, P.C. : Neutrality legislation - 1937. American journal of international law 31 : 306-313, April 1937.

KEPPLER, K. : Die neue Embargopolitik der Vereinigten Staaten vom Amerika und das Neutralitätsrecht (Contd.). Zeitschrift für Völkerrecht 21 : 389-419, Heft 4, 1937.

DOUKAS, A. : The non-recognition law of the United States. Michigan law review 35 : 1071-1098, May 1937.

CHALUFOUR, A. : États-Unis - La loi de neutralité du 1er mai 1937. Affaires étrangères 7 : 301-305, mai 1937.

HAZARD, H.B. : Immigration and naturalization, with special reference to the United States of America. International law and relations 6 : 1-22, 5 June 1937.

McREYNOLDS, S.D. : Our neutrality bill. World affairs 100 : 81-87, June 1937.

LARKIN, J.D. : The Trade Agreement Act in Court and in Congress. American political science review 31 : 498-507, June 1937.

LIPPMANN, W. : Rough-hew them how we will. Foreign affairs 15 : 587-594, July 1937.
The United States Neutrality Act.

KEPPLER, K. : Cash and carry. Völkerbund und Völkerrecht 4 : 201-206, Juli 1937.
The neutrality of the United States.

GREEN, J.C. : Supervising the American traffic in arms. Foreign affairs 15 : 729-744, July 1937.

ECKHARDT : Amerikas neuestes Neutralitätsgesetz. Marine - Rundschau 42 : 399-411, Juli 1937.

GARNER, J.W. : The United States Neutrality Act of 1937. American journal of international law 31 : 385-397, July 1937.

États-Unis - Loi sur la neutralité du 29 avril 1937. Revue de droit international 20 : 199-212, juillet-août-septembre 1937.
Texte annexé.

STRUPP, K. : De Forenede Staters Neutralitetslovgivning. Økonomi og Politik 11 : 238-248, Juli-September 1937.

VANDENBOSCH, A. : Die nieuwe Amerikaansche wetgeving inzake neutraliteit. Volkenbond 12 : 270-273, August-September 1937.

CASTLE, W.R. : Dangers d'une législation locale en matuère de neutralité. Revue économique internationale 3 : 557-570, septembre 1937.

REIFF, H. : The United States and international administrative unions - Some historical aspects. International conciliation : 627-655, September 1937.

RIESENFELD,S.A. : The power of Congress and the President in international relations - Three recent Supreme Court decisions. California law review 25 : 643-675, September 1937.

MITRANY, D. : The U.S.A. Neutrality Act of May 1, 1937. New Commonwealth quarterly 3 : 101-115, September 1937.

PREUSS, L., et KITCHIN, J.A. : Jurisprudence américaine en matière de droit international (1936). Revue générale de droit international public 44 : 561-585, septembre-octobre 1937.

MITRANY, D. : The U.S.A. Neutrality Act of 1 May 1937. New Commonwealth quarterly 6 : 4-6, October 1937.

BUELL, R.L. : The Neutrality Act of 1937. Foreign policy reports 13 : 166-177, 1 October 1937.

Positive neutrality. New republic 92 : 327-329, 27 October 1937.
The United States Neutrality Act.

MYERS, D.P., and RANSOM, C.F. : Reorganization of the State Department. American journal of international law 31 : 713-720, October 1937.

BUELL, R.L. : Zum Neutralitätsgesetz der USA. Monatshefte für auswärtige Politik 4 : 753-761, November 1937.

FRIEDE, W. : Das amerikanische Neutralitätsgesetz von 1937. Zeitschrift für ausländisches öffentliches Recht und Völkerrecht 7 : 769-792, November 1937.

GARNER, J.W. : Recent American neutrality legislation. International affairs 16 : 853-869, November-December 1937.

KUNZ, J.L. : Amerikanisches internationales Privatrecht. Zeitschrift für öffentliches Recht 17 : 648-654, 10. Dezember 1937.

McALLISTER, B. : The influence of Supreme Court decisions on the conduct of American foreign affairs. Institute of world affairs, Proceedings 15 : 157-161, 1937.

FRASER, H.S. : The constitutionality of the Trade Agreements Act of 1934. American Society of International Law, Proceedings : 55-67, 1937.

HYDE, C.C. : The Supreme Court of the United States as an expositor of international law. British year book of international law 18 : 1-16, 1937.

HYDE, C.C. : Constitutional procedures for international agreement by the United States. American Society of International Law, Proceedings : 45-55, 1937.

ECKHARDT, C. : Das neue Neutralitätsgesetz der Vereinigten Staaten von Amerika. Zeitschrift der Akademie für deutsches Recht 5 : 53-56, 15. Januar 1938.

JOBST, V. : The United States and international labor conventions. American journal of international law 32 : 135-138, January 1938.

PEPIN, E. : Récente réorganisation du "State Department". Affaires étrangères 8 : 24-36, janvier 1938.

OPPENHEIMER, R. : Recent developments in the deportation progress. Michigan law review 36 : 355-384, January 1938.
The deportation of aliens.

COURTNEY, K.D. : America and the neutrality legislation. Headway 20 : 16-17, January 1938.

HAMBRO, E. : Bemerkninger til den nye amerikanske noitralitetslovgivning. Nordisk tidsskrift for international Ret 9 : 110-118, Fasc. 1-2, 1938.

SPIEGEL, H.W. : American neutrality and the bill of 29 April 1937. Journal of comparative legislation and international law (Pt. 1) 20 : 80-84, February 1938.

BAGGE, A. : L'effet international de la législation américaine clause-or par rapport aux emprunts à obligation émises par des débiteurs non américains en valeur de dollars. Revue de droit international et de législation comparée 18 : 786-818, No. 4, 1938.

WEIDENBAUM, P. : Corporate nationality and the neutrality law. Michigan law review 36 : 881-905, April 1938.

THOMSON, I.L. : Flights abroad and the role of the Department of State. Journal of air law 9 : 220-250, April 1938.

TAYLER, W.L. : Maritime treaties submitted to the Senate. American journal of international law 32 : 352-354, April 1938.

STOWELL, E.C. : The joint resolution prohibiting the picketing of diplomatic and consular premises in the district of Columbia. American journal of international law 32 : 344-346, April 1938.

MATHEWS, J.M. : The joint resolution method. American journal of international law 32 : 349-352, April 1938.
Joint resolutions instead of treaties.

PAN, S.C.Y. : An analytical study of principles of American diplomacy - with an emphasis on their application in China. Chinese social and political science review 22 : 10-27, April-June 1938.

DEÁK, F. : The pitfalls of the new American neutrality. International conciliation : 179-192, May 1938.

NATIONAL LAW - COUNTRIES

ECKHARDT : Das Neutralitätsgesetz der Vereinigten Staaten von 1937, Zeitschrift für ausländisches öffentliches Recht und Völkerrecht 8 : 231-256, Mai 1938.

SCHEFTEL, J. : La reconnaissance internationale du Gouvernement soviétique et ses répercussions sur la jurisprudence américaine. Journal du droit international 65 : 433-467, mai-juin 1938.

WHITTON, J.B. : Le problème de la neutralité américaine 1938. Revue générale de droit international public 45 : 567-580, septembre-octobre 1938.

DULLES, A.W. , and ARMSTRONG, H.F. : Legislating peace. Foreign affairs 17 : 1-12, October 1938. The Neutrality Act.

BORCHARD, E. : Neutrality. Yale law journal 48 : 37-53, November 1938.

SIMPSON, W. H. : Legal aspects of executive agreements. Iowa law review 24 : 67-88, November 1938.

MORAN, C. : Appraising our neutrality. United States Naval Institute proceedings 64 : 1705-1715, December 1938.

The confusion about neutrality. United States in world affairs : 152-169, 1938.

GARNER, J.W. : The United States "neutrality" law of 1937. British year book of international law 19 : 44.66, 1938.

RAYMOND : Le "Neutrality Act". Revue de droit international et de législation comparée 66 : 159-166, No. 1, 1939.

BEARD, C.A. : Neutrality - Shall we have revision? The President's policy - and the people's. New republic 97 : 307-308, 18 January 1939.

JESSUP, P.C. : The Pacific Coast fisheries. American journal of international law 33 : 129-138, January 1939.

EAGLETON. C. : Revision of the Neutrality Axt. American journal of international law 33 : 119-126, January 1939.

International law - Power of a State to extend its boundary beyond the three mile limit. Columbia law review 39 : 317-326, February 1939.

BRIGGS, H.W. : Les États-Unis et la loi de 1935 sur la contrebande. Revue de droit internationale et de législation comparée 66 : 217-255, No. 2, 1939.

The neutrality Act of 1937 and proposed amendments. Congressional digest 18 : 77-78, March 1939.

United States neutrality. Amerasia 3 : 5-11, March 1939.

WOODWARD, C.H. : The relations between the Navy and the Foreign Service. American journal of international law 33 : 283-291, April 1939.

HEILMAN, R.J. : The enforceability of foreign awards in the United States. Arbitration journal 3 : 183-194, April 1939.

FENWICK, C.G. : The Monroe doctrine and the declaration of Lima. American journal of international law 33 : 257-268, April 1939.

SAYRE, F.B. : The constitutionality of the Trade Agreements Act. Columbia law review 39 : 751-775, May 1939.

BROWN, P.M. Neutrality, peace legislation and our foreign policy. World affairs 102 : 88-98, June 1939.

SALTER, A. : La législation américaine de neutralité. Esprit international 13 : 359-372, 1 juillet 1939.

CALLENDER, H. : Unneutral neutrality. Time and tide 20 : 979-980, 22 July 1939.

JESSUP, P.C. : The reconstruction of "neutrality" legislation in 1939. American journal of international law 33 : 549-557, July 1939.

BORCHARD, E. : Citizenship by birth in the United States not lost through naturalization abroad of minor's father. American journal of international law 33 : 534-538, July 1939.

STONE, W.T. : Will neutrality keep United States out of war? Foreign policy reports 15 : 166-176, 1 October 1939.

Should Congress amend the present neutrality law? Congressional digest 18 : 228-256, October 1939.

WOOLSEY, L.H. : The arbitration of the sabotage claims against Germany. American journal of international law 33 : 737-740, October 1939.

KEOPPLE, L.G. : Legislation affecting commerce enacted by the Seventy-sixth Congress, First Session. U.S. Department of Commerce, Comparative law series 2 : 447-452, October 1939.

WILCOX, F.O. : The neutrality fight in Congress : 1939. American political science review 23 : 811-825, October 1939.

FENWICK, C.G. : The revision of neutrality legislation in time of foreign war. American journal of international law 33 : 728-730, October 1939.

BROWN, P.M. : Neutrality. American journal of international law 33 : 726-727, October 1939.

Recent anti-alien legislative proposals. Columbia law review 39 : 1207-1223, November 1939.

U.S.A.

(Patents, Trademarks, Copyright)

La réforme du droit d'auteur aux États-Unis. Droit d'auteur 50 : 15-18, février 1937.

WOLFF, J. : Non-competing goods in trademark law. Columbia law review 37 : 582-608, April 1937.

LITTAUER-APT, R. : U.S.A. - The copyrights in Hitler's "Mein Kampf". Copy right 5 : 57-60, June-July 1930.

URUGUAY

Dekret der Regierung von Uruguay über den Abbruch der Beziehungen zur Sowjetunion vom 27.12.1935. Ost-Europa 11 : 254-256, Februar 1936.

HÉLIARD, M. : La constitution de l'Uruguay. Revue parlementaire 33 : 119-120, 1 juin 1937.

Projet de revision constitutionnelle (résumé). Informations constitutionnelles et parlementaires 2 : 224-225, 30 juin 1937.

SAMPAY, A.E. : El contralor jurisdiccional de la constitucionalidad de las leyes en la constitución uruguaya. Revista de derecho y legislación 27 : 77-110, octubre-diciembre 1938.

VATICAN STATE

FACCHINETTI, G. : I provvedimenti di amnista, d'indulto e di grazia in relazione all'art. 22 del trattato 11 febbraio 1929 fra la S. Sede e l'Italia. Echi e commenti 16 : 85-86, 25 gennaio1935.

AVACK, A. d' : La qualifica giuridica della Santa Sede nella stipulazione del trattato lateranense (Contd.). Rivista di diritto internazionale 27 : 83-124, 1 gennaio-30 giugno 1935.

D'AVAK, P.A. : La qualifica giuridica della Santa Sede nelle stipulazione del trattato lateranense (Contd.). Rivista di diritto internazionale 27 : 217-236, 1 luglio-31 dicembre 1935.

HOVER, E.v. : Die S. Romana Rota im Jahre 1935. Prager juristische Zeitschrift 16 : 526-534, 2. Septemberheft 1936.

LA BRIÈRE, Y. de : La souveraineté du Saint-Siège et le droit des gens. Revue de droit international 20 : 29-48, juillet-août-septembre 1937.

TRICAUD, M. : Le régime particulier de l'espace aérien au-dessus de la Cité du Vatican. Revue générale de droit aérien 7 : 197-200, avril-mai-juin 1938.

MIELE, M. : Persone giuridiche vaticane e l'art. 9 del Trattato del Laterano. Rivista di diritto unternazionale 30 : 457-465, 1 luglio-31 dicembre 1938.

CAPPELLO, M. : La figura giuridica dei coniugi e del promotore di giustizia nelle cause matrimoniali. Civiltà cattolica 90 : 3-16, 1 luglio 1939.

VENEZUELA

URBANEJA, A. : Breves comentarios al Código penal Venezolano di 1926. Revista jiurídica 6 : 137-156, agosto-setiembre 1935.

Boletin del Ministerio de Relaciones Exteriores de los Estados Unidos de Venezuela 11 : 5-323, 19 diciembre 1935.
Survey of twenty-five years' foreign relations.

New legislation in Venezuela. Bulletin of the Pan American Union 51 : 62-68, January 1937.
The political reconstruction.

BROWN, J.L. : Regulation of air navigation in Venezuela. Journal of air law 8 : 577-586, October 1937.

CRAWFORD, H.P. : The corporation law of Venezuela. Tulane law review 12 : 200-225, February 1938.

VIET NAM

LEVASSEUR, G. : Les conflits de lois et de juridictions intéressant les Chinois en Indochine. Revue indochinoise juridique et économique : 42-134, no. 4, 1937.

COUZINET, P. : La structure juridique de l'Union indochinoise. Revue indochinoise : 426-475, no. 3, 1938.

LEVASSEUR, G. : Contribution à l'établissement d'une bibliographie du droit indochinois. Revue indochinoise juridique et économique : 139-144, 1939.

YUGOSLAVIA

PÉRITCH, J. : L'"Angehörigkeit" provinciale en Yougoslavie. Bulletin de l'Institut juridique international 32 : 3-6, janvier 1935.

SAGADIN, S. : Die Verfassungsrechtliche Entwicklung Jugoslawiens seit 1926. Zeitschrift für osteuropäisches Recht 2 : 1-23, Juli 1935.

DNISTRJANSKYJ, S. : Die Rezeption des österreichischen Privatrechts in der Tschechoslowakei und in Jugoslavien. Zeitschrift für osteuropäisches Recht 1 : 463-490, März 1935.

Vorentwurf eines bürgerlichen Gesetzbuches für das Königreich Jugoslawien von 1933. Zeitschrift für ausländisches und internationales Privatrecht 9 : 516-519, Heft 3, 1935.

DNSTRJANSKYJ, S. : Die Rezeption des österreichischen Privatrechts in der Tschechoslowakei und in Jugoslawien (Contd.). Zeitschrift für osteuropäisches Recht 1 : 561-581, 618-634, Mai, Juni 1935.

Die Rechtsvereinheitlichung im Königreiche Yugoslavien. Zeitschrift der Akademie für deutsches Recht 2 : 464-472, Juli 1935.

Jugoslawien - Aus der Rechtsprechung zur Wechselordnung vom 29. November 1928. Zeitschrift für osteuropäisches Recht 2 : 163, September 1935.

ROSENBERG, W. : Le nouveau statut des étrangers en Yougoslavie. Écho de Belgrade 4 : 4, 20 novembre 1935.

FRANOLIC, V. : Droit budgétaire yougoslave. Revue de science et de législation financières 33 : 533-556, octobre-novembre-décembre 1935.

TAUBER, L. : Der siebente Juristentag des Königreichs Jugoslawien. Zeitschrift für osteuropäisches Recht 2 : 424-428, Januar 1936.

BLAGOYÉVITCH, V.O. : De l'influence du civil au criminel et du criminel au civil dans la législation yougoslave. Bulletin trimestriel de la Société de législation comparée 65 : 137-151, janvier-mars 1936.

ROSENBERGER, Z. : Die Gesetzgebung in Jugoslawien im Jahre 1935. Internationales Anwalsblatt 22 : 15-18, Februar 1936.

TAUBER, L. : Die jugoslawische Verordnung über den Schutz der Landwirte. Zeitschrift für osteuropäisches Recht 2 : 516-528, März 1936.

ROSENDORFF, R. : La réforme du droit des sociétés par actions en Yougoslavie. Annales de droit commercial 45 : 118-132, avril-juin 1936.

WERK, H. : Jugoslawisches Anwaltsrecht. Zeitschrift der Akademie für deutsches Recht 3 : 463-466, 15. Mai 1936.

DJERMEKOV, D. : Richter und Gerichte in Jugoslawien. Zeitschrift der Akademie für deutsches Recht 3 : 458-463, 15. Mai 1936.

Jugoslawien - Übersicht über die wesentliche Gesetzgebung im zweiten Halbjahr 1934 und im Jahr 1935. Zeitschrift für osteuropäisches Recht 2 : 671-676, Mai 1936.

DOLENC, M. : Die strafrechtliche Bekämpfung des Kommunismus im Königreiche Jugoslawien. Zeitschrift der Akademie für deutsches Recht 3 : 562-566, Juni 1936.

Tabelle der von Jugoslawien von 1926 bis 1936 geschlossenen Staatsverträge. Zeitschrift für osteuropäiches Recht 3 : 44-54, Juli 1936.

ROSENDORFF, R. : La réforme du droit des sociétés par actions en Yougoslavie (Contd.). Annales de droit commercial 45 : 193-218, juillet-septembre 1936.

BILIMOVIC, A. : Das Kartellrecht Jugoslawiens. Zeitschrift für osteuropäisches Recht 3 : 67-80, August 1936.

MAKLEZOW, A. : Der strafrechtliche Schutz des Staates in Jugoslawien. Zeitschrift für osteuropäisches Recht 3 : 149-164, September 1936.

PÉRITCH, J.-M. : Le droit yougoslave et la stérilisation. Bulletin trimestriel de la Société de législation comparée 65 : 451-458, octobre-décembre 1936.

GORŠIČ, F. : Die Rechtsstellung der Ausländer in Jugoslawien. Zeitschrift für osteuropäisches Recht 3 : 353-370, Dezember 1936.

PÉRITCH, J.M. : Des effets des jugements civils étrangers en Yougoslavie. Zeitschrift für schweizerisches Recht 56 : 105-139, Heft 1, 1937.

Jugoslawien - Übersicht über die wesentliche Gesetzgebung im Jahre 1936. Zeitschrift für osteuropäisches Recht 3 : 584-588, März 1937.

Die Gesetzgebung in Jugoslawien im Jahre 1936. Internationales Anwaltsblatt 23 : 29-31, März 1937.

BLAGOYÉVITCH, V.O. : Les preuves et l'assistance judiciaire devant les tribunaux yougoslaves. Annuaire de l'Association yougoslave de droit international 3 : 177-210, 1937.

MILIĆ, M. : Congrès des juristes du Royaume de Yougoslavie. Annuaire de l'Association yougoslave de droit international 3 : 435-449, 1937.

MITROVIC, P. Convention sur la pêche dans la mer Adriatique. Annuaire de l'Association yougoslave de droit international 3 : 98-104, 1937.

NICOLAYÉVITCH, R. : L'extradition en Yougoslavie. Annuaire de l'Association yougoslave de droit international 3 : 225-234, 1937.

Jurisprudence des tribunaux et des autorités yougoslaves en matière de droit international. Annuaire de l'Association yougoslave de droit international 3 : 237-257, 1937.

PRZIC, I.A. : Le problème des rapports entre le droit interne et le droit international et ses discussions dans la science juridique yougoslave. Annuaire de l'Association yougoslave de droit international 3 : 129-151, 1937.

PRZIC, I.A. : Bibliographie yougoslave de droit international (1930-1936). Annuaire de l'Association yougoslave de droit international 3 : 353-431, 1937.

SOUBBOTITCH, I.V. : Bibliographie des ouvrages et articles de revues parus en langue allemande dans les années 1930-1936 et concernant le droit yougoslave. Annuaire de l'Association yougoslave de droit international 3 : 307-313, 1937.

SOUBBOTITCH, I.V., et KORENIĆ, F. : Bibliographie française (1930-1936) concernant le droit yougoslave. Annuaire de l'Association yougoslave de droit international 3 : 323-332, 1937.

STRAZNICKY, M. : Les sources du droit maritime privé yougoslave. Annuaire de l'Association yougoslave de droit international 3 : 155-176, 1937.

TAUBERT, L. : La réglementation légale des cartels en Yougoslavie. Annales de droit commercial et industriel 46 : 198-211, juillet-september 1937.

EISNER, B. : Die einleitenden Bestimmungen, die Personen, die Familie und die dinglichen Rechte im Vorentwurf zu einem jugoslavischen Zivilgesetzbuch. Annuario di diritto comparato e di studi legislativi 14 : 1-64, fasc. 1, 1938.

Liste de lois, ordonnances, règlements organiques et décrets en matière pénale et pénitentiaire promulgués au cours du deuxième semestre de l'année 1936. Recueil de documents en matière pénale et pénitentiaire 7 : 124-137, janvier 1938.

EISNER, B. : Die Schuldverhältnisse, das Erbrecht, die Ersitzung und die Verjährung im Vorentwurf zu einem jugoslavischen Zivilgesetzbuch. Annuario di diritto comparato e di studi legislativi 14 : 137-200, fasc. 2, 1938.

TAUBER, L. : Jugoslawien - Übersicht über die wesentliche Gesetzgebung im Jahre 1937. Zeitschrift für osteuropäisches Recht 4 : 580-583, März 1938.

BUSSE, A. : Ein jugoslawisches Handelsgesetzbuch (Contd.). Deutsche Justiz 100 : 546-550, 8. April 1938.

GORŠIČ, F. : Der jugoslawische Verwaltungsschutz. Zeitschrift für osteuropäisches Recht 4 : 747-762, Juni 1938.

TAUBER, L. : Das neue Handelsgesetz des Königreichs Jugoslawien. Zeitschrift für osteuropäisches Recht 5 : 69-83, August 1938.

LAPAJNE : Entwurf eines Schadensersatzrechtes für das jugoslawische bürgerliche Gesetzbuch. Zeitschrift für osteuropäisches Recht 5 : 176-187, September 1938.

TAUBER, L. : Die Aktiengesellschaft und die Gesellschaft mit beschränkter Haftung nach dem neuen Handelsgesetz für das Königreich Jugoslawien. Zeitschrift für osteuropäisches Recht 5 : 217-234, Oktober 1938.

BISCOTTINI, G. : La formazione del Regno serbo-croato-sloveno (Contd.). Rivista di diritto internazionale 30 : 245-309, 1 luglio-31 dicembre 1938.

TAUBER, L. : Der achte Juristentag des Königreichs Jugoslawien. Zeitschrift für osteuropäisches Recht 5 : 399-404, Dezember 1938.

PÉRITCH, J.M. : Le mariage en droit international privé suivant la législation yougoslave. Bulletin de l'Institut juridique international 40 : 1-23, janvier 1939.

BAYER, V., et ZLATARIG, B. : Yougoslavie - année 1939. Istituto italiano di studi legislativi, Legislazione internazionale 8 : 919-1052, tomo II, 1939.
Index de législation et traductions.

PÉRITCH, J.-M. : Le mariage en droit international privé suivant la législation yougoslave (Contd.). Bulletin de l'Institut juridique international 40 : 186-195, avril 1939.

PÉRITCH, J.-M. : Le mariage en droit international privé suivant la législation yougoslave (Contd.). Bulletin de l'Institut juridique international 41 : 1-17, juillet 1939.

NATIONAL LAW - COUNTRIES

ALBANIA

CANSACCHI, G. : L'unione dell'Albania con l'Italia. Rivista di diritto internazionale 19 : 113-132, 1 aprile-30 settembre 1940.

KEMPNER, R.M.W. : The new constitution of Albania. Tulane law review 15 : 430-434, April 1941.

BASSANI, G.L. : Rassegna corporativa. Rivista d'Albania 2 : 301-304, settembre 1941.
Current notices.

VELENTINI, G. : Il clero cattolico e il diritto tradizionale albanese. Civiltà cattolica 95 : 73-81, 15 aprile 1944.

ARGENTINE

AZARA, A. : The project of the new Argentine civil code and agriculture. International bulletin of agricultural law 1 : 174-181, 1940.

RODA, J.J. : El régimen de extradición en la República Argentina. Revista del foro 27 : 79-82, enero-junio 1940.

CRAWFORD, H.P. : The Argentine limited liability company. Tulane law review 14 : 232-244, February 1940.

OSSORIO, A. : La reforma del Código civil Argentino. Universidad de la Habana : 167-192, mayo-junio-julio-agosto 1941.

IDELSON, V.R. : The Argentine civil code. Journal of comparative legislation and international law 23 : 174-176, November 1941.

ALSINA, H. : Reseña de la organización judicial en la República Argentina. Revista de derecho y legislación 30 : 267-284, noviembre-diciembre 1941.

BIELSA, R. : Sobre estudio de ciertos principios constitucionales. Revista parlamentaria 10 : 3-24, diciembre 1941.

L'accertamento della competenza del giudice argentino secondo la convenzione italo-argentina sull' esecuzione delle sentenze. Rivista di diritto internazionale 21 : 124-126, fasc. 1-2, 1942.

Leyes sancionadas en 1941. Revista parlamentaria 10 : 35-38, enero 1942.

GANDÍA, E. de : Limites internacionales de la República Argentina. Revista argentina de derecho internacional 5 : 5-39, enero-febrero-marzo 1942.

PICHETTO, J.R. : The present state of social legislation in the Argentine Republic. International labour review 46 : 383-419, October 1942.
(Also French edition).

SCHLESINGER, J.F. : El federalismo argentino - La centralización financiera. Revista parlamentaria 11 : 8-13, octubre 1942.

PALACIOS CABANILLAS, A.G. : El federalismo argentino. Revista parlamentaria 11 : 21-28, noviembre 1942.

FASSI, S.C. : De la inexistencia y de la nulidad del matrimonio. Anales de la Facultad de ciencias jurídicas y sociales de la Universidad de la Plata 13 : 27-132, 1942.

PARRY, A.E. : Las contribuciones por mejoras y las garantías constitucionales. Anales de la Facultad de ciencias jurídicas y sociales de la Universidad de la Plata 13 : 553-606, 1942.

Los privilegios parlamentarios. Revista parlamentaria 11 : 3-6, febrero 1943.

Demandas contra la nación o las entidades politicas que la componen en los paises de America. Revista de derecho y legislación 32 : 70-74, marzo-abril 1943.

SAYAGUES LASO, E. : Prescripción de la responsabilidad del estado. Revista de derecho y administración municipal : 427-442, mayo 1943.

Nomina de los tratados, convenions, etc. suscriptos por la República Argentina... 1941-1942. Revista argentina de derecho internacional 6 : 209-216, abril-mayo-junio 1943.

Catálogo de tratados, convenciones y demás actos internacionales celebrados por la República Argentina desde et 25 de mayo de 1810 hasta el 31 de diciembre de 1942. Informaciones argentinas : 36-64, 49-64, 60-64, 43-64, 15 marzo, 15 abril, 15 mayo, 15 junio 1943.

WASSERMANN, M. : La jurisprudence récente en matière de propriété industrielle. Propriété industrielle 59 : 91-99, juni 1943.

LOEWENSTEIN, K. : Legislation against subversive activities in Argentina. Harvard law review 56 : 1261-1306, July 1943.

Suspendiendo el otorgamiento de la carta de ciudadanía minetras dure el conflicto armado internacional. Revista parlamentaria 11 : 94-96, agosto 1943.

Demandas contra la nación o las entidades políticas que la componen en los paises de America - Argentina. Revista de derecho y legislación 32 : 205-212, setiembre-octubre 1943.

LINARES, J.F. : La garantía constitucional de razonabilidad. Revista de derecho y administración municipal: 957-988, octubre 1943.

SAN MILLAN ALMAGRO, J.N. : Reseña de jurisprudencia sobre derecho administrativo (1943). Revista de derecho y administración municipal : 873-919, octubre 1944.

AUSTRALIA

JANOUSEK, J.O. : The law of negotiable instruments in Australia. U.S. Department of commerce, Comparative law series 3 : 467-481, September 1940.

DODD, P. : The war and industrial arbitration in Australia. Arbitration journal 6 : 24-33, No. 1, 1942.

Australia. Journal of comparative legislation and international law 23 : 74-105, August 1941.
The legislation in 1939.

Compensation for war damage in Australia. Australasian insurance and banking record 66 : 25-26, 2 January 1942.

War damage to property. Australian law journal 15 : 333-336, 13 March 1942.

Compensation for war damage. Australasian insurance and banking record 64 : 147-148, 21 April 1942.

The commerce of power under the Australian Constitution. Columbia law review 42 : 660-681, April 1942.

The Constitutional Convention. Australian law journal 16 : 221-222, December 1942.

MITCHELL, R.E. : Delegated and subdelegated legislation. Australian law journal 17 : 75-79, 16 July 1943.

PHILLIPS, P.D. : Workers' compensation law and future. Australian law journal 17 : 110-114, 17 August 1943.

SUGERMAN, B., and DIGNAM, W.J. : The defence power and total war. Australian law journal 17 : 207-214, 12 November 1943.

BROADBENT, J.E. : Constitutional amendments in Australia. Journal of comparative legislation and international law 25 : 1-24, November 1943.

Imperium in imperio? - Powers of state premiers under national security regulations. Australian law journal 18 : 34-38, 16 June 1944.

AUSTRIA

Arrêt du Obergericht de Zurich du ler mars 1939 - Loi autrichienne du 13 avril 1938 - "Kommissarischer Verwalter". Bulletin de l'Institut juridique international 42 : 87-102, janvier 1940.

DEMELIUS, H. : Ubersicht über die Zivilrechtsprechung des österreichischen Obersten Gerichtshofes in den Jahren 1937 und 1938. Zeitschrift für ausländisches und internationales Privatrecht 13 : 924-965, Heft 5/6, 1942.

BALTIC STATES

Anordnungen des Reichskommissars für das Ostland 1941/42. Zeitschrift für osteuropäisches Recht 9 : 83-85, Juli-Septembre 1942.

SCHAFER, H. : Die Wiederherstellung des Privateigentums in den Generalbezirken Estland, Lettland und Litauen. Zeitschrift für osteuropäisches Recht 10 : 39-50, Januar/Juni 1943.

BELGIUM

RECHT, P. : La loi belge de 1929 sur le bail à ferme. Bulletin international de droit agricole 1 : 144-162, No. 2, 1940.

RECHT, P. : La legislation agricole en Belgique. Bulletin international de droit agricole 1 : 207-211, No. 2, 1940.

VAHLDIEK : Bestimmungen über die Wiedervereinigung der Gebiete von Eupen, Malmedy und Moresnet mit dem Deutschen Reich. Zeitschrift für ausländisches öffentliches Recht und Völkerrecht 10 : 919-934, No. 3/4, 1941.

WOLGAST, E. : Wiedergutmachung statt Amnestie - Erledigung der sog. Flamen-Amnestie-Klausel des Versailler Diktats. Zeitschrift für Völkerrecht 24 : 385-410, Heft 4, 1941.

ASCHENBRENNER, H. : Zu, belgischen Gesetz vom Jahre 1919. Archiv für das Recht der internationalen Organisationen 3 : 6-18, 1942.
The law on international unions.

MOSLER : Der Konflikt über die gerichtliche Nachprüfung der Verordnungen der Generalsekratäre in den belgischen Ministerien. Zeitschrift für ausländisches öffentliches Recht und Völkerrecht 11 : 610-620, Oktober 1943.

War criminals. Inter-Allied information committee (Documents) : 6-7, 12 October 1943.

FAYAT, H. : Legislation in exile. Belgium. Journal of comparative legislation and international law 25 : 30-40, November 1943.

BRAZIL

Código de processo civil brasileiro. Boletim da faculdade de direito, Coimbra 17 : 134-157, fasc. 1, 1940-41.

FALCAO, W. : Legislación social en el Brasil. Revista parlamentaria 10 : 4-15, octubre 1941.

CRAWFORD, H.P. : The 1940 corporation law of Brazil. Tulane law review 16 : 228-248, February 1942.

DUARTE, J. : O novo codigo penal. Revista de direito civil, comercial e criminal 140 : 26-47, abril 1942.

TOVAR, J. : Aplicação da lei estrangeira. Revista de direito civil, comercial e criminal 140 : 21-25, abril 1942.

VALLADÃO, H. : Lei nacional e lei do domicilio. Revista de direito civil, comercial e crominal 141 : 18-28, julho 1942.

MARCHANT, A. : The Brazilian writ of security, mandado de segurança, and its relationship to the extraordinary remedies of the Anglo-American common law - An object lesson in Latin American law-making. Tulane law review 19 : 213-228, December 1944.

BULGARIA

STAINOV, P. : Die neue Judengesetzgebung in Bulgarien. Zeitschrift für osteuropäisches Recht 7 : 553-558, Mai-Juni 1941.

KOJUCHAROFF, A. : Gesetz vom 21. Januar 1941 zum Schutze der Nation. Zeitschrift für osteuropäisches Recht 7 : 598-614, Mai-Juni 1941.

KOJUCHAROFF, A. : Gesetz vom 16. Dezember 1940 über die Staatsangehörigkeit. Zeitschrift für osteuropäisches Recht 8 : 316-330, November-Dezember 1941.

Bulgarien - Übersicht über die wesentliche Gesetzgebung im letzten Vierteljahr 1940 und in den ersten drei Vierteljahren 1941. Zeitschrift für osteuropäisches Recht 8 : 306-316, November-Dezember 1941.

KOJUCHAROFF, A. : Anerkennung und Vaterschaftsklage nach bulgarischen Recht. Zeitschrift für osteuropäisches Recht 8 : 443-478, März/April 1942.

Das bulgarische Gesetz zum Schutz der Nation. Glasul minoritatilor 20 : 88-93, Mai-Junie 1942.

STAINOV, P. : Der gegenwärtige Stand der Judengesetzgebung in Bulgarien. Zeitschrift für osteuropäisches Recht 9 : 51-59, Juli-September 1942.

ALTINOFF, I. : System und Probleme des bulgarischen internationalen Privatrechts. Zeitschrift für öffentliches Recht 23 : 137-172, Heft 2/3, 1943.

KRUSE : Das neue Aktienrecht in Bulgarien. Südost-Economist 5 : 52-54, 19. Februar 1943.

WLADIKIN, L. : Die Judengesetzgebung in Bulgarien. Reich, Volksordnung, Lebensraum 5 : 295-333, 1943.

VLAHOV, I.S. : Les nouveaux amendments du code de commerce bulgare relatifs aux sociétés par actions. Parole bulgare 8 : 2, 10 juillet 1943.

CANADA

MACDONALD, V.C. : The Constitution and the Courts in 1939. Canadian bar review 18 : 147-158, March 1940.

GETTYS, L. : Report of the Royal Commission on Dominion-Provincial relations. American political science review 35 : 100-107, February 1941.

GREENE, W.A. : War and the common law. Canadian bar review 19 : 438-452, June 1941.

CLOKIE, H. McD. : Basic problems of the Canadian Constitution. Canadian journal of economics and political science 8 : 1-32, February 1942.

CLOKIE, H. McD. : Basic problems of the Canadian Constitution. Canadian bar review 20 : 395-429, May 1942.

SCOTT, F.R. : Section 94 of the British North America Act. Canadian bar review 20 : 525-544, June-July 1942.
Uniformity of laws.

CLOKIE, H. McD. : Basic problem of the Canadian constitution (Contd.). Canadian bar review 20 : 817-840, December 1942.

CLAXTON, B. : Commercial arbitration under Canadian law. Canadian bar review 21 : 171-190, March 1943.

DAVIS, J.T.C. : Some observations on the Canadian constitution. Australian law journal 17 : 242-247, 10 December 1943.

CHILE

SCHWENK, H. : Labor arbitration in Chile. Arbitration journal 4 : 148-151, October 1940.

LOEWENSTEIN, K. : Legislation for the defense of the State in Chile. Columbia law review 44 : 366-407, May 1944.

CHINA

LÖWENTHAL, R. : The copyright in China. Yenching journal of social studies 3 : 145-173, August 1941.

The Chinese judicial system. Current notes on international affairs 14 : 244-245, 15 August 1943.

VECSEKLÖY, J. : Das Prüfungssystem in der chinesischen Verwaltung. Archiv des Öffentlichen Rechts 34 : 151-167, Juni 1944.

Foreigners in Chinese courts - An interview with China's minister of justice. Great Britain and the East 61 : 15-17, 9 September 1944.

COLOMBIA

La reforma del Código civil - Proyecto de ley. Estudios de derecho (Colombia) 2 : 401-426, noviembre 1940.

BOTERO, J.U. : Las sociedades ordinarias en la historia de la legislación minera. Estudios de derecho : 5-25, abril 1942.
Petroleum legislation. See also pp. 27-47.

LOZANO GARCES, R. : Critica de la posesión en el proyecto de nuevo código de minas. Estudios de derecho 4 : 201-228, agosto 1942.

GIBSON, W.M. : International law and Colombian constitutionalism. American journal of international law 36 : 614-620, October 1942.

GARCÉS, R.L. : Affirmación y negación de la posesión minera. Estudios de derecho : 353-377, noviembre 1942.

COMMONWEALTH

EVATT, H.V. : The discretionary authority of Dominion Governors. Canadian bar review 18 : 1-9, January 1940.

Native appellants to the Privy Council. Anti-slavery reporter and aborigines' friend 29 : 123-126, January 1940.

FRIEND, W.L. : A survey of Anglo-American legal bibliography. Law library journal 33 : 1-18, January 1940.

DALE, W.L. : War legislation in the Colonial Empire. Journal of comparative legislation and international law 22 : 1-11, February 1940.

KEITH, B. : Notes on imperial constitutional law. Journal of comparative legislation and international law 22 : 209-225, November 1940.

ASPINALL, A. : Constitutional changes in the British West Indies. Journal of comparative legislation and international law 22 : 129-135, November 1940.

Colonial constitutions. Economist 141 : 403-404, 4 October 1941.

HARRISON, W.N. : The statute of Westminster and Dominion sovereignty. Australian law journal 17 : 282-286, 314-318, 21 January, 18 February 1944.

Married women's nationality. Women in council newsletter : 2, June 1944.

NATIONAL LAW - COUNTRIES

LEWIN, J. : Native courts and British justice in Africa. Africa 14 : 448-453, October 1944.

LAWSON, F.H. : Uniformity of laws: a suggestion. Journal of comparative legislation and international law 26 : 16-27, November 1944.

CONGO (KINSHASA)

JENTGEN : Etudes sur le droit cambiaire, préliminaires à l'introduction au Congo belge d'une législation relative au chègue. Institut royal colonial be belge, Bulletin des séances 14 : 256-260, no. 2, 1943.
Premier article d'une série.

CUBA

CORTINA y CORRALES, Y.M. : El regimen de la nacionalidad en la constitución cubana de 1940. Revista de derecho internacional 19 : 151-189, junio 1940.

Proyecto de reforma del Código Civil para armonizario con la nueva Constitución de la República. Revista cubana de derecho 15 : 28-78, enero-marzo 1941.

QUINTANA, S.V.L. : La nueva Constitución politica de la República de Cuba. Boletin de la Unión Panamericana 76 : 259-263, mayo 1942.

CZECHOSLOVAKIA

SCELLE, G. : Le Gouvernement de la Tchécoslovaquie. Europe centrale 15 : 8-10, 10 janvier 1940.

FUCHS : Die deutsche Verwaltung im Protektorat Böhmen und Mähren. Zeitschrift der Akademie für deutsches Recht 7 : 91-93, 15. März 1940.

KLEIN, F. : Die Staats- und völkerrechtliche Stellung des Protektorats Böhmen und Mähren. Archiv des öffentlichen Rechts 31 : 255-277, 3. Heft 1940.

GUNTHER, E. : Slowakei - Übersicht über die wesentliche Gesetzgebung vom 14. März 1939 bis 31. Dezember 1939. Zeitschrift für osteuropäisches Recht 6 : 382-390, März-April 1940.

LUBY, S. : Das in der Slowakei geltende Privatrecht. Zeitschrift für osteuropäisches Recht 6 : 319-339, März-April 1940.

RABL, K.O. : Verfassungsrecht und Verfassungsleben in der neuen Slowakei. Zeitschrift für ausländisches öffentliches Recht und Völkerrecht 9 : 821-880, Heft 4, 1940.

GLOBKE, H. : Die Protektoratsangehörigkeit. Zeitschrift für osteuropäisches Recht 6 : 447-457, Mai-Juni 1940.

KARPAT, J. : Die Gauverfassung der Slowakei. Zeitschrift für osteuropäisches Recht 7 : 28-46, Juli-August 1940.

RABL, K.O. : Verfassungsrecht und Verfassungsleben in der neuen Slovakei. Zeitschrift für ausländisches öffentliches Recht und Völkerrecht 10 : 127-167, Oktober 1940.

KORKISCH, F. : Die Neuregelung der Staatsangehörigkeit in den Gebieten der früheren Tschechoslowakei. Zeitschrift für ausländisches öffentliches Recht und Völkerrecht 10 : 168-243, Oktober 1940.

GUNTHER, E. : Die Judengesetzgeburg in der Slowakei. Zeitschrift für osteuropäisches Recht 7 : 245-274, November-Dezember 1940.

GÜNTHER, E. : Slowakei - Übersicht über die wesentliche Gesetzgebung im Jahre 1940. Zeitschrift für osteuropäisches Recht 7 : 379-384, Januar-Februar 1941.

BISCOTTINI, G. : Sulla condizione giuridica del Protettorato di Boemia e Moravia. Rivista di diritto internazione 33 : 279-284, fasc. 4, 1941.

Abkommen vom 5. Februar 1941, zwischen dem Königreich Ungarn und der Slowakischen Republik über die gegenseitige Regelung einiger Fragen der Staatsangehörigkeit. Zeitschrift für osteuropäisches Recht 8 : 101-107, Juli-August 1941.

REINOLD, K. : Reichsrecht und Protektoratsrecht in Böhmen und Mähren in Zivilgerichtssachen. Zeitschrift für osteuropäisches Recht 8 : 113-143, September-Oktober 1941.

Slowakei - Übersicht über die wesentliche Gesetzgebung im Jahre 1941. Zeitschrift für osteuropäisches Recht 8 : 401-408, Januar-February 1942.

BÜRKLE : Der Aufbau der deutschen Rechtspflege in Böhmen und Mähren. Deutsches Recht 12 : 57-59, 15. März 1942.
See also pp. 59-62.

CASSIN, R. : La position internationale de la Tchécoslovaquie. Czechoslovak yearbook of international law : 60-66, March 1942.

WESTERMANN : Das Bodenrecht der Slowakei. Zeitschrift für osteuropäisches Recht 8 : 478-496, März-April 1942.

Das Recht in Böhmen und Mähren. Nation und Staat 15 : 295-298, Mai 1942.

DUKA-ZÓLYOMI, N. : Die Rechtsschöpfung in der Slowakei. Donaueuropa 2 : 742-745, Oktober 1942.

SCHWELB, E. : Czechoslovak legislation in exile. Central European observer 19 : 373-374, November 13, 1942.

DRUCKER, A. : The Czechoslovak Legal Council. Law journal 102 : 363, 14 November 1942.

SCHWELB, E. : Legislation in exile - Czechoslovakia. Journal of comparative legislation and international law 24 : 120-124, November 1942.

Slowakei - Verordnung vom 30. November 1940 über die jüdischen Unternehmungen. Zeitschrift für osteuropäisches Recht 10 : 112-123, Januar-Juni 1943.

TÁBORSKÝ, E. : The Czechoslovak juridical council. Modern law review 6 : 143-148, April 1943.

Slowakei - Verfassungsgesetz über den Verfassungssenat vom 4. Februar 1942. Zeitschrift für ausländisches öffentliches Recht und Völkerrecht 11 : 626-632, Oktober 1943.

Žaloby proti bÝv. Česko-slovenskej republike a bÝv. Slovenskej krajine pred slovenskÝmi súdmi. Hospodárstvo a právo 11 : 66-76, január 1944.

RONKE, M. : Fünf Jahre Rechtsentwicklung im Protektorat Böhmen und Mähren. Deutsches Recht 14 : 258-266, 22. u. 29. April 1944.

MATURA, A. : Základy verejnoprávneho hospodárstvo obci v Slovenskej republike. Hospodárstvo a právo 12 : 3-12, sept.-okt. 1944.

TABORSKY, E. : Czechoslovakia's experience with P.R. Journal of comparative legislation and international law 26 : 49-51, November 1944.

DENMARK

GÜNTHER, K. : Das Privatrecht in Dänemark. Zeitschrift für ausländisches und internationales Privatrecht 13 : 122-143, Heft 1/2, 1940.

CARSTENS, L. : Far den dansk Højesterets Praksis i 1940. Tidsskrift for rettsvitenskap 54 : 223-240, hefte 2, 1941.

BRÜEL, E. : Danmark og Island efter den 9. April 1940. Nordisk Tidsskrift for international Ret 13 : 29-39, Fasc. 1-2, 1942.

DRACHMANN BENTZON, A. : Fra den Danske Højesterets Praksis i 1941. Tidsskrift for rettsvitenskap 55 : 425-447, hefte 4, 1942.

DRACHMANN BENTZON, A., and KRARUP, O. : Fra den danske Højesterets Praksis i 1942. Tidsskrift for rettsvitenskap 56 : 527-549, hefte 5, 1943.

DOMINICAN REPUBLIC

MARCHANT, A. : Air carriers' liability for injury to passengers and goods in the Dominican Republic, Ecuador, Mexico and Venezuela. Air law review 12 : 283-298, No. 3, 1941.

TAVARES, F. : Notas de derecho procesal civil. Anales de la universidad de Santo Domingo 7 : 9-25, enero-marzo 1943.

ESTONIA

Anordnungen des Generalkommissars in Reval, 1942. Zeitschrift für osteuropäisches Recht 9 : 85-87, Juli-September 1942.

Estland - Übersicht über die wesentliche Gesetzgebung in den Jahren 1940 und 1941. Zeitschrift für osteuropäisches Recht 9 : 223-250, Oktober/Dezember 1942.

ETHIOPIA

Les arias d'une fondation ethiopienne en Terre-Sainte. Journal des tribunaux mixtes 21 : 4-5, 4 et 5 février 1942.

A proclamation relating to land acquired by the Italians. New times and Ethiopia news 7 : 4, 13 February 1943.

GUIRGUIS, T.T.W. : A proclamation to establish Kadis' courts. New times and Ethiopia news 7 : 1, 27 March 1943.

Ethiopian provincial administration. New Times and Ethiopia news : 3-4, 6 March 1943.

Enemy properties in Ethiopia. New times and Ethiopia news 8 : 3, 25 September 1943.

BENTWICH, N. : Law and justice in Ethiopia. Contemporary review 165 : 267-271, May 1944.

The new era - Establishment of law courts. New times and Ethiopia news 9 : 1-2, 15 July 1944.

FINLAND

SJÖSTRÖM, B. : Rassegna di letteratura giuridica finlandese, anni 1925-1928. Annuario di diritto comparato e di studi legislativi 10 : 1-28, parte prima, 1940.

HAATAJA, K. : Le droit agraire social en Finlande. Bulletin international de droit agricole 3 : 21-45, no. 1, 1942.

ARVELO, A.P. : Nouvelles dispositions législatives pénales en 1939-1942. Recueil de documents en matière pénale et pénitentiaire 10 : 237-242, mai 1943.

LINDMAN, S. : La constitution républicaine de la Finlande est en vigueur depuis 25 ans. Nord 7 : 259-266, no. 3-4, 1944.

GULDBERG, T. : Finns det någon folkrätt? Mellanfolkligt samarbete 14 : 134-136, no. 6, 1944.

FRANCE

RIPERT, G. : La réforme de l'adoption. Dalloz, Recueil hebdomadaire de jurisprudence 17 : 1-4, 11 janvier 1940.

BRODEUR, J. : The injunction in French jurisprudence. Tulane law review 14 : 211-224, February 1940.

HAMEL, J. : Le droit des sociétés par actions et la protection des actionnaires mobilisés. Revue politique et parlementaire 47 : 68-81, 10 avril 1940.

SUMIEN, P. : La législation de guerre des asurances terrestres. Dalloz, Recueil hebdomadaire de jurisprudence 17 : 13-16, 25 avril 1940.

ALIBERT, R. : The French Conseil d'État. Modern law review 3 : 257-271, April 1940.

Rénovation de la carrière préfectorale et réprganisation du ministère de l'Intérieur. Documents français 2 : 1-16, novembre 1940.

KIRCHHEIMER, O. : Decree powers and constitutional law in France under the Third Republic. American political science review 34 : 1104-1123, December 1940.

CORDONNIER, P. : Loi du 16 novembre 1940 relative aux sociétés anonymes. Dalloz, Recueil critique (Législation) : 1-19, 1er cahier 1941.

LALOU, H. : L'"incapacité" de l'homme marié. Dalloz, Recueil critique (Chronique) : 1-4, ler cahier 1941.

DESQUEYRAT, A. : La réforme des institutions départementales. Cité nouvelle : 747-760, 25 avril 1941.

PICARD, M. : L'assurance contre les risques de guerre et la réparation des dommages de guerre. Dalloz, Recueil critique (Chronique) : 13-16, 4e cahier 1941.

DESQUEYRAT, A. : La nouvelle loi sur le divorce. Cité nouvelle : 962-973, 25 mai 1941.

LEPOINTE, G. : Les crimes et délits contre la patrie. Dalloz, Recueil critique (Législation) : 42-52, 52 cahier 1941.

France - L'organisation corporative. Bulletin de législation comparée 1 : 648-667, 2e trimestre 1941.

DUCLOS, R. : La Charte du travail. Chronique sociale de France 50 : 265-279, octobre-novembre-décembre 1941.

GABOLDE, M. : L'activité législative en matière pénale et pénitentiaire du mois de juillet 1940 au mois de juillet 1941. Recueil de documents en matière pénale et pénitentiaire 9 : 313-319, novembre 1941.

DUVERGER, M. : La situation des fonctionnaires depuis la révolution de 1940. Revue du droit public et de la science politique 57 : 277-332, 417-539, juin, décembre 1941.

Remarques sur les constitutions. Revue des deux mondes 111 : 296-302, 1 décembre 1941.

BARTHELEMY, J. : Le ministre de la justice. Documents français 3 : 2-5, décembre 1941.
Voir aussi pp. 6-28.

ARRIGHI de CASANOVA, E. : Les réformes apportées par le code de la famille au code civil. Annales de la Faculté de droit d'Aix : 25-58, nouvelle série no. 33, 1941.

JARTOT, G. : Charte du travail et catholiques sociaux. Cité nouvelle : 26-42, 10 janvier 1942.

HEDEMANN, J.W. : Wirtschaftsrecht in Frankreich. Zeitschrift für ausländisches und internationales Privatrecht 14 : 116-155, Heft 1/2, 1942.

GROSSE, F. : Die neue französische Sozialverfassung. Neue internationale Rundschau der Arbeit 2 : 147-164, Heft 2, 1942.

OLIVIER, M. : A propos de la Charte du travail. Droit social 5 : 24-26, février 1942.
Voir aussi pp. 18-40.

L'administration du pays. Documents français 4 : 1-30, mars 1942.

The French Labour Charter. International labour review 45 : 269-285, March 1942.

DETEUF, A. : Problèmes de la corporation. Droit social 5 : 49-53, avril 1942.

BELIN, R. : La Charte du travail. Documents français 4 : 3-7, avril 1942.
Voir aussi pp. 8-15.

SHAETZEL, W. : Französisches Schrifttum zum Etat français. Zeitschrift für öffentliches Recht 22 : 383-394, Heft 4-5, 1942.

CHRÉTIEN, M. : Le nouveau régime des associations sans but pécuniaire ou professionel. Revue du droit public et de la science politique 58 : 125-148, avril-juin 1942.

DEMONDION, P. : La Charte du travail et l'artisanat. Droit social 5 : 96-102, juin 1942.

GROSSE, F. : La nouvelle charte sociale de la France. Nouvelle revue internationale du travail 2 : 146-162, 2me trimestre 1942.

BOUCAUD, C. : La tendance moderne à la socialisation du droit. Chronique sociale de France 51 : 288-294, septembre-octobre 1942.

BONNARD, R. : Les actes constitutionnels de 1940. Revue du droit public et de la science politique 58 : 46-90, 149-179, 258-279, 301-375, janvier-mars, avril-juin, juillet-septembre, octobre-décembre 1942.

DURAND, P. : Idéologie et technique de la Charte du travail. Collection droit social : 2-15, no. 13, 1942.

RIPERT, F. : Le régime administratif de la ville de Marseille. Annales de la Faculté de droit d'Aix : 135-160, nouville série, no. 35, 1942.

LALOU, H. : L'année législative française 1942. Dalloz, Recueil critique (Chronique) : 1-4, ler cahier 1943.

SOLUS, H. : Mari et femme sous la loi du 22 septembre 1942. Revue trimestrielle de droit civil 42 : 81-98, avril-juin 1943.

ROUX, M. de : La justice en échec sous la IIIe République. Revue universelle : 699-706, 10 mai 1943.

Comités sociaux - Organisation, fonctionnement, réalisations, projects. Documents français 5 : 1-31, mai 1943.
France.

LALOU, H. : Revue semestrielle de la législation française, ler semestre 1943. Dalloz, Recueil critique (Chronique) : 9-12, 7e cahier 1943.

VAUNOIS, L. : Lettre de France. Droit d'auteur 56 : 75-81, 15 juillet 1943.

VANDAMME, J. : Contribution à l'étude de le revendication des épaves terrestres. Revue trimestrielle de droit civil 42 : 157-171, juillet-septembre 1943.

La réforme du dépôt légal. Recueil de jurisprudence et d'études administratives 1 : 161-172, septembre 1943.

DURAND, P. : La notion de faute lourde du voitururier et la guerre. Bulletin des transports internationaux par chemins de fer 10 : 354-368, Oktober 1943.

VOIRIN, P. : Loi du 22 septembre 1942 sur les effets du mariage quant aux droits et devoirs des époux. Dalloz, Recueil critique (Législation) : 50-60, 10e cahier 1943.

LAMPUE, P. : Le contentieux de l'annulation devant les tribunaux administratifs locaux du premier degré. Recueil de jurisprudence et d'études administratives 1 : 3-48, 3-32, octobre-novembre 1943.

LÉCLUSIER, J. : Assurance et dommages de guerre. Journal de la marine marchande 25 : 1445-1447, 25 novembre 1943.

La charte du travail. Documents français 5 : 1-15, novembre 1943.

L'organisation professionnelle des assurances. Collection droit social 19 : 1-60, novembre 1943.

VERDIÉ, M. : La reconstitution des entreprises industrielles et commerciales sinistrées. Droit social 6 : 357-359, décembre 1943.

DELEBEZ, L. : La revision constitutionnelle de 1942. Revue du droit public et de la science politique 59 : 93-115, 1943.

BERLIA, G. : La loi constitutionnelle du 10 juillet 1940. Revue du droit public et de la science politique 60 : 45-57, janvier-mars 1944.

Bibliographie des ouvrages sur le droit civil. Revue trimestrielle de droit civil 43 : 20-24, janvier-mars 1944.

Ordonnances portant création d'un Bureau africain du droit d'auteur et du Bureau africain des gens de lettres (du 14 avril 1943). Droit d'auteur 57 : 37-41, 15 avril 1944.

KALL : Die Entwicklung des Privat- und Prozessrechts im Elsass seit Juni 1940. Deutsches Recht 14 : 266-271, 22. u. 29. April 1944.

MASPETIOL, R. : La notion de service d'intérêt public et la théorie juridique des institutions corporatives. Droit social 7 : 165-170, mai 1944.

MIRKINE-GUETZÉVITCH, B. : Le problème de la stabilité gouvernementale. Avenir 2 : 1-3, juillet 1944.

BAECQUE, F. de : Règles de la jurisprudence administrative relatives à la réparation du préjudice en cas de mise en oeuvre de la responsabilité de la puissance publique. Revue du droit public et de la science politique 60 : 197-230, juillet-septembre 1944.

BERLIA, G. : Ordonnance du 9 août 1944 relative au rétablissement de la légalité républicaine sur le territoire continental. Revue du droit public et de la science politique 60 : 315-321, octobre-décembre 1944.

JÈZE, G. : Contrôle juridictionnel de la légalité des mesures exceptionnelles prises par les autorités locales en exercice de leur compétence extraordinaire dans les circonstances de guerre. Revue du droit public et de la science politique 60 : 322-344, octobre-décembre 1944.

FRANCE
(International law, Aliens, Nationality)

BENOIST-MAUPAS, J. : La nouvelle législation française sur la nationalité. Nouvelle revue de droit international privé 8 : 7-68, 1941.

DOMKE, M.: Problems of international law in French jurisprudence 1939-1941. American journal of international law 36 : 24-36, January 1942.

BENOIST, J. : L'interprétation des traités. Nouvelle revue de droit international privé 9 : 7-36, 1942.

France : Das deutsche Strafrecht im Elsass. Deutsches Recht (Ausgabe B) 12 : 262, 15. Dezember 1942.

NIBOYET, J.-P. : Les mesures d'élimination des Français d'origine étrangère, et des étrangers dans le domaine des principales activités. Droit social 6 : 50-55, février 1943.

LA PRADELLE, A. de : Da la validité en France des mariages contractés en Espagne pendant la révolution. Nouvelle revue de droit international privé 11 : 94-112, janvier-mars 1944.

ANDRE-PRUDHOMME : La souveraineté actuelle de la loi française devant les juridictions étrangères. Journal du droit international 67-72: 13-22, janvier-mars 1945.

GERMANY

Überblick über die wichtigsten Gesetze und Verordnungen seit Kriegsbeginn. Deutsche Justiz 102 : 4-6, 4. Januar 1940.

HEFERMEHL : Kriegswirtschaftsrecht. Deutsche Justiz 102 : 85-88, 19. Januar 1940.

FRIESLER, R. : Zur Verordnung über asserordentliche Rundfunkmassnahmen. Deutsche Justiz 102 : 105-108, 26. Januar 1940.

WENGLER, W. : Das deutsche Privatrecht im Protektorat Böhmen und Mähren und im Generalgouvernement Polen. Zeitschrift der Akademie für deutsches Recht 7 : 105-108, 1. April 1940.

BORNHAK, C. : Weimarer Verfassung und Führerstaat. Zeitschrift für öffentliches Recht 20 : 573-593, Heft 4-6, 1940.

ROEDER, H. : Die Ueberwindung des individualistischen Rechtsdenken im Dritten Reich. Zeitschrift für öffentliches Recht 21 : 75-93, Heft 1, 1941.

HARMENING, R. : La législation relative aux domaines paysans héréditaires en Allemagne. Bulletin international de droit agricole 2 : 1-31, No. 1, 1941.

WEBER, W. : Führererlass und Führerverordnung. Zeitschrift für die gesamte Staatswissenschaft 102 : 101-137, 1. Heft 1941.

FRANK, H. : Technik des Staates. Zeitschrift der Akademie für deutsches Recht 8 : 2-6, 1. Januar 1941.

NATIONAL LAW - COUNTRIES

GROSSMANN-DOERTH, H. : Alte und neue Probleme des Handelsrechts und die heutige HGB-Erläuterung. Zeitschrift der Akademie für deutsches Recht 8 : 121 -124, 15. April 1941.

PFEIFER, H. : Die verfassungsrechtliche Einordnung der neuen Gebiete. Zeitschrift für öffentliches Recht 21 : 580-597, 5. Heft 1941.

KOHLRAUSCH, E. : Die Strafbarkeit der Umgehung des Blutschutzgesetzes. Zeitschrift der Akademie für deutsches Recht 8 : 185-188, 15. Juni 1941.

FRANK, H. : Das Reichsverwaltungsgericht. Deutsches Recht (Ausgabe B) 11 : 152-155, 15. Juni 1941.

KESSLER : Die Kriegsgesetzgebung und ihre Auswirkung. Deutsches Recht (Ausgabe B) 11 : 225-236, 15. September 1941.

BEST, W. : Die deutsche Militärverwaltung in Frankreich. Reich, Volksordnung, Lebensraum 1 : 29-76, 1941.

FREISLER, R. : Grundsätzliches zur Ministerratsverordnung über das Strafrecht gegen Polen und Juden. Deutsches Recht (Ausgabe B) 12 : 2-6, 15. Januar 1942.

RHODE, H. : Zur systematischen Stellung des deutschen Sozialrechtes. Neue internationale Rundschau der Arbeit 2 : 109-115, Heft 2, 1942.

RIESE, O. : La réforme actuelle du droit civil allemand et ses tendances dominantes. Zeitschrift für schweizerisches Recht 61 : 247-280, Heft 2, 1942.

COLLIARD, C.A. : Le régime disciplinaire des fonctionnaires allemands. Revue de droit public et de la science politique 58 : 1-45, janvier-mars 1942.

WENGLER, W. : Anwendungsbereich deutschen Erbrechts. Zeitschrift der Akademie für deutsches Recht 9 : 41-43, 1. Februar 1942.

The national-socialist conception of law. Polish fortnightly review : 1-8, 15 March 1942.
Series of articles.

WALZ, G.A. : Ius privatum oder ius arcanum? Zeitschrift der Akademie für deutsches Recht 9 : 99-101, 1. April 1942.

BEURMANN : Das Sondergericht Danzig, ain Sondergericht des deutschen Ostens. Deutsches Recht (Ausgabe B) 12 : 78-82, 15. April 1942.

BESSELMANN : Deutsches interlokales Ehescheidungsrecht - Zur Scheidung von Ehen zwischen deutschen Staatsangehörigen und Protektoratsangehörigen. Zeitschrift der Akademie für deutsches Recht 9 : 145-149, 15. Mai 1942.

Der Verwaltungsaufbau des Reichskommissariats Ostland und deine Voraussetzungen. Nation und Staat 15 : 262-269, Mai 1942.

BECHER : Von der Tätigkeit des Hanseatischen Sondergerichts. Deutsches Recht (Ausgabe B) 12 : 122-126, 15. Juni 1942.

BAUMBACH : Die neueste Vereinfachung des Zivilprozesses. Zeitschrift der Akademie für deutsches Recht 9 : 179-181, 15. Juni 1942.

SCHWARZ : Wandlung des Strafrechts im Kriege. Zeitschrift der Akademie für deutsches Recht 9 : 209-211, 15. Juli 1942.

SCHÖNKE : Die weitere Vereinfachung der Strafrechtspflege. Zeitschrift der Akademie für deutsches Recht 9 : 259-262, 15. September 1942.

BOCKELMANN, P. : Volksschädlingsverordnung und Tätertyp. Zeitschrift der Akademie für deutsches Recht 9 : 293-296, 15. Oktober 1942.

BRASS : Rechtsvergleichende Betrachtungen zu einem neuen Konkursrecht. Zeitschrift der Akademie für deutsches Recht 9 : 329-330, 15 November 1942.

SCHMIDT-LEICHNER : La loi du 4 Septembre 1941 portant modification du Code pénal du Reich. Recueil de documenzs en matière pénale et pénitentiaire 10 : 125-131, novembre 1942.

SCHWARZ : Richter und Staatsanwalt im neuen Strafprozessrecht. Zeitschrift der Akademie für deutsches Recht 9 : 337-340, 1. Dezember 1942.

Wert der Entwürfe - Arbeit am Volksgesetzbuch. Zeitschrift der Akademie für deutsches Recht 10 : 3-6, 1. Januar 1943.

THIERACK : Die Kriegsaufgaben der Akademie für deutsches Recht für die Gesetzgebung. Zeitschrift der Akademie für deutsches Recht 10 : 1-3, 1. Januar 1943.

OLCZEWSKI : Rassenpolitik im Rechtsleben. Deutsche Rechtspfleger 54 : 9, 15. Januar 1943.

LANGE, H. : Wesen und Gestalt des Volksgesetzbuchs. Zeitschrift für die gesamte Staatswissenschaft 103 : 208-259, Januar 1943.

STAUD : Die vierte Vereinfachungsverordnung in ihrer Bedeutung für die Entwicklung des Verfahrensrechts. Zeitschrift der Akademie für deutsches Recht 10 : 21-25, 1. Februar 1943.

DANCKELMANN, B. : Bedeutung des mitwirkenden Verschuldens im Kriegsschädenrecht. Zeitschrift der Akademie für deutsches Recht 10 : 81-84, 10. April 1943.

The place of law in Germany. Law quarterly review 59 : 134-149, April 1943.

ARNDT, J. : Der Begriff der "Deutschstämmigkeit". Nation und Staat 16 : 214-217, April-Mai 1943.

RYCZYNSKI, K. : Vornamen sind keine Modeartikel. Deutsche Rechtspfleger 54 : 104-105, 15. Mai 1943.
Control of Christian names.

KRATZ : Zweifelsfragen aus der Besteuerung geistlicher Order und Kongregationen. Deutsche Steuer-Zeitung 37 : 226-234, 19. Mai 1943.

SCHRODER, H. : Zum Aufbau der deutschen Gerichte. Zeitschrift der Akademie für deutsches Recht 10 : 175-177, 10. August 1943.

HAEGELE : Zur Todeserklärung von Kriegsvermissten. Deutsche Rechtspfleger 54 : 172-173, 15. August 1943.

PFEIFER, H. : Zur Neuordnung der Verwaltungsgerichtsbarkeit im Reich. Zeitschrift der Akademie für deutsches Recht 10 : 185-189, 10. September 1943.

WESTERMANN, H. : Die Neugestaltung des Liegenschaftsrechts als Teil des Bodenverfassung rechts. Zeitschrift der Akademie für deutsches Recht 10 : 189-193, 10. September 1943.

HAEGELE : Die Anordnung von Abwesenheitspflegschaften während des Krieges. Deutsche Rechtspfleger 54 : 192-193, 15. September 1943.

MEGOW, D. : Das System des Kriegsschädenrechts. Deutsche Volkswirtschaft 12 : 929-933, 3. Oktoberheft 1943.

KUMMER, H. : Öffentliches und privates Recht in der politischen Grundordnung. Zeitschrift für die gesamte Staatswissenschaft 104 : 29-74, Oktober 1943.

WAGNER, M. : Das Militärtestament. Zeitschrift der Akademie für deutsches Recht 10 : 223-226, 10. November 1943.

Die derzeitige Regelung der Verjährung. Deutsche Wirtschafts-Zeitung 41 : 9, 17. Januar 1944.

HAEGELE, K. : Zur Weiterentwicklung des Erbhofrechts. Deutsche Rechtspfleger 55 : 5-9, 15. Januar 1944.

HEINTZE, J. : Das Interregnum ohne Hauptversammlung. Bankwirtschaft: 68-71, 15. Februar 1944.
Joint stock companies.

MASON, J.B. : The judicial system of the Nazi party. American political science review 38 : 96-103, February 1944.

OLCZEWSKI, H. : Reformen und Kriegsnotrecht im Strafverfahren, der Strafvollstreckung und im Strafvollzuge. Deutsche Rechtspfleger 55 : 30-33, 15. Februar-15. März 1944.

HESSE, W. : Militärtestamente. Deutsche Justiz 12 : 109-117, 31. März 1944.

GRÜNHUT, M. : The development of the German penal system 1920-1932. Canadian bar review 22 : 198-252, March 1944.

WEBER, W. : Zuständigkeit und Zukunft der Verwaltungsgerichte. Zeitschrift für die gesamte Staatswissenschaft 104 : 424-450, Heft 4, 1944.

BÜHLER : Um die Prinzipien im Kriegssachsschädenrecht. Deutsches Recht 14 : 313-319, 6. u. 13. Mai, 1944.

WITTE : Vereinfachungen auf dem Gebiete des bürgerlichen Streitverfahrens. Deutsche Rechtspfleger 55 : 96-98, 15. Juni 1944.

HAAG : Der Staatsanwalt. Deutsche Justiz 12 : 209-213, 21. Juli 1944.

LÄMMLE : Aus der Rechtsprechung des Volksgerichtshofs zum allgemeinen Teil des Strafgesetzbuchs. Deutsches Recht 14 : 505-508, 22 u. 29 Juli 1944.

WILKE : Zur grundsätzlichen Regelung des Umfangs der Entaignungsentschädigung im künftigen Reichsrecht. Zeitschrift der Akademie für deutsches Recht 11 : 113-117, 10. Juli 1944.

KAHN-FREUND, O. : The Weimar constitution. Political quarterly 15 : 229-235, July-September 1944.

VOLKMAR : Abschied von der Verhandlungsmaxime? Zeitschrift der Akademie für deutsches Recht 11 : 136-140, August 1944.

WOLANY : Zur personen-, familien- und erbrechtlichen Stellung der deutschen Rückwanderer aus der Ukraine. Deutsches Recht 14 : 634-646, 2. u. 9. September 1944.

WEISE : Übersicht über die Spruch- und Verwaltungsentscheidungen in Kriegsschädensachen. Deutsches Recht 14 : 673-720, 16. u, 23. September 1944.

LEHMANN, H. : Der Entwurf des I. Buches des künftigen VGB im Vergleich mit neueren Kodifikationen. Zeitschrift der Akademie für deutschen Recht 11 : 153-155, September 1944.

BEHRENS : Richter und Staatsanwalt als politischer Leiter. Deutsches Recht 14 : 786-788, 15. Oktober 1944.

BABROWSKI, H. : Die Ausgabe von Ersatzstücken bei Kriegsschäden an Wertpapieren. Bankwirtschaft : 397-399, 1. November 1944.

OLSWALD, W.M. : Die Bestrafung der Naziverbrecher nach deutschen Recht. Zeitung 4 : 4, 1. Dezember 1944.

GERMANY
(Copyright, Patents, Trademarks)

KIRCHHOFF, H. : Sind Patente im Kriege überflüssig? Deutsche Volkswirtschaft 13 : 579-582, 2. Juliheft 1944.

SCHWABE : Vergeltungsmassnahmen im Urheberrecht. Deutsches Recht 14 : 566-570, 5. u. 12. August 1944.

GERMANY
(International law and practice, Aliens, Naturalization)

WEIDEN, P. : German confiscations of American securities. New York University law quarterly review 17 : 200-240, January 1940.

GLOBKE, H. : Die Staatsangehörigkeit der volksdeutschen Umsiedler. Deutsche Verwaltung 17 : 18-22, 25. Januar 1940.

HEFERMEHL : Die Behandlung des feindlichen Vermögens. Deutsche Justiz 102 : 165-170, 9. Februar 1940.

ROTHENBERGER, C. : Problems aus der Praxis des Deutschen Prisenhofs Hamburg. Zeitschrift der Akademie für deutsches Recht 7 : 73-74, 1. März 1940.

BRÜGMANN, U. : Die Verordnung über die Behandlung feindlichen Vermögens vom 15. Januar 1940. Deutsche Verwaltung 17 : 104-106, 10. April 1940.

MÖRRING, P. : Die Behandlung feindlichen Vermögens im Inland. Zeitschrift der Akademie für deutsches Recht 7 : 125-127, 15. April 1940.

Übersicht über die Verträge zur Regelung der handelspolitischen Beziehungen des Deutschen Reiches zu anderen Staaten nach dem Stande vom 31. Dezember 1939. Jahrbuch für auswärtige Politik 6 : 216-261, 1940.
See also pp. 262-266.

ROTHENBERGER, C. : Aus der Rechsprechung des deutschen Prisenhofs Hamburg im Jahre 1940. Zeitschrift der Akademie für deutsches Recht 8 : 12-15, 1. Januar 1941.

STREBEL : Die Behandlung des feindlichen Vermögens. Zeitschrift für ausländisches öffentliches Recht und Völkerrecht 10 : 887-919, Nr. 3/4, 1941.

STUCKART : Die Staatsangehörigkeit in den eingegliederten Gebieten. Zeitschrift der Akademie für deutsches Recht 8 : 233-237, 1. August 1941.

KÜLLER, H. : Kriegsschäden an deutschem Eigentum im Ausland. Deutsche Volkswirt 16 : 83-84, 17. Oktober 1941.

GLOBKE, H. : Der Zusatzvertrag zum deutsch-slowakischen Staatsangehörigkeitsvertrag. Zeitschrift für osteuropäisches Recht 8 : 278-283, November-Dezember 1941.

VOLKMAR : Der Rechtshilfeverkehr mit der Slowakei und Ungarn. Zeitschrift für osteuropäisches Recht 8 : 351-356, Januar-Februar 1942.

GLOBKE, H. : Die Verordnung zur Regelung von Staatsangehörigkeitsfragen gegenüber dem Protektorat Böhmen und Mähren. Zeitschrift für osteuropäisches Recht 8 : 373-380, Januar-Februar 1942.

SCHLEGELBERGER, F. : Wege und Ziele des deutschen internationalen interterritorialen und interpersonalen Familienrechts. Zeitschrift für ausländisches und internationales Privatrecht 14 : 1-17, Heft 1/2, 1942.

WOLFF, E. : Die Ausbürgerung der Juden. Zeitung : 4, 20. Februar 1942.
Decree of 25 November 1941.

GLEISPACH, von : Zur Erneuerung des Auslieferungsgesetzes. Zeitschrift der Akademie für deutsches Recht 9 : 65-68, 1. März 1942.

KAUFFMANN, A. : Denationalisation and expropriation - The German law depriving Jewish emigrants of nationality and property, and its effects. Law journal 92 : 93-94, 21 March 1942.

ABEL, P. : The new German denationalisation law. Free Austria 2 : 6, April 1942.

SATTER, K. : Die Anerkennung ausländischer Entscheidungen in Ehesachen. Zeitschrift der Akademie für deutsches Recht 9 : 132-134, 1. Mai 1942.

METTGENBERG, W. : Das deutsche Reich liefert einen Deutschen nicht aus. Zeitschrift der Akademie für deutsches Recht 9 : 227-228, 15. August 1942.

SCHOLZ, F. : Ausschliessung eines Gesellschaftes feindlicher Staatsangehörigkeit aus der GmBH. Zeitschrift der Akademie für deutsches Recht 10 : 71-73, 15. März 1943.

STUCKART, W. : Staatsangehörigkeit und Reichsgestaltung. Reich, Volksordnung, Lebensraum 5 : 57-91, 1943.

RICHTER, H. : Auslandsverflochtene Unternehmen im Kriegssachschädenrecht. Devisenarchiv 8 : 225-229, 251-253, 18. September, 23. Oktober 1943.

Auslieferungsstatistik für das Jahr 1943. Deutsche Justiz 12 : 186-187, 23. Juni 1944.

SCHECHTMANN, J.B. : The option in the Reich's treaties on the transfer of population. American journal of international law 38 : 356-374. July 1944.

GREAT BRITAIN

QUEKETT, A.S. : Divorce law reform in Northern Ireland. Journal of comparative legislation and international law 22 : 32-35, February 1940.

PERKINS, J.A. : Permanent advisory Committee to the British Government Departments. American political Science review 34 : 85-96, February 1940.

PAGE, L. : The reform of criminal law administration. Quarterly review 274 : 278-292, April 1940.

McNAIR, A.D. : Frustration of contract by war. Law quarterly review 56 : 173-207, April 1940.

HARTLEY, H. : British war controls : the legal framework. Manchester school 11 : 163-176, October 1940.

KEITH, A.B. : The war and the Constitution (Contd.). Modern law review 4 : 82-103, October 1940.

WADE, H.W.B. : The principle of impossibility in contract. Law quarterly review 56 : 519-556, October 1940.

CARR, C.T. : Crisis legislation in Britain. Columbia law review 40 : 1309-1325, December 1940.

KEETON, G.W. : The law of landlord and tenant - post-war problem. Political quarterly 12 : 29-39, January-March 1941.

HARTLEY, H. : English local government, the war and reform. Britain to-day : 4-8. 4 April 1941.

McILWAIN, C.H. : Our heritage from the law of Rome. Foreign affairs 19 : 597-608, April 1941.
Roman and English law.

LAWSON, H.B. : War damage Act 1941. Journal of the institute of bankers 62 : 35-46, April 1961.

FINER, M. : The War damage Act, 1941. Modern law review 5 : 54-63, July 1941.

MEGARRY, R.E. : "Actual military service" and soldiers' privileged wills. Law quarterlx review 57 : 481-489, October 1941.

STURGESS, H.A.C. : War and the Inns of Court. Canadian bar review 19 : 590-597, October 1941.
The library collection.

McNAIR, A.D. : Effect of war upon contracts. Transactions of the Grotius Society, Problems of peace and war 27 : 182-213, 1941.

CHASE, E.P. : The war and the English Constitution. American political science review 36 : 86-98, February 1942.

CARR, C.T. : A regulated liberty - War-time Regulations and judicial review in Great Britain. Columbia law review 42 : 339-355, March 1942.

NATIONAL LAW - COUNTRIES

JONES, R.W. : Notes on the War Damage Act, 1941, Part 1. Journal of the Institute of Bankers 63 : 60-68, April 1942.

KEETON, G.W. : The problem of law reforms after the war. Law quarterly review 58 : 247-256, April 1942.

War damage and equity. Investor's chronicle 162 : 543-544, 2 May 1942.

War damage. Economist 142 : 760, 30 May 1942.

Administration of aliens' estates in war-time. Law journal 92 : 230-231, 18 July 1942.

CAMPBELL, A.H. : A note on the word "jurisprudence". Law quarterly review 58 : 334-339, July 1942.

JONES, R.W. : The War damage (Amendment) Act, 1942. Journal of the Institute of bankers 63 : 171-176, October 1942.

STEWART, J. McG. : The abuse of freedom. Canadian bar review 20 : 649-658, October 1942.

Statute of Westminster. Current notes on international affairs 13 : 140-143, 16 November 1942.

Statutory rules and orders. Law journal 92 : 356-357, 364, 372-373, November 7, 14, 21, 1942.

HARVEY, C.P. : Law reforms after the war. Modern law review 6 : 39-46, December 1942.

Chancery decisions of 1942. Law journal 93 : 11-12, 19-21, 28-29, 36-37, January 9, 16, 23, 30, 1943.

Property and the war, 1942. Law journal 93 : 68-69, 27 February 1943.

Defence regulationa - Their amendment or annulment. Law journal 93 : 101-102, 27 March 1943.

The common law in 1942 - III. Contract. Law journal 93 : 131-133, 24 April 1943.

KAHN-FREUND, O. : Collective agreements under war legislation. Modern law review 6 : 112-143, April 1943.

War injuries to civilians. Law journal 93 : 174-175, 29 May 1943.

Lettre de Grande-Bretagne (contd.). Droit d'auteur 56 : 64-70, 15 juin 1943.

Company law reform. Economist 145 : 19-20, 3 July 1943.

Delegated legislation - Comments and illustrations arising out of a recent House of Commons debate (Contd.). Law journal 93 : 228-230, 17 July 1943.

Amendment of the companies act. Statist 140 : 521-522, 17 July 1943.

JONES, R.W. : Some further notes on war damage legislation. Journal of the institute of bankers 64 : 127-132, July 1943.

The exercise of emergency executive powers. Law journal 93 : 292-293, 11 September 1943.

FELLOWS, A. : The reform of company law. Fortnightly : 233-240, October 1943.

CROSSLEY VAINES, J. : Presumption of death. Law journal 93 : 356-357, 6 November 1943.

FRY, M. : The future treatment of the adult offender. Agenda 2 : 324-338, November 1943.

Company law reform. Statist 140 : 857-858, 4 December 1943.

Classification of war damage - An important stage reached. Law journal 93 : 397-398, 11 December 1943.

Interpretation sections and statutory definitions. Law journal 94 : 83-84, 92-93, March 11, 18, 1944.

ALLEN, C.K. : The 10,000 commandments : I. Spectator : 330-331, April 14, 1944.
Legislation of the future.

KAHN-FREUND, O. : Some reflections on company law reform. Modern law review 7 : 54-66, April 1944.

WORSLEY, J.W.B. : Developments in divorce. Quarterly review 282 : 163-177, April 1944.

Memorandum by the committee of London clearing bankers to the company law amendment committee. Journal of the institute of bankers 65 : 5077, April 1944.
See also pp. 78-130.

COHN, E.J. : Legal aid for the poor. Fortnightly 155 : 312-319, May 1944.

The Cohen committee hearing. Banker 70 : 69-75, May 1944.
Company law amendment.

Nuisance and war damage. Law journal 94 : 181-182, 3 June 1944.

QUILLA : Rules of practice of the judicial committee of the privy council. Law journal 94 : 179-181, 3 June 1944.

Delegated legislation. Round table : 204-210, June 1944.

SCHWARTZ, G.L. : Company law reform. Nineteenth century 135 : 257-265, June 1944.

La réparation des dommages de guerre... Grande Bretagne. Bulletin de législation comparée 4 : 193-314, 2e trimestre 1944.

LOGAN, D.W. : Post-war machinery of government - Delegated legislation (Contd.). Political quarterly 15 : 185-212, July-September 1944.

GREENE : Law and progress - The Haldane memorial lecture, 1944. Law journal 94 : 349-351, October 28 1944.

GREAT BRITAIN
(International law, Aliens)

WANG, H.K. : The "residence" of companies in the Income-Tax Act. Journal of comparative legislation and international law 22 : 166-177, November 1940.

JENNINGS, I. : The rule of law in total war. Yale law journal 50 : 365-386, January 1941.

NATIONAL LAW - COUNTRIES

COHN, E.J. : Legal aspects of internment. Modern law review 4 : 200-209, January 1941.
The internment of enemy aliens residing in Great Britain.

PARRY, C. : The Trading with the Enemy Act and the definition of an enemy. Modern law review 4 : 161-182, January 1941.

Diplomatic privilege. Law journal 91 : 107, 15 March 1941.
Foreign Governments in Great Britain.

FEIST, H.J. : The status of refugees. Modern law review 5 : 51-53, July 1941.

CHORLEY, R.S.T. : Allied Powers (Maritime Courts) Act, 1941. Modern law review 5 : 118-120, November 1941.

HOLDSWORTH, W.S. : The history of acts of State in English law. Columbia law review 41 : 1313-1331, December 1941.

The Allied maritime courts. Law quarterly review 58 : 41-52, January 1942.

SCHWELB, E. : The jurisdiction over the members of the Allied forces in Great Britain. Czechoslovak yearbook of international law : 147-171, March 1942.

HOLDSWORTH, W.S. : The treaty-making power of the Crown. Law quarterly review 58 : 175-183, April 1942.

McNAIR, A.D. : Procedural capacity of alien enemies - Statutes of limitation. Law quarterly review 58 : 191-231, April 1942.

Criminal jurisdiction and the American Forces. Law journal 92 : 267-268, 22 August 1942.

LACHS, R. : Allied Governments in exile - The effect of Allied legislation in Britain. Law journal 92 : 275-276, August 1942.

CREWE, W.G. : Die Rechtsstellung des amerikanischen Expeditionskorps in England. Auswärtige Politik 9 : 942-949, November 1942.

GRAUPNER, R. : Contractual stipulations conferring exclusive jurisdiction upon foreign courts in the law of England and Scotland. Law quarterly review 59 : 227-243, July 1943.

LACHS, R. : Foreign currencies in English courts. Law journal 93 : 299-300, 307, September 18, 25, 1943.

Alien enemy. Australasian insurance and banking record 67 : 414-415, 21 October 1943.

MANN, F.A. : Foreign investments and the law. Banker 68 : 62-65, November 1943.

SCHWELB, E. : The status of the United States forces in English law. American journal of international law 38 : 50-73, January 1944.

Claims against U.S. forces. Law journal 94 : 127, 15 April 1944.

MANN, F.A. : Judiciary and executive in foreign affairs. Transactions of the Grotius society 29 : 143-170, 1944.

GREECE

TSATSOS, C., and MIRASGHEZIS, D. : Rassegna di letteratura giuridica greca, anni 1925-1931. Annuario di diritto comparato e di studi legislativi 10 : 29-62, parte prima, (1940).

HELD, H.J. : Anwendung fremden Rechts in Griechenland (Internationales Privat- und Prozessrecht). Zeitschrift für öffentliches Recht 22 : 255-284, Heft 2-3, 1942.

SPIROPOULOS, J. : Griechisches internationales Privatrecht. Zeitschrift für öffentliches Recht 23 : 253-303, Heft 2/3, 1943.

GUATEMALA

SOLORZANO, R. : La letra de cambio, el pagaré y el cheque en Guatemala. Revista de derecho internacional 37 : 87-94, 31 marzo 1940.

Emergency legislation for the defense of personal economy. Revista de la economia nacional, Banco central de Guatemala 6 : 8-11, Mayo 1942.
See also pp. 27-34.

HUNGARY

ARATÒ, J. : Probleme der Wiedervereinigung der Ostungarischen und siebenbürgischen Gebiete mit Ungarn. Zeitschrift für osteuropäisches Recht 7 : 362-370, Januar-Februar 1941.

RÁCZ, G. : La constitution hongroise. Nouvelle revue de Hongrie 64 : 118-129, février 1941.

RÁCZ, G. : Le droit pénal hongrois 1920-1940. Nouvelle revue de Hongrie 64 : 208-215, mars 1941.

RONAY, F. : Die Privatgesetzgebung Ungarns seit 1925. Zeitschrift für ausländisches und internationales Privatrecht 13 : 536-572, Heft 3-4, 1941.

RÁCZ, G. : Le droit civil hongrois. Nouvelle revue de Hongrie 64 : 309-320, avril 1941.

HORVÁTH, K.R. : Gesetz vom 12. Juli 1940 über die Bestrafung einzelner Taten gegen die Sicherheit und die zwischenstaatlichen Interessen des ungarischen Staates. Zeitschrift für osteuropäisches Recht 7 : 618-623, Mai-Juni 1941.

KRUSCH, W. : Ungarns Privatrechtsgesetzbuch. Zeitschrift für osteuropäisches Recht 8 : 1-53, Juli-August 1941.

ARATÓ, I. : Rassenschutzmassnahmen in der ungarischen Ehegesetznovelle. Zeitschrift für osteuropäisches Recht 8 : 381-389, Januar-Februar 1942.
See also pp. 410-422.

Gesetzentwurf über die land- und forstwirtschaftlichen Liegenshaften der Juden in Ungarn. Glasul minoritatilor 20 : 82-88, Mai-Junie 1942.

CSIKY, J. : Die gesetzliche Regelungen der Judenfrage in Ungarn. Zeitschrift für osteuropäisches Recht 9 : 60-72, Juli-September 1942.

SZÁSZY, S. von : Das internationale Privatrecht Ungarns. Zeitschrift für öffentliches Recht 23 : 173-252, Heft 2/3, 1943.

Übersicht über die wesentliche Gesetzgebung im 4. Vierteljahr 1941 und im Jahr 1942. Zeitschrift für osteuropäisches Recht 10 : 131-134, Januar/Juni 1943.

VISKY, K. : Die Rechtsvereinheitlichung in Ungarn. Donaueuropa 3 : 270-279, April 1943.

HORVÁTH, E. : Die ungarische Rechtsakademie. Ungarn : 561-568, Dezemberheft 1943.

ICELAND

ARNÓRSSON, E. : Islandsk lovgivning i1938. Tidsskrift for Rettsvidenskap 53 : 98-105, I Hefte 1940.

BLOCH : Die Einwirkung des Krieges auf die Rechtsstellung Islands. Zeitschrift für ausländisches öffentliches Recht und Völkerrecht 10 : 804-815, Nr. 3/4, 1941.

INDIA

Constitutional difficulties bar legislation for Hindu women's right to property. Indian information 8 : 196 -198, 1 April 1941.

SINGH, G.N. : Constitutional reforms in Indian States. Indian journal of political science 3 : 90-107, July -September 1941.

British India. Journal of comparative legislation and international law 23 : 124-138, August 1941.
The legislation in 1939.

Quick reference to provincial legislation - Principal Acts passed by Legislatures, Governor's Acts, Bills introduced by Provincial Governments and Ordinances promulgated by Governors. Indian information 9 : 398-410, 15 October 1941.

AMERY : India's future constitution. Federal law journal of India 4 : 47-56, No. 11, 1941.

HOLLAND, R. : The Indian States and a Dominion Constitution. Asiatic review 38 : 61-65, January 1942.

MOITRA, A.C. : Position of the Federal Court in the constitutional system of India. Indian journal of political science 4 : 95-100, July-September 1942.

MAHAJAN, V.D. : The growth of administrative justice in the Punjab under provincial autonomy. Indian journal of political science 4 : 212-221, October-December 1942.

The India and Burma (temporary and miscellaneous provisions) Act, 1942. Federal law journal 5 : 63-66, Nos. 11-12, 1942.

SHARMA, B.M. : An interpretation of section 51 of the Government of India Act, 1935: a provincial Governor's power to dismiss his premier. Indian journal of political science 4 : 304-317, January-March 1943.

Quick reference to provincial legislation. Indian information 12 : 120-127, 1 February 1943.
Legislation in 1942.

CHAND, B. : The working of the Indian federal court. Indian journal of political science 4 : 354-362, April-June 1943.

Hindu women's right to property. Law member on Hindu law of intestate succession. Indian information 12 : 348-351, 15 April 1943.

RANKIN, G.C. : The Indian penal code. Law quarterly review 60 : 37-50, January 1944.

Merger of Indian States. Federal law journal 7 : 35-38, February 1944.

ERSKINE : Indian constitutional changes. Asiatic review 40 : 136-146, April 1944.

NAMBYAR, M.K. : Distribution of legislative powers in India. Federal law journal 7 : 51-75, April 1944.

CHATTERJEE, A.C. : Federalism and labour legislation in India. International labour review 49 : 415-445, April-May 1944.

NAMBYAR, M.K. : Distribution of legislative power in India. Federal law journal 7 : 79-102, May 194

BEAUMONT, J. : The Indian judicial system: Some suggested reforms. Asiatic review 40 : 275-286, July 1944.

Hindu law committee's draft code - Adoption, marriage and divorce, and succession. Indian information 15 : 251-254, 1 September 1944.

Das italienische Amtsblatt veröffentlicht. Commercio italo-Germanico 23 : 51-54, no. 4-6, 1944.
Summary of recent legislation.

IRAN

AGHABABIAN, R. : Le droit agricole de l'Iran. Revue internationale de droit agricole 2 : 70-85, No. 1, 1941.

GREENFIELD, J., et AGHABABOFF, R. : Droit des personnes, de famille, des successions et condition des étrangers dans la législation iranienne. Annuario di diritto comparato e di studi legislativi 15 : 243-314, fasc. 3, 1941.

IRELAND

Pre-union statutes of Ireland - Repeals and amendments since 1921. Irish jurist 9 : 34-35, July-September 1943.

ITALY

FERRARA, F. : Rinnovamento del diritto civile secondo i postulati fascisti. Archivio di studi corporativi 11 : 41-58, fasc. 1, 1940.

VENTURINI, G.C. : Osservazioni sulla configurazic dell'art. 1134 cod. civ. come norma di diritto in nazionale privato. Rivista di diritto internazionale 32 : 43-53, 1 gennaio - 31 marzo 1940.

I discorsi del Duce e di Grandi per la riforma de codici. Relazioni internazionali 6 : 243-244, 17 febbraio 1940.

FRASSOLDATI, C. : Le nouveau code de procédure c vile italien et la matière agricole. Bulletin international de droit agricole 1 : 197-206, No. 2, 1940.

NATIONAL LAW - COUNTRIES

MASSART, E. : La tutela economica del lavatore nel diritto internazionale privato italiano. Archivio di studi corporativi 11 : 391-426, fasc. 3, 1940.

GIOVENE, A. : Il "contratto d'albergo" (art. 565-659 del Progetto del IV libro del Codice Civile). Rivista del diritto commerciale 38 : 157-173, marzo-aprile 1940.

MOSCONE, G. : I limiti della giurisdizione italiana secondo il nuovo codice di procedura civile. Diritto internazionale 4 : 118-131, 1940.

DIENER, R. : Verwaltungsgerichtsbarkeit und Rechtsstaatsgedanke im faschistischen Italien. Deutsche Verwaltung 17 : 118-122, 20. April 1940.

MORTATI, C. : Esecutivo e legislativo nell'attuale fase del diritto costituzionale italiano. Rivista di diritto pubblico 32 : 301-332, giugno 1940.

FRAGOLA, G. : Il consiglio di Stato Tribunale delle prede di guerra. Rivista di diritto pubblico 32 : 425-437, agosto-settembre 1940.

COCO, N. : Possibilità e limiti di una trasformazione pubblicista del diritto privato. Rivista di diritto pubblico 32 : 565-577, novembre 1940.

LORDI, L. : Sul progetto del Codice di Commercio. Rivista del diritto commerciale 38 : 542-587, novembre-dicembre 1940.

MONTEL, A. : The first book of the new Italian civil code. Tulane law review 15 : 99-111, December 1940.

CAVARETTA, G. : La condizione giuridica dei funzionari dei Dicasteri della Santa Sede su territorio italiano. Rivista di diritto pubblico 32 : 625-632, dicembre 1940.

Elenco dei disegni di legge presentati dal Governo nall'anno 1940. Bollettino delle Assemblée legislative 14 : 625-762, dicembre 1940.

SPERL, H. : Die bürgerlichen Schiedsgerichte nach dem Rechte der italienische Zivilprozessordnung vom 28. Oktober 1940. Anuario di diritto comparato e di studi legislative 16 : 52-81, fasc. 1, 1941.

FERRARA, L. : La nuova legge italiani sul diritto d'autore. Rivista del diritto commerciale 39 : 1-23, gennaio-febbraio 1941.

GRANDI, D. : Valore giuridico della Carta del lavoro. Diritto del lavoro 15 : 3-8, gennaio-febbraio 1941.

QUADRI, R. : La giurisdizione sul cittadino nel nuovo codice di procedura civile. Rivista di diritto internazionale 20 : 3-13, fasc. 1-3, 1941.

MIELE, M. : Immunità delle sedi dei dicasteri pontifici in territorio italiano e immunità dei funzionari ecclesiastici ad essi addetti. Rivista di diritto internazionale 20 : 122-163, fasc. 1-3, 1941.

FERRARINI, S. : Introduzione al codice della navigazione. Archivio di studi corporativi 12 : 371-397, fasc. 3, 1941.

MARMO, I. : L'assistenza giudiziaria nella convenzione fra l'Italia e S. Marino. Rivista di diritto internazionale 33 : 346-359, fasc. 4, 1941.

SPERL, H. : Die Vollstreckung ausländischer Entscheidungen in Italien nach dem "Codice di procedura civile" vom 28. Oktober 1941. Annuario di diritto comparato e di studi legislativi 15 : 253-373, fasc. 4, 1941.

MONACO, R. : L'efficacia delle sentenze straniere secondo il nuovo Codice di procedura civile. Rivista di diritto internazionale 33 : 309-345, fasc. 4, 1941.

SARFATTI, M. : The new Italian civil code. Journal of comparative legislation 23 : 18-26, February 1941.

VITALI, A. : La riforma della costituzione del Tribunale delle Prede. Diritto marittimo 43 : 167-171, aprile 1941.

GIANNINI, T.C. : Osservazioni sull'ordinamento amministrativo e sulla proprietà ed armamento della nave bel progetto di codice della navigazione. Diritto marittimo 43 : 181-190, giugno-agosto 1941. See also pp. 191-233.

SANGIACOMO, V.O. : Norme costituzionali e parere del Gran Consiglio. Rivista di diritto pubblico 33 : 399-407, agosto-settembre 1941.

SBROCCA, A. : In materia di competenza sui ricorsi contro i decreti ministeriali di sequestro di aziende commerciali nemiche. Rivista di diritto pubblico 33 : 355-361, agosto-settembre 1941.

SOPRANO, E. : La società a responsibilità limitata nel nuovo codice civile. Rivista di diritto commerciale 39 : 394-420, settembre-ottobre 1941.

COSTAMAGNA, C. : Diritto pubblico e privato nel sistema del diritto italiano. Archivio di studi corporativi 13 : 47-69, fasc. 1, 1942.

MONACO, R. : Osservazioni sulla giurisdizione italiana delle prede. Rivista di diritto internazionale 21 : 90-98, fasc. 1-2, 1942.

LA LUMIA, I. : L'autonomia del nuovo diritto delle imprese commerciali. Rivista del diritto commerciale 40 : 1-9, gennaio-febbraio 1942.

GIESEKE, P. : Das Aktienrecht des Libro del lavoro. Zeitschrift für ausländisches und internationales Privatrecht 14 : 61-115, Heft 1/2, 1942.

GRANDI, D. : Il diritto di guerra e la sua formazione. Gerarchia 21 : 113-115, marzo 1942.

RAVA, P.B. : Italian administrative courts under Fascism. Michigan law review 40 : 654-678, March 1942.

ASQUINI, A., CARNELUTTI, F., and MOSSA, L. : Sulle nuove posizioni del diritto commerciale. Rivista del diritto commerciale 40 : 65-71, marzo-aprile 1942.

PAU, G. : Limiti di applicazione delle norme italiane concordatarie sul matrimonio. Rivista di diritto internazionale 34 : 293-308, fasc. 4, 1942.

Giurisprudenza del Tribunale delle prede. Diritto marittimo 54 : 276-287, maggio-dicembre 1942.

Italia, anni 1939-1940. Istituto italiano di studi legislativi, Giurisprudenza comparata di diritto internazionale privato 8 : 142-234, 15 giugno 1942.

CORDOVA, A. : Le traduzioni e la loro disciplina nella legge sui diritti di autore. Rivista di diritto pubblico 34 : 161-171, giugno 1942.

PIOLA CASELLI, E. : Les règles de droit international dans la nouvelle loi italienne sur le droit d'auteur. Droit d'auteur 55 : 100-103, 15 septembre 1942.

PUGLIATTI, S. : L'ordinamento corporativo e il codice civile. Rivista del diritto commerciale 40 : 358-375, novembre-dicembre 1942.

AROCA, A. : Die Organisation der Rechtspflege in Libyen. Koloniale Rundschau 33 : 327-338, Januar 1943.

VALERI, G. : Autonomia e limiti del nuovo diritto commerciale. Rivista del diritto commerciale 41 : 21-25, gennaio-febbraio 1943.

MICHELI, G.A. : Grundlinien des neuen italienischen Zivilprozesses. Zeitschrift für vergleichende Rechtswissenschaft 55 : 97-146, 2. Heft 1943.

SERENI, A.P. : Italian prize courts, 1866-1942. American journal of international law 37 : 248-261, April 1943.

Un commentaire de la nouvelle loi italienne sur le droit d'auteur. Droit d'auteur 56 : 49-53, 15 mai 1943.

BIONDI, P. : I principi generali del diritto della interpretazione e della codificazione fascista. Civiltà fascista 10 : 434-445, maggio 1943.

COSTAMAGNA, C. : Öffentliches Recht und Privatrecht im System des italienischen Rechts. Archiv des öffentlichen Rechts 33 : 97-121, August 1943.

La réparation des dommages de guerre... Italie. Bulletin de législation comparée 4 : 315-351, 2e trimestre 1944.

JAPAN

BÜNGER, K. : Zur Reform des japanischen Handelsgesetzbuches. Zeitschrift für ausländisches und internationales Privatrecht 13 : 144-159, Heft 1/2, 1940.

KOELLREUTER, O. : Zum Wesen des heutigen japanischen Verfassungsrechtes. Archiv des öffentlichen Rechts 32 : 1-6, September 1940.
See also pp. 7-71.

FURUTA, T. : The late Prince Saionji and the Genro system. Contemporary Japan 10 : 64-70, January 1941.

Japan - new national structure. Current notes on international affairs (Canberra) 10 : 111-114, 15 March 1941.

Japanisches Gesetz über die religiösen Körperschaften (Gesetz Nr. 717 vom 7. April 1939). Zeitschrift für vergleichende Rechtswissenschaft 55 : 83-91, 9. Juni 1942.

Legislation at 81st session of the Diet. Oriental economist 10 : 113-116, March 1943.

The new Japanese constitution. Current notes on international affairs 17 : 649-658, October 1946.
Text.

LATVIA

Lettland - Übersicht über die wesentlicher Gesetzgebung in den Jahren 1940/1941. Zeitschrift für osteuropäisches Recht 8 : 592-597, Mai/Juni 1942.

Anordnungen des Generalkommissars in Riga 1941/1942. Zeitschrift für osteuropäisches Recht 9 : 87-89, Juli-September 1942.

LASERSON, M.M. : The recognition of Latvia. American journal of international law 37 : 233-247, April 1943.

LITHUANIA

SWETSCHIN, A. : Litauen - Übersicht über die wesentliche Gesetzgebung im Jahre 1940. Zeitschrift für osteuropäisches Recht 7 : 371-378, Januar-Februar 1941.

Litauen - Übersicht über die wesentliche Gesetzgebung im Jahre 1941. Zeitschrift für osteuropäisches Recht 8 : 389-400, Januar-Februar 1942.

Verordnungen des Generalkommissars in Kauen' 1941/1942. Zeitschrift für osteuropäisches Recht 9 : 89-90, Juli-September 1942.

LUXEMBURG

Nouveau code pénal. Luxembourg bulletin 77-79, July-August 1943.

COHN, E.J. : Legislation in exile - Luxembourg. Journal of comparative legislation and international law 25 : 40-46, November 1943.

Arrêté grand-ducal du 13 juillet 1944, modifiant l'arrêté grand-ducel du 22 avril 1944, déterminant l'effet des mesures prises par l'occupant. Luxembour bulletin : 157, September-October 1944.

MEXICO

BROWN, P.M. : The "Cardenas Doctrine". American journal of international law 34 : 300-302, April 1940.
Rights of foreigners.

KUHN, A.K. : The Mexican Supreme Court decision in the oil companies expropriation cases. American journal of international law 34 : 297-300, April 1940.

CRAWFORD, H.P. : Arbitration procedure in Mexico. Arbitration journal 4 : 152-156, October 1940.

CLAGETT, H.L. : The sources of the commercial law of Mexico. Tulane law review 18 : 437-460, March 1944.

MONACO

LA PRADELLE, A. de : Les princes de Monaco devant la justice (Suite). Nouvelle revue de droit international privé 9 : 78-313, 1942.

NATIONAL LAW - COUNTRIES

NETHERLANDS

Dutch Court in England starts work - First of its kind in all of Britain's history. Netherlands news 2 : 21-22, No. 1, 1941.
High court for maritime cases.

KOCHS, H. : Deutsche Verwaltung in den Niederlanden. Zeitschrift für Politik 31 : 377-369 (sic), Juni 1941.

VAN RIJCKEVORSEL, J.J. : Wijsgeerige koloniale rechtsleer (Contd.). Koloniale studien 25 : 331-363, Augustus 1941.

Comité voor reconstuctie van het strafrecht. Vrij Nederland 3 : 813, 24 juli 1943.

FRANK, H.E.R.E.A. : Economische administratieve rechtspraak - Scheidsgerecht voor de voedselvoorziening. Economisch-statistische berichten 28 : 244-250, 11 augustus 1943.

ZEEMAN, J.H. : Legislation in exile: the Netherlands. Journal of comparative legislation and international law 26 : 4-11, November 1944.

NEW ZEALAND

MASON, H.G.R. : One hundred years of legislative development in New Zealand. Journal of comparative legislation 23 : 1-17, February 1941.

TUCK, W.R. : The Court of arbitration in New Zealand. Economic record 17 : 46-56, June 1941.

CHRISTIE, J. : New Zealand. Journal of comparative legislation and international law 23 : 105-113, August 1941.
The legislation in 1939-1940.

NORWAY

HANSSEN, E. : Noen bemerkinger angaende omregning til innelandsk mynt av forpliktelser uttryk i utenlandsk mynt. Tidsskrift for rettsvidenskap 54 : 569-593, hefte 5, 1941.

SCHNEIDER, H. : Staatsrechtliche Entwicklung und Verwaltungsgesetzgebung Norwegens seit 9. April 1940. Reich, Volksordnung, Lebensraum 2 : 379-405, 1942.

GRETTE, S. : Fra den norske hoyesteretts praksis i 1939 og 1940. Tidsskrift for rettsvitendskap 55 : 225-246, hefte 2, 1942.

WOLD, T. : The 1942 Enactment for the defence of the Norwegian State. Canadian bar review 20 : 505-509, June-July 1942.

ULRICH : Norwegens Verfassungslage. Auswärtige Politik 9 : 610-612, Juli 1942.

Legislation in exile - Norway. Journal of comparative legislation and international law 24 : 125-130, November 1942.

The work of the Norwegian ministry of Justice and Police. Norwegian fact service : 1-3, 11 August 1943.

WOLD, T. : Legislation promulgated by the Norwegian government. Norseman 1 : 430-438, November 1943.

PALESTINE

Powers of custodian enemy property. Current law reports (Jerusalem) 12 : 50-51, No. 6, 1942.

PANAMA

EDER, P.J. : The judicial status of non registered foreign corporations in Panama. Tulane law review 15 : 521-540, June 1941.

NELSON, E. : Economic theory implicit in the Panamian constitution of 1942. Tulane law review 16 : 562-572, June 1942.

FENWICK, C.G. : The Inter-American juridical committee. American journal of international law 37 : 5-29, January 1943.

PARAGUAY

GASPERI, L. de : La clausula oro en el Paraguay. Boletin del comité de abogados de los bancos de la capital federal 7 : 164-228, julio-diciembre 1940.

GROSS-BROWN, S.V. : First principles and the Paraguayan constitution. Review of politics 6 : 94-102, January 1944.

GROSS-BROWN, S.V. : Administrative justice in Paraguay. Tulane law review 18 : 610-618, June 1944.

PERU

PAZ-SALDAN, J.P. : Las inmunidades consulares - Su aplicación en el Perú. Revista de derecho internacional 37 : 5-33, 31 marzo 1940.

BARANDIARÁN, J.L. : Comentarios al código civil peruano. Revista de derecho y ciencias políticas 4 : 397-497, núm. 3, 1940.

VILLARÁN, M.V. : Posición constitutional de los ministros en el Perú. Revista de derecho y ciencias políticas 4 : 494-562, núm. 3, 1940.

Instalación de la nueva Junta directiva - Memoria del Decano cesante, Señor Doctor Ernesto de la Jara y Ureta. Revista del foro 27 : 8-17, enero-junio 1940.

La reforma del Código civil - Actas de las sesiones de la Comisión (Contd.). Revista del foro 27 : 121-251, 561-617, enero-junio, julio-diciembre 1940.

Das peruanische Gesetz zur Aufhebung der Finanz- und Handelsfreiheit für Angehörige der Achsenmächte. Devisenarchiv 7 : 373-376, 12. September 1942.
Law of April 10 and Decree of 15 April 1942.

Massnahmen betreffend das ausländische Eigentum. Devisenarchiv 8 : 13-16, 2. Januar 1943.
Texts of Laws of June 1942.

LÉON y LÉON, B. : Los tribunales del trabajo en el Perú. Revista parlamentaria 11 : 46-63, mayo 1943.

NATIONAL LAW - COUNTRIES

POLAND

Law and law courts in Poland, 1919-1939. Slavonic year-book 19 : 188-202, 1939-1940.

MIKLISZAŃSKI, J.K. : La guerre dans le droit polonais. Voix de Varsovie 1 : 152-157, 1 mars 1940.

HUBERNAGEL, G. : Die deutsche Gerichtsbarkeit im Generalgouvernement für die besetzten polnischen Gebiete. Zeitschrift für osteuropäisches Recht 6 : 483-501, Mai-Juni 1940.

HUBERNAGEL, G. : Das Wirtschaftsstrafrecht im Generalgouvernement. Zeitschrift für osteuropäisches Recht 7 : 1-28, Juli-August 1940.

ARNOLD, E. : Staatsangehörigkeitsfragen im Generalgouvernement. Zeitschrift für osteuropäisches Recht 7 : 148-153, September-Oktober 1940.

WEN, A. : Ein Jahr Generalgouvernement. Zeitschrift für osteuropäisches Recht 7 : 105-124, September-Oktober 1940.

RANKIN, G. : Legal problems of Poland after 1918. Transaction of the Grotius Society, Problems of peace and war 26 : 1-34, 1940.

GIESE, F. : Die gegenwärtige Staatsangehörigkeit der aus ehemals polnischen Gebieten stammenden Juden in Deutschland. Zeitschrift für öffentliches Recht 21 : 53-74, Heft 1, 1941.

HUBERNAGEL, G. : Das Kriminelle und das Verwaltungsstrafverfahren im Generalgouvernement. Zeitschrift für osteuropäisches Recht 7 : 345-361, Januar-Februar 1941.

KLEIN, F. : Zur Stellung des Generalgouvernements in der Verfassung des Grossdeutschen Reiches. Archiv des öffentlichen Rechts 32 : 227-267, Juni 1941.

KAULBACH : Das bürgerliche Recht in den eingegliederten Ostgebieten. Zeitschrift für osteuropäisches Recht 8 : 357-372, Januar-Februar 1942.

WOLANY : Bürgerliches Recht und Rechtspflege in den eingegliederten Ostgebieten. Zeitschrift der Akademie für deutsches Recht 9 : 51-55, 15. Februar 1942.

STAMM : Sozialversicherung im Generalgouvernement und ihre Einordnung in die Arbeits- und Gesundheitsverwaltung. Zeitschrift der Akademie für deutsches Recht 9 : 37-38, 1. Februar 1942.

WEH, A. : Die rechtlichen Grundlagen des Generalgouvernements und die Grundsätze der Generalgouvernementsverwalting. Europäische Revue 18 : 236-244, Mai 1942.

HELCZYNSKI, B. : The underlying principles of Polish commercial law. Polish science and learning : 28-34, June 1942.

Polonia, anni 1933-1934. Istituto italiano di studi legislativi, Giurisprudenza comparata di diritto internazionale privato 8 : 95-141, 15 giugno 1942.

PERNAU : Aufrechnung und Stundung bei Abwicklung der Forderungen und Schulden polnischer Vermögen. Deutsche Wirtschafts-Zeitung 39 : 427-428, 28. August 1942.

WILLE, K. : Drei Jahre Aufbauarbeit in der Justiz des Generalgouvernements. Deutsches Recht 12 : 229 232, 15. November 1942.

Generalgouvernement - Die nichtdeutsche Gerichtsbarkeit. Südost-Echo 13 : 12, 1. Jänner 1943.

RADISCHAT : Die Schulden des früheren polnischen Staates. Südost-Echo 13 : 15, 29. Jänner 1943.

SIEBERT : Deutsche Verwaltung im Generalgouvernement. Welzwirtschaft 31 : 70-71, März 1943.

BIRNBAUM, W. : Das Recht zur Aufsuchung und Gewinnung von Bodenschätzen im Generalgouvernement. Glückauf 70 : 340-344, 3. Juli 1943.

KUNKEL, G. : Das Staatsangehörigkeitsrecht in den eingegliederten Ostgebieten. Deutsche Rechtspfleger 55 : 28-29, 15. Februar/15. März 1944.

BIRNBAUM, W. : Neues Bergrecht im Generalgouvernement. Glückauf 80 : 250-252, 10. Juni 1944.

PORTUGAL

VILELA, M. : Notas sôbre a competência internacional no novo Código de processo civil. Boletim da Faculdade de direito da Universidade de Coimbra 17 : 274-346, fasc. 2, 1940-41.

MARTIN, K. : Die Rechtsverhältnisse der Eingeborenen in den afrikanischen Kolonien Portugals. Zeitschrift für vergleichende Rechtswissenschaft 54 : 137-167, 3. Heft 1941.

VILELA, M. : Notas sôbre a competência internacional no novo Código de processo civil (Contd.). Boletim da Faculdade de direito da Universidade de Coimbra 18 : 1-70, fasc. 1, 1941-42.

CARLOS MOREIRA, J. : Fiscalização da constituíção. Boletim da Faculdade de direito da Universidade de Coimbra 19 : 1-10, fasc. 1, 1943.

CAETANO, M. : Das neue öffentliche Recht Portugals Zeitschrift für vergleichende Rechtswissenschaft 55 : 163-176, 2. Heft 1943.

Le nouveau statut judiciaire. Portugal : 4-6, 31 mars 1944.

WYLER-SCHMID, M. : Kleine Skisse des portugiesisch Seerechts. Schiffahrts-Anzeiger 3 : 38-40, septembre-octobre 1944.

FONSECA, M.B.D. : O articulo 1236° do Código civil Boletim da faculdade de direito da universidade de Coimbra 17 (Suppl.) : 263-350, 1944. Inheritance law.

RUMANIA

IONASCU, A.R. : La nouvelle constitution roumaine. Revue de Transylvanie 5 : 421-447, octobre-décembre 1939.

WITTSTOCK, O. : Die Aufhebung der Stattshalterschaften in Rumänien nach dem Gesetz vom 21. September 1940. Zeitschrift für osteuropäisches Recht 7 : 156-158, September-Oktober 1940.

NATIONAL LAW - COUNTRIES

Le Stato legionario romeno e l'adeguamento della legislazione al nuovo ordine politico. Bollettino della Assemblee legislative 14 791-818, dicembre 1940.

Die internationalprivatrechtlichen Bestimmungen des revidierten rumänischen Zivilgesetzbuchs (1940). Zeitschrift für vergleichende Rechtswissenschaft 54 : 221-229, 3. Heft 1941.

GEORGESCU, I.L. : Das neue rumänische Handelsgesetzbuch in der europäischen Rechtsentwicklung. Zeitschrift für ausländisches und internationales Privatrecht 13 : 351-370, Heft 3-4, 1941.

KESCHMANN, F. : Dekretgesetz vom 4. September 1941 über die Organisierung Bessarabuens und des Buchenlandes. Zeitschrift für osteuropäisches Recht 8 : 203-214, September-Oktober 1941.
See also pp. 215-221.

Ubersicht über di wesentliche Gesetzgebung im Jahre 1941/1942. Zeitschrift für osteuropäisches Recht 8 : 502-515, März/April 1942.

AKERMAN, C. : La législation et la jurisprudence en matière de brevets d'invention et de marques de fabriques depuis 1930. Propriété industrielle 60 : 67-71, mai 1944.

SALVADOR

Ley organica del Servicio exterior de la República. Revista de hacienda (El Salvador) 5 : 3-24, octubre 1941.

SAN MARINO

GIANNINI, T.C. : La disciplina delle società commerciali nella Repubblica di San Marino. Rivista di politica economica 33 : 121-129, marzo 1943.

BIANCO, D.L. : In margine alla convenzione 31 marzo 1939 fra l'Italia e San Marino. Foro italiano 68 : 528, fasc. 9, 1943.

SPAIN

BRIGGS, H.W. : Relations officieuses and intent to recognize, British recognition of Franco. American journal of international law 34 : 47-57, January 1940.

SCOTTEN, R.M. : New Spanish law for the regulation and defense of industry. U.S. Department of commerce, Comparative law series 3 : 355-363, July 1940.
Text annexed.

BATISTA y ROCA, J.M. : The Constitution of the falangist state. Fortnightly 148 : 458-465, November 1940.

Zum spanischen Erbrecht - Interlokales Privatrecht - Katalanisches Foralrecht. Zeitschrift für ausländisches und internationales Privatrecht 13 : 646-669, Heft 3-4, 1941.

AVILA, M. : Rechtspflege in Spanisch Guinea. Koloniale Rundschau 33 : 338-341, Januar 1943.

GARRIGUES, J. : Verso un nuovo diritto commerciale della Spagna. Rivista del diritto commerciale 41 : 73-88, marzo-aprile 1943.

AYORA, F.H. : La Comisión de codificación y la mujer en el código. Nueva economia nacional : 12-13, 20 mayo, 1943.

ELZABURU, A. de : La législation sur la propriété industrielle et domaines voisins de 1936 à 1942. Propriété industrielle 59 : 109-114, juillet 1943.

CASTRO, F. de : La adquisición por vecindad de la nacionalidad española. Estudios juridicos 3 : 571-604, agosto 1943.

GIMENEZ-ARNAU, E. : Ley de reforma de la mayoría de edad civil. Economía mundial 3 : 13-14, 25 diciembre 1943.

La legislación en 1943. Economía mundial 4 : 7, 8 enero 1944.

OROZCO, F.M. : Restablecimiento de la jurisdicción contencioso-administrativa. Nueva economía nacional 8 : 7-9, 13 abril 1944.

ASENJO, E.J. : El derecho foral catalán ante la unidad codificadora. Estudios juridicos 4 : 3-25, no. 7, 1944.

SWEDEN

ROHTLIEB, K. : La législation sur la petite propriété de famille en Suède. Revue internationale de droit agricole 2 : 43-55, No. 1, 1941.

BLOCH, J.-D. : Die verfassungsrechtliche Bedeutung der schwedischen Krisengesetzgebung. Zeitschrift für ausländisches öffentliches Recht und Völkerrecht 11 : 35-50, Nr. 1/2, 1942.

REGNER, N. : La législation en matière de trahison, d'espionnage, etc. Recueil de documents en matière pénale et pénitentiaire 10 : 154-166, novembre 1942.

JÄGERSKIÖLD, S. : Något om jurisdiktionen över handelsfartyg. Nordisk Tidsskrift for international Ret 14 : 115-142, Fasc. 4, 1943.

BECKMAN, N. : Suède - La nouvelle loi sur les délits contre le patrimoine. Recueil de documents en matière pénale et pénitantiaire 10 : 331-346, novembre 1943.

SIMSON, G. : Das neue Schwedische Zivilprozessrecht. Zeitschrift für schweizerisches Recht 63 : 122-185, Heft 1, 1944.

Förslag till vissa ändringar i lagen om förenings- och förhandlingsrätt m. fl. lagar. Sociala meddelanden 54 : 474-486, nr. 6, 1944.

Ny svensk Aktieselskabslov. Udenrigsministeriets Tidsskrift 25 : 91-93, August 1944.

SWITZERLAND

WENGEN, M.C. : Die Umwandlung ainer Aktiengesellschaft in eine Gesellschaft mit beschränkter Haftung. Zeitschrift für schweizerisches Recht 59 : 1-52, Heft 1, 1940.

HUBER, H. : Die staatsrechtliche Bedeutung der Allgemeinverbindlicherklärung von Verbandsbeschlüssen und Vereinbarungen. Zeitschrift für schweizerisches Recht 59 : 331-414, Heft 3, 1940.

NATIONAL LAW - COUNTRIES

CHEVALIER, A., and FLÜGEL, W. : Übersicht über die schweizerische Rechtsgesetzgebung des Jahres 1939. Zeitschrift für schweizerisches Recht 59 : 443-569, Heft 4, 1940.

DES GOUTTES, R. : Les conditions du divorce pour aliénation mentale. Zeitschrift für schweizerisches Recht 60 : 266-317, Heft 2, 1941.

BOURGKNECHT, J. : Le recours au Tribunal fédéral en matière pénale, après l'entrée en vigueur du Code pénal suisse. Zeitschrift für schweizerisches Recht 60 : 1a-116a, Heft 3, 1941.

RIGGENBACH, B. : Übersicht der Literatur über schweizerisches Recht vom Jahre 1939. Zeitschrift für schweizerisches Recht 59 : 415-442, Heft 4, 1940.

CHEVALIER, A., und FLÜGEL, W. : Übersicht über die schweizerische Rechtsgesetzgebung des Jahres 1940. Zeitschrift für schweizerisches Recht 60 : 425-558, Heft 6, 1941.

SCHOCH, M. : Conflict of laws in a Federal State - The experience of Switzerland. Harvard law review 55 : 738-779, March 1942,

KISTLER, H. : Rechtsfragen aus dem Gebiete der Militärversicherung. Zeitschrift für schweizerisches Recht 61 : 1a-230a, Heft 3, 1942.

ROULLET, M. : Questions juridiques en matière d'assurance militaire. Zeitschrift für schweizerisches Recht 61 : 231a-392a, Heft 4, 1942.

MERZ, H. : Die Revision der Verträge durch den Richter. Zeitschrift für schweizerisches Recht 61 : 393a-508a, Heft 5, 1942.

Un interné militaire en Suisse peut-il y contracter mariage? Revue internationale de la Croix-Rouge 24 : 301-305, mai 1942.

ZIEGLER, A. : Die Rechtsprechung des Schweizerischen Bundesgerichtes auf dem Gebiete des gesamten Zivilrechtes und der Zwangsvollstreckung im Jahre 1938. Zeitschrift für ausländisches und internationales Privatrecht 13 : 853-923, Heft 5/6, 1942.

DESCHENAUX, H. : La revision des contrats par le juge. Zeitschrift für schweizerisches Recht 61 : 511a-636a, Heft 6, 1942.

Die Weiterziehung von Strafsachen an das Bundesgericht nach Inkraftreten des eidgenössischen Strafgesetzbuches. Zeitschrift für schweizerisches Recht 60 : 426a-473a, Heft 6, 1942.

RIGGENBACH, B. : Übersicht der Literatur über schweizerisches Recht vom Jahre 1941. Zeitschrift für schweizerisches Recht 61 : 379-412, Heft 8, 1942.

Übersicht über die schweizerische Rechtsgesetzgebung des Jahres 1941. Zeitschrift für schweizerisches Recht 61 : 413-555, Heft 8, 1942.

GIACOMETTI, Z. : Die gegenwärtige Verfassungslage der Eidgenossenschaft. Schweizerische Hochschulzeitung 16 : 139-154, September-Oktober 1942.

Message du Conseil fédéral à l'Assemblée fédérale à l'appui d'une nouvelle loi sur l'organisation judiciaire (du 9 février 1943). Feuille fédérale 95 : 101-232, 18 février 1943.

CAPITAINE, G. : Le statut des sociétés holdings en Suisse. Zeitschrift für schweizerisches Recht 62 : 1a-194a, Hft. 2, 1943.

STEIGER, W. v. : Die Rechtsverhältnisse der Holdinggesellschaften in der Schweiz. Zeitschift für schweizerisches Recht 62 : 195a-337a, Hft. 4, 1943.

LACHENAL, P. : La séparation des pouvoirs dans la Confédération Suisse spécialement au point de vue de la délégation du droit de légiférer. Zeitschrift für schweizerisches Recht 62 : 339a-401a, Hft. 5, 1943.

OSWALD, W. : Die Gewaltentrennung im schweizerischen Staatsrecht. Zeitschrift für schweizerisches Recht 62 : 403a-530a, Hft. 6, 1943.

Die Gewaltentrennung im Bund und in den Kantonen im besonderen vom Standpunkt der Delegation des Gesetzgebungsrechtes. Zeitschrift für schweizerisches Recht 62 : 625a-667a, Heft 7, 1943.

Die Rechtsverhältnisse der Holdinggesellschaften in der Schweiz. Zeitschrift für schweizerisches Recht 62 : 554a-597a, Heft 7, 1943.

Übersicht über die schweizerische Rechtsgesetzgebung des Jahres 1942. Zeitschrift für schweizerische Recht 62 : 383-511, Heft 7, 1943.

Rapport du Conseil fédéral à l'Assemblée fédérale sur le postulat du Conseil fédéral concernant la désignation d'une assemblée constituante (du 6 août 1943). Feuille fédérale 95 : 629-652, 19 août 1943.

TUASON, V. : Le statut juridique de l'adminitration des postes, des télégraphes et des téléphones suisses. Union postale 68 : 232-254, novembre-décembre 1943.

Loi fédérale d'organisation judiciaire (du 16 décembre 1943). Feuille fédérale 96 : 1-56, 6 janvier 1944.

RIGGENBACH, B. : Übersicht der Literatur über schweizerisches Recht vom Jahre 1943. Zeitschrift für schweizerisches Recht 63 : 347-369, Heft 6, 1944.

Übersicht über die schweizerische Rechtsgesetzgebung des Jahres 1943. Zeitschrift für schweizerisches Recht 63 : 395-496, Heft 6, 1944.

EGGER, A. : Die Ehescheidung nach dem schweizerischen ZGB und das Scheidungsverfahren nach kantonalem Prozessrecht. Schweizerische Zeitschrift für Gemeinnützigkeit 83 : 399-423, September 1944.

SWITZERLAND
(International law, Aliens)

PESTALOZZI, A. : Zivilprozessrecht und internationales Privatrecht der Schweiz im Jahre 1938. Zeitschrift für ausländisches und internationales Privatrecht 13 : 597-625, Heft 3-4, 1941.

KNAPP, C. : La division des effets du contrat dans le droit international privé de la Suisse. Zeitschrift für schweizerisches Recht 60 : 303a-358a, Heft 4, 1941.

Die Aufspaltung des Vertrages bezüglich seiner Wirkungen im schweizerischen internationalen Obligationenrecht. Zeitschrift für schweizerisches Recht 60 : 387a-420a, Heft 6, 1941.

La protection diplomatique des intérêts des Etats belligérants. Archives diplomatiques et consulaires 7 : 9, janvier 1942.

WEHBERG, H. : Sind Schiffe unter Schweizerflagge Bestandteil des Schweizerischen Territoriums? Friedens-Warte 42 : 175-178, Nr. 4/5, 1942.

NIEDERER, W. : Das Problem des ordre public in der neueren Rechtsprechung des Bundesgerichtes auf dem Gebiete des internationalen Privatrechts. Zeitschrift für schweizerisches Recht 62 : 1-24, Heft 1, 1943.

ITH, A. : Anwendbares Recht für internationale Verbände und Kongressorganisationen unter besonderer Berücksichtigung des schweizerischen Rechts. Archiv für das Recht der internationalen Organisationen 4 : 15-29, 1943.

Erwerb und Verlust des Schweizerbürgerrechtes. Archiv für schweizerische Politik und Volkwirtschaft 10 : 1847-1848, Februar 1943.

HAAB, R. : Das schweizerische Seerecht. Strom und See 38 : 77-79, Dezember 1943.

ETTER, O. : Gedanken zur kommenden Revision der schweizerischen Bürgerrechtsgesetzgebung. Schweiz 15 : 60-73, 1944.

SWITZERLAND
(Patents, Trademarks, Copyrights)

MARTIN-ACHARD, A. : Questions actuelles dans le domaine du droit et de la procédure en matière de brevets d'invention. Zeitschrift für schweizerisches Recht 63 : 127a-200a, Heft 3, 1944.
Voir aussi pp. 1a-126a.

La protection de la marque étrangère en Suisse. Propriété industrielle 60 : 154-157, octobre 1944.

SYRIA and LEBANON

Le nouveau code de commerce libanais. Journal des tribunaux mixtes 22 : 2, 16-17, juin 1943.

TURKEY

BEKTAS, G. : Study on agricultural legislation in Turkey. International bulletin of agricultural law 3 : 69-74, No. 5, 1942.

U.S.S.R.

Freund, H.A. : Soviet law under "Stalinism". Slavonic year-book 19 : 175-187, 1939-1940.

NAPOLITANO, T. : Il nuovo "Statuto sull'avvocatura dell'U.R.S.S.". Giustizia penale 46 : 2-3, gennaio-aprile 1940.

LABIN, S. : La peine de mort en Russie soviétique et les lois excessives. Mercure de France 297 : 546-554, 1er juin 1940.

HAZARD, J.N. : Soviet criminal procedure. Tulane law review 15 : 220-240, February 1941.

MARTYBOV, B. : Osnovnye problemy avtorskogo prava. Sovetskoe gosudarstvo i pravo : 21-37, No. 4, 1941.
Droit d'auteur.

BRANDENBURGSKY, J. : Courts and judicial procedure in the U.S.S.R. Moscow news 11 : 9, 15 May 1951.

Sowjetunion - Übersicht über die wesentlich Gesetzgebung 1939/40. Zeitschrift für osteuropäisches Recht 7 : 59-67, Juli-August 1940.

Sowjetunion. Übersicht über die wesentlich Gesetzgebung 1940-41. Zeitschrift für osteuropäisches Recht 8 : 74-84, Juli-August 1941.

SIHLE, R. : Die staatsrechtliche Gesetzgebung in der Sowjetunion seit der Verfassungsreform von 1936. Zeitschrift für osteuropäisches Recht 8 : 144-182, September-Oktober 1941.

WERTHER, K. : Verwaltungsaufbau und Verwaltungspraxis in der Sowjetunion. Zeitschrift für osteuropäisches Recht 8 : 283-306, November-Dezember 1941.

STANFIELD, B.M. : Private rights in Russia. International conciliation : 721-729, December 1941.

BRÄUTIGAM : Eigentumsfragen in den besetzten Ostgebieten. Ostwirtschaft 31 : 69-72, Mai 1942.

MAKAROV, A.N. : Das Privat- und Wirtschaftsrecht der Sowjet-Union. Zeitschrift für ausländisches und internationales Privatrecht 13 : 754-799, Heft 5/6, 1942.

Deutsches Recht und deutsche Gerichte im Reichskommissariat Ukraine. Ostwirtschaft 31 : 91-92, Juni/Juli 1942.

Anordnungen des Reichskommissars für die Ukraine 1941/42. Zeitschrift für osteuropäisches Recht 9 : 91-94, Juli-September 1942.

WEITNAUER : Der Aufbau der Rechtspflege in den besetzten Ostgebieten. Zeitschrift für osteuropäisches Recht 9 : 42-51, Juli-September 1942.

LABS : Der Verwaltungsaufbau in den besetzten Ostgebieten. Ostwirtschaft 31 : 109-111, August 1942.

SCHLESINGER, R. : Recent developments in Soviet legal theory. Modern law review 6 : 21-38, December 1942.

WEITNAUERT : Bürgerliches Recht und Bürgerliche Rechtspflege in den besetzten Ostgebieten. Zeitschrift für osteuropäisches Recht 10 : 26-38, Januar/Juni 1943.

HAZARD, J.N. : Soviet textbooks on law. Slavonic and East European review 21 : 211-222, March 1943.

LABS, W. : Die Verwaltung der Besetzten Ostgebiete. Reich, Volksordnung, Lebensraum 5 : 132-166, 1943.

Decree on rehabilitation of liberated areas. Soviet war news : 3, 24 August 1943.

The Soviet legal system. Law journal 94 : 13-14, 21-22, 30; 8, 15, 22 January 1944.

Decisions of tenth session of Supreme Soviet. Soviet war news : 3, 7 February 1944.
Text of laws amending constitution.

WILHELM, W. : Die Rechtspflege in den besetzen Ostgebieten. Zeitschrift der Akademie für deutsches Recht 11 : 21-24, 10. Februar 1944.

New Soviet law on mothers and children, marriage and divorce. Soviet war news : 2-4, 12 July 1944. Text.

LUCHAIRE, F. : La réforme constitutionnelle soviétique du 2 février 1944. Revue du droit public et de la science politique 60 : 310-314, octobre-décembre 1944.

U.S.S.R.
(International law and Practice, Aliens and Naturalization)

Tabelle der von der UdSSR von 1935-1940 abgeschlossenen Staatsverträge. Zeitschrift für osteuropäisches Recht 7 : 396-405, Januar-Februar 1941.

MAKAROV : Die Eingliederung der baltischen Staaten in die Sowjet-Union. Zeitschrift für ausländisches öffentliches Recht und Völkerrecht 10 : 682-707, Nr. 3/4, 1941.

TRAININ, I. : The constitutions of the Baltic Soviet Socialist Republics. American review on the Soviet Union 4 : 28-41, April 1941.

MAKAROV, A.N. : Die Einführung der Sowjetgesetzbücher in den der Sowjetunion neuangegliederten Gebieten. Zeitschrift für osteuropäisches Recht 7 : 423-441, März-April 1941.

UNITED ARAB REPUBLIC

Le contrôle des exportations et la notion de contrebande de guerre dans la législation égyptienne. Journal des tribunaux mixtes 19 : 3-4, 25 et 26 mars 1940.

L'unification de la législation pénale égyptienne. Journal des tribunaux mixtes 19 : 3, 27 et 28 mars 1940.

La liquidation, aboutissement de la séquestration des biens allemands en Egypte. Journal des tribunaux mixtes 19 : 3-4, 17 et 18 avril 1940.

De la nullité des clauses compromissoires tendant à un arbitrage à l'étranger lorsqu'elles ont été stipulées avant les accords de Montreux. Journal des tribunaux mixtes 19 : 4-5, 19 et 20 avril 1940.

BRINTON, J.Y. : Egypt - The transition period. American journal of international law 34 : 208-219, April 1940.
The Mixed Courts.

La signification des actes destinés aux personnes se trouvant en territoire occupé ou contrôle par l'ennemi. Journal des tribunaux mixtes 20 : 3-4, 11 et 12 décembre 1940.

LOEWENFELD, E. : The Mixed Courts in Egypt as a part of the system of capitulations after the Treaty of Montreux. Transactions of the Grotius Society, Problems of peace and war 26 : 83-123, 1940.

CHEVALLIER, J. : Jurisprudence des juridictions mixtes d'Egypte. Revue trimestrielle de droit civil 39-40 : 143-158, No. 1, 1940-1941.

La juridiction des tribunaux mixtes en matière de statut personnel des Italiens et des Allemands. Journal des tribunaux mixtes 20 : 3-4, 6-7 janvier 1941.

CHEVALLIER, J. : Le statut juridique des sociétés étrangères en Egypte. Journal des tribunaux mixtes 20 : 3-4, 1 mai 1941.

Le transfert aux tribunaux mixtes du pouvoir juridictionnel en matière de statut personnel des Italiens et Allemands. Journal des tribunaux mixtes 20 : 5, 19-20 mai 1941.

La monnaie de paiement des pensions de retraite servies par la Compagnie universelle du Canal maritime de Suez. Journal des tribunaux mixtes 20 : 5-6, 2 et 3 juin 1941.

La refonte de la législation de guerre relative aux personnes résident en pays occupés ou contrôlés par l'Allemagne ou l'Italie. Journal des tribunaux mixte 20 : 3-4, 23 et 24 juillet 1941.

L'Office des territoires occupées ou contrôlés. Journal des tribunaux mixtes 20 : 3-4, 22 et 23 septembre 1941.

Le prix de l'or. Journal des tribunaux mixtes 21 : 6-7, 4-5, 5-6, 19 et 20, 23 et 24, 26 et 27 janvier 1942.
Série d'articles concernant les obligations de la Compagnie Universelle du Canal Maritime de Suez.

Les problèmes juridictionnels relatifs au divorce des Suisses en Egypte. Journal des tribunaux mixtes 21 : 4-8, 4-7, 20 et 21, 23 et 24 février 1942.

Les nouvelles règles de compétence juridictionnelle établies par les Accords de Montreux et la chose jugée. Journal des tribunaux mixtes 21 : 3-4, 2 et 3 mars 1942.

Le transfert provisoire aux Tribunaux mixtes du pouvoir juridictionnel en matière de statut personnel des Français. Journal des tribunaux mixtes 21 : 4, 6, et 7 mars 1942.

Le régime juridictionnel des membres des forces helléniques en Egypte. Journal des tribunaux mixtes 21 : 4-7, 7-9, 3-5, 30 et 31 mars, 1 et 2 avril, 27 et 28 mai 1942.

Les problèmes juridictionnels relatifs au divorce des Suisses en Egypte. Journal des tribunaux mixtes 21 : 5-6, 3 et 4 avril 1942.

Le nouveau projet de Code civil égyptien. Journal des tribunaux mixtes 21 : 1-2, 11 et 12 mai 1942.

Les nouvelles règles de compétence juridictionnelle établies par les Accords de Montreux et la chose jugée. Journal des tribunaux mixtes 21 : 2-4, 29 e 30 mai 1942.

La réforme des codes. Journal des tribunaux mixtes 21 : 1-2, 3 et 4 juin 1942.

Le régime juridictionnel des membres des forces alliées en Egypte. Journal des tribunaux mixtes 21 3-4, 21 et 22 octobre 1942.

Le présentation du nouveau projet de révision et d'unification du code de procédure civile et commerciale. Journal des tribunaux mixtes 22 : 1-2, 9 et 10 novembre 1942.

NATIONAL LAW - COUNTRIES

L'application des dispositions législatives transférant aux Tribunaux mixtes le pouvoir juridictionnel des anciens Tribunaux consulaires allemands, italiens et français. Journal des tribunaux mixtes 22 : 1-2, 30 novembre et 1 décembre 1943.

Le caractère juridique de la qualité des séquestres des biens italiens ou allemands. Journal des tribunaux mixtes 21 : 4, 21 et 22 novembre 1942.

L'indemnisation des dommages de guerre et l'assurance obligatoire. Journal des tribunaux mixtes 21 : 3-4, 1 et 2 décembre 1942.
Voir aussi pp. 5-8.

Le régime juridictionnel des membres des Forces alliées en Egypte. Journal des tribunaux mixtes 22 : 3, 4 et 5 décembre 1942.

Des pouvoirs juridictionnels des tribunaux mixtes entre parties de nationalités différentes sur des questions de statut personnel lorsque la loi applicable n'est pas une loi étrangère. Journal des tribunaux mixtes 22 : 1-2, 25-26 janvier 1943.

Le régime juridictionnel des membres des forces alliées en Egypte. Journal des tribunaux mixtes 22 : 2-5, 19-20 février 1943.

La compétence des tribunaux mixtes à l'égard des sociétés de personnes formées entre étrangers ou entre étrangers et Egyptiens. Journal des tribunaux mixtes 22 : 1-3, 1-2 mars 1943.

La détermination de la monnaie de paiement dans les obligations contractuelles en Egypte et au Liban. Journal des tribunaux mixtes 22 : 1-2, 3-4 mars 1943.

La détermination de la monnaie de paiement dans les obligations contractuelles en Egypte et au Liban. Journal des tribunaux mixtes 22 : 1-3, 17-18 mars 1943.

Le régime juridictionnel des Forces Américaines en Egypte. Journal des tribunaux mixtes 22 : 1-4, 5 et 6 mars 1943.
Textes officiels pp. 4-5.

Le régime juridictionnel des Forces Américaines en Egypte (Contd.). Journal des tribunaux mixtes 22 : 2, 8 et 9 mars 1943.

Le régime juridictionnel des forces françaises combattantes en Egypte. Journal des tribunaux mixtes 22 : 15-16 mars 1943.

Le régime juridictionnel des Forces Françaises combattantes en Egypte. Journal des tribunaux mixtes 22 : 3-5, 8 et 9 mars 1943.

Le régime juridictionnel des forces amies ou alliées de la Grande-Bretagne. Journal des tribunaux mixtes 22 : 3-4, 10-11 mai 1943.

De la suspension des règles de procédure en raison de la cessation des communications entre l'Egypte et les pays ennemis ou occupés par l'ennemi. Journal des tribunaux mixtes 22 : 2-3, 23-24 juin 1943.

La situation faite aux tribunaux mixtes par les Accords de Montreux et par la guerre. Journal des tribunaux mixtes 22 : 1-2, 21 et 22 juillet 1943.

Le régime juridictionnel des marins français de la force X en Egypte et les immunités de juridiction des marines de guerre étrangères. Journal des tribunaux mixtes 22 : 3-5, 26 et 27 juillet 1943.

La nationalité et la situation juridique des sociétés de personnes constituées en Egypte sous une forme étrangère (Contd.). Journal des tribunaux mixtes 22 : 2-3, 30-31 août 1943.

L'administration future de la justice et les étrangers - La question de la langue. Journal des tribunaux mixres 22 : 1-2, 13 et 14 septembre 1943.

Les conditions de validité des wakfs constitués en Egypte par des étrangers. Journal des tribunaux mixtes 22 : 1-3, 6 et 7 septembre 1943.

Le règlement d'exécution de la loi no. 88 de 1942 sur la réparation des dommages de guerre. Journal des tribunaux mixtes 22 : 2-4, 24 et 25 septembre 1943.

Le problème de la nationalité égyptienne. Journal des tribunaux mixtes 22 : 3, 3et 4 septembre 1943.

VROONEN, E. : La juridiction gracieuse des tribunaux mixtes en matière de statut personnel (Contd,). Journal des tribunaux mixtes 22 : 1-2, 13 et 14 octobre 1943.

La compétence des tribunaux mixtes à l'égard des sociétés de personnes formées entre étrangers ou entre étrangers et égyptiens. Journal des tribunaux mixtes 22 : 3, 15 et 16 octobre 1943.

L'interprétation et l'application de la législation locative de guerre par les tribunaux mixtes. Journal des tribunaux mixtes 22 : 1-3, 20 et 21 octobre 1943.

L'application de la loi religieuse du "de sujus" à la dévolution héréditaire dans les successions "ab intestat" des Libanais et des Egyptiens non musulmans. Journal des tribunaux mixtes 23 : 2-4, 29 et 30 décembre 1943.

Le régime juridictionnel des membres des Forces Alliées en Egypte et la notion du service commandé.

Le projet de nouveau code civil. Journal des tribunaux mixtes 23 : 1-2, 7 et 8 février 1944.
ler article d'une série.

La compétence des tribunaux mixtes à l'égard des sociétés de personnes formées entre étrangers ou entre étrangers et Egyptiens (Suite). Journal des tribunaux mixtes 23 : 1-5, 24 et 25 avril 1944.

Le Parlement britannique et les atteintes aux pouvoirs juridictionnels des tribunaux mixtes. Journal des tribunaux mixtes 23 : 2, 12 et 13 mai 1944.

MOUSKHELI, M. : L'état de siège en Egypte et le régime des proclamations militaires. Journal des tribunaux mixtes 23 : 1-3, 5 rt 6 juin 1944.

BRINTON, J.Y. : Jurisdiction over members of allied forces in Egypt. American journal of international law 38 : 375-382, July 1944.

Le statut personnel des Egyptiens non-musulmans. Journal des tribunaux mixtes 23 : 1-2, 2 et 3 août 1944.

Le statut personnel des Egyptiens non-musulmans. Journal des tribunaux mixtes 24 : 1-3, 11 et 12 décembre 1944.

U.S.A.

McALLISTER, B.P. : Statutory roads to review of federal administrative orders. California law review 28 : 129-167, January 1940.

JAFFE, L. : Inter-Union disputes in search of a forum. Yale law journal 49 : 424-460, January 1940.

FRIEND, W.L. : A survêy of Anglo-American legal bibliography. Law library journal 33 : 1-18, January 1940.

ALBERTSWORTH, E.F. : Current constitutional fashions. Illinois law review 34 : 519-537, January 1940.

HAINES, C.G. : The adaptation of administrative law and procedure to constitutional theories and principles. American political science review 34 : 1-30, February 1940.

HART, H.M. : The business of the Supreme Court at the October terms, 1937 and 1938. Harvard law review 53 : 579-626, February 1940.

NUSSBAUM, A. : Fact research in law. Columbia law review 40 : 189-219, February 1940.

POWELL, T.R. : Some aspects of American constitutional law. Harvard law review 53 : 529-553, February 1940.

NORTHROP, E.H. : Small claims courts and conciliation tribunals - A bibliography. Law library journal 33 : 39-50, March 1940.

ALBERTSWORTH, E.F. : The constitution - Revised version. American bar association journal 26 : 324-328, 351, April 1940.

SUMNERS, H.W. : The constitution to-day. American bar association journal 26 : 285-289, 367, April 1940.

State legislation in the United States, 1935-1938. Journal of comparative legislation and international law 22 : 203-208, November 1940.

PINNEY, H. : The nature of government corporations. Tulane law review 15 : 51-74, December 1940.

Protection of intellectual property. Illinois law review 35 : 546-565, January 1941.

LILIENTHAL, D.E., and MARQUIS, R.H. : The conduct of business enterprises by the Federal Government. Harvard law review 54 : 545-601, February 1941.

WARNER, S.B. : The model Sabotage prevention Act. Harvard law review 54 : 602-631, February 1941.
See also pp. 632-646.

Corporate reorganizations. New York University law quarterly review 18 : 313-397, March 1941.
Series of articles.

The taking of proofs in arbitration proceedings. Arbitration journal 5 : 272-285, No. 3-4, 1941.

The final report of the Attorney general's committee on administrative procedure. Columbia law review 41 : 585-645, April 1941.

CUSHMAN, R.E. : Constitutional law in 1939-1940. American political science review 35 : 250-283, April 1941.
The constitutional decisions of the Supreme Court.

HAMILTON, W.H., and BRANDEN, G.D. : The special competence of the Cupreme Court. Yale law journal 50 : 1319-1375, June 1941.

AIKIN, C. : State constitutional law in 1940-1941. American political science review 35 : 683-700, August 1941.

PRITCHETT, C.H. : Divisions of opinion among justices of the U.S. Supreme Court, 1939-1941. American journal of international law 35 : 890-898, October 1941.

WHITEHEAD, W.C. : Admirality - Uniformity Rule. Michigan law review 40 : 260-267, December 1941.

MYERS, D.P. : Joint resolutions are laws. American bar association journal 28 : 33-37, January 1942.

MONTAGUE, G.H. : Reform of administrative procedure. Michigan law review 40 : 501-540, February 1942.

REED, D.D. and T.H. : Insurance for war damage. Survey graphic 31 : 68-71, February 1942.

ALBERTSWORTH, E.F. : Industrial law under the new constitutionalism. American bar association journal 28 : 106-112, February 1942.

Public laws enacted by the 77th Congress, first session (Contd.). Congressional digest 21 : 67-88, March 1942.

VANDERBILT, A.T. : The new Federal Criminal Rules. Yale law journal 51 : 719-722, March 1942.

BIDDLE, F. : Lawyers in the war effort. American bar association journal 28 : 232-235, April 1942.

CUSHMAN, R.E. : Constitutional law in 1940-1941. American political science review 36 : 263-289, April 1942.

FORRESTIER, R. : The nature of a "Federal question". Tulane law review 16 : 362-385, April 1942.

MORGAN, E.M. : Comments on the proposed Code of evidence of the American Law Institute. Canadian bar review 20 : 271-295, April 1942.

A symposium on the proposed Code of Civil Procedure for Missouri. Missouri law review 7 : 105-170, April 1942.

McDOUGAL, M.S. : Future interests restated - Tradition versus clarification and reform. Harvard law review 55 : 1077-1115, May 1942.
Restatement of the Law of Property, vol. III.

RIESMAN, D. : Democracy and defamation - Control of group libel. Columbia law review 42 : 727-780, May 1942.

FAIRMAN, C. : The law of martial rule and the national emergency. Harvard law review 55 : 1253-1302, June 1942.

ORFIELD, L.B. : A résumé of decisions of the United States Supreme Court of federal criminal procedure. Missouri law review 7 : 262-301, June 1942.

PATTERSON, E.W. : Constructive conditions in contracts. Columbia law review 62 : 903-954, June 1942.

CHANDLER, H.P. : The impact of the war upon the United States Courts. American bar association journal 28 : 460-466, July 1942.

AIKIN, C. : State constitutional law in 1941-1942. American political science review 36 : 667-688, August 1942.

COGHILL, E.H. : Recent American decisions. Australian law journal 16 : 356-358, 16 April 1943.

McGOVNEY, D.O. : A supreme court fiction - Corporations in the diverse citizenship jurisdiction of the federal courts. Harvard law review 56 : 853-898, May 1943.

LEWIS, W.D. : The American law institute. Journal of comparative legislation and international law 25 : 25-30, November 1943.

CARR, C.T. : Delegated legislation in the United States. Journal of comparative legislation and international law 25 : 47-54, November 1943.

NEMMERS, E.E. : Termination of war contracts. Columbia law review 44 : 864-898. November 1944.

HURST, W. : Treason in the United States. Harvard law review 58 : 226-272, November 1944.

U.S.A.
(International law, Aliens, Nationality)

DULLES, A.W. : Cash and carry neutrality. Foreign affairs 18 : 179-195, January 1940.

WURZEL, A. : Nonresident aliens and federal estate tax : a legislative problem. Columbia law review 40 : 52-84, January 1940.

WOOLSEY, L.H. : The sabotage claims against Germany. American journal of international law 34 : 23-35, January 1940.

JESSUP, P.C. : The "Neutrality Act of 1939". American journal of international law 34 : 95-99, January 1940.

FLOURNOY, R.W. : Revision of nationality laws of the United States. American journal of international law 34 : 36-46, January 1940.

Constitutionality of State legislation affecting aliens. New York University law quarterly review 17 : 242-254, January 1940.

De WOLFE HOWE, M. : The recognition of foreign divorce decrees in New York State. Columbian law review 40 : 373-403, March 1940.

ORFIELD, L.B. : Expatriation of American minors. Michigan law review 38 : 585-609, March 1940.

DEÁK, F. : The United States Neutrality Acts. International conciliation : 73-114, March 1940.

DEÁK, F. : The plea of sovereign immunity and the New York Court of Appeals. Columbia law review 40 : 453-465, March 1940.

WRIGHT, Q. : Rights and duties under international law as affected by the United States neutrality Act and the resolutions of Panama. American journal of international law 34 : 238-248, April 1940.

WRIGHT, Q. : The power to declare neutrality under American law. American journal of international law 34 : 302-310, April 1940.

LEVITAN, D.M. : Executive agreements: a study of the executive in the control of the foreign relations of the United States. Illinois law review 35 : 365-395, December 1940.

KNIGHT, G.S. : Nationality Act of 1940. American law association journal 26 : 938-940, December 1940.

Citizenship and expatriation of minors under the Nationality Act of 1940. Illinois law review 35 : 607-611, January 1941.

SCHIBSBY, M. : The new nationality code. Common ground 1 : 67-70, No. 2, 1941.

Protection of American holdings in foreign countries. Department of State bulletin 4 : 337-338, 22 March 1941.

The Nationality Act of 1940. Harvard law review 54 : 860-870, March 1941.

NUSSBAUM, A. : The problem of proving foreign law. Yale law journal 50 : 1018-1044, April 1941.

HYDE, C.C. : The Nationality Act of 1940. American journal of international law 35 : 314-319, April 1941.

GREWE, W.G. : Das Englandhilfsgesetz - Betrachtungen zum "Gesetz zur Verteidigung der Vereinigten Staaten" vom 11. März 1941 und zur amerikanischen Völkerrechtspolitik. Zeitschrift für die gesamte Staatswissenschaft 101 : 606-626, 4. Heft 1941.

O'CONNOR, B. : Constitutional protection of the alien's right to work. New York University law quarterly review 18 : 483-497, May 1941.

Foreign funds control through Presidential freezing orders. Columbia law review 41 : 1039-1071, June 1941.

The State Department assumes control of visa issuance. Interpreter releases 18 : 274-285, 1 July 1941.

JONES, H.W. : The President, Congress and foreign relations. California law review 29 : 565-585, July 1941.

RIESMAN, D. : The American constitution and international labour legislation. International labour review 44 : 123-193, August 1941.

KUHN, A.K. : Foreign funds control and foreign owned property. American journal of international law 35 : 651-654, October 1941.

NATIONAL LAW - COUNTRIES

SCHWARZENBERGER, G. : The "Aid Britain" Bill and the law of neutrality. Transactions of the Grotius Society, Problems of peace and war 27 : 1-29, 1941.

MILLS, D.N. : Aliens - Naturalization - Refusal to bear arms. Michigan law review 40 : 452-455, January 1942.

Re : Foreign funds control through presidential freezing orders. Columbia law review 42 : 105-106, January 1942.

WRIGHT, Q. : Repeal of the Neutrality Act. American journal of international law 36 : 8-23, January 1942.

WILSON, R.R. : Some aspects of the jurisprudence of national claims commissions. American journal of international law 36 : 56-76, January 1942.

RUPP, H. : Die Behandlung des ausländischen Vermögens in den Vereinigten Staaten von Amerika im Kriege. Zeitschrift für ausländisches und internationales Privatrecht 14 : 227-282, Heft 1/2, 1942.

HOFMANNSTHAL, E. von : "Austro-Hungarians". American journal of international law 36 : 292-294, April 1942.
Registration in the U.S.

Executive Agreements and the Treaty Power. Columbia law review 42 : 831-843, May 1942.

RUPP, H. : Die Behandlung deutscher Vermögenswerte in den Vereinigten Staaten. Bank-Archiv : : 202-204, 15. Mai 1942.

FITZHUGH, W.W. Jr., and HYDE, C.C. : The drafting pf neutral aliens by the United States. American journal of international law 36 : 369-382, July 1942.

McCLURE, W. : Copyright in war and peace. American journal of international law 36 : 383-399, July 1942.

TURLINGTON, E. : Vesting orders under the first War Powers Act, 1941. American journal of international law 36 : 460-465, July 1942.

WILSON, R.H. : Facilitation of naturalization through military service. American journal of international law 36 : 454-460, July 1942.

PREUSS, L. : Denaturalization on the ground of disloyalty. American political science review 36 : 701-710, August 1942.

SOMMERICH, O.C. : Recent innovations in legal and regulatory concepts as to the alien and his property. American journal of international law 37 : 58-73, January 1943.

BRIGGS, H.W. : The settlement of Mexican claims act of 1942. American journal of international law 37 : 222-232, April 1943.

DICKINSON, J. : Enemy-owned property, restitution or confiscation? Foreign affairs 22 : 126-142, October 1943.

Treaty-making power and ratification of treaties - Proposed amendment of provision of constitution which requires a two-thirds majority ih Senate for treaty ratification. Summary of congressional proceedings, U.S.A. 1 : 115-123, September 1943-January 1944.

FISCHER, P. : Die rechtlichen Grund lagen und Folgen der Behandlung des ausländischen Eigentums durch die Vereinigten Staaten. Zeitschrift für schweizerisches Recht 63 : 337-346, Heft 2, 1944.

WILSON, R.R. : Recent developments in the treatment of civilian alien enemies. American journal of international law 38 : 397-406, July 1944.

WRIGHT, Q. : The United States and international agreements. American journal of international law 38 : 341-355, July 1944.

BORCHARD, E. : Shall the executive agreement replace the treaty? American journal of international law 38 : 637-643, October 1944.

McNEIL, E.C. : United States army courts-martial in Britain. Law quarterly review 60 : 356-360, October 1944.

WRIGHT, H. : The two-thirds vote of the Senate in treaty-making. American journal of international law 38 : 643-650, October 1944.

WRIGHT, Q. : Constitutional procedure in the United States for carrying out obligations for military sanctions. American journal of international law 38 : 678-684, October 1944.

U.S.A.
(Patents, Trade-marks, Copyright)

HOLLAND, N.N. : An opportunity for the National Patents Planning Commission. American bar association journal 28 : 455-457, July 1942.

LÖWENBACH, J. : Les récents efforts entrepris aux Etats-Unis d'Amérique pour réformer la législation du copyright et pour la rallier à l'Union internationale. Droit d'auteur 57 : 86-89, août 1944.

URUGUAY

Demandas contra la nación o las entidades politicas que la componen en los paises de America. Revista de derecho y legislación 32 : 143-176, julio-agosto 1943.

La reforma constitucional en el Uruguay. Revista parlamentaria 11 : 14-26, octubre 1942.

VATICAN STATE

BASSANO, U. : Obbligo della manutenzione di Piazza S. Pietro e responsabilità vers o i terzi. Rivista di diritto pubblico 33 : 329-337, luglio 1941.

WRIGHT, H. : The status of the Vatican City. American journal of international law 38 : 452-457, July 1944.

VENEZUELA

MACHADO, J.E. : Historia del código civil venezolano. Revista de derecho y legislación 29 : 3-39, enero 1940.

Venezuela - Ley de naturalización (29 de mayo de 1940). Revista parlamentaria 10 : 49-54, agosto 1941.

ARCAYA, P.M. : Observaciones al proyecto de código civil. Revista de derecho y legislación 31 : 222-268, septiembre-noviembre 1942.

GOLDSTONE, J.L. : The judicial status of non-registered foreign corporations in Venezuela. Tulane law review 17 : 575-595, April 1943.

Ley sobre hidrocarburos de los Estados Unidos de Venezuela. Boletín de informaciones petroleras 21 : 73-92, abril 1944.

YUGOSLAVIA

SAGADIN, S. : Die staatsrechtliche Lösung der kroatischen Frage in Jugoslawien. Zeitschrift für osteuropäisches Recht 6 : 243-254, Januar-Februar 1940.

TOMAŠIĆ, D. : Constitutional changes in Yugoslavia. Political science quarterly 55 : 582-593, December 1940.

KUŠEY, G. : Die gegenwärtige staatsrechtliche Lage Kroatiens im Königreich Jugoslavien. Zeitschrift für öffentliches Recht 20 : 525-562, Heft 4-5, 1940.

KUŠEY, G. : Das Verhältnis zwischen Staat und Konfessionen in der jugoslavischen Religionsgesetzgebung. Zeitschrift für osteuropäisches Recht 7 : 315-345, Januar-Februar 1941.

SERENI, A.P. : The status of Croatia under international law. American political science review 35 : 1144-1151, December 1941.

La nuova Croatia - Discorso di Ante Pavelic al Sabor. Relazioni internazionali 8 : 332-335, 21 marzo 1942.

Jugoslawien - Ubersicht über die wesentliche Gesetzgebung im Jahre 1941. Zeitschrift für osteuropäisches Recht 8 : 496-497, März/April 1942.

Serbien - Ubersicht über die wesentliche Gesetzgebung im Jahre 1941. Zeitschrift für osteuropäisches Recht 8 : 497-502, März/April 1942.

LORKOVIC, M. : Ein Jahr unabhängiges Kroatien. Zeitschrift für Politik 32 : 205-208, April 1942.

PLIVERIC, M. : Das in Kroatien geltende allgemeine Privatrecht. Zeitschrift für osteuropäisches Recht 8 : 539-579, Mai/Juni 1942.

Kroatien - Uebersicht über die wesentliche Gesetzgebung im Jahre 1941/42. Zeitschrift für osteuropäisches Recht 8 : 580-591, Mai/Juni 1942.

SLADOVIC, E. : Der Unabhängige Staat Kroatien. Zeitschrift für osteuropäisches Recht 9 : 1-41, Juli-September 1942.
See also pp. 117-124.

Serbien - Ubersicht über die wesentliche Gesetzgebung im Jahre 1942. Zeitschrift für osteuropäisches Recht 9 : 204-206, Oktober/Dezember 1942.

La zagruda, communauté de famille en Serbie. Economie et humanisme 2 : 628-636, juillet-août 1943.

Jugoslavia, anni 1932-1938. Giurisprudenza comparata di diritto internazionale privato 9 : 1-77, 1943.

SLADOVIČ von SLADOEVIČKI, E. : Verfassungs- und Verwaltungsrecht des unabhängigen Staates Kroatien. Archiv des öffentlichen Rechts 33 : 222-282, August 1943.

AMLACHER, G. : Rechtspflege in der Untersteiermark. Deutsches Recht 14 : 271-278, 22. u. 29 April 1944.

Rechtspflege in der Untersteiermark. Deutsche Rechtspflege 55 : 151-153, 15. Juli 1944.

NATIONAL LAW - COUNTRIES

ARGENTINE

The impeachment of the justices of the Argentine Supreme Court. Review of the River Plate 101 : 14-16, 13 December 1946.

Declaration proclaiming sovereignty over the epicontinental sea and the continental shelf. American journal of international law, Official documents 41 : 11-12, January 1947.

LINARES QUINTANA, S.V. : République argentine - La théorie des gouvernements "de fait" dans la jurisprudence de la Cour suprême de justice de la République argentine. Revue du droit public et de la science politique 65 : 52-59, janvier-mars 1949.

The Argentine constitution - The complete text of the constitution of 1949. Review of the River Plate 105 : 19-27, 46-48, 25 March 1949.

Constitución de la Nación Argentina - Reformas introducidas por la Convención nacional constituyente año 1949. Ministerio de hacienda de la Nacion, Boletín (Argentine) 4 : 545-598, 26 marzo 1949.

La reforma de la Constitución nacional. Revista parlamentaria 17 : 1-27, marzo 1949.

Constitución de la Nación Argentina. Monitor de la educación común 67 : 3-24, enero-marzo 1949.

Constitución de la Nación Argentina. Revista de la Faculdad de ciencias económicas, comerciales y políticas (Rosario) : 5-39, enero-agosto 1949.

GONZALEZ BUSTAMANTE, J.J. : La reforma procesal en la Argentina. Criminalia 15 : 354-368, septiembre 1949.

GONZÁLEZ PÉREZ, J. : El proceso contencioso administrativo argentino. Revista de estudios políticos 28 : 250-277, noviembre-diciembre 1949.

La constitution argentine. Documentation française, Notes et études documentaires : 1-16, No. 1242, 8 décembre 1949.

AUSTRALIA

JONES, L. : Industrial arbitration in Australia. Modern law review 8 : 63-68, March 1945.

MITCHELL, R.E. : Australian aspects of government corporations. Canadian bar review 24 : 793-806, November 1946.

BAILEY, K.H. : Australia and the international labour conventions. International labour review 54 : 285-308, November-December 1946.

BAILEY, K.H. : L'Australie et les conventions internationales du Travail. Revue internationale du travail 54 : 329-356, novembre-décembre 1946.

SAWER, G. : The defence power of the Commonwealth in time of war. Australian law journal 20 : 295-300, 13 December 1946.

HOLMES, J.D. : Back to dual sovereignty. Australian law journal 21 : 162-169, 19 September 1947.

MORISON, W.L. : Extra-territorial enforcement of judgments within the Commonwealth of Australia. Australian law journal 21 : 298-302, 12 December 1947.

ZELLING, H. : Inconsistency between Commonwealth and state laws. Australian law journal 22 : 45-51, 20 May 1948.

COWEN, Z. : The separation of judicial power and the exercise of defence powers in Australia. Canadian bar review 26 : 829-844, May 1948.

Australian citizenship. Australian law journal 22 : 445, 17 February 1949.

BEASLEY, F.R. : The exercise of "judicial power" in the Commonwealth of Australia. Canadian bar review 27 : 686-701, June-July 1949.

Sixth legal convention of the Law council of Australia. Australian law journal 23 : 149-157, 24 August 1949.

Migratory divorce in Australia and the United States. University of Chicagi law review 17 : 134-148, autumn 1949.

WISEMAN, H.D. : Why not a criminal code? Australian law journal 23 : 347-252, 20 October 1949.
Victoria.

PARSONS, R. : English precedents in Australian courts. Annual law review 1 : 211-222, December 1949.

AUSTRIA

EHRENHAFT, R. : Conséquences législatives de la renaissance de l'Autriche à l'indépendance. Nouvelle revuee de droit international privé 13 : 159-163, no. 1-2, 1946.

KALTENBERGER, J. : Der Wirkungskreis des Bundespräsidenten. Osterreichs Monatshefte 1 : 143-145, Jänner 1946.

La constitution fédérale de la République d'Autriche, 1920-1929. France, Secrétariatd'état à la présidence du Conseil et à l'information, Notes documentaires et études : 1-24, No. 266, 21 mars 1946.

Nationalrat über Beschlagnahme deutschen Eigentums - Auszug aus dem Befehl des General Kurassow. Zeitspiegel 7 : 1-2, 20. Juli 1946.

CHAMRATH, G. : Das österreichische Volksgericht. Osterreichische Monatshefte 1 : 423-424, July 1946.

BOCK, F. : Die Sühne - Kommentar zum Nationalsozialistengesetz. Osterreichische Monatshefte 1 : 460-464, August 1946.

MARKOVICS, A. : Die belasteten Personen nach dem Nationalsozialistengesetz. Osterreichische Juristen-Zeitung 1 : 473-475, 22. November 1946.

WAHLE, K. : Der Regierungsentwurf des 3. Rückstellungsgesetzes. Osterreichische Volkswirt 33 : 2-6, 3. Jännerheft 1947.
Reparations.

KASTNER, W. : Zur Lage des wirtschaftlichen Gesellschaftsrechts in Osterreich. Juristische Blätter 69 : 4. Januar 1947.

DOLP, F. : Die Strafbarkeit der Denunziation nach dem Kriegsverbrechergesetz. Osterreichische Juristen-Zeitung 2 : 14-16, 24. Jänner 1947.

NATIONAL LAW - COUNTRIES

WERNER, L. : Das Wiedererstehen Österreichs als Rechtsproblem. Juristische Blätter 69 : 137-145, 161-164, 29. März, 12. April 1947.

BOCK, F. : Schlusswort zum Nationalsocialistengesetz. Österreichische Monatshefte 2 : 219-222, März 1947.

WOLFF, K. : Faschistisches Recht im demokratischen Österreich. Juristische Blätter 69 : 225-227, 24. Mai 1947.

THIERRY, A. : La loi d'interdiction du 8 février 1947. Bulletin d'information et de documentation, Haut-Commissariat de la République française en Autriche : 59-75, mai-juillet 1947.

BURKHART-SCHENK, P. : Das dritte Rückstellungsgesetz in der Praxis. Juristische Blätter 69 : 317-319, 19. Juli 1947.

WITT, G.A. : Restituierung der österreichischen Patentschutz-, Musterschutz- und Markenschutzgesetzgebung. Mitteilungen des Österreichischen Handelskammer in der Schweiz 1 : 46-68, September 1947.

GRÖSSWANG, W. : Die Präsumption der Rechtswidrigkeit bei Tatbeständen nach dem Kriegsverbrechergesetz. Österreichische Juristen-Zeitung 3 : 75-80, 20. Februar 1948,

Leidenschaftliche Debatte um die Arisierung - Diskussion über das Dritte Rückstellungsgesetz. Berichte und Informationen, Österreichisches Forschungsinstitut für Wirtschaft und Politik 3 : 3-7, 9. April 1948.
Reparation.

WOLFF, K. : Todeserklärung Staatenloser. Juristische Blätter 70 : 173-174, 24. April 1948.

HOYER, V. : Die Form der Eheschliessung nach österreichischem Recht im Inland und im Ausland, insbesondere Eheschliessung durch Stellvertretung. Österreichische JuristenZeitung 3 : 221-227, 14. Mai 1948.

WERNER, L. : Staatsbürgerschaftsrecht und Nationalsozialistengesetz. Juristische Blätter 70 : 249-256, 5. Juni 1948.

BECK, H. : Verletzungen der Menschenwürde nach paragraph 4 des Kriegsverbrechergesetzes und Ehrenbeleidigung. Österreichische Juristen-Zeitung 3 : 293-295, 25. Juni 1948.

VALTERS, N. : Österreichisches Recht und Verfügungen der Besatzungsmächte. Juristische Blätter 70 : 370-372, 4. September 1948.

BAECK, P.L. : Noch einmal: Das dritte Rückstellungsgesetz und die Praxis. Juristische Blätter 70 : 524-525, 13. November 1948.

Vier Beiträge zum Dritten Rückstellungsgesetz. Österreichische Juristen-Zeitung 3 : 509-512, 19. November 1948.

SEIDL-HOHENLINDERN, I. : Die Staatsbürgerschaft der Volksdeutschen im Licht österreichischer Urteile. Österreichische Juristen-Zeitung 3 : 516-519, 19. November 1948.

KÖSTLER, R. : Weg und Ziel einer Ehenrechtsreform. Juristische Blätter 70 : 577-581, 11. Dezember 1948.

SEIDL-HOHENVELDERN, I. : Österreichische Entscheidungen auf dem Gebiet des Internationalen Privatrechtes. Juristische Blätter 71 : 36-41, 22. Januar 1949.

SEIDL-HOHENVELDERN, L. : Le droit international privé en Autriche de 1939 à 1948. Revue critique de droit international privé 38 : 35-53, janvier-mars 1949.

SARADITSCH, H. : Die Todeserklärung kriegsverschollener Personen. Österreichische Juristen-Zeitung 4 : 151-152, 18. März 1949.

SEIDL-HOHENVELDERN, I. : Österreich - Das internationale Privatrecht 1945-1949. Zeitschrift für ausländisches und internationales Privatrecht 15 : 457-489, Heft 3/4, 1949.

SATTER, K. : Die Todeserklärung Staatenloser. Juristische Blätter 71 : 228-231, 30. April 1949.

PLANK, R. : Zur Anwendung des paragraph 4 (1) Verschollenheits G. auf Kriegsgefangenen. Österreichische Juristen-Zeitung 4 : 315, 10. Juni 1949.

MARKOVICS, A. : Der Ausschluss vom Wahlrecht. Österreichische Juristen-Zeitung 4 : 462-466, 23. September 1949.

BELGIUM

HEYSE, T. : Réplique au mémoire de M. Jentgen au sujet des pouvoirs des Secrétaires généraux pendant l'occupation, loi du 10 mai 1940. Institut royal colonial belge, Bulletin des sciences 17 ; 855-874, No. 3, 1946.

MOUREAU, L., et SIMONARD, A. : Le Conseil d'état de Belgique. Revue du droit public et de la science politique 64 : 159-203, avril-juin 1948.

VAN HOUTTE, J. : De Belgische oorlogsschaderegeling (Contd.). Economisch-statistische Berichten 33 : 506-510, 30 Juni 1948.

VIENNE, R. : La loi belge de défense sociale (Suite). Revue pénitentiaire et de droit pénal 72 : 244-286, juillet-décembre 1948.

LALOUX, P., et RENARD, C. : Chronique de droit belge - Jurisprudence en matière de droit civil, années 1946 et 1947. Revue trimestrielle de droit civil 1948 : 131-158, janvier-mars 1949.

BOLIVIA

REY-ARROJO, M.L. : Proyecto oficial del código penal para la República de Bolivia (Contd.). Revista de derecho (Concepción) 14 : 645-662, octubre-diciembre 1946.

BRAZIL

AZEVEDO, P. : Os tratados e os interêsses privados em face do direito brasileiro. Boletim da Sociedade brasileira de direito internacional 1 : 12-29, janeiro-junho 1945.

FERREIRA, W. : O crime politico e a fórma de seu julgamento na ditadura fascista brasiliera. Revista da Faculdade de direito (São Paulo) 40 : 29-69, 1945.

NASCIMENTO e SILVA, G.E. do : O código penal em face do direito das gentes. Boletim da Sociedade brasileira de direito internacional 2 : 22-39, janeiro-junho 1946.

VALLADÃO, H. : O direito internacional no projeto da constituição. Boletim da Sociedade brasileira de direito internacional 2 : 7-17, janeiro-junho 1946.

VALLADÃO, H. : Requisitos do processo de extradição. Boletim da Sociedade brasileira de direito internacional 2 : 27-46, julho-dezembre 1946.

A nova constituição do Brasil. Boletim da Sociedade brasileira de direito internacional 2 : 128-159, julho-dezembro 1946.

New constitution for Brazil. Bulletin of the Pan American union 81 : 22-28, January 1947.

BAMBERGER, E. : Die Gerichtsorganisation Brasiliens nach der neuen Verfassung. Österreichische Juristen-Zeitung 2 : 385-387, 26. September 1947.

CUNHA GONCALVES, L. da : Sugestões para a melhoria do código civil brasileiro. Revista acadêmica 55 : 113-130, 1947.

TENA, J.L. : Evolución del Brasil. Revista de estudios políticos 17 : 201-216, núms. 31-32, 1947.

HERZOG, J.B. : Peines et mesures de sûreté en droit brésilien. Revue de science criminelle et de droit pénal comparé : 53-72, janvier-mars 1948.

ACCIOLY, H. : A ratificação e a promulgação dos tratados, em face de constituição federal brasileira. Boletim da Sociedade brasileira de direito internacional 4 : 5-11, janeiro-junho 1948.

VALLADÃO, H. : Perda e reaquisição da nacionalidade brasileira. Boletim da Sociedade brasileira de direito internacional 4 : 139-145, julho-dezembro 1948.

WYLER, M. : The development of the Brazilian constitution, 1891-1946. Journal of comparative legislation and international law 31 : 63-60, parts 3-4, 1949.

Constitution des Etats-Unis du Brésil 1946. Cahiers de législation et de bibliographie juridique de l' Amérique latine : 155-224, No. 4, 1949.

BULGARIA

MEVORACH, N. : Le nouveau statut constitutionnel. Bulgarie nouvelle : 1, 3, 25 octobre 1946.

La costituzione bulgara. Politica estera 3 : 1429-1431, 1460-1462, 24 novembre, 1 dicembre 1946.

MEVORACH, N. : The new Bulgarian constitution. Changing epoch series : 54-62, No. 2, 1947.

Constitution de la République populaire de Bulgarie adoptée par la Grande assemblée nationale le 4 décembre 1947. Bulgarie nouvelle : 2-3, 17 décembre 1947.

La constitution bulgare. Documentation française, Notes documentaires et études : 1-15, No. 821, 4 février 1948.

HOYER, V. : Das bulgarische Ehegesetz vom 3. Mai 1945. Österreichische Juristen-Zeitung 3 : 313-316, 9. Juli 1948.

RADOÏLSKI, L. : Fundamental freedoms and human rights in PR Bulgaria. Free Bulgaria 4 : 333-335, 1 November 1949.

Constitution de la République populaire de Bulgarie adoptée le 4 décembre 1947. Informations constitutionnelles et parlementaires 2 : 4-24, no. unique 1949.

BURMA

MAUNG, E. : Enemy legislation and judgments in Burma. Journal of comparative legislation and international law 30 : 11-17, parts III and IV, 1948.

GLEDHILL, A. : Some aspects of the operation of international and military law in Burma, 1941-'945. Modern law review 12 : 191-204, April 1949.

CANADA

MORRIS, J.H.C. : Recognition of divorces granted outside the domicile. Canadian bar review 24 : 73-86, February 1946.

MACKENZIE, K.F. : Legal aid in war and peace. Canadian bar review 24 : 198-202, March 1946.

The latest amendments to the British North America act. Canadian bar review 24 : 609-613, August-September 1946.

STIKEMAN, H.H. : Descriptive outline of income tax law and administration in the dominion of Canada (Contd.). Bulletin for international fiscal documentation 1 : 247-258, No. 6, 1946-1947.

The Canadian citizenship act. Canadian bar review 25 : 364-372, April 1947.

MATAS, R.J. : Treaty making in Canada. Canadian bar review 25 : 458-477, May 1947.

PIGEON, L.P. : The necessity of law reform. Canadian bar review 25 : 955-966, November 1947.

ROGERS, S. : Copyright confusion. Canadian bar review 25 : 967-979, November 1947.

The Trade mark law revision committee. Canadian bar review 25 : 1135-1138, December 1947.

Anniversary number. Canadian bar review 26 : 1-361, January 1948.
Articles on many aspects of the law.

MacDONALD, V.C. : The constitution in a changing world. Canadian bar review 26 : 21-45, January 1948.

MANNING, H.E. : "Copyright confusion" reconsidered. Canadian bar review 26 : 671-682, April 1948.

The Joint committee on human rights and fundamental freedoms. Canadian bar review 26 : 706-714, April 1948.

OLLIVIER, M. : The revised statutes of Canada. Canadian bar review 26 : 797-811, May 1948.

NATIONAL LAW : COUNTRIES

HOW, W.G. : The case for a Canadian bill of rights. Canadian bar review 26 : 759-796, May 1948.

HARVEY, A.B. : Recent amendments to the criminal code. Canadian bar review 26 : 1319-1328, November 1948.

SHUMIATCHER, M.C. : Section 96 of the British North America act re-examined. Canadian bar review 27 : 131-152, February 1949.

SCOTT, F.R. : Dominion jurisdiction over human rights and fundamental freedoms. Canadian bar review 27 : 497-536, May 1949.

Penal reform in Canada. Canadian bar review 27 : 999-1110, November 1949.
Special issue.

CEYLON

JENNINGS, W.I. : The making of a dominion constitution. Law quarterly review 65 : 456-479, October 1949.

CHILE

MANDUJANO LÓPEZ, J.G. : Estudio comparativo entre el código civil approbado por le Congreso nacional en 1855 y el código promulgado en diciembre de ese año. Anales de la Facultad de ciencias jurídicas y sociales (Santiago) 13 : 105-134, nos. 52 al 59, 1948 y 1949.

DOMINGUEZ BENAVENTE, R. : La filiación en el proyecto que propone diversas modificaciones al código civil chileno. Revista de derecho (Concepción) 17 : 449-449 (sic) octubre-diciembre 1949.
Last of a series of articles.

BRAIN RIOJA, H. : Observaciones al proyecto de reforma del código penal chileno (Contd.). Revista de derecho (Concepción) 17 : 463-473, octubre-diciembre 1949.

CHINA

LOBINGIER, C.S. : The "corpus juris" of new China. Tulane law review 19 : 512-552, June 1945.

ESCARRA, J. : Le droit chinois moderne et son application par les tribunaux. Sinologica 1 : 97-107, No. 2, 1947.

TSENG YU-HAO : Comment on new constitution, historical background given. China weekly review 105 : 11-13, 1 March 1947.

Main features of China's constitution. China tomorrow 1 : 180-182, March 1947.

POUND, R. : The Chinese constitution. New York university law quarterly 22 : 194-232, April 1947.

China's courts. China weekly review 105 : 257-259, 3 May 1947.

CHAMBERLAIN, J.P. : Structure of China's constitution. Far Eastern survey 16 : 100-105, 7 May 1947.

POUND, R. : Law and courts in China - Progress in the administration of justice. American bar association journal 34 : 273-276, April 1948.

POUND, R. : Comparative law and history as bases for Chinese law. Harvard law review 61 : 749-762, May 1948.

Constitution de la République chinoise promulguée le 1 janvier 1947. Documentation française, Notes documentaires et études : 1-14, No. 906, 19 mai 1948.

POUND, R. : Development of a Chinese constitutional law. Law quarterly review 23 : 375-392, July 1948.

CHENG, T.H. : The development and reform of Chinese law. Current legal problems 1 : 170-187, 1948.

Textes constitutionnels et documents relatifs à la République populaire chinoise. Documentation française, Notes et études documentaires : 1-16, No. 1240, 6 décembre 1949.

COLOMBIA

BACKUS, R.C. : A guide to the law and legal literature of Colombia. Tulane law review 20 : 392-410, March 1946-

MORENO JARAMILLO, M. : Sociedades (Contd.). Estudios de derecho 8 : 67-119, mayo 1946.

RENDÓN, G.G. : Derecho penal colombiano. Estudios de derecho 8 : 7-65, mayo 1946.

RENDÓN, G.G. : Derecho penal colombiano. Estudios de derecho 10 : 219-254, julio 1948.

COMMONWEALTH

SCHWELB, E. : Legislation for enemy-occupied territory in the British Empire. Transactions of the Grotius society 30 : 239-259, 1945.

BOURDILLON, B. : The Nigerian constitution. African affairs 45 : 87-96, April 1946.

HARLOW, V. : Ceylon, experiment in oriental democracy. World affairs 109 : 123-127, June 1946.

CROSBY, J. : The constitutional position in Ceylon. Pacific affairs 19 : 272-279, September 1946.

BENTWICH, N. : A supreme commonwelath court. Fortnightly 160 : 191-195, September 1946.

GONIDEN, P.F. : L'évolution de la notion de citoyenneté dans la communauté des nations britanniques. Revue juridique et politique de l'Union française 1 : juillet-septembre 1947.

GANADO, J.M. : Maltese law. Journal of comparative legislation and international law 29 : 32-39, November 1947.

RAO, P.R. : The Commonwealth relationship. Federal law journal 12 : 57-61, May-June 1949.

RAO, P.R. : Citizenship rights for ceylon Indians. Hindustan review 85 : 22-25, July 1949.

FAWCETT, J.E.S. : Treaty relations of British overseas territories. British yearbook of international law 26 : 86-107, 1949.

JAMES, F.E.S. : Copyright law in the British Empire. British book news : 781-786, December 1949.

NATIONAL LAW - COUNTRIES

CUBA

El abuso de la intervenciones y el derecho de resistencia. Cuba económica y financiera 24 : 19-20, septiembre 1949.

CZECHOSLOVAKIA

MAXA, P. : From a state of occupation to freedom. Spirit of Czechoslovakia 6 : 5-6, No. 1, 1945.

POSVAR, J. : La nouvelle organisation de l'administration publique en Tchécoslovquie. Bulletin de droit tchécoslovaque 5 : 60-73, 1 mars 1947.

La constitution tchécoslovaque. France, Secrétariat d'état à la présidence du Conseil et à l'information, Notes documentaires et études : 1-12, No. 264, 19 mars 1946.

RADO, A.R. : Czechoslovak nationalization decrees - Some international aspects. American journal of international law 41 : 795-806, October 1947.

MATURA, A. : Nadbytok vyvlastnovacích noriem. Hospodárstvo a právo 13 : 91-93, september 1947.
Indemnity for expropriation.

SOLNAR, W. : Chronique tchécoslovaque, 1938-1947. Revue internationale de droit pénal 19 : 65-78, No. 1, 1938.

Czechoslovakia's new constitution. Czechoslovak life : 12-13, 15 May 1948.

WEISS-TESSBACH, A. : Zur Frage der jetzigen Staatsbürgerschaft der mittels Verfassungsdekret des Präsidenten der tschechoslowakischen Republik vom 2. VIII. 1945, Nr. 33 der Sammlung der Gesetze und Verordnungen der tschechoslowakischen Republik, ausgebürgerten Personen deutscher Volkszugehörigkeit. Juristische Blätter 70 : 381-385, 4. September 1948.

Constitution de la République Tchécoslovaque, 9 juin 1948. Documentation française, Notes documentaires et études : 1-19, no. 1005, 14 octobre 1948.

Czechoslovak act on private international law, 11 March 1948. Journal of comparative legislation and international law 31 : 78-88, part 3-4, 1949.

HOYER, V. : Das tschechoslowakische Gesetz über das internationale Privatrecht vom 11. März 1948. Österreichische Juristen-Zeitung 4 : 309-312, 10. Juni 1949.

ELÍAŠ, J. : La démocratisation de la justice en Tchécoslovaquie. Bulletin de droit tchécoslovaque 7 : 97-107, 1 octobre 1949.

MAGERSTEIN, W. : Die čsl. Jutizreform (Contd.). Juristische Blätter 71 : 496-499, 29. Oktober 1949.

DENMARK

ROSS, A. : Denmark's legal status during the occupation. Jus gentium 1 : 3-21, Fasc. 1, 1949.

SØRENSEN, M. : Den danske Grundlovs regler om parlamentarisk kontrol med udenrigspolitiken. Tidsskrift for rettsvitenskap 62 : 97-140, hefte 2-3, 1949.

SATZ, M. : Enemy legislation and judgments in Denmark. Journal of comparative legislation and international law 31 : 1-3, parts 3-4, 1949.

DOMINICAN REPUBLIC

Enmiendas a la constitución dominicana. Revista parlamentaria 16 : 15-16, diciembre 1947.

ECUADOR

KARGER, A. : Ecuador - Einführung der Adoption. Zeitschrift für ausländisches und internationales Privatrecht 15 : 557-567, Heft 3/4, 1949.

ETHIOPIA

BENTWICH, N. : Legal aspects of the restoration of Ethiopian Sovereignty. British year book of international law 22 : 275-278, 1945.

REITZER, H. : Recht und Juristenwesen in Abessinien. Juristische Blätter 69 : 127-129, 15. März 1947.

Ethiopian legislation. New times and Ethiopia news : 2. January 31, 1948.

ELWYN JONES, F. : Ethiopian justice. Spectator : 265-266, 27 August 1948.

FRANCE

JUGLART, M. de : L'obligation de renseignements dans les contrats. Revue trimestrielle de droit civil 44 : 1-22, janvier-mars 1945.

CASSIN, R. : Légalité et révolution républicaines. Cahiers politiques : 3-11, février 1945.

MORANGE, G. : Valeur juridique des principes contenus dans les déclarations des droits. Revue du droit public et de la science politique 60 : 229-250, avril-juin 1945.

DUPONT, F. : Référendum et proportionnelle. Revue politique et parlementaire 47 : 207-213, août-septembre 1945.
Voir aussi pp. 201-206.

Le projet de constitution du Comité général d'études. Cahiers politiques : 1-17, octobre 1945.

GARÇON, M. : Les tribunaux d'exception. Revue de Paris 52 : 18-28, novembre 1945.

SCELLE, G. : Réflexions sur la nouvelle constitution. Revue politique et parlementaire 47 : 102-113, novembre 1945.

La réparation des dommages de guerre. Collection droit social : 1-48, fasc. 28, décembre 1945.

SAUVAGEOT, A. : Pouvoir judiciaire et constitution. Cahiers politiques : 1-16, décembre 1945.

FABRE, M.H. : Les pouvoirs du commissaire régional de la République. Annales de la faculté de droit d'Aix : 3-67, No. 38, 1945.

MIRKINE-GUETZÉVITCH, B. : Les problèmes constitutionnels. Revue politique et parlementaire 48 : 17-27, janvier 1946.

La répression des faits de collaboration. France, Secrétariat d'état à l'information, Notes documentaires et études : 1-10, No. 245, 26 février 1946.

GIRAUD, E. : Le projet de constitution de la commission de l'Assemblée. Revue politique et parlementaire 48 : 97-128, février 1946.

RIVET, A. : Les garanties des droits indiviuels et le contrôle de la constitutionnalité des lois. Travaux : 21-35, fasc. 2, 1946.

VEDEL, G. : La technique des nationalisations. Droit social 9 : 49-58, février 1946.

MIRKINE-GUETZÉVITCH, B. : Some constitutional problems facing the French constituent assembly. Social research 13 : 24-32, March 1946.

BERLIA, G. : Le projet de constitution française du 19 avril 1946. Revue du droit public et de la science politique 62 : 209-250, avril-juin 1946.

La France d'outre-mer dans la constitution du 19 avril 1946. France, Secrétariat d'état à la présidence du Conseil et à l'information, Notes documentaires et études : 1-16, No. 314, 29 mai 1946.

PELLOUX, R. : La constitution du 19 avril 1946. Recueil Dalloz, Chronique : 45-48, 6 et 13 juin 1946.

MAZEAUD, H. : La renonciation à succession et à réduction en cas de confiscation des biens à venir pour indignité nationale ou infraction à la législation économique. Recueil Dalloz, Chronique : 49-52, 20 et 27 juin 1946.

La durée du droit d'auteur en France et les deux guerres mondiales. Droit d'auteur 59 : 62-65, juin 1946.

GIRAUD, E. : Corrections à la constitution écartée par le pays. Revue politique et parlementaire 48 : 7-19, juillet 1946.

La représentation des professions et la constitution. Droit social 9 : 261, juillet-août 1946.

Les projets constitutionnels français. France, Secrétariat d'état à la présidence du Conseil et à l'information, Notes documentaires et études : 1-43, No. 369, 3 août 1946.

THERY, R. : Indemnisation des dommages de guerre et reconstruction. Economiste européen 100 : 163-165, 22 septembre 1946.

Les dommages de guerre. France, Secrétariat d'état à la présidence du Conseil et à l'information, Notes documentaires et études : 1-24, No. 421, 28 septembre 1946.

Projet de constitution de la République française adopté le 29 septembre 1946 par l'Assemblée nationale constituante. France, Secrétariat d'état à la présidence du Conseil et à l'information, Notes documentaires et études : 1-10, No. 428, 1 octobre 1946.

BURDEAU, G. : Le régime des pouvoirs publics dans la constitution du 27 octobre 1946. Revue du droit public et de la science politique 62 : 545-592, octobre-décembre 1946.

LÉVY-BRUHL, H. : Une enquête sur la pratique juridique en France. Revue trimestrielle de droit civil 45 : 298-299, octobre-décembre 1946.

Les modes de scrutin. France, Secrétariat d'état à la présidence du Conseil et à l'information, Notes documentaires et études : 1-20, No. 461, 9 novembre 1946.

PELLOUX, R. : La nouvelle constitution de la France. Recueil Dalloz, Chronique : 81-84, 21-28 novembre 1946.

COT, P. : The new constitution of France. Journal of legal and political sociology 4 : 104-184, summer 1946-1947.

BÉRENGER, B., et RAZOULS, J. : Le problème du domicile des sociétés coloniales. Revue juridique et politique de l'Union française 1 : 40-51, janvier-mars 1947.

CHATELAIN : L'évolution du statut des populations d'outremer en droit public. Revue juridique et politique de l'Union française 1 : 83-96, janvier-mars 1947.

Dommages de guerre. Moniteur officiel du commerce et de l'industrie 65 : 274-282, 6 février 1947.

DUPUY, A.F. : La réparation des dommages corporels subis par les victimes civiles de la guerre. Recueil Dalloz, Chronique 25-28, 13 février 1947.

REUTER, P. : L'Union française et la constitution de 1946. Recueil Dalloz, Chronique : 33-36, 27 février 1947.

French constitution. Current history 12 : 161-173, February 1947.

LANGLET, M. : La charte des sinistrés. Revue politique et parlementaire 49 : 116-123, février 1947.
Reconstruction.

L'Assemblée de l'Union française. Bulletin d'information (Ministère de la France d'Outre-Mer) : 3-4, 24 mars 1947.

LAMPUÉ, P. : L'Union française d'après la constitution. Revue juridique et politique de l'Union française 1 : 1-39, 145-162, janvier-mars, avril-juin 1947.

BROUCHOT, J. : La Haute cour de justice, constitution de 1946. Revue de science criminelle et de droit pénal comparé: 317-340, juillet-septembre 1947.

Les divisions administratives du Territoire français - le projet de loi relatif à la réorganisation départementale (Suite). Services français d'information, Notes documentaires et études : 1-22, No. 751, 28 octobre 1947.

LAMPUÉ, P. : Le statut d'Algérie. Revue juridique et politique de l'Union Française 1 : 477-525, octobre-décembre 1947.

RIVERO, J. : Vers la fin du droit de la fonction publique? Recueil Dalloz, Chronique : 149-152, 13 novembre 1947.

L'Assemblée de l'Union française. Documentation française, Notes documentaires et études : 1-12, No. 768, 26 novembre 1947.

REUTER, P. : Le nouveau statut organique de l'Algérie. Recueil Dalloz, Chronique : 165-168, 11 décembre 1947.

REUTER, P. : Le nouveau statut organique de l'Algérie. Recueil Dalloz, Chronique : 165-168, 11 décembre 1947.

THERY, R. : Nécessité d'une réglementation légale de l'exercice du droit de grève. Economiste européen 102 : 323-326, 14 décembre 1947.

KAHN, J. : La collaboration économique pendant l'occupation. Nouvelle revue de droit international privé 14 : 28-59, 1947.

BERLIA, G. : La présidence de la République, magistrature morale du régime. Revue du droit publiq et de la science politique 64 : 53-58, janvier-mars 1948.

BONNEAU, H. : Les immunités parlementaires dans la constitution française du 27 octobre 1946. Revue du droit public et de la science politique 64 : 59-77, janvier-mars 1948.

NAUROIS, L. de : Diffamation et injures envers les collectivités. Revue de science criminelle et de droit pénal comparé : 1-23, janvier-mars 1948.

FOYER, J. : Le règlement de l'Assemblée de l'Union française. Revue juridique et politique de l'Union française 2 : 59-79, janvier-mars 1948.

BOURGUIGNON, P. : Le nouveau statut de l'Algérie. Etudes internationales 1 : 191-202, avril 1948.

COLLIARD, C.A. : La pratique de la question de confiance sous la IVe République. Revue du droit public et de la science politique 64 : 220-237, avril-juin 1948.

DUCLOS, P. : Progrès de la réforme administrative en France. Recueil Dalloz, Chronique : 97-104, 10 juin 1948.

JULLIOT de la MORANDIÈRE, L. : La réforme du code civil. Recueil Dalloz, Chronique : 117-124, 1 juillet 1948.

Les institutions algériennes, 1830 - 20 septembre 1947. Documents algériens, Série politique : No. 19, 27 août 1948.
Tableau.

TUNC, A. : La nouvelle forme des actions de société dans la législation française. Canadian bar review 26 : 1301-1318, November 1948.

BÉRAUD, R. : "La non-rétroactivité des lois nouvelles plus douces?" . Revue de science criminelle et de droit pénal comparé : 7-20, janvier-mars 1949.

SOULIER, A. : La délibération du Comité constitutionnel due 18 juin 1948. Revue du droit public et de la science politique 65 : 195-216, avril-juin 1949.

LAFERRIÈRE, J. : De l'authenticité du texte des los publiées au "Journal officiel". Revue du droit public et de la science politique 65 : 113-152, avril-juin 1949.

SAVATIER, R. : Une institution civile en euphorie: L'adoption devant le Parlement français. Recueil Dalloz, Chronique : 117-120, 30 juin 1949.

LAMPUÉ, P. : Le pouvoir réglementaire des représentants du Gouvernement dans les territoires d'outre-mer. Revue juridique et politique de l'Union française 3 : 257-275, juillet-septembre 1949.

BRUYAS, J. : L'évolution du Conseil de la République 8 décembre 1946 - 1 août 1949. Revue du droit public et de la science politique 65 : 541-582, octobre-décembre 1949.

LACHARRIÈRE, R. de : Le problème de l'organisation gouvernementale en vue de l'Union française. Revue juridique et politique de l'Union française 3 : 401-431, octobre-décembre 1949.

Liste de lois, ordonnances, règlements organiques et décrets en matiète pénale et pénitentiaire (Suite). Lois, etc., promulgués au cours de l'année 1948. Receuil de documents en matière pénale et pénitentiaire 14 : 466-482, novembre 1949.

FERNAND-JACQ : Un nouveau projet d'institution de la propriété scientifique. Propriété industrielle 65 : 177-180, novembre 1949.

FRANCE
(International law, Aliens, Nationality)

NIBOYET, J.P. : Le code de la nationalité. Dalloz, Recueil analytique et critique de doctrine, de jurisprudence et de législation, Chronique : 5-8, 17 et 24 janvier 1946.

LOUIS-LUCAS, P. : Le nouveau code de la nationalité française, ordonnance du 19 octobre 1945. Revue critique de droit international : 13-40, janvier-juin 1946.

NIBOYET, J.P. : L'ordonnance du 2 novembre 1945 relative aux conditions d'entrée et de séjour des étrangers en France. Dalloz, Recueil analytique et critique de doctrine, de juris prudence et de législation, Chronique : 13-16, 14 et 21 février 1946.

NIBOYET, J.P. : La constitution nouvelle et certaines dispositions de droit international. Recueil Dalloz, Chronique : 89-92, 19 et 26 décembre 1946.

PLAISANT, R. : A propos de la récente loi française sur la nationalité. Revue générale de droit international public 50 : 49-66, 1946.

NIBOYET, J.P. : La récente constitution française et le droit international. Comité français de droit international privé, Travaux 8-9 : 17-46, 1946/47-1947/48.

FRANCESCAKIS, P. : Effets en France des jugements étrangers indépendamment de l'exequatur. Comité français de droit international privé. Travaux 8-9, 129-155, 1946/47-1947/1948.

ROUAST, A. La loi sur les comités d'entreprise et les sociétés étrangères. Droit social 10 : 67-69, février 1947.

MORICE, J. : La réorganisation de la justice en Indochine. Revue juridique et politique de l'Union française 1 : 239-257, avril-juin 1947.

Le régime de propriété industrielle après l'accord franco-américain. Cahiers français d'information : 8-9, 15 mai 1947.

La nouvelle constitution du royaume du Cambodge promulguée le 5 mai 1947. Bulletin d'information (Ministère de la France d'outre-mer) : 3-10, 16 juin 1947.

LACHARRIÈRE, R. de : L'évolution du problème constitutionnel de l'Indochine. Revue juridique et politique de l'Union française 1 : 351-371, juillet-septembre 1947.

AYMOND, P. : La nouvelle loi française sur la nationalité- (Suite). Nouvelle revue de droit international privé 14 : 198-248, 1947.

ROUSSEAU, C. : Jurisprudence française en matière de droit international public, 1939-1941. Revue générale de droit international public 51 : 213-277, 1947.

DONNEDIEU de VABRES, J. : La constitution de 1946 et le droit international. Recueil Dalloz, Chronique : 5-8, 8 janvier 1948.

GERVAIS, A. : La jurisprudence française des prises maritimes dans la seconde guerre mondiale. Revue générale de droit international public 52 : 88-161, janvier-juin 1948.

LA CABEC, R. : L'expulsion des étrangers aux termes de l'ordonnance du 2.11.45 et du décret du 18.3.46. Revue critique de droit international privé 37 : 235-251, juillet-septembre 1948.

ROUSSEAU, C. : Jurisprudence française en matière de droit international public, 1942-1944. Revue générale de droit international public 52 : 423-454, juillet-décembre 1948.

DELAUME, G.R. : L'influence de la nationalité française sur la solution des conflits de lois en matière de droit des personnes. Revue critique de droit international privé 38 : 5-34, janvier-mars 1949.

Sur l'attribution de la nationalite française à l'enfant né hors de France d'une mère française et d'un père de nationalité étrangère ou apatride. Journal des tribunaux mixtes 28 : 1-2, 7 et 8 février 1949.

MIAJA de la MUELA, A. : La nueva escuela territorialista francesa en derecho internacional privado. Revista española de derecho internacional 2 : 403-443, No. 2, 1949.

MAKAROV, A.N. : Das französische Staatsangehörigkeitsgesetz von 1945. Zeitschrift für ausländisches und internationales Privatrecht 15 : 382-419, Heft 3/4 1949.

LACHARRIÈRE, R. de : Le changement de statut de la Cochinchine. Revue juridique et politique de l'Union française 3 : 146-173, avril-juin 1949.

LARCHÉ, J. : Le nouveau statut intérieur de l'Etat cambodgien. Revue juridique et politique de l'Union française 3 : 315-327, juillet-septembre 1949.

STARCK, B. : Preuve de la nationalité française et autorité absolue de la chose jugée. Revue critique de droit international privé 38 : 434-472, juillet-septembre 1949.

LINANT de BELLEFONDS, Y. : La fin des trois derniers tribunaux consulaires français à l'étranger. Recueil Dalloz, Chronique : 175-178, 24 novembre 1949.

TROTOBAS, L. : Le rattachement de Tende et La Brique. Annales de la Faculté de droit d'Aix : 5-17, No. 42, 1949.

SZLECHTER, E. : Le staut juridique des habitants des territoires réunis à la France par le Traité de Paris du 10 février 1947. Revue générale de droit international public 53 : 341-358, juillet-décembre 1949.

GERMANY

HEINKE : Die zweite Verordnung zur Änderung der Preisstrafrechts verordnung. Deutsches Recht 15 : 2-16, 15. Januar 1945.

HOEFER, F. : The Nazi penal system. Journal of criminal law and criminology 35 : 385-393, March-April 1945.

KELSEN, H. : The legal status of Germany according to the declaration of Berlin. American journal of international law 39 : 518-526, July 1945.

SAUSER-HALL, G. : L'occupation de l'Allemagne par les Puissances Alliées. Schweizerisches Jahrbuch für internationales Recht 3 : 9-64, 1946.

PETER, F.X. : Die völkerrechtliche Stellung Deutschlands unter dem Besetzungsregime. Schweizer Monatshefte 26 : 8-16, April 1946.

KEIL, W. : Un projet de constitution du Wurtemberg-Bade. France, Secrétariat d'état à la présidence du Conseil et à l'information, Articles et documents : 1-3, No. 619, 5 juillet 1946.
Publié dans "Neue Zeitung".

NOBLEMAN, E.E. : American military government courts in Germany. American journal of international law 40 : 803-811, October 1946.

SCHWELB, E. : The legal status of Germany. American journal of international law 40 : 811-812, October 1946.

MARSH, N.S. : Some aspects of the German legal system under national socialism. Law quarterly review 62 : 366-374, October 1946.

Die völkerrechtliche Stellung Deutschlands nach seiner bedingungslosen Kapitulation. Europa-Archiv 1 : 209-220, Oktober-November 1946.

HOYER, V. : Das deutsche Ehegesetz vom Jahre 1946. Österreichische Juristen-Zeitung 1 : 493-496, 6. Dezember 1946.

Constitution de l'état libre de Bavière. France, Secrétariat d'état à la présidence du Conseil et à l'information, Articles et documents : 1-16, No. 790, 22 décembre 1946.

GROS, A. : La condition juridique de l'Allemagne. Revue générale de droit international public 50 : 67-78, 1946.

L'organisation de la justice française en zone d'occupation en Allemagne. Services français d'information, Notes documentaires et études : 1-4, No. 564, 4 mars 1947.

HOYER, V. : Bemerkungen zur Verfassung des Freistaates Bayern vom 1. Dezember 1946. Österreichische Juristen-Zeitung 2 : 155-158, 18. April 1947.

The legal administration of Germany. British zone. Law journal 97 : 285, 6 June 1947.

MARTIN, M. : La législation française en Allemagne. Recueil Dalloz, Chronique : 109-112, 10 juillet 1947.

NOBLEMAN, E.E. : Military government courts - Law and justice in the American zone of Germany. American bar association journal 33 : 777-780, August 1947.

MANN, F.A. : The present legal status of Germany. International law quarterly 1 : 314-335, autumn 1947.

PARRY, C. : The status of Germany and of German internees. Modern law review 10 : 403-410, October 1947.

PLISCHKE, E. : Denazification law and procedure. American journal of international law 41 : 807-827, October 1947.

PREUSS, L. : International law in the constitutions of the Länder in the American zone in Germany. American journal of international law 41 : 888-899, October 1947.

MENZEL, E. : Zur völkerrechtlichen Lage Deutschlands. Europa-Archiv 2 : 1009-1016, Dezember 1947.

MANN, F.A. : The present legal status of Germany. Grotius society, Transactions 33 : 119-145, 1947.

MENZEL, E. : Deutschland - Ein Kondominium oder Koimperium? Jahrbuch für internationales und ausländisches öffentliches Recht 1 : 43-86, 1948.

MANN, F.A. : The present legal status of Germany. Jahrbuch für internationales und ausländisches öffentliches Recht 1 : 27-42, 1948.

LAUN, R. : Der gegenwärtige Rechtzustand Deutschlands. Jahrbuch für internationales und ausländisches öffentliches Recht 1 : 9-21, 1948.

IPSEN : Deutsche Gerichsbarkeit unter Besatzungshoheit. Jahrbuch für internationales und auslandisches öffentliches Recht 1 : 87-114, 1948.

DERNEDDE : Justiz und Besatzung in der Britischen Zone. Jahrbuch für internationales und ausländisches öffentliches Recht 1 : 115-122, 1948.

BUTZ : Die Rechtsgrundlagen für die Besatzungsleistungen. Jahrbuch für internationales und ausländisches öffentliches Recht 1 : 129-138, 1948.

STAPPERT : Die allierte Kontrollbehörde in Deutschland. Jahrbuch für internationales und ausländisches öffentliches Recht 1 : 139-159, 1948.

LUDERS, C.H. Das Schicksal der ehemaligen deutschen Auslandspatente. Zentral-Justizblatt für die Britische Zone 2 : 1-3, Januar 1948.

Wiedergutmachung - Deutschland. Informations-Dienst für Rück- und Weiterwanderung : 7-9, Januar 1948.

Military government, United States are of control, Germany - Law No. 59 : resisution of identifiable property. American journal of international law, Official documents 42 : 11-45, January 1948.

AUBRY, J.M. : Les nouvelles constitutions allemandes. Bulletin trimestriel de la Société de Législation comparée 71 : 49-76, janvier-mars 1948.
Zone française d'occupation.

LOEWENSTEIN, K. : Reconstruction of the administration of justice in American-occupied Germany. Harvard law review 61 : 419-467, February 1948.

SCHLOCHAUER, H.J. : Zur Frage eines Besatzungsstatuts für Deutschland. Archiv des Völkerrechts 1 ; 188-218, 2. Heft 1948.

STÖDTER, R. : Die völkerrechtliche Stellung Deutschlands. Friedens-Warte 48 : 111-123, Nr.3, 1948.

LOEWENSTEIN, K. : Law and legislative process in occupied Germany (Contd.). Yale law journal 57 : 994-1022, April 1948.

HARVEY, C.P. : Sources of law in Germany. Modern law review 11 : 196-213, April 1948.

Denazification. Office of Military government for Germany (U.S.), Report of the Military Governor : 1-167, 1 April 1947 - 30 April 1948.

GAUDEMET, P.M. : Allemagne - Les droits de l'homme dans les constitutions des "pays" allemands. Revue du droit public et de la science politique 64 : 204-219, avril-juin 1948.

VLACHOS, G. : La nouvelle constitution bavaroise. Bulletin trimestriel de la Société de législation comparée 71 : 265-293, avril-juin 1948.

PETERS, H. : Die Landesverfassungen in der sowjetischen Besatzungszone. Europa-Archiv 1 : 639-644, Juni 1947.

WENGLER, W. : Vorkämpfer der Völkerverständigung und Völkerrechtsgelehrte als Opfer des Nationalsozialismus (Contd.). Friedens-Warte 48 : 297-305, Nr. 6, 1948.
H.J. Graf von Moltke, 1906-1945.

SOLOVYEV, S. : Provincial constitutions in the Soviet occupation zone of Germany. Soviet news : 2-3, 31 July 1947.

WINDELS, D. : Wer ist Organisationsverbrecher? Spruchgerichte 2 : 202-205, July 1948.

Die Staatenlosigkeit der ausgewanderten deutschen Juden. Informations-Dienst für Rück- und Weiterwanderung : 5-6, Juli 1948.

Oberster Gerichtshof für due Britische Zone. Zentral-Justizblatt für die Britische Zone 2 : 149-151, Juli 1948.

COLLIARD, C.A. : Allemagne - L'organisation des pouvoirs publics dans les constitutions des "pays" allemands. Revue du droit public et de la science politique 64 : 452-471, juillet-septembre 1948.

WERNER, von : Die Ausführungsverordnung zum Ehegesetz vom 12. Juli 1948. Zentral-Justizblatt für die Britische Zone 2 : 169-171, August 1948.

SCHOUTEN, C. : Behandeling van Duitse merken bij het toekomstige vredesverdrag. Economisch-statistische berichten 33 : 749-752, 22 September 1948.

MITTELBACH, H. : Das Verbrechen gegen die Menschlichkeit in der Rechtsprechung des Obersten Spruchgerichtshofes. Spruchgerichte 2 : 262-267, September 1948.

NATIONAL LAW - COUNTRIES

ABENDROTH, W. : Die Justizreform in der Sowjetzone Deutschlands. Europa-Archiv 3 : 1539-1546, September 1948.

MOSLER, H. : Die Rechtsnatur der Jurisdiktion über das Organisationsverbrechen. Spruchgerichte 2 : 281-285, Oktober 1948.

RENGERT, J. : Rechtsgrenzen des Besatzungsregimes. Schweizer Monatsheft 28 : 496-502, November 1948.

RAAPE : Adoption eines deutschen Kindes durch einen Englander. Monatsschrift für deutsches Recht 2 : 382-384, November 1948.

FAHY, C. : Legal problems of German occupation. Michigan law review 47 : 11-22, November 1948.

RHEINSTEIN, M. : The legal status of occupied Germany. Michigan law review 47 : 23-40, November 1948.

HERZ, J.H. : The fiasco of denazification. Political science quarterly 63 : 569-594, December 1948.

Das Regierungs- und Verwaltungssystem der Besatzungsmächte in Deutschland als Treuhandverhältnis. Jahrbuch für internationales und ausländisches öffentliches Recht : 369-375, 1948.

MARQUORDT, G. : Zum heutigen interlokalen Privatrecht in Deutschland. Monatsschrift für deutsches Recht 3 : 5-8, Januar 1949.

HOLZT : Spruchgerichtsstatistik. Spruchgerichte 3 : 83-88, Februar/März 1949.

STEINIGER, A. : Zwei Verfassungsentwürfe. Neue Justiz 3 : 49-53, März 1949.

MANGOLDT, H. von : Grundrechte und Grundsatzfragen des Bonner Grundgesetzes. Archiv des öffentlichen Rechts 75 : 273-290, 3. Heft 1949.

MARQUORDT, G. : Zum heutigen interlokalen Privatrecht in Deutschland (Contd.). Monatsschrift für deutsches Recht 3 : 135-137, März 1949.

Die Konstituierung der "Deutschen Demokratischen Republik". Archiv des öffentlichen Rechts 75 : 452-464, 4. Heft 1949.

ULE, C.H. : Die neue Verwaltungsgerichtsbarkeit und das Verhältnis von Justiz und Verwalting. Deutsche Rechts-Zeitschrift 4 : 1-19, 10. Beiheft 1949.

KERN, E. : Zur Verfassungsentwicklung in den Ländern der britischen Zone. Deutsche Rechts-Zeitschrift 4 : 156-157, 5. April 1949.

HOYER, V. : Bemerkungen zur Fortentwicklung des Eherechts in Deutschland. Juristische BLätter 71 : 200-205, 16. April 1949.

ZIMMERREIMER, K. : Die Todeserklärung von Kriegsteilnehmern. Neue Justiz 3 : 83-85, April 1949.

HOEPFNER, W. : Die rechtliche Natur der bizonalen Wirtschaftsverwaltung. Monatsschrift für deutsches Recht 3 : 197-201, April 1949.

BERNAT : L'Allemagne occupée. Revue générale de droit international public 53 : 284-288, avril-juin 1949.

RUSCHEWEYH, H. : Richteranklage und Richterwahl im Bonner Grundgesetzentwurf. Monatsschrift für deutsches Recht 3 : 258-261, Mai 1949.

WOLFF, H.J. : Die verwaltungsgerichtliche Legitimation der Verwaltungen des Vereinigten Wirtschaftsgebietes. Monatsschrift für deutsches Recht 3 : 266-270, Mai 1949.

The Basic law. Information bulletin : 9-10, 28, 33, 14 June 1949.
With authorized Anglo-American text pp. 29-33.

GREWE, W. : Die verfassungsrechtlichen Grundlagen der Bundesrepublik Deutschland. Deutsche Rechts-Zeitschrift 4 : 265-270, 313-317, 20. Juni, 20. Juli 1949.

FRIEDRICH, C.J. : Rebuilding the German constitution. American political science review 43 : 461-482, June 1949.

Restitution of property - British zone. Law journal 99 : 410, 29 July 1949.

SPRECKELSEN, H. : Zur Todeserklärung von verschollenen Kriegsteilnehmern. Zentral-Justizblatt für die Britische Zone 3 : 121-123, Juli 1949.

GRAHAM, M.W. : The new fundamental law for the Western German federal republic. American journal of international law 43 : 494-498, July 1949.

FAIREN GUILLEN, V. : La jurisdicción civil y su ejercicio en la Alemania occupada. Revista juridica de Cataluña 60 : 331-366, julio-octubre 1949.

BECKER, I. : Zur Rückerstattungsrechtsprechung in der französischen Zone. Deutsche Rechts-Zeitschrift 4 : 352-356, 15. August 1949.

DREXELIUS, W. : Übergangsbestimmungen im Bonner Grundgesetzt. Monatsschrift für deutsches Recht 3 : 455-457, August 1949.

BOEHMER, G. : Die Einwirkung des zweiten Weltkrieges, der Nachkriegszeit und der Währungsreform auf privatrechtliche Verhältnisse. Deutsche Rechts-Zeitschrift 4 : 1-39, 8. Beiheft 1949.

ZUCKERMANN, L. : Atlantikpakt und Besatzungsstatut. Neue Justiz 3 : 177-178, August 1949.

FRIEDRICH, C.J. : Rebuilding the German constitution (Contd.). American political science review 43 : 704-720, August 1949.

SCHULZE : Das Rückerstattungsverfahren in der Britischen Zone. Zentral-Justizblatt für die Britische Zone 3 : 163-168, September 1949.

NIKISCH, A. : Die Neuregelung des Zivilprozessrechts in der sowjetischen Besatzungszone. Deutsche Rechts-Zeitschrift 4 : 439-441, 5. Oktober 1949.

ROTH, A. : Wirkungen der Verfassung der Deutschen Demokratischen Republik auf das Familienrecht. Neue Justiz 3 : 245-246, Oktober 1949.

HUBRECHT, G. : Le statut d'occupation de l'Allemagne occidentale. Revue internationale de droit comparé 1 : 418-427, octobre-décembre 1949.

GREWE, W. : Die Bundesrepublik als Rechtsstaat. Deutsche Rechts-Zeitschrift 4 : 392-395, 15. September 1949.

NATIONAL LAW - COUNTRIES

The new German constitution. Wiener library bulletin 3 : 30, 35, September-November 1949.

SCHMOLLER, G. von : Grundzüge das neuen Besatzungsregimes in Westdeutschland. Europa-Archiv 4 : 2535-2544, 20. Oktober 1949.

LENNHOFF, A. : The German (Bonn) constitution with comparative glances at the French and Italian constitutions. Tulane law review 24 : 1-50, October 1949.

SCHMID, K. : The work of Bonn. World affairs (London) 3 : 358-367, October 1949.

ERDSIEK : Vergleichende Überschau über das Rückerstattungsrecht der britischen un der amerikanischen Zone. Deutsche Rechts-Zeitung 4 : 487-490, 5. November 1949.

Dokumente zur Bildung der Deutschen Demokratischen Republik, Sowjetische Besatzungszone. Europa-archiv 4 : 2639-2640, 20. November 1949.
Published in "Tägliche Rundschau".

MAUNZ, T. : Rechtsfragen zur Neugliederung im Südwestraum. Deutsche Rechts-Zeitschrift 4 : 532-535, 5. Dezember 1949.
Bavaria, Württemberg, Baden; See also pp. 535-536.

BACHOF, O. : Geltung und Tragweite des Art. 131 des Bonner Grundgesetzes. Deutsche Rechts-Zeitschrift 4 : 553-557, 20. Dezember 1949.

Constitution de la République démocratique allemande, 7 octobre 1949. Documentation française, Notes et études documentaires : 1-16, No. 1249, 21 décembre 1949.

NATHAN, H. : Die obersten Rechtspflegeorgane der Deutschen Demokratischen Republik. Neue Justiz 3 : 303-305, Dezember 1949.

GERMANY
(International law and practice, Aliens and Naturalization)

SHAW, O.J. : Military government law and British subjects in Germany. International law quarterly 2 : 670-674, winter 1948-49.

BAGGE, A. : De allierade stormakternas folksrättsliga ställning i Tyskland. Jus gentium 1 : 23-42, Fasc. 1, 1949.
Legal position of the Allied Powers in Germany.

PAGENSTECHER, M. : Zur Geschäftsfähigkeit der Ausländer in Deutschland. Zeitschrift für ausländisches und internationales Privatrecht 15 : 189-239, Heft 2, 1949.

SEIDL-HOHENVELDERN, I. : Die staatsbürgerschaftsrechtliche Stellung der Volksdeutschen in Deutschland. Österreichische Juristen-Zeitung 4 : 253-255, 27. Mai 1949.

RAAPE, L. : Die Anerkennung eines ausländischen Ehenichtigkeitsurteils mit besonderer Berücksichtigung des Paragraph 24 der 4. EheV. Monatsschrift für deutsches Recht 3 : 586-590, Oktober 1949.

Deutsche Probleme des internationalen Rechts. Deutsche Rechts-Zeitschrift 4 : 1-23, 9. Beiheft 1949.

Foreign-owned industrial property rights in Germany. Law journal 99 : 689-690, 16 December 1949.

BINDSCHEDLER, R.L. : Die völkerrechtliche Stellung Deutschlands. Schweizerisches Jahrbuch für internationales Recht 6 : 37-64, 1949.

GERMANY
(Copyright, Patents, Trademarks)

ALBRECHT, H. : Neuordnung des gewerblichen Rechtsschutzes im Gebiete der Deutschen Bundesrepublik. Jahrbücher für Nationalökonomie und Statistik 161 : 411-427, Dezember 1949.

GREAT BRITAIN

RIX, M.S. : Company law - 1844 and to-day. Economic journal 55 : 242-260, June-September 1945.

Laying regulations before Parliament. Law journal 95 : 297-298, 15 September 1945.

Company law amendment - A note on the Cohen committee's report. Law journal 95 : 313-314, 29 September 1945.

Delegated legislation and executive powers. Law journal 95 : 332-334, 13 October 1945.

LAWSON, H.B. : The Cohen report in relation to banking. Journal of the Institute of bankers 67 : 7-33, January 1946.

SLESSER, H. : The crown as litigant. Fortnightly 159 : 1-5, January 1946.

HORRWITZ, W. : Company law reform and the ultra vires doctrine. Law quarterly review 62 : 66-76, January 1946.

COHN, E.J. : The Cohen report and company law. Fortnightly 159 : 49-58, January 1946.

CHORLEY : Law-making in Whitehall. Modern law review 9 : 26-41, April 1946.

DAVIES, A.E. : Shareholders' charter - The Cohen committee's report. Political quarterly 17 : 137-142, April-June 1946.

Litigation with nationalised industry - Immunities and privileges of the Crown. Law journal 96 : 297-300, 7 June 1946.

KAHN-FREUND, O. : Spare-time activities of employees Modern law review 9 : 145-153, July 1946.

MANNHEIM, H. : A new criminal justice bill? Fortnightly 160 : 77-83, August 1946.

KAHN-FREUND, O. : Company law reform. Modern law review 9 : 235-256, October 1946.

ROBSON, W.A. : Legislative draftmanship. Political quarterly 17 : 330-342, October-December 1946.

The companies bill. Economist 151 : 958-959, 14 December 1946.

The final report of the Denning committee. Law journal 97 : 100-101, 7 March 1947.
Matrimonial causes.

POLLARD, R.S.W. : A programme of law reform. Socialist commentary 11 : 606-610, April 1947.

Legal aid before litigation. Law journal 97 : 439-440, 22 August 1947.

British corporate law reform. Yale law journal 56 : 1383-1403, September 1947.

FRIEDMANN, W. : The new public corporations and the law (contd.). Modern law review 10 : 377-395, October 1947.

The abolition of appeals from the dominions to the Privy council. Law journal 97 : 601-602, 7 November 1947.

Criminal justice. Economist 153 : 750-751, 8 November 1947.

HARVEY, T.E. : Penal reform. Contemporary review 172 : 329-332, December 1947.

The companies act 1947 (Contd.). Law journal 98 : 34, 16 January 1948.

The National arbitration tribunal. Law journal 99 : 59-61, 4 February 1949.

GRIFFITH, J.A. : Delegated legislation - Some recent developments. Modern law review 12 : 297-318, July 1949.

The history of legal aid. Law journal 99 : 451, 19 August 1949.

The married woman (maintenance) bill. Law journal 99 : 481-482, 2 September 1949.

Supreme court practice and procedure. Law journal 99 : 493-494, 9 September 1949.

GREAT BRITAIN
(International law, Aliens)

ROWSON, S.W.D. : British prize law, 1939-1940. Law quarterly review 61 : 49-70, January 1945.

GRAUPNER, R. : British nationality and state succession. Law quarterly review 61 : 161-178, April 1945.

Naturalisation. Economist 149 : 406-407, 22 September 1945.

JONES, J.M. : Who are British protected persons? British year book of international law 22 : 122-129, 1945.

BATHURST, M.E. : Acquisition of British nationality through absentee marriages. British year book of international law 23 : 323-326, 1946.

LYONS, A.B. : The conclusiveness of the Foreign Office certificate. British year book of international law 23 : 240-281, 1946.
Existence of facts in international law.

LAUTERPACHT, H. : Allegiance, diplomatic protection and criminal jurisdiction over aliens. Cambridge law journal 9 : 330-348, No. 3, 1947.

BRESLAUER, W. : Foreign presumptions and declarations of death and English private international law. Modern law review 10 : 122-136, April 1947.

ROWSON, S.W.D. : British prize law, 1944-1946. Law quarterly review 63 : 337-354, July 1947.

WADE, E.C.S. : British nationality act, 1948. Journal of comparative legislation and international law 30 : 67-75, parts III-IV, 1948.

EVANS, W.V.J. : Decisions of English courts during 1947-8 involving points of public or private international law. British year book of international law 25 : 421-436, 1948.

JONES, J.M. : British nationality act, 1948. British year book of international law 25 : 158-179, 1948.

GERVAIS, A. : La jurisprudence britannique des prises maritimes dans la seconde guerre mondiale. Revue générale de droit international public 53 : 201-274, avril-juin 1949.

LÜHNING, H. : Das britische Staatsangehörigkeitsgesetz von 1948. Zeitschrift für ausländisches und internationales Privatrecht 15 : 420-438, Heft 3/4, 1949.

DURET AUBIN, C.W. : Enemy legislation and judgments in Jersey. Journal of comparative legislation and international law 31 : 8-11, parts 3-4, 1949.

GRAVESON, R.H. : The domicile of a widow in the English conflict of laws. British year book of international law 26 : 207-224, 1949.

GREECE

ZEPOS, P.J. : The new Greek civil code of 1946. Journal of comparative legislation and international law 28 : 56-71, parts 3-4, 1946.

ROCAS, C. : Il nuovo diritto ellenico delle obligazioni. Rivista del diritto commerciale 44 : 214-239, maggio-giugno 1946.

TÉNÉKIDÈS, G. : La nature juridique des gouvernements instituées par l'occupant en Grèce suivant la jurisprudence hellénique. Revue générale de droit international public 51 : 113-133, 1947.

ZEPOS, P.J. : Enemy legislation and judgments in liberated Greece. Journal of comparative legislation and international law 30 : 27-32, parts III-IV, 1948.

YOTIS, C.P. : L'extradition d'après le projet de code de procédure pénale de Grèce de 1948. Revue hellénique de droit international 1 : 226-238, juillet-septembre 1948.

RAMMOS, G. : A procedural problem encountered in the "exequatur" of foreign judgments in Greece. Revue hellénique de droit international 1 : 257-258, juillet-septembre 1948.

CORBOS, B. : Du séquestre des biens ennemis et de l'interdiction de commerce avec les ennemis en Grèce pendant la 2e guerre mondiale. Revue hellénique de droit international 1 : 239-249, juillet-septembre 1948.

CHRISTOPOULOS, T. : Requirements for the enforcement of foreign judgments in Greece. Revue hellénique de droit international 1 : 348-357, octobre-décembre 1948.

VALLINDAS, P.G. : Le droit international privé dans le code civil hellénique. Revue internationale de droit comparé 1 : 95-104, janvier-juin 1949.

GOGOS, D., and AUBIN, B.C.H. : Das internationale Privatrecht im griechischen Zivilgesetzbuch von 1940. Zeitschrift für ausländisches und internationales Privatrecht 15 : 240-285, Heft 2, 1949.
See also pp. 337-341.

CORBOS, B. : Conventions et accords signés entre la Grèce et des pays étrangers ou des organisations internationales, 1er janvier 1945 - 31 décembre 1948. Revue hellénique de droit international 2 : 270-276, avril-décembre 1949.

NICOLETOPOULOS, G.P. : Private international law in the new Greek civil code. Tulane law review 23 : 452-477, June 1949.

PAPAHADZIS, G.M. : The administrative litigation of prizes in Greece. Revue hellénique de droit international 2 : 136-152, avril-décembre 1949.

STASSINOPOULOS, M. : La responsabilité civile de l'Etat d'après le nouveau code civil grec de 1946. Revue du droit public et de la science politique 65 : 507-514, octobre-décembre 1949.

GUATEMALA

GRANT, J.A.C. : Due process for ex-dictators, a study of judicial control of legislation in Guatemala. American political science review 41 : 463-469, June 1947.

Decretos del Congresso de la República. Mes económico y financiero 1 : 9, 28, 31 julio 1947.

HUNGARY

Bilan des tribunaux du peuple. Informations hongroises : 7-10, 1er juillet 1946.

NEMES, L. : Die Reform des ungarischen Eherechts. Juristische Blätter 69 : 484-486, 29. November 1947.

SZASZY, M. : Le nouveau projet hongrois sur le droit international privé. Bulletin trimestriel de la Société de législation comparée 71 : 101-121, janvier-mars 1948.

RACZ, G. : L'évolution récente du droit pénal hongrois. Bulletin trimestriel de la Société de législation comparée 71 : 77-100, janvier-mars 1948.

ESZLARY, C. : La cour administrative hongroise. Revue du droit public et de la science politique 64 : 565-575, octobre-décembre 1948.

Constitution de la République de Hongrie - Loi I de 1946 sur la constitution de l'Etat hongrois. Documentation française, Notes documentaires et études : 1-4, no. 1020, 10 novembre 1948.

ARATÓ, I. : Hungarian jurisprudence relating to the application of international law by national courts. American journal of international law 43 : 536-541, July 1949.

A Magyar népköztársaság alkotmánya. Igazságügyi közlöny 58 : 415-419, augusztus 31, 1949.
Constitution.

Staatsangehörigkeit - Ungarn. Informations-Dienst für Rück- und Weiterwanderung : 6, Nr. 100/101, August 1949.
Nationality,

ZAJTAY, I. : Les régimes matrimoniaux du droit hongrois. Revue internationale de droit comparé 1 : 274-295, août-septembre 1949.

Constitution de la République populaire de Hongrie. Documentation française, Notes et études documentaires : 1-8, No. 1198, 14 septembre 1949.

INDIA

SINHA, K.P. : The legal and constitutional basis of the executive government in India under the government of India act, 1935. Federal law journal 8 : 5-15, February 1945.

Provincial legislation. Indian information 17 : 16-33, 1 July 1945.

The administration of civil justice in India - The need for reform. Capital 115 : 720, 22 November 1945.

RANKIN, G. : Hindu law to-day. Journal of comparative legislation and international law 27 : 1-17, November 1945.

The constitutional issue. International conciliation : 240-269, May 1946.

NAMBIAR, M.K. : The framework of the new constitution. Federal law journal 9 : 52-64, May-June 1946.

SHARMA, S.R. : Constitution-making for free India - The American example. Journal of the University of Bombay 15 : 14-20, July 1946.

APPADORAI, A. : The task before the constituent assembly. India quarterly 2 : 231-240, July-September 1946.

GADGIL, D.R. : The scope of union subjects. India quarterly 2 : 328-340, October-December 1946.

HODSON, H.V. : India's constitutional task. Asiatic review 43 : 48-59, January 1947.

NAMBYAR, M.K. : The States' declaration of independence. Federal law journal 10 : 121-131, May-September 1947.

Contemporary constitutional documents. Federal law journal 10 : 1-75, October-December 1947.

VESEY-FITZGERALD, S. : The projected codification of Hindu law. Journal of comparative legislation and international law 29 : 19-32, November 1947.

VENKATRAMAN, T.S. : The integration of Indian states. Federal law journal 11 : 1-12, January-February 1948.

DURGA DAS BASU : Suability of the State under the constitution of India. Federal law journal 12 : 1-9, February 1949.

DAS, D. : The seven freedoms of the constitution of India. Federal law journal 12 : 9-56, March-April 1949.

MITRA, D.N. : Indian appeals to the Privy council. Law journal 98 : 242, 30 April 1948.

East Bengal people and citizenship of the Indian union. Calcutta weekly notes 52 : 147-148, 16 August 1948.

BASU, D.D. : The President of India. Federal law journal 12 : 91-146, October 1949.

RAU, B.N. : The Indian constitution. India quarterly 5 : 293-303, October-December 1949.

The constitution of India. Gazette of India, Extraordinary : 2347-2597, 26 November 1949.

India's new constitution. Commerce 79 : 981-982, 3 December 1949.

IRELAND

The legal year in Eire. Law journal 98 : 32-33, 16 January 1948.

The Republic of Ireland Act, 1948. Irish jurist 14 : 55-59, part 4, 1948.

McCABE, E.W. : The need for a law of adoption. Statistical and social inquiry society of Ireland, Journal 18 : 178-191, 1948-49.

SULLIVAN, A.M. : Imperial constitutional developments - Eire. International law quarterly 2 : 660-666, winter 1948-49.

VILLERS, R. : La république d'Irlande. Revue du droit public et de la science politique 65 : 169-194, avril-juin 1949.

ISRAEL

ZANDER, H. : The Israeli draft constitution. Common cause 3 : 44-47, August 1949.

ITALY

PESCATORE, G. : Sulla nomina di pubblici funzionari da parte dell'autorità di occupazione. Foro italiano 71 : parte seconda, 50-53, fasc. 7-8, 1944-1946.

VALERI, G. : Il codice di commercio. Rivista di diritto commerciale 43 : 11-19, parte la, gennaio-dicembre 1945.

PLOSCOWE, M. : Purging Italian criminal justice of fascism. Columbia law review 45 : 240-264, March 1945.

AMATI, R. : Les nouvelles règles italiennes de droit international privé. Journal du droit international 67-72 : 330-342, avril-juin 1945.

LENER, S. : Diritto e politica nelle sanzioni contro il fascismo e nell'epurazione dell'amministrazione. Civiltà cattolica 96 : 289-300, 2 giugno 1945.
First of a series of articles.

MIGLIAZZA, S. : La legislazione nazifascita nei territori liberati. Stato moderno 3 : 8-9, 5 gennaio 1946.

CAMPBELL, A.H. : Fascism and legality. Law quarterly review 62 : 141-151, April 1946.

SABATINI, G. : Il sistema processuale per la repressione dei crimini fascisti (Contd.). Giustizia penale 51 : 97-106, parte 3a, aprile 1946.

VASSALI, G. : La collaborazione col tedesco invasore nella giurisprudenza della sezione speciale della cassazione (Contd.). Giustizia penale 51 : 257-283, parte 2a, maggio 1946.

VASSALI, G. : La collaborazione col tedesco invasore nella giurisprudenza della sezione speciale della Cassazione (Contd.). Giustizia penale 51 : parte 2a, 385-431, luglio-agosto 1946.

VASSALI, G. : La collaborazione col tedesco invasore nella giurisprudenza della Cassazione (Contd.). Giustizia penale 51 : parte 2a : 641-659, novembre 1946.

ROWSON, S.W.D. : Italian prize law, 1940-1943. British year book of international law 23 : 282-302, 1946.

BATTAGLIA, A. : La libertà personale dei cittadini nelle carte costituzionali. Stato moderno 4 : 80-83, 20 febbraio 1947.

Costituzione della Repubblica Italiana nel progetto approvato dalla Commissione dei 75 e presentato all' Assemblea costituente il 31-1-1947. Stato moderno, Supplemento 4 : 1-8, 20 febbraio 1947.

ARDIZZONE, U. : La validità degli atti emanati dal c.d. governo della repubblica sociale e la teoria degli atti di governo. Giustizia penale 52 : parte 2a, 81-93, febbraio 1947.

BALLADORE PALLIERI, G. : I rapporti internazionali nella nuova costituzione. Relazione internazionali 11 : 155-156, 1 marzo 1947.

MESSINEO, A. : Il progetto di costituzione della Repubblica Italiana. Civiltà cattolica 98 : 449-458, 15 marzo 1947.

SANDULLI, A.M. : Fatti dannosi della repubblica sociale e responsabilità della Stato italiano. Foro italiano 72 : parte la, 151-162, fasc. 3-4, 1947.

SATTA, S. : In difesa del codice di procedura civile. Foro italiano 72 : parte 4a, 45-52, fasc. 3-4, 1947.

CASALINUOVO, A. : Norme penali nel progetto di costituzione della Repubblica Italiana. Giustizia penale 52 : parte la, 49-60, aprile 1947.

GIANNINI, A. : Proprietà letteraria ed industriale nel trattato di pace. Rivista del diritto commerciale 45 : 89-99, aprile-giugno 1947.

ZANZUCCHI, M.T. : Sulla riforma del codice di procedura civile. Rivista del diritto commerciale 45 : 100-106, aprile-giugno 1947.

MARINA, F.A. : Il problema della soppressione dei tribunali militari. Giustizia penale 52 : parte la, 187-195, settembre 1947.

WEILLER, A. : In Tema di riforma della prodecura civile. Rivista bancaria 3 : 40-52, ottobre 1947.

GIANNINI, A. : Gli studi del diritto della navigazione in Italia, 1860-1947. Rivista del diritto commerciale 45 : 355-371, ottobre-dicembre 1947.

Costituzione della Repubblica Italiana. (Italy) Assemblea costituente : 1-19, seduta del 22 dicembre 1947.

La constitución de la República italiana. Revista de la Facultad de ciencias económicas, comerciales y politicas (Rosario) : 189-220, enero-agosto 1948.

Constitution de la République italienne. Documentation française, Notes documentaires et études : 1-16, No. 882, 17 avril 1948.

Constitution of the Italian Republic. Documents and State papers 1 : 46-63, April 1948.

La nouvelle constitution italienne. Fiches documentaires : VI.E.4/1-6, 15 mai 1948.

STANCIU, V.V. : Les délinquants par tendance dans le code italien. Revue de science criminelle et de droit pénal comparé : 521-528, juillet-septembre 1948.

La constitution de la République italienne. Revue du droit public et de la science politique 64 : 347-406, juillet-septembre 1948.

VASSALI, G. : La sentenza sull' "oro di Dongo". Giustizia penale 53 : parte 2a, 584-594, settembre 1948.
Legal position of partisans.

BARTOLOMEI, D.M. : Nullità di matrimonio concordatario e competenza internazionale. Foro italiano 73 : 154-160, monografie e varietà, fasc. XXI-XXII, 1948.

ORLANDO, V.E. : Il diritto di opzione della cittadinanza previsto dal trattato di pace e le sue ripercussioni nel diritto matrimoniale. Foro italiano 73 : IV/125-129, fasc. 17-18, 1948.

MARMO, L. : In tema di limiti di applicabilità dell' art. 16 del Trattato di pace. Giustizia penale 54 : parte 2a, 43-47, gennaio 1949.
Amnesty in peace treaty.

NEUHAUS, P.H. : Das internationale Privatrecht im italienischen Zivilgesetzbuch von 1942. Zeitschrift für ausländisches und internationales Privatrecht 15 : 22-35, Heft 1, 1949.

BERNARDI, G. : I diritti sul fondo e sul sottofondo dell'alto mare. Diritto marittimo 51 : 9-20, gennaio-marzo 1949.

GUELI, V. : Carattere e limiti della giurisdizione dell'Alta corte per la Regione siciliana. Foro italiano 74 : parte 1a, 113-122, fasc. III-IV, 1949.

NOVA, R. de : Sentenza inglese per i beni di Vittorio Emanuele III. Annali di diritto internazionale 7 : 116-119, 1949.

MANASSERO, A. : L'art. 16 del trattato di pace nel sistema del diritto penale italiano. Giustizia penale 54 : parte prima, 210-223, luglio 1949.

Trattati bilaterali conclusi dall'Italia prima della guerra ed ora rimessi in vigore. Rivista di studi politici internazionali 16 : 426-440, luglio-settembre 1949.

Cittadinanza - Alto Adige - Opzione per la cittadinanza germanica - Mancato trasferimento dell'optante in Germania. Foro italiano 74 : parte 1a, 332-334, fasc. VII-VIII, 1949.

FÜSSLEIN, R.W. : Die italienische Verfassung vom 27. Dezember 1947. Jahrbuch für internationales und ausländisches öffentliches Recht : 788-803, 194[illegible]

COLETTI, G. : Atti amministrativi emanati dall' autorità italiana sotto il Governo militare alleato e loro sindacato di legittimità. Foro italiano 74 : parte 1a, 1203-1206, fasc. 23-24, 1949.

JAPAN

ROWE, D.N. : The new Japanese constitution. Far Eastern survey 16 : 13-17, 29 January 1947.

La constitution japonaise du 3 novembre 1946. Services français d'information, Notes documentaires et études : 1-10, No. 596, 10 avril 1947.

QUIGLEY, H.S. : Japan's constitutions, 1890 and 1947. American political science review 41 : 865-874, October 1947.

GREEN, L.C. : Law and administration in present-day Japan. Current legal problems 1 : 188-205, 1948.

BLAKEMORE, T.L. : Recovery of Japanese nationality as cause for expatriation in American law. American journal of international law 43 : 441-459, July 1949.

JORDAN

Transjordan - the constitution of 7 December 1946. Revue égyptienne de droit international 3 : 227-241, 1947.

KUWAIT

Decree-law No. 2, regarding Kuwait nationality, 15 December 1948. British and foreign state papers 152 : 636-640, part 3, 1948.

LEBANON

TIMBAL, P. : Le chèque en droit libanais. Annales de l'Ecole française de droit de Beyrouth : 3-40, no. 1, 1946.

TYAN, E. : La règle "locus regit actum" et le régime international de la preuve en droit libanais. Revue critique de droit international privé 36 : 73-91, janvier-juin 1947.

MAZAS, A. : Divorces mixtes au Liban. Annales de l'Ecole française de droit de Beyrouth : 5-34, no. 2-3, 1947.

BAZ, J. : Les tribunaux mixtes au Liban. Annales de l'Ecole française de droit de Beyrouth : 25-42, No. 1, 1947.

Exposé des motifs du projet de code de commerce ma[illegible] time libanais. Annales de l'Ecole française de dro[illegible] de Beyrouth : 35-72, no. 2-3, 1947.

NATIONAL LAW - COUNTRIES

Constitution du 23 mai 1926 modifiée par les lois constitutionnelles des 17 octobre 1927, 8 mai 1929, 9 novembre, 7 décembre 1943 et 21 janvier 1947. Revue égyptienne de droit international 3 : 203-214, 1947.

MEXICO

MIGLIORATI, V. : La lotta intorno all'articolo terzo della costituzione messicana. Civiltà cattolica 98 : 228-238, 2 agosto 1947.

Reformas a la constitución de Mexico. Revista parlamentaria 16 : 27-32, noviembre 1947.

Loi fédérale sur le droit d'auteur, du 31 décembre 1947. Droit d'auteur 61 : 49-52, 15 mai 1948.

Il nuovo progetto di codice di commercio de Messico. Rivista di diritto commerciale 46 : 312-313, luglio-agosto 1948.

ECHANOVE TRUJILLO, C.A. : La procédure mexicaine d'Amparo. Revue internationale de droit comparé 1 : 229-248, août-septembre 1949.

TABÍO, E. : Algunas comentarios al ante proyecto de código penal para el distrito y territorios federales de México. Criminalia 15 : 369-390, septiembre 1949.

MOROCCO

BOULBES, R. : Le problème de l'application au Maroc du code de la nationalité française. Nouvelle revue de droit international privé 14 : 60-96, 1947.

LAUBADÈRE, A. de : Les réformes des pouvoirs publics au Maroc. Revue juridique et politique de l'Union française 2 : 1-28, janvier-mars 1948.

DECROUX, P. : La nationalité marocaine. Recueil Dalloz, Chronique : 111-116, 24 juin 1948.

JOFÉ, B. : Le statut international du Maroc. Revue de droit international et de droit comparé 26 : 35-51, nos. 1-4, 1949.

PATROCINIO GARCÍA, P. : Los matrimonios de musulmanes con no musulmanes en Marruecos. Revista juridica de Cataluña 60 : 367-378, julio-octubre 1949.

LA PLAZA, M. de : De nuevo sobre la nacionalidad marroquí. Revista de derecho privado 33 : 493-503, junio 1949.

NEPAL

Constitution of Nepal, Katmandu, 26 January 1948. British and foreign state papers 152 : 656-674, part 3, 1948.

NETHERLANDS

Eerste tribunaal ingesteld te Den Bosch. Vrij Mederland 5 : 9-10, 3 Februari 1945.

BODENHAUSEN, G.H.C. : Du droit international privé néerlandais dans le domaine de la propriété industrielle. Propriété industrielle 63 : 118-122, juillet 1947.

MEIJERS, E.M. : La réforme du code civil néerlandais. Bulletin trimestriel de la Société de législation comparée 71 : 199-215, avril-juin 1948.

Constitution du Royaume des Pays-Bas. Documentation française, Notes documentaires et études : 1-16, No. 1014, 30 octobre 1948.

STANISLAUS, K.H. : Das Recht der Kriegsverschollenheit in Holland. Informations-Dienst für Rück- und Weiterwanderung : 11-12, Nr. 84/85, 1948.

VEGTING, W.G. : Hollande - Les actes législatifs du gpuvernement néerlandais pendant l'occupation allemande et le juge. Revue du droit public et de la science politique 65 : 60-72, janvier-mars 1949.

NORWAY

MELLBYE, G. : Fra de tyske krigsdomstolers virksomhet i Norge under okkupasjonstiden. Tidsskrift for rettsvitenskap 58 : 162-180, hefte 1-2, 1945.

MELLBYE, J.C. : De strafferettslige og prosessuelle regler som anvendes i oppgjøret med de sivile landssvikere. Tidsskrift for rettsvidenskap 58 : 49-97, hefte 1-2, 1945.

SUND, H. : Krigsforbryterne i Norge og oppgjøret met dem. Tidsskrift for rettsvitenskap 59 : 1-29, Hefte 1, 1946.

SEYERSTED, F. : Okkupantens "Rettigheter" - Spesielt overfor offentlige tjenestemenn. Tidsskrift for rettsvitenskap 59 : 267-308, hefte 3, 1946.

LINDVIK, A. : Hoyesteretts stilling i norsk rettsliv. Tidsskrift for rettsvitenskap 59 : 361-380, hefte 4, 1946.

ANDENAES, J. : Okkupasjonstidens "likvidasjoner" i rettslig belysning. Tidsskrift for rettsvitenskap 61 : 1-31, hefte 1, 1948.

DONS, E. : Om tilbakevirkende lover om tap og erverv av norsk statsborgerrett. Tidsskrift for rettsvitenskap 61 : 274-284, hefte 3, 1948.

HAMBRO, E. : Some remarks about the relations between municipal law and international law in Norway. Nordisk tidsskrift for international ret, Acta scandinavica juris gentium 19 : 3-27, No. 1-2, 1949.

STABELL, P. : Enemy legislation and judgments in Norway. Journal of comparative legislation and international law 31 : 3-8, parts 3-4, 1949.

PALESTINE

GOITEIN, D. : Habeas corpus in Palestine. Jewish yearbook of international law : 240-247, 1948.

PHILIPPINE ISLANDS

PERKINS, E.A. : Enemy legislation and judgments in the liberated countries - The Philippines. Journal of comparative legislation and international law 30 : 17-27, parts III-IV, 1948.

POLAND

Verlassene und aufgegebene Vermögenswerte. Informations-Dienst für Rück- und Weiterwanderung : 4-5, Januar 1946.

GOLDENBERG, L., and METZGER, L. : The Polish nationalization law. Department of State bulletin 15 : 651-654, 13 October 1946.

ANCEL, M. : Un procès de criminel de guerre en Pologne. Revue de science criminelle et de droit pénal comparé : 213-220, avril-juin 1947.

FEDYNSKYJ, G. : Polnisches Personenrecht. Juristische Blätter 69 : 394-396, 4. Oktober 1947.

Reform of civil and criminal law. Review of Polish law 1 : 11-22, November 1947.

The small constitution. Review of Polish law 1 : 3-4, November 1947.
See also pp. 1-2.

Nationalisation of the larger industrial and commercial entreprises. Review of Polish law 1 : 8-10, November 1947.

Land reform. Review of Polish law 1 : 7-8, November 1947.

The legal position of persons who have repudiated their Polish nationality. Review of Polish law 2 : 9-12, April 1948.

FEDYNSKYJ, G. : Polnisches Familienrecht. Juristische Blätter 70 : 206-211, 8. Mai 1948.

The Highest national tribunal . Review of Polish law 2 : 1-10, October 1948.

Abandoned and ex-German property, decree of the 8 March 1946. Review of Polish law 2 : 21-29, October 1948.

The protection of inventions in Poland. Review of Polish law 2 : 1-9, December 1948.

The principles of the new Polish law of inheritance. Review of Polish law 2 : 10-18, December 1948.

DOBRAZAŃSKI, B. : Uwagido projektu Kodeksu Cywilnego Pokrewieństwo i powinowactwo (księga II - tytul II). Przeglad notarialny 1 : 98-130, styczen-luty 1949.
Family law in civil code draft.

JODLOWSKI, J. : Le nouveau droit de la famille en Pologne. Revue internationale de droit comparé 1 : 67-79, janvier-juin 1949.

The law on Polish citizenship. Review of Polish law 3 : 33-42, July 1949.

Décret du Gouvernement Polonais sur la défense de la liberté de conscience et de religion, 5 août. Bulletin quotidien de presse étrangère : 1-2, no. 1349, 12 août 1949.
Publié dans "Gazeta Polska".

MENZEL : Zur Frage der Danziger Staatsangehörigkeit. Jahrbuch für internationales und ausländisches öffentliches Recht : 886-894, 1949.

PORTO RICO

RAMOS, M.R. : Interaction of civil law and Anglo-American law in the legal method in Puerto Rico. Tulane law review 23 : 1-37, October 1948.

RAMOS, M.R. : Interaction of civil law and Anglo-American law in the legal method in Puerto Rico. Tulane law review 23 : 345-367, March 1949.

PORTUGAL

QUEIRO, A.R. : O novo direito constitucional português. Boletim da Faculdade de direito da universidade de Coimbra 22 : 44-66, fasc. 1, 1946.

PAES da SILVA VAZ SERRRA, A. : A revisão geral do código civil. Boletim da Faculdade de direito da Universidade de Coimbra 22 : 451-513, fasc. 2, 1946.

SEVILLA, D. : La reforma de la Constitución portuguesa. Revista de estudios políticos 16 : 128-153, septiembre-diciembre 1946.

ORTEGA PARDO, G.J. : La revisión del código civil portugues. Boletim da Faculdade de direito da Universidade de Coimbra 24 : 106-166, fasc. 1, 1948.

RUMANIA

The question of citizenship in Roumania. New Hungary 1 : 13, 9 June 1946.

The peoples' court in Rumania. New Hungary 1 : 14, 15 September 1946.

Constitution de la République populaire roumaine, 17 avril 1948. Documentation française, Notes documentaires et études : 1-17, no. 920, 4 juin 1948.

MIKIS, L. : Die Neugestaltung der rumänischen Gerichtsorganisation. Österreichische Juristen-Zeitung 3 : 385-386, 10. September 1948.

VOLANSCHI, A.A. : Legea pentru naţionalizarea intreprinderilor industriale bancare, de asigurări, miniere şi de transporturi. Probleme economice : 64-67, septembrie-octombrie 1948.

Constitution de la République populaire roumaine, adoptée en avril 1948. Informations constitutionnelles et parlementaires 2 : 145-161, no. unique 1949.

SALVADOR

Ley orgánica del Servicio consular de la República de El Salvador. Boletín de la Cámara de comercio e industria de El Salvador 23 : 15-54, marzo-abril 1949.

SAUDI ARABIA

Arabie Séoudite. Revue égyptienne de droit international 3 : 145-158, 1947.
Textes constitutionnels.

COUDERT, F.R. : Saudi Arabian offshore legislation American journal of international law 43 : 530-533 July 1949.

SOUTH AFRICA

South Africa - The citizenship act. Round table : 383-387, September 1949.

SPAIN

La reforma del código de comercio. España económica y financiera 49 : 406-407, 25 mayo 1946.

Loi minière espagnole. Annales des mines et des carburants, Documentation 135 : 1067-1099, 15 juillet 1946.
Texte.

BADENES GASSET, R. : Jurisprudencia civil. Revista jurídica de Cataluña 46 : 67-85, enero-marzo 1948.

COSSIO y CORRAL, A. de : El arrendamiento de solares y la nueva ley de arrendamientos urbanos. Anuario de derecho civil 1 : 473-492, abril-junio 1948.

MEZGER, E. : Derecho matrimonial español ante tribunales franceses. Revista de estudios políticos 21-22, 129-155, nos. 39-40, y 41-42, 1948.

CASTEJÓN y CHACÓN, C. : Código penal actualizado al 20 de septiembre 1938. Revista general de derecho 5 : 142-147, marzo 1949.

AGUILERA, C.R. : Influencia del protectorado en la evolución del derecho marroqui. Revista jurídica de Cataluña 47 : 141-156, marzo-abril 1949.

POLO DÍEZ, D.A. : Ante la reforma de la sociedad anónima. Comercio y navegación : 2-6, agosto-septiembre 1949.

MOSSA, L. : Para el proyecto español de ley sobre la sociedad anónima. Anuario de derecho civil 2 : 1307-1333, octubre-diciembre 1949.
See also pp. 1334-1415.

GASCÓN y MARÍN, J. : Necesidad de un código de procedimiento administrativo. Revista de estudios políticos 28 : 11-40, noviembre-diciembre 1949.
See also pp. 41-118.

SWEDEN

MATZ, S. : Den nya aktiebolagstiftningen. Kommersiella meddelanden 32 : 8-13, januari 1945.

SOLEM, E. : Østen Undén. Tidsskrift for rettsvitenskap 59 : 121-155, hefte 2, 1946.
Series of articles in honour of Østen Undén.

JÄGERSKIÖLD, S. : The immunity of state-owned vessels in Swedish judicial practice during world war II. American journal of international law 42 : 601-607, July 1948.

SCHMIDT, F. : Le droit international privé en Suède de 1939 à 1947. Revue critique de droit international privé 37 : 425-440, octobre-décembre 1948.

GIHL, T. : Svensk neutralitetsrättslig praxis under de båda världskrigen. Jus gentium 1 : 43-63, Fasc. 1, 1949.
Swedish neutrality-practice during the two world wars.

RAMEL, E. : Rättsfall i internationell rätt, avdömda av Högsta Domstolen i Sverige under åren 1944-1947. Nordisk tidsskrift for international ret 19 : 35-50, No. 1-2, 1949.

SCHÖNKE, A. : Die Strafrechtsreform in Schweden. Deutsche Rechts-Zeitschrift 4 : 49-52, 5. Februar 1949.

LINDEN, G. : Förslag till ny föreningslag. Från departement och nämnder 11 : 181-185, 27 maj 1949.
New company law.

FISCHLER, J. : Schweden - Das internationale Privatrecht 1942-1948. Zeitschrift für ausländisches und internationales Privatrecht 15 : 490-513, Heft 3/4, 1949.

SWITZERLAND

RIGGENBACH, B. : Übersicht der Literatur über schweizerisches Recht vom Jahre 1944. Zeitschrift für schweizerisches Recht 64 : 423-453, Heft 6, 1945.

Übersicht über die schweizerische Rechtsgesetzgebung des Jahres 1944. Zeitschrift für schweizerisches Recht 64 : 455-555, Heft 6, 1945.

GOETZINGER, F. : Die Rechtskraft von Zivilurteileb nach Rückzug der Appellation. Zeitschrift für schweizerisches Recht 65 : 177-184, Heft 2, 1946.

Message du Conseil fédéral à l'Assemblée fédérale concernant la publication d'un recueil des lois mis à jour, période de 1848 à 1947 (du 22 février 1946). Feuille fédérale 98 : 371-373, 28 février 1946.

COMTESSE, F.H. : Das Verhältnis des Bundesstrafrechts zum kantonalen Strafprozessrecht. Zeitschrift für schweizerisches Recht 65 : 62a-144a, Heft 3, 1946.

CAVIN, P. : Droit pénal fédéral et procédure cantonale. Zeitschrift für schweizerisches Recht 65 : 1a-60a, Heft 3, 1946.

ZWAHLEN, H. : Le fonctionnement de la justice administrative en droit fédéral et dans les cantons. Zeitschrift für schweizerisches Recht 66 : 95a-170a, Heft 3, 1947.

Message du Conseil fédéral à l'Assemblée fédérale à l'appui d'une nouvelle loi de procédure civile fédérale (du 14 mars 1947). Feuille fédérale 99 : 1001-1056, 20 mars 1947.

BÉGUIN, G. : Questions juridiques concernant le plan d'aménagement national et régional. Zeitschrift für schweizerisches Recht 66 : 350a-431a, Heft 4, 1947.

REICHLIN, P. : Rechtsfragen der Landesplanung. Zeitschrift für schweizerisches Recht 66 : 171a-342a, Heft 4, 1947.

Loi fédérale de procédure civile fédérale (du 4 décembre 1947). Feuille fédérale 100 : 237-258, 22 janvier 1948.

CLERC, F. : L'évolution du droit pénal suisse de 1938 à 1945. Revue de science criminelle et de droit pénal comparé : 37-51, janvier-mars 1948.

FELDMANN, M. : Zur Reform des schweizerischen Presserechtes. Zeitschrift für schweizerisches Recht 67 : 1a-122a, Heft 2, 1948.

JACCOTTET, G. : La réforme du droit de la presse en Suisse. Zeitschrift für schweizerisches Recht 67 : 123a-247a, Heft 2, 1948.

KEHL, R. : Bemerkungen zum schweizerischen Ehescheidungsrecht- Zeitschrift für schweizerisches Recht 67 : 225-246, Heft 4, 1948.

Message complémentaire du Conseil fédéral à l'Assemblée fédérale sur un projet de loi relative à la force obligatoire du Recueil systématique des lois et ordonnances mis à jour, 1848-1947, et à la nouvelle série du Recueil des lois (du 11 février 1948). Feuille fédérale 100 : 817-832, 19 février 1948.

RIGGENBACH, B. : Übersicht der Literatur über schweizerisches Recht 1947. Zeitschrift für schweizerisches Recht 67 : 297-338, Heft 5, 1948.

Übersicht über die schweizerische Rechtsgesetzgebung des Jahres 1947. Zeitschrift für schweizerisches ches Recht 67 : 337-485, Heft 6, 1948.

Message du Conseil fédéral à l'Assemblée fédérale à l'appui d'un projet de loi modifiant la loi sur le mode de procéder pour les demandes d'initiative populaire et les votations relatives à la revision de la constitution fédérale (du 16 novembre 1948). Feuille fédérale 100 : 913-943, 25 novembre 1948.

Message du Conseil fédéral à l'Assemblée fédérale concernant la revision de la loi sur le statut des fonctionnaires (du 20 décembre 1948). Feuille fédérale 100 : 1213-1268, 23 décembre 1948.

LEIMGRUBER, O. : La constitution de la Confédération suisse de 1848 à 1948. Revue internationale de droit comparé 1 : 9-22, janvier-juin 1949.

HENGEL, P.H. : Comment organiser les études de droit? Zeitschrift für schweizerisches Recht 68 : 273a-315a, Heft 3, 1949.
Voir aussi pp. 213a-271a.

Loi fédérale modifiant les dispositions du code des obligations sur la communauté des créanciers dans les emprunts par obligations (du ler avril 1949). Feuille fédérale 101 : 740-750, 14 avril 1949.

RIGGENBACH, B. : Bibliographie juridique suisse 1948. Zeitschrift für schweizerisches Recht 68 : 347-391, Heft 5, 1949.

GERMANN, O.A. : Präjudizielle Tragweite höchstinstanzlicher Urteile, insbesondere der Urteile des schweizerischen Bundesgerichts. Zeitschrift für schweizerisches Recht 68 : 297-332, Heft 5, 1949.

Message du Conseil fédéral à l'Assemblée fédérale à l'appui d'un projet de loi revisant partiellement le code pénal suisse (du 20 juin 1949). Feuille fédérale 101 : 1233-1290, 23 juin 1949.

Loi fédérale modifiant la loi du 30 juin 1927 sur le statut des fonctionnaires (du 24 juin 1949). Feuille fédérale 101 : 1310-1322, 30 juin 1949.

GERMANN, O.A. : Präjudzielle Tragweite höchstinstanzlicher Urteile, insbesondere der Urteile des schweizerischen Bundesgerichts (Contd.). Zeitschrift für schweizerisches Recht 68 : 423-456, Heft 6, 1949.

Message du Conseil fédéral à l'Assemblée fédérale concernant une révision partielle du code pénal militaire et de la loi sur l'organisation judiciaire et la procédure pénale pour l'armée fédérale (du 22 juillet 1949). Feuille fédérale 101 : 133-156, 4 août 1949.

Loi fédérale revisant la loi sur la poursuite pour dettes et la faillite (du 28 septembre 1949). Feuil fédérale 101 : 661-675, 20 octobre 1949.

DUBOIS, R. : L'expulsion en droit pénal et administratif. Revue de criminologie et de police technique 3 : 254-266, octobre-décembre 1949.

SWITZERLAND
(International law, Aliens)

IMER, F. : Le mariage d'un interné militaire ou d'un réfugié civil étranger en Suisse est-il possible? Revue internationale de la Croix-Rouge 27 : 226-234, mars 1945.

ZURBRÜGG, H. : Das internationale Flussschiffahrtsrecht in der Schweiz. Strom und See 40 : 74-80, Dezember 1945.

BÜHLER, R. : Zur Reform unseres Aussendienstes. Schweiz 17 : 52-61, 1946.
See also pp. 40-51.

SECRÉTAN, J. : Swiss constitutional problems and the International labour organisation. International labour review 56 : 1-20, July 1947.

Message du Conseil fédéral à l'Assemblée fédérale concernant une loi modifiant et complétant la loi sur le séjour et l'établissement des étrangers (du 8 mars 1948). Feuille fédérale 100 : 1277-1293, 25 mars 1948.

VISCHER-FREY, R. : Das Bürgerrecht der Gebürtigen Schweizerin. Echo 29 : 5-6, Oktober 1948.

Circulaire du Conseil fédéral aux gouvernements cantonaux concernant le nom de famille des femmes réintégrées dans la nationalité suisse (du 19 octobre 1948). Feuille fédérale 100 : 441-444, 21 octobre 1948.

GUGGENHEIM, P. : Rechtsstellung der international Verwaltungsunionen, die in der Schweiz ihren Sitz h ben. Schweizerisches Jahrbuch für internationales Recht 5 : 161-162, 1948.

Das neue Fremdenrecht der Schweiz. Informations-Dienst für Rück-und Weiterwanderung : 1-2, März 1949.

STAUFFER, W. : Form der Eheschliessung in der Schweiz und schweizerisches internationales Privatrecht. Schweizerisches Jahrbuch für international Recht 6 : 99-110, 1949.

BERTHOUD, P. : Les engagements internationaux con tractés par la Suisse, entrés en vigueur en 1948. Schweizerisches Jahrbuch für internationales Recht : 155-162, 1949.

VISCHER-FREY, R. : Erwerb und Verlust des Schweiz bürgerrechts durch Heirat. Schweiz 20 : 141-152, 1949.

NATIONAL LAW - COUNTRIES

SYRIA

RABBATH, E. : L'établissement du régime constitutionnel en Syrie et au Liban. Revue égyptienne de droit international 3 : 3-24, 1947.

GANNAGÉ, P. : La compétence des juridictions confessionnelles au Liban et en Syrie. Annales de la Faculté de droit, Université Saint Joseph de Beyrouth : 199-247, no. 1-2, 1948.

Al-kanoun al-Madani. Journal officiel de la République Syrienne 31 : 1407-1511, 31 mai 1949.
Code civil en vigueur à partir du 15 juin 1949. Texte arabe.

AL-JALKHI, I. : Le nouveau code civil syrien. Documentation française, Articles et documents : 4-5, no. 1602, 20 juillet 1949.

Kanoun el oukoubat. Journal officiel de la République Syrienne 31 : 2026-2100, 18 juillet 1949.
Code pénal en vigueur depuis le ler septembre 1949.

Kanoun al-tijarah. Journal officiel de la République Syrienne 31 : 2321-2403, 16 août 1949.
Code de commerce en vigueur à partir du ler septembre 1949.

THAILAND

Constitution du royaume du Siam, 23 mars 1949. Documentation française, Notes et études documentaires : 1-16, No. 1235, 24 novembre 1949.

TURKEY

KUNTER, N. : La répression des infractions économiques en Turquie et les problèmes y relatifs. Revue internationale de droit pénal 18 : 262-282, no. 3-4, 1947

U.S.S.R.

WALFORD, E.O. : Soviet courts and constitutional rights. Quarterly review 283 : 85-96, January 1945.

WALFORD, E.O. : Law and the citizen in the U.S.S.R. Contemporary review 167 : 100-104, February 1945.

DENISOV, A. : The presidium of the Supreme Soviet. Soviet news : 3, 26 September 1945.

How the U.S.S.R. will go to the polls - Regulations governing elections to the Supreme Soviet of the U.S.S.R., approved by decree of Presidium of Supreme Soviet of U.S.S.R. on October 11, 1945. Soviet weekly : 6-9, November 1, 1945.

DOBRIN, S. : Soviet federalism and the principle of double subordination. Transactions of the Grotius society 30 : 260-283, 1945.

OSSIPOW, P. : La propriété en droit soviétique. Zeitschrift für schweizerisches Recht 65 : 99-168, Heft 1, 1946.

DURMANOV, N. D. : How Soviet courts work - Soviet news : 3, 6 March 1946.

SCHWEIGL, G.M. : L'art. 124 della costituzione sovietica sulla libertà dei culti. Civiltà cattolica 97 : 225-230, 17 agosto 1946.

BERMAN; H.J. : Soviet family law in the light of Russian history and Marxist theory. Yale law journal 56 : 26-57, November 1946.

GSOVSKI, V. : Soviet law of inheritance. Michigan law review 45 : 291-320, 445-468, January, Februrary 1947.

ROTHSTEIN, A. : How the Soviet constitution works. Future : 94-104, no. 3, 1947.

VALTERS, N. : Sowjetstrafrecht, gestern und heute. Juristische Blätter 69 : 101-106, 1. März 1947.

KERBLAY, B. : Le régime juridique des brevets d'invention en U.R.S.S. Cahiers de l'économie soviétique : 3-10, avril-juin 1947.

Abolition of the death penalty. Soviet news : 1-2, 28 May 1947.
With article by A.Y. Vyshinsky.

BERMAN, H.J. : Principles of Soviet criminal law. Yale law journal 56 : 803-836, Nay 1947.

VYSHINSKYm A.Y. : The abolition of the death penalty. Soviet weekly : 4, 5 June 1947.
Published in "Pravda".

Protection of citizen's private property. Soviet news : 1, 6 June 1947.

Responsibility for disclosure of state secrets. Soviet news : 1, 11 June 1947.
Texts of decrees.

BERMAN, H.J. : Commercial contracts in Soviet law. California law review 35 : 191-234, June 1947.

SCHWEIGL, G.M. : Lo statuto ecclesiastico del 31 gennaio 1945 e l'art. 124 della costituzione societica. Civiltà cattolica 98 : 97-108, 19 luglio 1947.

VALTERS, N. : Reform der juristischen Bildung in der Sowjetunion. Oesterreichische Juristen-Zeitung 2 : 361-364, 12. September 1947.

Information constituting state secrets. American review on the Soviet Union 8 : 87-88, October 1947.
See also pp. 86-87.

AGARKOV, M.M. : The debtor's discharge from liability when performance is impossible. Journal of comparative legislation and international law 29 : 9-13, November 1947.

SVERDLOFF, G.M. : Modern Soviet divorce practice. Modern law review 11 : 163-175, April 1948.

GRAVEN, J. : Le droit pénal soviétique. Revue de science criminelle et de droit comparé : 231-273, avril-juin 1948.

POKROWSKI, J. : Schuld und Strafe im sowjetischen Strafrecht. Österreichische Juristen-Zeitung 3 : 217-219, 14. Mai 1948.

SVERDLOV, G.M. : Milestones in the development of Soviet family law. American review on the Soviet Union 9 : 3-27, August 1948.

NATIONAL LAW - COUNTRIES

GRAVEN, J. : Le droit pénal soviétique (Suite). Revue de science criminelle et de droit pénal comparé : 431-480, juillet-septembre 1948.

FRIDIEFF, M. : L'organisation du service public de la justice en U.R.S.S. Bulletin trimestriel de la Société de législation comparée 71 : 413-438, juillet-septembre 1948.

BAKAKIN, A., and MIRONOV, N. : K vyboram narodnykh sudov. Bolshevik 25 : 10-22, 30 noi͡abri͡a 1948.
Nationals courts.

GORSHENIN, K.P. : Vybory narodnykh sudov. Sovet͡skoe gosudarstvo i pravo : 1-9, dekabr' 1948.
National courts in U.S.S.R.

BRATUS', S.N. : Nekotorye voprosy proekta GK SSSR. Sovet͡skoe gosudarstvo i pravo : 10-23, dekabr' 1948.
Civil code.

BERMAN, H.J. : The challenge of Soviet law. Harvard law review 62 : 220-265, December 1948.

MEISSNER, B. : Die Verfassungsentwicklung der Sowjetunion seit dem zweiten Weltkrieg. Jahrbuch für internationales und ausländisches öffentliches Recht : 160-169, 1948.

NOVE, A. : Some aspects of Soviet constitutional theory. Modern law review 12 : 12-36, January 1949.

LACROIX, A. : La conception particulière du droit chez les Soviets et ses conséquences internationales. Revue politique et parlementaire 61 : 32-41, janvier 1949.

BERMAN, H.J. : The challenge of Soviet law. Harvard law review 62 : 449-466, January 1949.

La deuxième conférence juridique des savants et du corps enseignant des facultés et des instituts juridiques de l'U.R.S.S. Revue internationale de droit comparé 1 : 134-139, janvier-juin 1949.

CHKHIKVADZE, V.M. : Rol' sovetskogo suda v bor'be za preodolenie perezhitkov kapitalizma v soznanii li͡udeĭ. Sovetskoe gosudarstvo i pravo : 17-25, fevral' 1949.
Courts.

Sowjetischer Erfinderschutz für deutsche Erfinder. Verkehr (Berlin) 3 : 74-76, März 1949.

KOTOK, V.F. : K voprosu o predmete sovetskogo stroitel' stva. Sovetskoe gosudarstvo i pravo : 13-25, mart 1949.
Reconstruction of law.

WEISBERG, M.L. : The transformation of the collective agreement in Soviet law. University of Chicago law review 16 : 444-481, spring 1949.

Russian political penology - Article 58 of the Soviet penal code. Lithuanian bulletin 7 : 1-3, April-June 1949.

The results of the elections of people's courts. Soviet press translations 4 : 273-275, 1 May 1949.

MEISSNER, B. : Die verfassungsändernde Gesetzgebung des Obersten Sowjets der UdSSR und die Entwicklung der Ministerium 1947-1949 (Contd.). Europa-Archiv 4 : 2301-2306, 20. Juli 1949.

KARASS, V. : O soderzhanii prava gosudarstvennoi sot͡sialisticheskoĭ sobstvennosti. Sovetskoe gosudarstvo i pravo : 13-27, ii͡ul' 1949.
Socialist state property.

WOLFF, M.M. : Some aspects of marriage and divorce laws in Soviet Russia. Modern law review 12 : 290-296. July 1949.

IODOVSKY, A.N. : On the codification of Soviet laws. Current digest of the Soviet press 1 : 14-16, 9 August 1949.
Published in "Sovetskoye gosudarstvo i pravo".

GRIGOR'EV, V.K. : Administrativno-pravovye sposoby zashchity sot͡sialisticheskoĭ sobstvennosti. Sovetskoe gosudarstvo i pravo : 38-45, avgust 1949.
Protection of state property.

OSSIPOW, P. : Le droit successoral soviétique. Revue internationale de droit comparé 1 : 249-273, août-septembre 1949.

SCHLESINGER, R. : A glance at Soviet law. Law quarterly review 65 : 504-517, October 1949.

LIVSHIT͡S, V.I͡A. : Pravootnoshenii͡a i proet͡sssual' nai͡a dei͡atel'nost' v sovetskom ugolovnom prot͡sesse. Sovetskoe gosudarstvo i pravo : 48-56, noi͡abr' 1949.
Criminal procedure.

VENEDIKTOV, A.V. : Voprosy sot͡sialisticheskoĭ sobst vennosti v trudakh Iosifa Vissarionovicha Stalina. Sovetskoe gosudarstvo i pravo : 53-78, dekabr' 1949.
Stalin on state property.

U.S.S.R.
(International law and practice, Aliens and Naturalization)

HAZARD, J.N. : Soviet commercial arbitration. International arbitration journal 1 : 8-17, April 1945.

HILTON, H.J. : Commercial arbitration in the treaties and agreements of the U.S.S.R. Department of State bulletin 12 : 890-897, 13 May 1945.

RASHBA, E.S. : Settlement of disputes in commercial dealings with the Soviet Union. Columbia law review 45 : 530-555, July 1945.

PRINCE, C. : Current views of the Soviet Union on the international organization of security, economic coöperation and international law - A summary. American journal of international law 39 : 450-485, July 1945.

La saisie par le Gouvernement soviétique des avoirs russes aux Etats-Unis. Journal des tribunaux mixtes 24 : 2-4, 28 et 29 septembre 1945.

VERDROSS, A. : Die Völkerrechtssubjektivität der Gliedstaaten der Sowjetunion. Österreichische Zeitschrift für öffentliches Recht 1 : 212-218, Heft 1-2, 1946.

Statut de la representation commerciale de l'Union des République Socialistes Soviétiques en France, Moscou, 29 décembre 1945. Moniteur officiel du commerce et de l'industrie 64 : 1187-1188, 27 juin 194

CHAKSTE, M. : Soviet concepts of the state, international law and sovereignty. American journal of international law 43 : 21-36, January 1949.

MAURACH, R. : Das Kriegsrecht vom Blickfeld der Sowjetunion. Jahrbuch für internationales und ausländisches öffentliches Recht : 736-753, 1949.

UNITED ARAB REPUBLIC

Du contrôle judiciaire exercé sur la législation de guerre et son application. Journal des tribunaux mixtes 24 : 3, 23 et 24 février 1945.

La "war clause" et la belligérance de l'Egypte. Journal des tribunaux mixtes 24 : 3-4, 30 et 31 juillet 1945.

Le régime juridictionnel des membres des forces alliées en Egypte et la notion du service commandé. Journal des tribunaux mixtes 24 : 3-4, 24 et 25 août 1945.

Des questions que posent les successions testamentaires des Israélites algériens en Egypte. Journal des tribunaux mixtes 24 : 1-6, 26 et 27 septembre 1945.

A propos du projet de réforme du statut personnel des Egyptiens non musulmans. Journal des tribunaux mixtes 24 : 1-3, 3 et 4 octobre 1945.

PACE, U. : De la juridiction pénale des tribunaux mixtes à l'égard des members des forces armées alliées. Revue égyptienne de droit international : 87-94, 1945.

Le nouveau statut des Italiens d'Egypte. Journal des tribunaux mixtes 25 : 1, 27 et 28 mars 1946.

Le statut personnel des non musulmans en Egypte. Journal des tribunaux mixtes 25 : 1-3, 22 et 23 avril 1946.

Le statut des étrangers en Egypte. Journal des tribunaux mixtes 25 : 1-2, 29 et 30 juillet 1946.

BRINTON, J.Y. : The Egyptian moxed courts and foreign armed forces. American journal of international law 40 : 737-741, October 1946.

L'affaire des obligations de la Compagnie universelle du Canal maritime de Suez. Journal des tribunaux mixtes 26 : 3-4, 28 février - ler mars 1947.

L'affaire des obligations de la Compagnie du Canal de Suez (Suite). Journal des tribunaux mixtes 26 : 1-6, 16 et 17 avril 1947.

Le régime de la séquestration des biens italiens et les titres de sociétés égyptiennes déposés à l'étranger. Journal des tribunaux mixtes 26 : 4-6, 18 et 19 juin 1947.

CHEVALLIER, J. : Jurisprudence des juridictions mixtes d'Egypte. Revue trimestrielle de droit civil 46 : 364-369, juillet-septembre 1947.

Les clauses d'établissement et les accords de Montreux. Journal des tribunaux mixtes 27 : 1-2, 18 et 19 février 1948.

Le projet de modification de la loi sur la nationalité égyptienne. Journal des tribunaux mixtes 27 : 1-2, 17 et 18 mai 1948.

La "war clause" et la belligérance en Egypte. Journal des tribunaux mixtes 27 : 1-3, 2 et 3 juillet 1948.

Al kanoun al-Madani. Journal officiel du Gouvernement Egyptien 119 : 1-105, 29 juillet 1948.
Code civil en vigueur à partir du 15 octobre 1949. Texte arabe.

La réglementation du transfert des affaires mixtes à la Juridiction nationale. Journal des tribunaux mixtes 27 : 1-2, 18 et 19 août 1948.

La liquidation des procès pendants par devant les tribunaux mixtes. Journal des tribunaux mixtes 28 : 1-2, 8 et 9 novembre 1948.

La justice en Egypte d'Ismaïl à Farouk. Journal des tribunaux mixtes 28 : 1-4, 10 et 11 novembre 1948.

Le sort des fonctionnaires étrangers des juridictions mixtes. Journal des tribunaux mixtes 28 : 1-2, 8 et 9 décembre 1948.

McDOUGALL, A. : The terminations of the Egyptian mixed courts. British year book of international law 25 : 386-390, 1948.

BOULAD, G. : Où en sommes-nous de la question du statut personnel pour les non-musulmans? Journal des tribunaux mixtes 28 : 1-2, 2 et 3 mars 1949.

L'inadmissibilité de la mise en échec d'un certificat régulier de nationalité étrangère par l'application extensive de l'art. 22 de la loi sur la nationalité égyptienne. Journal des tribunaux mixtes 28 : 3-4, 6 et 7 avril 1949.

L'expiration du permis de séjour ne rend pas illégal le séjour en Egypte d'un étranger qui a droit à la résidence en vertue des Accords de Montreux. Journal des tribunaux mixtes 28 : 2-7, 8 et 9 juin 1949.

De l'indemnisation des dommages de guerre subis du fait de l'Italie par l'Egypte et ses habitants. Journal des tribunaux mixtes 28 : 3-4, 12 et 13 août 1949.

Le transfert aux juridictions nationales des fonctionnaires égyptiens des juridictions mixtes. Journal des Tribunaux mixtes 28 : 5-6, 10 et 11 octobre 1949.

L'heure de la séparation. Journal des Tribunaux mixtes 28 : 3-6, 12 et 13 octobre 1949.
Fin des tribunaux mixtes.

WALINE, M., et SOTO, L. de : Le conseil d'Etat égyptien. Revue du droit public et de la science politique 65 : 453-506, octobre-décembre 1949.

WÉE, M. de : Le régime juridictionnel des forces armées étrangères en Egypte. Revue de droit pénal et de criminologie 30 : 288-305, décembre 1949.

McDOUGALL, A. : The position of foreigners in Egypt on the termination of the mixed courts. British year book of international law 26 : 358-379, 1949.

U.S.A.

SCHWARTZ, B. : The war power in Britain and America (Contd.). New York university law quarterly review 20 : 465-498, October 1945.

NATIONAL LAW - COUNTRIES

BERNHARD, R.S. : A rationalization of the Illinois conflict of laws and rules applicable to contracts. Illinois law review 40 : 165-184, November-December 1945.

OPPENHEIM, L. : The civil liberties doctrines of Mr. Justice Holmes and Mr. Justice Cardozo. Tulane law review 20 : 177-219, December 1945.

MOSCOWITZ, G.M. : Trends in federal law and procedure. New York university law quarterly review 21 : 1-27, January 1946.

The question of amending the presidential succession act. Congressional digest 25 : 67-96, March 1946.

ORFIELD, L.B. : The federal rules of criminal procedure. New York university law quarterly review 21 : 167-224, April 1946.

DESSION, G.H. : The new federal rules of criminal procedure. Yale law journal 55 : 694-714, June 1946.

MULLINS, C. : Judicial reformers in the U.S.A. Quarterly review 284 : 286-297, July 1946.
Criminal jurisdiction.

WILDING-WHITE, A.M. : The American legal system. Law journal 96 : 453-454, August 23 1946.

SCHWARTZ, B. : Executive power and the disappearance of law. New York university law quarterly review 21 : 487-505, October 1946.

HALE, R.L. : Unconstitutional acts as federal crimes. Harvard law review 60 : 65-109, November 1946.

WADE, J.W. : Legal status of property transferred under an illegal transaction. Illinois law review 41 : 487-505, November-December 1946.

DYKES, J.A., and KEEFE, A.J. : The 1940 amendment to the diversity of citizenship clause. Tulane law review 21 : 171-191, December 1946.

SHERWOOD, F.H. : Mandamus to review state administrative action. Michigan law review 45 : 123-162, December 1946.

Negro disenfranchisement - A challenge to the constitution. Columbia law review : 76-98, January 1947.

Powers of the President, limitations of tenure and the line of succession. Congressional digest 26 : 1-2, January 1947.
See also pp. 3-32.

SCHLESINGER, A.M. : The Supreme court 1947. Fortune 35 : 73-79, 201-212, January 1947.

SCHWARTZ, B. : The American administrative procedure act, 1946. Law quarterly review 63 : 43-64, January 1947.

DESSION, G.H. : The new federal rules of criminal procedure (Contd.). Yale law journal 56 : 197-257, January 1947.

CONARD, A.F. : New ways to write laws. Yale law journal 56 : 458-481, February 1947.

The President's report. Arbitration journal 2 : 1-18, spring 1947.

Constitutional limitations on the Un-American activities committee. Columbia law review 47 : 416-431, April 1947.

RADIN, M. : Popular legislation in California, 1936-1946. California law review 35 : 171-190, June 1947.
Initiative and referendum.

HARPER, F. : The Supreme court and the conflict of laws. Columbia law review 47 : 883-913, September 1947.

The 1946 term of the Supreme court. Columbia law review 47 : 883-1008, September 1947.

KALLENBACH, J.E. : The new presidential succession act. American political science review 41 : 931-946, October 1947.

Survey of New York law, 1946-1947. New York university law quarterly review 22 : 523-920, October 1947.

POUND, R. : Annual survey of law - Decisions of courts show some dangerous trends. American bar association journal 33 : 1093-1098, November 1947.

MEANY, G. : The Taft-Hartley act. American federationist 54 : 8-9, 29, December 1947.

The Taft-Hartley law in operation. Information service 27 : 1-4, 31 January 1948.

WALLSTEIN, L.M. : The revision of the army court-martial system. Columbia law review 48 : 219-236, March 1948.

WITTE, E.E. : An appraisal of the Taft-Hartley act. American economic review 38 : 368-382, May 1948.

GREEN, J.R. : The bill of rights, the fourteenth amendment and the Supreme court. Michigan law review 46 : 869-910, May 1948.

MEYER, J. : Labor under the Taft-Hartley act. Social research 15 : 194-210, June 1948.

To amend the constitution - Curbs on dangerous centralization are proposed. American bar association journal 34 : 649-651, August 1948.

GILMORE, G. : On the difficulties of codifying commercial law. Yale law journal 57 : 1341-1359, August 1948.

ADELMAN, M.A. : Effective competition and the anti-trust laws. Harvard law review 61 : 1289-1350, September 1948.

FRANK, J.P. : The United States supreme court, 1947-48. University of Chicago law review 16 : 1-55, autumn 1948.

Survey of New York law, 1947-1948. New York university law quarterly review 23 : 573-919, October 1948.

Reorganization of the executive branch. Columbia law review 48 : 1211-1225, December 1948.

NATIONAL LAW - COUNTRIES

EMERSON, T.I., and HELFELD, D.M. : Loyalty among government employees. Yale law journal 58 : 1-143, December 1948.

The proposed commercial code. Illinois law review 43 : 820-822, January-February 1949.

HOOVER, J.E. : A comment on the article "Loyalty among government employees". Yale law journal 58 : 403-411, February 1949.

BERGER, M. : The Supreme court and group discrimination since 1937. Columbia law review 49 : 201-230, February 1949.

SILVA, R.C. : The presidential succession act of 1947. Michigan law review 47 : 451-476, February 1949.

TRUMAN, H.S. : Taft-Hartley act repeal. Vital speeches of the day 15 : 290-292, 1 March 1949.

LUND, T.G. : The legal aid and advice scheme. Record of the Association of the Bar of the City of New York 4 : 77-99, March 1949.

COLLINS, C.W. : Constitutional aspects of the Truman civil rights program. Illinois law review 44 : 1-12, March-April 1949.

SCOTT, A.W. : The Supreme court's control over state and federal criminal juries. Iowa law review 34 : 577-604, May 1949.

CONNOR, J.T. : The work of the National conference of commissioners on uniform state laws. Tulane law review 23 : 518-530, June 1949.

DONOVAN, W.J., and JONES, M.G. : Program for a democratic counter attack to communist penetration of government service. Yale law journal 58 : 1211-1241, July 1949.

AGAR, H. : Evolution of U.S. constitution. Freedom and union 4 : 3-5, July-August 1949.

SHERWOOD, F.H. : State constitutional law in 1948-49. American political science review 43 : 735-765, August 1949.

Congress weighs plans to reform the presidential election procedure. Congressional digest 28 : 193-224, August-September 1949.

FINER, H. : The Hoover commission reports. Political science quarterly 64 : 405-419, September 1949.

Summary of reports of the Hoover commission. Public administration 27 : 195-210, autumn 1949.

FRANK, J.P. : The United States Supreme court, 1948-49. University of Chicago law review 17 : 1-55, autumn 1949.

AARON, B., and KOMAROFF, M.I. : Statutory regulation of internal union affairs. Illinois law review 44 : 425-466, September-October 1949.

HARTMANN, P. : Racial and religious discrimination by innkeepers in U.S.A. Modern law review 12 : 449-453, October 1949.

ILLIG, C. : Tidelands - An unsolved problem. Tulane law review 24 : 51-65, October 1949.

MING, W.R. : Racial restrictions and the Fourteenth amendment - The restrictive covenant cases. University of Chicago law review 16 : 203-238, winter 1949.

1948-1949 survey of New York law. New York university law quarterly review 24 : 965-1340, December 1949.

DEAN, W.T. : Conflicts of laws. New York university law quarterly review 24 : 1008-1019, December 1949.
New York State.

U.S.A.
(International law, Aliens, Nationality)

LEVY, A.G.D. : Acquisition of nationality in the emergency refugee shelter. American journal of international law 39 : 13-19, January 1945.

ALEXANDROFF, L., et KLINE, E.M. : Le développement de la jurisprudence de l'état de New York en droit international, 1939 à 1944. Journal du droit international 67-72 : 309-329, avril-juin 1945.

GARVER, F.H. : The treaty veto of the United States senate (Contd.). World affairs interpreter 16 : 137-154, July 1945.

ATWATER, E. : Recent legislation affecting the American foreign service. American journal of international law 39 : 559-565, July 1945.

BORCHARD, E. : The proposed constitutional amendment on treaty-making. American journal of international law 39 : 537-541, July 1945.

HELMICK, M.J. : United States court for China. Far Eastern survey 14 : 252-255, 12 September 1945.

BORCHARD, E. : The charter and the constitution. American journal of international law 39 : 767-771, October 1945.
The United Nations charter.

KUHN, A.K. : The extension of sovereign immunity to government-owned commercial corporations. American journal of international law 39 : 772-775, October 1945.

Concerning the naturalization privileges extended to aliens serving with our armed forces. Interpreter releases 23 : 167-169, 26 July 1946.

TIMBERG, S. : Corporate fictions - Logical social and international implications. Columbia law review 46 : 533-580, July 1946.

FAIRMAN, C. : The Supreme Court on military jurisdiction - martial rule in Hawaii and the Yamashita case. Harvard law review 59 : 833-882, July 1946.

LENHOFF, A. : Attacks of vulnerable foreign divorces - Outposts of resistance. New York university law quarterly review 21 : 457-486, October 1946.

BATHURST, M.E. : Recognition of American divorce and nullity decrees. British year book of international law 23 : 168-177, 1946.

BORCHARD, E. : Nationalization of enemy patents. American journal of international law 37 : 92-97, January 1947.

American citizenship - Can applicants qualify their allegiance? American bar association journal 33 : 95-98, February 1947.

Judicial determination of the end of the war. Columbia law review 47 : 255-268, March 1947.

KAMPELMAN, M.M. : The United States and international copyright. American journal of international law 41 : 406-429, April 1947.

TORRE, G.J. : Aliens- Denaturalization for fraud. California law review 35 : 449-453, September 1947.

The Inter-American copyright convention - Its place in United States copyright law. Harvard law review 60 : 1329-1339, October 1947.

LYONS, A.B. : The conclusiveness of the "suggestion" and certificate of the American State department. British yearbook of international law 24 : 116-147, 1947.

LENHOF, A. : Über einige Grundfragen des amerikanischen Internationalen Privatrechts. Juristische Blätter 70 : 31-36, 31.Januar 1948.

BISHOP, W.W. : Recent American judicial decisions involving international law. American journal of international law 42 : 194-200, January 1948.

MARX, F.M. : Effects of international tension on liberty under law. Columbia law review 48 : 555-573, May 1948.

SAYRE, P. : Shelley v. Kraemer and United Nations law. Iowa law review 34 : 1-11, November 1948.

Seizure of disputed enemy claims by the alien property custodian. Columbia law review 49 : 403-408, March 1949.

BISHOP, J.W. : Judicial construction of the trading with the enemy act. Harvard law review 62 : 721-759, March 1949.

Renunciations of citizenship by Japanese Americans. Illinois law review 44 : 106-112, March-April 1949.

LEFLAR, R.A. : The new Uniform foreign judgments act. New York university law quarterly review 24 : 336-355, April 1949.

U.S.A.
(Patents, Trade-marks, Copyright)

CALLMANN, R. : The new trade-mark act of 5 July 1946. Columbia law review 46 : 929-950, November 1946.

BORDEN, N.H. : The new trade-mark law. Harvard business review 25 : 289-305, spring 1947.

STOUGHTON, L.B. : A review of the new trade-mark manual. Michigan law review 45 : 865-874, May 1947.

KILLIPS, D. : The new trade-mark registration statute. Illinois law review 42 : 204-222, May-June 1947.

URUGUAY

La capacidad jurídica de la mujer. Boletin del Banco hipotecario del Uruguay: 8-12, octubre 1946. See also pp. 5-7.

VATICAN STATE

BERNARDINI, C. : Motu proprio de ordine iudiciali et de ratione procedendi in causis civilibus in statu Civitatis Vaticanae servendis. Apollinaris 19 : 212-219, num. 3-4, 1946.

BRULLIARD, G. : Le code de procédure civile de la Cité du Vatican. Bulletin trimestriel de la Société de législation comparée 71 : 237-264, avril-juin 1948.

CUMBO, H.F. : The Holy See and international law. International law quarterly 2 : 603-620, winter 1948-49.

Creazione e diffusione di falsi notiziari sull' attività politica dello Stato della Città del Vaticano. Foro italiano 74 : parte 2a, 49-57, fasc. V-VI, 1949.

VENEZUELA

PIETRI, L.G. : Sociedades extranjeras - De la emisión de acciones preferidas por suscripción pública. Revista de derecho y legislación 34 : 29-32, marzo-abril 1945.

Decreto no. 219 sobre expropriación por causa de utilidad pública o social. Revista de derecho y legislación, Decretos de la Junta revolucionaria de gobierno 35 : 3-8, enero-febrero 1946.

GONZALEZ, G. : Derecho minero venezolano (Contd). Revista de hacienda 12 : 73-155, diciembre 1947.

Ley de expropriación por causa de utilidad pública o social. Revista de derecho y legislación, Collección de leyes vigentes 37 : 1-16, enero-abril 1948.

HERZ, W. : Über die Rechtsverhältnisse in Venezuela. Österreichische Juristen-Zeitung 3 : 151-153, 16. April 1948.

COLBORN, P.A. : The new constitution of Venezuela. Bulletin of the Pan American Union 82 : 219-224, April 1948.

Constitución de Venezuela. Revista parlamentaria 17 : 55-59. agosto 1948.

Constitución de Venezuela (Contd.). Revista parlamentaria 17 : 46-52, setiembre 1948.

YUGOSLAVIA

Le projet de sonstitution de la République fédérative populaire de Yougoslavie. Documentation yougoslave : 19-25, 20 décembre 1945.

La constitution yougoslave. France, Secrétariat d'état à l'information, Notes documentaires et études : 1-12, no. 246, 27 février 1946.

PERITCH, J.M. : Le centenaire du code civil serbe, 1844-1944. Zeitschrift für schweizerisches Recht 65 : 407-421, Heft 6, 1946.

La constitution du 31 janvier 1946. Revue du droit public et de la science politique 62 : 454-489, juillet-septembre 1946.
Texte annexé.

The judicature in Tito's Yugoslavia. Tablet 188 : 240-242, 9 November 1946.

MAJTIN, Z. : Das jugoslawische Ehegesetz vom 3. April 1946. Juristische Blätter 69 : 36-38, 18. Januar 1947.

PETROVITCH, M.B. : The Central government of Yugoslavia. Political science quarterly 62 : 504-530, December 1947.

Föderative Volksrepublik Jugoslawien. Juristische Blätter 70 : 489-492, 16. Oktober 1948.
Annotated index to 1946 constitution and selected index to laws 1945-1948.

Verzeichnis der neuen ausländischen Rechtsnormen - Föderative Volksrepublik Jugoslawien. Juristische Blätter 70 : 629-632, 24. Dezember 1948.

Constitution de la République fédérative populaire de Yougoslavie promulguée le 31 janvier 1946. Informations constitutionnelles et parlementaires 1 : 142-170, no. unique 1948.
Voir l'édition anglaise pour le texte anglais.

Zakonodavni rad Narodne skupshtine FHRJ na chetvertom vanrednom zasedanju. Arkhiv za pravne i drushtvene nauke 36 : 41-46, januar-mart 1949.
Legislative council.

Pregled zakonodavstva nashikh narodnikh republika u 1948 godini. Arkhiv za pravne i drushtvene nauke 36 : 47-74, januar-mart 1949.
Legislation in 1948.

PROKOP, A. : Postoji li po našem zakonodavstvu mogućnost naknade štete zbog umanjenog izgleda na udaju. Arkhiv za pravne i drushtvene nauke 36 : 467-471, iuli-september 1949.

DORDEVIĆ, J., and SRZENTIĆ, N. : O sistemu posebnog dela krivichnog zakonika FNRJ. Arkhiv za pravne i drushtvene nauke 36 : 571-626, Oktobar-detsembar 1949.
Draft of criminal code.

NATIONAL LAW - COUNTRIES

AFGHANISTAN

HUFFMAN, A.V. : The administrative and social structure of Afghan life. Royal Central Asian journal 38 : 41-48, January 1951.

ALBANIA

La République populaire d'Albanie (Suite) - Constitution de la République Populaire d'Albanie, juillet 1950. Documentation française, Notes et études documentaires : 1-8, no. 1844, 4 mars 1954.

ARGENTINA

SATANOWSKY, M. : Per l'unificazione del diritto delle obbligazione e dei contratti civili e commerciali in Argentina. Rivista del diritto commerciale 48 : 30-49, gennaio-febbraio 1950.

La nueva constitución de la Provincia de Buenos Aires. Hacienda, economía y previsión 2 : 13-16, enero-febrero 1950.

LISBONNE, J. : Bulletin de jurisprudence de la République Argentine. Journal du droit international 77 : 324-329, janvier-mars 1950.

LEVENE, R. : La situation actuelle de la procédure pénale en Argentine. Revue internationale de droit pénal 21 : 441-447, no. 3, 1950.

La constitution de la République Argentine. Archives internationales Pharos 7 : 1-10, section B, no. 957, octobre 1950.

PODETTI, J.R. : Esame del progetto di codice processuale civile argentino. Annuario di diritto comparato e di studi legislativi 26 : 319-332, fasc, 2-3, 1950.

BREGI, C.A. : Los territorios nacionales - Régimen legal - Proyectos de reformas. Revista de la Facultad de ciencias económicas, comerciales y políticas : 637-669, setiembre 1949-abril 1950.

GOLDSCHMIDT, W. : Separación y disolución del matrimonio en el derecho internacional privado argentino. Revista española de derecho internacional 4 : 83-111, núm. 1, 1951.

Argentina - Ley de organización de la justicia nacional. Información jurídica : 289-303, marzo 1951.

SAMPAY, A.E. : L'esprit de la réfrome constitutionnelle en Argentine. Cahiers de législation et de bibliographie juridique de l'Amérique Latine 2 : 11-23, octobre-décembre 1951.

LAFAILLE, H. : La Cour de cassation en Argentine et la nouvelle constituion. Cahiers de législation et de bibliographie juridique de l'Amérique Latine 2 : 41-46, octobre-décembre 1951.

ARECHA, W. : La propriété commerciale en Argentine. Cahiers de législation et de bibliographie juridique de l'Amérique Latine 3 : 39-42, janvier-mars 1952.

GOLDSCHMIDT, W. : Codificación del derecho internacional privado argentino. Revisto española de derecho internacional 5 .: 499-528, no. 2, 1952.

GOLDSCHMIDT, R. : Einführung der Adoption in Argentinien. Zeitschrift für ausländisches und internationales Privatrecht 17 : 260-268, Heft 2, 1952. Text pp. 281-283.

ROGERS, F.D. : Similarities and differences in letter and spirit between the constitutions of the United States and Argentina. Georgetown law journal 40 : 582-607, May 1952.

LISBONNE, J. : Bulletin de jurisprudence de la République Argentine. Journal du droit international 79 : 934- 951, juillet-septembre 1952.

RIPOLLÈS, A.Q. : Argentina - Nuevo proyecto del Código penal. Anuario de derecho penal y ciencias penales 5 : 478-482, septiembre-diciembre 1952.

Argentina - Reformas civiles y procesales. Información jurídica : 1175-1189, diciembre 1952.

JIMENEZ de ASUA, L. : Argentine - Les projets d'un nouveau code pénal. Revue de droit pénal et de criminologie 33 : 956-959, juillet 1953.

GOWLAND, N. : Control de la constitucionalidad de las leyes. Revistas jurídica de Cataluña 52 : 58-63, enero-febrero 1953.

GOWLAND, N. : Control de la constitucionalidad de las leyes. Revista jurídica de Cataluña 52 : 58-63, enero-febrero 1953.

CABRERA, J.M., and REMORINO, J. : El derecho laboral argentino ante el derecho comparado. Revista del Instituto de derecho comparado : 36-60, enero-junio 1954.

AUSTRALIA

ELSE-MITCHELL, R. : Transitional and post-war powers in the Commonwealth of Australia. Canadian bar review 28 : 407-421, April 1950.

FLEMING, J.G. : Recent Australian decisions on private international law. International law quarterly 3 : 426-431, July 1950.

STONE, J. : A government of laws and yet of men, being a survey of half a century of the Australian commerce power. New York university law review 25 : 45[illegible]-512, July 1950.

McINERNEY, M.V. : Procedural aspects of a Royal commission. Australian law journal 24 : 386-392, 15 February 1951.

DERHAM, D.P. : Australian communist party v. the Commonwealth. Journal of comparative legislation and international law 33 : 40-49, parts 3-4, 1951.

BEASLEY, F.R. : Australia's communist party dissolution act. Canadian bar review 29 : 490-514, May 1951.

BAILEY, K.H. : Fifty years of the Australian constitution. Australian law journal 25 : 314-343, September 20, 1951.

GROVES, M.C. : The criminal jurisdiction of the Supreme Court of Papua, New Guinea (Contd.). Australian law journal 25 : 636-641, 21 February 1952.

SMITH, E. : The restoration of lost titles in New Guinea. Australian law journal 25 : 712-715, 17 April 1952.
Records destroyed during the war.

EWENS, J.Q. : Parliamentary drafting in the Commonwealth of Australia. International and comparative law quarterly 1 : 363-368, July 1952.

FLEMING, J.G. : Inter-state enforcement of maintenance and alimony decrees. Australian law journal 26 : 407-412, 15 December 1952.

JOSKE, P.E. : Decisions under the Commonwealth matrimonial causes act. Australian law journal 26 : 642-645, 21 April 1953.

The eighth legal convention of the Law council of Australia. Australian law journal 27 : 133-124, 30 July 1953.
Soecial issue.

Australia and the continental shelf. Australian law journal 27 : 458-461, 19 November 1953.

O'CONNEL, D.P. : L'Australie et sa plateforme sous-marine. Revue de droit international, de sciences diplomatiques et politiques 32 : 63-66, janvier-mars 1954.

LEYSER, J. : Die australische Gesetzgebung auf dem Gebiete des Privatrechts 1939-1953. Zeitschrift für ausländisches und internationales Privatrecht 19 : 538-553, Heft 3, 1954.

PIETRI, A. : Une sentencia argentina en materia cambiaria. Revista de derecho y legislación 43 : 211-216, agosto-setiembre 1954.
See also pp. 217-244.

GOWLAND, N. : Las nuevas reformas en el Código de procedimientos civil y comercial de la Capital de la República argentina. Revista de derecho y legislación 43 : 279-294, octubre-diciembre 1954.

COWEN, Z. : Constitution of the Commonwealth of Australia, 9 July 1900. Jahrbuch des öffentlichen Rechts der Gegenwart 3 : 271-312, 1954.

GOLDIE, L.F.E. : Australia's continental shelf - Legislation and proclamations. International and comparative law quarterly 3 : 535-575, October 1954.
With map.

CARTER, P.B. : Some impressions of private international law in Australia. Annual law review 3 : 67-86, December 1954.

AUSTRIA

HELLBLING, E. : Das österreichische Staatsbürgerschaftsrecht nach dem Stande von 1949. Juristisches Blätter 72 : 3-7, 7. Januar 1950.

TONCIC-SORIN, L. : Die falsche Annexionstheorie. Österreichs völkerrechtliche Struktur von 1968 bis 1945. Österreichische Monatshefte 6 : 232-237, April 1950.

Gilt das Konkordat? - War der "Anschluss" Annexion oder Okkupation? Österreichische Monatshefte 6 : 195-231, April 1950.

LOEBENSTEIN, E. : Der Verfassungsgerichtshof seit seiner Wiederrichtung. Österreichische Juristen-Zeitung 5 : 173-175, 22. April 1950.

SCHÄRF, A. : Gilt das Konkordat? Zukunft : 117-125, Mai 1950.

Gilt das Konkordat? - War der "Anschluss" Annexion oder Okkupation. Österreichische Monatshefte 6 : 418-437, Juli-August 1950.

HOYER, V. : Anerkennung österreichischer Entscheidungen in Ehesachen im Ausland. Österreichische Juristen-Zeitung 5 : 442-444, 14. Oktober 1950.

MIELE, M. : La restaurazione dell'Austria. Annali di diritto internazionale 8 : 67-73, 1950.

EHRENZWEIG, A.A. : Österreichische Erben amerikanischer Verlassenschaften. Juristische Blätter 73 : 127-127, 17. März 1951.

BRASSLOFF, E. : Ausscheiden des Staatsoberhauptes aus seiner Funktion vor Ablauf der Amtsperiode. Juristische Blätter 73 : 201-203, 28. April 1951.

SÄTTLER, G. : Probleme der Unterhaltspflicht deutscher Väter gegenüber unehelichen österreichischen Kindern. Juristische Blätter 73 : 230-232, 12. Mai 1951.

HOYER, V. : Anerkennung österreichische Entscheidungen in Ehesachen im Ausland (Contd.). Österreichische Juristen-Zeitung 6 : 320-325, 29. Juni 1951.

URBAN, E. : Aus der Praxis der Verstaatlichung nach dem 2. Verstaatlichungsgesetz. Österreichische Juristen-Zeitung 6 : 372-376, 27. Juli 1951.

KAFKA, G.E. : Git die Bundesverfassung 1929? Österreichische Furche 7 : 3, 4. August 1951.

SCHIMA, H. : Zur Lage im internationalen Verfahrensrecht. Juristische Blätter 73 : 522-528, 10. November 1951.

SEIDL-HOHENVELDERN, I. : Entschädigung für Besatzungsschäden in Österreich. Journal du droit international 79 : 562-599, avril-juin 1952.

APPEL, K. : Besatzungskosten in der US-Zone Österreichs. Juristische Blätter 74 : 311-314, 21. Juni 1952.

SPANNER, H. : Landesbürgerschaft und Bundesbürgerschaft - Eine offene Verfassungsfrage. Österreichische Juristen-Zeitung 7 : 449-454, 12. September 1952.

HOYER, V. : Bemerkungen zum Verlust der österreichischen Staatsbürgerschaft nach dem Staatsbürgerschaftsgesetz 1949. Österreichische Juristen-Zeitung 7 : 505-508, 10. Oktober 1952.

WERNER, L. : Die Beseitigung der Landesbügerschaft. Juristische Blätter 75 : 277-280, 23. Mai 1953.
See also pp. 280-283.

SEIDL-HOHENVELDERN, I. : Austria - Restitution legislation. American journal of comparative law 2 : 383-389, summer 1953.

WERNER, L. : Vom Erwerb der österreichischen Staatsbürgerschaft durch Erklärung. Juristische Blätter 76 : 5-9. 2. Januar 1954.

SPANNER, H. : Die Prüfung von Gesetzen und Verordnungen durch den Verfassungsgerichtshof in der Zeit von 1950-1952. Österreichische Zeitschrift für öffentliches Recht 6 : 152-184, Februar 1954.

SCHWIND, F. : Probleme des österreichischen internationalen Familienrechts. Zeitschrift für ausländisches und internationales Privatrecht 19 : 242-259, Heft 2, 1954.

KAFKA, G.E. : Österreich, die Besatzung und die Grundlagen der Völkerrechtsgemeinschaft. Österreichische Zeitschrift für öffentliches Recht 6 : 348-377, Heft 3, 1954.

MAKAROV, A.N. : Die deutsche Staatsangehörigkeit der Österreicher nach 1945. Juristenzeitung 9 : 280-282, 5. Mai 1954.

BAECK, P.L. : Status and autonomy of Austrian attorneys at law. Tulane law review 28 : 468-479, June 1954.

HORROW, M. : L'évolution du droit criminel autrichien depuis 1945. Revue de science criminelle et de droit pénal comparé : 467-495, juillet-septembre 1954.

HELLAUER, E. : Das österreichische Entschädigungsgesetz. Zeitschrift für das gesamte Kreditwesen 7 : 514-516, 1. August 1954.

BELGIUM

VISSCHER, P. de Chronique de jurisprudence administrative étrangère - Belgique, 1948-1949. Revue di droit public et de la science politique 66 : 43-57, janvier-mars 1950.

GANSHOF van der MEERSCH, W.J. : Des rapports entre le chef de l'Etat et le gouvernement en droit constitutionnel belge. Revue de droit international et de droit comparé 27 : 181-197, no. spécial 1950.

VLIEBERGH, H. : De l'effet de l'assentiment des Chambres aux traités conclus par le Roi. Revue de droit international et de droit comparé 28 : 7-22, No. 1, 1951.

BIZET, J. : Législation coloniale, 1940-1950. Revue de droit international et de droit comparé 28 : 48-56, No. 1, 1951.

ABRAHAMS, R. : La réglementation des activités lucratives des étrangers en Belgique et les conventions d'établissement. Journal du droit international 78 : 482-507, avril-juin 1951.

La crise du droit d'auteur en Balgique. Union européenne de radiodiffusion, Bulletin de documentation et d'information 3 : 1-3, 15 mars 1952.

HERREMANS, M.P. : Le problème des nationalités en Belgique. Revue de l'Institut de sociologie : 389-404, no. 3, 1952.

MEYER, J. de : La décentralisation territoriale dans les états de Benelux. Revue du droit public et de la science politique en France et à l'étranger 68 : 367-395, avril-juin 1952.

RENARD, C., et GRAULICH, P. : Chronique de droit belge. Revue trimestrielle de droit civil 52 : 183-207, janvier-mars 1953.

ROLLAND, M. : L'organisation de la justice au Congo belge. Revue internationale de droit comparé 5 : 97-112, janvier-mars 1953.

RENARD, C., et GRAULICH, P. : Chronique de droit belge. Revue trimestrielle de droit civil 52 : 183-199, janvier-mars 1954.

ORBAN, P.M. : L'intégration européenne et la revision de la constitution belge. Revue internationale d'histoire politique et constiutionnelle 4 : 21-33, janvier-mars 1954.

IVe congrès de l'Académie internationale de droit comparé, Paris, août 1954 - Rapports des juristes belges. Revue de droit international et de droit comparé 31 : 1-340, no. spécial 1954.

BOLIVIA.

DURAN, P.M. : Bolivie, Annuaire de législation étrangère. Nouvelle série 2 : 62-69, 1950-51.

DURAN, P.M. : Résumé de la bibliographie juridique de la Bolivie. Cahiers do législation et de bibliographie juridique de l'Amérique Latine 2 : 223-229, octobre-décembre 1951.

ORTIZ, M.P. : Evolution du droit de la famille en Bolivie. Cahiers de législation et de bibliographie juridique de l'Amérique Latine 3 : 29-34. avril-juin 1952.

BRAZIL

FERREIRA, W. : Il centenario del codice commercial del Brasile. Rivista del diritto commerciale 48 : 367-381, settembre-ottobre 1950.

MEDEIROS da FONSECA, M.A. : La forza obbligatoria dei cpntratti e le sue modificazione nei diritti positivi moderni. Rivista del diritto commerciale 48 437-449. novembre-dicembre 1950.

NEHRU, S.S. : La constitution de l'Inde et le constitution du Brésil comparées. Revue de droit international et de droit comparé 28 : 161-164, Nos. 3-4, 1951.

FERREIRA, W. : A federação e o presidencialismo no sistema constitucional brasileiro. Revista da Faculdade de direito (São Paulo) 46 : 61-142, 1951.

HERZOG, J.B. : La loi brésilienne du 18 septembre 1949 sur la nationalité. Cahiers de législation et de bibliographie juridique de l'Amérique Latine 3 : 91-93, janvier-mars 1952.

AZULAY, F. : La conception brésilienne du fonds de commerce. Cahiers de législation et de bibliographie juridique de l'Amérique Latine 3 : 43-50, janvier-mars 1952.

PENNA MARINHO, I. : Da reaquisição da nacionalida[illegible] brasiliera. Sociedade brasiliera de direito internacional, Boletim 7 : 5-19, janeiro-dezembro 1951.

Loi no. 818 du 18 septembre 1949 réglant l'acruisition, la perte et le recouvrement de la nationalité ainsi que la perte des droits politiques. Textes législatifs étrangers 3 : 3-19, no. 3, 1953.

FERREIRA, W. : A personalidade juridica das sociedades mercantis no direito brasileiro. Revista da Faculdade de direito (São Paulo) 48 : 26-49, 1953.

CESARINO, A.F. : Evolución del derecho social brasileño. Revista de la Facultad de derecho de México 4 : 147-163, enero-marzo 1954.

BRABDÂO CAVALCANTI, T. : Le droit municipal au Brésil. Revue internationale des sciences administratives 20 : 393-411, no. 2, 1954.

BULGARIA

KUTIKOV, V. : Brachniîat rezhim na chuzhdentsite v NR Búlgariîa spored noviîa zakon za lisata i semeîstvoto. Godishnik na Sofiîskiîa universitet. Îuridicheski fakultet 44 : VI/1-43, 1949-1950.

STAINOV, P. : Prinos kům uchenieto za pravilnika i naredbata pri republikanskata konstutsiîa. Godishnik na Sofiîskiîa universitet, Îuridicheski fakultet 44 : 1/1-77, 1949-1950.

VASSILEV, L. : Caractères et principes fondamentaux du nouveau droit des obligations. Izvestiîa na Ikonomicheskiîa i pravniîa instituti : 213-222, kniga 3-4, 1950.

NICOLOFF, A.M. : An "Act for the protection of peace" in Bulgaria. American journal of international law 45 : 353-354, April 1941.

TCHIRKOVITCH, S. : Un nouveau code de la famille en Bulgarie. Revue internationale de droit comparé 3 : 304-306, avril-juin 1951.

République Populaire de Bulgarie - "Informations du Président de l'Assemblée nationale", no. 93 du 20 novembre 1951. Documentation juridique étrangère 3 : 1, no. 5-6, 1951.
Abrogation des lois antérieures au 9 septembre 1941.

Lois sur la propriété du 8/11/51. Textes législatifs étrangers : 3-24, no. 3, 1952.

PUNDEFF, M. : Bulgarian decree on territorial waters. American journal of international law 46 : 330-333, April 1952.

GROBOVENKO, ÎA. : Nov'yî ugolovno-protsessual'nyî kodeks narodnoî Respubliki Bolgarii. Sovetskoe gosudarstvo i pravo : 73-76, iîun' 1952.
Criminal procedure code.

Le code pénal bulgare. Documentation française, Notes et études documentaires : 1-28, no. 1638, 30 juillet 1952.

GALLARDO RUEDA, A. : Ordenación de la propiedad en la República Popular de Bulgaria. Anuaria de derecho civil 5 : 1362-1366, octubre-diciembre 1952.

Le Code du travail bulgare de 1951. Documentation française, Notes et études documentaires : 1-22, no. 1695, 12 janvier 1953.

DOLAPCHIEV, N. : Law and human rights in Bulgaria. International affairs 29 : 59-68, January 1953.

UKASE no. 544 - Le Code du travail voté le 9 novembre 1951. Documentation juridique étrangère : 9-65, no. 1, 1953.

KATZAROV, C. : Die Entwicklung des öffentlichen Rechtes in Bulgarien seit dem 2. Weltkrieg. Jahrbuch des öffentlichen Rechts 2 : 283-300, 1953.

Législation bulgare sur les personnes et la famille. Documentation juridique étrangère 5 : 3-47, no. 2, 1953.

Loi sur la nationalité bulgare. Textes législatifs étrangers 3 : 23-28, No. 3, 1953.

TCHIRKOVITCH, S. : Le régime matrimonial des étrangers en Bulgarie d'après la nouvelle loi sur les personnes et la famille. Revue internationale de droit comparé 5 : 714-717, octobre-décembre 1953.
Analyse de l'étude de Coutikov.

DROBNIG, U. : Das bulgarische Gesetz über das Eigentumsrecht vom 8.11.1951. Zeitschrift für ausländisches und internationales Privatrecht 18 : 692-698, Heft 4, 1953.

BURMA

Constitution de l'Union Birmane, 24 septembre 1947. Documentation française, Notes et études documentaires : 1-28, no. 1303, 28 mars 1950.

CHRISTIAN, W. : Burma's new constitution and Supreme court. Tulane law review 26 : 47-59, December 1951.

GLEDHILL, A. : The Burmese constitution. Indian year book of international affairs 2 : 214-224, 1953.

CAMEROON

CACAN, R. : La Cour criminelle du Cameroun. Penant, Recueil général de jurisprudence, de doctrine et de législation d'outre-mer, Doctrine 64 : 67-78, juillet-août 1954.

CANADA

NICHOLLS, G.V.V. : Legal periodicals and the Supreme court of Canada. Canadian bar review 28 : 422-445, April 1950.

NICHOLAS, H.S. : The Statute of Westminster and the constitution of Canada. Australian law journal 24 : 147-149, 17 August 1950.

KENNEDY, G.D. : Recent Canadian decisions on private international law. International law quarterly 3 : 431-437, July 1950.

LIVINGSTON, W.S. : Abolition of appeals from Canadian courts to the Privy Council. Harvard law review 64 : 104-112, November 1950.

CARTER, A.N. : Some merits and defects of the administration of justice in Canada. Canadian bar review 28 : 941-950, November 1950.

NATIONAL LAW - COUNTRIES

TURGEON, J. : De la revision du code civil québécois. Canadian bar review 29 : 70-77, January 1951.

Conflicts of law - Divorce - Canadian choice of law. Michigan law review 49 : 1039-1048, May 1951.

NELLIGAN, J.P. : Legal aid in Canada - Existing facilities. Canadian bar review 29 : 589-620, June-July 1951.

Nationhood and the constitution. Canadian bar review 29 : 1019-1179, December 1951.
Special issue.

FABRE-SURVEYER, E. : Le code civil canadien et le droit anglais en matière de testament. Revue de droit international et de droit comparé 30 : 73-73, no. 2, 1953.

The MacQuarrie report and the reform of combines legislation. Canadian bar review 30 : 549-607, June-July 1952.

GOWLING, E.G. : The new Canadian trade marks act. Canadian bar review 31 : 664-677, June-July 1953.

MUNDELL, D.W. : Tests for validity of legislation under the British North America act. Canadian bar review 32 : 813-843, October 1954.

The thirty-sixth annual meeting of the Canadian bar association. Canadian bar review 32 : 994-1008, November 1954.

CEYLON

KHADER NAWAZ, M. : The constitution of Ceylon. Indian year book of international affairs 2 : 237-246, 1953.

L'évolution constitutionnelle de Ceylan. Documentation française, Notes et études documentaires : 1-23, no. 1936, 18 octobre 1954.

CHILE

SILVA-BASCUÑAN, A. : La physionomie constitutionnelle du Chili. Revue internationale de droit comparé 2 : 91-107, janvier-mars 1950.

BRAIN RIOJA, H. : Observaciones al proyecto de reforma del código penal chileno (Contd.). Revista de derecho 19 : 167-172, abril-junio 1951.

ALESSANDRI, A. : La réforme du code civil chilien. Cahiers de législation et de bibliographie juridique de l'Amérique Latine 3 : 137-140, juillet-décembre 1952.

ALESSANDRI, A. : Chili. Annuaire de législation étrangère 3 : 123-129, 1952-1954.

CHINA

BÜNGER, K. : China - Das Ehegesetz der Volksrepublik von 1950. Zeitschrift für ausländisches und internationales Privatrecht 16 : 112-120, Heft 1, 1950.
Text pp. 121-126.

WU, J.C. : Raffronto fra la costituzione italiana e la costituzione cinese. Annuario di diritto comparato e di studi legislativi 26 : 1-12, fasc.1, 1950.

The marriage law of the People's Republic of China promulgated... on 1 May 1950. People's China 1 : 28-30, 16 June 1950.

VALTERS, N. : Das neue Staatsrecht in China. Juristische Blätter 72 : 407-410, 16. September 1950.

GILPATRICK, M.G. : The status of law and law-making procedure under the Kuomintang 1925-1946. Far Eastern quarterly 10 : 38-55, November 1950.

GAMBA, C. : Constitution making in China - A socio-historical analysis. Annual law review 1 : 409-432, December 1950.

KIRFEL, H. : Das Gewohnheitsrecht in China. Sinologica 3 : 52-64, Nr. 1, 1951.

BÜNGER, K. : Die Verfassung der Chinesischen Volksrepublik von 1949. Zeitschrift für ausländisches öffentliches Recht und Völkerrecht 13 : 759-785, Nr. 4, Juni 1951.
See also pp. 808-858.

SUDARIKOV, N.G. : Stroitel'stvo i ukreplenie organov gosudarstvennoĭ vlasti Kitaĭskoĭ Narodnoĭ Respubliki. Sovetskoe gosudarstvo i pravo : 23-42, avgust 1951.
Administration.

Disposition portant contrôle de l'état civil des résidents étrangers de Shanghai, 1951. Textes législatifs étrangers : 3-9, no. 1, 1952.

KIRICHENKO, V.F. : Zakonodatel'nye akty Kitaĭskoĭ Narodnoĭ Respubliki o bor'be gosudarstvennymi preszupleniîami. Sovetskoe gosudarstvo i pravo : 65-69, fevral' 1952.
Law against political crimes.

FRANKENSTEIN, M. : Formose, son statut juridique et sa situation politique. Revue politique et parlementaire 54 : 51-60, janvier 1952.

The new legal system in China. Far Eastern economic review 13 : 38-40, 10 July 1952.

SCHIBOR, L. : Über die Rechtsentwicklung in der Volksrepublic China. Neue Justiz 7 : 137-138, 5. März 1953.

Electoral law of the People's Republic of China for the All-China people's congress and local people's congresses of all levels - TENG, H.P. : An explanation on the electoral law. People's China, Supplement : 1-16, 1 April 1953.

Volksgericht in China. Ost-Probleme 5 : 817-820, 14. Mai 1953.

Chine - Loi relative à l'élection de l'Assemblée populaire nationale et des assemblées populaires locales (1er mars 1953). Informations constitutionnelles et parlementaires : 121-126, 15 juin 1953.
Extraits.

Verfassungsentwurf der Volksrepublik China. Neue Welt 9 : 2273-2290, Heft 18, September 1954.
Text.

Constitution of the Peolple's Republic of China. New times, Supplement : 1-13, no. 40, 2 October 1954.
Text.

Constitution de la République populaire chinoise, 20 septembre 1954. Documentation française, Notes et études documentaires : 1-11, no 1943, 14 octobre 1954.

Constitution de la République populaire chinoise, 20 septembre 1954. Informations constitutionelles et parlementaires 4 : 133-155, 1 novembre 1954.
Texte.

COLOMBIA

Régimen legal de la sociedad anónima - Decreto de 27 de julio de 1950. Información jurídica : 1248-1260, diciembre 1951.
Text of law.

Proyecto de reforma presentado por la Comisión de estudios constitucionales de Antioquia y exposición de motivos. Estudios de derecho 14 : 326-369, mayo 1953.
Constitution; See also pp. 371-387.

ESCALLON CAYZEDO, B. : Las sucesiones ante el derecho internacional privado colombiano. Información jurídica : 3-27, enero 1954.

COMMONWEALTH

GONIDEC, P.F. : Métamorphoses du Commonwealth. Revue juridique et politique de l'Union française 4 : 229-263, avri.-juin 1950.

An ordinance to amend and consolidate the Penal code. Uganada gazette, Supplement 43 : 11 May 1950.
See also pp. 32-39.

Eight dominion legal conference. New Zealand law journal 27 : 394-397, 18 December 1951.
Dunedin, 1951.

IWI, E.F. : The evolution of the Commonwealth since the statute of Westminster. Grotius society, Transactions 37 : 83-97, 1951.

HANBURY, H.G. : The territorial limits of criminal jurisdiction. Grotius society, Transactions 37 : 171-184, 1951.

BARTHOLOMEW, G.W. : Polygamous marriages. Modern law review 15 : 35-47, January 1952.

CLARENCE SMITH, J.A. : Eastern marriages in English law. International and comparative law quarterly 1 : 301-312, July 1952.

O'CONNELL, D.P. : Change of sovereignty and the doctrine of act of state. Australian law journal 26 : 201-205, 21 August 1952.

CARNELL, F.G. : Malayan citizenship legislation. International and comparative law quarterly 1 : 505-518, October 1952.

RAMPHAL, S.S. : Federal constitution-making in the British West Indies. International and comparative law quarterly 2 : 192-206, April 1953.

MATSON, J.N. : Internal conflicts of laws in the Gold Coast. Modern law review 16 : 469-481, October 1953.

PARRY, C. : Plural nationality and citizenship with special reference to the Commonwealth. British year book of international law 30 : 244-292, 1953.

JENNINGS, R.Y. : The Commonwealth and international law. British year book of international law 30 : 320-351, 1953.

FRANCK, T. : The Governor general and the head of state functions. Canadian bar review 32 : 1084-1099, December 1954.

CONGO
(Kinshasa - formerly Belgian)

RUBBENS, A. : Les différents statuts des habitants du Congo. Institut royal colonial belge, Bulletin des séances 24 : 423-439, no. 2, 1953.

MERCKAERT, D. : Le droit pénal congolais. Revue de droit pénal et de criminologie 33 : 819-828, juin 1953.
Voir aussi pp. 829-851.

HISLAIRE-GUISLAIN, A. : Législation coloniale, 1953-1954. Revue de droit international et de droit comparé 31 : 169-180, no. 4, 1954.

COSTA RICA

Ley de extranjería y naturalización. Boletín del Instituto de derecho comparado de México 3 : 147-152, septiembre-diciembre 1950.

SINJANSKI, D., et CASTANOS, S. : De la constitution de la République de Costa-Rica du 7 novembre 1949. Cahiers de législation et de bibliographie juridique de l'Amérique Latine 3 : 77-84, janvier-mars 1952.

CUBA

BUSTAMENTE y SIRVÉN, A.S. de : La letre de cambio. Revista jurídica de Cataluña 49 : 141-155, marzo-abril 1950.

ENTEZA JOVA, P.J. : El código procesal civil Montagú. Revista cubana de derecho 24 : 117-176, julio-diciembre 1950.

CABRERA SAQUI, M. : El problema del ingreso en el Servicio exterior de la República. Revista de derecho internacional 58 : 573-583, 31 diciembre 1950.

Los estatutos constitucionales de la República. Cuba económica y financiera 27 : 9, abril 1952.

Código de defensa social (Contd.). Información jurídica : 338-432, abril 1953.
Criminal law.

Législation cubaine en matière d'état civil. Documentation juridique étrangère 5 : 87-91, no. 12, 1953.
Mariage, 1953.

CZECHOSLOVAKIA

ČEPIČKA, A. : L'édification de la législation nouvelle en Tchécoslovaquie. Bulletin de droit tchécoslovaque 8 : 2-22, 1 janvier 1950.

RASCHE : Das neue Staatsangehörigkeitsrecht der tschechoslowakischen Republik. Deutsche Rechts-Zeitschrift 5 : 178-179, 20. April 1950.

BRÜGEL, J.W. : Justizreform in der Tschechoslowakei - Die Demokratisierung der Justiz in der Tschechoslowakei. Europa-Archiv 5 : 2943-2950, April 1950.

MANN, F.A. : Nazi spoliation in Czechoslovakia. Modern law review 13 : 206-212, April 1950.

REINER, P. : New Czechoslovak legislation on acquisition and loss of nationality. American journal of international law 44 : 387-390, April 1950.
Text pp. 77-81, Official documents.

HADEK, P. : Das neue Familienrecht in der ČSR. Juristische Blätter 72 : 306-311, 24. Juni 1950.

Code de la famille. Bulletin de droit tchécoslovaque 8 : 109-126, 1er avril 1950.
Voir aussi pp. 97-109, 126-132, Texte anglais pp. 199-212.

VIKTORY, J. : La démocratisation de la procédure civile. Bulletin de droit tchécoslovaque 8 : 226-232, 1 octobre 1950.

TOLAR, J. : La nouvelle procédure pénale. Bulletin de droit tchécoslovaque 8 : 251-276, 1 octobre 1950.

ŠIMÁK, J. : Les principes du nouveau droit pénal tchécoslovaque. Bulletin de droit tchécoslovaque 8 : 237-251, 1 octobre 1950.

KŘÍŽKOVSKÝ, L. : Le nouveau droit pénal administratif protège notre passage au socialisme. Bulletin de droit tchécoslovaque 8 : 276-289, 1 octobre 1950.

Un nouveau code de la famille en Tchécoslovaquie. Revue internationale de droit comparé 2 : 701-703, octobre-décembre 1950.

SLAPNICKA, H. : Die Strafrechtskodifikation in der Tschechoslowakei. Juristische Blätter 72 : 575-577, 23. Dezember 1950.

HUBER, M. : Die neue tschechische Strafprozessordnung. Juristische Blätter 73 : 104-106, 3. März 1951.

KORKISCH, F. : Die verfassungsrechtliche Entwicklung in der Tschechoslowakei bis zur Verfassung vom 9. Mai 1948. Zeitschrift für ausländisches öffentliches Recht und Völkerrecht 13 : 670-687, März 1951.

HUBER, M. : Die neue tschechische Strafprozessordnung. Juristische Blätter 73 : 104-106, 3. März 1951.

DE LUCA, L. : Il nuovo diritto matrimoniale cecoslovacco. Annuario di diritto comparato e di studi legislativi 27 : 371-380, fasc. 3, 1951.

FIERLINGER, Z. : La loi tchécoslovaque sur la protection de la paix. Bulletin de droit tchécoslovaque 9 : 1-6, 1 avril 1951.

STAJGR, F. : Rapports juridiques avec l'étranger dans la loi sur la procédure en matière civile. Jus gentium 3 : 193-211, settembre-dicembre 1951.

Penal code. Bulletin de droit tchécoslovaque 9 : 343-424, 1er octobre 1951.

FISCHER, H. : The foreign compensation, Czechoslovakia, order in Council. International and comparative law quarterly 1 : 97-102, January 1952.

Gesetz über den Erwerb und Verlust der tschechoslowakischen Staatsangehörigkeit vom 13.7. 49. Zeitschrift für ausländisches und internationales Privatrecht 17 : 476-479, Heft 3, 1952.

KORKISCH, F. : Das neue internationale Privatrecht der Tschechoslowakei. Zeitschrift für ausländisches und internationales Privatrecht 17 : 410-450, Heft 3, 1952.
See also pp. 457-466.

Etude comparative de l'ancien et du nouveau code civil. Textes législatifs étrangers : 83-123, no. 3, 1952.

BYSTRICKÝ, R. : Le remaniement de la législation tchécoslovaque sur les brevets. Bulletin de droit tchécoslovaque 10 : 21-31, 1 avril 1952.

SZIRMAI, Z. : Le droit du mariage dans les codes de la famille tchécoslovaque et polonais. Revue internationale de droit comparé 4 : 281-293, avril -juin 1952.

Das Strafgesetz der Tschechoslowakischen Republik. Bulletin de droit tchécoslovaque 10 : 235-318, 1 juillet 1952.

SOLNAŘ, V. : Les principes progressistes du nouveau droit pénal tchécoslovaque. Bulletin de droit techécoslovaque 10 : 156-164, 1er juillet 1952.

Le régime constitutionnel tchécoslovaque - Evolution historique, analyse de la constitution du 9 juin 1948. Archives internationales Pharos 9 : 1-2, no 1076, septembre 1952.
Texte no.1077, pp. 1-14.

BENEŠ, V. : The new legal system of Czechoslovakia. Journal of Central European affairs 12 : 215-235, October 1952.

MALOVSKÝ-WENIG, A. : La nouvelle loi tchécoslovaque concernant les marques de fabrique et de commerce (marques déposées) et les modèles industriels. Bulletin de droit techécoslovaque 10 : 333-343, 1er décembre 1952.

Civil code - Law no. 141 of October 25, 1950. Bulletin de droit tchécoslovaque 10 : 511-582, 1er décembre 1952.

BOURA, F. : A propos de la loi révisant le code de procédure civile. Bulletin de droit tchécoslovaque 11 : 129-134, no. 2-3, 1953.

MAGERSTEIN, W. : Die Frage des staatsbürgerrechtlichen Status der in der Tschechoslowakischen Republik mit Verfassungsdekret des Präsidenten der Republik vom 2. August 1945, Zahl 33/1945 Slg., ausgebürgerten "Personen deutscher Nationalität". Österreichische Zeitschrift für öffentliches Recht 5 : 338-409, Heft 3, 1953.

BYDŽOVSKÝ, L. : Les modifications apportées au code de procédure pénale. Bulletin de droit tchécoslovaque 11 : 134-140, no. 2-3, 1953.

OSWALD : Nochmals zur Frage - Staatsangehörigkeit der Sudetendeutschen. Monatschrift für deutsches Recht 7 : 151-152, März 1953.

Aperçu des normes les plus importantes publiées en 1953 au Recueil des lois de la République tchécoslovaque. Bulletin de droit tchécoslovaque 11 : 320-323, no. 4, 1953.

Législation tchécoslovaque sur les mariages entre ressortissants tchécoslovaques et les étrangers. Documentation juridique étrangère 5 : 119-121, no. 6-7, 1953.

BOURA, F. : Les principes fondamentaux du nouveau droit tchécoslovaque. Revue progressiste de droit français : 131-136, novembre 1953.

MAYDA, J. : Lawyers under communism - A "new" legal order in Czechoslovakia. American bar association journal 39 : 1071-1074, December 1953.

SLAPNICKA, H. : Neuerungen im Verwaltungsaufbau und in der Behördenorganisation der Tschechoslowakei. Juristische Blätter 76 : 218-220, 24. April 1954.

SCHMIED, E. : Das neue Rechtssystem der Tschechoslowakei. Zeitschrift für Ostforschung 3 : 567-589, Heft 4,1954.

TABORSKY, E. : The legal profession in a People's democracy. Tulane law review 28 : 362-370, April 1954.

SCHÄTZEL, W. : La nationalité des Allemands des Sudètes. Journal du droit international 81 : 625-635, juillet-septembre 1954.
Texte en allemand, anglais et français.

KVASNIČKA, V. : Modifications importantes dans le droit pénal de la Tchécoslovaquie démocratique populaire. Bulletin de droit tchécoslovaque 12 : 8-14, 1 octobre 1954.

Loi du 22 décembre 1953, no. 115 du Recueil des lois de la République tchécoslovaque sur le droit d'auteur, promulguée le 31 décembre 1953, entrée en vigueur le 1er janvier 1954. Bulletin de droit tchécoslovaque 12 : 335-356, 1 décembre 1954.

SLAPNICKA, H. : Die Loslösung der tschechischen Rechtswissenschaft vom abendländischen Rechtsdenken. Europa-Archiv 9 : 7166-7170, 20. Dezember 1954.

DENMARK

HURWITZ, S. : L'analogie dans le droit danois. Revue de science criminelle et de droit pénal comparé : 1-5, janvier-mars 1950.

Grønlanske retsproblemer. Finanstidende 36 : 967, 30. maj 1951.

FROST, J.L. : Fra den danske højesterets praksis i aaret 1950. Tidsskrift for rettsvitenskap 64 : 488-532, hefte 5, 1951.

Loi, du 27 mai 1950, sur la nationalité danoise. Textes législatifs étrangers : 13-18, no. 1, 1952.
Voir aussi pp. 19-20.

USSING, H. : Le transfert de la propriété en droit danois. Revue internationale de droit comparé 4 : 5-12, janvier-mars 1952.

FROST, J.L. : Fra den danske højesterets praksis i aaret 1951. Tidsskrift for rettsvitenskap 65 : 296-352, hefte 3, 1952.

Danemark. Annuaire de législation étrangère 3 : 130-143, 1952-54.
Suite d'articles.

FROST, J.L. : Fra den danske hojesterets praksis i aaret 1952. Tidsskrift for rettsvitenskap 66 : 418-462, hefte 4, 1953.

GAUDEFROY-DEMONBYNES, R. : Le mariage et le divorce au Danemark. Revue internationale de droit comparé 4 : 461-478, juillet-septembre 1952.

ERIKSEN, E. : Denmark's new constitution. Danish foreign office journal : 1-4, no. 8, 1953.

MARCUS, F. : Die dänische Verfassung vom 5. Juni und das Rhronfolgegesetz vom 27. März 1953. Zeitschrift für ausländisches öffentliches Recht und Völkerrecht 15 : 211-217, Nr. 1-2, Oktober 1953.

Constitution du Royaume de Danemark, 5 juin 1953 - Loi de succession au trône, 27 mars 1953. Informations constitutionnelles et parlementaires : 181-196, 1 novembre 1953.

ROBERT, J. : Danemark - La constitution du 5 juin 1953. Revue du droit public et de la science politique en France et à l'étranger 60 : 64-85, janvier-mars 1954.
Textes en annexe.

FROST, J.L., and LORENZEN, A. : Fra den danske højesterets praksis i aaret 1953. Tidsskrift for rettsvitenskap 67 : 297-343, hefte 3, 1954.

DOMINICAN REPUBLIC

MARINAS, L. : Santo Domingo - Constitución de la República Dominicana. Información jurídica : 455-464, abril 1951.

ECUADOR

LEON, B. : Algunas sugerencias para la reforma penal ecuatoriana. Criminalia 16 : 103-113, marzo 1950.

CORNEJO, R. : La nueva ley de inquilinato. Boletín de la Sección de investigaciones de derecho comparado, Universidad central del Ecuador 1 : 8-24, abril-julio 1951.

Ecuador - Decreto no. 985, sobre naturalización, extradición y expulsión de extranjeros. Boletín del Instituto de derecho comparado de México 4 : 155-164, mayo-agosto 1951.

PEREZ GUERRERO, A. : Breve análisis de la legislación cambiaria en el Ecuador. Boletín del Instituto de derecho comparado de México 4 : 37-45, septiembre-diciembre 1951.

ERITREA

WICKSTRÖM, H. : FN : s domstol i Eritrea. Svensk juristtidning 38 : 56-57, januari-februari 1953.

Erythrée - Acte de fédération avec l'Ethiopie (11 septembre 1952). Informations constitutionnelles et parlementaires : 127-129, 15 juin 1953.

Constitution de l'Erythrée (11 août 1952). Informations constitutionnelles et parlementaires : 129-151, 15 juin 1953.

SCHILLER, A.A. : Eritrea - Constitution and federation with Ethiopia. American journal of comparative law 2 : 375-383, summer 1953.

ETHIOPIA

BENTWICH, N. : Private international law in Ethiopia. International law quarterly 4 : 111-115, January 1951.

Important new legislation in Ethiopia. Public rights proclamation No. 139 of 1953. New times and Ethiopia news : 3-4, December 19, 1953.

FINLAND

SUONTAUSTA, T. : Presidentens ställning inom Finlands statsförfattning. Tidsskrift for rettsvitenskap 63 : 63-72, hefte 1-2, 1950.

TAXELL, L.E. : Juridisk litteratur i Finland 1947-1949. Svensk juristtidning 36 : 118-129, februari 1951.

SUONTAUSTA, T. : La situation juridique des îles d'Aland. Zeitschrift für ausländisches öffentliches Recht und Völkerrecht 13 : 741-752, Nr. 4, Juni 1951.

Loi sur l'acquisition et la perte de la nationalité finlandaise, promulguée à Helsinki le 9 mai 1941. Textes législatifs étrangers : 33-38, no. 1, 1952. Voir aussi pp. 39-44.

GODENHIELM, B. : Arvsrättsreformen i Finland. Tidsskrift for rettsvitenskap 66 : 241-266, hefte 3, 1953.

SCHWINDT, B. : Från Högsta Domstolen i Finland 1949 och 1950. Tidsskrift for rettsvitenskap 67 : 557-577, hefte 5, 1954.

Constitution finlandaise du 17 juillet 1919 et modifications ultérieures. Documentation française, Notes et études documentaires : 1-10, No. 1957, 7 décembre 1954.

FRANCE

WALINE, M. : Cinquante ans de jurisprudence administrative. Recueil Dalloz, Chronique : 21-24, 9 février 1950.

JULLIOT de la MORANDIÈRE, L. : La révision du code civil français. Zeitschrift für schweizerisches Recht 69 : 149-164, Heft 2, 1950.

VOUIN, R. : Le projet de réforme du code d'instruction criminelle. Recueil Dalloz, Chronique : 37-40, 9 mars 1950.

HAMSON, C.J. : Civil procedure in France and in England. Cambridge law journal 10 : 411-418, No. 3, 1950.

LAMPUÉ, P. : Les lois applicables en Algérie. Revue juridique et politique de l'Union française 4 : 1-23, janvier-mars 1950.

MALLET, L., et VERRIER, M. : Les travaux de la Commission de refonte du code civil français. Canadian bar review 28 : 247-266, March 1950.

BEYSSADE, J. : Evolution du statut juridique des musulmans. Documents algériens, Série politique : 1-6, 25 octobre 1950.

HOUIN, R. : Les travaux de la Commission de réforme du code civil. Revue trimestrielle de droit civil 50 : 34-50, janvier-mars 1951.

ARDANT, G. : La codification permanente des lois, règlements et circulaires. Revue du droit public et de la science politique en France et à l'étranger 57 : 35-70, janvier-mars 1951.

PASCAL, R.A. : A report on the French civil code revision project. Tulane law review 25 : 205-213, February 1951.

ANCEL, M. : The revision of the French civil code. Tulane law review 25 : 435-445, June 1951.

TOURY, J. : La réorganisation de l'appareil judiciaire. Revue de l'Action populaire : 451-460, juin-juillet 1951.

RAVANEL, J. : Le Conseil d'Etat et les Assemblées des territoires d'Outre-Mer. Penant, Recueil général de jurisprudence, de doctrine et de législation d'Outre-Mer, Doctrine 61 : 6378, juillet-août 1951.

CALEB, M. : Considérations sur le nouveau projet de code d'instruction criminelle. Revue de science criminelle et de droit pénal comparé : 19-33, janvier-mars 1952.

LAUBADÈRE, A. de : Des "pleins pouvoirs" aux "demi-décrets-lois". Recueil Dalloz, Chronique : 35-40, 6 mars 1952.

ANCEL, M. : Chronique de droit pénal français, 1938-1949. Zeitschrift für die gesamte Strafrechtswissenschaft 64 : 490-513, Heft 4, 1952.

LADHARI, N. : La liberté individuelle et ses garanties constitutionnelles. Recueil Dalloz, Chronique : 101-106, 24 juillet 1952.

MacDONALD, A. : The French law of marriage and matrimonial régimes. International and comparative law quarterly 1 : 313-324, July 1952.

MONTANÉ de la ROQUE : Essai sur la responsabilité du juge administratif. Revue du droit public et de la science politique en France et à l'étranger 68 : 609-661, juillet-septembre 1952.

MURDOCK, J.O. : Le droit français comme bas d'étude du droit comparé dans les écoles de droit américaines. Revue internationale de droit comparé 4 : 698-701, octobre-décembre 1952.

L'assistance judiciaire a cent ans. Etudes 275 : 345-359, décembre 1952.

The 1952 Congress of l'Association Henri Capitant. Canadian bar review 31 : 65-76, January 1953.

NATIONAL LAW - COUNTRIES

LAMPUÉ, P. : Nature juridique de l'Union française. Revue juridique et politique de l'Union Française 7 : 1-22, janvier-mars 1953.

DROUHET, R. : De l'unification de l'état-civil dans les territoires d'Outre-Mer. Recueil général de jurisprudence, de doctrine et de législation d'Outre-Mer, Doctrine 63 : 41-46, avril 1953.

MORANGE, G. : La réparation des accidents de personnes imputables à l'Administration. Recueil Dalloz, Chronique : 91-98, 25 juin 1953.

TERROU, P. : Le statut juridique de l'entreprise de presse en France (Suite). Etudes de presse 5 : 341-357, hiver 1953.

DESQUEYRAT, A. : Retour aux décrets-lois - Petite histoire constitutionnelle des décrets Laniel. Revue de l'Action populaire : 918-925, décembre 1953.

BESSON, A. : La réforme de la procédure pénale. Revue de science criminelle et de droit pénal comparé : 1-20, janvier-mars 1954.

LAMPUÉ, P. : Les conflits de lois interrégionaux et interpersonnels dans le système juridique français. Revue critique de droit international privé 43 : 249-324, avril-juin 1954.

BIAYS, P. : Les obligations du fonctionnaire en dehors de son service. Recueil Dalloz, Chronique : 105-112, 19 juin 1954.

LIET-VEAUX, G. : Du loyalisme des fonctionnaires - A propos de "l'affaire de l'E.N.A." (Ecole nationale d'administration). Revue administrative 7 : 393-399, juillet-août 1954.

GONZÁLEZ PÉREZ, J. : Consideraciones sobre el contencioso francés. Revista de administración pública 5 : 11-90, septiembre-diciembre 1954.

Le cent-cinquantenaire du code civil. Revue internationale de droit comparé 6 : 633-815, octobre-décembre 1954.
Numéro spécial.

WESER, M. : Faut-il reviser la convention franco-italienne du 3 juin 1930 sur l'exécution des jugements (Suite?). Revue critique de droit international privé 43 : 693-718, octobre-décembre 1954.

GOUET, Y. : Remarques sur une réorganisation éventuelle de l'état civil dans les parties d'outre-mer de la France qui connaissent le régime de la pluralité des états civils et dans les territoires sous tutelle. Revue juridique et politique de l'Union française 8 : 492-586, octobre-décembre 1954.

SCHWARZ, B. : Public tort liability in France. New York university law review 29 : 1432-1461, November 1954.

La réforme de la constitution française. Archives internationales Pharos 12 : 1-4, no. 1188, 1er décembre 1954.

FRANCE
(International law, Aliens, Nationality)

MOUSKHÉLY, M. : Le traité et la loi dans le système constitutionnel français de 1946. Zeitschrift für ausländisches öffentliches Recht und Völkerrecht 13 : 98-117, Nr. 1, 1950.

Actes définissant les rapports des Etats associés du Viet-Nam, du Cambodge et du Laos avec la France. Penant, Recueil général de jurisprudence, de doctrine et de législation coloniales et maritimes, Législation 60 : 1-28, mars 1950.

MIRKINE-GUETZÉVITCH, B. : La "guerre juste" dans le droit constitutionnel français, 1790-1946. Revue générale de droit international public 54 : 225-250, avril-juin 1950.

CHABAS, J. : L'organisation de la justice civile et commerciale devant les tribunaux mixtes du Viet-nam. Revue juridique et politique de l'Union française 4 : 351-378, juillet-septembre 1950.

LAMPUÉ, P. : La citoyyeneté de l'Union Française. Revue juridique et politique de l'Union Française 4 : 305-336, juillet-septembre 1950.

MARTIN, M. : La responsabilité de la puissance publique d'occupation en ce qui concerne les dommages causés en zone française d'occupation. Journal du droit international 77 : 798-849, juillet-septembre 1950.

PREUSS, L. : The relation of international law to internal law in the French constitutional system. American journal of international law 44 : 641-669, October 1950.

PONSARD, A. : Les conflits de lois et de juridictions dans les récents accords franco-vietnamiens. Journal du droit international 77 : 1086-1139, octobre-décembre 1950.

EISELE, A. : Réflexions sur les procès de criminels de guerre en France. Revue de droit pénal et de criminologie 31 : 305-317, décembre 1950.

HAMSON, J. : Immunity of foreign states - The policy of the French courts. British year book of international law 27 : 293-331, 1950.

PLANTEY, A. : La justice répressive et le droit pénal chérifien. Revue juridique et politique de l'Union Française 5 : 55-93, janvier-mars 1951.

Citizenship of the French Union. Civilisations 1 : 1-3, avril 1951.

PONSARD, A. : Les conflits de lois et de juridictions dans les récents accords franco-vietnamiens. Journal du droit international 78 : 374-463, avril-juin 1951.

CALEB, M. : Le sort des jugements rendus en Alsace-Lorraine pendant l'occupation allemande. Revue critique de droit international privé 40 : 245-264, avril-juin 1951.

PATIN, M. : La France et le jugement des crimes de guerre. Revue de science criminelle et de droit pénal comparé : 393-405, juillet-septembre 1951.

LOUIS-LUCAS, P. : Les principes directeurs posés par le projet de codification du droit international privé français. Revue critique de droit international privé 40 : 393-415, juillet-septembre 1951.

BOULBÈS, R. : L'exception de nationalité française devant les juridictions de droit commun autres que la juridiction civile. Revue critique de droit international privé 40 : 417-447, juillet-septembre 1951.

NATIONAL LAW - COUNTRIES

DELAUME, G.R. : A codification of French private international law. Canadian bar review 29 : 721-747, August-September 1951.

NGUYEN Q.D. : La question du statut de l'Etat associé d'après la Constitution. Revue juridique et politique de l'Union Française 5 : 466-502, octobre-décembre 1951.

LOUIS-LUCAS, P. : Les principes directeurs posés par le projet de codification du droit international privé français (Suite). Revue critique de droit international privé 40 : 597-618, octobre-décembre 1951.

SARRAUTE, T., et TAGER, P. : Hier et aujourd'hui - Les effets en France des nationalisations étrangères. Journal du droit international 79 : 496-561, avril-juin 1952.

BOULBÈS, R. : La portée et les limites du principe de la spécialité des lois coloniales en matière de nationalité. Revue critique de droit international privé 41 : 413-434, juillet-septembre 1952.

VOIRIN, P. : A propos de la confiscation générale des biens. Revue trimestrielle de droit civil 51 : 324-336, juillet-septembre 1952.

RACINE, J. : Mesures législatives et réglementaires prises par les autorités en exercice au Maroc (Suite). Revue juridique et politique de l'Union française 6 : 364-382, juillet-septembre 1952.

LOISEL, M. : La politique française en matière de naturalisation depuis la libération. Revue de défense nationale 8 : 301-309, octobre 1952.

SARRAUTE, R., et TAGER, P. : Hier et aujourd'hui - Les effets en France des nationalisations étrangères. Journal de droit international 79 : 1138-1190, octobre-décembre 1952.

PALLARD, R. : La filiation illégitime en droit international privé français. Revue critique de droit international privé 41 : 623-659, octobre-décembre 1952.

SAVATIER, R. : A propos des cartes de commerçants, les traités d'établissement et l'individualisation de la condition des étrangers. Recueil Dalloz, Chronique : 21-26, 22 janvier 1953.

Avis du comité juridique de l'Union Française, no. 82 du 19 avril 1950, concernant l'application des traités internationaux aux différents éléments de l'Union Française. Revue juridique et politique de l'Union Française 7 : 124-126, janvier-mars 1953.

SAMMARCELLI, M. : Quelques aspects particuliers de la fonction juridictionnelle dans les Etats associés du Viet-Nam, et du Laos. Revue juridique et politique de l'Union Française 7 : 106-123, janvier-mars 1953.

CASTEL, J.G. : Le principe de la réciprocité et l'exécution de droit international privé 42 : 317-328, avril-juin 1953.

BENOIST, J. : L'interprétation des traités d'après la jurisprudence française. Revue hellénique de droit international 6 : 103-116, avril-juin 1953.

PILENKO, A. : Le droit spatial et le droit international privé dans le projet du nouveau code civil français. Revue hellénique de droit international 6 : 319-355, octobre-décembre 1953.

ROUGIER, L. : Les traités diplomatiques et les constitutions. Revue : 417-424, ler décembre 1953.

ROUSSEAU, C. : Le régime actuel de publication des traités en France. Recueil Dalloz, Chronique : 169-174, 3 décembre 1953.

PERASSI, T. : La cittadinanza dell'attore come criterio di competenza giurisdizionale nell relazioni italo-francesi. Rivista di diritto internazionale 37 : 228-242, fasc. 2-3, 1954.

LASSALLE, C. : La responsabilité civile de la puissance publique française d'occupation en Allemagne. Revue du droit public et de la science politique en France et à l'étranger 70 : 352-416, avril-juin 1954.

FRANCESCAKIS, P. : Le divorce d'époux de nationalité différente - Après l'arrêt Rivière. Revue critique de droit international privé 43 : 325-347, avril-juin 1954.

ROTONDI, M. : The proposed Franco-Italian code of obligations. American journal of comparative law 3 : 345-359, summer 1954.

WESER, M. : Faut-il reviser la convention franco-italienne du 3 juin 1930 sur l'exécution des jugements? Revue critique de droit international privé 43 : 451-476, juillet-septembre 1954.

SIMON-DEPITRE, M. : L'activité professionnelle des étrangers en France et l'article 11 du Code civil. Revue critique de droit international privé 43 : 477-486, juillet-septembre 1954.

GERMANY
(Federal Republic)

KAULBACH : Zur Kritik des Rückerstattungsrechts. Deutsche Rechts-Zeitschrift 5 : 6-9, 5. Januar 1950.

WOLFF, E. : Wie weit gilt nach Artikel 123 bis 126 des Grundgesetzes bisheriges Recht fort? Deutsche Rechts-Zeitschrift 5 : 1-6, 5. Januar 1950.

SIMSON, G. : Die staatsrechtlichen Grundlagen der Westdeutschen Bundesrepublik. Zeitschrift für schweizerisches Recht 69 : 67-76, Heft 1, 1950.

NOBLEMAN, E.E. : American military government courts in Germany. Annals of the American academy of political and social science : 87-97, January 1950.

KLEIN, F. : Bonner Grundgesetz und Rechtsstaat. Zeitschrift für die gesamte Staatswissenschaft 106 : 390-411, 3. Heft 1950.

BAUR : Richterliches Prüfungsrecht und Besatzungsrecht. Deutsche Rechts-Zeitschrift 5 : 150-152, 5. April 1950.

SCHULTE, H.W. : Gesetzgebungskompetenz des Landes Nordrhein-Westfaken auf dem Gebiete des Bergrechts. Glückauf 86 : 289-292, 15. April 1950.

SCHMID, R. : Das politische Strafrecht. Deutsche Rechts-Zeitschrift 5 : 337-341, 15. August 1950.

NATIONAL LAW - COUNTRIES

HERLAN, W. : Immunitätsfragen. Monatsschrift für deutsches Recht 4 : 517-521, September 1950.

KERN, E. : Die Wiederherstellung der Rechtseinheit auf dem Gebiet der Strafgerichtsverfassung und des Strafverfahrens. Monatsschrift für deutsches Recht 4 : 582-588, Oktober 1950.

SCHMIDT, E. : Das neue Westdeutsche Wirtschaftsstrafrecht. Deutsche Rechts-Zeitschrift : 1-85, 11. Beihefte 1950.

ENGLER, W. : Die jüdische Rückerstattungs-Nachfolgeorganisation der amerikanischen Zone. Deutsche Rechts-Zeitschrift 5 : 531-533, 5. Dezember 1950.

ROSSBACH, M. : Wiedergutmachung nach dem Entschädigungsgesetz. Volkswirt 5 : 12-14, 12. Januar 1951.

DELBRUCK, H. : Vom Obersten Gerichtshof zum Bundesgerichtshof. Monatsschrift für deutsches Recht 5 : 20-21, Januar 1951.

MARTINSTETTER, H. : Die Zollgrenze. Zeitschrift für die gesamte Staatswissenschaft 107 : 173-183, Heft 1, 1951.

MARTIN : Das Gesetz zur Änderung von Vorschriften des Verschollenheitsrechts vom 15. Januar 1951. Juristenzeitung 6 : 104-107, 20. February 1951.

SPRECKELSEN, H. von : Die neuen Vorschriften des Verschollenheitsrechts. Deutsche Richterzeitung 29 : 29-32, Februar 1951.

Das neue Flaggenrechtsgesetz. Hansa 88 : 362-364, 3. März 1951.

SCHLICHTING, W. : Zum interzonalen Familienrecht. Monatsschrift für deutsches Recht 5 : 138-141, März 1951.

SCHÖNKE, A. : Die Entwicklung des Strafrechts und des Strafprozessrechts in Deutschland seit dem Jahre 1945. Revue pénale suisse 66 : 465-482, 4. Heft 1951.

HEYDTE, F.A. von der : Deutschlands Rechtslage. Friedens-Warte 50 : 323-336, Nr. 4, 1951.

ROEMER, W. : Das Gesetz über das Bundesverfassungsgericht. Juristenzeitung 6 : 193-199, 15. April 1951.

LAUN, K. von : The legal status of Germany. American journal of international law 45 : 266-285, April 1951.

ARNOLD, E. : Todeserklärung der Verschollenen des letzten Kriegs. Monatsschrift für deutsches Recht 5 : 202-204, April 1951.

DÖLLE, H. : Das Bundesgesetz über die Rechtswirkungen der nachträglichen Eheschliessung. Juristenzeitung 6 : 291-295, 20. Mai 1951.

INGLIS, L.M. : The occupation courts in Germany. New Zealand law journal 27 : 172-175, 19 June 1951.

ALEXANDER-KATZ, G. : Der wirkliche Restitutionsgläubiger und der fonds im Restitutionsverfahren der französischen Zone. Juristenzeitung 6 : 678-682, 5. November 1951.

Entwurf eines Gesetzes für die Durchführung gesamtdeutscher Wahlen zur Nationalversammlung. Neue Justiz 6 : 3-7, Januar 1952.

ARNOLD, E. : Toldeserklärung der in Konzentrations- oder Internierungslagern Verschollenen. Monatsschrift für deutsches Recht 6 : 11-13, Januar 1952.

MEHREN, A.T. von : Constitutionalism in Germany - The first decision of the new Constitutional court. American journal of comparative law 1 : 70-94, winter and spring 1952.

ALBERS, J. : Beschränkungen der Zivilrechtspflege durch Besatzungsrecht in der Britischen Zone. Monatsschrift für deutsches Recht 6 : 79-82, Februar 1952.

KLEIN, F. : Bundesverfassungsgericht und Südweststaatfrage. Archiv des öffentlichen Rechts 77 : 452-464, 4. Heft 1952.

WEILL, A., et VIRALLY, M. : Du contrôle exercé par la Cour de cassation sur l'interprétation des lois du Conseil de contrôle en Allemagne. Revue critique de droit international privé 41 : 253-275, avril-juin 1952.

LASSALLE, C. : Le Tribunal fédéral constitutionnel et la réorganisation des Länder de l'Allemagne du sudouest. Revue du droit public et de la science politique en France et à l'étranger 68 : 396-420, avril-juin 1952.

BÖGELSACK : Der volkseigene Betrieb als juristische Person. Deutsche Finanzwirtschaft 6 : 566-570, 1. Juniheft 1952.

DOMKE, M. : Zur Ausschlagung von Rechten Deutscher an amerikanischen Nachlässen. Juristenzeitung 7 : 741-744, 20. Dezember 1952.

NAUMANN, R. : Der verwaltungsgerichtliche Rechtsschutz nach Inkrafttreten des Gesetzes über das Bundesverwaltungsgericht (BVGG). Monatsschrift für deutsches Recht 6 : 705-708, Heft 12, 1952.

LASSALLE, C. : Les limites du contrôle de la constitutionalité des lois en Allemagne occidentale. Revue du droit public et de la science politique en France et à l'étranger 69 : 106-120, janvier-mars 1953.

SCHLOCHAUER, H.J. : Fragen zur Neuordnung der Verwaltungsgerichtsbarkeit. Archiv des öffentlichen Rechts 79 : 185-207, Heft 2, 1953.

BENJAMIN, H. : Bemerkungen zu der Lehre von der Gerichtsverfassung und ihrer Bedeutung für Theorie und Praxis. Staat und Recht 2 : 25-48, Februar 1953. Eastern Germany.

MARCIC, R. : Die Judikatur des Bayerischen Verfassungsgerichtshofes. Juristische Blätter 75 : 112-116, 28. Februar 1953.

SPANNER, H. : Über die Verfassungsgerichtsbarkeit im Bonner Grundgesetz. Österreichische Zeitschrift für öffentliches Recht 5 : 312-337, Heft 3, 1953.

KALISCH, W. : Grundrechte und Berufsbeamtentum nach dem Bonner Grundgesetz. Archiv des öffentlichen Rechts 78 : 334-354, Heft 3/4, 1953.

COHN, E.J. : German legal science today. International and comparative law quarterly 2 : 169-191, April 1953.

BALLREICH, H. : The legal capacity of international nongovernmental organizations in the German Federal Republic. Bulletin ONG - NGO bulletin 5 : 261-265, juin-juillet 1953.

BACHOF, O. : German administrative law with special reference to the latest developments in the system of legal protection. International and comparative law quarterly 2 : 368-382, July 1953.

EHMKE, H. : Verfassungsänderung und Verfassungsdurchbrechung. Archiv des öffentlichen Rechts 79 : 385-418, Heft 4, 1953/54.

Zur Entwicklung der Rückerstattung. Restitution 5 : 217-226, Januar 1954.

KLEIN, F. : Die Todeserklärung von Vermissten oder Verschollenen und die Wiederverheiratung der Überlebenden. Caritas 55 : 76-80, März 1954.

Code civil allemand en vigueur dans la République Fédérale d'Allemagne. Minorité, mariage, divorce, adoption, tutelle. Documentation juridique étrangère 6 : 1-107, no. 3, 1954.

FEDERER, J. : Die Rechtsprechung des Bundesverfassungsgerichts zum Grundgesetz für die Bundesrepublik Deutschland. Jahrbuch des öffentlichen Rechts der Gegenwart 3 : 15-66, 1954.

Législation allemande sur les sociétés à responsabilité limitée. Textes législatifs étrangers 4 : 3-40, no. 4, 1954.

MEZGER, E. : L'état actuel du droit pénal allemand. Revue de science criminelle et de droit pénal comparé : 457-465, juillet-septembre 1954.

Die bindende Wirkung der Entscheidungen des Bundesverfassungsgerichts. Juristenzeitung 9 : 525-533, 5. September 1954.
Two articles by G. Willms and D. Jesch.

CUELLO CALÓN, E. : La reforma del derecho penal en Alemania - Tercera ley de reforma penal de 4 de agosto de 1953. Anuario de deracho penal y ciencias penales 7 : 493-497, septiembre-diciembre 1954.

GERMANY
(International law and practice, Aliens and Naturalization)

MEISTER, U. : Stimmen des Auslands zur Rechtslage Deutschlands. Zeitschrift für ausländisches öffentliches Recht und Völkerrecht 13 : 173-185, Nr. 1, 1950.

FICKER, H.G. : Der Name der geschiedenen Ehefrau im deutschen internationalen Privatrecht. Zeitschrift für ausländisches und internationales Privatrecht 16 : 32-43, Heft 1, 1950.

MUENCH, F. : Droit international et droit interne d'après la constitution de Bonn. Revue internationale française du droit des gens 15 : 5-20, janvier -juin 1950.

HELM, R. : Das deutsche Auslandsstrafregister. Neue Justiz 4 : 396-397, Oktober 1950.
East and West Germany.

DUDEN, K. : Die privaten Vorkriegsverträge Deutscher mit dem Ausland. Zeitschrift für ausländisches und internationales Privatrecht 16 : 533-546, Heft 4, 1951.

JAHN, E. : Das Gesetz über die Rechtsstellung heimatloser Ausländer im Bundesgebiet. Juristenzeitung 6 : 326-329, 5. Juni 1951.

JESCHEK, H.H. : L'activité des tribunaux français d'occupation en Allemagne en matière civile. Revue internationale française du droit des gens 16 : 305-319, septembre-décembre 1951.

GERVAIS, A. : La jurisprudence allemande des prises maritimes dans la seconde guerre mondiale. Revue générale de droit international public 55 : 481-546, octobre-décembre 1951.

CONSTANTOPOULOS, D.S. : The relation of the law of nations to constitutional law and the new constitutions of Germany. Revue hellénique de droit international 5 42-62, janvier-juin 1952.

WEBER, W. : Die Vereinbarkeit des Verteidigungsbeitrags mit dem Grundgesetz, Archiv des öffentlichen Rechts 78 : 129-148, Heft 2, 1952.

KRAUS, H. : Die Zuständigkeit der Länder der Bundesrepublik Deutschland zum Abschluss von Kulturabkommen mit auswärtigen Staaten nach dem Bonner Grundgesetz. Archiv des Völkerrechts 3 : 414-427, 4. Heft 1952.

MAKAROV, A.N. : Zur Behandlung von deutschen Zwangseinbürgerungen 1938 bis 1945. Juristenzeitung 7 : 403-407, 15. Juli 1952.

REDSLOB, R. : La Charte de Bonn, son caractère en doctrine constitutionnelle. Revue internationale d'histoire politique et constitutionnelle : 157-170, juillet-septembre 1952.

RASCHHOFER, H. : "Sudetendeutsche sind deutsche Staatsbürger". Berichte und Informationen des Österreichischen Forschungsinstituts für Wirtschaft und Politik 7 : 819-820, 17. Oktober 1952.

INGLIS, L.M. : Military government courts in Germany. New Zealand law journal 28 : 315-318, 4 November 1952.

NEUMAYER, K.H. : Über die Fortgeltung deutsch-italienischer Staatsverträge privatrechtlichen Inhalts. Juristenzeitung 7 : 682-683, 20. November 1952.

KUNZ, J.L. : The contractual agreements with the Federal Republic of Germany. American journal of international law 47 : 106-114, January 1953.

POTRYKUS, G. : Ausländerpolizeiverordnung und Grundgesetz. Juristenzeitung 8 : 76-77, 5. Februar 1953.

SCHENK, D.v. : Die 11. Verordnung zum Reichsbürgergesetz im Rückerstattungsrecht. Juristenzeitung 8 : 134-137, 5. März 1953.

MEYER, H. : Neues zum Asylrecht. Monatsschrift für deutsches Recht 7 : 534-536, September 1953.

Zum Entwurf eines Gesetzes zur Regelung von Fragen der Staatsangehörigkeit. Deutsche Richterzeitung 32 : 11-13, Januar 1954.

DROBNIG, U. : Interzonale Kollisionsnormen in der Gesetzgebung Deutschlands. Zeitschrift für ausländisches und internationales Privatrecht 19 : 463-476, Heft 3, 1954.

MAIER, H. : Gerichtsbarkeit über Angehörige der Allierten Streitkräfte in der US-Zone. Juristenzeitung 9 : 72-73, 5. Februar 1954.

MAIER, H. : Nochmals - Gerichtsbarkeit über Angehörige der Allierten Streitkräfte. Juristenzeitung 9 : 185-186, 20. März 1954.

BÜLOW : Die deutschen Vorkriegsverträge auf dem Gebiete des internationalen Rechtsverkehrs in Zivil- und Handelssachen. Recht der internationalen Wirtschaft 1 : 3-5, 25. Juli 1954.

MAIER, H. : Haftung der Bundesrepublik für Eingriffe fremder Mächte in Privateigentum? Juristenzeitung 9 : 405-410, 15. Juli 1954.

McCAULEY, W.B. : American courts in Germany - 600,000 cases later. American bar association journal 40 : 1041-1045, 1101-1103, December 1954.

GERMANY
(Democratic Republic)

SCHULTES, K. : Zur deutschen Verfassungsentwicklung. Neue Justiz 4 : 2-5, Januar 1950.

ABENDROTH, W. : Zwiespältiges Verfassungsrecht in Deutschland - Die Verfassung der "Deutschen Demokratischen Republik" im Vergleich zum Bonner Grundgesetz. Archiv des öffentlichen Rechts 76 : k-25, 1. Heft 1950.

BOURTHOUMIEUX, C. : La magistrature populaire dans la zone soviétique d'occupation. Revue internationale de droit comparé 2 : 515-519, juillet-septembre 1950.

NATHAN, H. : Das neue Patentrecht der Deutschen Demokratischen Republik. Neue Justiz 4 : 430-433, November 1950.

SCHUMANN, K. : Ein Jahr Oberstes Gericht der Deutschen Demokratischen Republik. Neue Justiz 4 : 477-479, Dezember 1950.

REINARTZ, R. : Einheitliches Strafrecht für die Deutsche Demokratische Republik. Neue Justiz 5 : 18-20, Januar 1951.

WEISS, W. : Das Gesetz zum Schutze des Friedens. Neue Justiz 5 : 10-16, Januar 1951.

JOËL, C. : Die Rechtsprechung des Staatsgerichtshofs für das Deutsche Reich. Archiv des öffentlichen Rechts 77 : 129-167, Heft 2/3, 1951.

NATHAN, H. : Zwei Jahre Oberstes Gericht und Oberste Staatsanwaltschaft der Deutschen Demokratischen Republik. Neue Justiz 5 : 544-548, Dezember 1951.

POLAK, K. : Bericht über die theoretische Konferenz über Fragen der Staats- und Rechtswissenschaft in Leipzig am 15. und 16. Dezember 1951. Neue Justiz 6 : 7-12, Januar 1952.

LOEWENSTEIN, K. : L'Allemagne soviétique. Revue du droit public et de la science politique en France et à l'étranger 58 : 145-163, janvier-mars 1952.

NATHAN, H. : Die Gesetzgebung der Deutschen Demokratischen Republik. Neue Justiz 6 : 112-116, März 1952.

NATHAN, H. : Bericht über die theoretische Zivilrechtskonferenz in Berlin am 15. März 1952. Neue Justiz 6 : 155-159, April 1952.

Gerichtsverfassungsgesetz. Neue Justiz 6 : 434-446, 5. Oktober 1952.
Special issue.

Strafprozessordnung. Neue Justiz 6 : 465-495, 20. Oktober 1952.
Special issue.

BRANDT, H. : Das neue Verfahren in Todeserklärungssachen. Neue Justiz 7 : 40-41, 20. Januar 1953.

SCHÖNBERG, von : Zum Gerichtswesen in der Sowjetzone. Monatsschrift für deutsches Recht 7 : 143-144, März 1953.

BENJAMIN, H. : Unsere Justiz, ein wirksames Instrument bei der Durchführung des neuen Kurses. Neue Justiz 7 : 477-480, 5. August 1953.

RODIG : Die Ehescheidung in der sowjetischen Besatzungszone, ein Problem des interzonalen Rechts. Monatsschrift für deutsches Recht 7 : 460-462, August 1953.

HEINRICH, W., and KLAR, H. : Die Rechtsprechung des Obersten Gerichts auf dem Gebiete des Familienrechts. Neue Justiz 7 : 537-542, 5. September 1953.
Democratic Republic.

BREHME, G. : Über die normativen Akte der Regierung der Deutschen Demokratischen Republik. Staat und Recht 2 : 592-605, Oktober 1953.

BENJAMIN, H. : Die Staatsverbrechen im Zusammenhang mit der wirtschaftlichen und politischen Entwicklung seit 1945. Neue Justiz 8 : 33-37, 20. Januar 1954.

DROBNIG, U. : Extraterritoriale Reflexwirkungen ostzonaler Enteignungen. Zeitschrift für ausländisches und internationales Privatrecht 18 : 657-689, Heft 4, 1953.

Code civil allemand en vigueur dans la Zone soviétique d'Allemagne. Documentation juridique étrangère 6 : 1-86, no. 5, 1954.

Prinzipien und Wortlaut des Familiengesetzentwurfs. Neue Justiz 8 : 349-388, 30. Juni 1954.
Special issue.

TOEPLITZ, H. : Die Vorbereitung des neuen Damilienrechts durch die Rechtsprechung. Neue Justiz 8 : 658-663, 20. November 1954.

WIEMANN, H. : Die Bedeutung des internationalen Privatrechts in der Deutschen Demokratischen Republik. Staat und Recht 3 : 743-760, Dezember 1954.

RANKE, H. : Der Entwurf des neuen Familiengesetzbuches der Deutschen Demokratischen Republik, ein Dokument der demokratischen Gesetzlichkeit. Staat und Recht 3 : 733-742, Dezember 1954.

NATIONAL LAW - COUNTRIES

GOLD COAST

LOVERIDGE, A.J. : Wills and the customary law in the Gold Coast. Journal of African administration 2 : 24-28, October 1950.

GREAT BRITAIN

The legal aid scheme and the profession. Law journal 100 : 536-537, 29 September 1950.

HOLDEN, J.M. : Suggested reform of the law relating to cheques. Modern law review 14 : 33-52, January 1951.

BONTECOU, E. : The English policy as to communists and fascists in the Civil Service. Columbia law review 51 : 564-586, May 1951.

BROWN, H.J.J. : Questions of law in the assessment of compensation for compulsory acquisition. Journal of planning law : 444-455, August 1951.

LAWSON, F.H. : Le droit administratif anglais. Revue internationale de droit comparé 3 : 412-426, juillet-septembre 1951.

WILKINSON, G.S. : Reform of the criminal law. Modern law review 14 : 437-445, October 1951.

HORNSEY, G. : Tendances récentes du droit anglais des sociétés. Revue de droit international et de droit comparé 29 : 9-17, nos. 1-2, 1952.

DURET AUBIN, C.W. : Recent constitutional changes in Jersey. International and comparative law quarterly 1 : 491-503, October 1952.

GARDINER, G. : The machinery of law reform in England. Law quarterly review 69 : 46-62, January 1953.

PREVEZER, S. : Peacetime espionage and the law. Current legal problems 6 : 82-103, 1953.

BENTWICH, N. : The law of domicile. Law journal 104 : 198-199, 26 March 1954.

CLARK, C.E. : The Evershed report and English procedural reform. New York university law review 29 : 1046-1060, May 1954.

THOMPSON, C.S. : Developments in the British legal aid experiment. Columbia law review 53 : 789-803, June 1953.

Final report of the Evershed committee. Law journal 103 : 471-473, 24 July 1953.
The Supreme Court practice.

GRAVESON, R.H. : Reform of the law of domicile. Law quarterly review 70 : 492-513, October 1954.

PREVEZER, S. : Divorce in the English conflict of laws. Current legal problems 7 : 114-138, 1954.

GREAT BRITAIN
(International law, Aliens)

CARTER, P.B. : Immunity of foreign sovereigns from jurisdiction - Two recent decisions. International law quarterly 3 : 78-86, January 1950.

CARTER, P.B. : Recent English decisions - Immunity of foreign sovereigns from jurisdiction. International law quarterly 3 : 410-413, July 1950.

CARTER, P.B. : Recent English decisions - Municipal courts and the enforcement of international agreements. International law quarterly 3 : 413-417, July 1950.

HOLLAND, D.C. : Diplomatic immunity in English law. Current legal problems 4 : 81-106, 1951.

JOHNSON, D.H.N. : Control of exploitation of natural resources in the sea off the United Kingdom. International law quarterly 4 : 445-453, October 1951.

GRAVESON, R.H. : Choice of law and choice of jurisdiction in the English conflict of laws. British year book of international law 28 : 273-290, 1951.

GRAVESON, R.H. : The recognition of foreign divorce decrees. Grotius society, Transactions 37 : 149-170, 1951.

FISCHER, H. : The foreign compensation, Czechoslovakia, order in Council. International and comparative law quarterly 1 : 97-102, January 1952.

LIPSTEIN, K. : Jurisdiction to wind up foreign companies. Cambridge law journal 11 : 198-208, No. 2, 1952.

LATEY, W. : Problems of divorce jurisdiction. International and comparative law quarterly 1 : 229-235, April 1952.

SCAMMELL, E.H. : Nationalisation in legal perspective. Current legal problems 5 : 30-54, 1952.

LAWSON, F.H. : The handling of foreign law by English practitioners - A problem of supply and training. Grotius society, Transactions 38 : 93-108, 1952.

PARRY, C. : British nationality law and the history of naturalisation. Istituto di diritto internazionale e straniero della Università di Milano, Comunicazioni e studi 5 : 2-107, 1953.

SINCLAIR, I.M. : Decisions of English courts during 1952-53 involving questions of public or private international law. British year book of international law 30 : 513-537, 1953.

BORM-REID, M. : Recognition and enforcement of foreign judgments. International and comparative law quarterly 3 : 49-92, January 1954.

BLOM-COOPER, L.J. : Enforcement of foreign awards in England. Arbitration journal 9 : 198-209, No. 4, 1954.

The notion of political offences and the law of extradition. British year book of international law 31 : 430-436, 1954.
Polish trawler case, 1954.

SINCLAIR, I.M. : Polygamous marriages in English law. British year book of international law 31 : 248-272, 1954.

WORTLEY, B.A. : Proposed changes in the law of domicile, with reference to the Wynn-Parry report. Grotius society, Transactions 40 : 121-140, 1954.
Discussion pp. 140-145.

GREECE

YOTIS, C.P. : Chronique hellénique 1939-1948. Revue internationale de droit pénal 21 : 85-96, no. 1, 1950.

BENDERMACHER-GEROUSSIS, A. : Les effets du mariage sur la nationalité. Revue hellénique de droit international 3 : 72-81, janvier-mars 1950.

MAMOPOULOS, P. : L'état actuel de l'unification du droit en Grèce. Revue hellénique de droit international 3 : 14-19, janvier-mars 1950.

KYRIAKOPOULOS, E.G. : Le contrôle de la constitutionnalité des lois en Grèce. Revue hellénique de droit international 3 : 114-119, janvier-mars 1950.

ZEPOS, P.J. : Les solutions du code civil hellénique en matière de responsabilité civile. Revue internationale de droit comparé 2 : 297-304, avril-juin 1950.

CHRYSSANTHOPOULOS, T.L. : The nationality of the Dodecanesians and the peace treaty with Italy. Revue hellénique de droit international 3 : 224-233, avril-décembre 1950.

VALLINDAS, P.G. : Le droit international privé de la Loi civile grecque de 1856 et le Code de Zurich de 1854. Zeitschrift für schweizerisches Recht 69 : 401-410, Heft 6, 1950.

Chronique de législation, jurisprudence et bibliographie helléniques concernant le droit privé. Revue trimestrielle de droit civil 49 : 407-428, juillet-septembre 1950.
1944-1949.

La répression des crimes de guerre en Grèce. Revue de droit pénal et de criminologie 31 : 318, décembre 1950.

FRAGISTAS, C.N. : Contribution à l'étude de la technique du code civil grec. Revue hellénique de droit international 4 : 40-63, janvier-mars 1951.

VALLINDAS, P.G. : Le principe du droit unique en droit international privé grec. Jus gentium (Roma) 3 : 1-9, gennaio-aprile 1951.

MICHAÉLIDÈS-NOUAROS, G. : L'oeuvre créatrice de la jurisprudence grecque en cas de silence de la loi. Revue hellénique de droit international 4 : 163-180, avril-juin 1951.

PAPALAMBROU, A. : Le problème de la "transformation" et la question de la validité des actes étatiques "contraires" au droit international. Revue hellénique de droit international 3 : 234-269, avril-décembre 1950.

BOURNIAS, A. : La méthode depuis le code civil de 1804 au point de vue des sources du droit positif hellénique. Revue hellénique de droit international 4 : 323-340, juillet-décembre 1951.

KARANICAS, D.J. : Le nouveau code pénal hellénique. Revue de science criminelle et de droit pénal comparé : 633-646, octobre-décembre 1951.

CALOGEROPOULOS STRATIS, S. : A propos du livre de M. Maridakis Georges. Revue générale de droit international public 56 : 85-92, janvier-mars 1952.
Droit international privé.

Grèce - Constitution du 22 décembre 1951. Informations constitutionnelles et parlementaires : 55-80, 1er avril 1952.

YOTIS, C.P. : Le droit pénal hellénique, 1951. Revue de droit pénal et de criminologie 32 : 953-954, juin 1952.

STASSINOPOULOS, M. : La nouvelle loi hellénique sur le statut des fonctionnaires. Revue internationale de droit comparé 4 : 479-486, juillet-septembre 1952.

Grecia - Constitución de 22 de diciembre de 1951. Información jurídica : 977-983, octubre 1952.

MARIDAKIS, G. : Le mariage des Grecs orthodoxes hors de Grèce. Revue critique de droit international privé 41 : 661-671, octobre-décembre 1952.

PAPAHADJIS, G.M. : Algunos rasgos característicos de la nueva constitución griega de 1952. Revista de estudios políticos : 73-78, marzo-abril 1953.

YOTIS, C.P. : Le droit pénal hellénique, 1952. Revue de droit pénal et de criminologie 33 : 870-871, juin 1953.

PAPAHADJIS, G.M. : L'institution du conflit positif d'attributions et la mission du Préfet hellène. Revue du droit public et de la science politique en France et à l'étranger 69 : 608-614, juillet-september 1953.

Conventions etc. signées entre la Grèce et des pays étrangers ou des organisations internationales et ratifiées par la Grèce, 1er janvier 1949-31 décembre 1952. Revue hellénique de droit international 6 : 256-266, juillet-septembre 1953.

TÉNÉKIDÈS, G. : L'occupation pour cause de guerre et la récente jurisprudence grecque. Journal du droit international 80 : 822-858, octobre-décembre 1953.
Texte anglais aussi.

YOTIS, C. : La non-extradition du "civis novus" d'après la législation hellénique en vigueur. Revue de droit international, de sciences diplomatiques et politiques 31 : 383-385, octobre-décembre 1953.

ZISSIADIS, J. : Le nouveau code de procédure criminelle hellénique. Revue de science criminelle et de droit pénal comparé : 83-89, janvier-mars 1954.

PAPAHADJIS, G.M. : L'institution du recours pour excès de pouvoir en Grèce, 1928-1953. Jahrbuch des öffentlichen Rechts der Gegenwart 3 : 359-365, 1954.

KYRIACOPOULOS, E.G. : Die griechische Verfassung vom. 1. Januar 1952. Jahrbuch des öffentlichen Rechts der Gegenwart 3 : 313-358, 1954.
With text.

BENDERMACHER-GEROUSSIS, A. : Anerkennung und Vollstreckung ausländischer Entscheidungen über die Sorge der Person der Kinder und die Unterhaltspflicht nach griechischem Recht. Österreichische Juristen-Zeitung 9 : 105-107, 12. März 1954.

TRIANTAPHYLLIDIS, C. : Le nouveau code pénal hellénique. Revue de science criminelle et de droit pénal comparé : 275-297, avril-juin 1954.

MANESSIS, A. : La nouvelle constitution hellénique. Revue internationale de droit comparé 6 : 291-308, avril-juin 1954.

La constitution grecque, 1er janvier 1952. Documentation française, Notes et études documentaires : 1-15, no. 1894, 12 juillet 1954.

YOTIS, C.P. : Le droit pénal hellénique, 1953. Revue de droit pénal et de criminologie 34 : 926-928, juillet 1954.

TÉNEKIDÈS, G. : L'occupation pour cause de guerre et la récente jurisprudence grecque (Suite). Journal du droit international 81 : 636-689, juillet-septembre 1954.
Texte en anglais et français.

GREENLAND

SÖRENSEN, M. : Le statut juridique du Groenland. Revue juridique et politique de l'Union Française 7 : 425-442, octobre-décembre 1953.

GOLDSCHMIDT, V. : Den grønlandske kriminallov og dens sociologiske baggrund. Nordisk tidsskrift for kriminalvidenskab 42 : 242-268, 3. hefte 1954.

GUATEMALA

Guatémala - Loi concernant le droit d'auteur sur les oeuvres littéraires, scientifiques et artistiques, du 8 février 1954. Droit d'auteur 67 : 105-108, juin 1954.
Voir aussi pp. 114-116.

HAITI

Constitution de la République d'Haïti, 25 novembre 1950. Documentation française, Notes et études documentaires : 1-20, no. 1457, 30 mars 1951.

El empleo de extranjeros en Haiti. Nueva economia nacional 18 : 12-14, 29 abril 1954.
Law of September 25, 1953.

HONDURAS

Código de Comercio (1940 edition). "La Gaceta" for May 5 to 24, 1950 inclusive.

SOLA CANIZARES, F. de : Le nouveau code de commerce de Honduras. Cahiers de législation et de bibliographie juridique de l'Amérique Latine 3 : 141-144, juillet-décembre 1952.

OLAVARRIA, J. : Honduras - A new code of commerce. American journal of comparative law 2 : 66-69, winter 1953.

HUNGARY

SANTA, J.J. : El problema de la continuidad jurídica en Hungría. Revista de la Facultad de ciencias económicas (Córdoba) 3 : 76-84, nos. 1-2, 1950.

SZÁSZY, S. : Ungarischer Gesetzentwurf über das internationale Privatrecht. Österreichische Zeitschrift für öffentliches Recht 3 : 202-227, Heft 2, 1950.

BENKÖ, I. : Staatsangehörigkeitsrecht. Zeitschrift für ausländisches und internationales Privatrecht 16 : 293-298, Heft 2, 1951.
Texts pp. 302-312.

ARATÓ, I. : Ungarn - Die Entwicklung des bürgerlichen und Zivilprozessrechts in den Jahren 1945-1948. Zeitschrift für ausländisches und internationales Privatrecht 16 : 281-292, Heft 2, 1951.

ZAJTAY, I. : Les délinquants d'habitude dans le droit pénal hongrois. Revue de science criminelle et de droit pénal comparé : 257-264, avril-juin 1951.

ARATÓ, I. : Zur Kodifikationstechnik des internationalen Privatrechts besonders im ungarischen Entwurf von 1948. Zeitschrift für ausländisches und internationales Privatrecht 17 : 1-19, Heft 1, 1952.

GAULTIER, J.P. : Le nouveau code de la famille en Hongrie. Pour la vie : 42-49, 1er trimestre 1953.

Législation hongroise sur le mariage, la famille et la tutelle. Textes législatifs étrangers 3 : 29-69, no. 3, 1953.
Voir aussi pp. 71-89.

STEINIGER : Organisation und Arbeitsmethoden ungarischer Juristen. Staat und Recht 2 : 501-508, August 1953.

ARATÓ, I. : Neue Kollisionsnormen in Ungarn. Zeitschrift für ausländisches und internationales Privatrecht 19 : 100-104, Heft 1, 1954.

NÉVAL, L. : Une loi nouvelle sur l'organisation judiciaire de la République populaire hongroise. Revue de la législation hongroise : 13-18, no. 1, 1954.

ZAJTAY, I. : Le droit du mariage dans le nouveau code hongroise de la famille. Revue internationale de droit comparé 6 : 491-503, juillet-septembre 1954.

ICELAND

ANORSSON, E. : Islandsk straffelov af 12. februar 1940. Tidsskrift for rettsvitenskap 63 : 73-95, heft 1-2, 1950.

Constitution de la République d'Islande. Documentation française, Notes et études documentaires : 1-8, No. 1329, 19 mai 1950.

Islande, 1938-1951 - JOHANNESSON, O. : Droit public - SIGURJONSSON, B. : Droit privé. Annuaire de législation étrangère, Nouvelle série 2 : 233-244, 1950-51.

Icelandic fishery limits. International and comparative law quarterly 1 : 71-73, January 1952.

Loi islandaise no. 64, du 28 janvier 1935, sur l'acquisition et la perte de la nationalité. Textes législatifs étrangers : 61-64, no. 1, 1952.

NATIONAL LAW - COUNTRIES

Islande - Constitution de la République d'Islande, 17 juin 1944. Informations constitutionnelles et parlementaires : 83-93, 1er avril 1952.

Icelandic fishery limits. International and comparative law quarterly 1 : 350-354, July 1952.

INDIA

WADE, E.C.S. : Rights and privileges of Indians in the U.K. Calcutta weekly notes 54 : xlv-xlvi, 23-30 January 1950.

India's new constitution. Calcutta weekly notes 54 : lii-liv, 13 February 1950.

EDDY, J.P. : India and the Privy council. The last appeal. Law quarterly review 66 : 206-215, April 1950.

NICHOLAS, H.S. : The constitution of India. Australian law journal 23 : 638-640, 20 April 1950.

SINGH, S.B. : India, Central legislature. Journal of comparative legislation and international law 32 : 123-127, May 1950.

RAMASWAMY, M. : The constitutional position of the President of the Indian Republic. Canadian bar review 28 : 648-660, June-July 1950.

VARADACHARIAR, S. : The Indian constitution - A brief study. India quarterly 6 : 213-227, July-September 1950.

BOURNE, F. : Constitutional governors before and after the transfer of power. Asiatic review 46 : 1111-1118, October 1950.

Inde - Constitution du 26 novembre 1949. Informations constitutionnelles et parlementaires : 4-75, 15 janvier 1951.

MUKHARJI, P.B. : The march of statutory laws in India. Indian law review 5 : 13-25, no. 1, 1951.

La constitution de l'Inde. Documentation française, Notes et études documentaires : 1-73, No. 1454, 23 mars 1951.

SENGUPTA, N.C. : The first amendment of the constitution. Indian law review 5 : 135-142, Nos. 3-4, 1951.

Companion to the Constitution of India (Contd.). Indian law review 5 : 53-169, Nos. 3-4, 1951.
Alphabetical guide.

NEHRU, S.S. : La constitution de l'Inde et la constitution du Brésil comparées. Revue de droit international et de droit comparé 28 : 161-164, Nos. 3-4, 1951.

SCHWARTZ, B. : Delegation of legislative power - A comparison of Indian and American law. Indian law review 6 : 19-26, No. 1, 1952.

MURDESHWAR, B.G. : The Supreme Court of India. Australian law journal 25 : 634-636, 21 February 1952.

BANERJEE, D.N. : Freedom of speech and expression in India. Indian law review 6 : 90-103, No. 2, 1952.

Independent Republic of India, a member of British Commonwealth - An unusual situation. Calcutta weekly notes 56 : CI-CII, 16 June 1952.

ALEXANDER, C.H. : International law in India. International and comparative law quarterly 1 : 289-300, July 1952.

RAMASWAMY, M. : The Supreme court of India. Annual law review 2 : 215-244, December 1952.

BASU, K.K. : Constitution of India. Indian law review 7 : 15-29, No. 1, 1953.

Section 107 of the Government of India act. Supreme court journal 16 : 1-8, January 1953.
Provincial law.

SINHA, B.S. : Codification of the personal law. Supreme court journal 16 : 9-20, February 1953.

BISWAS, C.C. : Public international law and conflict of laws. Calcutta weekly notes 57 : lxvii-lxx, 16 March 1953.

DIWAN, P. : Nationalisation under the Indian constitution. Supreme court journal 16 : 21-50, March 1953.

VENKATARAMAN, S. : Equal protection of the laws and classification. Supreme court journal 16 : 51-66, April-May 1953.

DIWAN, P. : Kashmir and the Indian Union - The legal position. International and comparative law quarterly 2 : 333-353, July 1953.

MARKOSE, A.T. : The judiciary and the executive in India - Some suggestions for reform. Supreme court journal 16 : 111-134, August 1953.

DIWAN, P. : Hindu law of mixed marriages. Supreme court journal 16 : 232-249, December 1953.

DAHM, G. : Das Strafrecht in Indien und Pakistan. Zeitschrift für die gesamte Strafrechtswissenschaft 66 : 135-150, Heft 1, 1954.

TRIPATHI, P.K. : Directive principles of State policy. Supreme court journal 17 : 7-36, February 1954.

MUKHERJI, S.S. : Criminal peocedure reforms. Supreme court journal (Madras) 17 : 77-84, March 1954.

PALANISWAMI, A. : The law of extradition in India. Indian year book of international affairs 3 : 328-340, 1954.

DAHM, G. : Gerichtsverfassung und Strafverfahren in Indien und Pakistan. Zeitschrift für die gesamte Strafrechtswissenschaft 66 : 593-621, Heft 4, 1954.

PARRY, C. : Citizenship in the Commonwealth with special reference to India. India quarterly 10 : 101-125, April-June 1954.

RAMACHANDRAN, V.C. : The need for legal aid in India. Supreme court journal (Madras) 17 : 103-120, May 1954.

ALEXANDROWICZ, C.H. : Is India a federation? International and comparative law quarterly 3 : 392-403, July 1954.

NAMBIYAR, M.K. : American borrowings in the Indian constitution. Supreme court journal (Madras) 17 : 151-154, August 1954.

MARKOSE, A.T. : The administrative jurisdiction of the Indian judiciary - The nature and scope of the remedies under articles 226 and 32 of the constitution of India. Supreme court journal (Madras) 17 : 155-179, September 1954.

ALEXANDROWICZ-ALEXANDER, C.H. : Delegation of legislative power in India. American journal of comparative law 3 : 72-79, winter 1954.

INDONESIA

Constitution provisoire de la République des Etats-Unis d'Indonésie, 14 décembre 1949. Dpcumentation française, Notes et études documentaires : 1-22, no. 1287, ler mars 1950.

Indonesia - Constitución provisional de la República. Información jurídica : 859-868, junio 1950.

COLLIARD, C.A. : La création d'une union internationale - L'union Hollando-Indonésienne (Suite). Revue juridique et politique de l'Union Française 4 : 534-553, octobre-décembre 1950.

BONN, E. : Het Openbaar Ministerie in Indonesië van 15.8.1945 tot 27.12.1949. Tijdschrift voor strafrecht 60 : 111-124, afl. 2, 1951.

Constitution provisoire de la République d'Indonésie promulguée le 15 août 1950 à Djakarta. Documentation française, Notes et études documentaires : 1-14, no. 1589, 18 mars 1952.

LÉVY, D. : La constitution de la République d'Indonésie. Revue internationale de droit comparé 4 : 268-280, avril-juin 1952.

SRINAVASAMURTHY, A.K. : The Indonesian constitution. Indian year book of international affairs 2 : 225-236, 1953.

BOS, M. : Le premier procès de la République des Moluques du Sud contre la S.A. "Koninklijke Paketvaart Maatschappij". Journal du droit international 80 : 286-309, avril-juin 1953.

LEYSER, J. : Legal developments in Indonesia. American journal of comparative law 3 : 399-411, summer 1954.

IRAN

FARMANFARMA, A. : Constitutional law of Iran. American journal of comparative law 3 : 241-247, spring 1954.

IRAQ

Constitution de l'Iraq. Documentation française, Notes et études documentaires : 1-12, No. 1466, 19 avril 1951.

IRELAND

A matter of nomenclature - "The name of the State is Eire..." Irish jurist 16 : 5-6, part 1, 1950.

LEE, G.A. : The President of Ireland. Canadian bar review 28 : 1087-1103, December 1950.

VILLERS, R. : Irlande - L'Ireland Act de 1949 et l'aspect actuel de la question irlandaise. Revue du droit public et de la science politique en France et à l'étranger 57 : 168-181, janvier-mars 1951.

What is an "Irish national?" Irish jurist 18 : 36-38, Part 3, 1952.

SHERIDAN, L.A. : Irish private law and the English lawyer. International and comparative law quarterly 1 : 196-212, April 1952.

McWHINNEY, E. : The courts and the constitution in catholic Ireland. Tulane law review 29 : 69-86, December 1954.

ISRAEL

HIRSCHBERG, H.Z. : The problems of the Shari'a (Muslim law) in the State of Israel. New East 1 : 97-108, January 1950.
Hebrew text with English summary.

COHN, H.H. : The new law in the country of the law. United Nations world 4 : 62-63, September 1950.

ROSENNE, S. : Israël et les traités internationaux de la Palestine. Journal du droit international 77 : 1140-1173, octobre-décembre 1950.

SUSSMANN, J. : Law and juridical practice in Israel. Journal of comparative legislation and international law 32 : 29-31, November 1950.

SINGH, H. : The constitution of Israel. Modern review 90 : 29-33, July 1951.

GOTTSCHALK, R. : Personal status and religious law in Israel. International law quarterly 4 : 454-461, October 1951.

Documents sur l'Etat d'Israël - Les lois sur la citoyenneté israélienne, 1950-1952. Documentation française, Notes et études documentaires : 1-8, no. 1644, 14 août 1952.

YADIN, U. : Les problèmes juridiques en Israël. Synthèses 7 : 188-193, août-septembre 1952.

Loi sur la nationalité du 1/4/52. Textes législatifs étrangers : 25-33, no. 3, 1952.

MARGALITH, H. : Enactment of a nationality law in Israel. American journal of comparative law 2 : 63-66, winter 1953.

SCIAKY, I. : Lo sviluppo costituzionale in Israele. Politico 18 : 183-192, luglio 1953.

La compétence des tribunaux rabbiniques en matière de mariage et de divorce en Israël. Documentation juridique étrangère 6 : 67-71, no. 1, 1954.
Loi du 26 août 1953.

ROSENNE, S. : La loi israélienne sur la nationalité 5712-1952 et la loi du Retour 5710-1950. Journal du droit international 81 : 4-62, janvier-mars 1954.
Texte anglais aussi.

LEVONTIN, A.V. : Foreign judgments and foreign status in Israel. American journal of comparative law 3 : 199-211, spring 1954.

GIANNINI, A. : Le leggi israeliane sulla cittadinanza. Oriente moderno 34 : 409-413, ottobre 1954.

VITTA, E. : Stato d'Israele, anni 1948-1949. Giurisprudenza comparata di diritto internazionale privato 11 : 451-465, 1954.

JACOBSON, D. : The legal system of Israel. American bar association journal 40 : 1067-1068, December 1954.

ITALY

ORLANDO, V.E. : Divorce and the Italian courts. International law quarterly 3 : 104-110, January 1950.

SANDIFORD, R. : Les droits de l'homme dans la nouvelle constitution italienne. Revue de droit international et de droit comparé 27 : 105-109, no. 2, 1950.

CAPOTORTI, F. : Sulla efficacia in Italia di sentenze eritree posteriori al Trattato di pace. Foro italiano 75 : parte la, 227-236, fasc. 3-4, 1950.

SERENI, A.P. : The legal profession in Italy. Harvard law review 63 : 1000-1008, April 1950.

GERVAIS, A. : La jurisprudence italienne des prises maritimes dans la seconde guerre mondiale. Revue générale de droit international public 54 : 251-316, avril-juin 1950.

NOVA, R. de : La jurisprudence italienne en matière de conflits de lois de 1935 à 1949. Revue critique de droit international privé 39 : 159-178, avril-juin 1950.

GERVAIS, A. : La jurisprudence italienne des prises maritimes dans la seconde guerre mondiale (Suite). Revue générale de droit international public 54 : 433-504, juillet-septembre 1950.

LENER, S. : L'interpretazione dottrinale dell' articolo 7 della costituzione. Civiltà cattolica 101 : 357-368, 19 agosto 1950.
Church and state.

GARBAGNATI, E. : Sull'efficacia delle decisioni della Corte costituzionale. Jus (Milano) 1 : 232-250, ottobre 1950.

McCUSKER, P.D. : The Italian rules of conflict of laws. Tulane law review 25 : 70-87, December 1950.

PALMERINI, M. : L'efficacia delle sentenze dei Tribunali militari alleati. Giustizia penale 55 : parte Ia, 353-365, dicembre 1950.

Riforma del codice civile e del codice della navigazione. Annuario di diritto comparato e di studi legislativi, Collana della ricostruzione 24 : 1-342, 1950.

ARRIGO, B.E. : Il problema della pena nel codice, nella costituzione e nel progetto preliminare di riforma. Giustizia penale 56 : parte prima, 98-110, marzo 1951.

LENER, S. : Religione di Stato e principio democratico nella costituzione italiana. Civiltà cattolica 102 : 394-405, 18 agosto 1951.

ETTORI, C. : Le contrôle juridictionnel de l'administration en Italie. Revue du droit public et de la science politique 67 : 997-1035, octobre-décembre 1951.

RIVALTA, M. : La nouvelle organisation administrative italienne. Revue internationale de droit comparé 3 : 606-615, octobre-décembre 1951.

BARTOLOMEI, D.M. : Un aspetto della giuridizione internazionale nel regime matrimoniale concordatario. Foro italiano 77 : parte 4a, 24-30, fasc. 1-2, 1952.

Inaugurazione dell'anno giudiziario - Discorso del Procuratore Generale presso la Corte suprema di cassazione. Giustizia penale 57 : parte Ia, 33-53, febbraio 1952.

PIERANDREI, F. : Osservazioni intorno alle attività di pubblica amministrazione nella Regione siciliana. Foro italiano 77 : parte la, 317-325, 19 marzo 1952.

CANSACCHI, G. : L'évolution depuis 1945 du droit italien en matière de reconnaissance et d'exécution des décisions étrangères d'annulation du mariage et de divorce. Revue critique de droit international privé 41 : 241-252, avril-juin 1952.

BARDA, E. : Quelques aspects du nouveau code civil italien. Revue internationale de droit comparé 4 : 225-255. avril-juin 1952.

SERENI, A.P. : Basic features of civil procedure in Italy. American journal of comparative law 1 : 373-389, autumn 1952.

NEUMAYER, K.H. : Über die Fortgeltung deutsch-italienischer Staatsverträge privatrechtlichen Inhalts. Juristenzeitung 7 : 682-683, 20. November 1952.

CURATOLA, M. : Conditions et tendances de la vie constitutionnelle italienne dpuis le Statut Albertin jusqu'à la proclamation de la République. Revue de droit international et de droit comparé 30 : 7-24, no. 1, 1953.

The political, legislative and judicial structure of the Italian Republic. Italian affairs 2 : 18-19, April 1953.

CAPOTORTI, F. : Problemi di diritto internazionale nella giurisprudenza italiana recente, parte terza, anno 1952. Istito di diritto internazionale e straniero della Università di Milano, Comunicazioni e studi 5 : 387-435, 1953.

BARILE, G. : Recenti tendenze della dottrina italiana di diritto internazionale pubblico, 1952-1953. Istituto di diritto internazionale e straniero della Università di Milano, Comunicazioni e studi 5 : 467-566, 1953.

BELLONI, G.A. : Per un regolamento della posizione giudiziaria dei condannati per diserzione nel periodo 8 settembre 1943-49 maggio 1945. Giustizia penale 58 : parte Ia, 265-270, luglio 1953.

CASCIO, S.O. : Lo Statuto siciliano, l'Alta corte per la Sicilia e la Corte di cassazione. Foro italiano 78 : parte la, 1486-1487, fasc. 21-22, 1953.

SATTA-FLORES, B. : Sulla revisione delle sentenze del Tribunale italiano delle prede e sulla presunzione del caratere "nemico" della merce in tempo di guerra. Foro italiano 79 : parte 3a, 20-27, 31 gennaio 1954.

LESSONA, S. : La ejecución de sentencias y decisiones en la justicia administrativa italian. Revista de administración pública 5 : 103-120, enero-abril 1954.

BARRERA GRAF, J. : La empresa en el nuevo derecho mercantil italiano, su influencia en el derecho mexicano. Boletín del Instituto de derecho comparado de México 7 : 85-108, enero-abril 1954.

MIGLIAZZA, A. : Arbitrati nazionali ed arbitrati esteri. Rivista di diritto internazionale 37 : 203-227, fasc. 2-3, 1954.

PERASSI, T. : La cittadinanza dell'attore come criterio di competenza giurisdizionale nelle relazioni italo-francesi. Rivista di diritto internazionale 37 : 228-242, fasc. 2-3, 1954.

MONACO, R. : Die internationalen Verträge und die neue italienische Verfassung. Österreichische Zeitschrift für öffentliches Recht 6 : 285-302, Heft 3, 1954.

Code civil italien, livre 1 - Des personnes et de la famille. Documentation juridique étrangère 6 : 1-126, no. 8-9, 1954.

Italian administrative law. International and comparative law quarterly 3 : 421-453, July 1954.

ROTONDI, M. : The proposed Franco-Italian code of obligations. American journal of comparative law 3 : 345-359, summer 1954.

WESER, M. : Faut-il reviser la convention franco-italienne du 3 juin 1930 sur l'exécution des jugements? Revue critique de droit international privé 43 : 451-476, juillet-septembre 1954.

WESER, M. : Faut-il reviser la convention franco-italienne du 3 juin 1930 sur l'exécution des jugements (Suite)? Revue critique de droit international privé 43 : 693-718, octobre-décembre 1954.

Trattati ed accordi. Istituto per gli studi di politica internazionale, Annuario di politica internazionale 11 : 862-872, 1954.

BORGHESE, S. : Il progetto di riforma del codice di procedura penale. Rassegna di studi penitenziari (Italy) 4 : 753-790, novembre-dicembre 1954.

JAPAN

MEYERS, H. : The Japanese inquest of prosecution. Harvard law review 64 : 279-286, December 1950.

Establishing a business under the laws of Japan. International reference service 7 : 1-8, December 1950.

Législation japonaise en matière de nationalité, 1950. Textes législatifs étrangers : 33-36, no. 3, 1951.

Japan - Staatsangehörigkeitsgesetz vom 4.5.1950. Zeitschrift für ausländisches und internationales Privatrecht 16 : 496-499, Heft 3, 1951.

AZUMA, M. : Labour legislation in Japan. Far Eastern economic review 11 : 390-396, 27 September 1951.

Japan-American commercial arbitration agreement. Arbitration journal 7 : 237-240, No. 4, 1952.

OPPLER, A.C. : Courts and law in transition. Contemporary Japan 21 : 19-55, 30 May 1952.

GARDINER, H.A. : Japanese arbitration law. Arbitration journal 8 : 89-93, No. 2, 1953.

KAWAMURA, M. : The Japanese judiciary - A step toward democracy. American bar association journal 39 : 213-215, 253-256, March 1953.

TANAKA, La democratización de la justicia japonesa. Revista de la Facultad de derecho de México 3 : 267-278, abril-junio 1953.

TAKESHITA, K.L. : Recent works on the new Japanese constitution. Quarterly journal of current acquisitions 10 : 143-146, May 1953.

BLAKEMORE, T.L., and YAZAWA, W. : Japanese commercial code revisions concerning corporations. American journal of comparative law 2 : 12-24, winter 1953.

DANDO, S. : Strafrechtsentwicklung in Japan nach dem Kriege. Zeitschrift für die gesamte Strafrechtswissenschaft 66 : 151-166, Heft 1, 1954.

SUZUKI, R. : Die Modernisierung des japanischen Familien- und Erbrechtes. Zeitschrift für ausländisches und internationales Privatrecht 19 : 104-120, Heft 1, 1954.

Japon - Constitution, 3 novembre 1946. Informations constitutionnelles et parlementaires : 55-71, 1er avril 1954.

JORDAN

Doustour al-mamlakah al-Ourdoumilleh al-Hachimillah. Al-jaridah al-Rasmillah : 3-15, no. 1093, 8 Jan. 1952.
Constitution.

Constitution of the Hashemite Kingdom of Jordan. MiddleEast journal 6 : 228-237, No. 2, spring 1952.

MOGANNAM, E.T. : Developments in the legal system of Jordan. Middle East journal 6 : 194-206, spring 1952.

Constitution du Royaume de Jordanie Hachémite, 1er janvier 1952. Documentation française, Notes et études documentaires : 1-11, no. 1613, 14 mai 1952.

Jordania - Constitución del reino. Información jurídica : 880-884, septiembre 1952.

Jordanie - Constitution du Royaume de Jordanie Hachémite, 1er janvier 1952. Informations constitutionnelles et parlementaires : 72-94, 1er avril 1954.

LEBANON

DIB, P. : Liban. Annuaire de législation étrangère, Nouvelle série 2 : 276-287, 1950-1951.

NATIONAL LAW - COUNTRIES

CHAMAS, S. : Retour à l'unité libano-syrienne du droit commercial - Tendances générales. Annales de la Faculté de droit, Université Saint Joseph de Beyrouth : 19-46, no. 1, 1951.

GANNAGÉ, P. : Jurisprudence libanaise récente en matière de conflits de juridictions confessionelles. Annales de la Faculté de droit, Université Saint Joseph de Beyrouth : 79-94, no. 1, 1951.

MALEK, C. : Etude critique de la théorie parlementaire dans son application au Liban. Revue de droit international pour le Moyen-Orient 1 : 66-87, mai-juin 1951.

GANNAGÉ, P. : Les difficultés du contrôle de la compétence des juridictions confessionnelles dans un système juridique incomplètement laïcisé. Revue critique de droit international privé 40 : 227-243, avril-juin 1951.

Convention judiciaire entre le Liban et la Syrie signée à Damas le 25 février 1951. Revue judiciaire libanaise 7 : 27-35, juin 1951.

MIDANI, R. : Al-Ittifak al Kadaï baina Sourilla wa Loubnan. Al-Kanoun 3 : 1-11, January 1952.
Convention judiciaire syro-libanaise.

RABBATH, E. : Bulletin de jurisprudence libanaise. Journal du droit international 79 : 900-933, juillet-septembre 1952.

HATEM, C. : Kismat al-wakf wa Intihaouh. Revue judiciaire libanaise 8 : 43-48, août-septembre 1952.
Wakf legislation.

GAUNLETT, J.H. : Syro-Lebanese extradition treaty. Revue égyptienne de droit international 8 : 129-131, 1952.

GANNAGÉ, P. : L'évolution de la législation du statut personnel au Liban et ses dangers. Revue égyptienne de droit international 8 : 60-71, 1952.

MALEK, C. : Les aspects juridiques de la réélection ainsi que la démission du Président de la République libanaise, M.B. Khoury. Revue de droit international pour le Moyen-Orient 2 : 99-104, novembre 1952.

LIBYA

Constitution of Libya. Official gazette of the United Kingdom of Libya : 35-54, 7 October 1951.

La costituzione del Regno unito della Libia del 7 ottobre 1951. Oriente moderno 31 : 177-192, ottobre-dicembre 1951.

L'indépendance de la Libye et la constitution libyenne. Documentation française, Notes et études documentaires : 1-32, no. 1606, 28 avril 1952.

Libia - Constitución de 7 de octubre de 1951. Información jurídica : 616-618, junio 1952.
Summary.

MORELLI, G. : Il tribunale delle Nazioni Unite in Libia. Rivista di diritto internazionale 36 : 105-108, fasc. 1-2, 1953.

QASEM, A.M. : A juridical experiment in Libya - Unification of Civil and Shariat courts. International and comparative law quarterly 3 : 134-137, January 1954.

GIANTURCO, V. : La Corte suprema federale del Regno unito di Libia. Libia, Rivista trimestrale di studi libici 2 : 15-50, aprile-giugno 1954.

LUXEMBOURG

MEYER, J. de : La décentralisation territoriale dans les états de Benelux. Revue du droit public et de la science politique en France et à l'étranger 68 : 367-395, avril-juin 1952.

METZ, R. : La réparation des dommages de guerre au Grand-Duché de Luxembourg, loi du 25 février 1950. Bulletin d'information (Luxembourg) 6 : 63-69, 31 mai 1950.

BORJA y BORJA, R. : La constitución de Luxemburgo. Revista de estudios políticos : 149-176, septiembre-octubre 1954.

MEXICO

ECHANOVE TRUKILLO, C.A. : La nacionalidad de los nacidos en México de padres extranjeros, a partir de 1857. Revista de la Escuela nacional de jurisprudence 12 : 81-87, enero-marzo 1950.

TRIGUEROS, E. : La nouvelle loi mexicaine sur la nationalité. Journal du droit international 77 : 850-853, juillet-septembre 1950.

Curso colectivo acerca del anteproyecto de código procesal civil para el Distrito Federal. Revista de la Escuela nacional de jurisprudencia 12 : 9-266, julio-diciembre 1950.
Series of articles.

PORTE PETIT, C. : El anteproyecto del código penal. Criminalia 16 : 317-331, agosto 1950.

ARILLA BAS, F. : Breve ensayo crítico sobre el anteproyecto de reformas al código penal. Criminalia 16 : 394-401, octubre 1950.

PALACIOS, R. : Las reformas al código penal para el D.F. y territorios federales. Criminalia 16 : 478-491, diciembre 1950.

BERNALDO de QUIRÓS, C. : Observaciones al anteproyecto de cófigo penal para el distrito y territorios federales. Criminalia 17 : 45-54, enero 1951.

ARGÜELLES, F. : Las reformas al código penal vigente. Criminalia 17 : 75-82, febrero 1951.

HERNANDEZ, C.C. : El concepto del delito continuado en el anteproyecto de código penal mejicano de 1949. Información jurídica : 357-366, abril 1951.

CAMARGO HERNANDEZ, C. : El concepto del delito continuado en el anteproyecto del código mejicano de 1949 para el Distrito y Territorios Federales. Criminalia 17 : 337-345, junio 1951.

MOLINA PASQUEL, R. : Algunos problemas relacionados con el rezago en la Supreme corte - Ensayo de solúción. Revista de la Facultad de derecho de México 1 : 11-40, julio-diciembre 1951.

NATIONAL LAW - COUNTRIES

AHUMADA, R.C. : Le fonds de commerce dans la législation mexicaine. Cahiers de législation et de bibliographie juridique de l'Amérique Latine 3 : 51-56, janvier-mars 1952.

El régimen presidencial mexicano. Revista de la Facultad de derecho de México 2 : 11-73, abril-junio 1952.

ALCALA-ZAMORA y CASTILLO, N. : Examen del enjuiciamento mercantil mexicano, y conveniencia de su reabsorción por el civil. Revista de la Facultad de derecho de México 2 : 19-93, julio-septiembre 1952.

CRAWFORD, H.P. : The capital structure of Mexican corporations. Tulane law review 28 : 45-74, December 1953.

SIQUEIROS, P.J.L.: Las sociedades extranjeras en el proyecto del nuevo código de comercio. Boletín del Instituto de derecho comparado de México 6 : 9-31, septiembre-diciembre 1953.

BARRERA GRAF, J. : La empresa en el nuevo derecho mercantil italiano, su influencia en el derecho mexicano. Boletín del Instituto de derecho comparado de México 7 : 85-108, enero-abril 1954.

MANTILLA MOLINA, R.L. : El proyecto de código de comercio papa la República mejicana. Revista de la Facultad de derecho de México 4 : 143-173, julio-septiembre 1954.

CERVANTES AHUMADA, R. El libro 4e del proyecto para el nuevo código de comercio. Revista de la Facultad de derecho de México 4 : 159-168, octubre-diciembre 1954.

MONACO

GAUDEFROY, P. : De l'exécution des jugements rendus par les tribunaux français dans la principauté de Monaco et des jugements monégasques en France. Journal du droit international 81 : 910-953, octobre-décembre 1954.
Texte anglais aussi.

MOROCCO

BRÉMARD, F. : La procédure législative au Maroc depuis 1912. Revue juridique et politique de l'Union Française 5 : 228-250, avril-juin 1951.

Le nouveau code pénal marocain. Bulletin d'information du Maroc 4 : 216-217, 20 juin 1951.

RIVIÈRE, P.L. : A propos du nouveau code pénal du Maroc. Recueil Dalloz, Chronique : 173-175, 20 décembre 1951.

DECROUX, P. : L'état civil et les Marocains. Revue juridique et politique de l'Union Française 6 : 1-19, janvier-mars 1952.

PLANTEY, A. : La justice coutumière marocaine. Revue juridique et politique de l'Union Française 6 : 20-56, janvier-mars 1952.

DECROUX, P. : Le pouvoir d'expulsion au Maroc. Penant, Recueil général de jurisprudence, de doctrine et de législation d'Outre-Mer, Doctrine 63 : 53-56, juin 1953.

FOUGÈRE, L. : Le statut juridique international du Maroc. Revue économique franco-suisse 33 : 473-476, décembre 1953.

Code pénal marocain du 24 octobre 1953. Documentation juridique étrangère 5 : 3-82, no. 12, 1953.

RODRÍGUEZ AGUILERA, C. : Ante una posible reforma de la justicia marroqui en la Zona española de Protectorado en Marruecos. Cuadernos de estudios africains : 43-49, no. 24, 1953.

LÉRIS, P. : La Cour de cassation et le Maroc. Recueil Dalloz, Chronique : 17-19, 23 janvier 1954.

Documents relatifs aux réformes du Maroc (Suite) - Réforme judiciaire. Documentation française, Notes et études documentaires : 1-39, no. 1828, 28 janvier 1954.

RIVIÈRE, P.L. : Les nouveaux codes marocains. Recueil Dalloz, Chronique : 27-34, 6 février 1954.

FOUGÈRE, L. : Le problème judiciaire marocain et la réforme de 1953. Fédération 11 : 259-268, mars-avril 1954.

MALAVAL, L. : La réforme de la justice pénale au Maroc. Revue de science criminelle et de droit pénal comparé : 299-327, avril-juin 1954.

NETHERLANDS

Vergoeding van oorlogsschade. Economischstatistische berichten 35 ; 44-46, 18 Januari 1950.
War damages.

CZAPSKI, G. : Die Kriegs- und Nachkriegsbestimmungen über Verlust und Erwerb der Staatangehörigkeit und ihre Auswirkungen auf Deutsche. Zeitschrift für ausländisches und internationales Privatrecht 16 : 108-112, Heft 1, 1950.

CURTIUS, F.D. : La position jurisprudentielle néerlandaise en matière de loi applicable aux contrats- Revue critique de droit international privé 39 : 1-10, janvier-mars 1950.

HOLLANDER, F. : Chronique de droit pénal néerlandais. Revue de droit pénal et de criminologie 30 : 1098-1100, juillet 1950.

WIARDA, J. : Wesenzüge des niederländischen Privatrechts. Zeitschrift für ausländisches und internationales Privatrechts 16 : 216-228, Heft 2, 1951.

Législation néerlandaise en matière de sociétés anonymes. Textes législatifs étrangers : 47-92, no. 2, 1952.
Traduction de textes.

CZAPSKI, G. : Niederländische Rechtsprechung zum internationalen Privatrecht. Zeitschrift für ausländisches und internationales Privatrecht 17 : 618-642, Heft 4, 1952.

MEYER, J. de : La décentralisation territoriale dans les états de Benelux. Revue du droit public et de la science politique en France et à l'étranger 68 : 367-395, avril-juin 1952.

Législation sur le mariage et le divorce aux Pays-Bas. Textes législatifs étrangers 3 : 67-93, no. 1, 1953.

NATIONAL LAW - COUNTRIES

POT, C.W. van der : Die Entwicklung des öffentlichen Rechts in den Niederlanden seit 1930. Jahrbuch des öffentlichen Rechts 2 : 251-281, 1953.

La revision constitutionnelle aux Pays-Bas en 1953. Bulletin de droit des gens 2 : 165-175, no. 2, 1953. Texte pp. 173-175.

PANHUYS, H.F. van : The Netherlands constitution and international law. American journal of international law 47 : 537-558, October 1953.

ZIMMERMANN, E. : Die Neuregelung der auswärtigen Gewalt in der Verfassung der Niederlande. Zeitschrift für ausländisches öffentliches Recht und Völkerrecht 15 : 164-210, Nr. 1-2, Oktober 1953.

CZAPSKI, G. : Gesetzgebung der Niederlande auf dem Gebit des Privatrechts 1940-1953. Zeitschrift für ausländisches und internationales Privatrecht 19 : 516-538, Heft 3, 1954.

BOR, A.W. : Rechtspraak in Nieuw-Guinea, met inbegrip van de ontwikkeling in voormalig Nederlands Oost-Indië, waaruit zij is voortgekomen. Tidjschrift voor strafrecht 63 : 236-268, afl. 3-4, 1954.

WINKEL, H. : Nederlands interregionaal strafrecht. Tijdschrift voor strafrecht 63 : 188-220, afl. 3-4, 1954.

KOLLEWIJN, R.D. : Le droit interrégional privé du Royaume des Pays-Bas. Nederlands tijdschrift voor internationaal recht : 269-297, Juli 1954.

DOMKE, M. : Dutch war-time legislation before American courts, 1953. Nederlands tijdschrift voor internationaal recht - Netherlands international law review : 365-373, October 1954.

NEW ZEALAND

The proceedings of the eight Dominion legal conference, Dunedin, March 27-30, 1951. New Zealand law journal 27 : 79-132, 1 May 1951.

NORTHEY, J.F. : Curial review of the determinations of administrative tribunals. New Zealand law journal 28 : 89-91, 8 April 1952.

"The Queen of this realm" - Some constitutional aspects of the royal visit. New Zealand law journal 30 : 17-20, 2 February 1954.

DAVIS, A.G. : Judicial precedent in New Zealand - Judgments of courts of first instance. New Zealand law journal 30 : 305-306, 12 October 1954.

NICARAGUA

Constitución política. Gaceta (Nicagua) 54 : 2209-2243, 6 noviembre 1950.

NORWAY

Norvège - HIORTHÖY, F. : Droit public, droit privé - AULIE, A. : Droit pénal. Annuaire de législation étrangère, Nouvelle série 2 : 376-392, 1950-1951.

BAHR, H. : Den nye beredskapslovgivning i Norge. Nordisk tidsskrift for kriminalvidenskab 39 : 35-55, 1. hefte 1951.

LOUS, K. : Forandringer i norsk straffelov. Nordisk tidsskrift for kriminalvidenskab 39 : 348-356, 4. hefte 1951.

GAARDER, K. : Fra den norske høyesteretts praksis i 1950. Tidsskrift for rettsvitenskap 64 : 533-552, hefte 5, 1951.

Loi sur le droit au titre de citoyen norvégien, du 8 décembre 1950. Textes législatifs étrangers : 109-114, no. 1, 1952.

GAARDER, K. : Fra den norske høyesteretts praksis i 1951. Tidsskrift for rettsvitenskap 65 : 504-525, hefte 5, 1952.

BREMER, J. : Etterundersøkelser av legalt kastrerte personer i Norge i 15 års perioden 1935-49. Nordisk tidsskrift for kriminalvidenskab 41 : 201-230, 3. hefte 1953.

HIORTHÖY, F. : Den norske lovgivning om fiendegods - Forholdet til grunnloven og folkerretten. Tidsskrift for rettsvitenskap 66 : 379-393, hefte 4, 1953.

GAARDER, K. : Fre den norske Høyesteretts praksis i 1952. Tidsskrift for rettsvitenskap 66 : 511-540, hefte 5, 1953.

GAARDER, K. : Fra den norske Hoyesteretts praksis i 1953. Tidsskrift for rettsvitenskap 67 : 537-556, hefte 5, 1954.

PAKISTAN

Pakistan citizenship act. Commonwealth survey : 5-6, 8 June 1951.

GREEN, L.C. : The status of Pakistan. Indian law review 6 : 65-77, no. 2, 1952.

KESAVA RAO, C. : The constitution of Pakistan. Indian year book of international affairs 2 : 247-276, 1953.

DAHM, G. : Das Strafrecht in Indien und Pakistan. Zeitschrift für die gesamte Strafrechtswissenschaft 66 : 135-150, Heft 1, 1954.

DAHM, G. : Gerichtsverfassung und Strafverfahren in Indian und Pakistan. Zeitschrift für die gesamte Strafrechtswissenschaft 66 : 593-621, Heft 4, 1954.

GLEDHILL, A. : The judiciary in Pakistan. Indian year book of international affairs 3 : 257-267, 1954.

GLEDHILL, A. : Pakistan. Annuaire de législation étrangère 3 : 336-343, 1952-54.

PANAMA

RICORD, H.E. : El derecho panameño ante la cuestión del régimen matrimonial. Boletín del Instituto de derecho comparado de México 3 : 9-67, enero-abril 1950.

TORRES GUDIÑO, S. : Panorama del derecho procesal civil panameño. Revista de la Facultad de derecho de México 4 : 79-130, enero-marzo 1954.

NATIONAL LAW - COUNTRIES

PERU

BARANDIARÁN, J-L. : Comentarios al Código Civil Peruano (Contd.). Revista de derecho y ciencias políticas 14 : 3-44, nos. 1-3, 1950.

AYASTA GONZALEZ, J. : Información jurídica del Perú. Revista de la Escuela nacional de jurisprüdencia 12 : 219-222, enero-marzo 1950.

BARANDIARÁN, J.L. : Comentarios al código civil peruano (Contd.). Revista de derecho y ciencias políticas 15 : 197-273, no. 2, 1951.

BOGGIO, M.S. : Políca minera nacional y el Código de minería de 1950. Minería 1 : 7-13, febrero 1953.

SOMMARUGA, A.V. : La legítima defensa en la doctrina y en el código penal peruano. Revista de derecho y ciencias políticas 15 : 520-555, tercer cuatrimestre 1951.

Congreso internacional de juristas. Revista de derecho y ciencias políticas (Lima) 16 : 1-799, no. 1-3, 1952.
Lima, December 1951 ; special issue.

PHILIPPINES

MERRILL, F.T. : The outlook for Philippine independence. Foreign policy reports 15 : 154-164, 15 September 1939.

CASTRO, F. de : Las reglas sobre derecho internacional privado en el proyecto de código civil de las Islas Filipinas. Revista española de derecho internacional 3 : 77-88, núm. 1, 1950.

Annual survey of 1951 decisions. Philippine law journal 27 : 197-343, April 1952.
Series of articles.

HERNAEZ, R., and PONCIANO, A.M. : Criminal law, 1952. Philippine law journal 28 : 41-68, February 1953.

FERNANDO, E.M. : Another year of constitutional law, 1952. Philippine law journal 28 : 1-40, February 1953.

CASTRO, G. de : 1952 survey of civil law in the Philippines. Philippine law journal 28 : 159-209, April 1953.

FELICIANO, F.P. : The belligerent occupant and the returning sovereign - Aspects of the Philippine law of belligerent occupation. Philippine law journal 28 : 645-703, October 1953.

PADILLA, A. : An appraisal of the proposed code of crimes. Philippine law journal 28 : 895-909, December 1953.

Annual survey of 1953 Supreme court decisions - Public law. Philippine law journal 29 : 1-158, February 1954.
Series of articles.

Philippine judiciary - A symposium. Philippine law journal 29 : 567-643, October 1954.
Series of articles.

PIÑAR LOPEZ, B. : La adopción en el nuevo código civil filipino. Anuario de derecho civil 7 : 1175-1186, octubre-diciembre 1954.

ARMOVIT, R.A. Emergency powers. Philippine law journal 29 : 686-724, December 1954.

POLAND

BALICKA, J. : Le nouveau code de la famille. Documentation française, Articles et documents : 5-7, no. 1948, 28 août 1950.
Publié dans "Trybuna ludu".

KORBE, H. : Zwei polnische Gesetzwürfe zur Reform des Nichtehelichenrechts. Neue Justiz 4 : 441-442, November 1950.

PODLASKI, H. : Über die aktuellen Aufgaben der Staatsanwaltschaft des volksdemokratischen Polen. Neue Justiz 5 : 54-57, Februar 1951.

Code polonais de la famille. Textes législatifs étrangers : 40-67, no.1, 1951.

SIENNICKI, L. : Projekt konstytucji Polskiej Rzeczypospolitej Ludowej. Życie gospodarcze 7 : 163-165, 9 lutego 1952.
Draft constitution.

ROZMARYN, S. : Konstytucje socjalistyczne a konstytucje burżuazyjne. Nowe drogi 5 : 64-84, listopa -grudzień 1951.
Constitution.

SZWAJCER, S. : Pologne, 1946-1951. Annuaire de législation étrangère, Nouvelle série 2 : 412-433, 1950-51.

Poland is shaping its new constitution. New Central European observer 5 : 58-62, 16 February 1952.

Le nouveau projet de constitution polonaise. Cahier internationaux 4 : 83-93, février 1952.

Constitution of the Polish people's republic. Polis facts and figures : 5-9, 9 February 1952.

MUSKKAT, M. : Projekt konstytcji Polskiej Rzeczypos politej Ludowej - Nowy akt oskarżenia faszyzmu. Pánstwo i prawo 7 : 563-574, kwiecień 1952.

JABLÓNSKI, H. : Konstytucje Polskie. Pánstwo i prawo 7 : 367-405, 1952.

Z przebiegu dyskusji nad projektem części ogólnej kodeksu karnego Polski Ludowej. Państwo i prawo 7 : 87-98, styczeń 1952.
Criminal code.

Pologne - Projet de constitution, 23 janvier 1952. Informations constitutionnelles et parlementaires: 116-133, 15 juin 1952.

ZAKRZEWSKI, W. : System organów wladzy i administra państwowej wedlug orojektu Konstytucji Polskiej Rzez pospolitej Ludowej. Państwo i prawo 7 : 4-30, lipi 1952.

SZIRMAI, Z. : Le droit du mariage dans les codes de la famille tchécoslovaque et polonais. Revue internationale de droit comparé 4 : 281-293, avril-juin 1952.

NATIONAL LAW - COUNTRIES

Konstytucja Polskiej Rzeczypospolitej Ludowej. Państwo i prawo 7 : 185-203, luty 1952.

MAKAROV, A.N. : Das polnische Staatsangehörigkeitsgesetz. Zeitschrift für ausländisches und internationales Privatrecht 17 : 407-409, Heft 3, 1952.
Text pp. 453-457.

BIERUT, B. : O konstytucji Polskiej Rzeczypospolitej Ludowej. Nowe drogi 6 : 3-18, sierpień 1952.

KRÖGER, H. : Die neue Verfassung der Polnischen Volksrepublic - Der Ausdruck der gesellschaftlichen und ökonomischen Umwälzung. Einheit 7 : 962-973, Oktober 1952.

ROZMARYN, S. : Some problems of the electoral law in the Polish People's Republic. Państwo i prawo, English summary 7 : 1-7, October 1952.

Constitution de la République Populaire de Pologne. Textes législatifs étrangers : 47-74, no. 3, 1952.
1952.

Loi sur la nationalité du 8/1/51. Textes législatifs étrangers : 75-82, no. 2, 1952.

OLLERO, C. : Evolución políticoconstitucional de Polonia y constitución del 22 de julio de 1952. Revista de estudios políticos 5 : 151-172, no. 65, septiembre-octubre 1952.

Constitution de la République Populaire de Pologne promolguée le 22 juillet 1952. Dpcumentation française, Notes et études documentaires : 1-20, no. 1680, 20 novembre 1952.

Questions des mesures illégales des autorités britanniques, françaises et américaines d'occupation en Allemagne rejetant la compétence de la législation polonaise dans le domaine du droit personnel en ce qui concerne les citoyens polonais. Zbiór dokumentów : 2334-2344, nr. 9, 1952.

SOBOLEWSKI, M. : Systematyka zasad konstytucji Polskiej Rzeczypospolitej Ludowej. Państwo i prawo 7 : 613-633, listopad 1952.
Constitution.

STEMBROWICZ : Die Verfassung der polnischen Volksrepublik. Neue Justiz 6 : 599-602, 20. Dezember 1952.

Übersicht über die Veröffentlichungen in der Zeitschrift "Państwo i prawo", Jahrgänge 1948/51. Staat und Recht 1 : 162-172, Dezember 1952.

JEDRYKA, Z. : La récente réforme constitutionnelle en Pologne. Revue internationale de droit comparé 4 : 702-732, octobre-décembre 1952.

Législation intérieure, Pologne - Lois sur le droit d'auteur du 10 juillet 1952. Droit d'auteur 66 : 13-18, 15 février 1953.

WOLTER, W. : Zakres mocy obowiązującej ustawy karnej co do miejsca, podmiotu i przedmioti przestępstwa na tle projektu kodeksu karnego Polskiej Rzeczypospolitej Ludowej. Państwo i prawo 8 : 211-230, luty 1953.

PIĄTOWSKI, J.S. : Wspólny majątek małżonków w Kodeksie Rodzinnym. Państwo i prawo 8 : 560-578, kriecień 1953.

WOLTER, W. : Zakres mocy obowiązującej ustawy karnej co do miejsca, podmiotu i przedmiotu przestępstwa na tle projektu kodeksu karnego Polskiej Rzeczypospolitej Ludowej. Państwo i prawo 8 : 211-230, luty 1953.

ROSADA, S., and GWOZDZ, J. : Sources of legal information in Poland. Law library journal 46 : 120-130, May 1953.

SIEDLECKI, W. : Ciężar dowodu w polskim procedie cywilnym. Państwo i prawo 8 : 56-75, lipiec 1953.
Evidence in civil procedure.

GEILKE, G. : Die Entwicklung des polnischen Justizrechts seit Kriegsende, 1944-1951. Zeitschrift für Ostforschung 2 : 107-130, Heft 1, 1953.

WALIGÓRSKI, M. : Gwarancje wykrycia prawdy w procesie cywilnym. Państwo i prawo 8 : 254-280, sierpień-wrzesień 1953.
Civil procedure.

Législation polonaise sur la compétence des autorités en matière de nationalité. Documentation juridique étrangère 5 : 31-34, no. 6-7, 1953.

Własność spoleczna w świetle konstytucji Polskiej Rzeczypospolitej Ludowej (Contd.). Państwo i prawo 8 : 407-434, październik 1953.
Law of property.

NAMITKIEWICZ, J. : O wlasności osobistej w świetle naszej Konstytucji. Państwo i prawo 9 : 141-149, styczeń 1954.
Law of property.

WOLTER, W. : Niektóre zagadnienia prawa karnego w świetle konstytucji Polski Ludowej. Państwo i prawo 9 : 238-251, luty 1954.
Criminal law.

KOROWICZ, M.S. : Justice in Poland today. Record of the Association of the Bar of the City of New York 9 : 287-299, June 1954.

KĄKOL, K. : Obowiązek zapewnienia warunków sprzyjajacych wydajności pracy w świetle prawa pracy. Państwo i prawo 9 : 295-314, wrzesień 1954.
Labour law.

CERETELLI, T.W., and MAKASZWILI, W.G. : Stan przęstepstwa podstawą odpowiedzialności karnej. Państwo i prawo 9 : 483-498, październik-listopad 1954.
Criminal law.

SCHULTZ, L. : Die Verfassungsentwicklung Polens seit 1944. Jahrbuch des öffentlichen Rechts der Gegenwart 3 : 367-397, 1954.
With text.

LERNELL, L. : Niektóre zagadneinia kodyfikacji prawa karnego. Państwo i prawo 9 : 693-723, grudzień 1954.
Criminal law codifications.

PORTUGAL

Naturalização - Seus effeitos - Formalidades a observar para a sua produção. Boletim do Ministerio da iustiça : 102-110, setembro 1951.

NATIONAL LAW - COUNTRIES

CASTRO MENDES, J. de : Portugal, 1938-1951. Annuaire de législation étrangère, Nouvelle série 2 : 434-460, 1950-51.

JARDIM, A.V. : Opção de nacionalidade. Boletim do Ministerio da iustiça : 218-224, julho 1952.

BARBOSA de MAGALHAES : Reseña de legislación, doctrina y jurisprudencia portuguesas en 1953. Revista de derecho privado 38 : 1188-1202, diciembre 1954.

PUERTO RICO

FRAGA IRABARNE, M. : Las constituciones de Puerto Rico, 1812-1952. Información jurídica : 1021-1062, noviembre 1952.

GALINDEZ, J. de : Une nouvelle formule d'auto-détermination politique à Puerto-Rico. Revue internationale de droit comparé 5 : 117-120, janvier-mars 1953.

GALINDEZ, J. de : Nueva fórmula de autodeterminación política en Puerto Rico. Boletín del Instituto de derecho comparado de México 6 : 43-54, enero-abril 1953.

Constitution du Commonwealth de Porto-Rico, 25 juillet 1954. Informations constitutionnelles et parlementaires : 109-132, 15 juin 1954.

VELÁZQUEZ, G. : El derecho puertorriqueño de las obligaciones durante la primera mitad del siglo XX. Revista jurídica de la Universidad de Puerto Rico 23 : 285-306, marzo-abril 1954.

RUMANIA

Législation roumaine en matière de nationalité. Textes législatifs étrangers : 68-75, no. 1, 1951.

RAZI, G.M. : La constitution de la République Populaire de Roumanie. Revue internationale de droit comparé 3 : 262-298, avril-juin 1951.

Législation roumaine en matière de filiation par adoption, 1951. Textes législatifs étrangers : 123-126, no. 1, 1952.

GHEORGHIU-DEJ, G. : Raportul tovarasului Gh. Gheorghiu-Dej aspura projectulüi de Constitutie a R.P.R. Probleme economice 5 : 55-72, septiembrie 1952.
Text pp. 73-86.

Constitution de la République Populaire Roumaine votée par la Grande assemblée nationale le 24 septembre 1952. Roumanie nouvelle, Supplement 5 : 1-16, 1er octobre 1952.

Constitution de la République populaire roumaine. Informations constitutionnelles et parlementaires 4 : 9-27, 15 janvier 1953.
24 septembre 1952.

Loi roumaine concernant l'élection de députés à la grande assemblée nationale (du 25 septembre 1952). Documentation juridique étrangère 5 : 79-100, no. 2, 1953.

UNGER, O. : Die Verfassung der Rumänischen Volksrepublik, eine Verfassung des sozialistischen Aufbaus. Staat und Recht 2 : 79-96, Februar 1953.

UNGER, O. : Die Verfassung der Rumänischen Volksrepublik, eine Verfassung des sozialistischen Aufbaus. Staat und Recht 2 : 79-96, Februar 1953.

La nouvelle constitution de la République Populaire de Roumanie, 24 septembre 1952. Documentation française, Notes et études documentaires : 1-15, no. 1714, 5 mars 1953.

SCHULZ, L. : Die neue Verfassung Rumäniens, eine Entwicklungsstufe zum "Vollsozialismus". Europa-Archiv 8 : 5585-5590, 5. April 1953.

Rumania - Nueva constitución de la Republica Popular. Información jurídica : 515-520, mayo 1953.

Constitution de la République Populaire Roumaine. Documentation juridique étrangère 5 : 5-36, no. 5, 1953.

Roumanie - Loi relative à l'élection des députés à la grande Assemblée nationale (25 septembre 1952). Informations constitutionnelles et parlementaires : 157-165, 15 juin 1953.
Extraits.

Code pénal roumain - Modifications. Documentation juridique étrangère 5 : 55-98, nos. 8-9, 1953.

ALBANESI, A. : Le costituzioni romene del 1948 e del 1952. Annuario di diritto comparato e di studi legislativi 29 : 329-373, 1953.

BRAHAM, R.L. : The new constitution of Rumania. American journal of comparative law 3 : 418-427, summer 1954.

SAAR VALLEY

LIEBISCH, A. : Zwei Fragen zur saarländischen Familienrechtsreform. Annales Universitatis saraviensis - Droit, économie 3 : 192-222, no. 3-4, 19

SALVADOR

GALLARDO. R. : Commentaire à la constitution politique de ElSalvador du 14 septembre 1950. Cahiers de législation et de bibliographie juridique de l'Amérique Latine 4 : 7-13, no. 15-16, juillet-décembre 1953.
Texte pp. 83-125.

SAUDI ARABIA

The Saudi Arabian nationality ordinance - High Royal decree No. 7/1/47 of the 13th shawal, 1357 a. H. Revue de droit international pour le Moyen-Orient 3 : 235-238, janvier 1954.
1357i.e. 1938.

SOUTH AFRICA

The prohibition of mixed mariages act, 1949, and South African conflict of laws. International law quarterly 3 : 91-96, January 1950.

KAHN, E. : Notes on South African private international law. International law quarterly 3 : 437-443, July 1950.

VANE, M. : Restrictive legislation in South Africa. Quarterly review 289 : 304-317, July 1951.

PARSONS, R.W. : Modern South African law as a field of comparative study. Annual law review 2 : 56-64, December 1951.

GRISWOLD, E.N. : The "coloured vote case" in South Africa. Harvard law review 65 : 1361-1374, June 1952.

COWEN, D.V. : Reflections on the constitutional issues in South Africa. Modern law review 15 : 282-296, July 1952.

McWHINNEY, E. : The Union Parliament, the Supreme Court, and the "Entrenched clauses" of the South Africa act. Canadian bar review 30 : 692-722, August-September 1952.

CURREY, C.H. : The franchise question in South Africa. Australian outlook 6 : 153-165, September 1952.

McWHINNEY, E. : Court versus legislature in the Union of South Africa - The assertion of a right of judicial review. Canadian bar review 31 : 52-64, January 1953.

GRISWOLD, E.N. : The demise of the High Court of Parliament of South Africa. Harvard law review 66 : 864-872, March 1953.

BEINART, B. : Testamentary form and capacity and the Wills act, 1953. South African law journal 70 : 159-179, May 1953.

KEETON, G.W. : The constitutional crisis in South Africa. Current legal problems 6 : 22-38, 1953.

COWEN, D.V. : Legislature and judiciary - Reflections on the constitutional issues in South Africa (Contd.). Modern law review 16 : 273-298, July 1953.

McWHINNEY, E. : La crise constitutionnelle de l'Union Sud-Africaine. Revue internationale de droit comparé 5 : 542-563, juillet-septembre 1953.

COWEN, D.V. : The entrenched sections of the South Africa act. South African law journal 70 : 238-265, August 1953.

UNVERZAGT, K. : Der Verfassungsstreit in der Südafrikanischen Union um das Wahlgesetz von 1951. Zeitschrift für ausländisches öffentliches Recht und Völkerrecht 15 : 217-255, Nr. 1-2, Oktober 1953.
See also pp. 255-259.

McWHINNEY, E. : Race relations and the courts in the Union of South Africa. Canadian bar review 32 : 44-74, January 1954.

HAHLO, H.R. : First impressions of the Matrimonial affairs act, 1953. South African law journal 71 : 32-43, February 1954.

HENOCHSBERG, E.S. : The passing of the Natal native high court. South African law journal 71 : 221-231, August 1954.

SPAIN

España - El Instituto nacional de estudios jurídicos. Información jurídica : 563-571, abril 1950.

MONTANÉ de la ROQUE : Chronique constitutionelle étrangère - Espagne 1936-1949. Revue du droit public et de la science politique 66 : 307-348, avril-juin 1950.

Reforma de la sociedad anónima (Contd.). Estudios sociales y económicos : U/1-U/16, julio 1950.

CASTRO y BRAVO, F. de : Crisis de la sociedad anónima? - Reflexiones sobre la proyectada reforma legislativa de la sociedad anónima. Revista de estudios políticos 29 : 51-105, no. 49, 1950.

LASALA SAMPER, J.M. de : La norma española de conflicto sobre régimen legal de bienes del matrimonio. Revista española de derecho internacional 4 : 13-58, núm. 1, 1951.

GREÑO VELASCO, J.E. : Readquisición de la nacionalidad española por la mujer casada en los supuestos de separación indefinida y divorcio vincular. Revista española de derecho internacional 4 : 557-578, núm. 2, 1951.

LOZANO SERRALTA, M. : La pérdida de la nacionalidad. Revista española de derecho internacional 4 : 521-555, núm. 2, 1951.

FAIREN, V. : Innovazioni nella legislazione processuale spagnola. Annuario di diritto comparato e di studi legislativi 26 : 257-318, fasc. 2-3, 1950.

APELLANIZ y VALDERRAMA, F.S. : Reconocimiento y ejecución de sentencias extranjeras (Contd.). Información jurídica : 617-643, junio 1951.

PÉREZ, J.G. : La emancipación plena de los indígenas de Guinea. Información jurídica : 1129-1137, noviembre 1951.

BARREIRO, L. : Nueva ley de sociedades anónimas. Boletín minero e industrial 31 : 1-12, enero 1952.

LOZANO SERRALTA, M. : La prueba de la nacionalidad. Revista española de derecho internacional 5 : 181-229, núm. 1, 1952.

GAY de MONTELLÁ, R. : La nouvelle loi sur les sociétés anonymes en Espagne. Revue de droit international et de droit comparé 29 : 18-27, nos. 1-2, 1952.

NO LOUIS, E. de : El código de justicia militar español y los prisoneros de guerra. Revista española de derecho internacional 5 : 839-856, no. 3, 1952.

LUNA, A. de : Reconnaissance et exécution des sentences arbitrales étrangères en Espagne. Revue de droit international et de droit comparé 29 : 154-165, nos. 3-4, 1952.

Loi du 17 juillet 1951 instituant le régime juridique des sociétés anonymes en Espagne. Textes législatifs étrangers : 5-107, no. 4, 1952.

PLAZA, M. de la : La casación criminal española, su origen - Desarrollo en el mundo hispánico y posibles reformas. Anuario de derecho penal y ciencias penales 5 : 189-205, mayo-agosto 1952.

NATIONAL LAW - COUNTRIES

LOZANO SERRALTA, M. : La naturalización en el derecho español. Información jurídica : 687-716, julio-agosto 1952.

Índice alfabético de colaboradores y de sus trabajos publicados en la "Revista jurídica de Cataluña" desde 1895 hasta 1952. Revista jurídica de Cataluña 51 : 611-635, noviembre-diciembre 1952.

SOLA CANIZARES, F. de : Le droit civil catalan. Revue internationale de droit comparé 5 : 76-96, janvier-mars 1953.

Decreto de 23 de enero de 1953 (rectificado), organico de la administración de justicia en el Africa occidental española. Información jurídica : 382-387, abril 1953.

Législation espagnole sur les sociétés à responsabilité limitée. Textes législatifs étrangers 3 : 119-131, no. 4, 1953.
Loi du 17 juillet 1953.

LOZANO SERRALTA, M. : La nacionalidad de la mujer casada. Información jurídica : 567-593, junio 1953.

MOSSA, L. : El proyecto español de ley sobre las sociedades de responsabilidad limitada. Revista jurídica de Cataluña 52 : 497-502, noviembre-diciembre 1953.
See also pp. 503-557.

PERÉ RALUY, J. : Proyección del Concordato de 1953 sobre el derecho civil y procesal español. Revista jurídica de Cataluña 53 : 75-88, enero-febrero 1954.

MALDONADO y FERNANDEZ del TORCO, J. : La exigencia del matrimonio canónico en nuestra legislación civil. Annuario de derecho civil 7 : 149-166, enero-marzo 1954.

CARRERAS, J. : Estudio comparativo de la ley española de arbitraje. Revista del Instituto de derecho comparado : 104-116, anero-junio 1954.

NÚÑEZ HERNÁNDEZ, J. : Derecho contractual español en materia de privilegios consulares. Revista española de derecho internacional 7 : 365-409, núm. 2-3, 1954.

SERRALTA, L. : La nacionalidad originaria en el derecho español. Información jurídica : 217-243, marzo 1954.

Modifications au code civil espagnol - "Des Espagnols et des étrangers". Textes législatifs étrangers : 61-68, no. 3, 1954.

LÓPEZ RODÓ, L. : Die Gemeindeverwaltung in Spanien. Zeitschrift für ausländisches öffentliches Recht und Völkerrecht 15 : 661-680, Nr. 4, 1954.

HERRERO RUBIO, A. : Nuevo regimen de la nacionalidad en el código civil español. Istituto di diritto internationale e straniero della Università di Milano, Communicazioni e studi 6 : 1-18, 1954.

GAY de MONTELLA, R. : La loi espagnole du 17 juillet 1953 sur les sociétés à responsabilité limitée. Revue de droit international et de droit comparé 31 : 75-84, no. 2-3, 1954.

PRIETO CASTRO, L. : Una nueva regulación del arbitraje. Revista de derecho privado 38 : 709-733, septiembre 1954.

La ley de nacionalidad. Información jurídica : 697-707, septiembre 1954.

Orden de 22 de julio de 1954, por la que se aprueba el reglamento de la Comisión general de codificación. Información jurídica : 852-858, octubre 1954.

VILLAR y RAMERO, J.M. : Unificación de fueros - El problema de las jurisdicciones especiales. Revista de derecho privado 38 : 992-1003, noviembre 1954.

GONZÁLEZ RUIZ, M.E. : La seguridad social española y los tratados internacionales. Cuadernos de política social : 49-69, no. 23, 1954.

SWEDEN

SIMSON, G. : Lehren der schwedischen Strafrechtspflege. Monatsschrift für deutsches Recht 4 : 281-282, Mai 1950.

FISCHLER, J. : Neues schwedisches Prozessrecht. Österreichische Juristen-Zeitung 5 : 493-495, 11. November 1950.

SCHMIDT, F. : Nationality and domicile in Swedish private international law. International law quarterly 4 : 39-52, January 1951.

LECH, H., and BECKMAN, N. : Från Sveriges högsta domstol 1950. Tidsskrift for rettsvitenskap 64 : 251-271, hefte 3, 1951.

Loi du 22 juin 1950 sur la nationalité suédoise. Textes législatifs étrangers : 129-134, no. 1, 1952.

FISCHLER, J. : Die schwedische Gesetzgebung auf dem Gebiete des Privatrechts 1942-1950. Zeitschrift für ausländisches und internationales Privatrecht 17 : 73-85, Heft 1, 1952.

SIMSON, G. : Schweden 1941-1951. Zeitschrift für die gesamte Strafrechtswissenschaft 64 : 346-378, Heft 3, 1952.

LECH, H., and BECKMAN, N. : Från Sverige Högsta Domstol 1951. Tidsskrift for rettsvitenskap 65 : 435-453, hefte 4, 1952.

HJERNER, L. : Om trust receipt och trust i svensk internationell privaträtt. Nordisk tidsskrift for international ret og jus gentium 22 : 216-239, fasc. 4, 1952.

SIMSON, G. : Sorgerechts-Statut bei Ehetrennung. Zeitschrift für ausländisches und internationales Privatrecht 18 : 138-145, Heft 1, 1953.

HERLITZ, N. : Le droit administratif suédois. Revue internationale des sciences administratioves 19 : 533-570, no. 3, 1953.

JETTMAR, O. : Grundzüge des schwedischen Verfassungsrechtes. Österreichische Zeitschrift für öffentliches Recht 5 : 483-506, Heft 4, 1953.

HERLITZ, N. : Swedish administrative law. International and comparative law quarterly 2 : 224-237, April 1953.

LECH, H., and BECKMAN, N. : Från Sveriges Hogsta Donstol 1952. Tidsskrift for rettsvitenskap 66 : 498-510, hefte 5, 1953.

RUDHOLM, S. : Der Entwurf eines schwedischen Kriminalgesetzbuchs. Zeitschrift für die gesamte Strafrechtswissenschaft 66 : 304-320, Heft 2, 1954.

LECH, H., and BECKMAN, N. : Fran Sveriges Högsta Domstol 1953. Tidsskrift for rettsvitenskap 67 : 418-431, hefte 4, 1954.

SIMSON, G. : Der Schutz des Völkerrechts im schwedischen Strafrecht. Zeitschrift für ausländisches öffentliches Recht und Völkerrecht 15 : 551-559, Nr. 3, Mai 1954.

SWITZERLAND

PANCHAUD, A. : Les garanties de la constitutionnalité et de la légalité en droit fédéral. Zeitschrift für schweizerisches Recht 69 : 1a-131a, Heft 3, 1950.

Message complémentaire du Conseil fédéral à l'Assemblée fédérale concernant la revision partielle du code pénal militaire et de la procédure pénale militaire, adaptation aux conventions de Genève du 12 août 1949 (du 19 juin 1950). Feuille fédérale 102 : 262-267, 22 juin 1950.

The constitution of Switzerland. External affairs 2 : 212-217, June 1950.

DUBACH, W. : Das Disziplinarrecht der freien Berufe. Zeitschrift für schweizerisches Recht 70 : 1a-135a, Heft 3a, 1951.

GRISEL, A. : Des rapports entre le droit civil fédéral et le droit public cantonal. Zeitschrift für schweizerisches Recht 70 : 293-323, Heft 5, 1951.

KÄGI, W. : Zur Entwicklung des schweizerischen Rechtsstaates seit 1848 - Rückblick und Ausblick. Zeitschrift für schweizerisches Recht 71 : 173-236, 1. Halbband 1952.

ROOS, G. : Übersicht über die Gesetzgebung des Jahres 1951. Zeitschrift für schweizerisches Recht 71 : 567-579, Heft 5, 1952.

RIGGENBACH, B. : Übersicht der Literatur über schweizerisches Recht - Bibliographie juridique suisse, 1951. Zeitschrift für schweizerisches Recht 71 : 581-618, Heft 5, 1952.

Message du Conseil fédéral à l'Assemblée fédérale concernant la modification de la loi sur le statut des fonctionnaires (du 2 mai 1952). Feuille fédérale 104 : 1-8, 8 mai 1952.

RIGGENBACH, B. : Übersicht der Literatur über schweizerisches Recht - Bibliographie juridique suisse. Zeitschrift für schweizerisches Recht 70 : 419-466, Heft 6, 1951.

PANCHAUD, A. : Die finanzielle Haftung der Eidgenossenschaft und ihrer Beamten. Schweizer Monatshefte 32 : 434-439, Oktober 1952.

L'espionnage en droit suisse. Revue pénale suisse 68 : 59-68, no. 1, 1953.
Voir aussi pp. 47-58.

KAUFMANN, O. : Die Verantwortlichkeit der Beamten und die Schadenersatzpflicht des Staates in Bund und Kantonen. Zeitschrift für schweizerisches Recht 72 : 201a-380a, Heft 4, 1953.

RIGGENBACH, B. : Übersicht der Literatur über schweizerisches Recht - Bibliographie juridique suisse 1952. Zeitschrift für schweizerisches Recht 72 : 237-286, Heft 5, 1953.

GÖTZ, E. : Erfahrungen mit dem neuen Bürgerrechtsgesetz. Echo 33 : 13-15, August 1953.

FELDMANN, M. : Recht und Freiheit (Contd.). Schweizer Erziehungs-Rundschau 26 : 121-126, Oktober 1953.
Human rights convention and Swiss constitution.

BINDSCHEDLER, R. : Switzerland - Recent trends in international law. International and comparative law quarterly 3 : 93-100, January 1954.

REYMOND, C. : Le trust et le droit suisse. Zeitschrift für schweizerisches Recht 73 : 119a-214a, Heft 4, 1954.

GUBLER, F.T. : Besteht in der Schweiz ein Bedürfnis nach Einführung des Instituts der angelsächsischen Treuhand (trust)? Zeitschrift für schweizerisches Recht 73 : 215a-476a, Heft 5, 1954.

ROOS, G. : Übersicht über die schweizerische Gesetzgebung des Jahres 1953. Zeitschrift für schwiezerisches Recht 73 : 522-534, Heft 8, 1954.

Message du Conseil fédéral à l'Assemblée fédérale concernant l'état des fonctions dont les titulaires ont qualité de fonctionnaires fédéraux (du 3 septembre 1954). Feuille fédérale 106 : 329-336, 9 septembre 1954.

SWITZERLAND
(Patents, trade-marks)

Message complémentaire du Conseil fédéral à l'Assemblée fédérale concernant le projet de revision de la loi sur les brevets d'invention (du 28 décembre 1951). Feuille fédérale 104 : 1-28, 3 janvier 1952.

SWITZERLAND
(International law, Aliens)

MOSER, R. : Die Rechtsprechung auf dem Gebiet des internationalen Personen- und Familienrechts, 1939-1949. Zeitschrift für ausländisches und internationales Privatrecht 16 : 69-97, Heft 1, 1950.

GUGGENHEIM, P. : Abschluss von Staatsverträgen Genehmigungspflicht der Bundesversammlung. Schweizerisches Jahrbuch für internationales Recht 7 : 123-127, 1950.

THÉVENAZ, H. : Les engagements internationaux contractés par la Suisse, entrés en vigueur en 1950. Schweizerisches Jahrbuch für internationales Recht 8 : 205-216, 1951.

Message du Conseil fédéral à l'Assemblée fédérale relatif à un projet de loi sur l'acquisition et la perte de la nationalité suisse (du 9 août 1951). Feuille fédérale 103 : 665-718, 23 août 1951.

Le droit de cité suisse. Zeitschrift für schweizerisches Recht 71 : 695-863, Heft 6, 1952.
Numéro spécial.

LACHENAL, J.A. : Conséquences de la loi fédérale du 29 septembre 1952, sur l'acquisition et la perte de la nationalité suisse, en ce qui concerne le divorce ou la séparation de corps d'époux ayant une double nationalité. Schweizerisches Jahrbuch für internationales Recht 9 : 105-122, 1952.

Loi fédérale sur l'acquisition et la parte de la nationalité suisse (du 29 septembre 1952). Feuille fédérale 104 : 137-151, 30 septembre 1952.

RICE, W.G. : The position of international treaties in Swiss law. American journal of international law 46 : 641-666, October 1952.

LAVARINO, E. : La nationalité de la femme suisse mariée à un étranger. Schweiz 23 : 120-127, 1952.

SCHULTZ, H. : Übersicht über die neueste Rechtsprechung des Bundesgerichtes in Auslieferungssachen und über die räumliche Geltung des StrGB. Revue pénale suisse 68 : 111-128, no. 1, 1953.

LA RÜE, P.A. de : Das neue Staatsangehörigkeitsgesetz der Schweiz. Zeitschrift für ausländisches und internationales Privatrecht 18 : 80-83, Heft 1, 1953.

COHN, E.J. : The new Swiss nationality act. International and comparative law quarterly 2 : 427-430, July 1953.

MORGELI, E. : Das neue Bürgerrechtsgesetz. Schweiz 24 : 90-94, 1953.

MOSER, R. : Die Rechtsprechung der Schweiz auf dem Gebiete des internationalen Privatrechts, 1950-1953. Zeitschrift für ausländisches und internationales Privatrecht 19 : 651-706, Heft 4, 1954.

SCHNITZER, A.F. : Le droit international privé suisse. Revue hellénique de droit international 7 : 143-163, avril-décembre 1954.

MEYER, H.H. : Obtaining evidence in Switzerland for use in foreign courts. American journal of comparative law 3 : 412-418, summer 1954.

DIEZ, E. : Les engagements internationaux contractés par la Suisse, entrés en vigueur en 1952 et 1953. Schweizerisches Jahrbuch für internationales Recht - Annuaire suisse de droit international 11 : 231-246, 1954.

ZELLWEGER, E. : Die völkerrechtliche Anerkennung nach schweizerischer Staatenpraxis. Schweizerisches Jahrbuch für internationales Recht - Annuaire suisse de droit international 11 : 11-42, 1954.

SECRÉTAN, R. : Evolution récente de la jurisprudence suisse relative aux conflits de lois en matière de contrats. Revue hellénique de droit international 7 : 137-142, avril-décembre 1954.

SYRIA

Kanoun ousoul al- mouhakamat al- jazaillah. Journal officiel de la République Syrienne 32 : 1513-1554, 13 avril 1950.
Code de procédure pénale, en vigueur à partir du 1er juin 1950.

La constitution syrienne. Recueil des lois syriennes et de législation financière 2 : 1-32, août 1950.

La constitution syrienne. Documentation française, Notes et études documentaires : 1-16, no. 1413, 20 décembre 1950.

La constitution de la République Syrienne adoptée par l'Assemblée constituante le 5 septembre 1950. Archives internationales Pharos 7 : 1-10, section B, no. 981, décembre 1950.

ASSIOUN, F. : Syrie, 1938-1951. Annuaire de législation étrangère, Nouvelle série 2 : 501-533, 1950-51.

CHAMAS, S. : Retour à l'unité libano-syrienne du droit commercial - Tendances générales. Annales de la Faculté de droit, Université Saint Joseph de Beyrouth : 19-46, no. 1, 1951.

SULTAN, A.R. : La nationalisation dans la législation syrienne. Al-Kanoun 2 : 33-44, mars 1951.
Texte arabe.

Convention judiciaire entre le Liban et la Syrie signee à Damas le 25 février 1951. Revue judiciaire libanaise 7 : 27-35, juin 1951.

LATRABE, J. : La constitution récente de la Syrie. Revue de droit international pour le Moyen-Orient 1 : 88-98, mai-juin 1951.

SIBAÏ, N. : Al-Ashkhas al-ítibarillah fil Kanoun al-Madaini al-Souri. Majallat-nakabat al-Mouhamine 15 : 393-402, juillet 1951.
Corporations.

TARAZI, S.E.D. : La nouvelle constitution syrienne. Revue du droit public et de la science politique 67 : 788-814, juillet-septembre 1951.

ASSIOUN, F. : Syrie. Annuaire de législation étrangère 3 : 424-439, 1952-54.

MIDANI, R. : Al-Ittifak al-Kadaï baina Sourilla wa Loubnan. Al-Kanoun 3 : 1-11, January 1952.
Convention judiciaire syro-libanaise.

ABOUL-CHAMAT, M. : Al-ittijahat al-a'mmah lil kanoun al-madani al-souri al-jadid. Majallat Nakabat al-Mouhamine 16 : 103-108, July 1952.
Features of the new civil code.

GAUNTLETT, J.H. : Syro-Lebanese extradition treaty. Revue égyptienne de droit international 8 : 129-131, 1952.

MANLEY, M.L. : The Syrian constitution of 1953. Middle East journal 7 : 520-521, autumn 1953.
text pp. 521-538.

BAROUDI, M. : Bahth Moujaz fil Kada' al-idari al-souri. Majallat Nakabat al-Mouhamine 17 : 1-56, September 1953.
Administrative jurisdiction.

La constitution syrienne du 10 juillet 1953. Documentation française, Notes et études documentaires : 1-19, No.1785, 22 septembre 1953.

HOUIN, R. : Le code de commerce syrien de 1949. Revue internationale de droit comparé 5 : 675-681, octobre-décembre 1953.

MALEK, C. : L'organisation des pouvoirs publics en Syrie, d'après la Constitution récente du 11 juillet 1953. Revue de droit international pour le Moyen-Orient 3 : 185-204, janvier 1954.

Syrie - Constitution, 21 juin 1953. Informations constitutionnelles et parlementaires : 20-51, 15 janvier 1954.

La costituzione siriana dell' 11 luglio 1953. Oriente moderno 34 : 49-66, febbraio 1954.

TANGIER

Tanger - Ordenanza de 17 de abril de 1954, sobre la entrada de personas. Información jurídica : 571-573, junio 1954.

THAILAND

MARIÑAS, L. : Tailandia - La constitución. Información jurídica : 77-83, enero 1951.

Législation thailandaise en matière d'enregistrement des étrangers, 1950. Textes législatifs étrangers : 103-112, no. 3, 1951.

TRIESTE

Status internazionale del territorio libero di Trieste. Jus gentium (Roma) 3 : 31-37, gennaio-aprile 1951.

CAMMARATA, A.E. : Le sentenze triestine in Corte di cassazione. Foro italiano 76 : parte prima, 281-283, fasc. 5-6, 1951.

FAIRMAN, C. : Asserted jurisdiction of the Italian court of cassation over the Court of appeal of the Free Territory of Trieste. American journal of international law 45 : 541-548, July 1951.

TUNISIA

SILVERA, V. : Les réformes tunisiennes de février 1951. Revue juridique et politique de l'Union Française 5 : 1-54, janvier-mars 1951.

LUCHAIRE, F. : L'institution d'un tribunal administratif en Tunisie. Annales Universitatis saraviensis 1 : 37-48, No. 1, 1952.

SILVERA, V. : Les conditions de l'évolution de la nationalité tunisienne. Revue juridique et politique de l'Union Française 6 : 356-363, juillet-septembre 1952.

SILVERA, V. : Les réformes institutionnelles tunisiennes, mars 1954. Revue juridique et politique de l'Union française 8 : 25-'03, janvier-mars 1954.

TURKEY

KEMAL ELBIR, I. : Réflexions sur l'adoption, en Turquie, des règles du code civil suisse. Revue de droit international et de droit comparé 27 : 5-12, no. 1, 1950.

Loi sur le Conseil d'Etat turc. Annales de la Faculté de droit d'Istanbul 1 : 229-255, no. 1, 1951.

TANER, T. : Türkei. Zeitschrift für die gesamte Strafrechtswissenschaft 64 : 120-122, Heft 1, 1952.
Criminal law.

DÖNMEZER, S. : La nouvelle loi sur la presse. Annales de la Faculté de droit d'Istanbul 1 : 317-332, no. 2, 1952.

Loi sur les oeuvres intellectuelles et artistiques. Annales de la Faculté de droit d'Istanbul 1 : 582-635, no. 2, 1952.
Texte.

Législation turque - Nomenclature. Annales de la Faculté de droit d'Istanbul 1 : 439-463, no. 2, 1952.
1950-1951.

BASGIL, A.F. : Le droit de pétition devant la Grande assemblée nationale. Annales de la Faculté de droit d'Istanbul 1 : 277-298, no. 2, 1952.

Turquie - Loi sur les oeuvres intellectuelles et artistiques, no. 5846, du 10 décembre 1951. Droit d'auteur 65 : 85-96, 15 août 1952.

Turquie, années 1950-1954. Annuaire de législation étrangère 3 : 440-460, 1952-54.
Suite d'articles.

POSTACIOǦLU, I.E. : Le pouvoir judiciaire dans la constitution turque actuelle. Annales de la Faculté de droit d'Istanbul 2 : 116-135, no. 3, 1953.

Modification du code pénal turc - Activités subversives. Documentation juridique étrangère 6 : 85-89, no. 1, 1954.

ONAR, S.S. : The analysis and the criticism of the causes of appearance of the public corporations in Turkey and the legal and administrative structures of these corporations. Revue internationale des sciences administratives 20 : 23-66, No. 1, 1954.

TURKEY
(International law, Aliens)

Loi sur le séjour et le déplacement des étrangers en Turquie. Annales de la Faculte de droit d'Istanbul 2 : 344-354, no. 3, 1953.

U.S.S.R.

SCHEUERLE, W.A. : L'arbitrato statale sovietico. Annuario di diritto comparato e di studi legislativi 26 : 13-24, fasc. 1, 1950.

MOKICHEV, K. : Svi͡ashchennye prava i obi͡azannosti sovetskikh grazhdan. Bolshevik 26 : 59-67, fevral' 1950.
Rights and duties of Soviet citizens.

KIRICHENKO, V.F. : Voprosy sovetskogo ugolovnogo prava v svete rabot i vyskazyvaniǐ tovarishcha I.V. Stalina. Sovetskoe gosudarstvo i pravo : 16-23, fevral' 1950.
Criminal law.

SCHEUERLE, W.A. : I principii del diritto fondiario e dell'utilizzazione del suolo nell' U.R.S.S. Annuario di diritto comparato e di studi legislativi 26 : 335-344, fasc. 2-3, 1950.

NATIONAL LAW - COUNTRIES

SERGEEVA, T.L. : Voprosy prichinnoi sviazi v sudebnoi praktike po ugolovnym delam verkhovnogo suda SSSR. Sovetskoe gosudarstvo e pravo : 26-37, mart 1950.
Criminal law.

VALTERS, N. : Die Todesstrafe in der Sowjetunion. Juristische Blätter 72 : 209-212, 29. April 1950.

HAZARD, J.N. : Socialism, abuse of power, and Soviet law. Columbia law review 50 : 448-474, April 1950.

HAZARD, J.N. : Quelques aspects du droit soviétique tel qu'il apparaît à un juriste anglo-saxon. Revue internationale de droit comparé 2 : 237-249, avril -juin 1950.

FRIDIEFF, M. : Le mariage et le divorce d'après la législation actuelle de l'U.R.S.S. Revue internationale de droit comparé 2 : 347-355, avril-juin 1950.

FED'KIN, G.I. : O rukovodiashchei roli VKP(b) v razvitii sovetskogo sotsialisticheskogo prava. Sovetskoe gosudarstvo i pravo : 11-21, iiun' 1950.

KAMINSKAIA, V.I. : V chem znachie protsessual'nykh garantiĭ v sovetskom ugolovnom protsesse. Sovetskoe gosudarstvo i pravo : 46-56, mai 1950.
Criminal law.

SEREBROVSKIĬ, V.I. : Priniatie nasledstva. Sovetskoe gosudarstvo i pravo : 35-50, iiun' 1950.
Inheritance law.

HAZARD, J.N. : Soviet socialism and private enterprise. New York university law review 25 : 533-551, July 1950.

GENERALOV, V.F. : Ob osnovnykh chertakh mezhdunarodno-pravovogo sotrudnichestva Sovetskogo Soiuza i stran narodnoĭ demokratii. Sovetskoe gosudarstvo i pravo : 14-26, iiul' 1950.
Collaboration with Eastern Europe.

KRUPSKIĬ, N.V. : Sovetskaia federatsiia, forma sovetskogo gosudarstvennogo ustroĭstva. Vestnik Moskovskogo universiteta, Seriia obshchestvennykh nauk : 61-77, iiul' 1950.
Constitution.

KILLIAN, F.W., and ARENS, R. : Use of psychiatry in Soviet criminal proceedings. Journal of criminal law and criminology 41 : 136-149, July-August 1950.

Un manuel officiel de procédure civile soviétique. Revue internationale de droit comparé 2 : 519-523, juillet-septembre 1950.

RIPOLLES, A.Q. : El novisimo pensamiento jurídico en la U.R.S.S. Revista de derecho internacional 58 : 339-364, 30 septiembre 1950.

NIKOLAEV, N.P. : L'organisation judiciaire soviétique. Monde français 19 : 397-430, septembre 1950.

PAVLOV, I.V. : Za boevuiu tvorcheskuiu rabotu v oblasti sovetskoĭ pravovoĭ nauki. Izvestiia Akademii nauk SSSR., Otd. ékonomiki i prava : 340-346, sentiabr'-oktiabr' 1950.
Legal studies.

ARENS, R., and KILLIAN, F.W. : Use of psychiatry in Soviet criminal proceedings. Journal of criminal law and criminology 41 : 423-434, November-December 1950.

PETROV, G.I. : Voprosy teorii sovetskogo administrativnogo prava. Sovetskoe gosudarstvo i pravo : 57-65, dekabr' 1950.
Administrative law.

GSOVSKI, V. : Elements of Soviet labor law. Monthly labor review 72 : 257-262, March 1951.

TRAĬNIN, A. : Zakon o zashchite mira. Sovetskoe gosudarstvo i pravo : 17-25, aprel' 1951.
Peace defence law.

KIRALFY, A. : The Soviet Supreme court as a source of law. Soviet studies 2 : 356-363, April 1951.

GERTSENZON, A. : Razoblachenie prestupleniĭ imperialisticheskoĭ burzhuazii - Odna iz aktual'nykh zadach sovetskoĭ iuridicheskoĭ nauki. Sovetskoe gosudarstvo i pravo : 34-48, maĭ 1951.

TRAININ, A.N. : Das Gesetz zum Schutze des Friedens. Neue Justiz 5 : 248-252, Juni 1951.

SCHLESINGER, R. : "Justice in Russia" - A dissent. Yale law journal 60 : 976-985, June 1951.

The Soviet Bar and ethics of the lawyer. Current digest of the Soviet press 3 : 10-12, 14 July 1951.
Published in "Literaturnaya gazeta".

BOGORAD, V. : La planification soviétique et les obligations civiles. Problèmes de planification : 70-105, (no. hors série, juillet 1951).

LEPESHKIN, A. : Stalinskaia konstitutsiia, konstitutsiia pobedivshego sotsializma. Izvestiia Akademii nauk SSSR, Otdelenie ékonomiki i prava : 393-406, noiabr'-dekabr' 1951.
Comparison with other constitutions.

SIMON, J. : Le code pénal de l'URSS. Revue de droit international et de droit comparé 29 : 28-31, nos. 1-2, 1952.

RAD'KOV, V. : K voprosu o stabil'nosti zakonov. Izvestiia Akademii nauk SSSR, Otd. ékonomiki i prava : 25-34, ianvar'-fevral' 1952.

HAZARD, J.N. : Personal injury and Soviet socialism Harvard law review 65 : 545-581, February 1952.

FRIDIEFF, M. : A la recherche d'une définition parfaite du droit soviétique. Revue internationale de droit comparé 4 : 81-88, janvier-mars 1952.

El delito de malversación de fondos en la Rusia soviética. Información jurídica : 310-316, marzo 1952.

LINDENCRONA, F.: Rättsstillämpningen i Sovjet. Tidsskrift for rettsvitenskap 65 : 278-295, hefte 3, 1952.

BOGORAD, V. : Le statut juridique des entreprises soviétiques et la responsabilité pénale de leurs dirigeants. Problèmes de planification : 324-350, no. 4, 1952.

Constitution de l'Union des Républiques Socialistes Soviétiques, avec les modifications et additions approuvées par les Ire, IIe, IIIe, IVe, Ve, VIe sessions du Soviet Suprême de l'U.R.S.S. Archives internationales Pharos 9 : 1-8, no. 1061, avril 1952

NATIONAL LAW - COUNTRIES

SCHEUERLE, W.A. : Sowjetrussische Theorie der Rechtsquellen. Archiv des öffentlichen Rechts 77 : 435-451, 4. Heft 1952.

BOGORAD, V. : La législation soviétique de la famille et son évolution. Cahiers du Musée social : 151-156, nos. 5-6, 1952.

SCHEUERLE, W.A. : Les personnes morales en droit soviétique. Revue internationale de droit comparé 4 : 443-460, juillet-septembre 1952.

BENJAMIN, H. : Deutsche Juristen in der Sowjetunion. NeueJustiz 6 : 345-348, August 1952.

MOSTOVAC-MATIEV, M. : La justice soviétique. Revue de droit pénal et de criminologie 33 : 30-34, octobre 1952.

SCHEUERLE, W.A. : Lo sviluppo del diritto della Russia sovietica. Annuario di diritto comparato e di studi legislativi 28 : 231-297, 1952.
See also pp. 299-253.

Ubersicht über die Veröffentlichungen in der Zeitschrift "Sowjetstaat und Sowjetrecht", Jahrgänge 1949/51. Staat und Recht 1 : 152-161, Dezember 1952.

Sot͡sialisticheskai͡a zakonnost' i okhrana prav sovetskikh grazhdan, vazhneĭshai͡a osnova dal'neĭshego razvitii͡a i ukreplenii͡a sovetskogo gosudarstva. Sovetskoe gosudarstvo i pravo : 17-21, no. 2-3, 1953.
Civil rights.

Zakony i postanovlenii͡a prini͡atye Verkhovnym sovetom SSSR. Sovetskoe gosudarstvo i pravo : 11-16, no. 2-3, 1953.

Umgruppierungen in der Sowjethierarchie. Ost-Probleme 5 : 544-547, 26. März 1953.
Texts of laws.

MULLER, L. : Ce qu'il faut savoir du code pénal soviétique. Observateur 4 : 10-11, 9 avril 1953.

HAZARD, J. : Le droit et l'évolution sociale en U.R.S.S. Revue internationale de droit comparé 5 : 241-254, avril-juin 1953.

Ein Institut ohne Selbstkritik. Ost-Probleme 5 : 832-836, 14. Mai 1953.
The Law institute of the Academy; Published in "Sowjetskoje gossudarstwo i prawo".

AVALIANI, G. : The law and judical practice in the USSR. United Caucasus : 19-23, may 1953.

RAIGORODSKII, N.A. : Rol' izobretatel'skogo prava SSSR v razvitii peredovoi sovetskoi tekhniki. Sovetskoe gosudarstvo i pravo : 66-79, no. 6, 1953.
Patent law.

MOTOVAC-MATIEV, M. : La justicia soviética. Revista de la Escuela de estudios penitenciarios 9 : 27-33, junio 1953.

DAVID, R. : Garantie des libertés individuelles et contrôle de légalité des actes administratifs dans l'U.R.S.S. France, Conseil d'Etat, Etudes et documents : 139-150, no. 7, 1953.

La constitution de la R.S.S. du Kazakhstan et documents annexes. Documentation française, Notes et études documentaires : 1-16, No. 1771, 21 août 1953.

KULSKI, W.W. : Les tendances contemporaines dans le droit international soviétique. Revue de droit international, de sciences diplomatiques et politiques 31 : 272-280, juillet.septembre 1953.

CHAMBRE, H. : L'évolution de la législation familiale soviétique de 1917 à 1952. Revue de l'Action populaire : 801-818, novembre 1953.

TIMASCHEFF. N.S. : The impact of the penal law of imperial Russia on Soviet penal law. American Slavic and East European review 12 : 441-462, December 1953.

LUZZATO, F. : Osservazioni sul codice penale russo. Scuola positiva 8 : 250-262, fasc. 1-2, 1954.

KOROVIN, S.T. : Izviratel'nye prava sovetskikh grazhidan. Sovetskoe gosudarstvo i pravo : 1-13, no. 2, 1954.
Election law.

FRIDIEFF, M. : La procédure de cassation et de surveillance judiciaire dans la procédure criminelle soviétique. Revue de science criminelle et de droit pénal comparé : 90-98, janvier-mars 1954.

FRIDIEFF, M. : La jurisprudence du Tribunal suprême de l'U.R.S.S. dans les affaires concernanted le mariage et le divorce, années 1949 à 1951. Revue internationale de droit comparé 6 : 66-74, janvier-mars 1954.

STUDENIKIN, S.S. : Die Gewährleistung der Gesetzlichkeit in der sowjetischen staatlichen Verwaltung. Sowjetwissenschaft, Gesellschaftswissenshaftliche Abteilung : 335-354, Nr. 3, 1954.

FARBER, I.E. : O primenenii norm sovetskogo sot͡sialisticheskogo prava. Sovetskoe gosudarstvo i pravo : 15-26, no. 4, 1954.
Application of legal norms.

TADEVOSI͡AN, V.S. : K razrabotke proekta ugolovnogo kodeksa SSSR. Sovetskoe gosudarstvo i pravo : 72-80, no. 4, 1954.
Draft criminal code; See also pp. 59-71.

TAĬMANOV, G.T. : Kazakhskai͡a SSR v sovetskom mnogo nat͡sional'nom gosudarstve. Sovetskoe gosudarstvo i pravo : 27-38, no. 4, 1954.
Khazakstan.

SUCH, H. : Das Lehrbuch des sowjetischen Zivilrechts, ein unentbehrlicher Helfer für Theorie und Praxis. Neue Justiz 8 : 260-266, 5. Mai 1954.

OLLERO, C. : La organización constitucional del poder en la U.R.S.S. y Europa oriental. Información jurídica : 405-426, mayo 1954.

LE MAY, G.H.L. : Law and politics in Soviet Russia. South African law journal 71 : 137-144, May 1954.

TARCHOW, V.A. : Zur Frage der Subjekte von Rechtsverhältnissen im sowjetischen Zivilrecht. Staat und Recht 3 : 299-312, Juni 1954.

OLLERO, C. : La organización constitucional del poder en la U.R.S.S. y Europa Oriental (Contd.). Información jurídica : 609-635, julio-agosto 1954.

FRIDIEFF, M. : L'appréciation des preuves au cours de la procédure de cassation et de surveillance judiciaire en Russia soviétique. Revue de science criminelle et de droit pénal comparé : 523-534, juillet-septembre 1954.

GENTZ, J. : Die schöpferische Rolle des Sowjetstaates und des Sowjetrechts. Neue Justiz 8 : 588-592, 20. Oktober 1954.

ROMEUF, J. : Propos sur le droit soviétique. Cahiers économiques : 18-20, octobre 1954.

Un articles du procureur soviétique P. Roudenko sur la légalité en U.R.S.S. Revue socialiste : 529-543, décembre 1954.
Publié dans "Partiinaia jizn".

QUIASON, C.D. : A brief examination of fundamental Soviet legal principles. Philippine law journal 29 : 668-685, December 1954.

Où en est la révision du code pénal soviétique? Commission internationale contre le régime concentrationnaire, Bulletin d'information : 30-35, décembre 1954.

U.S.S.R.
(International law and Practice, Aliens and Naturalization)

Die UdSSR und das Völkerrecht. Orientierung 15 : 4-7, 15. Januar 1951.

KIRALFY, A.K.R. : A Soviet approach to private international law. International law quarterly 4 : 120-125, January 1951.

MAKAROV, A.N. : Die Einführung der Sowjetgesetzbücher in den der Sowjetunion neuangegliederten Gebieten. Zeitschrift für osteuropäisches Recht 7 : 423-441, März-April 1951.

KULSKI, W.W. : Soviet comments on international law and international relations. American journal of international law 45 : 556-564, July 1951.

ZHUKOVA, T.I. : The concept of Soviet citizenship. Current digest of the Soviet press 3 : 12-13, August 18 1951.
Published in "Sovetskoe gosudarstvo i pravo".

KOSHEWNIKOV, F.I. : Einige Fragen des Völkerrechts im Licht der Arbeit J.W. Stalins "Der Marxismus und die Fragen der Sprachwissenschaft". Neue Justiz 5 : 396-402, September 1951.

KOZHEVNIKOV, F. : Nekotorye osnovnye zadachi sovetskoi nauki mezhdunarodnogo prava. Sovetskoe gosudarstvo i pravo : 34-44, no. 10, 1952.
Study of international law.

LISSITZYN, O.J. : Recent Soviet literature on international law. American Slavic and East European review 11 : 257-273, December 1952.

KULSKI, M. : Soviet comments on international law and international relations. American journal of international law 47 : 125-135, January 1953.

KULSKI, W.W. : Present trends in Soviet international law. American society of international law, Proceedings 47 : 59-89, 1953.

Abrogation de l'ordonnance de l'URSS sur l'interdiction des mariages entre les citoyens de l'URSS et les étrangers. Documentation juridique étrangère 6 : 91-93, no. 1, 1954.
26 novembre 1953.

SCHULTZ, L. : Die sowjetische Völkerrechtslehre. Jahrbuch für internationales Recht 5 : 78-92, Heft 1, 1954.

UNITED ARAB REPUBLIC

BARAKAT, G.D. : Aliens and the end of the transitional period in Egypt. International law quarterly 3 : 112-115, January 1950.

BECHMANN, H.G. : Méditations à l'occasion de la suppression d'une institution de collaboration internationale. Nordisk tidsskrift for international ret, Acta scandinavica juris gentium 20 : 1-22, fasc. 1-2, 1950.
La juridiction mixte.

Le nouveau code civil. National bank of Egypt, Economic bulletin 3 : 148-156, no. 3, 1950.

SAFWAT, A. : Le Conseil des prises égyptien. Revue égyptienne de droit international 6 : 24-32, 1950.

GAUDEMET, P.M. : Actes de souveraineté. Bulletin de législation et de jurisprudence égyptiennes 2 : 1-4, no. 1, 1951.
Conseil d'Etat.

CASTRO y BRAVO, F. de : La nacionalidad egipcia - Ley de 18 de septiembre de 1950. Revista española de derecho internacional 4 : 69-82, núm. 1, 1951.

BAGHDADI, H. : Les conflits entre le droit musulman et le code civil. Bulletin de législation et de jurisprudence égyptiennes 2 : 21-24, no. 2, 1951.

La nouvelle loi égyptienne sur la nationalité égyptienne - Journal du droit international 78 : 654-666, avril-juin 1951.
Commentaire de J. Saidenberg pp. 666-670.

MOHAMED SOLIMAN, S. : Egypte - L'exécution par l'administration des arrêts du Conseil d'Etat. Revue du droit public et de la science politique en France et à l'étranger 67 : 369-374, avril-juin 1951.

BRAUN, F. : La nouvelle loi égyptienne sur la nationalité. Revue de droit international pour le Moyen-Orient 1 : 99-103, mai-juin 1951.

SMYRNIADIS, B. : Considérations sur le mariage en Egypte. Revue égyptienne de droit international 7 : 16-29, 1951.

Territorial waters. Revue égyptienne de droit international 7 : 91-96, 1951.

PERRET, H. : Les clauses des contrats internationaux attributives de compétence à un tribunal étranger et à la jurisprudence égyptienne. Bulletin de législation et de jurisprudence égyptiennes 2 : 165-173, no. 7, 1951.

EMILIANIDES, A.C. : A case of collective statelessness - The Cypriots in Egypt. Revue hellénique de droit international 4 : 312-322, juillet-décembre 1951.

LE BALLE, R. : La notion de lésion en droit égyptien positif. Bulletin de législation et de jurisprudence égyptiennes 2 : 197-208, no. 8, 1951.

QUADRI, R. : Rattachement religieux et rattachement national. Bulletin de législation et de jurisprudence égyptiennes 2 : 285-288, no.11, 1951.

CHLALA, J. : Un nouveau code égyptien de procédure pénale. Revue de science criminelle et de droit pénal comparé : 591-598, octobre-décembre 1952.

DRAGO, R. : Le contrôle de la constitutionnalité des lois et des décrets-lois par le Conseil d'Etat. Bulletin de législation et de jurisprudence égyptiennes 4 : 1-8, no. 1, 1953.

CHLALA, J. : La suppression du "wakf ahli" en Egypte. Revue internationale de droit comparé 5 : 682-685, octobre-décembre 1953.

LINANT de BELLEFONDS, Y. : Immutabilité du droit musulman et réformes législatives en Egypte. Revue internationale de droit comparé 7 : 5-34, janvier-mars 1955.

Constitution provisoire égyptienne. Documentation juridique étrangère 5 : 57-60, no. 2, 1953.

CHEHATA, C. : Volonté réelle et volonté déclarée dans le nouveau code civil égyptien. Revue internationale de droit comparé 6 : 241-249, avril-juin 1954.

SMYRNIADIS, B. : La compétence internationale dans la nouvelle législation égyptienne. Revue égyptienne de droit international 10 : 24-37, 1954.

U.S.A.

PINTO, R. : Les pouvoirs du Sénat américain en matière de traités. Revue internationale de droit comparé 2 : 5-26, janvier-mars 1950.

KELLOR, F. : The American pattern of arbitration. Arbitration journal 5 : 91-95, no. 2, 1950.

HARBRECHT, P.P. : What are the liberties of citizens of Puerto Rico under the constitution? Georgetown law journal 38 : 471-484, March 1950.

NEWMAN, F.C. : Government and ignorance - A progress report on publication of federal regulations. Harvard law review 63 : 929-956, April 1950.

CORBIN, A.L. : The uniform commercial code-sales - Should it be enacted? Yale law journal 59 : 821-836, April 1950.

KINEVAN, M.E. : Alaska and Hawii - From territoriality to statehood. California law review 38 : 273-292, June 1950.

ROSE, G. : The right to strike - Is it an inalienable right of free men? American bar association journal 36 : 439-442, 518-521, June 1950.

PORTER, C.O. : Minimum standards of judicial administration - The extent of their acceptance. American bar association journal 36 : 614-618, August 1950.
With charts and maps.

FRANK, J.P. : The United States Supreme court, 1949-50. University of Chicago law review 18 : 1-54, autumn 1950.

SUTHERLAND, A.E. : Freedom and internal security. Harvard law review 64 : 383-416, January 1951.

BLONDEEL, J.L. : L'organisation judiciaire aux Etats-Unis. Revue de droit international et de droit international et de droit comparé 28 : 23-32, no. 1, 1951.

EDER, P. : Projet de code de commerce aux Etats-Unis d'Amérique. Revue internationale de droit comparé 3 : 75-80, janvier-mars 1951.

SURRENCY, E.C. : A bibliography of the tentative drafts of the restatements. Law library journal 44 : 11-25, February 1951.

CRAWFORD, J.D. : Free speech and the Internal security act of 1950. Georgetown law journal 39 : 440-465, March 1951.

CRAWFORD, E.T. : The legislative status of an unconstitutional statute. Michigan law revue 49 : 645-666, March 1951.

SCHWARTZ, B. : La procédure administrative aux Etats-Unis. Revue internationale de droit comparé 3 : 251-261, avril-juin 1951.

Congressional investigations - A symposium. University of Chicago law review 18 : 421-597, spring 1951.

Security and civil liberties. Columbia law review 51 : 545-660, May 1951.

GIBSON, R.M. : Congressional concurrent resolutions - An aid statutory interpretation? American bar association journal 37 : 421-424, 479-483, June 1951.

NATHANSON, N.L. : Central issues of American administrative law. American political science review 45 : 348-385, June 1951.

TEN BROEK, J. : Thirteenth amendment to the constitution of the United States. California law review 39 : 171-203, June 1951.
Personal freedom.

LANDGROD, G. : Aperçu sur la situation légale des Indiens aux Etats-Unis d'Amérique - Enseignement à tirer d'une évolution sociale et juridique. Revue générale de droit international public : 343-416, juillet-septembre 1951.

The Supreme court, 1950 term. Harvard law review 65 : 107-183, November 1951.
Introduction by L.L. Jaffe.

DONNELLY, R.C. : Judicial control of informants, spies, stool pigeons, and agents provocateurs. Yale law journal 60 : 1091-1131, November 1951.

BERNARD, B.C. : Avoidance of constitutional issues in the United States Supreme court; liberties of the first amendment. Michigan law review 50 : 261-296, December 1951.

1951 survey of New York law. New York university law review 26 : 745-1069, December 1951.
Series of articles.

NATIONAL LAW - COUNTRIES

TUNC, A. : La technique législative du projet de code de commerce des Etats-Unis. Recueil Dalloz, Chronique : 9-12, 17 janvier 1952.

STURGES, W.A. : The need for modern arbitration laws. Arbitration journal 7 : 130-133, No. 3, 1952.

CRIMI, C.F. : Proposed legislation affecting the Supreme Court. Georgetown law journal 40 : 442-451, March 1952.

FELLMAN, D. : Constitutional law in 1950-1951. American political science review 46 : 158-199, March 1952.

BEUTEL, F.K. : The proposed uniform(?) commercial code should not be adopted. Yale law journal 61 : 334-363, March 1952.
See also pp. 364-379

GANDON, A. : La législation "anti-trust" aux Etats-Unis. Revue d'économie politique 62 : 217-228, mars-avril 1952.

NADELMANN, K.H. : Des conflits de lois aux Etats-Unis d'Amérique en matière de successions insolvables. Revue critique de droit international privé 41 : 201-220, avril-juin 1952.

TUNC, A. : Les tendances récentes de la Cour suprême des Etats-Unis en matière de libertés publiques. Revue du droit public et de la science politique en France et à l'étranger 68 : 421-442, avril-juin 1952.

WECHLER, H. : The challenge of a model penal code. Harvard law review 65 : 1097-1133, May 1952.

ROGERS, F.D. : Similarities and differences in letter and spirit between the constitutions of the United States and Argentina. Georgetown law journal 40 : 582-607, May 1952.

SURRENCY, E.C. : Preliminary drafts of the restatements (Contd.). Law library journal 45 : 96-111, May 1952.

GOODMAN, L.E. : Should California adopt federal civil procedure? California law review 40 : 184-191, June 1952.

FRANK, J.P. : The United States Supreme court, 1951-52. University of Chicago law review 20 : 1-68, autumn 1952.

O'BRIAN, J.L. : New encroachments on individual freedom. Harvard law review 66 : 1-27, November 1952.

FREUND, P.A. : The Supreme court, 1951 term. Harvard law review 66 : 89-184, November 1952.

FRANK, J.P. : The United States supreme court, 1950-51. University of Chicago law review 19 : 165-236, winter 1952.

KAUPER, P.G. : The steel seizure case - Congress, the President and the Supreme court. Michigan law review 51 : 141-182, December 1952.

1952 survey of New York law. New York university law review 27 : 895-1253, December 1952.

MULLALLY, M. : Military justice - The uniform code in action. Columbia law review 53 : 1-27, January 1953.

Constitution of the Commonwealth of Puerto Rico. Annals of the American academy of political and social science : 153-166, January 1953.
Text.

MERIKOSI, V. : A European view of legal education in the United States. Journal of legal education 6 : 209-213, no. 2, 1953.

FELLMANN, D. : Constitutional law in 1951 - 1952. American political science review 47 : 126-170, March 1953.

1952 annual survey of American law section. New York university law review 28 : 451-740, 771-875, March, April 1953.
Series of articles.

SCHWARTZ, B. : A decade of administrative law, 1942-1951. Michigan law review 51 : 775-862, April 1953.

BONASSIES, P. : Strudture fédérale et conflits internes de lois - L'exemple des Etats-Unis d'Amérique. Revue critique de droit international privé 42 : 289-316, avril-juin 1953.

NADELMANN, K.H. : Une révision, aux Etats-Unis d'Amérique, des règles de conflit de lois dans la loi sur la faillite. Bulletin de législation et de jurisprudence égyptiennes 4 : 121-127, no. 5, 1953.

MURRAY, J.M. : The privilege against self-incrimination versus immunity - Proposed statutes. Georgetown law journal 41 : 511-524, May 1953.

MALONE, R.L. : The Department of justice - The world's largest law office. American bar association journal 30 : 381-384, May 1953.

Judicial administration and the common man. Annals of the American academy of political and social science : 1-243, May 1953.
Series of articles.

Proposed revisions in the Illinois criminal code. North-western university law review 48 : 198-263, May-June 1953.

FRANTZ, L.B., and REDLICH, N. : Does silence mean guilt? Nation 176 : 471-477, 6 June 1953.
5th amendment to Constitution.

HART, H.M. : The power of Congress to limit the jurisdiction of federal courts - An exercise in dialectic. Harvard law review 66 : 1362-1402, June 1953.

BROEK, J. Ten : Wartime power of the military over citizen civilians within the country. California law review 41 : 167-208, summer 1953.

The use and meaning of the Fifth amendment. University of Chicago round table : 1-12, no. 802, 23 August 1953.
Protection against self-incrimination; See also pp. 13-21.

TELLER, J.S. : The legal maze created by forgeries of checks. Banking law journal 70 : 421-443, August 1953.

GOSSETT, W.T. : Human rights and the American bar. American scholar 22 : 411-422, autumn 1953.

NATIONAL LAW - COUNTRIES

The Supreme court, 1952 term. Harvard law review 67 : 91-179, November 1953.

ZORTHIAN, B. : The "two jurisdictions" doctrine as related to the self-incrimination privilege in New York State. Intramural law review 9 : 34-54, November 1953.

1953 survey of New York law. New York university law review 28 : 1351-1618, December 1953.
Special issue.

MAYERS, L. : Ex parte divorce - A proposed federal remedy. Columbia law review 54 : 54-69, January 1954.

WALKER, D. : An evaluation of the United States Court of military appeals. Northwestern university law review 48 : 714-733, January-February 1954.

Committee report - Report on the proposed uniform commercial code. Record of the Association of the Bar of the City of New York 9 : 67-71, February 1954.

PERSIG, M.E. : Toward a Uniform arbitration act. Arbitration journal 9 : 115-119, no. 3, 1954.

RUPRECHT, I. : Das Recht des Warenkaufs im amerikanischen Uniform Commercial Code. Zeitschrift für ausländisches und internationales Privatrecht 19 : 427-462, Heft 3, 1954.

1953 annual survey of American law (Contd.) - Commercial law, torts and family law. New York university law review 29 : 541-731, March 1954.

MEHREN, A. von : The legal session of the Salzburg seminar. Harvard law review 67 : 829-834, March 1954.
European lawyers and American law.

HORACK, F.E. : Congressional investigations - A plan for legislative review. American bar association journal 40 : 191-194, March 1954.

HUARD, L.A. : The fifth amendment - An evaluation. Georgetown law journal 42 : 345-377, March 1954.

CARTER, J.W. : The fifth amendment - "A barrier interposed between the individual and the power of the government". Vital speeches of the day 20 : 366-369, 1 April 1954.

BROWN, R.S. : Lawyers and the Fifth Amendment - A dissent. American bar association journal 40 : 404-407, May 1954.

McWHINNEY, E. : An end to racial discrimination in the United States? - The school-segregation decisions. Canadian bar review 32 : 545-566, May 1954.

BOUDIN, L.B. : The immunity bill. Georgetown law journal 42 : 497-528, May 1954.
The fifth amendment.

SCHUBERT, G.A. : Politics and the constitution - The Bricker amendment during 1953. Journal of politics 16 : 257-298, May 1954.

FARRELL, J.E. : The trial of Alger Hiss (Contd.). New Zealand law journal 30 : 194-197, 22 June 1954.

MASLOW, W. : Fair procedure in congressional investigations - A proposed code. Columbia law review 54 : 839-892, June 1954.

GRISWOLD, E.N. : The fifth amendment - An old and good friend. American bar association journal 40 : 502-505, 533-536, June 1954.

COLEMAN, S.C. : L'organisation judiciaire des Etats-Unis d'Amérique et plus particulièrement la juridiction de la Cour suprême des Etats-Unis d'Amérique. Revue internationale de droit comparé 6 : 477-490, juillet-septembre 1954.

GRISWOLD, E.N. : The Fifth amendment - The privilege against self-incrimination. Australian quarterly 26 : 25-42, September 1954.

WIENER, F.B. : The Supreme court's new rules. Harvard law review 68 : 20-94, November 1954.

SACKS, A.M. : The Supreme court, 1953 term. Harvard law review 68 : 96-103, November 1954.
See also pp. 104-193.

Governmental tort liability symposium. New York university law review 29 : 1321-1415, November 1954.
Series of articles.

1954 survey of New York law. New York university law review 29 : 1511-1763, December 1954.
Series of articles.

Estados Unidos de Norteamerica - Código uniforme de justicia militar. Información jurídica (Spain) : 1007-1050, diciembre 1954.

KLEPS, R.N. : The revision and codification of California statutes 1849-1953. California law review 42 : 766-802, December 1954.

U.S.A.
(International law, Aliens, Nationality)

WARD, W., and ROSENTHAL, M.S. : The need for the uniform commercial code in foreign trade. Harvard law review 63 : 589-592, February 1950.

HAUSSMANN, W.R. : Die Staatshaftung der Vereinigten Staaten von Amerika für Besatzungsschäden. Deutsche Rechts-Zeitschrift 5 : 121-126, 20. März 1950.

Foreign corporations - State boundaries for national business. Yale law journal 59 : 737-758, March 1950.

RIX, C.B. : Genocide convention and the U.S. constitution. Vital speeches of the day 16 : 369-372, 1 April 1950.

WEISS, T. : A flight on the fantasy of estoppel in foreign divorce. Columbia law review 50 : 409-432, April 1950.

Revocation of citizenship and the void ab initio concept. Columbia law review 50 : 674-686, May 1950.

REESE, W.L.M. : The status in this country of judgment rendered abroad. Columbia law review 50 : 783-800, June 1950.

HUDSON, M.O. : Charter provisions on human rights in American law. American journal of international law 44 : 543-548, July 1950.

NATIONAL LAW - COUNTRIES

REIFF, H. : The proclaiming of treaties in the United States. American journal of international law 44 : 572-576, July 1950.

PINTO, R. : La constitutionnalité des dispositions de fond des traités devant la Cour suprême des Etats -Unis. Technique et les principes du droit public; Etudes en l'honneur de Georges Scelle 1 : 439-457, 1950.

BRINTON, J. : Point IV, the law and its background. Egypte contemporaine 42 : 6-12, janvier 1951.

WILSON, R.R. : Property-protection provisions in United States commercial treaties. American journal of international law 45 : 83-107, January 1951.

Habeas corpus protection against illegal extra-territorial detention. Columbia law review 51 : 368-378, March 1951.

ROCHE, J.P. : Loss of American nationality - The years of confusion. Western political quarterly 4 : 268-294, June 1951.

Universal military training and service act defines responsibilities of aliens - Extends Lodge act. Interpreter releases 28 : 196-198, 3 July 1951.

DEUTSCH, E.P. : The treaty-making clause - A decision for the people of America. American bar association journal 37 : 659-662, 712, September 1951.

WILSON, R.R. : The international law standard in statutes of the United States. American journalf international law 45 : 732-740, October 1951.

State regulation of nonresident alien inheritance - An anomaly in foreign policy. University of Chicago law review 18 : 329-337, winter 1951.

MARTIN, C.E. : Presidential discretion in world affairs through executive agreements. American society of international law, Proceedings 45 : 10-20, 1951.

HAZARD, H.B. : Administrative naturalization abroad of members of the armed forces of the United States. American journal of international law 46 : 259-271, April 1952.

FINCH, G.A. : The treaty-clause amendment, the case for the association. American bar association journal 38 : 467-470, 527-530, June 1952.

SUTHERLAND, A.E. : Restricting the treaty power. Harvard law review 65 : 1305-1338, June 1952.

DEUTSCH, E.P. : The need for a treaty amendment - A restatement and a reply. American bar association 38 : 735-742, September 1952.
See also pp. 731-734.

DOMKE, M. : Zur Ausschlage von Rechten Deutscher an amerikanischen Nachlässen. Juristenzeitung 7 : 741-744, 20. Dezember 1952.

WILSON, R.R. : Access-to-courts provisions in United States commercial treaties. American journal of international law 47 : 20-48, January 1953.

BISHOP, W.W. : New United States policy limiting sovereign immunity. American journal of internatio-nal law 47 : 93-106, January 1953.

HOFFMANN, S. : Système fédéral et accords internationaux. Revue du droit public et de la science politique en France et à l'étranger 69 : 121-156, janvier-mars 1953.

La loi d'immigration américaine. Perspectives 9 : IV/1-9, 21 février 1953.

Developments in the law - Immigration and nationality. Harvard law review 66 : 643-745, February 1953.

HECKMAN, J.H. : Our immigration laws, a continuing affront to the administrative procedure act. Georgetown law journal 41 : 364-393, March 1953.

HAMBRO, L.H. : Constitutional law - Denaturalisation under the Immigration and nationality act of 1952. Michigan law review 51 : 881-902, April 1953.

GORDON, E.L. : Loss of citizenship by continuous residence abroad. Columbia law review 53 : 451-475, April 1953.

FENWICK, C.G. : Proposed limitations upon executive agreements. American journal of international law 47 : 284-287, April 1953.

SCHWARTZ, B. : Civil liberties and the "cold war" in the United States. Canadian bar review 31 : 392-427, April 1953.

HOFFMANN, S. : Accords internationaux et séparation des pouvoirs. Revue du droit public et de la science politique en France et à l'étranger 69 : 374-414, avril-juin 1953.

AUERBACH, F.L. : The visa function under the Immigration and nationality act. Department of State bulletin 28 : 642-646, 4 May 1953.

GARRETT, G. : Nullification by treaty. Freeman 3 : 549-550, 4 May 1953.

PARKER, J.J. : The American constitution and world order based on law. Record of the Association of the Bar of the City of New York 8 : 267-285, June 1953.

YOUNG, W.H. : The Passport office views the new Immigration and nationality act. I and N reporter 2 : 5-7, July 1953.

HOFFMANN, S. : Etats-Unis - Accords internationaux et prohibitions constitutionnelles. Revue du droit public et de la science politique en France et à l'étranger 69 : 649-679, juillet-septembre 1953.

HOLMAN, F.E. : American rights vs. "Treaty law". Freeman 3 : 803-805, 10 August 1953.

PEARSON, T., and BACKUS, D.C. : Save the peace power, don't strait-jacket treaties. American bar association journal 39 : 804-808, September 1953.

WILSON, R.R. : The international law standard in recent statutes of the United States. American journal of international law 47 : 669-678, October 1953.

RODE, Z.R. : The International claims commission of the United States, 28 August 1950 - 30 June 1953. American journal of international law 47 : 615-637, October 1953.

NATIONAL LAW - COUNTRIES

HOUCK, J. : Neutral aliens who sought relief from military service barred from becoming United States citizens. Michigan law review 52 : 265-276, December 1953.

MARCY, C. : A note on treaty ratification. American political science review 47 : 1130-1133, December 1953.

EVANS, A.E. : Self-executing treaties in the United States of America. British year book of international law 30 : 178-205, 1953.

DANIEL, P. : The Congress and international law - The treaty-making power and continental shelf. American society of international law, Proceedings 47 : 171-180, 1953.
See also pp. 21-37.

WHITTON, J.B., and FOWLER, J.E. : Bricker amendment - Fallacies and dangers. American journal journal of international law 48 : 23-56, January 1954.

ALAGIA, D.P. : A case for the Bricker amendment. Georgetown law journal 42 : 262-289, January 1954.

FINCH, G.A. : The need to restrain the treaty-making power of the United States within constitutional limits. American journal of international law 48 : 57-82, January 1954.

HOFFMAN, P.G. : The United Nations and the Bricker amendment. World affairs interpreter 24 : 348-356, winter 1954.

The Bricker amendment. University of Chicago round table : 1-15, no. 826, 7 February 1954.

LENHOFF, A. : Die Anerkennung und Vollstreckung ausländischer Urteile in den USA. Zeitschrift für ausländisches und internationales Privatrecht 19 : 201-241, Heft 2, 1954.

NADELMANN, K.H. : The United States of America and agreements on reciprocal enforcement of foreign judgments. Nederlands tijdschrift voor internationaal recht : 156-172, Februari 1954.

PARRY, C. : A conflicts myth, the American "consular" marriage. Harvard law review 67 : 1187-1212, May 1954.

ROYALL, K.C. : American freedom and the law - Fighting the communist menace. American bar association journal 40 : 559-562, July 1954.

WHITTON, J.B. : Etats-Unis - L'amendment Bricker. Revue du droit public et de la science politique en France et à l'étranger 70 : 714-721, juillet-septembre 1954.

FAIRMAN, C. : Extradition to a country under control of the United States. American journal of international law 48 : 612-616, October 1954.

ZIMMERMAN, G. : Judicial versus administrative determination of controverted claims to United States citizenship. Georgetown law journal 43 : 19-51, November 1954.

McCAULEY, W.B. : American courts in Germany - 600,000 cases later. American bar association journal 40 : 1041-1045, 1101-1103, December 1954.

URUGUAY

CARBALLA, J.B. : Die strafrechtliche Entwicklung in Uruguay. Zeitschrift für die gesamte Strafrechtswissenschaft 64 : 123-126, Heft 1, 1952.

OLLERO, C. : Uruguay - La reforma constitucional de 16 de diciembre de 1951, el ejecutivo "Colegiado". Revista de estudios políticos 42 : 139-155, marzo-abril 1952.

GALINDEZ, J. de : Poder ejecutivo colegiado en el Uruguay. Revista de la Facultad de derecho de México 2 : 141-147, abril-junio 1952.

COUTURE, E.J. : La constitution uruguayenne de 1952. Cahiers de législation et de bibliographie juridique de l'Amérique Latine 3 : 5-50, juillet-décembre 1952.
Texte pp. 51-118.

VAZ FERREIRA, E. : Uruguay. Annuaire de législation étrangère 3 : 465-470, 1952-54.

KRASKE, E. : Das kollegiale Staatshaupt in der Verfassung der Republik Uruguay vom 26. Oktober 1951. Zeitschrift für ausländisches öffentliches Recht und Völkerrecht 15 : 259-264, Nr. 1-2, Oktober 1953.

VAZ FERREIRA, E., et ZATJAY, I. : La légitimation adoptive en France et en Uruguay. Revue internationale de droit comparé 6 : 51-65, janvier-mars 1954.

VATICAN STATE

HEYDTE, F.A. v.d. : Die Stellung und Funktion des Heiligen Stuhls im heutigen Völkerrecht. Österreichische Zeitschrift für öffentliches Recht 2 : 572-586, Heft 5, 1950.

CIPROTTI, P. : Cité du Vatican, 1939 à 1950. Revue de droit international et de droit comparé 28 : 195-199, nos. 3-4, 1951.

VENEZUELA

RAISBECK, J.W. : Mining legislation of Venezuela. Tulane law review 25 : 345-352, April 1951.

De SOLA, R. : Les fonds de commerce en droit vénézuélien. Cahiers de législation et de bibliographie juridique de l'Amérique Latine 3 : 57-59, janvier-mars 1952.

Ley orgánica de la Corte federal y de casación. Revista de derecho y legislación 41 : 55-73, febrero-abril 1952.

Venezuela - Estatuto orgánico del Poder judicial. Información jurídica : 396-411, abril 1952.

CUENCA, H. : Aspectos fundamentales del proceso civil venezolano. Revista de la Facultad de derecho de México 2 : 97-111, octubre-diciembre 1952.

Un caso de negativa de extradición. Revista de derecho y legislación 42 : 49-72, enero-febrero 1953.

GOLDSCHMIDT, R. : Reforma de la legislación comercial venezolana. Revista del Ministerio de justicia (Caracas) 1 : 31-41, enero-marzo 1953.

Constitución de la República de Venezuela. Revista de derecho y legislación, Colección de leyes y reglamentos vigentes 42 : 3-46, marzo-abril 1953.
15 abril 1953.

RENGEL ROMBERG, A. : La justicia civil venezolana. Revista del Ministerio de justicia (Venezuela) 2 : 33-56, abril-junio 1953.

SIDJANSKI, D., et CASTANOS, S. : Aperçu de la nouvelle constitution vénézuélienne. Revue internationale de droit comparé 6 : 311-314, avril-juin 1954.
Avril 1953.

Venezuela - Código civil. Información jurídica : 658-675, julio-agosto 1954.
16 julio 1943.

GOLDSCHMIDT, R. : Problemas de la reforma del derecho mercantil venezolano. Revista del Instituto de derecho comparado : 25-44, julio-diciembre 1954.

SIDJANSKI, D. : La constitution vénézuélienne de 1953 face à la constitution française de 1946. Cahiers de législation et de bibliographie juridique de l'Amérique latine 5 : 19-33, no. 19-20, juillet-décembre 1954.

VIET-NAM

PHUONG, H.V. : La négociation et la signature des accords commerciaux par le Viet-Nam. Revue politique et juridique de l'Union Française 7 : 492-499, octobre-décembre 1953.

POMPËÏ, P. : Etude préliminaire au projet de code civil vietnamien. Revue juridique et politique de l'Union Française 8 : 347-359, juillet-septembre 1954.

YUGOSLAVIA

DORDEVIĆ, J. : Prilog pitanju sistema sotsijalistichkog prava FHRJ. Arkhiv za pravne i drushtvene nauke 37 : 7-64, januar-mart 1950.
Socialist legislation.

KIDRIČ, B. : Govor o reorganizatsiji drzhavne uprave u FNRJ. Arkhiv za pravne i druchtvene nauke 37 : 202-207, april-juni 1950.
Reorganisation of administration.

Reorganizacija državne uprave u Federativnoj Narodnoj Republici Jugoslaviji. Arkhiv za pravne i drushtvene nauke 37 : 403-414, juli-september 1950.
Reorganisation of administration.

KALEMBER, V. : Organisation de la justice dans la République populaire fédérative de Yougoslavie. Nouveau droit yougoslave 1 : 11-18, octobre-décembre 1950.

KANGRA, M. : Les unités autonomes en Yougoslavie. Nouveau droit yougoslave 1 : 29-33, octobre-décembre 1950.

KARDELJ, E. : Les caractéristiques de la nouvelle loi sur les Comités populaires. Nouveau droit yougoslave 1 : 1-10, octobre-décembre 1950.
Texte pp. 34-40.

Loi sur la nationalité du 1er juillet 1946. Textes législatifs étrangers : 76-90, no. 1, 1951.

Les lois relatives à la tutelle et à l'adoption. Nouveau droit yougoslave 2 : 17-22, janvier-mars 1951.
Résumé pp. 31-41.

Loi fondamentale sur le mariage. Nouveau droit yougoslave 2 : 5-16, janvier-mars 1951.
Résumé pp. 23-27, 41-45.

GIVANOVITCH, T. : Quelques considérations sur le droit criminel en Yougoslavie et sur l'influence de l'Union internationale de droit pénal. Revue internationale de droit pénal 22 : 201-208, nos.2-3, 1951.

Le nouveau code pénal de Yougoslavie. Revue internationale de droit pénal 22 : 639-645, 4e trimestre 1951.

FROL, F. : Exposé des motifs du projet de code pénal. Nouveau droit yougoslave 2 : 4-29, avril-septembre 1951.
Texte pp. 45-125.

VUKOVIĆ, M. : Gradanskopravna rasmatranja povodom zakona o upravljanju državnim privredim poduzećima. Arkhiv za pravne i drushtvene nauke 37 : 386-404, juli-septembar 1951.

TCHIRKOVITCH, S. : Le code de la famille en Yougoslavie. Revue internationale de droit comparé 3 : 616-628, octobre-décembre 1951.

El nuevo código penal yugoslavo. Anuario de derecho penal y ciencias penales 5 : 61-64, enero-abril 1952.

EISNER, B. : Das Privatrecht Jugoslawiens 1945-1951. Zeitschrift für ausländisches und internationales Privatrecht 17 : 244-259, Heft 2, 1952.

MUNDA, A. : Jugoslawien. Zeitschrift für die gesamte Strafrechtswissenschaft 64 : 379-392, Heft 3, 1952.
1940-1950.

CARTON de WIART, X. : Le nouveau code pénal yougoslave. Revue de droit pénal et de criminologie 32 : 619-622, mars 1952.

DONNELLY, R.C. : The new Yugoslav criminal code. Yale law journal 61 : 510-539, April 1952.

TCHIRKOVITCH, S. : Les dispositions du droit international privé du code de la famille yougoslave. Revue critique de droit international privé 41 : 221-239, avril-juin 1952.

BAKATSOULAS, M. : O neos Giougkoslauïkos poinikos kodix. Sophronistikē epitheorēsis 5 : 106-113, Iounios-Augoustos 1952.
Le nouveau code pénal yougoslave.

ANDRASSY, J. : Völkerrechtliche Elemente im jugoslawischen Strafrecht. Zeitschrift für ausländisches öffentliches Recht und Völkerrecht 14 : 549-560, Juli 1952.

The structure of the Federal People's Republic of Yugoslavia. New Yugoslav law 3 : 52-64, July-December 1952.
With charts.

The preparation of new laws in Yugoslavia. New Yugoslav law 2 : 49-62, October-December 1952.

NATIONAL LAW - COUNTRIES

STAJIČ, A. : Nacela legaliteta i individualizacije kazne u krivicnom pravu FNRJ. Arhiv za pravne i društvene nauke 39 : 433-451, oktobar-decembar 1952.
Criminal law.

MINIĆ, M. : The constitutional law of the People's Republic of Serbia. New Yugoslav law 4 : 4-17, January-June 1953.
Text pp. 36-67.

La loi constitutionnelle sur les fondements de l' organisation sociale et politique de la République Fédérative Populaire de Yougoslavie et sur les organes fédéraux du pouvoir. Questions actuelles du socialisme : 74-122, janvier-février 1953.

BARTOŠ, M. : La représentation internationale de la Yougoslavie selon la nouvelle loi constitutionnelle. Revue de la politique mondiale 4 : 9-10, ler février 1953.

La nouvelle loi constitutionnelle de la République fédérative populaire de Yougoslavie, 13 janvier 1953. Documentation française, Notes et études documentaires : 1-28, no. 1726, 16 avril 1953.

BAUER, E. : Die neue und die alte Staatsverfassung Jugoslawiens. Berichte und Informationen des Österreichischen Forschungsinstituts für Wirtschaft und Politik 8 : 439-441, 5. Juni 1953.

CRNOGORČEVIĆ, J. : O potrebi noveliranja Krivčnog zakonika. Naša zakonitost 7 : 321-340, broj 6-7, 1953.
Criminal law.

Von der Volksdemokratie zur sozialistischen Demokratie - Zwei Beiträge zum neuen Verfassungsgesetz Jugoslawiens. Europa-Archiv 8 : 5843-5851, 20. Juli-5. August 1953.

PIJADE, M. : Sur le code de procédure pénale et l'activité des organes judiciaires. Nourveau droit yougoslave 4 : 3-25, juillet-décembre 1953.
Textes en annexe.

ĐORĐEVIĆ, J. : Quelques principes fondamentaux de la nouvelle loi électorale yougoslave. Revue de la politique mondiale 4 : 12-13, 16 septembre 1953.

DJORDJEVIĆ, J. : Le nouveau code de procédure criminelle yougoslave yougoslave. Revue de la politique mondiale 4 : 21-22, ler octobre 1953.

VASSALLI, G. : Il nuovo codice penale jugoslavo. Annuario di diritto comparato e di studi legislativi 29 : 1-48, 1953.
English summary pp. 49-50.

MARCIC, R. : Die neue jugoslawische Verfassungsordnung. Juristische Blätter 76 : 37-41, 16. Januar 1954.

STYÉPANOVITCH, N. : Les réformes constitutionnelles et administratives en Yougoslavie, 1950-1953. Revue internationale des sciences administratives 20 : 119-142, no. 1, 1954.

ZLATARIĆ, B. : Neki problemi prethodnog postupka u novom Zakoniku o krivičnom postupku. Naša zakonitost 8 : 9-20, broj 1, 1954.
Criminal law.

ČULINOVIĆ, F. : Porota u Jugoslaviji. Zbornik Pravnog fakulteta u Zagrebu 4 : 40-58, broj 1-2, 1954.
Jury ; Summary in French.

BAYER, V. : Akuzatorni i inkvizitorni elementi u našem novom krivičnom postupku. Zbornik Pravnog fakulteta u Zagrebu 4 : 20-39, broj 1-2, 1954.
Criminal procedure; Summary in French.

DURAND, C. : Yougoslavie - La réforme de la constitution de la République fédérative populaire de Yougoslavie, 13 janvier 1953, et le droit constitutionnel de la doctrine marxiste-léniniste. Revue du droit public et de la science politique en France et à l'étranger 60 : 86-122, janvier-mars 1954.
Textes en annexe.

BLAGOJEVIC, B.T. : La nationalité d'origine en Yougoslavie. Revue critique de droit international privé 43 : 29-37, janvier-mars 1954.

Law on the rights and duties, election and recall of the Federal People's deputies. New Yugoslav law 5 : 51-83, January-June 1954.
Text.

Law on the legal status of religious communities - General provisions. New Yugoslav law 5 : 84-87, January-June 1954.

Code of criminal procedure (Contd.). New Yugoslav law 5 : 27-50, January-June 1954.

EISNER, B. : Die Zivilrechtsprechung der ordentlichen Gerichte Jugoslawiens 1945-53. Zeitschrift fr ausländisches und internationales Privatrecht 19 : 296-321, Heft 2, 1954.

MUNDA, A. : Das neue jugoslawische Strafprozessgesetzbuch vom 10. September 1953. Zeitschrift für die gesamte Strafrechtswissenschaft 66 : 321-337, Heft 2, 1954.

JAKSIĆ, S. : O ustanovi renvoi u jugoslovenskom medunarodnom privatnom pravu. Jugoslovenska revija za medunarodno pravo 1 : 59-68, broj 3, 1954.
Summary in French.

STJEPANOVIC, N. : L'organisation et le fonctionnement du Conseil exécutif fédéral en Yougoslavie. Revue internationale des sciences administratives 20 : 674-697, no. 3, 1954.

STJEPANOVIC, N., et KOVAC, P. : L'administration fédérale en Yougoslavie. Revue internationale des sciences administratioves 20 : 907-916, no. 4, 1954.

STOYANOVITCH, K. : Quelques aspects du droit civil yougoslave. Revue internationale de droit comparé 6 : 272-290, avril-juin 1954.

BRNČIĆ, J. : Metod rada sudova. Naša zakonitost 8 : 241-250, broj 5, 1954.
Courts in Croatia.

VRAŽALIĆ, M. : Prejudicijelna pitanja u krivičnom postupku. Naša zakonitost 8 : 305-316, broj 6-7, 1954.
Criminal procedure.

HOLLEAUX, A. : L'organisation du contentieux administratif en Yougoslavie. Conseil d'Etat, Etudes et documents (Paris) : 227-233, no. 8, 1954.

SRZENTIĆ, N. : The organization of the juridicature in Yugoslavia. New Yugoslav law 5 : 24-32, December 1954.

EUROPE
(European Communites, EFTA)

MONACO, R. : La struttura giridica della Comunità europea del carbone e dell' acciaio. Annali di diritto internazionale 8 : 45-66, 1950.

ESSEN, J.L.F. van : Het Gerechtshof van de Europese kolen- en staal-gemeenschap. Economisch-statistische berichten 36 : 641-645, 29 Augustus 1951.

BAYER, W.F. : Das Privatrecht der Montanunion. Zeitschrift für ausländisches und internationales Privatrecht 17 : 325-381, Heft 3, 1952.

SCHLOCHAUER, H.J. : Die Gerichtsbarkeit der Europäischen Gemeinschaft für Kohle und Stahl. Archiv des Völkerrechts 3 : 385-414, 4. Heft 1952.

DURIEUX, J. : Les recours des entreprises devant la Cour de justice du plan Schuman. Industrie 6 : 511-516, août 1952.

VIGNES, D. : I ricorsi giuridizionali delle imprese private contro le decision dell'Alta autorità del piano Schuman. Rivista di studi politici internazionali 19 : 657-670, ottobre-dicembre 1952.

DURANTE, F. : La Corte di giustizia della Comunità europea del carbone e dell'acciaio. Rivista di diritto internazionale 36 : 143-153, fasc. 1-2, 1953.

REUTER, P. : Le droit de la Communauté européenne du carbon et de l'acier. Journal du droit international 80 : 4-23, janvier-mars 1953.

ANTOINE, A. : La Cour de justice de la C.E.C.A. et la Cour internationale de justice. Revue générale de droit international public 57 : 210-261, avril-juin 1953.

SCHWEIZER, J. : La Cour de justice du Pool charbon-acier. Echo des mines et de la métallurgie : 315-317, mai 1953.

MOTTARD, J., et LAURENT-NEUPREZ, J. : La Cour de justice du pool charbon-acier devra-t-elle statuer sur la constitutionnalité de son règlement de procédure? Industrie 7 : 584-587, septembre 1953.

BEBR, G. : The European coal and steel community - A political and legal innovation. Yale law journal 63 : 1-43, November 1953.

SCHWARZ-LIEBERMANN von WAHLENDORF, H.A. : Die Europäische Gemeinschaft (Contd.) - Der Gerichtshof der Europäischen Gemeinschaft. Archiv des Völkerrechts 4 : 436-450, 4. Heft 1954.

LAGRANGE, M. : La Cour de justice de la Communauté européenne du charbon et de l'acier. Revue du droit public et de la science politique en France et à l'étranger 70 : 417-435, avril-juin 1954.

MATTHIES, H. : Das Recht der Europäischen Gemeinschaft für Kohle und Stahl und die nationalen Gerichte der Mitgliedstaaten. Juristenzeitung 9 : 305-309, 20. Mai 1954.

JEANTET, F.C. : Les intérêts privés devant la Cour de justice de la Communauté européenne du charbon et de l'acier. Revue du droit public et de la science politique en France et à l'étranger 70 : 684-713, juillet-septembre 1954.

ABRAHAM, J.P. : Les entreprises comme sujets de droit dans la Communauté charbon-acier. Cahiers de Bruges - Bruges quarterly 4 : 255-263, octobre 1954.

EUROPE
(European Convention of Human Rights)

MOSER, B. : Die Europäische Konvention zum Schutze der Menschenrechte und Grundfreiheiten. Juristische Blätter 76 : 449-453, 479-482, 2., 16. Oktober 1954.

NATIONAL LAW - COUNTRIES

ALBANIA

VOKOLOLA, K. : Albania - Reorganization of the Bar. Highlights of current legislation and activities in Mid-Europe 3 : 169-172, July 1955.

GODIN, M.A. von. : Das albanische Gewohnheitsrecht (Contd.). Zeitschrift für vergleichende Rechtswissenschaft 58 : 121-166, 2. Heft 1956.
See also pp. 166-198.

Albania. Library of Congress, Quarterly journal of current acquisitions 14 : 208-214, August 1957.
Law library survey.

VOKOPOLA, K. : Sovietization of civil law in Albania, (Contd.). Highlights of current legislation and activities in Mid-Europe 6 : 49-55, February 1958.

KLOSI, B. : Kuvendi popullor aprovoi Kodin e procedures civile të R.P.Sh. Drejtësia popullore (Albania) 11 : 1-7, mars-prill 1958.
Civil procedure code.

TAUSHANI, R. : Zgjedhjet e rcja të gjykatave popullore. Drejtësia popullore (Albania) 11 : 1-8. nr. 4, 1958.
Courts.

PAPAJANI. L. : Mbi prezumimin e pafajesise ne proceduren penale Shqiptare. Universitet shtetëror të Tiranës; Buletin, Seria shkencat shoqërore 13 : 112-133, nr. 1, 1959.
Criminal procedure.

CEVI, K. : Konventat mbi ndihmën juridike burim i së drejtës ndërkombëtare private. Drejtësia popullore (Albania) 12 : 1-6, nr. 4, 1959.
Judicial assistance.

Konferenca e IV-t¨e Shoqatës së juristëve të Shqupërisë. Drejtësia popullore (Albania 12 : 69-78, majqershor 1959.
Conference of jurists.

PANARITI, S. : Karakteri thellësisht demokratik i sistemit tonë gjyqësor dhe roli gjykatave në forcimin e vazhdueshëm të pushtetit popullor dhe të shtetit tonë socialist. Drejtësia popullore (Albania) 12 : 20-26, nr. 5, shtator-tetor,1959.
Judicial system.

ELEZI, I. : 15 vjet të së drëjtes penale dhe procéduriale penale në R.P.Sh. Drejtësia popullore (Albania) 12 : 42-50, nr. 5, shtator-tetor 1959.
Criminal law.

MEKSI, V. : Për një terminollogji më të saktë juridike shqipe. Drejtësia popullore (Albania) 12 : 52-60, no. 6, nendor-dhjetor 1959.
Legal terminology.

ALGERIA

CANAC, A. : L'évolution de l'organisation judiciaire en Algérie depuis 1830. Revue algérienne, tunisienne et marocaine de législation et de jurisprudence, Doctrine 72 : 191-210, septembre-octobre 1956.

ARABIAN STATES

LIEBESNY, H.J. : Administration and legal development in Arabia - Aden colony and protectorate. Middle East journal 9 : 385-396, autumn 1955.

ARGENTINA

Argentina - Ley orgánica de los ministerios del poder ejecutivo. Información jurídica (Spain) : 142-158, febrero 1955.

LISBONNE, J. : L'inexistence du mariage contracte à l'étranger en violation du droit ergentin. Journal du droit international 82 : 108-116, janvier-mars 1955.
Texte en anglais aussi.

Norme sulla naturalizzazione e la cittadinanza argentina, legge n. 14359 del 15 octobre 1954. Rivista di diritto internazionale 38 : 421-424, fasc. 2-3, 1955.

MIRANDA GONZÁLEZ, J. : La reforma constitucional de Argentina de 1949. Boletín del Instituto de derecho comparado de México 8 : 23-34, septiembre-diciembre 1955.

COLL, J.E. : El delito político y delitos comunes conexos. Revista de la Facultad de derecho y ciencias sociales (Buenos Aires) 10 : 885-894, setiembre-diciembre 1955.

GOLDSCHMIDT, W. : Einführung in das argentinische internationale Privatrecht. Jahrbuch für internationales Recht 7 : 283-314, Heft 2/3, 1956.

PORTE PETIT, C. : Breves consideraciones sobre el proyecto de código penal de 1951 para la República Argentina. Criminalia 22 : 248-261, mayo 1956.

GOLDSCHMIDT, W. : Zum geltenden argentinischen Familienrecht. Ehe und Familie im privaten und öffentlichen Recht 3 : 208-210, Juli/August 1956.

MIRANDA, A.M. : El derecho administrativo en la próxima reforma constitucional. Revista de ciencias económicas (Buenos Aires) 45 : 129-135, abril-junio 1957.

Message du Conseil fédéral à l'Assemblée fédérale concernant l'approbation de l'accord entre la Suisse et l'Argentine au sujet des obligations militaires des doubles nationaux nés en Argentine (du 10 mars 1958), Feuille fédérale (Switzerland) 110 : 565-570, 13 mars 1958.

SANTA PINTER, J.J. : Legislación nacional argentina - Versus tratados internacionales. Revista española de derecho internacional 11 : 587-597, núm. 3, 1958.

RAMELLA, P.A. : Panorama constitucional argentino. Revista de estudios políticos : 277-287, noviembre 1958 - febrero 1959.

Leyes y decretos de interés general nacionales, provinciales y extranjeros publicados en los diarios y boletines oficiales clasificados en la Seccion legislación y documentos parlamentarios, del Servicio de referencia. Boletín de la Biblioteca del Congreso de la nación : 484-709, noviembre-diciembre 1959.
A current index to legislation.

AUSTRALIA

O'CONNELL, D.P. : Sedentary fisheries and the Australian continental shelf. American journal of international law 49 : 185-209, April 1955.

The ninth legal convention of the Law council of Australia. Australian law journal 29 : 189-272, August 19, 1955.
Brisbane, July 1955.

DIXON, O. : Marshall and the Australian constitution. Australian law journal 29 : 420-427, December 15, 1955.

SAWYER, G. : Councils, ministers and cabinets in Australia. Public law : 110-138, spring-summer 1956.

TAMMELO, I. : The tests of inconsistency between Commonwealth and state laws. Australian law journal 30 : 496-501, 22 February 1957.

HART, G.L. : Some aspects of the section 92 of the constitution. Australian law journal 30 : 551-563, 21 March 1957.

The Australian states and Dominion status. Australian law journal 31 : 42-45, 20 June 1957.

VILE, M.J.C. : Judicial review and politics in Australia. American political science review 51 : 386-391, June 1957.

The Tenth legal convention of the Law council of Australia. Australian law journal 31 : 229-344, 29 August 1957.
Melbourne, July 1957.

O'CONNELL, D.P. : Problems of Australian coastal jurisdiction. British year book of international law 34 : 199-259, 1958.

The eleventh legal convention of the Law council of Australia. Australian law journal 33 : 101-192, 27 August 1959.
Series of articles.

AUSTRIA

VEITER, T. : Wegweiser durch die Rechtsquellen für Nichtjuristen. Berichte und Informationen des Österreichischen Forschungsinstituts für Wirtschaft und Politik 10 : 27-28, 14. Jänner 1955.

WERNER, L. : Rechtsfragen aus dem Gebiet des Staatsbürgerschaftsrechtes. Juristische Blätter 77 : 162-166, 2. April 1955.

MATOUSCHEK, A. : Die Amnestie 1955. Österreichische Juristen-Zeitung 10 : 217-222, 22. April 1955.

LINKE, R. : Aktuelle Fragen der Auslieferung nach Österreich. Österreichische Juristen-Zeitung 10 : 243-247, 6. Mai 1955.

MERKL, A. : Das Deutsche Eigentum und vermögensrechtliche Ansprüche Österreichs. Juristische Blätter 10 : 243-247, 14. Mai 1955.

BRAUN, R. : Staatsvertrag und Wiedergutmachung. Juristische Blätter 77 : 302-303, 11. Juni 1955.

ERMACORA, F. : Der Staatsvertrag und die österreichische Bundesverfassung - Eine staatsrechtstheoretische Information. Juristische Blätter 77 : 317-321, 25. Juni 1955.

SCHWIMM, M. : Über die Verluststatbestände des österreichischen Staatsbürgerschaftsrechtes. Österreichische Juristen-Zeitung 10 : 381-391, 29. Juli 1955.

Die Grundsätze für die Regelung aller Fragen des deutschen Eigentums. IW - Internationale Wirtschaft : 1-3, 2. September 1955.

SEIDLER, H. : Probleme des Deutschen Eigentums. Juristische Blätter 77 : 386-388, 3. September 1955.

VEITER, T. : Ein offenes Wort über die Alliierten Militärgerichte. Berichte und Informationen des Österreichischen Forschungsinstitut für Wirtschaft und Politik 10 : 765-768, 7. Oktober 1955.

SEIDL-HOHENVELDERN, I. : Relation of international law to internal law in Austria. American journal of international law 49 : 451-476, October 1955.

GROHS, F. : Privatrechtliche Auswirkungen des Staatsvertrages. Juristische Blätter 77 : 585-589, 10. Dezember 1955.

LINKE, R. : Der neue Vertrag zwischen Österreich und Jugoslawien über den wechselseitigen rechtlichen Verkehr und seine strafrechtlichen Bestimmungen. Österreichische Juristen-Zeitung 10 : 667-670, 16. Dezember 1955.
December 1954.

MOSER, B. : Die Auswirkungen der dauernden Neutralität auf das Straf- und Zivilrecht. Österreichische Juristen-Zeitung 11 : 85-88, 24. Februar 1956.

MAGERSTEIN, W. : Ist Österreich legitimiet, die vermögensrechtlichen Ansprüche der vormals tschechoslowakischen Deutschen, die nach der Konfiskation ihres Vermögens in Österreich eingebürgert wurden, gegenüber der Tschechoslowakei im Rahmen des österreichischen Staatsvertrags geltend zu machen? Juristische Blätter 78 : 224-226, 28. April 1956.

KUNZ, J.L. : Austria's permanent neutrality. American journal of international law 50 : 418-425, April 1956.

ESZLARY, C. d' : L'organisation administrative autrichienne. Revue politique et parlementaire 219 : 285-298, juin 1956.

MOSING, F. : Zustellungen und Beweisaufnahmen in den Vereinigten Staaten für österreichische Verfahren. Österreichische Juristen-Zeitung 11 : 337-344, 13. Juli 1956.

MATSCHER, F. : Anerkennung und Vollstreckung österreichischer Urteile in Frankreich. Juristische Blätter 78 : 459-463, 6. Oktober 1956.

HARRER, K.G. : Zur Entstehung und Problematik des ersten Staatsvertragsdurchführungsgesetzes. Österreichische Juristen-Zeitung 11 : 477-484, 5. Oktober 1956.
See also pp. 489-496.

ZIGEUNER, G. : Zehn Jahre Verfassungsgerichtshof in der Zweiten Republik. Juristische Blätter 78 : 629-633, 29. Dezember 1956.

LIEBSCHER, V. : Österreichs Neutralität und ihr strafrechtlicher Schutz. Juristische Blätter 78 : 597-600, 633-637, 15., 29. Dezember 1956.

MOSER, B. : Die Erweiterung der inländischen Zivilgerichtsbarkeit durch die Konvention über die Rechtsstellung der Flüchtlinge. Österreichische Juristen-Zeitung 12 : 58-62, 8. Februar 1957.

MERKL, A.J. : War Österreich von 1938 bis 1945 Bestandteil des Deutschen Reiches? Archiv des öffentlichen Rechts 82 : 480-490. Heft 4, 1957.
See also pp. 490-492.

LINKE, R. : Einige bedeutsame Fragen des Auslieferungsverfahrens. Österreichische Juristen-Zeitung 12 : 343-346, 5. Juli 1957.

VEITER, T. : Österreichischer Staatsvertrag und Asylrecht. Integration 4 : 40-43, Nr.1, 1957.

MEYER, R. : Die staatsrechtliche Stellung der Österreicherin nach ihrer Eheschliessung mit einem deutschen Staasangehörigen. Österreichische Juristen-Zeitung 12 : 366-368, 26. Juli 1957.

ERMACORA, F. : Über das Wesen des österreichischen Bundesstaats in Theorie und Praxis. Juristische Blätter 79 : 521-525, 26. Oktober 1957.

ERMACORA, F. : Die Entwicklung des österreichischen Verfassungsrechtes seit dem Jahre 1951. Jahrbuch des öffentlichen Rechts der Gegenwart 6 : 319-390, 1957.

SCHEUCHER, L. : Zur Anerkennung einer im Ausland erfolgten Entmundigung eines österreichers. Jurististische Blätter 80 : 112-113, 8. März 1958.

VEITER, T. : Der Nachweis der deutschen Staatsangehörigkeit bei deutschem Eigentum in Österreich. Österreichische Juristen-Zeitung 13 : 168-173, 4. April 1958.

PFEIFER, H. : Volksbegehren und Volksabstimmung im österreichischen Bundesrecht. Juristische Blätter 80 : 161-168, 5. April 1958.

HELIBLING, E.C. : Die Neuerungen in der Verfassungsgerichtsbarkeit. Österreichische Juristen-Zeitung 13 : 281-284, 30. Mai 1958.

SCHWIND, F. : Eherechtliche Probleme des österreichischen Konkordats. Ehe und Familie im privaten und öffentlichen Recht 5 : 263-266, Juli 1958.

BAECK, P.L. : Gedanken über das österreichische Eherecht und seine Reform. Österreichische Juristen-Zeitung 13 : 453-458, 5. September 1958.

JANOWSKY, N. : Auswirkungen der Europäischen Konvention zum Schutze der Menschen rechte und Grund freiheiten auf das österreichische Recht. Juristische Blätter 81 : 145-148, 21. März 1959.

VEITER, T. : Südtiroler Umsidler im öffentlichen Dienst. Berichte und Informationen des Österreichischen Forschungsinstituts für Wirtschaft und Politik 14 : 9-11, 8. Mai 1959.

LIEBSCHER, V. : Die Grundzüge eines Völkerstrafrechts in der österreichischen Rechtsordnung. Juristische Blätter 81 : 385-396, 29. August 1959.

ERMACORA, F. : Die Menschenrechtskonvention als Bestandteil der östereichischen Rechtsordnung. Juristische Blätter 81 : 396-405, 29. August 1959.

ERMACORA, F. : Die österreichische Verfassungsgerichtsbarkeit seit 1945. Jahrbuch des öffentlichen Rechts der Gegenwart 8 : 49-99, 1959.

BELGIUM

Conventions d'extradition conclues par la Belgique avec les pays étrangers. Bulletin de droit des gens 4 : 1-128, no. 1, 1955.
Textes.

GOOSSENS, C. : La Communauté européenne du charbon et de l'acier et le régime constitutionnel de la Belgique. Revue du droit public et de la science politique en France et à l'étranger 71 : 98-115, janvier-mars 1955.

RENARD, C., et GRAULICH, P. : Chronique de droit belge. Revue trimestrielle de droit civil 53 : 197-210, janvier-mars 1955.

Union Belge et luxembourgeoise de droit pénal. Revue de droit pénal et de criminologie 35 : 531-541, mars 1955.

SOHIER, A. : L'extension de la compétence de la Cour de cassation aux affaires pénales coloniales. Revue de droit pénal et de criminologie 35 : 579-588, avril 1955.

RENARD, C., et GRAULICH, P. : Chronique de droit belge. Revue trimestrielle de droit civil 54 : 213-227, janvier-mars 1956.

Union belge et luxembourgeoise de droit pénal, séance du 18 février 1956. Revue de droit pénal et de criminologie 36 : 736-750, avril 1956.

DIEVOET, E. van : Aspects techniques et pratiques de la revision du code civil en Belgique. Revue internationale de droit comparé 8 : 363-370, juillet-septembre 1956.

RENARD, C., et GRAULICH, P. : Chronique de droit belge. Revue trimestrielle de droit civil 56 : 202-219, janvier-mars 1957.

Conventione d'extradition conclues par la Belgique avec les pays étrangers (Suite). Bulletin de droit des gens 7 : 577-711, no. 1, 1958.
Textes en français.

RENARD, C. : La réforme du statut de la femme mariée en Belgique. Revue internationale de droit comparé 10 : 56-64, janvier-mars 1958.

Ve congrès international de droit comparé de l'Académie internationale de droit comparé..., Bruxelles, 419 août 1958 - Rapports des juristes belges. Revue de droit international et de droit comparé 35 : 1-536, nos. 2-3, 1958.

LIEVENS, R. : The Conseil d'Etat in Belgium. American journal of comparative law 7 : 572-588, autumn 1958.

JORION, E. : Le statut juridique de l'Exposition universelle et internationale de Bruxelles en 1958. Revue internationale des sciences administratives 25 : 43-50, no. 1, 1959.

BRAZIL

SÄ FREIRE, C. de : Eficacia del acto administrativo del derecho brasileño. Revista del Instituto de derecho comparado (Barcelona) : 49-60, enero-junio 1955.

VALLADAO, H. : Bul.etin de jurisprudence brésilienne. Journal du droit international 84 : 158-167, janvier-mars 1957.
Texte en anglais aussi.

NASCIMENTO e SILVA, G.E. do : As atribuições diplomáticas e consulares. Revista do serviço público (Brazil) 77 : 28-48, octubro 1957.

ARAGÃO, J.G. de : le problème actual de la juridiction administrative au Brésil. France, Conseil d'Etat, Etudes et documents 11 : 167-180, 1957.

GALVÃO de SOUSA, J.P. : Verfassungsrechtsentwicklung in Bralien. Jahrbuch des öffentlichen Rechts der Gegenwart 7 : 353-365, 1958.
Text of constitution in English, pp. 366-393.

FERREIRA, W. : Il diritto cambiario brasiliano e la legge uniforme di Ginevra. Revista da Faculdade de direito (São Paulo) 54 : 46-75, fasc. 1, 1959.

FERRIERA, W. : Il diritto cambiario brasiliano e la legge uniforme di Ginevra. Rivista del diritto commerciale e del diritto generale delle obbligazioni 57 : 1-12, gennaio-febbraio 1959.

BETTI, E. : Cultura giuridica brasiliana nelle impressioni di un viaggio giuridico. Jus, Rivista di scienze giuridiche 10 : 266-275, giugno 1959.

BULGARIA

PUBDEFF, M. : Indexes to Bulgarian law. Highlights of current legislation and activities in Mid-Europe 3 : 101, April 1955.

SAJOVIC, R. : O pripozmavi in izvrsbi civilnih odlocb pogodbi o vzajemni pravni pomoci med Federativno Ljudsko Republiko Jugoslavijo in Ljudsko Republiko Bolgarijo. Zbornik Pravnog faculteta u Zagrebu 6 : 187-196, Nos. 3-4, 1956.
Legal assistance with Yugoslavia.

SIPKOV, I. : Bulgaria - Government arbitration. Highlights of current legislation and activities in Mid-Europe 5 : 185-194, May 1957.

ZONEW, D. : Zur Strafprozessnovelle Bulgariens 1956. Osteuropa-Recht 3 : 110-111, Oktober 1957.

SIPKOV, I. : Postwar nationalizations and alien property in Bulgaria. American journal of international law 52 : 469-494, July 1958.

VLAHOFF, I.S. : Le tribunal d'arbitrage d'Etat dans la République Populaire de Bulgarie. Revue internationale de droit comparé 11 : 733-742, octobre-décembre 1959.

BURMA.

SUBRAMANIAN, N.A. : Some aspects of Burmese constitutional law. Indian year book of international affairs 5 : 123-155, 1956.

MAUNG, M. : Burma's constitution comes to life. Indian year book of international affairs 7 : 173-164, 1958.

SUBRAMANIAN, N.A. : Judicial power in Burmese constitutional law. Indian year book of international affairs 8 : 59-67, 1959.

CAMBODIA

Constitution du Royaume du Cambodge, 14 janvier 1956. Informations constitutionnelles et parlementaires : 197-215, octobre 1956.
Texte.

Constitution du Royaume du Cambodge du 6 mai 1947, modifiée le 14 janvier 1956. Revue internationale d'histoire politique et constitutionnelle : 218-231, juillet-septembre 1956.

Constitution du Royaume du Cambodge, 14 janvier 1956. Documentation française, Notes et études documentaires : 1-10, no. 2268, 5 mars 1957.

CAMEROUN

BOUVENET, G.J., et BOURDIN, R. : Un précurseur, l'arrêté du 16 décembre 1954 portant code de procédure civile et commerciale du Cameroun. Penant, Recueil général de jurisprudence, de doctrine et de législation d'outre-mer, Doctrine 65 : 21-32, mars-avril 1955.

CANADA

McLEOD, A.J., and MARTIN, J.C. : The revision of the criminal code. Canadian bar review 33 : 3-19, January 1955.
See also pp. 20-62.

KENNEDY, G.D. : The legal effets of adoption. Canadian bar review 33 : 751-875, August-September 1955.
Special issue.

BAUDOUIN, L. : Chronique de droit canadien, province de Québec. Revue trimestrielle de droit civil 53 : 733-740, octobre-décembre 1955.

SZABLOWSKI, G.J. : Creation and implementation of treaties in Canada. Canadian bar review 34 : 28-59, January 1956.

BAUDOUIN, L. : Chronique de droit canadien. Revue trimestrielle de droit civil 54 : 621-626, juillet-septembre 1956.

PIOTROWSKI, G. : La structure fédérative de l'Etat dans la jurisprudence canadienne en matière de droit international public. Journal du droit international 83 : 824-885, octobre-décembre 1956.

Report of the Committee on legal research. Canadian bar review 34 : 999-1064, November 1956.

BRADY, A. Le Canada moderne - Le problème de sa nationalité. Société belge d'études et d'expansion, Bulletin bimestriel 55 : 939-944, novembre-décembre 1956.

CASTEL, J.G. : De la forme des actes juridiques et instrumentaires en droit international privé québecois. Canadian bar review 35 : 654-696, June-July 1957.

BAUDOUIN, L. : Cjronique de droit canadien - Province de Québec. Revue trimestrielle de droit civil 56 : 602-608, juillet-septembre 1957.

JOHNSON, W.S. : Foreign judgments in Quebec. Canadian bar review 35 : 911-949, October 1957.

NATIONAL LAW - COUNTRIES

BAUDOUIN, L. : Chronique de droit civil canadien. Revue trimestrielle de droit civil 57 : 468-474, juillet-septembre 1958.

CASTEL, J.G. : Canadian private international law rules relating to domestic relations. McGill law journal 5 : 1-35, no. 1, 1958.

An act for the recognition and protection of human rights and fundamental freedoms. Canadian bar review 37 : 1-3, March 1959.
See also pp. 4-216.

CENTRAL AFRICAN REPUBLIC

MANGIN, G. : République Centrafricaine. Annuaire de législation française et étrangère 8 : 91-98, 1959.

CEYLON

GUPTA, A.K. : The Ceylon citizenship question and the Indian problem. Modern review 100 : 61-63, July 1956.

KRISHNA SHETTY, K.P. : The law of citizenship for Indian and Pakistani residents in Ceylon. Indian year book of international affairs 7 : 165-185, 1958.

KRISHNA SHETTY, K.P. : Judicial review and prerogative writs in Ceylon. Indian year book of international affairs 8 : 68-109, 1959.

CHAD

MANGIN, G. : Tchad. Annuaire de législation française et étrangère 8 : 495-500, 1959.

CHILE

PECCHI CROCE, C. : Entrada y expulsión de los extranjeros. Revista de derecho (Concepción) 23 : 191-221, abril-junio 1955.

RODRIGUEZ, A.A. : El código civil chileno. Información jurídica (Spain) : 657-670, noviembre-diciembre 1955.

TAPIA ARQUEROS, H. : Las personas jurídicas en el código civil chileno. Revista de derecho (Concepción) 24 : 465-487, octubre-diciembre 1956.

OTAROLA AQUEVEQUE, H. : Chile ante las nuevas jurisdicciones de mar territorial. Revista de derecho (Concepción) 25 : 430-442, julio-septiembre 1957.

MATUS VALENCIA, J.G. : The centenary of the Chilean civil code. American journal of comparative law 7 : 71-88, winter 1958.

ROMÁN VIDAL, S.M. : El derecho penal militar y el código de justicia militar de Chile. Revista española de derecho militar : 115-125, julio-diciembre 1959.

CHINA

Neues Familienrecht im Sowjetspiegel. Ost-Probleme 7 : 353-357, 4. März 1955.
Published in "Sowjetskoje gosudarstwo i prawo".

SCHULTZ, L. : Die neue Verfassung der Volksrepublik China. Osteuropa-Recht 1 : 43-55, März 1955.

The Sino-Indonesian treaty on dual nationality. Far Eastern survey 24 : 75-76, May 1955.

Traité sino-indonésien sur le problème de la double nationalité. Légation de la République Populaire de Chine. Bulletin d'information (Berne) : 3-6, 7 juin 1955.
Texte.

HOUN, F.W. : Communist China's new constitution. Western political quarterly 8 : 199-233, June 1955.

CUNHA GONÇALVES, L. da : Evolução das instituições jurídicas da China antes e depois do comunismo. Boletim da Sociedade de geogragia de Lisboa 73 : 349-365, julho-setembro 1955.
Summary in English.

PURCELL, V. : The dual nationality of the Chinese in South-East Asia. India quarterly 11 : 344-354, October-December 1955.

DIWAN, P. : Constitutional developments in China. Supreme court journal (Madras) 18 : 305-374, December 1955.

SIU, K.-P. : La nouvelle constitution de la Chine communiste du 20 septembre 1954. Etude comparative. Revue internationale de droit comparé 8 : 399-411, juillet-septembre 1956.

YEE, F.S.H. : Chinese Communist police and courts. Journal of criminal law, criminology and police science 48 : 83-92, May-June 1957.

Gesetzgebung der Ostblockstaaten (Contd.) - Vhina. Osteuropa-Recht 3 : 34-35, Juni 1957.
1955-56.

MONTADER, P. : Evolution de la justice en Chine. Saturne 4 : 134-146, janvier-mars 1958.

WRIGHT, W.T. : Gesetzgebung und Rechtsprechung in der Volksrepublik China. Osteuropa-Recht 4 : 189-197, Juli 1958.

GREENFIELD, D.E. : Marriage by Chinese law and custom in Hongkong. International and comparative law quarterly 7 : 437-451, July 1958.

LIU, C.-s. : The Chinese council of grand justices. American journal of comparative law 7 : 402-408, summer 1958.

CORINTH, B. : Die Organisation der Gerichte in der Volksrepublik China. Aussenpolitik 9 : 526-531, August 1958.

JAIN, H.M. : Some aspects of the Chinese constitution. India quarterly 14 : 373-379, October-December 1958.

MAURER, E. : Legal problems regarding Formosa and the Offshore islands. Department of State bulletin (United States) 39 : 1005-1011, 22 December 1958.

CORINTH, B. : Das Erbrecht ver Volksrepublik China. Zeitschrift für ausländisches und internationales Privatrecht 24 : 719-728, Heft 4, 1959.

LOEBER, D.A. : Das Erbrecht in der Volksrepublik China. Osteuropa-Recht 5 : 122-126, Oktober 1959.

COLOMBIA

Colombia - Código penal. Información jurídica (Spain) : 433-488, julio-agosto 1955.

COMMONWEALTH

PHILLIPS, O.H. : The making of a colonial constitution. Law quarterly review 71 : 51-78, January 1955.
Singapore.

Consultation et coopération au sein du Commonwealth. Revue juridique et politique de l'Union française 9 : 123-146, janvier-mars 1955.

The Commonwealth and Empire law conference. Law journal 105 : 516-518, August 19 1955.
London.

CHUBB, J.A. : Some notes on the Commonwealth and Empire law conference, 1955, and an address on the jury system. South African law journal 73 : 191-202, May 1956.
London, July 1955.

RIAD, F.A.M. : Foreign jurisdictional acts - A comparative study with special reference to the common law system. Revue égyptienne de droit international 12 : 1-20, 2e semestre 1956.

HAWKE, R.J. : The Commonwealth arbitration court - Legal tribunal or economic legislature? Annual law review 3 : 422-478, December 1956.

O'CONNELL, D.P. : The crown in the British Commonwealth. International and comparative law quarterly 6 : 103-125, January 1957.

Nationality and citizenship laws of countries of the Commonwealth. Central office of information, Reference division (Bulletin) - London : 1-17, no. R 3413, January 1957.

HOLLAND, D.C.: Constitutional experiments in British West Africa. Public law : 42-57, spring 1957.

MATSON, J.N. : The conflict of legal systems in the Federation of Malaya and Singapore. International and comparative law quarterly 6 : 243-262, April 1957.

The tenth Dominion legal conference. New Zealand law journal 33 : 93-164, 21 May 1957.
Christchurch, April 1957.

WILSON, R.R. : Some questions of legal relations between Commonwealth members. American journal of international law 51 : 611-617, July 1957.

WILLIAMS, A.A. : Administrative adjustment of a colonial government to meet constitutional change. Public administration 25 : 267-288, autumn 1957.

FITZGERALD, R.C. : The changing Commonwealth. Current legal problems 10 : 229-247, 1957.

The Channel Islands, a foreign jurisdiction. Law journal 108 : 51-52, 24 January 1958.

LANE, P.H. : The judicial power of the Commonwealth - Recent cases. Australian law journal 32 : 3-7, 23 May 1958.

CLUTE, R.E., and WILSON, R.R. : The Commonwealth and favored-nation usage. American journal of international law 52 : 455-468, July 1958.

WISEMAN, H.V. : The Cabinet in the Commonwealth. Public law : 326-340, winter 1958.

SMITH, S.A. de : Judicial independence in the Commonwealth. Listener 111 : 93-95, 15 January 1959.

READ, J.S. : Constitutions on the move - Constitutional and political developments in 1958. Journal of African law 3 : 39-64, spring 1959.

CAMPBELL, E.M. : The decline of the jurisdiction of the Judicial committee of the Privy council. Australian law journal 33 : 196-209, 24 September 1959.

CLUTE, R.E. : Law and practice in Commonwealth extradition. American journal of comparative law 8 : 15-28, winter 1959.

CONGO(Brazzaville)

MANGIN, G. : Congo. Annuaire de législation française et étrangère 8 : 110-118, 1959.

CONGO (Kinshasa)

SOHIER, A. : Le statut civil coutumier des Congolais. Civilisations 7 : 33-44, no. 1, 1957.

HISLAIRE-GUISLAIN, A. : Législation du Congo belge et du Ruanda-Urundi, ler août 1957 - 31 décembre 1958. Revue de droit international et de droit comparé 36 : 47-58, no. 1-2, 1959.

HISLAIRE-GUISLAIN, A. : Législation du Congo belge et du Ruanda-Urundi, ler janvier 1959 - 31 octobre 1959. Revue de droit international et de droit comparé 36 : 217-228, nos. 3-4, 1959.

CUBA

BLANCO, A. : Renseña de la jurisprudencia cubana durante los años 1952 y 1953. Revista de derecho privado 38 : 1203-1209, diciembre 1955.

DIHIGO, E. : Valor de los tratados ante los tribunales nacionales. Revista cubana de derecho 28 : 32-54, julio-septiembre 1956.

BLANCO, A. : Resumen de la legislación, la doctrina y la jurisprudencia cubanas durante el año 1957. Revista de derecho privado (Madrid) : 1089-1094, diciembre 1958.

CYPRUS

EMILIANIDÈS, A.C. : Interracial and interreligious law in Cyprus. Revue hellénique de droit international 11 : 286-306, juillet-décembre 1958.

NATIONAL LAW - COUNTRIES

CZECHOSLOVAKIA

ANKENBRANK, K. : Die Rechtswirksamkeit der Eingliederung des Sudetenlandes in das Deutsche Reich. Archiv des öffentlichen Rechts 80 : 191-202, Heft 1/2, 1955.

SKILLING, H.G. : The Soviet impact on the Czechoslovak legal revolution. Soviet studies 6 : 361-381, April 1955.

VYBÍRAL, B. : K otázce rozlišení spolupachatelství a pomoci čs. trestním právu. Právník 95 : 20-34, číslo 1, 1956.
Criminal law.

Seznam československých mezinárodních smluv dvoustranných podle stavu ze dne 1. ledna 1956. Studie z mezinárodního práva : 233-255, číslo 2, 1956.
Treaties.

RADVANOVÁ, S. : Modifications apportées au droit de famille tchécoslovaque. Bulletin de droit tchécoslovaque 14 : 318-323, no. 3-4, 1956.

MAGERSTEIN, W. : Ist Österreich legitimiert, di vermögensrechtlichen Ansprüche der vormals tschecoslowakischen Deutschen, die nach der Konfiskation ihres Vermögens in Österreich eingebürgert wurden, gegenüber der Tschechoslowakei im Rahmen des österreichischen Staatsvertrags geltend zu machen? Juristische Blätter 78 : 224-226, 28. April 1956.

STAJGER, F. : Der Staatsanwalt im Zivilprozess nach tschechoslowakischen Recht. Staat und Recht 5 : 468-484, No. 4, 30. Juni 1956.

BYDZOVSKÝ, L. : Rechtshilfevertrag zwischen der Tschechoslowakei und der Deutschen Demokratischen Republik. Neue Justiz (Germany) 10 : 613-614, 20.Oktober 1956.

LANDA, A. : Vente internationale au point de vue du droit tschécoslovaque. Bulletin de droit tchécoslovaque 14 : 133-163, no. 1-2, 1er octobre 1956.

JIRA, J. : Czechoslovak administration of justice since 1952. Highlights of current legislation and activities in Mid-Europe 4 : 303-316, October 1956.
See also pp. 315-318.

KANDA, A. : Uvaha o právu státní arbitráže založit, změnit nebo zrušit právní poměr mezi stranami. Právník 95 : 962-978, číslo 10, 1956.
Commercial arbitration.

La constitution de la République tchécoslovaque. Bulletin de droit tchécoslovaque 14 : 245-279, 1er décembre 1956.
Texte.

PROCHÁZKA, V. : L'origine de la constitution du 9 mai et son évolution ultérieure. Bulletin de droit tchécoslovaque 14 : 229-244, 1er décembre 1956.

LITERA, J. : Principes fondamentaux du nouveau code tchécoslovaque d'instruction criminelle. Droit au service de la paix : 47-51, décembre 1956.

Novelle zm Strafgesetzbuch und neue Strafprozessordnung der CSR. Neue Justiz (Germany) 11 : 70-72, 5. Februar 1957.

MANČAL, J., and TIBITANZL, K. : Nový trestní řád. Právnik 96 : 217-236, číslo 3, 1957.
Criminal code.

Seznam československých mezinárodních smluv mnohostranných podle stavu ze dne 1. července 1956. Stduie 7 mezinárodního práva : 277-295, číslo 3, 1957.
International conventions.

SLAPNICKA, H. : Der Weg der tschechischen Rechtswissenschaft von Wien nach Moskau. Donauraum 2 : 188-199, 3./4, Heft 1957.

Loi du 19 décembre 1956, no. 63 du Recueil des lois de la République tchécoslovaque, portant amendement et complètement du code pénal. Bulletin de droit tchécoslovaque 15 : 215-231, no. 3-4, 1957.
Texte.

Loi du 19 décembre 1956, no. 64 du Recueil des lois de la République tchécoslovaque, sur la procédure pénale judiciaire. Bulletin de droit tchéchoslovaque 15 : 233-330, no. 3-4, 1957.
Texte.

Loi du 19 décembre 1956, no. 65 du Recueil des lois de la République tchécoslovaque, sur le ministère public. Bulletin de droit tchécoslovaque 15 : 331-352, no. 3-4, 1957.
Texte.

VASILEV, L. : K povinnosti uzavřit smlouvu ve shodě s plánem a k předsmluvní arbitráži. Právník 96 : 712-724, číslo 8, 1957.
Commercial arbitration.

BYDŽOVSKÝ, L. : Pomoc sovětské právní vědi při tvorbě československého právniho řádu. Právnik 96 : 819-824, číslo 9, 1957.
Czechoslovakia and Soviet law.

KNAPP, W. : Z zagadnień stosowania i wykladni prawa ciwilnego w obrocie socjalistycznym Czechoslowacji. Państwo i prawo 12 : 325-336, wrzesień 1957.
Application of civil law; Summaries in English, French and Russian.

SLAPNICKA, H. : Richterwahlen in der Tsechoslowakei. Juristische Blätter 79 : 641-642, 21. Dezember 1957.

HANAK, S. : Exécution des sentences arbitrales égyptiennes en Tchécosloyaquie. Revue égyptienne de droit international 13 : 41-48, 1957.

PLUNDR, O. : Volba soudců a soudců z lidu. Právnik 97 : 13-28, cislo 1, 1958.
People's judges.

DONNER, T. : Les accords tchécoslovaques sur l'assistance juridique. Bulletin de droit tchécoslovaque 16 : 103-110, no. 1, 1958.

Code de la famille, loi no. 265. Bulletin de droit tchécoslovaque 16 : 245-259, no. 2, 1958.
Texte.

PROCHÁZKA, V. : He vzniku Ústavy 9. května. Právník 97 : 365-376, číslo 5, 1958.
Constitution; See also pp. 376-399.

LACO, K. : Ústava v predmníchovskej ČSR a ústava 9. mája (Contd.). Právnícké štúdie 7 : 106-146, číslo 1, 1959.
The constitution.

FRITZSCHE, H. : K otázkám řízení o vydání mezi Československou republikou a Německou demokratickou republikou. Časopis pro mezinárodní právo 3 : 130-142, číslo 2, 1959.
Extradition with Western Germany.

NATIONAL LAW - COUNTRIES

DONNER, B. : Lze se z hlediska čs. práva podrobit mezinárodní obchodní arbitráži, v níž by bylo rozhodnuto na základě ekvity nebo podle obchodních zvyklostí? Časopis pro mezinárodní právo 2 : 284-294, číslo 4, 1958.
Commercial arbitration; Summary in English.

KNAPP, V. : Le concept de personne morale dans le droit tchécoslovaque. Revue internationale de droit comparé 11 : 519-532, juillet-septembre 1959.

STAJGR, F. : Dix années de juridiction populaire en Tchécoslovaquie. Bulletin de droit tchécoslovaque 17 : 16-28, no. 1-2, 30 septembre 1959.

RABL, K. : Die verfassungsrechtliche Entwicklung der Tschechoslowakei seit 1944/45. Jahrbuch des öffentlichen Rechts der Gegenwart 8 : 293-363, 1959.

DONNER, T. : Le droit international successoral en vigueur dans la République tchécoslovaque. Bulletin de droit tchécoslovaque 17 : 258-275, 31 octobre 1959.

SCHMIED, E. : Das neue tschechoslowakische Staatsbürgerschaftsgesetz von 1958. Osteuropa-Recht 5 : 119-121, Oktober 1959.

BYDŽOVSKÝ, L. : Les amendements au code de procédure civile. Bulletin de droit tchécoslovaque 17 : 421-427, décembre 1959.

DENMARK

MARCUS, F. : Das dänische Kriminalgesetzbuch für Grönland. Zeitschrift für die gesamte Strafrechtswissenschaft 67 : 323-343, Heft 2, 1955.

MARCUS, F. : Dänische Gesetzgebung auf dem Gebiete des Privatrechts bis 1954. Zeitschrift für ausländisches und internationales Privatrecht 20 : 504-507, Heft 3, 1955.

MARCUS, F. : Die dänische Rechtsprechung auf dem Gebiete des internationalen Privatrechts 1945-1954. Zeitschrift für ausländisches und internationales Privatrecht 20 : 507-518, Heft 3, 1955.

HIMMELSTRUP, J. : Das öffentliche Recht Dänemarks von 1932 bis 1953. Jahrbuch des öffentlichen Rechts der Gegenwart 4 : 255-267, 1955.

HARDER, E. : La constitution danoise de 1953. Revue internationale des sciences administratives - International review of administrative sciences 22 : 115-124, no. 1, 1956.

MARCUS, F. : Die Rechtsprechungsmethode des Dänischen Obersten Gerichtshofs. Zeitschrift für ausländisches und internationales Privatrecht 21 : 243-256, Heft 2, 1956.

ANDERSON, S.V. : Article twenty of Denmark's new constitution. American journal of international law 50 : 654-659, July 1956.
Possible delegation of sovereignty to international organizations.

MARCUS, F. : Die Einführung der "starken" Adoption in Dänemark. Juristenzeitung 12 : 113-116, 20. Februar 1957.
Consequences of adoption.

FROST, J.L., and LORENZEN, A. : Fra den danske Højesterets praksis i året 1956. Tidsskrift for rettsvitenskap 70 : 305-360, hefte 4, 1957.

PHILIP, A. : Commercial arbitration in Denmark. Arbitration journal 13 : 16-22, no. 1, 1958.

DOMINICAN REPUBLIC

DRITO MATA, F.A. : Las nuevas orientaciones del derecho civil en la República Dominicana. Anales de la Universidad de Santo Domingo 25 : 157-170, enero-diciembre 1959.

Código penal de la República Dominicana. Información jurídica (Spain) : 1717-1786, septiembre-octubre 1959.

Constitution de la République Dominicaine, 1955. Documentation française, Notes et études documentaires : 1-15, no. 2612, 18 décembre 1959.

ECUADOR

KARGER, A. : Reformen des bürgerlichen Rechts in Ecuador. Zeitschrift für ausländisches und internationales Privatrecht 22 : 525-532, Heft 3, 1957.

ALARCON FALCONI, R. : Las constituciones de México y Ecuador. Revista mexicana del trabaho (Mexico) 5 : 12-22, enero-febrero 1958.

GONZÁLEZ BUSTAMANTE, J.J. : El código de ejecución penal del Ecuador. Criminalia 24 : 352-378, junio 1958.

Ecuador - Código penal. Información jurídica (Spain) : 1191-1281, noviembre-diciembre 1958.

ETHIOPIA

The new Ethiopian constitution - Universal suffrage in Ethiopia. New times and Ethiopia news : 1-4, 14 January 1956.
Text.

LEWIS, W.H. : Ehtiopia's revised constitution. Middle East journal 10 : 194-199, spring 1956.
With condensed text.

NORDSTRÖM, H.E. : Svensk juristverksamhet i Etiopien, 1946-1955. Svensk juristtidning 41 : 550-562, oktober 1956.

Ethiopie - Constitution révisée de l'Empire éthiopien, 4 novembre 1955. Informations constitutionnelles et parlemantaires 8 : 1-26, janvier 1957.
Texte.

GRAVEN, J. : L'Ethiopie moderne et la codification du nouveau droit. Schweizerische Zeitschrift für Strafrecht 72 : 397-407, Heft 4, 1957.

Constitution de l'Empire éthiopien, 4 novembre 1955. Documentation française, Notes et études documentaires : 1-12, no. 2282, 13 avril 1957.
Texte.

QUINTANO RIPOLLÉS, A. : Código penal del Imperio de Ethiopia. Anuario de derecho penal y ciencias penales 11 : 347-351, mayo-agosto 1958.

PANKHURST, S. : The new Ethiopian penal code - a survey. Ethiopia observer 2 : 257-270, July 1958.

OSTINI, F. : La condition juridique des étrangers en Erythrée. Civilisations 9 : 343-353, no. 3, 1959.

RUSSELL, F. F. : Eritrean customary law. Journal of African law 3 : 99-104, summer 1959.

FINLAND

Loi finlandaise du 5 décembre 1929 réglant certains rapports de droit familial de caractère international. Documentation juridique étrangère 7 : 13-25, no. 6-7, 1955.
Décret pp. 27-31.

PHILIP, D. : L'administration publique en Finlande. Revue internationale des sciences administratives - International review of administrative sciences 22 : 147-179, no. 3, 1956.

RYTKÖLÄ, O. : Die leitenden Prinzipien und die Organisation der finnischen Kommunalverwaltung. Österreichische Zeitschrift für öffentliches Recht 7 : 465-481, Heft 4, 1956.

MERIKOSKI, V. : La position juridique des langues nationales en Finlande. Revue internationale des sciences administratives 23 : 156-165, no. 2, 1957.

CASTRÉN, E. : Die Selbstverwaltung Alands. Internationales Recht und Diplomatie : 105-112, Heft 2, 1957.

SCHWINDT, B. : Från Högsta domstolen i Finland 1953 och 1954. Tidsskrift for rettsvitenskap 70 : 246-256, hefte 3, 1957.

JANSSON, J.M. : Die Verfassungsentwicklung in Finnland seit dem Jahre 1939. Jahrbuch des öffentliches Rechts der Gegenwart 6 : 285-318, 1957.

SCHWINDT, B. : Från Högsta domstolen i Finland 1955 och 1956. Tidsskrift for rettsvitenskap : 80-90, hefte 1, 1959.

FRANCE

DRAGO, R. : L'état d'urgence, lois des 3 avril et 7 août 1955, et les libertés publiques, Revue de droit public et de la science politique en France et à l'étranger 71 : 670-708, juillet-septembre 1955.

PADILLA SERRA, A. : La reforma de la constitución francesa. Archivo de derecho público (Granada) 8 : 143-174, 1955.
Texts pp. 175-179.

HOUIN, R. : Reform of the French civil code and the code of commerce. American journal of comparative law 4 : 485-505, autumn 1955.

LIMPENS, J. : L'expansion du code civil dans le monde. Revue de droit international et de droit comparé 33 : 59-77, nos. 2-3, 1956.

MICHEL, M. : La loi du 25 juin 1956 et l'évolution des territoires d'outre-mer. Revue administrative 9 : 366-368, juillet-août 1956.

HERZOG, J.B. : Observations sur les réformes apportées à l'instruction préparatoire du premier degré par le projet de code de procédure pénale. Revue de science criminelle et de droit pénal comparé : 465-478, juillet-septembre 1956.

HAMSON, C.J. : Vues anglaises sur le Conseil d'Etat français. Revue du droit public et de la science politique en France et à l'étranger 72 : 1049-1057, septembre-octobre 1956.

QUERMONNE, J.L. : La réforme de structure des territoires d'outre-mer et des territoires selon la loi-cadre du 23 juin 1956. Recueil Dalloz, Chronique : 5-12, 12 janvier 1957.

LAMPUÉ, P. : L'étendue d'application du statut personnel des autochtones dans les territoires français d'outre-mer. Civilisations 7 : 1-13, no. 1, 1957.

GOUET, Y. : L'article 82, paragraphe I, de la constitution relatif à l'option de statut et l'élaboration de la "théorie des statuts civils" du droit français moderne. Penant, Recueil général de jurisprudence, de doctrine et de législation d'outre-mer, Doctrine 67 : 1-36, janvier-février 1957.

DURAND, P.M.F. : Où en est la réforme du code de procédure pénale? Revue de l'action populaire : 223-230, février 1957.

GARRAUD, P. : Insuffisances de la procédure pénale française. Chronique de France 65 : 211-222, 30 mai 1957.

BONNECHOSE, H. de : Thémis et le droit d'auteur. Revue des deux mondes : 417-428, 1er juin 1957.

DEVAUX-CHARBONNEL, J. : Le régime juridique de la recherche et de l'exploitation des hydrocarbures dans les territoires d'Outre-Mer. Revue française de l'énergie 9 : 4-12, octobre 1957.

GULDNER, E. : Le rôle du Gouvernement dans la procédure de révision de la constitution du 27 octobre 1946. France, Conseil d'Etat, Etudes et documents 11 : 41-50, 1957.
Textes pp 51-52.

HOUIN, R. : The method of reform of the French codes of private law. Tulane law review 32 : 1-20, December 1957.

RAZI, G.M. : Guided tour in a civil law labrary - Sources and basic materials in French civil and commercial law. Michigan law review 56 : 375-400, January 1958.

Troisièmes journées de droit franco-espagnol, Toulouse, mai 1957 - Rapports. Annales de la Faculté de droit de Toulouse 6 : 43-191, fasc. 1, 1958.

Quatrièmes journées franco-espagnoles de droit comparé, Barcelone, avril 1958 - Rapports. Annales de la Faculté de droit de Toulouse 6 : 131-313, fasc. 2, 1958.

La nouvelle loi française sur le propriété littéraire et artistique. Bibliographie de la France, Chronique 147 ; i-xvi, 14 mars 1958.

BASTID, P. : La nouvelle constitution de la France. Bulletin interparlementaire 38 : 156-173, no. 4, 1958.

NATIONAL LAW - COUNTRIES

LUCHAIRE, F. : Les institutions politiques et administratives des territoires d'outre-mer après la loi cadre. Revue juridique et politique de l'Union française 12 : 221-294, avril-juin 1958.

GROSHENS, J.C. : La codification par décret des lois et règlements. Recueil Dalloz, Chronique 23 : 157-164, 18 juin 1958.

Texte de la constitution du 4 octobre 1958. Revue du droit public et de la science politique en France et à l'étranger 74 : 940-971, septembre-octobre 1958.

La nouvelle constitution. Chroniques d'outre-mer (France) : 37-46, octobre 1958.
Texte.

GONIDEC, P.F. : Introduction à l'étude de la Communauté. Recueil Penant, Doctrine 68 : 185-200, novembre 1958.
Voir aussi pp. 201-211.

France - Constitution, 4 octobre 1958. Informations constitutionnelles et parlementaires : 1-23, janvier 1959.
Texte ; Lois organiques pp. 24-30.

MORANGE, G. : La hiérarchie des textes dans la constitution du 4 octobre 1958. Recueil Dalloz, Chronique : 21-26, 28 janvier 1959.

PICKLES, D. : The constitution of the Fifth French republic. Modern law review 22 : 1-20, January 1959.

GALLARDO RUEDA, A. : El nuevo código de procedimiento penal francés. Información jurídica (Spain) : 1287-1293, enero-febrero 1959.

LIONS SIGNORET, M. : La constitución francesa de 4 de octubre de 1958. Boletín del Instituto de derecho comparado de México 12 : 73-98, enero-abril 1959.

Remise en ordre 1959 - Les nouvelles réformes. Banque 28 : 73-80, février 1959.

BONNICHON, A. : Une réforme judiciaire. Etudes 300 : 174-184, février 1959.

LANGROD, G. : Initial administrative tendencies of the Fifth French Republic. Revue internationale des sciences administratives 25 : 332-345, no. 3, 1959.

CASAMAYOR : La réforme judiciaire. Esprit 27 : 454-472, mars 1959.

ECHTERHÖLTER, R. : Die verfassungsmässige Ordnung der Fünften französischen Republik. Archiv des öffentlichen Rechts 84 : 330-358, Heft 3, 1959.

GRZYBOWSKI, K. : The new French constitution. American journal of comparative law 8 : 214-217, spring 1959.
See also pp. 218-225.

LETOURNEUR, M. : Reflections on the role of the French administrative judge. University of Chicago law review 26 : 436-440, spring 1959.

Les grandes lignes de la réforme de la justice française de 1958. Documentation française, Notes et études documentaires : 1-15, no. 2527, 2 avril 1959.

ROUSSIER, J. : L'ordonnance du 4 février 1959 sur le mariage et le divorce des Français de statut local algérien. Recueil Sirey, Chronique : 7-11, avril 1959.

BASTID, P. : Les principes généraux de la nouvelle constitution française. Revue internationale de droit comparé 11 : 334-364, avril-juin 1959.

BESSON, A. : L'origine, l'esprit et la portée du code de procédure pénale. Revue de science criminelle et de droit pénal comparé 14 : 271-289, avril-juin 1959.
Voir aussi pp. 291-361.

MIMIN, P. : Vue d'ensemble sur les caractères généraux du code de procédure pénale. Recueil Sirey, Chronique : 17-24, juin 1959.

NEVILLE BROWN, L. : The reform of the French administrative courts. Modern law review 22 : 357-380, July 1959.

De l'applicabilité des lois aux départements algériens sous la Ve République. Revue algérienne, tunisienne et marocaine de législation et de jurisprudence, Doctrine 75 : 86-90, juillet-août 1959.

PICKLES, W. : The French constitution of 4 October 1958 - A new translation and a commentary. Public law : 228-276, autumn1959.

KOVAR, R., et BLOCH, G.P. : Exécutif et législatif dans la constitution de la Ve République. Jahrbuch des öffentlichen Rechts der Gegenwart 8 : 215-266, 1959.

LIONS SIGNORET, M. : Algunos aspectos del constitucionalismo francés contemporaneo. Boletin del Instituto de derecho comparado de México 12 : 31-64, septiembre-diciembre 1959.

HERZOG, J.B. : Tableau des réformes apportées au code pénal par les ordonnances de 1958. Revue de science criminelle et de droit pénal comparé 14 : 785-804, octobre-décembre 1959.

FRANCE
(International law, Aliens, Nationality)

BOULBES, R. : La question de la double allégeance. Evolution à cet égard du droit français de la nationalité. Comité français de droit international privé Travaux 16-18 : 67-94, 1955-1957.

DONNIER, M. : La convention judiciaire franco-vietnamienne du 16 septembre 1954 au regard du droit international privé français - Conditions des étrangers, conflit de lois, conflit de juridictions. Penant, Recueil général de jurisprudence, de doctrine et de législation d'outre-mer, Doctrine 65 : 1-20, janvier-février 1955.

LEHMANN, R. : Du domaine d'application des lois de nationalité en droit français. Journal de droit international 82 : 4-44, janvier-mars 1955.
Texte en anglais aussi.

MORICE, J. : Le domaine d'application sur le territoire du Royaume du Cambodge de la législation française. Revue juridique et politique de l'Union française 9 : 183-186, janvier-mars 1955.

NATIONAL LAW - COUNTRIES

LEHMANN, R. : Du domaine d'application des lois de nationalité en droit français (Suite). Journal du droit international 82 : 324-383, avril-juin 1955.
Texte en anglais aussi.

BIAL, L.C. : Some recent French decisions on the relationship between treaties and municipal law. American journal of international law 49 : 347-355, July 1955.

ROTONDI, M. : Per un diritto uniforme italo-francese delle obbligazioni. Riviste del diritto commerciale e del diritto generale delle obbligazioni 53 : 415-425, settembre-ottobre 1955.

BATIFFOL, H. : Recognition in France of foreign decrees divorcing spouses of different nationality. American journal of comparative law 4 : 574-581, autumn 1955.

Convention franco-vietnamienne sur la nationalité, 16 août 1955. Documentation française, Notes et études documentaires : 1-6, no. 2112, 13 décembre 1955.

BATIFFOL, H. : Problemas de la ley aplicable al régimen matrimonial de bienes en el derecho internacional privado francés. Revista española de derecho internacional 9 : 71-86, num. 1-2, 1956.

FRANCESCAKIS, P. : Une extension discutable de la jurisprudence Rivière - L'application de la loi du domicile commun à la filiation légitime. Journal du droit international 83 : 254-291, avril-juin 1956.
Texte en anglais aussi.

BOISDON, D. : Du sort des articles 81 et 82 de notre constitution de 1946. Revue juridique et politique de l'union française 10 : 233-256, avril-juin 1956.
Citoyenneté de l'Union française.

LOUSSOUARN, Y. : French draft on private international law and the French conference on codification of private international law. Tulane law review 30 : 523-538, June 1956.
Paris, May 1955.

LOUSSOUARN, Y. : The French draft on private international law and the French conference on codification of private international law. International and comparative law quarterly 5 : 378-394, July 1956.

LOUIS-LUCAS, P. : Le colloque des 20 et 21 mai 1955 sur la codification du droit international privé français. Revue critique de droit international privé 45 : 391-407, juillet-septembre 1956.

SERVOS, J. : Die Vollstreckung ausländischer Urteile und Schiedssprüche in Frankreich. Monatsschrift für deutsches Recht 11 : 75-77, Februar 1957.

SIEG, K. : Aktuelle Fragen der französischen Schiedsgerichtsbarkeit, verglichen mit dem deutschen Recht. Deutsche Richterzeitung 35 : 27-29, Februar 1957.

CAPITANT, R. : La constitutionnalité des traités européens.. Année politique et économique 30 : 274-279, août-octobre 1957.

BARDA, E., et PRATIS, C.M. : De la condition juridique des Italiens en France en matière de loyers, avant et après la mise en vigueur de la convention d'établissement du 23 août 1951. Revue critique de droit international privé 46 : 605-638, octobre-décembre 1957.

ROBERT, J. : Le recours en France contre la sentence étrangère. Revue de l'arbitrage : 122-131, octobre-décembre 1957.

BATIFFOL, H. : L'interprétation des traités diplomatiques par les tribunaux judiciaires. Comité français de droit international privé, Travaux 19-20 : 99-113, 1958-59.
Discussion pp. 113-121.

BARDA, E., and PRATIS, C.M. : Il trattamento giuridico degli Italiani in Francia in Materia di locazione e di contratta agrari. Rivista di diritto internazionale 41 : 561-584, fasc. 4, 1958.

DUPARC, P. : Engagements internationaux en vigueur souscrits par la France. Revue générale de droit international public 62 : 277-296, avril-juin 1958.
Liste.

PICARD, R. : La double nationalité en droit international et en droit français. Annales de la Faculté de droit d'Istanbul 7 : 67-81, no. 8, 1958.

HOLLEY, D.L. : Enforcement of American awards in France. Arbitration journal 14 : 83-92, no. 2, 1959.

DERRUPPÉ, J. : La nationalité étrangère devant le juge français. Revue critique de droit international privé 48 : 201-235, avril-juin 1959.

ROUSSEAU, C. : L'affaire franco-hellénique des phares et la sentence arbitrale du 24 juillet 1956. Revue générale de droit international public 63 : 248-292, avril-juin 1959.

KISS, A.C. : L'extinction des traités dans le pratique française. Annuaire français de droit international 5 : 784-798, 1959.

NGUYEN QUOC DINH : La constitution de 1958 et le droit international. Revue de droit public et de la science politique en France et à l'étranger 75 : 515-564, mai-juin 1959.

LOUIS-LUCAS, P. : Existe-t-il une compétence générale du droit français pour le règlement des conflits de lois? Revue critique de droit international privé 48 : 405-441, juillet-septembre 1959.

RICCI, D. de : Niederlassungen ausländischer Gesellschaften in Frankreich. Aussenwirtschaftsdienst des Betriebs-Beraters 5 : 165-167, August 1959.

SCHLACHTER, E. : Un nouvel aspect de l'exequatur des jugements étrangers en France. Association des auditeurs de l'Académie de droit international de La Haye, Annuaire 29 : 93-95, 1959.

FRANCE
(France Community)

Les pays d'outre-mer de la République française, la Communauté et les accords d'association. Revue juridique et politique d'outre-mer 13 : 3-17, janvier-mars 1959.

GONIDEC, P.F. : Notes sur la nationalité et les citoyennetés dans la Communauté. Annuaire français de droit international 5 : 748-761, 1959.

GONIDEC, P.F. : Les constitutions des Etats de la Communauté. Receuil Penant, Doctrine 69 : 483-495, septembre 1959.

KIRSCH, M. : La Cour arbitrale de la Communauté. Recueil Penant, Doctrine 69 : 645-653, décembre 1959.

GERMANY
(Federal Republic)

JESCHEK, H.H. : L'évolution du droit pénal en Allemagne depuis 1945. Revue de droit pénal et de criminologie 35 : 361-376, janvier 1955.

SCHÖNHERR, K. : Das Bonner Ermächtigungsgesetz vom 26. März 1954. Staat und Recht 4 : 99-116, Januar 1955.

Code civil allemand. Textes législatifs étrangers 5 : 1-49, no. 1, 1955.
Livre I.

Code civil allemand (Suite). Textes législatifs étrangers 5 : 51-108, no. 2, 1955.

WUSTENBERG : Die Rechtsprechung des Bundesgerichtshofes auf dem Gebiete des Eherechts. Deutsche Richterzeitung 33 : 278-281, Dezember 1955.

Code civil allemand (Suite) - Droit de famille. Textes législatifs étrangers 6 : 249-357, no. 1, 1956.

Code civil allemand - Lois diverses. Textes législatifs étrangers 6 : 457-565, no. 3, 1956.

PANZER, R. : Die westdeutsche Strafrechtslehre u. -praxis über die Verantwortlichkeit für Handeln auf Begehl. Neue Justiz (Germany) 10 : 244-248, 20. April 1956.

Code civil allemand (Suite). Textes législatifs étrangers 5 : 179-248, no. 4, 1955.

MAIER, H. : Bereinigung der Besatzungsgesetzgebung. Juristenzeitung 11 : 396-399, 5. Juli 1956.

LOEN, E. van : Soldatengesetz und Kriegsverbrechen. Zeitschrift für Geopolitik 27 : 51-56, August 1956.
Military law.

JARCK, C. : Abänderung und Aufhebung sowjetzonaler gerichtlicher Entscheidungen durch Gerichte der Bundesrepublik. Ehe und Familie im privaten und öffentlichen Recht 3 : 296-298, Oktober 1956.

DRATH, M. : Die staatsrechtliche Stellung Berlins. Archiv des öffentlichen Rechts 82 : 27-75, Heft 1, 1957.

BUERSTEDDE, W. : La Cour constitutionnelle de la République fédérale allemande. Revue internationale de droit comparé 9 : 56-72, janvier-mars 1957.

MEZGER, E. : Orientation de la jurisprudence allemande en matière d'arbitrage. Revue de l'arbitrage : 8-13, janvier-mars 1957.

SIEG, K. : Aktuelle Fragen der französischen Schiedsgerichtsbarkeit, verglichen mit dem deutschen Recht. Deutsche Richterzeitung 35 : 27-29, Februar 1957.

Der Status des Bundesverfassungsgerichts. Jahrbuch des öffentlichen Rechts der Gegenwart 6 : 109-221, 1957.

MERKATZ, H.J. von : Die Rechtsentwicklung auf deutschem Boden. Aussenpolitik 8 : 412-429, Juli 1957.
West and East.

Das neue Wehrstrafgesetz. Juristenzeitung 12 : 393-410, 15. Juli 1957.
Series of articles.

BERNHARDT, R. : Der Begriff der "Anerkennung der Bundesrepublik" in deutschen Gesetzen. Juristenzeitung 12 : 561-564, 20. September 1957.

Troisième loi modifiant la loi fédérale complémentaire portant indemnisation des victimes de la persécution national-socialiste, du 29 juin 1956. Documentation juridique étrangère 8 : 3-104, no. 10, 1956.

WEBER, H. von : Hochverrat und Staatsgefährdung. Monatsschrift für deutsches Recht 11 : 584-585, Oktober 1957.

BEITZKE, G. : La loi allemande sur l'égalité de l'homme et de la femme. Revue internationale de droit comparé 10 : 39-55, janvier-mars 1958.

COLE, T. : The West German federal constitutional court - An evaluation after six years. Journal of politics 20 : 278-307, May 1958.

BUCHHOLZ, E. : Quelques caractéristiques du développement du droit pénal en Allemagne occidentale. Revue de droit contemporain 5 : 90-103, juin 1958.

TROUSSE, P.E. : La réforme du droit pénal allemand. Revue de droit pénal et de criminologie 38 : 943-969, juillet 1958.

FICKER, H.G. : L'état du droit comparé en Allemagne. Revue internationale de droit comparé 10 : 701-718, octobre-décembre 1958.

Articles sur la République fédérale d'Allemagne. Revue internationale des sciences administratives 25 : 135-200, no. 2, 1959.
Suite d'articles sur le droit administratif.

HOFFMEYER, V. : Aberkennung der deutschen Staatsangehörigkeit und Erbstatut in Entschädigungssachen. Juristenzeitung 14 : 81-85, 6. Februar 1959.

COLE, T. : The Bundesverfassungsgericht, 1956-1958 - An American appraisal. Jahrbuch des öffentlichen Rechts der Gegenwart 8 : 29-47, 1959.

SCHWALM, G. : Der Stand der Strafrechtsreform. Monatsschrift für deutsches Recht 13 : 797-801, 884-887, Oktober, November 1959.

LEISNER, W. : Le président de la République et le gouvernement dans la constitution de Bonn. Revue du droit public et de la science politique en France et à l'étranger 74 : 1033-1072, novembre-décembre 1958.

GERMANY
(International law and practice, Aliens and Naturalization)

MAKAROV, A.N. : Gesetzliche Normen des internationalen Privat- und Zivilprozessrechts in Deutschland 1945-1954. Zeitschrift für ausländisches und internationales Privatrecht 20 : 105-121, Heft 1, 1955.

MOSLER, H. : Kulturabkommen des Bundesstaats - Zur Frage der Beschränkung der Bundesgewalt in auswärtigen Angelegenheiten. Zeitschrift für ausländisches öffentliches Recht und Völkerrecht 16 : 1-34, Januar 1955.

LOEWENSTEIN, K. : The Bonn constitution and the European defense community treaties. Yale law journal 64 : 805-839, May 1955.

HOFFMANN, E. von : Zur Regelung der Staatsangehörigkeit in Deutschland. Berichte und Informationen des Österreichischen Forschungsinstituts für Wirtschaft und Politik 10 : 395-397, 3. Juni 1955.

LOEWENSTEIN, K. : La constitutionnalité des traités instituant la Communauté européenne de défense, aux termes de la constitution de Bonn. Revue du droit public et de la science politique en France et à l'étranger 71 : 632-669, juillet-septembre 1955.

COHN, E.J. : Ausländische Juden und Verfolgungsvermutung. Juristenzeitung 10 : 631-634, 20. Oktober 1955.

BRILL, H.L. : Rechtsfragen der Wiedervereinigung. Gewerkschaftliche Monatshefte 6 : 607-614, Oktober 1955.

WOHLFARTH, E. : Gerichtsbarkeit über fremde Streitkräfte. Deutsche Richterzeitung 33 : 232-234, Oktober 1955.

RABINOVITCH, L.A. : Les traités de Bonn et le problème des dommages d'occupation. Journal du droit international 82 : 844-873, octobre-décembre 1955.
Texte en anglais aussi.

SCHWENK, E.H. : Deutsche und ausländische Gerichtsbarkeit nach den Pariser Verträgen. Monatsschrift für deutsches Recht 9 : 703-707, Dezember 1955.

MEYER, H. : Der Schutz vor Überstellung an das Ausland nach dem Grundgesetz. Juristenzeitung 11 : 6-14, 5. Januar 1956.

ALLEN, C.G. : Revision of German war-time judgments under the Bonn-Paris agreement. International and comparative law quarterly 5 : 40-60, January 1956.

KREKELER, H.L. : German legal problems, national and international. Vital speeches of the day 22 : 632-635, August 1, 1956.

HEIDELMEYER, W. : Schiedsvereinbarungen in Verträgen der Bundesrepublik Deutschland. Zeitschrift für ausländisches öffentliches Recht und Völkerrecht 16 : 567-590, Nr. 3/4, 1956.

Das Gesetz zur Regelung von Fragen der Staatsangehörigkeit vom 22. Februar 1955. Zeitschrift für ausländisches öffentliches Recht und Völkerrecht 16 : 646-676, Nr. 3/4, 1956.

SCHÄTZEL, W. : Der heutige Stand des deutschen Staatsangehörigkeitsrechts. Archiv des öffentlichen Rechts 81 : 265-300, Heft 3/4, 1956.

MAKAROV, A.N. : Das Gesetz über die deutsch-österreichischen Staatsangehörigkeitsfragen. Juristenzeitung 11 : 744-749, Nr. 23/24, 1956.

BRACHT, H.W. : Zum Problem der völkerrechtlichen und staatsrechtlichen Kontinuität Deutschlands nach 1945. Zeitschrift für Ostforschung 6 : 293-297, Heft 2, 1957.

GECK, W.K. : Der Anspruch des Staatsbürgers auf Schutz gegenüber dem Ausland nach deutschem Recht. Zeitschrift für ausländisches öffentliches Recht und Völkerrecht 17 : 476-545, Nr. 3/4, 1957.

MAKAROV, A.N. : Die Behandlung der deutschen Sammeleinbürgerungen 1938-1945 in der ausländischen Rechtsprechung. Zeitschrift für ausländisches öffentliches Recht und Völkerrecht 18 : 329-344, Nr. 2, Dezember 1957.

NEUHAUS, H. : Die internazionale Zustandigkeit in Ehesachen nach dem Gleichberechtigungsgesetz. Ehe und Familie im privaten und öffentlichen Recht 5 : 13-14, Januar 1958.

KAISER, J.H. : Die Erfüllung der völkerrechtlichen Verträge des Bundes durch die Länder - Zum Konkordatsurteil des Bundesverfassungsgerichts. Zeitschrift für ausländisches öffentliches Recht und Völkerrecht 18 : 526-558, Nr. 3, Februar 1958.

STREBEL, H. : Das Österreichergesetz vom Blickpunkt des Völkerrechts. Zeitschrift für ausländisches öffentliches Recht und Völkerrechts 19 : 483-511, Nr. 1/3, August 1958.

PATEY, J. : L'adaptation pour l'Allemagne fédérale de la convention de Londres sur le statut des forces de l'OTAN. Annuaire français de droit international 5 : 727-747, 1959.

GERMANY
(Democratic Republic)

BENJAMIN, H., and MELSHEIMER, E. : Zehn Jahre demokratischer Justiz in Deutschland. Neue Justiz (Germany) 9 : 259-266, 5. Mai 1955.

Ordonnance concernant la formation et la dissolution du mariage, du 24 novembre 1955. Documentation juridique étrangère 7 : 1-6, no. 6-7, 1955.
Publié dans "Journal officiel de la République Démocratique Allemande".

ZIEGLER, W. : Verbrechen gegen die Deutsche Demokratische Republik. Neue Justiz (Germany) 9 : 677-679, 20. November 1955.

BRUNN, W. : Das neue Eherecht der Sowjetzone. Ehe und Familie im privanten und öffentlichen Recht 3 : 3-5, Januar 1956.

Die Leipziger Konferenz der Richter und Staatsanwälte - Ein erster Bericht. Neue Justiz (Germany) 10 : 2-7, 5. Januar 1956.
December 1955; See also pp. 8-11.

ARTZT, W. : Zur Rolle des Zivilrechts beim Aufbau des Sozialismus in der Deutschen Demokratischen Republik. Neue Justiz (Germany) 10 : 65-67, 5. Februar 1956.

BENJAMIN, H. : Zu einem Entwurf zur Ergänzung des Strafgesetzbuchs. Neue Justiz (Germany) 10 : 321-324, 5. Juni 1956.

NATIONAL LAW - COUNTRIES

DORNBERGER, G. : Zehn Jahre Volkseigentum in der Deutschen Demokratischen Republik. Staat und Recht 5 : 435-449, Nr. 4, 30. Juni 1956.

WIEMANN, H. : Aus der Praxis des Schiedsgerichts bei der Kammer für Aussenhandel. Neue Justiz (Germany) 10 : 436-439, 20. July 1956.

KUHLIG, G. : Zu den Tatbeständen der Spionage und der Verleitung zur Republikflucht. Neue Justiz (Germany) 10 : 428-433, 20. Juli 1956.

STORSBERG, G. : Sowjetisiertes Eherecht. SBZ (Sowjetische Besatzungszone) - Archiv 7 : 258-260, 10. September 1956.

BYDŽOVSKÝ, L. : Rechtshilfevertrag zwischen der Tschechoslovakischen Republik und der Deutschen Demokratischen Republik. Neue Justiz (Germany) 10 : 613-614, 20. Oktober 1956.

SCHULTES, K. : Verfassungsrecht und Verfassungswirklichkeit in der Sowjetischen Besatzungszone Deutschlands. Gewerkschaftliche Monatshefte 8 : 129-137, März 1957.

FRITZSCHE, H. : Zum räumlichen Geltungsbereich der Strafgesetz der Deutschen Demokratischen Republik. Staat und Recht 6 : 391-399, April 1957.

CUKIERSKI, K. : Rechtshilfevertrag zwischen der Volksrepublik Polen und der Deutschen Demokratischen Republik. Neue Justiz (Germany) 11 : 353-354, 20. Juni 1957.

BEYER, K.H., and CHEIM, H.G. : Das Lehrbuch des Zivilprozessrechts der DDR. Neue Justiz (Germany) 11 : 503-506, 20. August 1957.

HARHAMMER, L. : Das Konsulargesetz der DDR. Deutsche Aussenpolitik 2 : 758-761, September 1957.

RENNEBERG, J. : Die neuen Strafbestimmungen zum Schutze der Deutschen Demokratischen Republik. Neue Justiz (Germany) 12 : 6-12, 5. Januar 1958.

GRAEFRATH, B. : Zur Neugestaltung des Konsularrechts. Staat und Recht 7 : 12-28, Januar 1958.
German Democratic Republic.

SCHILLE, A. : Die Bedeutung der Strafrechtsnormen über die Verbrechen gegen die militärische Disziplin. Neue Justiz (Germany) 12 : 153-156, 5. März 1958.

BREYMANN, H. : Die Sicherung ausländischer insbesondere amerikanischer Erbschaften von SBZ-Bewohnern gegen sowjetische Zugriffsversuche. Recht in Ost und West 2 : 54-58, 15. März 1958.

OSTMANN, H. : Die Rechtshilfeverträge der Deutschen Demokratischen Republik. Neue Justiz (Germany) 12 : 545-550, 20. August 1958.

POLAK, K. : Die Entwicklung des deutschen volksdemokratischen Staates 1945 bis 1958. Neue Justiz (Germany) 12 : 581-584, 5. September 1959.

MAURACH, R. : Zur Problematik der Rechtsbeugung durch Anwendung sowjetzonalen Recht. Recht in Ost und West 2 : 177-181, 15. September 1958.

LEIM, E. : Abgrenzung der Hetze von der Staatsverleumdung. Neue Justiz (Germany) 12 : 694-697, 20. Oktober 1958.

Wissenschaftliche Beratung im Ministerium der Justiz über die Schaffung eines Zivilgesetzbuches. Neue Justiz (Germany) 12 : 738-741, 5. November 1958.

SUCH, H. : Über die Konzeption eines neuen Zivilgesetzbuches der Deutschen Demokratischen Republik. Staat und Recht 7 : 1096-1117, November 1958.

KIRCHHEIMER, O. : The administration of justice and the concept of legality in East Germany. Yale law journal 68 : 705-749, March 1959.

KOHL, M. : Zur Frage des Beitritts zu mehrseitigen offenen Verträgen in seiner aktuellen Problematik für die Deutsche Demokratische Republik. Časopis pro mezinárodni právo 3 : 329-348, čislo 4, 1959.

PINTO, R. : Le statut international de la République Démocratique Allemande. Journal du droit international 86 : 312-425, avril-juin 1959.
Texte en anglais aussi.

GENTZMANN, C. : Zur Rechtslage des in der SBZ und in Ost-Berlin Befindlichen Vermögens von Ausländern Recht in Ost und West 3 : 101-104, 15. Mai 1959.

ENDERLEIN, F. : Wir brauchen ein Zivilgesetzbuch neuer Art. Staat und Recht 8 : 598-615, Mai 1959.

SPITZNER, O. : Fünf Jahre Schiedegericht bei der Kammer für Aussenhandel der Deutschen Demokratische Republik. Aussenhandel, Recht im Aussenhandel : 1-4, Nr. 18, 29. September 1959.

BENJAMIN, H. : Zehn Jahre Justiz im Arbeiter- und Bauern-Staat - Rückblick und Ausblick. Neue Justi (Germany) 13 : 656-663, 5. Oktober 1959.

GHANA

DAVIES, S.G. : The growth of law in the Gold Coast. Journal of Africam administration (Great Britain) 9 : 88-92, April 1957.

Constitution du Ghana, 6 mars 1957. Informations constitutionnelles et parlementaires : 99-150, juillet 1957.
Texte.

The legislation providing for the grant of indeper dence to Ghana. Journal of African law 1 : 99-112 summer 1957.

Constitution du Ghana, 6 mars 1957. Documentatior française, Notes et études documentaires : 1-22, no. 2343, 26 octobre 1957.
Texte.

GOLD COAST

Ordonnance royale portant constitution de la Gold Coast, 5 mai 1954. Informations constitutionnelles et parlementaires : 2-39, 15 janvier 1956.

DAVIS, P.D. : Transition from primitive to modern law in the African Gold Coast - A student apprais Intramural law review of New York University 11 : 118-130, January 1956.

NATIONAL LAW - COUNTRIES

GREAT BRITAIN

DELL-SOURIAU, V. : La loi anglaise sur l'adoption. Femme dans la vie sociale 27 : 13-16, avril-juin 1955.

JOHNSON, D.H.N. : Arbitration in English law and in international law. Grotius society, Transactions 41 : 91-101, 1955.

ANTON, A.E. : Les conflits de lois et de juridictions entre l'Angleterre et l'Ecosse. Revue critique de droit international privé 45 : 191-221, avril-juin 1956.

GOWER, L.C.B. : Some contrasts between British and American corporation law. Harvard law review 69 : 1369-1402, June 1956.

CARR, C. : Parliamentary control of delegated legislation. Public law : 200-217, autumn 1956.

KAHN-FREUND, O. : Divorce law reform? Modern law review 19 : 573-600, November 1956.

WINDER, G. : A twentieth century problem - Administrative law in Great Britain. American bar association journal 43 : 621-623, 665 ; July 1957.

HONIG, F. : Reciprocal recognition and enforcement of foreign judgments. Law journal 107 : 787-789, 13 December 1957.

MANN, M. : The Royal commission on marriage and divorce - Jurisdiction on the English courts and recognition of foreign decrees. Modern law review 21 : 1-18, January 1958.

Human rights in the United Kingdom. Central office of information, Reference division, Bulletin (London) : 1-32, No. R 3980, October 1958.

FRANK, W.F. : The State and industrial arbitration in the United Kingdom. Louisiana law review 19 : 617-643, April 1959.

BIRKETT : The freedom of the individual under British law- New Zealand law journal 35 : 231-232, August 18 1959.

MARSHALL, G. : The recent development of English administrative law. Politico 24 : 637-645, December 1959.

GREAT BRITAIN
(International law, Aliens)

GARLAND, B. : Recognition of foreign decrees. Law journal 105 : 179-180, 25 March 1955.

HANBURY, H.G. : The position of the foreign sovereign before English courts. Current legal problems 8 : 1-23, 1955.

DRUCKER, A. : Compensation for nationalized property - The British practice. American journal of international law 49 : 477-486, October 1955.

LAUTERPACHT, E. : The contemporary practice of the United Kingdom in the field of international law - Survey and comment. International and comparative law quarterly 5 : 405-446, July 1956.

LATEY, W. : Jurisdiction in divorce and nullity - Proposed British code of international private law. International and comparative law quarterly 5 : 499-510, October 1956.

JOHNSON, D.H.N. : Recent developments in international law studies in England. Journal of legal education 10 : 29-46, No. 1, 1957.

HONIG, F. : Die Immunität ausländischer Staaten gegenüber der englischen Gerichtsbarkeit. Annales Universitatis saraviensis - Rechts- und Wirtswissenschaften : Droit, économie 5 : 77-91, Fasc. 2, 1956/57.

LEFEBURE, M. : The application of international law in the English courts. Zeitschrift für ausländisches öffentliches Recht und Völkerrecht 17 : 586-612, Nr. 3/4, 1957.

WEDDERBURN, K.W. : Sovereign immunity of foreign public corporations. International and comparative law quarterly 6 : 290-300, April 1957.

ABEL, P. : Die Rechtsprechung in Grossbritannien auf dem Gebiet des internationalen Rechts. Juristische Blätter 79 : 497-503, 12. Oktober 1957.

WEBB, P.R.H. : Recognition in England of non-domiciliary divorce decrees. International and comparative law quarterly 6 : 608-624, October 1957.

WORTLEY, B.A. : Great Britain and the movement for the unification of private law since 1948. Tulane law review 32 : 541-554, June 1958.

MANN, F.A. : The enforcement of treaties by English courts. Grotius society, Transactions 44 : 29-62. 1958-1959.

ZIEGLER, J.S. : Confiscation in English private international law. McGill law journal 6 : 1-29, No. 1, 1959.

Foreign divorce decrees. Law journal 109 : 116-118, 20 February 1959.

BLOM-COOPER, L.J. : Jurisdiction to wind up a foreign company in England. Journal du droit international 86 : 686-775, juillet-septembre 1959. Text also in French.

SNYDER, E. : Military law abroad - The status of Forces agreement in England. American bar association journal 45 : 1033-1036, 1117-1118, October 1959.

GRAVESON, R.H. : La récente législation anglaise en matière d'adoption et de filiation légitime et le droit international privé. Revue critique de droit international privé 48 : 651-659, octobre-décembre 1959.

GREECE

TSOUTSOS, A.G. : La fonction publique en Grèce. Revue internationale des sciences administratives 21 : 79-85, no. 1, 1955.

FRAGISTAS, C.N. : Griechische Rechtsprechung auf dem Gebiete des internationalen Privatrechts 1946-1953. Zeitschrift für ausländisches und internationales Privatrecht 20 : 144-157, Heft 1, 1955.

KYRIACOPOULOS, E. : De la séparation des juridictions administratives et des juridictions judiciaires en Grèce. Revue hellénique de droit international 8 : 74-100, janvier-mars 1955.

PAPALAMBROU, A. : The "actes de gouvernement" in Greek law. Revue hellénique de droit international 8 : 101-108, janvier-mars 1955.

STASSINOPOULOS, M. : Le 25e anniversaire du Conseil d'Etat hellénique. Revue internationale des sciences administratives 21 : 275-282, no. 2, 1955.

FRAGISTAS, C.N. : Die Garantien der richterlichen Unabhängigkeit in Griechenland. Deutsche Richterzeitung 34 : 46-48, März 1956.

YOTIS, C.P. : Le droit pénal hellénique, 1955. Revue de droit pénal et de criminologie 36 : 1025-1026, juillet 1956.

La ley griega de nacionalidad. Anuario de derecho civil 9 : 913-914, julio-septiembre 1956.

Conventions, etc., signées entre la Grèce et des pays étrangers ou des organisations internationales et ratifiées par la Grèce, ler janvier 1953 - 31 décembre 1955. Revue hellénique de droit international 9 : 126-138, janvier-décembre 1956.

SCHINAS, G. : Das griechische Gesetz über die Gesellschaft mit beschränkter Haftung. Zeitschrift für ausländisches un öffentliches Privatrecht 22 : 311-323, Heft 2, 1957.
Text pp. 334-356.

FRAGISTAS, C.N. : L'exécution en Grèce des sentences arbitrales étrangères. Revue de l'arbitrage : 74-88, juillet-septembre 1957.

YOTIS, C.P. : Le droit pénal hellénique, 1956. Revue de droit pénal et de criminologie 38 : 114-116, octobre 1957.

BALTATZIS, M. : Das internationale Szrafrecht im neuen griechischen Strafgesetzbuch. Internationales Recht und Diplomatie : 131-135, Heft 2, 1958.

PHILIPPIDES, T. : Das griechische Strafgesetzbuch vom 1.1.1951. Zeitschrift für die gesamte Strafrechtswissenschaft 69 : 580-590, Heft 4, 1957.

YOTIS, C.P. : Le droit pénal hellénique, 1957. Revue de droit pénal et de criminologie 38 : 903-905, juin 1958.

VALLINDAS, P.G., et KOKKINI-IATRIDOU, D. : Grèce. Revue de droit international et de droit comparé 36 : 78-85, no. 1-2, 1959.

PAPAHATZIS, G. : La notion de la légalité en Grèce. Revue hellénique de droit international 12 : 45-57, janvier-décembre 1959.
Voir aussi pp. 57-73.

KOKKINI-IATRIDOU, D. : L'exécution des sentences arbitrales étrangères en Grèce. Revue hellénique de droit international 12 : 119-130, janvier-décembre 1959.

STEFANOPOULOS, K.G. : Die Ehescheidung in Griechenland. Zeitschrift für ausländisches und internationales Privatrecht 24 : 470-488, Heft 3, 1959.

ROUSSEAU, C. : L'affaire franco-hellénique des phares et la sentence arbitrale du 24 juillet 1956. Revue générale de droit international public 63 : 248-292, avril-juin 1959.

STEFANOPULOS, K.G. : Die Eheschliessung nach griechischem Recht. Österreichische Juristen-Zeitung 14 : 451-457, 4. September 1959.

VLACHOS, G. : Remarques sur l'entrée en vigueur et la présomption de connaissance des lois en droit hellénique. Revue internationale de droit comparé 11 : 720-732, octobre-décembre 1959.

GREENLAND

WAABEN, K. : En kriminalloy for Grønland. Svensk juristtidning 40 : 69-74, januari 1955.

GUATEMALA

Guatemala - Constitución de la República. Boletín de la Biblioteca del Congreso (Buenos Aires) : 143-174, enero-abril 1957.

HALL LLOREDA, C. : Estudios sobre el tratado entre las repúblicas de Guatemala y El Salvador para el aprovechiamento de las aguas del Lago de Güija, de 15 abril de 1957... Revista de la Facultad de ciencias jurídicas y sociales de Guatemala 6 : 14-33, enero-junio 1958.

VILLAGRÁN KRAMER, F. : Principales reglas de conexión de conflicto del derecho internacional privado guatemalteco. Asociación guatemalteca de derecho internacional, Revista 3 : 31-74, enero 1959.

HONDURAS

LIONS SIGNORET, M. : Nueva constitución de la República de Honduras. Boletín del Instituto de derecho comparado de México 11 : 77-87, septiembre-diciembre 1958.
Text.

HUNGARY

SZABÓ, A. : Vita büntetőjogunk kodifikációjának elvi kérdéseiről. Jogtudományi közlöny : 442-453, július 1955.
Criminal law.

VILÁGHY, M. : A Magyar Népköztársaság polgári törvénykönyvének rendszeréről. Jogtudományi közlöny : 457-487, augusztus 1955.
Civil code.

Administration of justice in the Hungarian People's Republic. Revue de la législation hongroise : 1-31, special issue : 1955.

BENKŐ, G. : A Magyar népköztársaság legfelsőbb bíróságának irányíto szerepe. Jogtudományi közlöny 11 : 65-75, február 1956.
Supreme court.

LOVASS, L. : Die Rechtslage der Anwaltschaft in Ungarn. Osteuropa-Recht 2 : 202-206, Mai 1956.

LENARD, L. : Hungary - "Abandoned" property. Highlights of current legislation and activities in Mid-Europe 4 : 201-204, June 1956.

BEDO, A.K. : Hungary - Communist justice in Hungarian criminal courts. Highlights of current legislation and activities in Mid-Europe 4 : 349-362, November 1956.

TORZSAY-BIBER, G. : The Hungarian law of inheritance Highlights of current legislation and activities in Mid-Europe 4 : 435-451, December 1956.

NATIONAL LAW - COUNTRIES

TORZSAY-BIBER, G. : The Hungarian law of inheritance (Contd.). Highlights of current legislation and activities in Mid-Europe 5 : 115-130, March-April 1957.

SZIGETI, P. : Notes sur la loi hongroise LX de 1948 sur la nationalité. Journal de droit international 84 : 378-390, avril-juin 1957.
Texte en anglais aussi.

Gesetzgebung der Ostblockstaaten (Contd.). - Ungarn. Osteuropa-Recht 3 : 40-45, Juni 1957.
1956 - Jan. 1957.

Ungarn - Staatsbürgerschaftsgesetz von 1957. Osteuropa-Recht 3 : 114-119, Oktober 1957.
Published in "Magyar közlöny".

Ungarn - Gesetz über Eheschliessung und Adoption von Ausländern von 1957. Osteuropa-Recht 3 : 120-121, Oktober 1957.
Published in "Magyar közlöny".

SÓLYOM FAKETE, W. : Hungary - Changes in criminal procedure after the revolution of October 1956. Highlights of current legislation and activities in Mid-Europe 5 : 451- 453, November 1957.

NEVAI, L. : Das Gerichtsverfassungsgesetz der Ungarischen Volksrepublik. Staat und Recht 7 : 29-47, Januar 1958.

KATONA-SOLTÉSZ, M. : Caractéristiques de la nouvelle législation hongroise sur la nationalité. Revue de droit hongrois : 23-32, no. 1, 1958.
Texte pp. 58-63.

La nouvelle législation de la République populaire hongroise. Revue de droit hongrois : 75-78, no. 2, 1958.

EÖRSI, G. : Le projet 1957 du code civil de la République populaire hongroise. Revue de droit hongrois : 5-18, no. 2, 1958.

DOROGHI, E. : Internationales Personen- und Familienrecht Ungars. Osteuropa-Recht 4 : 186-188, Juli 1958.

Ungarn - Durchführungsverordnung zum Staatsbürgerschaftsgesetz von 1957. Osteuropa-Recht 4 : 224-227, Juli 1958.
Published in "Magyar közlöny".

KISS, G. : Észrevételek a Magyar polgári törvénykönyv tervezete kötelmi jogának általános reszéhez. Jogtudományi közlöny 13 : 261-272, julius-augusztus 1958.
Civil code project.

TALLOS, J. : Les traités d'assistance judiciaire de la République populaire hongroise. Revue de droit hongrois : 21-31, no. 1, 1959.

MARTONYI, J. : La loi hongroise sur les règles générales des actes administratifs de l'Etat. Revue internationale des sciences administratives 24 : 319-332, no. 3, 1958.

PÁRIS, L. : Arbitrage en Hongrie. Revue de droit hongrois : 32-41, no. 1, 1959.

KRIVICKAS, D. : The civil code of the Hungarian People's Republic. Highlights of current legislation and activities in Mid-Europe 7 : 371-382, October 1959.

KNEIF, T. : Die Entwicklung des Verfassungsrechts in Ungarn seit 1945. Jahrbuch des öffentlichen Rechts der Gegenwart 8 : 365-397, 1959.

ICELAND

SIGURJÓNSSON, B. : Fra den islandske Højesterets praksis i årene 1950-1954. Tidsskrift for rettsvitenskap 70 : 73-96, hefte 1, 1957.

INDIA

VENKOBA RAO, K. : Indian arbitration law. Arbitration journal 10 : 138-139, no. 3, 1955.

AGARWALA, S.K. : Standards of "reasonableness" in article 19 of the Indian constitution. Supreme court journal (Madras) 18 : 151-162, March 1955.

PYLEE, M.V. : The constitution of India. Jahrbuch des öffentlichen Rechts de Gegenwart 4 : 155-182, 1955.
Text pp. 183-254.

Who may be citizen? Eastern economist 24 : 956, 17 June 1955.

RAMACHANDRAN, V.G. : The significance of directive principles of state policy in the Indian constitution. Supreme court hournal (Madras) 18 : 233-242, July 1955.

GHOSH, A.C. : The law of the Indian constitution. Modern review 98 : 112-113, August 1955.

SRINIVASACHARYA, R.S. : The Law commission. Supreme court journal (Madras) 18 : 253-256, September 1955.

RAO, T.S.R. : Private international law in India. Indian year book of international affairs 4 : 219-274, 1955.

TOPE, T.K. : Provisions of the Indian constitution regarding international relations. Supreme court journal (Madras) 18 : 305-311, November 1955.

LOOPER, R.B. : The treaty power in India. British year book of international law 32 : 300-307, 1955-6.

RAMALINGAM, T. : The Supreme court of India and the doctrine of "stare decisis". Supreme court journal (Madras) 2 : 9-13, February 1956.

GUPTESWAR, K. : The rule against double jeopardy under the Indian constitution. Supreme court journal (Madras) 19 : 53-66, April 1956.

TOPE, T.K. : Power of President of India to consult the Supreme court of India - How far is this provision desirable? Supreme court journal (Madras) 19 : 118-122, August 1956.

DIWAN, P. : Recognition and execution of foreign judgments and decrees. Supreme court journal (Madras) 19 : 122-176, August 1956.

VENKATARAMAN, S. : The Hindu succession act, 1956 - A study. Supreme court journal (Madras) 19 : 195-204, September 1956.

REINTANZ, G. : Die Verfassung der Indischen Union. Staat und Recht 5 : 789-804, Heft 6, 30. September 1956.

DIWAN, P. : The Hindu succession act, 1956. Supreme court journal (Madras) 19 : 251-318, December 1956.

ARUNACHALAM, N. : Public international law - Indian interpretation. Supreme court journal (Madras) 20 : 1-18, January 1957.

Los problemas de la recepción de los derechos extranjeros en la India. Instituto de derecho comparado, Revista (Barcelona) : 67-212, enero-diciembre 1957.
Series of articles.

MAKAROV : Das indische Staatsangehörigkeitsgesetz vom 30. Dezember 1955. Zeitschrift für ausländisches öffentliches Recht und Völkerrecht 17 : 631-633, Nr. 3/4, 1957.
Text pp. 634-642.

APPADORAI, A. : The constitutional development of India since 1953. Internationale spectator 11 : 175-186, 8 maart 1957.

GLEDHILL, A. : La constitución de la India. Revista de estudios políticos : 13-29, marzo-abril 1957.

DIWAN, P. : The Hindu marriage act, 1955. International and comparative law quarterly 6 : 263-272, April 1957.

DERRETT, J.D.M. : The codification of personal law in India, Hindu law. Indian year book of international affairs 6 : 189-211, 1957.

RAMA RAO, T.S. : Some problems of international law in India. Indian year book of international affairs 6 : 3-45, 1957.

DIWAN, P. : The new Hindu law of maintenance. Supreme court journal (Madras) 20 : 97-130, July 1957.

ISMAIL, M.M. : The legal status of non-governmental international associations in India. Associations internationales - International associations 9 : 152-160, mars 1957.

Inde - Loi sur le droit d'auteur no. 14 du 4 juin 1957. Droit d'auteur 70 : 177-184, octobre 1957.

SIVARAMAYYA, B. : Some aspects of the Indian succession act. Supreme court journal (Madras) 20 : 221-230, December 1957.

BANERJEE, D.N. : Some aspects of our constitution - Fundamental rights, right to property. Modern review 103 : 25-39, January 1958.
First of a series of articles.

TRIPATHI, P.K. : Free speech in the Indian constitution - Background and prospect. Yale law journal 67 : 384-400, January 1958.

BANSAL, G.L. : The practice of commercial arbitration in India. Arbitration journal 13 : 23-29, no. 1, 1958.

RAMA RAO, T.S. : Conflict of laws in India. Zeitschrift für ausländisches und internationales Privatrecht 23 : 259-279, Heft 2, 1958.

BASU, D.D. : Protection par la constitution des droits civils en Inde. Commission internationale de juristes, Revue 1 : 167-211, printemps-été 1958.

EBB, L.F., and MARKROSE, A.T. : Conference of the Indian law institute. American journal of comparative law 7 : 219-233, spring 1958.
New Delhi, December 1957; Text of finalreport pp. 233-238.

PANDE, D.C. : Offences against religion. Supreme court journal (Madras) 21 : 93-98, May 1958.

GLEDHILL, A. : Inde. Annuaire de législation française et étrangère 7 : 175-200, 1958.

SINHA, A.N. : Law of citizenship and aliens in India. India quarterly 14 : 253-269, July-September 1958.

DERRETT, J.D.M. : Statutory amendments of the personal law of Hindus since Indian independence. American journal of comparative law 7 : 380-393, summer 1958.

SHARMA, S.R. : The Supreme court in the Indian constitution. Public law : 119-134, summar 1958.

VENKATARAMAN, S. : Remarriage after divorce under the Hindu marriage act. Supreme court journal (Madras) 21 : 251-258, December 1958.

RAMACHANDRAN, V.G. : Is the constitution of India federal? Supreme court journal (Madras) 22 : 97-108, April 1959.

DERRETT, J.D.M. : The role of Roman law and continental laws in India. Zeitschrift für ausländisches und internationales Privatrecht 24 : 657-685, Heft 4, 1959.

VENKATARAMAN, S. : Some reflections on the fourteenth report of the Law commission. Supreme court, journal (Madras) 22 : 121-132, June 1959.

VENKATARAMAN, S. : Matrimonial reliefs under the Hindu marriage act and their operation. Supreme court journal (Madras) 22 : 133-142, July 1959.

GOPALAKRISHNAN, P. : The constitutional implications of president's rule in Kerala. Supreme court journal (Madras) 22 : 161-176, August 1959.

AGARWALA, R. : Hindu divorce law, its history. Supreme court journal (Madras) 22 : 242-252, December 1959.

INDONESIA

PANHUYS, H.F. van : La succession de l'Indonésie aux accords internationaux conclus par les Pays-Bas avant l'indépendance de l'Indonésie. Nederlands tijdschrift voor internationaal recht 2 : 55-75, Januari 1955.

The Sino-Indonesian treaty on dual nationality. Far Eastern survey 24 : 75-76, May 1955.

Traité sino-indonésian sur le problème de la double nationalité. Légation de la République populaire de Chine, Bulletin d'information (Berne) : 3-6, 7 juin 1955.
Texte.

SUMARJO : The position of Adat law vis-à-vis the Universal declaration of human rights, as embodied in the provisional constitution. Indonesia (Indonesia) 2 : 10-11, 27-30,

McNAIR : The seizure of property and enterprises in Indonesia. Nederlands tijdschrift voor internationaal recht - Netherlands international law review 6 : 218-256, juli 1959.
See also articles by H. Rolin and A. Verdross, pp. 260-287.

VOGEL, F.J. : Die Nationalisierung niederländischen Eigentums in Indonesien. Europa-Archiv 14 : 787-790, 5./20. Dezember 1959.

IRAN

GRAVEN, J. : La modernisation du droit pénal iranien. Schweizerische Zeitschrift für Strafrecht 74 : 331-339, Hefte 3/4, 1959.

HEDAYATI, M.A. : L'évolution moderne du droit pénal iranien. Revue internationale de criminologie et de police technique 13 : 173-178, juillet-septembre 1959.

IRAQ

CURTI GIALDINO, A. : La dichiarazione dello Strato iracheno sul letto e sul sottosuolo marino. Rivista di diritto internazionale 41 : 99-110, fasc. 1, 1958.

Constitution de la Fédération arabe irako-jordanienne, proclamée le 19 mars 1958. Monde arabe en fin de chaque semaine, Annexe documentaire 1 : 1-10, no. 96, ler-6 avril 1958.
Texte.

La costituzione della Federazione Araba, 19 marzo 1958. Oriente moderno 38 : 299-307, aprile 1958.
Text in Italian.

Constitution de la Fédération arabe, Iraq et Jordanie, 19 mars 1958. Documentation française, Notes et études documentaires : 1-8, no. 2413, 17 mai 1958.
Texte.

BAZZAZ, A.R. : Nazarat fil doustour al Iraki. Majallat Nakabat al-mouhamine 22 : 116-121, April-June 1958.
Constitution; Text in Arabic.

Fédération arabe - Constitution, 19 mars 1958. Informations constitutionnelles et parlementaires 9 : 117-133, juillet 1958.
Texte.

La costituzione provvisoria della Repubblica irachena, 27 luglio 1958. Oriente moderno 38 : 665-667, agosto-settembre 1958.
Text.

Constitution provisoire de la République iraquienne, 27 juillet 1958. Documentation française, Notes et études documentaires : 1-4, no. 2500, 15 janvier 1959.

Constitution provisoire de la République iraquienne, 27 juillet 1958. Informations constitutionnelles et parlementaires : 70-72, avril 1959.

IRELAND

PHELAN, A. : The Republic of Ireland and extradition. Law journal 106 : 39, 20 January 1956.

O'HIGGINS, P. : Irish extradition law and practice. British year book of international law 34 : 274-311, 1958.

ISRAEL

KISCH, I. : Internationaal erfrecht voor Israël. Nederlands tijdschrift voor internationaal recht 2 : 47-54, Januari 1955.

GORNEY, U. : American precedent in the Supreme court of Israel. Harvard law review 68 : 1194-1210, May 1955.

BOASSON, C. : Some theoretical and practical considerations of the Israel nationality law. Nederlands tijdschrift voor internationaal recht - Netherlands international law review 2 : 375-383, October 1955.

MIGDAL, R. : La loi israélienne sur la nationalité. Revue de droit international pour le Moyen-Orient 4 : 415-422, décembre 1955.

SAMUEL, E. : Control of the executive in Israel. South African law journal 73 : 171-180, May 1956.

AKZIN, B. : Codification in a new state - A case study of Israel. American journal of comparative law 5 : 44-77, winter 1956.

WARSOFF, L.A. : Citizenship in the State of Israel - A comment. New York university law review 33 : 857-861, June 1958.

GRAJEVSKY, A.L. : Le mariage et le divorce en Israël. Revue internationale de droit comparé 10 : 567-573, juillet-septembre 1958.

ROSENNE, S. : La codificación del derecho en Israel. Revista jurídica de Buenos Aires : 27-41, julio-septiembre 1958.

RODIÈRE, R. : Un projet de loi israélien sur les sociétés par actions. Revue internationale de droit comparé 10 : 773-776, octobre-décembre 1958.

Israel - Loi fundamentale du 22 février 1958. Informations constitutionnelles et parlementaires : 31-36, janvier 1959.
Texte.

LAPIDOTH, R. : De la valeur interne des traités internationaux dans le droit israélien. Revue générale de droit international public 63 : 65-93, janvier-mars 1959.

LAPIDOTH, R. : De la valeur interne des traités internationaux dans le droit israélien (Suite). Revue générale de droit international public 63 : 221-247, avril-juin 1959.

ITALY

Code civil italien, livre I. Documentation juridique étrangère 7 : 1-106, no. 1, 1955.

NATIONAL LAW - COUNTRIES

BENTIVOGLIO, L.M. : La dottrina italiana di diritto internazionale privato, 1954-1955. Istituto di diritto internazionale e straniero della Università di Milano, Comunicazioni e studi 7 : 437-516, 1955.

MALINTOPPI, A. : La dottrina italiana di diritto internazionale pubblico, 1954-1955. Istituto di diritto internazionale e straniero della Università di Milano, Comunicazioni e studi 7 : 517-577, 1955.

RUINI, A. : L'interpretazione delle convenzioni internazionali e delle norme straniere in genere da parte del giudice interno. Foro italiano 80 : parte la, 518-534, fasc. 7-8, 1955.

CONSALVO, A. : Adeguamento della legislazione vigente nel Territorio di Trieste alla legislazione italiana. Foro italiano 80 : parte 4, 168-175, 30 settembre 1955.

ROTONDI, M. : Per un diritto uniforme italo-francese delle obbigazioni. Rivista del diritto commerciale e del diritto generale delle obbligazione 53 : 415-415-425, settembre-ottobre 1955.

Trattati ed accordi. Istituto per gli studi di politica internazionale, Annuario di politica internazionale 12 : 906-919, 1955.

AMBROSINI, G. : Decentramento, federalismo ed autonomia con speciale riguardo alla riforma regionale en Italia. Annuario di diritto comparato e di studi legislativi 30 : 425-444, 1955.

Atti internazionali fra l'Italia ed altri Stati resi esecutivi nel 1955. Rivista di diritto internazionale 39 : 141-146, fasc. 1, 1956.

THOMAS, E. : Italien - Der neue Verfassungsgerichtshof. Zeitschrift für ausländisches öffentliches Recht und Völkerrecht 17 : 327-343, Nr. 2, 1956.

FERRARI BRAVO, L. : Le controversie in materia d'impiego presso enti internazionali e la giurisdizione italiana. Rivista di diritto internazionale 39 : 550-567, fasc. 4, 1956.

SEIDL-HUHENVELDERN, I. ; Schiedsgerichtliche Entscheidungen zu vermögensrechtlichen Fragen des Italienischen Friedensvertrags. Juristische Blätter 78 : 252-256, 12. Mai 1956.
Franco-Italian conciliation commission.

FABOZZI, C. : Problemi di diritto internazionale nella giurisprudenza italiana, 1955. Istituto di diritto internazionale e straniero della Università di Milano, Comunicazrioni e studi 8 : 369-415, 1956.

BRULLIARD, G. : L'évolution de la notion de juridiction dite "gracieuse" ou "volontaire" et de celle de juridiction, d'après les récents travaux de la doctrine italienne. Revue internationale de droit comparé 9 : 5-26, janvier-mars 1957.

Atti internazionali fra l'Italia ed altri Stati resi esecutivi nel 1956. Rivista di diritto internazionale 40 : 171-175, fasc. 1, 1957.

SCIASCIA, G. : Die Rechtsprechung des Verfassungsgerichtshofs der Italienischen Republik. Jahrbuch des öffentlichen Rechts der Gegenwart 6 : 1-33, 1957.

FINA, S. de : Lo statuto siciliano e la costituzione. Foro italiano 82 : parte 4a, 50-68, fasc. 7-8, 1957.

LENER, S. : Alcuni aspetti politico e giuridico costituzionali dei rapporti tra stato e Chiese oggi in Italia. Civiltà cattolica 108 : 238-250, 2 novembre 1957.

RENGEL ROMBERG, A. : La reforma procesal italiana de 1942. Revista de la Facultad de derecho (Caracas): 25-79, no. 13, 1957.

SAILIS, E. : Lo scioglimento dei Consigli regionali. Studi economico-giuridici, Università di Cagliari 40 : 281-397, 1957-58.

BARILE, P. : La costituzione italiana nel suo nascere e nel suo divebire. Studi senesi 70 : 36-46, fasc. 1, 1958.

ERMACORA, F. : Die Autonomie Südtirols im Lichte der italienischen Rechtsordnung. Donauraum 3 : 74-96, 2. Heft 1958.

SCARANGELLA, G. : Il divorzio in Italia, in relazione ai limiti della giurisdizione ecclesiastica e dell'ordine pubblico. Jus gentium 6 : 161-167, no. 3, 1958.

CRISAFULLI, V. : Aspetti problematici del sistema parlamentare vigente in Italia. Jus, Rivista di scienze giuridiche 9 : 151-190, giugno 1958.

LOBIN, Y. : Le code de procédure civile italien. Revue internationale de droit comparé 10 : 525-539, juillet-septembre 1958.

BISCARETTI di RUSSIA, P. : The first two years of functioning of the Italian constitutional court. Politico 23 : 468-483, settembre 1958.

JAEGER, N. : La Corte sotituzionale nei primi tre anni della sua attività. Jus, Rivista de scienze giuridiche 9 : 446-464, dicembre 1958.

KOJANEC, G. : La dottrina italiana di diritto internazionale pubblico negli anni 1957-1958. Università di Milano, Istituto di diritto internazionale e straniero; Communicazioni e studi 10 : 393-468, 1958-1959.

BIANCHI, F. : La giurisprudenza italiana di diritto internazionale privato e processuale, 1957. Università di Milano, Istituto di diritto internazionale e straniero; Comunicazioni e studi 10 : 691-744, 1958-1959.

SCELSI, F. : L'oggetto del giudizio sui conflitti di attribuzione fra Stato e regioni. Jus, Rivista di scienze giuridiche 10 : 113-118, marzo 1959.

GIANNINI, A. : La prassi arbitrale italiana. Rivista di diritto commerciale 57 : 95-111, marzo-aprile 1959.

Note sul regime dell'arbitrato estero. Jus gentium 6 : 248-269, no. 4, 1959.

TREVES, G. : Judicial review in Italian administrative law. University of Chicago law review 26 : 419-435, spring 1959.

NATIONAL LAW - COUNTRIES

TRACANNA, L. : Sulla natura giuridica della pretesa del cittadino italiano agli indennizzi in base agli art. 76 e 79 del trattado di pace 10 febbraio 1947. Foro italiano 84 : parte la, 1156-1159, 30 luglio 1959.

CASSANDRO, G. : The Constitutional court of Italy. American journal of comparative law 8 : 1-14, winter 1959.

MARRÈ, E. : In tema di matrimonio canonico celebrato all'estero. Foro italiano 84 : parte 4a, 235-239, 31 ottobre 1959.

AZZARITI, G. : Die Stellung des Verfassungsgerichtshofs in der italienischen Staatsordnung. Jahrbuch des öffentlichen Rechts der Gegenwart 8 : 13-27, 1959.

CICCHITTI-SURIANI, A. : Il Concordato del 1929 non era in vigore nelle colonie italiane. Foro italiano 23 : parte 4a, 293-294, 31 dicembre 1959.

SCELSO, F. : Natura ed effetti delle decisioni della Corte costituzionale sui conflitti di attribuzione fra Stato e regioni. Jus, Rivista di scienze giuridiche 10 : 526-539, dicembre 1959.

IVORY COAST

Constitution de la République de Côte d'Ivoire du 26 mars 1959. Recueil Penant, Législation 69 : 148-158, mai-juin 1959.

MANGIN, G. : Côte d'Ivoire. Annuaire de législation française et étranger 8 : 119-125, 1959.

JAPAN

TANAKA, H.W. : Enforcement of American awards in Japan. Arbitrazion journal 10 : 88-93, No. 2, 1955.

YAMADA, Y. : The new Japanese constitution. International and comparative law quarterly 4 : 197-206, April 1955.

MIYASAWA, T. : Exposé sommaire de l'évolution récente du droit public japonais. France, Conseil d'Etat, Etudes et documents : 139-145, no. 9, 1955.

TAKAYANAGI, K. : Contact of the common law with the civil law in Japan. American journal of comparative law 4 : 60-69, winter 1955.

RABINOWITZ, R.W. : Materials on Japanese law in Western languages. American journal of comparative law 4 : 97-104, winter 1955.

SUZUKI, H. : Judicature of past ten years. Contemporary Japan 23 : 676-685, Nos. 10-12, 1955.

OHGUSHI, T. : Die japanische Verfassung vom 3. November 1946. Jahrbuch des öffentlichen Rechts der Gegenwart 5 : 301-328, 1956.

RABINOWITZ, R.W. : The historical development of the Japanese bar. Harvard law review 70 : 61-81, November 1956.

MIKAZUKI, A. : Wesen und Kompetenz des japanischen Obersten Gerichtshofes. Annales Universitatis saraviensis - Rechts- und Wirtschaftswissenschaften ; Droit, économie 5 : 12-22, fasc. 1, 1956/57.

UKAI, N. : The individual and the rule of law under the new Japanese constitution. Northwestern university law review 51 : 733-744, January-February 1957.

RÖHL, W. : Der japanische Richter. Deutsche Richterzeitung 35 : 31-33, Februar 1957.

NATHANSON, N.L. : On teaching law in Japan. Journal of legal education 9 : 300-310, no. 3, 1957.

SISSONS, D.C.S. : Japanese opinion regarding the United States-Japan security treaty. Australia's neighbours : 1-2, July 1957.

TSUDA, M. : Jurisdiction over foreign military personnel. Oriental economist 25 : 413-415, August 1957.

FUETO, T. : Japan - Revision of the new civil code. American journal of comparative law 6 : 559-565, autumn 1957.

ABE, H. : Criminal procedure in Japan. Journal of criminal law, criminology and police science 48 : 359-368, November-December 1957.

SUZUKI, R. : Die Entwicklung des japanischen Familienrechts unter dem Einfluss des europäischen Rechts. Zeitschrift für vergleichende Rechtswissenschaft 59 : 181-234, 1957.

KIMURA, K. : Evolution et tendances du droit pénal japonais, à propos du cinquantième anniversaire du code pénal japonais. Revue de science criminelle et de droit pénal comparé 13 : 65-72, janvier-mars 1958.

MIKAZUKI, A. : Das japanische Familiengericht. Ehe und Familie im privaten und öffentlichen Recht 5 : 53-57, Februar 1958.

MEHREN, A.T. von : Some reflections on Japanese law. Harvard law review 71 : 1486-1496, June 1958.

MATSUDA, J. : The Japanese legal training and research institute. American journal of comparative law 7 : 366-379, summer 1958.

WOODARD, W.P. : Study on religious juridical persons law. Contemporary Japan 25 : 418-440, September 1958.

GELLHORN, W. : Impressions of Japanese legal training. Columbia law review 58 : 1239-1251, December 1958.

MATSUDA, J. : Das neue japanische Aktienrecht. Zeitschrift für ausländisches und internationales Privatrecht 24 : 115-132, Heft 1, 1959.

TANIGUCHI, T. : La révision du code civil japonais et les conditions actuelles du mariage au Japon. Revue internationale de droit comparé 11 : 67-76, janvier-mars 1959.

FUKASE, T. : Le fonctionnement de la constitution japonaise de 1946. Revue internationale de droit comparé 11 : 365-382, avril-juin 1959.

JORDAN

Constitution de la Fédération arabe irako-jordanienne, proclamée le 19 mars 1958. Monde arabe en fin de chaque semaine, Annexe documentaire 1 : 1-10, no. 96, 1-6 avril 1958.
Texte.

La costituzione della Federazione Araba, 19 marzo 1958. Oriente moderno 38 : 299-307, aprile 1958.
Text in Italian.

Constitution de la Fédération arabe, Iraq et Jordanie, 19 mars 1958. Documentation française, Notes et études documentaires : 1-8, no. 2413, 17 mai 1958.
Texte.

Fédération arabe - Constitution, 19 mars 1958. Informations constitutionnelles et parlementaires 9 : 117-133, juillet 1958.
Texte.

Mining law in Jordan. Middle East review 1 : 151-165, July 1958.
Text.

KOREA

STOREY, R.G. : Korean law and lawyers - The new Korean legal center. American bar association journal 41 : 629-630, 641; July 1955.

LÓPEZ-REY, M. : El nuevo código penal de Corea. Boletín del Instituto de derecho comparado de México 9 : 9-29, mayo-agosto 1956.

KICHYUN RYU, P. : The new Korean criminal code of 3 October 1953 - An analysis of ideologies embedded in it. Journal of criminal law, criminology and police science 48 : 275-295, September-October 1957.

Corée - Loi sur le droit d'auteur, no 432, du 28 janvier 1957. Droit d'auteur 72 : 154-160, septembre 1959.

KIM, C.-s. : A study of marriage and divorce in the new civil code of Korea. Korean research center bulletin : 35-49, fall 1959.

LAOS

Constitution du Royaume du Laos, 11 mai 1947 - 29 septembre 1956. Informations constitutionnelles et parlementaires : 151-169, juillet 1957.
Texte.

Constitution du Royaume du Laos, 11 mai 1947 - 29 septembre 1956. Documentation française, Notes et études documentaires : 1-6, no. 2340, 19 octobre 1957.
Texte.

LEBANON

La constitution du Liban. Documentation française, Notes et études documentaires : 1-8, no. 2018, 12 mai 1955.
Avec modifications.

GANNAGÉ, P. : Observations sur l'évolution du droit de la famille chrétienne au Liban. Revue internationale de droit comparé 8 : 549-560, octobre-décembre 1956.

FARHAT, A. : La condition des étrangers au Liban. Civilisations 7 : 357-376, no. 3, 1957.

Exequatur des jugements étrangers. Revue judiciaire libanaise (Lebanon) 13 : 7-20, août 1957.

L'extradition. Revue judiciaire libanaise (Lebanon) 13 : 34-35, novembre 1957.

EL-HAKIM, J. : La diya et les atteintes aux personnes physiques dans le droit syrien et libanais. Annales de la Faculté de droit de Beyrouth : 249-287, 1957.

GANNAGÉ, P. : Observations sur les effets des jugements étrangers de divorce dans un système juridique non laïcisé. Revue critique de droit international privé 47 : 673-691, octobre-décembre 1958.

LIBERIA

KONVITZ, M.R. : The Liberian code of laws. Journal of African law 2 : 116-118, summer 1958.

WARD, P. : Liberia gives West Africa a law school. Journal of legal education 10 : 491-493, no. 4, 1958.

LIBYA

KHALIDI, I. : The origins of the constitution of the United Kingdom of Libya. Revue de droit international pour le Moyen-Orient 5 : 57-63, juin 1956.

Khalidi, I.R. : The origin of the constitution of the United Kingdom of Libya (Contd.). Revue de droit international pour le Moyen-Orient 5 : 178-183, décembre 1956.

CHILLEMI, A. : La condition juridique des étrangers en Libye. Civilisationa 7 : 327-341, No. 3, 1957.

CAPOTORTI, F. : Sulla sorte dei beni degli enti pubblici italiani in Libia. Rivista di diritto internazionale 40 : 362-383, fasc. 3, 1957.

Cittadinanza italiana libica ed eventi successivi al trattato pace. Diritto internazionale 13 : 347-350, no. 3, 1959.

LIECHTENSTEIN

HAGENS, W. von : Die Exterritorialität der fürstlich liechtensteinschen Kunstsammlung in Wien. Archiv des Völkerrechts 5 : 284-295, 3. Heft 1955.

LUXEMBOURG

Union belge et luxembourgeoise de droit pénal. Revu[e] de droit pénal et de criminologie 35 : 531-541, mar[s] 1955.

BROUWER, J. : La nationalité de la femme mariée au Grand-Duché de Luxembourg. Nederlands tijdschrift voor international recht - Netherlands international law review 3 : 262-271, juli 1956.

LOESCH, F. : Bulletin de jurisprudence luxembourgeoise. Journal du droit international 83 : 898-963, octobre-décembre 1957.
Texte en anglais aussi.

GOERENS, F. : El derecho penal militar del Gran Ducade de Luxembourgo. Revista española de derecho militar : 109-113, julio-diciembre 1959.

NATIONAL LAW - COUNTRIES

MALAYA

Fédération de Malaisie - Constitution, 31 août 1957. Informations constitutionnelles et parlementaires 9 : 134-172, juillet 1958.
Texte.

Fédération de Malaisie - Constitution, 31 août 1957 (Contd.). Informations constitutionnelles et parlementaires 9 : 173-213, octobre 1958.

Constitution de la Fédération de Malaisie, 31 août 1957. Documentation française, Notes et études documentaires : 1-48, no. 2516, 3 mars 1959.

MALI

MANGIN, G. : Mali. Annuaire de législation française et étrangère 8 : 356-367, 1959.

MAURITANIA

Constitution de la République Islamique de Mauritanie. Recueil Penant, Législation 69 : 167-176, mai-juin 1959.

MEXICO

ZAVALA ALVAREZ, A., and TRIGUEROS, E. : Boletín de jurisprudencia mexicana. Journal du droit international 82 : 412-444, avril-juin 1955.
Text also in English and French.

DE PINA, R. : Jurisprudencia de la Suprema corte de justicia de la nación. Revista de la Facultad de derecho de México 5 : 275-289, octubre-diciembre 1955.

FERNÁNDEZ del CASTILLO, G. : El arbitraje comercial en la legislación de México. Boletín del Instituto de derecho comparado de México 9 : 55-62, mayo-agosto 1956.

PLASILOVA, M.V. : Le statut juridique des organisations internationales non gouvernementales au Mexique. Associations internationales - International associations 8 : 503-505, août 1956.

ANAYA MONROY, F. : El código penal de 1931 y la realidad mexicana. Criminalia 22 : 784-809, noviembre 1956.

MANTILLA MOLINA R.L., and LUNA VILLANUEVA, B. : Reseña de legislación, literatura y jurisprudencia mejicanas en el año 1955. Revista de derecho privado (Madrid) : 1270-1278, diciembre 1956.

MANTILLA MOLINA, R. L. : L'influenza della scienza giuridica italiana sul diritto commerciale messicano. Rivista del diritto commerciale e del diritto generale delle obbligazioni 55 : 81-91, marzo-aprile 1957.

ALARCON FALCONI, R. : La constituciones de México y Ecuador. Revista mexicana del trabajo (Mexico) 5 : 12-22, enero-febrero 1958.

ALACALÁ-ZAMORA c CASTILLO, N. : Le ejecución de las sentencias arbitrales en México. Boletín del Instituto de derecho comparado de México 11 : 45-64, mayo-agosto 1958.

MANTILLA MOLINA, R.L. : Reseña de legislación, literatura y jurisprudencia mejicanas en el año de 1957. Revista de derecho privado (Madrid) : 590-598, junio 1958.

Anteproyecto de código penal para el Distrito y territorios federales. Criminalia 24 : 598-671, octubre 1958.

DORANTÉS-TAMAYO, L. : La procédure du "concurso civil" en droit mexicain. Revue internationale de droit comparé 10 : 753-769, octobre-décembre 1958.

PAVÓN VASCONCELOS, F.H. : El delito de traicón a la patria. Criminalia 25 : 136-153, marzo 1959.

MANTILLA MOLINA, R. L. : Reseña de la legislación, la literatura y la jurisprudencia mejicanas en el año 1958. Revista de derecho privado (Madrid) : 696-702, julio-agosto 1959.

MONACO

AUREGLIA, L. : La nationalité en droit monégasque. Journal du droit international 85 : 74-121, janvier-mars 1958.
Texte en anglais aussi.

MOROCCO

DURAND, E. : La réforme politique et administrative du gouvernement chérifien depuis 1912. Revue juridique et politique de l'Union française 9 : 83-122, janvier-mars 1955.

LÉAUTÉ, J. : L'application de la loi d'amnistie du 6 août 1953 au Maroc. Penant, Recueil général de jurisprudence, de doctrine et de législation d'outre-mer, Doctrine 66 : 1-4, février-mars 1956.

NADELMANN, K.H. : American consular jurisdiction in Morocco and the Tangier international jurisdiction. American journal of international law 49 : 506-517, October 1955.

DECROUX, P. : La question de la double nationalité au Maroc. Revue juridique et politique de l'Union française 9 : 669-696, octobre-décembre 1955.

AZZUZ HAQUIM, M.I. : La capacitación técnico-administrativa de los marroquies en la zona jalifiana de Marruecos. Cuadernos africanos y orientales : 27-36, no. 31, 1955.

DECROUX, P. : Le mariage des Français et des étrangers au Maroc. Recueil Dalloz, Chronique 32 : 109-116, 6 octobre 1956.

DURAND, E. : Souveraineté et pouvoirs publics dans le Maroc nouveau. Revue juridique et politique de l'Union française 11 : 478-500, juillet-septembre 1957.

THEIS, J. : Le contentieux administratif au Maroc. Revue du droit public et de la science politique en France et à l'étranger 74 : 401-409, mai-juin 1958.

BUISKOOL, J.A.E. : L'influence du rétablissement de l'indépendance sur l'organisation judiciaire au Maroc. Nederlands tijdschrift voor internationaal recht - Netherlands international law review 5 : 311-320, juli 1958.

ANDERSON, J.N.D. : Reforms in family law in Morocco. Journal of African law 2 : 146-159, autumn 1958.

DECROUX, P. : Le divorce en droit international privé marocain. Revue juridique et politique de l'Union française 12 : 637-652, octobre-décembre 1958.

LAPANNE-JOINVILLE, J. : Le code marocain de statut personnel. Revue Juridique et politique d'outre-mer 13 : 75-99, janvier-mars 1959.

DECROUX, P. : Le régime des biens en droit international privé marocain. Revue juridique et politique d'outre-mer 13 : 437-443, juillet-septembre 1959.

NETHERLANDS

Charte du Royaume des Pays-Bas, 29 décembre 1954. Informations constituionnelles et parlementaires: 19-34, 15 janvier 1955.

CZAPSKI, G. : Niederländische Rechtsprechung zum internationalen Privat- und Prozessrecht - Veröffentlichungen der Jahre 1952-1954. Zeitschrift für ausländisches und internationales Privatrecht 20 : 315-339, 2. Heft 1955.

Das Statut des Königreichs der Niederlande, in Kraft getreten am 29. Dezember 1954. Zeitschrift für ausländisches öffentliches Recht und Völkerrecht 16 : 304-330, April 1955.
See also pp. 299-303.

PANHUYS, H.F. van : Pays-Bas - La révision des dispositions constitutionnelles relatives aux relations internationales. Revue du droit public et de la science politique en France et à l'étranger 71 : 330-354, avril-juin 1955.
Annexes pp. 335-356.

OFFERHAUS, J. : L'évolution du droit commercial spécialement aux Pays-Bas. Revue internationale de droit comparé 7 : 296-310, avril-juin 1955.

Pays-Bas - Loi du 26 janvier 1956 tendant à introduire la possibilité d'adoption et modifiant en conséquence le code civil, le code de procédure civile et le code pénal. Documentation juridique étrangère 7 : 19-30, no. 11, 1955.

ERADES, L. : De invloed, die de Nederlandse rechtspraak met betrekking tot verdragen aan de oorlog toekende. Nederlands tijdschrift voor internationaal recht - Netherlans international law review 3 : 105-128, april 1956.
War and treaties.

DAINOW, J. : Civil code revision in the Netherlands - The fifty questions. American journal of comparative law 5 : 595-610, autumn 1956.

HELSDINGEN, W.H. van : La charte du Royaume des Pays-Bas. Revue juridique et politique de l'Union française 10 : 641-674, octobre-décembre 1956.
Texte pp. 674-686.

SCHUURMANS, J. : Aperçu du droit militaire néerlandais. Revue de science criminelle et de droit pénal comparé : 765-773, octobre-décembre 1956.

Pays-Bas - Modifications de la constitution 10 septembre 1956. Informations constitutionnelles et parlementaires 8 : 27-31, janvier 1957.
Texte.

LEVY, D. : Le nouveau statut constitutionnel du royaume des Pays-Bas. Revue internationale de droit comparé 9 : 539-549, juillet-septembre 1957.

BAUER, R. : Die niederländische Verfassungsänderung von 1956 betreffend die auswärtige Gewalt. Zeitschrift für ausländisches öffentliches Recht und Völkerrecht 18 : 137-155, Oktober 1957.

PANHUYS, H.F. van : The international aspects of the reconstruction of the Kingdom of the Netherlands in 1954. Nederlands tijdschrift voor internationaal recht - Netherlands international law review 5 : 1-31, januari 1958.

DOURHOT MEES, T.J. : Le projet d'un nouveau code civil néerlandais. Zeitschrift für schweizerisches Recht 77 : 389-394, Heft 8, 1958.

CZAPSKI, G. : Niederländische Rechtsprechung zum internationalen Privat- und Prozessrecht - Veröffentlichungen der Jahre 1955-1958. Zeitschrift für ausländisches und internationales Privatrecht 24 : 270-325, Heft 2, 1959.

BAADE, H.W. : The Netherlands private international law of succession and the German courts. Nederlands tijdschrift voor internationaal recht - Netherlands international law review 6 : 174-190, april 1959.

KOLLEWIJN, R.D. : Bulletin de jurisprudence néerlandaise. Journal du droit international 86 : 472-511, avril-juin 1959.
Texte en anglais aussi.

SANDERS, P. : Exécution des sentences arbitrales étrangères aux Pays-Bas. Revue de l'arbitrage : 45-47, avril-juin 1959.

NEW ZEALAND

BRAYBROOKE, E.K. : New Zealand - The divorce and matrimonial causes amendment act, 1953. International and comparative law quarterly 4 : 209-219, April 1955.

Alien's application for admission as barrister. New Zealand law journal 31 : 289-291, 18 October 1955.

INGLIS, B.D. : Annulment of foreign marriages and recognition of foreign divorces. New Zealand law journal 31 : 343-346, 6 December 1955.

EDDY, J.P. : New Zealand and the law of copyright. New Zealand law journal 33 : 190-192, 18 June 1957.

DAVIES, J.W., and INGLIS, B.D. : Divorce, the Royal commission and the conflict of laws. American journal of comparative law 6 : 215-234, spring-summer 1957.

ADAMS, E.C. : The new Companies act 1955. New Zealand law journal 33 : 221-223, 23 July 1957.

DAVIES, J.W., and INGLIS, B.D. : Divorce, the Royal commission, and the conflict of laws. New Zealand law journal 33 : 218-221, 23 July 1957.

NATIONAL LAW - COUNTRIES

NIGER

Constitution de la République du Niger du 25 février. Recueil Penant, Législation 69 : 176-184, mai-juin 1959.

NORWAY

HAMBRO, E. : Folkerettsanvendelse ved norske domstoler. Tidsskrift for rettsvitenskap 68 : 48-56, hefte 1, 1955.

GOLDSCHEIDER, R. : Enforcement of American awards in Norway. Arbitration journal 10 : 39-43, no. 1, 1955.

HAMBRO, E. : Bulletin de jurisprudence norvégienne. Journal du droit international 82 : 446-471, avril-juin 1955.
Texte en anglais aussi.

GAARDER, K. : Fra den norske Høyesteretts praksis i 1954. Tidsskrift for rettsvitenskap 68 : 535-561, hefte 5, 1955.

GAARDER, K. : Fra den norske Høyesteretts praksis i 1955. Tidsskrift for rettsvitenskap 69 : 449-475, hefte 5, 1956.

HAMBRO, E.I. : Ordre public and fraus legis in Norwegian conflict law. Internationales Recht und Diplomatie : 315-326, Heft 4, 1957.

GAARDER, K. : Fra den norske Høyesteretts praksis i 1956. Tidsskrift for rettsvitenskap 70 : 433-454, hefte 5, 1957.

RAMNDAL, L. : Naturalisation etter norsk statsrett. Tidsskrift for rettsvitenskap : 28-29, hefte 1, 1958.

HAMBRO, E. : The legal position of aliens in Norway. Revue internationale des sciences administratives 24 : 141-147, no. 2, 1958.

GAARDER, K. : Fra den norske Høyesteretts praksis i 1958. Tidsskrift for rettsvitenskap : 421-442, hefte 5, 1959.

PAKISTAN

Pakistan - Seeking a foundation for law. Round table : 282-285, June 1955.

GLEDHILL, A. : The Pakistan constitution. Indian year book of international affairs 5.: 110-122, 1956.

Pakistan - Constitution de la République islamique du Pakistan, 23 mars 1956. Informations constitutionnelles et parlementaires : 137-192, juillet 1956.
Extraits.

GLEDHILL, A. : The Pakistan constitution. Public law : 350-367, winter 1956.

MARIÑAS, L. : La constitución del Pakistan. Información jurídica (Spain) : 239-246, mayo-junio 1957.

La costituzione della Repubblica Islamica del Pakistan, 29 febbraio 1956. Oriente moderno 37 : 493-551, agosto-settembre 1957.

GLEDHILL, A. : The Islamic Republic - The first two years. Indian year book of international affairs 7 : 143-152, 1958.

GLEDHILL, A. : Pakistan. Annuaire de législation française et étrangère 7 : 247-269, 1958.

PANAMA

RODRIGUEZ-ARIAS BUSTAMENTE, L. : El principio de la proximidad de grado en el orden de los colaterales ordinarios en el código civil panameño y en la legislación comparada. Revista del Instituto de derecho comparado (Barcelona) : 81-93, julio-diciembre 1955.

PERU

Leyes, decretos y resoluciones. Industria peruana, Suplemento 27 : 37-66, enero 1957.

GARCÍA RADA, D. : Comentarios al código de procedimentos penales. Revista de derecho y ciencias políticas 23 : 196-270, nos. 1-3, 1959.

PHILIPPINES

TANSINSIN, L.G. : Survey of 1955 casis in international law. Philippine law journal 31 : 307-313, April 1956.

Annual survey of 1955 Philippine Supreme court decisions (Contd.). Philippine law journal 31 : 335-482, July 1956.
Series of articles.

NAVARRO, E.R. : The law of treason in the Philippines. Philippine law journal 30 : 719-750, October 1955.

Survey of 1955 Supreme court decisions. Philippine law journal 31 : 1-131, February 1956.
Series of articles.

CUSTODIO, A. : For a stringent application of Philippine naturalization laws. Philippine law journal 31 : 643-646, November 1956.

SAN PEDRO, A.S. : International law. Philippine law journal 32 : 141-145, January 1957.

NARAYANA RAO, K. : The constitution of the Philippines. Indian year book of international affairs 6 : 219-276, 1957.

ANGARA, E.J. : The Anti-subversion act. Philippine law journal 32 : 397-402, July 1957.

GUEVARA, S. : Rights, powers, and liabilities of foreign corporations in the Philippines. Philippine law journal 32 : 832-652, November 1957.

ESPEJO, C.R. : The enforcement of American awards in the Philippines. Arbitration journal 13 : 150-156, No. 3, 1958.

CONCEPCION, P. : The constitution of the Philippines and the proposed amendments thereto. Philippine law journal 33 : 603-611, November 1958.

PEDROSA, J.B.H. : International law, 1958. Philippine law journal 34 : 136-139, January 1959.

FERNANDO, E.M. : Brief survey of the legal status of aliens in the Philippines. Civilisations 9 : 173-183, No. 2, 1959.

FRANCISCO, V.J. : L'indépendance du pouvoir judiciaire aux Philippines. Commission internationale de juristes, Revue 2 : 163-168, printemps-été 1959.

FRANCISCO, V.J. : Independencia del poder judicial en las Filipinas. Revista de derecho y legislación 48 : 207-216, octubre-noviembre 1959.

LOMBARDO, G.C. : Il sistema giuridica delle Filippine. Diritto negli scambi internazionali 2 : 153-155, dicembre 1959.

POLAND

LITWIN, J. : Projekt kodeksu cywilnego a prawo administracyjne. Przegląd ustawodawstwa gospodarczego 8 : 1-9, styczeń 1955.

SIEDLECKI, W. : Fikcyjny proces cywilny. Państwo i prawo 10 : 212-236, luty 1955.

NOWAKOWSKI, K. : Kilka uwag o sprzedaży w zwiazku z projektem kodeksu cywilnego. Państwo i prawo 10 : 611-634, kwiecień-maj 1955.
Civil code draft.

ROSADA, S. : Draft of a civil code for the People's Republic of Poland. Highlights of current legislation and activities in Mid-Europe 3 : 231-235, August-September 1955.

TYCZKA, M. : Droga postepowania arbitrazowego. Państwo i prawo 10 : 558-584, październik 1955.
Commercial arbitration.

STREIT, J. : Der IV. Kongress der Vereinigung polnischer Juristen. Neue Justiz (Germany) 10 : 52-53, 20. Januar 1956.

SKUBISZEWSKI, K. : Poland's constitution and the conclusion of treaties. Jahrbuch für internationales Recht 7 : 213-228, Heft 2/3, 1956.

PODLASKI, H. : Zmiany w postepowaniu sądowym karnym. Państwo i prawo 11 : 680-701, kwiecień 1956.
Criminal procedure.

RUDZINSKI, A.W. : Soietization of civil law in Poland. American Slavic and East European review 15 : 216-243, April 1956.

ŚLIWIŃSKI, S. : Przegląd orzecznictwa Sądu najwyższego - Prawo karne procesowe, rok 1955. Państwo i prawo 11 : 963-978, maj-czerwiec 1956.
Criminal procedure.

BACHRACH, M. : Problèmes de législation et de codification en Pologne. Droit au service de la paix : 87-98, juin 1956.

La constitution de la République populaire de Pologne. Archives internationales Pharos 13 : 1-6, no. 1300, 30 août 1956.

PLAWSKI, S. : Kodifizierung des Strafrechts in der Polnischen Volksrepublik. Neue Justiz (Germany) 10 : 554-558, 20. September 1956.

HOGHBERG, L. : Amnestia 1956 roku. Państwo i prawo 11 : 648-654, październik 1956.
The 1956 amnesty.

SEGOT, A. : Poland - The 1956 Polish amensty law. Highlights of current legislation and activities in Mid-Europe 4 : 407-413, November 1956.
Text pp. 414-420.

WASILKOWSKA, Z. : Zadania Komisji kodyfikacynej. Państwo i prawo 12 : 3-9, styczeń 1957.
Codification commission; Summaries in English, French and Russian.

SIEKANOWICZ, P. : Poland - Sources of law. Highlights of current legislation and activities in Mid-Europe 5 : 73-77, February 1957.

STEMBROWICZ, J. : Uwagi o Radzie Państwa de lege lata i de lege ferenda. Państwo i prawo 12 : 247-284, luty 1957.
State council; Summaries in English, French and Russian.

WOLTER, A. : Kodeks cywilny a "prawo rodzinne". Państwo i prawo 12 : 475-479, marzec 1957.
Family law to be a part of the civil code; With summaries in English, French and Russian.

ZAKREWSKI, W. : Zagadnienie rewizji konstytucji. Panstwo i prawo 12 : 717-728, kwiecień-maj 1957.
Revision of the constitution; Summaries in English, French and Russian.

CUKIERSKI, K. : Rechtshilfevertrag zwischen der Volksrepublik Polen und der Deutschen Demokratischen Republik. Neue Justiz (Germany) 11 : 353-354, 20. Juni 1957.

PORALLA, C. : Der Oktoberumbruch und die jüngste Rechtsentwicklung in Polen. Osteuropa-Recht 3 : 1-7, Juni 1957.

MURZYNOWSKI, A. : Zaliczenie aresztu tymczasowego na poczet kary w procesie karnym PRL. Państwo i prawo 12 : 70-85, lipiec-sierpień 1957.
New criminal code; Summaries in English, French and Russian.

RESICH, Z. : Zasada dyspozycyjnosci i kontradyktoryjności w procesie cywilnym PRL. Państwo i prawo 12 : 56-69, lipiec-sierpień 1957.
Principles of civil procedure; Summaries in English, French and Russian.

Les juristes polonais à la recherche de la légalité. Commission internationale de juristes, Revue 1 : 7-22, automne 1957.

NAGORSKI, Z. : The legislation of the Polish People's Republic 1945-1957. Law in Eastern Europe : 6-53, no. 2, 1958.

PLAWSKI, S. : Quelques aspects du nouveau droit pénal polonais. Revue de science criminelle et de droit pénal comparé 13 : 341-356, avril-juin 1958.

GRZYBOWSKI, K. : Reform and codification of Polish laws. American journal of comparative law 7 : 393-402, summer 1958.

BABINSKI, L. : Les travaux de codification en Pologne après 1945. Revue hellénique de droit international 11 : 307-319, juillet-décembre 1958.

WOLTER, A. : Kierunki zmian polskiego prawa rodzinnego. Panstwo i prawo 13 : 269-291, sierpień-wrzień 1958.
Family law; Summaries in English, French and Russian.

SOBCZAK, K. : Nowe prawo wywłaszczeniowe. Państwo i prawo 13 : 292-302, sierpień-wrzesień 1958.
New expropriation law; Summaries in English, French and Russian.

SZWAJCER, S. : La législation pénale en Pologne. Est et Ouest 10 : 10-12, 1-15 octobre 1958.

HAMON, L., et JAROSZYNSKI, M. : Sur le droit de la Pologne moderne. France, Conseil d'Etat, Etudes et documents 12 : 219-239, 1958.
Deux articles.

ROZMARYN, S.: Podpisanie i ogloszenie ustawy w Polskiej Rzeczypospolitej Ludowej. Państwo i prawo 14 : 3-26, styczeń 1959.
Summaries in English, French and Russian.

PRZYBYŁOWSKI, K. : Odeslanie w polskim prawie międzynarodnowym prywatnym. Państwo i prawo 14 : 44-52, styczeń 1959.
Summaries in English, French and Russian.

SOBOLEWSKI, M. : Die verfassungspolitische Entwicklung in Polen seit 1952. Jahrbuch des öffentlichen Rechts der Gegenwart 8 : 267-291, 1959.

PORTUGAL

CUELLO CALÓN, E. : La reforma penal portuguesa introducida por decreto-ley de 5 de junio de 1954. Anuario de derecho penal y ciencias penales 8 : 73-75, enero -abril 1955.

PIRES de LIMA, F.A. : Anteprojecto de dois títulos do novo código civil referentes às relações pessoais entre os cônjugés e à sua capacidade patrimonial. Boletim do Ministerio da justiça (Portugal) : 5-25, maio 1956.

MASCARENAS, C.E. : Las denominaciones de origen en el derecho portugués. Informacion jurídica (Spain) : 415-420, julio-agosto 1955.

DUARTE GOMES DA SILVA, M. : O direito de família no futuro código civil. Ministério da justiça, Boletim (Portugal) : 25-101, abril 1957.

PIRES de LIMA, F.A. : Enfiteuse - Anteprojecto de um título do futuro código civil. Ministério da justiça, Boletim (Portugal) : 5-41, maio 1957.

FERRER CORREIA, A. : Pessoas colectivas - Anteprojecto de um capítulo du novo código civil. Ministério da justiça, Boletim (Portugal) : 247-281, junho 1957.

Constitution politique de la République portugaise. Archives internationales Pharos 14 : 1-14, no. 1353, 30 septembre 1957.

Nacionalidade. Ministério da justiça, Boletim (Portugal) : 335-339, dezembro 1957.

DUARTE GOMES da SILVA, M. : O direito de família no futuro código civil (Contd.). Ministério da justiça, Boletim (Portugal) : 63-92, julho 1959.
Text pp. 93-137.

JACONS, A.J. : Constitutional development in Portugal since 1926. Jahrbuch des öffentlichen Rechts der Gegenwart 8 : 388-434, 1959.

Boletim informativo dos trabalhos preparatórios do codigo civil. Ministério da justiça, Boletim (Portugal) : 223-225, dezembro 1959.

PUERTO RICO

ELLIOTT, S.D. : "Our faith in justice" - Puerto Rico shows the way to better courts. American bar association journal 42 : 24-28, January 1956.

MOUCHET, C. : La constitución del nuevo estado libre de Puerto Rico. Revista cubana de derecho 30 : 3-32, enero-marzo 1958.

FRANCIS, R. : Foreign corporations doing business in the Commonwealth of Puerto Rico. Revista juridica de la Universidad de Puerto Rico 26 : 347-356, marzo-abril 1957.

TRÍAS MONGE, J. : El funcionamiento de los tribunales bajo la constitución de Puerto Rico, 1925-1958. Revista jurídica de la Universidad de Puerto Rico 28 : 21-45, septiembre-octubre 1958.

RUMANIA

Code roumain de la famille, loi no. 4, du 21 décembre 1953. Documentation juridique étrangère 7 : 33-59, no. 11, 1955.

MIESS, H. : Esame delle norme di legge che regolano la materia editoriale in Romania. Annuario di diritto comparato e di studi legislativi 30 : 14-23, 1955.

LADISLAU, M. : Reglementarea infracţiunii de huliganism in legislaţia penală a R.P.R. Buletinul Universităţilor "V. Babeş" şi "Bolyai", Seria ştiinţe sociale 1 : 121-132, nr. 1-2, 1956.
Hooliganism.

Rumänien 1955. Osteuropa-Recht 2 : 303-305, Oktober 1956.
Legislation.

POPESCO, F.R. : Les principes fondamentaux du code roumain de la famille. Revue juridique et économique du Sud-Ouest, Série juridique 8 : 27-43, nos. 1-2, 1957.

BRAGA, S. : Rumänien - Überblick über die Rechtsprechung 1952-1954. Osteuropa-Recht 3 : 59-61, Juni 1957.

Das Justizwesen der Rumänischen Volksrepublik. Wissenschaftlicher Dienst Südosteuropa 7 : 20-21, Januar/Februar 1958.

15 ani de dezvoltare a ştiintei juridice în Romînia democrat-populară. Studii şi cercetări juridice 4 : 493-521, nr. 2, 1959.

Modifications apportées au code pénal de la République populaire roumaine. Documentation française, Notes et études documentaires : 1-10, No. 2583, 28 octobre 1959.

SAAR VALLEY

GUITARD, H. : Les aspects juridiques du traité franco-allemand sur la Sarre. Banque 26 : 70-74, février 1957.

NATIONAL LAW - COUNTRIES

BRAGA, S. : Die Eingliederung des Saarlandes. Ehe und Familie im privaten und öffentlichen Recht 4 : 37-40, Februar 1957.

FOLZ, H.E. : Bibliographie zum Recht des Saarlandes seit 1945. Annales Universitatis saraviensis - Rechts- und Wirtschaftswissenschaften; Droit, économie 7 : 39-79, fasc. 1, 1959.

SALVADOR

HALL LLOREDA, C. : Estudios sobre el tratado entre las repúblicas de Guatemala y El Salvador para el aprovechamiento de las aguas del Lago de Güija, de 15 abril de 1957... Revista de la Facultad de ciencias jurídicas y sociales de Guatemala 6 : 14-33, enero-junio 1958.

SAUDI ARABIA

Textes constitutionnels sur l'organisation des pouvoirs publics en Arabie Séoudite, règlement du 4 mai 1958. Documentation française, Notes et études documentaires : 1-4, no. 2465, 30 septembre 1958.

SALEM, A. : La justice et la législation en Arabie Séoudite. Egypte contemporaine 50 : 5-44, octobre 1959.
Texte en arabe.

SOUTH AFRICA

WEBER, H. von : Vom Strafrecht der Südafrikanischen Union. Zeitschrift für die gesamte Strafrechtswissenschaft 67 : 163-169, Heft 1, 1955.

Constitutional law. Annual survey of South African law : 1-36, 1955.

LEWIN, J. : The struggle for law in South Africa. Political quarterly 27 : 176-181, April-June 1956.

KAHN, E. : Choice of law in succession in the South African conflict of laws. South African law journal 73 : 303-318, August 1956.

Constitutional law. Annual survey of South African law : 1-39, 1956.

LE MAY, G.H.L. : Parliament, the constitution and the "doctrine of the mandate". South African law journal 74 : 33-42, February 1957.

KERR, A.J. : The application of native law in the Supreme court. South African law journal 74 : 313-330, August 1957.

McWHINNEY, E. : Laws and politics and the limits of the judicial process - An end to the constitutional contest in South Africa. Canadian bar review 35 : 1203-1212, December 1957.

STEINBERG, K. : The nationality of adopted children under South African law. South African law journal 75 : 318-324, August 1958.

BEINART, B. : The South African appeal court and judicial review. Modern law review 21 : 587-608, November 1958.

WARMELO, P. van : The function of Roman law in South African law. Tulane law review 33 : 565-576, April 1959.

SPAIN

CILLÁN APALATEGUI, A. : Jurisdicción y competencia de la Iglesia católica en las uniones civiles de los bautizados. Revista general de derecho 11 : 11-24, enero 1955.

ROSAL, J. del : Überblick über die Entwicklung der Strafrechtswissenschaft in Spanien während der letzten fünfzig Jahre. Zeitschrift für die gesamte Strafrechtswissenschaft 67 : 145-162, Heft 1, 1955.

GUAITA, A. : Los actos políticos o de gobierno en el derecho español. Revista del Instituto de derecho comparado (Barcelona) : 74-98, enero-junio 1955.

FERNÁNDEZ VIAGAS, P. : Los matrimonios de españoles en el extranjero. Revista general de derecho 11 : 101-105, febrero 1955.

LÓPEZ RODÓ, L. : Evolución y estado actual del recurso contencioso administrativo en España. Revista del Instituto de derecho comparado (Barcelona) : 61-73, enero-junio 1955.

XIMENEZ de EMBÚN y OSEÑALDE, F. : La necesaria revisión del código civil. Revista jurídica de Cataluña 54 : 327-332, julio agosto 1955.

Decreto sobre nacionalidad. Información jurídica (Spain) : 421-424, julio-agosto 1955.

LÓPEZ ALARCÓN, M. : El metrimonio civil como subsidiario del canónico. Revista general de derecho 11 : 594-603, septiembre 1955.

OGAYAR AYLLÓN, T. : Adquisición de la nacionalidad y de la regionalidad. Revista jurídica de Cataluña 54 : 519-538, noviembre-diciembre 1955.

VERDERA y TUELLS, E. : La emisión de titulos en la nueva ley española de sociedades anónimas. Annuario di diritto comparato e di studi legislativi 30 : 29-74, 1955.

GONZALEZ de ANDIA, M. : La loi espagnole de 22 décembre 1953 sur les arbitrages de droit privé. Revue de l'arbitrage : 6-9, no. 1, 1956.

Información española para el extranjero - Crónicas de legislación, jurisprudencia y bibliogragía, julio-diciembre 1955. Revista del Instituto de derecho comparado (Barcelona) : 559-621, enero-diciembre 1956.

D'un congrès à l'autre, Madrid 1930 - Madrid 1956 - La science administrative espagnole. Revue internationale des sciences administratives - International review of administrative sciences 22 : 3-192, no. 2, 1956.
Numéro spécial.

MARÍN LÓPEZ, A. : El reenvío en el derecho español. Revista española de derecho internacional 9 : 677-687, núm. 3, 1956.

PERÉ RALUY, J. : Derivaciones actuales de los regímenes matrimoniales de la II República y Zona roja. Revista jurídica de Cataluña 55 : 87-111, marzo-abril 1956.

MARTÍN-BALLESTERO y COSTEA, L. : La unificación del derecho privado en España. Anuario de derecho civil 9 : 505-532, abril-junio 1956.

RUBIÓ y TUDURÍ, M. : La legitimación por países extranjeros de hijos que, según nuestra legislación, serían adulterinos - Efectos de dicha legitimación en la sucesion du un español, abierta en España. Revista jurídica de Cataluña 55 : 218-227, mayo-junio 1956.

BROWN, L.N. : The sources of Spanish civil law. International and comparative law quarterly 5 : 364-377, July 1956.

De la aplicación del derecho civil especial de Cataluña. Revista jurídica de Cataluña 73 : 9-151, septiembre-diciembre 1956.

RAUCHHAUPT, F.W. von : Die Geschichte der spanischen Gesetzgebung. Annales Universitatis saraviensis - Rechts- und Wirtschaftswissenschaften; Droit, économie 5 : 135-194, fasc. 3, 1956-57.

VECIANA de la CUADRA, R.W. de : El llamado parentesco por afinidad naturel en el código civil español y su relación con la doctrina canńica. Revista jurídica de Cataluña 56 : 499-515, noviembre-diciembre 1957.

Troisièmes journées de droit franco-espagnol, Toulouse, mai 1957 - Rapports. Annales de la Faculté de droit de Toulouse 6 : 43-191, fasc. 1, 1958.

CONDOMINES, F. de A. : La reciente reforma del código civil. Revista jurídica de Cataluña 58 : 295-311, mayo-junio 1959.

Quatrièmes journées franco-espagnole de droit comparé, Barcelone, avril 1958 - Rapports. Annales de la Faculté de droit de Toulouse 6 : 131-313, fasc. 2, 1958.

SUÑER, J.M.P. : The reorganisation of the central administration in Spain. Tulane law review 32 : 595-598, June 1958.

DOCAVO, M. : La reforma del procedimiento administrativo en España. Revista de derecho y legislación 47 : 326-343, noviembre 1958.

GARCIA CANTERO, G. : Un nouvel aspect du problème de la double nationalité, la loi espagnole du 15 juillet 1954. Association des auditeurs et anciens auditeurs de l'Académie de droit international de La Haye, Annuaire 28 : 50-58, 1958.

RIPOLLÉS, A.Q. : Glosas a la nueva ley española de extradición pasiva, 26 de diciembre de 1958. Revista española de derecho internacional 12 : 99-118, núm. 1-2, 1959.

MARÍN LÓPEZ, A. : La conclusión del matrimonio en derecho internacional privado español. Revista española de derecho internacional 12 : 31-66, núm. 1-2, 1959.

MARTÍN RETORTILLO, C. : La nueva ley de la jurisdicción contencioso-administrativa. Revista de la Facultad de derecho de la Universidad de Madrid 3 : 29-61, núm. 5, 1959.

SUDAN

Soudan - Constitution transitoire, 1 janvier 1956. Informations constitutionnelles et parlementaires : 224-249, octobre 1956.
Texte.

FAWZI, S. : The status of foreigners in the newly independent Sudan. Civilisations 7 : 343-354, no. 3, 1957.

GUTTMANN, E. : The reception of the common law in the Sudan. International and comparative law quarterly 6 : 401-417, July 1957.

SWEDEN

HESSLER, H. : Svensk rättspraxis - Växel-och checkrätt 1945-1953. Svensk juristtidning 40 : 36-44, januari 1955.

PHILIP, D. : L'administration publique suédoise et ses rapports avec l'administration sociale. Revue internationale des sciences administratives 21 : 283-303, no. 2, 1955.

Die Entwicklung des öffentliches Rechts Schwedens in den Jahren 1933 bis 1953. Jahrbuch des öffentlichen Rechts der Gegenwart 4 : 299-353, 1955.

MALMSTRÖM, A. : Svensk rättspraxis - Sakrätt 1948 -1954. Svensk juristtidning 40 : 593-617, november-december 1955.

BECKMAN, N. : Les infractions dans la législation pénale suédoise (Suite). Revue de science criminelle et de droit pénal comparé : 251-275, avril-juin 1956.

BECKMAN, N. : Svensk rättspraxis - Familjerätt 1950-1955. Svensk juristtidning 41 : 289-308, maj-juni 1956.

KARLGREN, H. : Svensk rättspraxis - Internationell privat-, straff- och processrätt 1949-1955. Svensk juristtidning 41 : 401-410, juli-august 1956.

MALMSTRÖM, A. : The legal status of international non-governmental organizations in Sweden. Associations internationales - International associations 8 : 501-502, 505 ; août 1956.

FISCHLER, J. : Das internationale Privatrecht Schwedens, 1949-1955. Zeitschrift für ausländisches und internationales Privatrecht 22 : 276-300, Heft 2, 1957.

SIMSON, G. : Internationales Strafrecht und Verbrechen gegen das Völkerrecht in schwedischer Sicht und Gesetzgebung. Internationales Recht und Diplomatie : 113-125, Heft 2, 1957.

WELAMSON, L. : Svensk rättspraxis - Civil- och Straffprocessrätt 1953-1957. Svenskjuristtidning 44 : 225-274, april 1959.

LECH, H., and BECKMAN, N. : Fran Sveriges högsta domstol 1958. Tidsskrift for rettsvitenskap : 322-342, hefte 4, 1959.

MALMSTRÖM, A. : Some aspects of the personal law in Swedish private international law. Association des auditeurs et anciens auditeurs de l'Académie de droit international de La Haye, Annuaire 29 : 120-127, 1959.

SWITZERLAND

BARDE, E. : Le procès en divorce. Zeitschrift für schweizerisches Recht 74 : 453a-556a, Heft 3, 1955.

DUPRAZ, L. : De l'initiative en revision de la constitution dans les Etats suisses en particulier de l'initiative populaire. Zeitschrift für schweizerisches Recht 75 : 263a-590a, Heft 4, 1956.

Aktuelle Verfassungsprobleme - A propos de la constitution fédérale - Problemi costituzionali. Zeitschrift für schweizerisches Recht 74 : 111-347, Hefte 4 und 5, 1955.
Special issue.

CLERC, F. : Les travaux de rēvision du code pénal suisse. Revue de science criminelle et de droit pénal comparé : 277-285, avril-juin 1956.

ROOS, G. : Ubersicht über die schweizerische Gesetzgebung des Jahres 1954. Zeitschrift für schweizerisches Recht 74 : 489-500, Heft 7, 1956.

RIGGENBACH, B. : Ubersicht der Literatur über schweizerisches Recht - Bibliographie juridique suisse, 1955. Zeitschrift für schweizerisches Recht 75 : 439-490, Heft 10, 1956.

GERMANN, O.A. ; Wirtschaftlicher Nachrichtendienst nach Art. 273 des schweizerischen Strafgesetzbuches. Wirtschaft und Recht 9 : 12-23, Heft 1, 1957.

VUILLEUMIER, J. : Vers un régime juridique propre à la recherche et à l'exploitation des gisements de pétrole - Contribution à l'étude du droit minier suisse. Zeitschrift für schweizerisches Recht 76 : 185a-326a, Heft 4, 1957.

STOCKER, W. : Zum Schweizerischen Ehegüterrecht. Zeitschrift für schweizerisches Recht 76 : 329a-414a, Heft 5, 1957.

DESCHENAUX, H. : Revision du régime matrimonial. Zeitschrift für schweizerisches Recht 76 : 419a-594a, Heft 6, 1957.

Propositions de révision et questions d'interprétation concernant le régime matrimonial suisse - Zum Schweizerischen Ehegüterrecht, Revisionspostulate und Auslegungsfragen. Zeitschrift für schweizerisches Recht 76 : 616a-661a, Heft 9, 1957.
Une discussion.

Ubersicht der Literatur über schweizerisches Recht - Bibliographie juridique suisse 1956. Zeitschrift für schweizerisches Recht 76 : 491-530, Heft 10, 1957.

Loi fédérale sur la responsabilité de la Confédération, des membres de ses autorités et de ses fonctionnaires (du 14 mars 1958). Feuille fédérale (Switzerland) 110 : 677-685, 27 mars 1958.

RIGGENBACH, B. : Ubersicht der Literatur über schweizerisches Recht - Bibliographie juridique suisse 1957. Zeitschrift für schweizerisches Recht 77 : 531-581, Heft 10, 1958.

PATRY, R. : Les accords sur l'exercice des droits de l'actionnaire. Zeitschrift für schweizerisches Recht 78 : 1a-137a, Heft 3, 1959.
Bibliographie pp. 138a-140a.

USTERI, M. : Ausübung des Stimm- und Wahlrechtes nach freiheitsstaatlichen Prinzipien. Zeitschrift für schweizerisches Recht 78 : 357a-509a, Heft 5, 1959.

KLEIN, F.E. : L'application de la méthode comparative dans la jurisprudence du Tribunal fédéral suisse en matière de droit privé. Revue internationale de droit comparé 11 : 321-333, avril-juin 1959.

CASTELLA, J. : L'exercice du droit de vote. Zeitschrift für schweizerisches Recht 78 : 511a-618a, Heft 6, 1959.

RIGGENBACH, B. : Ubersicht der Literatur über schweizerisches Recht - Bibliographie juridique suisse 1958. Zeitschrift für schweizerisches Recht 78 : 531-580, Heft 10, 1959.

SWITZERLAND
(International law, Aliens)

PFENNIGER, H.F. : Die Immunität der Gesandten und das schweizerische Strafrecht - Zum Uberfall auf die rumänische Gesandtschaft. Neue Zürcher Zeitung 176 : 7, Nr. 468, 22. Februar 1955.

SCHNITZER, A.F. : Bedarf das schweizerische internationale Privatrecht eines neuen Gesetzes? Schweizerisches Jahrbuch für internationales Recht 12 : 55-74, 1955.

DIEZ, E. : Les engagements internationaux contractés par la Suisse, entrés en vigueur en 1954 et 1955. Schweizerisches Jahrbuch für internationales Recht 12 : 199-222, 1955.

Die Militärdienstpflicht von Schweizern im Ausland. Echo 36 : 13-14, März 1956.

Rapport du Conseil fédéral à l'Assemblée fédérale sur le rétablissement dans la nationalité suisse des femmes suisses par naissance, art. 58 de la loi sur la nationalite, et message relatif à un projet de loi complétant la loi sur acquisition et la perte de la nationalité suisse (du 8 juin 1956). Feuille fédérale (Switzerland) 108 : 1173-1202, 14 juin 1956.

PROBST, R. : International demarcation of compulsory military service with special emphasis on the Swiss-United States situation. Georgetown law journal 45 : 60-74, fall 1956.

HUBER, M. : Krise der Neutralität? Schweizer Monatshefte 37 : 1-13, April 1957.

LACHENAL, J.A. : Le droit applicable aux mariages mixtes célébrés à l'étranger. Schweizerisches Jahrbuch für internationales Recht 14 : 33-42, 1957.

FOËX, G. : A propos de l'expulsion des étrangers. Schweizerische Zeitschrift für Strafrecht 73 : 131-140, Heft 1/2, 1958.

Message du Conseil fédéral à l'Assemblée fédérale concernant l'approbation de l'accord entre la Suisse et l'Argentine au sujet des obligations militaires des doubles nationaux nés en Argentine (du 10 mars 1958). Feuille fédérale (Switzerland) 110 : 565-570, 13 mars 1958.

LOOPER, R.B. : The treaty power in Switzerland. American journal of comparative law 7 : 178-194, spring 1958.

NATIONAL LAW - COUNTRIES

AUBERT, J.F. : Le statut des étrangers en Suisse. Zeitschrift für schweizerisches Recht 77 : 215-253, Heft 7, 1958.

Die Wiedereinbürgerung der Schweizerin. Echo 38 : 12-14, August 1958.

RUEGGER, P. : Die Schweiz, die Genfer Seerechtskonventionen von 1958 und die Bestrebungen der Vereinigten Nationen zur Kodifikation des internationalen Rechts. Schweizerisches Jahrbuch für internationales Recht 15 : 9-38, 1958.

MAEDER, E. : Die Rechtsstellung des Ausländers in der Schweiz. Schweiz 30 : 191-197, 1959.

SWITZERLAND
(Patents, Trade-marks)

WALDKIRCH, E. v. : Das neue schweizerische Patentgesetz. Zeitschrift für schweizerisches Recht 75 : 221-249, Heft 7, 1956.

SYRIA

ANTAKI, G. : Al-fihras al-hijaï li kanoun al-mouhakamat al-houkoukïa. Majallat Nakabat al-mouhamine 19 : 18-23, September-October 1955.
Index to legal procedure code.

KOUATLY, M. : Rakabat al-kåda ala doustouriat al-kawanine. Al-Kanoun (Syria) 8 : 41-55, April 1957.
Constitutionality of laws.

EL-HAKIM, J. : La diya et les atteintes aux personnes physiques dans le droit syrien et libanais. Annales de la Faculté de droit de Beyrouth : 249-287, 1957.

TAIWAN

POUND, R. : The Chinese civil code in action. Tulane law review 29 : 277-291, February 1955.

TANGIER

BLIX, H. : The rule of unanimity in the revision of treaties - A study of the treaties governing Tangier (Contd.). International and comparative law quarterly 5 : 581-596, October 1956.

THAILAND

LYMAN, A. : The judicial system of Thailand. Far Eastern economic review 18 : 809-812, 30 June 1955.

Constitution du Royaume de Thaïlande, 8 mars 1952. Informations constitutionnelles et parlementaires : 108-127, avril 1956.
Texte.

SUCHARITKUL, S. : Le régime juridique de la Thaïlande et l'état de droit. Commission internationale de juristes, Revue 1 : 23-43, automne 1957.

SRIKHASIBANDH, S. : Aperçu sur l'influence du droit français dans l'oeuvre de codification en Thaïland. France-Asie 13 : 390-392, octobre-décembre 1956.

Siam - Ley sobre conflicto de leyes de 10 de marzo de 1938. Revista de la Facultad de derecho (Caracas) : 197-204, no. 12, 1957.
Text.

Constitution provisoire due Royaume de Thaïlande, 28 janvier 1959. Informations constitutionnelles et parlementaires 10 : 201-203, octobre 1959.

TRIESTE

CONFORTI, B. : L'attuale situazione giuridica del Territorio di Trieste. Rivista di diritto internazionale 38 : 568-583, no. 4, 1955.

TURKEY

ONAR, S.S. : Les transformations de la structure administrative et juridique de la Turquie et son état actuel. Revue internationale des sciences administratives 21 : 741-785, no. 4, 1955.

BERKIN, N. : Grundbegriffe des türkischen Zwangsvollstreckungs- und Konkursrechtes. Annales de la Faculté de droit d'Istanbul 4 : 93-154, no. 5, 1955.

DURAN, L. : Questions de droit administratif turc. Annales de la Faculté de droit d'Istanbul 4 : 77-92, no. 5, 1955.

POSTACIOGLŬ, I.E. : Aperçu sur l'organisation judiciaire en Turquie et son fonctionnement. Annales de la Faculté de droit d'Istanbul 4 : 155-161, no. 5, 1955.

HAMSON, C.J. : The Istanbul conference of 1955. International and comparative law quarterly 5 : 26-39, January 1956.
Reception of European law.

KEMAL ELBIR, H.: Perturbaciones producidas por la adopción del código civil suizo por Turquía, y reflexiones sobre la reforma del código civil turco en vigor. Revista del Instituto de derecho comparado (Barcelona) : 9-23, julio-diciembre 1955.

Le colloque d'Istanbul, septembre 1955. Annales de la Faculté de droit d'Istanbul 5 : v-xii, 1-251, no. 6, 1956.
Numéro spécial sur la réception des lois et codes étrangers.

ANSAY, T. : Commercial arbitration in Turkey. Arbitration journal 12 : 31-37, no. 1, 1957.

The reception of foreign law in Turkey. International social science bulletin, Unesco 9 : 7-81, no. 1, 1957.
Series of articles.

PRITSCH, E. : Das schweizerische Zivilgesetzbuch in der Türkei - Seine Rezeption und die Frage seiner Bewährung. Zeitschrift für vergleichende Rechtswissenschaft 59 : 123-180, 1957.

HIRSCH, E.E. : Die Gesetzgebung der Türkei auf dem Gebiete des Privatrechts 1939-1956. Zeitschrift für ausländisches und internationales Privatrecht 23 : 81-110, Heft 1, 1958.

DIBLAN CARLSON, S. : The liability of the governmrnz for service faults in Turkey, compared with France and Switzerland. Revue internationale des sciences administratives 24 : 152-164, No. 2, 1958.

DIBLAN CARSON, S. : The liability of the government for service faults in Turkey, compared with France and Switzerland. Revue internationale des sciences administratives 24 : 152-164, no. 2, 1958.

Colloque sur le code civile suisse, sa réception et son application en Turquie, organisé les 19-21 août 1957... Mukayeseli hukuk arastirmalari dergesi - Revue de recherches juridiques comparées 2 : 1-331, no. 2, 1958.
Texte en Turque.

HIRSCH, E. : Le nouveau code de commerce turc. Revue internationale de droit comparé 10 : avril-jiun 1958.

PRITSCH, E. : Das Schweizerische Zivilgesetzbuch in der türkischen Praxis. Zeitschrift für ausländisches und internationales Privatrecht 24 : 686-718, Heft 4, 1959.

GÜRBASKAN, S. : Les éléments matériels de la diffamation publique en droit turc et comparé. Annales de la Faculté de droit d'Istanbul 8 : 204-284, nos. 9-11, 1959.

TURKEY
(International law, Aliens)

SEVIĞ, V.R. : Le système des conflits de lois particuliers en droit international privé truc. Annales de la Faculté de droit d'Istanbul 4 : 175-190, no. 5, 1955.

Law on residence and travel of aliens in Turkey. Istanbul ticaret odasi mecmuasi - Journal of the Istanbul chamber of commerce 74 : 53-58, March-April 1957.
Text.

REDDEN, K. : Strengthening the ties of free nations. The first Turkish-American law conference. American bar association journal 43 : 1111-1112, December 1957.
Ankara, April 1957.

SEVIG, V. : La condition actuelle des étrangers en Turquie. Annales de la Faculté de droit d'Istanbul 6 : 34-55, no. 7, 1957.

SEVIG, V.R. : Les cas de double nationalité en droit turc. Annales de la Faculté de droit d'Istanbul 7 : 82-92, no. 8, 1958.
Texte pp. 93-97.

Loi turque sur l'expropriation. Annales de la Faculté de droit d'Istanbul 7 : 156-174, no. 8, 1958.
Texte.

ERDENER, N. : L'application de la règle "locus regit actum" en droit international privé turc. Annales de la Faculté de droit d'Istanbul 8 : 158-203, nos. 9-11, 1959.

TUNISIA

LUCHAIRE, F. : La justice en Tunisie. Revue juridique et politique de l'Union française 9 : 221-290, avril-juin 1955.

LADHARI, N. : La nationalité tunisienne. Revue juridique et politique de l'Union française 9 : 785-798, octobre-décembre 1955.

Code de la nationalité tunisienne - Décret du 26 janvier 1956 (12 djoumada II 1375), portant promulgation du code de la nationalité tunisienne. Documentation juridique étrangère 7 : 1-13, no. 11, 1955.
Texte.

JAMBU-MERLIN, R. : Le décret du 26 janvier 1956 sur la nationalité tunisienne. Revue tunisienne de droit 4 : 3-10, janvier-mars 1956.

MARTEL, P.A. : Le code de la nationalité tunisienne. Evidences 7 : 13-17, mars 1956.

JAMBU-MERLIN, R. : Le droit privé en Tunisie depuis l'entrée en vigueur des conventions franco-tunisiennes. Revue tunisienne de droit 4 : 117-125, avril-juin 1956.

SILVÉRA, V. : Le statut des fonctionnaires et agents français des services publics tunisiens depuis les conventions franco-tunisiennes. Revue administrative 9 : 487-495, septembre-octobre 1956.

SILVÉRA, V. : De l'autonomie interne à l'indépendance de la Tunisie. Revue juridique et politique de l'Union française 10 : 687-704, octobre-décembre 1956.

LUCHAIRE, F. : La mort des tribunaux français de Tunisie- Recueil Dalloz, Chronique : 61-64, 13 avril 1957.

SILVÉRA, V. : La justice française et l'indépendance de la Tunisie. Revue juridique et politique de l'Union française 12 : 1-17, janvier-mars 1958.

ANDERSON, J.N.D. : The Tunisian law of personal status. International and comparative law quarterly 7 : 262-279, April 1958.

JAMBU-MERLIN, R. : La disparition des juridictions françaises de Tunisie. Revue critique de droit international privé 46 : 213-228, avril-juin 1957.

ROUSSIER, J. : Le code tunisien du statut personnel. Revue juridique et politique de l'Union française 11 : 213-230, avril-juin 1957.

The Tunisian code of personal status. Middle East journal 11 : 309-318, summar 1957.
Text.

LESCURE, M. : L'évolution du système des conflits de lois tunisien - L'exemple du mariage. Revue critique de droit international privé 48 : 31-78, janvier-mars 1959.

La costituzione della Repubblica tunisina. Relazioni internazionali 23 : 1027-1028, 4 luglio 1959.
1 June 1959; See also pp. 999-1000.

SFEIR, G. : The Tunisian constitution. Middle East journal 13 : 443-448, autumn 1959.

Constitution de la République tunisienne, 1 juin 1959. Informations constitutionnelles et parlementaires 10 : 204-213, octobre 1959.

DEBBASCH, C. : La constitution de la République tunisienne du 1 juin 1959. Revue juridique et politique d'outre-mer 13 : 573-585, octobre-dédembre 1959.
Texte pp. 586-590.

Código de la nacionalidad tunecina. Información jurídica (Madrid) : 1833-1843, noviembre-diciembre 1959.

U.S.S.R.

BERMAN, H.J. : The law of the Soviet State. Soviet studies 6 : 225-237, January 1955.

FRIDIEFF, M. : Les héritiers dans le droit soviétique actuel. Revue internationale de droit comparé 7 : 74-92, janvier-mars 1955.

HAZARD, J.N. : The future of codification in the U.S.S.R. Tulane law review 29 : 239-248, February 1955.

GOLJAKOW, I.T. : Das sowjetische Gericht - Das demokratischste Gericht der Welt. Sowjetwissenschaft, Gesellschaftswissenschaftliche Abteilung : 177-195, Heft 2, 1955.

RIISMANDEL, V. : Soviet law and codes in Estonia. Highlights of current legislation and activities in Mid-Europe 3 : 59-72, February-March 1955.

GORSCHENIN, K. : Die Wahl der Richter und Schöffen in der Sowjetunion. Neue Justiz (Germany) 9 : 133-134, 5. März 1955.
Published in "Pravda".

Sowjetische Gesetzestexte in westlichen Bibliotheken. Osteuropa-Recht 1 : 64-66, März 1955.

CHKHIKVADZE, V.M. : Poniatie i znachenie sostava prestupleniia v sovetskom uglovnom prave. Sovetskoe gosudarstvo i pravo : 53-62, no. 4, 1955.
Criminal law.

JOHNSON, E.L. : Some aspects of the Soviet legal system. Soviet studies 6 : 351-358, April 1955.

TSCHCHIKWADSE, W.M. : Reformvorschläge... Ost-Probleme 7 : 797-803, 20. Mai 1955.
Criminal code; Published in "Sowjetskoe gosudarstwo i pravo".

HOGAN, J.C. : Justice in the Soviet Union - The trial of Beria and aides doe treason. American bar association journal 41 : 408-412, 477-479, May 1955.

La réforme du code pénal et le fonctionnement de la justice en U.R.S.S. Documentation française, Chroniques étrangères, U.R.S.S. : 8-11, 30 juin 1955.

BERMAN, H.J. : Soviet justice and Soviet tyranny. Columbia law review 55 : 795-807, June 1955.

Mise en vigueur du code des lois sur le mariage, la famille et la tutelle. Pour la vie : 210-229, jiun 1955.

GUINS, G.C. : Towards an understanding of Soviet law. Soviet studies 7 : 14-30, July 1955.

GRZYBOWSKI, K. : Public policy and Soviet law in the West after world war II. American journal of comparative law 4 : 365-387, summer 1955.

COLLARD, D. : State arbitration in the U.S.S.R. Modern law review 18 : 474-483, September 1955.

CHAMBRE, H. : Le projet de code pénal de l'U.R.S.S. Revue de l'action populaire : 931-942, septembre-octobre 1955.

SANTA PINTER, J.J. : El concepto sovietico del derecho. Boletiń del Instituto de derecho comparado de México 8 : 63-69, septiembre-diciembre 1955.

MOUSKHÉLY, M. : La notion soviétique de constitution. Revue du droit public et de la science politique en France et à l'étranger 71 : 894-908, octobre-décembre 1955.

KISELEV, IA. L. : Nektorye voprosy okhrany truda v sovetskom trudovom prave. Vestnik Moskovskogo universiteta, Seriia obshchestvennykh nauk 10 : no. 11, 1955.
Labour laws.

BISCARETTI di RUFFIA, P. : Recenti studi sull' ordinamento giuridico-costituzionale sovietico. Politico 20 : 396-415, dicembre 1955.

SCHULTZ, L. : Die Entwicklung der Rechtswissenschaft in der UdSSR seit Stalins Tod. Osteuropa -Recht 1 : 100-109, Dezember 1955.

SCHEUERLE, W.A. : Il divorzio e il procedimento di divorzio secondo il diritto sovietico. Annuario di diritto comparato e di studi legislativi 30 : 377-396, 1955.

GSOVSKI, V. : New trend in Soviet justice? Problems of communism (United States) 5 : 25-30, January-February 1956.

ALEXEJEW, N.S. : Einige Fragen des Allgemeinen Teils des Strafrechts im Zusammenhang mit der Ausarbeitung des Entwurfs eines Strafgesetzbuches der UdSSR. Staat und Recht 5 : 166-184, 31. März 1956.

BERESOWSKAJA, S. : Die Aufsicht der Staatsanwaltschaft in der sowjetischen staatlichen Verwaltung. Staat und Recht 5 : 154-165, 31. März 1956.

BERNARD, T. : Vers un cours nouveau juridique en U.R.S.S.? Saturne 2 : 8-15, mars-mai 1956.

BERMAN, H.J. : Law reform in the Soviet Union. American Slavic and East European review 15 : 179-189, April 1956.

ALEXEJEW, N.S. : Die Aufsicht des Staatsanwalts in der UdSSR. Neue Justiz (Germany) 10 : 298-301, 20. Mai 1956.

TIMASHEFF, N.S. : Das Strafprozessrecht der Sowjetunion in seinen Verhältnis zum kaiserlich-russischen Recht. Osteuropa-Recht 2 : 194-199, Mai 1956.

MEDER, W. : Die Hierarchie der Rechtsquellen in der Sowjetunion. Osteuropa-Recht 2 : 167-175, Mai 1956.

LAJAUNIE, J.J. : L'organisation et le fonctionnement de la justice en U.R.S.S. Documentation française, Notes et études documentaires : 1-40, no. 2178, 22 mai 1956.

FRIDIEFF, M. : L'acceptation et la répudiation des successions dans le droit soviétique actuel. Revue internationale de droit comparé 8 : 249-263, avril-juin 1956.

BERMAN, H.J. : Soviet legal reforms - Steps toward justice. Nation 182 : 546-548, 30 June 1956.

NATIONAL LAW - COUNTRIES

Revision of laws and codes - A roundup of articles. Current digest of the Soviet press 8 : 9-15, 34; 25 July 1956.

MIRONENKO, Y. : Changes in Soviet criminal law procedure since the twentieth Party congress. Institute for the study of the USSR, Bulletin 3 : 21-26, July 1956.

Der XX. Parteitag der KpdSU und die Aufgaben der sowjetischen Rechtswissenschaft. Sowjetwissenschaft, Gesellschaftswissenschaftliche Beiträge : 861-876, Juli 1956.
Published in "Sovetskoe gosudarstvo i pravo".

JURTSCHENKO, A. : Die staatsrechtliche Lage der Ukrainischen SSR als eines Bestandteiles der UdSSR. Sowjet Studien : 138-158, Juli 1956.

KUCHEROV, S. : The legal profession in pre- and postrevolutionary Russia. American journal of comparative law 5 : 443-470, summer 1956.

LOGINOV, P.V. : O sisteme grazhdanskogo protsessual'nogo kodeksa RSFSR i nekotorykh voprosakh grazhdanskogo protsessa. Sovetskoe gosudarstvo i pravo : 51-61, no. 8, 1956.
Criminal procedure.

TARASENKO, F.G. : Sovershenstvovanie sudebnogo upravleniia v SSSR. Sovetskoe gosudarstvo i pravo : 38-44, no. 9, 1956.
System of Courts.

DRUCKER, A. : Soviet corporations. International and comparative law quarterly 5 : 597-599, October 1956.

Sowjetische Gesetzblätter in westlichen Bibliotheken. Ost-Europa-Recht 2 : 309-311, Oktober 1956.

RAKHOUNOV, R.D. : Valeur de l'aveu dans la procédure criminelle soviétique. Droit au service de la paix : 14-24, décembre 1956.

PERLOV, I.D. : Do kontsa zavershit' reformu sudebnogo upravleniia v SSSR. Sovetskoe gosudarstvo i pravo : 13-26, no. 1, 1957.

POLJANSKI, N.N. : Die Grundzüge der sowjetischen Strafprozesswissenschaft, Staat und Recht 6 : 105-124, 20. Februar 1957.

Laws and decrees of the Supreme Soviet of the U.S.S.R., its Presidium, and the Council of ministers, published in 1956. Highlights of current legislation and activities in Mid-Europe 5 : 83-99, February 1957.

KAREV, D. : O kodifikatsii sovershenstvovanii sovetskogo zakonodatel'stva. Sovetskaia iustitsiia (U.S.S.R.) : 11-14, no. 2, aprel' 1957.
Codification of Soviet law.

ANASHKIN, G. : Nekotorye voprosy kodifikatsii ugolovno-protsessual'nogo zakonodatel'stva RSFSR. Sovetskaia iustitsiia (U.S.S.R.) : 34-38, no. 2, aprel' 1957.
Criminal law.

GOLIAKOV, I. : K proektu ugolovnogo kodeksa RSFSR. Sovetskaia iustitsiia (U.S.S.R.) : 30-33, no. 2, aprel' 1957.
Draft of criminal code.

PERLOV, I. : Ob organizatsii ustroistve sudebnoi sistemy Rossilskoi Federatsii. Sovetskaia iustitsiia (U.S.S.R.) : 39-44, no. 2, aprel' 1957.
Courts.

Les constitutions soviétiques. Documentation française, Notes et études documentaires : 1-24, no. 2297, 29 mai 1957.

SHARMA, S.P. : The constitution of the U.S.S.R., its nature. Supreme court journal (Madras) 20 : 79-83, May 1957.

FRIDIEFF, M. : Les récentes modifications introduites dans l'organisation du service public de la justice en U.R.S.S. Revue internationale de droit comparé 9 : 398-403, avril-juin 1957.

Westliches Schrifttum zum Sowjetrecht. Osteuropa-Recht 3 : 72-76, Juni 1957.

POLL, H.W. : Sowjetunion - Entscheidungen in Zivilsachen 1956. Osteuropa-Recht 3 : 48-58, Juni 1957.

KIRALFY, A.K.R. : Recent legal changes in the U.S.S.R. Soviet studies 9 : 1-19, July 1957.

HAMMER, D.P. : Legal education in the USSR. Soviet studies 9 : 20-27, July 1957.

BERMAN, H.J. : Soviet law reform - Dateline Moscow 1957. Yale law journal 66 : 1191-1215, July 1957.

BOLDYREV, V. : Za vysokoe kachestvo sudebnogo nadzora i kontrolia. Sovetskaia iustitsiia (U.S.S.R.) : 8-12, no. 6, avgust 1957.
Court of justice.

GOL'ST, G.R. : Osnovnye zadachi predvaritel'nogo rassledovaniia v sovetskom ugolovnom protsesse. Sovetskoe gosudarstvo i pravo : 70-80, no. 8, avg. 1957.
Criminal procedure.

LOEBER, D.A. : La Prokouratoura soviétique et les droits de l'individu envers l'Etat. Commission internationale de juristes, Revue 1 : 61-110, automne 1957.

HAZARD, J.N. : Soviet codifiers receive new orders. American journal of comparative law 6 : 540-546, autumn 1957.

LEVITSKY, S.L. : Richtlinien des Obersten Gerichts der UdSSR als Rechtsquelle. Osteuropa-Recht 3 : 92-99, Oktober 1957.

KIRALFY, A.K.R. : The campaign for legality in the U.S.S.R. International and comparative law quarterly 6 : 625-642, October 1957.

POLL, H.W. : Sowjetunion - Entscheidungen in Strafsachen 1956. Osteuropa-Recht 3 : 136-148, Oktober 1957.

RUBICHEV, A. : Verkhovnyi sud Rossiiskoi Federatsii i ego zadachi. Sovetskaia iustitsiia (U.S.S.R.) : 17-22, no. 9, noiabr' 1957.
Supreme court.

DIRNECKER, B. : Die Entwicklung des sowketischen Strafverfahrens- und Justizverfassungsrechts seit Stalins Tod. Recht in Ost und West 1 : 225-237, 15. November 1957.

NATIONAL LAW - COUNTRIES

GAIDUKOV, D.A. : Razvitie sovetskoĭ konstitut͡sii. Sovetskoe gosudarstvo i pravo : 61-73, no. 11, noi͡abr' 1957.
Constitution.

PAVLOV, I.V. : 40 years of development of Soviet legal science. Current digest of the Soviet press 9 : 3-9, 8 January 1958.
See also pp. 9-10.

RANKE, H. : Die Wahlen zu den Volksgerichten in der Sowjetunion. Neue Justiz (Germany) 12 : 50-52, 20. Januar 1958.

BERMAN, H.J. : Soviet law and government. Modern law review 21 : 19-26, January 1958.

BOITER, A. : Das neue sowjetische Gesetz gegen Parasiten. Osteuropa 8 : 10-16, January 1958.

ROMASHKIN, P. : Primenenie amnistii. Sot͡sialisticheskai͡a zakonnost (U.S.S.R.) 35 : 5-14, no. 1, i͡anvar' 1958.
Amnesty.

MAKOHON, S. : Rozvytol radi͡ans'koĭ pravovoĭ nauky na Ukraïni za 40 rokiv. Radi͡ans'ke pravo (U.S.S.R.) : 19-27, no. 1, 1958.

ANANOV, I.N. : Science of administrative law in the Soviet Union. Revue internationale des sciences administratives 24 : 355-363, no. 3, 1958.

MANDEL'SHTAM, L.I., and KIRIN, V.A. : Voprosy rasshirenii͡a prav soi͡uznykh respublik v zakonodatel'noĭ dei͡atel'nosti Verkovnogo soveta SSSR. Sovetskoe gosudarstvo i pravo : 32-42, no. 3, mart 1958.
The legislative role of the union republics.

ZELLWEGER, E. : Diktatur des Proletariats und Unions-gesetzgebung in der UdSSR. Recht in Ost und West 2 : 96-100, 15. Mai 1958.

SOUKHOMLINE, V. : Quarante ans de justice soviétique - Le développement et le renforcement de la légalité socialiste. Cahiers internationaux 10 : 18-32, 19-34, mai, juin 1958.

Code de procédure pénale de la République socialiste fédérative de Russie, R.S.F.S.R. - Texte official de l'édition de 1956. Documentation française, Notes et études documentaires : 1-43, no. 2432, 2 juillet 1958.

BAKSHEEV, S. : Proekt osnonykh nachal ugolovnogo zakonodatel'stva Soi͡uza SSR i soi͡uznykh respublik. Sovetskai͡a i͡ustit͡sii͡a (U.S.S.R.) : 5-10, no. 7, ii͡ul' 1958.

BELLON, J. : Quelques aspects de la procédure pénale soviétique. Revue de science criminelle et de droit pénal comparé 13 : 599-621, juillet-septembre 1958.

Appendice au code de procédure pénale de la République socialiste fédérative de Russia. Documentation française, Notes et études documentaires : 1-50, no. 2464, 27 septembre 1958.

GOUSKOVA, I. et MIKLINE, A. : La pratique judiciaire et arbitrale en U.R.S.S. en 1957. Revue de droit contemporain 5 : 158-168, décembre 1958.

RABINOVITCH, N.V. : Praktika Verkhovnogo suda SSSR i Verkhovnykh sudov soi͡uznykh respublik po grazhdanskim delam za 1956-1958 gody. Vestnik Leningradskogo univeritata, Serii͡a ékonomiki, filosofii i prava 13 : 77-90, no. 4, 1958.
Jurisprudence; Summary in English.

BOGUSLAVSKII, M.M., and RUBANOV, A.A. : Pravovoe sotrudnichestvo SSSR so stranami narodnoĭ demokratii. Sovetskiĭ ezhegodnik mezhdunarodnogo prava - Soviet year-book of international law : 254-272, 1958.
Legal cooperation with people's democracies.

Basic principles of the criminal procedure of the USSR and the Union republics. Law in Eastern Europe 3 : 112-151, 1959.
Text also in Russian.

MIRONENKO, Y.P. : The campaign to extend the death penalty. Institute for the study of the USSR, Bulletin 6 : 25-30, January 1959.

TARAS, T. : Problems of revision and retrial - The rights of the defendant in the light of the draft basic principles of Soviet criminal provedure. Soviet studies 10 : 213-227, January 1959.

SMIRNOV, V.G. : Novyĭ étap v razvitii ugolovnogo zakonodatel'stva Soi͡uza SSR i soi͡uznykh respublik. Pravovedenie (U.S.S.R.) 3 : 65-77, no. 2, 1959.

GUINS, G.C. : Révision de la législation pénale en Union Soviétique. Problèmes soviétiques 2 : 33-51, 1959.

GSOVSKI, V. : Soviet Union - Reform of the criminal law in the Soviet Union (Contd.). Highlights of current legislation and activities in Mid-Europe 7 : 49-142, February-March 1959.

Die neue Militärstrafgesetzgebung. Ost-Probleme 11 : 205-207, 20. März 1959.
Published in "Sowjetskij flot".

GRIBANOV, V.P. : K voprosu o poni͡atii prava sobstvennosti. Vestnik Moskovskogo universiteta, Serii͡a ékonomiki, filosofii, prava 14 : 173-190, no. 3, 1959.
Private property.

Law on the criminal responsibility for crimes against the state. Law in Eastern Europe 3 : 72-85, 1959.
Text also in Russian.

SOUKHOMLINE, V. : Après le XXIe congrès du P.C. de l'U.R.S.S. (Suite) - Réforme de la justice pénale. Cahiers internationaux 11 : 57-71, avril-mai 1959.

LUKASCHEWITSCH, W.S. : Die Veränderungen im Gerichtsverfassungsrecht der UdSSR und der Unionsrepubliken. Neue Justiz (Germany) 13 : 331-334, 20. Mai 1959.

LOEBER, D.A. : Die sowjetische Rechtsreform von 1958. Osteuropa 9 : 355-359, Mai/Juni 1959.

MIRONENKO, Y.P. : The new laws on criminal responsibility for state crimes. Institute for the study of the USSR, Bulletin 6 : 26-33, June 1959.

KLESMENT, J. : Promulgation, publication and codification of laws in the Estonian SSR. Highlights of current legislation and activities in Mid-Europe 7 : 289-292, July-August 1959.

RAGUINSKI, M., et MINKOVSKI, G. : Principes fondamentaux du système judiciaire de l'Union Soviétique et des Républiques fédérées et autonomes. Revue de droit contemporain 6 : 117-122, juin 1959.
Voir aussi pp. 128-132.

GRIGORYAN, L. : The part played by the public in strengthening Soviet law. Modern review 106 : 128-129, August 1959.

NIKIFOROV, B.S. : The fundamentals of Soviet criminal legislation. Anglo-Soviet journal 20 : 26-30, autumn 1959.

JOHNSON, E.L. : Commercial arbitration in the USSR since the decentralization of industrial management. Soviet studies 11 : 134-142, October 1959.

GSOVSKI, V. : Publications and effective date of Soviet federal laws - Secret laws. Highlights of current legislation and activities in Mid-Europe 7 : 387-394, October 1959.

KUDRJAVCEV, P.I. : Une importante étape dans l'évolution de la législation soviétique. Revue internationale de droit comparé 11 : 667-671, octobre-décembre 1959.
Organisation judiciaire.

U.S.S.R.
(International law and Practice, Aliens and Naturalization)

GRZYBOWSKI, K. : The Soviet doctrine of mare clausum and policies in Black and Baltic seas. Journal of Central Europeab affairs 14 : 339-353, January 1955.

MARGOLIS, E. : Soviet views on the relationship between national and international law. International and comparative law quarterly 4 : 116-128, January 1955.

FREY, G. : Das Strafverfahren gegen deutsche Kriegsgefangene in der Sowjetunion. Osteuropa-Recht 1 : 31-37, März 1955.

DRUCKER, A. : Soviet views on private international law. International and comparative law quarterly 4 : 384-389, July 1955.

KULSKI, W.W. : The Soviet interpretation of international law. American journal of international law 49 : 518-534, October 1955.

MEISSNER, B. : Sowjetunion and Haager Landkriegsordnung. Osteuropa-Recht 1 : 96-99, Dezember 1955.

SCHEUERLE, W.A. : L'arbitrato sovietico riguardante il commercio estero e la giurisprudenza relativa. Annuario di diritto comparato e di studi legislativi 30 : 148-170, 1955.

SETON-WATSON, H. : Soviet nationality policy. Russian review 15 : 3-13, January 1956.

SUONTAUSTA, T. : Den sovjetiska uppfattningen om folkrätten. Nordisk tidsskrift for international ret og jus gentium 26 : 3-11, fasc. 1, 1956.

HALAJCUZ, B.T. : Las doctrinas soviéticas de derecho internacional. Revista española de derecho internacional 9 : 689-704, núm. 3, 1956.

KOROVIN, E. Respect for sovereignty, an unchanging principle of Soviet foreign policy. International affairs (Moscow) : 31-41, November 1956.

LOEBER, D.A. : Bibliographie zum sowjetischen Völkerrecht 1956. Internationales Recht und Diplomatie : 86-88, Heft 1, 1957.

Reglement betr. die diplomatischen und konsularischen Vertretungen fremder Staaten auf dem Gebiet der Union der Sozialistischen Sowjetrepubliken bestätigt durch Verordnung des Zentralen Exekutivkomitees und des Rates der Volkskommissare der UdSSR vom 14. Januar 1927. Internationales Recht und Diplomatie : 181-185, Heft 2, 1957.

PISAR, S. : Soviet conflict of laws in international commercial transactions. Harvard law review 70 : 593-656, February 1957.

UCHIDA, H. : On the Soviet theory of territorial waters. Journal of international law and diplomacy 55 : 617-641, March 1957.
Text in Japanese.

ŽOUREK, J. : Sovětská definice agrese, veliký přínos rozvoji mezinárodního práva. Časopis pro mezinárodní právo 1 : 310-326, číslo 4, 1957.
Soviet definition of aggression.

SLUSSER, R.M., and TRISKA, J.F. : Professor Krylov and Soviet treaties. American journal of international law 51 : 766-770, October 1957.
Annex pp. 771-773.

BRACHT, H.W. : Co-existence and international law - The development of the modern idea of international law in the Soviet Union. Association des auditeurs et anciens auditeurs de l'Académie de droit international de La Haye, Annuaire 27 : 50-58, 1957.

RAMZAITSEY, D.F. : La jurisprudence en matière de droit international privé de la Commission arbitrale soviétique pour le commerce extérieur. Revue critique de droit international privé 47 : 459-478, juillet-septembre 1958.

GAFUROV, B. : Uspekhi nat͡sional'noĭ politiki KPSS i nektorye voprosy internat͡sional'nogo vospitanii͡a. Kommunist 35 : 10-24, no. 11, avgust 1958.

BOBROV, R.L. : Pŭrvo godishno sŭbranie na Sŭvetskata asotsiatsii͡a za mezhdunarodno pravo. Pravna misŭl 2 : 78-83, kn. 5, 1958.
Soviet association of international law, 1958 meeting.

BYKOV, D.V. : Soglashenii͡a o pravovom statuse sovetskikh voĭsk za granit͡sei. Sovetskiĭ ezhegodnik mezhdunarodnogo prava - Soviet year-book of international law : 381-386, 1958.
Soviet troops abroad; Summary in English.

TRISKA, J.F., and SLUSSER, R.M. : Ratification of treaties in Soviet theory, practice and policy. British year book of international law 34 : 312-333, 1958.

BISHOP, D.G. : Immunity of diplomatic establishment - Soviet law and practice. Osteuropa-Recht 5 : 8-14, Mai 1959.

KUCHEROV, S. : Das Problem der Küstenmeere und die Sowjetunion. Osteuropa-Recht 5 : 15-24, Mai 1959.

NATIONAL LAW - COUNTRIES

GRZYBOWSKI, K. : The extraterritorial effect of Soviet criminal law after the reform of 1958. American journal of comparative law 8 : 515-518, autumn 1959.

KLESMENT, J. : New Soviet position on the nationality of Estonians abroad. Highlights of current legislation and activities in Mid-Europe 7 : 347-348, September 1959.

BENJAMIN, P. : Soviet treaty practice on commercial arbitration since 1940. American journal of international law 53 : 882-889, October 1959.

TUNKIN, G. : The Soviet Union and international law. International affairs (Moscow) 5 : 40-45, November 1959.

UNITED ARAB REPUBLIC

The Egyptian constitution of 16 January 1956 (Contd.). New East 7 : 152-159, no. 2, 1956.
Text in Hebrew.

The Egyptian constitution announced 16 January 1956. Middle Eastern affairs 7 : 68-81, February 1956.
Text.

BADR, G.M. : The new Egyptian civil code and the unification of the laws of the Arab countries. Tulane law review 30 : 299-304, February 1956.

Constitution de la République d'Egypte, 16 janvier 1956. Informations constitutionnelles et parlementaires : 72-95, avril 1956.
Texte.

MONACO, R. : La nuova costituzione egiziana. Oriente moderno 36 : 281-288, maggio 1956.
16 January 1956; Text pp. 289-300.

LINANT de BELLEFONDS, Y. : La suppression des juridictions de statut personnel en Egypte. Revue internationale de droit comparé 8 : 412-425, juillet-septembre 1956.

SAÏD, N.A. : La technique de la codification en matière de droit privé en Egypte. Revue internationale de droit comparé 8 : 371-375, juillet-septembre 1956.

Constitution de la République d'Egypte, 16 janvier 1956. Documentation française, Notes et études documentaires : 1-16, no. 2203, 10 août 1956.
Texte p. 3-12.

LINANT de BELLEFONDS, Y. : Le droit musulman et le nouveau code civil égyptien. Revue algérienne, tunisienne et marocaine de législation et de jurisprudence, Doctrine 72 : 211-222, novembre-décembre 1956.

EMILIA, A. D' : Il diritto musulmano e il nuovo codice civile egiziano. Annuario di diritto comparato e di studi legislativi 31 : 114-136, 1956.

Egipto - Constitución de 16 de enero 1956. Información jurídica (Spain) : 129-137, marzo-abril 1957.

KHAFAGUI, A.R. : La corruption en droit égyptien. Egypte contemporaine 48 : 5-45, avril 1957.

KHAFAGUI, A.R. : La qualification juridique de la corruption en droit égyptien. Egypte contemporaine 48 : 5-63, octobre 1957.

The Egyptian revolution and the structure of government - A review of constitutional developments 1952-1957. Revue égyptienne de droit international 13 : 76-85, 1957.

Constitution provisoire de la République Arabe Unie proclamée le 5 mars 1958 simultanément à à Damas et au Caire. Monde arabe en fin de chaque semaine, Annexe documentation 1 : 1-6, no. 87, 319 mars 1958.

Constitution provisoire de la République arabe unie, 5 mars 1958. Documentation française, Articles et documents, Textes du jour : 1-4, no. 629, 13 mars 1958.

Charte de la création des Etats arabes, 8 mars 1958. Informations constitutionnelles et parlementaires 9 : 98-101, avril 1958.

The charter of the United Arab states. Egyptian economic and political review 4 : 21-22, April 1958.
March 1958; Text.

Constitution provisoire de la République Arabe Unie, Egypte-Syrie, 5 mars 1958. Documentation française, Notes et études documentaires : 1-16, no. 2420, 4 juin 1958.

Législations se rapportant aux tribus en Syrie. Monde arabe en fin de chaque semaine, Annexe documentaire 2 : 1-5, no. 174, 20 septembre-5 octobre 1958.

Sequestration of enemy property in Egypt. Revue égyptienne de droit international 14 : 137-153, 1958.

COTRAN, E. : Some legal aspects of the formation of the United Arab Republic and the United Arab states. International and comparative law quarterly 8 : 346-372, April 1959.
Documents pp. 372-390.

U.S.A.

HUNT, A.R. :Federal supremacy and state anti-subversive legislation. Michigan law review 53 : 407-438, January 1955.

Administration of claims against the sovereign. A survey of state techniques. Harvard law review 68 : 506-517, January 1955.

LENHOFF, A. : Reciprocity - The legal aspect of a perennial idea (Contd.) - The reciprocity idea in the American private international law. Northwestern university law review 49 : 752-779, January-February 1955.

HOFFMANN, S. : La discrimination contre les Noirs et le droit constitutionnel des Etats-Unis. Revue du droit public et de la science politique en France et à l'étranger 71 : 116-163, janvier-mars 1955.

JACOBSTEIN, J.M. : The statutes of the forty-eight states by subject - An annotated bibliography. Law library journal 48 : 40-58, February 1955.

1954 survey of American law (Contd.). Government regulation and taxation. New York university law review 30 : 227-476, February 1955.
Series of articles.

NATIONAL LAW - COUNTRIES

O'CONOR, J.F. : The Fifth amendment - Should a good friend be abused? American bar association journal 41 : 307-310, 369-370, April 1955.

PAGENSTECHER, M. : Renvoi in the United States - A proposal. Tulane law review 29 : 379-395, April 1955.

The Communist control act of 1954. Yale law journal 64 : 712-765, April 1955.

McWHINNEY, E. : Conflits philosophiques dans la Cour suprême des Etats-Unis - Le dilemme sur l'élaboration d'une politique jurisprudentielle. Revue internationale de droit comparé 7 : 281-295, avril-juin 1955.

Report of the Attorney general's national committee to study the anti-trust laws. Michigan law review 53 : 1033-1152, June 1955.
A symposium.

HARRIS, W.R. : The Hoover commission report - Improvement of legal services and procedure. American bar association journal 41 : 497-500, 558-562, June 1955.

RHEINSTEIN, M. : The constitutional bases of jurisdiction. University of Chicago law review 22 : 775-824, summer 1955.

HARRIS, W.R. : The Hoover commission report (Contd.). Improvement of legal services and procedure. American bar association journal 41 : 713-717, August 1955.

VRIES, H.P. de : Universalisme et unification du droit aux Etats-Unis d'Amérique. Revue internationale de droit comparé 7 : 542-547, juillet-septembre 1955.

Adoption - Symposium. Iowa law review 40 : 225-363, winter 1955.
Series of articles.

The Supreme court, 1954 term. Harvard law review 69 : 119-209, November 1955.

Hoover commission and task force reports on legal services and procedure. New York university law review 30 : 1267-1417, November 1955.
A symposium.

Immunity from statutes of limitations and other doctrines favoring the United States as plaintiff. Columbia law reviewing 55 : 1177-1192, December 1955.

HOFSTADTER, S.H. : The fifth amendment and the Immunity act of 1954. Record of the Association of the bar of the city of New York 10 : 453-497, December 1955.

1955 survey of New York law. New York university law review 30 : 1469-1713, December 1955.

1955 annual survey of American law - Part I, Public law in general. New York university law review 31 : 1-195, January 1956.

BOUDIN, L.B. : The constitutional right to travel. Columbia law review 56 : 47-75, January 1956.

WALKER, H. : Commercial arbitration in United States treaties. Arbitration journal 2 : 68-84, no. 2, 1956.

MASON, A.T. : Inter arma silent leges - Chief justice Stone's views. Harvard law review 69 : 806-838, March 1956.
Military proceedings.

FELLMAN, D. : Constitutional law in 1954-1955. American political science review 50 : 43-100, March 1956.

TONNDORF, I. : Das Entscheidungsrecht in der Ehe nach dem Recht der Vereinigten Staaten von Amerika. Zeitschrift für ausländisches und internationales Privatrecht 21 : 512-549, Heft 3/4, 1956.

PRUGH, G.S. : The code of conduct for the armed forces. Columbia law review 56 : 678-707, May 1956.

Law and the future - A symposium. Northwestern university law review 51 : 163-296, May-June 1956.

WALSH, W.F. : Military law - Return to drumhead justice? American bar association journal 42 : 521-525, June 1956.

PITTMAN, R.C. : The Fifth amendment, yesterday, today and tomorrow. American bar association journal 42 : 509-512, 588-594, June 1956.

KELLY, A.H. : The Fourteenth amendment reconsidered - The segregation question. Michigan law review 54 : 1049-1086, June 1956.

GOWER, L.C.B. : Some contrasts between British and American corporation law. Harvard law review 69 : 1369-1402, June 1956.

Five years of legal aid. Banker 106 : 510-514, August 1956.

JAFFE, L. L.: The American administrative procedure act. Public law : 218-232, autumn 1956.

JAFFE, L. L. : The right to travel - The passport problem. Foreign affairs 35 : 17-28, October 1956.

PARKER, J.J. : Dual sovereignty and the Federal courts. Northwestern university law review 51 : 407-423, September-October 1956.

AUERBACH, C.A. : The Communist control act of 1954 - A proposed legal-political theory of free speech. University of Chicago law review 23 : 173-220, winter 1956.

The Supreme court 1955 term. Harvard law review 70 : 83-188, November 1956.

1956 survey of New York law. New York university law review 31 : 1349-1580, December 1956.

CRAYHON, J.B. : The doctrine of the international shoe case and its limited vitality in our federal system. Intramural law review of New York university School of law 12 : 127-145, January 1959.

1956 annual survey of American law - Part one, Public law in general. New York university law review 32 : 1-145, January 1957.

VAGTS, D.F. : Free speech in the armed forces. Columbia law review 57 : 187-218, February 1957.

1956 annual survey of American law (Contd.), government regulation, torts and family law. New York university law review 32 : 231-349, February 1957.

KORT, F. : Predicting Supreme court decisions mathematically - A quantitative analysis of the "right to counsel" cases. American political science review 51 : 1-12, March 1957.

HECKE, M.T. van : Racial desegregation in the law schools. Journal of legal education 9 : 283-289, no. 3, 1957.

DAVEY, G.W. : An English view of the American bar. Law journal 107 : 231-232, 12 April 1957.

SUTHERLAND, A.E. : The American judiciary and racial desegregation. Modern law review 20 : 201-219, May 1957.

PAPALE, A.E. : Judicial enforcement of desegregation, its problems and limitations. Northwestern university law review 52 : 301-319, July-August 1957.

Policy-making in a democracy - The role of the United States Supreme court - A symposium. Journal of public law 6 : 275-508, fall 1957.

SUTHERLAND, A.E. : The citizen's immunities and public opinion. Harvard law review 71 : 85-93, November 1957.

1957 survey of New York law. New York university law review 32 : 1327-1528, December 1957.

SULLIVAN, J.P., and WEBSTER, D.N. : Some constitutional and practical problems of the Subversive activities control act. Georgetown law journal 46 : 299-314, winter 1957-58.

Legal problems in the Tidelands - A symposium. Tulane law review 32 : 173-290, February 1958.

FELLMAN, D. : Constitutional law in 1956-1957. American political science review 52 : 140-192, March 1958.

The Federal rules of civil procedure, 1938-1958. Columbia law review 58 : 435-515, April 1958.
Series of articles.

BRAUCHER, R. : The legislative history of the Uniform commercial code. Columbia law review 58 : 798-814, June 1958.

Symposium on the uniform commercial code and Illinois law. Northwestern university law review 53 : 315-426, July-August 1958.

HELLENTHAL, J.S. : Alaska's heralded constitution - The forty-ninth state sets an example. American bar association journal 44 : 1147-1150, December 1958.

DOOMS, M. : The role of the Supreme court in ending school segregation. Internationale spectator 13 : 78-103, nr. 4, 22 februari 1959.
United States.

FELLMAN, D. : Constitutional law in 1957-1958. American political science review 53 : 138-180, March 1959.

MALONE, R.L. : The Communist resolutions - What the House of delegates really did. American bar association journal 45 : 343-347, April 1959.

MEADOW, M.J. : Freedom to travel under the constitution. Intramural law review of New York university School of law 14 : 277-298, May 1959.

Racial integration and academic freedom (Contd.). New York university law review 34 : 899-938, May 1959.

EHRENZWEIG, A.A. : The statute of frauds in the conflict of laws - The basic rule of validation. Columbia law review 59 : 874-881, June 1959.

LOSOS, J.O. : The Supreme court and its critics - Is the Court moving left? Review of politics 21 : 495-510, July 1959.

KINGSLEY, R. : The protection of the family in American law. South African law journal 76 : 290-295, August 1959.

SPALIŃSKI, M. : Uwagi o statusie prawnym misji wojskowych Stanów Zjednoczonych. Państwo i prawo 14 : 598-613, październik 1959.
Summaries in English, French and Russian.

RIESENFELD, S.A. : The United States Supreme court and the recent constitutional tempest. Annual law review 4 : 421-441, December 1959.

U.S.A.
(International law, Aliens, Nationality)

MATHEWS, C. : The constitutional power of the President to conclude international agreements. Yale law journal 64 : 345-389, January 1955.

KOROVIN, E. : U.S. violation of the principle of freedom of the seas. International affairs (Moscow) : 57-65, no. 3, 1955.

GREEN, S.W. : Applicability of American laws to overseas areas controlled by the United States. Harvard law review 68 : 781-812, March 1955.

HOFSTEIN, G. : The returning resident alien. Intramural law review of New York university 10 : 271-284, May 1955.

SUTHERLAND, A.E. : The flag, the constitution and international agreements. Harvard law review 68 : 1374-1381, June 1955.
Occupational claims.

WILSON, R.R. : "Treaty-investor" clauses in commercial treaties of the United States. American journal of international law 49 : 366-370, July 1955.

The Expatriation act of 1954. Yale law journal 64 : 1164-1200, July 1955.

OLIVER, C.T. : Executive agreements and emanations from the fifth amendment. American journal of international law 49 : 362-366, July 1955.

JAMES, M. : The United States and the movement for universal copyright, 1945-1952. Library quarterly 25 : 219-234, July 1955.

La nationalité aux Etats-Unis. Revue de droit international, de sciences diplomatiques et politiques 33 : 253-260, juillet-septembre 1955.

HYNNING, C.J. : Treaty law for the private practitioner. University of Chicago law review 23 : 36-75, autumn 1955.

ROSENFIELD, H.N. : Consular non-reviewability - A case study in administrative absolutism. American bar association journal 41 : 1109-1112, 1181-1183, December 1955.
Immigration.

NIMMER, M.B. : Copyright 1955. California law review 43 : 791-808, December 1955.

New regulations for hearing procedure published by Immigration and naturalization service. Interpreter releases 33 : 13-18, 23 January 1956.
January 1956.

NADELMANN, K.H. : Les Etats-Unis d'Amérique et l'exécution de jugements étrangers. Bulletin de législation et de jurisprudence égyptiennes 7 : 1-11, no. 1, 1956.

Immigration and naturalization in Congress. Interpreter releases 33 : 38-47, 9 February 1956.
See also pp. 48-59.

MASLOW, W. : Recasting our deportation law - Proposals for reform. Columbia law review 56 : 309-366, March 1956.

Passport appeals procedure. Interpreter releases 33 : 127-133, 30 April 1956.

KUNZ, J.L. : Der heutige Stand der Wissenschaft und des Unterrichts des Völkerrechts in den Vereinigten Staaten. Osterreichische Zeitschrift für öffentliches Recht 7 : 401-427, Heft 4, 1956.

WEINSTEIN, J.B. : Recognition in the United States of the privilege of another jurisdiction. Columbia law review 56 : 535-549, April 1956.

SCHEIB, P.M. : Fraud in derivative citizenship. Intramural law review of New York university 11 : 271-279, May 1956.

Supreme court decisions on immigration and naturalization during the 1955-1956 term. Interpreter releases 33 : 195-202, 20 June 1956.

PHLEGER, H. : United States treaties - Recent developments. Department of State bulletin (United States) 35 : 11-18, 2 July 1956.

Amendments to the regulations under the Immigration and nationality act. Interpreter releases 33 : 293-301, 24 August 1956.

PROBST, R. : International demarcation of compulsory military service with special emphasis on the Swiss-United States situation. Georgetown law journal 45 : 60-74, fall 1956.

COERPER, M.G. : The foreign claims settlement commission and judicial review. American journal of international law 50 : 868-879, October 1956.

WILSON, R.R. : A decade of new commercial treaties. American journal of international law 50 : 927-933, October 1956.

HENKIN, L. : The treaty makers and the law makers - The Niagara reservation. Columbia law review 56 : 1151-1182, December 1956.

DOMKE, M. : Fragen des öffentlichen Rechts in der amerikanischen Feindvermögenspraxis 1956. Zeitschrift für ausländisches öffentliches Recht und Völkerrecht 17 : 655-668, Nr. 3/4, 1957.

KUNZ, J.L. : The new U.S. army field manual on the law of land warfare. American journal of international law 51 : 388-396, April 1957.

SCHÖNHERR, K. : Die Entrechtung des amerikanischen Senats im Treaty-Making-Verfahren. Staat und Recht 6 : 471-485, Mai 1957.

HEYMAN, A. : The nonresident alien's right to succession under the Iron curtain rule. Northwestern university law review 52 : 221-240, May-June 1957.

OLIVER, C.T. : Treaties, the Senate, and the constitution - Some current questions. American journal of international law 51 : 606-611, July 1957.

DOMKE, M. : Osteuropäische Erbrechtsinteresseb vor amerikanischen Gerichten. Osteuropa-Recht 3 : 85-91, Oktober 1957.

McCUSKER, P.D. : Some United States practices in international judicial assistance. Department of State bulletin (United States) 37 : 808-812, November 18, 1957.

Constitutionality of restrictions on alien's right to work. Columbia law review 57 : 1012-1028, November 1957.

Liability for registration and military service of aliens in the United States temporarily. Interpreter releases 34 : 322-324, 5 December 1957.

DOMKE, M. : Deutsche Statusfragen vor amerikanischen Gerichten. Juristenzeitung 13 : 14-15, 5. Januar 1958.

SHAW, D.J. : New United States immigration act, public law 85-316. Migration news 7 : 9-11, January-February 1958.

DOMKE, M. : Enforcement of foreign arbitral awards in the United States. Arbitration journal 13 : 91-97, no. 2, 1958.

EHRENZWEIG, A.A. : American private international law and the "restatement". Nordisk tidsskrift for international ret og jus gentium 28 : 229-237, fasc.3-4, 1958.

CZYZAK, J.J., and SULLIVAN, C.H. : American arbitration law and the UN convention. Arbitration journal 13 : 197-213, no. 4, 1958.

YIANNOPOULOS, A.N. : Wills of movables in American international conflicts law - A critique of the domiciliary rule. California law review 46 : 185-264, May 1958.

The status of international organizations under the law of the United States. Harvard law review 71 : 1300-1324, May 1958.

HONNOLD, J. : A uniform law for international sales. University of Pennsylvania law review 107 : 299-330, January 1959.

NATIONAL LAW - COUNTRIES

WHITTON, J.B. : L'exercice de la compétence pénale à l'égard des forces américaines à l'étranger. Revue générale de droit international public 63 : 5-20, janvier-mars 1959.

SUKIJASOVIĆ, M. : Sudski imunitet u medunarodnom pomorskom pravu u praksi američkih sudova. Jugoslovenska revija za medunarodno pravo 6 : 262-269, broj 2, 1959.
Summary in English.

BAECK, P.L. : Übersetzungsfragen im Rechtsverkehr mit den USA. Juristische Blätter 81 : 230-233, 2. Mai 1959.

PEARCY, G.E. : Measurement of the U.S. territorial sea. Department of state bulletin (United States) 40 : 963-971, 29 June 1959.
With maps.

SCHLESINGER, R.B. : The uniform commercial code in the light of comparative law. Inter-American law review - Revista jurídica interamericana 1 : 11-58, January-June 1959.

HOWARD, J.B. : International legal studies. University of Chicago law review 26 : 577-596, summer 1959.

DOMKE, M. : L'exécution des sentences arbitrales étrangères aux Etats-Unis. Revue de l'arbitrage : 70-77, juillet-septembre 1959.

DOMKE, M. : Osteuropäische Ansprüche auf Amerikanische Erbschaften. Recht in Ost und West 3 : 177-179, 15. September 1959.

SNYDER, E. : Military law abroad. The status of Forces agreement in England. American bar association journal 45 : 1033-1036, 1117-1118, October 1959.

SULTAN, A. : The United Nations arbitration convention and United States policy. American journal of international law 53 : 807-825, October 1959.

MYERS, D.P. : Contemporary practice of the United States relating to international law. American journal of international law 53 : 896-922, October 1959.

HESSE, S. : The constitutional status of the lawfully admitted permanent resident alien - The inherent limits of the power to expel. Yale law journal 69 : 262-297, December 1959.

U.S.A.
(Patents, Trade-marks, Copyright)

Developments in the law - Trade-marks and unfair competition. Harvard law review 68 : 816-920, March 1955.

SOMMERICH, O.C. : Treatment by United States of world war I and II enemy-owned patents and copyrights. American journal of comparative law 4 : 587-600, autumn 1955.

SHERMAN, P.J. : The Universal copyright convention - Its effect on United States law. Columbia law review 55 : 1137-1175, December 1955.

Trademarks and trade names - A symposium. California law review 44 : 437-546, July 1956.
Series of articles.

SARGOY, E.A. : UCC protection in the United States - The coming into effect of the Universal copyright convention. New York university law review 33 : 811-856, June 1958.

URUGUAY

SÁNCHEZ FONTÁNS, J. : Réseña de legislación, jurisprudencia y bibliografía uruguayas en 1954. Revista de derecho privado : 728-737, julio-agosto 1955.

SÁNCHEZ FONTÁNS, J. : Reseña de legislación, jurisprudencía y bibliografía uruguayas en 1955. Revista de derecho privado (Madrid) : 762-771, julio-agosto 1956.

SÁNCHEZ FONTÁNS, J. : Reseña de legislación, jurisprudencia y bibliografía uruguayas en 1957. Revista de derecho privado (Madrid) : 339-404, abril 1958.

GELSI BIDART, A. : La prova della sentenza straniera, con particolare riguardo al diritto uruguayano. Rivista di diritto internazionale 42 : 469-474, fasc. 3, 1959.

SÁNCHEZ FONTÁNS, J. : Reseña de legislación, jurisprudencia y bibliografía uruguayas en 1958. Revista de derecho privado (Madrid) : 448-454, mayo 1959.

VATICAN STATE

BACHELET, V. : L'organisation administrative du Saint-Siège et de la Cité du Vatican. Revue internationale des sciences administratives 21 : 231-274, no. 2, 1955.

CANSACCHI, G. : La continuità dello Stato Pontificio. Istituto di diritto internazionale e straniero della Università di Milano, Comunicazioni e studi 7 : 97-142, 1955.

MARKOVIĆ, M. : Položaj Vatikana, odnosno pape i katoličke crkve u medunarodnom pravu. Jugoslovenska revija za medunarodno pravo 3 : 245-257, broj 2, 1956.
Summary in French.

VENEZUELA

Venezuela - Código civil. Información jurídica (Spain) : 165-180, febrero 1955.

GOLDSCHMIDT, R. : Problemi della riforma del diritto commerciale venezuelano. Rivista del diritto commerciale e del diritto generale delle obbligazioni 53 : 181-197, marzo-aprile 1955.

Vénézuela - Loi de naturalisation. Cahiers de législation et de bibliographie juridique de l'Amérique latine 6 : 79-81, no. 23-24, juillet-décembre 1955.

Venezuela - Código civil, 3ª edición oficial, 16 julio 1943 (Contd.). Información jurídica (Spain) : 680-744, noviembre-diciembre 1955.
Text.

Venezuela - Ley de naturalización. Jus gentium 6 : 119-121, no. 2, 1956.

Ley de reforma parcial del código de comercio de 26 de julio de 1955. Revista de la Facultad de derecho (Caracas) : 159-171, no. 7, 1956.

Ley organica de la Corte de casación. Revista de la Facultad de derecho (Caracas) : 53-62, no. 9, 1956.

LORETO, L. : La sentencia extranjera en el sistema venezolano del exequátur. Studia iuridica (Caracas) 1 : 187-215, 1957.
See also pp. 346-368.

BAKER, W.R. : The formation and operation of a Venezuelan corporation. Tulane law review 31 : 261-282, February 1957.

GOLDSCHMIDT, R. : Vénézuela. Revue de droit international et de droit comparé 33 : 261-266, no. 4, 1956.

GOLDSCHMIDT, R. : El fideicomiso en la reciente legislación venezolana. Boletín del Instituto de derecho comparado de México 10 : 9-30, mayo-agosto 1957.

GOLDSCHMIDT, R. : La ley de fideicomiso de 1956. Revista de la Facultad de derecho (Caracas) 89-113, no. 11, 1957.

Legal provisions on nationality and imagination. Venezuela up-to-date (Venezuela) 8 - 9-10, 15; February 1958.

GOLDSCHMIDT, R. : Le ley venezolana de propriedad horizontal de 1958. Bolrtín del Instituto de derecho comparado de México 12 : 99-116, enero-abril 1959.

VIETNAM

DONNIER, M. : La convention judiciaire franco-vietnamienne du 16 septembre 1954 au regard du droit international privé français - Condition des étrangers, conflit de lois, conflit de juridictions. Penant, Recueil général de jurisprudence, de doctrine et de législation d'outre-mer, Doctrine 65 : 1-20, janvier -février 1955.

Convention franco-vietneamienne sur la nationalité, 16 août 1955. Documentation française, Notes et études documentaires : 1-6, no. 2112, 13 décembre 1955.

Le régime constitutionnel de la République du Viet-nam - Analyse, texte intégral de la constitution du 26 octobre 1956. Archives internationales Pharos 13 : 1-8, no. 1318, 10 décembre 1956.

Viet-Nam - Constitution de la République du Viet-nam, 26 octobre 1956. Informations constitutionnelles et parlementaires 8 : 32-50, janvier 1957.

Constitution de la République du Viet-Nam, 26 octobre 1956. Documentations française, Notes et études documentaires : 1-10, no. 2278, 2 avril 1957.
Texte.

FALL, B. : Die Rechtslage in der Demokratischen Republik Viet-Nam. Osteuropa-Recht 4 : 198-211, Juli 1958.

VOLTAIC REPUBLIC

Constitution de la République de Haute-Volta du 15 mars 1959. Recueil Penant, Législation 69 : 158-167, mai-juin 1959.

WEST INDIES

RAMPHAL, S.S. : The West Indies - Constitutional bacjground to federation. Public law : 128-151, summer 1959.

McPETRIE, J.C. : The constitution of the West Indies. Public law : 293-309, autumn 1959.

YEMEN

The charter of the United Arab states. Egyptian economic and political review 4 : 21-22, April 1958.
March 1958; Text.

Charte de la création des Etats arabes, 8 mars 1958. Informations constitutionnelles et parlementaires 9 : 98-101, avril 1958.

YUGOSLAVIA

EISNER, B. : Die Gesetzgebung jugoslawiens auf dem Gebiete des Privatrechts 1952-1954. Zeitschrift für ausländisches und internationales Privatrecht 20 : 158-167, Heft 1, 1955.

FABRE, M.H. : Les nouveaux principes titistes du droit public. Annales de la Faculté de droit d'Aix-en-Provence : 188-259, no. 48, 1955.

ČULINOVIĆ, F. : Problem o višedržavnosti jugoslavenske federacije. Zbornik Pravnog fakulteta u Zagrebu 5 : 119-133, broj 3-4, 1955.
Constitution.

BLAGOJEVIĆ, B.T. : Die Ausbürgerung nach dem Recht der Föderativen Volksrepublik Jugoslawien, im Lichte der allgemeinen Theorie der Staatsangehörigkeit. Österreichische Zeitschrift für öffentliches Recht 6 : 611-629, Heft 4/5, 1955.

POTCHEK, S. : La nouvelle loi yougoslave sur les successions. Revue internationale de droit comparé 7 : 368-371, avril-juin 1955.

PAVIĆ, D. : Nekoliko problema iz krivičnog pravosuda. Naša zakonitost 9 : 285-292, broj 6-7, 1955.
Criminal law.

KARDELJ, E. : The new organization of municipalitie and districts. New Yugoslav law 6 : 3-27, July-September 1955.
Texts annexed pp. 28-39.

DJORDJEVIC, J. : Le droit constitutionnel de la RPF de Yougoslavie et son évolution. Revue internationale de droit comparé 7 : 551-559, juillet-septembre 1955.

LINKE, R. : Der neue Vertrag zwischen Österreich ur Jugoslawien über den wechselseitigen rechtlichen Verkehr und seine strafrechtlichen Bestimmungen. Österreichische Juristen-Zeitung 10 : 667-670, 16. Dezember 1955.
December 1954.

NATIONAL LAW - COUNTRIES

Numéro publié en langues anglaise et française en l'honneur de la 47e conférence de l'International law association, tenue à Dubrovnik du 26 août au 2 septembre 1956. Jugoslovanska revisja za medunarodno pravo 3 : 1-236, broj 1, 1956.
Divers secteirs du droit yougoslave.

ZLATARIĆ, B. : L'organisation de l'assistance judiciaire internationale en Yougoslavie. Nouveau droit yougoslave 7 : 39-45, janvier-mars 1956.

PUSIC, E. : La réforme des pouvoirs locaux en Yougoslavie. Revue hellénique de droit international 9 : 93-102, janvier-décembre 1956.

BLAGOJEVIC, B. : Les droits successoraux du conjoint survivant en droit yougoslave. Revue hellénique de droit international 9 : 102-115, janvier-décembre 1956.

BARTOŠ, M. : Zastupanje stranih privrednih preduzéca u Jugoslaviji. Jugoslovanska revija za medunarodno pravo 3 : 237-243, broj 2, 1956.

EISNER, B. : Internationales Privat- und Verfahrensrecht im neuen jugoslawischen Gesetz über das Erbrecht. Zeitschrift für ausländisches und internationales Privatrecht 21 : 346-350, Heft 2, 1956.

SAJOVIC, R. : O pripoznavi in izvršbi civilnih odločb po pogodbi o vzajémni pravni pomoči med Federativno Ljudsko Republiko Jugoslavijo in Ljudsko Republiko Bolgarijo. Zbornik Pravnog facultata u Zagrebu 6 : 187-196, nos. 3-4, 1956.
Legal assistance with Bulgaria.

GOLDŠTAJN, A. : Die Rechtslage der Wirtschaftsunternehmen in Jugoslawien. Wirtschaft und Recht 8 : 280-287, Heft 4, 1956.

Novo sudsko zakonodavstvo i neka pitanja daljeg razvoja sudskog sistema. Naša zakonitost 10 : 145-151, broj 4, 1956.
Interview with J. Hrnčevićem; Courts.

L'organisation de l'administration d'Etat fédérale. Nouveau droit yougoslave 7 : 22-38, avril-juin 1956.
Voir aussi pp. 3-21.

KARDELJ, E. : Our State administration under the new conditions. New Yugoslav law 7 : 3-20, April-June 1956.
Text of laws and comments pp. 21-55.

LINKE, R. : Das jugoslawische Gesetz über des Strafverfahren vom 10. September 1953. Österreichische Juristen-Zeitung 11 : 227-230, 4. Mai 1956.

RANKOVIĆ, A. : The new law relating to the organs of internal affairs. New Yugoslav law 7 : 3-11, July-December 1956.

EISNER, B. : Die Entwicklung des Privatsrechts Jugoslawiens seit Ende des Weltkriegs bis Ende 1954. Annuario di diritto comparato e di studi legislativi 31 : 202-239, 1956.

MAKSIMOVICH, B., and JASZENKO, K. : Survey of laws and treatises for 1955-1956. Highlights of current legislation and activities in Mid-Europe 5 : 27-46, January 1957.

KRBEK, I. : Law of general administrative procedure. New Yugoslav law 8 : 12-20, January-March 1957.

KALODERA, M. : Medunarodne arbitražne klauzule prema našem novom procesnom pravu. Jugoslovanska revija za medunarodno pravo 4 : 237-249, br. 2, 1957.
Summary in French.

STJEPANOVIC, N. : La réforme du conseil exécutif fédéral de Yougoslavie. Revue international des sciences administratives 23 : 318-328, no. 3, 1957.

STJEPANOVIC, N. : Judicial review of administrative acts in Yugoslavia. American journal of comparative law 6 : 94-105, winter 1957.

LOUSSOUARN, Y. : De l'exequatur des sentences arbitrales étrangères non motivées. Recueil Dalloz, Chronique : 191-194, 9 novembre 1957.

GEILKE, G. : Zur Rückwirkung des jugoslawischen Erbrechtsgesetzes 1955. Zeitschrift für ausländisches und internationales Privatrecht 23 : 44-50, Heft 1, 1958.

BESAROBIC, M. : La reconnaissance et l'exécution des sentences arbitrales étrangères en République Populaire Fédérative de Yougoslavie. Jugoslovenska revija za medunarodno pravo 5 : 133-146, broj 1, 1958.

AVRAMOV, S. : Application of international law in the Yugoslav law. Jugoslovenska revija za medunarodno pravo 5 : 192-205, broj 1, 1958.

KALOGJERA, M. : La reconnaissance et l'exécution des décisions judiciaires étrangères. Jugoslovenska revija za medunarodno pravo 5 : 124-132, broj 1, 1958.

STJEPANOVIC, N. : La loi yougoslave sur la procédure administrative non contentieuse. Revue internationale des sciences administratives 24 : 181-198, no. 2, 1958.

BAYER, V. : Le droit pénal, l'organisation judiciaire et la procédure pénale dans la Yougoslavie nouvelle. Revue de droit pénal et de criminologie 38 : 557-581, février 1958.

MILENKOVIC, M. : La nouvelle loi yougoslave sur le droit d'auteur. Revue de l'U.E.R. (Union européenne de radiodiffusion), Cahier B : 42-44, no. 47, février 1958.

Drugi kongres pravnika Jugoslavije. Arhiv za pravne i društvene nauke 45 : 177-738, broj 2-4, 1958.
Zagreb, May 1958; Special issue.

JEVREMOVIĆ, B. : Sveopsta deklaracija o pravima coveka u jugoslovenskoj praksi. Jugoslovenska revija za medunarodno pravo 5 : 431-433, broj 3, 1958.
Declaration of human rights; Summary in English.

STOYANOVITCH, K. : La nouvelle loi yougoslave sur le droit d'auteur, loi du 28 août 1957. Revue internationale de droit comparé 10 : 776-781, octobre-décembre 1958.

TROFENIK, R. Die Grundsätze des jugoslawischen Asyl- und Auslieferungsrechts. Recht in Ost und West 2 : 224-228, 15. November 1958.

CIGOJ, S. : Anerkennung und Vollstreckung ausländischer Urteile in Jugoslawien. Osteuropa-Recht 4 : 315-325, Dezember 1958.

CIGOJ, S. : Jugoslawische Gesetzgebung auf dem Gebiet des Privatrechts 1955-1958. Zeitschrift für ausländisches und internationales Privatrecht 24 : 488-502, Heft 3, 1959.

CIGOJ, S. : Die Zivilrechtsprechung der ordentlichen Gerichte Jugoslawiens, 1953-1958. Zeitschrift für ausländisches und internationales Privatrecht 24 : 728-738, Heft 4, 1959.

PESELJ, B. : International aspect of the recent Yugoslav nationalization law. American journal of international law 53 : 428-432, April 1959.

STOYANOVITCH, K. : Bulletin de jurisprudence yougoslave. Journal du droit international 86 : 512-529, avril-juin 1959.
Texte en anglais aussi.

STJEPANOVIC, N.S. : The new Yugoslav law on administrative procedure. American journal of comparative law 8 : 358-371, summer 1959.

BESAROVIC, M. : L'exécution des sentences arbitrales étrangères en République Populaire Fédérative de Yougoslavie. Revue de l'arbitrage : 78-84, juillet-septembre 1959.

JEZDIĆ, M. Medunarodno privatno pravo stare i nove Jugoslavie. Arhiv za pravne i društvene nauke 46 : 413-427, oktobar-decembar 1959.
International private law.

EUROPE
(European Communites, EFTA)

BREITNER, F. : Zwei Jahre Montangerichtsbarkeit. Eine Darstellung der Funktionen und des Wirkens des Gerichtshofes der Europäischen Gemeinschaft für Kohle und Stahl. Europa-Archiv 10 : 7243-7250, 20. Januar 1955.

ELBIR, H.K. : L'idée d'un droit civil européen. Annales de la Faculté de droit de l'Université de Bordeaux 6 : 71-86, no. 1, 1955.

Cour de justice de la Communauté européenne du charbon et de l'acier. Revue de droit public et de la science politique en France et à l'étranger 71 : 54-97, janvier-mars 1955.
Arrêts commentés par L. Kopelmanas.

MATTHIES, H. : Der Gerichtshof der Montanunion und dritte Länder. Österreichische Juristen-Zeitung 10 : 75-76, 11. Februar 1955.

MAMOPOULOS, P. : La Convention européenne d'établissement. Revue hellénique de droit international 8 : 170-185, avril-décembre 1955.

SCHÜLE, A. : Grenzen der Klagebefugnis vor dem Gerichtshof der Montanunion. Zeitschrift für ausländisches öffentliches Recht und Völkerrecht 16 : 227-255, April 1955.

DAIG, H.W. : Die vier ersten Urteile des Gerichtshofes der Europäischen Gemeinschaft für Kohle und Stahl. Juristenzeitung 10 : 361-371, 20. Juni 1955.

Cour de justice de la Communauté européenne du charbon et de l'acier. Revue du droit public et de la science politique en France et à l'étranger 71 : 570-631, juillet-septembre 1955.
Suite d'articles.

RIPHAGEN, W. : The case law of the European coal and steel community court of justice. Nederlands tijdschrift voor international recht - Netherlands international law review 2 : 384-408, October 1955.

STEIN, E. : The European coal and steel community - The beginning of its judicial process. Columbia law review 55 : 985-999, November 1955.

LUDOVICY, J. : La jurisprudence de la Cour de justice de la C.E.C.A. Revue générale de droit internationale public 60 : 111-130, janvier-mars 1956.

HOUTTE, A. van : La Cour de justice de la Communauté auropéenne du charbon et de l'acier. Annuaire européen - European yearbook 2 : 183-222, 1956.

GOES van NATERS, M. van der : Les fondements du droit parlementaire européen. Nederlands tijdschrift voor internationaal recht - Netherlans internatioinal law review 3 : 324-341, October 1956.

RIGAUD, L. : La Convention européenne d'établissement. Revue générale de droit international public 61 : 5-50, janvier-mars 1957.

VALENTINE, D.G. : The first judgments of the Court of justice of the European coal and steel community. Modern law review 20 : 596-619, November 1957.

HÖGTUN, G. : Incorporation of international treaties in a state's legal system with special reference to the Council of Europe. Nordisk tidsskrift for international ret og jus gentium 28 : 62-69, fasc. 1, 1958.

MORELLI, G. : La Corte di giustizia delle Comunità europee come giudice interno. Rivista di diritto internazionale 41 : 3-8, fasc. 1, 1958.

HÉRAUD, G. : Observations sur la nature juridique de la Communauté économique européenne. Revue générale de droit international public 62 : 26-56, janvier-mars 1958.

MÜNCH, F. : Die Abgrenzung des Rechtsbereiches der supranationalen Gemeinschaft gegenüber dem innerstaatlichen Recht. Deutsche Gesellschaft für Völkerrecht, Berichte : 73-92, Heft 2, 1958.
Discussion pp. 116-138.

The Court of the European community. Law journal 108 : 102-103, February 14, 1958.

CARRILLO SALCEDO, J.A. : Jurisprudence del Tribunal de justicia de la Comunidad europea del carbón y del acero. Revista española de derecho internacional 11 : 599-635, núm. 3, 1958.

CARTOU, L. : Le Marché commun et la technique du droit public. Revue du droit public et de la science politique en France et à l'étranger 74 : 186-219, mars-avril 1958.

GALLARDO RUEDA, A. : Integración jurídica europea. Información jurídica (Spain) : 973-977, julio-agosto 1958.

MORELLI, G. : La Cour de justice des communautés européennes en tant que juge interne. Zeitschrift für ausländisches öffentliches Recht und Völkerrecht 19 : 269-274, Nr. 1/3, August 1958.

NATIONAL LAW - COUNTRIES

LAGRANGE, M. : L'ordre juridique de la C.E.C.A. vu à travers la jurisprudence de sa Cour de justice. Revue du droit public et de la science politique en France et à l'étranger 74 : 841-865, septembre-octobre 1958.

GRASSETTI, C. : La giurisprudenza della Corte di giustizia della Comunità europea del carbone e dell' acciaio. Diritto negli scambi internazionale 1 : 147-150, ottobre 1958.

AGUILAR NAVARRO, M. : La Comunidad económica europea y el derecho internacional. Asociación Francisco de Vitoria, Anuario 12 : 149-157, 1958-1959.

MIGLIAZZA, A. : L'attività interpretativa della Corte di giustizia delle Comunità sopranazionali europee. Università di Milano, Istituto di diritto internazionale e straniero; Comunicazioni e studi 10 : 351-391, 1958-1959.

DOHRENDORF, H.: Niederlassungsrecht im Handel und Recht der Zulassung. Europäische Wirtschaftsgemeinschaft 2 : 28-31, 15. Januar 1959.

MONACO, G. : La giurisprudenzia della Corte di giustizia della Comunità europea del carbone e dell' acciaio nell'anno 1957. Diritto internazionale 13 : 77-94, no. 1, 1959.

STEINDORF, E. : Die Europäischen Gemeinschaften in der Rechtsprechung. Archiv der Völkerrechts 8 : 50-70, Heft 1, 1959.

CARRILLO SALCEDO, J.A. : La figura del abogado general en las comunidades supranacionales europeas - Naturaleza jurídica y función. Revista española de derecho internacional 12 : 119-129, núm. 1-2, 1959.

SALMON, J. : La convention européenne pour le règlement pacifique des différends. Revue générale de droit international public 63 : 21-54, janvier-mars 1959.
Texte pp. 55-64.

LAUN, R. : Bemerkungen zur ausschliesslichen Zuständigkeit der Staaten im Falle einer Integration Europas. Internationales Recht und Diplomatie : 276-287, Heft 2, 1959.

KUNZMANN, K.H. : Die Europäische Konvention über die friedliche Beilegung von Streitigkeiten. Europa-Archiv 14 : 125-148, 5. Marz 1959.

Cour de justice des communautés européennes - Règlement de procédure. Journal officiel des communautés européennes 2 : 349-378, 21 mars 1959.

UDINA, M. : L'armonizzazione delle legislazioni nazionali dei paesi membri delle comunità europee. Annuario di diritto comparato e di studi legislativi 33 : 192-197, fasc. 3, 1959.

PERCIN, de : Le droit d'établissement dans la Communauté économique européenne. Bulletin de la Chambre de commerce de Paris : 115-127, mars 1959.
Texte du traité pp. 128-130.

SEIDL-HOHENVELDERN, I. : European companies. Journal of business law : 120-131, April 1959.

LUSSAN, C. : Les sociétés dans le Marché commun. Echanges internationaux et Marché commun 7 : 41-6, mai 1959.

LOUSSOUARN : Droit d'établissement des personnes physiques. Echanges internationaux et Marché commun 7 : 51-54, mai 1959.

La situation juridique des représentants de commerce dans les pays du Marché commun. Revue franco-Belge 69 : 136-140, mai 1959.

DAUSSIN, A. : Vers une fonction publique européenne. Annuaire européen - European yearbook 6 : 112-142, 1959.

FRANÇOIS, J.P.A. : La convention européenne pour le règlement pacifique des différends, 29 avril 1957. Annuaire européen - European yearbook 6 : 54-64, 1959.

LUSSAN, C. : Le droit d'établissement outre-mer des ressortissants des Six. Revue du Marché commun : 291-296, juillet-août 1959.

BÄRMANN, J. : Die Europäischen Gemeinschaften und die Rechtsangleichung. Juristenzeitung 14 : 553-560, 18. September 1959.

MEYER-MARSILIUS : Angleichung des Niederlassungsrechts im EWG-Raum. Berichte und Informationen des Österreichischen Forschungsinstituts für Wirtschaft und Politik 14 : 11-12, 30. Oktober 1959.

Statut du Personnel de la Communauté européenne du charbon et de l'acier. Annales de la Faculté de droit d'Istanbul 8 : 429-520, nos. 9-11, 1959.

WESER, M. : Les conflits de juridictions dans le cadre du Marché commun - Difficultés et remèdes. Revue critique de droit international privé 48 : 613-649, octobre-décembre 1959.
Premier article d'une série.

AUDINET, J. : Le droit d'établissement dans la Communauté économique européenne. Journal du droit international 86 : 982-1049, octobre-décembre 1959.
Texte en anglais aussi.

DIETRICH, P. de : Le recours en annulation devant la Cour de justice de la Communauté européenne du charbon et de l'acier. Annales de la Faculté de droit et des sciences économiques d'Aix-en-Provence : 7-19, no. 51, 1959.

EUROPE
(European Convention of Human rights)

BRÜGEL, J.W. : Der Konflikt zwischen Menschenrecht und Souveränität - Tragweite der Europäischen Konvention. Aussenpolitik 6 : 650-659, Oktober 1955.

GOLSONG, H. : Die Verfahrensordnung der Europäischen Kommission für Menschenrechte. Europa-Archiv 10 : 8349-8355, 6. November 1955.
Text pp. 9355-8360.

MODINOS, P. : La convention européenne des droits de l'homme. Revue générale de droit international public 60 : 87-92, janvier-mars 1956.
Avec table des ratifications.

COBLENTZ, W.K., and WARSHAW, R.S. : European convention for the protection of human rights and fundamental freedoms. California law review 44 : 94-104, March 1956.

ECHTERHÖLTER, R. : Die Europäische Menschenrechtskonvention in der juristischen Praxis. Juristenzeitung 11 : 142-146, 15. März 1956.

PARTSCH, K.J. : Die europäische Menschenrechtskonvention vor den nationalen Parlamenten. Zeitschrift für azsländisches öffentliches Recht und Völkerrecht 17 : 93-132, Nr. 1, 1956.

ROLIN, H. : Le rôle du requérant dans la procédure prévue par la Commission européenne des droits de l'homme. Revue hellénique de droit international 9 : 3-14, janvier-décembre 1956.

PADIRAC, R.: La convention européenne des droits de l'homme et les réticences de la France. Chronique sociale de France 65 : 231-233, 30 mai 1957.

TRISKA, J.F. : The individual and his rights in the European community - An experiment in international law. Tulane law review 31 : 283-302, February 1957.

PAPCOSTAS, A.N. : Le problème de l'établissement d'une Cour internationale des droits de l'homme. Association des auditeurs et anciens auditeurs de l'Académie de droit international de La Haye, Annuaire 28 : 11-18, 1958.

WALDOCK, C.H.M. : The European convention for the protection of human rights and fundamental freedoms. British year book of international law 34 : 356-363, 1958.

MOSER, B. : Die Europäische Menschenrechtskonvention und die Bestimmungen der St PO. über die Verwahrungs- und Untersuchungshaft. Österreichische Juristen-Zeitung 14 : 11-15, 9. Jänner 1959.

MÖBIUS, T. : Die Europäische Menschenrechtskonvention und Österreich. Zukunft : 82-84, März 1959.

CASSIN, R. : La cour européenne des droits de l'homme. Annuaire européen - European yearbook 7 : 75-92, 1959.

ROBERTSON, A.H. : The European court of human rights. International and comparative law quarterly 8 : 396-403, April 1959.

WIEBRINGHAUS, H. : Ein internationaler Gerichtshof zum Schutz der Menschenrechte. Friedens-Warte 55 : 1-25, Nr. 1, 1959.

NATIONAL LAW - COUNTRIES

ADEN

Constitution de l'Etat d'Aden, 9 octobre 1962. Documentation fran;aise, Notes et études documentaires : 1-20, no. 3125, 6 octobre 1964.
Texte.

ALBANIA

SCHWANKE, R. : Das geltende Recht in Albanien. Österreichische Ost-Hefte 2 : 126-133, 2. Heft 1960.

ALY VOKOPOLA, K. : Le gouvernement, les lois et les tribunaux de la République Populaire d'Albanie. Documentation française, Notes et études documentaires : 1-18, no. 2820, 2 octobre 1961.

LAMANI, A. : Ekzekutimi i vendimeve të gjykatave të huaja në R.P.S.H. sipas konventava me B.R.S.S. dhe demokracitë popullore. Drejtësia popullore (Albania) 14 : 45-57, nr 4, 1961.
Execution of judgments.

SCHWANKE, R. : Die Gerichtsorganisation Albaniens. Osteuropa-Recht 8 : 60-68, März 1962.

PAPULI, N. : Organizimi i shtetit të parë shqiptar dhe aktet e tij të para legjislative. Drejtësia popullore (Albania) 15 : 23-34, nr. 5, shtator-tetor 1962.

MEKSI, V. : Shtetësia shqiptare sipas dispozitave në fuqi - Shtetësia në të drejtën ndërkombëtare. Drejtësia popullore (Albania) 16 : 4-19, nr. 2, 1963.
Nationality law.

SCHWANKE, R. : Das Erbrecht in der Volksrepublik Albanien. Osteuropa-Recht 10 : 106-114, Juni 1964.

QIRJAQI, S. : 20 vjet ligjëshmëri socialiste. Drejtësia popullore (Albanie) 17 : 10-20, nr. 5, shtatortetor 1964.

ALGERIA

TOUSCOZ, J. : La réforme communale en Algérie. Revue juridique et politique d'outre-mer 15 : 111-141, janvier-mars 1961.
Bibliographie pp. 142-144.

La première constitution algérienne. Europe France outre-mer 40 : 57-59, no. 403-404, août-septembre 1963.
Septembre 1963; Text.

CHARNAY, J.P. : Le rôle du juge français dans l'élaboration du droit musulman algérien. Revue internationale de droit comparé 15 : 705-721, octobre-décembre 1963.

Algeria's new constitution. Middle East fprum 39 : 10-12, December 1963,
Text.

LECA, J. : L'organisation provisoire des pouvoirs publics de la République Algérienne, septembre 1962-septembre 1963. Revue algérienne des sciences juridiques, politiques et économiques : 7-45, janvier 1964.
Textes pp. 47-49.

Constitution de la République Algérienne Démocratique et Populaire, 8 septembre 1963. Documentation française, Notes et études documentaires : 1-9, no. 3063, 13 février 1964.

ROBERT, J. : La République algérienne, démocratique et populaire. Revue du droit public et de la science politique en France et à l'étranger 80 : 293-379, mars-avril 1964.
Texte de la constitution pp. 380-388.

ALTUG, Y. : Le nouveau code de la nationalité algérienne. Annales de la Faculté de droit d'Istanbul 14 : 123-138, no. 20, 1964.

ANDORRA

ANGLADA VILARDEBÓ, J. : La cláusula hereditaria de confianza en la jurisprudencia del Principado de Andorra. Revista jurídica de Cataluña 62 : enero-marzo 1963.

Jurisprudencia de los tribunales del principado de Andorra - Une sentencia sobre derecho de servidumbre. Revista jurídica de Cataluña 62 : 420-425, abril-junio 1963.
Commentary by F. Soto Nieto pp. 425-428.

ARABIAN STATES

Constitution de la Fédération des Emirats arabes du Sud, 11 février 1959. Informations constitutionnelles et parlementaires : 59-73, avril 1960.

Constitución de la Federation de los Emiratos Arabes del Sur, 11 febrero 1959. Información jurídica (Spain) : 47-57, mayo-junio 1960.

ARGENTINA

MELO, A.L. : El caso Eichmann y la soberanía argentina. Revista de derecho internacional y ciencias diplomaticas 8 : 99-119, enero-diciembre 1960.

CONTI, G.T., and SUGASTI, T.O. : Análisis y alcance de las reformas proyectdas en materia de legislación consular. Revista de derecho internacional y ciencias diplomáticas 8 : 41-54, enero-diciembre 1960.

MALAGARRIGA, C.C. : El derecho argentino en 1961. Boletín del Instituto de derecho comparado de México 14 : 363-374, mayo-agosto 1961.

WIESNER, D.A. : Enactment and suspension of absolute divorce in Argentina. American journal of comparative law 9 : 94-104, winter 1960.

WINIZKY, I. : Le plan des réformes législatives en Argentine - Exposé et commentaire. Revue internationale de droit comparé 12 : 719-731, octobre-décembre 1960.

MARQUARDT, E.H., et SOLER, S.: La privation de la liberté individuelle en droit argentin. Commission internationale de juristes, Revue 3 : 20-42, 2e semestre 1961.

SANTA-PINTER, J.J. : El estado de derecho en la Argentina. Revista jurídica de la Universidad de Puerto Rico 30 : 223-248, núms. 3-4, 1961.

MacLEAN, R. : La personas jurídicas en el derecho internacional privado argentino y peruano. Boletín del Instituto de derecho comparado de México 15 : 299-343, mayo-agosto 1962.

ANGULO, M.R. : Comments on the status of foreign business corporations under the commercial codes of Argentina and Venezuela. Inter-American law review - Revista juridica interamericana 4 : 159-185, July-December 1962.

Derecho constitucional y parlamentario - Provincia del Neuquén, Provincia de Corrientes, Provincia de Santiago del Estero, Provincia de La Pampa. Boletín de la Biblioteca del Congreso de la nación : 151-383, mayo-agosto 1962.

FARINA, J.M. : Unificación del derecho comercial entre Argentina y Uruguay. Revista de la Facultad de ciencias, comerciales y políticas (Rosario) 5 : 13-17, nos. 9-12, 1962-1963.

MATTES, H. : Der argentinische Entwurf zu einem St Strafgesetzbuch von 1960. Zeitschrift für die gesamte Strafrechtswissenschaft, Mitteilungsblatt der Fachgruppe Strafrecht 13 : 57-104, Heft 2, 1963.

GOLDSCHMIDT, W. : Problemas de derecho internacional privado sucesorio argentino. Revista de derecho internacional y ciencias diplomáticas (Rosaria) 13 : 77-81, enero-diciembre 1964.

RAMELLA, P.A. : Los derechos sociales en la constitución argentina- Bolétin del Instituto de derecho comparado de México 17 : 321-340, mayo-agosto 1964.

CAMARÁ, H. : Las reformas del año 1963 al código de comercio de la República Argentina. Boletín del Instituto de derecho comparado de México 17 : 629-646, septiembre-diciembre 1964.

AUSTRALIA

DONOVAN, F.P. : Law reform in Victoria. Journal of business law : 62-69, January 1960.

KAVASS, I.I. : Proof of foreign marriages in Australian divorce proceedings. Australian law journal 33 : 425-438, 21 April 1960.

BARWICK, G. : Some aspects of the new Matrimonial causes act. Sydney law review 3 : 410-438, March 1961.

LEYSER, J. : Das neue australische Gesetz in Ehe-Sachen. Rabels Zeitschrift für ausländisches und internationales Privatrecht 26 : 481-501, Heft 3, 1961.

The twelfth legal convention of the Law council of Australia. Australian law journal 35 : 93-204, 31 August 1961.
Special issue.

McCLEMENS : The legal position and procedure before a Royal commissioner. Australian law journal 35 : 271-278, 30 November 1961.

CASTLES, A.C. : The paramount force of Commonwealth legislation since the Statute of Westminster. Australian law journal 35 : 402-407, 29 March 1962.

CASTLES, A.C. : Limitations on the autonomy of the Australian states. Public law : 175-201, summer 1962.

PARSONS, R.W. : Uniform company law in Australia. Journal of business law : 235-246, July 1962.

NYGH, P.E. : Problems of Federal legislative power over the Australian dependent territories. American journal of comparative law 11 : 601-611, autumn 1962.

NYGH, P.E. : Problems of nationality and expatriation before English and Australian courts. International and comparative law quarterly 12 : 175-188, January 1963.

The thirteenth legal convention of the Law council of Australia. Australian law journal 38 : 273-388, 28 February 1963.
Hobart, January 1963; Special issue.

LEACH, R.H. : The uniform law movement in Australia. American journal of comparative law 12 : 206-223, spring 1963.

AUSTRIA

TSCHADEK, O. : Probleme des österreichischen Ehe- und Familienrechts. Ehe und Familie im privaten und öffentlichen Recht 7 : 41-42, Februar 1960.

WINKLER, G. : Der Verfassungsrang von Staatsverträgen. Österreichische Zeitschrift für öffentliches Recht 10 : 514-539, Heft 3/4, 1960.

RILL, H.P. : Der Rang der allgemeinen anerkennten Regeln des Völkerrechtes in der österreichischen Rechtsordnung. Österreichische Zeitschrift für öffentliches Recht 10 : 439-451, Heft 3/4, 1960.

MATSCHER, F. : Der neue östereichisch-deutsche Vertrag über die Anerkennung und Vollstreckung von gerichtlichen Entscheidungen im Lichte der allgemeinen Lehren des Internationalen Zivilprozessrechts. Juristische Blätter 82 : 265-279, 28. Mai 1960.

VERDROSS, A. : Österreich, die europäische Wirtschaftsintegration und das Völkerrecht. Europa-Archiv 15 : 442-448, 5./20. Juli 1960.

WINKLER, G. : Zur Frage der unmittelbaren Anwendbarkeit von Staatsverträgen. Juristische Blätter 83 : 8-15, 14. Januar 1961.

Message du Conseil fédéral à l'Assemblée fédérale concernant l'approbation de la nouvelle convention entre la Confédération suisse et la République d'Autriche relative à la reconnaissance et à l'exécution de décisions judiciaires (du 19 juin 1961). Feuille fédérale (Switzerland) 113 : 1585-1600, 29 juin 1961.

LOZICZKY, K. : L'assistance aux victimes de la lutte pour une Autriche libre et décmocratique, et aux victimes de persécutions politiques. Cahiers de législation comparée des anciens combattants et victimes de guerre : 91-93, août 1961.

VEITER, T. : Bemühungen des Habsburger-Chefs und die Rechtslage. Berichte und Informationen des Österreichischen Forschungsinstituts für Wirtschaft und Politik 17 : 4-5, 19. Jänner 1962.

PFEIFFER, H. : Der Verfassungsrang von Staatsverträgen. Österreichische Juristen-Zeitung 17 : 29-34, 30. Jänner 1962.

NATIONAL LAW - COUNTRIES

PFEIFER, H. : Die paralmentarische Genehmigung von Staatsverträgen in Österreich - Ihre innerstaatliche Wirksamkeit. Österreichische Zeitschrift für öffentliches Recht 12 : 1-70, Heft 1/2, 1962.

KUNST, G. : Zur Frage einer Wiederverlautbarung der Bundesverfassung- Österreichische Juristen-Zeitung 17 : 169-172, 10. April 1962.

MATSCHER, F. : Zur Entwicklung der Rechtsbeziehungen mit der Schweiz auf dem Gebiet des Privat- und Prozessrechts - Der neue österreichisch-Schweizerische Vollstreckungsvertrag vom 16. Dezember 1960. Juristische Blätter 84 : 356-366, 30. Juni 1962.

GSCHNITZER, F. : Hundertfünfzig Jahre allgemeines bürgerliches Gesetzbuch. Juristische Blätter 84 : 405-407, 1. September 1962.

VEITER, T. : Der Bodensee und die Vorarlberger Rechtsordnung. Berichte und Informationen des Österreichischen Forschungsinstituts für Wirtschaft und Politik 17 : 11-12, 28. September 1962.

ERMACORA, F. : Die Bedeutung von Entscheidungen der Menschenrechtskommission für die österreichische Rechtsordnung. Juristische Blätter 84 : 621-623, 15. Dezember 1962.

MATSCHER, F. : Die Anerkennung und Vollstreckung gerichtlicher Entscheidungen im Verhältnis zwischen Österreich und Grossbritannien. Juristische Blätter 85 : 229-236, 11. Mai 1963.

LIEBSCHER, V. : L'Autriche et la convention européenne de sauvegarde des droits de l'homme et des libertés fondamentales. Commission internationale de juristes, Revue 4 : 292-304, 2e semestre 1963.

LINKE, R. : Der neue Auslieferungsvertrag mit Grossbritannien v. 9. Jänner 1963. Österreichische Juristen-Zeitung 18 : 565-572, 5. November 1963.

ERMACORA, F. : Der Föderalismus in Österreich. Jahrbuch des öffentlichen Rechts der Gegenwart 12 : 221-248, 1963.

SMOLE, A. : Unterschiede zwischen dem österreichischen und dem jugoslawischen Erbrecht. Österreichische Juristen-Zeitung 19 : 4-11, 14 Jänner 1964.

KASTNER, W. : Gesellschafterwechsel und ähnliche Änderungen bei der stillen Gesellschaft. Juristische Blätter 86 : 113-118, 14. März 1964.

KUNST, G. : Die Menschenrechtskonvention als Bestandteil der Bundesverfassung. Österreichische Juristen-Zeitung 19 : 197-199, 21. April 1964.

BRODA, C. : Einige Probleme der österreichischen Strafrechtsreform. Österreichische Juristen-Zeitung 19 : 281-286, 2. Juni 1964.

WAHLE, K. : Ist die vorgeschlagene Reform des ehelichen Güterrechtes für dir Wirtschaft tragbar? Juristische Blätter 86 : 341-349, 4. Juli 1964.

BELGIUM

Chronique de droit belge. Revue trimestrielle de droit civile 59 : 199-216, janvier-mars 1960.

RENAULD, J.G. : Les fusions de sociétés en droit belge. Revue de droit international et de droit comparé 38 : 69-97, no. 2, 1961.

HARRIES, H. : Das deutsch-belgische Anerkennungs- und Vollstreckungsabkommen. Rabels Zeitschrift für ausländisches und internationales Privatrecht 26 : 629-667, Heft 4, 1961.

SERICK, L., and HARRIES, H. : Belgisches internationales Privatrecht nach der neueren Rechtsprechung. Zeitschrift für ausländisches und internationales Privatrecht 25 : 544-567, Heft 3/4, Mai 1961.

VIe congrès international de droit comparé de l'Académie internationale de droit comparé, Hambourg, 30 juillet- 4 août 1962. Rapports des juristes belges. Revue de droit international et de droit comparé 39 : v-vii, 1-471, no. 2, 1962.
Numéro spécial.

FRANCESCAKIS, P., et GOTHOT, P. : Une réglementation inachevée du divorce international - La loi belge du 27 juin 1960. Revue critique de droit international privé 51 : 247-282, avril-juin 1962.

BECK, W. : Le refus de service militaire par objection de conscience en Belgique. Revue de droit pénal et de criminologie 43 : 296-328, janvier 1963.

HORION, P. : L'évolution des sanctions pénales en droit social belge. Revue du travail (Belgium) 64 : 1133-1159, décembre 1963.

RIGAUX, F. : La reconnaissance et l'exécution des décisions judiciaires étrangères d'après le droit conventionnel en vigueur en Belgique. Nederlands tijdschrift voor internationaal recht 11 : 244-270, juli 1964.

JESCHEK, H.H. : Les principes de politique criminelle du projet d'un code pénal allemand en comparaison avec l'évolution du droit pénal en Belgique. Revue de droit pénal et de criminologie 45 : 205-233, décembre 1964.

BORNEO, BRITISH

Constitution de l'Etat de Brunéi, 1959. Documentation française, Notes et études documentaires : 1-23, no. 2867, 9 mars 1962.
Texte.

BRAZIL

CASTRO REBELLO, E. de : Il diritto cambiario brasiliano e la tradizione della dottrina italiana. Rivista del diritto commerciale e del diritto generale delle obbligazioni 58 : 1-12, gennaio-febbraio 1960.

FERREIRA, W. : O estatuto das sociedades anônimas brasileiras. Revista da Faculdade de direito (São Paulo) 55 : 41-58, 1960.

MAROTTA RANGEL, V. : La procédure de conclusion des accords internationaux au Brésil. Revista da Faculdade de direito (São Paulo) 55 : 253-271, 1960.

BUZAID, A. : A crise do Supremo tribunal federal. Revista da Faculdade de direito (São Paulo) 55 : 327-372, 1960.

PENNA MARINHO, I. : Adoção de nacionalidade no direito brasileiro. Sociedade brasileira de direito internacional, Boletim 17 : 59-71, janeiro-dezembro 1961.

CAVALCANTI, T. : A ratificação parcial dos tratados. Revista de direito público e ciência política 4 : 5-16, jan.-abr. 1961.

GARCIA, B. : La détention provisoire et préventive au Brésil. Commission internationale de juristes, Revue 3 : 43-53, 2e semestre 1961.

PENNA MARINHO, I. : Adoção de nacionalidade no direito brasileiro. Revista brasileira de política internacional 4 : 36-50, dezembro 1961.

SCHEMAN, L.R. : The social and economic origin of the Brazilian judges. Inter-American law review - Revista jurídica interamericana 4 : 45-72, January-June 1962.

WALD, A. : La réforme du droit brésilien. Revue internationale de droit comparé 14 : 713-723, octobre-décembre 1962.

RÍOS ESPINOZA, A. : Presupuestos constitucionales del mandato de seguridad. Boletín del Instituto de derecho comparado de México 16 : 71-96, enero-abril 1963.

GOMES CARNEIRO, M.T. : La organización de la justicia militar en el Brasil. Revista española de derecho militar : 93-120, enero-junio 1963.

FERREIRA, W. : O estatuto da mulher casada brasileira. Boletim da Faculdade de direito (Coimbra) 39 : 13-30, 1963.

Código de processo penal brasileira - Anteprojecto ... Ministério da justiça, Boletim (Portugal) : 5-251, junho 1964.

MONIZ de ARAGÃO, E.D. : The Brazilian judicial organization. Inter-American law review - Revista jurídica interamericana 6 : 239-264, July-December 1964.

BULGARIA

RADOILSKI, L. : Pravnoto polozhenie na osŭdenii͡a na propravitelen trud bez lishavane ot svobodo. Pravna misŭl 4 : 41-62, kn. 6, 1960.
Legal statute of correctional labour.

KUTIKOV, V. : Nasledstvenopravni problemi v dogovorite za sŭdebna (pravna) pomosht mezhdu NR Bŭlgarii͡a i drugite sot͡sialisticheski strani. Pravna misŭl 5 : 34-50, kn. 2, 1961.
Succession law.

SPASOV, B. : Izmenenieto na konstitutsii͡ata, Pravna misŭl 6 : 16-28, kn. 2, 1962.

STALEV, J. : L'arbitrage d'Etat en République Populaire de Bulgarie. Revue de droit contemporain 9 : 117-131, décembre 1962 - mars 1963.

SPASSOV, B. : Les organes représentatifs en République Populaire de Bulgarie. Revue de droit contemporain 11 : 130-140, no. 1, 1964.

I͡ANKOV, A. : Po vŭprosa za pravnii͡a rezhim na chuzhdentsite, vremenno prebivavashti v NR Bŭlgarii͡a, i iziskvanii͡ata na mezhdunarodnoto pravo. Pravna misŭl 8 : 14-32, kn. 4, 1964.

LILLICH, R.B. : The United States-Bulgarian claims agreement of 1963. American journal of international law 58 : 686-706, July 1964.

STALEV, Zh. : Kŭm nov grazhdanski protsesualen kodeks na Narodna Republika Bŭlgarii͡a. Pravna misŭl 8 : 77-98, kn. 5, 1964.

SPASOV, B., and DIMITROV, D. : Razvitie na dŭrzhavnite organi i na sotsialisticheskata demokratsii͡a v NRB. Pravna misŭl 8 : 3-33, kn. 5, 1964.

BURMA

MYINT SOE, U. : The constitutional development in Burma. Jahrbuch des öffentlichen Rechts der Gegenwart 11 : 365-415, 1962.

CAMBODIA

MORICE, J.C. : L'organisation judiciaire du Cambodge. Penant, Revue de droit des pays d'Afrique 72 : 7-35, janvier-mars 1962.

CAMEROUN

Constitution du Cameroun, 21 février 1960. Documentation française, Notes et études documentaires : 1-8, no. 2682, 9 juillet 1960.

Constitution de la République du Cameroun, 21 février 1960. Informations constitutionnelles et parlementaires 11 : 93-109, juillet 1960.
Texte.

MANGIN, G. : Cameroun. Annuaire de législation française et étrangère 9 : 91-96, 1960.

BIÉVILLE, M. de : La naissance d'une nouvelle nationalité en Afrique, la nationalité camerounaise. Revue juridique et politique d'outre-mer 15 : 600-609, octobre-décembre 1961.

Relations de la France et des Etats accédant à l'indépendance - Traités et accords conclus entre la France et le Cameroun, signés à Yaoundé le 13 novembre 1961. Journal du droit international 88 : 1202-1235, octobre-décembre 1961.
Texte en anglais aussi.

Constitution de la République Fédérale du Cameroun, 1 octobre 1961. Informations constitutionnelles et parlementaires 13 : 1-16, janvier 1962.

Constitución de la République Federal de Camerún, 1 de septiembre de 1961. Información jurídica (Spain) : 41-71, enero-febrero 1964.

Organigrammes des institutions judiciaires - République fédérale du Cameroun. Penant, Revue de droit des pays d'Afrique 72 : 153-156, janvier-mars 1962.

CAGAN, G. : La Cour criminelle au Cameroun oriental. Penant, Revue de droit des pays d'Afrique 74 : 309-320, juillet-septembre 1964.

NATIONAL LAW - COUNTRIES

CANADA

NADELMANN, K.H. : Enforcement of foreign judgments in Canada. Canadian bar review 38 : 68-88, March 1960.

RAND, I.C. : Some aspects of Canadian constitutionalism. Canadian bar review 38 : 135-162, May 1960.

BAUDOUIN, L. : Chronique de droit civil canadien, province de Québec. Revue trimestrielle de droit civil 59 : 559-568, juillet-september 1960.

LA FOREST, G.V. : May the provinces legislate in violation of international law? Canadian bar review 39 : 78-91, March 1961.

HENDRY, J.M. : Canada and modern international law. Canadian bar review 39 : 59-77, March 1961.

BEAULIEU, M.I. : Québec et la formation d'un droit canadien. Revue internationale de droit comparé 13 : 300-306, avril-juin 1961.

WILLIS, J. : Administrative law in Canada. Canadian bar review 39 : 251-265, May 1961.

ZIEGEL, J.S. : Uniformity of legislation in Canada - The conditional sales experience. Canadian bar review 39 : 165-231, May 1961.

PAYNE, J.D. : Recognition of foreign divorce decrees in the Canadian courts. International and comèarative law quarterly 10 : 846-850, October 1961.

BRUTON, P.W. : The Canadian bill of rights - Some American observations. McGill law journal 8 : 106-120, no. 2, 1962.

LASKIN, B. : Canada's bill of rights - A dilemma for the courts? International and comparative law quarterly 11 : 519-536, April 1962.

GRENON, J.Y. : De la conclusion des traités et de leur mise en oeuvre au Canada. Canadian bar review - La revue du Barreau canadien 40 : 151-164, May 1962.

MORIN, J.Y. : Les eaux territoriales du Canada au regard du droit international. Canadian yearbook of international law - Annuaire canadien de droit international 1 : 82-148, 1963.
Avec cartes.

GELINAS, A. : Judicial control of administrative action - Great Britain and Canada. Public law : 140-171, summer 1963.

MEYER, P. : The new Quebec code of civil procedure - Some comments and suggestions. McGill law journal 10 : 361-368, no. 4, 1964.

CASTEL, J.G. : Jurisdicción en materia de divorcio y reconocimiento de sentencias extranjeras en el Canadá. Boletín del Instituto de derecho comparado de México 17 : 341-365, mayo-agosto 1964.

CENTRAL AFRICAN REPUBLIC

Constituciones de los Estados miembros de la Comunidad francesa - República Centro-Africana, constitución del 16 de febrero de 1959. Información jurídica (Spain) : 3-12, marzo-abril 1960.
Spanish text.

Constitution de la République centrafricaine. Documentation française, Notes et études documentaires : 39-43, no. 2733, 19 décembre 1960.

MANGIN, G. : République Centraficaine. Annuaire de législation française et étrangère 9 : 97-101, 1960.

Código penal de la República Centroafricana. Información jurídica (Spain) : 1-76, noviembre-diciembre 1963.

CEYLON

THAMBIAH, H.W. : The draft civil procedure code. Ceylon law society journal 6 : ixxii-ixxx, March-June 1960.

RADHAKRISHNAN, N. : The stateless in Ceylon. Indian year book of international affairs 12 : 487-563, 1963.

BASNAYAKE, H.H. : Some legal aspects of marriage. Ceylon law society journal 8 : ixxviii-lxxxi, June-December 1964.

CHAD

Constitution de la République du Tchad, 31 mars 1959. Documentation française, Notes et études documentaires : 58-63, no. 2696, 31 août 1960.
Texte.

MANGIN, G. : Tchad. Annuaire de législation française et étrangère 9 : 352-356, 1960.

Les constitutions des Etats africains d'expression française (Suite) - République du Tchad. Revue juridique et politique d'outre-mer 15 : 471-481, juillet-septembre 1961.
Novembre 1960.

CHILE

MIAJA de la MUELA, A. : El convenio hispano-chileno de doble nacionalidad de 24 de mayo de 1958. Política internacional : 85-108, núm. 47, enero-febrero 1960.

ROMÁN VIDAL, S.M. : El delito militar en el código de justicia militar chileno. Revista española de derecho militar : 177-210, enero-junio 1960.

SILVA CIMMA, E. : La "Controleria general" de la République chilienne. Revue du droit public et de la science politique en France et à l'étranger 77 : 286-291, mars-avril 1961.

PESCIO, V. : Les règles de droit international privé dans le code chilien. Revue de droit international et de droit comparé 40 : 181-191, nos. 3-4, 1963.

CHINA

Código de procedimiento penal, 1938. Información juridica (Spain) : 3-176, julio-agosto 1963.

DAI, S.-y. : Government and law in Communist China. Current history 41 : 164-170, 177; September 1961.

NATIONAL LAW - COUNTRIES

BUXBAUM, D.C. : Preliminary trends in the development of the legal institutions of Communist China and the nature of the criminal law. International and comparative law quarterly 11 : 1-30, January 1962.

MICHAEL, F. : The role of law in traditional, nationalist and communist China. China quarterly : 124-148, January-March 1962.

LEE, L.T. : Chinese communist law, its background and development. Michigan law review 60 : 439-472, February 1962.

LENG, S.-t. : Le barreau dans la République Populaire de Chine. Commission internationale de juristes, Revue 4 : 36-54, 1er semestre 1962.

VALK, M.H. van der : Movables and immovables and connected subjects in Chinese law. Law in Eastern Europe : 167-206, no. 7, 1962.

FOCSANEANU, L. : Les grands traités de la République Populaire de Chine. Annuaire français de droit international 8 : 139-177, 1962.

McALEAVY, H. : The People's courts in Communist China. American journal of comparative law 11 : 52-65, winter 1962.

PFEFER, R.M. : The institution of contracts in the Chinese People's Republic. Harvard international law club journal 4 : 1-47, 1-47, December 1962.

Chinesisches Recht. Osteuropa-Recht 9 : 169-236, September 1963.
Series of articles.

BUXBAUM, D.C. : Horizontal and vertical influences upon the substantive criminal law in China - Some preliminary observations. Osteuropa-Recht 10 : 31-51, März 1964.

BEAUTÉ, J. : La République Populaire de Chine et le droit international. Revue générale de droit international public 35 : 350-412, avril-juin 1964.

LIN, F.-s. : Communist China's emerging fundamentals of criminal law. American journal of comparative law 13 : 80-93, winter 1964.

COMMONWEALTH

MITCHELL, J.D.B. : The flexible constitution. Public law : 332-350, winter 1960.

SMITH, S.A. de : Fundamental rights in the new Commonwealth. International and comparative law quarterly 10 : 83-102, January 1961.

Termination of membership of the Commonwealth and British nationality. Law journal 111 : 269-270, 28 April 1961.

Nationality and citizenship laws of countries of the Commonwealth. Central office of information, Reference division, Bulletin (London) : 1-25, No. 5024, December 1961.

COORAY, E.J. : A Commonwealth court. Journal of the parliaments of the Commonwealth 43 : 347-353, October 1962.

WILSON, R.R. : Commonwealth citizenship and common status. American journal of international law 57 : 566-587, July 1963.

SMITH, S.A. de : Political asylum and the Commonwealth. Parliamentary affairs 16 : 396-403, autumn 1963.

MARSHALL, H.H. : Statute law revision in the Commonwealth. International and comparative law quarterly 13 : 1407-1432, October 1964.

CONGO (BRAZZAVILLE) :

República del Congo - Ley constitucional de 28 de noviembre de 1958. Información jurídica (Spain) : 13-18, marzo-abril 1960.
Spanish text.

République du Congo - Constitution de 2 mars 1961. Revue juridique et politique d'outre-mer 15 : 245-254, avril-juin 1961.

La constitution de la République du Congo (Brazzaville). Semaine africaine et malgache : 5-19, 2 décembre 1963.

JOUHAUD, Y. : La nouvelle constitution de la République du Congo. Revue juridique et politique - Indépendance et coopération 18 : 143-146, janvier-mars 1964.
1963; Texte pp. 147-156.

CONGO (KINSHASA)

RUBBENS, A. : La décolonisation du droit et de l'organisation judiciaire dans la République du Congo. Académie royale des sciences d'outre-mer, Bulletin des séances (Bruxelles) 7 : 798-808, no. 6, 1961.

DEBBASCH, C. : Le problème constitutionnel congolais. Revue de droit public et de la science politique en France et à l'étranger 78 : 25-45, janvier-février 1962.

RAË : Le ministère public en République du Congo. Académie royale des sciences d'outre-mer, Bulletin des séances - Koninklijke academie voor overzeese wetenschappen, Mededelingen der zittingen (Bruxelles) 8 : 396-403, no. 3, 1962.

RYCKBOST, J. : Le régime des libertés publiques en droit congolais. Etudes congolaises 2 : 1-22, no. 4, 1962.

MURACCIOLE, L. : Loi fundamentale du 19 mai 1960 relative aux structures du Congo. Revue juridique et politique d'outre-mer 16 : 279-285, avril-juin 1962.
Texte pp. 285-311.

ROUGEVIN-BAVILLE, M. : Le sort des droits et obligations de l'ancienne colonie du Congo Belge d'après la jurisprudence des juridictions de Belgique. Revue judiciaire congolaise 2 : 1-3, 1er trimestre 1963.

RIVES, G. : Quelques aspects du droit pénal congolais. Annales de la Faculté de droit de Toulouse 11 : 169-192, fasc. 2, 1963.

NATIONAL LAW - COUNTRIES

COPPENS, P. : Le droit privé congolais de demain. Académie royale des sciences d'outre-mer. Bulletin des séances - Koninklijke academie voor overzeese wetenschappen, Mededelingen der zittingen (Bruxelles) : 630-647, no. 4, 1963.

RAE, M. : La constitution de la République démocratique du Congo et la lexloci delicti commissi. Académie royale des sciences d'outre-mer, Bulletin des séances - Koninklijke academie voor overzeese weteschappen, Mededelingen der zittingen (Bruxelles) : 1476-1484, no. 6, 1964.

DECHEIX, P. : La nouvelle constitution du Congo-Léopoldville (avec texte). Revue juridique et politique - Indépendance et coopération 18 : 605-645, octobre-décembre 1964.

PAUWELS, J.M. : La constitution du Congo et le droit coutumier. Etudes congolaise 7 : 1-26, novembre 1964.

Constitution de la République du Congo du ler août 1964. Etudes congolaises 7 : 1-55, décembre 1964.

CUBA

ALCALÁ ZAMORA y CASTILLO, N. : Ley cubana de procedimiento laboral. Boletín del Instituto de derecho comparado de México 13 : 95-99, septiembre-diciembre 1960.

GARREAU de LOUBRESSE, C. : Les nationalisations cubaines. Annuaire français de droit international 7 : 215-226, 1961.

LÁZARO, A. : Cuba - Las leyes constitucionales de la revolución. Revista de estudios políticos : 199-215, septiembre-octubre 1961.

Loi fondamentale de la République Socialiste de Cuba, promulguée le 7 février 1959. Documentation française, Notes et études documentaires : 1-36, no. 2855, 29 janvier 1962,

MESA LAGO, C. : El neo-derecho laboral de la República Socialista Cubana. Revista de la Facultad de derecho de la Universidad de Madrid 6 : 59-118, núm. 13, 1962.

The Castro government in American courts - Sovereign immunity and the Act of state doctrine. Harvard law review 75 : 1607-1621, June 1962.

CYPRUS

Constitución de la República de Chipre, 16 de agosto de 1960. Información jurídica (Spain) : 1-124, enero-febrero 1963.
Spanish text.

Constitution de la République de Chypre, 16 août 1960. Informations constitutionnelles et parlementaires 11-12 : 145-192, 1-46, octobre 1960, janvier 1961.

Constitution de la République de Chypre, 16 août 1960. Documentation française, Notes et études documentaires : 1-44, no. 2761, 17 mars 1961.
Texte.

TÉNÉKIDÈS, G. : La République de Chypre et le droit international. Politico 27 : 69-88, marzo 1962.

VLACHOS, G. : L'organisation constitutionnelle de la République de Chypre. Revue internationale de droit comparé 13 : 525-559, juillet-septembre 1961.

Constitution of the Republic of Cyprus. Revue égyptienne de droit international, Documents 19 : 263-359, 1963.
Text; See also pp. 257-262.

CZECHOSLOVAKIA

BYSTRICKÝ, R. : Konzulární snňatek podle čs. mezinárodního práva soukromého. Časopis pro mezinárodní právo 4 : 118-129, číslo 2, 1960.
Consular marriage.

KUČERA, Z. : Význam zákona č. 46/1959 Sb. pro naše mezinárodní právo procesní. Časopis pro mezinárodní právo 4 : 257-265, čislo 3, 1960.
International civil procedure.

KNAP, K. : Přístup Československa k Všeobecné úmluvě o právu autorském a jeho význam pro mezinárodní ochranu československých děl. Časopis pro mezinárodní právo 4 : 330-341, číslo 4, 1960.

COLOTKA, P., and MATOUŠEK, S. : K novej socialistickej ústave Československej socialistickej republiky. Právnické štúdie 8 : 503-566, číslo 4, 1960.
Constitution.

COLOTKA, P. : Významné vývojové obdobie nášho občianskeho a rodinného práva. Právny obzor 43 : 271-280, číslo 5, 1960.
Civil and family law.

Entwurf der Verfassung der Tschechoslowakischen Republik. Staat und Recht 9 : 1025-1046, Juni 1960.
Published in "Rudé Právo".

La nuova costituzione cecoslovacca. Relazioni internazionali 24 : 1085-1092, 13-20, agosto 1960.
Text.

LEVIT, P. : Les organes suprêmes de l'Etat dans la nouvelle constitution. Bulletin de droit tchécoslovaque 18 : 69-83, no. 1-2, 30 septembre 1960.

Constitution tchécoslovaque, 11 juillet 1960. Documentation française, Notes et études documentaires : 1-15, no. 2723, 3 décembre 1960.

Constitution de la République Socialiste Tchécoslovaque, 11 juillet 1960. Informations constitutionnelles et parlementaires 12 : janvier 1961.

KNAPP, V. : La réglementation juridique des rapports mutuels entre les entreprises nationales en droit tchécoslovaque. Revue de droit international et de droit comparé 38 : 7-17, no. 1, 1961.

PLUNDR, O. : L'organisation des tribunaux dans la République socialiste tchécoslovaque. Bulletin de droit tchécoslovaque 19 : 22-51, no. 1-2, 1961.

PESKA, P., and RATTINGER, B. : Die neue Verfassung der Tschechoslowakischen Sozialistischen Republik. Neue Justiz (Germany) 15 : 81-88, 5. Februar 1961.

WIERER, R. : Die tschechoslowakische Verfassung vom 11. Juli 1960. Donauraum 6 : 113-132, 2. Heft 1961.

NATIONAL LAW - COUNTRIES

KNAPP, V. : Algunos aspectos del derecho civil checoslovaco desde el punto de vista comparativo. Instituto de derecho comparado, Revista (Barcelona) : 127-152, enero-diciembre 1961.

KALVODA, J. : Czechoslovakia's socialist constitution. American Slavic and East European review 20 : 220-236, April 1961.
1960.

SLAPNICKA, H. : Die Organisation der Gerichte in der CSSR. Osteuropa-Recht 7 : 191-198, September 1961.

SCHULZ, W. : Grundzüge der Verfassung des Tschechoslowakei von 1960. Recht in Ost und West 6 : 45-54, 15. März 1962.

KNAPP, V. : Verträge im tschechoslowakischen Recht - Ein Beitrag zur Rechtsvergleichung zwischen Ländern mit verschiedener Gesellschaftsordnung. Rabels Zeitschrift für ausländisches und internationales Privatrecht 27 : 495-518, Heft 3, 1962.

CEPL, V. : Náleži mezinárodní právo do systému československého socialistického práva? Časopis pro mezinárodní prvo 6 : 258-264, číslo 3, 1962.

VYBIRAL, B. : Le nouveau code pénal de la République Socialiste Tchécoslovaque. Revue de droit contemporain 9 : 82-95, juin 1962.

TOLAR, J., et PRENOSIL, G. : Le nouveau code pénal et le nouveau code de procédure pénale de la République Socialiste Tchécoslovaque. Revue internationale de droit comparé 14 : 747-755, octobre-décembre 1962.

LUBY, Š. : Predchádzanie škodám v osnove Občianskeho zákonníka a v návrhu Hospodárskeho kódexu. Právnické štúdie 11 : 29-64, číslo 1, 1963.
Summary in Russian.

RŮŽEK, A. : Die neue Strafprozessordnung der Tschechoslowakischen Sozialistischen Republik. Staat und Recht 12 : 327-344, Februar 1963.

BYSTRICKÝ, R., and KALENSKÝ, P. : K některým otázkám navrhované osnovy zákona o mezinárodním právu soukromén. Časopis pro mezinárodní právo 7 : 214-229, číslo 3, 1963.

SOLNAŘ, V. : Die Grundgedanken des neuen tschechoslowakischen Strafrechts. Zeitschrift für die gesamte Strafrechtswissenschaft, Mitteilungsblatt der Fachgruppe Strafrecht in der Gesellschaft für Rechtsvergleichung 13 : 163-180, Heft 4, 1963.

HROMADA, J. : K niektorým úlohám práva v d'alšom roznoji našej socialistickej spoločnosti. Právny obzor 46 : 193-202, číslo 4, 1963.

KNAPP, V. : Introduction au droit tchécoslovaque. Pays communistes 4 : 7-26, avril 1963.

KNAPPOVÁ, M. : Tři poznámky k osnově hospodářského zákoníku. Právník 102 : 554-564, číslo 7, 1963.
Draft economic code; See also pp. 565-577.

STEINER, V. : K některým otázkám osnovy nového občanskho soudního řádu. Právník 102 : číslo 8, 1963.

LACHOUT, V. : K vývoji československého trestního procesu. Právny obzor 46 : 449-463, číslo 8, 1963.

RABL, K. : Die tschechoslowakische Verfassungsurkunde vom 11. Juli 1960 in Theorie und Praxis. Jahrbuch des öffentlichen Rechts der Gegenwart 12 : 353-389, 1963.
Texts pp. 390-416.

FRANKOWSKI, S. : Nowy kodeks karny Czechoslowackiej Republiki Socjalistycznej. Państwo i prawo 19 : 82-91, styczeń 1964.

KRATOCHVÍL, Z. : La nouvelle législation civile dans la République socialiste tchécoslovaque. Bulletin de droit tchécoslovaque 22 : 1-26, no. 1-2, 1964.
Texte du code civil 1964 pp. 46-155.

ŽOUREK, J. : Nouvelle réglementation de l'arbitrage commercial en Tchécoslovaquie. Bulletin de droit tchécoslovaque 21 : 256-272, no. 4, 1964.

KALENSKY, P. : A propos de la nouvelle codification tchéchoslovaque du droit international privé. Revista española de derecho internacional 17 : 225-240, abril-junio 1964.

STEINER, V. : Zu den neuen Vorschriften des Tschechoslowakischen Zivilprozessrechts. Staat und Recht 13 : 889-902, Mai 1964.

BYSTRICKÝ, R. : Nový československy zákon o medzinárodnom práve súkromnom a procesnom. Právny obzor 47 : 513-531, číslo 9, 1964.

KNAPP, V. : La nouvelle législation civile en Tchécoslovaquie. Revue internationale de droit comparé 16 : 753-766, octobre-décembre 1964.

DAHOMEY

República del Dahomey - Constitución del 15 de febrero de 1959. Información jurídica (Spain) : 19-28, marzo-abril 1960.
Spanish text.

MANGIN, G. : Dahomey. Annuaire de législation française et étrangère 9 : 123-126, 1960.

République du Dahomey - Constitution du 26 novembre 1960. Revie juridique et politique d'outre-mer 15 : 263-272, avril-juin 1961.

JOUHAUD, Y. : La nouvelle constitution de la République du Dahomey. Revue juridique et politique - Indépendance et coopération 18 : 157-161, janvier-mars 1964.
Texte pp. 161-172.

Constitution, 11 janvier 1964. Informations constitutionnelles et parlementaires 15 : 142-160, juillet 1964.

DENMARK

Ley penal para Groenlandia. Información jurídica (Spain) : 11-32, noviembre-diciembre 1960.

MARCUS, F. : Dänische Rechtsprechung auf dem Gebiet des internationalen Privatrechts 1955-1960. Rabels Zeitschrift für ausländisches und internationales Privatrecht 26 : 255-267, Heft 2, 1961.

PAONE, P. : Due provvedimenti del Governo danese circa i mari della Groenlandia. Rivista di diritto internazionale 46 : 388-390, fasc. 3, 1963.

NATIONAL LAW - COUNTRIES

MARCUS, F. : Rechtsprechung des dänischen Obersten Gerichtshofs auf dem Gebiete des Privatrechts 1954-1961. Rabels Zeitschrift für ausländisches und internationales Privatrecht 28 : 263-317, Heft 2, 1964.

DOMINICAN REPUBLIC

CORNIELLE, C. : Trujillo, creador de un derecho moderno dominicano. Renovación 7 : 17-29, julio-septiembre 1960.

HERRERA BILLINI, H. : La era de Trujillo y la jurisprudencia dominicana. Renovación 42 : 66-77, enero-marzo 1961.

Constitution de la République Dominicaine, 2 décembre 1960. Documentation française, Notes et études documentaires : 1-22, no. 2831, 10 novembre 1961.

ECUADOR

Código de procedimiento penal del Ecuador. Información jurídica (Spain) : 1-69, septiembre-octubre 1962.

ETHIOPIA

ARNOLD, H. : Die Zivilrechtspflege in Äthiopien. Zeitschrift für ausländisches und internationales Privazrecht 25 : 53-68, Heft 1, 1960.

GRAVEN, J. : La personalità del delinquente nel codice penale etiopico. Scuola positiva 65 : 392-401, fasc. 3, 1960.

ALTAVILLA, E. : Esame critico del codice penale etiopico del 23 giugno 1957. Rassegna di studi penitenziari (Italy) 11 : 7-21, gennaio-febbraio 1961.

LIONS SIGNORET, M. : Código penal para el imperio de Etiopía. Boletín del Instituto de derecho comparado de México 14 : 85-88, enero-abril 1961.

HILGERT, R. : Le nouveau code pénal éthiopien. Revue moderne de la police 9 : 14-17, mars-avril 1961.
Texte en anglais aussi.

DAVID, R. : Les sources du code civil éthiopien. Revue international de droit comparé 14 : 497-506, juillet-septembre 1962.

AGUILAR GUTIÉRREZ, A. : El código civil del Imperio de Etiopía. Boletín del Instituto de derecho comparado de México 15 : 621-628, septiembre-diciembre 1962.

GRAVEN, P. : La nouvelle procédure pénale éthiopienne. Schweizerische Zeitschrift für Strafrecht 79 : 70-82, Heft 1, 1963.

DAVID, R. : A civil code for Ethiopia - Considerations on the codification of the civil law in African countries. Tulane law review 37 : 187-204, February 1963.

KRZECZUNOWICZ, G. : The Ethiopian civil code - Its usefulness, relation to custom and applicability. Journal of African law 7 : 172-177, autumn 1963.

COPPENS, P. : Réflexions sur le code civil éthiopien. Académie royale des sciences d'outre-mer, Bulletin des séances - Koninklijke academie overzeese wetenschappen, Mededelingen der zittingen (Bruxelles) : 632-651, no. 4, 1964.

SEDLER, R.A. : The chilot jurisdiction of the Emperor of Ethiopia - A legal analysis in historical and comparative perspective. Journal of African law 8 : 59-76, summer 1964.

FINLAND

SCHWINDT, B. : Från Högsta Domstolen i Finland 1957. Tidsskrift for rettsvitenskap : 62-68, hefte 1, 1960.

KASTARI, P. : The constitutional protection of fundamental rights in Finland. Tulane law review 34 : 695-710, June 1960.

SCHWINDT, B. : Från Högsta domstolen i Finland 1958. Tidsskrift for rettsvitenskap : 63-69, hefte 1, 1961.

SCHWINDT, B. : Fran Högsta domstolen i Finland 1959. Tidsskrift for rettsvitenskap : 81-86, hefte 1, 1962.

SAARIO, V. : Control of the constitutionality of laws in Finland. American journal of comparative law 12 : 194-205, spring 1963.

FRANCE

AUBERT, J.F. : La constitution française du 4 octobre 1958. Zeitschrift für schweizerisches Recht 79 : 17-45, Heft 1, 1960.

LEVASSEUR, G. : Liberté de la presse et justice pénale - La solution française. Schweizerische Zeitschrift für Strafrecht 76 : 251-280, Heft 3, 1960.

FOULON-PIGANIOL, C. : Le mariage "simule". Revue trimestrielle de droit civil 59 : 217-251, avril-juin 1960.

La femme et le code civil. Fiches documentaires d'action sociale et civique : 1-19, mai-juin 1960.

SIRAT, C. : La loi organique et la constitution de 1958. Recueil Dalloz, Chronique : 153-160, 31 août 1960.

LAUBADÈRE, A. de : La constitution française de 1958. Zeitschrift für ausländisches und internationales Recht und Völkerrecht 20 : 506-561, August 1960.

BONNAUD-DELAMARE, R. : Le préfet dans le cadre de la constitution française de 1958. Revue internationale des sciences administratives 27 : 5-15, no. 1, 1961.

HÉBRAUD, P. : La réforme de la procédure civile - Le décret du 22 décembre 1958. Annales de la Faculté de droit de Toulouse 9 : 3-48, fasc. 1, 1961.

NATIONAL LAW - COUNTRIES

DOEKER, G. : The Fifth French Republic - A legal and constitutional analysis. Inter-American law review - Revista jurídica interamericana 3 : 129-148, January-June 1961.

JULLIOT de la MORANDIÈRE, L. : Où en est la réforme du code civil? Revue des travaux de l'Académie des sciences morales et politiques et comptes rendus de ses séances 114 : 92-102, 2e semestre 1961.
Discussion pp. 102-106.

LEGARET, J. : L'article 16 : Revue des deux mondes : 385-402, 1er juin 1961.
Pouvoirs du président de la République.

QUERMONNE, J.L. : L'article 16 et la défense de la République. Revue de l'Action populaire : 701-712, juin 1961.

GIRAUD, E. : La constitution du 4 octobre 1958 et la pratique de cette constitution. Revue du droit public et de la science politique en France et à l'étranger 77 : 1006-1014, septembre-octobre 1961.

GONFREVILLE, M. : La réforme de la procédure arbitrale en France. Revue de l'arbitrage: 3-16, janvier-mars 1963.

BREWSTER, R.W. : The "Tribunaux administratifs" of France - A venture in adjudicative reorganization. Journal of public law 11 : 236-259, no. 2, 1962.

PEISER, G. : La dissolution par décret des associations et groupements politiques français, loi du 10 janvier 1936. Recueil Dalloz, Chronique : 59-66, 13 mars 1963.

JULLIOT de la MORANDIÈRE, L. : Second report of the Civil code reform commission of France. Louisiana law review 23 : 506-517, April 1963.

GASSIN, R. : Les destinées du principe de l'autorité de la chose jugée au criminel sur le criminel dans le droit pénal contemporain. Revue de science criminelle et de droit pénal comparé 18 : 239-278, avril-juin 1963.

Ordenanza de 23-12-59, que modifica y completa el código de procidimiento penal francés. Información jurídica (Spain) : 3-127, septiembre-octubre 1963.

WALINE, M. : The constitutional council of the French Republic. American journal of comparative law 12 : 483-493, autumn 1963.

BECKER, L.E. : The société anonyme and the société à responsabilité limitée in France. New York university law review 38 : 835-889, November 1963.

LARGUIER, J. : French penal law and the duty to aid persons in danger. Tulane law review 38 : 81-90, December 1963.

Constitution de la République Française, 4 octobre 1958 - Mise à jour au 31 décembre 1963. Documentation française, Notes et études documentaires : 1-16, no. 3059, 30 janvier 1964.

DESCAMPS de BRAGELONGNE, H. : Le problème de statut des départements d'outre-mer, Guadeloupe et Martinique. Revue juridique et économique du Sud-Ouest, Série juridique 15 : 61-107, nos. 1-2, 1964.

VITU, A. : Une nouvelle juridiction d'exception, la Cour de sûreté de l'Etat. Revue de science criminelle et de droit pénal comparé 19 : 1-51, janvier-mars 1964.

ENGEL, S. : Judicial view and political pre-view of legislation in post-war France. Inter-American law review - Revista jurídica interamericana 6 : 53-72, January-June 1964.

STILLMUNKES, P. : La classification des actes ayant force de loi en droit public français. Revue de droit public et de la science politique en France et à l'étranger 80 : 261-292, mars-avril 1964.

ISAAC, G. : Le "domaine réservé" du Président de la République - Contribution à l'étude de la première législature de la Ve République. Annales de la Faculté de droit de Toulouse 12 : 21-137, fasc. 2, 1964.
Textes pp. 138-141.

TOWE, T.E. : Criminal pretrial procedure in France. Tulane law review 38 : 469-496, April 1964.

LANGROD, G. : La reforma administrativa en Francia, 1964. Documentación administrativa (Spain) : 9-26, agosto 1964.

DRAGO, R. : Some recent reforms of the French Conseil d'Etat. International and comparative law quarterly 13 : 1282-1299, October 1964.

FRANCE
(International law, Aliens, Nationality)

TOMASI, A. : La convention franco-allemande d'établissement du 27 octobre 1956. Journal du droit international 87 : 94-108, janvier-mars 1960.
Texte en anglais aussi.

WALKER, H. : Convention of establishment between the United States and France. American journal of international law 54 : 393-398, April 1960.

LEPAULLE, P. : Réflexions sur la convention d'établissement franco-américaine du 25 novembre 1959. Revue critique de droit international privé 50 : 291-304, avril-juin 1961.

MANGIN, G. : L'assistance technique judiciaire dans les Etats de la Communauté. Recueil Penant, Doctrine 70 : 213-224, mai 1960.

VIGOR, P. : Le statut des étrangers en France. Revue politique et parlementaire 228 : 609-616, juin 1960.

DESBOIS, H. : La protection des oeuvres littéraires et artistiques étrangères en France - Questions d'actualité. Comité français de droit international privé, Travaux 21-23 : 177-196, 1960-1962.
Discussion pp. 196-210.

BILBAO, R. : La nationalité française et l'accession à l'indépendance des anciens territoires d'outre-mer. Penant, Revue de droit des pays d'Afrique 71 : 517-522, septembre-octobre 1961.

Relations de la France et des Etats accédant à l'indépendance - Traités et accords conclus entre la France et le Cameroun, signés à Yaoundé le 13 novembre 1961. Journal du droit international 88 : 1202-1235, octobre-décembre 1961.
Texte en anglais aussi.

LOUIS-LUCAS, P. : La fraude à la loi étrangère. Revue critique de droit international privé 51 : 1-17, janvier-mars 1962.

FISCHER-DIESKAU, T. : Die französische Rechtsprechung zum internationalen Privatrecht 1945-1960. Rabels Zeitschrift für ausländisches und internationales Privatrecht 27 : 666-697, Heft 4, 1962.

CHEVALLIER, R.M. : Le droit de la Communauté européenne et les juridictions françaises. Revue du droit public et de la science politique en France et à l' étranger 78 : 646-663, juillet-août 1962.

MANGIN, G. : Les accords de coopération en matière de justice entre la France et les Etats africains et malgache. Revue juridique et politique d'outre-mer 16 : 339-364, juillet-septembre 1962.

LESAGE, M. : Les procédures de conclusion des accords internationaux de la France sous la Ve République. Annuaire français de droit international 8 : 873-888, 1962.

La publication des engagements internationaux de la France. Annuaire français de droit internatipnal 8 : 888-905, 1962.

VERDIER, J.M. : Décolonisation et développement en droit international privé - Essai d'une systématisation à partir de l'expérience française. Journal de droit international 89 : 904-973, octobre-décembre 1962.
Texte en anglais aussi.

LAMPUÉ, P. : Les bases juridiques du système coopératif franco-africain. Penant, Revue de droit des pays d'Afrique 72 : 645-663, novembre-décembre 1962.

GEOUFFRE de la PRADELLE, P. de : Juridiction administrative et droit international. France, Conseil d'Etat; Etudes et documents 16 : 13-40, 1962.

FRANCESCAKIS, P. : La loi étrangère à la Cour de cassation. Recueil Dalloz, Chronique : 2-14, 16 janvier 1963.

GAUDIN de LAGRANGE, E. de : Nationalité française 1963. Recueil Dalloz, Chronique : 107-112, ler mai 1963.

MALAURIE, P. : La contrôle des jugements étrangers - La règle du roi Carol. Recueil Dalloz, Chronique : 129-132, 22 mai 1963.

LOITRON, B. : L'exécution en France des sentences arbitrales étrangères et plus spécialement européennes. Droit européen 6 : 177-188, mai 1963.

MOTULSKY, H. : L'internationalisation du droit français de l'arbitrage. Revue de l'arbitrage : 110-122, octobre-décembre 1963.

MOTAIS de NARBONNE, L. : La double nationalité dans le cas où la nationalité française est en cause. Annales de la Faculté de droit d'Istanbul 13 : 170-185, no. 19, 1963.

FRANCE
(French Community)

MANGIN, G. : Problèmes judiciaires dans les Etats africains de la Communauté. Commission internationale de juristes, Revue 2 : 76-95, hiver 1959-printemps/ été 1960.

La révision constitutionnelle relative à la Communauté. Revue juridique et politique d'outre-mer 14 : 457-477, octobre-décembre 1960.

LAMPUÉ, P. : La diversité des statuts de droit privé dans les Etats africains. Penant, Revue de droit des pays d'Afrique 71 : 1-10, janvier-mars 1961.

JOUHAUD, Y. : L'évolution du contentieux administratif. Penant, Revue de droit des pays d'Afrique 71 : 25-46, janvier-mars 1961.

TERRE, F. : La reconnaissance de la nationalité française. Penant, Revue de droit des pays d'Afrique 71 : 17-23, janvier-mars 1961.

GABON

República del Gabón - Constitución del 19 de febrero de k959. Información jurídica (Spain) : 29-37, marzo-abril 1960.
Spanish text.

MANGIN, G. : Gabon. Annuaire de législation française et étrangère 9 : 231-237, 1960.

République Gabonaise - Constitutions du 14 novembre 1960 et du 21 février 1961. Revue juridique et politique d'outre-mer 15 : 272-294, avril-juin 1961.

GERMANY
(Federal Republic)

RUHRMANN : Die Behandlung innerdeutscher (interlokaler) Kollisionsfälle auf dem Gebiet des Staatsschutzstrafrechts. Zeitschrift für die gesamte Strafrechtswissenschaft 72 : 124-179, Heft 1/2, 1960.

BRAGA, S. : Das Grundgesetz und die (gesamtdeutsche) Staatsangehörigkeit. Annales Universitatis saraviensis - Rechts- und Wirtschaftswissenschaften; Droit, économie 8 : 75-86, fasc. 1-2, 1960.

HALLIER, H.J. : Die Ausfertigung und Verkündung von Gesetzen und Verordnungen in der Bundesrepublik Deutschland. Archiv des öffentlichen Rechts 85 : 391-422, Heft 4, 1960.

PAPPE, H.O. : On the validity of judicial decisions in the Nazi era. Modern law review 23 : 260-274, May 1960.

KAUPER, P.G. : The constitutions of West Germany and the United States - A comparative study. Michigan law review 58 : 1091-1184, June 1960.

HAAK, V. : Quelques aspects du contrôle de la constitutionnalité des lois exercé par la Cour constitutionnelle de la République Fédérale d'Allemagne. Revue internationale de droit comparé 13 : 78-88, janvier-mars 1961.

PETERS, K. : Probleme der deutschen Strafrechtsreform. Schweizerische Zeitschrift für Strafrecht 77 : 162-181, Heft 2, 1961.

VASAK, K. : Das Rechts- und Amtshilfegesetz der Bundesrepublik Deutschland vor der Europäischen Menschenrechtskommission. Recht in Ost und West 5 : 107-110, 15. Mai 1961.

HAY, P. : Frustration and its solution in German law. American journal of comparative law 10 : 345-373, autumn 1961.

McWHINNEY, E. : Judicial restraint and the West German constitutional court. Harvard law review 75 : 5-38, November 1961.

HASS, K. : Réforme de la législation allemande de protection des victimes de guerre. Cahiers de législation comparée des anciens combattants et victimes de guerre : 103-105, novembre 1961.

WÄGENBAUR, R. : Le régime de l'adoption en Allemagne d'après la loi de 1961. Revue internationale de droit comparé 14 : 63-67, janvier-mars 1962.

SCHULE, E. : Die Zentrale der Landesjustizverwaltungen zur Aufklärung nationalsozialistischer Gewaltverbrechen in Ludwigsburg. Juristenzeitung 17 : 241-244, 19. April 1962.

FELD, W. : The German administrative courts. Tulane law review 36 : 495-506, April 1962.

PFANNENSCHWARZ, K. : The norms of high treason, endangerment of the state and treason laid down in the West German government draft for a new criminal code. Law and legislation in the German Democratic Republic : 22-42, no. 2, 1963.

PFANNENSCHWARZ, K., and SCHNEIDER, T. : The draft laws of the West German government for the establishment of a military dictatorship. Law and legislation in the German Democratic Republic : 35-49, no. 2, 1963.

KLEIN, F. : Das Verhältnis von Gesetzgebungzuständigkeit und Verwaltungszuständigkeit nach dem Grundgesetz. Archiv des öffentlichen Rechts 88 : 377-410, Heft 4, 1963.

GOTTSCHLING, E. : Die Grundgesetzwidrigkeit der geplanten "Notstandsverfassung". Neue Justiz (Germany, Democratic Republic) 18 : 244-248, 277-279, 2. Aprilheft, 1. Maiheft 1964.

DUQUE, J.F. : La uniones de empresas en la reforma alemana del derecho de sociedades por acciones. Anuario de derecho civil 17 : 383-436, abril-junio 1964.

TROMBETAS, T.P. : The U.S. Supreme Court and the Federal constitutional court of Germany - Some comparative observations. Revue hellénique de droit international 17 : 281-298, juillet-décembre 1964.

JESCHEK, H.H. : Les principes de politique criminelle du projet d'un code pénal allemand en comparaison avec l'évolution du droit pénal en Belgique. Revue de droit pénal et de criminologie 45 : 205-233, décembre 1964.

GERMANY
(International law and practice, Aliens and Naturalization)

TOMASI, A. : La convention franco-allemande d'établissement du 27 octobre 1956. Journal du droit international 87 : 94-108, janvier-mars 1960.
Texte en anglais aussi.

KEGEL, G. : Reform des deutschen internationalen Eherechts. Zeitschrift für ausländisches und internationales Privatrecht 25 : 201-221, Heft 2, 1960.

MATSCHER, F. : Der neue österreichisch-deutsche Vertrag über die Anerkennung und Vollstreckung von gerichtlichen Entscheidungen im Lichte der allgemeinen Lehren des Internationalen Zivilprozessrechts. Juristische Blätter 82 : 265-279, 28. Mai 1960.

MÜNSCH, F. : Zur anwendung der Menschenrechtskonvention in der Bundesrepublik Deutschland. Juristenzeitung 16 : 153-155, 17. März 1961.

HARRIES, H. : Das deutsch-belgische Anerkennungs- und Vollstreckungsabkommen. Rabels Zeitschrift für ausländisches und internationales Privatrecht 26 : 629-667, Heft 4, 1961.

SKOWRONSKI, A. : Problèmes juridiques relatifs au statut d'occupation du Grand-Berlin. Revue de droit contemporain 8 : 75-89, juin 1961.

WENGLER, W. : Conflict of laws problems relating to restitution of property in Germany. International and comparative law quarterly 11 : 1131-1152, October 1962.

NEUHAUS, P.H. : Um die Reform des deutschen internationalen Eherechts. Zeitschrift für das gesamte Familienrecht 9 : 415-418, Oktober 1962.

KEGEL, G. : La réforme du droit international du mariage en Allemagne. Revue critique de droit international privé 51 : 641-665, octobre-décembre 1962.

KLEIN, F. : Die Europäische Menschenrechts-Konvention und Artikel 25 des Bonner Grundgesetzes. Jahrbuch für internationales Recht 11 : 149-177, 1962.

SCHAEFER, R. : Das Asylrecht in der Bundesrepublik Deutschland. Vereinte Nationen 11 : 44-50, April 1963.

VEITER, T. : Neues Fremdenrecht in der Bundesrepublik Deutschland. Berichte und Informationen des Österreichischen Forschungsinstituts für Wirtschaft und Politik 18 : 9-11, 17. Mai 1963.

DREYER : L'exécution en Allemagne des sentences arbitrales de la Cour arbitrale européenne de C.E.A. Droit européen 6 : 217-233, juin-septembre 1963.

Völkerrechtliche Praxis der Bundesrepublik Deutschland in den Jahren 1949 bis 1955, 1960 und 1961. Zeitschrift für ausländisches öffentliches Recht und Völkerrecht 23 : 173-472, Juli 1963.
Special issue.

MÜNCH, F. : Immunität fremder Staaten in der deutschen Rechtsprechung bis zu den Beschlüssen des Bundesverfassungsgerichts vom 30. Oktober 1962 und 30. April 1963. Zeitschrift für ausländisches öffentliches Recht und Völkerrecht 24 : 265-278, April 1964.
See also pp. 279-316.

GERMANY
(Copyright, Patents, Trademarks)

MERTHA, B. : La réforme du droit d'auteur en République Fédérale Allemande. Revue de l'U.E.R. (Union européenne de radiodiffusion), Cahier B : 21-25, mai 1960.

GERMANY
(Democratic Republic)

BENJAMIN, H. : The system of law courts in the German Democratic Republic. Law and legislation in the German Democratic Republic : 5-23, no. 1, 1960.

LÜBCHEN, G.A. : Die Durchführung von gerichtlichen Verfahren in Familiensachen, an denen Bürger der Tschechoslowakischen Republik oder der Volksrepublik Polen beteiligt sind. Neue Justiz (Germany) 14 : 12-14, 5. Januar 1960.

GRANZOW, C. : Familienrechtsreform in der Deutschen Demokratischen Republik. Ehe und Familie im privaten und öffentlichen Recht 7 : 85-93, März 1960.

ZIEGER, G. : Die Regierung der SBZ als Organ der Gesetzgebung. Recht in Ost und West 4 : 51-56, 15. März 1960.

Gedanken zur Konzeption eines sozialistischen Zivilgesetzbuchs. Neue Justiz (Germany) 14 : 790-794, 5. Dezember 1960.

BEIN, H., and CREUZBERG, H. : Zur Problematik des Strafensystems im künftigen Strafgesetzbuch. Neue Justiz (Germany) 15 : 20-24, 5. Januar 1961.

PÜSCHEL, H. : Work in progress on new civil code of the German Democratic Republic. Law and legislation in the German Democratic Republic : 40-57, no. 1, 1962.

ROSENTHAL, W. : Le pouvoir judiciaire dans le zone soviétique d'Allemagne. Commission internationale de juristes, Revue 4 : 143-160, ler semestre 1962.

REINTANZ, G., and HAALCK, J. : Die Territorialgewässer der DDR. Neue Justiz (Germany) 16 : 372-375, 2. Juniheft 1962.

DROBNIG, U. : Anerkennung und Rechtswirkungen sowjetzonaler Ehescheidungen. Ehe und Familie im privaten und öffentlichen Rechts 8 : 341-352, August/September 1961.

GRUNEWALD, J. : Grundzüge der sowjetzonalen Eigentumsordnung. Recht in Ost und West 7 : 5-10, 15. Januar 1963.

SCHIRMER, G. : Zur Völkerrechtssubjektivität der Staaten und zum Problem ihrer völkerrechtlichen Rechtmässigkeit. Staat und Recht 12 : 647-663, April 1963.
German Democratic Republic.

SARGE, G. : Die sozialistische Militärgerichtsbarkeit in der DDR. Neue Justiz (Germany) 17 : 364-367, 2. Juniheft 1963.

RIEGE, G. : Staatsbürgerschaft und nationale Frage. Staat und Recht 13 : 56-79, Januar 1964.

STREIT, J. : Character and functions of the Procurator's office of the German Democratic Republic. Law and legislation in the German Democratic Republic : 5-10, no. 1, 1964.

WEBER, H. : Zu den gesellschaftlichen Eigenschaften der Straftaten in der Deutschen Demokratischen Republik. Staat und Recht 13 : 649-667, April 1964.

WEICHELT, W. : The right to vote and the electoral system of the German Democratic Republic. Law and legislation in the German Democratic Republic : 5-16, no. 2, 1964.

SUCH, H. : The economic contracts of socialist firms. Law and legislation in the German Democratic Republic : 17-26, no. 2, 1964.

MAMPEL, S. : Die Entwicklung der Verfassungsordnung in der Sowjetzone Deutschlands von 1945 bis 1963. Jahrbuch des öffentlichen Rechts der Gegenwart 13 : 455-557, 1964.
Texts pp. 558-579.

GHANA

Ghana - Loi relative à l'Assemblée nationale, 9 décembre 1959. Informations constitutionnelles et parlementaires : 74-91, avril 1960.

Constitution de la République du Ghana, ler juillet 1960. Informations constitutionnelles et parlementaires 11 : 121-139, juillet 1960.
Texte.

Constitution du Ghana, ler juillet 1960. Documentation française, Notes et études documentaires : 1-10, no. 2709, 22 octobre 1960.
Texte.

ATIYAH, P.S. : Commercial law in Ghana. Journal of business law : 430-437, October 1960.

SCHWELB, E. : The republican constitution of Ghana. American journal of comparative law 9 : 634-656, autumn 1960.

Amendement au projet de constitution de la République du Ghana, ler juillet 1960. Informations constitutionnelles et parlementaires 12 : 47-48, janvier 1961.
Texte.

La loi sur l'internement administratif au Ghana. Commission internationale de juristes, Revue 3 : 69-102, 2e semestre 1961.

MIKHLIN, A.S. : Ugolovnoe zakonodatel'stvo Respubliki Gana. Sovetskoe gosudarstvo i pravo 32 : 127-131, no. 9, sentiabr' 1962.

HARVEY, W.B. : The evolution of Ghana law since independence. Law and contemporary problems 27 : 581-604, autumn 1962.

ALLOT, A. : Development of the law of Ghana. Annales de la Faculté de droit d'Istanbul 12 : 210-217, no. 18, 1962.

GREAT BRITAIN

Law reform. Modern law review 24 : 1-143, January 1961.
Series of articles.

DAVIS, K.C. : The future of judge-made public law in England. A problem of practical jurisprudence. Columbia law review 61 : 201-220, February 1961.

DELANEY, V.T.H. : Charitable trusts and the conflict of laws. International and comparative law quarterly 10 : 385-400, July 1961.

McCLINTOCK, F.H. : Crimes against the person. Manchester statistical society, Transactions : V/1-32, 1962/63.
With map and diagrams.

BRITTAN, L. : The right of privacy in England and the United States. Tulane law review 37 : 235-268, February 1963.

De FUNIAK, W.Q. : The legal system of Scotland. Tulane law review 38 : 91-102, December 1963.

GELINAS, A. : Judicial control of administrative action - Great Britain and Canada. Public law 140-171, summer 1963.

A symposium on English law and the Common Market. Current legal problems 16 : 1-231, 1963.

KOCK, G.L. : Criminal appeals in England - The Court that isn't. Journal of public law 13 : 95-103, no. 1, 1964.

Legal aid act 1964. Law journal 114 : 248-250, 17 April 1964.

DIPLOCK : La procédure civile en Engleterre. Revue de droit international et de droit comparé 41 : 189-202, no. 4, 1964.

DIPLOCK : La procédure pénale anglaise. Revue de droit pénal et de criminologie 44 : 617-628, avril 1964.

LASOK, D. : Les tendances récentes du droit anglais en matière de mariage et de divorce. Revue internationale de droit comparé 16 : 493-514, juillet-septembre 1964.

YARDLEY, D.C.M. : The British constitution and the rule of law. Jahrbuch des öffentlichen Rechts der Gegenwart 13 : 129-138, 1964.

GREAT BRITAIN
(International law, Aliens)

JOHNSON, D.H.N. : The English tradition in international law. International and comparative law quarterly 11 : 416-445, April 1962.

RICE, D.G. : Foreign companies in Great Britain. Journal of business law : 155-168, April 1962.

KEENAN, P.B. : Some legal consequences of Britain's entry into the European common market. Public law : 327-343, autumn 1962.

The sovereignty of the Queen. Time and Tide 43 : 5-7, 7-8; 6-13, 13-20 September 1962.
Consequences of Britain's entering the Common Market.

LASOK, D. : British nationality and statelessness. Law journal 113 : 35-36, 18 January 1963.

NIGH, P.E. : Problems of nationality and expatriation before English and Australian courts. International and comparative law quarterly 12 : 175-188, January 1963.

THORNBERRY, C.H.R. : Dr. Soblen and the Alien law of the United Kingdom. International and comparative law quarterly 12 : 414-474, April 1963.

SINCLAIR, I.M. : The principles of treaty interpretation and their application by the English courts. International and comparative law quarterly 12 : 508-551, April 1963.

MATSCHER, F. : Die Anerkennung und Vollstreckung gerichtlicher Entscheidungen im Verhältnis zwischen Österreich und Grossbritannien. Juristische Blätter 85 : 229-236, 11. Mai 1963.

MARSH, N.S. : Le Royaume-Uni devant les problèmes juridiques du Marché commun. Revue internationale de droit comparé 15 : 649-661, octobre-décembre 1963.

Thai-U.K. treaty of extradition. Foreign affairs bulletin (Thailand) 3 : 268-274, December 1963-January 1964.

COWAN, A. : Immunity of sovereign and diplomatic tenants. Journal of planning and property law : 246-251, April 1964.

DEVAUX-CHARBONNEL, J. : Le plateau continental du Royaume-Uni et la convention internationale de Genève de 1958. Annuaire français de droit international 10 : 705-717, 1964.

GREECE

BALTATZIS, A. : La non-extradition des nationaux. Revze hellénique de droit international 13 : 190-212, janvier-décembre 1960.

VLACHOS, G. : Les décrets législatifs et la loi formelle en droit constitutionnel hellénique. Revue du droit public et de la science politique en France et à l'étranger 76 : 233-302, mars-avril 1960.

VLACHOS, G. : La réforme de l'Etat et la codification de la législation en Grèce. Revue internationale de droit comparé 12 : 595-605, juillet-septembre 1960.

ECONOMOU, D.B. : The supremacy of law in the Greek government. Revue hellénique de droit international 14 : 148-165, janvier-décembre 1961.

ZEPOS, P.J. : The Greek legal system. Revue hellénique de droit international 14 : 1-13, janvier-décembre 1961.

MARKIANOS, D.J. : Griechische Rechtsprechung zum Familien- und Erbrecht des ZBG, 1946-1959. Zeitschrift für ausländisches und internationales Privatrecht 25, 26 : 69-148, 267-349, Heft 1, Heft 2, 1960, 1961.

STEFANOPOULOS, K.G. : Die Testamentserrichtung in Griechenland. Österreichische Juristen-Zeitung 16 : 376-383, 21. Juli 1961.

ZEPOS, P.J. : The historical and comparative background of the Greek civil code. Inter-American law review - Revista jurídica interamericana 3 : 285-299, July-December 1961.

ZEPOS, P.J. : Quinze années d'application du code civil hellénique, 1946-1961. Revue internationale de droit comparé 14 : 281-308, avril-juin 1962.

STEFANOPOULOS, K.G. : Gültigkeit, Eröffnung und Vollstreckung der Testamente in Griechenland. Österreichische Juristen-Zeitung 17 : 375-382, 17. Juli 1962.

PATRAS, L.P. : L'autorité en droit interne hellénique des traités internationaux. Revue hellénique de droit international 15 : 348-361, juillet-décembre 1962.

RAMMOS, G. : I mezza di impugnazione secondo il progetto del codice di procedura civile greco. Jus, Rivista di scienze giuridiche 13 : 572-583, luglio-dicembre 1962.

PAPAHATZIS, G. : La notion de la légalité en Grèce. Revue du droit public et de la science politique en France et à l'étranger 79 : 5-19, janvier-février 1963.

STEFANOPULOS, K.G. : Der Testamentsinhalt nach griechischem Rechte. Österreichische Juristen-Zeitung 18 : 233-236, 7. Mai 1963.

STEFANOPOULOS, K.G. : Die hereditatis petitio im griechischen Rechte. Österreichische Juristen-Zeitung 19 : 146-150, 172-176, 24. März, 7. April 1964.

GUAM

BARRETT, W.S., and FERENZ, W.S. : Peacetime martial law in Guam. California law review 48 : 1-30, March 1960.
With map.

GUATEMALA

VITERI, E.R. : Sociedades extranjeras - Requisitos para operar en el pais. Revista de la Facultad de ciencias jurídicas y sociales de Guatemala : 191-203, enero-junio 1961.

MURRAY, D.E. : The proposed code of criminal procedure of Guatemala. Louisiana law review 24 : 728-782, June 1964.

GUINEA

MANGIN, G. : Guinée. Annuaire de législation française et étrangère 9 : 238-240, 1960.

Constitution de la République de Guinée, 10 novembre 1958. Informations constitutionnelles et parlementaires 12 : 111-118, avril 1961.
Texte.

HAITI

LAMARRE, J.M. : Evolution et état du droit d'extradition en Haiti. Revue international de police criminelle 16 : 98-104, avril 1961.

HUNGARY

TIMÁR, I. : Příprava nového trestního zákoníka Mad'arské lidové republiky. Právník 99 : 40-55, číslo 1, 1960.
Penal code.

KATONA, Z. : Quelques traits généraux de la nouvelle loi sur le ministère public. Revue de droit hongrois : 5-12, no. 1, 1960.
Texte pp. 21-30.

La législation hongroise d'exception, 4 novembre 1956-31 décembre 1957. Documentation française, Notes et études documentaires : 1-26, no. 2657, 12 avril 1960.

EÖRSI, G. : A Magyar Népköztársaság polgári törvénykönyvének életbélépéséhez. Jogtudományi közlöny 15 : 312-319, június 1960.
Civil code.

Code civil de la République populaire hongroise. Revue de droit hongrois : 1-192, no. 2, 1960.

TIMÁR, I. : Le projet du code pénal de la République Populaire Hongroise. Revue de droit hongrois : 19-33, no. 3, 1960.

EÖRSI, G. : Réflexions autour de l'entrée en vigueur du code civil de la République Populair Hongroise. Revue de droit hongrois : 5-17, no. 3, 1960.

VILÁGHY, M. : A polgári jog szocialista elveinek alakulása a felszabadulás óta. Jogtodományi közlöny 15 : 349-361, július-augusztus 1960.
Civil law.

LEH, T. : La codification du droit coutumier hongrois. Revue internationale de droit comparé 12 : 559-573, juillet-septembre 1960.

BARACS, G. : Dissolution of marriage in Hungarian law. American journal of comparative law 9 : 471-481, summer 1960.

MIHALY, Z.M. : The role and activity of arbitration commissions in a communist economy - The Hungarian experience. American journal of comparative law 9 : 670-680, autumn 1960.

KHORVAT, T. : Nekotorye voprosy kodifikat͡sii ugolovnogo prava Vengrii. Pravovedenie (U.S.S.R.) 5 : 95-101, no. 1, 1961.

KÁDÁR, M. : Quelques remarques au sujet d'un article sur les aspects juridiques de la situation actuelle en Hongrie. Revue de droit hongrois : 42-53, no. 1, 1961.

KIRÁLY, T. : Les droits du prévenu dans la procédure pénale hongroise. Revue de droit hongrois : 31-41, no. 1, 1961.

TIMÁR, I. : La partie spéciale du projet du code pénal de la République Populaire Hongroise. Revue du droit hongrois : 5-18, no. 1, 1961.

VILÁGHY, M. : La première année du code civil dans la jurisprudence. Revue de droit hongrois : 5-20, no. 2, 1961.

SZÁSZY, S. : Das neue Zivilgesetzbuch der Ungarischen Volksrepublik. Rabels Zeitschrift für ausländisches und internationales Privatrecht 26 : 553-573, Heft 3, 1961.

SZIGETI, P. : Note sur la loi hongroise V de 1957 sur la nationalité. Journal du droit international 88 : 400-403, avril-juin 1961.
Texte en anglais aussi.

TIMÁR, I. : Le projet de code pénal de la République Populaire Hongroise. Revue de droit contemporain 8 : 97-113, juin 1961.

BARNA, P., and KHORVAT, T. : O puti͡akh razviti͡ia vengerskogo ugolovnogo prava. Sovetskoe godudarstvo i pravo 32 : 80-85, no. 1, i͡anvar' 1962.

MOLNÁR, L. : Les délits contre l'économie populaire dans le nouveau code pénal de la République Populaire Hongroise. Revue de droit hongrois : 17-31, no. 1, 1962.

Exposé ministériel des motifs accompagnant le projet du code pénal de la République Populaire Hongroise. Revue de droit hongrois : 13-31, no. 2, 1962.

Code pénal de la République Populaire Hongroise. Revue de droit hongrois : 1-129, no. 2, 1962.

MARTONYI, J. : La juridiction au service de la légalité de l'administration hongroise. Revue internationale des sciences administratives 28 : 269-281, no. 3, 1962.

FARAGÓ, L. : Das neue ungarische Erbrecht. Juristische Blätter 84 : 177-193, 7. April 1962.

NAGY, L. : Büntetö fellebbezési rendszerünk módosítása. Jogtudományi közlöny 17 : 439-450, szeptember 1962.

RACZ, G. : Le nouveau code pénal hongrois. Revue de science criminelle et de droit pénal comparé 17 : 705-721, octobre-décembre 1962.

SZABÓ, I. : Les traits généraux du système juridique de la démocratie populaire hongroise. Revue de droit international et de droit comparé 40 : 126-143, no. 2, 1963.

KIRÁLY, T. : Le rôle du défenseur dans la procédure pénale hongroise. Revue de droit hongrois : 5-12, no. 2, 1963.

KUSSBACH, F. : Besonderheiten im Ungarischen Zivilgesetzbuch. Osteuropa-Recht 9 : 43-52, März 1963.

SZIGLIGETI, V. : Protection de la famille dans la jurisprudence relative à la dissolution du mariage. Revue de droit hongrois : 57-75, no. 1, 1964.

TRAYTLER, E. : Les attentats aux moeurs dans le code pénal hongrois. Revue de droit hongrois : 19-41, no. 1, 1964.

MARCZALI, T.A. : Criminal law in Communist Hungary. Slavic review 23 : 92-102, March 1964.

LÉH, T. : Le droit international privé hongrois à la lumière des conventions bilatérales d'entraide judiciaire. Journal du droit international 91 : 523-540, juillet-septembre 1964.

LÁSZLÓ, J., and SCHÖNWALD, P. : A Btk. elötti büntetö ítélkezési gyakorlat az új büntetö törvény tükrében. Magyar jog 11 : 385-387, szeptember 1964.

ICELAND

THORARINSSON, T. : Les eaux territoriales de l'Islande. Revue de droit contemporain 7 : 251-263, juin 1960.

BAADE, H.W. : Das internationale uneheliche Kindschaftsrecht Islands. Ehe und Familie im privaten und öffentlichen Recht 7 : 341-344, August/September 1960.

INDIA

CADOUX, C. : Les droits fondamentaux de l'individu dans la constitution indienne et l'interprétation judiciaire. Revue du droit public et de la science politique en France et à l'étranger 76 : 544-615, mai-juin 1960.

RAO, K.V. : The companies amendment bill, 1959 - Joint select committee's report. Supreme court journal (Madras) 23 : 231-240, November 1960.

Marriage and divorce in India - Conflicting laws. Northwestern university law review 55 : 624-647, November-December 1960.

RAO, K.N. : Parliamentary approval of treaties in India. Indian year book of international affairs 9-10 : 22-39,1960-1961.

NATHANSON, N.L. : Indian constitutional laws in American perspective. Northwestern university law review 56 : 190-204, May-June 1961.

Amendements à la constitution de l'Inde. Documentation française, Notes et études documentaires : 1-17, no. 2796, 13 juillet 1961.

CHOWDHURY, S.R. : Equality before the law in India. Cambridge law journal: 223-238, November 1961.

ARORA, R.S. : Rise of the public corporation in India. Some constitutional aspects. Public law : 362-385, winter 1961.

MATHUR, R.N. : The constitutional position and powers of the president of the Indian Union. Supreme court journal (Madras) 26 : 15-18, January 1962.

SINGH, R. : Towards the better administration of divorce laws - a blue-print for marriage guidance and conciliation in India. Supreme court journal (Madras) 26 : 19-28, February 1962.

NAWAZ, M.K. : The problem of jurisdictional immunities of foreign states with particular reference to Indian state practice. Indian journal of international law 2 : 164-199, April 1962.

SAKENA, J.N. : The Extradition bill, 1961 - A critical study. Supreme court journal (Madras) 26 : 51-63, April 1962.

SATHE, S.P. : Some problems regarding the determining of citizenship in India. Supreme court journal (Madras) 26 : 67-78, May 1962.

MAHADEVAN, N. : The centenary of the Indian penal code. Supreme court journal (Madras) 26 : 100-102, June 1962.

SEERVAL, H.M. : Constitutional law of India. Law quarterly review 78 : 388-406, July 1962.

AGRAWALA, S.K. : Law of nations as interpreted and applied by Indian courts and legislature. Indian journal of international law 2 : 431-478, October 1962.

McDONALD, A.C. : An American looks at the Indian conflicts law of contracts. Indian year book of international affairs 11 : 76-87, 1962.

KAPUR, L.J. : The Supreme court of India. Jahrbuch des öffentlichen Rechts der Gegenwart 11 : 1-42, 1962.

FYZEE, A.A.A. : The impact of English law on the Shariat in India. Revue égyptienne de droit international - Egyptian review of international law 18 : 1-27, 1962.

SINGH, N., and NAWAZ, M.K. : The contemporary practice of India in the field of international law, 1961. International studies 4 : 74-101, 281-297; July 1962, January 1963.

BHARADVAJA, B. : Delegated legislation in India. Supreme court journal (Madras) 28 : 26-35, February 1963.

BANERJEE, D.N. : The Indian legislatures and the development of legislative power. Modern review 113 : 271-281, April 1963.

Company law reform. Calcutta weekly notes 67 : cxli-cxliv, 29 July 1963.

NAMBIYAR, M.K. : Seventeenth amendment of the constitution. Supreme court journal (Madras) 29 : 1-8, Pctober 1963.

RAMASESHAN, V. : Effect of war on contracts in Indian law. Indian year book of international affairs 12 : 231-255, 1963.

NAWAZ, M.K. : International law in the contemporary practice of India - Some perspectives. American society of international law, Proceedings 57 : 275-290, 1963.
Discussion pp. 290-293.

SAXENA, J.N. : India - The Extradition act, 1962. International and comparative law quarterly 13 : 116-138, January 1964.

GHOUSE, M. : Emergency provisions in the constitution of India - An appraisal. Modern review 115 : 97-106, February 1964.

JAIN, M.P. : Parliamentary control of delegated legislation in India. Public law : 33-59, 152-179 spring, summer 1964.

SINGH, N., and NAWAZ, M.K. : The contemporary practice of India in the field of international law, 1962. International studies 6 : 69-86, July 1964.
First of a series of articles.

JENA, B.B. : Thirteenth to sixteenth amendments of the Indian constitution - An autopsy. Modern review 116 : 112-118, August 1964.

RAMASESHAN, V. : State contracts in Indian law. Indian year book of international affairs 13/1 : 275-292, 1964.

INDONESIA

DOMKE, M. : Indonesian nationalization measures before foreign courts. American journal of international law 54 : 305-323, April 1960.

LEYSER, J. : Indonesia's nationalisation of Dutch enterprises and international law. Australian outlook 14 : 200-210, August 1960.

La costituzione della Repubblica Indonesiana, 1945. Oriente moderno 40 : 552-555, settembre 1960.

BAADE, H.W. : Indonesian nationalization measures before foreign courts - A reply. American journal of international law 54 : 801-835, October 1960.

GOUWGIOKSIONG : Law reform in Indonesia. Rabels Zeitschrift für ausländisches und internationales Privatrecht 26 : 535-553, Heft 3, 1961.

MOZINGO, D. : The Sino-Indonesian dual nationality treaty. Asian survey 1 : 25-31, December 1961.

LEV, D.S. : The Supreme court and adat inheritance law in Indonesia. American journal of comparative law 11 : 205-225, spring 1962.

IRAN

SARSHAR, M. : Law and lawyers and judicial institutions in Iran. Kanoun vokala dadgostari, Majaleye 14 : 1-8, no. 81, 1962.

Iranian civil code. Kanoun vokala dadgostari, Majaleye 14 : 22-30, no. 81, 1962.
First of a series of articles; Text also in French.

The Iranian commercial code. Kanoun vokala dadgostari, Majaleye - Iranian bar association journal 15 : 70-83, July-August 1963.
English text; First of a series of articles.

Code pénal. Kanoun Vokala dadgosti, Majaleye 15 : 33-40, no. 83, 1963.
Premier article d'une série.

Code de procédure civile iranien (suite). Kanoon vokala dadgosti, Majaleye - Iranian bar association journal 15 : 51-56, January-February 1964.

IRAQ

Al-WAHAB, I. : Tribal customary law and modern law in Iraq. International labour review, I.L.O. 89 : 19-28, January 1964.

The provisional Iraqi constitution. Hamizrah hehadash - The new East 14 : 379-386, no. 4, 1964.
Text in Hebrew.

The temporary constitution of the Republic of Iraq. Middle East forum 40 : 12-14, June 1964.

Constitution provisoire irakienne. Cahiers de l'Orient contemporain 21 : 345-353, no. 55, 1964.
29 avr. 1964.

IRELAND

HENCHY, S. : Precedent in the Irish supreme court. Modern law review 25 : 544-558, September 1962.

KNIGHT, M. : The Criminal justice act, 1964. Irish jurist 30 : 29-32, no. 3, 1964.

ISRAEL

GOTTSCHALK, R. : The development of the law of torts in Israel. Modern law review 24 : 345-354, May 1961.

SEARA VÁZQUEZ, M. : La ley no. 5710, de 1950 de Israel, sobre castigo a los nazis y sus colaboradores. Boletín del Instituto de derecho comparado de México 14 : 651-654, septiembre-diciembre 1961.

KLINGHOFFER, H. : Die Entstehung des Staates Israel. Jahrbuch des öffentlichen Rechts der Gegenwart 10 : 439-484, 1961.

MERON, T. : Public international law problems of the jurisdiction of the State of Israel. Journal du droit international 88 : 986-1063, octobre-décembre 1961.
Text also in French.

YADIN, U. : Reception and rejection of English law in Israel. International and comparative law quarterly 11 : 59-72, January 1962.

La ley de justicia militar de Israel. Revista española de derecho militar : 139-192, enero-junio 1962.

KLEYFF, M. : Le développement de la législation israélienne des anciens combattants et victimes de guerre et son influence sur la législation sociale en Israël. Cahiers de législation comparée des anciens combattants et victimes de guerre : 193-198, décembre 1962.

MARTÍN-RETORTILLO BAQUER, S. : La legislación de aguas en el Estado de Israel. Instituto de derecho comparado, Revista (Barcelona) : 7-31, enero-junio 1963.

LEHMANN, R. : Nationalité et religion en Israël - A propos de l'affaire Rufeisen (Le Père Daniel). Journal du droit international 90 : 694-717, juillet-septembre 1963.
Texte en anglais aussi.

PELLEY-KARP, J. : The Israeli statement of reasons act, 1958. American journal of comparative law 12 : 72-81, winter 1963.

LAUFER, J. : Israel's Supreme court - The first decade. Journal of legal education 17 : 43-62, no. 1, 1964.

BENTWICH, N. : The legal system of Israel. International and comparative law quarterly 13 : 236-255, January 1964.

EISENBERG, Y. : Independence of judges in the State of Israel. International commission of jurists, Journal 5 : 74-84, summer 1964.

ZELTNER, W. : The emerging legal system of Israel. Record of the Association of the bar of the city of New York 19 : 470-481, November 1964.

ITALY

MALTOPPI, A. : La delimitazione della zona di pesca riservata nella legislazione marittima italiana. Diritto marittimo 62 : 3-13, gennaio-marzo 1960.

MOSCONI, F. : La giurisprudenza italiana del dopoguerra in tema di espropriazioni estere. Diritto internazionale 14 : 170-187, no. 2, 1960.

BERNARDINI, A. : La reciprocità rispetto agli atti esecutivi e cautelari contro Stati esteri. Rivista di diritto internazionale 43 : 449-464, fasc. 3, 1960.

BRACCI, A. : Le norme di attuazione degli statuti per le regioni autonomia speciale. Studi senesi 72 : 212-245, no. 2, 1960.

CANSACCHI, G. : Osservazioni sul disegno di legge sulla cittadinanza italiana. Rivista di diritto internazionale 43 : 648-656, fasc. 4, 1960.

BALLARINO, T. : La doctrine italienne de droit international privé, 1958-1960. Università di Milano, Istituto di diritto internazionale e straniero ; Communicazioni e studi 11 : 507-619, 1960-1962.

LAMBERTI ZANARDI, P. : Les problèmes de droit international dans la jurisprudence italienne, 1958-1960. Università di Milano, Istituto di diritto internazionale e straniero ; Comunicazioni e studi 11 : 671-744, 1960-1962.

MIELE, M. : L'esecuzione nell'ordinamento italiano degli atti internazionali istitutivi della Comunità economica europea e dell'Euratom. Diritto internazionali 15 : parte la, 17-25, no. 1, 1961.

DEAN, F. : Il delitto di cui all'art. 244 c.p. e la nozione di atti ostili. Scuola positiva 66 : 301-339, fasc. 2, 1961.
Hostile acts against a foreign state.

UDINA, M. : Sull'efficacia delle norme delle comunità europee nell'ordinamento italiano. Diritto internazionale 15 : 123-131, no. 2, 1961.

UDINA, M. : Gli accordi internazionali in forma semplificata e la costituzione italiana. Rivista di diritto internazionale 44 : 201-219, fasc. 2, 1961.

CAVALLA, G.L. : Il delinquente per tendenza nella legislazione penale italiana. Rassegna di studi penitenziari (Italy) 11 : 153-163, marxo-aprile 1961.

SEIDL-HOHENVELDERN, I. : Die Vergleichskommissionen gemäss Art. 83 des Friedensvertrages mit Italien von 1947. Archiv des Völkerrechts 9 : 278-288, 3. Heft, September 1961.

KOJANEC, G. : La doctrine italienne de droit international public en 1959-1961. Università di Milano, Istituto di diritto internazionale e straniero; Comunicazioni e studi 11 : 355-506, 1960-1962.

GARCÍA CALDERÓN, M. : Sistema italiano de derecho internacional privado. Revista de derecho y ciencias políticas (Lima) 26 : 545-568, no. 3, 1962.

SESSO, R. : Osservazioni in tema di responsabilità penale del Presidente della Repubblica per reati comuni. Scuola positiva 67 : 459-467, fasc. 3, 1962.

CARPI, L. : I cittadini italiani del Dodecanesi e la nuova legge sulla cittadinanza italiana. Rivista di diritto internazionale 45 : 570-573, fasc. 4, 1962.

NATIONAL LAW - COUNTRIES

MORELLI, G. : Interpretazione del Concordato e irretroattività dell'articolo 5. Jus, Rivista di scienze giuridiche 13 : 228-238, giugno 1962.

BERNARDINI, A. : Accordo e contratto di sede tra Italia e FAO (Food and agriculture organisation). Rivista di diritto internazionale 46 : 26-40, fasc. 1, 1938.

BISCOTTINI, G. : I diritti fondamentali dello straniero. Diritto internazionale 17 : parte la, 10-29, no. 1, 1963.

TELCHINI, I. : La Cour constitutionnelle en Italie. Revue internationale de droit comparé 15 : 33-53, janvier-mars 1963.

PAU, G. : Deroga convenzionale alla giurisdizione italiana e competenza internazionale del giudice straniero. Rivista di diritto internazionale 46 : 576-587, fasc. 4, 1963.

PIZZI, A. : La défense de la liberté et des droits fondamentaux de l'homme dans la jurisprudence de la Cour constitutionnelle d'Italie. Commission internationale de juristes, Revue 4 : 305-326, 2e semestre 1963.

De NOVA, R. : New trends in Italian private international law. Law and contemporary problems 28 : 808-821, autumn 1963.

BOSCO, G. : La riforma dei codici. Nuova antologia 489 : 289-301, novembre 1963.

NUVOLONE, P. : Problemi concernenti la riforma del processo penale italiano. Schweizerische Zeitschrift für Strafrecht 80 : 1-7. Heft 1, 1964.

SANSO, B. : Sobre la exclusión de la responsabilidad contractual y de la responsabilidad por vicios ocultos en la legislación italiana y en la venezolana. Revista de la Facultad de derecho (Caracas) : 113-118, no. 28, 1964.

IVORY COAST

Constitution de la République de Côte d'Ivoire, 26 mars 1959. Informations constitutionnelles et parlementaires 11 : 13-26, janvier 1960.

MANGIN, G. : Côte d'Ivoire. Annuaire de législation française et étrangère 9 : 117-122, 1960.

Etudes juridiques sur la Côte d'Ivroire. Penant, Revue de droit des pays d'Afrique 71 : 629-785, novembre-décembre 1961.
Numéro spécial.

JAPAN

YOKOTA, K. : Renunciation of war in the new Japanese constitution - As interpreted by the Supreme court in the Sunakawa judgment. Japanese annual of international law 4 : 16-31, 1960.

TANAKA, K. : La démocratie et la justice au Japon. Commission internationale de juristes, Revue 2 : 7-19, hiver 1959-printemps/été 1960.

BLAKENEY, B.B. : A sketch of the development of Japanese law. Japan quarterly 7 : 491-506, October-December 1960.

YAMADA, R. : Some problems of recent Japanese precedents concerning foreign corporations. Japanese annual of international law 5 : 31-38, 1961.

A chronological list of treaties and other international agreements concluded by Japan in 1960. Japanese annual of international law 5 : 150-153, 1961.

SALWIN, L.N. : The new commercial code of Japan, symbol of gradual progress toward democratic goals. Georgetown law journal 50 : 478-512, spring 1962.

EGAWA, H. : Progress of revision of the private international law of Japan. Japanese annual of international law 6 : 1-6, 1962.

TAKANO, Y. : Post-war studies in public international law in Japan. Japanese annual of international law 6 : 79-94, 1962.

Post-war studies in private international law in Japan. Japanese annual of international law 6 : 95-106, 1962.

MATSUMOTO, K. : Problems of constitutional revision in Japan. Japanese annual of international law 6 : 63-78, 1962.

OUCHI, K. : Defamation and constitutional freedoms in Japan. American journal of comparative law 11 : 73-81, winter 1962.

KURIBAYASHI, T. : The Japanese legal system. Australian law journal 36 : 437-449, 30 April 1963.

MEHREN, A.T. von : The legal order in Japan's changing society - Some observations. Harvard law review 76 : 1170-1205, April 1963.

IKEHARA, S. : Nationality in the private international law of Japan. Japanese annual of international law 7 : 8-19, 1963.
Text pp. 20-23.

PREUSCHEN, D. von : Die Vollstreckung ausländischer Schiedssprüche in Japan nach dem Inkrafttreten des UN-Übereinkommens. Aussenwirtschaftsdienst des Betriebs-Beraters 10 : 112-113, 30. April 1964.

EGAWA, H. : International divorce jurisdiction in Japan. Japanese annual of international law 8 : 1-18, 1964.

TAKANO, Y. : Conclusion and validity of treaties in Japan - Constitution requirements. Japanese annual of international law 8 : 9-23, 1964.

KENYA

Constitution de Kenya - Ordonnance royale portant constitution du Kenya, prise en Conseil privé de 1958. Documentation française, Notes et études documentaires : 1-22, no. 2711, 3 novembre 1960.

ROWLANDS, J.S.S. : Notes on native law and custom in Kenya. Journal of African law 6 : 192-209, autumn 1962.

NYAMWEYA, J. : The constitution of Kenya. Civilisations 14 : 331-338, no. 4, 1964.
December 1963.

NATIONAL LAW - COUNTRIES

KUWAIT

Constitution de lEtat de Koweït, 11 novembre 1962. Informations constitutionnelles et parlementaires 15 : 169-193, octobre 1964.

KOREA

Constitution de la République de Corée, 17 juillet 1948-29 novembre 1960. Informations constitutionnelles et parlementaires 12 : 83-110, avril 1961. Texte.

KIM, C. : Les articles concernant la famille (parenté) - Code civil de la République de Corée. Seoul law journal 3 : 1-49, (176-224), July 1961.

Constitution de la République de Corée, 17 juillet 1948-29 novembre 1960. Documentation française, Notes et études documentaires : 1-15, no. 2815, 14 septembre 1961. Texte.

Constitución de la República de Corea, 17 de julio de 1948-29 noviembre de 1960. Información jurídica (Spain) : 23-42, noviembre-diciembre 1962.

KWAK, Y.-c. : The Korean new civil code. Journal of social sciences and humanities : 1-23, December 1962.

HAHM, P.-c. ; The function of law in an underdeveloped Asian country - An interpretation of the Korean situation. Journal of sciences and humanities : 29-44, June 1963.

HAHM, P.-c. : The Korean people and their property rights. American journal of comparative law 12 : 61-71, winter 1963.

YUN, K.-s. : Die Verfassungsentwicklung der Republik Korea seit 1948. Jahrbuch des öffentlichen Rechts der Gegenwart 12 : 461-491, 1963. English text of constitution pp. 492-503.

ROE, M.-j.: The problem of proving foreign law in Korean courts - A comparative study. Indian year book of international affairs 13/1 : 151-173, 1964.

LEBANON

Statuts personnels pour les communautés non musulmanes. Revue judiciaire libanaise (Lebanon) 19 : 1-428, janvier-avril 1963. Texte en arabe.

FAYAD, A. : Le fondement de la responsabilité de la puissance publique en droit libanais. Annales de la Faculté de droit des sciences économiques de Beyrouth, Etudes de droit libanais 45 : 468-481, juillet-décembre 1964.

HABACHY, S. : The republican institutions of Lebanon, its constitution. American journal of comparative law 13 : 594-604, autumn 1964.

LIBERIA

PIERRE, J.A.A. : Schéma de l'organisation judiciaire du Libéria. Penant, Revue de droit des pays d'Afrique 71 : 503-505, septembre-octobre 1961.

LIBYA

GAJA, G. : Cittadinanza - Italiani libici, residenza in Italia, cittadinanza italiana. Foro italiano 87 : parte la, 2128-2132, dicembre 1962.

LIECHTENSTEIN

SIMONIN, P.H. : De certains aspects de droit civil de la Principauté de Liechtenstein. Société belge d'études et d'expansion, Revue 59 : 148-156, janvier-février 1960.

SIMONIN, P.H. : De certains aspects du croit civil de la principauté de Liechtenstein. Revue de science financière 52 : 590-598, juillet-septembre 1960.

LUXEMBOURG

BERNECKER, D. : Internationales Privat- und Prozessrecht im Grossherzogtum Luxemburg. Rabels Zeitschrift für ausländisches und internationales Privatrecht 27 : 263-346, Heft 2, 1962.

La constitution du Grand-Duché de Luxembourg du 17 octobre 1868, modifiée par les lois des 15 mai 1919... et 25 octobre 1956. Documentation française, Notes et études documentaires : 53-61. no. 3134, 6 novembre 1964. Texte.

MALAGASY REPUBLIC

MANGIN, G. : Madagascar. Annuaire de législation française et étrangère 9 : 256-276, 1960.

Constitution de la République Malgache, 29 avril 1959. Documentation française, Notes et études documentaires : 52-61, no. 2737, 23 décembre 1960.

BILBAO, R. : L'organisation judiciaire dans la République Malgache. Penant, Revue de droit des pays d'Afrique 71 : 47-55, janvier-mars 1961.

TERRÉ, F. : A propos de la nationalité malgache. Penant, Revue de droit des pays d'Afrique 71 : 339-346, juin-août 1961.

BLANC, P. : Les réformes malgaches. Revue de droit despays d'Afrique 71 : 445-458, juin-août 1961. Régime domanial et foncier.

BILBAO, R. : Les tendances du droit pénal malgache. Penant, Revue de droit des pays d'Afrique 71 ; 459-462, juin-août 1961.

RAMANGASOAVINA, A. : Du droit coutumier aux codes modernes malgaches. Penant, Revue de droit des pays d'Afrique 72 : 327-347, juin 1962.

MURACCIOLE, L. : La révision de la constitution malgache réalisée pa la loi du 6 juin 1962. Revue juridique et politique d'outre-mer 16 : 425-429, juillet-septembre 1962. Texte des articles modifiés pp. 428-435.

BILBAO, R. : Droit pñal et procédure pénale malgaches. Penant, Revue de droit des pays d'Afrique 74 : 441-457, octobre-décembre 1964.

NATIONAL LAW - COUNTRIES

MALAWAI

ROBERTS, S. : Matrilineal family law and custom in Malawi - A comparison of two systems. Journal of African law 8 : 76-90, summer 1964.

MALAYSIA

ATHULATHMUDALI, L.W. : L'internement administratif dans la Fédération de Malaisie. Commission internationale de juristes, Revue 3 : 103-115, 2e semestre 1961.

BARTHOLOMEW, G.W. : The application of Shari'a in Singapore. American journal of comparative law 13 : 385-413, summer 1964.

SHERIDAN, L.A. : Constitutional problems of Malaysia. International and comparative law quarterly 13 : 1349-1367, October 1964.

MALI

MANGIN, G. : Mali. Annuaire de législation française et étrangère 9 : 277-280, 1960.

Constitution de la République du Mali. Documentation française, Notes et études documentaires : 59-65, no. 2739, 13 janvier 1961.

Les constitutions des Etats africains d'expression française (Suite) - République Soudanaise. Revue juridique et politique d'outre-mer 15 : juillet-septembre 1961.
Juillet 1960.

Les constitutions des Etats africains d'expression française (Suite) - Fédération du Mali. Revue juridique et politique d'outre-mer 15 : 489-512, juillet-septembre 1961.
Janvier 1959 et juin 1960.

DECHEIX, P. : Le code de la nationalité malienne. Penant, Revue de droit des pays d'Afrique 73 : 300-314, juin-septembre 1963.

MAURITANIA

La constitution de la Républiqe Islamique de Mauritanie, 22 mars 1959. Documentation française, Notes et études documentaires : 46-59, no. 2687, 29 juillet 1960.
Texte.

MANGIN, G. : Mauritanie. Annuaire de législation française et étrangère 9 : 281-283, 1960.

BLANC, P. : La réforme mauritanienne. Penant, Revue de droit des pays d'Afrique 71 : 312-319, avril-mai 1961.
Régime domanial et foncier.

Les constitutions des Etats africains d'expression française (Suite) - République Islamique de Mauritanie. Revue juridique et politique d'outre-mer 15 : 439-445, juillet-septembre 1961.
Mai 1961.

JEOL, M. : La réforme de la justice en République Islamique de Mauritanie. Penant, Revue de droit des pays d'Afrique 72 : 193-204, avril-mai 1962.

MEXICO

OUENTE y F., A. : La situación legal de la plataforma continental mexicana y de los zócolos submarinos de sus islas. Crédito 19 : 11-16, mayo 1960.

ALCALA ZAMORA y CASTILLO, N. : Unificación de los códigos procesales mexicanos tanto civiles como penales. Criminalia 26 : 594-628, septiembre 1960.

BARRERA GRAF, J. : La sociedad anónima - Evolución y algunos problemas en derecho mexicano. Boletín del Instituto de derecho comparado de méxico 14 : 3-28, enero-abril 1961.

BERKE, J.R. : Efectus de las sentencias de divorcio pronuniadas por tribunales mexicanos en el Estado de Nueva York. Boletín del Instituto de derecho comparado de México 14 : 281-291, mayo-agosto 1961.

SEPULVEDA, C. : Peculiaridades de las licencias de uso de marcas en el derecho mexicano. Boletín del instituto de derecho comparado de México 14 : 629-648, septiembre-diciembre 1961.

MANTILLA MOLENA, R. L. : Reseña de la legislación, la literatura y la jurisprudencia mejicanas en 1960. Revista de derech privado (Madrid) 45 : 997-1004, noviembre 1961.

SIQUEIROS, J.L. : Ley aplicable al estado civil de los extranjeros en México - Federal o estatal? Boletín del Instituto de derecho comparado de México 15 : 345-354, mayo-agosto 1962.

PIÑA y PALACIOS, J. : El ministerio público en México. Criminalia 29 : 196-208, 30 abril 1963.

CABRERA, L., and HEADRICK, W.C. : Notes on judicial review in Mexico, and the United States. Inter-American law review - Revista jurídica interamericana 5 : 253-276, July-December 1963.

CARRANCÁ y TRUJILLO, R. : Un nuevo código penal local a la vista y urgencia de un código penal federal. Criminalia 29 : 868-895, 31 diciembre 1963.

PLOSCOWE, M. : La validez de los divorcios mexicanos. Boletín del Instituto de derecho comparado de México 17 : 367-377, mayo-agosto 1964.

MONACO

Constitution de la Principauté de Monaco, 17 décembre 1962. Informations constitutionnelles et parlementaires 14 : 65-79, avril 1963.

Constitution de la Principauté de Monaco, 17 decembre 1962. Documentation française, Notes et études documentaires : 1-10, 14 octobre 1963.

FRANÇOIS, N.P. : Réflexions sur le nouveau code de procédure pénale monégasque. Revue de science criminelle et de droit pénal comparé 19 : 317-323, avril -juin 1964.

MONGOLIA

SCHULTZ, L. : Die neue Verfassung der Mongolischen Volksrepublik. Osteuropa-Recht 8 : 45-59, März 1962.
July 1960.

Verfassung der Mongolischen Volksrepublik von 1960. Osteuropa-Recht 6 : 249-263, Dezember 1960.
Text in Russian.

DAMDIN, M. : Le caractère démocratique de la législation en République populaire de Mongolie. Revue de droit contemporain 7 : 118-125, décembre 1960.

GINSBURGS, G. : A comparative commentary on the criminal code of the Mongolian People's Republic, General part. Osteuropa-Recht 7 : 42-65, Januar-Juni 1961.

GINSBURGS, G., and PIERCE, R.A. : Revolutionary law reform in Outer Mongolia - A study in the impact of Soviet legal doctrine on a backward society. Law in Eastern Europe : 207-252, No. 7, 1962.

MARKELOW, W.N. : Über das neue Strafgesetzbuch der Mongolischen Volksrepublik. Staat und Recht 11 : 2028-2042, November 1962.

OLIVIER, J. : La première constitution de la République populaire Mongole. Est et Ouest 16 : 17-18, 16-31 décembre 1964.

MOROCCO

BARREDA TREVIÑO, C. : El código de justicia militar de las fuerzas armadas reales de Marruecos. Revista española de derecho militar : 211-252, enero-junio 1960.

DECROUX, P. : Quelques réflexions sur le code de la nationalité marocaine. Revue juridique et politique d'outre-mer 15 : 63-74, janvier-mars 1961.

COLOMER, A. : La tutelle des mineurs dans la Moudawwana ou code du statut personnel marocain. Revue internationale de droit comparé 13 : 327-337, avril-juin 1961.

Fundamental law of Morocco. Middle East journal 15 : 326-328, summer 1961.

COLOMER, A. : Le code du statut personnel marocain, la Moudawwana. Revue algérienne, tunisienne et marocaine de législation et de jurisprudence : Doctrine 77 : 79-82, juillet-août 1961.

Loi fondamentale du royaume du Maroc, 2 juin 1961. Informations constitutionnelles et parlementaires 13 : 106-108, avril 1962.

BOURELY, M. : Le droit international privé du Maroc indépendant. Revue critique de droit international privé 51 : 211-246, avril-juin 1962.

La costituzione del Marocco. Oriente moderno 42 : 909-916, dicembre 1962.
Approved the 7 December 1962.

Constitution du Royaume du Maroc, 7 décembre 1962. Informations constitutionnelles et parlementaires 14 : 5-19, janvier 1963.
Texte.

La constitution du Royaume du Maroc, 7 décembre 1962. Documentation française, Notes et études documentaires : 1-11, no. 2962, 9 février 1963.

LAZARÓ, A. : La nueva constitución del reino de Marruecos. Revista de estudios políticos : 127-138, septiembre-octubre 1963.

DECROUX, P. : Condition civile actuelle des étrangers au Maroc. Revue juridique et politique - Indépendance et coopération 18 : 585-604, octobre-décembre 1964.

NEPAL

MISRA, R.K. : The constitution of Nepal. Supreme court journal (Madras) 23 : 207-224, October 1960.

NETHERLANDS

CZAPSKI, G. : Gesetzgebung der Niederlande auf dem Gebiet des Privatrechts 1954-1959. Zeitschrift für ausländisches und internationales Privatrecht 25 : 289-304, Heft 2, 1960.

POELJE, G.A. van : Le Conseil d'Etat néerlandais, un exemple pour les Etats nouveaux. Revue internationale des sciences administratives 28 : 406-414, no. 4, 1962.

DORHOUT MEES, T.J. : Le projet d'un nouveau code civil néerlandais. Zeitschrift für schweizerisches Recht 81/1 : 533-539, Heft 4, 1962.

EMDE BOAS, M.J. van : La Convention européenne de sauvegarde des droits de l'homme et des libertés fondamentales dans la jurisprudence néerlandaise. Annuaire européen - European yearbook 10/1 : 226-257, 1962.

RÖLING, B.V.A. : Het volkenrecht en het nationale strafrecht. Tijdschrift voor strafrecht 72 : 378-398, afl- 5-6, 1963.

PANHUYS, H.F. van : The Netherlands constitution and international law. American journal of international law 58 : 88-108, January 1964.

ALEXANDER, W. : L'adoption d'enfants grecs aux Pays-Bas. Revue hellénique de droit international 17 : 50-61, janvier-juin 1964.

NEW GUINEA

DERHAM, D.P. : Law and custom in the Australian territory of Papua abd Bew Guinea. University of Chicago law review 30 : 495-506, spring 1963.

MATTES, J.R. : Sources of law in Papua and New Guinea. Australian law journal 37 : 148-153, September 26, 1963.

NEW ZEALAND

The proceedings of the eleventh Dominion legal conference, Wellington, April 19-22, 1960. New Zealand law journal 36 : 96-207, 24 May 1960.

DAVIS, A.G. : Le Commissaire parlementaire en Nouvelle-Zélande. Commission internationale de juristes, Revue 4 : 55-67, ler semestre 1962.

New Zealand law conference, Auckland, 16-19 April 1963. New Zealand law journal : 153-344, 4 June 1963.
Special issue.

NIGER

MANGIN, G. : Niger. Annuaire de législation française et étrangère 9 : 284-287, 1960.

Les constitutions des Etats africains d'expression française (Suite) - République du Niger. Revue juridique et politique d'outre-mer 15 : 445-452, juillet-septembre 1961.
November 1960.

NIGERIA

AJAYI, F.A. : The interaction of English law with customary law in Western Nigeria. Journal of African law 4 : 40-50, spring 1960.

Criminal law reform in Northern Nigeria. Modern law review 24 : 604-615, September 1961.
Series of articles.

Constitution de la Fédération du Nigéria, ler octobre 1960. Informations constitutionnelles et parlementaires 13 : 109-153, avril 1962.

La constitution de la Fédération du Nigéria, ler octobre 1960. Documentation française, Notes et études documentaires : 1-50, no. 2891, 31 mai 1962.
Texte.

DAVIES, S. G. : Nigeria - Some recent decisions on the constitution. International and comparative law quarterly 11 : 919-936, October 1962.

ANDERSON, J.N.D. : Return visit to Nigeria - Judicial and legal developments in the Norther Region. International and comparative law quarterly 12 : 282-294, January 1963.

SCHÜTZE, R.A. : Die Anerkennung und Vollstreckung ausländischer Zivilurteile in Nigeria. Juristische Blätter 85 : 563-565, 16. November 1963.

COLE, R.T. : Die Unabhängigkeits-Verfassung des Bundesstaates Nigeria. Jahrbuch des öffentlichen Rechts der Gegenwart 12 : 417-435, 1963.
English text of constitution pp. 436-459.

RICHARDSON, S. S. : "Opting out ", an experiment with jurisdiction in Northern Nigeria. Journal of African law 8 : 20-28, spring 1964.

NWOGUGU, E.I. : Legitimacy in Nigerian law. Journal of African law 8 : 91-105, summer 1964.

SERTORIO, G. : L'evoluzione costituzionale della Nigeria. Africa (Rome) 19 : 120-132, luglio-settembre 1964.

NORWAY

CASTBERG, F. : Die Entwicklung des Verfassungsrechtes in Norwegen. Jahrbuch des öffentlichen Rechts der Gegenwart 10 : 427-437, 1961.

WILBERG, I. : Some aspects of the principle of ministerial responsibility in Norway. Scandinavian studies in law 8 : 243-264, 1964.

PAKISTAN

Constitution du Pakistan, 27 octobre 1959. Documentation française, Notes et études documentaires : 1-28, no. 2703, 28 septembre 1960.
Texte.

COURBE COURTEMANCHE, N. : La nueva ley pakistaní de la familia musulmana. Revista de estudios políticos : 201-209, marzo-abril 1962.

GUDOSHNIKOV, L.M. : Novaîa konstitutsiîa Pakistana. Sovenskoe gosudarstvo i pravo 32 : 129-133, no. 10, oktîabr' 1962.

ISLAM, K. : Pakistan's new dispensation. Commonwealth journal 5 : 279-283, November-December 1962.

La costituzione della Republica del Pakistan, 1 marzo 1962. Oriente moderne 43 : 223-281, aprile-maggio 1963.
Text.

COURBE, N. : La constitution de la République du Pakistan du ler mars 1962. Revue du droit public et de la science politique en France et à l'étranger 79 : 453-476, mai-juin 1963.

NEWMAN, K.J. : Entstehung und verfassungsrechtliche Entwicklung von Pakistan, 1947-1963. Jahrbuch des öffentlichen Rechts der Gegenwart 13 : 139-221, 1964.
Text of the constitution, 1st March 1962, pp. 222-242.

PAPUA

DERHAM, D.P. : Law and custom in the Australian territory of Papua and New Guinea. University of Chicago law review 30 : 495-506, spring 1963.

MATTES, J.R. : Sources of law in Papua and New Guinea. Australian law journal 37 : 148-153, September 26 1963.

PERU

SANCHEZ PALACIOS, M. : Las sentencias expedias en el extranjero en la ley peruana. Revista de derecho y ciencias políticas 24 : 5-18, nos. 1-2, 1960.

RADA, D.G. : Comentarios al código de procedimentos penales (Contd.). Revista de derecho y ciencias políticas (Lima) 26 : 5-43, no. 1, 1962.

MacLEAN, R. : Las personas jurídicas en el derecho internacional privado argentino y peruano. Boletín del Instituto de derecho comparado de México 15 : 299-343, mayo-agosto 1962.

CASTANEDA, J.E. : Teoría genereal de los contratos - Los contratos. Revista de derecho y ciencias políticas (Lima) 28 : 249-316, núm. 1, 1964.
First of a series of articles.

Código de procidimiento penal de Perú. Información jurídica (Spain) : 3-65, mayo-junio 1964.

PHILIPPINES

BAUTISTA, E.B. : International law. Philippine law journal 35 : 754-760, January 1960.

FERNANDEZ, P.V. : Sixty years of Philippine law. Philippine law journal 35 : 1389-1411, November 1960.

AQUINO, R.C. : The Filippino dream or national progress through law since the inauguration of the Republic. Philippine law journal 36 : 314-360, July 1961.

GUEVARA, S. : The Philippine corporation law viewed from the outside. Phillipine law journal 36 : 530-555, November 1961.

Is Philippine legislative action necessary on twelve ECAF-listed problems of commercial arbitration ? Philippine law journal 38 : 648-727, December 1963.
Texts pp. 728-735.

VENTURINI, V.G. : Joint stock companies under Philippine law journal 39 : 371-443, September 1964.

SOLIDUM, A. : Changes in criminal procedure under the new rules of court. Philippine law journal 39 : 463-473, September 1964.

POLAND

LASOK, D. : A legal concept of marriage and divorce - A comparative study of Polish and Western family law. International and comparative law quarterly 9 : 53-95, January 1960.

SIEDLECKI, W. : Projekt kodeksu postepowania cywilnego PRL. Państwo i prawo 15 : 447-458, marzec 1960.
Summaries in English, French and Russian.

GRODECKI, J.K. : State economic arbitration in Poland. International and comparative law quarterly 9 : 177-190, April 1960.

BREDIN, J.D. : Table ronde sur "Les problèmes de l'organisation judiciaire en Pologne." Revue internationale de droit comparé 12 : 385-395, avril-juin 1960.
Conférence de J. Jodlowski.

JODLOWSKI, J. : Les principes de la procédure civile polonaise. Revue internationale de droit comparé 12 : 369-384, avril-juin 1960.

WASILKOWSKI, J. : Codification du droit civil en Pologne. Perspectives polonaises 3 : 12-20, juillet 1960.

PIATOWSKI, J.S. : L'égalité des droits des époux et le régime de la communauté en droit polonais. Revue internationale de droit comparé 12 : 500-523, juillet-septembre 1960.

ROZMARYN, S. : La loi, le règlement et l'arrêté dans le droit constitutionnel polonais. Revue internationale de droit comparé 13 : 494-506, juillet-septembre 1961.

CASTAGNÉ, J. : La règle de la double subordination dans la république populaire de Pologne. Revue du droit public et de la science politique en France et à l'étranger 77 : 59-98, janvier-février 1961.

RODE, Z.R. : The American-Polish claims agreement of of 1960. American journal of international law 55 : 452-459, April 1961.

PLAWSKI, S. : Il diritto penale della Repubblica Popolare di Polonia. Scuola positiva 67 : 39-48, fasc. 1, 1962.

NAHLIK, S.E. : Osobowe klauzule dyplomatyczne - Konwencja wiedeńska 1961 a ustawodawstwo polskie. Państwo i prawo 17 : 236-256, luty 1962.
Personal diplomatic clauses; Summaries in English, French and Russia.

Gesetz über den Obersten Gerichtshof der Vr Polen vom 15-Februar 1962. Wiener Quellenhefte zur Ostkunde, Recht; Aktuelle Texte : 21-32, Heft 2, 1962.

JAKUBOWSKI, J. : Zobowiązania z umów w projekcie nowej ustawy o prawie prywatnym miedzynarodnowym. Państwo i prawo 17 : 445-453, marzec 1962.
Contractual obligations in draft new international private law act; Summaries in English, French and Russia.

RESICH, Z. : Ustawa o Sądzie najwyższym. Państwo i prawo 17 : 773-781, maj-czerwiec 1962.
Supreme court act; Summaries in English, French and Russian.

SAWICKI, J. : Vers une nouvelle codification pénale. Perspectives polonaises 5 : 12-19, juin 1962.

GELBERG, L. : Nowa ustawa o obywatelstwie polskim. Państwo i prawo 17 : 334-342, sierpień-wrzesień. 1962.
New nationality act; Summaries in English, French and Russian.

NAHLIK, S.E. : Les clauses diplomatiques personnelles - La Convention de Vienne 1961 et la législation polonaise. Annuaire polonais des affaires internationales : 121-154, 1962.

ROZMARYN, S. : Organisation des travaux de codification dans la République Populaire de Pologne. Revue de droit international et de droit comparé 39 : 570-588, no. 3, 1962.

CZACHORSKI, W. : Nouveau projet de code civil polonais, rédaction de 1961. Pays communistes 3 : 413-427, décembre 1962.

USCHAKOW, A. : Das System der Volksräte in Polen. Osteuropa-Recht 8 : 265-291, Dezember 1962.

GÓRECKI, J. : Matrimonial property in Poland. Modern law review 26 : 156-173, March 1963.

SZPUNAR, A. : La responsabilité civile dans le projet de nouveau code polonais. Revue internationale de droit comparé 15 : 19-29, janvier-mars 1963.

CASTAGNÉ, J. : Les défenseurs de l'intérêt social dans la procédure administrative non contenieuse de la République Populaire de Pologne. Revue du droit public et de la science politique en France et à l'étranger 79 : 177-204, mars-avril 1963.

KAFARSKI, A. : Na marginesie "Przestepstw gospodarczych" w projekcie kodeksu karnego. Przglad ustawodawstwa gospodarczego 16 : 125-128, maj 1963.

SAWICKI, J. : Projekt Kodeksu Karnego z 1962 r, - Założenia, technika, zasady. Państwo i prawo 18 : 214-224, luty 1963.
Draft criminal code; Summaries in English, Fremch amd Russian; See also pp. 225-239.

MODLINSKI, E. : Les tribunaux ouvriers dans les pays socialistes et l'expérience polonaise. Revue internationale de droit comparé 15 : 669-686, octobre-décembre 1963.

RESICH, Z. : The organization of courts in the Polish people's Republic. Droit polonais contemporain : 9-16, no. 3, 1964.

LITWIN, J. : Kodeks cywilny a prawo administracyjne. Przeglad ustawodawstwa gospodarczego 17 : 241-248, paźziernik 1964.

Schrifttum ausserhalb des Ostblocks zum Recht der Volksrepublik Polen, seit 1954. Osteuropa-Recht 10 : 300-310, Dezember 1964.

PORTUGAL

Portugal - Amendements à la constitution, 29 août 1959. Informations constitutionnelles et parlementaires 11 : 47-52, janvier 1960.

RAU, H. : Portugal - Scheidung kanonischer Ehen von Ausländern. Rabels Zeitschrift für ausländisches und internationales Privatrecht 26 : 114-136, Heft 1, 1961.

Discurso proferido por Sua Excelência o Ministro da justiça... em 11 de junho de 1961. Ministério da justiça, Boletim (Portugal) : 5-15, julho 1961.
Reform of civil code.

Código de processo civil. Ministério da justiça, Boletim (Portugal) : 5-84, dezembro 1962.
Revised text.

Nota informativa sobre o projecto do código penal. Ministério de justiça, Boletim (Portugal) : 5-143, junho 1963.

The revision of the organic law of the overseas provinces. Centre portugais d'informations : 1-6, 31 July 1963.

RUMANIA

GEILKE, G. : Rechtsprobleme Nordsieben bürgens im Lichte des rumänischen Gesetzes Nr. 260 vom 4. April 1945. Jahrbuch für internationales Recht 9 : 240-248, Heft 2/3, 1961.
Legal texts pp. 249-263.

ILIESCU, N. : Infracţiunile ce privesc avutul obştesc în sistemul codului penal al R.P.R. Studii şi cercetări juridice 5 : 657-679, no. 4, 1960.
Summaries in French and Russian.

CHRISTENSON, A.G. : The United States-Rumanian claims settlement agreement of 30 March 1960. American journal of international law 55 : 617-636, July 1961.

VENIAMIN, V. : Le droit public et l'organisation judiciaire de la Roumanie d'après-guerre. Law in Eastern Europe : 82-166, no. 7, 1962.

EREMIA, M.I. : Numele de familie al persoanei căsătorite, precum şi cel al persoanei a cărei căsătorie s-a desfăcut. Studii şi cercetări juridice 8 : 169-181, nr. 2, 1963.
Names of married and formerly married persons; Summaries in French and Russian.

Caracterul profund reacţionar al legislaţiei dictaturi militare-fasciste din Romînia - Influente naziste asupra acestei legislaţii. Studii şi cercetări judice 8 : 347-382, nr. 3, 1963.
Summaries in French and Russian.

POPESCU, T.R. : Das eheliche Güterrecht in der Rumänischen Volksrepublik. Zeitschrift für das gesamte Familienrecht 10 : 275-278, Juli 1963.

RADEL, S. : Corelaţia dintre esenţa şi forma statului democrat-popular romîn in fazele sale successive de dezvoltare. Studii şi cercetări juridice 9 : 7-31, no. 1, 1964.

LEPADATESCO, M. : La Grande assemblée nationale, organe suprême du pouvoir d'Etat dans la République populaire roumaine. Revue roumaine des sciences sociales, Série de sciences juridiques 8 : 19-36, no. 1, 1964.

IONASCO, T. : La transmission du droit de propriété, la constitution et la transmission des autres droits réels de type nouveau en droit roumain. Revue roumaine des sciences sociales, Série de sciences juridiques 8 : 3-18, no. 1, 1964.

SALVADOR

ENRIQUE SILVA, J. : La reforma penal en El Salvador. Criminalia 30 : 690-693, noviembre 1964.

SAMOA

KELM, H. : Die Eigentumsrechte auf Samoa, Polynesien. Zeitschrift für vergleichende Rechtswissenschaft 64 : 131-228, 1962.
Bibliography pp. 228-230.

SENEGAL

MANGIN, G. : Sénégal. Annuaire de législation française et étrangère 9 : 314-321, 1960.

Constitution de la République du Sénégal, 25 août 1960. Documentation française, Notes et études documentaires : 42-48, no. 2754, 22 février 1961.

ARBOUSSIER. G. d' : Le Sénégal - Exemple africain d'organisation judiciaire. Penant, Revue de droit des pays d'Afrique 71 : 171-180, avril-mai 1961.

M'BAYE, K. : L'attribution de la nationalité "Jure soli" et l'option de nationalité dans la loi sénégalaise du 7 mars 1961. Penant, Revue de droit des pays d'Afrique 71 : 347-353, juin-août 1961.

GUILLABERT, A. : La Cour suprême du Sénégal. Penant, Revue de droit des pays d'Afrique 71 : 496-502, septembre-octobre 1961.

AURILLAC, M. : La Cour suprême du Sénégal. France, Conseil d'Etat; Etudes et documents 15 : 207-222, 1961.
Textes pp. 223-250.

DECOTTIGNIES, R. : Réflexions sur le projet de code sénégalais des obligations. Annales africaines : 171-180, no. 1, 1962.

AURILLAC, M. : Les aspects juridiques du socialisme sénégalais. Annales africaines : 93-112, no. 1, 1962.

DECOTTIGNIES, R. : Réflexions sur le projet de code sénégalais des obligations. Penant, Revue de droit des pays d'Afrique 72 : 497-507, septembre-octobre 1962.

FORSTER, I. : La place de la coutume indigène dans le droit moderne de la République du Sénégal. Boletim da faculdade de direito (Coimbra) 38 : 91-115, 1962.

GAUTRON, J.C. : Sur quelques aspects de la succession d'Etats au Sénégal. Annuaire française de droit international 8 : 836-863, 1962.

MURACCIOLE, L. : La constitution de la République du Sénégal du 7 mars 1963. Revue juridique et politique d'outre-mer 17 : 138-148, janvier-mars 1963.
Texte pp. 148-160.

LAVROFF, D.G. : Sénégal - La constitution du 3 mars 1963. Revue du droit public et de la science politique en France et à l'étranger 79 : 207-228, mars-avril 1963.
Texte pp. 229-242.

Constitution de la République du Sénégal, 3 mars 1963. Informations constitutionnelles et parlementaires 14 : 80-97, avril 1963.
Texte.

FARNSWORTH, E.A. : Le nouveau code des obligations du Sénégal. Annales africaines : 73-90, 1963.

FORSTER, J. : La place de la coutume indigène dans le droit moderne de la République du Sénégal. Zeitschrift für vergleichende Rechtswissenschaft 66 : 1-18, Januar 1964.

FARNSWORTH, E.A. : Law reform in a developing country - A new code of obligations for Senegal. Journal of African law 8 : 6-19, spring 1964.

DECOTTIGNIES, R. : L'apport européen dans l'élaboration du droit privé sénégalais. Annales africaines : 79-113, 1964.

SOMALIA

MALINTOPPI, A. : La costituzione somala e il diritto internazionale. Rivista di diritto internazionale 44 : 270-275, fasc. 2, 1961.

Constitution de la République de Somalie, ler juillet 1960. Documentation française, Notes et études documentaires : 1-14, no. 3132, 30 octobre 1964.
Texte.

MUHAMMAD, N. : The rule of law in the Somali Republic. International commission of jurists, Journal 5 : 275-302, winter 1964.

SOUTH AFRICA

CORNELL, M. : The statutory background of apartheid - A chronological survey of South African legislation. World to-day 16 : 181-194, May 1960.

ABRAMOWITZ, N. : Legal aid in South Africa. South African law journal 77 : 351-367, August 1960.

HAHLO, H.R. : ...And save us from codification. South African law journal 77 : 432-437, November 1960.

HAHLO, H.R. : The trust in South African law. Inter-American law review - Revista jurídica interamericana 2 : 229-242, July-December 1960.

KAHN, E. : The new constitution. South African law journal 78 : 244-281, August 1961.

MILLNER, M.A. : Apartheid and the South African courts. Current legal problems 14 : 280-306, 1961.

KAHN, E. : Constitutional and administrative law. Annual survey of South African law : 1-67, 1961.

LANDIS, E.S. : South African apartheid legislation. Yale law journal 71 : 1-52, 437-500, November 1961, January 1962.

GEY van PITTIUS, E.F.W. : The Transvaal's experiment in local government. Public administration 40 : 65-68, spring 1962.

Constitution de la République d'Afrique du Sud, 31 mai 1961. Documentation française, Notes et études documentaires : 1-23, no. 2928, 15 octobre 1962.

KAHN, E. : Constitutional and administrative law. Annual survey of South African law : 1-73, 1962.

KAHN, E. : Some thoughts on the competency of the Transkeian legislative assembly and the sovereignty of the South African parliament. South African law journal 80 : 473-382, November 1963.

STRAUSS, S.A. : Neuere Entwicklung im Strafrecht von Süd-Afrika. Zeitschrift für die gesamte Strafrechtswissenschaft, Mitteilungsblatt der Fachgruppe Strafrecht in der Gesellschaft für Rechtsvergleichung 14 : 39-68, Heft 1, 1964.

WULFSOHN, J.G. : Separation of church and state in South African law. South African law journal 81 : 90-101, 226-236, February, May 1964.

SPAIN

TRÍAS de BES, J.M. : Las reglas de competencia general - Ensayo de derecho procesal internacional español. Revista jurídica de Cataluña 59 : 7-19, enero-febrero 1960.

EICHLER, H. : Das spanische Gesetz über die Gesellschaften mit beschränkter Haftung. Zeitschrift für ausländisches und internationales Privatrecht 25 : 304-312, Heft 2, 1960.

PORTERO SÁNCHEZ, L. : Matrimonios de españoles en el extranjero y de extranjeros en España. Annuario de derecho civil 13 : 501-518, abril-junio 1960.

TERUEL CARRALERO, D. : Los delitos contra la religión entre los delitos contra el Estado. Anuario de derecho penal y ciencias penales 13 : 208-228, mayo-agosto 1960.

PASTOR RIDRUEJO, J.A. : Los delitos contra el derecho de gentes en el código de justicia militar. Revista española de derecho militar : 9-20, julio-diciembre 1960.

FENECH, M. : Principes d'organisation judiciaire espagnole. Annales de la Faculté de droit de Toulouse 8 : 83-98, fasc. 1, 1960.

MEDINA ORTEGA, M. : La recepción en el derecho español de las sanciones por infracción al derecho de la guerra. Anuario de derecho penal y ciencias penales 14 : 69-77, enero-abril 1961.

ALLENDESALAZAR, J.M. : El derecho de petición en España. Revue internationale des sciences administratives 27 : 192-194, no. 2, 1961.

ESPÍN CÁNOVAS, D. : Die jüngsten spanischen Bestimmungen über die bürgerliche Wirksamkeit der kanonischen Ehe. Ehe und Familie im privaten und öffentlichen Recht 8 : 199-203, Mai 1961.

HERNÁNDEZ-CANUT y ESCRIVÁ, J. : La compilación del derecho civil especial de Baleares. Anuario de derecho civil 14 : 659-690, julio septiembre 1961.

Ley de 19 abril de 1961 por la que se aprueba la compilación del derecho civil especial de las Islas Baleares. Información jurídica (Spain) : 51-67, septiembre-octubre 1961.

QUINTANO RIPOLLES, A. : La reforma del código penal español. Anuario de derecho penal y ciencias penales 14 : 453-461, septiembre-diciembre 1961.

SANCHEZ AGESTA, L. : Die Entwicklung der spanischen Verfassung seit 1936. Jahrbuch des öffentlichen Rechts der Gegenwart 10 : 397-426, 1961.

GARCÍA CANTERO, G. : Matrimonio de los funcionarios de la carrera diplomática. Anuario de derecho civil 14 : 897-908, octubre-diciembre 1961.

MURO de la VEGA, M. : La clause compromissoire en droit espagnol. Revue de l'arbitrage : 227-232, octobre-décembre 1961.

MEDINA ORTEGA, M. : Reconsideración del divorcio en el derecho español de conflictos. Revista española de derecho internacional 15 : 445-463, núm. 3, 1962.

ESPIN, D. : La réforme du code civil espagnol par la loi du 24 avril 1958. Revue de droit international et de droit comparé 39 : 545-569, no. 3, 1962.

CREMADES y SANZ-PASTOR, J.A. : Les régimes matrimoniaux légaux du droit espagnol. Revue internationale de droit comparé 14 : 341-367, avril-juin 1962.

PANTOJA BAUZA, R.E. : El Consejo de Estado español. Revue internationale des sciences administratives 29 : 30-43, no. 1, 1963.

MEDINA ORTEGA, M. : Derecho de pesca y mar territorial español. Revista española de derecho internacional 16 : 61-73, núm. 1-2, 1963.

MARTÍNEZ MORCILLO, A.E. : Validez de la forma local extranjera en los matrimonios civiles de españoles acatólicos. Revista española de derecho internacional 16 : 81-93, núm. 1-2, 1963.

PECOURT GARCÍA, E. : Rassegna di giurisprudenza spagnola di diritto internazionale privato, 1960-61. Diritto internazionale 18 : parte la, 179-198, no. 2, 1963.

MURRAY, D.E. : A survey of civil procedure in Spain and some comparisons with civil procedure in the United States. Tulane law review 37 : 399-452, April 1963.

MIAJA de la MUELA, A. : Riflessioni sull'elaborazione di un nuovo sistema spagnolo di diritto internazionale privato e di diritto interregionale. Diritto internazionale 17 : parte la, 307-340, no. 4, 1963.

BELTRAN de HEREDIA, J. : Efectos civiles del matrimonio de conciencia. Revista de derecho privado (Madrid) : 533-563, junio 1963.

BUEN ARÚS, F. : La reforma del código español, de 1963 - Exposición y anotaciones. Revista de estudios penitenciarios 19 : 511-571, julio-septiembre 1963.

Ley de bases de los funcionarios civiles del Estado. Revista de la Facultad de derecho (Caracas) : 109-124, no. 26, 1963.

PARRA BORDETAS, F. : La révision du code pénal espagnol - Les délits contre le droit d'auteur. Droit d'auteur 77 : 150-152, juin 1964.
Publié dans "Boletín de la Sociedad general de autores de España".

CEREZO MIR, J. : La conciencia de la antijuricidad en el código penal español. Revista de estudios penitenciarios 20 : 449-466, julio-setiembre 1964.

CORDOBA RODA, J. : El delito de detenciones ilegales en el código penal español. Anuario de derecho penal y ciencias penales 17 : 383-404, septiembre-diciembre 1964.

MANZENEDO MATEOS, J.A. : La responsabilidad civil de los funcionarios del Estado. Documentación administrativa (Spain) : 35-48, octubre 1964.

SUDAN

RANNAT, S.M.A. : The relationship between Islamic and customary law in the Sudan. Journal of African law 4 : 9-16, spring 1960.

SWEDEN

FISCHLER, J. : Die schwedische Gesetzgebung auf dem Gebiete des Privatrechts 1951-1962. Rabels Zeitschrift für ausländisches und internationales Privatrecht 28 : 113-134, Heft 1, 1964.

AGGE, I. : Das neue schwedische Strafgesetzgebuch. Zeitschrift fürdie gesamte Strafrechtswissenschaft, Mitteilungsblatt der Fachgruppe Strafrecht in der Gesellschaft für Rechtsvergleichung 14 : 3-39, Heft 1, 1964.

BEXELIUS, A. : The Swedish institution of the justitieombudsman. Revue internationale des sciences administratives 27 : 243-256, no. 3, 1961.

BECKMAN, N. : Das internationale Privat- und Prozessrecht in der schwedischen Rechtsprechung und Literatur. Zeitschrift für ausländisches und internationales Privatrecht 25 : 496-543, Heft 4/3, Mai 1961.

FRYKHOLM, L., and BYSTRÖM, T. : Swedish legal publications in English, French and German. Scandinavian studies in law 5 : 155-127, 1961.

GINSBURG, R., and BRUZELIUS, A. : Professional legal assistance in Sweden. International and comparative law quarterly 11 : 997-1026, October 1962.

STRAHL, I. : Les grandes lignes du nouveau code pénal suédois. Revue de science criminelle et de droit pénal comparé 19 : 527-544, juillet-septembre 1964.

SWITZERLAND

GUYET, J. : L'arbitrage en matière de société et ses sources en droit suisse. Revue de l'arbitrage : 2-16, janvier-mars 1960.

RIGGENBACH, B. : Übersicht der Literatur über schweizerisches Recht - Bibliographie juridique suisse 1959. Zeitschrift für schweizerisches Recht 79 : 533-575, Heft 10, 1960.

VOYAME, J. : Droit privé fédéral et procédure civile cantonale. Zeitschrift für schweizerisches Recht 80/2 : 67-192, Heft 1, 1961.

SUNGURBEY, I. : Le système d'acquisition par prescription extraordinaire du droit suisso-turc. Zeitschrift für schweizerisches Recht 80/1 : 269-285, Heft 3, 1961.

RIGGENBACH, B. : Übersicht der Literatur über schweizerisches Recht - Bibliographie juridique suisse 1960. Zeitschrift für schweizerisches Recht 80/1 : 493-541, Heft 5, 1961.

SCHULTZ, H. : Zwanzig Jahre Schweizeriches Strafgesetzbuch. Schweizerische Zeitschrift für Strafrecht 78 : 3-30, Heft 1, 1962.

PERRIN, R. : Le code pénal suisse dans la jurisprudence du Tribunal fédéral. Schweizerische Zeitschrift für Strafrecht 78 : 134-149, Heft 2/3, 1962.

KELLER, R. : Zur Revision der Militärstrafgerichtsordnung und des Militärstrafgesetzes. Schweizerische Zeitschrift für Strafrecht 79 : 121-148, Heft 2, 1963.

Protokoll der 97. Jahresversammlung des Schweizerischen Juristenvereins vom 7., 8. und 9. September 1963 in Basel. Zeitschrift für schweizerisches Recht 82/II : 425-548, Heft 5, 1963.

DARBELLAY, J. : L'initiative populaire et les limites de la revision constitutionnelle. Revue du droit public et de la science politique en France et à l'étranger 79 : 714-742, juillet-août 1963.
Texte de la constitution relatif à la revision pp. 743-744.

Message du Conseil fédéral à l'Assemblée fédérale concernant l'approbation du statut organique de l'Institut international pour l'unification du droit privé (du 6 septembre 1963). Feuille fédérale (Switzerland) 115 : 349-355, 12 septembre 1963.
Statut de l'Institut pp. 356-362.

GRAVEN, J. : Organisation et fonction du ministère public en Suisse - Rapport pour le congrès de Mexico sur le ministère public, 13-20 juillet 1963. Revue de science criminelle et de droit pénal comparé 19 : 53-90, janvier-mars 1964.
Bibliographie pp. 91-92.

FRIEDRICH, H.P. : Zur sozialdemokratischen Verfassungsinitiative betreffend Bekämpfung der Bodenspekulation. Wirtschaft und Recht 16 : 85-109, Heft 2, 1964.

RIGGENBACH, B. : Übersicht der Literatur über schweizerisches Recht - Bibliographie juridique suisse, 1963. Zeitschrift für schweizerisches Recht 83/1 : 469-515, Heft 5, 1964.

HERNÁNDEZ OROZCO, J. : Notas sobre el derecho penal militar suizo. Revista española de derecho militar : 57-90, julio-diciembre 1964.

SWITZERLAND
(International law, Aliens)

PROBST, R. : Die Schweiz und die internationale Schiedsgerichtsbarkeit. Schweizerisches Jahrbuch für internationales Recht 17 : 99-146, 1960.

Message du Conseil fédéral à l'Assemblée fédérale concernant l'approbation de la nouvelle convention entre la Confédération suisse et la République d'Autriche relative à la reconnaissance et à l'exécution de décisions judiciaires (du 19 juin 1961). Feuille fédérale (Switzerland) 113 : 1585-1600, 29 juin 1961.

Message du Conseil fédéral à l'Assemblée fédérale proposant l'adhésion de la Suisse à la convention de La Haye pour la protection des biens culturels en cas de conflit armé (du 11 décembre 1961). Feuille fédérale (Switzerland) 113 : 1197-1214, 21 décembre 1961.
Texte de la convention pp. 1215-1248.

AUBERT, J.F. : Les contrats internationaux dans la doctrine et la jurisprudence suisses. Revue critique de droit international privé 51 : 19-52, janvier-mars 1962.

MATSCHER, F. : Zur Entwicklung der Rechtsbeziehungen mit der Schweiz auf dem Gebiet des Privat- und Prozessrechts - Der neue österreichisch-schweizerische Vollstreckungsvertrag vom 16. Dezember 1960. Juristische Blätter 84 : 356-366, 30. Juni 1962.

SCHINDLER, D. : Neutralität und Völkergemeinschaft. Schweiz in der Völkergemeinschaft 17 : 65-67, Nr. 4, Dezember 1962.
Commentary on H. Haug's book.

CARABIBIER, C. : L'exécution en Suisse des sentences arbitrales internationales. Revue de l'arbitrage : 78-88, juillet-september 1963.

GUGGENHEIM, P. : Droit international public - La pratique suisse, 1962. Schweizerisches Jahrbuch für internationales Recht 20 : 65-120, 1963.

DIEZ, E. : Les engagements internationaux conclus par la suisse, entrés en vigueur en 1963. Schweizerisches Jahrbuch für internationales Recht 20 : 121-134, 1963.

SWITZERLAND
(Patents, Trade-marks)

Message du Conseil fédéral à l'Assemblée fédérale concernant les actes adoptés à Nice, en matière de marques de fabrique et de commerce (du 5 juin 1961). Feuille fédérale (Switzerland) 113 : 1241-1262, 15 juin 1961.
Textes des arrangements de Madrid et de Nice pp. 1263-1279.

NATIONAL LAW - COUNTRIES

Message du Conseil fédéral à l'Assemblée fédérale concernant les actes convenus par la conférence de Lisbonne de l'Union internationale pour la protection de la propriété industrielle (du 5 juin 1961). Feuille fédérale (Switzerland) 113 : 1280-1303, 15 juin 1961.
Textes officiels pp. 1303-1333.

TROLLER, A. : Brennpunkte der schweizerischen Urheberrechts-Revision. Zeitschrift für schweizerisches Recht 82/II : 1-86, Heft 1, 1963.

POINTET, P.J. : La protection de la marque - Propositions en vue de la revision de la loi fédérale sur les marques de fabrique et de commerce. Zeitschrift für schweizerisches Recht 82/II : 87-220, Heft 2, 1963.

TAIWAN

WOODSWORTH, K.C. : The legal system of the Republic of China. Canadian bar journal 4 : 299-311, August 1961.

TANZANIA

COTRAN, E. : Some recent developments in the Tanganyika judicial system. Journal of African law 6 : 19-28, spring 1962.

THAILAND

Constitution provisoire du Royaume de Thaïlande, 28 janvier 1959. Documentation française, Notes et études documentaires : 1-4, no. 2635, 23 février 1960.

Constitución provisional del Reino de Tailandia, 28 enero 1959. Información jurídica (Spain) : 59-61, mayo-junio 1960.

ERICKSON, D.H. : Enforcement of American arbitral awards in Thailand. Arbitration journal 16 : 143-146, no. 3, 1961.

TOGO

MANGIN, G. : Togo. Annuaire de législation française et étrangère 9 : 366-368, 1960.

Les constitutions des Etats africains d'expression française (Suite) - République Togolaise. Revue juridique et politique d'outre-mer 15 : 481-489, juillet-septembre 1961.
Avril 1961.

Constitution de la République du Togo, 11 mai 1963. Informations constitutionnelles et parlementaires 15 : 194-213, octobre 1964.

TUNISIA

Constitution de la République tunisienne, 1er juin 1959. Documentation française, Notes et études documentaires : 1-6, no. 2633, 20 février 1960.

Code de procédure civile et commerciale. Revue algérienne, tunisienne et marocaine de législation et de jurisprudence; Législation 76 : 123-146, mars-avril 1960.

LUCAS, P.L. : La République tunisienne et les traités antérieurs à l'indépendance. Journal du droit international 88 : 86-119, janvier-mars 1961.
Texte en anglais aussi.

ANABI, M. : L'évolution de la législation sur le statut personnel en Tunisie. Revue judiciaire libanaise (Lebanon) 18 : 75-80, août 1962.
Texte en arabe.

GAUDIN de LAGRANGE, E. de : Les notions de commerçant et d'actes de commerce dans les articles 1er à 4 du code de commerce tunisien. Revue tunisienne de droit : 13-23, 1963-1965.

TURKEY

La costituzione provvisoria turca, 12 giugno 1960. Oriente moderno 40 : 425-428, luglio-agosto 1960.
Text.

Déclaration de la Commission chargée de préparer un avant-projet de constitution. Annales de la faculté de droit d'Istanbul 10 : vii-x, no. 15, 1960.

SUNGURBEY, I. : Le système d'acquisition par prescription extraordinaire du droit suisso-turc. Zeitschrift für schweizerisches Recht 80/I : 269-285, Heft 3, 1961.

Colloque sur la réception des droits occidentaux en Turquie, Luxembourg, 27-30 juillet 1959. Annales de la Faculté de droit d'Istanbul 11 : 1-402, no. 16-17, 1961.
Suite d'articles.

Constitution de la République Turque, 9 juillet 1961. Informations constitutionnelles et parlementaires 13 : 18-63, janvier 1962.

VELIDEDEOGLU, H.V. : Erfahrungen mit dem Schweizerischen Zivilgesetzbuch in der Türkei. Zeitschrift für schweizerisches Recht 81/1 : 51-74, Heft 1, 1962.

AZRAK, A.Ü. : Verfassungsgerichtsbarkeit in der Türkei. Jahrbuch des öffentlichen Rechts der Gegenwart 11 : 73-92, 1962.

BALTA, T.B. : L'administration publique et le droit privé en Turquie. Annales de la Faculté de droit d'Istanbul 12 : no. 18, 77-145, 1962.

La costituzione della Repubblica di Turchia, 9 luglio 1961. Oriente moderno 43 : 1-28, gannaio-febbraio 1963.
English text.

MIMAROGLU, S.K. : Quelques considérations sur le droit civil et le droit commercial en Turquie. Revue de droit international et de droit comparé 40 : 85-104, no. 2, 1963.

ELBİR, H.K. : La fusion des sociétés en droit turc. Annales de la Faculté de droit d'Istanbul 13 : 131-136, no. 19, 1963.

VERSAN, V. : Evolution of the rule of law and the new constitution of Turkey. Pakistan horizon 17 : 122-129, 2nd quarter 1964.

ARSLANLI, H. : Le contrôle de l'Etat dans les sociétés anonymes en droit turc. Annales de la Faculté de droit d'Istanbul 14 : 1-26, no. 20, 1964.

ABADAN, Y. : Die türkische Verfassung von 1961. Jahrbuch des öffentlichen Rechts der Gegenwart 13 : 325-411, 1964.
Text pp. 412-436.

AZRAK, A.Ü. : Der türkische Verfassungsgerichtshof und seine Rechsprechung. Annales de la Faculté de droit d'Istanbul 14 : 90-111, no. 20, 1964.

Constitution de la République Turque - Rapport de la Commission de la constitution à la Haute présidence de l'Assemblée représentative. Annales de la Faculté de droit d'Istanbul 14 : 241-309, no. 20, 1964.
Adoptée de 9 juillet 1961; Avec texte.

TURKEY
(International law, Aliens)

KORAL, R.N. : L'exécution des sentences arbitrales étrangères en Turquie. Revue de l'arbitrage : 38-43, avril-juin 1960.

SEVIG, V.R. : Le Marché Commun et le droit d'établissement adopté par la Turquie. Annales de la Faculté de droit d'Istanbul 14 : 39-62, no. 20, 1964.

U.S.S.R.

BILINSKY, A. : Das sowjetische Eherecht. Ehe und Familie im privaten und öffentlichen Recht 7 : 1-6, Januar 1960.

NIKIFOROV, B.S. : Fundamental principles of Soviet criminal law. Modern law review 23 : 31-42, January 1960.

LEVITSKY, S.L. : Der Schutz der Urheberrechte im Sowjetrecht. Osteuropa 10 : 124-140, Februar/März 1960.

KRIVICKAS, D. : Laws and courts in Soviet-occupied Lithuania. Baltic review : 31-42, no. 19, March 1960.

MORGAN, G,G. : The "proposal" of the Soviet procurator - A means for rectifying administrative illegalities. International and comparative law quarterly 9 : 191-207, April 1960.

BILINSKY, A. : Die "gesellschaftliche Rechtspflege" in der Sowjetunion. Recht in Ost und West 4 : 89-97, 15. Mai 1960.

BINKLEY, J.T. : The rule of law - The new Soviet criminal procedure. American bar association journal 46 : 637-639, June 1960.

MORGAN, G.G. : Les fonctions de surveillance générale de la Prokouratoura dans l'Union Soviétique. Commission internationale de juristes, Revue 2 : 119-133, hiver 1959 - printemps/été 1960.

KERIMOW, A., and NIKOLAJEWA, L.A. : Die Allgemeine Aufsicht der Staatsanwaltschaft über die Gesetzlichkeit in der sowjetischen staatlichen Verwaltung. Neue Justiz (Germany) 14 : 413-418, 5. Juli 1960.

GRZYBOWSKI, K. : The Powers trial and the 1958 reform of Soviet criminal law. American journal of comparative law 9 : 425-440, summer 1960.

Osnovy grazhdanskogo zakonadatel'stva Soi͡uza SSR i soi͡uznykh respublik. Sot͡sialisticheskai͡a zakonnost' (U.S.S.R.) 37 : 4-20, no. 8, avgust 1960.
Draft civil code.

ANDREJEW, N.D., and KERIMOW, D.A. : Der Paragraphenautomat als Rechtsinstanz. Ost-Probleme 12 : 593-596, 16. September 1960.
Published in Woprosy filosofi".

Entwurf der Grundlagen für das zivilgerichtliche Verfahren der Union der SSR und der Unionsrepubliken. Staat und Recht 9 : 1583-1596, September 1960.
Published in "Sowjetskoje gossudarstwo i prawo".

Entwurf der Grundlagen für die Zivilgesetzgebung der Union der SSR und der Unionsrepubliken. Staat und Recht 9 : 1563-1583, September 1960.
Published in "Sowjetskoje gossudarstwo i prawo".

SOUKHOMLINE, V. : L'Etat et l'essor de la justice populaire en U.R.S.S. Cahiers internationaux : 21-36, novembre-décembre 1960.

DOBROVOL'S'KA, T., and MIN'KOVS'KII, G. : Prot͡sessual'ne stanovishche pidozri͡uvanogo pid chas poperedn'ogo slidstva i diznanni͡a. Radi͡ans'ke (Ukraine) : 29-35, no. 6, listopad-gruden' 1960.
Ukrainian inheritance law.

Schrifttum ausserhalb des Ostblock zum Sowjetrecht. Osteuropa-Recht 6 : 275-295, Dezember 1960.

FRENDL, L. : La conception soviétique du droit international. Justice dans le monde 2 : 201-222, décembre 1960.

Chronologische Gesetzessammlungen der Sowjetunion 1945-1960 - Bibliographie mit Standortangabe. Osteuropa-Recht 6 : 265-269, Dezember 1960.
Text in Russian.

Ugolovno-prot͡sessual'nyi kodeks RSFSR, 1.1.1961. Sovetskai͡a i͡ustit͡sii͡a (U.S.S.R.) : 16-62, no. 15-16, 1960.
Text.

Ugolovnyĭ kodeks RSFSR, 1.1.1961. Sovetskai͡a i͡ustit͡sii͡a (U.S.S.R.) : 5-32, no. 17, 1960.
Text.

Novye zakon o sudoustroĭstve, Ugolovnyĭ i Ugolovno-prot͡sessual'nyĭ kodeksy Rossiĭskoĭ Federat͡sii. Sovetskoe gosudarstvo i pravo 31 : 24-36, no. 1, i͡anvar' 1961.
New penal and criminal procedure codes.

TIKHOMIROV, I͡U. A. : K voprosu o pravovom polozhenii vedomstv v SSSR. Pravovedenie (U.S.S.R.) 5 : 15-27, no. 1, 1961.

GINSBURGS, G. : Objective truth and the judicial process in post-Stalinist Soviet jurisprudence. American journal of comparative law 10 : 53-75, winter-spring 1961.

Kriminal'niĭ kodeks Ukraīns'koī RSR. Radi͡ans'ke pravo (Ukraine) : 13-54, no. 1, sichen'-li͡utiĭ 1961.
Text.

O pori͡adke vvedenii͡a v deĭstvie novogo Uglovnogo kodeksa RSFSR. Sovetskai͡a i͡ustit͡sii͡a (U.S.S.R.) : 8-10, no. 5, mart 1961.

NATIONAL LAW - COUNTRIES

Kriminal'no-protsessual'nii kodeks Ukrainskoi RSR. Radians'ke pravo (Ukraine) : 57-133, no. 1, sichen'-liutii 1961.
Text.

Obsuzhdenie proektov osnov grazhdanskogo zakonodatel'stva Soiuza SSR i soiuznykh respublik i osnov grazhdanskogo sudoproizvodstva Soiuza SSR i soiuznykh respublik. Sovetskoe gosudarstvo i pravo 31 : 86-114, no. 2, fevral' 1961.
Civil law and civil procedure.

MIRONENKO, Y. : The new Soviet law on death sentences. Analysis of current developments in the Soviet Union : 1-5, 6 June 1961.

BOLDYREW, W.A. : Die neue Strafgesetzgebung der RSFSR. Neue Justiz (Germany) 15 : 401-405, 20. Juni 1961.

SCHLESINGER, R. : Zum Abschluss der Kodifikation des sowjetischen Strafrechts. Osteuropa-Recht 7 : 28-42, Januar-Juni 1961.

KERIMOV, D.A., and SHARGORODSKII, M.D. : Aktual'nye problemy teorii sovetskogo prava. Pravovedenie (U.S.S.R.) 5 : 22-33, no. 2, 1961.

ZAICHUK, V. : Novyi kryminal'nyi kodeks Ukrains'koi RSR. Radians'ke pravo (Ukraine) : 9-17, no. 3, berezen'kviten' 1961.

BRACHT, H.W. : Die clausula rebus sic stantibus in der sowjetischen Völkerrechtslehre. Internationales Recht und Diplomatie : 191-203, Heft 3/4, 1961.

YURCHENKO, A. : The latest trends in communist constitutional law. Institute for the study of the USSR, Bulletin 8 : 50-56, May 1961.

LAPENNA, I. : The new Russian criminal code and code of criminal procedure. International and comparative law quarterly 10 : 421-453, July 1961.

Ley sobre responsabilidad penal por delitos militares en la U.R.S.S. de 25 de diciembre de 1958. Revista española de derecho militar : 211-233, julio-diciembre 1961.

FRENDL, L. : Les droits d'auteur en U.R.S.S. Est et Ouest 13 : 17-20, 16 juillet 1961.

LIEBSCHER, V. : Die neuen Justizgesetze der UdSSR. Monatsschrift für deutsches Recht 15 : 637-643, August 1961.

NIKIFOROV, B. : Whither the Soviet criminal code? Anglo-Soviet journal 22 : 19-27, autumn 1961.

RZEPKA, W. : Sowjetische Gesetzestechnik. Recht in Ost und West 5 : 177-180, 15. September 1961.

ROGOVIN, E.B. : Social conformity and the comradely courts in the Soviet Union. Crime and delinquency 7 : 303-311, October 1961.

RAD'KOV, V. : Poniatie i soderzhanie sotsialisticheskoi zakonnosti. Sotsialisticheskaia zakonnost (U.S.S.R.) 38 : 21-30, no. 11, noiabr' 1961.

HASTRICH, A. : Zum Ehegüterrecht der RSFSR. Osteuropa-Recht 7 : 258-265, Dezember 1961.

New Soviet civil legislation and the problem of private property in a communist state. Analysis of current developments in the Soviet Union : 1-6, 9 January 1962.

GINSBURGHS, G. : Structural and functional evolution of the Soviet judiciary since Stalin's death, 1953-1956. Soviet studies 13 : 281-302, January 1962.

BRATUS', S. : Ob osnovakh grazhdanskogo zakonodatel'stva Soiuza SSR i soiuznykh respublik. Sovetskaia iustitsiia (U.S.S.R.) : 2-6, No. 2, ianvar' 1962.

Osnovy grazhdanskogo zakonodatel'stva Soiuza SSR i soiuznykh respublik. Sovetskaia iustitsiia (U.S.S.R.) : 4-19, no. 1, ianvar' 1962.

FRIDIEFF, M. : Le nouveau code pénal de la R.S.F.S.R. de 1960. Revue de science criminelle et de droit pénal comparé 17 : 75-82, janvier-mars 1962.

Ley orgánica de los tribunales militares de la U.R.S.S., de 25 de diciembre de 1958. Revista española de derecho militar : 133-138, enero-junio 1962.

NIETHAMMER, F. : Einführende Bemerkungen zu den Grundlagen für die Zivilgesetzgebung der UsSSR und der Unionsrepubliken. Staat und Recht 11 : 347-349, Februar 1962.
See also pp. 350-368.

IOFFE, O.S. : Vazhnyi étap novoi kodifikatsii sovetskogo grazhdanskogo zakonodatel'stva. Pravovedenie (U.S.S.R.) 6 : 52-65, no. 2, 1962.

GERTSENZON, A. : Voprosy nauki ugolovnogo prava v svete reshenii XXII s''ezda KPSS. Sotsialisticheskaia zakonnost'(U.S.S.R.) 39 : 35-42, no. 3, mart 1962.

KIRIN, V. : Zakony SSSR za chetyre goda. Sotsialisticheskaia zakonnost'(U.S.S.R.) 39 : 7-11, no. 3, mart 1962.

LAPENNA, I. : State and law in the programmes of the Jugoslav and Soviet parties. Politico 27 : 92-111, marzo 1962.

AZOV, L. : Avtorskoe pravo v Osnovakh grazhdanskogo zakonodatel'stva. Sovetskaia iustitsiia (U.S.S.R.) : 7-9, no. 5, mart 1962.

Gesetz der Russischen Sozialistischen Föderativen Sowjetrepublik über die Bestätigung der Rechtsanwaltsordnung der RSFSR. Wiener Quellenhefte zur Ostkunde, Recht; Beilage : 41-52, Heft 4, 1962.
Text.

DAVLETSHIN, T. : Reform of Soviet civil law. Institute for the study of the USSR, Bulletin 9 : 41-50, April 1962.

DAVLETCHINE, T. : Au sujet de la réforme du code civil soviétique. Problèmes soviétiques : 35-46, no. 5, 1962.

PETROV, G.I. : O kodifikatsii sovetskogo administrativnogo prava. Sovetskoe gosudarstvo i pravo 32 : 27-33, no. 5, mai 1962.

The new laws on the judicial system, the criminal code, and the code of criminal procedure of the Russian Federation. Soviet law and government 1 : 33-42, summer 1962.
Published in "Sovetskoe gosudarstvo i pravo".

LUNTS, L.A. : Voprosy primeneniia inostrannykh zakonov v osnovakh grazhdanskogo zakonodatel'stva Soiuza SSR i soiuznykh respublik. Sovetskoe gosudarstvo i pravo 32 : 100-107, no. 6, iiun' 1962.

POUTCHINSKI, V.K. : Principes de procédure civile de l'U.R.S.S. et des républiques fédérales. Revue de droit contemporain 9 : 72-81, juin 1962.

BRATOUS, S.N. : Principes de la législation civile de l'U.R.S.S. et des républiques fédérées. Revue de droit contemporain 9 : 62-71, juin 1962.

KHALFINA, R.O. : Property right of Soviet citizens and the right to inherit property in the U.S.S.R. Ceylon law society journal 7 : xci-c, June-December 1962.

GINSBURGS, G., and RUSIS, A. : Soviet criminal law and the protection of State secrets. Law in Eastern Europe : 3-48, no. 7, 1962.

Loi de l'Union des Républiques Socialistes Soviétiques sur l'adoption des principes du croit civil de l'Union Soviétique et des Républiques fédérées. Pays communistes 3 : 167-219, juillet-1962.

KUCHEROV, S. : Property in the Soviet Union. American journal of comparative law 11 : 376-392, summer 1962.

TIKHOMIROV, IU. A. : Les tendances fondamentales du déceloppement des organes locaux du pouvoir d'Etat en U.R.S.S. à l'époque contemporaine. Revue internationale de droit comparé 14 : 507-518, juillet-septembre 1962.

BOLDYREV, V.A. : O proekte Grazhdanskogo kodeksa RSFSR. Sovetskoe gosudarstvo i pravo 32 : 15-25, no. 8, avgust 1962.

FLEISHITS, E. : The fundamentals of Soviet civil law. Anglo-Soviet journal 23 : 25-29, autumn 1962.

Principes de procédure civile de l'Union Soviétique et des Républiques fédérées. Pays communistes 3 : 301-328, septembre 1962.

VAHTER, L. : Some questions on fundamentals of the civil code of the U.S.S.R. and of the Union republics. Baltic review : 12-20, October 1962.

FRIDIEFF, M. : L'organisation judiciaire soviétique. Revue internationale de droit comparé 14 : 725-745, octobre-décembre 1962.

KROKHOTKIN, A.M. : Postoiannye predstavitel'stva - organy sviazi Sovetov ministrov soiuznykh respublik s Sovetom ministrov SSSR. Sovetskoe gosudarstvo i pravo 32 : 89-97, no. 11, noiabr' 1962.

BILINSKY, A. : Das Problem der materiellen Wahrheit im sowjetischen Strafprozess. Recht in Ost und West 6 : 232-238, 15. November 1962.

Les fondements de la législation et de la procédure civiles en U.R.S.S. Documentation française, Notes et études documentaires : 1-49, no. 2942, 3 décembre 1962.

BILINSKY, A. : Kameradschaftsgerichte in der UdSSR. Osteuropa-Recht 8 : 306-330, Dezember 1962.

K itogam obsuzhdeniia proekta Grazhdanskogo protsessualnogo kodeksa RSFSR. Sovetskaia iustitsiia (U.S.S.R.) : 13-15, no. 2, ianvar' 1963.

LUNC, L.A. : Otázky mezinárodního práva soukromého v Základech občanského zákonodárství a Základech občanského soudního řízení Svazu SSR a Svazových republik. Časopis pro mezinárodní právo 7 : 111-121, číslo 2, 1963.

VOEVODIN, L.D. : Teoreticheskie voprosy pravovogo polozheniia lichnosti v Sovetskom obshchenarodnom gosudarstve. Sovetskoe gosudarstvo i pravo 33 : 12-22, no. 2, fevral' 1963.

BERMAN, H.J. : The dilemma of Soviet law reform. Harvard law review 76 : 929-951, March 1963.

DAVLETSHIN, T. : Law and the State. Studies on the Soviet Union 2 : 89-97, no. 3, 1963.

MIRONENKO, Y. : Changes in criminal legislation. Studies on the Soviet Union 2 : 83-88, no. 3, 1963.

MEDER, W. : Die Lokalverwaltung in der Sowjetunion. Archiv des öffentlichen Rechts 88 : 428-450, Heft 4, 1963.

DAVLETSHIN, T. : Property law in the Soviet Union. Studies on the Soviet Union 2 : 11-22, no. 4, 1963.

IOFFE, O.S. : The new codification of civil law and protection of the honor and dignity of the citizen. Soviet law and government 1 : 37-45, spring 1963.
Published in "Sovetskoe gosudarstvo i pravo".

BABUKHIN, N., and KOROLEV, IU. : Predlozheniia trudiashchikhsia k zakonou o brake i sem'e. Sovetskaia iustitsiia (U.S.S.R.) : 4-6, no. 7, aprel' 1963.

GENKIN, D. : Operativnoe upravlenie kak institut sovetskogo grazhdanskogo prava. Sovetskaia iustitsiia (U.S.S.R.) : 3-5, no. 9, mai 1963.

VLADIMIROV, V. : Unichtozhenie ili povrezhdenie gosudarstvennogo ili obshchestvennogo imushchestva libo lichnogo imushchestva grazhdan. Sovetskaia iustitsiia (U.S.S.R.) : 17-19, no. 11, iiun 1963.

Results of the discussion of the draft civil code of the RSFSR. Soviet law and government 2 : 18-22, summer 1963.
Published in "Sovetskaia iustitsiia".

PLATTS-MILLS, J. : Law in the Soviet Union. Anglo-Soviet journal 24 : 8-11, summer 1963.

BILINSKY, A. : Kontradiktorische Verhandeln und Parteiprinzip im sowjetischen Strafprozess. Recht in Ost und West 7 : 190-196, 15. September 1963.

ORLOVSKII, P.E. : Pravo lichnoi sobstvennosti v "Osnovakh grazhdanskogo zakonadatel'stva Soiuza SSR i soiuznykh respublik. Vestnik Moskovskogo universiteta Seriia : pravo 18 : 12-19, no. 4, oktiabr'-dekabr' 1963.

MAURACH, R. : Todesstrafe in der Sowjetunion. Osteuropa 13 : 745-753, November-Dezember 1963.

Novyi étap v dei͡atel'nosti tovarishcheskikh sudov. Sovetskai͡a i͡ustitsii͡a (U.S.S.R.) : 1-4, no. 23, dekabr' 1963.
Law relating to social courts pp. 5-6.

BELZ, H.G. : Das Prinzip des Föderalismus in der Spwjetunion. Jahrbuch des öffentlichen Rechts der Gegenwart 12 : 249-293, 1963.

SEMENOV, V.M. : Printsipy sovetskogo sotsialisticheskogo obshchenarodnogo prava. Pravovedenie (U.S.S.R.) 8 : 16-26, no. 1, 1964.

KUTAFIN, O.E. : Pravovoe polozhenie postoi͡annykh komissiĭ palat Verkhovnogo soverta SSSR. Vestnik Moskovskogo universiteta, Serii͡a : pravo 19 : 23-33, no. 1, i͡anvar'mart 1964.

SANTUCCI, G. : La riforma penale sovietica. Annuario di diritto comparativo e di studi legislativi 38 : ea serie, 244-257, fasc. 3, 1964.

IOFFE, O.S., and TOLSTOĬ, I͡U. K. : Novyĭ grazhdanskiĭ kodeks RSFSR. Pravovedenie (U.S.S.R.) 8 : 3-21, no. 3, 1964.

ISHUTINA, A. : Praktika primenenii͡a st. 61 Osnov grazhdanskogo zakonodatel'stva. Sovetskai͡a iustitsii͡a (U.S.S.R.) 28 : 4-8, no. 6, mart 1964.

RAKHMILOVICH, V.A. : O protivopravnosti kak osnovanii grazhdanskoĭ otvetstvennosti. Sovetskoe gosudarstvo i pravo 34 : 53-62, no. 3, mart 1964.

VITRUK, N.V. : O i͡uridicheskikh sredstvakh obespechenii͡a realizatsii i okhrany prav sovetskikh grazhdan. Pravovedenie (U.S.S.R.) 8 : 29-38, no. 4, 1964.

Verkhovnomu sudu SSSR - Sorok let. Sovetskai͡a i͡ustitsii͡a (U.S.S.R.) 28 : 4-5, no. 8, aprel' 1964.

RANDALU, Kh. : O nauchnom issledovanii teoreticheskikh voprosov sovershenstvovanii͡a zakonodatel'stva. Eesti NSV teaduste akadeemia toimetised, Uhiskonnateaduste seeria - Akademii͡a nauk Éstonskoĭ SSR; Izvestii͡a, Serii͡a obshchestvennykh nauk 13 : 295-305, no. 4, 1964.
Theoretical research in legislation; Summaries in Estonian and German.

IVANOV, O.V. : Grazhdanskie protsessual'nye pravootnoshenii͡a. Vestnik Moskovskogo universiteta, Serii͡a : pravo 18 : 26-34, no. 2, aprel'-ii͡un' 1963.

STROGOVITCH, M.S. : La protection des droits des citoyens en U.R.S.S. Revue internationale de droit comparé 16 : 297-306, avril-juin 1964.

HAZARD, J.N. : Le droit pénal soviétique et"l'Etat du peuple entier". Revue de science criminelle et de droit pénal comparé 19 : 293-305, avril-juin 1964.
Voir aussi pp. 353-357.

VILLORO TORANZO, M. : Principios filosófico-políticos del sistema soviética de derecho. Boletín del Instituto de derecho comparado de México 17 : 261-314, mayo-agosto 1964.
Bibliography pp. 314-319.

Grazhdanskiĭ kodeks RSFSR. Sovetskai͡a iustitsii͡a (U.S.S.R.) 28 : 4-57, no. 13-14, ii͡ul' 1964.
Text.

DAVYDENKO, V. : New course of Soviet nationality policy in USSR. Ukrainian quarterly 20 : 144-151, summer 1964.

Economic crimes in the Soviet Union. International commission of jurists, Journal 5 : 3-47, summer 1964.

DAVLETCHINE, T. : La situation juridique du Turkestan soviétique. Problèmes soviétiques : 14-23, no. 8, 1964.

FLEĬSHITS, E.A., and MAKOVSKIĬ, A.L. : O grazhdanskom kodekse RSFSR. Sovetskoe gosudarstvo i pravo 34 : 14-23, no. 8, avgust 1964.

KOZLOV, IU. M. : The relationship between collegial and one-man management in Soviet State administration at the present stage of development. Soviet law and government 3 : 8-12, fall 1964.

BARRY, D.D. : The specialist in Soviet policy-making - The adoption of a law. Soviet studies 16 : 152-165, October 1964.

SVERDLOV, G.M. : Zakon o razvode i statistika. Sovetskoe gosudarstvo i pravo 34 : 31-41, no. 10, oktiabr' 1964.

LUNZ, L.A. : Les règles de conflit dans les "Principes de droit civil" de l'Union Soviétique et des Républiques fédérées. Revue critique de droit international privé 53 : 629-646, octobre-décembre 1964.

BURCHELL, R.A. : Soviet military law. Intramural law review of New York university School of law 20 : 22-36, November 1964.

DANIELI͡AN, D. : Za dal'neĭshee ukreplenie sotsialisticheskoĭ zakonnosti. Sotsialisticheskai͡a zakonnost'(U.S.S.R.) 41 : 6-12, no. 11, noi͡abr' 1964.

Sovershenstvovanie sledstvennoĭ raboty - vazhnoe uslovie dal'neĭshego ukreplenii͡a sotsialisticheskoĭ zakonnosti. Sovetskoe gosudarstvo i pravo 34 : 3-11, no. 11, noi͡abr' 1964.

KHANGEL'DYEV, B.B. : O kodifikatsii sovetskogo administrativnogo prava. Sovetskoe gosudarstvo i pravo 34 : 38-47, no. 12, dekabr' 1964.

U.S.S.R.
(International law and practice, Aliens and Naturalization)

Soviet contribution to the evolution of international law. Economic weekly, Annual number 12 : 113-116, January 1960.

GINSBURGS, G. : Laws of war and war crimes on the Russian front during World War II - The Soviet view. Soviet studies 11 : 253-285, January 1960.

Soviet law and East-West trade. Record of the Association of the bar of the city of New York 16 : 26-41, January 1961.
Series of articles; Bibliography pp. 63-67.

MEISSNER, B. : Völkerrechtswissenschaft und Völkerrechtskonzeption der UdSSR. Recht in Ost und West 5 : 1-5, 15. Januar 1961.

BRACHT, H.W. : Die Auslegung internationaler Verträge in der sowjetischen Völkerrechtslehre. Osteuropa-Recht 7 : 66-81, Januar-Juni 1961.

SLUSSER, R., and GINSBURGS, G. : A calendar of Soviet treaties, January-December 1958. Osteuropa-Recht 7 : 100-131, Januar-Juni 1961.

NATIONAL LAW - COUNTRIES

KORODOV, A.A., and SOKOLOV, K.A. : Imushchestvennye prava inostrantsev v praktike sovetskogo suda i notariata. Sovetskii ezhegodnik mezhdunarodnogo prava - Soviet year-book of international law : 361-361, 1961.
Property rights of aliens; Summary in English.

GINSBURGS, G. : Option of nationality in Soviet treaty practice, 1917-1924. American journal of international law 55 : 919-946, October 1961.

LAPENNA, I. : International law viewed through Soviet eyes. Year book of world affairs 15 : 204-232, 1961.

GINSBURGS, G. : The Soviet Union, the neutrals and international law in World War II. International and comparative law quarterly 11 : 171-230, January 1962.

STOYANOVITCH, K. : Le droit international public en U.S.S.R. Journal du droit international 89 : 52-113, janvier-mars 1962.
Texte en anglais aussi.

Kollisionsrechtliche Bestimmungen der Grundlagen für die Zivilgesetzgebung vom 8. Dezember 1961. Rabels Zeitschrift für ausländisches und internationales Privatrecht 27 : 719-723, Heft 4, 1962.
Text also in Russian.

RUBANOV, A.A. : Fragen des internationalen Privatrechts in den Grundlagen für die Zivilgesetzgebung der Union der SSR und der Unionsrepubliken. Rabels Zeitschrift für ausländisches und internationales Privatrecht 27 : 698-718, Heft 4, 1962.

TUNKIN, G.I. : XXII s''ezd KPSS i zadachi sovetskoi nauki mezhdunarodnogo prava. Sovetskoe gosudarstvo i pravo 32 : 3-17, no. 5, mai 1962.

KURYLEV, S., and IUKHO, L. : Osnovy grazhdanskogo sudoproizvodsta SSSR i GPK soiuznykh respublik. Sotsialisticheskaia zakonnost' (U.S.S.R.) 39 : 24-30, no. 7, iiul' 1962.

KUNZMANN, K.H. : Die friedliche Koexistenz im sowjetischen Völkerrecht. Europa-Archiv 17 : 741-748, 10. November 1962.

ZAKHAROVA, N.V. : Otkaz Sovetskogo gosudarstva ot dogorov tsarskoi Rossii, narushavshikh prava narodov vostochnykh stran. Sovetskii ezhegodnik mezhdunarodnogo prava - Soviet year-book of international law : 126-134, 1962.
Renunciation of Tsarist treaties; Summaries in English.

LUNTS, L. : Legal position of foreigners in the U.S.S.R. under the new civil legislation. Soviet law and government 1 : 29-32, winter 1962-63.
Published in "Sovetskaia iustitsiia".

TUNKIN, G.I. : The 22nd Congress of the CPSU and the tasks of the Soviet science of international law. Soviet law and government 1 : 18-28, winter 1962-63.
Published in "Sovetskoe gosudarstvo i pravo".

RAMUNDO, B.A. : Soviet criminal legislation in implementation of The Hague and Geneva conventions relating to the rules of land warfare. American journal of international law 57 : 73-84, January 1963.

GARNEFSKY, A. : Das Europäische Übereinkommen über die internationale Handelsschiedsgerichtsbarkeit und das Sowjetrecht. Osteuropa-Recht 9 : 14-25: März 1963.

LISSITZYN, O.J. : The Soviet Union and international law. International conciliation : 14-36, no. 452, March 1963.

GINSBURGS, G. : A calendar of Soviet treaties, January-December 1960. Osteuropa-Recht 9 : 120-159, Juni 1963.

NILIN, V. : Shestoe ezhegodnoe sobranie Sovetskoi assotsiatsii mezhdunarodnogo prava. Sovetskoe gosudarstvo i pravo 33 : 141-144, no. 7, iiul' 1963.
Soviet association of international law.

RAMZAITSEV, D. : The law of international trade in the new Soviet legislation. Journal of business law : 229-237, July 1963.

GARNEFSKY, A. : Some problems of Soviet international law of civil procedure. Nederlands tijdschrift voor internationaal recht 10 : 256-274, juli 1963.
Bibliography pp. 270-273.

FÜNER, A. von : Das sowjetische Erfinderrecht und der Schutz ausländischer Erfindungen in der UdSSR. Recht in Ost und West 7 : 185-190, 15. September 1963.

FRENZKE, D. : Die Rechtstellung der sowjetischen Handelsvertretungen nach der Vertragspraxis der UdSSR. Osteuropa-Recht 9 : 269-300, Dezember 1963.

GREVTSOVA, T.P. : Mezhdunarodnyi dogover v sisteme istochnikov sovetskogo vnutrigosudarstvennogo prava. Sovetskii ezkegodnik mezhdunarodnogo prava - Soviet year-book of international law : 171-179, 1963.
International treaties as a source of national law ; Summary in English.

RZEPKA, W. : Die Rechtsstellung der Ausländer in der UdSSR. Recht in Ost und West 8 : 49-55, 15. März 1964.

ZILE, Z.L. : A Soviet contribution to international adjudication - Professor Krylov's jurisprudential legacy. American journal of international law 58 : 359-388, April 1964.

DOBRIANSKY, L.E. : The second treaty of Moscow. Ukrainian quarterly 20 : 318-330, winter 1964/65.
U=S.S.R.-United States Consular convention, 1 June 1964.

GINSBURGS, G. : Option of nationality in Soviet treaty law - The war-time and post-war record. Iowa law review 49 : 1130-1176, summer 1964.

MANELIS, B.L. : Edinstvo suvereniteta Soiuza SSR i suvereniteta soiuznykh respublik v period razvernutogo stroitel'stva kommunizma. Sovetskoe gosudarstvo i pravo 34 : 17-26, no. 7, iiul' 1964.

GARNEFSKY, A. : Soviet private international law relating to carriage by sea. Modern law review 27 : 412-433, July 1964.

MARESCA, A. : La convenzione consolare russo-americana del 1° giugno 1964. Comunità internazionale 19 : 409-423, luglio 1964.

NATIONAL LAW - COUNTRIES

TRISKA, J.F. : Soviet treaty law - A quantitative analysis. Law and contemporary problems 29 : 896-909, autumn 1964.

MEISSNER, B. : La position soviétique concernant l'annexion et la prescription. Internationales Recht und Diplomatie : 106-110, 1964.

UNITED ARAB REPUBLIC

CHLALA, J. : Die Rechtsstellung der Ausländer in Ägypten. Aussenwirtschaftsdienst des Betriebs-Beraters 6 : 63-65, 30. März 1960.

République Arabe Unie - Loi concernant l'emploi de la lange arabe, no. 115, du 11 août 1958. Propriété industrielle 76 : 121-122, juillet 1960.

ABDEL-WAHAB, S.E., and BRINSLEY, J.H. : The stipulation for a third person in Egyptian law. American journal of comparative law 10 : 76-86, winter-spring 1961.

Texte de la loi électorale de la République Arabe Unie, du 16 novembre 1963. Orient 7 : 215-221, 4e trimestre 1963.

La nouvelle constitution provisoire. Observateur arabe : 20-26, 30 mars 1964.
Mars 1964; Texte.

La nouvelle constitution. Al-Ahram al-iktisadi: 384-385, ler avril 1964.
Mars 1964; Texte en arabe.

JOUHAUD, Y. : La nouvelle constitution égyptienne. Revue juridique et politique - Indépendance et coopération 18 : 307-318, avril-juin 1964.

La nuova costituzione della Repubblica Araba Unita. Relazioni internazionali 28 : 727-731, 9 maggio 1964.
March 1964; Text.

Constitution, 23 mars 1964. Informations constitutionnelles et parlementaires 15 : 120-141, juillet 1964.

AYAD, M. : L'évolution du droit civil sous le régime socialiste arabe. Egypte contemporaine 55 : 5-18, juillet 1964.
Texte en arabe.

U.S.A.

BLACK, C.L. : The lawfulness of the segregation decisions. Yale law journal 69 : 421-430, January 1960.

CARROW, M.M. : Sovereign immunity in administrative law - A new diagnosis. Journal of public law 9 : 1-23, spring 1960.

HILL, A. : Governmental interest and the conflict of laws - A reply to Professor Currie. University of Chicago law review 27 : 463-504, spring 1960.

SAKS, J.H., and RABKIN, S. : Racial and religious discrimination in housing - A report of legal progress. Iowa law review 45 : 488-524, spring 1960.

GOLDSTEIN, A.S. : The state and the accused - Balance of advantage in criminal procedure. Yale law journal 69 : 1149-1199, June 1960.

HARTMAN, P. : The United States Supreme court and desegregation. Modern law review 23 : 353-372, July 1960.

The reform of real property law - A symposium. New York university law review 35 : 1236-1342, November 1960.

WOLLETT, D.H. : Race relations. Louisiana law review 21 : 85-108, December 1960.
Louisiana.

SCHNADER, W.A. : Report on the status of the uniform commercial code. Banking law journal 78 : 21-27, January 1961.

WEINSTEIN, J.B. : Notes on proposed revision of the New York arbitration law. Arbitration journal 16 : 61-78, no. 2, 1961.

FELLMAN, D. : Constitutional law in 1959-1960. American political science review 55 : 112-135, March 1961.

BOSHKOFF, D. : Documents of title - A comparison of the uniform commercial code and other uniform acts, with emphasis on Michigan law. Michigan law review 59 : 711-754, March 1961.

The Louisiana code of civil procedure. Tulane law review 35 : 473-607, April 1961.
Series of articles.

POLLITT, D.H. : The President's powers in areas of race relations - An exploration. North Carolina law review 39 : 239-281, April 1961.

Administrative regulation. Law and contemporary problems 26 : 179-346, spring 1961.
Special issue.

WEINTRAUB, R.J. : The contracts proposals of the second restatement of conflict of laws - A critique. Iowa law review 46 : 713-731, summer 1961.

MERWIN, J.D. : The U.S. Virgins come of age - A saga of progress in the law. American bar association journal 47 : 778-781, August 1961.
Virgin Islands code.

OPPENHEIM, L. : Judicial review in the United States - Religion and race. South African law journal 78 : 392-420, November 1961.

FINMAN, T. : The request for admissions in federal civil procedure. Yale law journal 71 : 371-436, January 1962.

Migratory divorce - The Alabama experience. Harvard law review 75 : 568-575, January 1962.

GAYNOR, J.K. : Military law source material. Law library journal 55 : 16-32, February 1962.

Commercial arbitration in the United States - A bibliography. Arbitration journal 17 : 227-234, no. 4, 1962.

FARNSWORTH, A. : Le droit commercial aux Etats-Unis d'Amérique. Revue internationale de droit comparé 14 : 309-320, avril-juin 1962.

NATIONAL LAW - COUNTRIES

PENNEY, N. : New York revisits the code - Some variations in the New York enactment of the Uniform commercial code. Columbia law review 62 : 992-1016, June 1962.

Judicial review - Its role in intergovernmental relations. Georgetown law journal 50 : 653-783, summer 1962.
A symposium.

LOISEAUX, P.R. : Domestic obligations in bankruptcy. North Carolina law review 41 : 27-48, fall 1962.

MILLER, A.S. : The changing role of the United States Supreme court. Modern law review 25 : 641-653, November 1962.

FUCHS, R.F. : The United States Supreme court - Pioneer in social policy. Indian year book of international affairs 11 : 88-102, 1962.

MALCOLM, W.D. : The Uniform commercial code in the United States. International and comparative law quarterly 12 : 226-246, January 1963.

ROWE, J.W. : Algunos aspectos de las relaciones entre los poderes legislativo y ejecutivo en Estados Unidos. Boletín de la Biblioteca del Congreso de la nación (Buenos Aires) : 13-46, enero-abril 1963.

MUELLER, G.O.W. : Codification pénale aux Etats-Unis d'Amérique. Revue de droit pénal et de criminologie 43 : 383-417, février 1963.

BRITTAN, L. : The right of privacy in England and the United States. Tulane law review 37 : 235-268, February 1963.

The New York arbitration law, article 75, civil practice law and rules - Commentary and text. Arbitration journal 18 : 132-146, no. 3, 1963.

DOUGLAS, W.O. : The Bill of rights is not enough. New York university law review 38 : 207-242, April 1963.

SPEIDEL, R.E. : Implied duties of cooperation and the defense of sovereign acts in government contracts. Georgetown law journal 51 : 516-557, spring 1963.

McKAY, R.B. : Congressional investigations and the Supreme court. California law review 51 : 267-295, May 1963.

Pre-induction availability of the right to claim conscientious objector exemption. Yale law journal 72 : 1459-1468, June 1963.

MEADOR, D.J. : Judicial determinations of military status. Yale law journal 72 : 1293-1325, June 1963.

CABRERA, L., and HEADRICK, W.C. : Notes on judicial review in Mexico and the United States. Inter-American law review - Revista jurídica interamericana 5 : 253-276, July-December 1963.

Symposium - Arbitration and the courts. Northwestern university law review 58 : 466-582, September-October 1963.

Civil rights and the South - A symposium. North Carolina law review 42 : 1-178, December 1963.

ALTUĞ, Y. : Party autonomy in choice of governing law and adhesion contracts in American conflict of laws. Annales de la Faculté de droit d'Istanbul 13 : 24-44, no. 19, 1963.
Bibliography pp. 45-46.

Religion and the constitution - A symposium on the Supreme court decisions on prayer and Bible reading in the public schools. Journal of public law 13 : 245-503, no. 2, 1964.

TROMBETAS, T.P. : The U.S. Supreme court and the Federal constitutional court of Germany - Some comparative observations. Revue hellénique de droit international 17 : 281-298, juillet-décembre 1964.

BICKEL, A.M. : The Civil rights act of 1964. Commentary 38 : 33-39, August 1964.

SILVEIRA, A. : La Suprema corte en el amoldamiento de la democracia norteamericana. Boletín del Instituto de derecho comparado de México 17 : 543-595, septiembre-diciembre 1964.

GREENAWALT, K.A. : Legal aspects of civil rights in the United States and the Civil rights act of 1964. International commission of jurists, Journal 5 : 247-274, winter 1964.

Government contracts. Law and contemporary problems 29 : 1-274, winter 1964.
A symposium.

HARLAN, J.M. : The Bill of rights and the constitution. American bar association journal 50 : 918-920, October 1964.

EMERSON, T.I. : Freedom of association and freedom of expression. Yale law journal 74 : 1-35, November 1964.

Constitutional problems in the administration of criminal law - Symposium. Northwest university law review 59 : 610-714, November-December 1964.

SPIES, E.G. : Due process and the American criminal trial. Australian law journal 38 : 223-237, November 30, December 31, 1964.

BARTHOLOMEW, P.C. : The Supreme court of the United States, 1963-1964. Western political quarterly 17 : 595-607, December 1964.

LOEWENSTEIN, K. : Staatspolitik und Verfassungsrecht in den Vereinigten Staaten, 1955-1964. Jahrbuch des öffentlichen Rechts der Gegenwart 13 : 1-116, 1964.

U.S.A.
(International law, Aliens, Nationality)

DEAN, A.H. : Department seeks Senate approval of conventions on law of sea. Department of State bulletin (United States) 42 : 251-261, 15 February 1960.

WALKER, H. : Convention of establishment between the United States and France. American journal of international law 54 : 393-398, April 1960.

BOUDIN, L.B. : Involuntary loss of American nationality. Harvard law review 73 : 1510-1531, June 1960.

NATIONAL LAW - COUNTRIES

BARNES, W. : Diplomatic immunity from local jurisdiction, its historical development under international law and application in United States practice. Department of State bulletin (United States) 43 : 173-182, 1 August 1960.

BISHOP, W.W., and MYERS, D.P. : Unwarranted extension of Connally-amendment thinking. American journal of international law 55 : 135-145, January 1961.
Jurisdiction affecting domestic law.

RODE, Z.R. : The American-Polish claims agreement of 1960. American journal of international law 55 : 452-459, April 1961.

OLIVER, C.T. : The American law institute's draft restatement of the foreign relations law of the United States. American journal of international law 55 : 428-440, April 1961.

LEPAULLE, P. : Réflexions sur la convention d'établissement franco-américaine du 25 novembre 1959. Revue critique de droit international privé 50 : 291-304, avril-juin 1961.

QUINGLEY, L.V. : Accession by the United States to the United Nations convention on the recognition and enforcement of foreign arbitral awards. Yale law journal 70 : 1049-1082, June 1961.

SMIT, H. : International aspects of federal civil procedure. Columbia law review 61 : 1031-1072, June 1961.

VOLCHKOV, A.F., and RUBANOV, A.A. : Imushchestvennye prava sovetskikh grazhdan v Soedinennykh Shtatakh Ameriki. Sovetskoe gosudarstvo i pravo 31 : 83-83, no. 6, iiun' 1961.

VAGTS, D.F. : The corporate alien - Definitional questions in federal restraints on foreign enterprise. Harvard law review 74 : 1489-1551, June 1961.

CHRISTENSON, G.A. : The United States-Rumanian claims settlement agreement of 30 March 1960. American journal of international law 55 : 617-636, July 1961.

BOYD, W.L. : Constitutional, treaty, and statutory requirements of probate notice to consuls and aliens. Iowa law review 47 : 29-103, fall 1961.

HARRIS, C.W. : International relations and the disposition of alien enemy property seized by the United States during World War II - A case study on German properties. Journal of politics 23 : 641-666, November 1961.

EVANS, A.E. : Observations on the practice of territorial asylum in the United States. American journal of international law 56 : 148-157, January 1962.

BERMAN, H.J. : Soviet heirs in American courts. Columbia law review 62 : 257-274, February 1962.

LUBMAN, S. : The unrecognized government in American courts - Upright vs. Mercury business machines. Columbia law review 62 : 275-310, February 1962.

STILLEY, V.A. : Recognition in New York of foreign nation divorce decrees. Intramural law review of New York university School of law 17 : 239-254, May 1962.

NELSON, R.H. : The subject-matter limitation upon the treaty-making power. Journal of public law 11 : 122-155, spring 1962.

ALEXY, H. : Der Einfluss der Exekutive und innerstaatlicher Rechtsgrundsätze auf die amerikanische Rechtsprechung zur Immunität fremder Staaten. Zeitschrift für ausländisches öffentliches Recht und Völkerrecht 22 : 661-696, Oktober 1962.

WETTER, J.G. : Diplomatic assistance to private investment - A study of the theory and practice of the United States during the twentieth century. University of Chicago law review 29 : 275-326, winter 1962.

SMIT, H. : Assistance rendered by the United States in proceedings before international tribunals. Columbia law review 62 : 1264-1276, November 1962.

Fifty-fifth annual meeting American association of law libraries - Panel on foreign law, Wednesday, 4 July 1962. Law library journal 55 : 311-424, November 1962.
Including bibliographies.

Executive discretion in extradition. Columbia law review 62 : 1313-1329, November 1962.

GARDNER, P. : Extraterritorial application of the trademark laws of the United States. Harvard international law club journal 4 : 48-99, December 1962.

HEINI, A. : Neuere Strömungen im amerikanischen internationalen Privatrecht. Schweizerisches Jahrbuch für internationales Recht 19 : 31-70, 1962.

DOMKE, M. : The War claims act of 1962. American journal of international law 57 : 354-372, April 1963.

McPHAIL, I.D. : Security for costs and its treatment in United States treaties. Tulane law review 37 : 461-480, April 1963.

United States jurisdiction over representatives to the United Nations. Columbia law review 63 : 1066-1085, June 1963.

GRÄBER, F. : Die Scheidung der Ehe von USA-Bürgern, die sich in Deutschland befinden. Zeitschrift für das gesamte Familienrecht 10 : 493-495, Oktober 1963.

LEANZA LAURIA, F. : Confische cubane innanzi a Corti statunitensi - Il caso Sabbatino. Diritto internazionale 18 : parte 1a, 66-84, no. 1, 1964.

HENKIN, L. : The foreign affairs power of the Federal courts - Sabbatino. Columbia law review 64 : 805-832, May 1964.

GORDON, C. : Finality of immigration and nationality determinations - Can the Government be estopped? University of Chicago law review 31 : 433-466, spring 1964.

DOBRIANSKY, L.E. : The second treaty of Moscow. Ukrainian quarterly 20 : 318-330, winter 1964/65.
U.S.S.R.-United States Consular convention, 1 June 1964.

LILLICH, R.B. : The United States-Bulgarian claims agreement of 1963. American journal of international law 58 : 686-706, July 1964.

MARESCA, A. : La convenzione consolare russo-americana del 1° giugno 1964. Comunità internazionale 19 : 409-423, luglio 1964.

SMIT, H. : L'assistenza prestada dagli Stati Uniti nei procedimenti di fronte ai tribunali internazionali. Jus, Rivista di scienze giuridiche 15 : 550-564, otoobre-dicembre 1964.

EVANS, A.E. : Acquisition of custody over the international fugitive offender, alternatives to extradition - A survey of United States practice. British year book of international law 40 : 77-104, 1964.

UPPER VOLTA

Constitution de la République de Haute-Volta, 28 février 1959. Documentation française, Notes et études documentaires : 55-59, no. 2693, 19 août 1960.
Texte.

MANGIN, G. : Haute-Volta. Annuaire de législation française et étrangère 9 : 241-245, 1960.

République de Haute Volta. Constitution du 30 novembre 1960. Revue juridique et politique d'outre-mer 15 : 299-307, avril-juin 1961.

MOUSSA, K. : La justice en Haute-Volta. Penant, Revue de droit des pays d'Afrique 74 : 49-51, janvier-mars 1964.

URUGUAY

SÁNCHEZ FONTÁNS, J., and SORIANO, O.R. : Reseña de legislación, jurisprudencia y bibliografía uruguayas durante el año 1960. Revista de derecho privado (Madrid) 45 : 879-885, octubre 1961.

FARINA, J.M. : Unificación del derecho comercial entre Argentina y Uruguay. Revista de la Facultad de ciencias económicas, comerciales y políticas (Rosario) 5 : 13-17, nos. 9-12, 1962-1963.

VATICAN STATE

MALINTOPPI, A. : La protezione speciale della Città del Vaticano in caso di conflitto armato. Rivista di diritto internazionale 43 : 607-629, fasc. 4, 1960.

IGINO : Le Saint Siège et le droit consulaire. Osservatore romano, Edition hebdomadaire en langue française 14 : 3-4, 22 mars 1963.
Premier article d'une série.

VENEZUELA

Venezuela - Constitución de 23-1-1961. Documentos, Revista de información política : 434-478, enero-marzo 1961.
Text.

Constitution de la République de Venezuela, 23 janvier 1961. Documentation française, Notes et études documentaires : 1-33, no. 2766, 4 avril 1961.

LIONS SIGNORET, M. : Nueva constitución de la République de Venezuela. Boletín del Instituto de derecho comparado de México 14 : 375-393, mayo-agosto 1961.

Constitution de la République de Venezuela, 23 janvier 1961. Informations constitutionnelles et parlementaires : 125-185, juillet 1961.
Texte.

ANGULO, M.R. : Comments on the status of foreign business corporations under the commercial codes of Argentina and Venezuela. Inter-American law review - Revista jurídica interamericana 4 : 159-185, July-December 1962.

AGUERREVERE, A.D. : Del régimen dominical en el derecho (Caracas) : 9-17, no. 24, 1963.

SANSO, B. : Sobre la exclusion de la responsabilidad contractual y de la responsabilidad por vicios ocultos en la legislación italiana y en la venezolana. Revista de la Facultad de derecho (Caracas) : 113-118, no. 28, 1964.

FEO, R.F. : Revista de la Facultad de derecho (Caracas) : 39-59, no. 29, 1964.

Ley de reforma parcia del código penal. Revista de la Facultad de derecho (Caracas) : 111-124, no. 30, 1964.

VIET-NAM

Democratic Republic of Vietnam constitution of 1960. Osteuropa-Recht 6 : 222-238, August 1960.
Text.

DERRIDA, F. : Un code de la famille au Sud-Viet-Nam. Revue internationale de droit comparé 13 : 57-77, janvier-mars 1961.

PERERA, V.S. : Justice in South Viet-Nam. Ceylon law society journal 7 : xxv-xxvi, March 1961.

TRIN DINH TIEU : L'adoption dans la loi vietnamienne du 2 janvier 1959 sur la famille. Revue internationale de droit comparé 13 : 602-615, juillet-septembre 1961.

Constitution de la République Démocratique du Viet-Nam, 31 décembre 1959. Documentation française, Notes et études documentaires : 1-14, no. 2989, 10 mai 1963.
Texte.

République Démocratique du Viet-Nam - Constitution, 31 décembre 1959. Informations constitutionnelles et parlementaires 14 : 169-190, octobre 1963.
Texte.

WEST INDIES

PATCHETT, K.W. : English law in the West Indies - A conference report. International and comparative law quarterly 12 : 922-988, July 1963.

McFARLANE, D. : A comparative study of incentive legislation in the Leeward Islands, Windward Islands, Barbados and Jamaica. Social and economic studies, Supplement 13 : 1-63, no. 3, 1964.

YEMEN

La nouvelle constitution yéménite. Monde arabe en fin de chaque semaine : 1-2, annexe no. 643, 29 octobre-4 novembre 1962.

Constitución de la República de Yemen (1963) - Parte dispositiva. Documentos, Revista de información política : 277-284, octubre-diciembre 1963.

The constitution of the Arab-Yemenite Republic. Hamizrah hehadash - The new East 14 : 369-378, no. 4, 1964.
Text in Hebrew.

YUGOSLAVIA

GROL, V.M. : The condition of aliens and the conflict of laws in the Yugoslav law of succession. American journal of comparative law 9 : 249-253, spring 1960.

LJUBISA, L. : Chronique yougoslave - Loi portant modification du code pénal yougoslave et le complétant. Revue pénitentiaire et de droit pénal 84 : 439-451, juillet-septembre 1960.

SRZENTIĆ, N. : Teorija i praksa u oblasti krivičnog prava. Naša zakonitost 14 : 473-587, broj 11-12, 1960.

PEŠELJ, B.M. : The socialist character of Jugoslav law. Study centre for Jugoslav affairs, Review 2 : 94-131, no. 2, 1961.

BARTOŠ, M. : Doprinos nove Jugoslavije razvoju medunarodnog prava. Jugoslovenska revija za medunarodno pravo 8 : 180-186, broj 2, 1961.
Summary in French.

BAYER, V. : La réforme du code pénal yougoslave. Revue de science criminelle et de droit pénal comparé 16 : 293-309, avril-juin 1961.

STAMENOVIĆ, V. : Mesni odbori u komunalnom sistemu. Pravni zbornik 10 : 105-122, nroj 2, jun 1961.
Local government in Montenegro.

ČULINOVIĆ, F. : Nastajanje novog jugoslovenskog prava. Naša zakonitost 16 : 477-484, broj 11-12, 1961.

PRETNAR, S. : Das Unternehmen in Jugoslawien und seine Rechtsstellung. Osteuropa-Recht 7 : 233-257, Dezember 1961.

El capítulo XXV del código penal yugoslavo. Revista española de derecho militar : 117-132, enero-junio 1962.
Crimes against the armed forces.

NITSCHE, P. : Jugoslawische Amtsblätter, Rechts- und Verwaltungszeitschriften. Osteuropa-Recht 8 : 72-86, März 1962.

LAPENNA, I. : State and law in the programmes of the Jugoslav and Soviet parties. Político 27 : 92-111, marzo 1962.

CICOJ, S. : Das jugoslawische Kollisions- und internationale Urheberrecht. Osteuropa-Recht 8 : 111-120, Juni 1962.

L'avant-projet de la constitution devant l'Assemblée nationale. Questions actuelles du socialisme (Beograd) : 1-123, octobre-décembre 1962.
Texte pp. 131-247, Numéro spécial.

GERSKOVIC, L. : Osnove odredbe i intencije novog Ustava. Ekonomski pregled 13 : 915-927, broj 12, 1962.

Diskusija o principima i problemima prednacrta Ustava socijalističke Jugoslavie. Arhiv za pravne i društvene nauke 50 : 77-307, januar-juni 1963.

ALCALÁ-ZAMORA, N. : Ley yugoeslava sobre procedimiento general administrativo. Boletín del Instituto de derecho comparado de México 16 : 127-138, enero-abril 1963.

DJORDJEVIC, J. : The Socialist federation and the Republic. New Yugoslav law 14 : 3-20, January-September 1963.
See also pp. 20-49; Draft of the constitution pp. 50-104.

LEVI, M. : Becka konvencija o konzularnim odnosima i jugoslovenska praksa. Jugoslovenska revija za medunarodno pravo 10 : 215-242, broj 2, 1963.
See also pp. 161-173.

STEFANOVIĆ, J. : Neke bitne karakterne crte naših novih ustava. Zbornik Pravnog fakulteta u Zagrebu 13 : 87-97, broj 2-4, 1963.
New constitution; Summary in French.

La constitution de la République Socialiste Fédérative de Yougoslavie. Questions actuelles du socialisme (Beograd) : 1-133, juin 1963.
Texte intégral; Numéro spécial.

CIGOJ, S. : Development of torts law in Yugoslavia. American journal of comparative law 12 : 396-404, summer 1963.

Constitution de la République Socialiste Fédérative de Yougoslavie, 9 avril 1963. Informations constitutionnelles et parlementaires 14 : 114-161, juillet 1963.
Texte.

SRZENTIĆ, N. : Zaštita prava ličnosti u jugosloven skom krivičnom pravu. Arhiv za pravne i društvene nauke 50 : 321-343, juli-septembar 1963.

FERRETJANS, J.P. : La constitution du 7 avril 1963 de la République Socialiste Fédérative de Yougoslavie et l'unité marxiste du pouvoir d'Etat. Revue du droit public et de la science politique en France at à l'etranger 79 : 939-962, septembre-octobre 1963.

DJORDJEVIC, J. : Les caractéristiques fondamentales de la nouvelle constitution yougoslave. Revue internationale de droit comparé 15 : 689-703, octobre-décembre 1963.

GEORGIJEVIĆ, R. : Novi institut brisanja osude našeg krivičnopravnog sistema. Naša zakonitost 17 : 504-514, broj 11-12, 1963.

Constitución de la República Socialista Federativa de Yugoslavia. Revista de la Facultad de derecho (Caracas) : 95-140, no. 27, 1963.
Text; See also pp. 93-94.

MAGARAŠEVIĆ, A. : Theory of international law in Yugoslavia - A comment on status and approaches. American society of international law, Proceedings 57 : 270-275, 1963.
Discussion pp. 290-293.

SMOLE, A. : Unterschiede zwischen dem österreichischen und dem jugoslawischen Erbrecht. Österreichische Juristen-Zeitung 19 : 4-11, 14. Jänner 1964.

NATIONAL LAW - COUNTRIES

SCHULTZ, L. : Der sowjetische Begriff des Revisionismus und das jugoslawische Verfassungsrecht. Recht in Ost und West 8 : 1-7, 15. Januar 1964.

Constitution de la République Socialiste Fédérative de Yougoslavie. Documentation française, Notes et études documentaires : 1-43, no. 3055, 16 janvier 1964.
1963.

SRZENTIĆ, N. : On the new constitutional judicature of Yugoslavia. New Yugoslav law 15 : 20-28, January-September 1964.

SINGER, M. : Nehat "kamen smutnje" u teoriji krivičnog prava. Naša zakonitost 18 : 73-83, 169-193; broj 3-4, broj 5-6, 1964.

TADIĆ, L. : Opste karakteristike i osnovni izvori sloboda, prava i dužnosti čovjeka i gradanina u ustavu SFRJ. Pravni zbornik 12 : 1-8, broj 1, april 1964.

GRUJOSKI, T. : Neki problemi uskladivanja saveznih zakona sa ustavom i dalja izgradnja pravnog sistema. Arhiv za pravne i društvene nauke 51 : 185-192, juli-septembar 1964.

GOLUBOVIC, M. : Samoupravljanje u privrednoj organizaciji prema Ustavu Socijalističke Federativne Republike Jugoslavije. Pravni zbornik 12 : 1-50, broj 2, avgusta 1964.

SIMIĆ, V. : Problemi zakonodavstva i izgradnje pravnog sistema. Arhiv za pravne i društvene nauke 51 : 313-419, oktobar-decembar 1964.

SPASOJEVIĆ, M. : Princip ustavnosti i zakonitosti i njegovo obezbjedenje u našem ustavnom sistemu. Pravni zbornik 12 : 19-35, broj 3, decembar 1964.

SIMIĆ, V. : Problems of legislation and development of the legal system. New Yugoslav law 15 : 17-26, October-December 1964.

SEPAROVIĆ, Z. : Der neue jugoslawische Strafvollzug. Zeitschrift für strafvollzug 13 : 340-349, Dezember 1964.

KRBEK, I. : Die Verfassung der Sozialistischen Föderativen Republik Jugoslawien vom 7.4.1963. Jahrbuch des öffentlichen Rechts der Gegenwart 13 : 243-283, 1964.
Text pp. 284-324.

EUROPE
(Economic Community, EFTA)

SANDERS, P. : Auf dem Wege zu einer europäischen Aktiengesellschaft? Aussenwirtschaftsdienst des Betriebs-Beraters 6 : 1-5, 30. Januar 1960.

SPERDUTI, G. : L'organizzazione e le funzioni di governo della Comunità europea del carbone e dell' acciaio (Contd.). Comunità internazionale 15 : 3-20, gennaio 1960.

WOHLFARTH, E. : Europäisches Recht - Von der Befugnis der Argane der Europäischen Wirtschaftsgemeinschaft zur Rechtsetzung. Jahrbuch für internationales Recht 9 : 12-32, Heft 1, 1960.

SCHLOH, B. : Eine Entscheidung des Bundesgerichtshofs über das Verhältnis von Recht der Montanunion und deutschem Zivilrecht. Jahrbuch für internationales Recht 9 : 92-101, Heft 1, 1960.

Les effets du jugement déclaratif de faillite et du jugement homologuant un concordat au sein des six pays membres de la Communauté économique européenne - Rapport de la Commission belge. Annuario di diritto comparato e di studi legislativi 34 : 32-35, fasc. 1, 1960.

MIGLIAZZA, A. : Su alcuni caratteri della Corte di giustizia delle Comunità europee. Rivista di diritto internazionale 43 : 229-256, fasc. 2, 1960.

KERN, E. : Der Europäische Dienst und das Europäische Dienstrecht. Europäische Wirtschaft 3 : 90-92, 15. März 1960.

WOLTERS, A. : Les recours en annulation devant la Cour de justice des communautés européennes. Revue de droit international et de droit comparé 37 : 165-184, no. 3, 1960.

GORI, P. : Sui poteri d'investigazione dell'Alta autorità della CECA. Rivista di diritto internazionale 43 : 630-647, fasc. 4, 1960.

Les recours en annulation et en cas de carence dans le droit de la CECA à la lumière de la jurisprudence de la Cour de justice des communautés. Chronique de politique étrangère 13 : 287-396, mai 1960.

GAUDET, M. : Legal problems of the European common market. Record of the Association of the bar of the city of New York 15 : 218-229, May 1960.

REIBSTEIN, E. : Das Europäische Öffentliche Recht 1648-1815 - Ein institutionengeschichtlicher Überblick. Archiv des Völkerrechts 8 : 385-420, 4. Heft 1960.

Le fonds de commerce et la propriété commerciale dans la Communauté économique européenne. Recueil Dalloz, Chronique : 109-112, 1 juin 1960.

STEIN, E., and HAY, P. : Legal remedies of enterprises in the European economic community. American journal of comparative law 9 : 375-424, summer 1960.

THOMÄ, K.E. : Das Auskunftsverlangen im Recht der Europäischen Wirtschaftsgemeinschaft. Europäische Wirtschaft 3 : 423-431, 15. August 1960.

FRIAUF, K.H. : Die Notwendigkeit einer verfassungskonformen Auslegung im Recht der westeuropäischen Gemeinschaften. Archiv des öffentlichen Rechts 85 : 224-235, Heft 2, August 1960.

Um ein gemeinsames Gesellschaftsrecht in der EWG. Berichte und Informationen des Österreichischen Forschungsinstituts für Wirtschaft und Politik 15 : 9-10, 14. Oktober 1960.

THOMÄ, K.E. : Le droit de communication dans la Communauté économique européenne. Revue du Marché commun : 345-356, octobre 1960.

CONARD, A.F. : Forming a subsidiary in the European common market. Michigan law review 59 : 1-48, November 1960.

NATIONAL LAW - COUNTRIES

ERADES, L. : Recht en rechter in Nederland en in de Europese gemeenschappen. Nederalns tijdschrift voor international recht - Netherlands international law review 7 : 334-358, oktober 1960.
Summary in French.

SCHLACHTER, E. : Nouveaux aspects de la liberté d'établissement dans le traité de Rome. Revue du Marché commun : 392-396, novembre 1960.

VALENTINE, D.G. : The jurisdiction of the Court of justice of the European communities to annul executive action. British year book of international law 36 : 174-222, 1960.

DAVID, R. : L'unification des droits européens. Boletim da Faculdade de direito (Coimbra) 36 : 44-54, 1960.

MIGLIAZZA, A. : La Cour de justice des Communautés européennes et l'ordre des Etats membres - Analyse de la jurisprudence de la C.I.C.E. Università di Milano, Istituto di diritto internazionale e straniero; Comunicazioni e studi 11 : 199-220, 1960-1962.

SAVATIER, R. : Les aspects de droit international privé de la Communauté économique européenne. Comité français de droit international privé, Travaux 21-23 : 17-34, 1960-1962.
Discussion pp. 34-37.

VEITER, T. : Wer kann den Europäischen Gerichtshof anrufen? Berichte und Informationen des Österreichischen Forschungsinstituts für Wirtschaft und Politik 16 : 5, 27. Jänner 1961.

LAGRANGE, M. : Le rôle de la Cour de justice des communautés européennes tel qu'il se dégage de sa jurisprudence. Droit social 24 : 1-11, janvier 1961.

ZANNINI, W. : Dell'uniformità nell'interpretazione dei sistemi di diritto delle comunità europee. Diritto internazionale 15 : parte la, 26-43, no. 1, 1961.
See also pp. 43-47.

ROBERTSON, A.H. : The legal work of the Council of Europe. International and comparative law quarterly 10 : 143-166, January 1961.

LAGRANGE, M. : Les pouvoirs de la Haute autorité et l'application du Traité de Paris. Revue du droit public et de la science politique en France et à l'étranger 77 : 40-58, janvier-février 1961.

CATALANO, N. : La Communauté économique européenne et l'unification, le rapprochement et l'harmonisation des droits des Etats membres. Revue internationale de droit comparé 13 : 5-17, janvier-mars 1961.

ALCALÁ-ZAMORA y CASTILLO, N. : Reglamento de la Corte europea de derechos humanos. Boletín del Instituto de derecho comparado de México 14 : 89-99, anero-abril 1961.

CASTANOS, S. : Les nouveaux principes du fonctionnalisme dans la C.E.C.A. Revue hellénique de droit international 13, 14 : 213-245, 60-91; janvier-décembre 1960, janvier-décembre 1961.

ROHNFELDER, G. : Eine europäische Konsularkonvention? Europa-Archiv 16 : 141-148, 25. März 1961.

MONACO, R. : Natura ed efficacia dei regolamenti delle Comunità europee. Rivista di diritto internazionale 44 : 393-408, fasc. 3, 1961.

VELU, J. : Le problème de l'application aux juridictions administratives des règles de la Convention européenne des droits de l'homme relatives à la publicité des audiences et des jugements. Revue de droit international et de droit comparé 38 : 129-171, nos. 3-4, 1961.

GRISOLI, A. : Alcune considerazione sulla responsabilità aquiliana delle comunità economiche europee. Rivista del diritto commerciale e del diritto geneale delle obbligazioni 59 : parte la, 104-136, marzo-aprile 1961.

BARILE, G. : La Carta sociale europea il diritto internazionale. Rivista di diritto internazionale 44 : 624-644, fasc. 4, 1961.

DUCLOS, P. : L'Européen - Exploration d'une catégorie juridique naissante. Revue générale de droit international public 65 : 260-300, avril-juin 1961.

KNOPP, W. : Über die Pflicht deutscher Gerichte zur Vorlage von Auslegungsfragen an den Gerichtshof der Europäischen Gemeinsxhaften nach Art. 177 des EWG-Vertrages. Juristenzeitung 16 : 305-312, 19. Mai 1961.

L'exequatur des jugements et la Communauté économique européenne. Banque 36 : 276-279, mai 1961.

LEGROS, R. : Effets internationaux des jugements répressifs et communautés européennes. Revue de droit pénal et de criminologie 41 : 795-823, juin 1961.

VIGNES, D. : Le droit d'établissement et les services dans la Communauté économique européenne. Annuaire français de droit international 7 : 668-725, 1961.

European regional communities. Law and contemporary problems 26 : 347-588, summer 1961.
A symposium.

BUERGENTHAL, T. : Appeals for annulment by enterprises in the European coal and steel community. American journal of comparative law 10 : 227-252, summer 1961.

WESER, M. : Bases of judicial jurisdiction in the Common market countries. American journal of comparative law 10 : 323-344, autumn 1961.

HONIG, F. : Entry into the Common market - Some legal problems. Law journal 111 : 593-596, 15 September 1961.

LOEWE, R., and ZEMBSCH, A. : Europäische Übereinkommen über die Internationale Handelsschiedsgerichtsbarkeit. Österreichische Ost-Hefte 3 : 345-351, September 1961.

Die Rechtsfragen der europäischen Einigung. Europa-Archiv 16 : 595-600, 25. Oktober 1961.

THOMPSON, D. : The project for a commercial company of European type. International and comparative law quarterly 10 : 851-876, October 1961.

Droit d'établissement dans la Communauté économique européenne. Revue du Marché commun : 410-413, novembre 1961.

NATIONAL LAW - COUNTRIES

ROBERT, J. : La convention européenne sur l'arbitrage commercial international signée à Genève le 21 avril 1961. Recueil Dalloz, Chronique : 173-176, 177-184, 1er, 8 novembre 1961.

WAGNER, W.J. : La codificazione del diritto in Europa ed il movimento per la codificazione degli Stati Uniti intorno alla metà del diciannovesimo secolo. Jus, Rivista di scienze giuridiche 12 : 519-533, dicembre 1961.

BENJAMIN, P. : The European convention on international commercial arbitration. British year book of international law 37 : 478-495, 1961.

McMAHON, J.F. : The Court of the European communities - Judicial interpretation and international organization. British year book of international law 37 : 320-350, 1961.

GUGGENHEIM, P. : Droit international général et droit public européen. Schweizerisches Jahrbuch für internationales Recht 18 : 9-28, 1961.

MIGLIAZZA, A. : La jurisprudence de la Cour de justice des Communautés auropéennes et le problème des sources du droit. Association des auditeurs et anciens auditeurs de l'Académie de droit international de La Haye, Annuaire 31 : 96-107, 1961.

GLAESNER, H.J. : Treaty making power and legislation of the European communities. Association des auditeurs et anciens auditeurs de l'Académie de droit international de La Haye, Annuaire 31 : 147-154, 1961.

DRAETTA, U. : Il ravvicinamento delle legislazioni nel trattato istitutivo della Comunità economica europea. Diritto internazionale 16 : parte 1a, 43-72, no. 1, 1962.

McMAHON, J.F. : The Court of the European communities. Journal of Common market studies 1 : 1-21, 1962.

TELCHINI, I. : Rapporti di coesistenza fra la Corte di giustizia delle Comunità europee e le giurisdizioni nazionali. Diritto internazionale 16 : parte 1a, 114-121, no. 1, 1962.

DURANTE, F. : I privilegi ed immunità dei funzionari della C.E.C.A. e la competenza della Corte di giustizia delle Comunità europee. Rivista di diritto internazionale 45 : 54-63, fasc. 1, 1962.

HAHN, H.J. : Die Organisation für Wirtschaftliche Zusammenarbeit und Entwicklung (OECD) - Entstehung und Rechtsordnung. Zeitschrift für ausländisches öffentliches Recht und Völkerrecht 22 : 49-112, Nr. 1/2, 1962.

BAUGNIET, J. : Las sociedades por acciones en los seis paises de la Comunidad europea. Instituto de derecho comparado, Revista (Barcelona) : 7-54, enero-junio 1962.

MONCAYO, G.R. : Esquema jurídico de las Comunidades europeas. Revista jurídica de Buenos Aires : 167-192, enero-junio 1962.

MARSH, N.S. : The Common market and the common law. Listener 67 : 455-457, 15 March 1962.

MUNRO, H. : The Common market and English courts. Law journal 112 : 165-168, 16 March 1962.

ZANNINI, W. : La giurisdizione della Corte di giustizia delle Comunità europee in rapporto agli ordinamenti degli Stati membri. Diritto internazionale 16 : parte 1a, 242-259, no. 3, 1962.
Texts pp. 259-264.

MIGLIAZZA, A. : La jurisprudence de la Cour de justice des Communautés européennes et le problème des sources du droit. Österreichische Zeitschrift für öffentliches Recht 12 : 332-343, Heft 3, 1962.

SECHE, J.C. : La notion d'intérêt à agir dans le droit de la Communauté européenne du charbon et de l'acier. Revue générale de droit internationale public 66 : 299-356, avril-juin 1962.

DUMON, F. : La Cour de justice des Communautés européennes et les juridictions des Etats membres. Revue internationale de droit comparé 14 : 369-398, avril-juin 1962.

DONNER, A.M. : The Court of justice of the European communities. Record of the Association of the bar of the city of New York 17 : 232-243, May 1962.

HAMMES, C.L. : Le droit des Communautés européennes sous l'aspect de son application juridictionnelle. Revue de l'Université de Bruxelles 14 : 253-272, mai-juin 1962.

BENEDUCE, A. : Per una disciplina europea delle società per azioni - Il bilancio. Rivista del diritto commerciale e del diritto general delle obbligazioni 60 : parte 1a, 186-231, giugno 1962.

BUERGENTHAL, T. : The private appeal against illegal state activities in the European coal and steel community. American journal of comparative law 11 : 325-347, summer 1962.

THOMPSON, D. : The Bosch case. International and comparative law quarterly 11 : 721-737, July 1962.

WAELBROECK, M. : Le problème de la validité des ententes économiques dans le droit privé du Marché commun. Revue critique de droit international privé 51 : 415-443, juillet-septembre 1962.

BREBAN, J. : Revue de jurisprudence de la Cour de justice des Communautés européennes. Revue du droit public et de la science politique en France et à l'étranger 78 : 873-930, septembre-octobre 1962.

SEIDL-HOHENVEKDERN, I. : Harmonisation of legislation in the Common market and the heritage of the common law. Journal of business law : 247-252, 363-372, July-October 1962.

KLEIN, F.E. : La convention européenne sur l'arbitrage commercial international. Revue critique de droit international privé 51 : 621-640, octobre-décembre 1962.

The law report of the Common market. Law journal 112 : 711-714, 2 November 1962.

MÜNCH, F. : Die Entwicklung der europäischen Gerichtsbarkeit. Jahrbuch für internationales Recht 11 : 324-338, 1962.

TREZISE, P.H. : The Common market and industrial property. Department of state bulletin (United States) 47 : 925-927, 17 December 1962.
E.E.C. patent convention.

NATIONAL LAW - COUNTRIES

HOUIN, R. : Les sociétés de type européen. Comité français de droit international privé, Travaux 23-25 : 19-59, 1962-1964.

CHEVAL, C. : De l'opportunité de créer une Cour européenne de justice pour les litiges de droit privé. Droit européen 5 : 27-32, janvier 1963.

Droit européen. Revue de droit international et de droit comparé 40 : 7-71, no. 1, 1963.
Suite d'articles.

SCHLOCHAUER, H.J. : Das Verhältnis des Rechts der Europäischen Wirtschaftsgemeinschaft zu den nationalen Rechtsordnungen der Mitgliedstaaten. Archiv des Völkerrechts 11 : 1-34, 1. Heft 1963.

FELD, W. : The civil service aspect of the European communities - Legal and political aspects. Journal of public law 12 : 68-85, no. 1, 1963.

GRAUPNER, R. : Some recent aspects of the recognition and enforcement of foreign judgments in Western Europe. International and comparative law quarterly 12 : 367-386, April 1963.

HESS, G. : Zehn Jahre Rechtsprechung des Gerichtshofes der Europäischen Gemeinschaften - Ergebnisse einer Arbeitstagung des Instituts für das Recht der Europäischen Gemeinschaften der Universität Köln. Europa-Archiv 18 : 497-501, 10. Juli 1963.

DURRY, G. : Ouragan européen sur les contrats d'exclusivité? Recueil Dalloz, Chronique : 177-183, 10 juillet 1963.

CATALANO, N. : La Corte costituzionale e le Comunità europee. Foro italiano 88 : parte 4a, 67-71, 31 luglio 1963.

PÉPY, A. : L'article 177 du traité de Rome et les juridictions françaises - Compétence préjudicielle de la Cour de justice des Communautés. Revue critique de droit international privé 52 : 475-501, juillet-septembre 1963.

PELLICER VALERO, J.A. : El Tribunal de justicia de las Comunidades europeas. Revista de derecho y ciencias sociales (Concepción) 31 : 63-81, julio-septiembre 1963.

STOLFI, M. : Diritto europeo in materia di concorrenza. Rivista del diritto commerciale e del diritto generale delle obbligazioni 61 : parte la, 332-350, settembre-ottobre 1963.

BRODA, C. : Auf dem Wege zur europäischen Rechtsvereinheitlichung. Österreichische Juristen-Zeitung 18 : 477-482, 24. September 1963.

ESSÉN, E. : Europarådets rättssamarbete. Svensk juristtidning 48 : 507-520, september 1963.

GOFFIN, L. : La responsabilité civile de la C.E.E. et de l'Euratom. Industrie (Bruxelles) 17 : 597-599, septembre 1963.

ELLIS, J.J.A. : L'interprétation du mot "affecter" dans l'article 85, para. 1, du traité de la Communauté économique européenne par rapport aux mots "empêcher", "restreindre", ou "fausser le jeu de la concurrence". Recueil Dalloz, Chronique : 221-228, 9 octobre 1963.

BALLADORE PALLIERI, G. : Les pouvoirs des organisations économiques européennes à l'intérieur des Etats membrs. Zeitschrift für ausländisches öffentliches Recht un Völkerrecht 23 : 473-484, Oktober 1963.

HAY, P. : Federal jurisdiction of the Common market court. American journal of comparative law 12 : 21-40, winter 1963.

BREDIN, J.D. : Les conflits de lois en matière de contrats dans la Communauté economique européenne. Journal du droit international 90 : 938-963, octobre-décembre 1963.
Texte en anglais aussi.

UNDÉN, Ö. : Om FN:s och Europarådets domstolar. Svensk juristtidning 48 : 657-661, november-december 1963.

LECOURT, E., et CHEVALLIER, R.M. : Chances et malchances de l'harmonisation des législations européennes. Recueil Dalloz, Chronique : 273-283, 18 décembre 1963.

FELD, W. : The Court of justice of the European communities, emerging political power? - An examination of selected decisions of the Court's 1961-1962 term. Tulane law review 38 : 53-80, December 1963.

SIZARET, L. : La Cour de justice des Communautés européennes. Annuaire european yearbook ii/I : 88-100, 1963.

LLOYD, D. : The Court of justice of the European economic community. Current legal problems 16 : 34-53, 1963.

SCAMELL, E.H. : The Common market and the legal profession. Current legal problems 16 : 54-67, 1963.

GUREEV, S. : Evropeĭskaia konventsiia o vneshnetorgovom arbitrazhe. Sovetskiĭ ezhegodnik mezhdunarodnogo prava - Soviet year-book of international law : 533-537, 1963.
Geneva, April 1961.

MOSER, R. : Direito internacional privado, unificação do direito e Comunidade econômica européia. Revista da Facultade de direito (São Paulo) 58 : 93-105, 1963.

LAGRANGE, M. : La Cour de justice des Communautés européennes. France, Conseil d'Etat; Etudes et documents 17 : 55-79, 1963.

STEIN, E. : Assimilation of national laws as a function of European integration. American journal of international law 58 : 1-40, January 1964.

BARILE, G. : Sulla struttura delle Comunità europee. Rivista di diritto internazionale 47 : 17-22, fasc. 1, 1964.

PARLAVANTZAS, P.B. : Les rapports juridiques entre le Conseil de l'Europe, l'Union de l'Europe occidentale et l'O.T.A.N. Revue hellénique de droit international 17 : 62-87, janvier-juin 1964.

NERI, S. : Sulla natura giuridica delle Comunità europee. Rivista di diritto internazionale 47 : 231-265, fasc. 2, 1964.

NATIONAL LAW - COUNTRIES

PELLICER VALERO, J. : Los recursos de anulación en las Comunidades europeas. Estudios de derecho 23 : 47-67, marzo 1964.

VELU, J. : Action accomplie en 1963 par le Conseil de l'Europe dans le domaine du droit. Revue de droit international et de droit comparé 41 : 125-156, no. 3, 1964.

VIGNES, D.H. : Chronique sur le droit européen - I. A propos des recours des particuliers contre les décisions communautaires - II. Les organes arbitraux créés par les accords d'association. Revue de droit international et de droit comparé 41 : 109-124, no. 3, 1964.

CONFORTI, B. : La personalità della Comunità economica europea nel diritto statale. Rivista di diritto internazionale 47 : 566-572, fasc. 4, 1964.

ADLER, G.M. : The E.E.C. court of justice. Canadian bar journal 7 : 102-127, April 1964.

ZWEIGERT, K. : Der Einfluss des europäischen Gemeinschaftsrechts auf die Rechtsordnungen der Mitgliedstaaten. Rabels Zeitschrift für ausländisches und internationales Privatrecht 28 : 601-643, Heft 4, 1964.

RUEFF, J. : La Corte di giustizia delle Comunità europee e i rapporti economici. Rivista del diritto commerciale e del diritto generale delle obbligazione 62 : 221-232, maggio-giugno 1964.

REISNER, R. : National regulation of the movement of workers in the European community. American journal of comparative law 13 : 360-384, summer 1964.

BONN, F. : Les problèmes juridico-linguistiques dans les Communautés européennes. Revue générale de droit international public 68 : 708-718, juillet-septembre 1964.

LA GRAVIÈRE, E. : De quelques problèmes posés par le droit d'établissement dans le Marché commun. Revue politique des idées et des institutions 53 : 380-395, novembre 1964.

ROBERT, J. : De la place de l'arbitrage dans le jeu des traités instituant les Communautés européennes. Revue de l'arbitrage : 111-121, octobre-décembre 1964.

MEGRET, J. : Le pouvoir de la Communauté économique européenne de conclure des accords internationaux. Revue du Marché commun : 529-536, décembre 1964.

MULLER, R. : L'évolution de la coopération en matière juridique dans le cadre du Conseil de l'Europe. Annuaire européen - European year-book 12/I : 26-45, 1964.

LORENZ, W. : General principles of law, their elaboration in the Court of justice of the European communities. American journal of comparative law 13 : 1-29, winter 1964.

EUROPE
(Economic Community - Patents, trade-marks)

NEUMEYER, F. : Unification of European patent legislation on the Common market. Modern law review 24 : 725-737, November 1961.

GUTTMAN, F.G. : Towards a European patent. Journal of business law : 309-314, July 1962.

SAINT-GAL, Y. : Marque et réglementation de la concurrence dans le C.E.E. Revue du Marché commun : 250-255, juin 1963.
Voir aussi pp. 256-266.

FROSCHMAIER, F. : Some aspects of the draft convention relating to a European patent law. International and comparative law quarterly 12 : 886-897, July 1963.

PLAISANT, R. : Les projets de convention européenne sur les brevets d'invention. Receuil Dalloz, Chronique : 195-202, 18 septembre 1963.

FRISCH, A. : Das Patent in der Europapolitik. Wirtschaftsdienst (Hamburg) 43 : 475-478, November 1963.

EUROPE
(European Convention of Human rights)

BALLADORE PALLIERI, G. : Il regolamente della Corte dei diritti dell'uomo. Diritto internazionale 14 : 126-135, no. 2, 1960.

GOLSONG, H. : Der Europäische Gerichtshof für Menschenrechte. Juristenzeitung 15 : 193-198, 1. April 1960.

MOSLER, H. : Organisation und Verfahren des Europäischen Gerichtshods für Menschenrechte. Zeitschrift für ausländisches öffentliches Recht und Völkerrecht 20 : 415-449, August 1960.

WEIL, G.L. : Decisions on inadmissible applications by the European commission of human rights. American journal of international law 43 : 874-881, October 1960.

ROBERTSON, A.H. : The European court of human rights. American journal of comparative law 9 : 1-28, winter 1960.

La grande réalisation du Conseil de l'Europe, la Convention européenne des droits de l'homme. Monde diplomatique 7 : 3, décembre 1960.
Suite d'articles.

VERDROSS, A. : Der europäische Schutz der Menschenrechte. Österreichische Zeitschrift für Aussenpolitik 1 : 91-103, Dezember 1960.

La Convention européenne des droits de l'homme a dix ans. Nouvelles du Conseil de l'Europe 10 : 109-113, décembre 1960.

MORVAY, W. : Rechtsprechung nationaler Gerichte zur Europäischen Konvention zum Schutze der Menschenrechte und Grundfreiheiten vom 4. November 1950 (MRK) nebst Zusatzprotokoll vom 20. März 1952 (ZP) (I). Zeitschrift für ausländisches öffentliches Recht und Völkerrecht 21 : 89-112, Nr. 1, Januar 1961.

KERSON, D.L.A. : The European convention for the protection of human rights and fundamental freedoms. California law review 49 : 172-186, March 1961.

MATTHIES, H. : Das erste Urteil des Europäischen Gerichtshofs für Menschenrechte - Verfahrensfragen in der Sache Lawless. Zeitschrift für ausläbdisches öffentliches Recht und Völkerrecht 21 : 249-258, Nr. 2, April 1961.

NATIONAL LAW - COUNTRIES

HUBER, H. : Der Hauptentscheid des Europäischen Gerichtshofs für Menschenrechte in der Sache Lawless. Zeitschrift für ausländisches öffentliches Recht und Völkerrecht 21 : 649-666, Nr. 4, 1961.
See also pp. 727-763.

HERZOG, R. : Das Grundrecht auf Freiheit in der Europäischen Menschenrechtskonvention. Archiv des öffentlichen Rechts 86 : 194-244, Heft 2/3, September 1961.

MESSINEO, A. : Dalla Convenzione sui diritti dell' uomo alla Carta sociale europea. Civiltà cattolica 112 : 29-41, 7 ottobre 1961.

WIESLER, L. : Der Beginn der Tätigkeit des Europäischen Gerichtshofes für Menschenrechte. Europe-Archiv 16 : 735-742, 25. Dezember 1961.

PFUEL, C.C.v. : Die Bedeutung der Europarats-Konvention für Menschenrechte. Europäische Wirtschaft 5 : 29-32, 31. Januar 1962.

KASAK, K. : Les droits de la défense dans la convention européenne des droits de l'homme. Droit européen 5 : 41-45, février 1962.

COMTE, P. : L'application de la Convention européenne des droits de l'homme dans l'ordre juridique interne. Commission internationale de juristes, Revue 4 : 102-138, 1er semestre 1962.

EISSEN, M.A. : The European convention on human rights and the duties of the individual. Nordisk tidsskrift for international ret og jus gentium 32 : 230-253, fasc. 3-4, 1962.

BOESS, W. : Die Europäische Menschenrechtskonvention und das materielle Strafrecht. Österreichische Juristen-Zeitung 17 : 293-294, 5. Juni 1962.

SUY, E. : De zaak "Lawless" voor het Europees gerechtshof voor de mensenrechten. Nederlands tidjschrift voor internationaal recht 9 : 273-291, juni 1962.
The Lawless case befor the European court of Human rights; Summary in French.

MODINOS, P. : Effects and repercussions of the European conevention on human rights. International and comparative law quarterly 11 : 1097-1108, October 1962.

VASAK, K. : The European convention of human rights beyond the frontiers of Europe. International and comparative law quarterly 12 : 1206-1231, October 1963.

WEIL, G.L. : The evolution of the European convention on human rights. American journal of international law 57 : 804-827, October 1963.

GREENBERG, J., and SHALIT, A.R. : New horizons for human rights - The European convention, court and commission of human rights. Columbia law review 63 : 1384-1412, December 1963.

GURADZE, H. : Die Allgemeine Erklärung der Menschenrechte und die europäische Konvention zum Schutz der Menschenrechte und Grundfreiheiten. Vereinte Nationen 11 : 189-191, Dezember 1963.

GOLSONG, H. : Protection internationale des droits de l'homme en Europe. Revue de l'Action populaire : 302-310, mars 1964.

PAHR, W.P. : Das 4. Zusatzprotokoll zur Europäischen Menschen rechtskonvention. Juristische Blätter 86 : 187-196, 11. April 1964.

GIANZURCO, M. : I diritti dell'uomo in Europa e nel mondo. Nuova antologia 491 : 386-391, luglio 1964.

SCHWELB, E. : On the operation of the European convention on human rights. International organization 18 : 558-585, summer 1964.

SCHWELB, E. : The protection of the right of property of nationals under the first protocol to the European convention on human rights. American journal of comparative law 13 : 518-541, autumn 1964.

TIWARI, S.C. : The European convention for the protection of human rights. Indian journal of international law 4 : 509-521, October 1964.

SAND, M. : Le quatrième protocole additionnel à la Convention européenne des droits de l'homme. Annuaire français de droit international 10 : 569-575, 1964.

NATIONAL LAW - COUNTRIES

AFGHANISTAN

Constitution de l'Afghanistan, ler octobre 1964. Documentation française, Notes et études documentaires : 1-16, no. 3170, 11 mars 1965.

Constitución de Afghanistán, 1.10.1964. Información júridica (Spain) : 49-76, mayo-junio 1965.
Text in Spanish.

SIRAT, A.S. : The modern legal system of Afghanistan. American journal of comparative law 16 : 563 -569, no. 4, 1968.

MODJAZ, M.E. : Die neue Verfassung von Afghanistan (1964) unter besonderer Berücksichtigung des Rechtswesens. Verfassung und Recht in Übersee 2 : 169-179, 2. Quartal 1969.

ALBANIA

NOVA, K. : Garancitë proceduriale penale të zhvillimit demokratik të gjykimit. Drejtësia popullore (Albania) 18 : 26-38, no. 6, nendordhjetor 1965.

VOKOPOLA, K.A. : The nationality law of Albania. Osteuropa-Recht 13 : 241-260, Dezember 1967.

Constitution de la République populaire d'Albanie. Documentation française, Notes et études documentaires : 1-13, no. 3504, 28 juin 1968.
Texte.

PFAFF, D. : Die Aussenhandels-Schiedsgerichtsbarkeit in der Volksrepublik Albanien. Aussenwirtschaftsdienst des Betriebs-Beraters 16 : 261-266, Juni 1970.

STATOVCI, E. : Učešće trećih osoba u parnici po albanskom Građanskom parničnom kodeksu i jugoslavenskom Zakonu o parnicnom postupku. Naša zakonitost 24 : 108-118, broj 2, ožujak-travanj 1970.

ALGERIA

GARREAU de Loubresse, C. : Structures et réalités juridiques des nationalisations algériennes. Revue internationale de droit comparé 17 : 73-89, janvier-mars 1965.

ETIENNE, B. : Fin du délai accordé aux Français d'Algérie ou bilan de 3 ans d'option, ler juillet 1962 - ler juillet 1965. Revue juridique et politique - Indépendance et coopération 19 : 579-604, octobre-décembre 1965.

MATHÈTES, O. : La réforme judiciaire algérienne. Annuaire de l'Afrique du Nord 5 : 111-119, 1966.

BORELLA, F. : Le droit public économique algérien. Revue algérienne des sciences juridiques, politiques et économiques : 499-562, septembre 1966.

TIMSIT, G. : La fonction publique algérienne en 1966. Revue algérienne des sciences juridiques, politiques et économiques : 563-592,septembre 1966.

FENAUX, H. : Un problème de procédure pénale algérienne, requalification et compétence. Revue algérienne des sciences juridiques, politiques et économiques : 855-859, décembre 1966.

VERDIER, J.M. : L'indépendance de l'Algérie et le droit international privé. Comité français de droit international privé. Travaux 27-30, 35-64, 1966-1969.

SBIH, M. : Le statut général de la fonction publique. Revue algérienne des sciences juridiques, politiques et économiques : 5-21, mars 1967.

CHARDENON, P. : Dettes des rapatriés et nationalisations algériennes. Journal du droit international 94 : 290-322, avril-juin 1967.

LOURDJANE, A. : Les musulmans originaires d'Algérie peuvent-ils bénéficier de la double nationalité, française et algérienne? Revue juridique et politique - Indépendance et coopération 21 : 295-300, avril-juin 1967.

TIMSIT, G. : Le statut général de la fonction publique algérienne. Revue algérienne des sciences juridiques, Politiques et économiques : 203-292, juin 1967.

ROBERT-DUVILLIERS, P. : Le statut de la fonction publique algérienne. Revue administrative 20 : 404-412, juillet-août 1967.

FENAUX, H. : Eléments de droit judiciaire algérien (A suivre). Revue algérienne des sciences juridiques, politiques et économiques : 483-544, septembre 1967.

LAMPUÉ, P. : La justice administrative en Algérie. Revue juridique et politique - Indépendance et coopération 23 : 167-182, avril-juin 1969.

SALAHEDDINE, A. : De quelques aspects du nouveau droit judiciaire algérien. Revue algérienne des sciences juridiques, économiques et politiques 6 : 435-447, juin 1969.

SOULIER, G. : Le droit constitutionnel algérien - Situation actuelle et perspectives. Revue algérienne des sciences juridiques, économiques et politiques 6 : 793-820, septembre 1969.

MOHAMED-CHERIF, S.B. : La justice en Algérie (A suivre). Dossiers documentaires (Algeria) : 1-24, no. 3, décembre 1969.

BADR, G.M. : La relance du droit islamique dans la jurisprudence algérienne depuis 1962. Revue internationale de droit comparé 22 : 43-54, janvier-mars 1970.

HAZARD, J.N. : The residue of Marxist influence in Algeria. Columbia journal of transnational law 9 : 194-225, fall 1970.

ANDORRA

SOTO NIETO, F. : Jurisprudencia de Andorra. Revista jurídica de Cataluña 67 : 51-68, enero-marzo 1968.

GARCÍA ARIAS, L. : El nuevo decreto sobre la nacionalidad andorrana. Revista española de dercho internacional 23 : 99-101, núm. 1, 1970.

ARABIAN STATES

KASSIM, A.F. : Conflicting claims in the Persian Gulf. Journal of law and economic development 4 : 282-337, no. 2, 1969.

NATIONAL LAW - COUNTRIES

ARGENTINA

VANOSSI, J.R.A. : El Ministerio de justicia y el poder judicial. Revista jurídica de Buenos Aires : 45-131, enero-agosto 1965.

GORDILLO, A.A. : Acerca de la revision judicial de los actos administrativos - Confusiones que origina lo contenciosadministrativo. Revisza jurídica de Buenos Aires : 111-137, septiembre-diciembre 1965.

KALLER de ORCHANSKY, B. : Régimen de los contratos en derecho internacional privado argentino. Revista española de derecho internacional 19 : 519-533, octubre-diciembre 1966.

CIURO, M.A. : La filiación extramatrimonial en el derecho international privado argentino no convencional. Revista de derecho internacional y ciencias diplomáticas (Rosairo) 15-16 : 14-29, nos. 29-32, 1966-67.

REVYEN, J.J. : Das neue argentinische Wechselrecht. Rabels Zeitschrift für ausländisches und internationales Privatrecht 32 : 63-124, Heft 1, 1968.

GUERRERO, G.H. : Reforma del código penal. Revista de la Unión industrial (Buenos Aires) : 77-86, julio-septiembre 1968.

DOMINGUEZ AGUILA, R.H., and DOMINGUEZ BENAVENTE: R. : Reformas al código civil argentino. Revista de derecho y ciencias sociales (Concepción) 36 : 41-73, julio-septiembre 1968.

Código procesal civil y comercial de la nación argentina de 20 de septiembre de 1967, (To be continued). Información jurídica (Spain) : 115-136, octubre-diciembre 1968.

BIDART CAMPOS, G.J. : La concepción del derecho en la Constitución argentina. Revista de estudios políticos : 153-162, noviembre-diciembre 1968.

SÊVE de GASTON, A. : Los tratados ejecutivos en la República Argentina - Su análisis tridimensional. Revista de derecho internacional y ciencias diplomáticas (Rosaria) 17 : 135-191, nos. 33-34, 1968.

PUIG, J.C. : Derecho de la comunidad internacional y derecho interno - A propósito del caso ESSO. Revista de derecho internacional y ciencias diplomáticas (Rosaria) 17 : 114-134, nos. 33-34, 1968.

WINIZKY, I. : La unificación de las obligaciones y de los contratos en la República Argentina. Revista de la Facultad de derecho (Caracas) : 9-18, núm. 41, 1968.

REYVEN, J.J. : Das Namensrecht der Frau und der Kinder im Privatrecht und internationalen Privatrecht Argentiniens. Rables Zeitschrift für ausländisches und internationales Privatrecht 33 : 711-733, Heft 4, 1969.

WINIZKY, I., et BACQUÉ, J.A. : La nouvelle loi argentine sur l'offre publique des valeurs. Revue internationale de droit comparé 21 : 565-575, juillet-septembre 1969.

RAMELLA, P.A. : Die Entwicklung des Verfassungsrechts in Argentinien. Jahrbuch des öffentlichen Rechts der Gegenwart 18 : 579-680, 1969.

REYVEN, J.J. : Der Grundrechtsschutz (habeas corpus, recurso de amparo) im argentinischen Recht. Verfassung und Recht in Übersee 3 : 179-193, 2. Quartal 1970.

Constitution de la nation argentine (texte). Notes et études documentaires : 1-24, no. 2738, 16 novembre 1970.

AUSTRALIA

COWEN, Z. : Some observations on the law of criminal contempt. University of Western Australia law review 7 : 1-39, June 1965.

MOFFAT, R.C. L. : Philosophical foundations of the Australian constitutional tradition. Sydney law review 5 : 59-88, September 1965.

HARBICH, H. : Gedanken zur Amnestie 1965. Österreichische Juristen-Zeitung 20 : 589-596, 621-628, 16. November, 30. November 1965.

LANE, P.H. : Judicial review or government by the high court. Sydney law review 5 : 203-220, no. 2, 1966.

SELBY, D.M. : The development of divorce law in Australia. Modern law review 29 : 473-491, September 1966.

DRUMMOND, D.P. : Section 92 (of the Commonwealth constitutional) and burden of proof. Australian law journal 40 : 384-391, 31 March 1967.

RICHARDSON, J.E., and ROSE, D.J. : An analysis of the Australian trade practices act. McGill law journal 13 : 383-423, no. 3, 1967.

DAVIES, W.E.D. : Section 17 of the Married women property act - Law or palm tree justice? University of Western Australia law review 8 : 48-60, June 1967.

CAMPBELL, E. : Public access to government documents. Australian law journal 41 : 73-89, July 1967.

DURACK, P.D., and WILSON, R.D. : Do we need a new constituent for the Commonwealth? Australian law journal 41 : 231-250, 30 November 1967.

NICHOLSON, R.D. : Constitutional guarantees of the rule of law - A judicial service commission for Papua and New Guinea? Australian law journal 42 : 10-17, 31 May 1968.

HAMBLY, D. : Adoption of children - An appraisal of the uniform Acts. University of Western Australia law review 8 : 281-318, June 1968.

CAMPBELL, E. : The federal spending power - Constitutional limitations. University of Western Australia law review 8 : 443-458, December 1968.

SAWYER, G. : The Commonwealth copyright act 1968. Australian law journal 43 : 8-12, January 1969.

MASON, K. : Judicial review of inquiries in administrative law. Sydney law review 6 : 206-218, no. 2, 1969.

LAHORE, J.C. : Industrial designs and the Copyright act 1968 - The problem of dual protection. Australian law journal 43 : 139-148, 30 April 1969.

FINLAY, H.A. : The dual nature of the territories power of the Commonwealth. Australian law journal 43 : 256-264, 31 July 1969.

REABURN, N.S. : Conscientious objection and the particular war. Australian law journal 43 : 317-329, 29 August 1969.

SHEWCROFT, J. : La loi australienne de 1968 sur le droit d'auteur entrée en vigueur le ler mai 1969. Revue de l'U.E.R. (Union européenne de radiodiffusion), Cahiers B : 46-69, septembre 1969.

LUMB, R.D. : Sovereignty and jurisdiction over Australian coastal waters. Australian law journal 43 : 421-449, 31 October 1969.

CAMPBELL, E. : Commonwealth contracts. Australian law journal 44 : 14-33, 30 January 1970.

BARWICK, G. : Precedent in the Southern Hemisphere. Israel law review 5 : 1-41, January 1970.

PETERSSON, K.B. : La nouvelle loi australienne sur les brevets. Propriété industrielle 86 : 60-63, février 1970.

PALFREEMAN, A.C. : Political asylum in Australia. Australian quarterly 42 : 52-61, March 1970.

O'CONNELL, D. P. : The Australian maritime domain. Australian law journal 44 : 192-208, 29 May 1970.

BENNETT, J.M. : Historical trends in Australian law reform. University of Western Australia law review 9 : 211-241, June 1970.

COOPER, E.J. : The quasi-criminal federal jurisdiction. The Australian law journal 44 : 365-380, 31 August 1970.

HOGG, P.W. : Suits against the Commonwealth and the States in the federal jurisdiction. The Australian law journal 44 : 425-436, 30 September 1970.

Australie; loi de 1968 sur le droit d'auteur (A suivre). Le Droit d'auteur 83 : 232-237, octobre 1970.

MARKS, B. : Choice of law and conflicts avoidance in Australia/Japanese transactions (to be contd.). The Australian law journal 44 : 528-541, November 1970.

TATZ, C. : Aborigines - Law and political development. The Australian quarterly 42 : 33-46, December 1970.

AUSTRIA

GRUNIGEN, M. von : Die österreichische Verfassungsnovelle über Staatsverträge vom 4. März 1964 (with text). Zeitschrift für ausländisches öffentliches Recht und Völkerrecht 25 : 76-99, Januar 1965.

SCHNEIDER, F. : Die rechtliche Stellung der Lebensgefährten. Österreichische Juristen-Zeitung 20 : 174-179, 6. April 1965.

KLEIN, H. : Rechtsprechungsprobleme um das Amnestiegesetz 1965. Juristische Blätter 87 : 355-357, 3. Juli 1965.

SCHÄFFER, H. : Der Zivilrechtsbegriff der Menschenrechtskonvention - Einige Auswirkungen des Art. 6 MRK auf die österreichische Rechtsordnung. Österreichische Juristen-Zeitung 20 : 511-520, 5. Oktober 1965.

MAKAROV, A.N. : Das österreichische Bundesgesetz vom 15. Juli 1965 über die Staatsbürgerschaft. Zeitschrift für ausländisches öffentliches Recht und Völkerrecht 25 : 693-716, Dezember 1965. Text pp. 717-734.

STÜTTLER, J.A. : Die Stellung der Familie im österreichischen Recht in kritischer Sicht. Österreichische Juristen-Zeitung 21 : 225-228, 4. Mai 1966.

NOVAK, F. : Österreichs grosse Rechtsreform und die Zivilgerichtsbarkeit. Juristische Blätter 89 : 171-179, 8. April 1967.

Código civil general austriaco. Información jurídica (Spain) : 3-35, mayo-junio 1967.

BRECCIA, A. : L'amministratione della giustizia in Austria. Rivista di studi politici internazionali 35 : 94-115, gennaio-marzo 1968.

ROEDER, H. : Gibt es "absolut nichtige" Strafurteile? Österreichische Juristen-Zeitung 23 : 141-149, 26. März 1968.

ZEMANEK, K. : Das Problem der Beteiligung des immerwährend neutralen Österreich an Sanktionen der Vereinten Nationen, besonders im Falle Rhodesiens. Zeitschrift für ausländisches öffentliches Recht und Völkerrecht 28 : 16-30, März 1968.

VEITER, T. : Völkerrechtsnormen und Völkerrechtsgrundsätze zum Schut nationaler Minderheiten. Österreichische Juristen-Zeitung 23 : 225-234, 7. Mai 1968.

SPANNER, H. : Probleme der Verfassungsgerichtsbarkeit. Österreichische Juristen-Zeitung 23 : 337-343, 2. Juli 1968.

TLAPEK, L. : Rechtsmittelreform im Strafverfahren. Österreichische Juristen-Zeitung 23 : 565-572, 5. November 1968.

SCHÄFFER, H. : Legal restraints on personal liberties in Austria. Österreichische Zeitschrift für öffentliches Recht 19 : 36-58, Heft 1, 1969.

PFEIFER, H. : Das neue österreichische Asylrechtsgesetz. Juristische Blätter 91 : 57-61, 8. Februar 1969.

NOVAK, R. : Grundsätze des österreichischen Staatsbürgerschaftsrechts. Österreichische Zeitschrift für öffentliches Recht 19 : 145-186, Heft 2/3, 1969.

ANTONIOLLI, W. : Die österreichische Verfassungsgerichtsbarkeit 1945-1969. Archiv des öffentlichen Rechts 94 : 576-601, Heft 4, 1969.

PERNTHALER, P. : Der österreichische Bundesstaat im Spannungsfeld von Föderalismus und formalem Rechtspositivismus. Österreichische Zeitschrift für öffentliches Recht 19 : 361-379, Heft 4, 1969.

PERNTHALER, P. :Die Grundrechtsreform in Österreich. Archiv des öffentlichen Rechts 94 : 31-84, April 1969.

NATIONAL LAW - COUNTRIES

Betrachtungen zur Judikatur des Verfassungsgerichtshofes - Sig. 1967 (To be contd.). Österreichische Juristen-Zeitung 24 : 318-320, 17. Juni 1969.

SPERL, W. : Die Struktur der Gerichtshöfe des öffentlichen Rechts im Vergleich zur ordentlichen Gerichtsbarkeit. Österreichische Juristen-Zeitung 24 : 365-369, 15. Juli 1969.

OBERNDORFER, P. : Grundrechte und staatliche Wirtschaftspolitik. Österreichische Juristen-Zeitung 24 : 449-458, 9. September 1969.

SCHWIMM, M. : Zur Lage im internationalen Privatrecht Österreichs. Juristische Blätter 91 : 544-549, 11. Oktober 1969.

KRZIZEK, F. : Probleme des österreichischen Enteignungsrechtes (To be contd.). Österreichische Juristen-Zeitung 24 : 561-569, 4. November 1969.

KORINEK, K. : Kammern und Verbände in der österreichischen Rechtsordnung. Wirtschaftspolitische Blätter 17 : 3-10, Nr. 1/2, 1970.

BARFUSS, W. : Kollegialbehörden und Bundesverfassung. Österreichische Juristen-Zeitung 25 : 57-63, 10. Februar 1970.

REINDL, P. : Änderungen im Recht der Geschäftsfähigkeit? Juristische Blätter 92 : 57-67, 7. Februar 1970.

WENGER, K. : Der Verbraucherschutz im österreichischen Verwaltungsrecht. Juristische Blätter 92 : 230-238, 2. Mai 1970.

JAKUSCH, W. : Okkupationstheorie, Annexionstheorie und das ius postliminii. Österreichische Juristen-Zeitung 25 : 258-263, 19. Mai 1970.

KANIAK, G. : Die Monarchie in der Republik. Österreichische Juristen-Zeitung 25 : 309-315, 16. Juni 1970.

SCHANTL, G., and WELAN, M. : Betrachtungen über die Judikatur des Verfassungsgerichtshofes zur Menschenrechtskonvention (To be contd.). Österreichische Juristen-Zeitung 25 : 617-625, 1. Dezember 1970.

BELGIUM

CORNIL, P. : Sursis et probation - La loi belge du 29 juin 1964. Revue de science criminelle et de droit pénal comparé : 51-71, janvier-mars 1965.

WAELBROECK, M. : Le juge belge devant le droit international et le droit communautaire. Revue belge de droit international : 348-368, no. 2, 1965.

MEEUS, A. : La loi du 7 avril 1964 relative à l'effacement des condamnations et à la réhabilitation en matière pénale. Revue de droit pénal et de criminologie 45 : 607-634, avril 1965.

DROOGHENBROECK, P. van : Commentaire de la loi du 29 juin 1964 concernant la suspension, le sursis et la probation. Revue de droit pénal et de criminologie 45 : 731-795, mai 1965.

DEPELCHIN, L. : Considérations sur l'article 2 du code pénal. Revue de droit pénal et de criminologie 47 : 191-226, décembre 1965.

DEKKERS, R. : L'évolution du droit civil belge depuis le code Napoléon. Revue juridique du Congo 41 : 7-24, no. spécial, 1965.

MERTENS, P. : Le droit d'asile en Belgique à l'heure de la revision constitutionnelle. Revue belge de droit international : 218-247, no. 1, 1966.

MAROY, P. : L'évolution de la législation linguistique belge. Revue du droit public et de la science politique en France et à l'étranger 82 : 449-501, mai-juin 1966.

FLAMME, M.A. : The legislation governing commercial and industrial activity carried on by public authorities in Belgium and in other countries. Annals of public and cooperative economy 37 : 343-367, September-December 1966.

ABRAHAMS, R., et PUTTERS, J. : La loi belge du 27 juin 1960 sur l'admissibilité du divorce lorsqu'un conjoint au moins est étranger. Journal du droit international 93 : 765-782, octobre-décembre 1966.

CLOSE, R. : Etude juridique des accidents sur le chemin du travail. Bulletin des assurances 46 : 805-848, novembre-décembre 1966.

Colloque sur l'autonomie communale en droit belge, Huy, 8-11 septembre 1966. Crédit communal de Belgique, Bulletin trimestriel 20 : 163-175, octobre 1966.
Suite d'articles.

FLAMAND, G. : Considérations sur les délais en matière de procédure pénale. Revue de droit pénale et de criminologie 47 : 243-282, décembre 1966.

LOUIS, J.V. : L'accession du Congo belge à l'indépendance - Problèmes de succession d'Etats dans la jurisprudence belge. Annuaire française de droit international 12 : 731-756, 1966.

LOX, F. : Le droit de protection des mineurs. Enfant : 15-22, No. 1, 1967.

VERSEE, M.T. : La privation de la liberté dabs la procédure pénale belge. Revue de droit pénal et de criminologie 47 : 343-382, janvier 1967.

HOVEN, H.M. : La protection des droits de la défense en droit belge. Revue de droit pénal et de criminologie 47 : 461-492, février 1967.

SUY, E. : Immunity of states before Belgian courts and tribunals. Zeitschrift für ausländisches öffentliches Recht und Völkerrecht 27 : 660-692, Nr. 4, 1967.

MARCHAL, A. : De l'état de légitime défense en droit pénal belge. Revue de droit pénal de criminologie 47 : 943-991, juillet 1967.
Bibliographie pp. 992-994.

CONSTANT, J. : Les "choses dandereuses" face au droit pénal belge. Revue internationale de criminologie et de police technique 21 : 263-270, octobre-décembre 1967.

Centenaire du code pénal belge 1867-1967. Revue de droit pénal et de criminologie 48 : 75-342, novembre 1967.
Suite d'articles.

LE COURT, E. de : L'évolution de la chambre du conseil dans les lois pénales belges. Revue de droit pénal et de criminologie 48 : 345-371, décembre 1967.

NATIONAL LAW - COUNTRIES

VENNMAN, R. : La pratique belge en matière de traités dans le domaine consulaire. Revue belge de droit international 4 : 365-396, no. 2, 1968.

VERHOEVEN, J. : La Convention européenne des droits de l'homme dans la jurisprudence belge. Revue de droit contemporain 15 : 27-52, no. 2, 1968.

CORNIL, P. : Une réforme de la loi belge du 9 avril 1930 de défense sociale à l'égard des anormaux - Loi du ler juillet 1964. Revue de science criminelle det de droit pénal comparé 23 : 263-273, avri-juin 1968.

MÉGRET, C.C. : La loi du 6 août 1967 et l'exécution forcée de certains arrêts communautaires. Revue belge de droit international 5 : 69-79, no. 1, 1969.

GANSHOF van der MEERSCH, W.J. : Réflexions sur le droit international et la revision de la constitution belge. Revue belge de droit international 5 : 1-43, no. 1, 1969.

TROCLET, L.E. : Les droits ēconomiques et sociaux dans la constitution belge, (A suivre). Revue du travail (Belgium) 70 : 485-507, avril 1969.

NISOT, J. : A propos du processus de la conclusion des traités par la Belgique. Revue générale de droit international public 74 : 107-110, janvier-mars 1970.

GANSHOF van der MEERSCH, W.J. : Le juge belge et le droit international. Revue belge de droit international 6 : 409-461, no. 2, 1970.

HUYS, M. : Evolution du droit des sociétés en Belgique et dans les pays du Marché commun (A suivre). Energie (Bruxelles) : 9-21, ler et 2e trimestre 1970.

LOUIS, J.V. : L'article 25 bis de la constitution belge (l'attribution de pouvoirs à des organisations internationles). Revue du Marché commun : 410-416, septembre 1970.

BOLIVIA

CAMACHO OMISTE, E., and CÉSPEDES TORO, A. : Notes on Bolivian legislation relating to international judicial cooperation. Inter-American law review - Revista judídica interamericana 7 : 281-301, July-December 1965.
Text also in Spanish pp. 255-280.

BOTSWANA

CRAWFORD, J.R. : The history and nature of the judicial system of Botswana, Lesotho and Swaziland - Introduction and the Superior courts (To be contd.). South African journal 86 : 476-485, November 1969.

BRAZIL

BERGAMINI MIOTTO, A. : Les effets des jugements pénaux étrangers au Brésil. Revue de droit pénal et de criminologie 45 : 532-545, mars 1965.

O projeto e a constituição do Brasil. Revista de ciência política (Rio de Janeiro) 1 : 149-238, janeiro-março 1967.

BARROS MONTEIRO, W. de : Da nacionalidade e da cidadania em face da nova constitução. Revista da Faculdade de direito (São Paulo) 62 : 319-334, fasc. 2, 1967.

MOSER, R. : Emancipação e paridade de direitos da Mulher casada no Brasil e nos outros países do sistema jurídico francês. Revista da Faculdade de direito São Paulo) 61 : 14-38, fasc. 2, 1966.

HERZOG, J.B. : L'avant-projet de code d'exécution des peines du Brésil. Revue de science criminelle et de droit pénal comparé 20 : 637-645, juillet-septembre 1965.

LIMA, V.F.C. : A principio da isonomia do direito no regime das constituções de 1946 e 1967. Revista do serviço público (Brazil) 99 : 73-82, julho-dezembro 1967.

Brésil, constitution promulguée le 24 janvier 1967 - Titre I. Informations constitutionnelles et parlementaires 19 : 2-40, janvier 1968.

RUSSOMANO, R. : A discriminação de rendas na nova Constituição federal. Revista brasileira de estudos políticos : 165-181, julho 1968-janeiro 1969.

La consitution du Brésil, 24 janvier 1967. Documentation française, Notes et études documentaires : 1-39, no. 3512, 31 août 1968.
Texte.

Código da propriede industrial do Brasil - Decreto-lei no. 254, de 28 de fevreiro de 1967. Ministério da justiça, Boletim (Portugal) : 231-316, outubro 1968.

ROSAS, R. : Dos direitos políticos. Revista de informação legislativa (Brazil) 5 : 43-52, outobro-dezembro 1968.

FILHO, H.L. : Contrôle financeiro das autarquias e emprêsas públicas. Revista de informação legislativa (Brazil) 6 : 62-72, janeiro-março 1969.

ROSAS, R. : Abuso de poder das comissoes parlamentares de inquérito. Revista de informação legislativa (Brazil) 6 : 47-52, janeiro-março 1969.

ROSAS, R. : Aspectos do contrôle da constitucionalidad das leis. Revista de informação legislativa (Brazil) 6 : 25-30, julho-setembro 1969.

MARINHO, J. : Inconstitucionalidade de decretos-leis sôbre ineligibilidades. Revista de informação legislative (Brazil) 6 : 3-10, outubro-dezembro 1969.

ROSAS, R. : Poder de iniciativa das leis. Revista de informação legislativa (Brazil) 7 : 25-65, abril-junho 1970.
Bibliography pp. 65-68.

Simpósio de conferências e debates sobre o novo Código penal e o nôvo Código penal militar. Revista de informação legislativa (Brazil) 7 : 3-210, julho-setembre 1970.

BULGARIA

VASILEV, L. : Usŭvŭrshenstvuvane na zakonodatelstvoto i povishavane ne negovata efektivnost v sitsialisticheskoto stroitelstvo. Novovreme 41 : 32-74, kn. 1 Ĭanuari 1965.

SPASOV, B. : Nîakoi cherti na razvitieto na dŭrzhavnoto pravo v NR Bŭlgariîa. Pravna misŭl 10 : 3-13 kn. 1, 1936.

VLAHOV, I. : La législation bulgare en matière de successions. Centre d'étude des pays de l'Est (et) Centre national pour l'étude des Etats de l'Est, Bulletin 7 : 93-120, no. 1, 1966.

VLAHOV, I. : La leglación búlgara en materia de sucesiones. Bolétin del instituto de derecho comparado de México 19 : 489-515, mayo-dicembre 1966.

VASILEV, L. : Devetiîat kongres na Bŭlgarskata komunisticheska partiîa, zakonodatelstvoto i pravnata nauka. Pravna misŭl 11 : 3-32, kn. 1, 1967.

VLAHOV, I.S. : La responsabilité matérielle des travailleurs, ouvriers et employes, dans la legislation bulgare. Centre d'étude des pays de l'Est (et) Centre nationale pour l'étude des Etats de l'Est, Bulletin 8 : 97-108, no. 1, 1967.

KUCHEV, S.I. : Aktŭt za nachet v Nakazatelniîa protses pri osŭshtestvîavane na nakazatelnata otgovornost. Pravna misŭl 11 : 16-34, kn. 3, 1967.

Convention between the Union of Soviet Socialist Republics and the People's Republic of Bulgaria concerning the prevention of dual nationality, signed at Sofia, 6 July 1966. International legal materials, Current documents 6 : 493-496, May-June 1967.

GENOVSKI, M. : Das Problem der virtualen Entwicklung des Rechts und insbesondere der bulgarischen Verfassung von Tarnowo. Osteuropa-Recht 13 : 97-107, Juni 1967.

MARINOV, M. : Uslovnoe osuzdenie po bolgarskomu sotsialisticheskomu ugolovnomu pravu. Sovetskoe gosudarstvo i pravo : 107-111, no. 5, maĭ 1968.

La nouvelle loi sur la nationalité bulgare, du 8 octobre 1968. Centre d'étude des pays de l'Est et Centre national pour l'étude des Etats de l'Est, Revue 10 : 229-239, no. 1, 1969.

PETKOV, P.I. : Vŭrkhu niakoi strani ot razvitieto na obshtonarodnata sobstvenost. Narodnostopanski arkhiv 22 : 270-282, kn. 3, 1969.
Socialist property; summaries in German and Russian.

Das bulgarische Patentgesetz, vom 8. Oktober 1968. Jahrbuch für Ostrecht 10 : 237-252, Juli 1969.

Bulgaria; law on citizenship, 8 October 1968. International legal materials, Current documents 8 : 1165-1174, November 1969.

DAMÎANOV, Ts. : Belezhki vŭrkhu razporedbite za priznavane i dopuskane izpŭlnenie na chuzhdestranni sŭdebni i arbitrazhni resheniîa po proekta na grazhdanskiîa protsesualen kodeks. Pravna misŭl 14 : 54-58, kn. 2, 1970.

NENOV, I. : Le nouveau code pénal de la R.P. de Bulgarie. Revue de science criminelle et le droit pénal comparé 25 : 13-28, janviers-mars 1970.

BURUNDI

Constitution du Royaume du Burundi, octobre 1962. Documentation française, Notes et études docmentaires : 8-14, no. 3175, 26 mars 1965.

Burundi - Constitution du Royaume du Burundi, 16 octobre 1962. Informations constitutionnelles et parlementaires : 66-80, avril 1965.

CAMBODIA

MORICE, J.C. : L'évolution depuis un siècle de la procédure criminelle au Cambodge. Annales de la Faculté de droit d'Istambul 17 : 280-296, 26-28, 1967.

CAMEROUN

Le code pénal camerounais, code africain et franco-anglais. Revue de science criminelle et de droit pénal comparé 22 : 339-384, avril-juin 1967.

SMITH, J.A.C. : The Cameroon penal code - practical comparative law. International and comparative law quarterly 17 : 651-671, July 1968.

MARTICOU RIOU, A. : L'Organisation judiciaire du Cameroun. Penant, Revue de droit des pays d'Afrique 79 : 33-86, janvier-mars 1969.

CANADA

LASKIN, B. : Amendment of the constitution - Applying the Fulton-Favreau formula. McGill law journal 11 : 2-18, no. 1, 1965.

HONSBERGER, J.D. : Bi-lingualism in Canadian statutes. Canadian bar review - La revue du Barreau canadien 43 : 314-336, May 1965.

AZARD, P. : La Cour suprême du Canada et l'application du droit civil de la Province de Québec. Canadian bar review - La revue du Barreau canadien 43 : 553-560, December 1965.

NORMANDEAU, A. : La peine de mort au Canada. Revue de droit pénal et de criminologie 46 : 547-559, mars 1966.

Constitutional amendment in Canada. McGill law journal 12 : 337-613, no. 4, 1966.
Series of articles.

Québec - Le code civil, 1866-1966. Canadian bar review - la revue du Barreau canadien 44 : 389-522, September 1966.
Suite d'articles.

VALIQUETTE, A. : Le nouveau code de procédure civile. McGill law journal 13 : 161-168, no. 1, 1967.

CASTEL, J.G. : Canada and The Hague conference on private international law, 1893-1967. Canadian bar review - Le revue du Barreau canadien 45 : 1-34, March 1967.

BOILARD, J.G. : La détention préventative du repris de justice en droit criminel canadien. McGill law journal 13 : 557-600, no. 4, 1967.

GROSMAN, B.A. : The right to counsel in Canada. Canadian bar journal 10 : 189-211, June 1967.

NATIONAL LAW - COUNTRIES

CARDINAL, J.G. : Le droit civil au Québec - Ses sources, son évolution, son originalité. Revue juridique et politique - Indépendance et coopération 21 : 417-424, juillet-septembre 1967.

DAWSON, W.F. : Privilege in the Senate of Canada. Public law : 212-229, autumn 1967.

Canada, 1867-1967. Canadian bar review - La revue du Barreau canadien 45 : 391-626, September 1967.
Series of articles.

Canada 1867-1967. Canadian bar review - La revue du Barreau canadien 45 : 627-874, December 1967.
Series of articles.

BARBE, R.P. : Le statut des juges de la Cour des sessions de la paix. McGill law journal 14 : 84-98, February 1968.

PINEAU, J. : La législation maritime canadienne et le code civil québécois. McGill law journal 14 : 26-58, February 1968.

CASTEL, J.G. : Some legal aspects of human organ transplantation in Canada. Canadian bar review - La revue du Barreau canadien 46 : 345-405, September 1968.

FETZER, E.C. : The rape of Canada's constitution. Canadian bar journal 11 : 461-468, October 1968.

BRIERLEY, J.E.C. : Quebec's civil law codification. McGill law journal 14 : 521-589, December 1968.

MENDES DA COSTA, D. : The Canadian divorce law of 1968 and its provisions on conflicts, American journal of comparative law 17 : 214-238, no. 2, 1969.

McDONALD, B.C. : Constitutional aspects of Canadian anti-combines law enforcement. Canadian bar review - La revue du Barreau canadien 47 : 161-240, May 1969.

HUCKER, J., and McDONALD, B.C. : Securing human rights in Canada. McGill law journal 15 : 220-243, June 1969.

MCWHINNEY, E. : Canadian federalism, and the Foreign affairs and treaty power - The impact of Quebec's "quiet revolution". The Canadian yearbook of international law 7 : 3-32, 1969.

SMILEY, D.V. : The case against the Canadian charter of human rights. Canadian journal of political science - Revue canadienne de science politique 2 : 277-291, September 1969.

The Canadian legal system. A panel. Law library journal 62 : 365-380, November 1969.

MARX, H. : The emergency power and civil liberties in Canada. McGill law journal 16 : 39-91, March 1970.

MEWETT, A.W. : Law enforcement and the conflict of values. McGill law journal 16 : 1-18, March 1970.

KONAN, R.W. : The "Manhattan"'s Arctic conquest and Canada's respose in legal diplomacy. Cornell international law journal 3 : 189-204, spring 1970.

HARTLEY, T.C. : Race relations law in Ontario (To be contd.). Public law : 20-35, spring 1970.

Living resources of the sea - Protective legislation announced by Canada. External affairs (Canada) 22 : 130-160, May 1970.

COHEN, M. : The juridical process and national policy - A problem for Canadian federalism. McGill law journal 16 : 297-311, June 1970.

LEIGH, L.H. : The Indian act, the supremacy of Parliament, and the equal protection of the laws. McGill law journal 16 : 389-398, June 1970.

MacDONALD, J. : The new Canadian declaration of acceptance of the compulsory jurisdiction of the International court of justice. The Canadian yearbook of international law. Annuaire canadien de droit international 8 : 3-38, 1970.

MORIN, J.Y. : Le progrès technique, la pollution et l'évolution récente du droit de la mer au Canada, particulièrement à l'égard de l'Arctique. The Canadian yearbook of international law. Annuaire canadien de droit international 8 : 158-248, 1970.

POWE, L.A. : The "Georgia Straight" and freedom of expression in Canada. Canadian bar review, La revue du Barreau canadien 48 : 410-438, September 1970.

BILDER, R.B. : The Canadian Arctic waters pollution prevention act - New stresses on the law of the sea. Michigan law review 69 : 1-54, November 1970.

CENTRAL AFRICAN REPUBLIC

DECHEIX, P. : La nouvelle constitution de la République centrafricaine. Revue juridique et politique - Indépendance et coopération 19 : 142-147, janvier-mars 1965.
Adoptée le 18 novembre 1964.

DECHEIX, P. : La constitution provisoire de la République centrafricaine. Revue juridique et politique - Indépendance et coopération 20 : 359-360, avril-juin 1966.
Texte pp. 361-362.

CEYLON

MUDALL, L.W.A. : Ceylon - Current constitutional problems. Indian year book of international affairs 14 : 301-322, 1965.

AMERASINGHE, C.F. : The legal sovereignty of the Ceylon parliament. Public law : 65-96, spring 1966.

CHAD

L'Organisation judiciaire au Chad. Penant, Revue de droit des pays d'Afrique 78 : 65-76, janvier-mars 1968.

DURAND, C. : La nouvelle organisation judiciaire du Tchad et le renforcement des pouvoirs des magistrats au pénal. Penant, Revue de droit des pays d'Afrique 80 : 181-190, avril-juin 1970.

CHILE

Código de procedimient civil de Chile. Información jurídica (Spain) : 3-88, enero-febrero 1965.

NATIONAL LAW - COUNTRIES

ILLANES BENITEZ, O. : The Supreme court of justice of Chile. International commission of jurists, Journal 7 : 269-277, winter 1966.

CASTÁN VÁZQUEZ, J.M. : La sucesión forzosa del cónyuge viudo en el derecho chileno. Anuario de derecho civil 19 : 829-841, octubre-diciembre 1966.

PECCHI CROCE, C. : La participación del juez en el proceso civil - Su aplicación en el código de procedimiento civil chileno. Revista de derecho y ciencias sociales (Concepción) 35 : 35-79, abril-junio 1967.

GRISOLIA, F. : La reforma penal en Chile. Anuario de derecho penal y ciencias penales 20 : 289-332, enero-agosto 1967.

CASTÁN VÁZQUEZ, J.M. : La sucesión forzosa del cónyuge viudo en el derecho chileno. Revista de derecho y ciencias sociales (Concepción) 35 : 25-42, octubre -diciembre 1967.

PRIEUR KOELLING, W. : Die Entwicklung des Verfassungsrechtes in Chile. Jahrbuch des öffentlichen Rechts der Gegenwart 16 : 411-444, 1967.
Text of the Constitution pp. 445-463.

PENAILILLO AREVALO, D. : El principio de la igualdad en el derecho sucesorio. Revista de derecho y ciencias sociales (Concepción) 36 : 59-109, enero-marzo 1968.

TRONCOSO LARRONDE, H. : El principio de la propiedad privada en el código civil y sus transformaciones. Revista de derecho y ciencias sociales (Concepción) 36 : 31-58, enero-marzo 1968.

MORAL-LOPEZ, P. : Problèmes constitutionnels de la réforme agraire - La réforme de la constitution du Chili en matière de droit de propriété, dans une perspective de droit comparé. Revue internationale de droit comparé 21 : 545-564, juillet-septembre 1969.

CHINA

LENG, S.-c. : Post-constitutional development of people's justice in China. International commission of jurists, Journal 6 : 103-128, summer 1965.

CHIU, H. : The theory and practice of Communist China with respect to the conclusion of treaties. Columbia journal of transnational law 5 : 1-13, no. 1, 1966.

COHEN, J.A. : The criminal process in the People's Republic of China - An introduction. Harvard law review 79 : 469-533, January 1966.

CHIU, H. : Communist China's attitude toward international law. American journal of international law 60 : 245-267, April 1966.

COHEN, J.A. : Chinese mediation on the eve of modernization. California law review 54 : 1201-1226, August 1966.

STAHNKE, A. : The background and evolution of party policy on the drafting of legal codes in Communist China. American journal of comparative law 15 : 506-525, no. 3, 1966/67.

ENGELBORGHS-BERTELS, M. : L'assimilation de l'esprit du droit occidental en Chine. Co-existence 4 : 77-92, January 1967.

WOODSWORTH, K.C. : Family law and resolution of domestic disputes in the People's Republic of China. McGill law journal 13 : 169-177, no. 1, 1967.

CHUA, I.L.-e. : Communist China and international law. Library of Congress, Quarterly journal 24 : 319-334, October 1967.

LEE, L.T. : Treaty relations of the People's Republic of China - A study of compliance. University of Pennsylvania law review 116 : 244-314, December 1967.

The People's Republic of China and international law - Observations. American society of international law, Proceedings 61 : 108-140, 1967.
A panel.

VALK, M.H. van der : Voluntary surrender in Chinese law. Law in Eastern Europe : 359-394, no. 14, 1967.
Index p. 407.

ENGELBORGHS-BERTELS, M. : Le pluralisme juridique en République populaire de Chine. Centre d'étude des pays de l'Est et Centre national pour l'étude des Etats de l'Est, Revue 9 : 125-146, nos. 1-2, 1968.

FINKELSTEIN, D. : The language of Communist China's criminal law. Journal of Asian studies 27 : 503-521, May 1968.

HSIA, T.-t., and MURRAY, D. : Communist Chinese legal development. Library of Congress, Quarterly journal 25 : 290-298, October 1968.

FOCSEANU, L. : L'attitude de la Chine à l'égard du droit international à l'époque de la révolution culturelle. Annuaire français de droit international 14 : 43-86, 1968.

CHENG, T. : Communist China and the law of the sea. American journal of international law 63 : 47-73, January 1969.

TAY, A.E.-s. : Law in Communist China (To be contd.). Sydney law review 6 : 153-172, no. 2, 1969.

LUBMAN, S. : Form and function in the Chinese criminal process. Columbia law review 69 : 535-575, April 1969.

SPITZ, A. : Maoism and the people's courts. Asian survey 9 : 255-263, April 1969.

SU, J.-h. : Wesen und Funktion von Staat, Recht und Regierung im kommunistischen China. Osteuropa-Recht 15 : 154-168, September 1969.

CHIU, H. : Suspension and termination of treaties in Communist China's theory and practice. Osteuropa-Recht 15 : 169-190, September 1969.

CRESPI REGHIZZI, G. : Il processo penale in Cina. Est, Rivista trimestrale di studi sui paesi dell'Est: 137-145, 30 giugno 1970.

WEGEL, O. : Die Gesetzgebung in der Volksrepublik China. Verfassung und Recht in Ubersee 3 : 139-165, 2. Quartal 1970.

TAO, L.-s. : Communist China's criminal jurisdiction over aliens. International and comparative law quarterly 19 : 599-625, October 1970.

LI, V.H. : The role of law in Communist China. The China quarterly : 66-111, October-December 1970.

NATIONAL LAW - COUNTRIES

COLOMBIA

Legislación fundamental de la función pública colombiana. Documentación administrativa (Spain) : 55-58, octubre 1967.

El estatuto legal de los funcionarios diplomáticos en Colombia. Documentación administrativa (Spain) : 65-69, diciembre 1967.

RESTREPO ARTEAGA, F. : El estado de emergencia económica y social. Estudios de derecho 27 : 325-335, septiembre 1968.

VILLA ZEA, O. : Manual de instrumentos negociables. Estudios de derecho 28 : 269-465, septiembre 1969.

ARIAS MONTOYA, R. : Las fronteras de Colombia en la América Central y en el Caribe y el problema de la plataforma submarina. Estudios de derecho 31 : 5-30, marzo 1970.

COMMONWEALTH

IRVINE, C.N. : The third Commonwealth and Empire law conference. New Zealand law journal : 433-434, 19 October 1965.
Sydney, August 1965; First of a series of articles.

MARSHALL, H.H. : The legal relationship between the State and its servants in the Commonwealth. International and comparative law quarterly 15 : 150-174, January 1966.

Supreme court for the Commonwealth. Calcutta weekly notes 70 : lxxxiii-lxxxv, May 2-9 1966.

FRIDMAN, G.H.L. : Change of domicile during divorce. New law journal 116 : 1160-1162, 11 August 1966.

NETTHEIM, G. : Legislative interference with the judiciary. Australian law journal 40 : 221-231, 30 November 1966.

AVINS, A. : Involuntary servitude in British Commonwealth law. International and comparative law quarterly 16 : 29-55, January 1967.

HOWELL, J.M. : The Commonwealth and the concept of domestic jurisdiction. The Canadian yearbook of international law 5 : 14-44, 1967.

LAWFORD, H.J. : The practice concerning treaty succession in the Commonwealth. The Canadian yearbook of international law 5 : 3-13, 1967.

GREENWELL, J.H. : Administration tribunals and the rule of law. Ceylon law society journal 9 : iii-xv, June-August 1967.

Nationality and citizenship laws of countries of the Commonwealth. Central office of information, Reference division, Bulletin (London) : 1-36, no. R, 5024, September 1967.

STONE, O.M. : Recent developments in family law in British common law jurisdictions. Columbia law review 67 : 1241-1249, November 1967.

DOEKER, G. : Der Abschluss völkerrechtlicher Verträge im traditionellen Commonwealth of nations. Archiv des Völkerrechts 14 : 1-56, 1. Heft 1968.

ROBERTS-WRAY, K. : Human rights in the Commonwealth. International and comparative law quarterly 17 : 908-925, October 1968.

HAHLO, H.R. : The Privy council and the "gentle revolution". South African law journal 86 : 419-437, November 1969.

SMILLIE, J.A. : Jurisdictional review of abuse of discretionary power. Canadian bar review - La revue du Barreau canadien 47 : 623-642, December 1969.

JACKSON, D. : The judicial Commonwealth. The Cambridge law journal 28 : 257-279, November 1970.

CONGO (BRAZZAVILLE)

Constitution de la République du Congo-Brazzaville, décembre 1963. Documentation française, Notes et études documentaires : 34-42, 26 mars 1965.

Congo-Brazzaville; constitution, décembre 1963. Informations constitutionnelles et parlementaires 16 : 174-190, octobre 1965.

Constitución de la República de Congo-Brazzaville, diciembre 1963. Información jurídica (Spain) : 47-63, noviembre-diciembre 1966.

La nouvelle constitution de la République populaire du Congo. Semaine (Brazzaville) 19 : 8-9, 11 janvier 1970.
Promulguée le 3 janvier 1970.

DECHEIX, P. : La constitution de la République populaire du Congo du 3 janvier 1970. Revue juridique et politique - Indépendance et coopération 24 : 111-126, janvier-mars 1970.
Texte et commentaire.

MARDEK, H. : Gedanken zur Verfassung der Volksreoublik Kongo. Staat und Recht 19 : 825-833, Heft 5, Mai 1970.

ROGGE, H. : Die Verfassung der Volksrepublik vom 3.1.1970 und ihre Vorläufer. Verfassung und Recht in Ubersee 3 : 461-468, 4. Quartal 1970.

CONGO (KINSHASA)

RAË, M. : Propos sur la constitution de la République démocratique du Congo. Académie royale des sciences d'outre-mer, Bulletin des séances - Koninklijke academie voor overzeese wetenschappen, Mededelingen der zittingen (Bruxelles) : 1023-1051, no. 4, 1965.
Bibliographie p. 1052.

SALMON, J. : Les attributions normatives du président de la République. Revue juridique du Congo 41 : 177-186, juillet-septembre 1965.

VIGNERON, R. : La lésion en droit civil congolais - Essai d'interprétation du décret du 26 août 1959. Revue juridique du Congo 41 : 289-305, octobre-décembre 1965.

BUREN, R. : L'usurpation de fonctions publiques en droit pénal congolais, commentaire de l'article 123. Revue juridique du Congo 41 : 306-312, octobre-décembre 1965.

GANSHOF, L.F. : La faillite en droit international privé congolais. Revue juridique du Congo 41 : 25-44, no. spécial, 1965.

RAË, M. : La constitution de la République démocratique du Congo et la lex loci delicti commissi. Revue juridique du Congo 41 : 235-241, no. spécial 1965.

JULEMONT, P.V. de : La nouvelle constitution de la République démocratique du Congo. Revue juridique du Congo 41 : 57-134, no. spécial, 1965.

RUBBENS, A. : La justice militaire. Revue juridique du Congo 42 : 3-12, janvier-mars 1966.

DEVAUX, V. : Les lacunes de la loi dans le droit de l'ancien Congo belge. Revue juridique du Congo (Lubumbashi) 42 : 195-209, juillet-septembre 1966.

FOURRÉ, J. : Le pouvoir exécutif dans la République démocratique du Congo. Revue juridique et politique - Indépendance et coopération 20 : 523-534, octobre-décembre 1966.

YOUNG, M.C. : Constitutionalism and constitutions in the Congo. Jahrbuch des öffentlichen Rechts der Gegenwart 15 : 645-682, 1966.

FOURRÉ, J. : Les sources du droit public et du droit administratif congolais. Penant, Revue de droit des pays d'Afrique 77 : 33-52, janvier-mars 1967.

VIGNERON, R. : L'évolution du droit civil congolais depuis l'indépendance. Revue juridique du Congo (Lubumbashi) 43 : 222-240, 2e semestre 1967.

La nouvelle constitution congolaise. Remarques africaines 9 : 282-291, ler juin 1967.

FOURRÉ, J. : Décentralisation et fédéralisme au Congo Kinshasa. Penant, Revue de droit des pays d'Afrique 77 : 301-309, juillet-septembre 1967.

ROUGENIN-BAVILLE, M. et FOURRÉ, J. : Les rapports entre le gouvernement central et les provinces dans la République démocratique du Congo. Revue juridique et politique - Indépendance et coopération 22 : 131-140, janvier-mars 1968.

Constitution de la République démocratique du Congo. Ambassade de la République démocratique du Congo, Bulletin d'information (Berne) : 1-22, no. 7, 1968.
5 avril 1967; Text.

MULUMBA, C. : Le pouvoir législatif dans la constitution congolaise du 24 juin 1967. Cahiers économiques et sociaux 7 : 119-131, mars 1969.

RUBBENS, A. : La réforme judiciaire du 10 juillet 1968 en République démocratique du Congo. Cahiers économiques et sociaux 7 : 411-429, décembre 1969.

COIPEL, M. : Le divorce d'époux de nationalité différente en droit international privé congolais. Revue juridique du Congo (Lubumashi) 46 : 105-119, mai-août 1970.

COSTA RICA

VARGAS SOLERA, M.E. : La jurisdicción tutelar de menores en Costa Rica. Instituto interamericano del niño, Boletín 39 : 286-294, junio 1965.

RETANA SANDÍ, G. : Exposición de motivos del proyecto de ley reguladora de la jurisdicción contencioso-administrativa en Costa Rica. Boletín del Instituto de derecho comparado de México 18 : 749-759, septiembre-diciembre 1965.

HUNG-VAILLANT, F. : La empresa individual de responsabilidad limitada en el Congo de comercio vigente en Costa Rica. Revista de la Facultad de derecho (Caracas) : 38-58, nos. 37-38, 1967.

CUBA

LE-RIVEREND, E. : El divorcio, derechos cubano y puertorriqueño. Revista jurídica de la Universidad de Puerto Rico 35 : 535-634, núm. 4, 1966.

SCHREIBER, A. P. : Human rights in revolutionary Cuba - The work of the Inter-American commission on human rights. Revue des droits de l'homme - Human rights journal 2 : 139-158, no. 1, 1969.

DORTICÓS TORRADO, O. : Cuban hikacking law, September 16, 1969. International legal materials, Current documents 8 : 1175-1186, November 1969.

BERMAN, J. : The Cuban popular tribunals. Columbia law review 69 : 1317-1354, December 1969.

CYPRUS

TORNARITIS, C.G. : Notes by the Attorney-general of the Republic of Cyprus. Revue hellénique de droit international 19 : 286-300, janvier-décembre 1966.

TORNARITIS, C.G. : The right to petition the authorities especially under the law of Cyprus. Revue des droits de l'homme - Human rights journal 1 : 518-529, no. 4, 1968.

TORNARITIS, C.G. : The inviolability of correspondence and communication, especially under the law of the Republic of Cyprus. Revue des droits de l'homme - Human rights journal 3 : 83-99, mars 1970.

CZECHOSLOVAKIA

STUNA, S. : L'évolution de la législation économique dans la République socialiste tchécoslovaque et l'objet de la réglementation portée par le code économique. Bulletin de droit tchécoslovaque 23 : 1-12, no. 1-2, 1965.
Code économique du 4 juin 1964 pp. 43-162.

GLOS, J. : Na okraj civilistických kodexů. Právnik 104 : 323-335, cislo 4, 1965.

ELÍÁS, : Probleme der Neuregelung des tschechoslowakischen Familienrechts. Staat und Recht 14 : 1077-1091, Juli 1965.

LUBY, Š. : Nové československé autorské právo. Právnik 104 : 696-707, čislo 8, 1965.

MOLČAN, T. : Niekel'ko úvah nad uplatňovaním para.62 zákona o rodine. Právny obzor 48 : 490-494, čislo 8, 1965.

RŮŽEK, A. : Novela k trestnímu řádu. Právník 104 : 805-814, čislo 9, 1965.

NATIONAL LAW - COUNTRIES

KANDA, A. : La nouvelle réglementation de la responsabilité en droit civil tchécoslovaque. Revue internationale de droit comparé 17 : 895-907, octobre-décembre 1965.

CESKA, Z. : La nouvelle réglementation de la procédure civile tchécoslovaque. Bulletin de droit tchécoslovaque 23 : 169-208, 31 décembre 1965.
Texte du code pp. 209-295.

BREIER, Š., and PANÍČEK, F. : Novela trestného zákona. Právny obzor 49 : 5-11, číslo 1, 1966.

RUZEK, A. : Les modifications de la législation pénale tchécoslovaque en 1965. Revue internationale de droit pénal 36 : 187-196, 1er-2e trimestre 1965.

LUBY, Š. : Aktuálne právnopolitické problémy v občianskom práve. Právnické študié 14 : 209-292, číslo 2, 1966.
Summaries in German and Russian.

PIASECKI, K. : Czechoslowacki kodeks cywilny. Nowe prawo 22 : 181-190, luty 1966.

ELIÁŠ, J. : Základní zásady socialistického občanského práva. Právnické štúdie 14 : 463-502, číslo 3, 1966.
Civil law; Summaries in German and Russian.

LUBY, S. : La protection des droits des auteurs dans la République socialiste tchécoslovaque. Bulletin de droit tchécoslovaque 24 : 171-184, no. 3, 1966.
Voir aussi pp. 213-228.

SPIŠIAK, J. : Vybrané teoretické aspekty novej učebnice občianskeho práva. Právny obzor 49 : 344-357, číslo 4, 1966.

LEVIT, P. : K některým otázkam zákonnosti ve státní správě. Právník 105 : 322-332, číslo 4, 1966.

PEŠKA, P. : O perspektivách ústavního práva a konstitucionalismu. Právník 105 : 407-419, číslo 5, 1966.
Summary in Russian.

KUCERA, Z. : La loi tchécoslovaque du 4 décembre 1963, no. 97 du Recueil des lois, sur le droit international privé et de procédure. Journal du droit international 93 : 783-804, octobre-décembre 1966.

NEZKUSIL, J. : La modification du code pénal tchécoslovaque et la nouvelle réglementation de la poursuite, devant les tribunaux de district, des infractions et contraventions en cas de récidive. Bulletin de droit tchécoslovaque 24 : 275-294, décembre 1966.

HUSAR, E. : Les modifications apportées à la procédure pénale en République socialiste tchécoslovaque. Bulletin de droit tchécoslovaque 24 : 295-309, décembre 1966.

L'évolution du droit dans les différents pays - LUKEŠ, Z. : Tchécoslovaquie. Annuaire de législation française et étrangère 15 : 502-511, 1966.

SLAPNICKA, H. : Die neueste Rechtsentwicklung in der Tschechoslowakei. Österreichische Osthefte 9 : 1-10, Jänner 1967.

PAVLÍČEK, V. : La conception de la liberté d'association et de réunion en République socialiste tchécoslovaque. Bulletin de droit tchécoslovaque : 85-105, no. 1-4, 1967.

LUBY, Š. : Les droits sur les oeuvres d'auteur, les prestations artistiques, les découvertes et les inventions et leur protection dans la législation tchécoslovaque. Bulletin de droit tchécoslovaque : 170-196, no. 1-4, 1967.

SCHMIED, E. : Leyes de procedimiento penal y de la organización judicial de la Eépublica Socialista de Checoslovaquia. Boletín del Instituto de derecho comparado de México 20 : 251-257, enero-agosto 1967.

RASLA, A. : Vývojové tendencie v československom trestnom zákondarstve. Právny obzor 50 : 560-571, číslo 6, 1967.

ULČ, O. : Class struggle and socialist justice - The case of Czechoslovakia. American political science review 61 : 727-743, September 1967.

STEPAN, J. : L'étendue de la procédure préliminaire dans la procédure pénale tchécoslovaque et son rapport avec l'audience. Revue internationale de droit pénal 38 : 353-374, 3e-4e trimestre 1967.

KOPAC, L. : Le code tchécoslovaque du commerce international. Journal du droit international 94 : 789-818, octobre-décembre 1967.

KUNZ, O. : Některé kolizní otázky smluv v oblasti autorského práva. Studie z mezinárodního práva 12 : 169-190, 1967.
Copyright and conflict of laws; Summary in French.

PEŠKA, P. : Zur gegenwärtigen Verfassungsentwicklung in der Tschechoslowakei. Jahrbuch des öffentlichen Rechts der Gegenwart 16 : 295-323, 1967.

GROSPIČ, J., and JIČÍNSKÝ, Z. : Ústava 9. května a některé otázky československého konstitucionalismu. Právník 107 : 380-392, číslo 5, 1968.

SOLNAR, V. : Quelques problèmes fondamentaux du droit pénal tchécoslovaque. Revue de droit pénal et de criminologie 48 : 829-846, juin 1968.

SPIŠIAK, J. : Hospodárskoprávne aspekty československej federácie. Právny obzor 51 : 708-719, číslo 8, 1968.

POTOČNÝ, M. : Kodifikace zásady pokojného řešení sporů. Časopis pro mezinárodní právo 13 : 33-45, číslo 1, 1969.

LUBY, Š. : Právne úkony v československom Občianskom zákonníku. Právnické štúdie 17 : 5-79, číslo 1, 1969.
Legal acts in civil code; Summaries in French and Russian.

BYSTRYCKY, R. : Nekalá soutěž z hlediska československého mezinárodního práva soukromého. Časopis pro mezinárodní právo 13 : 230-238, číslo 3, 1969.

KUNZ, O. : Postayení cizinců v oblasti československého autorského práva. Časopis pro mezinárodní právo 13 : 345-353, číslo 4, 1969.

CHOVANEC, J. : Zásady československej socialistickej federácie. Právny obzor 52 : 310-315, číslo 4, 1969.

PEŠKA, P. : Ustavní situace Československa, též se zřetelem na českou státoprávní politiku. Právník 108 : 297-305, číslo 5, 1969.
Constitutional situation: Summary in French.

SOLTYSINSKI, S.J. : New forms of protection for intellectual property in the Soviet Union and in Czechoslovakia. Modern law review 32 : 408-419, July 1969.

PEŠKA, P. : Několik námětů a poznámek k přípravě zákona o ústavním soudu ČSSR. Právník 108 : 543-551, čislo 7, 1969.

PLANK, K. : Problém dvojitého štátneho občianstva v československej federácii. Právny obzor 52 : 695-711, čislo 8, 1969.

GROSPIČ, J., and JIČÍNSKÝ, Z. : K problematice zákonodárství podle ústavního zákona č. 143/1968 Sb., o československé federaci. Právník 108 : 649-657, čislo 9, 1969.

LUBY, S. : Právo predchádzajúceho uživatel'a vynálezu. Právny obzor 52 : 809-818, čislo 9, 1969.

FATRANSKÝ, R. : Vývoj právnej úpravy dôvodov rozvodu manželstiev. Právny obzor 52 : 884-892, čislo 10, 1969.

FABRY, V. : Ownership and other property rights in respect of land in Czechoslovakia. International and comparative law quarterly 18 : 970-980, October 1969.

Loi constitutionnelle sur la Fédération tchécoslovaque, 27 octobre 1968. Notes et études documentaires : 1-32, no. 3647, 17 décembre 1969.

BOBEK, J. : Zur gegenwärtigen Verfassungssituation in der ČSSR. Jahrbuch des öffentlichen Rechts der Gegenwart 18 : 295-301, 1969.

FIALA, J., and STEINER, V. : Teoretické otázky určení mateřství podle československého právna. Právník 109 : 33-43, čislo 1, 1970.

TURČÁNI, J. : Príspevok pravidiel administratívneho konania k humanizácii rozhodovacej činnosti orgánov štátnej správy. Právny obzor 53 : 89-104, čislo 2, 1970.

FIALA, J., and ŠVESTKA, J. : Úvaja nad teoretickým systémem čs. občanského práva. Právnik 109 : 77-95, čislo 2, 1970.

KNAP. K. : Lizenzverträge im Handelsverkehr mit der Tschechoslowakei. Aussenwirtschaftsdienst des Betriebs-Beraters 16 : 167-171, April 1970.

CHOVANEC, J. : Ústavné zásady československej socialistickej federácie. Právny obzor 53 : 577-588, čislo 7, 1970.

DAHOMEY

Constitution de la République du Dahomey, janvier 1964. Documentation française, Notes et études documentaires : 42-51, no. 3175, 26 mars 1965.

DECHEIX, P. : Le code de la nationalité dahoméenne. Revue juridique et politique - Indépendance et coopération 19 : 605-608, octobre-décembre 1965.
Texte pp. 609-622.

ADANDÉ, A. : L'organisation judiciaire et l'évolution législative générale au Dahomey. Penant, Revue de droit des pays d'Afrique 75 : 429-445, octobre-décembre 1965.

L'évolution du droit dans les différents pays - MANGIN, G. : Dahomey. Annuaire de législation française et étrangère 15 : 152-160, 1966.

DECHEIX, P. : La nouvelle constitution du Dahomey. Revue juridique et politique - Indépendance et coopération 22 : 919-922, juillet-septembre 1968.
Texte de la constitution, adoptée le 31 mars 1968, pp. 923-935.

Constitution, adoptée par référendum du 31 mars 1968. Informations constitutionnelles et parlementaires 20 : 135-156, juillet 1969.

DENMARK

PEDERSEN, I.M. : Matrimonial property law in Denmark. Modern law review 28 : 137-153, March 1965.

GELLHORN, W. : The Ombudsman in Denmark. McGill law journal 12 : 1-40, no. 1, 1966.

L'évolution du droit dans les différent pays - Danemark. Annuaire de législation française et étrangère 15 : 161-178, 1966.
Suite d'articles.

CHRISTENSEN, B. : Public regulation of private real property. Scandinavian studies in law 13 : 73-106, 1969.

ECUADOR

VILLEGAS, D.R. : De la terminación del matrimonio en la legislación ecuatoriana. Estudios de derecho 24 : 403-411, septiembre 1965.

Código de procedimiento penal del Ecuador, 25 de marzo de 1938. Información jurídica (Spain) : 3-84 marzo-abril 1967.

EQUATORIAL GUINEA

Constitución de la Guinea ecuatorial (To be contd.). Africa (Madrid) 25 : 27-28, agosto 1968.
Text presented by the Spanish delegation, 22 June 1968.

Constitución de Guinea Ecuatorial de 11 de agosto de 1968. Información jurídica (Spain) : 59-72, abril-junio 1969.

ETHIOPIA

MARY, G.T. : Die Eigentumsrechte der Kaffitscho in Äthiopien. Zeitschrift für vergleichende Rechtswissenschaft 68 : 216-232, 2. Heft 1966.

AHOOJA, K. : Law and development in Ethiopia - A report on Haile Selassie I university Faculty of law seminar. Ethiopia observer 10 : 152-163, no. 2, 1966.

VANDERLINDEN, J. : An introduction to the sources of Ethiopian law from the 13th to the 20th century. Journal of Ethiopian law 3 : 227-255, June 1966.
Bibliography pp. 256-283.

HABTE SELASSIE, B. : Constitutional development in Ethiopia. Journal of African law 10 : 74-91, summer 1966.

Development and legislation in Ethiopia. Ethiopia observer 10 : 233-234, no. 4, 1967.
Series of articles; Bibliography p. 235.

SINGER, N.J. : The dissolution of religious marriages in Ethiopia. Journal of Ethiopian law 4 : 205-210, June 1967.

DAVID, R. : Administrative contracts in the Ethiopian civil code. Journal of Ethiopian law 4 : 143-153, June 1967.

KRZECZUNOWICZ, G. : The nature of marriage under the Ethiopian civil code, 1960 - An exegesis. Journal of African law 11 : 175-180, autumn 1967.

SEDLER, R.A. : The development of legal systems - The Ethiopian experience. Iowa law review 53 : 562-635, December 1967.

McCARTHY, P. : "De facto" and customary partnerships in Ethiopian law. Journal of Ethiopian law 5 : 105-122, June 1968.

MEANS, R.C. : The Eritrean employment act of 1958 - Its present status. Journal of Ethiopian law 5 : 139-150, June 1968.

SAND, P.H. : Die Reform des äthiopischen Erbrechts - Problematik einer synthetischen Rezeption. Rabels Zeitschrift für ausländisches und internationales Privatrecht 33 : 413-454, Heft 3, 1969.

KRZECZUNOWICZ,G. : The present role of equity in Ethiopian civil law. Journal of African law 13 : 145-157, autumn 1969.

GERAGHTY, T. : People, practice, attitudes and problems in the lower courts of Ethiopia. Journal of Ethiopian law 6 : 427-512, December 1969.

La constitution éthiopienne (1955) - Traduite et annotée par Jean Doresse. Revue juridique et politique - Indépendance et coopération 24 : 267-288, avril-juin 1970.

VANDERLINDEN, J. : Quelques aspects fondamentaux du développement juridique éthiopien. Verfassung und Recht in Ubersee 3 : 167-178, 2. Quartal 1970.

SINGER, N.J. : Modernization of law in Ethiopia - A study in process and personal values. Harvard international law journal 11 : 73-125, winter 1970.

FINLAND

SIPPONEN, K.: Some aspects of the delegation of legislative power in Finland. Scandinavian studies in law 9 : 159-176, 1965.

Constitution de la Finlande, 17 juillet 1919. Documentation française, Notes et études documentaires : 1-11, no. 3233, 3 novembre 1965.

SUNDSTRÖM, G.O.Z. : Die finnische Gesetzgebung auf dem Gebiete des Privatrechts 1945-1965. Rabels Zeitschrift für ausländisches und internationales Privatrecht 31 : 275-318, Heft 2, 1967.

KASTARI, P. : Le chef de l'Etat dans les institutions finlandaises. Revue du droit public et de la science politique en France et à l'étranger 83 : 861-883, septembre-octobre 1967.

BLOMSTEDT, Y. : From elected magnates to state-appointed professionals. Aspects of the history of the Finnish judiciary. Scandinavian studies in law 13 : 9-57, 1969.

FRANCE

SCHNEYDER, P. : La divulgation du secret militaire et la presse. Revue administrative 18 : 26-30 janvier-février 1965.

KING, J.B. : Constitutionalism and the judiciary in France. Political science quarterly 80 : 62-87, March 1965.

CHAVANNE, A. : La loi du 31 décembre 1964 sur les marques de fabrique, de commerce ou de service. Recueil Dalloz Sirey, Chronique : 83-90, 7 avril 1965.

MAZEAUD, H. : La communauté réduite au bon vouloir de chacun des époux - Réflexions sur le nouveau projet de loi portant réforme des régimes matrimoniaux. Recueil Dalloz Sirey, Chronique : 91-94, 14 avril 1965.

JOZEAU-MARIGNÉ, L. : La réforme des dispositions du code civil relatives à la tutelle et à l'émancipation. Revue politique des idées et des institutions 54 : 15-19, avril 1965.

LEBACQZ, A. : La réforme de la législation sur les sociétés. Revue politique des idées et des institutions 54 : 36-44, avril 1965.

CARTERON, M. : Quelques remarques sur le projet de réforme des sociétés commerciales. Revue adminitrative 18 : 261-265, mai-juin 1965.

PETOT, J. : Quelques remarques sur les notions fondamentales du droit administratif français. Revue du droit public et de la science politique en France et à l'étranger 81 : 370-398, mai-juin 1965.

SAVATIER, R. : La finance ou la gloire, option pour la femme mariée? - Réflexions sur la réforme des régimes matrimoniaux. Recueil Dalloz Sirey, Chronique : 135-140, 16 juin 1965.

LE BRIS, R.F. : L'effet du divorce sur le nom des époux. Recueil Dalloz Sirey, Chronique : 141-146, 23 juin 1965.

BROWN, L.N. : The reform of French matrimonial property law. American journal of comparative law 14 : 308-322, spring 1965.

PLAISANT, R. : Statut fiscal de la propriété industrielle en droit français. Fiscalité du Marché commun - Europäische Steuer-Zeitung : 300-306, juin 1965.
Texte en allemand aussi.

LARGUIER, J. : The civil action for damages in French criminal procedure. Tulane law review 39 : 687-700, June 1965.

COSTA-NOBLE, P. da : Une erreur politique et sociale, le rachat des greffes des Cours et Tribunaux. Revue politique des idées et des institutions 54 : 121-131, juillet 1965.
Textes pp. 132-142.

NATIONAL LAW - COUNTRIES

BARALE, J. : Le régime juridique de l'eau, richesse nationale, loi du 16 décembre 1964. Revue du droit public et de la science politique en France et à l'étranger 81 : 587-630, juillet-août 1965.

MAURY, J. : La séparation de fait entre époux. Revue trimestrielle de droit civil 64 : 515-544, juillet-septembre 1965.

AMSELEK, P. : Les vicissitudes de la compétence juridictionnelle en matière d'atteintes administratives à la liberté individuelle. Revue du droit public et de la science politique en France et à l'étranger 81 : 801-855, septembre-octobre 1965.

WEIL, P. : The strength and weakness of French administrative law. Cambridge law journal : 242-259, November 1965.

STARR, R.I. : Protection of stockholders' rights in the French "société anonyme". Tulane law review 40 : 57-96, December 1965.

BOUZAT, P. : Le droit pénal et les transformations sociales en France. Annales de la Faculté de droit d'Istanbul 15 : 71-98, nos. 21-22, 1965.

LENOIR, Y. : La notion de responsabilité politique. Recueil Dalloz Sirey, Chronique : 5-8, 12 janvier 1966.

GONFREVILLE, M. : L'évolution de la jurisprudence française en matière d'arbitrage et les projets de réforme. Revue de l'arbitrage : 55-64, no. 2, 1966.

ROBINO, P. : La gestion des biens communs sous le régime de la communauté légale. Revue juridique et économique du Sud-Ouest, Série juridique 17 : 143-162, no. 3-4, 1966.

DERRUPPÉ, J. : Le nouveau visage de la société à responsabilité limitée dans la loi du 24 juillet 1966. Revue juridique et économique du Sud-Ouest, Série juridique 17 : 163-176, no. 3-4, 1966.

AUBRUN, C. : Le nouveau droit des conjoints - Application à la banque. Banque 41 : 175-181, 247-251, mars, avril 1966.

BOCKEL, A. : La condition juridique du stagiaire dans le régime français de la fonction publique. Revue du droit public et de la science politique en France et à l'étranger 82 : 265-294, mars-avril 1966.

STURM, F. : Das französische Familienrechtsänderungsgesetz vom 13. Juli 1965. Zeitschrift für das gesamte Familienrecht 13 : 161-169, April 1966.

CEDIE, R., and LEONNET, J. : El Consejo constitucional francés. Revista de estudios políticos : 65-87, marzo-abril 1966.

CATALA, P. : La transformation du patrimoine dans le droit civil moderne. Revue trimestrielle de droit civil 65 : 185-215, avril-juin 1966.

LÉAUTÉ, J. : Pour une responsabilité de la puissance publique en cas de détention préventive abusive. Recueil Dalloz Sirey, Chronique : 61-64, 11 mai 1966.

BOURELY, M. : De la compétence respective de la Cour de sûreté de l'Etat et des tribunaux des forces armées. Recueil Dalloz Sirey, Chronique : 65-70, 18 mai 1966.

LACHAUME, J.F. : Le détachement d'un fonctionnaire auprès d'un organisme privé - A propos de l'arrêt du 13 octobre 1965 de la Cour de cassation. Droit social 28 : 324-336, juin 1966.

BELLAS, M. : Un nouveau couple? Projet; Civilisation, Travail, économie : 697-708, juin 1966.
Réforme des régimes matrimoniaux, loi du 13 juillet 1965.

RENDEL, M. : How the Conseil d'Etat supervises local authorities. Public law : 213-238, autumn 1966.

AUBY, J.M. : Revue du droit public et de la science politique en France et à l'étranger 82 : 864-883, septembre-octobre 1966.

BOULANGER, F. : Réflexions sur le problème de la charge de la preuve. Revue trimestrielle de droit civile 65 : 736-754, octobre-décembre 1966.

DOMINGUEZ AGUILA, R.H. : La reforma de los regímenes matrimoniales en el código civil francés (To be contd.). Revista de derecho y ciencias sociales (Concepción) 34 : 3-24, octubre-diciembre 1966.

DOLL, P.J. : La répression de "l'alcool au volant". Revue de science criminelle et de droit pénal comparé 21 : 827-850, octobre-décembre 1966.

PALMERO, F. : L'indemisation des rapatriés, légitime et utile. Revue politique des idées et des institutions 56 : 449-456, novembre 1966.
Rapatriés d'Algérie.

ROUGIER, L. : Du contrôle de la constitutionnalité des lois - Pourquoi une Cour suprême de justice? Revue internationale du droit des gens 31 : 15-39, 1966.

FAVOREU, L. : Le Conseil constitutionnel régulateur de l'activité normative des pouvoirs publics. Revue du droit public et de la science politique en France et à l'étranger 83 : 5-120, janvier-février 1967.

HAMON, L., et VAUDIAUX, J. : Chronique constitutionnelle et parlementaire française. Revue du droit public et de la science politique en France et à l'étranger 83 : 290-328, mars-avril 1967.
1965-1966.

RASSAT, M.L. : Père de droit et père de fait. Revue trimestrielle de droit civil 66 : 249-309, avril-juin 1967.

HOUIN, R., et GORÉ, F. : La réforme des sociétés commerciales. Recueil Dalloz Sirey, Chronique : 121-176, 14 juin 1967.

PARISOT, B. : Les droits d'auteur et l'oeuvre d'art en régime de communauté. Recueil Dalloz Sirey, Chronique : 189-194, 12 juillet 1967.

CHEMILLIER-GENDREAU, M. : Le détachement dans la fonction publique. Revue de droit public et de la science politique en France et à l'étranger 83 : 647-693, juillet-août 1967.

FENAUX, H. : Le changement de régime matrimonial et les droits des tiers. Revue trimestrielle de droit civil 66: 545-580, septembre 1967.

OPPETIT, B. : Les fins de non-recevoir à l'action en recherche de paternité naturelle. Revue trimestrielle de droit civil 66 : 749-781, octobre-décembre 1967.

FRANÇON, A. : Le décret d'application de la loi du 8 juillet 1964 en matière de protection du droit d'auteur. Revue critique de droit international privé 56 : 667-681, octobre-décembre 1967.

JOZEAU-MARIGNÉ, L. : La réforme de la faillite. Revue politique des idées et des institutions 56 : 357-362, no. 18, novembre 1967.

KLEIN, C. : Les dépens devant les juridictions administratives. Revue du droit public et de la science politique en France et à l'étranger 83 : 1073-1111, novembre-décembre 1967.

BERLIA, G. : Les travaux préparatoires de la constitution. Revue du droit public et de la science politique en France et à l'étranger 83 : 1190-1200, novembre-décembre 1967.

PEPY, D. : Les changements de nom dans le droit français. France, Conseil d'Etat; Etudes et documents 20 : 31-40, 1967.

MOTULSKY, H. : Pour une délimitation plus précise de l'autorité de la chose en matière civile. Recueil Dalloz Sirey, Chronique : 1-8, 9-14; 3 janvier, 10 janvier 1968.

MARTÍNEZ SARRIÓN, A. : Del viejo al nuevo estatuto jurídico francés del matrimonio y de la familia - En torno a la ley de 13 de julio de 1965. Revista de derecho privado : 15-45, enero 1968.

CHIROUX, R. : Le nouveau statut du Territoire français des Afars et des Issas. Penant, Revue de droit des pays d'Afrique 78 : 1-47, janvier-mars 1968.

BOURGEOIS, A.M. : La loi du 13 juillet 1965 et les séquelles du statut d'infériorité juridique de la femme mariée. Revue trimestrielle de droit civil 67 : 68-101, janvier-mars 1968.

HABSCHEID, W.J. : Les cours supérieures en République fédérale d'Allemagne et la distinction du fait et du droit devant les juridictions suprêmes en France et en Allemagne. Revue internationale de droit comparé 20 : 79-94, janvier-mars 1968.

CONTIN, R. : L'arrêt Fruehauf et l'évolution du droit des sociétés (A suivre). Recueil Dalloz Sirey, Chronique : 45-48, 21 février 1968.

La pensée du doyen Maurice Mauriou et son influence. Annales de la Faculté de droit et des sciences économiques de Toulouse 16 : 1-282, fasc. 2, 1968.
Journées Hauriou, Toulouse, mars 1968.

IMBERT, J. : La France et les droits de l'homme. Documentation française, Notes et études documentaires : 1-57, no. 3481, 15 avril 1968.

La justice en France. Documentation française illustrée : 1-63, juin-juillet 1968.

Les peines non privatives de liberté - PIONTKOVSKIJ, A.A. : Rapport sur le droit pénal soviétique - MAZARD, J. : Rapport sur le droit pénal français Revue de science criminelle et de droit comparé 23 : 585-601, juillet-septembre 1968.
Ire rencontre franco-soviétique, Paris, mars 1967.

ROUJOU de BOUBÉE, G. : La loi nouvelle et le litige. Revue trimestrielle de droit civile 67 : 479-501, juillet-septembre 1968.

LAGRANGE, M. : The French Council of State (Conseil d'Etat). Tulane law review 43 : 46-57, December 1968.

POMEY, M. : L'acte de fondation en droit français. France, Conseil d'Etat; Etudes et documents 21 : 27-40, 1968.

GIANVITI, F. : Temps de paix et temps de guerre en droit pénal français. Revue de science criminelle et de droit pénal comparé 24 : 47-78, janvier-mars 1969.

AGUILAR BENÍTEZ de LUGO, M. : El divorcio de españoles ante los tribunales franceses. Revista española de derecho internacional 22 : 721-741, número 4, 1969.

WARREN, L.B., and WILLARD, C.L. : A comparative view of the new French approach to corporate conflicts of interest - The law of 24 July 1966. Business lawyer 24 : 809-822, April 1969.
Text pp. 822-824.

BRIN, H.L. : La survie des titres de noblesse dans le droit moderne. Revue trimestrielle de droit civil 68 : 205-229, avril-juin 1969.

WIEDERKEHR, G. : Le régime matrimonial légal, l'égalité des époux et la protection de l'homme marié contre la femme. Revue trimestrielle de droit civil 68 : 230-280, avril-juin 1969.

BLANDINO, P. : La nouvelle loi française sur les brevets d'invention. Revue de défense nationale 25 : 1220-1232, juillet 1969.

POISSON, E. : Le changement de régime matrimonial article 1397 du code civil. Revue trimestrielle de droit civil 68 : 469-507, juillet-septembre 1969.

ABBOUD, A. : L'aval des effets de commerce. Proche-Orient; études juridiques : 345-460, juillet-décembre 1969.
Comparison entre le droit syrien et le droit français.

WILL, M.R. : Recent modifications in the French law of commercial companies. International and comparative law quarterly 18 : 980-997, October 1969.

HONORAT, J. : Rôle effectif et rôle concevable des quasi-contrats en droit actuel. Revue trimestrielle de droit civil 68 : 653-691, octobre-décembre 1969.

SOULIER, G. : Réflexion sur l'évolution et l'avenir du droit de la responsabilité de la puissance publique. Revue du droit public et de la science politique en France et à l'étranger 85 : 1039-1103, novembre-décembre 1969.

WATRIN, G. : Le domaine législatif et le domaine réglementaire dans la coutume constitutionnelle française. Annales de la Faculté de droit d'Istanbul 19 : 1-20, nos. 33-35, 1969.

FOYER, J. : La protection de la liberté individuelle et la répression des infractions contre la sûreté de l'Etat. Revue des travaux de l'Académie des sciences morales et politiques et comptes rendus de ses séance (Paris) 123: 37-59, ler semestre 1970.

FRENISY, A.M. : La preuve de la propriété et des pouvoirs dans les régimes matrimoniaux depuis la loi du 13 juillet 1965. Revue trimestrielle de droit civil 69 : 64-112, janvier-mars 1970.

LEVY, G. : Recherches sur quelques aspects de la garantie des vices cachés dans la vente des véhicules neufs et d'occasion. Revue trimestrielle de droit civil 69 : 1-63, janvier-mars 1970.

AUBY, J.M. : The abuse of power in French administration law. American journal of comparative law 18 : 549-564, no. 3, 1970.

CHRISTIAENS, L. : Un nouvel homme de loi? - La réforme des professions judiciaires et juridiques. Etudes : 376-385, mars 1970.

L'exécution des directives de la CEE en France. Cahiers de droit européen 6 : 274-302, no. 3, 1970.

TOUSCOZ, J. : La situation juridique des coopérants techniques et la jurisprudence française. Revue du droit public et de la science politique en France et à l'étranger 86 : 287-303, mars-avril 1970.

La France devant la Convention européenne des droits de l'homme - Colloque de Besançon, 5-7 novembre 1970. Revue des droits de l'homme. Human rights journal 3 : 550-738, no. 4, 1970.

VINEY, G. : Réflexions sur l'article 489-2 du code civil. Revue trimestrielle de droit civil 69 : 251-267, avril-juin 1970.
Réforme du droit des incapables mineurs.

CATRICE, R.L., and SCOTT, D.M.M. : Business associations under French law. New law journal 120: 590-592, 25 June 1970.

HENRIQUEZ, P.C. : La nouvelle loi française sur les brevets d'invention. Propriété industrielle 86 : 194-203, juin 1970.

Le TARNEC, A. : La réforme du droit des brevets d'inventaire. Usine nouvelle, Edition supplémentaire : 295-302, juin 1970.

JODLOWSKI, J., et PONSARD, A. : La convention franco-polonaise du 5 avril 1967 relative à la loi applicable, à la compétence et à l'exéquatur dans le droit des personnes et de la famille. Journal du droit international 97 : 545-631, juillet-septembre 1970.

LOUSSOUARN, Y. : La mise en oeuvre du droit d'établissement en France. Revue trimestrielle de droit européen 6 : 499-506, juillet-septembre 1970.

SIMLER, P. : Le conflit des présomptions en régime de communauté. Revue trimestrielle de droit civile 69 : 478-525, juillet-septembre 1970.

NICHOLAS, B. : Loi, règlement and judicial review in the Fifth Republic. Public law : 251-276, autumn 1970.

FOULON-PIGANIOL, J. : Réflexions sur la diffamation reciale - Eléments constitutifs du délit et imperfections du taxe actuel. Recueil Dalloz Sirey, Chronique : 133-136, 30 septembre 1970.

WOOLDRIDGE, F. : The private company in French law- The Journal of business law : 317-331, October 1970.
See also pp. 313-317.

CHEVALLIER, J. : La coutume et le droit constitutionnel français. Revue de droit public et de la science politique en France et à l'étranger 86 : 1375-1416, novembre-décembre 1970.

FRANCE
(International law, Aliens, Nationality)

FRANÇON, A. : La loi du 8 juillet 1964 sur l'application du principe de réciprocité en matière de droit d'auteur. Revue critique de droit international privé 54 : 279-303, mai-juin 1965.

LE TARNEC, A. : La loi du 8 juillet 1964 sur l'application du principe de réciprocité en matière de protection du droit d'auteur. Journal du droit international 92 : 883-893, octobre-décembre 1965.

HARTINGH, F. de : La position française à l'égard de la convention de Genève sur le plateau continental. Annuaire français de droit international 11 : 725-734, 1965.

FRANÇON, A. : La nouvelle loi française sur les marques et le droit international. Journal du droit international 93 : 5-25, janvier-mars 1966.

TALLON, D., and KOVAR, R. : The application of community law in France. Common market law review 4 : 64-77, June 1966.

BLECKMANN, A. : Die Mitwirkung des französischen Parlaments bei Abschluss, Aufhebung und Änderung von Verträgen. Zeitschrift für ausländisches Öffentliches Recht und Völkerrecht 26 : 310-349, September 1966.

DALIMIER, G. : L'évolution récente du droit fiscal international en France. Journal du droit international 93 : 805-816, octobre-décembre 1966.

ANSELME-RABINOVITCH, L. : Clauses monétaires dans un contrat international. Banque 41 : 839-843, décembre 1966.

LAGARDE, P. : La disparition de la faculté pour les Algériens de statut musulman de se faire reconnaitre la nationalité française. Revue critique de droit international privé 56 : 55-67, janvier-mars 1967.
Loi no. 66-945, du 20 décembre 1966.

JUSSEAU, P. : Le problème de la réparation des dommages subis par les Français d'outre-mer à la suite de la décolonisation. Revue politique des idées et des institutions 56 : 80-88, nos. 3-4, février 1967.

SPITERI, P. : La fraude à la loi étrangère. Annales de la Faculté de droit et des sciences économiques de Toulouse 15 : 37-51, fasc. 2, 1967.

LOURDJANE, A. : Musulmans originaires d'Algérie, peuvent-ils bénoficier de la double nationalité, française et algérienne? Revue juridique et politique - Indépendance et coopération 21 : 295-300, avril-juin 1967.

CHARDENON, P. : Dettes de rapatriation et nationalisations algériennes. Journal du droit international 94 : 290-322, avril-juin 1967.

DROZ, G.A.L. : Les nouvelles règles de conflit françaises en matière de forme des testaments - Entrée en vigueur de la convention de La Haye sur les conflits de lois en matière de forme des dispositions testamentaires. Revue critique de droit international privé 57 : 1-23, janvier-mars 1968.

PRATS, Y. : Incidences des dispositions du traité instituant la Communauté économique européenne sur le droit administratif français. Revue trimestrielle de droit européen 4 : 19-49, janvier-mars 1968.

STASSINOPOULOS, M. : Remarques sur la jurisprudence française relative à l'interprétation des traités internationaux. Revue générale de droit international public 73 : 5-29, janvier-mars 1969.

KOZYRIS, P.J. : Equal joint-venture corporations in France - Problems of control and resolution of deadlocks. American journal of comparative law 17 : 503-528, no. 4, 1969.

GINATTA, F. : Sull'interpretazione dell'art. 14 della convenzione italo-francese del 3 giugno 1930 sull'esecuzione delle sentenze in materia civile e commerciale. Rivista di diritto internazionale privato e processuale 5 : 453-461, aprile-giugno 1969.

BRULLIARD, G. : Les solutions du droit international privé français commun et conventionnel en matière de reconnaissance et d'exécution des jugements étrangers. Rivista du diritto internazionale privato e processuale 5 : 285-320, aprile-giugno 1969.

GINATTA, F. : La convenzione italo-francese sull' esecuzione delle sentenze e la sua applicazione giurisprudenziale, 1945-1967. Rivista di diritto internazionale privato e processuale 5 : 661-695, luglio-settembre 1969.

FRANCESCAKIS, P. : Remarques critiques sur le rôle de la constitution dans le conflit entre le traité et la loi interne devant les tribunaux judiciaires, Revue critique de droit international privé 58 : 425-446, juillet-septembre 1969.

COLOMÈS, M. : La liberté communautaire d'établissement et son application en France. Revue franco-belge 79 : 244-253, novembre 1969.

RUILOBA SANTANA, E. : El convenio hispano-francés de 28 de mayo de 1969 sobre reconocimiento de sentencias extranjeras y actas auténticas en materias civil y mercantil. Revista española de derecho internacional 23 : 42-75, núm. 1, 1970.

DUMAS, J.P. : Effets de la décolonisation sur la nationalité française des métis. Revue juridique et politique - Indépendance et coopération 24 : 35-50, janvier-mars 1970.

BOTTINI, R. de : La convention franco-polonaise relative à la loi applicable, la compétence et l' exequatur dans le droit des personnes et de la famille. Revue critique de droit international privé 59 : 1-43, janvier-mars 1970.

DROZ, G.A.L. : Saisine héréditaire et administration de la succession en droit international privé français et comparé. Revue critique de droit international privé 59 : 183-225, avril-juin 1970.

SIMON-DEPITRE, M. : L'application en France des mesures communautaires en matière de liberté d'établissement. Revue critique de droit international privé 59 : 227-245, avril-juin 1970.

GABON

Constitution du 21 février 1961, modifié le 31 mai 1963. Informations constitutionnelles et parlementaires 16 : 15-32, janvier 1966.

GERMANY
(Federal Republic)

OSTERMEYER,G. : La protection du nom commercial (firme) en droit allemand. Revue juridique et économique du Sud-Ouest, Série juridique 16 : 125-133, nos. 3-4, 1965.

RUPP, H.H., and ZEZSCHWITZ, F. von : Ehrengerichtsbarkeit und Grundgesetz. Juristenzeitung 20 : 399-403, 2. Juli 1965.

MÜHLHAUS, H. : Die Strafzumessung bei den unter Alkoholeinschluss begangenen Verkehrsdelikten. Deutsches Autorecht 34 : 141-145, Juni 1965.

MÜLLER, G. : The Federal constitutional court of the Federal Republic of Germany. International commission of jurists, Journal 6 : 191-218, winter 1965.

MENDELSOHN, B. : Les infractions commises sous le régime nazi sont-elles des crimes au sens du droit commun? Revue de droit international, de sciences diplomatiques et politiques 43 : 333-341, octobre-décembre 1965.

SIEGERT, K. : Le ultime riforme del codice di procedura penale germanico. Scuola positiva 71 : 25-37, fasc. 1, 1966.

Loi fondamentale pour la République fédérale d'Allemagne adoptée par le Conseil parlementaire le 8 mai 1949, texte en vigueur le 1er janvier 1966. Documentation française, Notes et études documentaires : 1-22, no. 3274, 21 mars 1966.

LEIBHOLZ, G. : El Tribunal constitucional de la República federal alemana y el problema de la apreciación judicial de la política. Revista de estudios políticos : 89-98, marzo-abril 1966.

JAKOBS, O.W. : Das Eigentum als Rechtsinstitut im deutschen und sowjetischen Recht. Rabels Zeitschrift für ausländisches und internationales Privatrecht 29 : 694-724, Heft 4, 1965.

ROXIN, C. : Zur Dogmatik der Teilnahmelehre im Strafrecht. Juristenzeitung 21 : 293-299, 6. Mai 1966.

KUNST, G. : Eine kritische Stimme zur deutschen Strafrechtsreform. Österreichische Juristen-Zeitung 21 : 589-600, 16. November 1966.

WEBER, H. : Die Reform des westdeutschen politischen Strafrechts und das Bonner Grundgesetz. Staat und Recht 15 : 2013-2026, Dezember 1966.

NATIONAL LAW - COUNTRIES

JESCHEK, H.H. : Zur Reform des politischen Strafrechts. Juristenzeitung 22 : 6-13, 6. Januar 1967.

MAYER, H. : Les fondements du droit pénal allemand actuel. Revue internationale de droit pénal 38 : 61-76, ler-2e trimestre 1967.

PATZIG, W. : Gegenwartsfragen des Finanzverfassungsrechts. Archiv des öffentlichen Rechts 92 : 297-357, Heft 3, 1967.

PLEYER, K. : Propriété et contrat, instruments de l'ordre économique dans la République fédérale d'Allemagne. Revue internationale de droit comparé 19 : 373-392, avril-juin 1967.

MERTENS, P. : La prescription des crimes de guerre en Allemagne fédérale à la lumière des événements récents. Année politique et économique 40 : 159-170, juillet 1967.

MATTES, H. : La réforme du droit des infractions réglementaires dans la République fédérale d'Allemagne. Revue internationale de droit pénal 38 : 437-481, 3e-4e trimestre 1967.

ROBINSON, C.D. : Le droit du prévenu au silence et son droit à être assisté par un défenseur au cours de la phase préjudiciaire en Allemagne et aux Etats-Unis d'Amérique. Revue de science criminelle et de droit pénal comparé 22 : 567-618, juillet-septembre 1967.

BOBERACH, H., and MEYER, B. : Gesetzliche Bestimmungen und Verwaltungsvorschriften für das staatliche Archivwesen und zur Archivpflege in der Bundesrepublik Deutschland 1966 und 1967, bis April. Archivar 20 : 407-436, November 1967.

RAMM, T. : La situation actuelle du droit du travail en Allemagne. Droit social : 624-630, décembre 1967.

BOGS, W. : Die Rechtsprechung des Bundessozialgerichts zum Grundgesetz. Jahrbuch des öffentlichen Rechts der Gegenwart 16 : 129-162, 1967.

HABSCHEID, W.J. : Les cours supérieures en République fédérale d'Allemagne et la distinction du fait et du droit devant les juridictions suprêmes en France et en Allemagne. Revue internationale de droit comparé 20 : 79-94, janvier-mars 1968.

ROGGEMANN, H. : Zur Entwicklung des politischen Strafrechts in Deutschland. Recht in Ost und West 12 : 50-63, 15. März 1968.

FRIESENHAHN, E. : Die verfassungsrechtliche Stellung der Parteien in der Bundesrepublik Deutschland. Zeitschrift für schweizerisches Recht 87/1 : 245-282, Heft 3, 1968.

PAKUSCHER, E.K. : Administrativ law in (Western) Germany - Citizen v. state. American journal of comparative law 16 : 309-331, no. 3, 1968.

BICKELHAUPT, H. : Schutz der Persönlichkeitsrechte be Benutzung von Archiven. Archivar 21 : 209-215, Juli 1968.

SCHULTZ, H. : Un tournant nouveau de la réforme du droit allemand. Revue internationale de droit comparé 20 : 493-509, juillet-septembre 1968.

SIMSON, G. : Grenzen des Sexualstrafrechts in Deutschland und Schweden. Juristenzeitung 23 : 481-487, 9. August 1968.

BECKER, W. : Das jugendgefährdende Opus in der Rechtsprechung. Monatsschrift für deutsches Recht 22 : 881-884, November 1968.

GREZER, J.O. : Zur Reform des Wahlrechts. Blätter für deutsche und internationale Politik 13 : 1181-1189, November 1968.
Western Germany.

FISCHER, A. : La justice administrative (ouest) allemande. Revue du droit public et de la science politique en France et à l'étranger 84 : 1032-1068, novembre-décembre 1968.

FALLER, H.J. : Die Rechtsprechung des Bundesgerichtshofes zum Grundgesetz vom 1.1.1962 bis zum 31.12.1967. Jahrbuch des öffentlichen Rechts der Gegenwart 17 : 407-435, 1968.

MÜLLER, G. : Die Grundrechte, ihr Wesen und ihre Grenzen. Zeitschrift für das gesamte Familienrecht 16 : 4-10, Januar 1969.

ENDER, K. : La réforme du code de procédure pénale en Allemagne fédérale et ses premiers effets (A suivre). Chronique internationales de police - International police chronicle 17 : 23-32, janvier-février 1969.
Texte français/allemand/anglais.

BENNHOLD, M. : Die Vorbeugehaft und ihre Funktion in der gegenwärtigen Phase der Entwicklung der B.R.D. Blätter für deutsche und internationale Politik 14 : 131-143, Februar 1969.

LENCKNER, T. : Die Strafrechtsreform in der Bundesrepublik Deutschland und der Alternativ-Entwurf eines Strafgesetzbuches. Tijdschrift voor Strafrecht 78 : 57-84, afl. 2, 1969.

SCHICK, W. : Bonner Grundgesetz und Weimarer Verfassung, heute. Archiv des öffentlichen Rechts 94 : 353-387, Heft 3, 1969.

GRUHL, K.E. : Zum gegenwärtigen Stand der Wehrdienstverweigerung. Blätter für deutsche und internationale Politik 14 : 309-316, März 1969.

FROMONT, M. : L'évolution du droit public allemand en 1968 - Le problème de l'état de crise (A suivre). Revue du droit public et de la science politique en France et à l'étranger 85 : 197-224, mars-avril 1969.
Allemagne de l'Ouest.

FROWEIN, J.A. : Der freundschaftliche Ausgleich im Individualbeschwerdeverfahren nach der Menschenrechtskonvention und das deutsche Recht. Juristenzeitung 24 : 213-217, 4. April 1969.

TIEDEMANN, K. : Zur legislatorischen Behandlung des Verbotsirrtums im Ordnungswidrigkeiten- und Steuerstrafrecht. Zeitschrift für die gesamte Strafrechtswissenschaft 81 : 869-885, Heft 4, 1969.

WALLENBERG, I. : Restitution av egendom till nazismens offer. Svensk juristtidning 54 : 477-515, April 1969.

NATIONAL LAW - COUNTRIES

BARMANN, J. : Tendances nouvelles dans l'évolution du droit des sociétés et du droit économique de la République fédérale d'Allemagne. Revue internationale de droit comparé 21 : 337-352, avril-juin 1969.

NOLL, P. : Le contre-projet d'un code pénal allemand. Revue de droit pénal et de criminologie 49 : 751-767, mai 1969.
Allemagne de l'Ouest; Voir aussi pp. 768-777.

KROPHOLLER, J. : Die Rechtsnatur der Familienmitarbeit und die Ersatzpflicht bei Verletzung oder Tötung des mitarbeitenden Familienangehörigen. Zeitschrift für das gesamte Familienrecht 16 : 251-251, Mai 1969.
Western Germany.

DIECKMANN, A. : Bemerkungen zum Beschluss des Bundesverfassungsgerichts vom 29.1.1969 betreffend die Neuordnung des Unehelichenrechts. Zeitschrift für das gesamte Familienrecht 16 : 297-304, Juni 1969.

Recent emergency legislation in West Germany. Harvard law review 82 : 1704-1737, June 1969.

PREECE, R.J.C. : Federal German emergency powers' legislation. Parliamentary affairs 22 : 216-225, summer 1969.

RANDELZHOFER, A. : Probleme des Parteienrechts. Juristenzeitung 24 : 533-541, 4. September 1969.
Western Germany.

FROMONT, M. : L'évolution du droit public allemand en 1968. Revue du droit public et de la science politique en France et à l'étranger 85 : 897-906, septembre-octobre 1969.
République fédérale d'Allemagne.

SCHUSTER, L. : Deutsche Investmentgesetzgebung 1969. Österreichisches Bank-Archiv 17 : 366-376, Oktober 1969.
Federal Republic of Germany.

TIEDEMANN, K. : Bemerkungen zur Rechtsprechung in den sog. Demonstrationsprozessen. Juristenzeitung 24 : 717-726, 21. November 1969.
Federal Republic of Germany.

ERMACORA, F. : 20 Jahre Bonner Grundgesetz. Juristische Blätter 91 : 633-639, 6. Dezember 1969.

SCHMID, W. : Zur Heilung gerichtlicher Verfahrensfehler durch den Instanzrichter. Juristenzeitung 24 : 757-766, 12. Dezember 1969.
Federal Republic of Germany.

SCHWAB, D. : Die Mitarbeitspflicht der Ehegatten nach para. 1356 Abs.2 BGB. Juristenzeitung 25 : 1-7, 2. Januar 1970.

MANKIEWICZ, R.H. : Products liability - A judicial breakthrough in West Germany. International and comparative law quarterly 19 : 99-117, January 1970.

SCHMIDT, E. : Zur Reform der sogenannten "Demonstrationsdelikte". Zeitschrift die gesamte Strafrechtswissenschaft 82 : 1-24, Heft 1, 1970.

SCHAUMANN, W. : Der Auftrag des Gesetzgebers zur Verwirklichung der Freiheitsrechte. Juristenzeitung 25 : 48-54, 16. Januar 1970.

SCHMIDT, E. : Amtsbezeichnung der Richter und Präsidialverfassung. Zeitschrift für die gesamte Strafrechtswissenschaft 82 : 329-343, Heft 2, 1970.

JESCHEK, H.H. : Der Strafprozess - Aktuelles und Zeitloses. Juristenzeitung 25 : 201-207, 3. April 1970.

ZEZSCHWITZ, F. v. : Das Gewissen als Gegenstand des Beweises. Juristenzeitung 25 : 233-240, 17. April 1970.

SCHEUNER, U. : Das Grundgesetz in der Entwicklung wzeier Jahrzehnte. Archiv des öffentlichen Rechts 95 : 353-408, September 1970.

HARTMANN, D.D. : Verwirkung von Grundrechten. Archiv des öffentlichen Rechts 95 : 567-580, Dezember 1970.

RIEGERT, R.A. : The West German civil code, its origin and its contract provisions. Tulane law review 45 : 48-99, December 1970.

GERMANY
(International law and practice, Aliens and Naturalization)

BOTHE, M. : Völkerrechtliche Praxis der Bundesrepublik Deutschland im Jahre 1963. Zeitschrift für ausländisches öffentliches Recht und Völkerrecht 25 : 223-351, Mai 1965.

STEINMANN, H.G. : Ein Beitrag zu Fragen der zivilrechtlichen Immunität von ausländischen Diplomaten, Konsuln und anderen bevorrechtigten Personen sowie von fremden Staaten, die durch ihre Missionen oder auf ähnliche Weise in der Bundesrepublik Deutschland tätig werden. Monatsschrift für deutsches Recht 19 : 706-712, September 1965.

DOERRING, K. : Neuregelungen des deutschen Fremdenrechts durch das Azsländergesetz von 1965. Zeitschrift fr ausländisches öffentliches Recht und Völkerrecht 25 : 478-498, Oktober 1965.
Text of law pp. 499-515.

BUSCHBECK, K. : Völkerrechtliche Praxis der Bundesrepublik Deutschland im Jahre 1964. Zeitschrift für ausländisches öffentliches Recht und Völkerrecht 26 : 85-170, Juni 1966.

ARZINGER, R. : Das völkerrechtliche Selbstbestimmungsrecht und seine Subjekte in Deutschland. Deutsche Aussenpolitik 11 : 910-921, August 1966.

MANN, F.A. : Deutschlands Rechtslage 1947-1967. Juristenzeitung 22 : 585-591, 6. Oktober 1967.

BÖHMERT, V. : Natur und Umfang der der Bundesrepublik Deutschland am Kontinentalschelf zustehenden Rechte - Eine Analyse des Ert.2, 1 des Genfer Kontinentalschelfabkommens von 1958. Internationales Recht und Diplomatie : 101-129, 1967.

GAMILLSCHEG, F. : Das Verlöbnis im deutschen internationalen Privatrecht. Rabels Zeitschrift für ausländisches und internationales Privatrecht 32 : 473-486, Heft 3, 1968.

TOMUSCHAT, C. : Deutsche Rechtsprechung in völkerrechtlichen Fragen, 1958-1965. Tel A. Allgemeines Friedensvölkerrecht 28 : 48-147, März 1968.

SODER, J. : Der Grundrechtskatalog der Menschenrechtskonventionen der UN als innerdeutsches Recht (To be contd.). Vereinte Nationen 16 : 69-55, Juni 1968.

NATIONAL LAW - COUNTRIES

KIMMINICH, O. : Das Völkerrecht in der Rechtsprechung des Bundesverfassungsgerichts. Archiv des öffentlich Rechts 93 : 485-537, Dezember 1968.

BAUR, W. : On the juridical character of the Bonn government's presumptuous claim to exclusive representation. Law and legislation in the German Democratic Republic : 5-26, no. 1, 1969.

LUTTER, M. : Die erste Angleichungs-Richtlinie zu Art. 54 Abs.3 Lit.g) EWGV und ihre Bedeutung für das geltende deutsche Unternehmensrecht. Europarecht 4 : 1-19, Januar/März 1969.

ROELLECKE, G. : Die Staatsangehörigkeit ausgebürgeter Juden. Juristenzeitung 24 : 97-102, 7. Februar 1969.

CONSTANTINESCO, L. : L'introduction et le contrôle de la constitutionnalité des traités et en particulier des traités européens en droit (ouest)-allemand. Revue belge de droit international 5 : 425-459, no. 2, 1969.

GAMILLSCHEG, F. : Gleichberechtigung der Frau und Reform des internationalen Eherechts. Rabels Zeitschrift für ausländisches und internationales Privatrecht 33 : 654-710, Heft 4, 1969.

HOLCH, G. : Der Bundesrat zur Rechtsetzung der Europäischen Gemeinschaften. Europarecht 4 : 213-230, Juli/September 1969.

WULFFERT, N. von : Asylsuche und Asylrecht in der Bundesrepublik Deutschland. Osteuropa 20 : 37-45, Januar 1970.

NEUHAUS, P.H. : Um die Reform des deutschen internationalen Erbrechts. Zeitschrift für das gesamte Familienrecht 17 : 12-14, Januar 1970.

BROGGINI, G. : Convenzioni attributive di giurisdizione nel commercio italo-tedesco. Rivista di diritto internazionale privato e processuale 6 : 5-26, gennaio-marzo 1970.

PFAFF, D. : Probleme der Anerkennung und Vollstreckung jugoslawischer Schiedssprüche in der Bundesrepublik. Aussenwirtschaftsdienst des Betriebs-Beraters 16 : 55-60, Februar 1970.

GANSKE, J. : Der deutsch-tunesische Rechtshilfe- und Vollstreckungsvertrag in Zivil- und Handelssachen vom 19.7.1966. Aussenwirtschaftsdienst des Betriebs-Beraters 16 : 145-156, April 1970.

KNUTH, H. : Zur völkerrechtlichen Exemption Ostberliner Regierungsdelegationen und Emissäre in der Bundesrepublik. Juristenzeitung 25 : 539-542, 4. September 1970.

RAMBOW, G. : L'exécution des directives de la Communauté économique européenne en République fédérale d'Allemagne. Cahiers de droit européen 6 : 379-411, no. 4, 1970.

SOELL, H. : Verfassungsrechtliche Probleme bei der Abtretung von Bundesgebiet. Archiv des öffentlichen Rechts 95 : 423-448, September 1970.

WENGLER, W. : Der Moskauer Vertrag und das Völkerrecht. Juristenzeitung 25 : 632-637, 16. Oktober 1970.

GERMANY
(Copyright, Patents, Trade-marks)

HILLIG, H.P. : Le nouveau droit d'auteur dans la République fédérale d'Allemagne, considéré du point de vue de la Radiodiffusion. Revue de l'U.E.R. (Union européenne de radiodiffusion)

GERMANY
(Democratic Republic)

KUNZE, K. : The penal system of the German Democratic Republic. Law and legislation in the German Democractic Republic : 38-45, no. 1, 1965.

EINHORN, H. : On the draft family code. Law and legislation in the German Democratic Republic : 23-37, no. 2, 1965.

Beschluss des Plenums des Obersten Gerichts über die erzieherische Tätigkeit der Gerichte zur Erhaltung von Ehen. Neue Justiz (Germany, Democratic Republic) 19 : 309-311, 2. Maiheft 1965.

MÜLLER-RÖMER, D. : Die Rechtsnatur der Grundrechte in der SBZ. Recht in Ost und West 9 : 107-114, 15. Mai 1965.

RANKE, H. : Einige Ergebnisse soziologischer Untersuchungen zur Vorbereitung des Entwurfs eines Zivilgesetzbuchs. Neue Justiz (Germany, Democratic Republic) 19 : 373-376, 2. Juniheft 1965.

HAARLAND, H. : Entwicklung und Bekämpfung der Kriminalität in der DDR im Spiegel der Statistik. Neue Justiz (Germany, Democratic Republic) 19 : 401-406, 435-438, 1. Juliheft, 2. Juliheft 1965.

GRANDKE, A. : Familienrecht und Soziologie. Staat und Recht 14 : 1054-1061, Juli 1965.
Eastern Germany; See also pp. 1062-1077, 1092-1100.

SZKIBIK, H. : Zur Entwicklung der Szrafvollzugswissenschaft in der DDR. Staat und Recht 14 : 1701-1712, Oktober 1965.

GRANDKE, A., and KUHRIG, H. : Das neue Familiengesetzbuch der DDR. Einheit 20 : 13-21, November 1965.

SCHRADER, H. : Das Prinzip der sozialistischen Gesetzlichkeit in der Rechtstheorie der Sowjetischen Bestzungszone Deutschlands. Jahrbuch des öffentlichen Rechtes der Gegenwart 14 : 77-85, 1965.

FRIEDMAN, P. : Social courts and law reforms in East Germany. Columbia essays in international affairs: the dean's papers : 107-125, 1965.

PÜSCHEL, H. : A new copyright code in the GDR. Law and legislation in the German Democratic Republic : 31-43, no. 1, 1966.

STROHBACH, H. : Commercial arbitrage in the GDR. Law and legislation in the German Democratic Republic : 57-65, no. 1, 1966.

Grundrechte und Grundpflichten der Bürger in der DDR. Staat und Recht 15 : 563-577, April 1966.

ROST, R. : Die führende Rolle der SED bei der Entwicklung des sozialistischen Staates und Rechts in der Deutschen Demokratischen Republik. Staat und Recht 15 : 721-747, Mai 1966.

NATIONAL LAW - COUNTRIES

STREIT, J. : L'évolution de la justice en République démocratique allemande. Synthèses 21 : 200-205, juin 1966.

République démocratique allemande - Loi sur le droit d'auteur, du 13 septembre 1965. Droit d'auteur 79 : 162-173, juin 1966.

HARRLAND, H., and STILLER, G. : Entwicklung eines umfassenden Systems der Kriminalitätsvorbeugung in der DDR Staat und Recht 15 : 1609-1629, Oktober 1966.

BUCHHOLZ, E. : The development of economic criminal law. Law and legislation in the German Democratic Republic : 17-27, no. 1, 1967.

TREVES, T. : Les nationalisations en Allemagne de l'Est et la fondation Carl Zeiss. Revue critique de droit international privé 56 : 23-54, janvier-mars 1967.

BENJAMIN, H. : The new criminal law of the German Democratic Republic. Law and legislation in the German Democratic Republic : 5-10, no. 2, 1967.

RENNEBERG, J. : Die Grundsätze des sozialistischen Strafrechts der DDR. Neue Justiz (Germany, Democratic Republic) 21 : 105-109, 2. Februarheft 1967.

LOOSE, W. : Zu den sozialen und weltanschaulichen Grundlagen des Entwurfs des sozialistischen Strafgesetzbuches der DDR. Staat und Recht 16 : 604-614, Heft 4, 1967.

RANKE, H. : Neues ökonomisches System und aktuelle Probleme des sozialistischen Zivilrechts. Neue Justiz (Germany, Democratic Republic) 21 : 201-205, 1. Aprilheft 1967.

ULBRICHT, W. : Die sozialistische Staats- und Rechtsordnung in der DDR. Staat und Recht 16 : 852-862, Juni 1967.

STREICH, R. : The legal status of nationally-owned industries in the GDR. Law and legislation in the German Democratic Republic : 35-46, no. 1, 1968.

LEICHTFUSS, H. : Verfassungsentwicklung und Volkssouveränität - Eine Studie zu einer bedeutsamen Phase der Verfassungsgeschichte der DDR. Staat und Recht 17 : 194-211, Februar 1968.

KUNZ, F. : Neue sozialistische Verfassung - Bilanz und Perspektive des Arbeitsrechts der DDR. Arbeit und Arbeitsrecht 23 : 134-139, 2. Märzheft 1968.

HAUPT, L. , and HAFEMANN, W. : Das Volk in der DDR gibt sich eine neue Verfassung. Deutsche Aussenpolitik 13 : 259-267, März 1968.

ULBRICHT, W. : Die Verfassung des sozialistischen Staates deutscher Nation. Staat und Recht 17 : 340-375, März 1968.

MÜLLER-RÖMER, D. : Zur sozialistischen Verfassung der DDR. Juristenzeitung 23 : 313-318, 17. Mai 1968.

WÜNSCHE, K. : Das neue, sozialistische Strafrecht der Deutschen Demokratischen Republik und das Völkerrecht. Deutsche Aussenpolitik 13 : 537-545, Mai 1968.

BUCHHOLTZ : Le nouveau droit pénal de la République démocratique allemande. Revue de droit pénal et de criminologie 48 : 954-966, juillet 1968.

WESTEN, K. : Zur Situation des Rechts in der DDR. Deutschland Archiv 1 : 337-350, Juli 1968.

Constitution de la République démocratique allemande, 8 avril 1968. Documentation française, Notes et études documentaires : 1-19, no. 3523, 3 octobre 1968.

MARKOVITS, I.S. : Civil law in East Germany - Its development and relation to Soviet legal history and ideology. Yale law journal 78 : 1-51, November 1968.

MÜLLER-RÖMER, D. : Ziele und Methoden der Rechtsvergleichung zwischen beiden Teilen Deutschlands. Recht in Ost und West 13 : 1-8, 15. Januar 1969.

BUCHHOLZ, E., and SEIDEL, D. : Justified economic risk. Law and legislation in the German Democratic Republic : 27-39, 27-39, no. 1, 1969.

HOFMANN, M. : The activities of the Law office for international civil law matters. Law and legislation in the German Democratic Republic : 35-56, no. 1, 1969.

STROHBACH, H. : The election of arbitrators for proceedings before the Arbitration court of the Chamber of foreign trade. Law and legislation in the German Democratic Republic : 40-44, no. 1, 1969.

PÜSCHEL, H. : Zum System des Geschmacksmusterrechts und zur Gewährleistung des Rechtsschutzes auf diesem Gebiet. Neue Justiz (Germany, Democratic Republic) 23 : 12-16, 1. Januarheft 1969.

BOTHE, M. : The 1968 constitution of East Germany - A codification of Marxist-Leninist ideas on state and government. American journal of comparative law 17 : 268-291, no. 2, 1969.

BECHTOLD, I. : Gerechtigkeit und sozialiszische Gesetzlichkeit im neuen StrafverfahRen der DDR - Untersuchungen zur StPO vom 12.1.1968. Zeitschrift für die gesamte Strafrechswissenschaft 81 : 277-328, Heft 2, 1969.

ZIEGER, G. : Die Organisation der Staatsgewalt in der Verfassung der DDR von 1968. Archiv des öffentlichen Rechts 94 : 185-223, Nr. 2, 1969.

KAUL, F.F., and NOACK, J. : Anwendung des Völkerstrafrechts gegen Nazi-System-Verbrechen. Neue Justiz (Germany, Democratic Republic) 23 : 97-102, 2. Februarheft 1969.

SCHMIDT, A. : Der Rechtsschutz der Arbeitnehmererfindung. Wochenblatt für Papierfabrikation 97 : 163-168, Mitte März 1969.

NOWOTKA, W., and PANZER, W. : Volkseigentumsrecht und sozialistische Patentinhaberschaft. Wirtschaftswissenschaft 17 : 516-530, April 1969.

ROGGEMAN, H. : Das Strafgesetzbuch der DDR von 1968 (To be contd.). Recht in Ost und West 13 : 97-113, 15. Mai 1969.

WÜNSCHE, K. : Das völkerrechtliche Gebot der Betrafung der Nazi- und Kriegsverbrecher und die Gesetzgebubg in den beiden deutschen Staaten. Staat und Recht 18 : 660-666, Mai 1969.

NATIONAL LAW - COUNTRIES

MOCKEL, E. : Das Warenzeichen als Schutzrecht der sozialistischen Wirtschaft. Zellstoff und Papier : 184-188, Juni 1969.

SCHMIDT, H.T. : Straf- und Strafverfahrensrecht. Deutschland Archiv (Köln) 2 : 728-734, Juli 1969.
Eastern Germany; A bibliography.

WESTEN, K. : Neuere Entwicklungen im Zivilrecht der DDR. Deutschland Archiv (Köln) 2 : 681-697, Juli 1969.

LÜBCHEN, G.A. : Aufgaben und Gegenstand des Künftigen Zivilgesetzbuches. Neue Justiz (Germany, Democratic Republic) 23 : 547-553, 2. Septemberheft 1969.

WESTEN, K. : Die Rechtsentwicklung in der DDR. Deutschland Archiv (Köln) 2 : 905-918, September 1969.

WOLFF, F. : Aufgaben und Stellung des Rechtsanwalts im entwickelten gesellschaftlichen System des Sozialismus. Neue Justiz (Germany, Democratic Republic) 23 : 615-620, 1. Oktoberheft 1969.

MÜLLER-RÖMER, D. : Gesellschaftspolitische Vorstellungen im Verfassungsrecht der DDR. Deutschland Archiv (Köln) 2 : 1018-1037, Oktober 1969.

SCHMIDT, H.T. : Wesen und Entwicklung der Konflikt- und Schiedskommissionen in der DDR, 1952-1969. Jahrbuch für Ostrecht 10 : 57-86, Dezember 1969.

MAMPEL, S. : Die neue Verfassungsordnung in Mitteldeutschland. Jahrbuch des öffentlichen Rechts der Gegenwart 18 : 333-452, 1969.
Text of the constitution of 6 April 1968, pp. 453-466.

HACKER, J. : Zum Problem der Staaten-Sukzession in der Sicht der DDR. Recht in Ost und West 14 : 1-16, 15. Januar 1970.

PLAT, W. : Probleme des Strafrechts der DDR. Zeitschrift für die gesamte Strafrechtswissenschaft 82 : 76-107, Heft 1, 1970.

TOEPLITZ, H. : The code of criminal procedure of the German Democratic Republic. Law and legislation in the German Democratic Republic : 5-12, no. 2, 1970.
Text pp. 13-87.

SCHMIDT, H.T. : Die Strafgesetzgebung des Allierten Kontrollrats und ihre Anwendung in der Rechtsprechung der SBZ. Internationales Recht und Diplomatie : 63-79, 1. Halbband 1970.

OSTERLAND, R., and HUMMI, M. : Der Vertrag über den Austausch wissenschaftlich-technischer Ergebnisse innerhalb der sozialistischen Staatengemeinschaft. Sozialistische Aussenwirtschaft, Recht in Aussenwirtschaft 20 : 1-8, Heft 3, 1970.

BECHTOLD, U. : Der Kampf gegen Konfliktursachen in der Zivil- und Familienrechtspflege der DDR. Jahrbuch für Ostrecht 11 : 49-83, Juli 1970.

BRUHN, H.H. : Die Regelung des räumlichen Geltungsbereichs im Strafrecht der Bundesrepublik und der DDR unter besonderer Berücksichtigung ihres Verhältnisses zueinander. Monatsschrift für deutsches Recht 24 : 638-644, August 1970.

FRENZKE, D. : De-jure-, De-facto- und faktische Anerkennung in der Völkerrechtslehre der DDR und der UdSSR. Recht in Ost und West 14 : 181-190, 15. September 1970.

MÜLLER-RÖMER, D. : Die Entwicklung des Verfassungsrechts in der DDR seit 1949. Archiv des öffentlichen Rechts 95 : 528-567, Dezember 1970.

GHANA

ASANTE, S.K.B. : Interests in land in the customary law of Ghana - A new appraisal. Yale law journal 74 : 848-885, April 1965.

RUBIN, L. : The constitution of Ghana. Jahrbuch des öffentlichen Rechts der Gegenwart 14 : 585-624, 1965.

HARVEY, W.B. : The judiciary in Ghana. Record of the Association of the bar of the City of New York 21 : 222-235, April 1966.

UCHE, U.U. : Changes in Ghana law since the military take-over. Journal of African law 10 : 106-111, summer 1966.

WOODMAN, G.R. : Developments in pledges of land in Ghanian customary law. Journal of African law 2 : 8-26, spring 1967.

AFREH, K. : Ghana's legal muddles (To be contd.). West Africa : 572-573, 18 May 1968.

MENSAH-BROWN, A.K. : Chiefs and the law in Ghana. Journal of African law 13 : 57-63, summer 1969.

WOODMAN, G.R. : Estoppel by judicial decision in Ghana. Journal of African law 13 : 80-97, summer 1969.

AMANKWAH, H.A. : Ghanaian law - Its evolution and interection with English law. Cornell international law journal 4 : 37-57, fall 1970.

GREAT BRITAIN

GINOSSAR, S. : Eléments du système anglais de la preuve judiciaire. Revue de droit international et de droit comparé 42 : 9-19, nos. 1-2, 1965.

POWELL-SMITH, V. : The mystique of crown privilege. Law journal 115 : 84-86, February 1965.

DEMIERRE, E. : Le problème de la peine de mort en Grande Bretagne. Revue internationale de criminologie et de police technique 19 : 39-46, janvier-mars 1965.

SCHMITTHOFF, C.M. : Law reform in England. Journal of business law : 219-238, July 1965.

GANZ, G. : Estoppel and res judicata in administrative law. Public law : 237-255, autumn 1965.

SAMUELS, A. : Maintenance of stepchildren. New law journal 116 : 6-7, 28 October 1965.

UPJOHN : Evolution of the English legal system. American bar association journal 51 : 918-921, October 1965.

NATIONAL LAW - COUNTRIES

UPJOHN : Evolution of the English legal system. American bar association journal 51 : 918-921, October 1965.

MILSOM, S.F.C. : Reason in the development of the common law. Law quarterly review 81 : 496-517, October 1965.

NORTH, P.M. : Disclosure of confidential information. Journal of business law : 307-316, October 1965.

MITCHELL, J.D.B. : The state of public law in the United Kingdom. International and comparative law quarterly 15 : 133-149, January 1966.

GOODHARDT, A.L. : The Burmah oil case and the War damage act 1965. Law quarterly review 82 : 97-114, January 1966.

ANDREWS, J.A. : Estoppels against statutes. Modern law review 29 : 1-15, January 1966.

BARAK, A. : The nature of vicarious liability in English law. Annuario di diritto comparato e di studi legislativi 40 : 1-29, fasc. 1, 1966.

FRIDMAN, G.H.L. : Termination of contract of employment. New law journal 116 : 551-552, 600-601, 10 March, 24 March 1966.

DAWTRY, F. : The abolition of the death penalty in Britain. British journal of criminology 6 : 183-192, April 1966.

KING, H. : The impartiality of the speaker. Parliamentarian 47 : 125-131, April 1966.

GRAVESON, R.H. : L'unification des différents systèmes juridiques en vigueur dans les îles Britanniques. Revue internationale de droit comparé 18 : 385-412, avril-juin 1966.

STONE de MONTPENSIER, R. : The British doctrine of parliamentary sovereignty - A critical enquiry. Louisiana law review 26 : 753-787, June 1966.

HARTWIG, H.J. : Infants' contracts in English law, with Commonwealth and European comparisons. International and comparative law quarterly 15 : 780-834, July 1966.

COOPER, H.H.A. : La jurisprudencia inglesa. Revista de derecho y ciencias sociales (Concepción) 34 : 3-16, julio-septiembre 1966.

YARDLEY, D.C.M. : The progress of law reform in the United Kingdom. Irish jurist 1 : 66-83, summer 1966.

WILSON, W.A. : Scottish commercial law. Journal of business law : 320-325, October 1966.

LOEWENSTEIN, K. : L'investiture du premier ministre en Angleterre. Revue du droit public et de la science politique en France et à l'étranger 82 : 1063-1115, novembre-décembre 1966.

HOSKINS, B.C. : Fatal accidents - Damages. New law journal 117 : 4-6,, 5 January 1967.

MacKENNA, B. : Divorce by consent snd divorce for breakdown of marriage. Modern law review 30 : 121-138, March 1967.

WALEFFE, B. : Réflexions au sujet de l'investiture du Premier ministre en Angleterre. Res Publica 9 : 661-676, no. 4, 1967.

LUPOI, M. : Il contratto a favore di terzo in diritto inglese. Rivista del diritto commerciale e del diritto generale delle obbligazioni 65 : parte la, 171, 240, maggio-giugno 1967.

DAVIES, W.E.D. : Section 17 of the Married women property act - Law or palm tree justice? University of Western Australia law review 8 : 48-60, June 1967.

BAKER, C.D. : Liability for damage by fire. New law journal 117 : 789-790, 20 July 1967.

LANGROD, G. : L'option britannique en faveur de l'Ombudsman. Revue administrative 20 : 453-461, juillet-août 1967.

ROSE, P.L. : Matrimonial homes act 1967. New law journal 117 : 824-826, 3 August 1967.

BICKNELL, B.A. : The age of majority. New law journal 117 : 955-956, 7 September 1967.

CLARK, D.H. : Administrative control of judicial action - The authority of Duncan v. Cammell Laird. Modern law review 30 : 489-513, September 1967.

CORAPI, D. : Il Companies act 1967. Rivista del diritto commerciale e del diritto generale delle obbligazioni 65 : parte la, 407-413, settembre-ottobre 1967.

LANGROD, G. : Vers une réprientation de la fonction publique anglaise - La Commission Fulton, genèse et perspectives. Stato sociale 11 : 869-887, ottobre 1967.

MARC, G. : Le "Murder act" de 1965 et le droit anglais de l'homicide. Revue de science criminelle et de droit pénal comparé 22 : 843-850, octobre-décembre 1967.

Human rights in the United Kingdom. Central Office of information, Reference division, Bulletin (London) : 1-32, no. R. 5625, November 1967.

NANCE, J. : Interpreting Matrimonial homes act 1967. New law journal 117 : 1360-1362, 28 December 1967.

BOTTOMLEY, A.K. : The granting of bail - Principles and practice. Modern law review 31 : 40-54, January 1968.

GILMOUR, D.R. : The sovereignty of Parliament and the European commission of human rights. Public law : 62-73, spring 1968.

FRANK, B. : The British parliamentary commissioner for administration - The Ombudsman. Federal bar journal 28 : 1-24, winter 1968.

HUGHES, G.E.F. : England's great leap backward - The Abortion act, 1967. Australian law journal 43 : 12-19, January 1969.

LANGROD, G. : La jurisprudence de l'Ombudsman britannique. Revue administrative 22 : 79-83, janvier-février 1969.

HARTLEY, T.C. : Polygamy and social policy. Modern law review 32 : 155-173, March 1969.

NATIONAL LAW - COUNTRIES

SIMMONDS, K.R. : The British islands and the community (Jersey, the Isle of Man, Guernsey)(To be contd.). Common market law review 6 : 156-169, March 1969.

LEGRAND, A. : Le Commissaire parlementaire pour l'administration, ombudsman britannique. Revue du droit public et de la science politique en France et à l'étranger 85 : 225-258, mars-avril 1969.

JONES, E. : The office of Attorney-general. Cambridge law journal 27 : 43-53, April 1969.

WILLIAMS, J.E.H. : Changing British criminal law. Tijdschrift voor strafrecht 78 : 239-253, afl. 5, 1969.

MARSH, N.S. : La réforme du droit en Grande-Bretagne - Quelques développements récents. Revue internationale de droit comparé 21 : 485-497, juillet-septembre 1969.

The Beeching Royal commission's report. New law journal 119 : 905-906, 2 October 1969.
Reform of assizes; See also pp. 889-890.

STONE, J. : 1966 and all that ! - Losing the chains of precedent. Columbia law review 69 : 1162-1202, November 1969.
House of Lords and reversal of decisions.

MARSHALL, R. : Legislation and racial equality. Current legal problems 22 : 46-60, 1969.

YARDLEY, D.C.M. : The abuse of powers and its control in English administrative law. American journal of comparative law 18 : 565-574, no. 3, 1970.

TOPPING, M.R., and VANDENLINDEN, J.P.M. : Ibi renascit jus commune. Modern law review 33 : 170-176, March 1970.
Codification of English law.

HEPPLE, B.O. : Intention to create legal relations. Cambridge law journal 28 : 122-137, April 1970.

WILLIAMS, D.G.T. : Protest and public order. Cambridge law journal 28 : 96-121, April 1970.

MORRIS, J.H.C. : The Family law reform act 1969, sections 14 and 15. International and comparative law quarterly 19 : 328-333, April 1970.
Intestate succession and gifts by dded or will.

LEIGH, L.H. : Recent developments in the law of search and seizure. Modern law review 33 : 268-280, May 1970.

BARTON, J.L. : Questions on the Divorce reform act 1969. Law quarterly review 86 : 348-356, July 1970.

CARSON, J. : Defining and protecting civil liberties. Political quarterly 41 : 316-327, July-September 1970.

SCHWARTZ, B. : The Parliamentary commissioner and his office - The British ombudsman in operation. New York university law review 45 : 963-994, November 1970.

GREAT BRITAIN
(International law, Aliens)

SWAMINATHAN, L. : Recognition of foreign unilateral divorces in the English conflict of laws. Modern law review 28 : 540-550, September 1965.

O'HIGGINS, P. : Anglo-Irish extradition. New law journal 116 : 69-70, 11 November 1965.

GRAVESON, R.H. : Divorce, separation and annulment of marriage in English private international law. Revue hellénique de droit international 18 : 253-267, juillet-décembre 1965.

BUCKLEY, M. : The effect of the Diplomatic priveleges act 1964 in English law. British year book of international law 41 : 321-367, 1965-1966.

FRIDMAN, G.H.L. : Recognition of foreign divorce decrees. New law journal 116 : 796-798, 841-843; 12 May, 19 May 1966.

FRIDMAN, G.H.L. : Foreign adoptions. New law journal116 : 1020-1022, 1055-1056, 7 July, 14 July 1966

WEBB, P.R.H. : Nullity and divorce - Recognition in New Zealand of English decrees and recognition in England of New Zealand decrees. New Zealand universities law review 2 : 145-161, October 1966.

LASOK, D.: Les traités internationaux dans le système juridique anglais. Revue générale de droit international public 70 : 961-994, octobre-décembre 1966.

GREIG, D.W. : The Carl-Zeiss case and the position of an unrecognised government in English law. Law quarterly review 83 : 96-145, January 1967.

STOEL, T.B. : The enforcement of foreign non-criminal penal and revenue judgments in England and the United States. International and comparative law quarterly 16 : 663-679, July 1967.

JACKSON, P. : Anglo-Irish extradition. Irish jurist 2 : 43-48, summer 1967.

FAWCETT, J.E.S. : The Judicial committee committee of the Privy council and international law. British year book of international law 42 : 229-263, 1967.

GRAVESON, R.H. : Le renvoi dans le droit anglais actuel. Revue critique de droit international privé 57 : 259-265, avril-juin 1968.

FAWCETT, J.E.S. : Customary international law in the courts of the United Kingdom. Revista española de derecho internacional 21 : 459-470, julio-septiembre 1968.

WOODLIFFE, J.C. : Consular relations act 1968. Modern law review 32 : 59-64, January 1969.

KATO, L.L. : Act of State in a protectorate - In retrospect. Public law : 219-235, autumn 1969.

RAY, R.P. : Foreign domicile and estate duty. New law journal 119 : 964-966, 23 October 1969.

MANN, F.A. : English procedural law and foreign arbitrations. International and comparative law quarterly 18 : 997-1001, October 1969.

FRANCESCAKIS, P. : Un bond de la jurisprudence anglaise en matière de reconnaissance des décisions étrangères - L'arrêt de la Chambre des Lords dans l'affaire du divor Indyka. Revue critique de droit international privé 58 : 601-637, octobre-décembre 1969.

PRINGSHEIM, M., and HAHNDORF, R.: Die Scheidung deutsch-englischer Ehen. Monatschrift für deutsches Recht 24 : 104-105, Februar 1970.

Foreign torts and English courts. International and comparative law quarterly 19 : 24-46, January 1970.

GREECE

ZAFIRIS, G. : La justicia militar en Grecia. Revista española de derecho militar : 89-96, enero-junio 1965.

TSOUTSOS, A.G. : To problema tēs dioikētikēs dikaiosynēs en Helladi. Nea oikonomia 19 : 228-230, Martios 1965.

KYRIACOPOULOS, E. : Der Staatsrat in Griechenland. Jahrbuch des öffentlichen Rechts der Gegenwart 14 : 409-423, 1965.

KOUTSOUBAKIS, G. : Traités et accords internationaux publiés au Journal officiel de la Grèce au cours des années 1956-1964. Revue hellénique de droit international 19 : 316-350, janvier-décembre 1966.

EUSTRATIADES, G.D. : Laïkē kyriarchia kai basilikes pronomies. Nea oikonomia 20 : 141-145, Phebrouarios 1966.

DAES, E.I.A. : Some points of Greek and foreign law on dissolution of adoption - A comparative study-Revue hellénique de droit international 21 : 49-91, janvier-décembre 1968.

PAPADOPOULOS, G. : La nouvelle constitution grecque - Le référendum du 20 septembre 1968. Europe Sud-Est : 3-9, octobre 1968.

BENDERMACHER-GEROUSIS, E. : Die gültige Eheschliessung im griechischen internationalen Privatrecht. Revue hellénique de droit international 22 : 1-16, juillet-décembre 1969.

SCHEFOLD, D. : Die griechische Verfassung vom 15. November 1968. Jahrbuch des öffentlichen Rechts der Gegenwart 18 : 303-306, 1969.
Text pp. 307-332.

Grèce; constitution, 1968. Informations constitutionnelles et parlementaires 21 : 2-54, janvier 1970.

TSOUTSOS, A. : La motivation des actes administratifs. Revue hellénique de droit international 23 : 126-132, janvier-décembre 1970.

MASSOURIDIS, P. : The enforcement of foreign judgments in Greece. Revue hellénique de droit international 23 : 186-224, janvier-décembre 1970.

Constitution de la Grèce, 29 septembre 1968. Notes et études documentaires : 1-26, no. 3687, 5 mai 1970.

GUATEMALA

ALACALA-ZAMORA y CASTILLO, N.: El nuevo código procesal civil de Guatemala. Boletín del Instituto de derecho comparado de México 18 : 155-192, enero-abril 1966.

MURRAY, D.E. : The new code of civil procedure of Guatemala. Inter-American law review - Revista jurídica interamericana 7 : 303-350, July-December 1965.
Text in Spanish pp. 351-393.

Código civil de Guatemala. Información jurídica (Spain) : 3-83, marzo-abril 1966.
See also subsequent issues.

GUYANA

HAZARD, J.N. : Guyamana's alternative to socialist and capitalist legal models. American journal of comparative law 16 : 507-523, no. 4, 1968.

HAITI

BARCLAY, B. : Le respect du droit dans la République d'Haïti. Revue de droit international, de sciences diplomatiques et politiques 45 : 333-338, octobre-décembre 1967.

HUNGARY

SZABÓ, L. : Népi demokratikus jogfejlődésünk fő vonásai. Magyar jog 12 : 145-150, április 1965.

EÖRSI, G. : Richterrecht und Gesetzesrecht in Ungarn. Zum Problem der Originalität eines Zivilrechts. Rabels Zeitschrift für ausländisches und internationales Privatrecht 30 : 117-140, Heft 1, 1966.

HALÁSZ, S. : Quelques questions théoriques et pratiques relatives à l'application du code pénal hongrois. Revue de droit hongrois : 20-31, no. 2, 1966.

MEZÖFY, L. : El enjuiciamento criminal húngaro, Boletín del Instituto de derecho comparado de México 19 : 541-559, mayo-diciembre 1966.

Two aspects of pre-trial procedure in Eastern Europe - TAYLOR, P.B. : The role of the investigator in Soviet criminal procedure - CSIZMÁS, M. : Remand in custody in Hungary. International commission of jurists, Journal 7 : 20-54, summer 1966.

KIRÁLY, T. : A buntető eljárás módosítása. Jogtudományi közlöny 21 : 633-642, december 1966.

KULCSÁR, K. : Az állampolgári jogok a mai társadalomban. Jogtudományi közlöny 22 : 1-6, január 1967.

VILÁGHY, M. : Les enseignements de la jurisprudence relative au code civil, 1960-1966. Revue de droit hongrois : 7-23, no. 1, 1967.

TAKACS, I. : A demokratikus választójog fejlődése Magyarországon. Társadalmi szemle 22 : 13-22, február 1967.

BIHARI, O. : A legfelsőbb Bíróság alkotmányos helyzete Magyarországon. Jogtudományi közlöny 22 : 186-191, március-április 1967.

KOVÁCS, I. : Les sources du droit de la République populaire hongroise. Revue internationale de droit comparé 19 : 655-674, juillet-septembre 1967.

SZABO-NAGY, T. : A szabálysértés elbírálása a büntető eljárásban. Jogtudományi közlöny 22 : 646-654, december 1967.

KIRÁLY, T. : A büntető eljárási kódex általános résének szerkezete. Magyar jog és külföldi jogi szemle 14 : 705-708, december 1967.

Constitution de la République populaire hongroise, 20 août 1949. Documentation française, Notes et études documentaires : 1-12, no. 3452, 9 janvier 1968.

HORVÁTH, T. : A feltételes elítélés a magyar büntetőjogban. Jogtudományi közlöny 23 : 13-24, január 1968.

BÉKÉSI, F. : Une loi sur le développement progressif de la propriété et de l'usage de la terre. Revue de droit hongrois : 5-19, no. 2, 1968.

BACSÓ, J., and FARKAS, J. : Tizenöt éves a polgári perrendtartás. Jogtudományi közlöny 23 : 79-88, február 1968.

TIMÁR, I. : A magyar-szovjet szerzői jogi egyezményről. Magyar jog és külföldi jogi szemle 15 : 129-132, március 1968.

SZILBEREKY, J. : A polgári eljárás reformjához. Magyar jog és külföldi jogi szemle 15 : 449-457, augusztus 1968.

KIRÁLY, T. : A terheltté nyilvánítás jövője. Magyar jog és külföldi jogi szemle 15 : 651-655, november 1968.

SZÉNÁSI, G. : A Magyar Tanacsköztársasag jogpolitikája. Magyar jog és külföldi jogi szemle 16 : 193-196, április 1969.

FARKAS, S. : A büntetőjog néhány időszerű kérdése. Magyar jog és külföldi jogi szemle 16 : 334-341, június-július 1969.
See also pp. 341-346.

KRATOCHWILL, F. : A tárgyalás bírói előkészítésének feledata és elhelyezkedése a magyar büntető eljárásban. Jogtudományi közlöny 24 : 376-383, július-augusztus 1969.

TIMAR, I. : Sovetsko-vengerskoe soglashenie o vzaimnoĭ okhrane avtorskikh prav. Sovetskore gosudarstvo i pravo ; 93-95, no. 8, avgust 1969.

PÁLOS, G. : La nouvelle loi hongroise sur les inventions. Propriété industrielle 85 : 265-270, septembre 1969.

A magyar nemzetközi magánjogi kodifikáció a siófoki jogászkongresszus napirendjén. Jogtudományi közlöny 24 : 451-477, szeptember 1969.
Siófok congress, 1969, on the codification of Hungarian private international law; Summaries in English, French and Russian.

SZILBEREKY, J. : Kormányhatározat a jogrendszer továbbfejlesztéséről. Magyar jog és külföldi jogi szemle 16 : 513-524, szeptember 1969.

NAGY, L. : Grundsatz- und Kodifikationsfragen aus dem Genossenschaftsrecht in der Ungarischen Volksrepublik. Staat und Recht 18 : 1889-1903, Heft 12, 1969.

NEMÉNYI, B. : Elméleti és gyakorlati kérdések a garázdaság bűnette köréből. Magyar jog és külföldi jogi szemle 16 : 705-715, december 1969.

TIMÁR, I. : La nouvelle loi hongroise sur le droit d'auteur. Droit d'auteur 82 : 242-247, décembre 1969.
Texte de la loi pp. 236-242.

BOYTHA, G. : Le nouveau droit d'auteur de la Hongrie. Revue de droit hongrois : 5-24, no. 2, 1969/no. 1, 1970.
Voir aussi pp. 25-38.

BENEDEK, K. : Jogrendszerünk és igazságszolgáltatásunk fejlődésének 25 éve. Magyar jog és külföldi jogi szemle 17 : 134-140, március 1970.

VILÁGHY, M. : A magyar civiljogtudomány 25 éve. Jogtudományi közlönyi 25 : 257-267, június 1970.
Twenty-five years of civil law science; Summaries in English, French, German and Russian.

INDIA

DEVI, D.L. : Private international law concerning negotiable instruments in India. Indian year book of international affairs 14 : 177-195, 1965.

BAXI, U. : Law of treaties in the contemporary practice of India. Indian year book of international affairs 14 : 137-176, 1965.

SINGH, H. : Powers and privileges of legislature in Inida. Journal of parliamentary information (India) 11 : 1-12, 1965.

MITTAL, J.K. : Right to equality and the Indian supreme court. American journal of comparative law 14 : 422-458, summer 1965.

NARAIN, J. : Nationalisation and the right to hold property under the Italian constitution - Lessons from comparable Australian and U.S. experiences. Public law : 256-267, autumn 1965.

NARAIN, J. : Equal protection guarantee and the right of property under the Indian constitution. International and comparative law quarterly 15 : 199-230, January 1966.

SRIVASTAVA, V.N. : Indian presidency. Supreme court journal 35 : 3-10, July 1966.

KUMAR, S. : Government contracts. Supreme court journal (Madras) 35 : 60-66, October 1966.

MISRA, K.P. : Territorial sea and India. Indian journal of international law 6 : 465-482, October 1966.

HARIANI, K.P. : Enforcement of foreign arbitration agreements and awards in India. Indian journal of international law 7 : 31-44, January 1967.

SRIVASTAVA, S.C. : Les problèmes de la définition du lock-out indien. Revue de droit contemporain 14 : 90-119, no. 1, 1967.

NAMBIAR, K.R. : The right to a passport. Indian journal of international law 7 : 526-534, October 1967.
The Passport act, 1967, pp. 569-584.

BHARADVAJA, B. : Delegation of powers under the Indian constitution. Supreme court journal (Madras) 38 : 7-12, no. 3, 1968.

SINGH, N. : India and international law. Revista española de derecho internacional 21 : 600-615, julio-septiembre 1968.

NARAIN, J. : Constitutional changes in India - An inquiry into the working of the Constitution. International and comparative quarterly 17 : 878-907, October 1968.

SUBRA RAO, K. : Property rights under the Constitution. Journal of the Indian merchants' chamber 42 : 21-25, December 1968.

GHOUSE, M. : The vicissitudes of freedom of exit in India. American journal of comparative law 17 : 559-572, no. 4, 1969.

BARAK, A. : Company law doctrines and the law of agency in Israel. International and comparative law quarterly 18 : 847-878, October 1969.

GADBOIS, G.H. : Indian judicial behaviour. Economic and political weekly, Annual number 5 : 149-166, January 1970.

MITTAL, J.K. : Right to equality in the Indian constitution (To be contd.). Public law : 36-72, spring 1970.

PANDE, G.S. : Parliament's power to abridge fundamental rights. Supreme court journal (Madras) 42 : 53-68, no. 7, 1970.

INDONESIA

DANUREDJO, S.L.S. : La formation du droit national en Indonésie. Revue de droit contemporain 12 : 121-136, no. 1, 1965.

LEV, D.S. : The lady and the banyan tree - Civil-law change in Indonesia. American journal of comparative law 14 : 282-307, spring 1965.

GOUWGIOKSIONG : De verhouding tussen internationaal privaatrecht en intergentiel recht in Indonesie. Nederlands tijdschrift voor internationaal recht 14 : 345-364, afl. 4, 1967.
Interpersonal law and private international law: Summary in English.

IRAN

SURATGAR, D. : Arbitration in the Iranian legal system. Arbitration journal 20 : 143-156, no. 3, 1965.

MATINE-DAFTARY, A. : Aperçu sur la constitution de l'Iran et l'évolution de son régime parlementaire, 1906-1966. Bulletin interparlementaire 46 : 131-145, 3e trimestre 1966.

SURATGAR, D. : Arbitration in the Iranian legal system. ECAFE (Economic commission for Asia and the Far East)centre for commercial arbitration, News bulletin : 16-31, December 1966.

IRAQ

La constitution intérimaire de la République d'Irak. Documentation française, notes et études documentaires : 1-9, no. 3205, 20 juin 1965.

La constitution provisoire irakienne du 21 septembre 1968. Orient 12 : 91-96, 3e et 4e trimestre 1968.
Texte dd. 325-336.

Constitution provisoire de la République d'Irak, 21 septembre 1968. Documentation française, Notes et études documentaires : 1-13, no. 3569, 3 mars 1969.

IRELAND

O'HIGGINS, P. : Anglo-Irish extradition. New law journal 116 : 69-70, 11 November 1965.

O'HIGGINS, P. : The Irish extradition act, 1965. International and comparative law quarterly 15 : 369-394, April 1966.

JACKSON, P. : Anglo-Irish extradition. Irish jurist 2 : 43-48, summer 1967.

JONES, C. : The non-recognition of foreign divorces in Ireland. Irish jurist 3 : 299-321, winter 1968.

KNIGHT, M. : The Irish court of criminal appeal, (To be contd.). Irish jurist 4 : 91-118, summer 1969.

GREER, D. : Legal services and the poor in Ireland. Irish jurist 4 : 270-292, winter 1969.

KELLY, J.M. : The malicious injuries code and the Constitution. Irish jurist 4 : 221-233, winter 1969.

ISRAEL

HECHT, A. : Entwicklungstendenzen im Privatrecht Israels. Rabels Zeitschrift für ausländisches und internationales Privatrecht 29 : 302-354, Heft 2, 1965.

DRAPKIN, I. : Algunas características del suicidio en Israel. Criminalia 32 : 729-745, diciembre 1966.

REIFEN, F. : New venture of law enforcement in Israel. Journal of criminal law, criminology and police science 58 : 70-74, March 1967.

HARNON, E. : Criminal procedure in Israel - Some comparative aspects. University of Pennsylvania law review 115 : 1091-1110, May 1967.

ELMAN, P. : Compulsory acquisition in Israel law. International and comparative law quarterly 17 : 215-221, January 1968.

ELON, M. : The sources and nature of Jewish law and its application in the State of Israel - Part II (To be contd.). Israel law review 3 : 88-126, January 1968.

BOIM, L. : The parliamentary control over the administration, including the Ombudsman. Annuario di diritto comparato e di studi legislativi 42 : 67-90, fasc. 1, 1968.

SASSOON, D.M. : The Israel legal system. American journal of comparative law 16 : 405-415, no. 3, 1968.

LIVNEH, E. : Some developments of human rights in Israel, 1948-1968. Revue des droits de l'homme - Human rights journal 1 : 582-608, no. 4, 1968.

ENGLAND, I. : The problem of Jewish law in a Jewish state. Israel law review 3 : 254-278, April 1968.

LIKHOVSKI, E. : The courts and the legislative supremacy of the Knesset. Israel law review 3 : 345-367, July 1968.

JACOBSON, D. : The standard contracts law of Israel. Journal of business law : 325-332, October 1968.

HECHT, A. : The Israel law on standard contracts. Israel law review 3 : 586-594, October 1968.

LIKHOVSKI, E. : Can the Knesset adopt a constitution whcih will be the "supreme law of the land"? Israel law review 4 : 61-69, January 1969.

BOIM, L. : The statement for administrative decisions in Israel. Annuario di diritto comparato e di studi legislativi 43 : 171-187, fasc. 2-3, 1969.

SHER, Z. : La nouvelle législation isrélienne sur les brevets - La loi sur les brevets 5727-1967. Propriété industrielle 85 : 102-106, avril 1969.

ALBERT, J.M. : Constitutional adjudication without a constitution - The case of Israel. Harvard law review 82 : 1245-1265, April 1969.

LAPIDOTH, A. : The tests for the determination of the scope of taxes - The territorial location of the object and the personal link of the taxpayer to the country. Israel law review 4 : 392-416, July 1969.

KLEIN, C. : Les problèmes constitutionnels de l'Etat d'Isräel et le contrôle de la constitutionnalité des lois. Revue du droit public et de la science politique eb France et à l'étranger 85 : 1105-1125, novembre-décembre 1969.

MERON, T. : Israel and the European extradition system. Israel law review 5 : 75-91, January 1970.

BIN-NUN, A. : Das Israelische Gesetz über den Kaufvertrag. Rabels Zeitschrift für ausländisches und internationales Privatrecht 34 : 76-85, Heft 1, 1970.

WWISMAN, J. : The Land law, 1969 - a critical analysis. Israel law review 5 : 379-456, July 1970.

NIMMER, M.B. : The uses of judicial review in Israel's quest for a constitution. Columbia law review 70 : 1217-1260, November 1970.

ITALY

BERUTTI, M. : Mariage et divorce en Italie. Revue de droit international et de droit comparé 42 : 20-40, nos. 1-2, 1965.

VITTA, E. : L'ordre public en matière de divorce et de nullités de mariage dans le jurisprudence italienne. Revue critique de droit international privé 54 : 267-278, mai-juin 1965.

REALE, O. : La Dichiarazione universale dei diritti dell'uomo e l'ordinamento giuridico italiano. Comunità internazionale 21 : 3-13, gennaio 1966.

DURANTE, F. : La cittadinanza per adozione. Rivista di diritto internazionale 49 : 162-166, fasc. 2, 1966.

COMBA, A. : Status familiari e cittadinanza italiana. Diritto internazionale 20 : parte la, 175-189, no. 2, 1966.

GALOPPINI, A.M. : Le problème du divorce en Italie. Revue de droit contemporain 13 : 81-107, no. 2, 1966.

BARILE, P., et CAPPELLETTI, M. : Les restrictions apportées par la loi aux libertés individuelles. Annuario di diritto comparato e di studi legislativi 40 : 254-270, fasc. 2-3, 1966.

GIANNINI, M.S. : Le régime des activités commerciales et industrielles des pouvoirs publics en Italie. Annuario di diritto comparato e di studi legislativi 40 : 163-173, fasc. 2-3, 1966.

GIULIANO, M. : Le determinazione del tribunale competente nel diritto internazionale privato italiano. Annuario di diritto comparato e di studi legislativi 40 : 192-225, fasc. 2-3, 1966.

SACCO, R. : L'évolution de la législation italienne sur la filiation naturelle. Annuario di diritto comparato e di studi legislativi 40 : 111-123, fasc. 2-3, 1966.

SICO, L. : Considerazioni sull'interpretazione dell' art. 11 della costituzione. Diritto internazionale 20 : parte la, 297-325, no. 3, 1966.

BALLADORE PALLIERI, G. : Competenza della Corte costituzionale riguardo al diritto delle Comunità europee. Diritto internazionale 20 : parte la, 255-267, no. 3, 1966.

CAPPELLETTI, M. : Il trattamento del diritto straniero nel processo civile italiano. Rivista di diritto internazionale 49 : 299-341, fasc. 3-4, 1966.

NERI, S. : Le droit communautaire et l'ordre constitutionnel italien. Cahiers du droit européen : 363-387,
no. 4, 1966.

FUMAGALLI, B. : Inviolabilità della corrispondenza e poteri istruttori. Jus, Rivista di scienze giuridiche 17 : 371-381, luglio-dicembre 1966.

SANDRELLI, E. : Il delitto di omicidio a causa d'onore. Rasegna di studi penitenziari (Italy) 16 : 359-376, luglio-ottobre 1966.

MERRYMAN, J.H., and VIGORITI, V. : When courts collide - Constitution and cassation in Italy. American journal of comparative law 15 : 665-686, no. 4, 1966/67.

BERNARDINI, A. : L'Italia e le convenzioni universali in materia di diritti dell'uomo. Rivista di diritto internazionale 50 : 107-125, fasc. 1, 1967.

NATIONAL LAW - COUNTRIES

GRISOLI, A. : Enquiry into periodical publications devoted to legal subjects and problems in Italy. Annuario di diritto comparato e di studi legislativi 41 : 85-103, fasc. 1, 1967.

ASQUINI, A. : Dal codice di commercio del 1865 al libro del lavoro del codice civil del 1942. Rivista del diritto commerciale e del diritto generale delle obbligazioni 65 : parte la, 1-8, gennaio-febbraio 1967.

BOGNETTI, G. : La Corte costituzionale italiana e la sua partecipazione alla funzione di indirizzo politico dello Stato nel presente momento storico. Jus, Rivista di scienze giuridiche 18 : 109-126, gennaio-giugno 1967.

ILARDI, A. : La posizione dei regolamenti comunitari nell'ordinamento giuridico italiano. Stato sociale 11 : 148-156, febbraio 1967.

MINOLI, E. : Adesione dell'Italia alla Convenzione di New York? Mondo aperto 21 : 13-23, febbraio 1967.

CALLERI, P. : Matrimoni acattolici ed ordine pubblico. Rivista di diritto internazionale 50 : 342-354, fasc. 2, 1967.

UDINA, M. : L'asilo politico territoriale nel diritto nazionale e secondo la costituzione italiana. Diritto internazionale 21 : parte la, 258-272, no. 3, 1967.

LEONE, G. : Points fondamentaux et points en discussion de la prochaine réforme du code pénal italian. Revue internationale de droit pénal 38 : 269-290, 3e-4e trimestre 1967.

CATTANEO, M.A. : Leggi penali e libertà del cittadino. Comunità 21 : 2-8, aprile 1967.

BLECKMAN, A. : Das Eigentum im italienischen Verfassungsrecht. Zeitschrift für ausländisches öffentliches Recht und Völkerrecht 27 : 94-120, Juli 1967.

DI FRANCIA, A. : Ancora sul problema della trasformazione delle società cooperativa in società ordinaria. Rivista del diritto commerciale e del diritto generale delle obbligazioni 65 : parte la, 323-328, luglio-agosto 1967.

VALIANTE, M. : La riforma del codice di procedura penale. Rassegna di studi penitenziari (Italy) 16 : 701-788, novembre-dicembre 1967.

MONACO, R. : Costituzione italiana e Comunità europee. Relazioni internazionali 32 : 9-11, 6 gennaio 1968.

CRISAFULLI, V. : Le systeme de contrôle de la constitutionnalité des lois en Italie. Revue du droit public et de la science politique en France et à l'étranger 84 : 83-132, janvier-février 1968.

ROTONDI, M. : L'unification du droit des obligations civiles et commerciales en Italie. Revue trimestrielle de droit civil 67 : 1-24, janvier-mars 1968.

CAMAÑO ROSA, A. : Reformas del código penal italiano. Criminalia 34 : 96-106, febrero 1968.

MOTZO, G., et DUNI, G. : Les choses dangereuses en droit public - Rapport pour l'Italie. Studi senesi 79 : 341-372, fasc. 3, 1967.

MONACO, R. : La ratifica dei trattati internazionali nel cudaro costituzionale. Rivista di diritto internazionale 51 : 641-668, fasc. 4, 1968.

ROMANELLI, A. : Aspetti giuridici e aspetti criminologici della recidiva. Giustizia penale 73 : parte la, 225-264, luglio-agosto 1969.

ROTONDI, M. : Zur Reform des Gesellschaftsrechts in Italien. Juristische Blätter 90 : 415-417, 17. August 1968.

LENER, S. : L'imposta "cedolare" e la Santa Sede. Civiltà cattolica 119 : 215-338, 2 novembre 1968.

SERRA, G. : Leggi dichiarate incostituzionali e "reviviscenza" di disposizioni abrogate. Studi senesi 81 : 208-255, fasc. 2, 1969.

UBERTAZZI, G.M. : La rappresentanza dello straniero in Italia come criterio di giurisdizione. Diritto internazionale 23 : parte la, 161-175, no. 2, 1969.

NAPOLITANO, A., and DI STEFANO, A. : Sul diritto di voto degli italiani all'estero. Studi emigrazione 6 : 1-28, febbraio 1969.

POLITI, M. : "Foro della reciprocità" e principi costituzionali in tema di giurisdizione. Rivista di diritto internazionale 52 : 258-288, fasc. 2-3, 1969.

MONTESANO, L. : Sur les arrêts d'inconstitutionnalité "interprétifs" rendus par la Cour constitutionnelle italienne. Annuario di diritto comparato e di studi legislativi 43 : 215-227, fasc. 2-3, 1969.

BISCOTTINI, G. : Sull'attribuzione della cittadinanza a figli di nostri connazionali e di "nativi" dell'Africa italiana. Diritto internazionale 23 : parte la, 373-383, no. 3, 1969.

LUTHER, G. : Die Ehetrennung nach italienisch Recht. Rabels Zeitschrift für ausländisches und internationales Privatrecht 33 : 476-498, Heft 3, 1969.

TULLIO, L. : L'accordo italo-jugoslavo per la delimitazione della piattaforma continentale dell' Adriatico. Rivista del diritto della navigazione 35 : parte la, 300-319, no. 3-4, 1969.

RODOTÀ, S. : Rapporti privati e leggi di nazionalizzazione. Rivista del diritto commerciale e del diritto general delle obbligazioni 67 : parte la, 95-117, marzo-aprile 1969.

PAU, G. : Limiti di applicazione del diritto straniero nell'ordinamento italiano. Rivista di diritto internazionale 52 : 477-508, fasc. 4, 1969.

BARSOTTI, R. : Piattaforma litorale e competenza delle regioni davanti alla corte costituzionale. Rivista di diritto internazionale privato e processuale 5 : 443-452, aprile-giugno 1969.

GINATTA, F. : Sull'interpretazione dell'art. 14 della convenzione italo-francese del 3 giugno 1930 sull'esecuzione delle sentenze in materia civile e commerciale. Rivista di diritto internazionale provato e processuale 5 : 453-461, aprile-giugno 1969.

SCIACCITANO, R. : La giustizia nella costituzione italiana. Aggiornamenti sociali 20 : 331-346, maggio 1969.

NATIONAL LAW - COUNTRIES

VALIANTE, M. : Disegno di legge di delega al governo per il nuovo Codice di procedura penale. Rassegna di studi penitenziari (Italy) 19 : 409-515, maggio-giugno 1969.

RANZI, G. : Der Schutz des gewerblichen Eigentums in Italien. Aussenwirtschaftsdienst des Betriebs-Beraters 15 : 258-262, Juli 1969.

GINATTA, F. : La convenzione itali-francese sull' esecuzione delle sentenze e la sua applicazione giurisprudenziale, 1945-1967. Rivista di diritto internazionale privato e processuale 5 : 661-695, luglio-settembre 1969.

NOBILI, R. : La mouvelle loi italienne sur les licences obligatoires. Propriété industrielle 85 : 229-234, août 1969.
Décret du 26 février 1968.

GAMBINO, A. : La disciplina del conflitto di interessi del socio. Rivista del diritto commerciale et del diritto generale delle obbligazioni 67 : parte la, 371-425, settembre-ottobre 1969.

RIGHETTI, M. : Trascrivabilità ed efficacia civile del matrimonio canonico dei cittadini italiana all' estero nella giurisprudenza italiana, 1957-1968. Rivista di diritto internazionale privato e processuale 5 : 939-966, ottobre-dicembre 1969.

CASSESE, A. : L'efficacia delle norme italiane di adattamento alla Convenzione europea dei diritti dell'uomo. Rivista di diritto internazionale privato e processuale 5 : 918-938, ottobre-dicembre 1969.

LIBONATI, : La "chiarezza" et la "precisione" nei bilanci delle società per azioni. Rivista del diritto commerciale e del diritto generale delle obbligazioni 67 : parte la, 477-533, novembre-dicembre 1969.

LIBONATI, B. : La "chiarezza" et la "precisione" nei bilanci delle società per azioni. Rivista del diritto commerciale e del diritto generale delle obbligazioni 67 : parte la, 477-533, novembre-dicembre 1969.

ROSSANO, C. : Der Gleichheitssatz und seine Bedeutung für die italienische Verfassung. Jahrbuch des öffentlichen Rechts der Gegenwart 18 : 201-254, 1969.

BALLARINO, T. : Costituzione e diritto internazionale privato. Diritto internazionale 24 : parte la, 18-47, no. 1, 1970.

MONACO, R. : La ratification des traités internationaux dans le cade constitutionnel italien. Revue générale de droit international public 74 : 1-26, janvier-mars 1970.

RODOTÀ, S., et CHELI, E. : Tendances et problèmes actuels de la "réforme du droit" en Italie. Revue internationale de droit comparé 22 : 21-33, janvier-mars 1970.

BROGGINI, G. : Convenzioni attributive di giurisdizione nel commercio italo-tedesco (Frederal Republic of Germany). Rivista di diritto internazionale privato e processuale 6 : 5-26, gennaio-marzo 1970.

MARTIN MATEO, R. : El consorcio como institución jurídica. Revista de administración pública : 9-42, enero-abril 1970.

DE CUPIS, A. : Problemi e tendenze attuali nella responsabilità civile. Rivista del diritto commerciale e del diritto generale delle obbligazioni 68 : parte la, 95-103, marzo-aprile 1970.

MALINTOPPI, A. : La dilimitazione della piattaforma continentale adriatica e l'art. 80 delle Costituzione. Rivista di diritto internazionale 53 : 506-525, fasc. 4, 1970.

IVORY COAST

ABITBOL, E. : La famille conjugale et le droit nouveau demariage en Côte d'Ivoire. Penant, Revue de droit des pays d'Aftique 76 : 303-316, 455-467, juillet-septembre, octobre-décembre 1966.

VANGAH, D. : Le statut de la femme mariée dans le nouveau droit de la famille en Côte d'Ivoire. Revue juridique et politique - Indépendance et coopération 21 : 96-104, janvier-mars 1967.

KOUAMÉ, P. : La Chambre administrative de la Cour suprême de la Côte d'Ivoire. Penant, Revue de droit des pays d'Afrique 77 : 279-288, juillet-septembre 1967.

EMANÉ, J. : Les droits patrimoniaux de la femme mariée ivoirienne. Annales africaines : 85-126, 1967.

WODIE, F. : Les attributions de la Chambre administrative de la Côte d'Ivoire. Revue juridique et politique - Indépendance et coopération 22 : 63-78, janvier-mars 1968.

JAPAN

AKIBA, J. : Proof of nationality and the legal status of koreans in Japan. Journal of international law and diplomacy (Tokyo) 64 : ..., March 1966.

ODA, S. : Admission, deportation and extradition of aliens under the Japanese laws. Japanese annual of international law 10 : 23-36, 1966.

L'évolution du droit dans les différent pays - Japon. Annuaire de législation française et étrangère 15 : 316-327, 1966.

HAYASHIDA, K. : Development of election law in Japan. Jahrbuch des öffentlichen Rechts der Gegenwart 15 : 471-511, 1966.

KIKKAWA, T. : Le sursis à l'exécution des peines, en particulier de l'amende, au Japon. Revue internationale de droit pénal 38 : 49-60, ler-2e trimestre 1967.

YAMAMOTO, K. : Revision of the copyright law - Report of the Copyright system in investigating council. Japanese annual of international law 11 : 61-67, 1967.

MATSUMOTO, K. : Development of parliamentary democracy and the modern party state in Japan up to 1945. Jahrbuch des öffentlichen Rechts der Gegenwart 16 : 513-565, 1967.

HIGUCHI, Y. : La protection des droits de l'homme au Japon. Revue des droits de l'homme - Human rights journal 1 : 609-623, no. 4, 1968.

KYOZUKA, S. : Internal enforcement and application of treaties in Japan. Japanese annual of international law 12 : 45-58, 1968.

KAWAKAMI, T. : Die Entwicklung des internationalen Privat- und Prozessrechts in Japan nach dem zweiten Weltkrieg. Rabels Zeitschrift für ausländisches und internationales Privatrecht 33 : 498-517, Heft 3, 1969.

TOYOTA NAKAGAWA, E.K.: El derecho japonés en general. Boletín mexicano de derecho comparado 2 : 69-73, enero-abril 1969.

DAVIS, P. : Legal problems of New Zealand-Japanese trade (to be contd.). New Zealand law journal : 537-540, 2 September 1969.
Japanese legal system.

YOKOTA, K. : Judicial review in Japan - Political and diplomatic questions. Japanese annual of international law 13 : 1-18, 1969.

NOMURA, Y. : Lettre du Japon. Droit d'auteur 83 : 49-57, mars 1970.
Projet sur le droit d'auteur, 1969.

ITOH, H. : How judges think in Japan. The American journal of comparative law 18 : 775-804, no. 4, 1970.

LEE, T.S. : Japanese law - A selective bibliographical guide. Law library journal 63 : 189-230, May 1970.

MARKS, B. : Choice of law and conflicts avoidance in Australian/Japanese transactions (to be contd.). The Australian law journal 44 : 528-541, November 1970.

JORDAN

Constitution du Royaume de Jordanie hachémite, texte mis à jour en 1965. Informations constitutionnelles et parlementaires 17 : 86-110, avril 1966.

Constitution du royaume de Jordanie Hachémite - Texte mis à jour en 1965. Documentation française, Notes et études documentaires : 1-13, no. 3329, 21 octobre 1966.

KENYA

SINGH, C. : The republican constitution of Kenya - Historical background and analysis. International and comparative law quarterly 14 : 878-949, July 1965.

Loi sur le droit d'auteur, 1966. Droit d'auteur 79 : 138-143, mai 1966.

Kenya, constitution - Mise à jour 3 janvier 1967. Informations constitutionnelles et parlementaires 18 : 118-133, juillet 1967.

ABEL, R.L. : Customary laws of wrongs in Kenya - An essay in research method. American journal of comparative law 17 : 573-626, no. 4, 1969.

KOREA

KIM, D.-c. : Constitutional law and the national unification issue. Seoul law journal 8 : 32-53, no. 2, 1966.
Text in Korean with summary in English.

Constitution de la République de Corée, 1962. Documentation française, Notes et études documentaires: 1-14, no. 3333, 2 novembre 1966.

HAHM, P.-c. : Ideology and criminal law in North Korea. American journal of comparative law 17 : 77-93, no. 1, 1969.

The issue of constitution amendment - YUN, T.-y. : Constitutional amendment is necessitated - KIM, C.-k. : Amendment of the constitution lacks logical foundation. Koreana quarterly (Seoul) 11 : 1-25, autumn 1969.

CHO, S.Y. : The structure and functions of the Nprth Korean court system. Library of Congress, Quarterly journal 26 : 216-226, October 1969.

KIM, C. : The legal status of aliens in Korea. Columbia journal of transnational law 8 : 220-245, winter 1969.

List of the treaties that the Republic of Korea entered into (1945-1968). Korea observer (Seoul) 2 : 120-148, July 1970.

KUWAIT

Constitution de l'Etat de Kuwait, 11 novembre 1962. Documentation française, Notes et études documentaires : 1-14, no. 3201, 17 Juni 1965.

LAOS

DORÉ, F. : Le Laos. Revue du droit public et de la science politique en France et ' l'étranger 82 : 295-323, mars-avril 1966.
Chronique constitutionnelle.

Constitution du royaume du Laos, 30 juillet 1961. Documentation française, Notes et études documentaires : 1-7, no. 3627, 10 octobre 1969.

LEBANON

GANNAGE, P. : Statut personnel. Annales de la Faculté de droit et des sciences économiques de Beyrouth, Etudes de droit libanais 45 : 69-77, janvier-mars 1965.

NAJJAR, I. : Le mariage et la nationalité de la femme en droit libanais. Etudes de droit libanais : 437-522, no. 3, juillet-décembre 1965.

SAFA, P. : Le président du conseil d'administration d'une société anonyme libanaise est-il révocable "ad nutum"? Etudes de droit libanais : 9-27, no. 7, janvier-mars 1966.

Texte intégral de la loi du 26 juillet 1966 relative a l'acquisition de biens-fonds par les étrangers. Syrie et monde arabe 13 : 109-113, juillet-août 1966.

EL-HAKIM, J. : Les atteintes mortelles sans intention de causer la mort en droit syrien et libanais. Proche-Orient, Etudes juridiques : 41-71, janvier-avril 1967.

CHEBATH, F. : Le statut personnel des non-musulmans en Syrie et au Liban - Etude comparée. Proche-Orient, Etudes juridiques : 4-7, janvier-avril 1967.
Texte en arabe avec résumé en français.

NAJJAR, I. : La validité des legs déguisés en droit libanais, communautés non musulmanes. Proche-Orient, Etudes juridiques : 321-340, mai-août 1967.

RIFAAT, H.T. : Les libertés locals en droit libanais. Proche-Orient, Etudes juridiques : 291-321, mai-décembre 1968.

CARDAHI, P. : De la représentation successorale en droit libanais. Proche-Orient, Etudes juridiques : 10-35, janvier-avril 1969.

MESNARD, A.H. : Les juridictions administratives face à la situation politique du Liban. Revue juridique et politique - Indépendance et coopération 23 : 403-433, juillet-septembre 1969.

CHAOUL, J. : L'interprétation de la loi fiscale en droit libanais. Proche-Orient; études juridiques : 97-127, janvier-avril 1970.

FABIA, C. : Valeur libératoire du chèque. Proche-Orient, études juridiques : 9-20, janvier-avril 1970.

RIFAAT, H.T. : Les rapports du pouvoir exécutif et du pouvoir judiciaire en droit libanais. Proche-Orient, études juridiques : 65-95, janvier-avril 1970.

DOUENCE, J.C. : Liban - L'expédition des affaires courantes par un gouvernement démissionnaire. Revue du droit public et de la science politique en France et à l'étranger 86 : 1115-1136, septembre-octobre 1970.

LESOTHO

POULTER, S. : The Common Law in Lesotho. Journal of African law 13 : 117-144, autumn 1969.

CRAWFORD, J.R. : The history and nature of the judicial system of Botswana, Lesotho and Swaziland - Introduction and the Superior courts (To be contd). South African law journal 86 : 476-485, November 1969.

LIBERIA

PARNALL, T. : Aliens and real property in Liberia. Journal of African law 12 : 64-80, summer 1968.

LIBYA

Constitution du Royaume de Libye, adoptée le 7 octobre 1951, revisée en 1963. Informations constitutionnelles et parlementaires 17 : 112-135, juillet 1966.

Constitución del Reino de Libia, adoptada el 7 de octubre de 1951 y revisada en 1963. Información jurídica (Spain) : 27-46, noviembre-diciembre 1966.

Loi relative à la protection du droit d'auteur. Droit d'auteur 82 : 116-121, juin 1969.

LIECHTENSTEIN

PAPPERMANN, E. : Der Amtsenthebungsantrag, parlamentarisches System oder konstitutionelle Monarchie in Liechtenstein? Juristische Blätter 92 : 607-613, 5. Dezember 1970.

LUXEMBOURG

Situation actuelle dans le domaine des droits de propriété industrielle (A suivre). Revue franco-belge 79 : 277-279, décembre 1969.

MALAGASY REPUBLIC

Constitution de la République malgache, mise à jour au 27 décembre 1962. Informations constitutionnelles et parlementaires 16 : 46-64, janvier 1965.

PASCAL, R. : Le législateur à Madagascar de 1895 à 1958. Bulletin de Madagascar (Malagasy Republic) 15 : 907-913, novembre 1965.

BARDONNET, D. : La succession aux traités à Madagascar. Annuaire français de droit international 12 : 593-730, 1966.

RANJEVA, R. : Aspects juridiques originaux de la commune malgache. Revue juridique et politique - Indépendance et coopération 22 : 249-362, avril-juin 1968.

Numéro spécial - Madagascar. Penant, Revue de droit des pays d'Afrique 78 : 421-576, octobre-décembre 1968.

MALAWI

ROBERTS, S. : A revolution in the law of succession of Malawi. Journal of African law 10 : 21-32, spring 1966.

ROBERTS, S. : The republican constitution of Malawi. Public law : 304-323, winter 1966.

ROBERTS, S. : The Malawi law of succession - Another attempt at reform. Journal of African law 12 : 81-88, summer 1968.

MALAYSIA

GLOS, G.E. : The administrative nature and legal system of Malaya. Zeitschrift für ausländisches öffentliches Recht und Völkerrecht 25 : 100-122, Januar 1965.

MILNE, R.S. : The constitution of Malaysia. Journal of the parliaments of the Commonwealth 46 : 419-424, October 1965.

VENTURINI, V.G. : Malaysia's new company law. Philippine law journal 40 : 408-454, July 1965.

BUXBAUM, D.C. : Chinese family law in a common law setting - A note on the institutional environment and the substantive family law of the Chinese in Singapore and Malaysia. Journal of Asian studies 25 : 621-644, August 1966.

HOOKER, M.B. : The interaction of legislation and customary law in a Malay state. American journal of comparative law 16 : 415-428, no. 3, 1968.

MALDIVE ISLANDS

HECKER, H. : Die Republik im Indischen Ozean - Verfassungsentwicklung und Rechtsstellung der Malediven. Verfassung und Recht in Ubersee 2 : 425-435, 4. Quartal 1969.

MALI

BOUBOU, D.O. : Le mariage et le divorce au Mali. Penant, Revue de droit des pays d'Afrique 75 : 319-329, juillet-septembre 1965.

HAZARD, J.N. : Mali's socialism and the Soviet legal model. Yale law journal 77 : 28-69, November 1967.

MALTA

Constitution de Malte, 21 septembre 1964. Documentation française, Notes et études documentaires : 1-30, no. 3229, 22 octobre 1965.

MAURITANIA

SY, S.M. : La loi mauritanienne du 11 juillet 1967 portant loi organique relative aux lois de finances. Revue sénégalaise de droit 3 : 5-32, septembre 1969.

MAURITIUS

DE SMITH, S.A. : Mauritius - Constitutionalism in a plural society. Modern law review 31 : 601-622, November 1968.

MOOLLAN, H. : Les difficultés d'application des codes français à l'île Maurice et les projets de codification. Annales de la Faculté de droit et des sciences économiques d'Aix-En-Provence : 137-150, no. 57, 1968.

MEXICO

GRAUE, D. : Consideraciones sobre algunos aspectos jurídicos del régimen familiar en México. Criminalia 31 : 376-396, 31 julio 1965.

FLORES BARROETA, B. : La voluntad contractual en el derecho mexicano. Boletín del Instituto de derecho comparado de México 18 : 699-722, septiembre-diciembre 1965.

FIX ZAMUDIO, H. : Algunas consideraciones respecto a las reformas constitucionales al poder federal. Boletín del Instituto de derecho comparado de México 19 : 3-63, enero-abril 1966.

CÁRDENAS, R.F. : La ejecución de las sanciones en México. Criminalia 32 : 60-79, 28 febrero 1966.

Constitution des Etats-Unis du Mexique, mise à jour au 28 décembre 1964. Informations constitutionnelles et parlementaires 17 : 136-184, juillet 1966.

GARCÍA RAMÍREZ, S. : Características del enjuiciamiento penal militar mexicano. Criminalia 32 : 660-677, noviembre 1966.

Código penal de méjico, 13 de agosto de 1931. Información jurídica (Spain) : 3-104, enero-febrero 1967.

NAVARRO, A. : El delito económico. Criminalia 33 : 428-486, 30 septiembre 1967.

SECCI, M. : Lineamientos constitucionales y procesales del juicio de amparo mexicano. Boletín del Instituto de derecho comparado de México 20 : 461-487, septiembre-diciembre 1967.

FIX ZAMUDIO, H. : Introduccion al estudio de la defensa de la constitución. Bolétin mexicano de derecho comparado 1 : 89-118, enero-abril 1968.

GARCÍA RAMÍREZ, S. : La libertad provisional del inculpado. Criminalia 34 : 463-483, agosto 1968.

Los delitos de disolución social - El Presidente de la República ante en articulo 145 del Código penal - Antecedentes del articulo... Criminalia 34 : 621-782, noviembre 1968.
Series of articles.

CARPIZO, J. : La interpretación del artćulo 133 constitutional. Boletín mexicano de derecho comparado 2 : 3-32, enero-abril 1969.
Constitutional supremacy.

MOLINA PASQUEL, R. : The Mexican fideicomiso - The reception, evolution and present status of the common law trust in a civil law country. Columbia journal of transnational law 8 : 54-78, spring 1969.

BUTTE, W.L. : Strict liability in Mexico. The American journal of comparative law 18 : 805- 830, no. 4, 1970.

MONACO

FRANÇOIS, N.P. : Le nouveau code pénal monégasque. Revue de science criminelle et de droit pénal comparé 23 : 275-300, avril-juin 1968.

MOROCCO

Le système judiciaire marocain. Maghreb : 31-37, mai-juin 1966.

ROUSSET, M. : Développements récents de l'exception d'illégalité au Maroc. Revue juridique et politique - Indépendance et coopération 20 : 379-388, juillet-septembre 1966.

ROUSSET, M. : Réflexions sur la compétence administrative du roi dans la constitution marocaine de 1962. Revue juridique et politique - Indépendance et coopération 21 : 525-538, octobre-décembre 1967.

DEFAULT, G. : A propos d'une expérience vécue - le rôle du juge rapporteur dans la procédure marocaine. Revue trimestrielle de droit civile 67 : 25-67, janvier-mars 1968.

FASSI-FIHRI, M. : La législation pénale du Maroc. Revue de science criminelle et de droit pénal comparé 23 : 301-308, avril-juin 1968.

DECROUX, P. : Le droit international privé marocain et les mariages mixtes. Revue juridique et polittique - Indépendance et coopération 22 : 893-908, juillet-septembre 1968.

DECROUX, P. : La délégation de pouvoir au Maroc. Revue juridique et politique - Indépendance et coopération 23 : 357-366, juillet-septembre 1969.

Código penal marroquí de 1962 (To be contd.). Información jurídica (Spain) : 44-63, julio-septiembre 1969.

ROBERT, J. : La constitution marocaine du 31 juillet 1970. Maghreb : 29-39, septembre-octobre 1970. Texte pp. 39-44.

NEPAL

Népal, loi destinée à réglementer les questions relatives au droit d'auteur. Droit d'auteur 79 : 255-259, octobre 1966.

Népal; constitution modifiée par le premier amendement à la constitution, le 27 janvier 1967. Informations constitutionnelles et parlementaires 20 : 169-216, octobre 1969.

Constitution du Royaume du Népal, 27 janvier 1967. Notes et études documentaires : 1-23, no. 3668, 3 mars 1970.

NETHERLANDS

LANGEMEIJER, G.E. : La réforme du code civil néerlandais. Revue internationale de droit comparé 17 : 55-72, janvier-mars 1965.

EMDE BOAS, M.J. van : The impact of the European convention of Human Rights and fundamental freedoms on the legal order of the Netherlands. Nederlands tijdschrift voor internationaal recht 13 : 337-373, afl. 4, 1966.
First of a series of articles.

Código civil holandés. Información jurídica (Spain) : 1-68, septiembre-octubre 1967.

MOONS, J.M.A.V. : Enige beschouwingen over artikel 117 van het Wetboek van strafrecht. Tijdschrift voor strafrecht 78 : 1-23, afl. 1, 1969.

BINSBERGEN, W.C., and KUITENBROUWER, F. : Neue Entwicklungen im holländischen Strafrecht seit dem Zweiten Weltkrieg. Schweizerische Zeitschrift für Strafrecht 85 : 1-48, Heft 1, 1969.

CONSTANTINESCO, L. : Droit communautaire et droit constitutional néerlandais. Revue générale de droit international public 73 : 378-420, avril-juin 1969.

KELLERMANN, A.E. : Les directives de la CEE dans l'ordre juridique néerlandais. Cahiers de droit européen 5 : 247-312, no. 3, 1969.

SCHAAFSMA, P.A. : Het Nederlandse vaartuig van artikel 3 Wetboek van strafrecht. Tijdschrift voor strafrecht 78 : 319-332, afl. 6, 1969.

DIJK, P. van : The implementation and application of the law of the European communities within the legal order of the Netherlands. Common market law review 6 : 283-308, July 1969.

THOMAS, H.F. : Die Anerkennung ausländischer, insbesondere deutscher Scheidungsurteile in den Neiderlanden. Rebels Zeitschrift für ausländisches und internationales Privatrecht 33 : 734-747, Heft 4, 1969.

ADHIN, J.H. : Het genocide-verdrag en de Surinaamse wetgeving. Tijdschrift voor strafrecht 79 : 86-98, afl. 2, 1970.

Unofficial translation of Book 6 of the draft of a new Netherlands civil code. Nederlands tijdschrift voor internationaal recht 17 : 225-274, afl. 3, 1970.

VERLOREN van THEMAAT, P. : Das innerstaatliche niederländische Wirtschaftsrecht nach der Fusion der Europäischen Gemeinschaften. Aussenwirtschaftsdienst des Betriebs-Beraters 16 : 253-258, Juni 1970.

NEW GUINEA

O'REGAN, R.S. : The reception of the common law and the authority of common law precedents in the Territory of Papua and New Guinea. International and comparative law quarterly 19 : 217-228, April 1970.

NEW ZEALAND

SHER, B.D. : Contracts and commercial law - Teaching and research in New Zealand. New Zealand law journal : 222-225, 248-250, 1 June, 22 June 1965.

GELLHORN, W. : The Ombudsman in New Zealand. Californian law review 53 : 1155-1211, December 1965.

BUIST, M. : The jurisprudence of issue estoppel. New Zealand universities law review 2 : 43-74, April 1966.

The New Zealand law conference 1966, Dunedin, 13-14 April. New Zealand law journal : 153-260, 7 June 1966.

WEBB, P.R.H. : Nullity and divorce - Recognition in New Zealand of English decrees and recognition in England of New Zealand decrees. New Zealand universities law review 2 : 145-161, October 1966.

PATERSON, D.E. : The New Zealand Ombudsman as a protector of citizens' rights. Revue des droits de l'homme - Human rights journal 2 : 395-430, no. 3, 1969.

BURROWS, J.F. : The cardinal rule of statutory interpretation in New Zealand. New Zealand universities law review 3 : 253-278, April 1969.

The New Zealand centennial law conference, Rotorua, 8-11, April 1969. New Zealand law journal : 155-404, 3 June 1969.

ROSS, S.D. : The future of legal aid in New Zealand. New Zealand law journal : 309-312, 21 July 1970.

NIGER

DANDOBI, M. : Le mariage au Niger. Revue juridique et politique - Indépendance et coopération 21 : 105-117, janvier-mars 1967.

Constitution du 8 novembre 1960, amendée des 12 juillet et 14 août 1961, et le 7 septembre 1965. Informations constitutionnelles et parlementaires 18 : 102-116, avril 1967.
Texte.

SÉRÉ de RIVIÈRES, E. : La chefferie au Niger. Penant, Revue de droit des pays d'Afrique 77 : 463-488, octobre-décembre 1967.

NIGERIA

UTTON, A.E. : Nigeria and the United States - Some constitutional comparisons. Journal of African law 9 : 40-59, spring 1965.

WILLIAMS, T.H. : The criminal procedure code of Northern Nigeria - The first five years. Modern law review 29 : 258-272, May 1966.

KEAY, E.A. : Legal and constitutional changes in Nigeria under the military government. Journal of African law 10 : 92-105, summer 1966.

WILLIAMS, F.R.A. : Fundamental rights and the prospect for democracy in Nigeria. University of Pennsylvania law review 115 : 1073-1090, May 1967.

WILLIAMS, F.R.A. : Legal development in Nigeria, 1957-67 - A practising lawyer's view. Journal of African law 11 : 77-85, summer 1967.

OLUYEDE, P.A. : Judicial approach to customary law. Nigeria lawyer's quarterly 3 : 11-21, nos. 1-2, 1968.

SCHRÖDER, D. : Die Bundesstaatlichkeit in Nigeria. Verfassung und Recht in Ubersee 1 : 30-42, 1. Quartal 1968.

NWOGUGU, E.I. : An examination of the position of illiterates in Nigerian law. Journal of African law 12 : 32-55, spring 1968.

OROJO, J.O. : Companies decree. Nigeria lawyers' quarterly 4 : 21-34, nos. 1-4, 1969.

OBILADE, A.O. : Reform of customary court systems in Nigeria under the military government. Journal of African law 13 : 28-44, spring 1969.

ILEGBUNE, C.U. : A critique of the Nigerian law of divorce under the matrimonial causes decree 1970. Journal of African law 14 : 178-197, autumn 1970.

NORWAY

HAMBRO, E. : Norwegian attitude to international arbitration. Archiv des Völkerrechts 12 : 369-398, 4. Heft 1965.

Constitution de la Norvège. Documentation française, Notes et études documentaires : 1-23, no. 3349, 27 décembre 1966.

BROCH, L.O. : The recognition of foreign decrees of divorce and separation in Norwegian law. Nederlands tijdschrift voor internationaal recht 14 : 259-274, afl. 3, 1967.

MEANS, I.N. : The Norwegian Ombudsman. Western political quarterly 21 : 624-650, December 1968.

BIERKHOLT, M. : Riksmeglingsmanninstitusjonen - Oppgaver og kompetanse. Sosialt arbeid 43 : 310-316, hefte 10, 1969.

OPSAHL, T. : Limitation of sovereignty under the Norwegian constitution. Scandinavian studies in law 13 : 151-177, 1969.

FARMER, J.A. : The Norwegian administration acts of 1967 and 1969. Nordisk tidsskrift for international ret 39 : 93-108, fasc. 3-4, 1969.

ANDERSEN, J.A. : Reform af den norske straffeproceslov. Tidsskrift for rettsvitenskap : 166-192, hefte 2, 1970.

PAKISTAN

KUNHI, M.K.M. : The Ayub constitution and after. Indian year book of international affairs 14 : 323-404, 1965.

PAPUA

O'REGAN, R.S. : The reception of the common law and the authority of common law precedents in the Territory of Papua and New Guinea. International and comparative law quarterly 19 : 217-228, April 1970.

PARAGUAY

MARIN IGLESIAS, A. : Derecho paraguayo y filosofía del derecho. Verfassung und Recht in Ubersee 3 : 75-86, 1. Quartal 1970.

PERU

Legislación del Ministerio de relaciones exteriores del Perú. Revista peruana de derecho internacional 24 : 1-449, nos. 64-65, 1964-1965.

BARANDIARAN, J.L. : Examen comparativo de los códigos civiles nacionales de 1852 y 1936. Revista de derecho y ciencias políticas (Lima) 30 : 121-147, nos. 1-3, 1966.

COOPER, H.H.A. : Habeas corpus in the Peruvian legal system. Revista de derecho y ciencias políticas (Lima) 31 : 296-334, núm. 2, 1967.

Perú, ley de sociedades mercantiles, 27.VII. 1966. Información jurídica (Spain) : 1-85, julio-agosto 1967.

ARIAS-SCHREIBER, P.A. : Fundamentos de la soberánia marítima del Perú. Revista de derecho y ciencias políticas (Lima) 34 : 35-36, nos. 1-2, 1970.

PHILIPPINES

PUGH, G.W. : Aspects of the administration of justice in the Philippines. Louisiana law review 26 : 1-24, December 1965.

PUGH, G.W. : Aspects of the administration of justice in the Philippines. Philippine law journal 40 : 519-540, September 1965.

REGALA, R. : The contributions of Philippine courts in the development of public international law. Philippine law journal 40 : 501-509, September 1965.

BONGCO, G.G. : The enforcement of foreign arbitration agreements and awards in the Philippines. Arbitration journal 21 : 34-46, no. 1, 1966.

DAENECKE, E. : Constitutional law in the Philippines. American bar association journal 52 : 161-164, February 1966.

PECK, C.J. : Nationalistic influences on the Philippine law of citizenship. American journal of comparative law 14 : 459-478, summer 1965.

TAGUINOD, T.C. : A reexamination of the position of foreign corporations under the Philippine corporation law. Philippine law journal 41 : 449-499, July 1966.

ABAD SANTOS, V. : The role of the judiciary in policy formulation. Philippine law journal 41 : 567-576, September 1966.

Survey of Philippine law and jurisprudence 1966. Philippine law journal 42 : i-vi, 1-146, January 1967.

Survey of Philippine law and jurisprudence 1966. Philippine law journal 42 : 1-146, 147-309, January, April, 1967.

Constitution des îles Philippines. Documentation française, Notes et études documentaires : 1-11, no. 3425, 6 octobre 1967.
Adoptée le 8 février 1935, amendée en 1940 et 1946.

TAGUINOD, T.C. : The problem of liability for nuclear incidents in the Philippines. Philippine law journal 42 : 555-602, December 1967.

DELLAPENNA, J.W. : The Philippines territorial water claim in international law. Journal of law and economic development 5 : 45-61, spring 1970.

POLAND

STELMACHOWSKI, A. : Klauzule generalne w kodeksie cywilnym. Pánstwo i prawo 20 : 5-20, styczeń 1965.
Summaries in English, French and Russian.

OHANOWICZ, A. : Zbieg norm w kodeksie cywilnym. Państwo i prawo 20 : 189-194, luty 1965.
Concurrence of norms in civil code; Summaries in English, French and Russian.

WASILKOWSKI, J. : La méthode d'élaboration et les principes du code civil. Droit polonais contemporain : 5-15, no. 4, 1965.

WYRWA, T. : La nouvelle codification civile en Pologne populaire et le problème du droit économique. Revue internationale de droit comparé 17 : 417-429, avril-juin 1965.

GWIAZDOMORSKI, J. : Prawo spadkowe w kodeksie cywilnym PRL. Państwo i prawo 20 : 707-725, maj-czerwiec 1965.
Law of succession in the civil code; Summaries in English, French and Russian.

SZUBERT, W. : Kodyfikacja prawa cywilnego a prawo pracy. Państwo i prawo 20 : 633-648, listopad 1965.
Civil code and labour law; Summaries in English, French and German.

GELLHORN, W. : Protecting citizens against administrators in Poland. Columbia law review 65 : 1133-1166, November 1965.

WŁODYKA, S. : Tagadnienia dowodowe w nowym kodeksie postępowania cywilnego. Nowe prawo 22 : 3-13, styczeń 1966.

PRZYBŁOWSKI, K. : Nowe polskie prawo prywatne międzynarodowe. Państwo i prawo 21 : 21-33, styczeń 1966.

WYRWA, T. : L'élaboration du nouveau code civil en Pologne populaire. Revue hellénique de droit international 19 : 247-256, janvier-décembre 1966.

ANDREJEW, I. : W drodze do nowego kodeksu karnego. Państwo i prawo 21 : 195-204, luty 1966.

RESICH, Z. : Podmioty procesu w nowym kodeksie postępowania cywilnego. Nowe prawo 22 : 139-150, luty 1966.

RAJSKI, J. : The new Polish private international law, 1965. International and comparative law quarterly 15 : 457-469, April 1966.

SZER, S. : La nouvelle loi polonaise sur le droit international privé. Journal du droit international 93 : 346-352, avril-juin 1966.

GWIAZDOMORSKI, J. : Dedičské právo v občianskom zákonníku Pol'skej l'udovej republiky. Právnické štúdie 14 : 684-700, čislo 4, 1966.
Right of inheritance; Summary in Russian.

GÓRECKI, J. : Recrimination in Eastern Europe - An empirical study of Polish divorce law. American journal of comparative law 14 : 603-629, no. 4, 1965-1966.

GRALLA, E. : Das polnische Zivilgesetzbuch. Osteuropa-Recht 12 : 81-119, Juni 1966.

RYBICKI, Z. : Problèmes juridiques relatifs au système de la gestion de l'économie nationale en la République populaire de Pologne. Droit polonais contemporain : 5-21, no. 6, 1966.

CHRYPINSKI, V.C. : Legislative committees in Polish lawmaking. Slavic review 25 : 247-258, June 1966.

JODLOWSKI, J. : La reconnaissance et l'exécution des décisions judiciaires étrangères en Pologne. Journal du droit international 93 : 539-570, juillet-septembre 1966.

USCHAKOW, A. : Das neue polnische Gesetz über das internationale Privatrecht. Recht in Ost und West 10 : 198-206, 15. September 1966.

NANOWSKI, Z.L. : L'arbitrage commerciale international en Pologne. Revue de l'arbitrage : 78-92, octobre-décembre 1966.

SZPUNAR, A. : The law of tort in the Polish civil code. International and comparative law quarterly 16 : 86-102, January 1967.

SOBOCIŃSKI, W. : Sad i prawo w Polsce pod zaborami. Państwo i prawo 22 : 220-234, luty 1967.

ROZMARYN, S. : L'exécution administrative dans le droit polonais. Revue du droit public et de la science politique en France et à l'étranger 83 : 433-456, mai-juin 1967.

NATIONAL LAW - COUNTRIES

BURDA, A. : Konstytucja PRL na tle tendencji rozwojowych konstytucjonalizmu socjalistycznego. Państwo i prawo 22 : 846-864, czerwiec 1967.
Constitution and development tendencies of socialist constitutionalism; Summaries in English, French and Russian.

PRZBYLOWSKI, K. : Remarques sur la loi polonaise du 12 novembre 1965 - Le droit international privé. Droit polonais contemporain : 25-30, no. 7-8, 1967.
Voir aussi pp. 31-43.

SZPUNAR, A. : La place de la responsabilité civile en droit polonais. Revue internationale de droit comparé 19 : 861-874, octobre-décembre 1967.

FRENDL, L. : La législation de la République populaire de Pologne de 1960 jusq'au 30 juin 1966 - Une revue. Law in Eastern Europe : 325-356, no. 14, 1967.
Index pp. 405-406.

DABROWA, J. : Odpowiednie ograniczanie rozmiarów obowiązku naprawienia szkody na tle kodeksu cywilnego. Państwo i prawo 23 : 91-101, styczeń 1968.

ZAWAKZKI, K. : Zadania i organizacja szkolenia pracowników wymiaru sprawiedliwości. Nowe prawo 24 : 5-16, styczeń 1968.

WALCZAK, S. : Projekt kodeksu karnego w Sejmie PRL. Nowe prawo 24 : 503-518, kwiecień 1968.

WALCZAK, S. : Z problematyki projektu kodeksu karnego wykonawczego. Przegląd penitencjarny (Poland) 5 : 3-10, nr. 4, 1968.

WALCZAK, S. : Niektoré problemy kodyfikacji prawa karnego. Państwo i prawo 23 : 585-605, kwiecień-maj 1968.
Codification of penal law; Summaries in English, French and Russian.

GRALLA, E. : Die Vernichtbarkeit und Scheidung einer Ehe nach polnischem Recht (To be contd.). Recht in Ost und West 12 : 97-105, 15. Mai 1968.

STEMBROWICZ, J. : Le Conseil d'Etat de la République populaire de Pologne. Revue du droit public et de la science politique en France et à l'étranger 84 : 801-831, juillet-octobre 1968.

GOLISZEWSKI, C. : La loi sur le service militaire obligatoire en Pologne populaire. Pologne contemporaine 2 : 34-36, août-septembre 1968.

ROZMARYN, S. : Une nouvelle codification de la procédure d'exécution administrative. Droit polonais contemporain : 5-18, no. 9, 1968.

GRZYBOWSKI, S. : Les principes et les idées directrices du droit polonais des brevets d'invention. Droit polonais contemporain : 19-31, no. 9, 1968.

WENGEREK, E. : Die Grundlagen des Zivilprozessrechts in Polen. Juristenzeitung 23 : 647-651, 18. Oktober 1968.

BURDA, A. : Une nouvelle loi sur le ministère public de la République populaire de Pologne. Droit polonais contemporain : 9-15, nó. 10, 1968.

ANDREJEW, I. : Systematyka projektu kodeksu karnego. Państwo i prawo 23 : 737-747, listopad 1968.
Draft penal code; Summaries in English, French and Russian.

WALCZAK, S. : Spoleczne aspekty kodyfikacji prawa. Nowe drogi 23 : 3-19, czerwiec 1969.

BILINSKY, A. : Die sozialistische juristische Person in der Rechtsordnung der UdSSR und Polens. Jahrbuch für Ostrecht 10 : 125-165, Juli 1969.

GRALLA, E. : Das polnische internationale Zivilverfahrensrecht. Jahrbuch für Ostrecht 10 : 167-235, Juli 1969.

DUDEK, W. : Regulowanie odszkodowań za przejete mienie na Ziemiach Zachodnich jako przyczynek do kwestii uznania suwerenności Polski na tym terenie. Państwo i prawo 24 : 53-59, lipiec 1969.

BAFIA, J. : Kodyfikacja prawa karnego PRL a Międzynarodowy pakt praw obywatelskich i politycznych. Państwo i prawo 24 : 41-52, lipiec 1969.
Penal law and International covenant on civil and political rights; Summaries in English, French and Russian.

JAKUBOWSKI, J. : Osoby prawne w polskim prawie prywatnym międzynarodowym. Państwo i prawo 24 : 268-279, sierpień-wresień 1969.
Juridical persons in Polish private international law; Summaries in English, French and Russian.

PRZETACZNIK, R. : L'immunité de juridiction des personnes physiques étrangères dans le code polonais de procédure civile. Revue critique de droit international privé 58 : 639-664, octobre-décembre 1969.

KAFTAL, A. : Niektoré zagadnienia prawa dowodowego w świetle k.p.k. 1969. Państwo i prawo 25 : 46-61, styczeń 1970.
Evidence in the new code of penal procedure; Summaries in English, French and Russian.

WRÓBLEWSKI, J. : Law, cybernetics and computers in Poland. Law and computer technology 3 : 9-13, January 1970.

BOTTINI, R. de : La convention franco-polonaise relative à la loi applicable, la compétence et l'exequatur dans le droit des personnes et de la famille. Revue critique de droit international privé 59 : 1-43, janvier-mars 1970.

GWIAZDOMORSKI, J. : Das gesetzliche Ehegüterrecht nach dem polnischen Familiengesetzbuch. Rabels Zeitschrift für ausländisches und internationales Privatrecht 34 : 264-288, Heft 2, 1970.

FRENDL, L. : Die sozialistischen juristischen Personen und die Rechtsnatur ihrer gegenseitigen Verträge im polnischen ZGB. Recht in Ost und West 14 : 56-61, 15. März 1970.

BADKOWSKI, J. : Die Anerkennung ausländischer Entscheidungen in Polen nach zivilprozessrechtlichen Vorschriften und nach internationalen Verträgen. Osteuropa-Recht 16 : 1-24, März 1970.

CIESLAK, M. : La nouvelle procédure pénale in Pologne. Revue de droit pénal et de criminologie 50 : 729-746, mai 1970.

ZAWADZKI, S., et KUBICKI, L. : L'élément populaire et le juge projessionel dans la procédure pénale en Pologne. Revue de droit pénal et de criminologie 50 : 919-935, juillet 1970.

ROT, H. : Uwagi o kodyfikacji prawa w PRL (Klauzule delegacyjne i derogacyjne). Państwo i prawo 25 : 714-722, listopad 1970.
Some remarks on the codification of law; Summaries in English, French and Russian.

JODLOWSKI, J., et PONSARD, A. : La convention franco-polonaise du 5 avril 1967 relative à la loi applicable, à la compétence et à l'exequatur dans le droit des personnes et de la famille. Journal du droit international 97 : 545-631, juillet-septembre 1970.

PORTUGAL

GARCIA, B. : Preservação da liberdade no anteprojeto de código de processo penal. Revista da Faculdade de direito (São Paulo) 60 : 132-147, 1965.

BAPTISTA MACHADO, J. : La compétence internationale en droit portugais. Boletim da Faculdade de direito (Coimbra) 41 : 97-115, 1965.

RODRIGUES QUEIRÓ, A.: Os limites do poder discricionário das autoridades administrativas. Boletim da Faculdade di direito (Coimbra) 41 : 83-96, 1965.

BRAGA da CRUZ, G. : Os pactos sucessórios na história do direito português. Revista da Faculdade de direito (São Paulo) 60 : 93-120, 1965.

O projecto definitivo do código civil. Ministério da justiça, Boletim (Portugal) : 5-65, maio 1966.
Series of articles.

Código penal, livro I, parte geral. Ministério da justiça, Boletim (Portugal) : 23-83, junho 1966.

ÁGUEDO de OLIVEIRA, A. : Regime jurídico da caça. Ministério da justiça, Boletim (Portugal) : 18-249, outubro 1966.

FERRER CORREIRA, A. : La question du renvoi dans le nouveau code civil portugais. Boletim da Faculdade de direito (Coimbra) 42 : 245-283, 1966.

SANTOS BRIZ, J. : El nuevo código civil portugués de 25 de noviembre de 1966. Revista de derecho privado : 13-25, enero 1967.

SOUSA FRANCO, A.L. de : Aspectos fiscais do novo código civil. Ciência e técnica fiscal (Portugal) : 7-85, fevereiro 1967.

Constitution politique de la République portugaise. Documentation française, Notes et études documentaires : 1-23, no. 3412, 21 juillet 1967.

ALBUQUERQUE, M. de : Para uma distinção do erro sobre o facto e do erro sobre a ilicitude em direito penal. Ciência e técnica fiscal (Portugal) : 59-126, agosto-setembre 1967.

La reforma administrativa en Portugal. Documentación administrativa (Spain) : 47-53, octubre 1967.

Portugal, décret-loi no. 46980 - Code du droit d'auteur. Droit d'auteur 80 : 311-322, décembre 1967.

SOUSA SANTOS, B. de : L'interruption de la grossesse sur indication médicale dans le droit pénal portugais. Boletim da Faculdade de direito (Coimbra) 43 : 163-221, 1967.

CORREIA, E. : La peine de mort - Réflexion sur la problématique et sur le sens de son abolition au Portugal. Revue de science criminelle et de droit pénal comparé 23 : 19-35, janvier-mars 1968.

LARREA HOLGUÍN, J. : El Código civil de Portugal. Estudios de derecho 27 : 77-83, marzo 1968.

ASCENSÃO, J. de O. : L'attribution originaire du droit d'auteur à l'entité qui finance une oeuvre ou qui la publie. Droit d'auteur 83 : 9-11, janvier 1970.

RUMANIA

CĂPAȚÎNĂ, O. : L'autorisation de l'exécution des jugements patrimoniaux rendus sur le territoire d'un autre Etat socialiste, dans le système des traités d'assistance juridique conclus par la République populaire roumaine. Revue roumaine des sciences sociales, Série de sciences juridiques 9 : 77-102, no. 1, 1965.

GLASER, E. : Contribuția politicii externe a Republicii socialiste româna la dezvoltarea progresistă a dreptului internațional contemporan. Studii și cercetări juridice 10 : 441-456, nr. 3, 1965.

IONAȘCO, T. : La constitution de la République socialiste de Roumanie. Documents, articles et informations sur la Roumanie 16 : 7-10, 15 septembre 1965.
1965.

Constitution de la République socialiste de Roumanie, août 1965. Informations constitutionnelles et parlementaires 16 : 191-213, octobre 1965.

IONASCO, T., et BARASCH, E.A. : Les contrats économiques dans le droit de la République socialiste de Roumanie. Revue internationale de droit comparé 17 : 887-893, octobre-décembre 1965.

SCHULZ, W. : Die neue Verfassung Rumäniens. Recht in Ost und West 10 : 20-22, 15. Januar 1966.

KAHANE, S., et CONESCO, R.M. : La compétence des juridictions pénales roumaines pour les infractions commises à l'étranger. Revue roumaine des sciences sociales, Série de sciences juridiques 10 : 73-79, no. 1, 1966.

IONASCO, T. : La notion de patrimoine et ses fonctions dans le droit civil de la République socialiste de Roumanie. Revue roumaine des sciences sociales, Série de sciences juridiques 10 : 3-18, no. 1, 1966.

IONASCO, T. : La constitution socialiste roumaine de 1965. Revue de droit contemporain 13 : 87-105, no. 1, 1966.

GEAMĂNU, G. : La contribution de Nicolae Titulesco au développement du droit international. Revue roumaine des sciences sociales, Série de sciences juridiques 10 : 167-177, no. 2, 1966.

CONESCO, R.M. : L'extradition dans les traités d'assistance juridique conclus par l'Etat socialiste roumain avec les autres Etats socialistes d'Europe. Revue roumaine des sciences sociales, Série de sciences juridiques 9 : 279-291, no. 2, 1965.

ELIESCU, M. : L'inexécution des obligations contractuelles, leur impossibilité d'exécution ainsi que leur exécution forcée en nature en droit civil roumain. Revue roumaine des sciences sociales, Série de sciences juridiques 10 : 215-232, no. 2, 1966.

DONGOROZ, V. : Restrîngerea treptată a domeniului dreptului penal socialist şi limitele acesteia. Studii şi cercetări juridice 11 : 533-549, no. 3, 1966.

Constitution de la République socialise de Roumanie, 1965. Documentation française, Notes et études documentaires : 1-13, no. 3314, 20 août 1966.

BRADEANU, S. : Otázky vlastníctva vo svetle ústavy Rumunskej socialistickej republiky. Právny obzor 49 : 773-785, čislo 9, 1966.

Constitución de la República socialista de Rumania de 1965. Información jurídica (Spain) : 3-25, noviembre-diciembre 1966.

L'évolution du droit dans les différent pays - Roumanie. Annuaire de législation française et étrangère 15 : 398-411, 1966.

SCHULTZ, L. : Die verfassungsrechtliche Entwicklung der Sozialistischen Republik Rumänien seit dem Zweiten Weltkrieg. Jahrbuch des öffentlichen Rechts der Gegenwart 15 : 407-458, 1966.
Text of Constitution of August 1965 pp. 459-470.

IONAŞCU, E.A., and BARASCH, E.A. : Concepţia dreptului civil al Republicii Socialiste România asupra nulităţii actului juridic. Studii şi cercetări juridice 12 : 19-40, nr. 1, 1967.

FILIP, I., et CĂPĂŢÎNĂ, O. : Les effets des sentences arbitrales étrangères en matière de rapports de commerce extérieur, conformément au droit de la République socialiste de Roumanie. Revue roumaine d'études internationales : 105-123, no. 1-2, 1967.

MILLER, L. : Les principes fondamentaux de la nouvelle loi des pensions. Revue roumaine des sciences sociales, Série de sciences juridiques 11 : 229-244, no. 2, 1967.

CISMARESCU, M. : Rumania's changing legal code. East Europe 16 : 16-17, August 1967.

CADERE, V.G. : Aperçu général sur le droit roumain du mariage et des régimes matrimoniaux. Revue internationale de droit comparé 19 : 675-688, juillet-septembre 1967.

NASHITZ, A.M. : Le perfectionnement du mécanisme législatif dans l'Etat socialiste roumain. Revue roumaine des sciences sociales, Série de sciences juridiques 12 : 87-103, no. 1, 1968.

La legge sulla censura. Documentazione sui paesi dell'Est 4 : 196-203, 15 febbraio 1968.
28 December 1967.

IONASCO, A. : Les conventions sur la preuve dans le droit socialiste roumain. Revue roumaine des sciences sociales, Série de sciences juridiques 12 : 231-239, no. 2, 1968.

GHECIU, M. : Efectele juridice ale intervenţiei terţelor persoane în procesul civil socialist român. Studii şi cercetări juridice 13 : 251-261, nr. 2, 1968.
Summary in French.

CAPATINA, O. : Regimul juridic al chestiunilor prealabile în dreptul international privat român. Studii si cercetari juridice 13 : 543-555, nr. 4, 1968.

PAPADOPOL, V. : Noul cod penal şi exigenţele democraţiei socialiste. Lupta de clasă 48 : 21-28, mai 1968.

DONGOROZ, V. : Sinteze asupra noului Cod penal al Republicii Socialiste România. Studii şi cercetări juridice 14 : 7-34, nr. 1, 1969.
Summary in French.

FODOR, I. : Le nouveau code pénal roumain. Revue roumaine des sciences sociales, Série de sciences juridiques 13 : 3-17, no. 1, 1969.

POPESCU, T.R. : L'applicazione delle legge straniere nel diritto romeno. Diritto internazionale 23 : parte la, 395-403, no. 3, 1969.

NESTOR, I. : Organisation et fonctionnement de l'arbitrage pour le commerce extérieur dans la République socialiste de Roumanie. Diritto negli scambi internazionali 8 : 235-287, giugno 1969.

FODOR, J. : Das neue Strafgesetzbuch der Sozialistischen Republik Rumänien. Jahrbuch für Ostrecht 10 : 21-44, Juli 1969.

DRAGANU, T. : L'interprétation de la constitution. Revue roumaine des sciences sociales; série de sciences juridiques 14 : 41-51, no. 1, 1970.

ANGHENE, M. : Les juridictions spéciales de l'administration d'Etat de la République socialiste de Roumanie. Revue roumaine des sciences sociales; série de sciences juridiques 14 : 209-219, no. 2, 1970.

ANGHEL, I.M. : La condition juridique de l'étranger en Roumanie, expression de l'humanisme socialiste. Revue roumaine d'études internationales : 85-147, nos. 3-4, 1970.

Constitution de la République socialiste de Roumanie, 13 mars 1969. Informations constitutionnelles et parlementaires 21 : 74-98, avril 1970.

MARINESCU, S. : Cessions et licences de marques en Roumanie. Propriété industrielle 86 : 132-134, avril 1970.

RUANDA

Constitution de la République rwandaise, novembre 1962. Documentation française, Notes et études documentaires : 15-24, no. 3175, 26 mars 1965.

RUHASHYANKIKO, N. : Le problème de l'interprétation authentique dans la pratique constitutionnelle rwandaise. Penant, Revue de droit des pays d'Afrique 77 : 417-423, octobre-décembre 1967.

SENEGAL

M'BAYE, K. : L'organisation judiciaire au Sénégal. Penant, Revue de droit des pays d'Afrique 75 : 27-34, janvier-mars 1965.

ARRIGHI, G. : Tradition adaptée au monde moderne - Le code de procédure civile au Sénégal. Penant, Revue de droit des pays d'Afrique 75 : 155-169, avril-juin 1965.

NATIONAL LAW - COUNTRIES

MADEMBA-SY, S. : Le régime des associations au Sénégal. Revue sénégalaise de droit 1 : 57-74, décembre 1967.

GAUTRON, J.C. : La révision constitutionnelle du 20 juin 1967 au Sénégal. Revue sénégalaise de droit 1 : 5-21, décembre 1967.

VERDUN, L.G. : Sénégal - La revision constitutionnelle du 20 juin 1967. Revue juridique et politique - Indépendance et coopération 22 : 89-108, janvier-mars 1968.

BA, A.C. : Quelques considérations sur la loi relative au domaine national au Sénégal. Revue sénégalaise de droit 2 : 56-63, juin 1968.

DIOP, M. : L'expérience sénégalaise du contrôle juridictionnel de l'administration. Revue sénégalaise de droit 2 : 5-30, décembre 1968.

AURILLAC, M. : La Cour suprême du Sénégal. Revue juridique et politique - Indépendance et coopération 23 : 65-98, janvier-mars 1969.

BILBAO, R. : Statuts civils et nationalité. Revue sénégalaise de droit 3 : 28-39, mars 1969.

Révision constitionnelle - Loi no. 67-32 du 20 juin 1967, modifiant la constitution du 3 mars 1963. Informations constitutionnelles et parlementaires 20 : 157-160, juillet 1969.

BOUREL, P. : La formation du contrat en droit sénégalais. Revue sénégalaise de droit 3 : 33-54, septembre 1969.

MOLLION, J. : La célébration du mariage des étrangers au Sénégal. Revue sénégalese de droit 3 : 55-72, septembre 1969.

M'BAYE, K. : L'expérience sénégalaise de la réforme du droit. Revue internationale de droit comparé 22 : 35-42, janvier-mars 1970.

DECHEIX, P. : La réforme du 26 février 1970 de la constitution du Sénégal. Revue juridique et politique - Indépendance et coopération 24 : 289-306, avril-juin 1970.

SIERRA LEONE

Sierra Leone, loi sur le droit d'auteur de 1965, no. 28, du 5 mai 1965 (A suivre). Droit d'auteur 81 : 131-142, juin 1968.

KASHOPÉ DIXON-FYLE, R. : Company law and economic development in Sierra Leone - A study in conflict. International and comparative law quarterly 19 : 447-467, July 1970.

Constitution de la Sierra Leone. Documentation française, Notes et études documentaires : 1-34, no. 3574, 21 mars 1969.

SINGAPORE

BUXBAUM, D.C. : Chinese family law in a common law setting - A note on the institutional environment and the substantive family law of the Chinese in Singapore and Malaysia. Journal of Asian studies 25 : 621-644, August 1966.

La constitution de Singapour. Informations constitutionnelles et parlementaires 19 : 67-93, avril 1968.
Extraits.

JAYAKUMAR, S. : Singapore and state succession - International relations and internal law. International and comparative law quarterly 19 : 398-423, July 1970.

SOMALIA

NOOR MUHAMMAD, H.N.A. : Judicial review of administrative action in the Somali Republic. Journal of African law 10 : 9-20, spring 1966.

CONTINI, P. : Integration of legal systems in the Somali Republic. International and comparative law quarterly 16 : 1088-1105, October 1967.

EGAL, M.H.I. : Somalia - Nomadic individualism and the rule of law. African affairs 67 : 219-226, July 1968.

SOUTH AFRICA

PROCULUS REDIVIVUS : South African law at the crossroads or what is our common law? South African law journal 82 : 17-25, February 1965.

République sud-africaine, loi sur le droit d'auteur, 1965. Droit d'auteur 79 : 27-50, février 1966.
Voir aussi pp. 60-68.

FELICE, J.J. de : Aspects juridiques récents de l'apartheid. Revue de droit contemporain 13 : 134-141, no. 2, 1966.

KAHN, E. : The rules of precedent applied in South African courts. South African law journal 84 : 43-55, February 1967.
First of a series of articles.

SUZMAN, A. : South Africa and the rule of law. South African law journal 85 : 261-271, August 1968.

MITTLEBEELER, E.V. : Race and injury in South Africa. Howard law journal 14 : 90-104, winter 1968.

DUGARD, C.J.R. : Foreign affairs and public international law. Annual survey of South African law : 49-65, 1968.

HAHLO, H.R. : Law of persons. Annual survey of South African law : 66-89, 1968.

SHEPHERD, H. : Necessity and the rule of law in Rhodesia and South Africa. Contemporary review 214 : 266-272, May 1969.

ROOME, K.P.S. : Discrimination in by-laws. South African law journal 86 : 319-324, August 1969.

SUTTNER, R.S. : Legal pluralism in South Africa - A reappraisal of policy. International and comparative law quarterly 19 : 134-153, January 1970.

DUGARD, J. : 1570 revisited - An examination of South African criminal procedure and the "Hiemstra proposals". The South African law journal 87 : 410-423, November 1970.

SPAIN

BELTRÁN de HEREDIA, J. : Reconocimiento de hijo natural en testamento. Revista de derecho privado 49 : 183-202, marzo 1965.

PUIG FERRIOL, L. : Problemas de sociedades mercantiles en la sustitución fideicomisaria. Revista jurídica de Cataluña 64 : 359-377, abril-junio 1965.

MORENO QUESADA, B. : La tutela de los hijos adoptivos. Anuario de derecho civil 18 : 435-469, abril-junio 1965.

LOS MOZOS, J.L. de : La sucesión abintestato en favor del Estado. Anuario de derecho civil 18 : 393-433, abril-junio 1965.

GULLÓN BALLESTEROS, A. : La disolución de la comunidad de bienes en la jurisprudencia. Anuario de derecho civil 18 : 365-391, abril-junio 1965.

TERUEL CARRALERO, D. : Teoria general de las infracciones contra el Estado. Anuario de derecho penal y ciencias penales 18 : 299-314, mayo-agosto 1965.
Bibliography pp. 314-315.

BOQUERA OLIVER, J.M. : Los órganes estatales titulares de poder reglamentario. Revista de administración pública : 79-93, mayo-agosto 1965.

PEÑA BERNALDO de QUIROS, M. : Antecedentes del código civil vigente. Anuario de derecho civil 18 : 911-920, octubre-diciembre 1965.

GUILARTE ZAPATERO, V. : Algunas consideraciones sobre la partición adicional del artículo 1.079 del código civil. Anuario de derecho civil 19 : 55-79, enero-marzo 1966.

ORTUN, F. : L'unification du droit civil espagnol. Revue internationale de droit comparé 18 : 413-421, avril-juin 1966.

PIÑAR, B. : Derecho turístico inmobiliario, problemas de titularidad, documentación y servidumbres. Anuario de derecho civil 19 : 315-335, abril-junio 1966.

CASTRO LUCINI, F. : Algunas consideraciones críticas sobre los requisitos de la adopción. Anuario de derecho civil 19 : 337-368, abril-junio 1966.

COSSÍO, A. de : La causalidad en la responsabilidad civil - Estudio del derecho español. Anuario de derecho civil 19 : 527-554, julio-septiembre 1966.

SALAS, J. : Los decretos-leyes en el ordenamiento jurídico español - En torno a la urgencia. Revista de administración pública : 41-96, septiembre-diciembre 1966.

GONZÁLEZ CASANOVA, J.A. : La distinción Estado-régimen político y la jurisprudencia penal del Tribunal supremo. Revista jurídica de Cataluña 65 : 979-1016, octubre-diciembre 1966.

PELLICER VALERO, J.A. : La sucesión extraordinaria en el derecho español. Revista de derecho y ciencias sociales (Concepción) 34 : 25-41, octubre-diciembre 1966.

MARTÍN MATEO, R. : La inamovilidad de los funcionarios públicos. Revista de administración pública : 9-40, septiembre-diciembre 1966.

La nouvelle loi organique de l'Etat. Documentation française, Chroniques étrangères; Espagne : 6-10, novembre 1966.
22 novembre 1966; Premier article d'une série; Voir aussi pp. 3-4.

SAINZ de BUJANDA, F. : La capacidad jurídica tributaria de los entes collectivos no dotados de personalidad. Revista de la Facultad de derecho de la Universidad de Madrid 10 : 623-757, núm. 27, 1966.

NO LOUIS, E. de : L'Espagne et le droit humanitaire de la guerre - Quelques considérations. Revue internationale de la Croix-Rouge 49 : 1-11, janvier 1967.

GARCÍA CALDERÓN, M. : Sistema español de derecho internacional privado. Revista de derecho y ciencias políticas (Lima) 31 : 105-127, no. 1, 1967.

PASTOR RIDRUEJO, J.A. : La ley aplicable al fondo de las obligaciones contractuales en el derecho internacional privado español. Revista española de derecho internacional 20 : 17-35, enero-marzo 1967.

VALLET de GOYTISOLO, J. : El deber de instituir herederos a legitimarios y el actual régimen de la preterición en los derechos civiles españoles. Anuario de derecho civil 20 : 3-115, enero-marzo 1967.

MARTÍN MATEO, R. : El estatuto de la propiedad inmobiliaria. Revista de administración pública : 101-150, enero-abril 1967.

La Ley orgánica del Estado. Revista de estudios políticos : 1-320, marzo-abril 1967.
text pp. 321-354; Series of articles.

MOURULLO, G.R. : La punition des actes préparatoires dans le droit pénal espagnol. Revue internationale de droit pénal 38 : 77-120, 1er-2e trimestre 1967.

UCELAY de MONTERO, J.A. : Personal contratado por la administración del Estado - Régimen jurídico en España. Revue internationale des sciences administratives 33 : 314-318, no. 4, 1967.

LÓPEZ JACOISTE, J.J. : Propiedad y contratación forestales en derecho civil. Revista de derecho privado : 277-303, abril 1967.

FERRER MARTÍN, D. : Sistema actual aspañol para determinar la filiación. Anuario de derecho civil 20 : 255-295, abril-junio 1967.

AGUILAR BENÍTEZ de LUGO, M. : Estatuto personal y orden público en el derecho internacional privado español. Revista española de derecho internacional 20 : 217-246, abril-junio 1967.

La loi organique de l'Etat espagnol, janvier 1967. Documentation française, Notes et études documentaires : 1-33, no. 3400, 12 juin 1967.

Bases para el anteproyecto de Código penal para España. Criminalia 34 : 7-18, enero 1968.

VALLET de GOYTISOLO, J.: El apartamiento y la desheredación. Anuario de derecho civil 21 : 3-107, enero-marzo 1968.

GARRIDO FALLA, F. : La evolución del recurso contencioso-administrativo en España. Revista de administración pública : 9-26, enero-abril 1968.

COBO, M. : Función y naturaleza del artículo 226 del Código penal. Anuario de derecho penal y ciencias penales 21 : 53-76, enero-abril 1968.

MONTULL LAVILLA, E. : Estudio comparativo del delito de traición militar y el de traición de derecho penal común. Revista española de derecho militar : 9-54, enero-diciembre 1968.

GARRIDO FALLA, F. : La empresa pública en el derecho español. Revista de derecho privado : 117-127, febrero 1968.

PUENTE EGIDO, J. : Algunas consideraciones en torno al principio de armonía institucional en las organizaciones europeas, con especial referencia al derecho español. Revista española de derecho internacional 21 : 570-582, julio-septiembre 1968.

GUAITA MARTORELLI, A. : La división territorial en la Ley orgánica del Estado. Documentación administrativa (Spain) : 11-33, septiembre-octubre 1968.

GALLEGO ANABITARTE, A. : Ley y reglamento en España. Revista de administración pública : 81-136, septiembre-diciembre 1968.
Bibliography pp. 137-140.

MARTÍNEZ-PEREDA RODRÍQUEZ, J.M. : Hacia un concepto criminológico del furtivo español. Anuario de derecho penal y ciencias penales 21 : 505-519, septiembre-diciembre 1968.

FERNÁNDEZ FLORES, J.L. : Principios que rigen la validez del matrimonio, con elemento extranjero, en derecho español. Revista española de derecho internacional 21 : 781-797, octubre-diciembre 1968.

RODRIGUEZ BEREIJO, A. : La limitación de la iniciativa parlamentaria en materia presupuestaria en el derecho positivo expañol. Revista de la Facultad de derecho de la Universidad de Madrid 12 : 437-491, núm. 33, 1968.

LOPEZ y LOPEZ, A.M. : Problemas jurídicos de los trasplantes de tejidos y órganos humanos. Anuario de derecho civil 22 : 145-161, enero-marzo 1969.

CAMAÑO ROSA, A. : El delito de rapiña. Anuario de derecho penal y ciencias penales 22 : 155-184, enero-abril 1969.

LUCAS FERNÁNDEZ, F. : Contratos traslativos del dominio y derechos reales sobre bienes inmuebles otorgados en España por personas naturales o jurídicas extranjeras. Revista de derecho privado 52 : 85-98, febrero 1969.

MARTÍNEZ CARO, S. : Delimitación de las aguas jurisdiccionales españolas. Revista española de derecho internacional 22 : 742-754, núm. 4, 1969.

ALEGRE GONZÁLEZ, J. : La excepción de orden público en derecho interregional privado español. Revista de derecho privado 53 : 260-268, abril 1969.

CLAVERO ARÉVALO, M.F. : Los derechos de preferencia frente a la administración y el sistema de licitación en la contratación de los entes públicos. Revista de administración pública : 9-39, mayo-agosto 1969.

SERRAMALERA, R.R. : La responsabilité du mineur en droit espagnol. Revue internationale de police criminelle 24 : 167-173, juin-juillet 1969.

CANO TELLO, C.A. : El concepto de finca agraria, dentro de la clasificación de los bienes inmuebles por naturaleza, en el derecho español. Anuario de derecho civil 22 : 529-543, julio-septiembre 1969.

ESCRIVA MONZO, V. : El articulo 235 del Código civil - El parentesco y la línea de parentesco en el protutor. Anuaria de derecho civil 22 : 545-595, julio-septiembre 1969.

CASTRO y BRAVO, F. de : El término derecho común en el Código de comercio - Estudio sobre la doctrina del Tribunal supremo. Anuario de derecho civil 22 : 839-873, octubre-diciembre 1969.

MULLERAT BALMANA, R.M. : Las patentes y el examen previo a su concesión. Revista jurídica de Cataluña 68 : 954-964, octubre-diciembre 1969.

ALVAREZ-LINERA y URÍA, C. : Tribunales competentes en las causas criminales contra autoridades y funcionarios públicos. Información jurídica (Spain) : 7-18, octubre-diciembre 1969.

RUILOBA SANTANA, E. : El convenio hispano-francès de 28 de mayo de 1969 sobre reconocimiento de sentencias extranjeras y actas auténticas en materias civil y mercantil. Revista española de derecho internacional 23 : 42-75, núm. 1, 1970.

GONZÁLEZ NAVARRO, F. : Notificaciones, auxilio administrativo y entes locales. Documentación administrativa (Spain) : 11-39, enero-febrero 1970.

ROSAL, J. del : Les délits de presse dans le droit pénal espagnol moderne. Revue de science criminelle et de droit pénal comparé 25 : 35-79, janvier-mars 1970.

VALLET de GOYTISOLO, J. : Contenido cualitativo de la legítima de los descendientes en el Código civil. Anuario de derecho civil 23 : 9-121, enero-marzo 1970.

MARTÍN MATEO, R. : El consorcio como institución jurídica. Revista de administración pública : 9-42, enero-abril 1970.

VALLET de GOYTISOLO, J. : Contenido cualitativo de la legítima vidual del Código civil. Revista de derecho privado 54 : 101-118, febrero 1970.

CLAVÉRO ARÉVALO, M.F. : Existen reglamentos autónomos en el derecho español? Revista de administración pública : 9-34, mayo-agosto 1970.

MEDINA MUÑOZ, M.A. : Los consejeros nacionales del movimiento, según la Ley orgánica del mismo y el reglamento del Consejo. Revista de estudios políticos : 117-139, mayo-agosto 1970.

BERCOVITZ, R. : La adquisición de la vecindad civil por navimiento en territorio distinto al de la vecindad de origen. Anuario de derecho civil 23 : 739-764, octubre-diciembre 1970.

SUDAN

La costituzione provvisoria del Sudan, 1964. Oriente moderno 47 : 341-375, maggio-luglio 1967.

AL-CHIBLI, A.T. : Le système judiciaire du Soudan. Al-Mouhamoune 32 : 329-332, juillet 1967.
Texte en arabe.

GRETTON, G. : The law and the Constitution in the Sudan. World today 24 : 314-323, August 1968.

SWAZILAND

RUBIN, N. : Swaziland - The marriage proclamation, 1964. Journal of African law 9 : 60-64, spring 1965.

RUBIN, N.N. : The Swazi law of succession - Restatement. Journal of African law 9 : 90-113, summer 1965.

CRAWFORD, J.R. : The history and nature of the judicial system of Botswana, Lesotho and Swaziland - Introduction and the Superior courts (To be contd.). South African law journal 86 : 476-485, November 1969.

SWEDEN

HOLMGREN, K. : Några reformfrågor rörande förvaltningsrättskipningen. Svensk juristtidning 50 : 569-580, oktober 1965.

Constitution de la Suède. Documentation française, Notes et études documentaires : 1-45, no. 3256, 21 janvier 1966.

SCREVENS, R. : Le nouveau code pénal suédois. Revue de droit pénal et de criminologie 46 : 618-634, avril 1966.

WALTER, H. : Die allgemeine Verfassungsrevision in Schweden und die Grundgesetzänderungen von 1965. Zeitschrift für ausländisches öffentliches Recht und Völkerrecht 26 : 59-81, Juni 1966.

FRIESEN, B. von : L'institution suédoise du Procureur parlementaire, moyen d'assurer le respect des droits des citoyens. Bulletin interparlementaire 48 : 17-27, 1er trimestre 1968.
L'Ombudsman.

SIMSON, G. : Grenzen des Sexualstrafrechts in Deutschland und Schweden. Juristenzeitung 23 : 481-487, 9. August 1968.

HOLMGREN, K. : La publicité des actes officiels en droit suédois. Revue du droit public et de la science politique en France et à l'étranger 84 : 1019-1031, novembre-décembre 1968.

HOLMGREN, K. : La protection des administrés en droit suédois et la charge de l'Ombudsman. Droit social : 69-74, février 1969.

MAHRER, I. : Die Öffentlichkeit amtlicher Akten in Schweden. Zeitschrift für schweizerisches Recht 88/1 : 317-343, Heft 3, 1969.

STJERNQUIST, N. : Die Entwicklung des öffentlichen Rechts Schwedens in den Jahren 1954 bis 1969. Jahrbuch des öffentlichen Rechts der Gegenwart 18 : 255-293, 1969.

HERLITZ, N. : Parteill författningsreform. Svensk juristtidning 55 : 1-32, januari 1970.

HENKOW, H. : Det reformerade JO-ämbetet. Svensk juristtidning 55 : 461-466, juli-august 1970.

WELAMSON, L. : Comments on the recognition and enforcement of foreign judgements. Scandinavian studies in law 14 : 251-266, 1970.

SWITZERLAND

WALDER, H. : Der Affekt und seine Bedeutung im schweizerischen Strafrecht. Schweizerische Zeitschrift fürStrafrecht 81 : 24-67, Heft 1, 1965.

LALIVE, P. : La révision du droit de la filiation illégitime. Zeitschrift für schweizerisches Recht 84/11 : 543-812, Heft 4, 1965.

CLERC, F. : Le projet de révision partielle du code pénal suisse. Revue de droit pénal et de criminologie 46 : 31-41, octobre 1965.

SCHULTZ, H. : Le sursis en droit suisse. Revue de science criminelle et de droit pénal comparé 20 : 801-821, octobre-décembre 1965.

GROSSEN, J.M. : Quelques remarques sur la situation et les méthodes du droit de la famille. Zeitschrift für schweizerisches Recht 85/I : 41-66, Heft 1, 1966.

HIRSCH, A. : Problèmes actuels du droit de la société anonyme - L'organisation de la S.A. : Zeitschrift für schweizerisches Recht 85/II : 1-84, Heft 1, 1966.

Message du Conseil fédéral à l'Assemblée fédérale à l'appui d'un projet de loi sur la protection des biens culturels en cas de conflit armé (du 4 février 1966). Feuille fédérale (Switzerland) 118 : 157-186, 17 février 1966.

CLERC, F. : Les avatars de la deuxième révision du code pénal suisse. Schweizerische Zeitschrift für Strafrecht 82 : 125-135, Heft 2, 1966.

HELG, R. : La haute surveillance du parlement sur le gouvernement et l'administration. Zeitschrift für schweizerisches Recht 85/II : 85-164, Heft 2, 1966.

BÄUMLIN, R. : Die Kontrolle des Parlaments über Regierung und Verwaltung. Zeitschrift für schweizerisches Recht 85/II : 165-319, Heft 3, 1966.

ROOS, G. : Übersicht über die schweizerische Gesetzgebung des Jahres 1965. Zeitschrift für schweizerisches Recht 85/I : 407-417, Heft 5, 1966.

Procès-verbal de la 100e assemblée annuelle de la Société suisse des juristes des 23, 24 et 25 septembre 1966 à Zoug. Zeitschrift für schweizerisches Recht 85/II : 539-776, Heft 5, 1966.

MÜLLER, A. : Übersicht der Literatur über schweizerisches Recht - Bibliographie juridique suisse 1965. Zeitschrift für schweizerisches Recht 85/I : 495-545, Heft 5, 1966.

ZELLWEGER, E. : The Swiss federal court as a constitutional court of justice. International commission of jurists, Journal 7 : 97-124, summer 1966.

GRAVEN, J. : Comment le droit suisse réprime-t-il les infractions par négligences? Revue internationale de criminologie et de police technique 20 : 171-200, juillet-septembre 1966.

MÜNCH, F. : Die schweizerische Initiative zu zweiseitigen Abmachungen über die friedliche Beilegung von Streitigkeiten. Zeitschrift für ausländisches öffentliches Recht und Völkerrecht 26 : 705-745, Dezember 1966.

GRAVEN, J. : Como reprime el derecho suizo las infracciones por negligencia? Anuario de derecho penal y ciencias penales 20 : 245-287, enero-agosto 1967.

GILLIARD, F. : Vers l'unification du droit de la responsabilité. Zeitschrift für schweizerisches Recht 86/II : 193-323, Heft 2, 1967.

ROHR, J. : Un parlement cantonal suisse, le Grand conseil genevois. Revue du droit public et de la science politique en France et à l'étranger 83 : 457-502, mai-juin 1967.

Rapport du Conseil fédéral à l'Assemblée fédérale sur l'initiative populaire contre la pénétration étrangère (du 29 juin 1967). Feuille fédérale (Switzerland) 119 : 69-122, 17 août 1967.

Message du Conseil fédéral à l'Assemblée fédérale concernant la revision des titres dixième et dixième bis du code des obligations - Du contrat de travail (du 25 août 1967). Feuille fédérale (Switzerland) 119 : 249-479, 5 octobre 1967.

KEMPF, J.C. : Quelques aspects du ministère public genevois. Revue internationale de criminologie et de police technique 21 : 293-296, octobre-décembre 1967.

PATRY, R. : Les accords entre actionnaires en droit suisse. Annales de la Faculté de droit d'Istanbul 17 : 159-179, nos. 26-28, 1967.

Message du Conseil fédéral à l'Assemblée fédérale concernant la modification de la loi sur le statut des fonctionnaires et des statuts des caisses d'assurance du personnel (du 7 février 1968). Feuille fédérale (Switzerland) 120 : 289-352, 23 février 1968.

PATRY, R. : Le problème de la revision du droit des sociétés en Suisse. Revue de droit international et de droit comparé 45 : 83-112, no. 2, 1968.

Quelques opinions sur la revision de la constitution fédérale. Zeitschrift für schweizerisches Recht 87/I : 371-592, Heft 4, 1968.

Message du Conseil fédérale à l'Assemblée fédérale concernant le renforcement de la protection pénale du domaine personnel secret (du 21 février 1968). Feuille fédérale (Switzerland) 120 : 609-623, 5 avril 1968.
Texte du projet de loi pp. 624-626.

Zur Vereinheitlichung des Zivilprozessrechts - Berichterstattung des Vorstandes des Schweizerischen Juristenvereins. Zeitschrift für schweizerisches Recht 88/II : 1-548, Heft 1, 1969.
Texts in French and German.

NEF, M. : Pressefreiheit und Zeugnisverweigerungsrecht im Strafprozess. Schweizerische Zeitschrift für Strafrecht 85 : 113-138, Heft 2, 1969.

KNECHT, H. : Erfahrungen bei der Untersuchung von Wirtschaftsdelikten. Schweizerische Zeitschrift für Strafrecht 85 : 352-369, Heft 4, 1969.

BURKHARD, W. : Rechtliche Fragen im Zusammenhang mit der Anerkennung des "Hirntodes". Schweizerische Zeitschrift für Strafrecht 84 : 362-377, Heft 4, 1968.

HUBER, H. : Die Rechtssprechung des Schweizerischen Bundesgerichts als Verfassungsgerichtshof von 1961 bis 1968. Jahrbuch des öffentlichen Rechts der Gegenwart 18 : 51-78, 1969.

GIGER, H. : Massenmedien, Informationsbetrug und Persönlichkeitsschutz als privatrechtliches Problem. Zeitschrift für schweizerisches Recht 89/I : 33-54, Heft 1, 1970.

GENTINETTA, J. : Konkordat der Schweizer Kantone zur Vereinheitlichung des Rechts der Schiedsgerichtsbarkeit. Aussenwirtschaftsdienst des Betriebs-Beraters 16 : 113-118, März 1970.

ARDINAY, H. : Der Betrug nach dem schweizerischen Strafgesetzbuch. Schweizerische Zeitschrift für Strafrecht 86 : 225-326, Heft 3/4, 1970.

HUG, B. : Le droit d'être entendu et la consultation du dossier en procédure administrative fédérale et genevoise. Revue genevoise de droit public 1 : 113-130, mai 1970.

SWITZERLAND
(International law, Aliens)

Message du Conseil fédéral à l'Assemblée féderale concernant l'octroi de nouveaux prêts à la fondation des immeubles pour les organisations internationales, à Genève (du 6 juin 1966). Feuille fédérale (Switzerland) 118 : 993-1000, 30 juin 1966.

MOSER, H.P. : Die Rechtsstellung des Ausländers in der Schweiz. Zeitschrift für schweizerisches Recht 86/II : 325-482, Heft 3, 1967.
Bibliography pp. 483-488.

VAUCHER, R.F. : Le statut des étrangers en Suisse, Selon le droit civil et en matière d'assurances sociales. Zeitschrift für schweizerisches Recht 86/II : 489-643, Heft 4, 1967.

BINDSCHEDLER, R.L. : Das Problem der Beteiligung der Schweiz an Sanktionen der Vereinigten Nationen, besonders im Falle Rhodesiens. Zeitschrift für ausländisches öffentliches Recht und Völkerrecht 28 : 1-15, März 1968.

HAURI, K. : Die Umwandlung schweizerischer Gesandtschaften in Botschaften. Zeitschrift für schweizerisches Recht 87/I : 283-321, Heft 3, 1968.

KNAPP, B. : Les particuliers et les traités internationaux devant les tribunaux internes. Zeitschrift für schweizerisches Recht 88/I : 259-315, Heft 3, 1969.

MUELLER, K. : The Swiss banking secret - From a legal view. International and comparative law quarterly 18 : 360-377, April 1969.

DUTOIT, B. : L'avenir possible du rattachement à la loi nationale en droit international privé suisse. Schweizerisches Jahrbuch für internationales Recht 26 : 41-64, 1969-1970.

SYRIA

Le statut personnel des non-musulmans. Al-Mouhamoune 31 : 35-135, février-mars 1966.
Suite d'articles; Texte en arabe.

EL-HAKIM, J. : Les atteintes mortelles sans intention de causer la mort en droit syrien et libanais. Proche-Orient, Etudes juridiques : 41-71, janvier-avril 1967.

CHEBATH, F. : Le statut personnel des non-musulmans en Syrie et au Liban - Etude comparée. Proche-Orient, Etudes juridiques : 4-7, janvier-avril 1967.
Texte en arabe avec résumé en français.

KAYALL, N. : L'arbitrage dans la législation syrienne. Al-Kanoun (Syria) 18 : 41-65, mars 1967.

ANTAKI, R. : La question du statut personnel en Syrie. Proche-Orient, Etudes juridiques : 1-12, janvier-avril 1968.

ABBOUD, A. : L'aval des effets de commerce. Proche-Orient; études juridiques : 345-460, juillet-décembre 1969.
Comparaison entre le droit syrien et le droit français.

Constitution provisoire de la République arabe syrienne, 1er mai 1969. Documentation française, Notes et études documentaires : 1-11, no. 3621, 22 septembre 1969.

TAIWAN

KIRKHAM, D.B. : The international legal status of Formosa. The Canadian yearbook of international law. Annuaire canadien de droit international 6 : 144-163, 1968.

NING, W.Y.F. : Due process and the Sino-American Status of forces agreement. American journal of comparative law 17 : 94-115, no. 1, 1969.
Presence of U.S. troops in Taiwan.

TANZANIA

READ, J.S. : Minimum sentences in Tanzania. Journal of African law 9 : 20-39, spring 1965.

BEIDELMAN, T.O. : Intertribal tensions in some local government courts in colonial Tanganyika. Journal of African law 10 : 118-130, summer 1966.

RABL, K. : Constitutional development and law of the United Republic of Tanzania. Jahrbuch des öffentlichen Rechts der Gegenwart 16 : 567-609, 1967.
Text of the interim constitution, 1965, pp. 610-637.

Tanzanie, loi sur le droit d'auteur de 1966. Droit d'auteur 81 : 40-45, février 1968.

SAWYER, G.F.A. : Discriminatory restrictions on private dispositions of land in Tanganyika - A second look. Journal of African law 13 : 2-27, spring 1969.

GROHS, G. : Traditionalismus und Sozialismis im tansanischen Strafrecht. Verfassung und Recht in Ubersee 2 : 449-455, 4. Quartal 1969.

DIAS, C. : Tanzanian nationalizations, 1967-1970. Cornell international law journal 4 : 59-79, fall 1970.

THAILAND

Thailand's legal system, bar association and legal profession. Foreign affairs bulletin (Thailand) 4 : 1189-1208, June-July 1965.

Constitution du royaume de Thaïlande, promulguée le 21 juin 1968. Informations constitutionnelles et parlementaires 19 : 159-188, octobre 1968.

DARLING, F.C. : The evolution of law in Thailand. Review of politics 32 : 197-218, April 1970.

TOGO

Constitution de la République togolaise, mai 1963. Documentation française, Notes et études documentaires : 25-34, no. 3175, 26 mars 1965.

TRINIDAD and TOBAGO

WOODING, W. : Law reform necessary in Trinidad and Tobago. Canadian bar journal 9 : 292-298, August 1966.

TUNISIA

BENATTAR, R. : La filiation dans le code de statut personnel tunisien. Revue tunisienne de droit : 25-29, 1963-1965.

Le système judiciaire tunisien. Maghreb : 26-30, septembre-octobre 1966.

SILVERA, V. : L'organisation judiciaire tunisienne. Documentation française, Notes et études documentaires : 27-37, no. 3331, 28 octobre 1966.

SNOUSSI, M. : Les droits de l'homme en Tunisie dix ans après l'indépendance. Association des auditeurs et anciens auditeurs de l'Académie de droit international de La Haye, Annuaire 36 : 141-149, 1966.

STRASCHNOV, G. : La loi tunisienne sur le droit d'auteur. Droit d'auteur 80 : 79-83, avril 1967.

LAGRANGE, E. de : Le législateur tunisien et ses interprètes. Revue tunisienne de droit : 11-24, 1968.

BENATTAR, R. : Les conflits de juridictions en matière de divorce - La compétence judiciaire générale des juridictions tunisiennes et les effets internationaux des jugements étrangers. Revue tunisienne de droit : 25-42, 1968.

BENATTAR, R. : L'évolution récente du droit international privé tunisien en matière de divorce. Revue critique de droit international privé 58 : 17-52, janvier-mars 1969.

ABDALLAH, R. : Du Secrétariat d'Etat à la présidence au Premier ministère. Revue tunisienne de droit : 69-97, 1969-1970.

CHARFI, M. : Les conditions de forme du mariage en droit tunisien. Revue tunisienne de droit : 11-37, 1969-1970.

MABROUK, M. : Sur la responsabilité de la puissance publique tunisienne. Revue tunisienne de droit : 139-183, 1969-1970.

GANSKE, J. : Der (west) deutsch-tunesische Rechtshilfe-und Vollstreckungsvertrag in Zivil- und Handelssachen vom 19-7.1966. Aussenwirtschaftsdienst des Betriebs-Beraters 16 : 145-156, April 1970.

LADHARI, M. : La révision de l'article 51 de la constitution tunisienne du 1er juin 1959. Revue juridique et politique - Indépendance et coopération 24 : 307-334, avril-juin 1970.
Problème de la succession du président de la République.

TURKEY

Constitución de Turquia, 9.VII. 1961. Informacíon jurídica (Spain) : 3-47, mayo-junio 1965.
Text in Spanish.

SEVIG, V.R. : L'élection de for en droit international privé turc. Annales de la Faculté de droit d'Istanbul 15 : 115-142, nos. 21-22, 1965.

MIMAROGLU, S.K. : Les modes de fondation des sociétés anonymes selon le droit commercial turc - Etude de droit comparé turc et suisse, Revue de droit international et de droit comparé 44 : 221-237, no. 4, 1967.

ERMAN, S. : Los delitos militares en el derecho turco. Revista española de derecho militar : 57-76, enero-junio 1967.

SAVCI, B. : Dokunulmazlik konusunda. Anayasa Mahkemesinin yeri ve rolü. Siyasal bilgiler fakültesi dergisi (Ankara) 22 : 73-81, Haziran 1967.

BILGE, A.S. : Türk hukukuna göre milletlerarasi andlaşmalarin akti. Siyasal bilgiler fakültesi dergisi (Ankara) 22 : 97-149, Haziran 1967.

UNAT, I. : Türk vatandaşliğindan koğulanlar miras hakkindan yoksun mudur? Siyasal bilgiler fakültesi dergisi (Ankara) 20 : 179-226, Eylül 1965.

YÜCEL, M-T. : Suçtan zarar gören kisinin Korunmasi. Forum 20 : 14-15, 1 Ekim 1967.

KUBALI, H.N. : Les traits dominants de la constitution de la seconde République turque. Revue internationale de droit comparé 17 : 855-872, octobre-décembre 1965.

YÜCEL, M.T. : Ceza adaleti, cezanin tayini sorunu (To be contd.). Forum 20 : 10-11, 15 Kasim 1967.

IMRE, Z. : La responsabilité civile provenant des choses dangereuses en droit privé turc. Annales de la Faculté de droit d'Istanbul 18 : 1-64, nos. 29-32, 1968.

Loi relative à la liberté de réunion et à la liberté de faire des marches de manifestation. Annales de la Faculté de droit d'Istanbul 18 : 367-376, nos. 29-32, 1968.

DURAN, L. : Loi sur le Conseil d'Etat. Annales de la Faculté de droit d'Istanbul 18 : 445-454, nos. 29-32, 1968.
Texte de la loi pp. 455-521.

BERKIN, N. : Parteivernehmung und Parteivorweisungspflicht im modernen türkischen Zivilprozessrecht. Annales de la Faculté de droit d'Istanbul 19 : 69-80, nos. 33-35, 1969.

Code de la presse. Annales de la Faculté de droit d'Istanbul 19 : 157-170, nos. 33-35, 1969.

Loi sur les fondations. Annales de la Faculté de droit d'Istanbul 19 : 184-192, nos. 33-35, 1969.

UGANDA

SHARMA, B.S. : The constitution of Uganda. Journal of the parliaments of the Comonwealth 46 : 171-176, April 1965.

MORRIS, H.F. : Uganda - Changes in the structure and jurisdiction of the courts and in the criminal law they administer. Journal of African law 9 : 65-73, spring 1965.

MORRIS, H.F. : The Uganda constitution, April 1966. Journal of African law 10 : 112-117, summer 1966.

MORRIS, H.F. : Two early surveys of native courts in Uganda. Journal of African law 11 : 159-174, autumn 1967.

UNITED ARAB REPUBLIC

ROBERT, J. : L'Egypte moderne et ses constitutions. Revue du droit public et de la science politique en France et à l'étranger 81 : 856-911, septembre-octobre 1965.
Statuts de l'Union socialiste arabe pp. 912-924; Proclamation constitutionnelle de la R.A.U., 23 mars 1964, pp. 925-941.

CHEHATA, C. : Les survivances musulmanes dans la codification du droit civil égyptien. Revue internationale de droit comparé 17 : 839-853, octobre-décembre 1965.

SOROUR, A.F. : A propos de l'application de la loi pénale dans le temps, la règle de l'unanimité dans la condamnation en RAU. Revue de science criminelle et de droit pénal comparé 21 : 821-825, octobre-décembre 1966.

SALAM, M.A. : Les aspects sociaux du nouveau projet de code pénal de la République arabe unie. Revue de science criminelle et de droit pénal comparé 22 : 101-125, janvier-mars 1967.

YOUNES, A. : L'oeuvre créatrice de la Cour de cassation de la République arabe unie. Revue internationale de droit comparé 19 : 363-372, avril-juin 1967.

MOSTAFA, M. : Les nouvelles tendances du projet de code pénal de la R.A.U. (A suivre). Proche-Orient, Etudes juridiques : 579-592, mai-août 1967.
Texte en arabe avec résumé en français pp. 341-346.

RIAD, F.A.M. : Le conflit de compétence en matière de nationalité en République arabe unie. Proche-Orient, Etudes juridiques : ... janvier-avril 1968.
Text en arabe avec résumé en français pp. 51-52.

EL-MIKAYIS, A.W. : Internationales und interreligiöses Personen-, Familien- und Erbrecht in der Vereinigten Arabischen Republik. Rabels Zeitschrift für ausländisches und internationales Privatrecht 33 : 517-543, Heft 3, 1969.

ABDALLA, E. : La philosophie du législateur égyptien en matière de conflit des lois. Egypte contemporaine 61 : 29-59, avril 1970.

HASSAN, S.O. : Emergency powers of the executive in the United Arab Republic. Cornell international law journal 3 : 45-62, winte4 1970.

ABBAS, H. : Lettre de la République arabe unie (sur la propriété industrielle). La Propriété industrielle 86 : 405-411, décembre 1970.

U.S.S.

REDLICH, N. : The Supreme court, 1833 term - Foreword : The Constitution, "A rule for the government of courts, as well as of the legislature". New York university law review 40 : 1-11, January 1965.

MANLEY, J.F. : The US civil rights act of 1964. Contemporary review 206 : 10-13, January 1965.

ABT, J.J. : La Cour suprême des Etats-Unis et les libertés publiques. Revue de droit contemporain 12 : 105-120, no. 1, 1965.

MARCUS-HELMONS, S. : L'expropriation, pouvoir souverain du Gouvernement fédéral des Etats-Unis d'Amérique. Revue de droit internationalet de droit comparé 42 : 41-72, nos. 1-2, 1965.

MILLER, A.S. : On the choice of major premises in Supreme court opinions. Journal of public law 14 : 251-275, no. 2, 1965.

Racial discrimination and the duty of fair representation. Columbia law review 65 : 273-287, February 1965.

FLEISCHER, A. : Federal corporation law - An assessment. Harvard law review 78 : 1146-1179, April 1965.

WAGNER, W.J. : Le droit à l'intimité aux Etats-Unis. Revue internationale de droit comparé 17 : 365-376, avril-juin 1965.

HINDELL, K. : Civil rights breaks the cloture barrier. Political quarterly 36 : 142-153, April-June 1965.

Symposium on the Warren commission report. New York university law review 40 : 403-524, May 1965.
Assassination of J.F. Kennedy.

PETERSON, C.H. : Some observations on provisional relief in American law. American journal of comparative law 14 : 266-281, spring 1965.

UTTON, A.E. : Nigeria and the United States - Some constitutional comparisons. Journal of African law 9 : 40-59, spring 1965.

WITHERSPOON, J.P. : Civil rights policy in the federal system - Proposals for a better use of administrative process. Yale law journal 74 : 1171-1244, June 1965.

FRANKLIN, M. : A précis of the American law of contract for foreign civilians. Tulane law review 39 : 635-686, June 1965.

Federal civil action againts private individuals for crimes involving civil rights. Yale law journal 74 : 1463-1471, July 1965.

POWER, R.W. : Wills - A primer of interpretation and construction. Iowa law review 51 : 75-106, fall 1965.

FRIENDLY, H.J. : The bill of rights as a code of criminal procedure. California law review 53 : 929-956, October 1965.

MEITUS, A.C., and MIETUS, N.J. : Criminal abortion, a failure of law or a challenge to society? American bar association journal 51 : 924-928, October 1965.

Proposed constitutional amendment abolishing electoral college and making other changes in election of President and Vice-President, by the Committee on federal legislation. Record of the Association of the bar of the City of New York 20 : 503-517, October 1965.

The uniform commercial code. Howard law journal 11 : 1-148, winter 1965.
A symposium.

MILLER, A.S. : On the need for impact analysis of Supreme court decision. Georgetown law journal 53 : 365-401, winter 1965.

OAKS, D.H. : Habeas corpus in the states, 1776-1865. University of Chicago law review 32 : 243-288, winter 1965.

FEERICK, J.D. : Proposed amendment on presidential inability and vice-presidential vacancy. American bar association journal 51 : 915-917, October 1965.

SCHWENK, E.H. : Zehn Jahre umwälzender Entscheidungen des Obersten Gerichts der Vereinigten Staaten von Amerika. Juristenzeitung 20 : 672-677, 5. November 1965.

MUELLER, G.O.E. : Uniformisation des droits de l'accusé dans la procédure pénale américaine. Revue internationale de police criminelle 20 : 250-257, novembre 1965.

WALTON, J. : Photocopying and the law. Library association record 67 : 397-403, November 1965.

Symposium on the"Griswold" case and the right of privacy. Michigan law review 64 : 197-288, December 1965.

AĆIMOVIĆ, M.M. : Conceptions of culpability in contemporary American criminal law. Louisiana law review 26 : 28-55, December 1965.

LEVIE, J.H. : Trade usage and custom under the common law and the Uniform commercial code. New York university law review 40 : 1101-1117, December 1965.

AIKIN, C. : Impact of the death of an American president on the exercise of executive power. Jahrbuch des öffentlichen Rechts der Gegenwart 14 : 45-55, 1965.

Power of U.S. congress to punish for contempt. Journal of parliamentary information (India) 11 : 41-47, 1965.

WELBORN, D.M. : Presidents, regulatory commissioners and regulatory policy. Journal of public law 15 : 3-29, no. 1, 1966.

La constitution des Etats-Unis d'Amérique. Documentation française, Notes et études documentaires : 1-19, no. 3267, 25 février 1966.
Comprend les articles additionnels et amendements votés jusqu'en 1965.

NATIONAL LAW - COUNTRIES

The uniform commercial code. Louisiana law review 26 : 189-316, February 1966.
Series of articles.

SCHARPF, F.W. : Judicial review and the political question - A functional analysis. Yale law journal 75 : 517-597, March 1966.

MENTSCHIKOFF, S. : The uniform commercial code. Rabels Zeitschrift für ausländisches und internationales Privatrecht 30 : 403-413, Heft 3, 1966.
See also pp. 414-433.

FELLER, P.B., and GOTTING, K.L. : The second amendment - A second look. Northwestern university law review 61 : 46-70, March-April 1966.

COLLINS, D.G. : Arbitration and the uniform commercial code. Arbitration journal 21 : 193-214, no. 4, 1966.

Theories of federalism and civil rights. Yale law journal 75 : 1007-1052, May 1966.

BEANEY, W.M. : The right to privacy and American law. Law and contemporary problems 31 : 253-271, spring 1966.

GOLDFARB, R.L. : Three conscientious objectors. American bar association journal 52 : 564-567, June 1966.

WRIGHT, A.L. : The effect of the fourth amendment on arrests without a warrant. Louisiana law review 26 : 789-802, June 1966.

KALVEN, H., and ZEISEL, H. : The American jury and the death penalty. University of Chicago law review 33 : 769-781, summer 1966.

COHN, S.L. : The new federal rules of civil procedure. Georgetown law journal 54 : 1204-1257, summer 1966.

MUTIGNON, P. : La loi fédérale du 6 août 1965 relative à la discrimination raciale en matière de droit public et de la science politique en France et à l'étranger 82 : 732-758, juillet-août 1966.

KAPLAN, J. : Equal justice in an unequal world, equality for the Negro - The problem of special treatment. Northwestern university law review 61 : 363-410, July-August 1966.

MUELLER, G.O.W. : Bibliography of local practice books on criminal law and procedure. Law library journal 59 : 295-299, August 1966.

MUTIGNON, P. : Le problème noir aux Etats-Unis depuis le Civil rights act du 2 juillet. Revue internationale de droit comparé 18 : 669-699, juillet-septembre 1966.

The conscientious objector and the first amendment - There but for the grace of God... University of Chicago law review 34 : 79-105, autumn 1966.

A symposium on the Supreme court and the police, 1966. Journal of criminal law, criminology and police science 57 : 237-311, September 1966.
Northwestern university School of law, Chicago, April 1966.

COLLINS, D.G. : Arbitration and the uniform commercial code. New York university law review 41 : 736-756, October 1966.

QUICK, C.W. : Constitutional rights in the Juvenile court. Howard law journal 12 : 76-109, winter 1966.

LOWNDES, C.L.B., and STEPHENS, R.B. : Identification of property subject to the federal estate tax. Michigan law review 65 : 105-144, November 1966.

DUKE, S. : Prosecutions for attempts to evade income tax - A discordant view of a procedural hybrid. Yale law journal 76 : 1-76, November 1966.

ISRAELS, C.L., and GUTTMAN, E. : The transfer agent and the uniform commercial code. Banking law journal 83 : 941-961, November 1966.

The Supreme court, 1965 term. Harvard law review 80 : 91-272, November 1966.

HASTINGS, J.S. : The Criminal justice act of 1964. Journal of criminal law, criminology and police science 57 : 426-429, December 1966.

KATZ, M. : The Supreme court and the States - An inquiry into Mapp v. Ohio in North Carolina - The model, the study and the implications. North Carolina law review 45 : 119-151, December 1966.

FRATCHER, W.F. : Toward uniform succession legislation. New York university law review 41 : 1037-1092, December 1966.

HENDERSON, E.G. : The background of the seventh amendment. Harvard law review 80 : 289-337, December 1966.
Civil procedure.

AIKIN, C. : The question of executive primacy - Thoughts on American experiences. Jahrbuch des öffentlichen Rechts der Gegenwart 15 : 1-8, 1966.

PYE, A.D. : American criminal procedure from a comparative viewpoint. The Indian year book of international affairs 15-16 : 300-327, 1966-1967.

LUINI del RUSSO, A. : L'oeuvre jurisprudentielle de la Cour suprême des Etats-Unis en matière d'égalité raciale. Revue belge de droit international 3 : 84-101, no. 1, 1967.

FARNSWORTH, E.A. : Documentary drafts under the uniform commercial code. Business lawyer 22 : 479-492, January 1967.

RUDER, D.S. : Corporate disclosures required by the federal securities laws - The codification implications of "Texas Gulf sulphur". Northwestern university law review 61 : 872-906, January-February 1967.

The civil rights and civil liberties decisions of the United States Supreme court for the 1965-1966 term. Revista jurídica de la Universidad de Puerto Rico 36 : 255-309, núm. 2, 1967.

BERNSTEIN, M.C. : The impact of the uniform commercial code upon arbitration - Revolutionary overthrow or peaceful existence? Arbitration journal 22 : 65-92, no. 2, 1967.

BENNETT, D.E. : The 1966 code of criminal procedure. Louisiana law review 27 : 175-230, February 1967.

BLACKBURN, O.M. : Warranties under the uniform commercial code. Arbitration journal 22 : 173-181, no. 3, 1967.

NATIONAL LAW - COUNTRIES

LÓPEZ-REY, M. : La reforma penal en Puerto Rico. Revista jurídica de la Universidad de Puerto Rico 36 : 419-510, núm. 3, 1967.

The United States Court of claims - A symposium. Georgetown law journal 55 : 393-553, 373-737, December 1966, March 1967.

LEVY, J.T. : Congressional power over the appellate jurisdiction of the Supreme court - A reappraisal. Intramural law review (New York) 22 : 178-207, Marxh 1967.

Electing the President - Recommendations of the American bar association's commission on electoral college reform. American bar association journal 53 : 219-224, March 1967.

BERNSTEIN, M.C. : The impact of the uniform commercial code upon arbitration - Revolutionary overthrow or peaceful coexistence? New York university law review 42 : 8-33, March 1967.

WHELAN, J.W., and DUNIGAN, T.L. : Government contracts - Apparent authority and estoppel. Georgetown law journal 55 : 830-849, April 1967.

Spying and slandering - An absolute privilege for the CIA agent? Columbia law review 67 : 752-772, April 1967.

Symposium on uniform commercial code. Michigan law review 65 : 1275-1488, May 1967.

GIANNELLA, D.A. : Religious liberty, nonestablishment, and doctrinal development. Harvard law review 80 : 1381-1431, May 1967.
First of series of articles.

UNDERWOOD, R.C. : The Fifth amendment and the lawyer. Northwestern university law review 62 : 129-136, May-June 1967.

ABRAMS, G.H. : Constitutional limitations on detention for investigation. Iowa law review 52 : 1093-1119, June 1967.

HILL, A. : The law-making power of the federal courts - Constitutional preemption. Columbia law review 67 : 1024-1081, June 1967.

WINTER, R.K. : Improving the economic status of negroes through laws against discrimination. A reply to Professor Sovern. University of Chicago law review 34 : 817-855, summer 1967.

ROBINSON, C.D. : Le droit du prévenu au silence et son droit à être assisté par un défenseur au cours de la phase préjudiciaire en Allemagne et aux Etats-Unis d'Amérique. Revue de science criminelle et de droit pénal comparé 22 : 567-618, juillet-septembre 1967.

BRAUCHER, R. : The law of contract in the uniform commercial code. Rabels Zeitschrift für ausländisches und internationales Privatrecht 31 : 589-605, Heft 4, 1967.

BRAEMER, R.J. : Recent developments in government contract law. Business lawyer 22 : 1057-1073, July 1967.

HARTLEY, T.C. : Bigamy in the conflict of laws. International and comparative law quarterly 16 : 680-703, July 1967.

LESHER, R.S. : The non-profit corporation - A neglected stepchild comes of age. Business lawyer 22 : 951-973, July 1967.

BARTHOLOMEW, P.C. : The Supreme court of the United States, 1956-1966. American bar association journal 53 : 729-731, August 1967.

LELEUX, P. : Corporation law in the United States and in the E.E.C. - Some comments on the present situation and future prospects. Common market law review 5 : 133-176, September 1967.

CARROLL, W.A. : The constitution, the Supreme court, and religion. American political science review 61 : 657-674, September 1967.

SUTTON, K.C.T. : The uniform commercial code and the law of contract. Sydney law review 5 : 398-424, October 1967.

GOULD, W.B. : Employment security, seniority and race - The role of title VII of the Civil rights act of 1964. Howard law journal 13 : 1-50, winter 1967.

CLARK, T.C. : Federal courts in the United States - Their work and administration. Australian law journal 41 : 251-260, 30 November 1967.

Freedom of information - The statute and the regulations. Georgetown law journal 56 : 18-57, November 1967.

LEIBOWITZ, A.H. : The applicability of federal law to the Commonwealth of Puetro Rico. Georgetown law journal 56 : 219-271, December 1967.

BYSE, C., and FIOCCA, J.V. : Section 1361 of the Mandamus and venue act of 1962 and "nonstatutory" judicial review of federal administrative action. Harvard law review 81 : 308-355, December 1967.

SANTA-PINTER, J.J. : Aviso de desatención en el derecho puertorriqueño de los instrumentos negociables. Revista de la Facultad de derecho (Caracas) : 19-29, núm. 35, 1967.

BURGESS, H. : The mental defective and the law. Intramural law review (New York) 23 : 115-134, January 1968.

WILNER, I. : Civil appeals - Are they useful in the administration of justice? Georgetown law journal 56 : 417-450, January 1968.

SCHWARTZ, H. : The legitimation of electronic eavesdropping - The politics of "law and order". Michigan law review 67 : 455-510, January 1969.

LELEUX, P. : Le droit des sociétés aux Etats-Unis et dans la C.E.E. - Perspectives de leur évolution. Revue trimestrielle de droit européen 4 : 50-91, janvier-mars 1968.

Threatening the president - Protected dissenter or potential assassin. Georgetown law journal 57 : 553-572, February 1969.

STRONG, F.R. : The persistent doctrine of "constitutional fact". North Carolina law review 46: 223-283, February 1968.

LEVY, L.W. : The right against self-incrimination - History and judicial history. Political science quarterly 84 : 1-29, March 1969.

NATIONAL LAW - COUNTRIES

ZIFF, H.L. : Recent abortion law reforms, or much ado about nothing. Journal of criminal law, criminology and police science 60 : 3-23, March 1969.

Must a Supreme court justice refuse to answer senators' questions? Yale law journal 78 : 696-712, March 1969.

ROBISON, J.B., and WALDMAN, L. : The civil rights and civil liberties decisions of the United States Supreme court for the 1966-1967 term. Revista jurídica de la Universidad de Puerto Rico 37 : 435-525, núm. 3, 1968.

Symposium on the Article V - Convention process. Michigan law review 66 : 837-1016, March 1968.

The "new" thirteenth amendment - A preliminary analysis. Harvard law review 82 : 1294-1321, April 1969.

MATHIOT, A. : La Cour suprême des Etats-Unis à la fin de l'administration Johnson. Revue française de science politique 19 : 261-285, avril 1969.

The Indian bill of rights and the constitutional status of tribal governments. Harvard law review 82 : 1343-1373, April 1969.

LEGH-JONES, P.N. : Products liability - Consumer protection in America. Cambridge law journal 27 : 54-80, April 1969.

TREECE, J.M. : American law analogues of the author's "moral right". American journal of comparative law 16 : 487-506, no. 4, 1968.

Human rights symposium. University of Pennsylvania law review 116 : 967-1117, April 1968.

BENNETT, J.V., and MATTHEWS, A.R. : The dilemma of mental disability and the criminal law. American bar association journal 54 : 467-471, May 1968.

AIKIN, C. : The role of dissenting opinions in American courts. Politico 33 : 262-269, giugno 1968.

NIMMER, M.B. : The right to speak from "Times" to "Times" - First amendment theory applied to libel and misapplied to privacy. California law review 56 : 935-967, August 1968.

SADLER, A.M., and SADLER, B.L. : Transplantation and the law - The need for organized sensitivity. Georgetown law journal 57 : 5-54, October 1968.

KOVARSKY, I. : Testing and the Civil rights act. Howard law review 15 : 227-249, winter 1969.

DORSEN, N. : The American aid on racial discrimination. Public law : 304-324, winter 1968.

On the justifications for civil commitment. University of Pennsylvania law review 117 : 75-96, November 1968.

Title II of the Omnibus crime control act - A study in constitutional conflict. Georgetown law journal 57 : 438-460, November 1968.

FELDMAN, F. : New protection for the art collector - Warranties, opinions and disclaimers. Record of the Association of the bar of the City of New York 23 : 661-668, December 1968.

WECHSLER, H. : Codification of criminal law in the United States - The model penal code. Columbia law review 68 : 1425-1456, December 1968.

Symposium, the Warren court. Michigan law review 67 : 219-358, December 1968.

MELADY, R.P., et MELADY, M.B. : Histoire de l'intérêt des Etats-Unis pour les droits de l'homme. Justice dans le monde 10 : 173-187, décembre 1968.

MASON, A.T. : The American Supreme court under fire. Jahrbuch des öffentlichen Rechts der Gegenwart 17 : 395-406, 1968.

Constitutional law and civil rights. Annual survey of American law : 155-186, 1968/69.

KURLAND, P.B. : Toward a political Supreme court. University of Chicago law review 37 : 19-46, no. 1, 1969.

POSNER, R.A. : The Federal trade commission. University of Chicago law review 37 : 47-89, no. 1, 1969.

KERR, J.R. : Constitutional rights, tribal justice, and the American Indian. Journal of public law 18 : 311-338, no. 2, 1969.

HOWARD, J.W. : Adjudication considered as a process of conflict resolution - A variation on separation of powers. Journal of public law 18 : 338-370, no. 2, 1969.

ROBISON, J.B., and COLEMAN, B. : The civil rights and civil liberties decisions of the United States Supreme court for the 1967-1968 term. Revista jurídica de la Universidad de Puerto Rico 38 : 211-320, núm. 2, 1969.
A summary and analysis.

Compulsory removal of cadaver organs. Columbia law review 69 : 693-705, April 1969.

Progress in family life. Annals of the American academy of political and social science : ix-xiii, 1-144, no. 383, May 1969.
United States; Series of articles.

FOSTER, H.H. : Divorce law reform - The choice for the States. State government 42 : 112-119, spring 1969.

"Jones v. Mayer" - The thirteenth amendment and the federal anti-discrimination laws. Columbia law review 69 : 1019-1056, June 1969.

FRIEDMAN, L. : Conscription and the constitution - The original understanding. Michigan law review 67 : 1493-1552, June 1969.

KURLAND, P.B. :, The Constitution and the tenure of federal judges - Some notes from history. University of Chicago law review 36 : 665-698, summer 1969.

MEHREN, A.T. von : Conflict of laws in a federal system - Some perspectives. International and comparative law quarterly 18 : 681-688, July 1969.

VLACHOS, G.S. : Aspects juridiques de l'intervention économique de l'Etat aux Etats-Unis. Revue du droit public et de la science politique en France et à l'étranger 85 : 587-620, juillet-août 1969.

NATIONAL LAW - COUNTRIES

Legislative politics and the criminal law. Northwestern university law review 64 : 277-358, July-August 1969.

CARLSON, R.L. : Jailing the innocent - The plight of the material witness. Iowa law review 55 : 1-25, October 1969.

MARTÍNEZ IRIZARRY, D. : El principio de inscripción y el principio de legitimación en Puerto Rico. Revista jurídica de la Universidad de Puerto Rico 38 : 193-210, núm. 2, 1969.

GARFIELD, F.R. : Pre-induction judicial review. California law review 57 : 948-994, October 1969.

MARSHALL, R. : Group action in the pursuit of justice. New York university law review 44 : 661-672, October 1969.

ZAMIR, I. : Administrative control of administrative action. California law review 57 : 866-905, October 1969.

REESE, W.L. M. : Recent developments in torts choice-of-law thinking in the United States. Columbia journal of transnational law 8 : 181-195, winter 1969.

MANDEL, K.A. : Toward state and municipal liability in damages for denial of racial equal protection. California law review 57 : 1142-1181, November 1969.

HILL, A. : Constitutional remedies. Columbia law review 69 : 1109-1161, November 1969.

MICHELMAN, F.I. : On protecting the poor through the Fourteenth amendment. Harvard law review 83 : 7-59, November 1969.

"Shapiro v. Thompson" - Travel, welfare and the Constitution. New York university law review 44 : 989-1013, November 1969.

Extraordinary majority voting requirements. Georgetown law journal 58 : 411-426, November 1969.

Constitutional rights and administrative investigations - Suggested limitations on the inquisitorial powers of the federal agencies. Georgetown law journal 58 : 345-368, November 1969.

REDLICH, N., and FEINBERG, K.R. : Individual conscience and the selective conscientious objector - The right not to kill. New York university law review 44 : 875-900, November 1969.

AVERILL, L.H. : Choice-of-law problems raised by sister-state judgments and the full-faith-and-credit mandate. Northwestern university law review 64 : 686-703, November-December 1969.

LOUISELL, D.W. : The procurement of organs for transplanting. Northwestern university law review 64 : 607-627, November-December 1969.

Mandatory "cy pres" and the racially restrictive charitable trust. Columbia law review 69 : 1478-1495, December 1969.

GREENE, R.J. : Hybrid state law in the federal courts. Harvard law review 83 : 289-326, December 1969.

Libel and the corporate plaintiff. Columbia law review 69 : 1496-1513, December 1969.

JOHNSON, F.M. : Civil disobedience and the law. Tulane law review 44 : 1-13, December 1969.

Symposium - Arbitration and antitrust. New York university law review 44 : 1069-1100, December 1969.

CLARK, J.M. : Guidelines for the free exercise clause. Harvard law review 83 : 327-365, December 1969.

AIKIN, C. : The United States Supreme court - The judicial dissent. Jahrbuch des öffentlichen Rechts der Gegenwart 18 : 467-474, 1969.

GELLHORN, W. : Protection of the citizen in American administrative procedures (excluding judicial review). Jahrbuch des öffentlichen Rechts der Gegenwart 18 : 539-577, 1969.

Defiance of unlawful authority. Harvard law review 83 : 626-647, January 1970.

CRAMTON, R.C. : Nonstatutory review of federal administrative action - The need for statutory reform of sovereign immunity, subject matter jurisdiction, and parties defendant. Michigan law review 68 : 387-470, January 1970.

LOSS, L. : The fiduciary concept as applied to trading by corporate "insiders" in the United States. Modern law review 33 : 34-52, January 1970.

MONAGHAN, H.P. : First amendment "due process". Harvard law review 83 : 518-551, January 1970.

SAX, J.L. : The public trust doctrine in natural resource law - Effective judicial intervention. Michigan law review 68 : 471-566, January 1970.

TECLAFF, L.A. : The coastal zone - Control over encroachments into the tidewaters. Journal of maritime law and commerce 1 : 241-290, January 1970.

WHITE, W.S., and GREENSPAR, R.S., : Standing to object to search and seizure. University of Pennsylvania law review 118 : 333-366, January 1970.

WADLINGTON, W. : Artificial insemination - The dangers of a poorly kept secret. Northwestern university law review 64 : 777-807, January-February 1970.

ROBINSON, G.O. : The making of administrative policy - Another look at rulemaking and adjudication and administrative procedure reform. University of Pennsylvania law review 118 : 485-539, February 1970.
See also pp. 540-611.

Antitrust enforcement against organized crime. Columbia law review 70 : 307-336, February 1970.

KATZ, L.R. : Gideon's trumpet, mournful and muffled. Iowa law review 55 : 523-569, February 1970.
Right to counsel in state felony prosecutions.

Dissenting servicemen and the First amendment. Georgetown law journal 58 : 534-568, February 1970.

LEVINSON, L.H. : Toward principles of public law. Journal of public law 19 : 327-369, no. 2, 1970.

CLARK, T.C. : Objectives for American justice. Journal of public law 19 : 169-178, no. 2, 1970.

Secret files - Legitimate police activity or unconstitutional restraint on dissent? Georgetown law journal 58 : 569-590, February 1970.

POWER, P.F. : On civil disobedience in recent American democratic thought. American political science review 64 : 35-47, March 1970.

Developments in the law - Federal habeas corpus. Harvard law review 83 : 1038-1280, March 1970.

ERICSON, R., and SNOW, D.R. : The Indian battle for self-determination. California law review 58 : 445-490, March 1970.

Extraordinary majority requirements and the equal protection clause. Columbia law review 70 : 486-503, March 1970.

The public trust in tidal areas - A sometimes submerged traditional doctrine. Yale law journal 79 : 762-789, March 1970.

ELLIS, D.D. : Vox populi v. suprema lex - A comment on the testimonial of the Fifth amendment. Iowa law review 55 : 829-863, April 1970.

KATZENBACH, N. de B. : Protest, politics and the First amendment. Tulane law review 44 : 439-451, April 1970.

SCALIA, A. : Sovereign immunity and nonstatutory review of federal administrative action - Some conclusions from the public-lands cases. Michigan law review 68 : 867-924, April 1970.

SIVE, D. : Some thoughts of an environment lawyer in the wilderness of administrative law. Columbia law review 70 : 612-651, April 1970.

CAHN, E.S., and CAHN, J.C. : Power to the people or the profession? - The public interest in public interest law. Yale law journal 79 : 1005-1048, May 1970.
See also pp. 1049-1152.

MOLTENO, D.B. : The "flexibility" of a "rigid" constitution. South African law journal 87 : 204-233, May 1970.

NATHANSON, N.L. : Freedom of association and the quest for internal security - Conspiracy from Dennis to Dr. Spock. Northwestern university law review 65 : 153-192, May-June 1970.

ELY, J.H. : Legislative and administrative motivation in constitutional law. The Yale law journal 79 : 1207-1341, June 1970.

Legislative purpose and federal constitutional adjudication. Harvard law review 83 : 1887-1903, June 1970.

TATE, A. : Civilian methodology in Louisiana. Tulane law review 44 : 673-680, June 1970.

The role and rule(s) of law in contemporary America. The Antioch review 30 : 151-239, summer 1970.

OAKS, D.H. : Studying the exclusionary rule in search and seizure. University of Chicago law review 37 : 665-757, summer 1970.

BLASI, V. : Prior restraints on demonstrations. Michigan law review 68 : 1481-1574, August 1970.

The impact of state constitutional right to bear arms provisions on state gun control legislation. The University of Chicago law review 38 : 185-210, fall 1970.

MILLER, P.E. : Preventive detention - A guide to the eradication of individual rights. Howard law journal 16 : 1-18, fall 1970.

Products liability - Economic analysis and the law - A symposium. The University of Chicago law review 38 : 1-141, fall 1970.

AMSTERDAM, A.G. : The Supreme court and the rights of suspects in criminal cases. New York university law review 45 : 785-815, October 1970.

Corporate assaults on the privacy of outside critics. The Georgetown law journal 59 : 190-208, October 1970.

KAUFMAN, I.R. : The medium, the message and the First amendment. New York university law review 45 : 761-784, October 1970.

HAZARD, G.C. : Law reforming in the anti-poverty effort. University of Chicago law review 37 : winter 1970.

FISH, P.G. : The Circuit councils - Rusty hinges of federal judicial administration. University of Chicago law review 37 : 203-241, winter 1970.

TIGAR, M.E. : Waiver of constitutional rights. Disquiet in the citadel. Harvard law review 84 : 1-28, November 1970.

A new approach to judicial review of conscientious objector claims. New York university law review 45 : 1037-1074, November 1970.

FARNSWORTH, E.A. : Legal remedies for breach of contract. Columbia law review 70 : 1145-1216, November 1970.

Conscientious objectors - Recent developments and a new appraisal. Columbia law review 70 : 1426-1441, December 1970.

KAUPER, P.G. Judicial review and "strict construction" of the Constitution - President Nixon and the Supreme court of the United States, Zeitschrift für ausländisches öffentliches Recht und Völkerrecht 30 : 631-645, Dezember 1970.

MARTIN, P.L. : The application clause of Article five (of the U.S. constitution). Political science quarterly 85 : 616-628, December 1970.

U.S.A.
(Patents, Trade-marks, Copyright)

McGEE, J.S. : Patent exploitation - Some economic and legal problems. Journal of law and economics 9 : 135-162, October 1966.

SELSKY, I.B. : Biography and the copyright law. Intramural law review (New York) 22 : 208-229, March 1967.

WOODWARD, W.R. : Changes in the patent system recommended by the President's commission. Federal bar journal 27 : 189-227, summer 1967.

NATIONAL LAW - COUNTRIES

DOBKIN, J.A. : Arbitrability of patent disputes under the U.S. arbitration act. Arbitration journal 23 : 1-17, no. 1, 1968.

SURRENCY, E.C. : The new Copyright act - Its implications for law libraries. Law library journal 61 : 16-19, February 1968.

Copyright law revision - A symposium. Iowa law review 53 : 805-890, February 1968.

RINGER, B.A. : The role of the United States in international copyright - Past, present and future. Georgetown law journal 56 : 1050-1079, June 1968.

BRADERMAN, E.M. : International patent cooperation. What it means for the United States. Department of State bulletin (United States) 59 : 143-147, 5 August 1968.

CLAPP, V.W. : The copyright dilemma - A librarian's view. Library quarterly 38 : 352-387, October 1968.

Can Copyright law respond to the new technology? Law library journal 61 : 387-420, November 1968. A panel.

GOLDSTEIN, P. : Federal system ordering of the copyright interest. Columbia law review 69 : 49-92, January 1969.

Symposium on copyright and patent law in honour of Professor Walter Julius Derenberg. New York university law review 44 : 447-588, May 1969.

STEDMAN, J.C. : The employed inventor, the public interest, and horse and buggy law in the space age. New York university law review 45 : 1-32, March 1970.

GAMBRELL, J.B. : Mechanical and design inventions - Double patenting rejections and the doctrine of election. New York university law review 45 : 441-486, May 1970.

GOLDSTEIN, P. : Copyright and the Frist amendment. Columbia law review 70 : 983-1057, June 1970.

U.S.A.
(International law, Aliens, Nationality)

EVANS, A.E. : The new extradition treaties of the United States. American journal of international law 59 : 351-362, April 1965.

SIMMONDS, K.R. : The Sabbatino case and the act of state doctrine. International and comparative law quarterly 14 : 452-492, April 1965.

Constitutional limitations on the power of Congress to confer citizenship by naturalization. Iowa law review 50 : 1093-1113, summer 1965.

FRIEDMANN, W. : United States policy and the crisis of international law. American journal of international law 59 : 857-871, October 1965.

LAY, S.H. : The United States-Soviet consular convention. American journal of international law 59 : 876-891, October 1965.

GORDON, C. : The citizen and the state - Power of Congress to expatriate American citizens. Georgetown law journal 53 : 315-364, winter 1965.

JUILLARD, P. : L'arrêt Banco nacional de Cuba c/ Sabbatino. Annuaire français de droit international 11 : 205-229, 1965.

COLLINS, L.A., and ETRA, A. : Policy, politics, international law and the United States investment guaranty program. Columbia journal of transnational law 4 : 240-296, no. 2, 1966.

A symposium on the restatement of the law (second) - Foreign relations law of the United States. New York university law review 41 : 1-147, March 1966.

NIMMER, M.B. : Le droit d'auteur aux Etats-Unis face à la Convention de Berne - Les implications contenues dans leurs projets de revision respectifs. Droit d'auteur 79 : 102-133, avril 1966.

RIGGS, J.H. : Termination of treaties by the executive without congressional approval - The case of the Warsaw convention. Journal of air law and commerce 32 : 526-534, autumn 1966.

GREBLER, L. : The naturalization of Mexican immigrants in the United States. International migration review 1 : 17-31, fall 1966.

SCOLES, E.F. : Interstate and international distinctions in conflict of laws in the United States. California law review 54 : 1599-1623, October 1966.

MADDEN, M.S., and COHN, S.L. : The legal status and problems of the American abroad. Annals of the American academy of political and social science : 119-131, no. 368, November 1966.

MILLER, A.R. : Federal rule 44.1 and the "fact" approach to determining foreign law - Death knell for a die-hard doctrine. Michigan law review 65 : 615-750, February 1967.

RODGERS, R.S. : The capacity of states of the Union to conclude international agreements - The background and some recent developments. American journal of international law 61 : 1021-1028, October 1967.

STOEL, T.B. : The enforcement of foreign non-criminal penal and revenue judgments in England and the United States. International and comparative law quarterly 16 : 663-679, July 1967.

HARRIS, L.J. : Diplomatic privileges and immunities - A new regime is soon to be adopted by the United States. American journal of international law 62 : 98-113, January 1968.

STONE, O.L. : United States legislation relating to the continental shelf. International and comparative law quarterly 17 : 103-117, January 1968.

MEZGER, E. : Vers la consécration aux Etats-Unis de l'autonomie de la clause compromissoire dans l'arbitrage international. Revue critique de droit international privé 57 : 25-45, janvier-mars 1968.

DEUTSCH, E.P. : International covenants on human rights and our constitutional policy. American bar association journal 54 : 238-245, March 1968.

Congress, the President, and the power to commit forces to combat. Harvard law review 81 : 1771-1805, June 1968.

NATIONAL LAW - COUNTRIES

Extraterritorial application of the Securities exchange act of 1934. Columbia law review 69 : 94-111, January 1969.

NING, W.Y.F. : Due process and the Sino-American Status of forces agreement. American journal of comparative law 17 : 94-115, no. 1, 1969.
Presence of U.S. troops in Taiwan.

HEADRICK, W.C. : El sistema normativo vigente en las aguas territoriales de los Estados Unidos y de Puerto Rico. Revista jurídica de la Universidad de Puerto Rico 38 : 329-349, núm. 2, 1969.

REMBAR, C. : Xenophilia in Congress - Ad interim copyright and the manufacturing clause. Columbia law review 69 : 770-796, May 1969.

Due process challenge to the Korean Status of forces agreement. Georgetown law journal 57 : 1097-1107, May 1969.

Citizenship - Statute making retention of citizenship of person born outside the United States conditional upon completing five years' residence in the United States held to violate due process clause of the Fifth amendment. New York university law review 44 : 824-835, October 1969.

LOWENFELD, A.F. : Claims against foreign states - A proposal for reform of United States law. New York university law review 44 : 901-938, November 1969.

DU FRESNE, E., and DU FRESNE, W. : Foreign migrant workers vs. sovereign immunity - Poverty law in a transnational context. Columbia journal of transnational law 8 : 196-219, winter 1969.

FREDMAN, H.S. : The offenses clause - Congress' international penal power. Columbia journal of transnational law 8 : 279-309, winter 1969.

MILLS, L.R. : Pendent jurisdiction and extraterritorial service under the federal securities laws. Columbia law review 70 : 423-446, March 1970.

BILDER, R.B. : East-West trade boycotts - A study in private, labor union, state, and local interference with foreign policy. University of Pennsylvania law review 118 : 841-938, May 1970.

KNOLL, A.P. : International executive agreements - Their constitutionality, scope and effect. Case Western Reserve journal of international law 2 : 94-119, spring 1970.

POLIER, J.W. : Western European sovereignty and American export and trade controls. The Columbia journal of transnational law 9 : 109-133, spring 1970.

FELLER, P.B. : U.S. customs aspects of seabed operations. Law and policy in international business 2 : 402-442, summer 1970.
See also pp. 443-478.

DOBRIANSKY, L.E. : The Genocide convention. The Ukrainian quarterly 26 : 237-250, autumn-winter 1970.
The question of its ratification by the U.S. Senate.

COHEN, H. : Nonenforcement of foreign tax laws and the act of state doctrine - A conflict in judicial foreign policy. Harvard international law journal 11 : 1-36, winter 1970.

HANEY, W. : Deportation and the right to counsel. Harvard international law journal 11 : 177-190, winter 1970.

FREEDMAN, J.O. : Administrative procedure and the control of foreign direct investment. University of Pennsylvania law review 119 : November 1970.

U.S.S.R.

FLEISHITS, E.A., and MAKOVSKII, A.L. : The RSFSR civil code. Soviet law and government 3 : 3-11, winter 1964/65.

KALLISTRATOVA, R.F. : The code of civil procedure of the Russian Federation. Soviet law and government 3 : 12-19, winter 1964/65.

SCHROEDER, F.C. : Das neue Bürgerliche Gesetzbuch der Russischen Sowjetrepublik. Recht in Ost und West 9 : 1-9, 49-58, 15. Januar, 15. März 1965.

SVERDLOV, G.M. : Considérations statistiques sur le divorce en Union Soviétique. Documentation française, Chroniques étrangères ; U.R.S.S. : 20-23, janvier 1965.

PRIANICHNIKOV, E. : L'activité législative en U.R.S.S. Revue de droit contemporain 12 : 137-158, no. 1, 1965.

FRIDIEFF, M. : Les nouveaux codes civils et de procédure civile de la R.S.F.S.R. Revue internationale de droit comparé 17 : 103-105, janvier-mars 1965.

O poni͡atii, predmete i istochnikakh gosudarstvennogo prava. Pravovedenie (U.S.S.R.) 9 : 28-33, no. 1, 1965.

CHEREPAKHIN, B.B. : Okhrana prav grazhdan v grazhdanskom kodekse RSFSR 1964 goda. Vestnik Leningradskogo universiteta, Serii͡a ékonomiki, filosofii i prava 20 : 78-86, vyp.2, 1965.

Law and legality in the USSR. Problems of communism (United States) 14 : 1-111, March-April 1965.
Series of articles; See also pp. 136-144.

SAMOSHCHENKO, I.S. : Nekotorye voprosy kodifikat͡sii zakonodatel'stva Soi͡uza SSR i soi͡uznakh respublik. Pravovedenie (U.S.S.R.) 9 : 34-42, no. 4, 1965.

JAKOBS, O.W. : Das Eigentum als Rechtsinstitut im deutschen und sowjetischen Recht. Rabels Zeitschrift für ausländisches und internationales Privatrecht 29 : 694-724, Heft 4, 1965.

MALEVILLE, G. : Sur quelques principes du droit soviétique. Revue socialiste : 483-501, mai 1965.

FERÓN, B. : L'homme soviétique devant la justice. Etudes (Paris) : 826-838, juin 1965.

NAPOLITANO, T. : Outline of modern Soviet criminal law. International commission of jurists, Journal 6 : 54-81, summer 1965.

POPOVA, V., and KHOLI͡AVCHENKO, A. : Rol' Sovetov v obespechenii sot͡sialisticheskoĭ zakonnosti i okhrane prav grazhdan. Sovety deputatov trudi͡ashchikhsi͡a : 8-19, no. 1, I͡anvar' 1966.

NATIONAL LAW - COUNTRIES

SANTORO, A. : Significato politico e valore tecnico del nuevo codice penale sovietico. Scuola positiva 71 : 3-24, fasc. 1, 1966.

BARINOVA, T.A. : Sovetskoe ugolovnoe pravo i sotsialisticheskaia ékonomiki. Vestnik Leningradskogo universiteta, Seriia ékonomiki, filosofii i prava 21 : 84-90, vyp. 2, 1966.
Influence of criminal law on economic relations; Summary in English.

IVANOV, O.V. : Zashchita sub''ektivnykh prav i problema istiny v grazhdanskom protsesse. Vestnik Moskovskogo universiteta, Seriia : pravo 21 : 15-25, no. 2, mart-aprel'1966.

Obespechenie svobody lichnosti i okhrany grazhdan SSSR. Sotsialisticheskaia zakonnost' (U.S.S.R.) : 40-47, no. 4, aprel' 1966.

MIRONENKO, Y. : The evolution of Soviet family law. Institute for the study of the USSR, Bulletin 13 : 33-40, May 1966.

DAVLETSHIN, T. : The legal position of the state-owned industrial enterprise in the USSR. Institute for the study of the USSR, Bulletin 13 : 3-9, May 1966.

GRIBANOV, V.P. : Printsipy osushchestvleniia grazhdanskikh prav. Vestnik Moskovskogo universiteta, Seriia : pravo 21 : 10-23, no. 3, mai-iiun' 1966.

FLEISHITS, E.A. : Nuevos códigos civiles de las Repúblicas Federadas Soviéticas. Boletín del Instituto de derecho comparado de México 19 : 5525-39, mayo-diciembre 1966.

RUDENKO, R. : XXIII s'ezd KPSS i zadachi organov prokuratury. Sotsialisticheskaia zakonnost' (U.S.S.R.) : 3-12, no. 6, iiun' 1966.

GELLHORN, W. : Review of administrative acts in the Soviet Union. Columbia law review 66 : 1051-1079, June 1966.

SINGH, B. : Le droit, instrument politique - L'exemple soviétique. Justice dans le monde 7 : 435-448, juin 1966.

Two aspects of pre-trial procedure in Eastern Europe - TAYLOR, P.B. : The role of the investigator in Soviet criminal procedure - CSIZMÁS, M. : Remand in custody in Hungary. International commission of jurists, Journal 7 : 20-54, summer 1966.

BILINSKY, A. : Die Grundzüge des sowjetrussischen Zivilprozesses. Recht in Ost und West 10 : 156-163, 15. Juli 1966.

ANASHKIN, G.Z. : O zadachakh i tendentsiiakh razvitiia sotsialisticheskogo pravosudiia. Vestnik Moskovskogo universiteta, Seriia: pravo 21 : 3-15, no. 4, iiul'-avgust 1966.

Decrees seek to stregthen public law and order. Current digest of the Soviet press 18 : 4-8, 17 August 1966.

SADIKOV, O.N. : Nekotorye polozheniia teorii sovetskogo grazhdanskogo prava. Sovetskoe gosudarstvo i pravo 36 : 15-24, no. 9, sentiabr' 1966.

Usilenie bor'by s prestupnost'iu i zadachi prokuratury. Sotsialisticheskaia zakonnost' (U.S.S.R.) : 3-10, no. 9, sentiabr' 1966.

The new civil code of the R.S.F.S.R. - YOFFE, O. S., and TOLSTOY, Y.K. : A Soviet view - KIRALFY, A.K.R. : A Western view. International and comparative law quarterly 15 : 1090-1134, October 1966.

ORLOVSKII, P.E. : K voprosu o razdel'nom i obschem imushchestve suprugov po sovetskomu semeinomu pravu. Vestnik Moskovskogo universiteta, Seriia: pravo 21 : 3-12, no. 6, noiabr'-dekabr' 1966.

ROGGEMANN, H. : Das sowjetische Zivilverfahrensrecht. Osteuropa-Recht 12 : 229-280, Dezember 1966.
First of a series of articles.

MAGGS, P.B., and WINKLER, K.F. : Libel in the Soviet press - The new civil remedy in theory and practice. Tulane law review 41 : 55-74, December 1966.

L'évolution du droit dans les différents pays - Union soviétique. Annuaire de législation française et étrangère 15 : 525-537, 1966.

MEDER, W. : Grundzüge der sowjetischen Staatstheorie. Jahrbuch des öffentlichen Rechts der Gegenwart 15 : 9-54, 1966.

BEGAUX-FRANCOTTE, C. : Les règles de la responsabilité civile dans la législation soviétique actuelle. Centre d'étude des pays de l'Est (et) Centre national pour l'étude des Etats de l'Est, Bulletin 8 : 69-93, no. 1, 1967.
Bibliographie pp. 93-95.

SAVITSKII, V. : Rol' praktiki v razvitii i sovershenstvovanii demokraticheskikh osnov sovetskogo pravosudiia. Sotsialisticheskaia zakonnost'(U.S.S.R.) : 22-28, no. 1, ianvar' 1967.

FARBER, I.E. : Prava cheloveka, grazhdanina i litsa v sotsialisticheskom obshchestve. Pravovedenie (U.S.S.R.) : 39-46, no. 1, ianvar-fevral' 1967.

VASILENKOV, P.T. : Pravovoe polozhenie i kompetentsiia Prezidiuma Verkhovnogo soveta SSSR. Vestnik Moskovskogo universiteta, Seriia : pravo 22 : 12-22, no. 1, ianvar'-fevral' 1967.

Les brevets en U.R.S.S. Revue de droit contemporain 14 : 66-76, no. 2, 1967.

CRESPI-REGHIZZI, G. : La comparazione giuridica nel' l'URSS e la sovietologia giuridica nell'Occidente. Est, Rivista trimestrale di studi sui paesi dell'Est : 132-143, no. 2, 1967.

BILINSKY, A. : Stellung der Parteien und Verfahren im sowjetrussischen Zivilprozess. Recht in Ost und West 11 : 49-58, 15. März 1967.

CRESPI-REGHIZZI, G. : La Corte suprema dell' URSS - Spunti da una recente modifica al suo regolamento. Est, Rivista trimestrale di studi sui paesi dell'Est : 198-214, no. 4, 1967.

GALPERIN, I.M. : Responsibility of recidivists under the penal legislation of the USSR and Union republics. McGill law journal 13 : 679-682, no. 4, 1967.

LUNTS, L.S. : Puti vospolneniia probelov sovetskogo zakonpdatel'stva po voprosam mezhdunarodnogo grazhdanskogo protsessa. Sovetskoe gosudarstvo i pravo : 55-64, no. 5, mai 1967.

NATIONAL LAW - COUNTRIES

DENISOV, A. : Some theoretical problems of the constitutional structure of the Soviet state - On the thirtieth anniversary of the USSR constitution of 1936. Soviet law and government 5 : 20-25, spring 1967.

TOWE, T.E. : Fundamental rights in the Soviet Union - A comparative approach. University of Pennsylvania law review 115 : 1251-1274, June 1967.

PIONTKOWSKY, A.A. : Les problèmes essentiels de la théorie de l'infraction d'après le droit pénal soviétique. Revue internationale de droit pénal 38 : 143-155, 1er-2e trimestre 1967.

WESTEN, K. : Probleme der sowjetischen Rechtswissenschaft. Juristenzeitung 22 : 391-398, 7. Juli 1967.

IVANOV, ÎU. A. : Nektorye voprosy del'neĭshego sovershenstvovaniîa sovetskogo ugolovno-protsessual'nogo zakonodatel'stva. Vestnik Moskovskogo universiteta, Seriîa: pravo 22 : 26-34, no. 4, iîul'-avgust 1967.

KURYLEV, S.V. : The application of Soviet law. Soviet law and government 6 : 21-28, summer 1967.

PANIUGIN, V. : Court practice in inheritance cases. Soviet law and government 6 : 37-42, summer 1967.

SHAFIR, G.M. : The right to defense in Soviet criminal procedure and possibilities for expanding it. Soviet law and government 6 : 29-36, summer 1967.

Zavorot'ko, P.P. : Nové zákonodarstvo USSR o spôsobe výkonu súdnych rozhodnutí. Právny obzor 50 : 707-712, číslo 8, 1967.

SHCHELOKOV, N. : Glavnoe-preduprezhdenie pravonarushenii. Sotsialisticheskaia zakonnost (U.S.S.R.) : 7-16, no. 8, avgust 1967.

SHEBANOV, A.F. : Razvitie formy sovetskogo prava. Sovetskoe gosudarstvo i pravo : 22-31, no. 9, sentîabr' 1967.

GRISHAEV, P. I. : Sovetskoe ugolovnoe pravo - pravo novogo, vysshego tipa. Pravovedenie (U.S.S.R.) : 105-112, no. 5, sentîabr'-oktîabr' 1967.

JOHNSON, E.L. : Matrimonial property in Soviet law. International and comparative law quarterly 16 : 1106-1134, October 1967.

RUDDEN, B. : Soviet tort law. New York university law review 42 : 583-630, October 1967.

MAKOVSKIĬ, A. : Rol' V.I. Lenina v kodifikatsii sovetskogo grazhdanskogo zakonidatel'stva. Sovetskaîa îustitsiîa (U.S.S.R.): 4-5, no. 19, oktîabr' 1967.

GORKIN, A. : Pîatidesîatiletie Sovietskoĭ vlasti sotsialisticheskoe pravosudie. Sotsialistischeskaîa zakonnost' (U.S.S.R.) : 15-23, no. 11, noîabr' 1967.

Loi de l'U.R.S.S. sur le service militaire obligatoire, 12 octobre 1967. Documentation française, Chroniques étrangères; U.R.S.S. : 18-31, novembre 1967.

GORKIN, A. : Usytuowanie Sądu najwyższego ZSRR w systemie radziekich organów pánstwowych. Nowe prawo 23 : 1399-1408, listopad 1967.

KONSTANTINOV, I.F. : K voprosu o pravovom regulirovanii narodnogo kontrolîa. Pravovedenie (U.S.S.R.) : 34-39, no. 6, noîabr'-dekabr' 1967.

ROZENBERG, IA. A. : Pravosob'' ektonost' i predstavitel'stvo obshchestvennosti v grazhdanskom protsesse. Pravovedenie (U.S.S.R.) : 58-64, no. 6, noiabr'-dekabr' 1967.

PIONTKOVSKIĬ, A.A. : O ponîatii ugolovnoĭ otvetstvennosti. Sovetskoe gosudarstvo i pravo : 40-48, no. 12, dekabr' 1967.

LEVITSKY, S.L. : The concept of civil defamation in the Soviet principles of civil legislation, 1961. Law in Eastern Europe : 15-65, no. 14, 1967. Index pp. 395-396.

RODITI, H.L. : Patent protection in the USSR and Eastern Europe. American review of East-West trade 1 : 12-18, January 1968.

BUTLER, W.E. : The legal regime of Russian territorial waters. American journal of international law 62 : 51-77, January 1968.

MANKHIN, V. M. : Pravovoe regulirovanie sovetskoĭ gosudarstvennoĭ sluzhby. Sovetskoe gosudarstvo i pravo : 33-40, no. 1, îanvar' 1968.

PFAFF, D.: Das Problem der Unterscheidung "Öffentliches und privates Recht" in der Entwicklung der Sowjetischen Rechtslehre. Zeitschrift für vergleichende Rechtswissenschaft 70 : 129-231, Nr. 1, 1968.

POPKOV, V.D. : Sovetskiĭ grazhdanin - pravovoĭ status i otvetstvennost'. Vestnik Moskovskogo universiteta, Seriîa: pravo 23 : 3-15, no. 1, îanvar'-fevral' 1968,

TCHKHIKVADZÉ, V.M. : L'évolution de la science juridique soviétique. Revue internationale de droit comparé 20 : 19-34, janvier-nars 1968.

DAVLETSHIN, T. : The vicissitudes of Soviet law. Analysis of current developments in the Soviet Union : 1-6, 19 Match 1968.

LUKASHEVA, E.A. : Sotsialisticheskaîa zakonnost' v sovremennyĭ period. Sovetskoe gosudarstvo i pravo : 3-12, no. 3, mart 1968.

GINSBURGS, G. : Judicial controls over administrative acts in the Soviet union - The current scene. Osteuropa-Recht 14 : 1-33, März 1968.

LOCKERETZ, S.W. : Legal professionnals and amateurs in the Soviet union - The People's court and the Comradely court. Columbia essays in international affairs: the dean's papers 4 : 126-149, 1968.

ERH-SOON TAY, A. : The law of inheritance in the new Russian civil code of 1964. International and comparative law quarterly 17 : 472-500, April 1968.

LESAGE, M. : Le Praesidium du Soviet suprême de l'U.R.S.S. Revue du droit public et de la science politique en France et à l'étranger 84 : 605-626, mai-juin 1968.

SCHRAMEYER, K. : Das sowjetische Warenzeichenrecht. Osteuropa-Recht 14 : 69-85, Juni 1968.

Les peines non privatives de liberté - PIONTKOVSKIJ, A.A. : Rapport sur le droit pénal soviétique - MAZADR, J. : Rapport sur le droit pénal français. Revue de science criminelle et de droit pénal comparé 23 : 585-601, juillet-septembre 1968.
1re rencontre juridique franco-soviétique, Paris, mars 1967.

JUKES, G. : Changes in Soviet conscription law. Australian outlook 22 : 204-217, August 1968.

BOGUSLAVSKII, M.M. : The purchase and sale of licenses in the USSR. Soviet law and government 7 : 46-53m fall 1968.

ORLOV, V.N., and ÉKIMOV, A.I. : TSel' v norme sovetskogo prava. Pravovedenie (U.S.S.R.) : 22-28, no. 5, sentiabr'-oktiabr' 1968.

HOLTZMANN, J.L. : Principes fondamentaux de la protection des inventions en Union soviétique. Documentation française, Notes et études documentaires : 1-25, no. 3527, 18 octobre 1968.

KAMINSKAIA, V.I. : Okhrana prav i zakonnykh interesov grazhdan v ugolovno-protsessual'nom prave. Sovetskoe gosudarstvo i pravo : 28-35, no. 10, oktiabr' 1968.
Safeguard of citizen's rights and legal interests in criminal procedure; Summary in English.

BARRY, D.D., and BERMAN, H.J. : The Soviet legal profession. Harvard law review 82 : 1-41, November 1968.

MELKUMOV, V.G. : Prokurorskoe pravo kak samostoiatel'naia otrasl' sovetskogo prava. Pravovedenie (U.S.S.R.) : 14-20, no. 6, noiabr'-dekabr. 1968.

CHERTKOV, V. : Vedenie advokatami sudebnykh del po sporam, vytekaiushchim iz avtorskogo prava. Sovetskaia iustitsiia (U.S.S.R.) : 11-13, no. 24, dekabr' 1968.

MIRONENKO, Y. : An extension of the powers of the Supreme court. Institute for the study of the USSR, Bulletin 15 : 23-29, December 1968.

PANCZUK, G. : Les droits de l'homme et l'Unio soviétique. Justice dans le monde 10 : 225-256, décembre 1968.

Principes de législation sur le régime de la terre de l'Union soviétique et des républiques fédérées. Centre d'étude des pays de l'Est et Centre national pour l'étude des Etats de l'Est, Revue 10 : 27-64, no. 1, 1969.

GORELIK, R. : Le droit d'auteur en U.R.S.S. Centre d'étude des pays de l'Est et Centre national pour l'étude des Etats de l'Est, Revue 10 : 19-29, no. 2, 1969.

WESTEN, K. : Die Rolle der Grundrechte im Sowjetstaat (To be contd.). Vereinte Nationen 17: 12-17, Februar 1969.

O sovershenstvovanii patentno-pravovykh uslug SSSR. Sovetskaia iustitsiia (U.S.S.R.) : 9-10, no. 3, fevral' 1969.

MAKAROV, A.N. : Kollisionsnormen in den "Grundlagen für die Zivilgesetzgebung der Sowjetunion und der Unionsrepubliken". Osteuropa-Recht 15 : 1-18, März 1969.

GORSHENEV, V.M. : Raznovidnosti protsessual'nykh norm v sovetskom prave. Pravovednie (U.S.S.R.) : 23-31, No. 2, mart-aprel' 1969.

PEÑARANDA LÓPEZ, A. : Autodeterminación y sucesión de Estados en la doctrina spviética. Revista española de derecho internacional 22 : 297-305, núm. 2, 1969.

GORELIK, R. : General study - Copyright in the U.S.S.R. Copyright bulletin, Unesco 3 : 32-37, no. 4, 1969.

ERH-SOON, A. : Principles of liability and the "source of increased danger" in the Soviet law of tort. International and comparative law quarterly 18 : 424-448, April 1969.

BARRY, D.D. : The USSR Supreme court - Recent developments. Soviet studies 20 : 511-522, April 1969.

GILLI, J.P. : Le régime juridique du sol urbain en Union soviétique. Revue internationale de droit comparé 21 : 353-371, avril-juin 1969.

ERSHOVA, N. : Rol' grazhdanskogo zakonodatel'stva v regulirovanii semeinykh otnoshenii. Sovetskaia iustitsiia (U.S.S.R.) : 4-5, no. 10, mai 1969.

POLENINA, S.V. : Analogiia v grazdanskom prave. Sovetskoe gosudarstvo i pravo : 29-36, no. 5, mai 1969.

Symposium on the study of Soviet law in the United States. Columbia law review 70 : 187-252, February 1970.
Columbia University, June 1969.

HASTRICH, A. : Volksrichter und Volksgerichte in der UdSSR, Osteuropa-Recht 15 : 121-142, Juni 1969.

Union des Républiques socialistes soviétiques - Dispositions concernant la formulation des demandes d'enregistrement des inventions, 28 juillet 1966. Propriété industrielle 85 : 171-179m juin 1969.

BILINSKY, A. : Die sozialistische juristische Person in der Rechtsordnung der UdSSR und Polens. Jahrbuch für Ostrecht 10 : 125-165, Juli 1969.

SOLTYSINSKI, S.J. : New forms of protection for intellectual property in the Soviet Union and Czechoslovakia. Modern law review 32 : 408-419, July 1969.

SANGIGLIO, C.G. : La teoria generale del diritto nell'l'U.R.S.S. Stato sociale 13 : 680-689, agosto 1969.

TIMAR, I. : Sovetsko-vengerskoe solashenie o vzaimnoi okhrane avtorskikh prav. Sovetskoe gosudarstvo y pravo : 93-95, no. 8, avgust 1969.

LEVIN, D.B. : Metodologiia sovetskoi nauki mezhdunarodnogo prava. Sovetskoe gosudarstvo i pravo : 59-66, no. 9, sentiabr' 1969.

EVSEEV, P.N. : Ispolnenie rechenii inostrannykh sudov na territorii Sovetskogo soiuza. Pravovedenie (U.S.S.R.) : 95-103, No. 5, sentiabr'-oktiabr'1969.

ZINO'EV, A.V. : O konstitut͡sionnom razgranichenii kompetent͡sii Soi͡uza SSR i soi͡uznykh respublik. Pravovedenie (U.S.S.R.) : 58-65, senti͡abr'-okti͡abr' 1969.

MADDOCK, C.S., and GRZYBOWSKI, K. : Law and communist reality in the Soviet Union. American bar association journal 55 : 938-942, October 1969.

MAKSAREV, Y.E. : Le rôle des inventions d'employés en URSS. Propriété industrielle 85 : 300-303, octobre 1969.

Sushchestvennye narusheniia ugolovno-protsessual'nogo zakona. Sovetskaia iustitsiia (U.S.S.R.) : 14-15, no. 20, oktiabrr' 1969.

NOCHVIN, D., and SHIRI͡AEV, I. : Sistematizat͡sii͡a zakonodatel'stva v organakh prokuratury. Sot͡sialisticheskai͡a zakonnost (U.S.S.R.) 46 : 22-26, no. 12, dekabr' 1969.

BEGAUX-FRANCOTTE, C. : La Prokurata soviétique (suite). Centre d'études des pays de l'Est et Centre national pour l'étude des Etats de l'Est. Revue 11 : 65-88, no. 2, 1970.
Bibliographie pp. 89-92.

NAGEL, H. : Das Revolutionäre im sowjetischen Zivilprozess. Svensk Juristtidning 55 : 177-197, mars 1970.

V.I. Lenin i sovetskoe pravo. Pravovedenie (U.S.S.R.) : 9-136, no.2, mart-aprel'1970.
Series of articles on Lenin and Soviet law; Summaries in English.

DENISOV, A.I. : Velichaĭshiĭ teoretik gosudarstva y prava. Vestnik Moskovskogo universiteta, Serii͡a: pravo 25 : 3-14, no. 2, mart-aprel' 1970.

GURVICH, M.A. : Obi͡azatel'nost i zakonnai͡a sila sudebnogo reshenii͡a. Sovetskoe godudarsvo i pravo : 37-45, no. 5, maĭ 1970.

Lo Stato e il diritto sovietico dopo Chruščev. Est, Rivista trimestrale di studi sui paesi dell'Est : 169-174, 30 giugno 1970.

SHKOL'NIKOV, A. : Rozhdenie zakona. Sovety deputatov trudi͡ashchikhsi͡a : 7-15, no. 6, ii͡un' 1970.

SCHMIDT, H.T. : Die Voraussetzungen für die Anordnung der Untersuchungshaft im sowjetischen Strafverfahren. Osteuropa-Recht 16 : 98-108, Juni 1970.

KUDRI͡AVTSEV, P. : Prokurir v sude pervoĭ instant͡sii. Sot͡sialisticheskai͡a zakonnost (U.S.S.R.) : 3-9, no. 7, ii͡ul'1970.

SCHMIDT, J. : Traits originaux du système soviétique de protection des inventions. Revue internationale de droit comparé 22 : 503-519, juillet-septembre 1970.

CHECHINA, N.A. : Normy sovetskogo grazhdanskogo prot͡sessual'nogo prava i normy morali. Pravovedenie (U.S.S.R.) : 68-74, no. 5, senti͡abr'-okti͡abr' 1970.
Soviet civil procedural law and morality; summary in English.

S.S.S.R.
(International law and Practice, Aliens and Naturalization)

BROVKA, I͡U. P. : Suverenitet i mezhdunarodnai͡a pravosub''ektnost' Belorusskoĭ Sot͡sialisticheskoĭ Respublik. Sovetskiĭ ezhegodnik mezhdunarodnogo prava - Soviet year-book of international law : 312-319, 1964-1965.

SMETS, P.F. : Les réserves aux conventions multilatérales - La conception soviétique. Centre d'étude des pays de l'Est (a) Centre national pour l'étude des Etats de l'Est, Bulletin 6 : 7-36, juin 1965.

GINSBURGS, G. : Inheritance by foreigners under Soviet law. Iowa law review 51 : 16-74, fall 1965.

LAY, S.H. : The United States-Soviet consular convention. American journal of international law 59 : 876-891, October 1965.

LISSITZYN, O.J. : Le droit international dans un monde divisé - L'Union soviétique et le droit international. Revue générale de droit international public 69 : 927-947, octobre-décembre 1965.

QUIGLEY, J.B. : The new Soviet approach to international law. Harvard international law club journal 7 : 1-32, winter 1965.

TOUSCOZ, J. : La notion de souveraineté effective dans la doctrine sovétique du droit international. Revue algérienne des sciences juridiques, politiques et économiques : 7-27, décembre 1965.

SHARMA, S.P. : Soviet view of peaceful coexistence and international law. Indian year book of international affairs 14 : 109-136, 1965.

GINSBURGS, G. : Soviet citizenship legislation and statelessness as a consequence of the conflict of nationality laws. International and comparative law quarterly 15 : 1-54, January 1966.

KHLESTOV, O.N. : Novoe polozhenie ob inostrannykh diplomaticheskikh i konsul'skikh predstavitel'stvakh. Sovetskoe gosudarstvo i pravo 36 : 30-38, no. 8, avgust 1966.

Statute concerning diplomatic and consular missions of foreign states on the territory of the Union of Soviet Socialist Republics. International legal materials, Current documentas 5 : 801-813, September 1966.

KHLESTOV, O.N. : The new state on foreign diplomatic and consular missions. Soviet law and government 5 : 51-58, fall 1966.

SCHULTZ, L. : Die sowjetische Konzeption der allgemeinen Grundsätze des Völkerrechts und deren Stellung in der sowjetische Rechts-Quellenlehre. Internationales Recht und Diplomatie : 11-27, 1966.

BLISHCHENKO, I., and PIRADOV, A. : The Soviet Union and diplomatic law. International affairs (Moscow) : 86-90, January 1967.

PEÑARANDA LÓPEZ, A. : Autodeterminación y sucesión de Estados en la doctrina jurid́ico-international soviética. Revista de estudios políticos : 79-88, enero-febrero 1967.

U.S.S.R. - BUTLER, W.E. : Soviet territorial waters. World affairs (Washington) 130 : 17-25, April-June 1967.

Convention between the Union of Soviet Socialist Republics and the People's Republic of Bulgaria concerning the prevention of dual nationality, signed at Sofia, 6 July 1967. International legal materials, Current documents 6 : 493-496, May-June 1967.

PENNAR, J. : Soviet nationality policy redefined. Analysis of current developments in the Soviet Union : 1-4, 20 June 1967.

BRACHT, H.W. : Die Haftung des Staates für Verletzungen des Völkerrechts in sowjetischer Sicht. Recht in Ost und West 11 : 154-164, 15. Juli 1967

RAMZAITSEV, D. : Principî fondamentali sull'arbitrato in materia di commercio estero nell-Unione Sovietica. Diritto negli scambi internazionali 7 : 1-14, marzo 1968.

TIMAR, I. : A magyar-szovjet szerzői egyezmenyről. Magyar jog és külföldi jogi szemle 15 : 129-132, március 1968.

PRZETACZNIK, F. : Principes du droit diplomatique et consulaire soviétique contemporain. Revue belge de droit international 4 : 397-415, no. 2, 1968.

GINSBURGS, G. : The Soviet Union and international cooperation in legal matters - The current phase, civil law. Iowa law review 53 : 1020-1073, April 1968.

FREEMAN, A.V. : Some aspects of Soviet influence on international law. American journal of international law 62 : 710-722, July 1968.

BUTLER, W.E. : The Soviet Union and the continental shelf. American journal of international law 63 : 103-107, January 1969.

LEFF, E.J. : The Foreign trade arbitration commission of the USSR and the West. Arbitration journal 24 : 1-34, no. 1, 1969.

HAFNER, G. : Die permanente Neutralität in der sowjetischen Völkerrechtslehre - Eine Analyse. Österreichische Zeitschrift für öffentliches Recht 19 : 215-258, Heft 2/3, 1969.

LOEBER, D.A. : Der hoheitlich gestalte Vertrag in sowjetischer Sicht. Recht in Ost und West 13 : 113-120, 15. Mai 1969.

DUTOIT, B. : Die friedliche Koexistenz in der heutigen sowjetischen Auffassung des Völkerrechts. Jahrbuch für Ostrecht 10 : 69-83, Juli 1969.

SHEVTSOV, V.S. : Sovetskoe grazhdanstvo i gosudarstvennyí suverenitet. Sovetskoe gosudarstvo i pravo : 39-47, no. 6, iiun' 1970.
Soviet citizenship and state sovereignty; Summary in English.

FRENZKE, D. : De-jure-, De-facto- und faktische Anerkennung in der Völkerrechtslehre der DDR und der UdSSR. Recht in Ost und West 14 : 181-190, 15. September 1970.

GINSBURGS, G. : The Soviet Union and international cooperation in legal matters - Criminal law, the current phase. International and comparative law quarterly 19 : 626, October 1970.

UPPER VOLTA

NIKYEMA, P. : Le projet de code du mariage et l'abandon du domicile conjugal en Haute-Volta. Revue juridique et politique - Indépendance et coopération 22 : 833-852, juillet-septembre 1968.

URUGUAY

Constitution de la République orientale de l'Uruguay. Documentation française, Notes et etudes documentaires : 1-38, no. 3426, 10 octobre 1967.
Entrée en vigueur le 15 février 1967.

GROS ESPIELL, H. : La integración económica de Latinamérica y la Constitución uruguaya. Verfassung und Recht in Übersee 2 : 55-64, 1. Quartal 1969.

BRUNO, J.L. : Las disposiciones transitorias y especiales en el derecho constitucional uruguayo. Revista de derecho, jurisprudencia y administración (Montevideo) 68 : 180-194, 17 diciembre 1969.

VATICAN STATE

NAVARRO VALLS, R. : Los representantes diplomáticos de la Santa Sede según la última legislacion canónica. Revista española de derecho internacional 23 : 91-97, núm. 1, 1970.

VENEZUELA

PARRA ARANGUREN, G. : La función de la reciprocidad en el sistema venezolano del exequatur. Revista de la Facultad de derecho (Caracas) : 39-119, 31, 1965.
Bibliography pp. 120-122.

BREWER-CARIAS, A.R., and PÉREZ OLIVARES, E. : El recurso contencioso-administrativo de interpretación en el sistema jurídico venezolano. Revista de la Facultad de derecho (Caracas) : 103-126, no. 32, 1965.

SANSO, B. : La conversión de la separación de cuerpos en divorcio. Revista de la Facultad de derecho (Caracas) : 127-133, no. 32, 1965.

Loi sur les mesures et son application - Venezuela. Organisation internationale de métrologie légale, Bulletin 7 : 13-24, juin 1966.

SANSÓ, B. : La repudiación de la herencia en el derecho venezolano. Revista de la Facultad de derecho (Caracas) : 133-155, no. 34, 1966.

CRISTÓBAL-MONTES, A. : La cesión de contrato en el derecho venezolano. Revista de la Facultad de derecho (Caracas) : 41-85, no. 36, 1967.

SANSO, B. : Exposición resumida sobre las disposiciones concernientes a las sociedades anónimas en Venezuela. Revista de la Facultad de derecho (Caracas) : 121-187, no. 39, 1968.

ARENAS CANDELO, O. : El delito de actos lascivos arbitrarios. Revista de la Facultad de derecho (Caracas) : 94-116, núm. 41, 1968.

KUMMEROW, G. : Noticias preliminar sobre los anteproyectos de unification de la obligaciones civiles y mercantiles en Venezuela. Boletín mexicana de derecho comparado 2 : 43-55, enero-abril 1969.

CARMONA, J. : Ante-proyecto de reforma del Código de comercio. Cámara de comercio de Caracas, Boletín 76 : 21937-21949, mayo 1969.

FRANCO GARCÍA, J.M. : La titulación jurídica de la propiedad y la reforma agraria venezolana. Boletín mexicano de derecho comparado 2 : 273-291, mayo-agosto 1969.

VIET-NAM

WESTERMAN, G.F., and McHUGH, J.L. : Reaching for the rule of law in South Vietnam. American bar association journal 53 : 159-164, February 1967.

Constitution of the Republic of Viet Nam. Jahrbuch des öffentlichen Rechts der Gegenwart 19 : 577-588, 1970.
Text, March 1967.

Constitution de la République du Vietnam, ler avril 1967. Informations constitutionnelles et parlementaires 18 : 134-157, juillet 1967.

Constitution de la République du Vietnam, ler avril 1967. Documentation française, Notes et études documentaires : 1-14, no. 3433, ler novembre 1967.

Aspects juridiques de la constitution du Gouvernement révolutionnaire provisoire du Sud Vietnam. Revue de droit contemporain 16 : 7-15, no. 1, 1969.

WEST INDIES

FORBES, U. : Subsidiary law-making process - Antigua, Dominica and St. Kitts, 1960-1968 - A critique. International and comparative law quarterly 18 : 533-558, July 1969.

YUGOSLAVIA

GJAKOVIĆ, D. : Savezni zakoni i njihova nadležnost. Zbornik Pravnog fakulteta u Zagrebu 15 : 14-25, broj 1-2, 1965.
Federal laws; Summary in French.

FINŽGAR, A. : Die grundlegenden Neuerungen des jugoslawischen Zivilrechts. Juristische Blätter 87 : 134-141, 13. März 1965.

BEKAVAC, S. : O Urebodavnim ovlastenjima i njihovu koristenju. Zbornik Pravnog fakulteta u Zagrebu 15 : 159-170, broj 3, 1965.
Government control in constitutional law; Summary in French.

LAZAREVIĆ, A. : Osvrt na ustnavna načela o sudovima Socijalističke federativne republike Jugoslavije. Arhiv za pravne i društvene nauke 52 : 194-211, broj 3-4, juli-decembar 1965.

LUKIĆ, R.D. : Društvena svojina i naše pravo. Arhiv za pravne i društvene nauke 52 : 167-182, broj 3-4, juli-decembar 1965.

SINGER, M. : O pojmu krivnje u krivičnom pravu. Naša zakonitost 19 : 391-404, rujan-listopad 1965.

ZLATARIC, B. : La nouvelle législation yougoslave concernant l'exécution des sanctions criminelles. Revue de science criminelle et de droit pénal comparé : 73-86, janvier-mars 1965.

GOLDSCHMIDT, R. : La teoría general de los usos mercantiles y los usos generales de comercio en Yugoslavia. Revista de la Facultad de derecho (Caracas) : 23-37, no. 31, 1965.

GELLHORN, W. : Citizens' grievances against administrative agencies - The Yugoslav approach. Michigan law review 64 : 385-420, January 1966.

BOSNIĆ, P. : Razvod braka s medunarodnim elementom u Jugoslaviji. Naša zakonitost 20 : 32-43, broj 1, siječanj-veljača 1966.

BLAGOJEVIĆ, B.T., and JOVIČIĆ, M. : The place and function of comparative law in Yugoslav jurisprudence. New Yugoslav law 17 : 26-40, January-December 1966.

BEITZKE, G. : Rechtsvergleichende Bemerkungen zur Anerkennung und Vollstreckung ausländischer zivilrechtlicher Entscheidungen in Jugoslawien. Rabels Zeitschrift für ausländisches und internationales Privatrecht 30 : 642-665, Heft 4, 1966.

BRNCIĆ, J. : Neki problemi pravosudnog sistema Jugoslavije. Arhiv za pravne i drustvene nauke 52 : 153-159, april-juni 1966.

FISK, W.M., and RUBINSTEIN, A.Z. : Yugoslavia's constitutional court. East Europe 15 : 24-28, July 1966.

STOYANOVITCH, K. : La nouvelle constitution yougoslave. Revue du droit public et de la science politique en France et à l'étranger 82 : 709-731, juillet-août 1966.
1963.

VENÉČEK, S. : Soudnictví v Socialistické federativní republice Jugislávii. Právník 106 : 40-50, číslo 1, 1967.

KATIČIĆ, N. : Načela revnopravnosti muža i žene i dobrobiti djeteta u jugoslavenskom medunarodnom porodičnom pravu. Jugoslovenska revija za medunarodno pravo 14 : 30-56, broj 1-3, 1967.
Equality of husband and wife and welfare of the child in family law; Summary in English.

JOVICIC, M. : Les rapports entre les organes représentatifs et les organes exécutifs notamment en Yougoslavie. Revue internationale des sciences administratives 33 : 130-138, no. 2, 1967.

MEICHSNER, V. : Der Zahlungsort bei Geldschulden nach jugoslawischem Recht. Osteuropa-Recht 13 : 81-88, Juni 1967.

ŽUPANIĆ, M. : Opći pojedinačni akti u ustavnosudskom postupku. Naša zakonitost 21 : 205-221, broj 3, svibanjlipanj 1967.

JONČIĆ, K.: Structure nationale et égalité des nationalités. Revue de la politique international (Belgrade) 18 : 21-24, no. 425, 20 décembre 1967.

Teze pravosudnog sistema, smjernice za unapredenje. Naša zakonitost 22 : 55-63, siječanj-veljača 1968.

GRUBIŠA, M. : Značenje novele zakonika o krivičnom postupku od 1967. godine i njezine osnove karakteristike. Zbornik Pravnog fakulteta u Zagrebu 18 : 122-145, broj 2, 1968.
Reform of criminal procedure; Summary in French.

NATIONAL LAW - COUNTRIES

DIMITRIJEVIĆ, V. : Verfassungsgerichtsbarkeit in Jugoslawien. Zeitschrift für ausländisches öffentliches Recht und Völkerrecht 28 : 170-196, März 1968.

GLOBEVNIK, J. : Savezno opšte zakonodavstvo i neki njegovi problemi. Arhiv za pravne i društvene nauke 55 : 147-160, broj 2, april-jun 1968.

JOVANOVIĆ, B. : Pet godina ustavnog sudstva. Arhiv za pravne i društvene nauke 54 : 315-324, broj 3, juli-septembar 1968.

BUDISAVLJEVIĆ, J. : Izmjene i dopune Zakona o eksproprijaciji i Zakon o odredivanju gradevinskog zemljišta. Naša zakonitost 22 : 345-353, rujan-listopad 1968.

VASILJEVIC, T. : Les nouveautés dans la procédure pénale yougoslave. Revue de droit pénal et de criminologie 49 : 308-314, janvier 1969.

DAMAŠKA, M. : Napomene o početku krivičnog postupka i početku primjene procesne norme. Zbornik Pravnog fakulteta u Zagrebu 19 : 21-35, br. 1, 1969.
Criminal procedure; Summary in English.

KOSOVAC, M. : Pred donošenjem zakona o izvršnom postupku. Naša zakonitost 23 : 1-15, siječanj-veljača 1969.

BAYER, V. : La réforme du code de procédure pénale yougoslave. Revue de science criminelle et de droit pénal comparé 24 : 79-97, janvier-mars 1969.

STOJANOVIĆ, M. : La nouvelle loi yougoslave sur le droit d'auteur. Revue de l'U.E.R. (Union européenne de radiodiffusion), Cahier B : 52-55, mars 1969.

TULLIO, L. : L'accordo italo-jugoslavo per la delimitazione della piattaforma continentale dell' Adriatico. Rivista de diritto della navigazione 35 : parte la, 300-319, no. 3-4, 1969.

PERAZIĆ, G. : La nouvelle loi sur la défense nationale. Revue de la politique internationale (Belgrade) 20 : 29-31, no. 454, 5 mars 1969.

DENKOVIČ, D. : Zachování zákonnosti a práva občanů v jugoslávském právu. Právník 108 : 330-342, čislo 5, 1969.

VASILJEVIC, T. : El procedimiento penal yugoslavo. Información jurídica (Spain) : 19-27, abril-junio 1969.

STOJANOVIĆ, D. : Das gesellschaftliche Eigentum in der jugoslawischen Doktrin und Rechtsprechung. Osteuropa-Recht 15 : 101-120, Juni 1969.

BULATOVIĆ, Ž. : Načelo legaliteta u krivičnom pravu. Pravni zbornik 18 : 35-57, broj 1-2, avgusta 1969.

KULIĆ, D. : The Constitutional Court of Yugoslavia. Jahrbuch des öffentlichen Rechts der Gegenwart 18 : 79-93, 1969.

ŽUPANIĆ, M. : Ustavni sudovi i pitanje praćenja pojava od interesa za ostvarivanje ustavnosti zakonitosti. Naša zakonitost 24 : 8-11, broj 1, siječanj-veljača 1970.

VILUS, J. : A projected civil code for Yugoslavia. International and comparative law quarterly 19 : 333-338, April 1970.

STATOVCI, E. : Učešće trećih osoba u parnici po albanskom Gradanskom parničnom kodeksu i jugoslavenskom. Zakonu o parničnom postupku. Naša zakonitost 24 : 108-118, broj 2, ožujak-travanj 1970.
ROMAC, A. : Vojno sudstvo i reforma našeg pravosudnog sistema. Naša zakonitost 24 : 170-181, broj 3, svibanj 1970.

LAZAREVIĆ, A.P. : Izvršilac testamenta i njegova funkcija. Naša zakonitost 23 : 265-274, srpanj-kolovoz 1969.

STOJANOVIĆ, D. : Das Privateigentum im jugoslawischen Recht. Osteuropa-Recht 16 : 170-182, September 1970.

DJURIŠIĆ, N. : Experience of the Constitutional court of Yugoslavia. Osteuropa-Recht 16 : 183-190, September 1970.
See also pp. 191-196.

KOZARČANIN, H., and LOVRIĆ, J. : Osnovni problemi upravnog spora - mesto u sistemu pravosuda. Naša zakonitost 23 : 441-472, studeni-prosinac 1969.

EUROPE
(Economic Community and EFTA)

ALEXANDER, W. : Questions préjudicielles - L'application récente de l'article 177 CEE par la cour de justice et par les juridictions nationales. Cahiers de droit européen : 47-58, no. 1, 1965.

DUMON, F. : L'afflux européen dans les droits et les institutions des Etats membres des Communautés européennes. Cahiers de droit européen : 10-44, no. 1, 1965.

BATINI, F., and PITTON, A. : Prospettive di unificazione della definizione di invalidità nell'ambito della Comunità economica europea. Previdenza sociale (Italy) 21 : 15-34, gennaio-febbraio 1965.

DUMON, F. : Conflits entre les normes résultant des traités ayant institué les Communautés européennes et celles des droits nationaux des Etats membres - Application des articles 85 et 86 du traité C.E.E. par les tribunaux nationaux. Revue internationale de droit comparé 17 : 21-52, janvier-mars 1965.

PELLICER VALERO, J.A. : Régimen jurídico de la actividad procesal en el ordenamiento de la Comunidades europeas. Boletín del Instituto de derecho comparado de México 18 : 65-87, enero-abril 1965.

MARCHAL, A. : Le problème de la supranationalité dans l'Europe des Six. Rivista internazionale di scienze economiche e commerciali 12 : 134-142, febbraio 1965.

GERVEN, W. van : Droit d'établissement. Cahiers de droit européen : 125-139, no. 2, 1965.
Dans le traité de Rome.

CATALANO, N. : Les voies de recours ouvertes aux personnes physiques ou morales contre les actes non réglementaires de la Commission C.E.E. Annuario di diritto
comparato e di studi legislativi 39 : 106-149, fasc. 2-3, 1965.

BÜLOW, A. : Vereinheitliches internationales Zivilprozessrecht in der Europäischen Wirtschaftsgemeinschaft. Rabels Zeitschrift für ausländisches und internationales Privatrecht 29 : 473-508, Heft 3, 1965.

NATIONAL LAW - COUNTRIES

PEPY, A. : Les questions préjudicielles dans les traités de Paris et de Rome et la jurisprudence de la Cour de justice des Communautés européennes. Cahiers de droit européen : 194-213, no. 3, 1965.
Premier article d'une série.

GOLSONG, H. : Action accomplie en 1964 par le Conseil de l'Europe dans le domaine du droit. Revue de droit international et de droit comparé 42 : 189-211, nos. 3-4, 1965.

MATSCHER, F. : Zur europäischen Integration auf dem Gebiet des Zivilprozessrechts. Juristische Blätter 87: 194-197, 10. April 1965.

CONARD, A.F. : Corporate fusion in the Common market. American journal of comparative law 14 : 573-602, no. 4, 1965-1966.

The legal programme of the Council of Europe. International and comparative law quarterly 14 : 646-653, April 1965.

RIESENFELD, S.A. : The decisions of the Court of Justice of the European communities, 1961-1963. American journal of international law 59 : 325-335, April 1965.

HOUIN, R. : Le groupement d'entreprises vu à l'échelle européenne - Rapport général présente au colloque de l'Association des juristes européens, Paris, 4 et 5 décembre 1964. Revue internationale de droit comparé 17 : 321-327, avril-juin 1965.

PAETOW, H. : EWG-Recht in der Anwaltspraxis. Monatsschrift für deutsches Recht 19 : 429-431, Juni 1965.

LAGRANGE, M. : The non-contractual liability of the Community in the E.C.S.C. (European coal and steel community) and in the E.E.C. (European economic community). Common market law review 3 : 10-36, June 1965.

ZAMPAGLIONE, G. : La fusione degli esecutivi nella prospettiva dell'integrazione europea. Comunità internazionale 20 : 297-313, aprile-luglio 1965.

LASSALLE, C. : Aspects de la fonction publique européenne. Revue générale de droit international public 69 : 682-741, juillet-septembre 1965.

EECKMAN, P. : L'application de l'article 85 du traité de Rome aux ententes étrangères à la C.E.E. mais causant des restrictions à la concurrence à l'intérieur du Marché commun. Revue critique de droit international privé 54 : 499-528, juillez-septembre 1965.

PELLICER VALERO, J.A. : La ententes de la C.E.E. ante el Tribunal de las Comunidades. Rivista jurídica de Cataluña 64 : 701-728, julio-septiembre 1965.

ASTOLFI, A. : La procedura secondo l'art. 177 del trattato istitutivo della Comunità secondo l'art.153-174, settembre 1965.
Bibliography pp. 174-177.

De PINNA, L.A. : Notifiable Common market transactions. Law journal 115 : 687-688, 15 October 1965.

BELLET, P. : L'élaboration d'une convention sur la reconnaissance des jugements dans le cadre du Marché commun. Journal du droit international 92 : 833-870, octobre-décembre 1965.

MEGRET, J. : La fusion des exécutifs des Communautés européennes. Annuaire français de droit international 11 : 692-709, 1965.

WIEBRINGHAUS, H. : Une nouvelle juridiction administrative en Europe, la Commission de recours du Conseil de l'Europe. Annuaire français de droit international 11 : 379-389, 1965.

FENELLI, N. : Il diritto comunitario e i diritto nazionali. Trasporti pubblici (Italy) 22 : 1372-1382, novembre 1965.

MATHIJSEN, P. : Some legal aspects of Euratom. Common market law review 3 : 326-343, December 1965.

MASHAW, J.L. : Federal issues in and about the jurisdiction of the Court of justice of the European communities. Tulane law review 40 : 21-56, December 1965.

BROWN, E.D. : International social law in Europe. Year book of world affairs 19 : 160-182, 1965.

PAPA, F.R. : The decision-making process in the European economic community. Columbia essays in international affairs : the dean's papers : 59-74, 1965.

LAGRANGE, M. : The Court of jsutice as a factor in European integration. American journal of comparative law 15 : 709-725, no. 4, 1966/1967.

WESER, M. : La libre circulation des jugements dans le Marché commun. Comité français de droit international privé. Travaux 27-30 : 353-377, 1966-1969.

NERI, S. : La giurisprudenza delle Corte di giustizia delle Comunità europee. Rivista di diritto internazionale 48, 49 : 416-427, 36-48, fasc. 3, 1965, fasc. 1, 1966.
1965.

ROSAUER, G. : L'orientamento della Commissione della Comunità economica europea in materia di contratti di esclusiva. Annuario di diritto comparato e di studi legislativi 40 : 43-65, fasc. 1, 1966.

TOMMASI di VIGNANO, A. : Inesistenza di un "ordinamento comunitario europeo". Annuario di diritto comparato e di studi legislativi 40 : 66-74, fasc. 1, 1966.

ERADES, L. : International law, European community law and municipal law of members states. International and comparative law quarterly 15 : 117-132, January 1966.

VIGNES, D. : Techniques employées et résultats atteints par la C.E.E. dans le domaine de l'unification du droit des Etats membres. Revue de droit international et de droit comparé 43 : 7-24, nos. 1-2, 1966.

DAMME, J. van : La mise en oeuvre des articles 85 et 86 du traité de Rome. Cahiers de droit européen : 35-51, no. 2, 1966.
Dispositions antitrust; Voir aussi pp. 52-58. Premier article d'une série.

VINCENT, F. : La présidence des assemblée européennes. Revue trimestrielle de droit européen 2 : 79-111, janvier-avril 1966.

NATIONAL LAW - COUNTRIES

LE TALLEC, G., et EHLERMANN, C.D. : La motivation des actes des Communautés européennes. Revue du Marché commun : 179-187, avril 1966.

BISCOTTINI, G. : Osservazioni sulla natura giuridica delle Comunità europee. Diritto internazionale 20 : parte 1a, 127-133, no. 2, 1966.

WARTBURG, W.P. von : Commercial arbitration and antitrust matters in the European economic community. Arbitration journal 21 : 65-92, no. 2, 1966.

ROBERT, J. : Arbitrage en matière internationale et au regard du Marché commun. Revue de l'arbitrage : 65-75, no. 2, 1966.

Travaux du 2e Congrès international de l'arbitrage, Rotterdam, 6-9 juillet 1966 - Arbitrage et Marché commun. Revue de l'arbitrage : 1-159, no. 3, 1966.
Suite d'articles.

ALTING von GEUSAU, F.A.M. : Problèmes institutionnels des Communautés européennes - Introduction à l'étude de la procédure de décision. Cahiers de droit européen : 227-248, no. 3, 1966.

WOLF, K. : Le recours en carence dans le droit des Communautés européennes. Revue du Marché commun : 111-124, mars 1966.

PANHUYS, H.F. van : Conflicts between the law of the European communities and other rules of international law. Common market law review 3 : 420-449, March 1966.

SCARANGELLA, G. : Comunità europée - Ordine costituzionale e norma comunitaria. Jus gentium 7 : 280-286, no. 3, 1966.

ILARDI, S. : La responsabilità extracontrattuale dell'Euratom. Economia internazionale delle fonti di energia 10 : 105-143, marzo-aprile 1966.

FINE, R.I. : Procedure under articles 85 and 86 of the E.E.C. treaty as interpreted by the Commission, the European court of justice and the courts of the member states. Diritto negli scambi internazionali 5 : 1-22, marzo-giugno 1966.

LE TALLEC, G., and EHLERMANN, C.D. : Die Begründungspflicht für Rechtsakte der Europäischen Gemeinschaften. Aussenwirtschaftsdienst des Betriebs-Beraters 12 : 149-155, 30. April 1966.

CONSTANTINESCO, L. : La spécificité du droit communautaire. Revue trimestrielle de droit européen 2 : 3-30, janvier-avril 1966.

SASSE, C. : The Common market, between international and municipal law. Yale law journal 75 : 695-753, April 1966.

PETERSEN, E. : L'influence possible du droit anglais sur le recours en annulation auprès de la Cour de justice des Communautés européennes. Revue trimestrielle de droit européen 2 : 256-266, avril-juin 1966.

SIZARET, L. : Une disposition curieuse, l'article 65 des statuts des fonctionnaires des Communautés européennes. Revue trimestrielle de droit européen 2 : 181-188, avril-juin 1966.

DEGAN, V.D. : Procédés d'interprétation tirés de la jurisprudence de la Cour de justice des Communautés européennes - Exposé comparatif avec la jurisprudence de la Cour internationale de justice. Revue trimestrielle de droit européen 2 : 189-227, avril-juin 1966.

PEPY, A. : Le rôle de la Cour de justice des Communautés européennes dans l'application de l'article 177 du traité de Rome. Cahiers de droit européen : 459-489, no. 5, 1966.

Le traité instituant un Conseil unique et une Commission unique des Communautés européennes devant la Chambre des députés luxembourgeois. Ministère d'Etat, Bulletin de documentation (Luxembourg, Grand Duchy) 22 : 1-21, 30 juin 1966.

BEBR, G. : Judicial remedy of private parties against normative acts of the European communities - The role of exception of illegality. Common market law review 4 : 7-31, June 1966.

TALLON, D. : Le droit communautaire - Réalités et illusions. Cahiers de droit européen : 571-580, no. 6, 1966.

Company law in the European economic community. European trends : 16-22, July 1966.

CATALANO, N. : La protection juridictionnelle indirecte dans le système des traités de Rome. Revue trimestrielle de droit européen 2 : 371-382, juillet-septembre 1966.

POLETTI, G. : La disciplina delle pratiche restrittive della concorrenza nell'E.F.T.A., art. 15 della convenzione di Stoccolma - Cenni di confronto con il regime in vigore nella C.E.E. Diritto negli scambi internazionali 5 : 185-193, settembre 1966.

EVERLING, U. : Legal problems of the common commercial policy in the European economic community. Common market law review 4 : 141-165, September 1966.

LOUIS, J.V. : La fusion des institutions des Communautés européennes. Revue du Marché commun : 843-856, décembre 1966.

BERRIOS MARTINEZ, R.A. : The nature and functioning of article 177 of the Rome treaty. Journal of Common market studies 5 : 113-139, December 1966.
Court of justice.

WIEBRINGHAUS, H. : L'interprétation uniforme des conventions du Conseil de l'Europe. Annuaire français de droit international 12 : 455-469, 1966.

OPSAHL, T. : The right of establishment in the EEC and EFTA. Association des auditeurs et anciens auditeurs de l'Académie de droit international de La Haye, Annuaire 36 : 87-97, 1966.

MOSLER, H. : European law - Does it exist? Current legal problems 19 : 168-191, 1966.

SLUSNY, M. : Les mesures provisoires dans la jurisprudence de la Cour de justice des Communautés européennes. Revue belge de droit international 3 : 127-153, no. 1, 1967.

CATALANO, N. : La jurisprudence de la Cour de justice à l'égard des contrats dits d'exclusivité. Cahiers de droit européen : 20-48, no. 1, 1967.

NATIONAL LAW - COUNTRIES

WEIL, G.L. : The merger of the institutions of the European communities. American journal of international law 61 : 57-65, January 1967.

FRANCESCHELLI, R. : Sistema delle impugnative nel diritto comunitario della concurrenza. Diritto internazionale 21 : parte la, 3-39, no. 1, 1967.

DROBNIG, U. : Conflict of laws and the European economic community. American journal of comparative law 15 : 204-229, nos. 1-2, 1966-1967.

LAGRANGE, M. : Le pouvoir de décision dans les Communautés européennes - Théorie et réalité. Revue trimestrielle de droit européen 3 : 1-29, janvier-avril 1967.

GOLDMAN, B. : Le projet de convention entre les Etats membres de la Communaute économique européenne sur le reconnaissance mutuelle des sociétés et personnes morales. Rabels Zeitschrift für ausländisches und internationales Privatrecht 31 : 201-232, Heft 2, 1967.

SCALABRINO, M. : La nozione di impresa nei trattati istitutivi delle Comunità europee. Diritto internazionale 21 : parte la, 176-202, 176-202, no. 2, 1967.

OVEN, A. van : The kaleidoscope of E.E.C. company law reform. Progress 52 : 60-64, no. 2, 1967.

CAHIER, P. : Le recours en constatation de manquements des Etats membres devant la Cour des Communautés auropéennes. Cahiers de droit européen : 123-159, no. 2, 1967.

VELU, J. : Action accomplie en 1965 par le Conseil de l'Europe dans le domaine du droit. Revue de droit international et de droit comparé 44 : 77-148, no. 2-3, 1967.

LECOURT, R. : La protection juridictionnelle des personnes en droit communautaire. Recueil Dalloz Sirey, Chronique : 51-56, 8 mars 1967.

SCHOLTEN, Y. : Company law in Europe (To be contd.). Common market law review 4 : 377-398, March 1967.

CONSTANTINESCO, L.. : Zur Vorlage nationaler Instanzgerichte an den Europäischen Gerichtshof, Art. 177 Abs. 2 EWGV. Aussenwirtschaftsdienst des Betriebs-Beraters 13 : 125-130, 15. April 1967.

TERRÉ, F. : La liberté d'établissement dans les professions judiciaires et la Communauté économique européenne. Journal du droit international 94 : 265-289, avril-juin 1967.

PELLICER VALERO, J.A. : La jurisdiction del tribunal de la Comunidades europeas en materia contractual y extracontractual. Revista jurídica de Cataluña 66 : 301-320, abril-junio 1967.

KNAUB, G. : La procédure devant la Cour de justice des Communautés européennes. Revue trimestrielle de droit européen 3 : 269-316, avril-juin 1967.
Bibliographie pp. 317-318.

GROEBEN, H. von der : Vers des sociétés anonymes européennes - Nécessité et possibilité de créer une société de type européen. Revue trimestrielle de droit européen 3 : 224-237, avril-juin 1967.
Voir aussi pp. 319-333.

FOCSANEANU, L. : Les prix imposés dans la Communauté économique européenne - Droits nationaux et droit communautaire. Revue trimestrielle de droit européen 3 : 173-223, avril-juin 1967.

BOUZAT, P. : Propositions pour la constitution d'une Cour pénale européenne. Revue internationale de droit pénal 38 : 179-194, ler-2e trimestre 1967.

Vers la société commerciale de type européen. Usine nouvelle 23 : 139-141, 4 mai 1967.
Congrès de Deauville, avril 1967.

RENAULD, J. : Aspects de la coordination et du rapprochement des dispositions relatives aux sociétés. Cahiers de droit européen : 611-652, no. 6, 1967.
Bibliographie pp. 611-613.

ANDRÉ, A. : Evidence before the European court of justice, with special reference to the Grundig/Consten decision. Common market law review 5 : 35-49, June 1967.

TOMUSCHAT, C. : Der Vorbehalt der Ausübung öffentlicher Gewalt in den Berufsfreiheitsregelungen des EWG-Vertrages und die freie Advokatur im Gemeinsamen Markt. Zeitschrift für ausländisches öffentliches Recht und Völkerrecht 27 : 53-92, Juli 1967.

SALTER, L.M. : Toward a supranational law - The Common market experience. American bar association journal 53 : 620-623, July 1967.

DUBOUIS, L. : Fonctionnaires des Communautés européennes. Revue trimestrielle de droit européen 3 : 684-664, juillet-septembre 1967.

KHEITMI, R. : La fonction consultative de la Cour de justice des Communautés européennes. Revue trimestrielle de droit européen 3 : 553-594, juillet-septembre 1967.

LIMPENS, A. : Harmonisation des législations dans le cadre du Marché commun. Revue internationale de droit comparé 19 : 621-653, juillet-septembre 1967.

MÉGRET, J. : La spécificité du droit communautaire. Revue internationale de droit comparé 19 : 565-577, juillet-septembre 1967.

Traité instituant un Conseil unique et une Commission unique des Communautés européennes. Revue trimestrielle de droit européen 3 : 703-718, juillet-septembre 1967.

PALK, W.L. : European court and the Common market. Canadian bar journal 10 : 290-309, August 1967.

LELEUX, P. : Corporation law in the United States and in the E.E.C. - Some comments on the present situation and future prospects. Common market law review 5 : 133-176, September 1967.

Treaty establishing a single Council and a single Commission of the European communities. Journal of Common market studies 6 : 60-87, September 1967.

NERI, S. : Le recours en annulation dans les Communautés européennes - Rôle et limites- Revue du Marché commun : 452-465, septembre 1967.

JACQUEMIN, A. : Pour une nouvelle approche du droit économique. Revue du Marché commun : 439-445, septembre 1967.

NATIONAL LAW - COUNTRIES

GREMENTIERI, V. : Le statut des juges de la Cour de justice des Communautés européennes. Revue trimestrielle de droit européen 3 : 817-830, octobre-décembre 1967.

FERRIERE, G. : Le contrôle de la légalité des actes étatiques par la Cour de justice des Communautés européennes. Revue générale de droit international public 71 : 879-1008, octobre-décembre 1967.

BLECHMAN, M.D. : Regional development in the EEC - A constitutional analysis. Harvard international law journal 8 : 32-77, winter 1967.

STORM, P.M. : Statute of a Societas europea. Common market law review 5 : 265-290, December 1967.

MODINOS, P. : Du droit conventionnel général du droit conventionnel européen - Quelques problèmes d'élaboration et d'application des conventions du Conseil de l'Europe. Cahiers de droit européen 4 : 3-36, no. 1, 1968.

LELEUX, P. : Le droit des sociétés aux Etats-Unis et dans la C.E.E. - Perspectives de leur évolution. Revue trimestrielle de droit européen 4 : 50-91, janvier-mars 1968.

TURANO, F. : Diritto e Comunità europee. Revue de droit international, de sciences diplomatiques et politiques 46 : 76-88, janvier-mars 1968.

STEVENS, L. : Linguistic equality in the Court of justice of the European communities. World affairs (Washington) 130 : 247-254, January-March 1968.

BELLANGER, F. : Contribution à l'étude de la nature juridique des "accords de Luxembourg" due 29 janvier 1966. Nederlands tijdschrift voor internationaal recht 15 : 179-196, afl. 2, 1968.
Texte pp. 234-236.

LELEUX, P. : Le rapprochement des législations dans la Communauté économique européenne. Cahiers de droit auropéen 4 : 129-160, no. 2, 1968.

BISCOTTINI, G. : La natura giuridica delle Comunità europee. Diritto internazionale 22 : parte la, 229-245, no. 3, 1968.

COSTONIS, J.J. : The treaty-making power of the European economic community - The perspectives of a decade. Common market law review 5 : 421-457, March 1968.

MASQUELIN, J., et RIGAUX, F. : Force obligatoire et application dans le temps des conventions internationales modifiant un des traités ayant institué les Communautés européennes. Cahiers de droit européen 4 : 276-288, no. 3, 1968.

CRAYENCOUR, J.P., de : Propos sur le droit d'établissement dans le traité de Rome. Cahiers de droit européen 4 : 420-435, no. 4, 1968.

HAY, P. : Supremacy of community law in national courts - A progress report on referrals under the EEC treaty. American journal of comparative law 16 : 524-551, no. 4, 1968.

PELLICER VALERO, J.A. : La jurisdicción del Tribunal de las Comunidades europeas en materia contractual y extracontractual. Revista jurídica de Cataluña 67 : 342-361, abril-junio 1968.

IGLESIAS BUIGUES, J.L. : La nature juridique du droit communautaire. Cahiers de droit européen 4 : 501-531, no. 5, 1968.

PICKERING, M. : The European company. Banker 118 : 519-525, June 1968.

SOLDATOS, P., et VANDERSANDEN, G. : L'admission dans la Communauté économique européenne - Essai d'interprétation juridique. Cahiers de droit européen 4 : 674-707, no. 6, 1968.

FERRI, G. : Le imprese comuni di diritti internazionale. Rivista del diritto commerciale e del diritto generale delle obbligazioni 66 : parte la, 277-287, luglio-agosto 1968.

SALMON, J.J.A., et TORRELLI, M. : La représentation juridique des Communautés européennes. Revue du Marché commun : 815-822, juillet-août 1968.

MOTZO, G. : Mesures répressives et sanczions administratives dans l'organisation de la Communauté européenne. Istituto di studi europei "Alcide de Gasperi", Bollettino 3 : 12-19, lugio-settembre 1968.

LOY, O. : L'application de la liberté d'établissement dans les Etats membres de la Communauté économique européenne. Journal du droit international 95 : 673-694, juillet-septembre 1968.

CHLOROS, A.G. : Principle, reason and policy in the development of European law. International and comparative law quarterly 17 : 849-877, October 1968.

Allocutions prononcées à l'audience solennelle du 23 octobre 1968 à l'occasion du Xe anniversaire de la Cour de justice des Communautés européennes. Revue trimestrielle de droit européen 4 : 746-762, octobre-décembre 1968.

NOEL, J., et LEMONTEY, J. : Aperçus sur le projet de convention européenne relative à la faillite, aux concordats et aux procédures analogues. Revue trimestrielle de droit européen 4 : 703-719, octobre-décembre 1968.

MARTIN, A. : The accession of the United Kingdom to the European community - Jurisdictional problems. Common market law review 6 : 7-49, November 1968.

HUNNINGS, N.M.: Constitutional implications of joining the Common market. Common market law review 6 : 50-66, November 1968.

KOHLER, R.: The new corporation laws in Germany, 1966, and France, 1967, and the trend towards a uniform corporation law for the Common market. Tulane law review 43 : 58-93, December 1968.

SUHR, E. : Die Verfassungsrechtsprechung des Europäischen Gerichtshofs. Jahrbuch des öffentlichen Rechts der Gegenwart 17 : 83-115, 1968.

GAUDET, M., et AMPHOUX, J. : La fusion des institutions des Communautés européennes. Annuaire européen. European yearbook 16 : 17-53, 1968.

SIDJANSKI, D. : Proceso de decisión en la Comunidad europea. Revista de la Facultad de derecho (Caracas) : 46-87, no. 39, 1968.

NATIONAL LAW - COUNTRIES

CIMOLINO, G.P. : Corte costituzionale e competenza pregiudiziale interpretiva della Corte di giustizia delle Comunità europee. Diritto internazionale 23 : parte la, 70-103, no. 1, 1969.

NAGY, N. : Le rapprochement des législations dans la C.E.E., compte tenu en particulier des art. 100 à 102, du traité de Rome. Wirtschaft und Recht 21 : 50-60, Heft 1, 1969.

Conferenza europea dei presidi delle Facoltà di giurisprudenza, Consiglio d'Europa, Strasburgo, novembre 1968. Annuario di diritto comparato e di studi legislativi 43 : iii-vi, 1-121, fasc. 1, 1969.

IPSEN, H.P. : Zur Verfassung der fusionierten Gemeinschaft. Integration; Vierteljahreshefte zur Europaforschung: 3-22, Nr. 1, 1969.

GARRON, R. : Réflexions sur la primauté du droit communautaire. Revue trimestrielle de droit européen 5 : 28-48, janvier-mars 1969.

VANDERSANDEN, G. : Le recours en intervention devant la Cour de justice des Communautés européennes. Revue trimestrielle de droit européen 5 : 1-27, janvier-mars 1969.

WÄGENBAUR, R. : Das Verbot steuerlicher Diskriminierung nach dem EWG-Vertrag im Lichte der Rechtsprechung des Gerichtshofs. Europarecht 4 : 20-36, Januar/März 1969.

BERNARDINI, A. : Regolamento comunitario e legge statale. Rivista di diritto internazionale 52 : 231-257, fasc. 2-3, 1969.

FUSS, E.W. : Rechtliche Aspekte einer gemeinsamen Wirtschaftspolitik in der EWG. Integration; Vierteljahreshefte zur Europaforschung : 137-152, Nr. 2, 1969.

STOLFI, M. : Il conflitto "norma comunitaria-legge interna". Rivista del diritto commerciale e del diritto generale delle obbligazioni 67 : parte la, 1-18, gannaio-febbraio 1969.

PENNINGTON, R.R. : European commercial law in the 1970's. Annuario di diritto comparato e di studi legislativi 43 : 202-214, fasc. 2-3, 1969.

KASTNER, W. : Zur Europäischen Aktiengesellschaft. Juristische Blätter 91 : 127-139, 8. März 1969.

IGLESIAS BUIGUES, J.L. : El tratado de fusión de los ejecutivos en el proceso de regresión comunitaria europea. Revista española de derecho internacional 22 : 496-517, núm.3, 1969.

ARNOLD, H. : Das EWG-Gerichtsstands- und Vollstreckungsübereinkommen vom 27.9.1968. Aussenwirtschaftsdienst des Betriebs-Beraters 15 : 89-93, März 1969.

EHLE, D. : The legal protection of enterprises of the Common market within the jurisdiction of the European court of justice and of national courts. Common market law review 6 : 193-204, March 1969.

SOLDATOS, P. : L'introuvable recours en carence devant la Court de justice des Communautés européennes. Cahiers de droit européen 5 : 313-334, no. 3, 1969.

LIMPENS, J., et LIMPENS, A. : Les problèmes actuels du rapprochement régional des droits nationaux - Expérience Benelux et considérations générales. Revue de droit international et de droit comparé 46 : 217-242, no. 4, 1969.

BURBAN, J.L. : Le problème de la dénonciation politique des accords d'association entre la Communauté économique européenne et les pays tiers. Revue du Marché commun : 188-192, avril 1969.

LAGRANGE, M. : Les obstacles constitutionnelles à l'intégration européenne. Revue trimestrielle de droit européen 5 : 240-254, avril-juin 1969.

OMMESLAGHE, P. van : La première directive du Conseil du 9 mars 1968 en matière de sociétés (A suivre). Cahiers de droit européen 5 : 495-563, no. 5, 1969.

STOLFI, C. : Cooperazione tra imprese e presupposti di ammissabilità nell'ambito delle Comunità europee. Rivista del diritto commerciale e del diritto generale delle obbligazioni 67 : parte la, 208-216, maggio-giugno 1969.

IOANNOU, K.M. : States as international judgment debtors within the European communities - Institutional enforcement mechanisms. Revue hellénique de droit international 22 : 17-44, juillet-décembre 1969.

FROMONT, M. : Der Rechtsschutz gegen Massnahmen der Verwaltung im Europa der Sechs. Europarecht 4 : 202-212, Juli/September 1969.

ANDRÉ, A. : Artikel 189 Abs. 3 EWG-Vertrag als politische Norm. Europarecht 4 : 191-201, Juli/September 1969.

RITTSTIEG, H. : Verpflichtende Aussenhandelslizenzen und ihre Absicherung durch Kautionen im EWG-Recht. Aussenwirtschaftsdienst des Betriebs-Beraters 15 : 305-313, August 1969.

AUBENAS, B. : Quelques considérations sur les infractions contre les traités de Paris et de Rome. Revue du Marché commun : 458-464, octobre 1969.

RAMBOW, G. : The end of the transitional period. Common market law review 6 : 434-450, October 1969. European economic community.

TORRELLI, M. : Les "habilitations" de la Commission des Communautés européennes. Revue du Marché commun : 465-472, octobre 1969.

LASSALLE, C. : Aspects communautaire de certains actes du droit international. Revue générale de droit international public 73 : 987-1017, octobre-décembre 1969.

PESCATORE, P. : L'application directe des traités européens par les juridictions nationales - La jurisprudence nationale. Revue trimestrielle de droit européen 5 : 697-723, octobre-décembre 1969.

SOLDATOS, P. : Durée et dénonciation des traités de Rome. Revue de droit international, de sciences diplomatiques et politiques 47 : 257-270, octobre-décembre 1969.

CORREIA, A. : O direito das sociedades na Comunidade económica europeia. Ministério da justiça, Boletim (Portugal) : 112-164, novembro 1969.

NATIONAL LAW - COUNTRIES

KALBE, P. : Niederlassungsfreiheit und freier Dienstleistungsverkehr der freien Berufe in der Europäischen Wirtschaftsgemeinschaft. Aussenwirtschaftsdienst des Betriebs-Beraters 15 : 433-435, November 1969.

MÖLLER, W. : Die Verordnung der Europäischen Gemeinschaften. Jahrbuch des öffentlichen Rechts der Gegenwart 18 : 1-50, 1969.

BRITO CORREIA, L. de : A Comunidade económica, europeia e a harmonização das legislações sobre sociedades. Ministério da justiça, Boletim (Portugal) : 248-274, no. 182, 1969.

GUNDERSEN, F.F. : Etableringsretten og frihandelsforbundet EFTA. Tidsskrift for rettsvitenskap : 1-66, hefte 1, 1970.

BEBR, G. : Les dispositions de droit communautaire directement applicables - Dévelopmment d'une notion communautaire. Cahiers de droit européen 6 : 3-49, no. 1, 1970.

HIRSCH, A. : Vers l'universalité de la faillite au sein du Marché commun? Cahiers de droit européen 6 : 50-60, no. 1, 1970.

LEGARET, J. : L'amorce d'une législation européenne. Revue politique des idées et des institutions 59 : 18-22, nos. 1-2, janvier 1970.

DAIG, H.W. : Die Rechtsprechung des Gerichtshofes der Europäischen Gemeinschaften zur unmittelbaren Wirkung von EWG-Bestimmungen auf die Rechtsbeziehungen zwischen Mitgliedstaaten und Gemeinschaftsbürgern. Europarecht 5 : 1-31, Januar-März 1970.

JAEGER, F. : Warum muss EWG- und EFTA-Recht GATT-konform sein? Wirtschaft und Recht 22 : 128-147, Heft 2, 1970.

CANSACCHI, G. : Il futuro trattato di fusione delle tre Comunità economiche europee. Diritto internazionale 24 : parte la, 309-318, no. 3, 1970.
See also pp. 319-334.

ESCH, B. van der : L'unité du Marché commun dans la jurisprudence de la Cour. Cahiers de droit européen 6 : 303-313, no. 3, 1970.

DROBNIG, U. : Verstösst das Staatsangehörigkeitsprinzip gegen das Diskriminierungsverbot des EWG-Vertrages? Rabels Zeitschrift für ausländisches und internationales Privatrecht 34 : 636-661, Heft 3-4, 1970.

HUYS, M. : Evolution du droit des sociétés en Belgique et dans les pays du Marché commun (A suivre). Energie (Bruxelles) : 9-21, ler et 2e trimestre 1970.

BEBR, G. : Directly applicable provisions of Community law - The development of a Community concept. International and comparative law quarterly 19 : 257-298, April 1970.

FICKER, H.C. : A project for aEuropean corporation (To be contd.). Journal of business law : 156-169, April 1970.

PESCATORE, P. : International law and Community law - A comparative analysis. Common market law review 7 : 167-183, April 1970.

CINTURA, P. : L'objectivisme juridique et la Cour de Luxembourg. Revue trimestrielle de droit européen 6 : 272-295, avril-juin 1970.

COLARD, D. : L'accord européen de Londres du 6 mai 1969. Revue générale de droit international public 74 : 421-435, avril-juin 1970.

SCHAUB, A., and BEUVE-MÉRY, J.J. : Die Beseitigung der technischen Handelshindernisse zwischen den EWG-Mitgliedstaaten durch Richtlinien gemäss Art.100 EWGV. Europarecht 5 : 135-160, April-Juni 1970.

L'apport du droit communautaire. Cahiers de droit européen 6 : 501-567, no. 5, 1970.
Suite d'articles.

MORAND, C.A. : Les recommandations, les résolutions et les avis du droit communautaire. Cahiers de droit auropéen 6 : 623-644, no. 6, 1970.

STEIN, E. : Conflict of rules by treaty - Recognition of companies in a regional market. Michigan law review 68 : 1327-1354, June 1970.
European economic community.

BOT, B.R. : Negotiating Community agreements - Procedure and practice. Common market law review 7 : 286-310, July 1970.

MANN, F.A. : The European company. International and comparative law quarterly 19 : 468-482, July 1970.

MASHAW, J.L. : Ensuring the observance of law in the interpretation and application of the EEC treaty - The role and functioning of the renvoi d'interprétation under article 177 (To be contd.). Common market law review 7 : 258-285, July 1970.

ROHDE-LIEBENAU, W. : Rechtsetzung auf Grund EWG-Richtlinien und OECD-Beschlüssen. Aussenwirtschaftsdienst des Betriebs-Beraters 16 : 304-308, Juli 1970.

COLESANTI. V. : Unità e universalità del fallimento nel progetto di convenzione della C.E.E. Rivista di diritto internazionale privato e processuale 6 : 522-556, luglio-septembre 1970.
See also pp. 501-521.

MERTENS de WILMARS, J. : Les enseignements communautaires des jurisprudences nationales. Revue trimestrielle de droit européen 6: 454-468, juillet-septembre 1970.

MARTENS, J. : Die rechtsstaatliche Struktur der Europäischen Wirtschaftsgemeinschaft. Europarecht 5 : 209-231, Juli-September 1970.

Proposition d'un statut des sociétés européennes. Communautés européennes. Bulletin, Supplément : 1-223, no. 8, 1970.

TUROT, P. : Le projet de société commerciale européenne. Notes et études documentaires : 1-46, no. 3719, 18 septembre 1970.

HELLMANN, R. : Nationale Souveränität und EWG-Vertragstreue - Die Probe in lebenswichtigen Fragen steht noch aus. Europa-Archiv 25 : 678-684, 25. September 1970.

MERTENS de WILMARS, J., and VEROUGSTRAETE, I.M. : Proceedings against ECE member states for failure to fulfil their obligations. Common market law review 7 : 385-406, October 1970.

MIGLIAZZA, A. : I problemi di diritto internazionale relativi alla creazione di una società commerciale europea. Rivista di diritto internazionale privato e processuale 6 : 761-789, ottobre-dicembre 1970.

PESCATORE, P. : Das Zusammenwirken der Gemeinschaftsrechtsordnung mit den nationalen Rechtsordnungen. Europarecht 5 : 307-323, Oktober-Dezember 1970.
See also pp.324-333.

DUBOIS, J.P. : Le projet de groupement d'intérêt économique sur le plan européen, le contexte institutionnel et l'intégration politique. Revue trimestrielle de droit européen 6 : 625-649, octobre-décembre 1970.

La profession d'avocat dans les six Etats membres des Communautés européennes. Revue trimestrielle de droit européen 6 : 607-624, octobre-décembre 1970.

MARCHINI-CAMIA, A. : Facilitating transnational business within the EEC - Progress to date. Cornell international law journal 3 : 9-31, winter 1970.

VANDERSANDEN, G. : Le rôle de la Cour de justice des Communautés européennes dans le processus d'intégration communautaire. Aussenwirtschaft 25 : 403-426, Dezember 1970.

EUROPE
(Economic Community, Patents, Trade-marks)

European lawyers at Leiden - TOOKEY, G.W. : The draft European patent convention. International and comparative law quarterly 14 : 281-287, January 1965.

MEGRET, J. : De l'accessibilité au droit européen des brevets. Journal du droit international 92 : 871-882, octobre-décembre 1965.

HOLSTEIN, P. von : International co-operation in the field of patent law with special reference to the activities of the Council of Europe. International and comparative law quarterly 16 : 191-206, January 1967.

MORERA, R., et ARGAN, F. : Les tendances actuelles en matière de brevet européen. Cahiers de droit européen : 491-512, no. 5, 1967.

SAINT-GAL, Y. : Importance des droits de propriété industrielle pour les firmes exportatrices plus specialement dans le cadre de la C.E.E. Revue trimestrielle de droit européen 3 : 799-816, octobre-décembre 1967.

PLAISANT, R. : Le principe de la territorialité des brevets d'invention et le traité de C.E.E. Recueil Dalloz Sirey, Chronique : 259-264, 6 décembre 1967.

SCHATZ, U. : Epuisement des droits conférés par les brevets et contrefaçon. Revue trimestrielle de droit européen 5 : 449-462, juillet-septembre 1969.

ZANDEN, J.W. van der : La loi uniforme Benelux sur les marques de produits. Benelux, Bulletin trimestriel économique et statistique - Economisch en statistisch kwartaalbericht : 36-40, décembre 1969.
Texte français/néerlandais.

SAINT-GAL, Y. : Aspect actuel de la réglementation de la concurrence et de la protection des droits de propriété industrielle dans le cadre communautaire européen. Revue trimestrielle de droit européen 6 : 43-67, janvier-mars 1970.

DEMARET, P. : Justification et problèmes d'élaboration d'un droit européen des brevets. Revue trimestrielle de droit européen 6 : 215-271, avril-juin 1970.

EUROPE
(European convention of Human rights)

VELU, J. : Le bilan politique de la Convention européenne des droits de l'homme. Cahiers de droit européen : 99-121, no. 2, 1965.

ALBERT-SOREL, J. : Le passé et l'avenir des droits de l'homme. Revue des deux mondes : 69-82, 1er mai 1965.
Convention européenne des droits de l'homme.

VASAK, K. : La Convention européenne des droits de l'homme, complément utile des conventions de Genève. Revue internationale de la Croix-Rouge 47 : 365-378, août 1965.

VERDROSS, A. : The status of the European convention for the protection of human rights and fundamental freedoms in the hierarchy of rules of law. Indian journal of international law 5 : 455-463, October 1965.

BUERGENTHAL, T. : The domestic status of the European convention on human rights - A second look. International commission of jurists, Journal 7 : 55-96, summer 1966.

CAPOTORTI, F. : Interferenze fra la Convenzione europea dei diritti dell'uomo ed altri accordi, e loro riflessi negli ordinamenti interni. Università di Milano, Istituto di diritto internazionale e straniero; Comunicazioni e studi 12 : 115-142, 1966.

FAVRE, A. : La Convention européenne des droits de l'homme. Schweizerisches Jahrbuch für internationales Recht 23 : 9-36, 1966.

SARHANE, A.A.M. : Application dans le temps de la Convention européenne des droits de l'homme et des libertés fondamentales. Revue égyptienne de droit international 22 : 133-169, 1966.
Texte en arabe.

BEDDARD, R. : The status of the European convention of human rights in domestic law. International and comparative law quarterly 16 : 206-217, January 1967.

RONZITTI, N. : L'accettazione della Convenzione europea dei diritti dell'uomo e delle sur clausole facoltative da parte degli Stati membri del Consiglio d'Europa. Rivista di diritto internazionale 50 : 357-366, fasc. 2, 1967.

ROBERTSON, A.H. : La Convention européenne des droits de l'homme. Société d'études et d'expansion, Revue 66 : 287-291, mars-avril 1967.

BUERGENTHAL, T., and KEWENIG, W. : Zum Begriff der Civil Rights in Artikel 6 Absatz 1 der Europäischen Menschenrechtskonvention. Archiv des Völkerrechts 13 : 393-411, 4. Heft 1967.

NATIONAL LAW - COUNTRIES

MARCUS-HELMONS, S. : L'article 64 de la Convention de Rome ou les réserves à la Convention européenne des droits de l'homme. Revue de droit international et de droit comparé 45 : 7-26, no. 1, 1968.

MÜLLER-RAPPARD, E. : Le droit d'action en vertu des dispositions de la Convention européenne des droits de l'homme. Revue belge de droit international 4 : 485-517, no. 2, 1968.

WIEBRINGHAUS, H. : Das Europarecht der Grundfreiheiten im Jahr der Menschenrechte. Vereinte Nationen 16 : 46-51, April 1968.

PESCATORE, P. : Les droits de l'homme et l'intégration européenne. Cahiers de droit européen 4 : 629-668, no. 6, 1968.

WALTER, H. : Der Grundsatz iura novit curia im Europäischen Menschenrechtsverfahren - Zur Teilabweisung von Individualbeschwerden wegen offensichtlicher Unbegründetheit. Zeitschrift für ausländisches öffentliches Recht und Völkerrecht 28 : 561-577, November 1968.

KNEUCKER, R.F. : Wirksame Rechtsmittel gegen Verletzung der Europäischen Menschenrechtskonvention. Juristische Blätter 90 : 598-609, 7. Dezember 1968.

ROBERTSON, A.H. : The United Nations covenant on civil and political rights and the European convention on human rights. British year book of international law 43 : 21-48, 1968-1969.

LODIGIANI, G. : I diritti dell'uomo nella comunità internazionale e la tutela azzuata dalla Commissione nelle Convenzione europea. Jus, Rivista di scienze giuridiche 20 : 38-107, gennaio-giugno 1969.

ZOTIADES, G.B. : Some aspects of the functions assigned to the European commission of human rights in the examination of the merits of the case. Revue hellénique de droit international 22 : 65-91, janvier-juin 1969.

PESCATORE, P. : Die Menschenrechte und die europäische Integration. Integration; Vierteljahreshefte zur Europaforschung : 103-136, Nr. 2, 1969.

Colloque international sur la Convention européenne des droits de l'homme, Szrasbourg, 18-19 novembre 1968. Revue des droits de l'homme - Human rights journal 2 : 195-373, no. 2, 1969.

ZANGHÌ, C. : La libertà di espressione nella Convenzione europea dei diritti dell'uomo e nel Patto delle Nazioni Unite sui diritti civili e politici. Rivista di diritto internazionale 52 : 295-308, fasc. 2-3, 1969.

TURANO, F. : La dichiarazione universale dei diritti dell'uomo e la Convenzione europea dei diritti dell'uomo (To be contd.). Stato sociale 13 : 157-161, marzo 1969.

TAJIMA, Y. : Protection of freedom of expression by the European convention. Revue des droits de l'homme - Human rights journal 2 : 658-695, no. 4, 1969.

GREMENTIERI, V. : La Convention européenne des droits de l'homme et le procès civil. Revue trimestrielle de droit européen 5 : 463-474, juillet-septembre 1969.

ECONOMOPOULOS, C.P. : Les éléments politiques et judiciaires dans la procédure instaurée par la Convention européenne des droits de l'homme. Revue hellénique de droit international 22 : 122-139, juillet-décembre 1969.

LIEBSCHER, V. : Strafverfolgung und Menschenrechte - Der Begriff des "délai raisonnable" in der Rechtsprechung der Europäischen Kommission und des Europäischen Gerichtshofes. Juristische Blätter 91 : 465-477, 13. September 1969.

PELLOUX, R. : La Cour européenne des droits de l'homme. France, Conseil d'Etat; Etudes et documents 22 : 83-102, 1969.

DAUBIE, C. : La Convention européenne des droits de l'homme et la raison d'Etat. Revue des droits de l'homme - Human rights journal 3 : 247-274, no. 2, 1970.

Human rights - The European convention and its national application. American journal of comparative law 18 : iv, 233-366, no. 2, 1970.
Series of articles.

CONDORELLI, L. : La proprietà nella Convenzione europea dei diritti dell'uomo. Rivista di diritto internazionale 53 : 175-232, fasc. 2-3, 1970.

RASENACK, C. : "Civil rights and obligations" or "droits et obligations de caractère civil" - Two crucial legal determinations in Art. 6 (1) of the European convention for the protection of human rights and fundamental freedoms. Revue des droits de l'homme - Human rights journal 3 : 51-81, mars 1970.

MacBRIDE, S. : The European court of human rights. New York university journal of international law and politics 3 : 1-17, spring 1970.

MORRISSON, C.C. : Restrictive interpretation of sovereignty-limiting treaties - The practice of the European human rights convention system. International and comparative law quarterly 19 : 361-375, July 1970.

ZANGHI, C. : La liberté d'expression dans la Convention européenne des droits de l'homme et dans le Pacte des Nations Unies relatif aux droits civils et politiques. Revue générale de droit international public 74 : 573-589, juillet-septembre 1970.

O'HANLON, R.J. : The Brussels colloquy on the European convention on human rights (September-October 1970). The Irish jurist 5 : 252-261, winter 1970.